W9-ANB-744

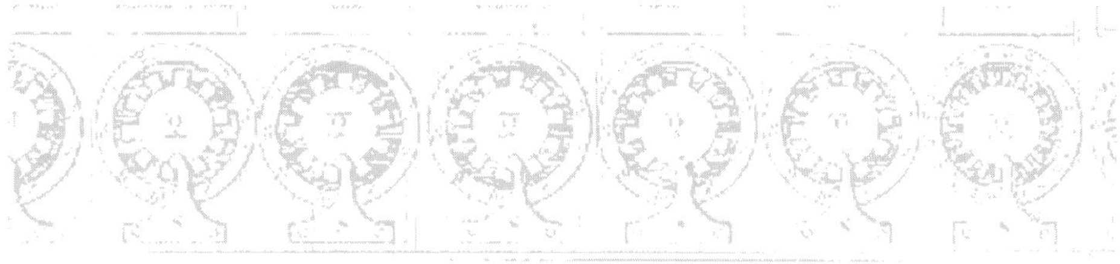

2nd edition

ENCYCLOPEDIA OF PHILOSOPHY

CABANIS – DESTUTT DE TRACY

volume 2

2nd edition

ENCYCLOPEDIA OF PHILOSOPHY

DONALD M. BORCHERT
Editor in Chief

MACMILLAN REFERENCE USA
An imprint of Thomson Gale, a part of The Thomson Corporation

Detroit • New York • San Francisco • San Diego • New Haven, Conn. • Waterville, Maine • London • Munich

Encyclopedia of Philosophy, Second Edition

Donald M. Borchert, Editor in Chief

For more information, contact
Macmillan Reference USA
An imprint of Thomson Gale
27500 Drake Rd.
Farmington Hills, MI 48331-3535
Or you can visit our internet site at
http://www.gale.com

LIBRARY OF CONGRESS CATALOGING-IN-PUBLICATION DATA

Encyclopedia of philosophy / Donald M. Borchert, editor in chief.—2nd ed.
p. cm.
Includes bibliographical references and index.—
ISBN 0-02-865780-2 (set hardcover : alk. paper)—
ISBN 0-02-865781-0 (vol 1)—ISBN 0-02-865782-9 (vol 2)—
ISBN 0-02-865783-7 (vol 3)—ISBN 0-02-865784-5 (vol 4)—
ISBN 0-02-865785-3 (vol 5)—ISBN 0-02-865786-1 (vol 6)—
ISBN 0-02-865787-X (vol 7)—ISBN 0-02-865788-8 (vol 8)—
ISBN 0-02-865789-6 (vol 9)—ISBN 0-02-865790-X (vol 10)
1. Philosophy–Encyclopedias. I. Borchert, Donald M., 1934-

B51.E53 2005
103–dc22

2005018573

This title is also available as an e-book.
ISBN 0-02-866072-2
Contact your Thomson Gale representative for ordering information.

Printed in the United States of America
10 9 8 7 6 5 4 3 2 1

contents

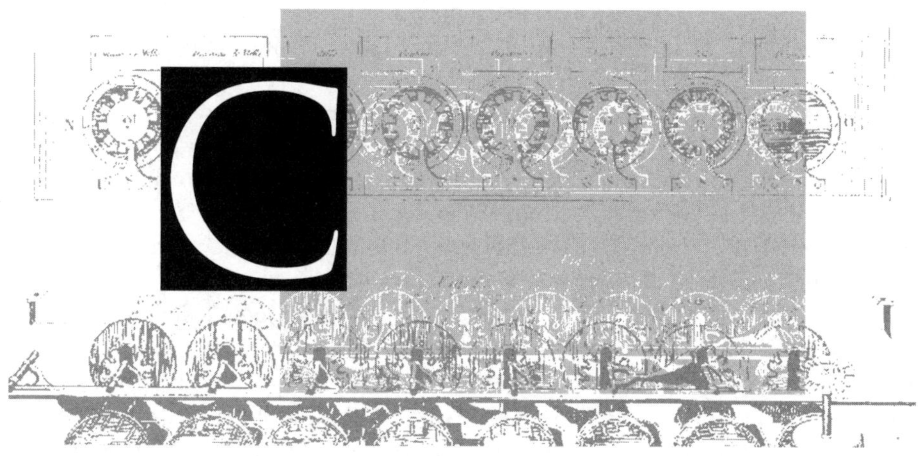

CABALA

See *Kabbalah*

CABANIS, PIERRE-JEAN GEORGES

(1757–1808)

Pierre-Jean Georges Cabanis was, with Comte Antoine Louis Claude Destutt de Tracy, the leader of the Idéologues. A precocious student of philosophy and of the classics, he chose medicine as a career, but he never practiced. As a protégé of Claude-Adrien Helvétius's widow, he frequented the company of Étienne Bonnot de Condillac, Baron d'Holbach, Benjamin Franklin, and Thomas Jefferson. When Voltaire disparaged his poetry in 1778, Cabanis turned to physiology and philosophy. During the Revolution, he collaborated with Mirabeau on public education and was an intimate of Marquis de Condorcet. Later, he backed the Directory and Napoleon Bonaparte's coup d'état of 18 Brumaire. Although Napoleon made him a senator, Cabanis opposed his tyrannical policies. Bitter and scornful, Napoleon dubbed Cabanis's group "Idéologues." Cabanis wrote on medical practice and teaching, but his fame and influence derive from one book, *Rapports du physique et du moral de l'homme* (12 memoirs written between 1796 and 1802, published in 1802).

The Idéologues (who also included Constantin Volney, Condorcet, Antoine Lavoisier, and Pierre de Laplace) were often scorned in their time, and later, as belated *philosophes* and purveyors of visionary speculations. In the rising tide of metaphysical idealism, their positivistic approach was held in disfavor. They suffered from the influence of the religious revival and the spell exercised by François René de Chateaubriand's *Le génie du Christianisme,* as well as from the popularity of "Illuminist" fads derived from Masonic practices. Their political activity during the Revolution also worked against them, and Napoleon's suppression of their movement left them without an outlet for publication.

Cabanis, like the others, sought a mechanistic explanation of the universe, nature, and human behavior—an approach later continued by Auguste Comte and Hippolyte-Adolphe Taine. Matter alone is real and eternal in its many transitory forms. As Lavoisier had applied analysis to chemistry, so—Cabanis declared—it could be applied to ideas, which could thereby be reduced to the original sensations whence they spring. Self-interest, the pursuit of happiness and pleasure, and self-preservation are the only motives of action. These notions, already advanced by the eighteenth-century materialists, were systematically developed by Cabanis and Destutt de Tracy. The study of man, they held, must be reduced to physics and physiology. Man must be observed and analyzed like any mineral or vegetable. The medical expert, said Cabanis, should play the part formerly taken by the moralist (an idea that harks back to René Descartes and Julien Offray de La Mettrie). "Physiology, analysis of ideas, and morals are three branches of one science which may be called the science of man." Consequently, Cabanis and his fellow theorists refused to recognize notions not based on phenomena or sensations, that is, not susceptible of exact knowledge and (ultimately, at least) of mathematical notation. An understanding of the "mechanism of language" was considered essential to the understanding of the "mechanism of the intellect" and to the meaning of ideas. Language itself, however, had to be illumined by analysis of the sensations which constitute an idea an by the functioning of the intellect.

In his preface to the *Rapports du physique et du moral de l'homme,* Cabanis insisted that both the moralist and the physician are interested in the whole man; that is, in the physical and the moral, which are inseparable, and incomprehensible taken separately. The moral sciences must be placed on a physical basis. The union of mind and body is the theme of the first "Mémoire." Sensation is the necessary cause of our ideas, feelings, needs, and will. Since sensitivity is the connection between biological life and mind, the mental is only the physical considered from a certain point of view. Cabanis makes a famous comparison between the brain and the stomach: As the latter is a machine for digesting food, so the former is a machine for digesting impressions, by "the secretion of thought." He then develops a genetic analysis of sensations and ideas. There are no causes except those which can act on our senses, no truths except in relation to "the general way of feeling" of human nature, which varies with such positive factors as age, sex, disposition, health, climate, and so on. Thus the state of the abdominal viscera may influence the formation of ideas.

The second "Mémoire" is a "physiological history of sensations." Cabanis defines life as feeling and, following the work of Albrecht von Haller and La Mettrie, discusses the difference between sensitivity and irritability. The latter, he maintains, is only a result of the former, which is the basic biological phenomenon; since both depend on the nerves, they are essentially the same. Voluntary movements come from perceptions, which arise from sensations. Involuntary movements are caused by the organs' sensitivity, which produces the unconscious (autonomic) impressions that determine many of our ideas and decisions. The action of the nervous system, moreover, is only a specialized application of the laws of physical motion, which are the source of all phenomena. The third "Mémoire" develops a theory of the unconscious. The nervous system is affected by internal changes, that is, by memory and imagination; thus within man exists "another internal man" in constant action, the effects of which are noticeable in dreams. The fourth "Mémoire" explores the influence of age on ideas and "moral affections." The organs, like all else in nature, are in constant motion, and are therefore involved in decomposition and recomposition. Consequently, variations in the cellular tissue produce physical and psychic changes due to chemical action. The fifth "Mémoire" takes up sexual differences. The generative organs are essentially glandular, and their secretions influence the brain and the whole body. Unknown primitive "dispositions" (structures), which cause the embryo to be male or female, are also the cause of sexual differences, both physical and psychic. The fact that women can be forced to reproduction and men only excited to it produces vast differences in habits and mental outlook. What the sexes have in common constitutes human nature.

The sixth "Mémoire" treats the influence of "temperament," that is, the determining effects of the inherited physical constitution. Thus a large heart and lungs produce an energetic character, small ones an intellectual character. Because of heredity, the human race could be improved by hygienic methods. Believing in the inheritance of acquired characteristics and in improvement of species through crossbreeding, Cabanis pleads for a program of eugenics that will do for the human species what human beings have done for dogs and horses. In the seventh "Mémoire" Cabanis explores emotional and mental perturbations caused by diseases. For instance, weakness and irritability of the stomach produce muscular enervation and rapid alternations between excitement and depression. The eighth "Mémoire" discusses such effects of diet, air pressure, humidity and temperature, as excitation and sedation. Cabanis analyzes the effects of different foods and drinks, but his information and conclusions are rather fantastic.

Climate is the subject of the ninth "Mémoire." Man, the most modifiable animal, responds to heat and cold with differences in sexual and physical activity, and consequently in mental and moral habits. The tenth "Mémoire" is the longest. It explores the phenomena of animal life, including sensitivity, instinct, sympathy, sleep, dreams, and delirium. The forces that cause matter to organize (a natural tendency) are unknown, and will always remain so. Nevertheless these forces are only physical, and life is only organization. Cabanis believed in spontaneous generation. Species have evolved through chance mutations ("fortuitous changes") and planned mutation ("man's experimental attempts"), which change the structures of heredity. Cabanis does not, however, develop a general theory of evolution. The eleventh "Mémoire" concerns the influence of the "moral" (mental) on the physical, which is merely the action of the brain on the body. The last "Mémoire," on "acquired dispositions," treats the influence of habituation and experience in general.

As a positivist, Cabanis was willing to renounce ultimate explanations. He was interested only in cause and effect on the level of phenomena. Unlike the other Idéologues, he was much influenced by La Mettrie and the man-machine school. He opposed the psychological method of Condillac and the sensationists, which was limited to external sensations. He preferred the physiological approach, which emphasized hereditary dispositions, the state of the organs, dreams, and automatic or unconscious impulses. These factors were more significant for him than experience (sensation) in determining the individual's behavior; for the tabula rasa concept ignored what the child or adult brings to experience. For the same reason, Condillac's statue is only an unreal abstraction from the reality of the unified, total, active organism. Cabanis was interested in the moral and social improvement of humankind, which he considered possible through an understanding of physiology—a science that he thought would eventually influence even positive law.

Cabanis and the Idéologues were one moment of a tradition that extends from Epicurus to the contemporary logical positivists (whose interest in linguistic analysis was prefigured by the Idéologues). Cabanis, like the others, has frequently been accused of impoverishing human experience by reducing it to the physical and mechanical level, and by denying the possibility of transcending internal and external sensations. On the other hand, the Idéologues considered man to be his own justification and the master of his own destiny. They had faith in his capacity to progress indefinitely by means of his own resources.

Bibliography

WORKS BY CABANIS

The *Oeuvres complètes* (Paris, 1823–1825) of Cabanis was edited by P. J. G. Thurot.

Cabanis, Pierre-Jean Georges. *On the Relations between the Physical and Moral Aspects of Man,* edited by George Mora. Translated by Margaret Duggan Saidi. Baltimore: Johns Hopkins Press, 1981.

WORKS ON CABANIS

The best study of the Idéologues (although it ignores Cabanis's connection with La Mettrie and the man-machine outlook) is Emile Cailliet, *La tradition littéraire des Idéologues* (Philadelphia: American Philosophical Society, 1943). See also Charles H. Van Duzer, *The Contribution of the Idéologues to French Revolutionary Thought* (Baltimore: Johns Hopkins Press, 1935), and the more apologetic F. Picavet, *Les idéologues* (Paris: Alcan, 1891).

Moravia, Sergio. "From 'Homme Machine' to 'Homme Sensible': Changing Eighteenth-Century Models of Man's Image." *Journal of the History of Ideas* 39 (1978): 45–60.

Other Recommended Titles

Richards, Robert J. "Influence of Sensationalist Tradition on Early Theories of the Evolution of Behavior." *Journal of the History of Ideas* 40 (1979): 85–105.

Staum, Martin S. *Cabanis: Enlightenment and Medical Philosophy in the French Revolution.* Princeton, NJ: Princeton University Press, 1980.

Wright, John P., and Paul Potter, eds. *Psyche and Soma: Physicians and Metaphysicians on the Mind Body Problem from Antiquity to Enlightenment.* Oxford: Clarendon Press, 2000.

L. G. Crocker (1967)
Bibliography updated by Tamra Frei (2005)

CAIRD, EDWARD

(1835–1908)

Edward Caird, a leading Scottish Hegelian, was born in Greenock, the fifth of seven boys. His eldest brother, John Caird, became well known as a preacher and theologian, and exercised considerable influence on the young Edward. Educated at Greenock Academy and Glasgow University (with a brief interlude at St. Andrews), Edward Caird went to Balliol College, Oxford, gaining first-class honors in Classical Moderations and in "Greats." From 1864 to 1866 he was a fellow and tutor of Merton, leaving to take the chair of moral philosophy at Glasgow, which he held until 1893. He then returned to Oxford to succeed Benjamin Jowett as master of Balliol. He resigned because of ill health in 1907, and died the year after.

Caird had a profound influence on his students, who regarded themselves as his disciples and included such distinguished philosophers as Henry Jones, J. H. Muirhead, J. S. Mackenzie, and John Watson. "The greatest theme of modern philosophy," Caird held, "is the problem of the relation of the human to the divine" (*The Evolution of Theology in the Greek Philosophers,* 1904). Many of his Glasgow students were destined for the church, and his liberalizing influence on religion was widely transmitted through them beyond the classroom.

Caird's philosophy was a form of speculative idealism, based on Immanuel Kant but going beyond him. It was essentially a philosophy of reconciliation. The need for philosophy, he held, arises from the apparently irreconcilable opposition between different elements in our spiritual life—between subject and object, religion and science, freedom and determination, reason and desire. Unless we reconcile these antagonisms in a higher unity, we cannot achieve the spiritual harmony without which the highest achievements of humanity are impossible.

Kant, he was convinced, had found the key to the problem, but had failed to grasp the implications of his own doctrine. Caird had first to clear away what he thought was a common misinterpretation of Kant and then to go further along the Kantian road, with G. W. F. Hegel as his guide. Kant had been held, according to Caird, to teach that the material of knowledge is given in sense perception and that the mind then goes to work on it, ordering it by concepts supplied by itself. But, in fact, for Kant there *are* no objects until thought has done its work. Thought enters into the very constitution of experience. And further, the process of knowing is dominated by an "idea of the Reason," which drives the mind to seek a form of experience in which all differences are seen as elements in a single system.

But instead of insisting that the larger the part played in knowledge by the mind's synthetic activity, the more adequate that knowledge is, Kant took the view that this activity confines us to appearances and bars us from things-in-themselves. He should have shown, Caird argued, that our knowledge of objects will be imperfect insofar as we fail to recognize that they are only partial aspects of the ideal whole toward which reason points.

Caird's ethical theory had close affiliations with that of his lifelong friend, T. H. Green. His main problem centered on the opposition of inclination and duty, and his solution lay in establishing the power of human beings to determine their conduct by reference to the self, as a permanent center, as distinct from its relatively isolated and transient desires. A self-conscious being seeks *self*-satisfaction, not just the satisfaction of this or that desire. And in this power of determining conduct by reference to the self lies human freedom.

The principle of evolution, Caird recognized, was of great value in reconciling differences, and in his Gifford Lectures, *The Evolution of Religion* (1891–1892), he traced the development of a single religious principle through its varied manifestations in the main religions of the world.

See also Green, Thomas Hill; Hegel, Georg Wilhelm Friedrich; Hegelianism; Kant, Immanuel;.

Bibliography

WORKS BY CAIRD

A Critical Account of the Philosophy of Kant. Glasgow: J. Maclehose, 1877.

Hegel. Edinburgh: Blackwood, 1883.

The Social Philosophy and Religion of Comte. New York: Macmillan, 1885.

The Critical Philosophy of Immanuel Kant. Glasgow: J. Maclehose, 1889.

Essays on Literature and Philosophy. Glasgow: J. Maclehose, 1892.

The Evolution of Religion. Glasgow, 1893: J. Moclehose.

The Evolution of Theology in the Greek Philosophers. Glasgow: J. Maclehose, 1904.

WORKS ON CAIRD

Jones, Sir Henry, and J. H. Muirhead. *The Life and Philosophy of Edward Caird.* Glasgow: Maclehose, Jackson, 1921.

Mackenzie, J. S. "Edward Caird as a Philosophical Teacher." *Mind* 18 (1909): 509–537.

Watson, John. "The Idealism of Edward Caird." *Philosophical Review* 18 (1909): 147–163, 259–280.

A. K. Stout (1967)

CAIRNS, DORION
(1901–1973)

Thomas Dorion Cairns was born on July 4, 1901. His father was a Methodist pastor. Cairns studied phenomenological theory of value with Winthrop Bell at Harvard in 1923 and 1924, used a traveling fellowship to study with Edmund Husserl for two years, returned later for over another year, and received his doctorate with *The Philosophy of Edmund Husserl* in 1933. After temporary positions in New York, Cairns taught psychology as well as philosophy at Rockford College from 1938 to 1950. During World War II, he won a Bronze Star as a prisoner of war interrogator in the Air Corps. He was invited to the New School for Social Research in 1954 by Alfred Schutz, taught there with Aron Gurwitsch during the 1960s, retired in 1969, and died on January 4, 1973. All who heard him considered him a brilliant teacher, but he published little. However, his translations of Husserl's *Cartesian Meditations* (1960) and *Formal and Transcendental Logic* (1969) played an important role. His *Conversations with Husserl and Fink* (1976), *Guide for Translating Husserl* (1973), and a dozen essays from his Nachlass have appeared posthumously. The editing of the manuscripts of his New School lecture courses began in 2003.

SOME RESULTS OF CAIRNS'S INVESTIGATIONS

Cairns's original project was to bring Husserl's earlier work up to the level of *Cartesianische Meditationen* (1931), but from attempting to repeat the investigations, he came to propose at least seven major revisions.

(1) Like many in modern philosophy, Husserl pursued a first philosophy that seeks grounds in consciousness for everything else. Hence, the positive sciences are grounded in a primal science called transcendental phenomenology. This first philosophy is transcendental because it refrains from accepting the intramundane status of consciousness in order to avoid trying to ground the world in part of itself. Cairns always accepted the transcendental *epochē* and agreed with his master that it was Husserl's chief contribution.

Husserl's publications emphasize the theory of science (*Wissenschaftstheorie*), especially the theory of logic, although there are remarks about valuation and action. Cairns revised Husserl so that the goal of phenomenological philosophy became not merely knowledge, but the integration of critically justified willing, valuing, and believing.

(2) There is a considerable shift in emphasis when Cairns follows his revision of Husserl's goal by affording value theory and theoretical ethics as much attention as epistemology within his presentation phenomenological first philosophy.

(3) Although many stop after defining intentionality (which Cairns came to call "intentiveness") as directedness toward objects, Cairns followed Husserl in using the concept of synthesis to make this insight fruitful—for example, a synthesis of intentive processes constituting an object as self-identical and different from other objects.

Although Husserl saw intentiveness more clearly than anybody previously, Cairns believed that Husserl still tended to reify the noema (i.e., the thing-as-intended-to in an intentive process), which is easy to do if one conceives of intentionality as a relation, whereas intentiveness is actually a property.

(4) Husserl held that there were sensuous hyletic data immanent in the stream of consciousness. These moments are themselves not intentive and no distinction was needed between sensing and sensa for Husserl, but for Cairns that distinction must be carefully maintained and sensa are transcendent of consciousness.

(5) Cairns held that Husserl left much to be done on the emotions and advanced the account by showing above all how emotion can be critically justified by the evidencing of objects valued in it. By contrast, rationality for most philosophers is wholly a matter of propositions conforming to the norms of logic.

(6) Cairns went beyond Husserl in developing the idea of ethics as a theory of critically justified willing (i.e., a theory of practical reason).

(7) Cairns's most radical revision of Husserl concerns the theory of the other. He objected to the reduction of the sphere of ownness introduced in the latter's Fifth Cartesian Meditation because the procedure described as a suspending acceptance of a noema without a suspending acceptance of the noesis is impossible to perform. Instead, Cairns asserted that a series of noetico-noematic strata of transcendental consciousness must be reflectively suspended through "unbuilding" (*Abbau*). Fields of sensa are ultimately reached. Through "building up" (*Aufbau*), one allows founded strata to be motivated once again, and thereby can reflectively observe how the intersubjective world is constituted.

A fundamental distinction for most European and North American philosophers holds between inanimate physical nature and the stratum of animate nature. A course in Indian philosophy with James Houghton Woods at Harvard in 1923 prepared Cairns to recognize that when the sense "animate body" is transferred from one's own body it transfers not to some but to all sensuous objects—rocks, trees, and sky included—and that animism follows. In class, Professor Cairns would say that chairs were rather stupid animals who stood in one place unless moved by somebody else. The distinction between inanimate and animate is then secondary, and may be recast as a distinction between animals with evident organs of sensation and locomotion and those without them. And phenomenology is clearly not merely about human consciousness.

In an era when practically all soi-disant phenomenologists devote themselves entirely to the interpretation of texts, Dorion Cairns is among the few who made a strict distinction between what may be called scholarship, which includes translation as well as interpretation of texts, and what may be called investigation, which is concerned not with texts, but with the "things themselves" in the signification whereby anything is a "thing." Like Husserl, Cairns regularly offered methodological reflections: he not only described the things reflectively observed, but also described how he had been able to analyze them, emphasizing reflection, analysis, "seeing," and description.

Furthermore, Cairns often began by describing the *psychological* phenomenological epochē and reduction—a methodological step whereby consciousness remains intramundane but is abstracted from other mundane things—before contrasting it with the specifically *transcendental philosophical* epochē and reduction that refrains from accepting the intramundaneity of consciousness and makes the grounding of the world and all sciences of it possible. Although investigation, methodology included, predominates overwhelmingly in the writings of Husserl, it may be hoped that the posthumous publications of his arguably closest critical continuer will also help phenomenologists remember what phenomenology is.

See also Consciousness; Consciousness in Phenomenology; Husserl, Edmund; Phenomenology.

Bibliography

WORKS BY CAIRNS

"An Approach to Phenomenology." In *Essays in Memory of Edmund Husserl*, edited by Marvin Farber, 3–18. Cambridge, MA: Harvard University Press, 1940.

"The Ideality of Verbal Expressions." *Philosophy and Phenomenological Research* 1 (1941): 453–462.

"Phenomenology." In *A History of Philosophical Systems*, edited by Vergilius Ferm, 353–364. New York: Philosophical Library, 1950.

"The Many Senses and Denotations of the Word *Bewusstsein* ('Consciousness') in Edmund Husserl's Writings." In *Life-World and Consciousness: Essays for Aron Gurwitsch*, edited by Lester E. Embree, 19–31. Evanston, IL: Northwestern University Press, 1972.

Guide for Translating Husserl. The Hague: Martinus Nijhoff, 1973.

"My Own Life," edited by Lester Embree. In *Phenomenology: Continuation and Criticism: Essays in Memory of Dorion Cairns*, edited by Frederick I. Kersten and Richard M. Zaner. The Hague: Martinus Nijhoff, 1973.

"Perceiving, Remembering, Image-Awareness, Feigning Awareness." In *Phenomenology: Continuation and Criticism. Essays in Memory of Dorion Cairns*, edited by Frederick I. Kersten and Richard M. Zaner, 251–262. The Hague: Martinus Nijhoff, 1973.

Conversations with Husserl and Fink, edited by Husserl-Archives. The Hague: Martinus Nijhoff, 1976.

"Philosophy as Striving toward Universal *sophia* in the Integral Sense," edited by Lester Embree. In *Essays in Memory of Aron Gurwitsch*, edited by Lester Embree, 27–43. Washington, DC: Center for Advanced Research in Phenomenology and University Press of America, 1984.

"Reason and Emotion," edited by Lester Embree, Fred Kersten, and Richard M. Zaner. *Husserl Studies* 17 (2000): 21–33.

"Theory of Intentionality in Husserl," edited by Lester Embree, Fred Kersten, and Richard M. Zaner. *Journal of the British Society for Phenomenology* 22 (2) (2001): 116–124.

"The First Motivation of Transcendental Epoch&emacron;," edited by Lester Embree, Fred Kersten, and Richard M. Zaner. In *One Hundred Years of Phenomenology*, edited by Dan Zahavi and Frederik Stjernfelt, 219–231. Dordrecht, Netherlands: Kluwer, 2002.

WORKS ABOUT CAIRNS

Embree, Lester. "Dorion Cairns: The Last Lecture Course on Ethics." In *Phenomenological Approaches to Moral Philosophy*, edited by John J. Drummond and Lester Embree, 139–160. Dordrecht: Kluwer, 2002.

Kersten, Fred. *Phenomenological Method: Theory and Practice*. Dordrecht, Netherlands: Kluwer, 1989.

Lester Embree (2005)

CAJETAN, CARDINAL

(1469–1534)

Cajetan (Tommaso de Vio), the most influential Renaissance Thomist, studied and taught in Italy, early distinguishing himself in teaching, commentaries, and debates as a philosopher and theologian. Rising to the leadership of the Dominican Order and becoming prominent in ecclesiastical politics, he was made cardinal in 1517. In 1518–1519 he disputed with Martin Luther.

Cajetan's works number more than a hundred titles. His later writing was primarily devoted to biblical exegesis; his primary contributions to Thomistic philosophy and theology are due to his earlier commentaries and treatises, most notably his commentary on St. Thomas Aquinas's *De Ente et Essentia* (On being and essence, 1495), his treatise *De Nominum Analogia* (On the analogy of names, 1498), and his formidable commentary on Aquinas's *Summa Theologiae* (1507–1522), which is printed with the pontifical (Leonine) edition of Aquinas's work. Other significant philosophical works include commentaries on Porphyry's *Isagoge* and on Aristotle's *Categories*, *Posterior Analytics*, *De Anima*, *Physics*, and *Metaphysics* (these last two have never been published), and a treatise on economics.

The *De Ente et Essentia* commentary is a sophisticated defense of Aquinas's metaphysics, loosely organized in question format, clarifying (inter alia) the Thomistic theses that being is the first object of cognition, that matter is the principle of individuation, and that essence and existence are really distinct in creatures. Sensitively attending to language, the work, with the *Categories* commentary, is also an important source for Cajetan's realist semantics.

De Nominum Analogia teaches a threefold classification and hierarchy of analogical signification. *Analogy of inequality* only counts as analogy from the metaphysician's perspective; logically, it is a form of univocation (as *body* is predicated equally of, though realized differently in, plant and stone). *Analogy of attribution* is Aristotle's *pros hen* equivocation; a term naming primarily one thing is extended to others by virtue of their relation to the first, as *healthy* denominates animal (intrinsically, as *subject* of health) and medicine (extrinsically, as *cause* of the animal's health). *Analogy of proportionality* is based not on a relation, but on a similarity of relations (as the body's ocular vision is proportional to the soul's intellectual vision). When proper and not merely metaphorical, denomination here is always intrinsic. Cajetan regards this as the most genuine form, a true mean between univocation and equivocation, and the majority of his treatise explores the implications (for abstraction, judgment, and reasoning) of proportionally similar concepts.

Cajetan's writings are shaped by the polemical context of Renaissance Thomism. Concerned to address the objections of humanists (such as Count Giovanni Pico Della Mirandola, whom he debated in 1495), Italian Averroists, and especially Scotists (foremost Anthony Trombetta, his contemporary at Padua and primary dialectical target of the *De Ente* commentary), Cajetan does not simply repeat formulas from Aquinas, he rearticulates Thomistic ideas in sometimes novel terminology. Despite this, and notwithstanding apparent departures from Aquinas on particular points (e.g., whether the soul's immortality is demonstrable), Cajetan was long regarded as a definitively authoritative expositor of Aquinas. When the twentieth-century Thomistic revival, distinguishing the historical Aquinas from longstanding scholastic traditions, emphasized differences between Cajetan and Aquinas, Étienne Gilson and others criticized Cajetan, especially on the topics of abstraction and existence. On analogy some scholars challenged whether the elements of Cajetan's comprehensive, systematic theory—especially the discussion of extrinsic versus intrinsic denomination, the preference for proportionality, and the threefold classification itself—are warranted from Aquinas's rather more dispersed and occasional reflections on the subject. Whether Cajetan's distinct philosophical vocabulary is a departure from the mind of his master, or a legitimate development of authentic Thomism in light of the innovations of the intervening centuries, remains a question, but the forcefulness of his mind has never been doubted.

See also Aristotle; Humanism; Thomas Aquinas, St.; Thomism.

Bibliography

WORKS BY CAJETAN

The Analogy of Names, and the Concept of Being. Translated by Edward A. Bushinski and Henry J. Koren. Pittsburgh, PA: Duquesne University Press, 1953.

Commentary on Being and Essence. Translated by Lottie H. Kendzierski and Francis C. Wade. Milwaukee, WI: Marquette University Press, 1964.

WORKS ABOUT CAJETAN

Reilly, John P. *Cajetan's Notion of Existence.* The Hague: Mouton, 1971.

Riva, Franco. *Analogia e univocità in Tommaso de Vio "Gaetano."* Milan, Italy: Vita e Pensiero, 1995.

Joshua P. Hochschild (2005)

CALDERONI, MARIO

(1879–1914)

Mario Calderoni ranks next to his teacher Giovanni Vailati as an Italian "Peircean pragmatist." He was graduated in law from the University of Pisa in 1901, and later lectured on the theory of values at the universities of Bologna and Florence.

Calderoni engaged in analyses of human behavior. These began with the interpretation of voluntary acts, which he regarded as the only nonmetaphysical problem of free will. In everyday life we all possess as good a criterion as is necessary to distinguish between voluntary and involuntary acts. To find out whether an act is to be called voluntary or not, we must modify the circumstances in which it usually occurs. If it still occurs in any case, we call it "involuntary"; if not, we call it "voluntary." The difference rests on the "plasticity" of voluntary acts, on their liability to modification by certain influences. A voluntary act "is liable not to be performed if the actor … is given some new information on its consequences." What determines his acting is some expectation, which we can modify "either by changing one of the actor's beliefs by means of persuasion or reasoning, or, so to say artificially, by adding to the consequences the act would bring about if it were performed" (*Scritti*, vol. 2, pp. 25–26.). This criterion would hold good even if it were proved that all our acts are subject to the principle of causality. In Calderoni's hands, it became an empirical, perfectible tool applied to the analysis of moral and legal responsibility.

In *Disarmonie economiche e disarmonie morali* (Florence, 1906) Calderoni viewed moral life as a "wide market where some men … make determinate demands on other men who oppose such demands with more or less resistance and claim in their turn … some sort of reward." Moral acts are judged not according to their total value, but according to their marginal or comparative value. We tend to confer the highest moral value not on common acts but on acts so rare that we would be obliged to repress them if their normal production increased. The moral value of actions is therefore related to their supply.

See also Peirce, Charles Sanders; Vailati, Giovanni; Value and Valuation.

Bibliography

ADDITIONAL WORKS BY CALDERONI

I postulati della scienza positiva ed il diritto penale (The postulates of positive science and penal law). Florence, 1901. His doctoral dissertation, containing his main ideas in brief.

Scritti. Edited by Odoardo Campa. 2 vols. Florence: Società anon. editrice "La voce," 1924. Preface by Giovanni Papini.

For joint papers by Calderoni and Giovanni Vailati, see the entry on Vailati.

WORKS ON CALDERONI

Bozzi, Paolo. "Il pragmatismo italiano: Mario Calderoni." *Rivista critica di storia della filosofia* 12 (3) (1957): 293–322.

Renauld, J.-F. "L'oeuvre inachevée de Mario Calderoni." *Revue de Métaphysique et de Morale* 23 (1918): 207–231.

Santucci, Antonio. *Il pragmatismo in Italia.* Bologna: Il Mulino, 1963. Ch. 5, 216–262.

Ferruccio Rossi-Landi (1967)

CALVIN, JOHN

(1509–1564)

John Calvin, the Protestant reformer and theologian, was born at Noyon, France. The son of middle-class parents of considerable local importance, Calvin was early directed toward an ecclesiastical career. From 1523 to 1528 he studied theology in Paris, there becoming acquainted with both the scholastic and humanist trends of his day. When he had achieved the master of arts degree, Calvin, in response to his father's wishes, left Paris to study law at Orléans, finishing his doctorate there by early 1532.

By 1534 Calvin had decisively broken with his Catholic heritage and had joined the Protestant reform movement in France. From this time on, all his efforts were devoted to the cause of the Reformation, and most of the remainder of his life was spent preaching, teaching, and writing in Geneva. He carried on a voluminous correspondence with thinkers and reformers all over Europe, and he had a powerful voice in the political and educational, as well as the ecclesiastical, institutions of Geneva.

Calvin's major work was the *Institutes of the Christian Religion,* first published in 1536 and originally addressed to King Francis I of France in defense of the French Protestants. It was extensively revised several times, and the last edition, published in 1559, provides a systematic presentation of virtually all the lines of thought found in Calvin's other mature works.

KNOWLEDGE OF GOD AND SELF

"Nearly all the wisdom we possess," wrote Calvin in the opening of the *Institutes,* "consists of two parts: the knowledge of God and of ourselves." The overarching question in the *Institutes* is how we acquire this twofold knowledge, and the answers to this question have proved to be the most influential part of Calvin's thought.

Thomas Aquinas had taught that the theologian should start with God and then consider creatures insofar as they relate to God as their beginning and end. Calvin broke decisively with this approach in claiming that knowledge of God is so interrelated with knowledge of ourselves that the one cannot be had without the other. He taught that when we accurately reflect on ourselves, we realize the excellence of our natural gifts; but we also realize that our exercise of these gifts yields "miserable ruin" and unhappiness, and that "our very being is nothing but subsistence in the one God." Without this realization of our misery and dependence—especially of our misery—none of us comes, or even tries to come, to a knowledge of God. On the other hand, there is also no knowledge of self without a knowledge of God. Without a standard by which to measure ourselves, we invariably yield to pride, overestimating the worth of our natural gifts and overlooking the corruption that has resulted from the exercise of those gifts. Calvin readily allowed that "the philosophers," without knowing God, can give us much accurate and worthwhile information concerning man's faculties and constitution (I, XV). Philosophy, however, cannot yield a true estimate of our worth and condition.

In any discussion of Calvin's views on how we can come to know ourselves and God, it is very important to understand what he meant by knowing God, for his views on this point are both original and subtle. The Scholastics tended to equate knowing God with knowing truths about God. Calvin invariably regarded this as inadequate. He did not deny, indeed he insisted, that knowing God presupposes knowing *about* God. But in addition to this he always maintained that an essential aspect of our knowledge of God is our acknowledgment of his attitude toward us, especially his attitude of benevolence and love. Again, Calvin never equated acknowledging God's benevolence toward us with believing *that* God is benevolent toward us. Rather, acknowledging God's benevolence presupposes worshiping and obeying him. Thus, as Calvin uses the concept "knowing God," there is no knowledge of God apart from worship of, and obedience to, him. For this reason E. A. Dowey (1952) said that Calvin conceived of knowledge of God as existential. It may be added that Calvin held, as did many of the Scholastics, that what can be known about God is never his nature (*quid est*), but only what he is like (*qualis est*); and more specifically, what he is like toward us.

How is knowledge of God to be achieved? Calvin always held that knowledge of God can, in principle, be achieved by nourishing one's subjective awareness of deity and its will, with reflection on the structure of the objective world.

"There is," he said, "within the human mind, and indeed by natural instinct, an awareness of divinity [*sensus divinitatis*]" (I, iii, 1). Although this concept of a sense of divinity played a significant role in Calvin's thought, he spent little time elucidating it. Apparently he thought of it as yielding a rudimentary conviction of dependence on some Maker, as well as a numinous awareness of the glory and majesty of the Creator. In support of his conviction that this sense is universal in humankind, Calvin frequently quoted Cicero. It is this universally innate sense of divinity in humankind that, according to Calvin, accounts for the universality of religion in human society. It is a seed of religion (*semen religionis*). Religion is intrinsic to human life; it was not "invented by the subtlety and craft of a few to hold the simple folk in thrall" (I, iii, 2).

In Calvin's thought, conscience (*conscientia*), as a subjective mode of revelation, was closely related to the sense of divinity. Conscience too, he said, is part of the native endowment of all men, written "upon the hearts of all." Typically he spoke of it as a sort of knowledge whose object is God's will; or, equivalently, the difference between good and evil, the law of God, or the law of nature. Thus it is by virtue of conscience that man is aware of his responsibility—aware of the moral demands to which he is subject with respect to God and man. Calvin did not state with any exactitude the actual principles that all men know by virtue of conscience. He did say, however, that "that inward law … written, even engraved, upon the hearts of all, in a sense asserts the very same things that are to be learned from the [Decalogue]" (II, viii, 1); and he said that what the Decalogue requires is perfect love of God and of our neighbor.

The subjective awareness of divinity and of its will can be supplemented, Calvin taught, by reflecting on the structure of the external world and the pattern of history. "[God has] not only sowed in men's minds that seed of religion of which we have spoken but revealed himself and daily discloses himself in the whole workmanship of the universe. As a consequence, men cannot open their eyes without being compelled to see him" (I, v, l). At various times Calvin called the universe at large a book, a mirror, and a theater for the display of God's attributes—preeminently for the display of his goodness to us but also of his glory, wisdom, power, and justice. In the course of expounding his view that God can be known through his works, Calvin explicitly opposed the view that God can be known by speculation concerning his essence. It is by nourishing his sense of divinity and his conscience, with the contemplation of God's works, that man can in principle arrive at a knowledge of God.

SIN. It was Calvin's persistent teaching, however, that in fact no one does come to know God in the manner described above. The positive demands placed on all men by God's internal and external revelation are rejected, and this rejection results in an endless series of spurious religions. This resistance to God's demands is what Calvin identified as sin. Thus sin is not primarily ignorance about God; although such ignorance, or blindness, as Calvin often called it, will always be a consequence. Rather, Calvin viewed sin as an active willful opposition to God, as a positive refusal to acknowledge his demands of worship and obedience and as a deliberate alienation from him. Its prime characteristic is perversity, and its root is ordinarily pride and self-love.

Thus, being in sin is just the opposite of knowing God. Calvin, however, was quite willing to allow that a person who does not know God because he refuses to worship and obey him can still know or believe a variety of propositions about God that happen to be true. This explains what has, to so many readers, proved to be such an infuriating feature of Calvin's thought—his insistence, sometimes in adjacent sentences, that the pagans do not at all know God but are not wholly ignorant of him. For example, Calvin, speaking of man's natural ability to know God, said, "the greatest geniuses are blinder than moles." In the very next sentence he said, "Certainly I do not deny that one can read competent and apt statements about God here and there in the philosophers" (II, ii, 18).

Not only was Calvin insistent that knowing or believing "competent and apt" propositions about God was not sufficient for knowing God; he was also profoundly convinced that man's proud refusal to worship and obey God leads him to resist acknowledging the truth about God. Sin, although primarily a matter of the will, infects man's reason as well. Perversity leads to blindness and distortion. Immediately after saying that the philosophers make competent and apt statements about God, Calvin added, "but these always show a certain giddy imagination… . They [the philosophers] saw things in such a way that their seeing did not direct them to the truth, much less enable them to attain it." Thus the consequence of man's willful alienation from God is not merely that he does not know God but also that his views about God are now so incomplete and distorted that nothing at all can be built on them. This is Calvin's judgment on natural theology.

It must be added that Calvin regarded the effects of sin as far more pervasive than have yet been indicated. Not only does sin disrupt man's relation to God; it thereby spreads corruption throughout the whole of human life. Of course, it does not impair our natural faculties as such. Calvin typically spoke of reason and will as man's chief faculties, and he held that the man in sin may be as intelligent and as capable of making decisions as the man who knows God. The corruption is to be found, rather, in the *use* we make of our native capacities.

Calvin maintained that if we are to state accurately what sin does to man's use of his native talents, we must distinguish between man's supernatural gifts, his abilities concerning heavenly things, and his natural gifts, his abilities concerning earthly things (II, ii, 12–13). The supernatural gifts comprise man's ability to know God, to worship him properly, and to obey him inwardly as well as outwardly. We have, however, been stripped of these gifts. The natural gifts pertain to matters of the present life, such as government, household management, all mechanical skills, and the liberal arts. Concerning these, said Calvin, our abilities have certainly not been destroyed. Not only are ancient law, medicine, and natural philosophy worthy of the highest admiration (II, ii, 15); but man, even in his estrangement from God, retains some sense of the laws that must be obeyed if human society is to be preserved. Man "tends through natural instinct to foster and preserve society. Consequently, we observe that there exist in all men's minds universal impressions of a certain civic fair dealing and order… . And this is ample proof that in the arrangement of this life no man is without the light of reason" (II, ii, 13). Calvin immediately added, however, that although man's abilities concerning earthly things have not been destroyed, they have been profoundly corrupted. In opposition to what he understood as the teaching of the Greek philosophers, he held that both reason and will have been gravely wounded; the mind "is both weak and plunged into deep darkness. And depravity of the will is all too well known" (II, ii, 12).

If man's natural gifts are to be healed and his supernatural gifts restored, his sin must be overcome; he must come to know God. We have already seen that for this purpose man's conscience, his sense of divinity, and his awareness of God's revelation in the objective world are all inadequate. Thus, if human life was to be renewed, it was necessary that God should choose some special means. This he did by revealing himself with special clarity in the history of the Jewish people, culminating in the life and words of Christ. When God leads man to respond to this revelation with faith, then man again knows God. Indeed, faith, consisting as it does in a clear knowledge about God coupled with proper worship and true obedience, is a certain sort of knowledge of God—that sort which focuses on Christ as interpreted in the Scriptures. Thus, in Calvin's thought there is never a contrast between faith in God and knowledge of God; rather, given man's prior perversity, faith is the only kind of knowledge of God available to men. Also, faith, in Calvin's teaching, is never understood in scholastic fashion as an assent to divinely revealed propositions. Rather, the object of faith is God as revealed in Christ.

SOCIAL AND POLITICAL TEACHINGS

Calvin's social and political theory has also proved most influential. Man, according to Calvin, is a creature of fellowship, created with tendencies that find their fulfillment in a variety of natural groupings, each concerned with a certain facet of man's life in society. One of these groupings is the church, another the state. Church and state are differentiated primarily by reference to their different tasks. The concern of the church is the spiritual realm, the life of the inner man; the concern of the state is the temporal realm, the regulation of external conduct. In regulating external conduct, the general aim of the state, in Calvin's view, is to insure justice or equity in society at large. This equity has two facets. Obviously the state must enforce restrictive justice, but Calvin also believed that the state should secure distributive justice, doing its best to eliminate gross inequalities in the material status of its members.

It is the duty of the church to seek the welfare of the state, but equally it is the duty of the state to seek the welfare of the church. Thus, part of the state's duty is to promote piety; and Calvin, along with most of his contemporaries, regarded blasphemy as a civil crime. It was Calvin's view, however, that church and state ought to be structurally independent of each other. Church officials are not, by virtue of their office, to have any official voice in the state; and state officials are not, by virtue of their office, to have any official voice in the church.

Although he thought that the best form of government would vary with circumstances, Calvin quite firmly believed that the ideal government would be a republic in which those of the aristocracy who are competent to rule are elected by the citizenry, and in which power is balanced and diffused among a number of different magistrates. The magistrate has his authority from God. In a sense his authority is God's authority; for magistrates, Calvin said, are ministers of Divine justice, vicegerents of God. Thus the duty of the magistrate is to apply the law of God, implanted on the hearts of all and clarified in the Scriptures, to the affairs of civil society. To what extent and under what circumstances Calvin regarded civil disobedience as justified is a matter of debate. What is clear is that Calvin regarded the law of nature as in some sense a standard by which the decisions of the magistrate are to be judged, and at the same time he regarded revolutions which rip apart the entire fabric of human society as not to be condoned.

INFLUENCE

Both the theological and social views of Calvin have had an enormous influence throughout history. The Reformed, churches of the Continent and the Presbyterian churches of England adhered fundamentally to his thought, and the dominant theological thought of the American colonies was Calvinistic. In the eighteenth and nineteenth centuries the impact of Calvinism on society and theological thought suffered a decline, but the twentieth century saw a resurgence in Calvin's influence. In the early part of the century in the Netherlands, Abraham Kuyper led a revival of Calvinism in politics and education as well as in theology. And the so-called neoorthodox theology, represented by such figures as Karl Barth and Emil Brunner, not only was accompanied by a renewed interest in the writings of Calvin but also in large measure marked a return to the main patterns of Calvin's theological thought.

See also Barth, Karl; Brunner, Emil; Thomas Aquinas, St.

Bibliography

The standard edition of Calvin's works is that by J. W. Baum, E. Cunitz, E. Reuss, et al., in the *Corpus Reformatorum,* 59 vols. (Brunswick, Germany, 1863–1900). Most of these were translated by the Calvin Translation Society as *Works,* 48 vols. (Edinburgh: Calvin Translation Society, 1843–1855). An especially fine annotated translation is J. T. McNeill, ed., *Calvin: Institutes of the Christian Religion,* translated by F. L. Battles, 2 vols. (Philadelphia; Fortress Press, 1959). The classic study of Calvin's life is Émile Doumergue, *Jean Calvin; les hommes et les choses de son temps,* 7 vols. (Lausanne: G. Bridel, 1899–1927).

For discussions of the sources of Calvin's thought, see François Wendel, *Calvin: Sources et évolution de sa pensée religieuse* (Paris: Presses Universitaires de France, 1950), translated by Philip Mairet as *Calvin* (New York: Harper & Row, 1963); and Josef Bohatec, *Budé und Calvin* (Graz, Austria, 1940). A good discussion of Calvin's theology as a whole is Wilhelm Niesel, *Die Theologie Calvins* (Munich: C. Kaiser, 1938), translated by Harold Knight as *The Theology of Calvin* (Philadelphia: Westminster Press, 1956). The most adequate discussion of Calvin's views on the knowledge of God is E. A. Dowey, *The Knowledge of God in Calvin's Theology* (New York: Columbia University Press, 1952). Calvin's doctrine of man is treated in Thomas Forsyth Torrance, *Calvin's Doctrine of Man* (London: Lutterworth, 1949). Calvin's social and political thought is well discussed in André Biéler, *La pensée économique et sociale de Calvin* (Geneva: Librairie de l'universityé, 1959); and Josef Bohatec, *Calvins Lehre von Staat und Kirche* (Breslau: M. and H. Marcus, 1937). The finest survey of the history of Calvinism is J. T. McNeill, *The History and Character of Calvinism* (New York: Oxford University Press, 1954).

Nicholas Wolterstorff (1967)

CALVIN, JOHN [ADDENDUM]

During the past few decades much scholarly work has been done on John Calvin by theologians, historians, and others. Some of this work has recognized the ways in which Calvin, despite his rejection of Scholasticism and his ostensibly purely scriptural approach to theology, does in fact use philosophical argument in his work and does engage implicitly with philosophical issues even in his decisions not to proceed philosophically (see Helm 2004). But the context in which philosophers are most likely to have encountered Calvin's ideas since the early 1980s has been that of so-called Reformed epistemology.

This is an approach to the philosophy of religion pioneered mainly, though not exclusively, by philosophers associated with the Reformed (i.e., Calvinist) tradition. It is noteworthy for combining some of Calvin's ideas on the understanding of God with the antifoundationalism that has become more or less orthodox in the mainstream of secular epistemology since the 1950s and 1960s.

The Reformed epistemologists start with a rejection of evidentialism—the claim that one is only justified in holding a belief if one can provide a rational justification for it. Reformed epistemologists such as Alvin Plantinga and Nicholas Wolterstorff (1983) repudiate evidentialism in epistemology generally, and the epistemology of religion in particular. One cannot refute a skeptic by giving a nonquestion-begging proof of the reality (or even probability) of the external world or of other minds; but there is no rational requirement that one should do so. These beliefs are "properly basic" (Plantinga 1981); one does not form them on the basis of argument and is only rationally required to defend them if good reasons for doubt are given in some particular case. Similarly, according to the Reformed epistemologists, with belief in God.

This account has been worked out most elaborately by Plantinga (1993). He argues that what is needed to turn true belief into knowledge is warrant, an externalist notion that he explicates in terms of proper function. A belief is warranted if it is formed by the proper functioning of a subject's cognitive apparatus. The internalist notion of justification is given only a secondary role; one is justified in holding a belief if one can defend it against specific claims that it is false or unreasonable. Applying this account to religious belief, Plantinga (2000) draws heavily on Calvin's notion of the *sensus divinitatis*. People have been so created that their minds, when functioning properly, are naturally led to a belief in God. This is not through argument, any more than their belief in other minds or physical objects is formed by argument. The obvious disanalogy is that religious skepticism is a live issue in a way that other forms of skepticism are not. Here, Plantinga turns again to Calvin, to his doctrine of sin and its noetic effects. Those who disbelieve in God (or who have inadequate, confused, or half-hearted beliefs) do so because, ultimately, they are repressing or distorting the operations of the *sensus divinitatis* in themselves. (Plantinga compares this with the error theories of religion advanced by Marxists and Freudians, who argue that religious beliefs are self-deceiving evasions of reality.) This tendency to repression is universal; those who escape from it do so through the operations of divine grace. Calvin is again the main source for Plantinga's account of how the "internal instigation of the Holy Spirit" is necessary for one to be brought to belief in the specifically Christian doctrines of sin and redemption and thus to a true belief in God, which the sin-damaged *sensus divinitatis* cannot now achieve alone. Hence, Plantinga, while seeing non-Christian religions as evidence of the universality of the *sensus divinitatis*, rejects the idea that they can give their adherents a true or adequate knowledge of God.

It is striking that what is perhaps the most discussed late twentieth/early twenty-first-century development in religious epistemology is so deeply indebted to a theologian often thought of as nonphilosophical (although Plantinga's interpretation of Calvin has itself been questioned, for example, see Jeffreys [1997]). Plantinga denies that his account is Calvinist in any narrowly denominational sense, and indeed appeals to St. Thomas Aquinas as well as to Calvin. But as a Catholic commentator notes (Zagzebski 1993), the Reformed epistemologists' characteristic externalism, and their focus on the beliefs of individuals rather than of communities, are both, for better or worse, deeply rooted in the thought and sensibility of the Reformed tradition.

Bibliography

Helm, Paul. *John Calvin's Ideas.* New York: Oxford University Press, 2004.

Jeffreys, Derek. "How Reformed Is Reformed Epistemology? Alvin Plantinga and Calvin's *Sensus Divinitatis*." *Religious Studies* 33 (1997): 419–431.

Plantinga, Alvin. "Is Belief in God Properly Basic?" *Nous* 15 (1981): 41–51.

Plantinga, Alvin. *Warrant and Proper Function.* New York: Oxford University Press, 1993.

Plantinga, Alvin. *Warranted Christian Belief.* New York: Oxford University Press, 2000.

Plantinga, Alvin, and Nicholas Wolterstorff, eds. *Faith and Rationality: Reason and Belief in God.* Notre Dame, IN: University of Notre Dame Press, 1983.

Zagzebski, Linda. "Religious Knowledge and the Virtues of the Mind." In *Rational Faith: Catholic Responses to Reformed Epistemology*, edited by Linda Zagzebski. Notre Dame, IN: University of Notre Dame Press, 1993.

Anthony Rudd (2005)

CAMBRIDGE PLATONISTS

The Cambridge Platonists were a group of seventeenth-century thinkers, associated with Cambridge University, who drew on the neoplatonic tradition and contemporary philosophical developments in order to combat voluntarism, materialism, and determinism, and promote a tolerant and inclusive understanding of Christianity.

The core members of this school were active from the late 1630s through the 1680s, and were associated either with Emmanuel or Christ colleges. The central thinkers in the movement were Ralph Cudworth (1617–1688), Henry More (1614–1687), John Smith (1618–1652), and Benjamin Whichcote (1609–1683), their founding figure. Other close associates at Cambridge included Peter Sterry (1613–1672), John Worthington (1618–1680), George Rust (1626–1670), and Nathanael Culverwell (1618–1651). Beyond Cambridge, thinkers with connections to the school include John Norris (1657–1711), Joseph Glanvill (1636–1680), and Anne Conway (1631–1679). Leading latitudinarian divines, including Simon Patrick (1626–1707), John Tillotson (1630–1694), Gilbert Burnet (1643–1715), and Edward Stillingfleet (1635–1699), can also be considered disciples of the Cambridge Platonists.

Although the movement was centered in Emmanuel College, long a stronghold for Calvinistic Puritanism, it constituted a repudiation of what the Cambridge Platonists took to be a central feature of Calvinist thought, its voluntaristic understanding of morality as a creation of the divine will. Against this voluntarism, which the Cambridge Platonists perceived as offering an unacceptable account of God as arbitrary tyrant, they argued for a form of moral realism. Good and evil are "eternal and immutable"; moral distinctions are ontologically real and unchanging. Influenced by Renaissance neoplatonism (and thus interpreting Plato through the lens of Plotinus and later Christian Platonism), the Cambridge Platonists conceived of God as the Good, the form of forms. The goodness that God wills is an expression of God's own nature. Thus, while what is good is not good by virtue of being willed by God, eternal moral distinctions also do not serve as constraints on God's will.

The Cambridge Platonists declared themselves opposed to any separation of the realms of reason and faith, of the rational and the spiritual. By this they meant most fundamentally to assert that God's ways are fair, and in this sense reasonable. Rejecting the doctrine of predestination, they insisted that God's decrees are not arbitrary or unfathomable but are objectively just. The Cambridge Platonists were staunch defenders both of freedom of the will and freedom of conscience. If God is just in holding us responsible for our actions, then these actions must be up to us and freely chosen. Furthermore, faith is reasonable, and reason must be persuaded; it cannot be forced. On matters that reason cannot determine, the Cambridge Platonists advocated tolerance of a diversity of opinion. They worked for a policy of broad comprehension in the Church of England, minimizing core doctrines and emphasizing moral truths. Their theology thus resembles that of the Dutch Arminians, although arrived at independently.

Reason served for the Cambridge Platonists, as for so much of Renaissance neoplatonism, as a substantial link between the human and divine natures. Whichcote often wrote of reason as the "candle of the Lord." Discounting the impact of the Fall on human nature, the Cambridge Platonists were optimistic about the capacity of human persons to know God and eternal moral truths through reason. Human knowledge of various moral goods is a participation in God's own self-knowledge. Although there is a mystical aspect to the Cambridge Platonists' assertion that God is present within human persons through reason, they were critical of claims to private communications from God, which they condemned as "enthusiasm." Despite their emphasis on access to divine truth through reason, the Cambridge Platonists did not seek to undermine the authority of revealed truths. They did, though, tend to blur the boundaries between reason and revelation. So, for instance, they entertained the possibility that Plato's wisdom derived from Moses or other ancient Hebrews, and thus that pagan wisdom was indebted to revelation. But they also argued that pagan anticipations of revealed doctrines, including the trinity, might have derived from the powers of reason, God within.

If Puritan theology was the target against which the Cambridge Platonist movement took shape, the Platonists (particularly Cudworth and More) soon took on new foes, notably Thomas Hobbes. Like the Calvinists, Hobbes was a voluntarist, who made morality dependent on will. That for Hobbes morality was dependent on the will of the human sovereign rather than the will of God rendered his thought no less problematic in their eyes. Hobbes was also attacked for his materialism, which the Cambridge Platonists regarded as a dangerous form of atheism.

Initially, the Cambridge Platonists perceived René Descartes as a valuable ally against both materialism and the old scholastic Aristotelianism. The Cambridge Platonists were among the first English thinkers to read Descartes, and More carried on an extensive correspondence with him. Like Descartes, the Cambridge Platonists were dualists and they regarded a dualism of spirit and matter as indispensable for their defense of the spiritual realm against materialistic reduction. (More's friend and pupil Anne Conway, author of *Principles of the Most Ancient and Modern Philosophy* [1692], parted ways with the Cambridge Platonists on this point, moving in the direction of a metaphysical monism).

The Cambridge Platonists came to think, though, that Descartes carried mechanistic explanations of the natural world too far. Arguing that matter is essentially passive and incapable of accounting for complex and orderly natural phenomena, they argued for a spiritual presence mediating between God and the physical universe. More termed this a *Spirit of Nature* or *Hylarchic Principle*, whereas Cudworth spoke of *Plastic Nature*. The eagerness to demonstrate the reality of immaterial substance reinforced in More and Glanvill a belief in witchcraft and a fascination with purported spiritual phenomena. Once seen as evidence of their credulity and backwardness, this feature of their thought is now understood as a further reflection of their support for the new experimental science. The Cambridge Platonists were familiar not only with the work of Hobbes, Descartes, and Benedict Spinoza, but also with Francis Bacon, Robert Boyle, and the Royal Society.

Whichcote's sermons were published by Anthony Ashley Cooper, third Earl of Shaftesbury. John Locke, Richard Price, and Thomas Reid were also indebted to the Cambridge Platonists, particularly Cudworth. Gottfried Wilhelm von Leibniz read both Cudworth and More, and Pierre Bayle critiqued Cudworth's *Plastic Nature*. Jonathan Edwards, John Wesley, Samuel Taylor Coleridge, and Matthew Arnold all admired the Cambridge Platonists. The lasting significance of the Cambridge Platonists resides in their success in carrying forward the insights of the tradition of Christian Platonism through a creative rapprochement with the philosophical revolution underway during their time. Within the heavily empiricist cast of English philosophy, they introduced a distinctive form of idealism.

See also Cudworth, Ralph; Culverwel, Nathanael; More, Henry; Whichcote, Benjamin.

Bibliography

Beiser, Frederick C. "Cambridge Platonism." In *The Sovereignty of Reason: The Defense of Rationality in the Early English Enlightenment*. Princeton, NJ: Princeton University Press, 1996.

Hutton, Sarah. "The Cambridge Platonists." In *A Companion to Early Modern Philosophy*, edited by Steven Nadler. Oxford, U.K.: Blackwell, 2002.

Patrides, C. A., ed. *The Cambridge Platonists*. Cambridge, MA: Havard University Press, 1970.

Rogers, G. A. J., J. M. Vienne, and Y. C. Zarka, eds. *The Cambridge Platonists in Philosophical Context: Politics, Metaphysics and Religion*. Dordrecht, Netherlands: Kluwer Academic Publishers, 1997.

Jennifer A. Herdt (2005)

CAMPANELLA, TOMMASO

(1568–1639)

Tommaso Campanella, a Renaissance philosopher and scholar, was born at Stilo, in Calabria, Italy. At an early age he entered the Dominican order and devoted himself to the study of philosophy. In 1599 he was arrested by order of the Spanish government on charges of heresy and conspiracy. Although he never confessed to either charge, he was considered to be a dangerous subject and was kept in prison at Naples for twenty-seven years. Released in 1626, he was arrested again and arraigned before the Holy Office in Rome to stand trial for certain suspect propositions found in his works. After regaining his freedom, he spent some time at the Dominican monastery of Minerva in that city. In 1634, fearing further persecution, because of the suspicion that he might be involved in a new conspiracy, he followed the advice of Pope Urban VIII and fled to France, where he was befriended by Cardinal Richelieu and King Louis XIII. He died in the quiet of the Dominican monastery of Rue St. Honoré in Paris.

Campanella wrote a great number of books dealing with subjects ranging from grammar and rhetoric to philosophy and theology, from apologetics to politics, and from medicine to magic and astrology. He conceived of philosophy as an all-embracing science to which all other sciences must be referred as their ultimate source and foundation. No subsidiary science deals with all things as they are, but only as they appear, whereas philosophy, and especially metaphysics, deals with all things as they are and insofar as they are. Philosophy is an inquiry after the truth of both human and divine things, based on the testimony of God, who reveals himself either through the world of created things or by direct teaching. Consequently, nature and the Scriptures are the two codes on which philosophy must be built.

EPISTEMOLOGY

In his actual approach to philosophy, Campanella discussed first the possibility and reality of knowledge, thus anticipating a common trend among later thinkers. He was the first philosopher (antedating René Descartes) to assert the need of positing a universal doubt at the beginning of his system and to state the principle of self-consciousness as the basis of knowledge and certitude. He distinguished between innate and acquired knowledge. Innate knowledge (*notitia innata*) is cognition through self-presence and belongs to the very essence of the soul; acquired knowledge (*notitia illata*) is the soul's cognition of external things. Innate knowledge is superior to, and more certain than, acquired knowledge; for the soul cannot be mistaken about what belongs to its nature. Knowledge of the external world can be obtained either by intuition or by abstraction. By intuition one grasps a thing immediately in its concrete reality, so that nothing of the object escapes the penetrating and all-embracing act of the intellect. By abstraction, one obtains only an indistinct and confused image of a thing. This image is what Campanella called the Aristotelian universal and is the object of both sense and intellect. The Platonic universal, on the contrary, is the idea as the formal cause of a thing and can be grasped exclusively by the intellect.

As to the essence and process of knowledge, Campanella gave a twofold explanation. A first explanation is contained in his early works and developed along the general lines of Bernardino Telesio's system. It represents his empirical approach to knowledge, which he reduced mainly to sensation and explained in terms of partial assimilation of the object known. This assimilation is made by contact between the knower and the sensible species of the object known. These species are neither the intentional species of the Aristotelians nor the corporeal images of Democritus. Although they may assume as many different forms as there are sensations, they are always something material that impinges on the senses and represents to a certain extent the external object.

A second and more advanced explanation of knowledge is what may be called the metaphysical approach from the standpoint of the soul as an essentially knowing nature. Here we meet Campanella's characteristic doctrine that to know is to be (*cognoscere est esse*). In this new approach, knowledge is still called sensation and assimilation, but the assimilation is carried so far as to mean a real transformation of the knower into the object known. This doctrine that to know is "being" or "to be" must not be understood in the idealistic sense of the absolute identity of object and subject. Campanella introduced a distinction between knowledge that a person has of himself in virtue of his own nature and knowledge that a person acquires from outside himself. Campanella called this the distinction between "innate" and "illate" knowledge. Both types of knowledge are said to belong to "being": But the former refers to knowledge of the original being of the knower, and the latter refers to the knowledge of being that is inferred by reasoning and is formally distinct from the being of the knower. In the first case, knowledge *is* the *esse*; in the second case, it becomes intentionally the *esse* in the possession of the extramental reality.

METAPHYSICS

For Campanella the object of metaphysics is "being," namely, whatever exists either within or outside our mind. He denied a real distinction between essence and existence in creatures, but admitted a real distinction between essence and extrinsic existence, or that type of existence that corresponds to the particular circumstances and environment wherein an essence happens to be in the physical world. All things, whether spiritual or material, consist ultimately, although in different degrees, of power, knowledge, and love as their transcendental principles. These are called "primalities" and are found in creatures as well as in God, of whom creatures are faint imitations. Whereas God is pure and infinite being, creatures are composites of finite being and infinite nonbeing. Being and nonbeing concur in making up finite things, not as physical components but as metaphysical principles. Just as a creature is essentially and necessarily a particular and limited entity, so it also is essentially and necessarily the nonbeing of all other things and of God himself.

PSYCHOLOGY

In psychology Campanella accepted the trichotomic theory, according to which man is a composite of three substances, body, spirit, and mind or *mens*. The spirit or sensitive soul is the corporeal principle that animates the body and serves as a link between body and mind. The mind or intellective soul is created and infused by God into the body already organized by the spirit; it is a spiritual substance and the form of the whole man. With the Platonists, Campanella defended the doctrine of a world soul, and developed the theory of universal animation by endowing all things with some kind of sensation.

PHILOSOPHY OF NATURE

Campanella was greatly influenced by Telesio's *De Rerum Natura,* which he defended against the attacks of G. A. Marta (1559–1628). He conceived of space as a primary and incorporeal substance having the capacity to receive all bodies. Space is the substratum of all things. In this space God placed matter, a body that is formless and inactive but capable of being molded into many forms, just as wax is acted upon by a seal. Matter is not pure potency, as Aristotle taught, but has a reality of its own distinct from the form. This, in turn, is not a substantial principle of material beings and is only improperly called an act. In short, Campanella dismissed the Aristotelian hylomorphic theory and substituted for it Telesio's naturalistic doctrine of heat and cold as the active principles and matter as the passive principle of all material beings. He also rejected Aristotle's notion of time as measure of movement and claimed that time is not something ideal and subjective, but something real. Time is the successive duration of things having a beginning and an end. Or, more concretely, time is the thing itself considered in its successive duration through change.

ETHICS

Following Telesio, Campanella taught that man's supreme good consists in self-preservation. However, this must not be understood in a purely egoistic sense, but rather as the conservation of one's existence in God in the next life. Whereas God is his own supreme good and does not look to another being outside himself for his preservation, so that to be and to be happy are for him one and the same thing, man depends entirely on God for his own preservation. God is therefore the supreme good toward which man must direct all his acts and operations.

POLITICAL THEORY

Campanella advocated a universal monarchy with the pope as its supreme temporal and spiritual ruler. This ambitious but hardly realistic plan is described in the *Monarchia Messiae* (The Messiah's Monarchy) and represented the dream of his entire life. *Civitas Solis* (*The City of the Sun*), on the other hand, contains the scheme of a state modeled after Plato's *Republic* and Sir Thomas More's *Utopia,* where people, who live in the pure order of nature, organize themselves into an ideal society ruled by philosophers and share everything. Many of the ideas expressed in this work have some practical value, inasmuch as they contain the germs of social, political, and educational reforms that would be beneficial to the state. In this respect, Campanella may be considered as an original thinker and a forerunner of various modern theories and practices.

Bibliography

PRINCIPAL WORKS BY CAMPANELLA

Philosophia Sensibus Demonstrata, in defense of Telesio. Naples, 1591.

Monarchia Messiae. Jesi, 1633.

Atheismus Triumphatus. Paris, 1636.

Disputationum in Quatuor Partes Suae Philosophiae Reales Libri Quatuor. Paris, 1637.

Philosophiae Rationalis Partes Quinque. Paris, 1638.

Universalis Philosophiae, seu Metaphysicarum Rerum Iuxta Propria Dogmata Partes Tres, Libri 18. Paris, 1638.

Del senso delle' cose e della magia, edited by A. Bruers. Bari, 1925.

Epilogo Magno, edited by C. Ottaviano. Rome: Reale Accademia d'Italia, 1939.

Theologicorum Libri XXX, edited by R. Amerio. Florence and Rome, 1949–.

Civitas Solis. Frankfurt, 1623. Translated by W. J. Gilstrap as *The City of the Sun.* New York, 1952.

WORKS ON CAMPANELLA

Amerio, Romano. *Campanella.* Brescia: "La Scuola" Editrice, 1947.

Bonansea, Bernardine M. "Campanella as Forerunner of Descartes." *Franciscan Studies* 16 (1–2) (1956): 37–59.

Bonansea, Bernardine M. "The Concept of Being and Nonbeing in the Philosophy of Tommaso Campanella." *New Scholasticism* 31 (1) (1957): 34–67.

Bonansea, Bernardine M. "Knowledge of the Extramental World in the System of Tommaso Campanella." *Franciscan Studies* 17 (2–3) (1957): 188–212.

Bonansea, Bernardine M. "The Political Thought of Tommaso Campanella." In *Studies in Philosophy and the History of Philosophy,* edited by John K. Ryan, Vol. II, pp. 211–248. Washington, DC: Catholic University of America Press, 1963.

Bonansea, Bernardino M. *Tommaso Campanella, Renaissance Pioneer of Modern Thought.* Washington, DC: Catholic University of America Press, 1969.

Corsano, Antonio. *Tommaso Campanella.* Bari: Laterza, 1961.

Di Napoli, Giovanni. *Tommaso Campanella, filosofo della restaurazione cattolica.* Padua: CEDAM, 1947.

Headley, John M. "On the Rearming of Heaven: The Machiavellism of Tommaso Campanella." *Journal of the History of Ideas* 49 (1988): 387–404.

Headley, John M. *Tommaso Campanella and the Transformation of the World.* Princeton, NJ: Princeton University Press, 1997.

Szentpeteri, Marton. "Il Transilvano: The Image of Zsigmond Bathory in Campanella's Political Thought." *Bruniana and Campanelliana* 9 (1) (2003): 217–225.

Bernardine M. Bonansea, O.F.M. (1967)
Bibliography updated by Tamra Frei (2005)

CAMPBELL, NORMAN ROBERT

(1880–1949)

Norman Robert Campbell, the English physicist and philosopher of science, was educated at Eton. From Eton he went as a scholar to Trinity College, Cambridge, and became a fellow there in 1904. From 1903 to 1910 he also worked as a research assistant at the Cavendish Laboratory, whose director, the celebrated J. J. Thomson, became the most important inspiration of his scientific work. In 1913 he became an honorary fellow for research in physics at Leeds University, but he left this post after the war and from 1919 to 1944 was a member of the research staff of the General Electric Company.

The writers who seem to have influenced him most are Ernst Mach and Henri Poincaré, apart from classical authors such as William Whewell, John Stuart Mill, and W. S. Jevons. On the other hand, such philosophers as Bertrand Russell and Alfred North Whitehead came too late to have much effect on him; the main outlines of his thought developed during the first decade of the century, and there are only occasional references to their writings.

Campbell exhibited the very rare combination of competence in both physics and philosophy, but while he preferred to think of himself primarily as an experimental physicist, it is as a philosopher of science that he made his mark. This point is brought out in the writings of F. P. Ramsey, R. B. Braithwaite, and Ernest Nagel, although these concentrate largely on the formal parts of Campbell's doctrines and pay scant attention to the more valuable contributions that he made to certain methodological ideas, particularly that of analogy. These philosophical views, shaped by Campbell's actual experiences and ideas as a physicist and expositor of physical theories, were meant to be construed as answers to intellectual pressures and problems that confronted him in the years that saw the rise of the twentieth-century atomic theory on the one hand and relativity and quantum mechanics on the other. In philosophy of science, his most important contributions were in the fields of the logic of theory construction and (to a lesser extent) the principles of physical measurement.

PHILOSOPHY OF THEORY CONSTRUCTION

Campbell's views were stated in systematic form for the first time in a popular book, *The Principles of Electricity.* Thereafter they were developed, with minor changes of emphasis and greater attention to the nature of "mathematical theories," in *Physics: The Elements.* In contrast with the usual textbook approach, his views were deeply interwoven with, and at times even explicitly discussed in, his more formal scientific treatises.

CONCEPTS AND IDEAS. Campbell distinguishes sharply between the laws and theories of a science. In the case of laws, the constituent terms (Campbell calls them concepts) designate entities whose magnitudes may be determined more or less directly by instrumental means; they are not unlike what later came to be called operational concepts. The explanatory part of theories, the hypotheses, involve terms that Campbell calls ideas. These lack the instrumental relations of concepts, for a variety of reasons that Campbell does not always clearly distinguish.

Sometimes the ideas refer to the unobservable infrastructure of a physical system, as in the case of the atoms and electrons of modern electrical theory or, more properly (as Campbell points out), to their adjectival aspects, such as their mass, velocity, and momentum. At other times, the ideas pertain to such interstructural devices as Michael Faraday's lines of force, or the carriers of the transfer of electrical and optical phenomena, such as light waves, light corpuscles (photons) or even the "aether," considered the substantival carrier of electromagnetic energy. (Infrastructural entities are unobservable in a sense different from interstructural ones, but the question is controversial.) A third case in which theories are said to involve unobservables is that of geological and evolutionary theories. And there is yet another case, for Campbell denominates certain notions "ideas" because they involve an amount of idealization and abstraction to which no physical entities could correspond. The most frequent and important cases are those ideas which involve infinitesimals, such as the differential coefficients in James Clerk Maxwell's equations or François Marie Charles Fourier's theory of heat.

It follows from the nature of ideas that the hypotheses in which they occur are not directly testable. Their function consists merely in systematically relating a set of corresponding laws, and, through extensions of the theory, in foreshadowing further laws and experiments. This foreshadowing is sometimes negative, for when the ideas are too narrowly framed, they demand not only extension but also the formulation of additional concepts and theories.

"DICTIONARY" OF A THEORY. Since the ideas of the hypotheses lack operational meaning, and since their deductive development can, in the first place, yield only statement forms containing either ideas or combinations of them, it is necessary to add certain rules (a kind of "dictionary") that will coordinate the ideas with those operational concepts which occur in the laws to be explained. Of course, not all ideas need dictionary entries. In the beta-ray theory, for instance, the velocity, *v*, of the hypothetical electrons *means* "the quantity that is defined by the relation $F = e[X+(v \cdot H)]$." This expression, however, is a hypothesis in Campbell's sense because v never occurs either alone or in combination in the testable derivations at all.

"MATHEMATICAL" THEORIES. All this provided Campbell with a means of distinguishing so-called mathematical theories from nonmathematical ones. In the former, each and every idea is separately coordinated with a corresponding concept by means of a dictionary entry. It follows that whether a theory is of the mathematical type depends partly on historical accidents: Maxwell's theory *became* a mathematical theory only *after* Heinrich Rudolf Hertz's experiment had demonstrated the existence of the displacement current.

Nonetheless, ideas so far have no meaning apart from their use in hypotheses and their coordination with concepts. In the mathematical cases this is often forgotten, but in the nonmathematical cases this fact is more difficult to overlook. Because of the lack of independent significance of ideas, Campbell held that a theory is not a real explanation unless certain additional requirements are satisfied. One of his reasons for this view was that it is always possible to construct an indefinite number of hypotheses that would account for a set of laws. In the case of mathematical theories, the additional element of consolidation that Campbell suggests is the regulative feature of simplicity and aesthetic elegance—for instance, through symmetrical arrangements of the parts of a theory. (Thus, it was the introduction of Maxwell's displacement current into the original equations of André Marie Ampère and Faraday that produced a symmetrical set of equations regarding the relations between the electrical and magnetic phenomena for the case of open circuits.) Furthermore, the hypotheses are not entirely arbitrary because their ideas mirror the corresponding concepts of the laws. There is, according to Campbell, a sort of analogy between ideas and concepts (*Physics: The Elements*, p. 141).

ANALOGY. Analogy plays a more central role in the case of the nonmathematical theories. As we have seen, their ideas frequently cannot be clarified at all by the concepts that occur in the laws. According to Campbell, it is an analogy of the hypotheses and their ideas with corresponding laws and concepts of some testable field of science that imparts the missing element of significance and logical strength to the theory. It follows that analogies are not merely aids to the establishment of theories; "they are an utterly essential part of theories, without which theories would be completely valueless and unworthy of the name" (ibid., p. 129).

Campbell's point is that "a theory is not a law" (ibid., p. 130); that hypotheses are, from the nature of the case, never directly testable; and, hence, that their addition to the corpus of scientific knowledge would make no difference to science at all if it were not for some additional features that make the hypotheses significant. He dismisses the fact that they supply a systematic relation between the laws of the theory on the grounds that an infinity of such hypotheses can be constructed.

Campbell's positive grounds for the necessity of analogies are of various kinds. The fundamental reason is that since hypotheses are not directly testable but are only instruments for deductive development, possessing a purely formal content, they lack the sort of meaning required for genuine explanatory power: Only analogy can supply this. Another ground of a more heuristic nature is that analogies aid in the extension of theories, especially when a new field is grafted onto the dictionary of an existing theory (as when optical conceptions were added to Maxwell's generalization of the electrical theories of Ampère and Faraday).

As mentioned, however, analogy must be supplemented by additional criteria, which are clearly needed for dealing with mathematical theories. These criteria are largely derived from Campbell's actual experience with the theories with which he had been dealing in his physical textbooks. In addition to simplicity and aesthetic elegance, there is "simplification in our physical conceptions," such as was produced by the early theories of Faraday, Thomson, and Hendrik Antoon Lorentz. Campbell insists on the importance of such regulative conceptions precisely because "scientific propositions are [not] capable of direct and irrefutable proof." An additional criterion is the "anticipative force" of a theory—for instance, the suggestiveness of Faraday's lines in the direction of the existence of electromagnetic radiation, of a motion that is displaced in time, with a given velocity, in empty space.

Finally, another regulative criterion is that of importance, or depth, of the ideas involved. This is invoked particularly in those cases where analogy is barely a relevant consideration, as in such mathematical theories as Maxwell's, or Albert Einstein's special theory of relativity.

METHODOLOGICAL CONTRIBUTIONS

Campbell's clear account of the logical structure of a theory, with its hypotheses, laws, and dictionary, offers an elegant means of formalizing the place of ideas (theoretical concepts) within theories. He emphasizes also the logical gap between hypotheses and laws even in cases where its existence had previously been practically overlooked—the mathematical theories. He uses this fact to question Mach's preference for such theories (called phenomenological by Mach), on the grounds that they employ hypotheses and hypothetical ideas just like any other theory. (Whether this does sufficient justice to the difference between the two types of theories must be left an open question.) The theoretical nature of such substantival entities as atoms and electrons seems to differ from that of lines of force on the one hand and, say, from the entropy functions on the other, in deeper ways not caught by Campbell's criteria of ideas.

The fact that the systematizing power of hypotheses is an insufficient criterion of their truth or explanatory power introduces the remaining feature of Campbell's doctrine—such regulative notions as the existence of a strong analogy, of simplicity, symmetry, anticipative force, and, finally, of importance. The most interesting of these is analogy, which in the end emerges as a metaphysical device in terms of which to formulate the special aspect of those theories that involve unobservables. The "absolute necessity" for an analogy is the result of the emasculation of the semantic power of hypotheses, coupled with the consideration that this emasculation entails the introduction of a special constraint that prevents such hypotheses from being mere arbitrary formulas.

THEORY OF MEASUREMENT

The second part of *Physics: The Elements* is a detailed discussion of the principles of physical measurement; this, like most of Campbell's ideas, was already contained in embryo in *The Principles of Electricity* (Ch. 2). His interest in measurement is not altogether removed from his main philosophical preoccupations mentioned so far. Just as he was concerned with a clear delineation of laws from theories, he was equally firm in stating the differences as well as the relations between laws and definitions. In *Measurement and Calculation* Campbell defines measurement "as the assignment of numerals to present properties in accordance with … laws." Thus, every measurable property must have a definite order; the systems to be measured must be capable of "addition," but what operation is considered "addition" must be carefully specified in a given situation; and whether the resultant quantities yield consistent measurements is a matter for lawlike experience. Campbell points out that the specification in question is usually tacitly adopted ab initio and is, indeed, often suggested by theory and the relevant analogy. Hence, he believes that "no new measurable quantity has ever been introduced into physics except as the result of the suggestion of some theory" (*The Principles of Electricity,* p. 41).

See also Ampère, André Marie; Braithwaite, Richard Bevan; Einstein, Albert; Faraday, Michael; Fourier, François Marie Charles; Hertz, Heinrich Rudolf; Jevons, William Stanley; Mach, Ernst; Maxwell, James Clerk; Mill, John Stuart; Nagel, Ernest; Poincaré, Jules Henri; Quantum Mechanics; Ramsey, Frank Plumpton; Relativity Theory; Russell, Bertrand Arthur William; Whewell, William; Whitehead, Alfred North.

Bibliography

Campbell's works include *Modern Electrical Theory* (Cambridge: Cambridge University Press, 1907; 2nd ed., 1913); *The Principles of Electricity* (London, 1912); *Physics: The Elements* (Cambridge, U.K.: Cambridge University Press, 1920), which was reprinted as *Foundations of Science* (New York: Dover, 1957); *Measurement and Calculation* (London: Longmans, Green, 1928); and *Photoelectric Cells,* written with Dorothy Ritchie (London: Pitman, 1929; 3rd ed., 1934).

As supplementary chapters of *Modern Electrical Theory,* the following monographs by Campbell were published in the Cambridge Physical Series: *Series Spectra,* Suppl. Ch. 15 (Cambridge, 1921); *Relativity,* Suppl. Ch. 16 (Cambridge, 1923); and *The Structure of the Atom,* Suppl. Ch. 17 (Cambridge, 1923).

For works with detailed references to Campbell, see Brian D. Ellis, *Basic Concepts of Measurement* (Cambridge: Cambridge University Press, 1966), Chs. 4, 5, and 8; Mary B. Hesse, *Models and Analogies in Science* (London, 1963), Ch. 1; and George Schlesinger, *Method in the Physical Sciences* (London: Routledge and Paul, 1963), Ch. 3, Sec. 5.

Gerd Buchdahl (1967)

CAMUS, ALBERT

(1913–1960)

Albert Camus, the French novelist and essayist, was born in Mondovi, Algeria, and was educated at the University of Algiers. From 1934 to 1939 he was active writing and producing plays for a theater group he had founded in Algiers. About the same time he began his career as a journalist, and in 1940 he moved to Paris. During the German occupation of France, Camus was active in the resistance movement, and after the liberation of Paris he became the editor of the previously clandestine newspaper *Combat.* His literary fame dates from the publication in 1942 of his first novel, *L'étranger* (*The Stranger*), and an essay titled *Le mythe de Sisyphe* (*The Myth of Sisyphus*). During the immediate postwar period Camus was deeply involved in political activity, and his name was for a time closely associated with that of Jean-Paul Sartre and with the existentialist movement. In 1947 he published a second major novel, *La peste* (*The Plague*), and, in 1951, *L'homme revolté* (*The Rebel*), an essay on the idea of revolt. The latter book provoked a bitter controversy between Camus and Sartre, which ended with a severance of relations between them. In 1957 Camus was awarded the Nobel Prize for literature. His last major work was *La chute* (*The Fall*), a novel that appeared in 1956. In 1960 Camus was killed in an automobile accident.

Although Camus studied philosophy for a number of years at the University of Algiers, he was not a philosopher in any technical or academic sense. Nevertheless, virtually all his literary work was deeply influenced by philosophical ideas, and in two major essays, *The Myth of Sisyphus* and *The Rebel*, he undertook a more or less systematic exposition and defense of the moral attitudes that had in each case found expression in his novels and plays. *The Myth of Sisyphus* can thus be regarded as in some sense a philosophical commentary on *The Stranger*, and *The Rebel* has clear affinities with *The Plague*. There can be no doubt that there are profound differences between the views set forth in these two essays. Camus's philosophical career was essentially a movement away from the nihilism of *The Myth of Sisyphus* toward the humanism of *The Rebel*. Ideas that had been present in his work from the beginning, in one form or another, were to retain their place there; but he progressively revised his views of their relative importance within the moral life.

Although Camus's name is often associated with contemporary European phenomenology and existentialism, there is no evidence that he was ever deeply influenced by, or very much interested in, the doctrines of Edmund Husserl or Martin Heidegger or even Sartre; and on occasion he expressed himself as having distinct reservations with respect to existentialism as a philosophy. In fact, his philosophical thought was formed on much more traditional models. His deepest interest was in those great figures in the Western philosophical tradition—among them Socrates, Blaise Pascal, Benedict de Spinoza, and Friedrich Nietzsche—whose lives and personalities were all reflected in their philosophizing. If he came, as he did, to reject the exaggerated claims that philosophers have made for human reason and subscribed to many of the criticisms that contemporary existentialists have made of the classical tradition, he continued to regard the striving of the great thinkers of the past to achieve a total conception of reality and of the human relation to the world as reflecting one of the deepest human aspirations and to view its inevitable failure as marking a crisis in man's relation to himself.

On the other hand, Camus does not appear to have had any theoretical interest in the analysis of philosophical problems. His interest in philosophy was almost exclusively moral in character; when he had come to the conclusion that none of the speculative systems of the past could provide any positive guidance for human life or any guarantee of the validity of human values, he found himself in the situation that he describes in *The Myth of Sisyphus*. This essay is ostensibly a consideration of the problem of suicide, which Camus describes as the only serious philosophical problem. The question he asks is whether it makes any sense to go on living once the meaninglessness of human life is fully understood and assimilated. Camus gives a number of somewhat different formulations of what this meaninglessness or "absurdity" comprises. At bottom, it is the failure of the world to satisfy the human demand that it provide a basis for human values—for our personal ideals and for our judgments of right and wrong.

It is very important for an understanding of Camus's point of view to see how closely he thought ordinary moral attitudes are dependent upon metaphysical belief in some kind of congruence between human values and the nature of reality. The external supports on which the validity of moral distinctions rested in the past were, of course, primarily religious in character; but Camus held, as do many others, that with the decline of religious belief in the modern period a number of secular religions—in particular, Hegelian and Marxist historicism—have attempted to tie values to reality by means of a postulated schedule of historical development that guarantees their eventual realization. In *The Myth of Sisyphus*, Camus presupposes, without very much argument, that none of these interpretations of reality as value-supporting can survive critical scrutiny; the tenability of any purposive or evaluative attitude on the part of human beings—the only moral beings—is thus called into question. It is this isolation of the human being as an evaluative and purposive being in a world that affords no support to such attitudes that Camus calls the absurdity of the human condition.

Camus maintained that suicide cannot be regarded as an adequate response to the experience of absurdity. The reason he gives is that suicide deals with absurdity simply by suppressing one of the two poles—the human being and the "world"—that together produce the tension described above. Suicide is thus an admission of incapacity, and such an admission is inconsistent with that human pride to which Camus openly appeals. Indeed, he goes so far as to say that "there is nothing equal to the spectacle of human pride." Only by going on living in the face of their own absurdity can human beings achieve their full stature. For Camus, as for Nietzsche, whose influence at this stage of Camus's thought is very marked, the conscious espousal of the metaphysical arbitrariness of human purpose and action transforms nihilism from a passive despair into a way of revolting against and transcending the world's indifference to man.

It is evident that in *The Myth of Sisyphus* Camus believed that absurdity, in the sense of recognition and acceptance of the fact that there are no metaphysically guaranteed directives for conduct, could by itself generate a positive ethic. In particular, the ideal of human fraternity was connected with Camus's heroic nihilism on the grounds that to accept oneself as the sole guarantor of one's own values would necessarily involve accepting a principle of respect for other human beings. It is here, however, that Camus encountered a very serious difficulty. He found it necessary to show by means of examples just what the specific implications for conduct of his doctrine of absurdity are and also make it plausible that these implications are consistent with the humanistic ideal to which he as an individual is clearly devoted. In *The Myth of Sisyphus*, however, the specimens that are offered of the mode of life appropriate to the "absurd" man bear only a rather remote affinity to that ideal or, for that matter, to any general social ethic. Camus did not demonstrate satisfactorily either that the kind of life that followed from an acceptance of nihilism bore any clear relation to his own moral ideals or that a life dedicated to these ideals could be adequately motivated by an acceptance of absurdity.

What is clear is that Camus, from the beginning, regarded certain responses to absurdity as morally unacceptable. In his "Letters to a German Friend" (1943–1944), he interpreted Nazism as one reaction to the very nihilistic vision of the world that he himself had come to accept. He then went on to condemn it in the severest terms for its denial of human fraternity. Even at this stage in the development of his thought, Camus insisted that an authentic revolt against the human condition had to be a revolt in the name of the solidarity of man with man.

In the character of Meursault, the "hero" of *The Stranger*, this tension between Camus's nihilistic vision and his ethical demands becomes particularly clear. Meursault is presented as a man characterized by the moral equivalent of achromatic vision. Although he is not at all given to philosophical reflection, he views the whole conventional human apparatus of moral distinctions, of justice and of guilt, as a kind of senseless rigmarole with no basis in reality. He stands, in fact, outside the whole moral world in a peculiar state that Camus describes as "innocence," apparently because in a world that affords no transcendental sanction for human judgments of right and wrong there can be no real guilt. His relationship to his mother and to his mistress are devoid of feeling, and he eventually kills an Arab for no particular reason. But at the very end of the novel, after Meursault, facing execution, has burst into a rage against a priest who tries to persuade him to accept the reality of his guilt and the possibility of redemption, there is a long semipoetic passage in which he declares his love of the world and its sensuous immediacy and speaks tenderly and almost lovingly of his fellow men and of their common fate, which he shares. As a number of critics have noted, there is nothing in the novel that prepares one for this passage. Camus, however, clearly wishes to persuade us that these two aspects of Meursault's character are not just consistent but intimately related to one another; but again he experienced difficulty in showing how a positive ethic of human fraternity can be generated by a nihilistic attitude toward all values.

There can be little doubt that in the years immediately following the publication of *The Stranger* and *The Myth of Sisyphus* Camus substantially revised his view of the moral significance of value-nihilism. Increasingly, it was the injustice and cruelty of man to man that aroused Camus to action; by comparison with the hideous but remediable evils of human society, the cosmic injustice of the human condition seems to have lost some of its obsessive hold on his mind. Like many of the existentialists, Camus still tried to present these two revolts—the revolt against the human condition and the revolt against human injustice—as essentially continuous with one another. Nevertheless, he came to feel that the relationship between these two revolts had been misconceived and that this misconception was at the heart of twentieth-century totalitarianism, to which he was as resolutely opposed in its communistic as in its Nazi version. Camus gradually came to believe that the reason for the extraordinary miscarriage of the Soviet revolution was that the revolutionary tradition had its roots in a revolt against the human condition as such, and that such a revolt can never lead to human fraternity but leads instead to a new enslavement of man by man. This radical revision of his earlier views found its full expression in Camus's second main philosophical essay, *The Rebel.*

The Rebel begins with a consideration of the problem of murder or, more exactly, with the problem of political justification for the killing of human beings. For Camus, political action is essentially violent revolt, and it thus inescapably raises the question of whether one has the right to take the life of another human being. Camus's answer is that taking a human life is inconsistent with true revolt since, as he now makes clear, that revolt involves the implicit assertion of a supraindividual value, the value of human life. It is not altogether clear how this rejection of violence is to be interpreted, but it is interesting to note the approval that Camus expresses in his play *The Just* (1950) of the Russian terrorist Kaliaev who murders the Grand Duke Serge but insists that he himself pay for his act with his life in order to affirm the moral inadmissibility of murder. In any case, the revolt that Camus still advocates in *The Rebel* is presented there as ethically inspired from its inception. He rejects, however, what he now calls "metaphysical revolt," which he sees as a radical refusal of the human condition as such, resulting either in suicide or in a demonic attempt to depose God and remake the world in the image of man. Its deepest motive is not a love for humankind but a desire to destroy the world as it is. The order it attempts to impose on the new world it constructs is informed by no ethically creative principle because, as Camus now declares, nihilism can yield no such principle. A nightmare state of power for power's sake is the ultimate fruit of metaphysical revolt.

In order to substantiate this thesis, Camus reviews the intellectual history of the past two hundred years and discusses in detail a number of poets, philosophers, and practicing revolutionaries whom he regards as the chief fomentors of metaphysical revolt. Among them are the Marquis de Sade, Max Stirner, Nietzsche, le Comte de Lautréamont, Baron de Saint-Just, and Sergei Nechaiev, to mention only a few. G. W. F. Hegel and Karl Marx are assigned a central role in the construction of a view of history and of the state that exempts man from all moral controls and that proposes as the only valid ideal man's total mastery of his own fate. The two political revolutions that Camus thinks were inspired by the ethos of metaphysical revolt are the French and the Russian, although the Nazi "revolution" represents some of the same tendencies in even purer form. Camus considers none of the modern revolutions that did not eventuate in political terrorism, and he makes no attempt to evaluate or even consider other kinds of explanation of the revolutions that he does discuss. As many critics have remarked, the apocalyptic character of the historical tableau that he presents is in good part due to a principle of selection that seems to reflect a personal predilection for extreme or crisis situations rather than any objective assessment of the real influence that the representatives of metaphysical revolt may have had on the course of events.

Camus's novel *The Plague*, which appeared four years before *The Rebel*, gives clear indications of his reevaluation of nihilism. The plague that descends on Oran symbolizes not just the Nazi occupation of France or even totalitarianism as a political system but all of the many forms that injustice and inhumanity can assume. A variety of reactions to this "plague" is presented; but it is Dr. Rieux, the organizer of the "sanitation squads" that fight the plague, who represents Camus's ideal of moral action. Rieux is not inspired by any dream of a total conquest of evil. Instead, his conception of himself is modest and limited; throughout the struggle he retains his sense of humanity and his capacity for love and for happiness. The doctor is in fact what many have said Camus aspired to be, a kind of "saint without a God."

If *The Rebel* and *The Plague* represent—as they seem to do—Camus's mature position, it would appear that this position differs from traditional nonreligious humanism mainly by virtue of the terminology of revolt that Camus retained even after he had so thoroughly moralized his conception of revolt as to make most of the normal connotations of that term inapposite. As he himself says in *The Rebel*, the true significance of nihilism is negative; it clears the ground for new construction but by itself provides no principle of action. As such it survives in Camus's view of the moral world mainly as a prophylactic against the kind of mystification, religious or metaphysical, by which a man tries to rid himself of his radical contingency and confer upon himself a cosmic status that makes it easier for him to be a human being. Camus was a pitiless critic of all such forms of shamming, and he was convinced that their general tendency was to enable their practitioners to evade the responsibility that goes with moral self-ownership and to confirm them in their inhumanity to their fellow men. Nihilism would seem, in Camus's final view, to be a kind of immunizing experience, although one with very considerable dangers of its own, by virtue of which one is enabled to grasp the ideal of human fraternity in its pure form without the entanglements of ideology and doctrine by which it has so often been disfigured. Camus's attitude toward life is thus, at bottom, simply a stubborn moral integrity and a deep sympathy with his fellow men, to which the somewhat meretricious rhetoric of revolt adds very little. At the same time, however, it must be conceded that the absence or unavailability of absolute values, whatever these might be, remains for Camus anything but trivial, and it pervades the atmosphere of the humanistic ethic that he erected in their place.

The work of Camus's last years reinforces one's impression that an essentially nonmetaphysical and strongly moralistic humanism was his final view of life. He drew away more and more from direct political action; his refusal to side unambiguously with the Algerian rebels brought him the bitter reproaches of many former associates, among them Sartre. In 1960 in *Réflexions sur la peine capitale* ("Reflections on the Guillotine"), Camus argued that society does not have the right to put its criminals to death, and one wonders in what circumstances Camus would have regarded war as morally defensible. Finally, in *The Fall*, he seems to have abandoned political and social action entirely in favor of a conception of evil that no longer situates it in unjust social institutions or in the terms on which man is permitted to exist but in the very heart of man himself. The protagonist, Clamence, is a man whose interior corruptness is concealed from the world—and for a long time from himself—by a life of philanthropy and active sympathy for his fellow men. He is, in fact, a sort of monster whose ultimate self-knowledge leads him to create a sense of guilt and unworthiness in others by advertising his own corruption. In this way he again feeds his obsessive need for superiority, which was the real motive of his earlier philanthropy. It is not justifiable to impute the unrelieved pessimism of this novel to Camus personally, or to suggest, as some have, that he had accepted the doctrine of original sin; but there can be little doubt that his treatment of the character of Clamence is indicative of a further shift in the locus of the struggle between good and evil. The shift, broadly speaking, is one that emphasizes our inner complicity with evil and our lack of the kind of innocence that Camus had always claimed for humanity. Whether this strain would have been developed further in Camus's thought if he had lived longer is a question to which there can be no answer.

See also Ethics, History of; Existentialism; Hegel, Georg Wilhelm Friedrich; Heidegger, Martin; Humanism; Husserl, Edmund; Life, Meaning and Value of; Literature, Philosophy of; Marx, Karl; Nietzsche, Friedrich; Nihilism; Pascal, Blaise; Phenomenology; Sartre, Jean-Paul; Socrates, Spinoza, Benedict (Baruch) de; Stirner, Max; Suicide.

Bibliography

WORKS BY CAMUS

L'etranger. Paris: Gallimard, 1942. Translated by S. Gilbert as *The Stranger*. New York: Knopf, 1946.

Le mythe de Sisyphe. Paris: Gallimard, 1942. Translated by J. O'Brien as *The Myth of Sisyphus*. New York: Knopf, 1955.

Lettres à un ami allemand. Paris: Gallimard, 1945. Translated by J. O'Brien as "Letters to a German Friend," in *Resistance, Rebellion and Death*. New York: Knopf, 1961.

La peste. Paris: Gallimard, 1947. Translated by S. Gilbert as *The Plague*. New York: Knopf, 1948.

Les justes. Paris: Gallimard, 1950. Translated by S. Gilbert as "The Just." In *Caligula and Three Other Plays*. New York: Knopf, 1958.

L'homme revolté. Paris: Gallimard, 1951. Translated by A. Bower as *The Rebel*. New York: Knopf, 1954.

La chute. Paris: Gallimard, 1956. Translated by J. O'Brien as *The Fall*. New York: Knopf, 1957.

Réflexions sur la peine capitale. Paris, 1960. Translated by J. O'Brien as "Reflections on the Guillotine." In *Resistance, Rebellion and Death*. New York: Knopf, 1961.

Carnets. Paris: Gallimard, 1962. Translated by P. Thody as *Notebooks 1935–42*. New York: Knopf, 1963.

BIOGRAPHIES

Lebesque, Morvan. *Portrait of Camus: An Illustrated Biography*. New York: Herder and Herder, 1971. Originally published in French, 1963.

Lottman, Herbert R. *Albert Camus: A Biography*. New York: Doubleday, 1979.

Todd, Oliver. *Albert Camus. A Life*. New York: Knopf, 1997.

CRITICAL STUDIES OF CAMUS

Brée, G. *Camus*. New Brunswick, NJ: Rutgers University Press, 1959.

Cruickshank, J. *Albert Camus and the Literature of Revolt*. London: Oxford University Press, 1959. Contains a detailed bibliography.

Knapp, Bettina L., ed. *Critical Essays on Albert Camus*. Boston: G.K. Hall, 1988.

McBride, Joseph. *Albert Camus: Philosopher and Littérateur*. New York: St. Martin's Press, 1992.

Rhein, Philip H. *Albert Camus*. Boston: Twayne, 1989.

Sprintzen, David. *Camus: A Critical Examination*. Philadelphia: Temple University Press, 1988.

Thody, P. *Albert Camus: A Study of His Work*. London: Hamilton, 1957.

Frederick A. Olafson (1967)
Bibliography updated by Thomas Nenon (2005)

CAN

What can be true or can be done varies with the meaning of "can." As far as philosophy is concerned, the important senses of this word ("could," past indicative) fall into five major groups. For convenience these groups, most of which are distinguished in *Webster's Third New Interna-*

tional Dictionary, may be singled out as the "can" of ability, of right, of inclination or probability, of opportunity, and of possibility.

"CAN" OF ABILITY

The "can" of ability has at least three subsenses: (1) to have the skill—"He can speak five languages or paint lifelike portraits"; (2) to have the requisite mental or physical power—"He can solve difficult problems, invent remarkable machines, or foretell the future" or "He can swim a mile or do one hundred push-ups"; (3) to have the requisite strength of character—"He can resist anything but pleasure, pass up a free drink, or bear criticism of his books."

"CAN" OF RIGHT

The "can" of right, which is often used interchangeably with "may," has at least four subsenses: (1) logically or axiologically can—"Equivalent formulas can be interchanged, *salva veritate,* in any extensional context" or "From this we can reasonably infer …"; (2) can in virtue of custom, agreement, law, and so on—"One can be prosecuted for saying that" or "An ambulance can disregard traffic lights"; (3) permission-giving "can"—"You can borrow my car if you'd like"; (4) be permitted by conscience or feeling—"I can condone no willful act of destruction" or "I can accept electrocution but not hanging."

"CAN" OF INCLINATION OR PROBABILITY

Examples of the "can" of inclination or probability are "I was so angry that I could have killed him" and "That car could hardly have made a trip across the desert."

"CAN" OF OPPORTUNITY

"He could have played chess had he known how," "Come in here where we can talk," and "The traffic was so heavy that I could not cross" illustrate the "can" of opportunity.

"CAN" OF POSSIBILITY

The "can" of possibility has at least five subsenses: (1) consistency with knowledge—"For all that I know, Jones could have been the one"; (2) whether it is possible for someone (compare with the "can" of opportunity)—"Can you get away for lunch?" (3) the "can" of physical possibility—"If such-and-such has to happen, then it cannot fail to happen" or "A man, properly equipped, can survive indefinitely in outer space"; (4) the "can" of logical possibility (compare with the logical or axiological use of the "can" of right)—"Nothing can be red all over and green all over at the same time"; (5) conditional possibility (logical or physical)—"If the conclusion of a valid argument is false, not all of the premises can be true" or "In a deterministic system everything that can occur is necessitated by something else."

CAN AND FREE WILL

Because the field of philosophical perplexity is virtually limitless, any one of the "cans" listed above is a possible source of trouble to the philosopher. Nevertheless, several of them (especially the "cans" of ability, opportunity, and possibility), have proved exceptionally potent in bewitching the philosophical imagination, mainly in connection with the age-old problem of free will. This problem is partly generated by the conviction that a man can be said to perform an action freely only if he did not have to perform it but he could have done something else instead. A conviction of this kind tends to generate a problem because if the metaphysical thesis of determinism is intelligible, tenable, and applicable to human actions, it becomes doubtful whether it is ever true that a man can do anything other than what he does do, at least in one of these three basic senses of "can."

"CAN" OF ABILITY. How the ability senses of "can" bear on the free will issue has received perhaps the largest share of attention in the recent literature, possibly because questions about a man's abilities are often so crucially relevant in moral contexts. Yet the decisive points about abilities in this connection are easily stated. In all of the subsenses of the "can" of ability, there is an essential distinction between the possession of an ability and the exercise of that ability. To show that a person lacks an ability is more complicated than to show that he does not exercise it. A failure to perform a certain action implies that a man lacks the corresponding ability only if both he wants, wills, intends, or chooses to perform that action and his failure to perform it occurs in relevantly normal conditions. This fact has tempted philosophers (for instance, P. H. Nowell-Smith) to analyze "He can" (in the sense of ability) as meaning "He will if … ." Important difficulties with such hypothetical analyses have been pointed out by Austin and others, but it has not been shown that there is anything wrong with the line of thought that prompted these analyses—namely, that our use of "can" in this sense is built on the idea that a man need not do what he can do and that in order to find out what he can do, we must find out what he will do if, in relevantly normal conditions, he wants, wills, intends, and so forth to do certain things. This line of thought is not, moreover, inconsistent with determinism, since determinism does not imply that if, under appropriate conditions, I wanted and were to try to perform an alternative action, I should certainly fail. On the contrary, it is presumably only because a measure of determinism does hold that my trying, in certain circumstances, to perform a particular action is likely to meet with consistent success.

"CAN" OF OPPORTUNITY. Although the truth of determinism does not imply that if a man performs a certain action, he could not (in the sense of the "can" of ability) have done otherwise, it might still be claimed that he would not, under these conditions, have the opportunity to do otherwise and, thus, that he could not do otherwise in the sense of the "can" of opportunity. But this claim is simply false, since in the ordinary sense of "opportunity" one can be said to have the opportunity to do many things that one is not presently doing, whether or not determinism holds. As the examples of the "can" of opportunity indicate, "having the opportunity to do *X*" does not mean anything like "being in a situation in which nothing physically essential for one's performance of *X* is lacking," which the claim in question seems to suppose (for more on this point see Taylor, *Metaphysics*). On the contrary, to have the opportunity to do something requires only that one be in a situation such that if, roughly speaking, one wanted to do it, it would be reasonable to expect that one would be successful in doing it if one were able to do it (that is, could do it in the sense of ability). And such a situation would normally be lacking in many things essential, in the required sense, to one's performing that action. Not only might it lack the essential interest or even ability on one's own part, but it might also fail to involve the means that one would have to take in order to accomplish that action if it were at all complex—for instance, walking across the room in order to grasp the vase that one "has the opportunity" to break, throwing it toward the floor with sufficient force, and so on.

"CAN" OF POSSIBILITY. In spite of all this, it still seems possible to argue that, given determinism, a man cannot do other than what he does do in the sense that any alternative action on his part is physically impossible. A claim of this sort is, however, false if taken literally, since what is physically possible *simpliciter* need be consistent only with the laws of nature, not consistent with the laws of nature *and* certain initial conditions. If, however, the claim is to be taken in a slightly different way—namely, that it is *conditionally* physically impossible for the man to perform some other action—then it is entirely unexceptionable if the thesis of determinism is tenable and applicable to human actions. The reason for this is simply that the notion of conditional possibility is a technical one, definable by reference to determinism: Roughly, "*A* is conditionally physically possible" is by definition equivalent to "Nothing has happened that physically determines non-*A*."

Because one is to make sense of "conditional physical possibility" by reference to determinism or something like it, it is clear that the hard-fought question whether determinism rules out human freedom is not the question whether determinism rules out the conditional possibility of a man's doing other than what he does do. There is, in fact, little that is controversial about the last question; it gets an analytic "Yes." What is controversial is the question whether the sense of "can" involved in the morally relevant query "Can he do otherwise?" is to be understood as the "can" of conditional possibility. For if, as both libertarians and sophisticated fatalists seem to think, this "can" *is* of basic moral significance, then free actions are possible only if determinism is false, untenable, or inapplicable to human actions. If, on the other hand, this sense of "can" is *not* the one that does concern us or should concern us when in a moral context we wonder whether a man can do other than what he does do—the opinion of the "reconcilers" of the empiricist tradition—then there is, perhaps, no incompatibility between determinism and human freedom after all.

NORMATIVE "CAN." How is this basic question about the "can" in the morally crucial use of "He can do otherwise" to be resolved? Only a few, admittedly feeble, hints can be given here. First, the idea that this "can" is that of conditional possibility seems extremely dubious, since this sense of the word is pretty clearly a contrived one, not mentioned even in unabridged dictionaries and thus hardly one that, like the "can" of ability and opportunity, is likely to be used in the familiar, everyday, morally compelling assessment of free, responsible actions. Second, the less heavy-handed and therefore far more tempting claim—that it is at any rate naive or unreasonable to describe an action as free if it is conditionally impossible for the agent to have done otherwise—seems very unsatisfactory when it is carefully pressed. For one thing, to think of free actions as differing from unfree ones in being conditionally undetermined is to make the very notion of a free action practically useless, since any question that might arise about the freedom of a given act would presumably then have to be settled by a fairly hopeless hunt for causes in the jungles of neurology. For another thing, to conceive of free actions in this way is to sever their ties with those complex principles of personal responsibility that incline us to excuse, rather than emphatically condemn, the kindly old parson who (we might imagine) suddenly, spontaneously, and without cause wills to, and does, brain the infant he is baptizing. The last point really seems to go to the heart of the matter: To conceive of free actions as conditionally physically indeterminate actions is to conceive of them in too naturalistic a way. After all, the very identity of an action—think of promising or murdering—is determined not just by the physical movements involved but also by a complex system of rules, laws, and so forth. Since it is the application of such rule concepts that distinguishes actions involving the same physical movements—murder and defensive or punitive acts—the basic vocabulary of action descriptions is essentially normative to a very large extent. (Actually, the vocabulary of action description is "intentional" in a way in which "scientific" language presumably is not.) Because the "can" in the morally crucial claim "He can do otherwise" plainly belongs to the family of words specifically used in connection with human actions, there is an inescapable force to the claim, made by many contemporary philosophers, that to identify this sense of the word with "conditional physical possibility" is to confuse a practical, largely normative "can" with an aseptic, scientific, theoretical one and thus to misconceive drastically the purpose, point, and import of the familiar, nontechnical statement "His action was done freely."

See also Determinism and Freedom; Possibility.

Bibliography

Aune, Bruce. "Abilities, Modalities, and Free Will." *Philosophy and Phenomenological Research* 23 (1963): 397–413.

Austin, J. L. "Ifs and Cans." In *Philosophical Papers,* edited by J. O. Urmson and G. J. Warnock. Oxford: Clarendon Press, 1961.

Baier, Kurt. "Could and Would." *Analysis* Supp. Vol. (1963): 20–29.

Edwards, Paul, and Arthur Pap, eds. *A Modern Introduction to Philosophy.* Glencoe, IL: Free Press, 1957. See Ch. 1; this book should also be consulted for more detailed bibliographical information.

Hook, Sidney, ed. *Determinism and Freedom in the Age of Modern Science.* New York: New York University Press, 1958.

Melden, A. I. *Free Action.* London, 1961.

Morgenbesser, Sidney, and James Walsh, eds. *Free Will: A Book of Readings.* Englewood Cliffs, NJ: Prentice-Hall, 1962.

Nowell-Smith, P. H. *Ethics.* London: Penguin, 1954.

Pears, D. F., ed. *Freedom and the Will.* New York: St. Martin's Press, 1963.

Raab, F. V. "Free Will and the Ambiguity of 'Could.'" *Philosophical Review* 64 (1955): 60–77.

Taylor, Richard. *Metaphysics.* Englewood Cliffs, NJ: Prentice-Hall, 1963. See Chs. 4–5.

Bruce Aune (1967)

CANTOR, GEORG

(1845–1918)

Georg Cantor, a mathematician who created set theory and a corresponding theory of transfinite numbers, revolutionized mathematics at the end of the nineteenth century with his ideas about the infinite, which were to be of profound significance not only for mathematics but for philosophy and many allied disciplines as well.

He was born on March 3, 1845, in St. Petersburg, Russia, to Georg Woldemar Cantor, a successful merchant and the son of a Jewish businessman from Copenhagen, and Maria Anna Böhm, who came from a family of notable musicians and was a Roman Catholic. But Cantor's father, raised in a Lutheran mission, was a deeply religious man and passed his own strong convictions on to his son. Later in life, Cantor's religious beliefs would play a significant role in his steadfast faith in the correctness of his controversial transfinite set theory, just as his mother's Catholicism may have made him particularly amenable to the substantial correspondence he undertook with Catholic theologians over the nature of the infinite from a theological perspective.

EARLY MATHEMATICAL STUDIES

Cantor received his doctorate in 1868 from the University of Berlin, where he had studied with Leopold Kronecker, Ernst Eduard Kummer, and Karl Weierstrass. His dissertation was devoted to number theory, as was his *Habilitationsschrift.* When Cantor began teaching as an instructor at the University of Halle, among his colleagues there was Eduard Heinrich Heine. Heine had been working on problems related to trigonometric series, and he urged Cantor to take up the challenging problem of whether or not, given an arbitrary function represented by a trigonometric series, the representation was unique. In 1870 Heine had established the uniqueness of such representations for almost-everywhere continuous functions, assuming the uniform convergence of the trigonometric series in question. Cantor succeeded in establishing increasingly general versions of the uniqueness theorem in a series of papers he published between 1870 and 1872, the most remarkable of which showed that even if an infinite number of exceptional points for the representation were allowed, the uniqueness could still be shown if such infinite sets of "exceptional" points were distributed in a particular way. Such sets of exceptional points constituted what Cantor called sets of the first species.

An infinite set of points P was said to be of the first species if its set of limit points P' was finite; if not, then P' must contain an infinite number of points and also have a derived set, the second derived set of P, P''. If for some finite number v the vth derived set P^v contains only a finite number of points, then its derived set will be empty, that is, $P^{v+1} = \emptyset$. It was for such first-species sets that he was able to establish the uniqueness of trigonometric series representations, even though there were an infinite number of exceptional points. Transfinite set theory would arise from Cantor's later consideration of point sets of the second species, all of whose derived sets were infinite. From these Cantor would eventually generate an endless hierarchy of what he came to call transfinite ordinal, and later their corresponding cardinal, numbers.

THE REAL NUMBERS

Cantor realized that to define the structure of point sets of the first species unambiguously required a rigorous definition of the real numbers, which he approached in terms of fundamental, convergent sequences of rational numbers in his last paper on trigonometric series of 1872. In the same year Richard Dedekind introduced his own rigorous definition of the real numbers in terms of "Dedekind cuts." Both approaches are concerned with the continuity of the real numbers in general, a subject that was to haunt Cantor for the rest of his life. In particular, he succeeded in proving just a few years later, in 1874, that the set of all real numbers was in fact nondenumerably infinite, that is, of a distinctly higher order of infinity than denumerably infinite sets like the whole, rational, or algebraic numbers. This fact soon led to the articulation of one of Cantor's most famous problems: his continuum hypothesis, that the infinite set of real numbers R is the next higher order of infinite sets following denumerably infinite sets like the set of all natural numbers N. Cantor became especially interested in the question of whether or not point sets of two and higher dimensions might furnish examples of increasingly infinite orders of infinity, something he answered negatively in 1877. This was another of Cantor's important early results, his proof (though faulty) of the invariance of dimension; the first correct proof was published by L. E. J. Brouwer in 1911.

Between 1879 and 1883 Cantor wrote a series of articles that culminated in an independently published monograph devoted to the study of linear point sets, *Grundlagen einer allgemeinen Mannigfaltigkeitslehre: Ein mathematisch-philosophischer Versuch in der Lehre des Unendlichen* (Foundations of a general theory of sets: A mathematico-philosophical investigation into the theory of the infinite). In addition to introducing such concepts as everywhere-dense sets, he showed that whereas everywhere-dense sets were necessarily of the second species, first-species sets could never be everywhere-dense.

TRANSFINITE NUMBERS

In his series of papers on linear point sets, and in the *Grundlagen*, Cantor introduced his new concept of transfinite numbers. At first, these were limited to the transfinite ordinal numbers that he generated from the point sets of the second species that he had introduced in 1872. Considering the entire sequence of derived sets P^v, none of which was empty (i.e., every derived set P^v contained an infinite number of limit points): $P', P'', \ldots, P^v, \ldots$, Cantor defined the intersection of all these sets as P^∞. This was an infinite set that in turn led to the next derived set $P^{\infty+1}$. If this set were infinite, and in fact every derived set thereafter, this led to an endless hierarchy of further infinite derived sets: $P', P'', \ldots, P^v, \ldots, P^\infty, P^{\infty+1}, \ldots, P^{\infty+v}, \ldots, P^{2\infty}, \ldots$

At first, Cantor only regarded the superscripts as "infinite symbols," but early in the 1880s he began to distinguish these indexes as numbers independently of point sets of the second species. By the time he wrote the *Grundlagen* in 1883, these infinite symbols had become transfinite ordinal numbers.

CONTROVERSY AND CRITICISM

Cantor understood that his new ideas would be controversial, and his work had already met with criticism, especially from Kronecker, his former teacher at the University of Berlin. Cantor was so concerned about the possible objections to his new ideas that he undertook a detailed analysis of the subject historically, which served his strategy in the *Grundlagen* to present a detailed analysis of the foundations of transfinite set theory from both a philosophical and theological perspective. It was in the *Grundlagen* that he made one of his most famous statements, that "the essence of mathematics lies precisely in its freedom" (1996, p. 182). As Cantor later confided to the mathematician David Hilbert, this statement was inspired by the negative criticism Kronecker had made of set theory and was a call for open-mindedness among mathematicians, especially in dealing with new and novel ideas proposed by younger mathematicians. But the opposition mounted by Kronecker served a useful purpose in stimulating Cantor's own philosophical reaction and his determination to provide the soundest possible foundations, both mathematically and philosophically, for transfinite set theory.

What Cantor did in the *Grundlagen* was to present the transfinite ordinal numbers as a direct extension of the real numbers. But because he generated these infinite real numbers as abstractions from sets of points, he rejected the possibility of there being actually infinitesimal numbers. He also knew that an important property of the transfinite ordinal numbers was their noncommutativity, that is:

$$2+\omega = (1, 2, a_1, a_2, \ldots , a_n, a_{n+1}, \ldots) \neq (a_1, a_2, \ldots , a_n, a_{n+1}, \ldots , 1, 2) = \omega+2,$$

$$2\omega = (a_1, a_2, a_3, \ldots ; b_1, b_2, b_3, \ldots) \neq (a_1, b_1, a_2, b_2, a_3, b_3, \ldots) = \omega 2.$$

Such distinctions brought new insights to the differences between finite and infinite sets. For finite sets and their corresponding ordinal numbers, addition and multiplication were commutative; infinite sets were more interesting because their corresponding ordinal numbers and transfinite arithmetic were not commutative. Cantor expected that understanding such differences would not only explain the seemingly paradoxical nature of the infinite but would also answer some of the long-standing objections to the infinite that historically had been so persuasive to mathematicians and philosophers alike.

TRANSFINITE CARDINALS AND CANTOR'S ALEPHS

Although the *Grundlagen* offered a systematic presentation of Cantor's transfinite ordinal numbers, there was no mention of his best-known innovation: the transfinite cardinal numbers, or alephs. Indeed, nowhere in the *Grundlagen* was there any indication that the power of an infinite set was to be equated with the concept of a transfinite cardinal number, a step he first took in a lecture he delivered at Freiburg in September 1883. Over the next decade he used a number of different notations for transfinite cardinal numbers, but did not decide on a definite symbol until Giulio Vivanti, an Italian mathematician who was writing an introductory monograph on set theory, asked Cantor about notation. Only then did he finally choose the Hebrew aleph for the transfinite cardinal numbers. In "Beiträge zur Begründung der transfiniten Mengenlehre" (Contributions to the founding of the theory of transfinite numbers) he designated the least transfinite cardinal number as $\aleph_0$.

It was also in "Beiträge" that Cantor offered an algebraic interpretation of his continuum hypothesis, based on his proof of 1891 that given any infinite set *P*, the set of all its subsets was of a higher power than *P*. Since the cardinality of the set of all real numbers could be written as $2^{\aleph_0}$, and if $\aleph_1$ was the next largest cardinal following $\aleph_0$, then the continuum hypothesis could now be expressed as $2^{\aleph_0} = \aleph_1$. Cantor hoped that with this new algebraic formulation of the hypothesis, he would soon manage to produce a proof that the power of the real numbers was indeed equal to $\aleph_1$. He never succeeded in doing so, for reasons that only became apparent in the twentieth century, thanks to the results of Kurt Gödel (who established that the continuum hypothesis was consistent with the basic axioms of Zermelo-Fraenkel set theory) and Paul Cohen (who showed, on the contrary, that the continuum hypothesis was independent of the same axioms), which meant that it was possible to conceive of consistent set theories in which Cantor's continuum hypothesis did not hold.

Cantor's last major publication appeared in two parts in the journal *Mathematische Annalen* in 1895 and 1897. "Beiträge" not only offered a complete account of both his transfinite ordinal and cardinal numbers but also his theory of order types, which investigated in detail the different properties of the sets of natural, rational, and real numbers, respectively. The well-ordered set of integers, taken in their natural order, he designated (ω; the set of rational numbers in their natural order, which were everywhere-dense but not continuous, he designated η; sets like the real numbers that were continuous he designated by the order-type θ. But the result he hoped to achieve in "Beiträge" but failed to produce, namely, proof of his continuum hypothesis, remained illusive.

CANTOR'S MANIC DEPRESSION

Much has been written about Cantor's unfortunate history of mental illness, which some writers have linked with the heavy criticism of Cantor's transfinite set theory from Kronecker. But recent studies suggest that what Cantor suffered from was manic depression, which would have afflicted him regardless of the controversies surrounding his mathematical work (see Grattan-Guinness 1971, Dauben 1979, Charraud 1994). Whereas the earliest serious breakdown occurred in 1884, as Cantor was encountering his first disappointments in trying to prove the continuum hypothesis (for a detailed account of what happened, see Schoenflies 1927), the manic depression became more serious as he grew older, and after 1900 he spent increasingly long periods under professional care, often at the Nervenklinik in Halle. Also, following the first attack in 1884, Cantor began to take up interests other than mathematics, including the idea that Francis Bacon was the real author of writings attributed to William Shakespeare and that Joseph of Arimathea was the natural father of Jesus. Cantor also began an extensive correspondence with Catholic theologians, and even wrote to Pope Leo XIII directly, in hopes that a correct understanding of the infinite mathematically, in terms of his transfinite set theory, would help the church avoid making any incorrect pronouncements on the subject, especially where the absolutely infinite nature of God was concerned, which Cantor took to be consistent with but wholly different from the concepts of transfinite set theory.

The mathematician Eric Temple Bell (1986) offers a Freudian analysis of Cantor's relationship with his father, whose initial opposition to Cantor's wish to become a mathematician Bell takes to be the source of his son's later mental problems; more recently, Nathalie Charraud (1994), a French psychoanalyst, examined the records of Cantor's treatment at the neurological clinic in Halle and offers a different, Lacanian assessment of the role Cantor's father played in his son's life. Equally important in understanding Cantor's tenacious defense of his controversial set theory is the role that religion played with respect to the transfinite numbers, which he took to have been communicated to him from God directly. For details of how his religious convictions and periods of manic depression may actually have played important, supportive roles in the battle to establish transfinite set theory as a fundamental part of modern mathematics, see Joseph Warren Dauben (2005).

One final aspect of Cantor's career as a mathematician deserves brief mention, because he was primarily responsible for the creation of the Deutsche Mathematiker-Vereinigung (German Mathematical Society), of which Cantor was elected its first president in 1891. He was also instrumental in promoting the idea of the first International Congresses of Mathematicians, beginning with Zürich in 1897, and then Paris in 1900 (Dauben 1979, pp. 163–165).

THE PARADOXES OF SET THEORY

To conclude with an assessment of Cantor's significance for philosophy, he was above all responsible for making the infinite a central part of modern mathematics. From the time of the Greeks, Zeno's discovery of the paradoxes of motion and Aristotle's opposition to the concept of completed infinities (as opposed to the potential infinite) led most mathematicians to avoid using the infinite in their work. Cantor faced the subject head-on and argued that there was nothing inherently contradictory in considering actually infinite collections of point sets or the infinite sets of integers, rational, and real numbers as unified, completed objects of thought. His contemplation of these eventually led to his development of transfinite set theory, transfinite arithmetic, and his fundamental concepts of transfinite ordinal and cardinal numbers. His greatest contribution was understanding the roles these played in establishing a proper foundation for mathematics, which he approached essentially on formalist terms. Consistency, for Cantor, was the only test a new mathematical theory needed to pass before he considered it legitimate as a subject for study and application.

When Cantor himself first realized the contradictions inherent in trying to decide the ordinal number of the set of all transfinite ordinal numbers, or the cardinality of the set of all transfinite cardinal numbers, his solution was to simply ban such "collections" from mathematics, saying they were too large to be considered legitimately as "sets." But as others like Cesare Burali-Forti and Jules Richard began to consider the antinomies of set theory, Bertrand Russell discovered a logical paradox at the heart of set theory involving the set of all sets that are not members of themselves. One solution to this dilemma was advanced by Ernst Zermelo, who sought to axiomatize set theory in such a way that the paradoxes would be excluded. Further developments along such lines were made by Russell and Alfred North Whitehead in their monumental *Principia Mathematica*; alternative axiomatizations were also advanced by Abraham Fraenkel and John von Neumann, among others.

By the end of his life, Cantor was a mathematician honored by the Royal Society with its Copley Medal for his outstanding contributions to mathematics. He was also granted an honorary degree by the University of St. Andrews (Scotland). Today, the highest award conferred by the German Mathematical Society is a medal honoring its first president, Georg Cantor.

See also Infinity in Mathematics and Logic; Set Theory.

Bibliography

Cantor, Georg, and Richard Dedekind. *Briefwechsel Cantor-Dedekind*, edited by E. Noether and J. Cavaillès. Paris: Hermann, 1937.

WORKS BY CANTOR

Gesammelte Abhandlungen mathematischen und philosophischen Inhalts, edited by Ernst Zermelo. Berlin: Springer, 1932.

"Über eine Eigenschaft des Inbegriffes aller reellen algebraischen Zahlen." In *Gesammelte Abhandlungen mathematischen und philosophischen Inhalts*, edited by Ernst Zermelo, 115–118. Berlin: Springer, 1932. This was originally published in the *Journal für die reine und angewandte Mathematik* in 1874.

"Foundations of a General Theory of Manifolds: A Mathematico-Philosophical Investigation into the Theory of the Infinite." Translated by W. B. Ewald. In *From Kant to Hilbert: A Source Book in the Foundations of Mathematics*, edited by W. B. Ewald, 2:878–920. New York: Oxford University Press, 1996. This was originally published under the title "Grundlagen einer allgemeinen Mannigfaltigkeitslehre: Ein mathematisch-philosophischer Versuch in der Lehre des Unendlichen" in 1883.

"Beiträge zur Begründung der transfiniten Mengenlehre." In *Contributions to the Founding of the Theory of Transfinite Numbers*. Translated by Philip E. B. Jourdain. Chicago: Open Court, 1915.

WORKS ABOUT CANTOR

Bell, Eric Temple. "Paradise Lost: Georg Cantor." In *Men of Mathematics*, 555–579. New York: Simon and Schuster, 1986.

Charraud, Nathalie. *Infini et inconscient: Essai sur Georg Cantor*. Paris: Anthropos, 1994.

Dauben, Joseph Warren. *Georg Cantor: His Mathematics and Philosophy of the Infinite*. Cambridge, MA: Harvard University Press, 1979.

Dauben, Joseph Warren. "The Battle for Cantorian Set Theory." In *Mathematics and the Historian's Craft. The Kenneth O. May Lectures*, edited by Micahel Kinyon and Glen van Brummelen. New York: Springer Verlag, Canadian Mathematical Society Books in Mathematics, 2005.

Fraenkel, Abraham A. "Georg Cantor." *Jahresbericht der Deutschen Mathematiker-Vereinigung* 39 (1930): 189–266.

Grattan-Guinness, Ivor. "Towards a Biography of Georg Cantor." *Annals of Science* 27 (1971): 345–391.

Hallett, Michael. *Cantorian Set Theory and Limitation of Size*. Oxford, U.K.: Clarendon Press, 1984.

Lavine, Shaughan. *Understanding the Infinite*. Cambridge, MA: Harvard University Press, 1994.

Meschkowski, Herbert. *Probleme des Unendlichen: Werk und Leben Georg Cantors*. Braunschweig, Germany: Vieweg and Sohn, 1967.

Purkert, Walter, and Hans Joachim Ilgauds. *Georg Cantor*. Leipzig, Germany: Teubner, 1985.

Purkert, Walter, and Hans Joachim Ilgauds. *Georg Cantor, 1845–1918*. Basel, Switzerland: Birkhäuser, 1987.

Schoenflies, Arthur. "Die Krisis in Cantor's mathematischem Schaffen." *Acta Mathematica* 50 (1927): 1–23.

Joseph W. Dauben (2005)

CAPREOLUS, JOHN

(c. 1380–1444)

John Capreolus, a French Dominican theologian, was born in Rodez. He studied at the University of Paris, receiving the magistrate in theology in 1411. Later he taught in Dominican houses of study at Toulouse and Rodez and came to be recognized as the "Leader of the Thomists" (*Princeps Thomistarum*). His chief work is *Defensiones Theologiae D. Thomae* (Defenses of the theology of St. Thomas). This is the first commentary that considers the *Summa Theologiae* more important than Thomas Aquinas's *Commentary on the Sentences,* a view which has persisted in later Thomism. The *Defensiones* is historically useful for its information on scholastic philosophical controversies of the fourteenth century and the views of John Duns Scotus, John of Ripa, Peter Aureolus, and Durandus of Saint-Pourcain. Capreolus' contributions to philosophy are in the field of metaphysics. On the then central question of the relation between essence and existence, he taught that they are distinguished as two different beings (an extreme real distinction) and used the terminology of Giles of Rome (*esse essentiae* and *esse existentiae*) to express his position. Capreolus regarded essences as eternal and uncreated entities, not efficiently produced by God but subject only to divine formal causality. On the other hand, he stressed the importance of existence in treating personality (divine and human), teaching that personality is the very subsistence of the act of existing (*esse actualis existentiae,* see *Defensiones,* Vol. V, pp. 105–107). Where other thinkers required some sort of formal or modal constituent of the person, Capreolus demanded nothing more than the act of existing as an intelligent individual nature. He taught that the intrinsic principle that individuates bodies is matter marked by quantity (*materia signata*), as did Thomas, but Capreolus insisted that the quantification must be actual (under definite dimensions) and not indeterminate (*Defensiones,* Vol. III, pp. 200–241).

See also Aristotelianism; Duns Scotus, John; Durandus of Saint-Pourçain; Peter Aureol; Thomas Aquinas, St.

Bibliography

WORKS BY CAPREOLUS

Defensiones Theologiae D. Thomae. Edited by Paban-Pègues, 7 vols. Turin, 1900–1908. There are no known English translations of Capreolus's work.

WORKS ON CAPREOLUS

Grabmann, M. "J. Capreolus, O.P., der Princeps Thomistarum und seine Stellung in der Geschichte der Thomistenschule." *Divus Thomas* (Freiburg) 22 (1944): 85–109, 145–170.

Wells, N. J. "Capreolus on Essence and Existence." *Modern Schoolman* 38 (1960): 1–24.

Vernon J. Bourke (1967)

CARD, CLAUDIA

(1940–)

Claudia Card, an American philosopher, has published work on a wide range of philosophical topics but is best known for her contributions to ethics and feminist philosophy. Card began her academic career at Harvard University, where she received a PhD for her dissertation on theories of punishment. Currently the Emma Goldman Professor of Philosophy and Senior Fellow at the Institute for Research in Humanities, Card has been a professor of philosophy at the University of Wisconsin at Madison since 1966. Card is also an affiliate professor in women's studies, environmental studies, Jewish studies, and lesbian, gay, bisexual, and transgendered studies. Extraordinarily active in various philosophical societies, Card was named the Distinguished Woman Philosopher of the Year in 1996 by the Eastern Society for Women in Philosophy. The author of numerous scholarly books and journal articles, Card has also given a number of media interviews and served on many editorial boards. Her research interests include feminist philosophy, lesbian ethics, and evil.

Card's work is striking not just for the range of areas of philosophy to which it makes a contribution but also for the connections it draws between them. In ethics Card's work is notable for showing how questions in mainstream moral philosophy are tied to pressing political issues. In *The Unnatural Lottery: Character and Moral Luck* (1996), for example, Card defends the concept of moral luck and explores how a person's opportunity to act morally is affected by such variables as gender, race, social class, and sexual identity. Card asks about the implications of moral luck for attributions of moral responsibility and in the course of her examination discusses the problems faced by survivors of childhood sexual abuse. Another notable feature of Card's contribution to philosophy is her attraction to difficult, troubling, and important questions. Her work on moral luck falls into this category, as does her later work on evil. Card's monograph *The Atrocity Paradigm: A Theory of Evil* (2004) explores the relationship between evil and other concepts/practices such as forgiveness, toleration, and hate. Card asks what distinguishes evils from ordinary wrongs. The theory of evil developed in the book is applied to such practices as war rape and violence against intimates. She also addresses the moral "gray zone," in which persons can occupy the dual role of the victim and the perpetrator of evil.

Within feminist philosophy Card argues that feminism is not a single, unified worldview, but rather a lively debate characterized by the belief that women's subordination is wrong and that one should pay close attention to women's lived experiences. She stresses the importance of enabling women to describe their experiences in their own terms and cautions against the tendency to gloss over the unique experiences of nonwhite and poor women. Card's work urges one to be alert to the dangers of internalized oppression and adaptive preferences, and, in particular, to the ways in which oppression can compromise the integrity of its victims. Under oppressive circumstances victims are often motivated to ease their burdens by collaborating with their oppressors and/or uncritically adopting oppressive practices. In such cases, she contends that the oppressed cannot elude all responsibility; bad luck, for Card, does not necessarily subvert moral culpability and she advises that "[w]e need to be alert to the dangers of becoming what we despise" (1991, p. 26).

Card believes that opposition to real evils, such as, for example, domestic violence, should be given priority to opposition to gender inequalities, such as pay equity for tenured professors. Equality feminism, she says, trivializes the feminist movement and takes attention away from the graver problems that women face. On its own, Card thinks that care ethics is ill equipped to handle real evils. She also impugns care ethics for the way in which it dichotomizes the values of justice and care. Justice, she says, is not only about impartiality and universal principles of fairness, but also about giving people what they deserve, including compassionate, caring responses such as gratitude, trust, loyalty, and forgiveness.

Rejecting the idea that there is an essential lesbian identity, Card believes that there are, nonetheless, some historical commonalities among the experiences of lesbians. In *Lesbian Choices* (1995) Card attempts to articulate a lesbian ethics, understood as a ethics that grows of out the histories and experiences of lesbians and draws on paradigms and archetypes common in lesbian culture.

See also Ethics; Feminist Ethics; Feminist Philosophy.

Bibliography

Card, Claudia, and Robert R. Ammerman, eds. *Religious Commitment and Salvation: Readings in Secular and Theistic Religion*. Columbus, OH: Merrill Press, 1974.

WORKS BY CARD

Feminist Ethics. Lawrence: University Press of Kansas, 1991.

Adventures in Lesbian Philosophy. Bloomington: Indiana University Press, 1994.

Lesbian Choices. New York: Columbia University Press, 1995.

The Unnatural Lottery: Character and Moral Luck. Philadelphia: Temple University Press, 1996.

On Feminist Ethics and Politics. Lawrence: University Press of Kansas, 1999.

The Cambridge Companion to Simone de Beauvoir. New York: Cambridge University Press, 2003.

The Atrocity Paradigm: A Theory of Evil. New York: Oxford University Press, 2004.

Amanda Porter (2005)
Samantha Brennan (2005)

CARLYLE, THOMAS

(1795–1881)

Thomas Carlyle, the essayist, historian, and philosopher of culture, was born in Ecclefechan, Scotland, the eldest son of a stern, puritanical stonemason. There can be little doubt that the often-hysterical extravagances of Carlyle's later social doctrines had a direct emotional origin in the Calvinism of his childhood. In 1809 he became a divinity student at Edinburgh University, but he soon stopped attending the university courses and read widely on his own in modern literature. After leaving Edinburgh in 1814, he taught school, at the same time broadening his already impressive span of reading. In addition to imaginative literature and German philosophy, Carlyle's serious interests at this time extended to Voltaire and François Fénelon, as well as to the scientific works of Isaac Newton and Benjamin Franklin. A reading of Edward Gibbon in 1817 immediately precipitated Carlyle's rejection of the Bible as a historical record and gave impetus to his growing interest in history and social institutions.

Convinced that he could never become a minister, he returned to Edinburgh in 1819 and began his literary career as a freelance journalist. The next three years were the most miserable in a generally agonized life. He was unknown; he was socially, ideologically, even stylistically antipathetic to the fashionable literary world. He was also very poor, desperately lonely, and because of his irregular eating habits, almost permanently dyspeptic. Religious doubts quickly darkened into unbelief, and in 1822 he experienced the spiritual crisis later hieroglyphically recorded in *Sartor Resartus* (1833–1834). Like the hero of *Sartor,* Diogenes Teufelsdröckh, Carlyle found a new (if decidedly secular) faith in the moral efficacy of work: "Doubt of any sort cannot be removed except by Action," extols Teufelsdröckh. Conviction is worthless until it is converted into activity, mere speculation being "endless, formless, a vortex amid vortices." Therefore, one must "Do the Duty which lies nearest thee … Work while it is called To-day; for the Night cometh wherein no man can work." Here, in a language persuasively familiar to his readers, Carlyle expressed the chief psychotherapeutic discovery of his youth—one which was more widely disseminated in the writings of Thomas Arnold, John Ruskin, John Henry Newman, and particularly the later prophetic Carlyle himself, and was to become a leitmotif of mid-Victorian culture. Soon Carlyle found a role in which his genuine talents could emerge. His translation of Johann Wolfgang von Goethe's *Wilhelm Meister* in 1824 and his *Life of Schiller,* which was published as a book in 1825, established him as the first interpreter of German literature to the British public.

Carlyle's marriage in 1826 to Jane Baillie Welsh, an attractive, high-strung, and unusually intellectual twenty-five-year-old woman, ended his loneliness without in any way soothing the more creative ontological anxieties upon which his work depended. Carlyle's long years of isolated reading now bore fruit in a series of remarkable articles published in the Great Reviews.

LITERARY CRITICISM

Carlyle's early essays, especially "Jean Paul Friedrich Richter" (1827), "The State of German Literature," "Goethe," "Burns" (1828), "Voltaire," and "Novalis" (1829), are masterpieces of literary and ideological exegesis. However, his critical method, which was uncompromisingly didactic even for its day, was much more a criticism of life than any technical analysis of words on a page; in effect, it was essentially romantic criticism. Carlyle viewed literature as a form of self-revelation and literary criticism as a heightened confrontation of personalities engaged in the quest for moral truth. He stressed the primary need for the "transposition of the critic into the author's point of vision," which is the prerequisite of all historical and biographical as well as literary studies. Like Samuel Taylor Coleridge before him, Carlyle recognized Germany as the great contemporary source of spirituality and inwardness. For Carlyle, however, Goethe rather than Immanuel Kant was Germany's spiritual leader. More than any other writer, Goethe triumphed over all doubts and denials and manifested the freedom of belief and activity. In this respect Carlyle believed that there was a significant contrast to be made between Goethe and Voltaire. In the essay "Voltaire," Carlyle argued that despite Voltaire's intellectual adroitness, his power of rapid, perspicuous arrangement of scientific and historical data, his humanity, and his universal susceptibility of mind, his real claim to greatness was that he "gave the death-stab to modern superstition." Such an achievement was, however, too negative: For Carlyle, Voltaire remained essentially a mocker, "the greatest of all Persifleurs," his chief fault being a terrible lack of earnestness.

This contrast between Voltaire and Goethe—between the pragmatic values of the eighteenth century and those of a new age of belief which was, if not actually beginning, at least imminent—ran through Carlyle's works in ever-widening applications. Moreover, it is symptomatic of the type of thinker Carlyle was that most of his later ideas were already contained embryonically in his very earliest writings (for example, in his first original publication in 1822 in the *New Edinburgh Review,* which was significantly a critique of Goethe's *Faust*). Had he stuck to literature and written more about the English classics, Carlyle would today no doubt be placed between Coleridge and Matthew Arnold as one of the major British literary critics of his age. But his interest in literature was only a steppingstone to a more vital concern with history and social diagnosis. He never really methodologically distinguished between criticism, biography, and historical and philosophical analysis. They were all used as media through which the current *crise de conscience* was to be more clearly seen and diagnosed. In this respect Carlyle may be thought of, in his early works, as an amateurish practitioner of *Geisteswissenschaften* (or "human studies"), in roughly the sense given to that term by Wilhelm Dilthey.

EARLY SOCIAL CRITICISM

"Signs of the Times" (1829), "On History" (1830), and particularly "Characteristics" (1831) were Carlyle's earliest communications in the self-assumed role of Victorian prophet. The early nineteenth century, he claimed, was a mechanical age, both externally and internally, its chief symptom being an excessive self-consciousness. With its inheritance of the largely negative contributions of the Enlightenment, it was an age of inquiry and doubt rather than of meditation and faith. Outwardly, social mechanization was more prized than individual vitality. Inwardly, morality no longer sprang from belief in a transcendental authority but arose out of prudential feeling grounded on mere calculation of consequences. The most grievous mistake of bourgeois liberalism was its doctrine that social welfare can be promoted solely through external politico-economic legislation, whereas, in truth, all human progress that is genuine ("dynamical") must emerge from the moral culture of individual men. According to Carlyle, although the present time is thus out of joint, there is nevertheless strong hope for the future. History is a cyclical but progressive (perhaps spiral) unfolding of human capabilities, and borrowing freely from Johann Gottfried Herder and the Saint-Simonians, he affirmed that the modern period is the end of a critical phase. Even as the darkest hour heralds the dawn, so the springtime of organic rebirth is now at hand.

As it happened, Carlyle was not the only British subscriber to this philosophy of history in the early 1830s. J. S. Mill's papers on "The Spirit of the Age," which appeared in the *Examiner* for 1831, propounded very similar views. These papers, which immensely impressed Carlyle, led to the formation of his somewhat precarious friendship with Mill. Doubtless the chief obstacle for Mill was Carlyle's blatantly authoritarian concept of morality and his notorious views on liberty and democracy, three notions that were soon to be dramatically embodied in Carlyle's theory of the hero.

THE HERO AND HISTORY

In the *French Revolution* (1837), Carlyle stereoscopically visualized the events between the death of Louis XV and the appointment of Napoleon Bonaparte as commander in chief of the Army of the Interior in 1795 as the accumulated result not so much of economic or social, but of moral and, in the last analysis, theological causes. The French Revolution, he sometimes seemed to suggest, was an upheaval ordained by the Creator to punish the sins of the world. Yet at the same time, and importantly for Carlyle's anthropomorphic imagination, it was an exhibition of individual personalities (of Honoré Gabriel Riqueti, Comte de Mirabeau, Georges-Jacques Danton, Maximilien-Francois-Marie-Isidore de Robespierre, etc.) in their most intense form. "History," he had written in 1830, "is the essence of innumerable Biographies." Biography, which is based on insight into human personality, is the foundation of all historical inquiry; hence, the true history of an age is the biography of its great men. Carlyle's main interest in history (as in literature) was in the moral psychology of specific individuals who seemed to him endowed with certain admirable traits of character that he felt to be chronically lacking in the contemporary *Zeitgeist.*

The lectures he delivered in 1840, *On Heroes, Hero Worship, and the Heroic in History,* blended mythology with metaphysics to produce an image of the ideal type of individual needed as the savior of humankind. The hero can take many forms: He can be a god (Odin), a prophet (Muḥammad), poet (Dante Alighieri and William Shakespeare), priest (Martin Luther and John Knox), a man of letters (Samuel Johnson, Jean-Jacques Rousseau, Robert Burns), or a political ruler (Oliver Cromwell and Napoleon). In fact the hero can be "what you will, according to the kind of world he finds himself born into": His ever-varying persona results from the deeper needs of society. He is directed not by the "mechanical" needs of men, but by their "dynamical," unseen, mystical needs. Thus, all heroes have discerned "truly what the time wanted" and have led it "on the right road thither." In this sense, the hero is a gift from heaven, or as Carlyle otherwise puts it, a force of nature; his essential quality is "Original Insight" into the "primal reality of things." Because of the hero's firm contact with the "great Fact of Existence," he cannot lie. "He is heartily in *earnest*"; an unconscious sincerity emanates from him turning his acts or utterances into "a kind of 'revelation'" which the ordinary, unheroic man is morally obliged to recognize and obey. For "all that is *right* includes itself in this of co-operating with the real tendency of the World." Indeed, the proper feelings of ordinary men toward the heroes of their age are loyalty (which is "akin to religious Faith"), reverence, admiration, and "an obedience which knows no bounds." Hero worship, Carlyle significantly concludes, is a basic and indestructible tendency of human nature: It is "the one fixed point in modern revolutionary history, otherwise as if bottomless and shoreless."

As with Friedrich Nietzsche's *Übermensch,* there was a tendency in the twentieth century to view Carlyle's theory of the hero far too much in terms of contemporary political experience—that is, to think of the hero as a direct ancestor of fascism. But Carlyle, like Nietzsche, was essentially a philosopher of culture, not a political theorist. The hero concept is best understood as a rather curious and obsessional example of a spiritual phenomenon that reached something of a climax in the nineteenth century, most notably in the thought of Ludwig Feuerbach, Auguste Comte, Karl Marx, and Nietzsche—namely, the uneasy substitution of purely secular objects of veneration for the traditional transcendental one. Worship of God gave way to worship of man and human society.

AFTER 1840

Beginning with *Chartism* (1839), and more disastrously in *Past and Present* (1843) and the *Latterday Pamphlets* (1850), Carlyle explicitly incorporated the hero concept within the central tenets of his early social criticism to produce not only a renewed attack upon the materialistic spirit of industrial society but also an indictment of political liberty and democracy. Once more he protested against laissez-faire, the irresponsible pursuit of wealth in which "cash payment" has become the "sole nexus" between men, thus displacing the traditional ties of obligation. But social justice, he now paradoxically asserted, can be achieved only through the enforcement of social inequality. Members of the aristocracy and those heroes of the business world, the "Captains of Industry," must assume their responsibilities as rulers of the masses: Freedom consists in "the right of the ignorant man to be guided by the wiser." In this instance, as in nearly all of Carlyle's writing after about 1840, it seems that genuine social criticism was lost sight of in an increasingly pathological obsession with power: Nothing could have been further from the spirit of Mill's *On Liberty* (1859) and *Representative Government* (1861). In *Oliver Cromwell's Letters and Speeches, with Elucidations* (1845) and the *History of Frederick the Great* (1858–1865), Carlyle tried to give some historical backing to his by now hopeless moral aberrations for which he ultimately received the Prussian Order of Merit in 1874.

It is impossible to exaggerate Carlyle's impact, for better and worse, upon all aspects of Victorian culture, ranging from the development of the novel (particularly as evidenced in the work of Charles Dickens), to the formation of social policy. Nietzsche described him as a man constantly misled by a craving for a strong faith that he lacked the necessary capacity to experience. But it was hardly the capacity Carlyle lacked; rather, like Nietzsche himself, he needed something to have faith in. In the absence of his father's God, he chose what seemed to him the best substitute—the hero.

See also Arnold, Matthew; Coleridge, Samuel Taylor; Comte, Auguste; Dante Alighieri; Dilthey, Wilhelm; Fénelon, François de Salignac de la Mothe; Feuerbach, Ludwig Andreas; Franklin, Benjamin; Gibbon, Edward; Goethe, Johann Wolfgang von; Johnson, Samuel; Kant, Immanuel; Luther, Martin; Marx, Karl; Mill, John Stuart; Newman, John Henry; Newton, Isaac; Nietzsche, Friedrich; Rousseau, Jean-Jacques; Ruskin, John; Social and Political Philosophy; Voltaire, François-Marie Arouet de.

Bibliography

WORKS BY CARLYLE

The Centenary Edition, edited by H. D. Trail, 30 vols. (London, 1896–1899; New York, 1896–1901) is the most complete edition of Carlyle's *Works.* Carlyle's correspondence, most notably with Goethe, Ralph Waldo Emerson, Mill, and John Stirling, is essential reading for anyone interested in Carlyle's thought or, indeed, in nineteenth-century intellectual history in general. See also *Correspondence of Emerson and Carlyle,* edited by J. Slater (New York: Columbia University Press, 1964).

WORKS ON CARLYLE

To date there exists no full-scale analysis of the whole range of Carlyle's thought. The best short account is given by Ernst Cassirer in *The Myth of the State* (New Haven, CT: Yale University Press, 1946), Chs. 15–16. J. A. Froude, *Thomas Carlyle 1795–1835,* 2 vols. (London: Longmans Green, 1882) and *Thomas Carlyle 1834–1881,* 2 vols. (London: Longmans Green, 1884) are still indispensable. Among the many important specialized studies are B. H. Lehmann, *Carlyle's Theory of the Hero* (Durham, NC: Duke University Press, 1928); C. F. Harrold, *Carlyle and German Thought: 1819–1834* (New Haven, CT: Yale University Press, 1934); René Wellek, "Carlyle and the Philosophy of History," *Philological Quarterly* 23 (1944): 55–76; and G. Holloway, *The Victorian Sage* (London: Macmillan, 1953), Chs. 1–3.

OTHER RECOMMENDED WORKS

Rigney, Ann. "Sublimity: Thomas Carlyle and the Aesthetics of Historical Ignorance." In *Imperfect Histories: The Elusive Past and the Legacy of Romantic Historicism.* Ithaca, NY: Cornell University Press, 2001.

Sussman, Herbert L. *Fact into Figure: Typology in Carlyle, Ruskin, and the Pre-Raphaelite Brotherhood.* Columbus: Ohio State University Press, 1979.

Vida, Elizabeth Maximiliana. *Romantic Affinities: German Authors and Carlyle: A Study in the History of Ideas.* Toronto: University of Toronto Press, 1993.

Michael Moran (1967)

Bibliography updated by Desirae Matherly Martin (2005)

CARNAP, RUDOLF

(1891–1970)

Rudolf Carnap was the philosophically most articulate member of the Vienna Circle in the 1920s and 1930s, and later of the movement that came to be known in the United States as logical empiricism. During his lifetime, he was respected among analytic philosophers as the proponent of a number of ambitious language projects, especially, in his later years, a system of inductive logic. The philosophical agenda underlying these technical projects, however, remained largely implicit; only disconnected fragments of this agenda, often reduced to superficial slogans, gained some currency. Subsequent generations, quite reasonably, discarded these fragments with some contempt. The coherent and powerful view that Carnap actually held (and partly articulated), of which the ambitious technical projects were manifestations and illustrations, but not explicit statements, has only begun to be unearthed. As a result, the view of Carnap held during his lifetime and since his death is under revision.

INFLUENCES AND EARLY AMBITIONS

Carnap was born on May 18, 1891, in the German town of Wuppertal At this time the region ("Bergisches Land") was known for its pietistical, even mystical, brand of Lutheranism, and the Carnap family was strongly imbued with this local tradition. Carnap's mother's family was more intellectual, in the German tradition of *Bildung.* Carnap's grandfather, Friedrich Wilhelm Dörpfeld, was a leading educational thinker and writer who championed the ideals of Johann Friedrich Herbart. When Carnap was eight, his father died. His mother taught him and his sister at home, following her father's educational program. Teaching was restricted to one hour a day, and the children were encouraged to work out the implications of what they had learned for themselves. His mother also emphasized the arbitrary nature of moral and linguistic conventions.

Carnap's mother was evidently the strongest influence on Carnap's early mental development. In many ways this influence probably derived from the religious and educational views of her father, of whom she wrote a biography. She was herself a highly literate person, at home in the German classics, who took a particular interest in the philosophical and religious writings of Theodor Gustav Fechner, the founder of psychophysics. When Carnap began to doubt the religious doctrines he had been brought up with, he turned first to Fechner's mystical pantheism as a more explicit and detailed version of the worldview embodied in the writings of Johann Wolfgang von Goethe. The ethical and practical convictions associated with the religion of his childhood never changed. Though he abandoned it, first for pantheism, then for atheism, this change was very gradual and took a long time. And it was an entirely doctrinal change; it did not affect his values. The pragmatist streak in educational Herbartianism allowed room for the replacement of its religious props by a scientific humanism of the kind Carnap imbibed from the popular writings of Hermann von Helmholtz, Ernst Haeckel, Wilhelm Ostwald, and others.

Ostwald in particular appears to have been an important early influence. A Nobel Prize–winning chemist, he had sketched in his popular writings a consistent and comprehensive worldview firmly anchored in the nineteenth-century positivist tradition of Auguste Comte and Ernst Mach. His wide-ranging interests also encompassed the German classics, the history of science, visual art, politics, and much else. He was perhaps the archetypal embodiment, during the first decade or so of the new century, of a thoroughly and uncompromisingly "scientific worldview." He was unusually cosmopolitan for a German of his generation and had traveled widely, including to the United States, where he was instrumental in establishing physical chemistry as a discipline.

Carnap advocated pacifism and internationalism, and campaigned for the use of an international language such as Esperanto, both among scientists and more widely. Many of these aspects appealed to Carnap; he even became an Esperantist in his teens, while still at school. He was especially influenced by Ostwald's conception of a "system of science" (*System der Wissenschaft*), modeled on Comte's system of unified science. In this conception, there was no fundamental distinction between human and physical sciences, of the kind that the German idealists and neo-Kantians had advocated. All knowledge was part of a single system, whose basic concepts were those of physics. This system was needed as a blueprint, Ostwald thought, for optimizing the hitherto rather aimless and chaotic output of the scientific disciplines; it would give them coherence and enable them to cooperate.

When Carnap studied at the University of Jena, from 1909, he encountered Gottlob Frege and learned modern logic from him. Though he did not immediately see the wider philosophical applications of Frege's logic, he was enthused by Frege's Leibnizian ideal of a universal language that could tie all knowledge together and display its deductive interrelations. Comte and Ostwald, like other nineteenth-century positivists, had been vague about the precise nature of the relations among the various sciences in their proposed "system of science." In Frege's logic, Carnap saw a tool for making these relations completely transparent and explicit, and making the "system of science" into something much more than a vague ideal. Logic could serve as a central discipline for bringing order to the rather chaotic and spontaneous growth of knowledge. This "system of science" could thus be a tool for coordinating and *organizing* knowledge-production on a large scale, in just the way Ostwald had envisaged.

But Jena also subjected Carnap to a quite different kind of influence, one much more at odds with anything in his background up to that time: the German Youth Movement (*Jugendbewegung*). This was a Romantic, back-to-nature rebellion of middle-class German teenagers against the materialistic and socially complacent values of their parents. There was a strong emphasis on a healthy life, especially long walks in the wilderness and avoidance of the "bourgeois" drugs (alcohol, tobacco, caffeine), as well as an idealization of peasant life and the customs of premodern times. The movement took many different local forms. In Jena, the publisher Eugen Diederichs organized the "Sera Circle," a group of university students and other young people who undertook outings with elaborate, medieval-style costumes and rituals, some improvised and some traditional. The annual midsummer celebration was a high point, when the group, with its banners, costumes, and pageantry walked in procession to a mountain some distance from town, accompanied by horse-drawn carriages. There they built a bonfire, danced, feasted, sang, and jumped over the flames two by two until sunrise. In the years just before the First World War, Carnap became very active in organizing these and similar events.

For Carnap, the lasting effect of this involvement was to give him the sense that the basic forms of human life are within human control; they do not have to be accepted from tradition or from existing conventions. This attitude of "voluntarism" would prove to be of fundamental importance to Carnap's philosophy through all its phases. And though the Youth Movement "did not leave any externally visible achievements," Carnap later wrote, "the spirit that lived in this movement, which was like a religion without dogmas, remained a precious inheritance for everyone who had the good luck to take an active part in it. What remained was more than a mere reminiscence of an enjoyable time; it was rather an indestructible living strength which forever would influence one's reactions to all practical problems of life" (Carnap 1956/7, pp. B34–B35). Moreover, it was something he missed throughout his subsequent life:

> After the war … the same spirit was still alive in the life of my newly founded family and in the relationships with friends. When I went to Vienna, however, the situation was different. I still preserved the same spirit in my personal attitude, but I missed it painfully in the social life with others. None of the members of the Vienna Circle had taken part in the Youth Movement, and I did not feel myself strong and productive enough to transform single-handedly the group of friends into a living community, sharing the style of life which I wanted. Although I was able to play a leading role in the

> philosophical work of the group, I was unable to fulfill the task of a missionary or a prophet. Thus I often felt as perhaps a man might feel who has lived in a strongly religious [and] inspired community and then suddenly finds himself isolated in the Diaspora and feels himself not strong enough to convert the heathen. The same feeling I had in a still greater measure later in America, where the power of traditional social conventions is much stronger than it was in Vienna and where also the number of those who have at least sensed some dissatisfaction with the traditional forms of life is smaller than anywhere on the European continent. (Carnap 1956/7, p. B35)

Into this idyllic dawn of a new world erupted the unheralded disaster of August 1914 and the Great War. Carnap and his Sera friends dutifully enlisted and were not even unwilling combatants, at first. Only when they witnessed the scale of the slaughter did doubts arise. Like Wittgenstein on the eastern front, Carnap participated in many of the bloodiest engagements on the western front. Both young philosophers were profoundly alienated by the culture of the officer corps. Both were wounded and were decorated for bravery. But their reactions could not have been more different. Wittgenstein withdrew into an inner life of mystical contemplation, inspired by Leo Tolstoy. Carnap, in contrast, came to appreciate that it was precisely an over-emphasis on the contemplative life, and a lack of interest in public life, that had made the German intelligentsia complicit in the bloodshed, and had allowed it to stand idly by while the political elites had started a world war. The only answer, he now decided, was active involvement in politics. Accordingly, he joined the anti-war independent socialist party, sent clandestine circular letters to friends with excerpts from the foreign press, and wrote well-informed articles about world government for underground newsletters.

The general conception behind this new commitment was a natural extension of the positivist idea of a "system of science" inherited from Comte and Ostwald, combined with the voluntarism Carnap derived from the Youth Movement. For the human race to survive and avoid disasters like the Great War, Carnap thought, it needed to take its fate into its own hand. Conflicts among nations and classes could not be left to an anarchic state of nature, but had to be subordinated to consciously chosen forms of civic cohabitation. These, of course, required highest-level conceptual planning and organization of knowledge; this too was part of the "politics" Carnap now regarded himself as involved in. For all the various social functions to work together, it was essential to arrive at a "structure of community" (*Gemeinschaftsgestalt*) that could serve to coordinate them so as "to remove [these tasks] from the realm of chaotic whim and subordinate them to goal-oriented reason" (Carnap 1918, p. 18).

Carnap's intention immediately after the war was to realize this ambition through teaching and direct political involvement. Before the war he had intended to become a physicist; now his first priority was to obtain the teaching certificate for secondary schools. The papers he wrote to qualify for the certificate show him at work, both within physics itself and in philosophical reflection about the foundations of geometry, on the construction of an Ostwaldian-Comtean "system of science" with Fregean logicist tools. In the course of these projects, he evidently came to realize that his vision of a "system of science" was anything but obvious. Though there had been much talk, among positivists (like Mach) and some systematic philosophers (like Richard Avenarius) of the reducibility of all knowledge to an empirical starting point, much work was still to be done. Like Comte in response to an earlier revolution, Carnap now realized that the reconstruction of society along the lines he had in mind, with its *Gemeinschaftsgestalt* to coordinate all productive activities within it, required the reconstruction of *knowledge* as the first and indispensable step. Though social reform could go ahead meanwhile, it could not be put on a genuinely rational basis until a "system of science" was developed, a conceptual system that was adequate to the scientific and conceptual revolutions of the past decades *and* that afforded a vantage point from which the whole of knowledge could be surveyed and organized, allowing individual claims or theories to be rationally judged. It was to the development of such a conceptual system that Carnap now single-mindedly devoted himself.

EARLY WRITINGS AND PROJECTS

This change in priorities also brought with it a change in career plans. Carnap now decided to pursue an academic career after all, but was faced with the quandary that the kind of work he planned fell between academic stools. The first project he chose for a dissertation topic was, like his 1920 paper on space and geometry, intended to work out a partial "system of science" for a subrealm of knowledge. This time it was to be an axiomatization of relativistic space-time kinematics, and the question Carnap particularly had in mind was much discussed then: Precisely what is the *empirical content* of general relativity, and precisely what parts of it were conventional? Even before the war, Carnap had read Henri Poincaré. Now he also encountered the "radical conventionalist" Hugo Dingler, who rejected relativity on the Poincaréan grounds that all the observations involved could be accommodated without giving up Euclidean geometry, whose axioms are much simpler. Carnap disagreed; the simplicity of the system as a whole should be maximized, he said, not just the simplicity of the axioms, though he admitted that this was itself a conventional decision.

However, his proposed project was rejected by the physics department in Jena as too philosophical, and the philosophers thought it was too scientific. So instead, he reworked his 1920 paper on space and geometry, and this was accepted. The result was Carnap's doctoral dissertation and first philosophical publication, *Der Raum* (Space; 1922). Here too the central question was the status of the empirical basis (*Tatbestand*) within our conceptions of space. The answer, Carnap said, depends on whether we have mathematical, intuitive, or physical space in mind. Formal or mathematical space, Carnap said, can be constructed from logic alone, in the way Bertrand Russell had suggested in *Principles of Mathematics*, and so it has no empirical content. Intuitive space is not constructed in this logicist way, but derives from axioms based on a pure phenomenological essence-perception (*Wesensschau*) of our spatial experience. These axioms concern not the metrical properties of space, as Immanuel Kant had thought, but only its topological properties. Physical space, finally, adds the empirical basis, which, however, as Carnap argued with the aid of an extended example, underdetermines the choice of metrical geometry (it fixes the choice only up to topological assumptions).

During this period, Carnap framed the basic epistemological questions in terms of an "idealistic conception" deriving from the "positivist idealism" of Hans Vaihinger, a neo-Kantian philosopher whose book *The Philosophy of As If* had generated a great deal of discussion after its publication in 1911. Vaihinger took an extreme positivist view of what we actually know: It is only the "chaos" of our immediately present sensations that we can rely on for certain. The "reality" we construct on this basis, whether in science or in everyday life, is not genuine knowledge but a tissue of useful *fictions* that we purposefully invent to get things done in the world and to serve our mental and social needs. These fictions include not just Kant's synthetic a priori propositions (the axioms of arithmetic, geometry, and mechanics, as well as the principles of causality and of the uniformity of nature), but also, for example, the fictions of religion, of natural justice and equal citizenship, of free will and moral reasons. This was essentially a pragmatist position, as Vaihinger himself recognized, though he thought William James wrong to make utility a *standard* of truth. There is genuine truth, Vaihinger maintained, however limited in scope, while the fictions, though useful, are *not* true. They are to be judged by practical results, not by cognitive standards.

Carnap sought to pursue his dream of a system of knowledge within the framework of such an "idealistic conception." He tried various ways of *deducing* aspects of physical "reality" from the "chaos" of experience, even using a makeshift fuzzy logic at one point, but these efforts led nowhere. It seemed impossible to break out of the phenomenal "chaos" convincingly. But amidst all his other projects, the preoccupation with this overall system did not let him go. "I worked on many special problems, always looking for new approaches and improved solutions," Carnap wrote of this period "But in the background there was always the ultimate aim of the total system of all concepts. I believed that it should be possible, in principle, to give a logical reconstruction of the total system of the world as we know it" (Carnap 1956/7, p. E4).

THE *AUFBAU* PROJECT AND VIENNA

In the winter of 1921/1922 Carnap read a book that showed him how to overcome the main obstacle to his project of a "total system of all concepts," Russell's *Our Knowledge of the External World as a Field for Scientific Method in Philosophy*. This book gave Carnap the crucial hint that the way to get from the chaos of experience to a "reality" was not by *analysis* of experience, but by *construction*, using what Russell called a "principle of abstraction": "When a group of objects have that kind of similarity which we are inclined to attribute to possession of a common quality, the principle [of abstraction] shows that membership of the group will serve all the purposes of the supposed common quality, and that therefore, unless some common quality is actually known, the group or class of similar objects may be used to replace the common quality, which need not be assumed to exist" (Russell, pp. 44–45). Experiences could be gathered into equivalence classes. For example, a series of experiences of "red," at a certain position in the visual field, could be defined as equivalent. For the purposes of constructing a "real" world, this class can be regarded as an objectand used in place of the quality. No actual quality, transcending momentary experience, need figure in subsequent steps to a "reality." The evanescence of "chaotic" experience is no longer a constraint. The problem of forcing the fluid character of lived experience into the straightjacket of deductive relations disappears.

Russell's principle also solved another problem. According to Vaihinger, the "chaos" of subjective experience has no structure; nothing is "given" but the undifferentiated chaos itself. No distinguishable "elements" present themselves as naturally discrete or isolable from the chaos, available unambiguously in themselves, without calling on externally imposed fictions. A somewhat less extreme version of this holistic starting point had just been articulated by a new school of "Gestalt" psychologists. Russell's principle of abstraction—his method of substituting "logical constructions for inferred entities" (such as qualities)—solved this problem as well. Instead of trying to isolate specific elements within the undifferentiated "chaos," Carnap could obtain the elements he sought by partitioning the entire "chaos" into just two sectors, which he called the "living" and "dead" parts of experience, corresponding essentially to David Hume's "impressions" and "ideas." This one distinction allowed Carnap to arrange experiences into a temporal sequence ("ideas" belong to the past; "impressions" are present), and thus made it possible to identify holistic "temporal cross-sections" of experience, in which the total experience of a given specious present remains intact as a momentary whole.

This chronological sequence of experiential time slices gave Carnap the basic framework he needed for identifying qualities as cross-temporal equivalence classes of particular aspects within certain time slices. The holistic time-slices of experience did not need to be *analyzed*. Rather, qualities and qualitative relations could be *constructed* by defining equivalence classes of sufficiently "similar" experience aspects (e.g., approximations to "red" at certain coordinates of the visual field) across a series of time slices. ("Similarity" could be defined as precisely as needed.) The result of this procedure—with "quality classes" standing in for qualities, and so on—was therefore essentially what empiricists (like Hume, John Stuart Mill, and Mach) had always hoped to achieve by analysis, but it was accomplished *without* analysis. Carnap called it "quasi-analysis." Once qualities had been constructed, physical objects could be constructed as classes of spatial relations among qualities, and the path to a "reality" was clear.

Carnap still followed Vaihinger in distinguishing sharply between the direct, genuine, first-hand knowledge of the "chaos" and the fictive, constructed nature of "reality." But he put the boundary between them in a different place. Phenomenology, Carnap thought, offered an escape route from Vaihinger's completely undifferentiated chaos. It gave certain basic distinctions *within* the chaos (such as that between "living" and "dead" experience) a degree of objectivity. These distinctions, then, were *not* "fictional" but actually extended the range of what could be genuinely *known*, even *without* fictions, just from the "chaos" itself. So Carnap put the boundary between the "chaos" and the fictions further out than Vaihinger had done. But fictions were still needed to get from this immediately known *primary world* (of "chaos" supplied with a minimal, phenomenologically justified structure) to a fictive *secondary world* of "reality"—be it the everyday world of physical objects and forces, the abstract scientific world of fields and space-time coincidences, or some other construction.

Carnap thought at this point that he could show on phenomenological grounds that the primary world was two-dimensional, in all sense modalities. So the stepping-off point from the fixed primary world up to a freely choosable secondary world was located at the point of ascent from two to three dimensions. Within the primary world, the construction proceeded entirely by explicit definition, beginning from the qualities obtained by quasi analysis. Secondary worlds are not uniquely determined by the one given primary world, so the construction of a secondary world proceeds by optimizing its "fit" to whichever fictions are chosen to guide the construction, subject to the constraint of the primary world.

Regarding the choice among fictions to guide this ascent, Carnap remained as radically pragmatist as Vaihinger. The choice of fictions was entirely a matter of what was practically useful for some purpose. To obtain the scientific secondary world, Carnap suggested, we need adopt only two fictions, corresponding roughly to Kant's categories of cause and substance: (1) a principle of induction or uniformity of nature and (2) a principle of "continuity" (as Mach had called it), the principle that a certain cluster of perceptions grouped into a physical object, say, remains constant while we are not perceiving it if it remains sufficiently similar (by defined standards) before and after the interruption.

It seemed then that the problems facing Carnap's dream of a "total system of all concepts" had been overcome. He could now go public with his grand plan to revolutionize the conceptual framework of knowledge. He immediately wrote up a sketch of the new "total system of all concepts" that he gave the Vaihinger-inspired title *Vom Chaos zur Wirklichkeit* (From the chaos to reality). He organized a conference for the following year (1923) to discuss it—the first conference of "scientific philosophy." The participants, who previously had each been working alone, became a like-minded community. Carnap also talked to Hans Reichenbach and others about starting a new journal to propagate the new ethos. The program of "conceptual politics" was well under way.

Carnap continued to work on his "total system of concepts" and in 1928 published *Der logische Aufbau der Welt* (*The Logical Construction of the World*), which became the programmatic bible of the Vienna Circle (Carnap had joined it in 1926, when he became a junior lecturer at the University of Vienna). The *Aufbau* exemplified the Vienna Circle's goal of "rational reconstruction," the replacement of vague, informal concepts by precise ones defined within a standard logical language in which all of knowledge could be expressed. The concept rationally reconstructed in the *Aufbau* was that of "empirical content" (or "empirical meaning"), which had long been of central importance for empiricists but had never been made logically precise.

Though the germ of the *Aufbau* is already contained in "From the Chaos to Reality," there were also some important changes. In the 1922 system, three components had worked somewhat uneasily together: (1) the *basis* of momentary time-slices of total experience, distilled from a chaotic primary world by phenomenological reflection; (2) the *fictions* that guided the construction of a secondary world from the primary world; and (3) the *logic* that connected the constructional steps. As Carnap worked on the system after 1922, these three parts came to seem less compatible with each other. Though he had greatly reduced the number of fictions from Vaihinger's heterogeneous jumble, the two he had chosen still seemed somewhat ad hoc. And phenomenological reflection, though also a kind of "thought," did not operate mechanically, without mental assistance, as the logical system of Frege and Russell did. Logic and phenomenology seemed to be fundamentally different kinds of constructional procedure that could not be reduced to each other. If Carnap was to take seriously Russell's dictum that "logic gives the method of research," then everything that *could* be done by logic alone *had* to be done by logic alone. Accordingly, by 1925 Carnap gave up the distinction between "primary" and "secondary" worlds (between a single determinate "given" reality and optional constructed "realities"). Instead, he extended the logical construction *downwards* as far as possible to perform the tasks that had previously been left to phenomenology.

This displacement of phenomenology by logic led Carnap to minimize the number of relations required for the construction. By 1925 the number of basic relations had been reduced to five, and in the published *Aufbau* there is only a *single* basic relation—that of "remembered similarity" of qualitative aspects across temporal slices of experience. Indeed, the imperative to eliminate the subjective element altogether and make the construction *entirely* logical led Carnap to the extreme of suggesting that even this one remaining basic relation might be eliminated if we define it "implicitly," that is, define it simply as "whatever basic relation leads to our existing body of scientific knowledge" (1928/2003, sec. 153).

Carnap did not, however, give up Vaihinger's pragmatist orientation. To make the fictions of cause and substance that guided the construction less ad hoc, Carnap suggested that they could be deduced from some "highest principle of constitution," which might in turn be deducible from "whatever it is that knowledge contributes to the more comprehensive context of life purposes" (1928/2003, sec. 105). And he emphasized that the *Aufbau* construction was not the only possible one, but that quite different approaches might be appropriate for different purposes.

The *Aufbau* construction gave the Vienna Circle a standard by which to judge any statement and determine whether it has meaning. Carnap gave a popular lecture around this time in which he depicted human intellectual history since the Greeks as a struggle between "critical intellect" and "poetic imagination." In the ancient world, he said, critical intellect had dealt poetic imagination a major blow with its concept of a single, all-encompassing physical space. In response to any mythical creature or entity the imagination might dream up, critical intellect could now ask, "Where is it located in space?" or, "Tell me exactly how I can get there from here." Imagination took to hiding its goblins and spirits in remote, inaccessible places, but this was only a stopgap. Eventually, imagination struck back more forcefully by inventing *metaphysics*. It hit on the idea of a *nonmaterial* God and other nonmaterial entities. This was plausible, Carnap explained, because we often refer, quite legitimately, to nonmaterial items like numbers, relations, and so on. Many thinking people were taken in. But now, he said, critical intellect has found a tool to combat this maneuver. Just as the ancients had hit upon the idea of an all-encompassing *physical* space, so now we, here in Vienna, have developed a single, all-encompassing *conceptual* space: the *Aufbau* system. This system puts the burden on the poetic imagination to specify exactly how to get to any supposed non-material entity from "here"—from my own immediate experience. This was how the *Aufbau* system provided the basis for the Vienna Circle's campaign against metaphysics and traditional obscurantism, and exemplified the circle's project of "rational reconstruction"—the piecemeal replacement of traditional, vague concepts by more precise and useful ones.

WITTGENSTEIN

When Carnap went to Vienna in 1926, the *Aufbau* was substantially complete. He assumed that its construction of physical objects and theoretical entities would all be of a piece, so that concrete and theoretical objects could also be cashed out again in terms of subjective experience. In 1926 he published the booklet *Physikalische Begriffsbildung* (Physicalconcept formation), in which he argued for the completely seamless intertranslatability of subjective experiences and the sets of 14-tuples of numbers in which, he said, the world could, against a set of background theories, be exhaustively described.

But on arriving in Vienna, Carnap was confronted with a new influence that disrupted this harmony. The Vienna Circle was just in the process of reading Wittgenstein's *Tractatus Logico-Philosophicus* line by line, and Carnap came to share their appreciation of it. The *Tractatus* solved what historically had been the severest problem for empiricism: its inability to account for mathematics. Frege's critique of empiricist efforts (by Mill, for instance) to found arithmetic on empirical generalizations had convinced members of the circle that a different approach was needed. But they also rejected Frege's and Russell's view that logic and mathematics were essentially like laws of nature, only of much greater generality, governing *everything*. Wittgenstein argued, rather, that logic and mathematics are about *nothing*; they are empty. They convey no information about the world, as they are "tautological" artifacts of the language itself and neither make nor exclude any assertions about anything that is or is not the case.

What gives a sentence meaning, Wittgenstein said, is that it is a logical "picture" of a fact. So all meaningful sentences have to be built up out of "atomic" sentences, picturing simplest facts, by truth-functional connectives. Since the number of observation sentences supporting a physical law can only ever be finite, this meant, to the Vienna Circle, that a *universal* law cannot, strictly speaking, have meaning. So in Wittgenstein's framework, a law could be nothing more than the body of evidence for it. This made theoretical science as it had been done for the past few centuries impossible, and it broke the seamless continuity Carnap had previously assumed between subjective experience and theoretical concepts. This was bad enough, but Wittgenstein's conception of meaning raised another problem for the circle. The very sentences expressing that conception fell victim to their own consequences. Wittgenstein confirmed this in the final sentences of the *Tractatus*, where he declared his own book meaningless. So although the Vienna Circle regarded the *Tractatus* as indispensable, they also realized that to do the job they relied on it to do, its conception of language would somehow have to be expanded to admit physical laws and metalinguistic "elucidations."

Carnap's first task, in this project, was an attempt to fit *axiomatic* concepts within Wittgenstein's constraints. During his first few years in Vienna, this was his main focus; he worked until 1930 on a large manuscripthe called *Untersuchungen zur allgemeinen Axiomatik* (Investigations in general axiomatics). Its main point was to show that David Hilbert's use of a "metamathematics" to prove the consistency of merely formal axiom systems, of which most mathematics consists, was ultimately not essential, but that only a single basic language would suffice. In the *Axiomatics*, Carnap takes a "foundation system" of logic, arithmetic, and set theory as the starting point, and stipulates that all axiom systems must be expressed in it; they derive their meaning from being anchored in this absolute system. Where does this "foundation system" itself come from? Carnaop gave a preliminary answer in a sketch entitled "Neue Grundlegung der Logik" (New foundation of logic), where he tried to expand the repertoire of what can be regarded as meaningful (and tautological) within Wittgenstein's picture theory by experimenting with arbitrarily long truth tables.

All this effort came to naught in early 1930 when Alfred Tarski visited the Vienna Circle. In private conversations, he convinced Carnap that the single-language approach of the *Axiomatics* did not really capture the metamathematical concepts that Carnap had wanted to account for in a single language. Later that year a young student of Carnap's, Kurt Gödel, showed that arithmetic was incomplete—that it contained sentences that, although true, could not be proved from its axioms. This contradicted one of the central theorems Carnap had arrived at in his *Axiomatics*.

By the end of 1930, then, the program of rational reconstruction had run aground. The efforts to expand Wittgenstein's restrictive conception of language to allow universal laws and axiomatic mathematics had come to nothing. And much of the damage had been done by mathematicians like Alfred Tarski and Kurt Gödel, who were using metalanguages in very precise ways, apparently flouting Wittgenstein's claim that it was impossible to speak about language *in* language. Could the Vienna Circle's program somehow be rescued?

SYNTAX

On January 21, 1931, Carnap came down with a bad flu. He hardly slept that night. As he lay awake an idea came to him, in a flash, that solved all his problems. The Wittgensteinian conception of meaning went overboard. We can forget about meaning, he realized, at least in our statements *about* the scientific language—our metalinguistic "elucidations." Though the scientific language itself had empirical meaning (in a way that remained to be clarified—this became the subject of the "protocol sentence debate"), in our elucidations of it we are not talking about anything extralinguistic; we are talking *always and only about language.* In these metalinguistic elucidations, we must be careful not to talk about "facts" or about "things," but always confine ourselves to talking rather about "sentences" or "thing names." As Carnap would soon put it, we should in principle restrict ourselves to the "formal mode of speech" (sentences and names) and indulge in the "material mode of speech" (facts and things) only if we are sure we can translate our statements into the formal mode. Carnap adopted the metalinguistic viewpoint of Hilbert, Tarski, and Gödel, and applied this hitherto purely mathematical method to the whole of knowledge. Philosophy itself was to be reconstructed in the formal mode of speech. What remained of philosophy was the metalinguistic "logic of science" (*Wissenschaftslogik*) that could be expressed in the formal mode.

Carnap immediately threw himself into creating the language for the formal mode of speech. Taking his cue from Hilbert's metamathematics, Carnap sought to strip this standard metalanguage of all problematic assumptions. It would consist simply of strings of dots on a page, and the basic laws of arithmetic would arise unambiguously in the metalanguage from the immediately evident patterns of dots (the commutative law, for instance, is immediately evident from the perceptible equivalence of the number of dots counted from the left and from the right). A few months later, when he was preparing to present his new ideas to the Vienna Circle in June of 1931, Carnap found that he could not express certain essential concepts in this limited language, and turned instead to a more usual axiomatized arithmetic. This also had the advantage that, by using Gödel's trick of arithmetizing syntax, Carnap could now express the syntax of the language (its logic) in the language itself. So the syntactic metalanguage collapses into its object language, and there is after all only one language again.

Though some details still needed working out, Carnap was convinced he had what he needed: a canonical language for the formal mode of speech. This gave him a new and different way of eliminating metaphysics, superceding the previous, Wittgensteinian way. The previous criterion had been a criterion for *meaning*. The new criterion was not. It required that any statement either be straightforwardly factual or be translatable into the formal mode of speech. In other words, an acceptable sentence had to be statable in a "correct" language—the canonical language or an equivalent. Assuming that the kinks in his canonical language could be ironed out, Carnap thought it would be capable of expressing the entire language of physics, as well as its own syntax in a sublanguage. Since the Vienna Circle's "unity-of-science" program held that all knowledge was expressible in the language of physics, Carnap put his canonical language forward as a *universal* language (though not as *the* universal language) for all knowledge. So another way of putting the new criterion was this: An acceptable statement must be expressible in the language of physics. The new ideas of January 1931 flowed into the stream of Carnap's discussions in the circle, particularly with Otto Neurath, to produce this new doctrine of *physicalism*.

But the demands on the "correct" language were exorbitant. Though Carnap had wanted to keep it weak and uncontroversial, it also had to be capable of expressing all the mathematics needed for physics. On the other hand, its arithmetized syntax had to be capable of expressing the basic concept of "analytic truth," or there would be no way of saying whether a formal-mode statement "holds." Gödel had shown that provability was not a sufficient criterion for mathematical or logical truth; there are true sentences that are not provable. So a different criterion was needed, one that would identify the logically true sentences solely by means of the formation and transformation rules of the language. Carnap did attempt such a criterion for "analyticity" in the first draft of his syntax book *Logische Syntax der Sprache* (*Logical Syntax of Language*), written between late 1931 and the spring of 1932. He sent the typescript to Gödel, who pointed out that the new criterion was defective, and that it is *impossible* to give a correct definition of analyticity or logical truth in *any* metalanguage that can be faithfully represented in the object language (e.g., by arithmetization). (This is the indefinability of truth we now associate with Tarski.) So it turns out that Carnap's single-language approach will not work after all.

But although Carnap, with Gödel's assistance, would later develop a new definition of analyticity, in a metalanguage, this definition no longer enjoyed the privileged status that one in the *same language* (had it been possible) could have claimed. And indeed, there is no basis for singling out any particular metalanguage as more "suitable" or "natural" than any other. One option may turn out to be more *useful* than another, but there is no basis for privileging one of the many possible candidates as "correct." So the new definition of analyticity hardly seemed to matter any more. Carnap was more impressed with the *language relativity* of any definition of truth or analyticity. The disputes about protocol sentences within the circle merged in his mind with the disputes among intuitionists, logicists, and formalists in the philosophy of mathematics. All these disputes, it suddenly seemed to him in October 1932, really just revolved around the question how to set up the *language*, and there was no right or wrong answer to such questions. He no longer saw any basis for choosing one solution as "correct." One could only try out different ways and see which ones worked better. This new attitude, which completed Carnap's "linguistic turn" and first appeared in his reply to Neurath about protocol sentences in late 1932, received its definitive statement in the "principle of tolerance," enunciated in *Logische Syntax der Sprache* (The Logical Syntax of Language) in 1934.

SEMANTICS, LATER PROJECTS, AND THE IDEAL OF EXPLICATION

Carnap's syntax period was characterized by two successive major ideas. The first, from January 1931, had been the rejection of Wittgenstein's picture theory of meaning and its replacement by (a) a sharp distinction between a language (a calculus or purely formal symbol system) and its interpretation, and (b) the requirement that a language be entirely specified by explicit rules. The second major idea, from October 1932, had been the principle of tolerance: No language is inherently definitive or "correct"; there is no logical "reality" for a language to "correspond to." In the published *Logical Syntax of Language*, these two ideas were enmeshed with a third idea: the restriction to the "formal mode of speech" and the avoidance of meaning. But within a year of the book's publication, that third idea was dropped; Carnap accepted Tarski's new semantical accounts of designation and truth. The first two major "syntax" ideas (those of January 1931 and October 1932), however, survived unscathed, though, for the rest of Carnap's career (so it is actually a bit misleading to call them "syntactic"). What did *not* survive was the overreaction against "meaning" that accompanied the original insight. In distinguishing between a language and its interpretation, Carnap's first response had been to restrict extra-linguistic interpretation to the object language (and there to physicalistic interpretation), and dispense with it entirely in the "elucidatory" metalanguage. But this restriction was loosened when he saw that interpretation could be completely specified by explicit rules (governing satisfaction, designation, and truth).

The remaining thirty-five years of Carnap's career were largely occupied with technical work on a number of of not very successful language projects, of which the best known were these: (1) He tried, in a series of semantic works, to develop a general definition of "analyticity" that would distinguish analytic from synthetic sentences in a natural and obvious way. The shortcomings of these successive attempts were pointed out by W. V. O. Quine, and were often taken to undermine other parts of Carnap's view, for example, the principle of tolerance itself. (2) Carnap also tried unsuccessfully to specify a strict logical relation between observation sentences and theoretical sentences. After he abandoned the *Aufbau* effort to construct theories directly from subjective experience, he offered a series of progressively looser definitions of "empirical content" or "empirical reducibility." These attempts were also subjected to searching criticism, above all by C.G. Hempel. The lesson derived from this failure has generally been to abandon the question altogether, instead of confining the pessimism to Carnap's particular approach. (3) The last three decades of Carnap's life were largely devoted to the creation of an inductive logic. This was intended as a tool for practicing scientists, to give them a way of measuring the objective probability of a theory with respect to the available evidence. It was intended to make precise the informal usage, in everyday *and* scientific life, by which the evidence is taken to "make" one hypothesis "more likely" than another. Carnap's proposals attained some currency in the 1950s and 1960s and were considered by R. B. Braithwaite, for instance, to be the most promising route to a fundamental justification of John Maynard Keynes's theory of probability. But with a few exceptions, Carnap's work on probability has not been in the mainstream of discussion since the 1980s.

Even if these language projects are written off as failures, though, this would not discredit the larger vision or ideal of explication and language engineering that guided Carnap after 1935. He devoted little time to making this ideal explicit, so it must be gleaned indirectly from his approach to the various language projects and from occasional statements, like the famous paper "Empiricism, Semantics, and Ontology" (1950), his replies to critics in the Schilpp volume, as well as unpublished papers and notes.

The basis of this ideal is the utopian conception of highest-level "conceptual politics" that never left him after 1918. He believed that those who are fortunate enough to be able to devote their lives to thought and reflection have a responsibility to devise conceptual frameworks for human knowledge (as a whole) that will maximize the usefulness of that knowledge for the human species—not for some particular use, but for the full spectrum of uses to which humans put knowledge, especially for the purpose of enlightenment, or liberation from unreflective tradition and conformity. In devising such frameworks we are constrained by certain obvious human limitations, but we should not allow ourselves to be overly constrained by the past—the languages handed down to us by our ancestors. Those give us a starting point, certainly, but we should not treat the puzzles and contradictions embedded in natural languages, or in historical languages of philosophy, with any undue reverence. In fact, we should liberate ourselves from them as far as possible when planning new and better frameworks of thought. Certainly our habitual ways of thinking and talking are deeply entrenched, and are hard for us to abandon, but in Carnap's view this is no reason to be constrained by them when we envision new ones.

In Carnap's mature conception, there are three levels of language engineering and language study: *Syntax* considers languages in isolation from anything extralinguistic that they might be thought of as indicating; *semantics* considers languages in relation to an extralinguistic world, but still in isolation from the actual uses of those languages by (human or machine) users; and *pragmatics* considers languages in relation to their use contexts and their users. Each of these three (syntax, semantics, pragmatics) can be considered as *engineering* activities (the creation or discussion of new or improved languages) or as *empirical* studies (of existing languages). The engineering activity Carnap called "pure" syntax, semantics, or pragmatics, while the empirical study he called "descriptive" syntax, semantics, or pragmatics. Linguists generally engage in the *descriptive* syntax, semantics, and pragmatics of already existing natural languages, while logicians generally engage in the *pure* syntax and semantics of constructed languages. Among the traditional sectors of philosophy, epistemology and methodology belong to pragmatics, while whatever remains of metaphysics and ontology belongs to semantics—though this now becomes a matter of *deciding* which entities to make fundamental to a language framework, given existing scientific knowledge, rather than *finding out* what those entities are or might be.

This voluntarist orientation remained fundamental for Carnap. The notion that something beyond the scope of science might actually *be the case* seemed to him a back door to the re-admission of traditional prejudices and conformities of all kinds. Certainly we need to make assumptions, he acknowledged, but we can *decide* on these and spell them out; they are not "out there" for us to *find*. On these grounds he deprecated Quine's preoccupation with ontology. It makes no sense to talk about "what there is," Carnap said, without specifying the language framework in which this is asserted; any such claim is intelligible only relatively to a language framework. It makes perfectly good sense to ask, *within* a framework that includes, say, the Zermelo-Frankel axioms for set theory, whether there are infinite numbers. Such "internal" questions have determinate answers. But it makes no sense, *outside* such a framework, to ask "just in general" whether "there are" infinite numbers. Not only is there no determinate answer, but there is no way to give such an "external" question itself any clear meaning. What we *can* ask instead is the *practical* question whether it is better (e.g., for use in science) to choose a linguistic framework that has infinite numbers or one that does not. But this is not a question of ontology or semantics; this is a question of pragmatics, a question of *which language* we *want*.

The process by which the human species upgrades its messy and imprecise inherited languages to newly built and more precise ones Carnap called *explication*. He acknowledged that this is a piecemeal process, not a revolutionary one. Humanity replaces its concepts a few at a time. Even the people working at the frontier of knowledge have to use a vernacular, a derivative of ordinary language, to discuss the application of the more precise calculi in which they frame their theories. Their vernacular will, of course, be cleaner and more precise than the vernacular of the society at large. In the scientific vernacular, all concepts used are intended in their scientifically rigorous meanings.

But many concepts even in this tidied-up vernacular have no such precise meanings. They may go on being used for generations before they are made precise. The mathematical concept of the derivative of a function, for instance, was put to good use for nearly two centuries before it was given a precise meaning by the work of Cauchy and Weierstrass. Another example Carnap often cited was the replacement of our vague, subjective, intuitive sense of "hot" and "cold" by the precise, quantitative concept of temperature, which we can define intersubjectively by reference to measurement devices. This concept not only takes the place of the former vague concepts for many purposes; it also gave us many capabilities the vague concepts lacked. For instance, it can provide an outside, objective framework or standard against which to judge subjective feelings; instead of just saying "I feel hot" or "I feel feverish," I can take my temperature and find out exactly how much higher it is than its ordinary level. So explication also provides a framework of objectivity that enables us to escape from a merely subjective view of the world. But the replacement of the vague, informal worldview by a framework of more objective concepts is iterative and never complete; temperature is not an ultimate constituent of our theory of nature.

Explication, which in Carnap's view is the main task of conceptual engineering, consists in the *replacement* of a vague concept in need of explication—the *explicandum*—by a more precise one, the *explicatum*. The first step is the *clarification* of the explicandum, the establishment of some basic agreement among those using the vague concept what they mean by it. The next step is a proposal for its replacement, a proposed *explicatum*. This should have the most important uses agreed on in the clarification stage, but need not have all of them. It should, if possible, be expressed in a language framework that makes clear its relation to a wide range of other concepts. Above all, it should be more precise and more useful than the explicandum. The (provisional) acceptance of an explicatum is just its use by the specific community to which it has been proposed and, ultimately, its wider use by the community of those who use the tidied-up scientific vernacular.

Explication differs in one critical respect from the previous Vienna Circle program of "rational reconstruction." Rational reconstruction was a one-way street; vernacular concepts were to be replaced, piece by piece, with more precise ones. It was assumed that there was a single, definitive logical language in which this reconstruction could be done. But under the new regime of tolerance, there is no longer a single correct language. There is an infinity of possible languages for the community to choose from. Explication is therefore *dialectical*, as Howard Stein, a student of Carnap's, has pointed out, in a way that rational reconstruction was not. Knowledge has obvious and far-reaching effects on our practical life (more and more so, it seems, as history advances). It can tell us, among other things, about the likely consequences of various value systems and courses of action, far more than we could have known a few centuries ago. On the other hand, the way we represent our knowledge to ourselves is language-relative. We can only know what we know in a particular language, and the form in which it presents itself to us is relative to that language. The choice *among* languages, though, is not a choice we make *within* a given language framework. It is a practical choice, involving values (as is the choice among explications for a given explicandum, at the local, piecemeal level.). These are *external* questions, in Carnap's terms. So knowledge and values are in a constant feedback relation to each other, in this dialectical ideal of explication; knowledge shapes values and values shape knowledge.

See also Analysis, Philosophical; Logical Positivism; Positivism; Quine, Willard Van Orman.

Bibliography

WORKS BY CARNAP

P. A. Schilpp, ed., *The Philosophy of Rudolf Carnap*, Vol. XI in the Library of Living Philosophers (La Salle, IL: Open Court, 1963), is indispensable. This 1,100-page volume contains Carnap's illuminating intellectual autobiography, 26 critical essays on various aspects of his philosophy, his replies to the critics, and an exhaustive bibliography through 1963. The manuscripts of the original, longer version of the autobiography is held by the Carnap collection of the Young Research Library, UCLA and cited above as "Carnap 1956/7. Another manuscript item cited above (as "Carnap 1918") is a newspaper editorial Carnap planned to publish in October 1918; it is held by the Carnap Collection of the Archive of Scientific Philosophy, University of Pittsburgh.

Carnap's major works include *Der Raum: Ein Beitrag zur Wissenschaftslehre*. Berlin: Reuther & Reichard, 1922; *Physikalische Begriffsbildung*. Karlsruhe, Germany: Braun, 1926; *Der Logische Aufbau der Welt* (1928); English translation by R. George as *The Logical Structure of the World*, 2nd ed. LaSalle, IL: Open Court, 2003; "Überwindung der Metaphysik durch die logische Analyse der Sprache." *Erkenntnis* 2 (1931–1932): 219–241, translated by Arthur Pap as "The Elimination of Metaphysics through Logical Analysis of Language." In A. J. Ayer, ed., *Logical Positivism*. Glencoe, IL: Free Press, 1959: 60–81; "Die physikalische Sprache als Universalsprache der Wissenschaft," in *Erkenntnis* 2 (1931–1932): 432–465, translated by Max Black as *The Unity of Science* (London: Routledge, 1934) *Logische Syntax der Sprache*. Vienna: Springer, 1934, translated by Amethe Smeaton as *Logical Syntax of Language*, 2nd edition. LaSalle, IL: Open Court 2002; "Testability and Meaning." *Philosophy of Science* 3 (1936): 419–471 and 4 (1937): 1–40; *Foundations of Logic and Mathematics*, Vol. I, no. 3, of *International Encyclopedia of Unified Science*. Chicago: University of Chicago Press, 1939; *Introduction to Semantics*. Cambridge, MA: Harvard University Press, 1942; *Meaning and Necessity: A Study in Semantics and Modal Logic*, 2nd ed. Chicago: University of

Chicago Press, 1956; "Empiricism, Semantics, and Ontology." *Revue internationale de philosophie* 4 (1950), 20–40, reprinted in *Meaning and Necessity*, 2d ed., op. cit., 205–221; *Logical Foundations of Probability*, 2nd edition (Chicago: University of Chicago Press,1962); and "The Methodological Character of Theoretical Concepts." In Herbert Feigl et al., eds., *Minnesota Studies in the Philosophy of Science*, Vol. I, Minneapolis: University of Minnesota Press, 1956: 38–76; "The Aim of Inductive Logic." In Ernest Nagel, Patrick Suppes, and Alfred Tarski, eds., *Logic, Methodology, and Philosophy of Science*, Stanford, CA: Stanford University Press, 1962: 303–318.

WORKS ON CARNAP

The best overview of Carnap's work is the collection of essays *Carnap Brought Home: The View from Jena*, edited by Steve Awodey and Carsten Klein (LaSalle, IL: Open Court, 2004). Also essential is Michael Friedman, *Reconsidering Logical Positivism* (Cambridge, U.K.: Cambridge University Press, 1999), which focuses on the early works. A. W. Carus, *Carnap in Twentieth-Century Thought: Explication as Enlightenment* (Cambridge, U.K.: Cambridge University Press, 2006) cites a range of unpublished sources.

The *Aufbau* was subject to close technical analysis by Nelson Goodman, *The Structure of Appearance*, 3rd ed. Boston, MA: Kluwer, 1977, and from a very different viewpoint, focused on its neo-Kantian origins, by Alan Richardson, *Carnap's Construction of the World: The Aufbau and the Emergence of Logical Empiricism*. Cambridge, U.K.: Cambridge University Press, 1998.

The *Syntax* has attracted a great deal of attention since 1990. Among the most important contributions are Thomas Ricketts, "Carnap's Principle of Tolerance, Empiricism, and Conventionalism." In *Reading Putnam*, edited by P. Clark and B. Hale. Oxford: Blackwell, 1994: 176–200; Warren Goldfarb and Thomas Ricketts, "Carnap and the Philosophy of Mathematics." In *Science and Subjectivity: The Vienna Circle and Twentieth-Century Philosophy*. Berlin: Akademie-Verlag, 1992: 61–78.

The debate between Carnap and Quine has also generated much secondary literature. The classic statements are in the Schilpp volume, as well as Quine's famous "Two Dogmas of Empiricism." Richard Creath has edited their correspondence, together with some very interesting documents, in *Dear Carnap—Dear Van: The Quine-Carnap Correspondence and Related Work*. Berkeley: University of California Press, 1990, with an introduction that gives a lucid overview of the controversy. Important contributions to the debate since then include Howard Stein, "Was Carnap Entirely Wrong, After All?" *Synthese* 93 (1992): 275–295; G.H. Bird, "Carnap and Quine: Internal and External Questions," *Erkenntnis* 42 (1995): 41–64; and Richard Creath "The Linguistic Doctrine and Conventionality: The Main Argument in 'Carnap and Logical Truth,'" In *Logical Empiricism in North America*, edited by Gary L. Hardcastle and Alan Richardson. Minneapolis: University of Minnesota Press, 2003: 234–256.

Among other topics in the vast literature, the posthumously published critique of Carnap by Kurt Gödel ("Is Mathematics Syntax of Language?" in Kurt Gödel, *Collected Works, vol. III: Unpublished Essays and Lectures*, Oxford: Oxford University Press, 1995: 324–363, with an introductory note by Warren Goldfarb) has aroused much interest; see Goldfarb and Ricketts (above); also Steve Awodey and A.W. Carus, "How Carnap Could Have Replied to Gödel." In Awodey and Klein (above). Finally, Richard Jeffrey addresses a central feature of Carnap's philosophy, in the context of the inductive logic, in his paper on "Carnap's Voluntarism," in *Logic, Methodology, and Philosophy of Science IX*, edited by D. Prawitz, B. Skyrms, and D. Westerståhl. Amsterdam: Elsevier, 1994: 847–866.

A.W. Carus (2005)

CARNEADES

(214–129/8 BCE)

Carneades became scholarch of the Academy (Plato's school) sometime before 155 BCE, when he was sent to Rome along with the leaders of the Stoa and the Peripatos (Aristotle's school) to represent the interests of Athens before the senate. It was during the embassy to Rome that the most notorious episode in his life took place. According to tradition, Carneades delivered public lectures on succeeding days, defending justice on the first and arguing that it is a form of folly on the second day.

He was renowned in antiquity above all for the argumentative virtuosity that he displayed in the skeptical examination of views of other philosophers. For this he was indebted to the example of Arcesilaus, who had inaugurated the skeptical turn in the Academy in the third century BCE, which saw the examination of other schools' theories, especially the Stoa's, replace the elaboration of its own positive doctrines as the school's principal occupation. By common consent, Carneades brought this practice to its highest level. Until the dissolution of the school, which probably occurred under the scholarch Philo of Larissa, who left Athens for Rome in 88 BCE, philosophy in the Academy and among the philosophers in its orbit was dominated by Carneades and his legacy. He also stimulated Stoics such as Antipater of Tarsus to modify and refine their positions.

CARNEADES AND THE ACADEMY

Like Arcesilaus and Socrates before him, Carneades wrote nothing, but exerted an influence on his students and contemporaries through his teaching and in-person practice of philosophical debate. What is known of him depends ultimately on works written by those who were in a position to observe him, especially Clitomachus, his student and, after an interval, successor as head of the Academy. None of these works have survived, but they were mined extensively by authors such as Cicero and Sextus Empiricus, whose books are available.

Carneades was credited in antiquity with founding the third or New Academy, which succeeded the second or Middle Academy of Arcesilaus and the old Academy of Plato and his immediate followers. Two new characteristics appear to set Carneades apart from his middle Academic predecessors. Ancient philosophers and modern historians of philosophy have credited him with a less skeptical attitude toward the possibility of well-founded beliefs, if not of certain knowledge. And the evidence shows that he tackled and sometimes defended views about a wider range of issues—not only epistemology, but logic, ethics, natural philosophy, and theology as well. If the first of these is correct, the second comes as no surprise. A moderation of the Academy's skepticism would have opened the way for the suitably circumspect adoption of views in ethics, natural philosophy, and other areas.

Caution is in order, however. The Academics' arguments were in the first instance dialectical. They aimed to deduce conclusions unwelcome to an opponent from assumptions to which that opponent was committed, either because they were already explicitly incorporated in the opponent's theories or because they were for some other reason difficult for the opponent to reject. Without committing their authors to a position themselves, such arguments expose difficulties within the opponent's position and show that the opponent's claims to knowledge were not secure.

Carneades's practice of defending positive views, which at first appears to be a departure from the Academic tradition of dialectical argument, may instead be viewed as a continuation of it by other means. Arguments between the Academy and other schools often reached an impasse. The powerful case brought by the Academics against Stoic epistemology, for instance, elicited a formidable response. If the burden of proof belonged to the Academy, it had not proved its case; the Stoics were not obliged to concede all the premises of the Academy's arguments on pain of self-contradiction. On the other hand, by rejecting those premises, the Stoics often committed themselves to theses that were highly disputable and implausible. And they were not content merely to exhibit the consistency of their theories; they claimed that these theories were true, and that open-minded and intelligent auditors could be persuaded of this.

To this end, the Stoics now argued that the consequences of rejecting their position were unacceptable and that no alternative could do justice to the relevant considerations. If an argument of this kind were successful, the Stoics' opponents would be compelled to reevaluate their doubts. At a minimum, Carneades's positive proposals served to counter arguments of this kind by showing that there remained alternatives that his opponents were not in a position to exclude. Thus, although they were his in the sense of being his creations, Carneades's proposals need not have been his in the sense of expressing his convictions. Some of his theories seem to have been meant only to serve polemical purposes, others were considerably more substantial and deserve to be taken seriously in their own right. It is obvious that some of Carneades's successors did adopt positions of his; It is obvious that some of Carneades's successors adopted some of his theories as their own positions; it is less clear whether Carneades committed himself to these or any other theories.

CARNEADES'S SKEPTICAL ARGUMENTS

Like his Academic predecessors, Carneades argued for the two epistemological propositions for which ancient skepticism is most famous: that nothing can be known and that one ought therefore to suspend judgment about all matters. Strictly speaking, they argued that there are no cognitive impressions. The cognitive impression (*kataleptikē phantasia*), the Stoics' criterion, is a perceptual impression that arises in conditions that both ensure that it is true and impart to it a clarity and distinctness that belong only to impressions produced in this way. By confining one's assent to cognitive impressions, one can avoid accepting any false perceptual impressions. Because this is a necessary condition for knowledge according to the Stoa, if there are no cognitive impressions, it follows for anyone who accepts Stoic epistemological views that nothing can be known. The Academy made its case by arguing that the special character of clarity and distinctness allegedly peculiar to the cognitive impression was not, in fact, confined to impressions that had arisen in the ideal conditions specified by the Stoa, but could in fact also belong to false impressions, which were therefore indistinguishable from impressions with the required truth-guaranteeing origin.

Carneades probably added to the stock of skeptical arguments that he had inherited, but the contribution to the debate for which he is best known came in response to the Stoics' counterarguments. In answer to their contention that, without cognitive impressions, human beings would be deprived of a basis for rational action as well as the possibility of wisdom, he developed a theory of probable impressions (from *probabilis*, that which invites approval, Cicero's Latin for the Greek *pithanos*, persuasive). The theory describes how one may discriminate among impressions by checking to see whether an initially persuasive impression agrees with one's other impressions or if there is anything about the conditions in which it arose that casts doubt on it. Depending on the amount of time available and the importance of the matter at issue, one may perform more or fewer such checks. No amount of checking is sufficient to eliminate the possibility of error, but it will be possible to achieve the degrees of confidence required in different circumstances to make rational action and theoretical inquiry possible. The theory is an early instance of fallibilism.

This account of probable impressions is behind the views that Carneades defended about assent. Sources reveal that he sometimes argued that the wise person will withhold assent, but be able to act and inquire by going along with probable impressions in a way that does not amount to assent; whereas on other occasions, Carneades maintained that the wise person will assent and so form opinions, but with the proviso that he may be wrong. The first view, championed by Clitomachus, is the classical skeptical stance that influenced the other ancient school of skeptics, the Pyrrhonists. The second, which was favored by Philo of Larissa among others, gave rise to a form of probabilism, which is the other legacy of the New Academy.

ETHICS

In ethics Carneades was famous for describing a framework that allegedly classified not only all the views about the goal of life that had been held, but also all those that could be held. He starts with the assumption that practical wisdom must have an object, and one toward which human beings have a natural impulse. He identifies three possibilities: pleasure, freedom from pain, and natural advantages such as health and strength. The principle of virtue is to act with a view to obtaining one of these. There are six simple views, depending on whether the goal is merely to act with a view to obtaining one of the three candidate objects or actually to obtain it. Three further combined views take the goal to be a combination of virtue and actually obtaining the corresponding object. The Stoic position, that virtue is the only good, appears third on the list as the view that the goal is acting with a view to obtaining the natural advantages whether one obtains them or not. At different times Carneades defended the view that the goal is actually to obtain the natural advantages or the view that it is a combination of virtue and pleasure. His aim seems to have been to challenge the Stoics by showing that the considerations captured by the framework do not all point to their view. Carneades's division influenced his successors and through Cicero the understanding of Hellenistic ethical theory.

Other issues that attracted Carneades's attention include Stoic and Epicurean views about fate and moral responsibility and Stoic theology, against the last of which he used a series of Sorites arguments to show that the Stoics could not consistently set any bounds to the divine, so that on their view everything threatened to become divine.

See also Ancient Skepticism; Arcesilaus; Greek Academy.

Bibliography

TEXTS OF CARNEADES

Mette, H. J. "Weitere Akademiker heute Von Lakydes bis zu Kleitomachos." *Lustrum* 27 (1985): 39–148.

STUDIES OF CARNEADES

Algra, Keimpe. "Chrysippus, Carneades, Cicero: The Ethical *Divisiones* in Cicero's *Lucullus*." In *Assent and Argument: Studies in Cicero's Academic Books*, edited by Brad Inwood and Jaap Mansfeld. Utrecht, Netherlands: Brill, 1997.

Allen, James. "Academic Probabilism and Stoic Epistemology." *Classical Quarterly*, n.s., 44 (1994): 85–113.

Allen, James. "Carneadean Argument in Cicero's Academic Books." In *Assent and Argument: Studies in Cicero's Academic Books*, edited by Brad Inwood and Jaap Mansfeld. Utrecht, Netherlands: Brill, 1997.

Bett, Richard. "Carneades' Distinction between Assent and Approval." *Monist* 73 (1990): 3–20.

Burnyeat, Myles. "Gods and Heaps." In *Language and Logos: Studies in Ancient Greek Philosophy Presented to G. E. L. Owen*, edited by Malcolm Schofield and Martha Craven Nussbaum. Cambridge, U.K.: Cambridge University Press, 1982.

Frede, Michael. "The Sceptic's Two Kinds of Assent and the Question of the Possibility of Knowledge." In *Philosophy in History*, edited by Richard Rorty, J. B. Schneewind, and Quentin Skinner. Cambridge, U.K.: Cambridge University Press, 1984. Reprinted in Michael Frede's *Essays in Ancient Philosophy*. Minneapolis: University of Minnesota Press, 1987.

Frede, Michael. "Stoics and Skeptics on Clear and Distinct Impressions." In *The Skeptical Tradition*, edited by Myles Burnyeat. Berkeley: University of California Press, 1983.

Schofield, Malcolm. "Academic Epistemology." In *The Cambridge History of Hellenistic Philosophy*, edited by Keimpe Algra, Jonathan Barnes, Jaap Mansfeld, and Malcolm Schofield. Cambridge, U.K.: Cambridge University Press, 1999.

Striker, Gisela. "Sceptical Strategies." In *Doubt and Dogmatism: Studies in Hellenistic Epistemology*, edited by Malcolm Schofield, Myles Burnyeat, and Jonathan Barnes. Oxford: Oxford University Press, 1980.

James Allen (2005)

CAROLINGIAN RENAISSANCE

The reign of Charlemagne (768–814) ended the long period of cultural decay and intellectual stagnation that had begun over three centuries before with the barbarian invasions of Western Europe. Despite the disintegration of the Carolingian Empire under Charlemagne's successors, the cultural revival that he inspired continued until the Vikings put an end to it, and even then something of the achievement of the eighth and ninth centuries survived to foster the renaissance of the eleventh and twelfth centuries.

The "Carolingian Renaissance" was dominated by two practical interests, ecclesiastical reform and social progress. Since Charlemagne depended on churchmen to implement his educational policy, the religious motives and ecclesiastical achievements—liturgical reform, monastic renewal, advancement of clerical education—inevitably predominated. Literary sensibility and intellectual curiosity were not, however, wholly lacking in the churchmen of the age, and some charming poems and substantial doctrinal treatises remain to testify to their intellectual versatility.

The chief agent, though not the finest mind, of the Carolingian Renaissance was the Englishman Alcuin (735–804). The Irishman John Scotus Erigena (c. 810–c. 877), the Lombard Paul Warnefrid (d. c. 800), the Spaniard Theodulf of Orleans (d. 821), the Frenchman Remigius of Auxerre (d. c. 908), and the German Rabanus Maurus (d. 856) exemplify the cosmopolitan character of the movement.

The centers of the revival were cathedral and monastic schools established by legislation throughout the Frankish dominions. In addition to a theology consisting mainly of traditional biblical exegesis, their curriculum included the seven liberal arts—the trivium of grammar, rhetoric, and logic and the quadrivium of arithmetic, geometry, astronomy, and music. The assimilation of ancient learning was stressed, and little original work was done; the chief forms of academic literature were commentaries and handbooks.

In philosophy the arts curriculum did not go beyond logic. Several scholars are known to have touched on the question of universal ideas, but the issue does not seem to have been widely debated. The Carolingian Renaissance produced very little speculative philosophy; the great exception, the work of Erigena, stands alone both in its systematic character and in its Neoplatonic inspiration. The few philosophically interesting ideas of the age emerged more or less incidentally in the course of theological reflection and debate.

Perhaps the most important single fragment of philosophical theology to survive from the ninth century is the *Dicta Candidi de Imagine Dei,* attributed to the monk Candidus, schoolmaster at Fulda in 822, which includes the earliest known dialectical demonstration of God's existence by a medieval author. The principle of the proof is the idea of the scale of perfection. Moving from that which simply exists through that which exists and lives and that which exists, lives, and possesses intelligence, the writer argues that the scale would be incomplete without the omnipotent intelligence which is God.

Another small work of some philosophical interest was obviously inspired by consideration of the problem of universals. Fredegisus of Tours (died 834), in his *Epistola de Nihilo et Tenebris,* assumes that every term has some real entity corresponding to it. He concludes that the "nothing" (*nihil*) of the orthodox Christian doctrine of creation "out of nothing" must be conceived as a preexistent, undifferentiated stuff out of which God created everything, including human souls and bodies. Fredegisus was evidently an early instance of a theological dialectician who found difficulty in reconciling the results of his logical analysis of the meaning of terms with doctrinal orthodoxy; the problem was not widely recognized as urgent until the eleventh century.

The outstanding intellectual issue of the Carolingian Renaissance was unquestionably the problem of predestination. The German monk Gottschalk (d. c. 868) was accused of teaching that from eternity God has infallibly predestined some men to salvation and others to damnation; that God therefore does not in any sense will the salvation of all men; that Christ's atoning sacrifice was offered only for the elect; and that each man's will is irresistibly determined either to good or to evil. The authority of Augustine and of his great disciples Fulgentius of Ruspe and Prosper of Aquitaine was invoked by Gottschalk and others in favor of these ideas. In opposition to this intransigent Augustinianism, Erigena expounded a libertarian doctrine, inspired by Greek thought; others sought a middle way within the Augustinian tradition. The controversy was long and heated, and its terms were not always clearly defined, but it is obvious that the crucial issue was the relation between divine immutability and omnipotence, on the one hand, and human freedom and moral responsibility, on the other. After a series of conflicting synodical decisions, the moderate Augustinians were officially vindicated, but the debate was to be repeatedly renewed in the later Middle Ages and the Reformation and Counter-Reformation.

A second vigorous controversy of the period had to do with the presence of Christ in the Eucharist. Paschasius Radbertus (d. c. 860), in his *De Corpore et Sanguine Domini,* the first technical elaboration of Eucharistic doctrine in theological history, asserted the identity of the sacramental elements with the historical body of Jesus crucified and glorified. Although he insisted at the same time on the spiritual and mystical manner of Christ's presence, some of his statements could be interpreted in a crudely materialistic sense, and Ratramnus (d. 868), in his *De Corpore et Sanguine Domini,* opposed an ostensibly symbolist doctrine to the realism of Radbertus; owing to vagueness of definition, however, it remains uncertain how far and in precisely what way the two doctrines were incompatible. The debate is significant primarily because it eventually issued in the definition of the dogma of transubstantiation by the Fourth Lateran Council (1215) and in the subtle metaphysical elaboration of that dogma in the theology of Thomas Aquinas.

See also Alcinous; Augustine, St.; Augustinianism; Determinism, A Historical Survey; Erigena, John Scotus; Libertarianism; Reformation; Thomas Aquinas, St.

Bibliography

TEXTS

Alcuin

Duemmler, E., ed. *Monumenta Germaniae Historica, Epistolae.* Vol. 4. Berlin: Weidmann, 1895.

Duemmler, E., ed. *Monumenta Germaniae Historica, Poetae Latini Aevi Carolini.* Vol. 1, 160–351. Berlin: Weidmann, 1881.

Migne, J.-P., ed. *Patrologiae cursus completus. Series Latina.* Paris, 1844–. Vols. 100–101.

Candidus: Dicta Candidi de Imagine Dei

Hauréau, B. *Histoire de la philosophie scolastique.* Vol. 1, 134–137. Paris, 1872.

John Scotus Eriugena

Sheldon-Williams, I. P. ed., and L. Bieler, col. *Johannis Scotti Eriugenae Periphyseon (De divisione naturae).* Dublin: Dublin Institute for Advanced Studies, 1968–.

Fredegisus of Tours: Epistola de Nihilo et Tenebris

Fredegisus. *Epistola de Nihilo et Tenebris.* In J. P. Migne, *Patrologia Latina.* 221 vols. Paris, 1844–1864. Vol. CV, cols. 751–756.

Gottschalk

Strecker, K., ed. *Monumenta Germaniae Historica, Poetarum Latiorumi Medii Aevi.* Vol. 6, 86–106. Munich, 1951.

Hrabanus Maurus

Duemmler, E., ed. *Monumenta Germaniae Historica, Poetae Latini Aevi Carolini.* Vol. 2, 154–258. Berlin: Weidmann, 1884.

Paschasius Radbertus

Paschasius Radbertus. Works Vol. CXX. Berlin: Weidmann, 1884.

Paulus, B. ed. *Pascasius Radbertus De corpore et sanguine Domini: cum appendice Epistola ad Fredugardum.* Turnhout, Belgium: Brepols, 1969.

Traube, L., ed. *Monumenta Germaniae Historica, Poetae Latini Aevi Carolini.* Vol. 3, 38–53. Berlin: Weidmann, 1896.

Paul the Deacon

Duemmler, E., ed. *Monumenta Germaniae Historica, Poetae Latini Aevi Carolini.* Vol. 1, 35–86. Berlin: Weidmann, 1881.

Waitz, G., ed. *Monumenta Germaniae Historica, Scriptores Rerum Langobardicarum et Italicarum.* Hannover: Weidmann, 1878.

Ratramnus

Migne, J.-P., ed. *Patrologiae cursus completus. Series Latina.* Paris, 1844–. Vol. 121, cols. 1–346, 1153–1156.

Ratramnus. Works. Vol. CXXI.

Remigius of Auxerre

Edwards, B., ed. *Remigii Autissiodorensis Expositio super Genesim.* Turnhout, Belgium: Brepols, 1999.

Lutz, C. E., ed. *Commentum in Martianum Capellam.* 2 vols. Leiden: Brill, 1962–1965.

Silk, E. T., ed. *Saeuli noni auctoris in Boetii Consolationem philosophiae commentarius.* Rome: American Academy in Rome, 1935.

Theodulf of Orleans

Duemmler, E., ed. *Monumenta Germaniae Historica, Poetae Latini Aevi Carolini.* Vol. 1, 437–581. Berlin: Weidmann, 1881.

STUDIES

Colish, M. L. *Medieval Foundations of the Western Intellectual Tradition, 400-1400.* New Haven, CT: Yale University Press, 1997.

Colish, M. L. *The Mirror of Language; A Study in the Medieval Theory of Knowledge.* New Haven, CT: Yale University Press, 1968.

Marenbon, J. *Early Medieval Philosophy (480–1150): An Introduction.* New York: Routledge, 1983.

Marenbon, J. *From the Circle of Alcuin to the School of Auxerre: Logic, Theology, and Philosophy in the Early Middle Ages.* Cambridge, U.K.: Cambridge University Press, 1981.

McCracken, G. E., ed. *Early Medieval Theology.* Philadelphia: Westminster Press, 1957.

McKitterick, R., ed. *Carolingian Culture: Emulation and Innovation.* Cambridge, U.K.: Cambridge University Press, 1994.

Moran, D. *The Philosophy of John Scottus Eriugena: A Study of Idealism in the Middle Ages.* Cambridge, U.K., and New York: Cambridge University Press, 1989.

Sullivan, R. E. "The Carolingian Age: Reflections on Its Place in the History of the Middle Ages." *Speculum: A Journal of Medieval Studies* 64 (1989): 267–306.

Waddell, Helen. *The Wandering Scholars*, 6th ed. London, 1932.

Eugene R. Fairweather (1967)
Bibliography updated by Joseph Pucci (2005)

CARROLL, LEWIS
(1832–1898)

Lewis Carroll is the pen name of Charles Lutwidge Dodgson. The eldest son of a large clerical family, he was born at Daresbury, Cheshire, was educated at Rugby School, and entered Christ Church, Oxford, in 1850. On obtaining first-class honors in mathematics in 1854, he was appointed student and mathematical lecturer of the college, and remained on its foundation until his death. In many ways an archetype of the pernickety bachelor don, Dodgson had a wholly uneventful academic career. Hampered by a stammer, he shone neither as lecturer nor as preacher (he took deacon's orders in 1861). He embroiled himself—often amusingly, although usually without effect—in academic politics, was for a time curator of the college common room, and visited Russia in 1867. His leisure was spent in gallery-going and theatergoing; in photography, at which he was an expert; in the writing of light verse; and in the patronage of an interminable succession of small girls. The last peculiarity has endeared him to psychoanalytical biographers, who would seem, however, to have enriched the literature of nonsense on the subject more often than they have been able to explain it.

Dodgson the mathematician published a number of books and pamphlets, none of any lasting importance. The best known is *Euclid and His Modern Rivals* (London, 1879); the most useful, probably his edition of *Euclid I & II* (London, 1882); and the most original, his contributions to the mathematical theory of voting, to which attention was drawn by D. Black in his *Theory of Committees* (Cambridge, U.K., 1958). Dodgson's mathematical outlook was, in general, conservative and provincial, aiming no higher than the improvement of elementary teaching or routine calculation. His talent found greater scope in the construction of puzzles contained in *A Tangled Tale* (London, 1885) and *Pillow Problems* (London, 1893), which at times show depth as well as ingenuity. The same can be said of his dabblings in symbolic logic, which otherwise make little advance on the work of Augustus De Morgan and John Venn. His *Game of Logic* (London, 1887) and *Symbolic Logic, Part I* (London, 1893) present logic merely as a mental recreation devoted to the solution of syllogistic problems by means of a square diagram and colored counters. His logical output was completed by nine papers on elementary logic and by two short pieces in *Mind* (n.s., 3, 1894 and n.s., 4, 1895). His influence is to be seen mainly in the attempts of later logicians to imitate the elegant absurdity of his examples. Their failure merely emphasizes the rarity of his own peculiar gift.

Needless to say, that gift finds its happiest exercise in his writings for children. *Alice in Wonderland* (London, 1865), *Through the Looking-Glass* (London, 1871), and *The Hunting of the Snark* (London, 1876) and, to a lesser extent, the two parts of *Sylvie and Bruno* (London, 1889 and 1893), are the only works that keep his name alive—or deserve to do so. Apart from *Pickwick,* and perhaps *Waverley,* they seem also to be the only works of fiction generally known to philosophers, and have been constantly pillaged for quotations. All five are dream narratives or have episodes depicting dreams, whose aberrant logic is responsible for much of their philosophic interest and fun. *Alice in Wonderland* exploits the idea of sudden variations in the size of the heroine; its sequel, the conception of a world in which time, space, and causality are liable to operate in reverse. The characters—a bizarre medley of nursery and proverbial figures, animals (fabulous or otherwise), plants, playing cards, and chessmen—are all much addicted to argument; and their humor, where it does not rely upon puns, is largely a matter of pursuing logical principles to the point of sophistry or absurdity. The frog, who supposes that an unanswered door must have been asking something, is a simple case in point. The King of Hearts and the White King, who both take "nobody" for a person, are victims of the same error and have often been cited as a warning to less venial, because less nonexistent, hypostatizers of the null class.

These books are further remarkable for their echoes—and pre-echoes—of philosophic controversy. Tweedledum and Tweedledee are Berkeleian metaphysicians, and the latter has notions of logic that bespeak the influence of Gottfried Wilhelm Leibniz. Alice herself, on the road to their house, is a step ahead of Gottlob Frege in discovering the difference between *Sinn* and *Bedeutung.* Humpty Dumpty has been taken, on anatomical grounds, for a Hegelian; but his ascription of fixed meaning to proper names and denial of it to general terms, plus his confident philology and shaky mathematics, proclaim him beyond doubt an early, if eccentric, linguistic analyst. The White Knight's reactionary views on the mind-body question give no hint of the metalinguistic virtuosity he later displays in the announcement of his song. The distinctions there enunciated have been formalized by Ernest Nagel in

"Haddocks' Eyes" (in J. R. Newman, *The World of Mathematics,* New York, 1956, Vol. III, pp. 1886–1890). They would not have troubled the Duchess, another adroit logician, although her primary interest is in morals. Her cat, on the other hand, although adept enough at defying the principle that an attribute must inhere in a substance, offers a regrettably invalid proof of its own madness, as does the pigeon of Alice's serpentinity. The Hatter, March Hare, and Dormouse are sounder reasoners; whatever their troubles with time, they know a fallacy of conversion when they see one, and it is no great wonder that Messrs. Bertrand Russell, George Edward Moore, and John McTaggart, who were supposed to resemble them, should have been known at one time as the "Mad Tea Party of Trinity."

Not even Nobody, in his senses, would venture to identify that other and more formidable trio, the Queen of Hearts and her chessboard cousins. The former's principle of government by decapitation scarcely ranks as a political theory; but the White Queen is respected by philosophers both for her abilities in believing the impossible and for her success in proving, for the special case of jam at least, that the future *will* resemble the past, if not the present. The Red Queen is no less celebrated, among physicists, for her anticipations of the theory of relativity. In this, however, she meets competition from the Bellman in the *Snark,* who has been acclaimed, on the strength of his map, as the first general relativist and is, in any case, the undisputed inventor of an interesting three-ply version of the semantic theory of truth (⊢p. ⊢p. ⊢p ≡ "p" is true). Of his crew members, the Baker, with his lost identity and Heideggerian premonitions of impending *Vernichtung,* has been plausibly represented as a protoexistentialist; but the other protagonists still abide the conjecture of commentators, as do the quest and the quarry itself. The Snark has been taken for everything from the Tichborne inheritance to the North Pole, and from a business depression to the atom bomb. F. C. S. Schiller's interpretation of it in *Mind!* (1901, pp. 87–101) as the Absolute is elaborately argued, and doubtless finds an echo in the *Oxford Dictionary*'s definition of the creature as a "chimerical animal of ill-defined characteristics and potentialities"; but its fondness for bathing machines is not really explained thereby, and the theory founders completely on the Bellman's explicit assertion, confirmed by the Baker's uncle, that Snarks are Many and not One. Nobody, it is true, has been more successful than Schiller on this point, and his views have been generally accepted; but the opinions of nonentities have no place in a grave work of learning such as the present, so neither use nor mention of them is appropriate here.

See also Berkeley, George; De Morgan, Augustus; Frege, Gottlob; Heidegger, Martin; Leibniz, Gottfried Wilhelm; Logic, History of; McTaggart, John McTaggart Ellis; Moore, George Edward; Nagel, Ernest; Russell, Bertrand Arthur William; Schiller, Ferdinand Canning Scott; Venn, John.

Bibliography

Apart from the standard *Life and Letters of Lewis Carroll* by his nephew, S. D. Collingwood (London: T.F. Unwin, 1899), the soberest accounts of Carroll's life are Derek Hudson, *Lewis Carroll* (London: Constable, 1954), and Roger Lancelyn Green, *Story of Lewis Carroll* (New York: Henry Schuman, 1950) and *Lewis Carroll* (London: Bodley Head, 1960).

The least incomplete version of Lewis Carroll's works is *The Complete Works of Lewis Carroll* (London and New York, 1939). The most philosophical editions are *The Annotated Alice* (New York: C.N. Potter, 1960) and *The Annotated Snark* (New York: Simon and Schuster, 1962), edited by Martin Gardner.

The pioneer work of logical investigation in this field is P. E. B. Jourdain, *The Philosophy of Mr B*rtr*nd R*ss*ll* (Chicago: Open Court, 1918). Further light on the subject may be obtained, inter alia, from R. B. Braithwaite, "Lewis Carroll as Logician," in *Mathematical Gazette* 16 (1932): 174–178; P. Alexander, "Logic and the Humour of Lewis Carroll," in *Proceedings of the Leeds Philosophical and Literary Society* 6, Part 8 (1951): 551–566; and, despite some inaccuracies, from W. Weaver, "Lewis Carroll, Mathematician," in *Scientific American* 194 (4) (1956): 116–128; and R. W. Holmes, "The Philosopher's *Alice in Wonderland,*" in *Antioch Review* 19 (2) (1959): 133–149.

P. L. Heath (1967)

CARROLL, LEWIS [ADDENDUM]

The success of the "Alice" books established Charles L. Dodgson's reputation as a gifted writer of children's literature. His admirers expected humor in everything he wrote from then on, an attitude that affected the reception of his serious pieces and prevented his work from contributing to the development of their subjects. For example, the more amusing *Euclid and His Modern Rivals* (1879) overshadowed his more important book, *Curiosa Mathematica. Part 1. A New Theory of Parallels* (1888).

Dodgson made significant contributions to linear algebra in *An Elementary Treatise on Determinants* (1867), a book that though marred by odd notation and unusual terminology, contains the first written proof of a standard theorem connecting the rank of a matrix with the existence of solutions to certain linear systems (chapter 4, proposition II). One of his techniques, condensation, was used in an early step of the solution to the alternating sign matrix problem (Bressoud 1999).

In the field of cryptology his five cipher systems, based on the three cipher paradigms of his time (Vigenère, Beaufort, Variant Beaufort) are not well known. These were: Key-Vowel, Matrix, Alphabet, Telegraph, and Memoria Technica. The first two (1858, unpublished) were unbreakable from a practical point of view. The third and fourth (1868) were secure by the standards of his time for ordinary telegrams and mailed postcards. The last (1875), directly tied to word games, was the most literary.

His publications on the theory of voting consisted of four pamphlets, three written between 1873 and 1876, and *The Principles of Parliamentary Representation* (1884). The pamphlets of the 1870s, an outcome of Dodgson's involvement with college and university affairs, reflect his independent rediscovery of Condorcet's cyclical majorities and include the first application of game theory to sophisticated voting. The argument of the 1884 pamphlet, written to influence the outcome of two electoral reforms, a goal it did not accomplish, is based on the zero-sum game. Dodgson was the first to treat formally apportionment (allocating seats to districts) and proportional representation (assigning seats to political parties) together.

Dodgson's contributions to logic have been widely recognized since William Warren Bartley, III's edition of *Lewis Carroll's Symbolic Logic* (1977) which includes the unpublished manuscript of part 2 of Dodgson's *Symbolic Logic*. Dodgson developed a formal logic where he set down intuitively valid rules for making inferences. A comparison of the two parts reveals the progress he made toward an automated approach to the solution of multiple connected syllogistic problems, many being humorous puzzle problems. The most important of his techniques, the method of trees, foreshadowed modern concepts and techniques in automated reasoning that were developed from the 1950s. Dodgson's use of existential import, abandoned in modern logical usage, marred the reception of part 1 of his book. He developed a method of diagrams as a visual proof system for syllogisms that he introduced in *The Game of Logic* (1887). Like his tree test, which is a proof system for soriteses, it is sound and complete. His self similar diagrams (invariant under a change of scale) are capable of handling existential statements and are easily extended to any number of sets using a linear iterative process. In this regard, they are superior to the diagrams described by John Venn in 1880.

See also Logic Diagrams; Logic, History of; Logic, Traditional; Venn, John.

Bibliography

Abeles, Francine F. "Lewis Carroll's Ciphers: The Literary Connections." *Advances in Applied Mathematics* 34(2005): 697–708.

Abeles, Francine F., ed. *The Mathematical Pamphlets of Charles Lutwidge Dodgson and Related Pieces.* New York: Lewis Carroll Society of North America; Charlottesville: Distributed by the University Press of Virginia, 1994.

Abeles, Francine F., ed. *The Political Pamphlets and Letters of Charles L. Dodgson and Related Pieces.* New York: Lewis Carroll Society of North America; Charlottesville: Distributed by the University Press of Virginia, 2001.

Bressoud, David M. *Proofs and Confirmations. The Story of the Alternating Sign Matrix Conjecture.* Washington, D.C.: The Mathematical Association of America; Cambridge, U.K.: Cambridge University Press, 1999.

Cohen, Morton N. *Lewis Carroll. A Biography.* New York: Knopf, 1995.

Francine F. Abeles (2005)

CARTESIANISM

According to one panoramic view of modern philosophy, René Descartes is the father and Cartesianism an inherited characteristic or family trait. With no disparagement intended of this assessment of Descartes's influence, the term *Cartesianism* will be used here in a less contentious way to refer to the multifarious, more or less self-conscious efforts on the part of his contemporaries and immediate successors to supply what they found lacking in his ambitious attempt to reconstitute human knowledge. Three directions of their activities can be distinguished and, corresponding to them, three particular applications of the term *Cartesianism.*

(1) It was evident that Descartes's project of a universal and all-encompassing science of nature was not fully realized. His intended *summa philosophiae, Principia Philosophiae* (*Principles of Philosophy,* Amsterdam, 1644), lacked the proposed parts on plants and animals and man; and his posthumously published and widely read *Traité de l'homme* (*Treatise on Man,* Paris, 1664) ended abruptly. Moreover, in his *Discours de la méthode* (*Discourse on Method,* Leiden, 1637) and in the letter prefacing the French translation of the *Principles* (Paris, 1647), he asked for assistance in carrying out his program for the sciences, suggesting that cooperative endeavor in the acquisition of *expériences* would be necessary to decide among equally possible explanations of the more partic-

ular facets of nature. His early admirers, attracted as much—and often far more—by his physics than by his metaphysics, accepted the invitation, and, working within the framework of his methodological prescriptions and cosmologic theory, distinguished themselves not only from their scholastic opponents of the academic establishment but also from other non-Aristotelian scientists of the time whose work went against views they had inherited. In the seventeenth century, *les cartésiens* were predominantly Descartes's followers in physics; and the term *Cartesianism* has acquired some of its less favorable associations from its application to this maligned movement in the history of science.

(2) A second line of development can be traced from Descartes's novel use of the term *idea* in presenting what has sometimes been considered the characteristically Cartesian view that knowledge is attained by way of ideas. These "as it were images of things" (*tanquam rerum imagines, veluti quasdam imagines*), as they were introduced in the *Third Meditation,* were variously described in his works, and a host of questions arose about their origin and nature. "Orthodox" Cartesians differed in their interpretations of Descartes's answers to these questions, while the more independently minded, accepting the thesis that knowledge is attained by way of ideas, produced deviant answers of great subtlety and originality. Since John Locke and his followers accepted Descartes's general thesis although they disagreed on the subject of innate ideas, Cartesianism, in a second application of the term, has been taken to cover a considerable domain, including family squabbles among rationalists and empiricists as well as more recent disputes, such as that about the genesis and status of sense data. (It should be noted that this use of "Cartesianism" to refer to the "way of ideas" differs from another use, in which "Cartesianism" and "rationalism" are roughly coextensive and connote a view or views about innate ideas or principles.)

(3) When Descartes was presented with objections to his metaphysics framed in terms of traditional categories and distinctions, a number of thorny problems became apparent; notably, concerning the substantiality and causal efficacy of his seemingly formless and inert corporeal things and concerning the union in man of a body and a soul, or mind, that is alleged to be really distinct from the body. In these sensitive areas, Descartes's teachings were interpreted and developed in various ways; and those who chose to follow the natural light rather than Descartes came to conclusions far removed from, and incompatible with, his. Yet, because of a common view concerning the distinction of mind and matter, Nicolas Malebranche and Benedict (Baruch) de Spinoza, as well as some less celebrated metaphysicians, have been called Cartesians; and Cartesianism, in a third acceptation of the term, comprises various monist, pluralist, and occasionalist variations on a common metaphysical theme. Within the limits of this general survey of Descartes's influence, Cartesianism will be mapped in each of the three general areas to which the term has been applied.

PHYSICS AND DERIVATIVE SCIENCES

Like Descartes, the Cartesians attracted to his program for the sciences thought of themselves as possessing a powerful method for investigating nature; and, though they disagreed with him and among themselves on particular applications, they accepted a general theory in physics, salient features of which were the laws of motion in Part II of the *Principles*; the theory of vortices in Part III; and the doctrine of subtle matter that underlies explanations of various phenomena, both celestial and terrestrial, in Parts III and IV of the *Principles.* Although Descartes's laws of motion became increasingly troublesome—Malebranche accepted them at first but was later forced to modify them beyond recognition—the cosmogonic picture of which they were part was altered but not effaced. It was an integral feature of the picture that Earth, like the other planets, was transported in a whirlpool that centered about the sun; and, while Descartes took pains in the *Principles* to distinguish his view from that of Nicolas Copernicus and to point out that, in his view and according to his definitions, Earth, though indeed a planet, was, strictly speaking, at rest, his followers were less concerned to establish a difference. They, too, rejected the possibility of unoccupied space or a vacuum, and claimed that apparently empty spaces—the heavens, the "pores" of bodies, and experimentally produced vacuums—were actually filled with subtle matter. Like Descartes, they made free use of the adaptable particles of subtle matter in their jigsaw-puzzle explanations of the workings of nature. There was some question as to what they conceived the vaunted "true" method to be, as evidenced by Gottfried Wilhelm Leibniz' skeptical queries. Nonetheless, some general characteristics of their practice were apparent.

Following the rule of evidence in the *Discourse,* they understood Descartes's injunctions against preconception and precipitancy as condemnations of merely accepted opinion and of idle speculation; and contrary to a popular conception of their apriorism, they were keenly interested in the detailed observation of nature and in experiments, thinking of themselves as countering the bookish physics of the Scholastics and the wanton practices of alchemists, astrologers, and the like. Lenses, Torricellian tubes, and sundry apparatus were much in evidence; and, like Descartes, many of them took pleasure in anatomical and physiological investigations. To what use they put their observations and experiments is one thing; their cult of *expériences,* another—and an indisputable fact. The requirement of clear and distinct ideas was met in the doctrine that matter is extension and the corollary that change is local motion, or *translatio.* The methodological implications of these complex views were manifold. Negatively, they ruled out explanations involving qualitative entities or "real" qualities, such as light, heat, and weight, in physics, and substantial forms, such as vegetative and sensitive souls, in biology. Also banished were final causes, including natural place, gravitation, and attraction; faculties, virtues, and powers as causes of change; and sensible qualities supposed to inhere in bodies and to be mysteriously purveyed to us by intentional species. Distinctly conceived, bodies were geometrical solids occupying parts of space and were subject to alteration by the crowding, or impact and pressure, of their neighbors. A vacuum, or void, was thought impossible, as were, at least for the "orthodox" Cartesians, indivisible particles or atoms. Sharing corpuscular and mechanistic assumptions with other nonscholastic scientists, they showed the mark of the master in their geometrical notions of—or, as some would have it, their lack of concepts of—mass and force. Quantity of matter was volume; weight was a centripetal reaction in a vortex of bodies of a certain size. Force, as effort or action on the part of bodies, was as suspect as were the powers and virtues of the Scholastics. Distinctly conceived, it was derived from a principle of inertia, and the force of a body in motion was reckoned as the product of mass (volume) and velocity.

HOLLAND: REGIUS AND CLAUBERG. During Descartes's long expatriation in Holland, he made a number of converts to his program for the sciences; and despite outbreaks of official opposition, Cartesianism made an impression on academic life that it did not make in France.

Regius. Of special note is Descartes's sometime friend and disciple Henry de Roy, or Regius (1598–1679), professor of medicine at the University of Utrecht, who typified Cartesian scientists in following the master more or less closely in physics and the derivative sciences while departing from his views in metaphysics. His *Fundamenta Physices* (Amsterdam, 1646), which appeared two years after the *Principles,* recapitulated the physics of Parts II, III, and IV, to which were added views from the earlier *Meteors* and *Dioptric* and also from unpublished work. Regius's physics, unlike Descartes's in the *Principles,* was not represented as derived from metaphysical principles. Moreover, in the concluding chapter on man, adverting to issues concerning the soul, he presented views to which Descartes could only take exception. In the preface to the French translation of the *Principles* (1647), Descartes disowned both the physics and the metaphysics of his disciple; and Regius in turn circulated a defense of his metaphysical theses, arguing for an empiricist view of the origin of ideas and against the necessity of a real distinction of mind and body. Descartes's reply to Regius, his *Notae in Programma* (1648), contained the prototype of later defenses of innate ideas against empiricist incursions. Innate ideas, he maintained, need not be *actually* present in the mind. Moreover, certain ideas—for example, of God—differ in kind from "adventitious" ideas; and even the latter do not, strictly speaking, come to us from the senses, that is, the sense organs.

Clauberg. From Holland, Cartesianism was taken to Germany by Johannes Clauberg, who attempted to explain and defend both Descartes's physics and his metaphysics. Working out apparent implications of the metaphysics in *De Cognitione Dei et Nostri …* (Duisberg, 1656), he too came to hold a deviant view of the relation of mind and body (though not Regius's), a view linking him with the occasionalists. Clauberg also faced the problem of the relation of traditional logic and Cartesian methodology, and his work in logic anticipated the more famous *Logique, ou L'art de penser* (*Port-Royal Logic,* 1662) of Antoine Arnauld and Pierre Nicole, which was the chief contribution of the Cartesians (Leibniz, of course, excluded) to logic.

FRANCE: ROHAULT AND RÉGIS. In France, Cartesianism, though it was not received in the universities and was, in effect, interdicted in 1671, flourished in extra-academic circles. Dissemination of Descartes's unpublished works and letters was in the hands of his devoted admirer Claude Clerselier (1614–1684), while leadership of his scientific enterprise devolved upon Jacques Rohault.

Rohault. The most gifted of the Cartesian scientists, Rohault devised ingenious experiments for his popular weekly meetings and presented the results of his work in his influential *Traité de physique* (Paris, 1671; translated by John Clarke as *System of Natural Philosophy,* London, 1723). Like Regius, he was inclined to separate Descartes's physics from his metaphysics; and, in line with this, he developed Descartes's notion of hypothesis or *supposition,* eliminating, however, any qualification to the effect that hypotheses were to be accepted for lack of something better.

Régis. Pierre-Sylvain Régis succeeded Rohault as leader of the Cartesian school. In his *Système de philosophie …* (Paris, 1690), a comprehensive work containing sections on logic, metaphysics, and moral philosophy as well as his extensive physics, he assimilated work that had been done since Descartes's death. The apogee of the Cartesian movement in physics has been set at about the time of Régis's *Système* and of Bernard Le Bovier de Fontenelle's imaginative exploration of the vortices in his *Entretiens sur la pluralité des mondes* (Paris, 1686).

CRITICAL RECEPTION. While receiving acclamation, the Cartesians were simultaneously threatened—and eventually discredited—by discoveries, such as that of the finite velocity of light, that contravened crucial parts of their system and by the objections and strictures of Leibniz and of Isaac Newton and his followers. These adverse judgments have been generally accepted. It is commonplace (and true) that Newton showed beyond the shadow of a doubt the incompatibility of the theory of vortices and Johannes Kepler's laws, while Leibniz neatly proved the inconsistency of Descartes's laws of motion with Galileo Galilei's. Citing Leibniz' derogatory characterization of the Cartesians, the not unsympathetic historian Charles Adam has reiterated comments on the paucity of equations in their work and on the uncontrolled play of their imagination in assigning jobs to the ubiquitous particles of subtle matter. His verdict was that Descartes's physics threatened to become as harmful to the progress of science as Aristotle's had been.

Yet, more recently, some less disparaging comments have been made. The picture is considerably brightened when Malebranche and especially Christiaan Huygens (1629–1695) are, by virtue of obvious influences, included among the Cartesians (as in Paul Mouy's [1934] account.) It has also been suggested that the attempted geometrization of physics was premature rather than perverse (Mouy; Max Jammer, *Concepts of Force,* Cambridge, U.K., 1957) and that the unstable and indeterminate particles of the Cartesians, not the billiard-ball atoms of the opposition, were in line with things to come (Geneviève [Rodis-] Lewis, *L'individualité selon Descartes,* Paris, 1950). Nonetheless, Descartes's followers in physics and the derivative sciences, Malebranche and Huygens aside, have not, on the whole, enhanced his reputation.

THEORY OF KNOWLEDGE

Proposing, in the *Third Meditation,* the term *idea* for those of his thoughts that are the "as it were images of things," Descartes proceeded to classify ideas according to their apparent origin—as innate or adventitious or made by him. He introduced distinctions bearing on their nature—between formal and material truth or falsity, and between objective and formal reality. Discussions generated by these passages concerned both Descartes's intent and the tenability of the views attributed to him. Four main problems can be distinguished, two relating to the tentative classification of ideas according to origin and two having to do with the distinctions bearing on their nature.

INNATE IDEAS. The contratraditional notion of innate ideas—that is, of ideas not derived in some way from the senses but instead having their source in the mind itself—presented an obvious difficulty; namely, how could such an idea, taken to be the form of a thought, exist or preexist in a person's mind if he did not in fact have the thought or indeed never had it? It seemed that Descartes's metaphor of a treasure house in which these ideas were stored needed to be cashed—a process that he attempted and that was carried out in various ways, in the face of some formidable difficulties, by supporters of his doctrine of innate ideas.

ADVENTITIOUS IDEAS. It was evident that ideas provisionally classified as adventitious—for instance, of a sound, the sun, or a fire—could not, strictly speaking, come to us from external objects; for, in Descartes's view, there was nothing in the objects or in the sense organs exactly like these ideas, or at least like many of them. Although these ideas could, in some sense, be said to be caused by external objects, they could not, strictly speaking, originate there; and some other cause or source more in keeping with their nature seemed to be necessary. Descartes suggested that the mind had the faculty or power of forming these ideas on the occasion of motions in the brain and that ideas seeming to come to us from without were in fact innate. Both suggestions were explored by his successors.

MATERIALLY FALSE IDEAS. Noting that falsity (formal falsity) was to be found in judgments and not in ideas, Descartes added that nonetheless certain ideas—for instance, the idea of cold—might be materially false; that is, if cold were a privation, then the idea of cold, representing a privation or what is not a thing, as if it were a thing would be materially false. The implications to be drawn from this remark were that, in his view, ideas of sensible qualities—of heat as well as cold, of sounds, colors, and the like—were materially false; and questions arose as to whether the notion of a materially false idea (literally, an idea misrepresenting what is not a thing) made sense, and whether sensations of heat, cold, and the like were, in a strict sense of the term, ideas. Two models seemed to be at work in Descartes's account of sense perception, and a problem bequeathed to his followers was that of specifying the latent distinction between the nonrepresentational and the representational elements—sensations and ideas properly so called—that were supposed to be ingredients of sense experience.

IDEAS OF EXTENDED THINGS. There was also a problem concerning ideas of extended things derived from the dual reality—objective and formal—accorded them. As representations, it seemed that they must have something in common with, or be in some respect like, the extended things they represented. Nevertheless, it was taken to follow from their formal reality as modes of thought that they were totally unlike extended things. A dilemma presented itself: Either ideas of extended things were totally unlike extended things, in which case they could not represent them; or, if they were in some respect like extended things, then they could not be accommodated in the mind.

MALEBRANCHE. Malebranche, among others, addressed himself to these problems; and, in his elaborate discussions of the nature and origin of ideas and in the numerous polemics to which they gave rise, various answers were surveyed and the major lines of development of Descartes's theory of knowledge were represented. Regarding the problem of materially false ideas and the difficulty concerning ideas of extended things, Malebranche, in the numerous editions of *De la Recherche de la vérité* (first published 1674–1675) and in the *Éclaircissements* added to them, drew a sharp distinction between the perception of heat, color, and the like and the perception of objects as extended. The former consisted in sensations or feelings (*sentiments*), nonrepresentational modifications of the mind conceived on the analogy of feelings of pain, and did not, in his precise use of the term, involve ideas (*idées*). The latter required ideas, which were distinguished from the mind's awareness of them and were not, in his view, modifications of the soul. Approaching the problem of the location or status of these ideas, Malebranche investigated a number of possibilities suggested by Descartes's tripartite classification (adventitious, made by the mind, and innate). Finding difficulties in the suggested sources, he concluded that ideas of extended things were neither adventitious nor made by the mind nor innate. The arguments against these possibilities served as indirect evidence for his own thesis: that these ideas were (as in a medieval use of the term) archetypes of created things in the Divine Understanding and that the human mind, intimately united with God, perceived created, extended things by way of ideas in him. Because, in this theory, ideas of extended things were not modifications of the human mind, the problem of their existence in an unextended mind did not arise, though, as became evident in the ensuing controversies, there was a related problem about the possibility of their existence in God.

FOUCHER. Two of the polemics were especially revealing. In his *Critique de la recherche de la vérité …* (Paris, 1675) and subsequent writings, Simon Foucher, though he misunderstood parts of Malebranche's tortuous theory, raised problems worthy of serious consideration. First, he urged that, if ideas of extended things had to have something in common with what they represented, they could not be, as he at first wrongly interpreted Malebranche, modifications of the mind or—as Malebranche in fact believed—inhabitants of the divine understanding. Second, granted that ideas of extended things were not modifications of the human mind but were divinely situated, could they be immediately perceived? The basis of the question was that, if immediate perception were tied to Descartes's views about indubitability and the *cogito,* then we could not be immediately aware of anything outside or apart from the mind. Third, he also questioned the distinction (to use Locke's terms) of primary and secondary qualities along lines that were continued by Pierre Bayle and George Berkeley, noting what, in Malebranche's distinction of sensation and idea, seemed to require explanation: that, when we perceive an object, we are aware of one uniform appearance of something having both shape and color. Unfortunately, Malebranche was inclined to dismiss Foucher's criticisms on the ground of misinterpretation, but Dom Robert Desgabets (d. 1678), in his *Critique de la Critique de la recherche de la vérité …* (Paris, 1675), attempted to defend Cartesian views (though not Malebranche's peculiar versions of them) against this attack.

ARNAULD. The most interesting controversy was with Arnauld, who, in *Des Vrayes et des Fausses Idées* (Cologne, 1683), attacked Malebranche's view of ideas as entities distinct from the mind's perception of them by tracing the source of this view to a misconceived analogy with ocular vision and a confusion of presence in the mind with local presence. For Arnauld, as for Descartes, ideas were modes of thought; and, as Descartes was content to explain the objective presence of objects in the mind as the way they were wont to be there, so Arnauld took it to be the nature of thought or mind, requiring no explanation of the kind Malebranche proffered, to represent objects—near or at a distance, present or absent, real or imaginary. Though Malebranche was not moved by this attempt to impugn his theory as the answer to a pseudo problem, in the course of the controversy he was forced to articulate his view that we perceive extended things in God, not by way of individual archetypes but by way of infinite, intelligible extension, which is the common archetype of all extended things, actual or possible.

LOCKE AND LEIBNIZ. A significant event in the annals of the Cartesian theory of knowledge was the publication of Locke's *An Essay concerning Human Understanding* (London, 1690). Locke's attack on innate ideas and principles and Leibniz' defense in his *Nouveaux essais sur l'entendement* (published posthumously, Amsterdam and Leipzig, 1765) are a long story, that cannot be told here. Suffice it to say that, in this division of Cartesianism into empiricism and rationalism, Leibniz used arguments like Descartes's in the *Notae in Programma* and, on this question, represented the orthodox Cartesian point of view.

METAPHYSICS

The occasionalist, monist, and pluralist developments included in the third application of the term *Cartesianism* were foreshadowed in Descartes's views about corporeal substance.

OCCASIONALISM. In the *Principles* (II, 36), maintaining that God was the primary and universal cause of motion, Descartes explained that, when God created matter or extension, he created it with motion and rest; and Descartes implied that, but for God's imparting motion to matter, it would have been motionless and undifferentiated, and that motion and rest, and the resulting differentiation of matter, did not follow necessarily from its nature or essence. He further explained that, in conserving matter from moment to moment, God preserved the same quantity of motion that He originally introduced; and it seemed to follow that God's continuing to impart motion to matter was a necessary condition of the continued existence of motion and that bodies of themselves did not have the power of remaining in motion or of producing motion in other bodies. The conclusion toward which Descartes was drawn was that, although motion (*translatio*) was a characteristic or mode of bodies, the moving force of bodies was not in bodies themselves but in God. He did not, however, draw this conclusion. In a letter to Henry More, he noted that he was reluctant to discuss the question of the moving force (*vis movens*) of bodies in his published works, for fear that his view might be confused with that of God as *anima mundi*; and the view that he apparently wished to maintain was that, though the moving force of bodies was from God and in a sense was in God, it was also a characteristic or mode of bodies.

The occasionalists, taking the views that matter was inert and that the motion ascribed to bodies was simply change of position, did not hesitate before the conclusion that the force required to move bodies was not in bodies themselves but in the primary and universal Cause of motion, God. According to their conclusion, when a billiard ball that was in motion came in contact with a second ball that was at rest, there was no power or force in the first ball capable of moving the second, and the movement of the second ball required the action of God, who, on the occasion of impact, moved the second ball in accordance with rules that he had established for the motion of bodies. By virtue of the uniformity of God's action, the first ball could be called the cause—the particular or occasional cause—of the second ball's moving; but, without God's action, it was inefficacious, and the primary and universal cause of motion, that is, God, was the effectual cause of the second ball's moving. The occasionalists took it to be true a fortiori that bodies of themselves lacked the power of producing, as in sense perception, changes in the mind; and they offered a number of arguments to show that the mind in turn lacked the power, as in volition, of moving the body. The true cause of both sensations and voluntary movements was God, who instituted laws for the union of mind and body and acted accordingly in particular instances.

The originators of the occasionalist movement were Louis de La Forge and Géraud de Cordemoy.

La Forge. In the *Traité de l'esprit de l'homme* (Paris, 1666), La Forge represented himself as continuing work that Descartes had left unfinished in his *Treatise on Man* and undertook to explain and develop the notion of a mind or soul distinct from, yet united to, the body. Facing problems concerning the possibility of the body acting on the mind and vice versa, he noted that these problems were not isolated and that there was a related problem concerning the possibility of one body acting on another. In his discussion of these problems, La Forge did not deny that bodies acted on one another or on the mind, or that the mind acted on the body; on the contrary, he insisted that God in his omnipotence could delegate the power of acting to created things. Yet, distinguishing two senses of "cause," he denied that created things were unambiguously the causes of the effects attributed to them and called them the "occasional" or "equivocal" causes.

Cordemoy. In *Le discernement du corps et de l'âme* (Paris, 1666), Cordemoy, unlike La Forge, was not concerned with presenting views necessarily in harmony with Descartes's, and he denied outright the action of bodies on one another or on the mind and the action of the human mind on the body. In his formally presented proof that God was the true cause of the movement of bodies, he made use of principles that Descartes would have accepted but drew conclusions from them that it would be safe to say would have greatly disturbed Descartes. Descartes had written of a motion in the brain as giving occasion (*donnera occasion*) to the soul to have a certain sensation or thought, and Cordemoy may have had these passages in mind in employing the expression *cause occasionelle* to refer to what, as in the case of a motion in the brain, might be thought to be the true cause of an event. But, unlike Descartes, he denied that the occasion or occasional cause was, strictly speaking, the cause of the event and maintained that the true cause was God.

Geulincx. Arnold Geulincx apparently developed his version of occasionalism independently of La Forge and Cordemoy. Illustrating the lack of causal relation between mind and body, he used the analogy of synchronized clocks, which was later taken up by Leibniz; and, to prove a lack of genuine causation, he made use of the principle that nothing can be done unless there is knowledge on the part of the putative agent or cause of how it is done.

Malebranche. Malebranche, the most celebrated of the occasionalists, was familiar with the work of Cordemoy and adapted, for his own purposes and with great originality, the theory of causation he found in Cordemoy. He added powerful arguments, extended the view to cover volitions not pertaining to bodily movements (such as the volition to form an idea), and presented it as an integral part of his theocentric vision of the universe.

MONISM AND PLURALISM. It has been argued that the dualisms and pluralism found in Descartes's statements about substance—of uncreated and created substance, corporeal and spiritual substance, and individual substances—contradicted his own definitions and principles and that Spinoza's doctrine of the unity of substance was the consistent and pure form of Cartesianism. It has also been maintained that Spinoza's monism and Leibniz' pluralism were the opposite poles to which philosophers accepting a notion of substance like that of Descartes were inescapably driven. Discussions of these views and of Spinoza's and Leibniz's metaphysics of substance is beyond the limits of this article, though it need hardly be added that the historical and logical relations of Descartes's assertions about substance and those of Spinoza and Leibniz have figured importantly in discussions of Cartesianism and that the essence of Cartesianism has sometimes been located in a common notion of, or presupposition about, substantiality.

It may be noted, however, that Descartes's assertions about corporeal substance also gave rise to conflicting theories among less renowned students of his metaphysics. On the one side, Geulincx, following Descartes's inclination to think of particular bodies as portions of a common stuff or substance, contended that "body itself" (*corpus ipsum*) was primary and substantial and that particular bodies were limitations or modes of corporeal substance. On the other side, Cordemoy, sharing Descartes's inclination to think of particular bodies as objects really distinct from one another, came to the unorthodox conclusion that body in general, or matter, was an aggregate and that the parts of which it was composed were indivisible extended substances, or atoms.

See also Arnauld, Antoine; Bayle, Pierre; Berkeley, George; Clauberg, Johannes; Copernicus, Nicolas; Cordemoy, Géraud de; Descartes, René; Desgabets, Robert; Dualism in the Philosophy of Mind; Fontenelle, Bernard Le Bovier de; Foucher, Simon; Geulincx, Arnold; Leibniz, Gottfried Wilhelm; Locke, John; Malebranche, Nicolas; Monism and Pluralism; Newton, Isaac; Nicole, Pierre; Régis, Pierre-Sylvain; Regius, Henricus (Henry de Roy); Rohault, Jacques.

Bibliography

Balz, Albert G. A. *Cartesian Studies.* New York: Columbia University Press, 1951.

Belaval, Yvon. *Leibniz critique de Descartes.* Paris: Gallimard, 1960.

Berthé de Besaucèle, Louis. *Les cartésiens d'Italie.* Paris: A. Picard, 1920.

Bohatek, Josef. *Die cartesianische Scholastik in der Philosophie und reformierte Dogmatik des 17. Jahrhunderts.* Leipzig, 1912.

Bordas-Demoulin, Jean Baptiste. *Le cartésianisme,* 2nd ed. Paris, 1874.

Bouillier, Francisque. *Histoire de la philosophie cartésienne,* 3rd ed. Paris: C. Delagrave, 1868. A standard work, to be used with caution.

Cousin, Victor. *Fragments philosophiques,* 5th ed. Paris, 1866.

Damiron, Jean Philibert. *Essai sur l'histoire de la philosophie en France au XVIIe siècle.* Paris: Hachette, 1846.

Dibon, Paul. *La philosophie néerlandaise au siècle d'or.* Paris: Elsevier, 1954.

Dijksterhuis, E. J. et al. *Descartes et le cartésianisme hollandais.* Paris: Presses universitaires de France, 1950.

Lemaire, Paul. *Le cartésianisme chez les bénédictins; Dom Robert Desgabets, son système, son influence et son école.* Paris: Alcan, 1901.

Monchamp, Georges. *Histoire du cartésianisme en Belgique.* Brussels: F. Hayez, 1886.

Mouy, Paul. *Le développement de la physique cartésienne, 1646–1712.* Paris: J. Vrin, 1934. An invaluable account—intelligent, informed, and judicious—of Cartesianism in physics.

Prost, Joseph. *Essai sur l'atomisme et l'occasionalisme dans la philosophie cartésienne.* Paris, 1907.

Sortais, Gaston. *Le cartésianisme chez les jésuites français au XVIIe et au XVIIIe siècle.* Paris: G. Beauchesne, 1929.

Thijssen-Schoute, Caroline Louise. *Nederlands cartesianisme.* Amsterdam: Noord-Hollandsche, 1954.

Vartanian, Aram. *Diderot and Descartes.* Princeton, NJ: Princeton University Press, 1953.

Willis Doney (1967)

CARTESIANISM [ADDENDUM]

Apparently, it was the Cambridge Platonist Henry More who introduced the term *Cartesianism*—from the Latin *Cartesius*—into the English language. The term itself now denotes either the views of René Descartes or the various defenses and developments of these views in the writings of les cartésiens, an eclectic group of seventeenth- and eighteenth-century European intellectuals.

SCIENCE AND THEOLOGY

Descartes is perhaps best known in the early twenty-first century both for his epistemological "method of doubt" and for his metaphysical doctrine of mind-body dualism. However, he was known in the early modern period primarily for his attempt to systematically displace explanations of natural phenomena, deriving from the work of Aristotle, that were then predominant in both Catholic and Protestant schools on the Continent. In *Principles of Philosophy* (1644) Descartes proposed as an alternative for Aristotelian explanations in terms of prime matter, substantial forms, and final causality his own more austere explanations in terms of extension, its modifications, and purely mechanistic laws. There were other critics of the Aristotelianism of the schools, most notably Pierre Gassendi and the Gassendists. Nevertheless, Descartes's followers proved to be more adept than the Gassendists at packaging the new mechanistic science. Even so, it is understandable that Cartesian science is not as prominent today given the decisive refutation of Descartes's particular brand of physics in the work of More's greatest student, Isaac Newton.

Theological issues also dominated discussions of Descartes's system in earlier centuries in a way that they no longer do today. Such issues were of immediate practical concern to Descartes himself, who encountered fierce theological resistance not only in France but also in the United Provinces (now Holland), where he lived for most of his adult life. He failed in his attempt to infiltrate the Catholic universities in France at least partly because Aristotelian traditionalists saw his system as a threat to the Catholic dogma of the miraculous conversion in the Eucharist of the substance of bread and wine into the body and blood of Christ.

Descartes did fare somewhat better in the Calvinist United Provinces, where his writings received an audience in the academy during his residence there. Even in this region, however, orthodox Calvinists urged that his insistence on the real distinction between mind and body conflicts with the Aristotelian position that the soul bears a natural relation to a certain body in virtue of being its substantial form. These critics emphasized the threat that his system posed to Christian doctrines such as the resurrection of the body and the unity of the incarnated Christ. Moreover, before and after Descartes's death critics attempted to gain an advantage over Cartesianism by linking it to heterodox theological views. In the United Provinces the connection was typically to the doctrinally tolerant Dutch Remonstrant Calvinists, who deviated from Reformed Orthodoxy in insisting on one's freedom to accept or reject divine grace. After his death, however, Descartes was linked in France to a different group, the rigoristic French Jansenists, who set themselves in opposition to a Jesuit theology that emphasizes the dependence of one's salvation on the activity of one's undetermined free will. That the Jansenists were linked to Descartes bespeaks the influence of Antoine Arnauld, who was a prominent defender of both Cartesianism and Jansenism.

CARTESIANISM AND AUGUSTINIANISM

There was a strong inclination among French Cartesians to counter theological objections by invoking the authority of St. Augustine. There were roughly two general approaches, which were reflected in the distinction of the scholar Henri Gouhier (1978) between "Cartesianism augustinized" and "Augustinianism cartesianized." The augustinized Cartesians, including Claude Clerselier, Descartes's literary executor, and the physician Louis de la Forge, were concerned to bolster Cartesian natural philosophy by stressing the ways in which Descartes's proofs of the existence of God and of the immateriality of mind complement Augustinian spiritualism. The defense of a cartesianized theology was pursued with disastrous consequences by the Benedictine Robert Desgabets, whose development of Descartes's account of the Eucharist provided the impetus for the official censorship of Cartesianism in France two decades after Descartes's death.

The cartesianized Augustinians tended to emphasize not Descartes's infrequent forays into theology, but his more common insistence that theological issues are outside of his jurisdiction insofar as their treatment requires recourse to revelation. This insistence allowed theologians such as Arnauld to appeal to Descartes to safeguard against Jesuit intrusion a "positive" or dogmatic theology devoted to providing a philosophical explication (or, for critics of the Jesuits, misrepresentation) of Augustinian views on matters of faith. Dutch Cartesians also attempted to insulate Cartesian philosophy from theology, though for them the concern was less to promote Augustinian purity in theology than to honor the distinction of the disciplines in the universities. This interest in making Descartes fit for the schools also explains the emphasis in the work of these Cartesians on the similarities between Aristotle and Descartes. It is this "scholasticized" Cartesianism that was exported from the United Provinces to Germany soon after Descartes's death by Dutch-trained Cartesians such as Johannes Clauberg.

MALEBRANCHE AND HIS CRITICS

The reception of Descartes was conditioned by the work of Nicolas Malebranche, a member of the Oratory in Paris. Malebranche attempted with other French Cartesians to link Descartes to Augustine. In Malebranche's case the result was a synthesis that stressed the dependence of creatures on God's rational activity. His system included the view, anticipated in the work of La Forge and others, that bodies serve as the noncausal occasion for God to distribute motion by means of the most economical laws. Malebranche further extended this sort of view to theology, arguing that God distributes grace in accord with simple general laws.

Malebranche's theological views upset Arnauld, his former ally, who took them to be an illustration of the dangers of philosophical incursions into theology. Nonetheless, the opening salvo in his protracted and increasingly bitter dispute with Malebranche was his critique of Malebranche's philosophical doctrine that "we see all things in God," that is, that one knows the bodies one sees through the idea of extension in God that represents them. Arnauld appealed to Descartes in defense of the alternative position that representative ideas are merely modes of one's soul. The French Cartesian Pierre-Sylvain Régis, who had earlier published a popularization of Cartesianism in his *System of Philosophy* (1690), defended Arnauld's account of ideas in a polemical exchange with Malebranche during the mid-1690s. Unlike Arnauld, however, but like Desgabets, whom he admired, Régis challenged Malebranche's claim that eternal essences that serve as the ground for eternal truths are identical to uncreated ideas in the divine reason. As Malebranche himself recognized, such a claim undermines Descartes's doctrine of the creation of the eternal truths. Régis and Desgabets were both concerned to defend this doctrine by claiming that eternal truths concerning creatures derive not from uncreated ideas in God, but from features of the world that God created with complete indifference.

See also Clauberg, Johannes; Descartes, René; Desgabets, Robert; Régis, Pierre-Sylvain; Regius (Henri de Roy); Rohault, Jacques.

Bibliography

Armogathe, Jean-Robert. *Theologia cartesiana: l'explication physique de l'Eucharistie chez Descartes et dom Desgabets.* The Hague: Nijhoff, 1977.

Clarke, Desmond M. *Occult Powers and Hypotheses: Cartesian Natural Philosophy under Louis XIV.* Oxford, U.K.: Clarendon Press, 1989.

Des Chene, Dennis. *Physiologia: Natural Philosophy in Late Aristotelian and Cartesian Thought.* Ithaca, NY: Cornell University Press, 1996.

Gaukroger, Stephen. *Descartes: An Intellectual Biography.* Oxford, U.K.: Clarendon Press, 1995.

Gouhier, Henri. *Cartésianisme et augustinisme au XVIIe siècle.* Paris: J. Vrin, 1978.

Lennon, Thomas M. *The Battle of the Gods and Giants: The Legacies of Descartes and Gassendi, 1655–1715.* Princeton, NJ: Princeton University Press, 1993.

Marion, Jean-Luc. *Sur la théologie blanche de Descartes: Analogie, création des vérités éternelles, et fondement.* Paris: Presses Universitaires de France, 1981.

Schmaltz, Tad M. *Radical Cartesianism: The French Reception of Descartes.* New York: Cambridge University Press, 2002.

Verbeek, Theo. *Descartes and the Dutch: Early Reactions to Cartesian Philosophy, 1637–1650.* Carbondale: Southern Illinois University Press, 1992.

Tad M. Schmaltz (2005)

CARTWRIGHT, NANCY
(1944–)

Nancy Cartwright, as of 2005, held several academic positions, including professor of philosophy in the Department of Philosophy, Logic, and Scientific Method at the London School of Economics (since 1991); director of the LSE Centre for Philosophy of Natural and Social Science (since 1993); and professor of philosophy in the Department of Philosophy at the University of California at San Diego (since 1998). She had also served on the faculty at the University of Maryland (1971–1973) and Stanford University (1973–1991). She is the recipient of a MacArthur Fellowship and is a Fellow of the British Academy.

Cartwright first became widely known for the radical thesis, presented in her landmark 1983 collection of essays *How the Laws of Physics Lie*, that the fundamental laws of physics did not state truths about the world. The thesis is radical because philosophers have generally assumed that there is some set of underlying physical laws which, ultimately, describe all natural events. This is probably still a majority opinion among philosophers of science, though a much more controversial one than when Cartwright wrote these essays. At the same time she also proposed (along with Ian Hacking) a cautious realism about theoretical entities, which did not depend on people's ability to formulate true laws about them.

Cartwright's argument is based on a distinction between phenomenological and theoretical—or fundamental—laws. Phenomenological laws are, unsurprisingly, the laws that apply to actually observable phenomena. Their application is generally tightly circumscribed by detailed specification of the situations to which they apply. While fundamental laws may play an essential role in the formulation of phenomenological laws, the former are not themselves true. This is because they abstract from all the detailed *ceteris paribus* conditions that give phenomenological laws a chance, at least, of being true within their specific domains.

In her most recent book, *The Dappled World* (1999), Cartwright continues her attack on fundamentalism, the idea—from realism—that there is one unique set of laws applying to everything. The attack on fundamentalism, however, is now more uncompromising, as she has become increasingly skeptical about the usefulness of fundamental laws for deriving phenomenological laws. At the same time, a positive theme that she has developed throughout her career is increasingly emphasized: The conception of science not as searching for laws at all, but as constructing models. For models, the question of truth does not arise. They may more or less adequately represent parts of reality, and they may be more or less useful in providing understanding, explanation, and prediction.

Another theme more strongly emphasized in the later book is the disunity of science. Whereas a majority of philosophers of science accept a disunified science in the sense that laws in different domains are not reducible to laws of a more fundamental science, a majority of these philosophers see this as a consequence only of practical problems of complexity or the limited cognitive capacities of humans. Cartwright, on the other hand, is a leading advocate of a more radical position: that the autonomy of theories is indicative of what there is to know about the world. The world itself does not have a unitary underlying lawlike pattern. Its nomological structure is dappled.

The other related topic to which Cartwright has been among the most prominent contributors is the nature of causality. The decentering of fundamental laws from the vision of science naturally engenders skepticism about the Humean program of reducing causes to instances of laws. A project introduced in her first book—and developed in detail in her 1989 work, *Nature's Capacities and their Measurement*—is that an understanding of causality in terms of laws should be replaced with one in terms of capacities. In parallel with the emphasis on models, this move contributes to doubts as to whether laws are needed at all. The central thesis of this book is that science cannot be understood without assuming real capacities in the world. As is well known, Hume argued that positing capacities violated a proper empiricism. Cartwright, a committed empiricist, insists that capacities are as empirically accessible as laws and more specifically, that their measurement is a defining activity of science. In a further anti-Humean move, she argues that singular rather than generic causes are fundamental. A paradigm for Cartwright of causal knowledge is that aspirins have the capacity to cure headaches. Yet the canonical evidence for this claim is that on some specific occasions an aspirin actually does cure a headache.

This also connects to a central topic of her earliest work: probabilistic causality. This topic arises because capacities are to be thought of as being displayed only under specific circumstances, so that the relation between a capacity and its exercise is typically probabilistic. Conversely, Cartwright explores the question whether probabilistic relations can provide evidence for causes. Her answer is that they can, but only on the assumption that the effects are indications of real capacities in objects.

This entry has described some main themes from Cartwright's work in fairly abstract terms, but it should be emphasized that she has been a leader of the move to focus philosophy of science on detailed examination of exemplary cases of scientific work. For the earlier part of her career most of this work was addressed to physics. From the late 1980s she increasingly switched her attention to examples from economics, and is now a leading figure in the philosophy of economics. Perhaps surprisingly to those who see the sciences as hierarchically arranged with physics secure at the top of the heap, Cartwright finds many themes in common to physics and economics. A central idea linking the two is her interest in machines, which can also be seen as concrete instantiations of models. A paradigm from her earlier work is the laser. The moral of this example is that the laser concretely embodies the *ceteris paribus* clauses emphasized in her critical discussion of fundamental laws by a range of actual mechanisms that ensure the proper conditions for the exercising of the crucial capacity—in this case the capacity for inversion in a population of atoms. Central to Cartwright's work on economics is the idea of a socioeconomic machine. As an example, she considers the mechanism by which a central bank increases the money supply. Like the laser, this does not reflect a law of nature, but a capacity of a certain kind of money, under properly controlled conditions, to have an important economic effect.

Cartwright claims as a philosophical hero Otto Neurath, a founding member of the Vienna Circle. Her admiration is of his commitment to seeing in science the capacity to change the world. A concern with the social impact of science and philosophy of science, while often beneath the surface, has been discernible in much of Cartwright's work.

See also Laws, Scientific; Scientific Realism.

Works by Cartwright

How the Laws of Physics Lie. Oxford: Oxford University Press, 1983.

Nature's Capacities and their Measurement. Oxford: Oxford University Press, 1989.

The Dappled World: A Study of the Boundaries of Science. Cambridge, U.K.: Cambridge University Press, 1999.

John Dupré (2005)

CARUS, CARL GUSTAV

(1789–1869)

Carl Gustav Carus, a German physician, biologist, and philosopher, was born in Leipzig and studied chemistry and then medicine at the University of Leipzig. In 1811 he became the first person to lecture there on comparative anatomy. Two years later he became director of the military hospital at Pfaffendorf and, in 1814, professor of medicine at the medical college of the University of Dresden, where he remained to the end of his life. He was appointed royal physician in 1827 and privy councilor in 1862.

Carus was widely known for his work in physiology, psychology, and philosophy, and was one of the first to do experimental work in comparative osteology, insect anatomy, and zootomy. He is also remembered as a landscape painter and art critic. He was influenced by Aristotle, Plato, Friedrich Wilhelm Joseph von Schelling, and Johann Wolfgang von Goethe, about whom Carus wrote several works, the most important of which is *Goethe dessen seine Bedeutung für unsere und die kommende Zeit* (Vienna, 1863). Carus's philosophical writings were more or less forgotten until the German philosopher and psychologist, Ludwig Klages, resurrected them.

Carus's philosophy was essentially Aristotelian in that it followed the unfolding or elaboration of an idea in experience from an unorganized multiplicity to an organized unity. This universal, unfolding unity or developing multiplicity within unity Carus called God. God, or the Divine, is not a being analogous to human intelligence; rather, it is the ground of being revealed through becoming, through the infinitely numerous and infinitely varying beings or organisms that come into being through the Divine in space and time.

Carus called his theory of a divine or creative force "entheism." The unknown Divine is revealed in nature through organization, structure, and organic unity. As the ground of being, it is outside space and time, unchanging, and eternal. As thought or insight, it is the God-idea of religion, found everywhere in life and the cosmos. As life, it is the sphere, the basic form taken by living cells and the heavenly stars. As matter, it is the ether exfoliating in infinitely varied things.

According to Carus, the body cannot be separated from the soul. Both are soul, but we speak of "body" when some unknown part of the soul affects the known part; and we speak of "soul" when the known part affects the unknown part.

Carus's metaphysics, and his important contribution to psychology, is a theory of movement from unconsciousness to consciousness and back again. Whatever understanding we can have of life and the human spirit hinges upon observation of how universal unconsciousness, the unknown Divine, becomes conscious. Universal unconsciousness is not teleological in itself; it achieves purpose only as it becomes conscious through conscious individuals. Consciousness is not more permanent than things; it is a moment between past and future. As a moment, it can maintain itself only through sleep or a return to the unknown.

See also Aristotle; Goethe, Johann Wolfgang von; Klages, Ludwig; Plato; Schelling, Friedrich Wilhelm Joseph von; Unconscious.

Bibliography

PRINCIPAL WORKS BY CARUS

Psyche: zur Entwicklungsgeschichte der Seele. Pforzheim, 1846; 3rd ed., Stuttgart, 1860.

Physis: zur Geschichte des leiblichen Lebens. Stuttgart: Scheitlin, 1851.

Symbolik der menschlichen Gestalt. Leipzig, 1853.

Natur und Idee. Vienna: W. Braumüller, 1861.

Lebenserinnerungen und Denkwürdigkeiten, 4 vols. Leipzig: F. A. Brockhaus, 1865–1866.

Vergleichende Psychologie. Vienna: W. Braumüller, 1866.

WORKS ON CARUS

Bernouilli, Christoph. *Die Psychologie von Carl Gustav Carus.* Jena, Germany: E. Diederichs, 1925.

Kern, Hans. *Carus: Personlichkeit und Werk.* Berlin, 1942.

Rubin Gotesky (1967)

CARUS, PAUL
(1852–1919)

Paul Carus, a philosopher and monist, was born at Ilsenburg, Germany, and died in La Salle, Illinois. After receiving his Ph.D. at Tübingen, in 1876, and completing his military service, he taught in Dresden. Censure of religious views he had expressed in pamphlets led him to leave Germany for England. He then went to New York, where in 1885 he published *Monism and Meliorism.* This book aroused the interest of a German chemist in La Salle, Illinois, Edward Carl Hegeler, who had started a periodical, the *Open Court.* He invited Carus to take over the editorship. In 1888 another and more technical journal, the *Monist,* was founded, and Carus became its editor. Carus also published a series of philosophical classics, edited by leading professors of philosophy, which are still widely used in classrooms. The Carus family operated the Open Court Publishing Company until 1996. Open Court publishes the volumes of the Carus Lectures, which are given at meetings of the American Philosophical Association. The *Monist* was revived in 1962 under the editorship of Eugene Freeman.

For the *Monist,* Carus chose articles on the history and philosophy of religion, archaeology, biblical criticism, and especially the philosophy of science, both philosophy for the scientifically minded and philosophy about the sciences. He invited contributions from France and Germany and arranged for their translation. Important articles by Bertrand Russell, Ernst Mach, David Hilbert, Jules Henri Poincaré, John Dewey, and Charles Sanders Peirce appeared in the *Monist.* Carus frequently published articles of his own in criticism of his contributors, but the debates seem not so much to have modified his own monistic philosophy as to have led him to explain in detail how it differed from other monisms, such as Ernst Haeckel's.

Monism, for Carus, was the doctrine that all the things that are—however varied, diverse, and independent of each other they may appear to be—are somehow one. What makes them one are certain eternal laws that reside in things and are discovered, not created, by the investigator. These laws of nature are asserted to be dependent on a single law, which Carus identified with God.

Carus viewed his metaphysics as a speculative generalization from the view of mathematics that he had learned from Hermann Grassmann, his teacher at the Stettin Gymnasium. Alfred North Whitehead, too, acknowledged the influence of Grassmann, in his *Universal Algebra.* Some of the similarities between the metaphysics of Carus and Whitehead may have resulted from this common influence.

Carus can be called a realist inasmuch as he rejected the notion that the laws of nature depend on the mind of the investigator. In this he found himself in opposition to the Kantians. Nor did he hold to a materialism. Rather, he insisted that every part of the world is both material (acting in accord with the laws of matter) and spiritual (acting in accord with the laws of mind). The characteristic of mind, or spirit, is the ability to mirror the world. Thus Carus was also a realist in his account of knowing. In ethics he held that the worth of any part of the world depends on the degree to which it knows—that is, mirrors—the whole. This is achieved through greater and greater knowledge of the laws of nature. Hence, devotion to knowledge is the way to greater goodness. Prayer is recommended as a means of changing the will of the man who prays so that he can mirror the one law in his actions.

See also Dewey, John; Hilbert, David; Mach, Ernst; Monism and Pluralism; Peirce, Charles Sanders; Poincaré, Jules Henri; Russell, Bertrand Arthur William; Whitehead, Alfred North.

Bibliography

Hay, William H. "Paul Carus: A Case-Study of Philosophy on the Frontier." *Journal of the History of Ideas* 17 (1956): 498–510.

Meyer, Donald Harvey. "Paul Carus and the Religion of Science." *American Quarterly* 14 (1962): 597–607.

Sheridan, James Francis. *Paul Carus: A Study of the Thought and Work of the Editor of the Open Court Publishing Company.* Ann Arbor, MI, 1957.

William H. Hay (1967)

CASO, ANTONIO

(1883–1946)

Antonio Caso, a Mexican philosopher and diplomat, was born in Mexico City in 1883 and died there in 1946. He was a professor of philosophy at the National University of Mexico, rector of that institution, lecturer at the Colegio Nacional, and ambassador to several South American nations. He wrote voluminously over a period of three decades and had great influence as a teacher. For his sources he turned especially to Henri Bergson but also to Immanuel Kant, Arthur Schopenhauer, and Edmund Husserl.

The metaphysics of Caso emphasizes process, freedom, life, and spirit. He conceived of reality as a fluent dynamism whose operations and forms are unified organically. The subject-predicate bias of traditional logic distorts reality by its apparatus of static terms related as in a closed machine. Modern science has more insight with its realization that even the physical world eludes a rigorous determinism. The individual particle has a factor of spontaneity; law is only statistical, applying to groups by virtue of the mutual compensation of individual irregularities. By the same token, living process has a unique character that cannot be reduced to the terms of physics and chemistry but stimulates and directs the material vehicle. A conscious living being discovers its own freedom in the simple act of willing a bodily movement: freedom coincides with causation from within. Consciousness is not passively derived from more primitive conditions by laws of association and evolution. On the contrary, the pure ego projects its own structures upon the data of raw feeling, thus supplying the objects of mature experience and the principles underlying those of association and evolution.

The ethics of Caso is concerned with two triads: that of things, individuals, and persons, and that of economy, disinterest, and love. Things are merely physical, are deficient in unity, are divisible, and are not subjects of value. Individuals are living beings that are indivisible but can be substituted for each other. The value of the merely biological is economy, found in egocentricity and utility and illustrated in nutrition, growth, reproduction, tool making, and death. Beyond individuals are persons, which add the character of spirit to life. Persons are capable of both disinterest and love. Disinterest suspends the mechanisms of selfishness and usefulness in the act of contemplation; love identifies the self with another in sympathy and service and is at its noblest in self-sacrifice. Persons are unique; they play a role as creators of values in society, and in them freedom is most advanced and responsible. Their interplay defines human culture, the enemies of which are individualism and totalitarianism; both are forms of egoism and of economic value. The error of totalitarian philosophy is to transfer the notion of the absolute from a universal principle of existence, where it is justified, to the state, where it does not exist. This philosophy has its source in Thomas Hobbes; it should not be imputed to G. W. F. Hegel, who placed art, religion, and philosophy above the state.

Caso's aesthetics begins with the concept of a surplus of energy, or vital excess, that is the basis of play, art, and the spirit of sacrifice. Art is distinguished from play and from the spirit of sacrifice by disinterest. In addition to the suspension of selfishness and usefulness, disinterest implies abstraction from questions of reality and goodness of the object contemplated. Disinterest preserves art from any possibility of immorality, which requires an interested attitude. It is associated with the intuitive nature of the aesthetic experience, since absorption in the object as an end favors appreciation of its full individuality. The nonconceptual nature of the experience is reconciled with the claim of universality, after the manner of Kant. The experience, however, does not terminate with an image within the mind. The conative tendency of psychic states leads to empathy, or projection of the state upon the outer world. Aesthetic empathy differs from the projection mentioned earlier in that it is emotional and concrete rather than logical and formal, and from that empathy and religious empathy in that it is disinterested. But natural objects do not readily satisfy the aesthetic need. Aesthetic empathy therefore leads to expression, or the creation of works of art, in which are consummated the empathic tendency and disinterested intuition. In his account of intuition and expression, Caso claimed to follow Benedetto Croce, but he did not do so without wavering.

See also Bergson, Henri; Croce, Benedetto; Hegel, Georg Wilhelm Friedrich; Husserl, Edmund; Kant, Immanuel; Schopenhauer, Arthur; Sympathy and Empathy.

Bibliography

MAIN WORKS BY CASO

La filosofía de la intuición (The philosophy of intuition). Mexico City, 1914.

La existencia como economía, como desinterés y como caridad (Existence as economy, as disinterest, and as love). Mexico City, 1919.

Discursos á la nación mexicana (Discourses to the Mexican Nation). Mexico City: Porrua huos., 1922.

El concepto de la historia universal (The concept of universal history). Mexico City: Ediciones Botas, 1923.

Principios de estética (Principles of aesthetics). Mexico City: Publicaciones de la Sria. de Edvcacion, 1925.

La Persona humana y el estado totalitario (The human person and the totalitarian state). Mexico City: Universidad Nacional Autónoma, 1941.

WORKS ON CASO

Berndtson, Arthur. "Mexican Philosophy: The Aesthetics of Antonio Caso." *Journal of Aesthetics and Art Criticism* 9 (4) (June 1951): 323–329.

Romanell, Patrick. *Making of the Mexican Mind.* Lincoln: University of Nebraska Press, 1952. Ch. 3.

Arthur Berndtson (1967)

CASSIRER, ERNST
(1874–1945)

Ernst Cassirer, the German neo-Kantian philosopher, was born in Breslau, Silesia. He studied at the universities of Berlin, Leipzig, Heidelberg, and Marburg and taught first at Berlin. From 1919 to 1933 he was professor of philosophy at Hamburg University; and he served as rector from 1930 to 1933. Cassirer, who was Jewish, resigned his post in 1933 and left Germany. He taught at Oxford from 1933 to 1935, at Göteborg, Sweden from 1935 to 1941, and at Yale from 1941 to 1944. He died in New York City while a visiting professor at Columbia University.

Cassirer was both a prolific historian of philosophy and an original philosopher. His philosophy is in many important respects a development and modification of Immanuel Kant's critical philosophy, idealistic in outlook and transcendental in method. Like Kant, he holds that the objective world results from the application of a priori principles to a manifold that can be apprehended only as differentiated and ordered by them. His method is transcendental in the sense that he investigates not so much the objects of knowledge and belief as the manner in which these objects come to be known or are constituted in consciousness. His work has to some extent also been influenced by G. W. F. Hegel and, of his own contemporaries, by his teacher Hermann Cohen and by Edmund Husserl.

Cassirer differs from Kant mainly in holding that the principles by which the manifold of experience receives its structure are not static, but developing; and that their field of application is wider than Kant supposed. Kant, according to Cassirer, assumed that the science and mathematics of his day admitted of no philosophically relevant alternatives, and therefore he conceived the synthetic a priori principles of the understanding to be unchangeable. He could not foresee the development of non-Euclidean geometry, of the modern axiomatic method, of the theory of relativity, or of quantum mechanics. Also, in Kant's day many areas of human culture had not yet been subjected to scientific investigation: There existed in particular no developed science of language and no scientific treatment of religion and myth. The idea of the humanities or moral sciences (*Geisteswissenschaften*) arose only in the nineteenth century. Cassirer's professed aim was to extend Kant's static critique of reason, that is, his critique of the organizing principles of natural science and morality, into a dynamic critique of culture, that is, of the organizing principles of the human mind in all its aspects. This aim is apparent in all his works, especially in his magnum opus, *Die Philosophie der symbolischen Formen.*

THE NATURE OF SYMBOLIC REPRESENTATION

A fundamental problem for the Kantian philosophy had been to understand the conceptualization of experience, in particular the relation between concepts and that to which they apply. For Cassirer, conceptualization, that is, the apprehension of the manifold of experience as instantiating general notions or as perceptual matter exhibiting a conceptual structure, is merely a special case of what he calls "symbolization," "symbolic representation," or simply "representation." Symbolic representation, according to Cassirer, is the essential function of human consciousness and is cardinal to our understanding not only of the structure of science, but also of myth and religion, of language, of art, and of history. Man is a symbolizing animal.

Symbolization creates, and exhibits within our consciousness, connections between perceptual signs and their significance or meaning. It is the nature of symbolic representation in general to constitute, or bring into being, a totality that both transcends the perceptual sign and provides a context for it. The unity of sign and signified allows for distinction in thought, but not in fact—just as color and extension are separable in thought but not in fact. The given always shows itself as a totality, one part of which functions as a representative of the rest. This basic self-differentiation of every content of consciousness is given a more enduring structure by the use of artificial signs that, as it were, articulate the stream of consciousness and impose patterns on it. The artificial signs or symbols, like the Kantian concepts and categories, do not mirror an objective world, but are constitutive of it. Scientific symbols constitute, or bring about, only one kind of objective world—the world of science. Mythical pictures constitute the reality of myths and religion; the words of ordinary language constitute the reality of common sense.

To the three symbolic systems that articulate three types of reality under different "symbolic forms" there correspond three modes of the one function of symbolic representation. The first and most primitive of these modes Cassirer calls the "expression function" (*Ausdrucksfunktion*). In the world it constitutes, the primitive world of myth, the sign and its significance merge into each other. The difference between them exists, but is not consciously noted. The thunder by which a primitive god shows his anger is not merely an external sign that the god is angry. It is the god's anger. In the same way, in ordinary perception we often not merely associate a smile with a kind intention, but also perceive a kindly smile.

The second mode of symbolic representation is "intuition function" (*Anschauungsfunktion*), which by the use of ordinary natural languages constitutes the world of common sense. The intuition function differentiates our perceptual world into spatially and temporally related material objects or substances that become the bearers of properties, the more permanent properties being apprehended as distinctive of the various kinds of substance, the less permanent being apprehended as accidental. Aristotle's philosophy represents, according to Cassirer, a prescientific stage of thinking about objects, based on the predominance of symbolic representation in the mode of the intuition function.

The third mode of symbolic representation, the "conceptual function" (*reine Bedeutungsfunktion*) constitutes the world of science, which is a system of relations as opposed to a system of substances with attributes. The particular, in this mode, is not subsumed under a universal but rather under a principle of ordering, which relates particulars to each other in ordered structures that, Cassirer seems to hold, are always serial in nature. He finds the prototype of this kind of symbolization in the works of Richard Dedekind, Giuseppe Peano, Gottlob Frege, and their successors.

The transcendental inquiry into the nature and function of symbolic representation is supported by a wealth of illustrations taken from the history of philosophy, the natural sciences, general linguistics, anthropology, and the humanities. Symbolic representation as a fundamental and logically primitive function must be seen at work in order to be understood. The philosophical analysis of symbolic representation can hardly do more than point out that in any symbolic representation two moments, the symbol and the symbolized, are united into an essential unity yet stand in polar relationship to each other. It has been objected that this analysis, by identifying a unity with an opposition of two different moments, results in a contradiction. Cassirer's answer to this objection, and to accusations that his professedly Kantian position is really Hegelian, is that his philosophy is not intended as a logic or a metaphysics, but as a phenomenology of consciousness.

PHILOSOPHY OF CULTURE

The highly general character of Cassirer's analysis of symbolic representation gives flexibility to a philosophy of culture. It does not force the variety of the ever-changing contents and structure of culture into rigid and artificial molds. But the very generality of Cassirer's conception makes it, perhaps, too easy to fit it to any situation and comparably difficult to test. It also makes it difficult to place the conclusions of Cassirer's special investigations in order of importance. The order here followed is in the main that of the summary given at the end of his *Essay on Man*, itself a synopsis of his *Philosophie der symbolischen Formen*.

Cassirer holds that the polarity that he finds in the relation between symbol and significance or meaning continually expresses itself in two opposing tendencies, a tendency toward stabilization and a tendency toward the breaking up of permanent symbolic patterns. In myth and the primitive religions the conservative tendency is stronger. Mythological explanation explains patterns of the present in terms of origins in a remote past—a type of explanation still regarded in the Platonic dialogues as containing important elements of truth. The more advanced religions exhibit the opposing evolutionary tendency at work. This is mainly the result of conceiving forces in nature as individuals and persons, and of the consequent emergence of the notion of morality as being rooted in personal responsibility.

In natural languages, through which the commonsense world of substances in public space and time is constituted, the conservative tendency shows itself in the rules to which a language must conform if communication is to be possible. The evolutionary tendency, which is equally essential, works through phonetic and semantic change. The psychology of the processes by which children acquire their language shows important similarities to the development of a language through succeeding generations in a community.

In the arts, the tendency toward new patterns, which has its source in the originality of the individual artist, predominates over the tendency to preserve a tradition. Yet traditional forms can never be entirely discarded, since this would imply the breakdown of communication, making art, which is a cultural and social phenomenon, impossible. The polarity in artistic creation is mirrored in the history of aesthetic theories. Theories of art as based on imitation and as based on inspiration have in one way or another continuously arisen in opposition to each other. Cassirer's own view of the nature of art is largely influenced by Kant's *Critique of Judgment*, in which the essence of artistic creation and aesthetic experience is held to lie in the interplay of the understanding, which imposes rules, and of the free imagination, which can never be completely subsumed under determinate concepts.

In science the stabilizing and objective tendency predominates over that toward change and subjective innovation. Cassirer's philosophy of science is recognizably Kantian, although Kant's absolute a priori is replaced in it by a relative a priori. Scientific theories contain, apart from empirical concepts and propositions, concepts that are a priori and propositions that are synthetic a priori with respect to a given theoretical system. This idea has proved both fruitful and influential and has been further developed by, among others, Arthur Pap, at one time a pupil of Cassirer. Relative a priori concepts and propositions are hardly distinguishable from the theoretical concepts and propositions admitted by logical positivist philosophers of science when it appeared that their original positions were not wholly tenable.

Cassirer regards language, art, religion, and science as aspects in a continuous development that although it is not predictable in advance, does show an organic unity. Every aspect expresses the fundamental function of symbolic representation in human consciousness and the power of man to build an "ideal" or symbolic world of his own, which is human culture. Cassirer's work depends to a very great extent on the illustrative power of his detailed analyses. For this reason it is difficult to do it justice in a brief survey, especially since philosophical disagreement with his critical idealism is quite compatible with a deep appreciation of his informed scholarship and his sensitive judgment as to what is and what is not important in the various symbolic and conceptual systems that he has investigated.

See also Aesthetic Experience; A Priori and A Posteriori; Cohen, Hermann; Frege, Gottlob; Hegel, Georg Wilhelm Friedrich; Husserl, Edmund; History and Historiography of Philosophy; Kant, Immanuel; Neo-Kantianism; Peano, Giuseppe.

Bibliography

SELECTED WORKS BY CASSIRER

Theoretical

Substanzbegriff und Funktionsbegriff. Berlin: Cassirer, 1910.

Zur Einsteinschen Relativitätstheorie. Berlin: Cassirer, 1921. These two works have been translated in one volume as *Substance and Function and Einstein's Theory of Relativity*. Chicago: Open Court, 1923; reprinted New York, 1953.

Philosophie der Symbolischen Formen. 3 vols. Berlin: Cassirer, 1923, 1925, 1929. *Index*, Berlin, 1931. Translated by Ralph Manheim as *Philosophy of Symbolic Forms*. 3 vols. New Haven, CT: Yale University Press, 1953, 1955, 1957.

Symbol, Myth, and Culture: Essays and Lectures of Ernst Cassirer, 1935–1945, edited by Donald Phillip Verene. New Haven, CT: Yale University Press, 1979.

Zur Logik der Kulturwissenschaften. Göteborg: Göteborgs Högskolas Årsskrift 47, 1942. Translated by S. G. Lofts as *The Logic of the Humanities*, New Haven, CT: Yale, 2001.

An Essay on Man. New Haven, CT: Yale University Press, 1944.

Historical

Leibniz's System in seinen wissenschaftlichen Grundlagen. Marburg: Elwert, 1902.

Das Erkenntnisproblem in der Philosophie und Wissenschaft der neueren Zeit. 3 vols. Berlin: Cassirer, 1906, 1907, 1920. Vol. 4 translated by W. H. Woglom and C. W. Hendel as *The Problem of Knowledge*. New Haven, CT: Yale University Press, 1950.

Freiheit und Form, Studien zur deutschen Geistesgeschichte. Berlin: Cassirer, 1916.

Kants Leben und Lehre. Vol. XI of *Immanuel Kant's Werke*, edited by Ernst Cassirer and Hermann Cohen. Berlin: Cassirer, 1918.

Individuum und Kosmos in der Philosophie der Renaissance. Leipzig: Teubner, 1927. Translated by Mario Domandi as *The Individual and the Cosmos in Renaissance Philosophy*. New York: Harper, 1964.

Die Platonische Renaissance in England und die Schule von Cambridge. Leipzig: Teubner, 1932. Translated by F. C. A. Koelln and James P. Pettegrove as *The Platonic Renaissance in England*. Austin: University of Texas Press, 1953.

Die Philosophie der Aufklärung. Tübingen: Mohr, 1932. Translated by F. C. A. Koelln and James P. Pettegrove as *The Philosophy of the Enlightenment*. Princeton, NJ: Princeton University Press, 1951.

WORKS ON CASSIRER

Cassirer, Toni. *Mein Leben mit Ernst Cassirer*. Hildesheim: Gerstenberg, 1981.

Itzkoff, S. W. *Ernst Cassirer: Scientific Knowledge and the Concept of Man*. Notre Dame, IN: University of Notre Dame Press, 1971.

Krois, J. *Cassirer: Symbolic Forms and History*. New Haven, CT: Yale University Press, 1987.

Lipton, D. *Ernst Cassirer: The Dilemmas of a Liberal Intellectual in Germany, 1914–1933*. Toronto: Toronto University Press, 1978.

Paetzold, H. *Ernst Cassirer—Von Marburg nach New York: eine philosophische Biographie*. Darmstadt: Wissenschaftliche Buchgesellschaft, 1995.

Schilpp, P. A., ed. *The Philosophy of Ernst Cassirer*. Evanston, IL: Library of Living Philosophers, 1949. Critical studies and full bibliography to 1949. For bibliography to 1964, see H. J. Paton and Raymond Klibansky, eds., *Philosophy and History, Essays Presented to Ernst Cassirer* (new ed., New York, 1964).

S. Körner (1967)
Bibliography updated by Thomas Nenon (2005)

CASTRO, ISAAC OROBIO DE

See *Orobio de Castro, Isaac*

CATEGORICAL IMPERATIVE

Immanuel Kant (1724–1804) introduced the term "categorical imperative" to characterize the fundamental principle of morality as it presents itself to beings. The principle is categorical, or unconditional, because it is valid for all humans, indeed, for all rational beings, independently of any particular desires or aims they may have. It presents itself as an imperative precisely because human beings have desires and aims that can be incompatible with the unconditional demands of the principle of morality and thus those demands often present themselves as obligations and constraints. Hence the propositional content of the fundamental principle of morality is identical for all rational beings, but its coloration as an imperative is distinctively human. For Kant, since there is a single fundamental principle of morality, there is, properly speaking, only a single categorical imperative, although more specific moral duties and obligations derivable from it are themselves unconditionally valid for any agent in the situation in which they arise. Kant contrasts the categorical imperative with "hypothetical imperatives," which express only the necessity of adopting certain means to achieve certain ends that are themselves merely conditional. Hypothetical imperatives can also present themselves to us as constraints, because we are not always sufficiently rational even to accept willingly the means to ends that we have willingly adopted, but in the case of hypothetical imperatives, we are not under any moral constraint to adopt the ends concerned.

Kant anticipated his mature distinction between categorical and hypothetical imperatives in his *Inquiry concerning the Distinctness of the Principles of Natural Theology and Morality* of 1764. There he wrote, "Every *ought* expresses a necessity of the action and is capable of two meanings. … Either I ought to do something (as a *means*) if I want something else (as an *end*), or I *ought immediately* to do something else (as an *end*) and make it actual." He argued that the former do not really express obligations at all; rather, they express only "recommendations to adopt a suitable procedure, if one wish[es] to attain a given end." Genuine obligations, by contrast, are "subordinated to an end which is necessary in itself." Kant's examples of ends that might be necessary in themselves were advancing the greatest total perfection and acting in accord with the will of God (Kant 1764; in Kant 1900, 2: 298; in Kant 1992, p. 272). The first of these is the ultimate end of morality according to Christian Wolff (1679–1754) and Alexander Baumgarten (1714–1762), and the latter the ultimate end of morality according to their Pietist opponent Christian August Crusius (1715–1775). In his *Anweisung, vernünftig zu leben* (Guide to living rationally; 1744/1964), Crusius himself anticipated the distinction that Kant made in the *Inquiry* by contrasting duties of prudence, which are grounded "only in certain ends already desired by us," with true obligations, which are grounded in "moral necessity" lying "in a law and in our owing fulfillment of it," and ultimately, in the case of "the obligation of virtue, or true obligation in a narrower sense," in divine law (§161). A widespread account of Kant's development of his mature conception of the categorical imperative is that he moved from the idea of an unconditional obligation grounded in a necessary end to the idea of an unconditional obligation that does not depend on any end whatever. Below, that will turn out to be misleading.

Kant first published his mature account of the categorical imperative in his *Groundwork for the Metaphysics of Morals* (1785). There Kant distinguished the categorical imperative from two kinds of hypothetical imperatives, namely, hypothetical imperatives of skill, which simply prescribe practically necessary means to realize entirely optional ends, and the hypothetical imperative of prudence, which prescribes means to an end that all human beings have as a matter of fact, namely happiness. Kant described the imperatives of skill as "problematic" (debatable, since the ends are optional) and the imperative of prudence as "assertoric" (impelled by the goal of happiness). Because the end of happiness is universal but not obligatory and because it is also indeterminate what will actually make anyone happy, the imperative of prudence can give rise only to "counsels of prudence." Finally, Kant stated, "There is one imperative that, without being based upon and having as its condition any other purpose to be attained by certain conduct, commands this conduct immediately. … It has to do not with the matter of the action and what is to result from it, but with the form and principle from which the action itself follows" (Kant 1785; in Kant 1900, 4:415–416; in Kant 1996, pp. 68–69). This is the categorical imperative, which is apodictic (certain).

In the *Groundwork*, Kant gave his first official formulation of the categorical imperative and the one to which he most frequently refers in subsequent works. This is that one "must act only in accordance with that maxim through which you can at the same time will that it become a universal law" (Kant 1785; in Kant 1990, 4:421; in Kant 1996, p. 73). He reached this formulation by different routes in the first and second sections of the book. In the first section, he began with the claim that only a good will is of unconditional value, and then argued that a good will is demonstrated in acting from the motive of duty, where "duty is the necessity of an action from respect for law" (Kant 1785; in Kant 1900, 4:400; in Kant 1996, p. 55), rather than in acting from any inclination toward a particular end or object. The good will having thereby been deprived of any inclination to realize it with action, nothing is left as its principle "but the conformity of actions as such with universal law" (Kant 1785; in Kant 1900, 4:402; in Kant 1996, p. 56).

In the second section, Kant argued that the formula of universal law follows from the very concept of the categorical imperative, since once it is stipulated that such an imperative "contains no condition to which it would be limited, nothing is left with which the maxim of action is to conform but the universality of a law as such" (Kant 1785; in Kant 1900, 4:420–421; in Kant 1996, p. 73). In his *Critique of Practical Reason* of 1788 (1996), Kant derives a similar formulation of the categorical imperative from the initial premises that any practical law must be necessary, but that any objective for action is empirical and contingent—a circumstance that leaves only the form of a law to furnish content for the categorical imperative (theorem III, Kant 1788, in Kant 1900, 5:27; in Kant 1996, p. 160).

In the *Groundwork*, Kant offers four further formulations of the categorical imperative. The first of these is "*Act as if your maxim were to become by your will a universal law of nature*" (Kant 1785; in Kant 1900, 4:421; in Kant 1996, p. 73), where a maxim is a proposal to perform a certain type of action for a certain end. H. J. Paton (1947) held that this introduces a teleological conception of nature into Kant's argument, and this is true in Kant's first illustration of how the imperative yields a prohibition of suicide. But since all that Kant explicitly meant by a law of nature is a law that is uniformly followed, this formulation, like the initial one, requires only that you consider whether you could act on your proposed maxim if in fact everyone else were also to act on it. In the second formulation, Kant said that "a possible categorical imperative" needs a ground in "something *the existence of which in itself* has an absolute worth, something which *as an end in itself* could be a ground of determinate laws," and stated that this ground is "the human being and in general every rational being" (Kant 1785; in Kant 1900, 4:428; in Kant 1997, p. 78). This leads Kant to reformulate the imperative as follows: "*So act that you use humanity, whether in your own person or in the person of any other, always as an end and never merely as a means*" (Kant 1785; in Kant 1900, 4:429; in Kant 1996, p. 80). By "humanity" Kant meant just the capacity to set and pursue ends (Kant 1785; in Kant 1900, 4:437; in Kant 1996, p. 86; Kant 1797; in Kant 1900, 6:387, 392; in Kant 1996, pp. 518, 522), so this requirement means that the human capacity to set and pursue ends should itself always be an end and never merely a means. Kant interpreted this requirement in turn to mean that the categorical imperative requires that you act only for ends that others can accept or even adopt for themselves. Third, Kant reformulated the imperative as "the *principle* of a human will *as a will giving universal laws through all its maxims*" (Kant 1785; in Kant 1900, 4:432; in Kant 1996, p. 82), which requires that any maxim be part of a universally acceptable *system* of maxims. Finally, he formulated the imperative as the requirement that "all maxims from one's own lawgiving are to harmonize into a possible kingdom of ends" (Kant 1785; in Kant 1900, 4:436; in Kant 1996, p. 86), which is "a whole both of rational beings as ends in themselves and of the ends of his own that each may set himself" (Kant 1785; in Kant 1900, 4:433; in Kant 1996, p. 83).

This formulation makes explicit that to treat everyone as an end involves not only acting only on universally acceptable maxims but also allowing and promoting the individual ends of each insofar as doing so is consistent with treating all as ends in themselves. This sequence of formulations thus shows that the normative force of the categorical imperative is grounded on recognition of a necessary end, thus that the distance between Kant's mature formulation and his initial formulation of twenty years earlier is not as great as it initially seems, and that far from proscribing actions in behalf of particular, contingent ends, the categorical imperative prescribes such actions to the extent that such ends are freely chosen and are consistent with universal law. This is the foundation for Kant's doctrine of duties.

G. W. F. Hegel famously charged that Kant's categorical imperative is an "empty formalism," that is, that it either presupposes some already accepted particular end or else licenses any action that anyone is willing to universalize. This is clearly false, since the imperative requires consistency between any maxim on which you are proposing to act and the universalization of that maxim. Moreover, as the analysis above shows, universalization includes the requirement that your maxim be universally acceptable. This means that it is not enough that *you* be willing for your maxim to be universalized; everyone must be willing. More recent authors, including Marcus G. Singer (1971), Onora O'Neill (1975, 1989), and Allen Wood (1999), have considered cases in which clearly permissible maxims seem to fail the test of universalizability while clearly impermissible maxims seem to pass it. This shows that considerable care is needed in properly formulating maxims to be tested by the categorical imperative. John Rawls (2000) has interpreted the categorical imperative as yielding a "CI-procedure," which can be directly applied to individual maxims or proposals of action, while Barbara Herman (1993) has argued that it rather yields "rules of moral salience," that is, general factors of moral relevance that need to be considered in undertaking any particular action. The latter seems closer to Kant's own use of "categorical imperative" in the *Metaphysics of Morals* (1797) to yield general categories of duty, although Kant himself sometimes interpreted the requirement of being universalizable to apply to very specific types of action, as in his notorious argument of 1798 that lying is always wrong, no matter what the circumstances.

In addition to these questions about the interpretation and application of the categorical imperative, it has been criticized from a number of other points of view. Philippa Foot (1972/1978) has argued that categorical form is not sufficient to show that a requirement is moral, since rules of etiquette are also stated in categorical form. She concluded that both etiquette and morality, in spite of their categorical form, are really systems of hypothetical imperatives, to be adopted only if one wants to be regarded as polite or moral respectively. Bernard Williams (1985) accepted the categorical imperative as formulating the demands of morality, but raised questions about whether these demands are "overriding," that is, whether one's own personal projects and goals must always be sacrificed to the demands of morality in cases of conflict between them. R. M. Hare (1971) likewise accepted that moral principles have the form of categorical imperatives, or universal prescriptions, while raising the question of whether such prescriptions must always be accepted. These latter objections suggest that Kant was correct to use the concept of the categorical imperative to characterize the demands of morality, but that there is room to debate both whether he correctly identified the ground of any possible categorical imperative and whether morality itself is overriding.

See also Deontological Ethics; Duty; Kant, Immanuel; Kantian Ethics; Moral Rules and Principles.

Bibliography

PRIMARY SOURCES

Crusius, Christian August. *Anweisung, vernünftig zu leben* (1744). In *Die philosophische Hauptschriften*, edited by Giorgio Tonelli. Hildesheim: Olms, 1964. Selection translated in *Moral Philosophy from Montaigne to Kant*, edited by J. B. Schneewind. Vol. 2, 568–585. Cambridge, U.K.: Cambridge University Press, 1990.

Hegel, Georg Wilhelm Friedrich. *Elements of the Philosophy of Right* (1821). Translated by H. B. Nisbet. Cambridge, U.K.: Cambridge University Press, 1991.

Hegel, Georg Wilhelm Friedrich. *The Scientific Ways of Treating Natural Law, Its Place in Moral Philosophy, and Its Relation to the Positive Sciences of Law* (1802). Translated b y T. M. Knox. Philadelphia: University of Pennsylvania Press, 1975.

Kant, Immanuel. *Critique of Practical Reason* (1788). In his *Practical Philosophy*, edited and translated by Mary J. Gregor, 137–271. Cambridge, U.K.: Cambridge University Press, 1996.

Kant, Immanuel. *Groundwork for the Metaphysics of Morals* (1785). In his *Practical Philosophy*, edited and translated by Mary J. Gregor, 37–108. Cambridge, U.K.: Cambridge University Press, 1996.

Kant, Immanuel. *Inquiry concerning the Distinctness of the Principles of Rational Theology and Morality* (1764). In his

Theoretical Philosophy, 1755–1770, edited and translated by David Walford, in collaboration with Ralf Meerbote, 243–275. Cambridge, U.K.: Cambridge University Press, 1992.

Kant, Immanuel. *Kants Gesammelte Schriften*, edited by the Königlich Preussischen (later Deutschen und Berlin-Brandenburgischen Akademie der Wissenschaften. 29 vols. Berlin: George Reimer (later Walter de Gruyter and Company), 1900–.

Kant, Immanuel. *Metaphysics of Morals* (1797). In his *Practical Philosophy*, edited and translated by Mary J. Gregor, 353–603. Cambridge, U.K.: Cambridge University Press, 1996.

Kant, Immanuel. "On a Supposed Right to Lie from Philanthropy" (1798). In his *Practical Philosophy*, edited and translated by Mary J. Gregor, 605–615. Cambridge, U.K.: Cambridge University Press, 1996.

SECONDARY SOURCES

Aune, Bruce. *Kant's Theory of Morals*. Princeton, NJ: Princeton University Press, 1979.

Ebbinghaus, Julius. "Interpretation and Misinterpretation of the Categorical Imperative." *Philosophical Quarterly* 4 (1954): 97–108.

Foot, Philippa. "Morality as a System of Hypothetical Imperatives." *Philosophical Review* 81 (1972): 305–316. Reprinted in her *Virtues and Vices*, 157–173. Berkeley: University of California Press, 1978.

Guyer, Paul. "The Possibility of the Categorical Imperative." *Philosophical Review* 104 (1995): 353–385. Reprinted in his *Kant on Freedom, Law, and Happiness*, 172–206. Cambridge, U.K.: Cambridge University Press, 2000.

Hare, R. M. *Practical Inferences*. Berkeley: University of California Press, 1971.

Herman, Barbara. *The Practice of Moral Judgment*. Cambridge, MA: Harvard University Press, 1993.

Höffe, Otfried. *Categorical Principles of Law: A Counterpoint to Modernity*. Translated by Mark Migotti. University Park: Pennsylvania State University Press, 2002.

Kerstein, Samuel J. *Kant's Search for the Supreme Principle of Morality*. Cambridge, U.K.: Cambridge University Press, 2002.

McDowell, John. "Are Moral Requirements Categorical Imperatives?" *Proceedings of the Aristotelian Society*, supp. vol. 52 (1978): 13–29. Reprinted in his *Mind, Value, and Reality*, 77–94. Cambridge, MA: Harvard University Press, 1998.

Nisters, Thomas. *Kants kategorischer Imperativ als Leitfaden humaner Praxis*. Freiburg, Germany: Verlag Karl Alber, 1989.

O'Neill, Onora. *Constructions of Reason: Explorations of Kant's Practical Philosophy*. Cambridge, U.K.: Cambridge University Press, 1989.

[O'Neill], Onora Nell. *Acting on Principle: An Essay on Kantian Ethics*. New York: Columbia University Press, 1975.

Paton, H. J. *The Categorical Imperative: A Study in Kant's Moral Philosophy*. London: Hutchinson, 1947.

Patzig, Günter. *Ethik ohne Metaphysik*. Göttingen, Germany: Vandenhoeck und Ruprecht, 1971.

Pogge, Thomas W. "The Categorical Imperative." In *Grundlegung zur Metaphysik der Sitten: Ein kooperativer Kommentar*, edited by Otfried Höffe, 172–193. Frankfurt am Main, Germany: Vittorio Klostermann, 1989. Reprinted in *Kant's Groundwork of the Metaphysics of Morals: Critical Essays*, edited by Paul Guyer, 189–214. Lanham, MD: Rowman and Littlefield, 1998.

Rawls, John. *Lectures on the History of Moral Philosophy*. Cambridge, MA: Harvard University Press, 2000.

Schnoor, Christian. *Kants kategorischer Imperativ als Kriterium der Richtigkeit des Handelns*. Tübingen, Germany: J. C. B. Mohr, 1989.

Schwaiger, Clemens. *Kategorische und andere Imperative: Zur Entwicklung von Kants praktischer Philosophie bis 1785*. Stuttgart, Germany: Fromann-Holzboog, 1999.

Schwemmer, Oswald. *Philosophie der Praxis: Verusch zur Grundlegung einer Lehre vom moralischen Argumentieren in Verbindung mit einer Interpretation der praktischen Philosophie Kants*. 2nd ed. Frankfurt am Main, Germany: Suhrkamp, 1980.

Singer, Marcus George. *Generalization in Ethics: An Essay in the Logic of Ethics, with the Rudiments of a System of Moral Philosophy*. New York: Atheneum, 1971.

Stratton-Lake, Philip. "Formulating Categorical Imperatives." *Kant-Studien* 83 (1993): 317–340.

Williams, Bernard. *Ethics and the Limits of Philosophy*. Cambridge, MA: Harvard University Press, 1985.

Williams, T. C. *The Concept of the Categorical Imperative: A Study of the Place of the Categorical Imperative in Kant's Ethical Theory*. Oxford, U.K.: Clarendon Press, 1968.

Wood, Allen W. *Kant's Ethical Thought*. Cambridge, U.K.: Cambridge University Press, 1999.

Paul Guyer (2005)

CATEGORIES

Philosophical categories are classes, genera, or types supposed to mark necessary divisions within our conceptual scheme, divisions that we must recognize if we are to make literal sense in our discourse about the world. To say that two entities belong to different categories is to say that they have literally nothing in common, that we cannot apply the same descriptive terms to both unless we speak metaphorically or equivocally.

ARISTOTELIAN THEORY

The word *category* was first used as a technical term in philosophy by Aristotle. In his short treatise called *Categories*, he held that every uncombined expression signifies (denotes, refers to) one or more things falling in at least one of the following ten classes: substance, quantity, quality, relation, place, time, posture, state, action, and passion. By "uncombined expression" Aristotle meant an expression considered apart from its combination with other expressions in a sentence, and he intended his account to apply only to those expressions we now call "descriptive" and "nonlogical." Logical expressions, such as "not," "or," "some," and "every," are excluded; these were called by medieval philosophers "syncategorematic," to distinguish them from the categorematic expressions covered by Aristotle's account of categories.

Each of the ten classes of entities signified constitutes a category, or genus, of entities, and each categorematic expression is said to be an expression in the category constituted by the class of entities it signifies. The nouns "plant" and "animal," for example, signify kinds of substances and are said to be expressions in the category of substance; the nouns "color" and "justice" signify kinds of qualities and are said to be expressions in the category of quality. On the other hand, the adjectives "colored" and "just" signify, respectively, colored and just things (substances) and also connote (consignify) the qualities color and justice. Aristotle labeled such expressions "derivative terms" or "paronyms" and held that instead of signifying substances simply, as expressions in the category of substance do, they signify substances derivatively by connoting accidents of substances.

Although Aristotle implied that his ten categories constitute the ten highest genera of entities and hence the only true genera—the only genera that cannot be taken as species of higher genera—he also implied that it is not essential to his theory that the categories be exactly ten in number or even that they be mutually exclusive and exhaustive. Categories are listed in various of Aristotle's writings, but the list usually stops short of ten without indication that categories have been omitted. He explicitly stated that no absurdity would result if the same items were included in both the category of quality and that of relation. He remarked that the expressions "rare," "dense," "rough," and "smooth" do not signify qualities, since they apply to a substance with reference to a quality it possesses, yet he did not specify in which category or categories these expressions are included. Despite these indications that his theory of categories is not entirely complete, medieval philosophers generally wrote as though Aristotle's list of ten provided a final, exhaustive enumeration of the highest genera of being.

What is essential to Aristotle's theory of categories is that substances be properly distinguished from accidents and essential predication from accidental predication. Any entity, regardless of the category in which it is included, can be an entity referred to by the subject term of an essential predication. "Man is an animal." "Red is a color." "Four is a number." "A year is twelve months." The subject terms denote entities that fall, respectively, in the categories of substance, quality, quantity, and time, and the predication in each case is essential. On the other hand, only entities in the category of substance can be entities referred to by subject terms of accidental predication. There is no such thing as an accident of an accident; accidents happen to substances and not to other accidents. "Red is darker than orange" does not assert something that happens to be, but need not be, true of red; it asserts what is essentially true of red, something that red must always be if it is to remain the color red. "Red is John's favorite color" does not assert anything that may happen to be true of red; rather, it asserts something that may happen to be true of John. To undergo change through time while remaining numerically one and the same thing is what principally distinguishes substances from entities in other categories. If John ceases to regard red as his favorite color, we say not that red has changed while remaining the same color but that John has changed while remaining the same person.

Categorematic expressions, for Aristotle, are technically "predicates," but they are not "predicates" in a sense that keeps them from serving as subject terms in essential predication. The minor term of an Aristotelian "scientific syllogism" occurs only as a subject, though Aristotle gave no examples in which it is a proper name. He regarded the ultimate subject terms in demonstration as common names marking species that are not further divided. Such expressions are still "predicates" in that like more generic terms they are applied to individuals in answer to the question What is it? But proper names are in a class by themselves; they are applied only in answer to the question Who? or Which? and are not "predicates" at all. Yet if proper names are thus not categorematic expressions, they are still fundamental to Aristotle's theory of categories. Without proper names there are no names for the subjects of accidental as distinct from essential predication. Man as such is an animal—"man" names every person indifferently if it names any, and the question of naming which one (or ones) does not arise. But only some man (or men) is (are) snub-nosed, and until the question Which? is answered by a proper name the subject of the accidental predication remains unnamed.

CATEGORY-MISTAKES. If we ask what, according to Aristotle's theory, would be the sort of thing often called today a "category-mistake," we must distinguish a mistake that violates what is essential to the theory from a mistake that violates a particular category-difference marked by the theory. Only a mistake of the first kind is strictly a category-mistake. Mistakes of the second kind form a subclass of equivocations. In his *Topics* (107a3–17), Aristotle listed as one example of equivocation the sentence

"The musical note and knife are sharp." That "sharp" is here used equivocally is shown by the fact that a musical note and a knife belong to different categories. A musical note is a kind of sound, and sounds are qualities. (Aristotle argued in *On the Soul,* 420a25–28, that we speak of the sound of a body as we speak of the color of a body.) A knife is a kind of substance, and one who believes that "sharp" applies in the same sense to musical notes and to knives may be said to have made the category-mistake of confusing a quality and a substance. Yet an appeal to category-differences is not necessary to expose the equivocation, and many equivocations cannot be exposed in this way because there is no violation of a category-difference. Aristotle claimed that the equivocal use of "sharp" in the example is also exposed by the fact (among others) that musical notes and knives are not compared with respect to their sharpness. Two notes may be equally sharp, or two knives, but not a note and a knife. Again, two flavors are equally sharp, but not a flavor and a note or a flavor and a knife. The equivocation in "The flavor and note are sharp" is exposed, although since flavors and sounds are both qualities there is no violation of a category-difference.

The appearance of absurdity produced by an equivocation can always be removed and literal meaning restored by distinction between the different senses of the crucial words. But with a genuine category-mistake there is no literal meaning to restore. In a passage in his *Posterior Analytics* (83a30–33), where he was discussing features of essential and accidental predication, Aristotle remarked that Plato's forms can be dismissed as mere sound without sense. The point is illustrated by a sentence like "The color white is white." The sentence may seem to make sense if one claims that since the color white is the standard by which we judge things to be white, it is itself white. But the sense is only apparent, because whatever is white remains numerically one and the same object even if its color changes. Such an object cannot be the quality, that is, the color white itself, as we then have the absurdity that the color white changes its color. Plato's theory of forms, as Aristotle interpreted it, makes the mistake of confusing accidental with essential predication. "The color white is the color white" is not an accidental but a trivially true essential predication; it is clearly not what is intended by the Platonic assertion that the color white is white. But the latter is just as absurd as the assertion that sitting sits.

Except in the passage in the *Posterior Analytics,* Aristotle did not refer to Plato's forms as mere sound without sense. Plato's theory has certain affinities with Aristotle's metaphysical account of substance as a composite of form and matter, and in his *Metaphysics,* Aristotle criticized Plato's forms, not as sound without sense, but as entities that fail to do the job they should, since they cannot be formal causes (991a11; 1033b26) and lead to an infinite regress (the third-man argument: 990b17). His criticism of the theory of forms receives attention in the history of philosophy mainly in this context of form, matter, and substance, and the passage in the *Posterior Analytics* that dismisses the forms as sound without sense is generally passed over or dismissed as a result of more than usual hostility toward Platonists. Yet apart from hostility, Aristotle was required by his theory to regard a sentence like "The color white is white" strictly as a category-mistake.

KANTIAN THEORY

Aristotle's theory dominated discussion of categories until the work of Immanuel Kant, where we find a radically new conception of a category. Kant professed in his theory of categories to have achieved what Aristotle had tried but failed to achieve in such a theory. Instead of beginning with uncombined expressions, Aristotle should have started with expressions of statements or judgments. Every statement is universal, particular, or singular in quantity; affirmative, negative, or infinite in quality; categorical, hypothetical, or disjunctive in the relation of its parts; and problematic, assertoric, or apodictic in modality (*Critique of Pure Reason,* "Transcendental Analytic," I, 2–3). Each of these twelve ways in which judgments are classified in logic corresponds to a function of the understanding indispensable to the formation of judgments, and each such function yields a category, or pure concept of the understanding, in one of the four major divisions of categories: quantity, quality, relation, and modality. The function, for example, of relating subject to predicate in a categorical judgment yields the relational category of substance and accident, and the function of relating antecedent to consequent in a hypothetical judgment yields the relational category of cause and effect.

Kant's conception of substance leads to important departures from Aristotle in the treatment of common names and paronyms. Whether an expression serves as a common name or as a paronym depends on its function in a given statement and not on its signification as an uncombined expression. "Stone," for example, serves as a common name of the substance in which a change occurs in "The stone grows warm," but it serves to specify a kind of change that occurs in a substance in "The sand becomes stone." In the second case "stone" serves as a paronym; it connotes certain properties, such as hardness and solidity, and denotes any substance, such as a certain amount of sand, that acquires these properties. For Aristotle the change from sand to stone is substantial change, or coming to be, rather than alteration; for Kant substantial change is impossible because substance is related to accident as that which undergoes alteration is related to that which becomes and ceases to be. A substance is altered when one of its accidents ceases to be and is followed by another accident, so accidents, not substances, become and cease to be.

With Kant's theory there are no ordinary equivocations that can be exposed as category-mistakes, since categories are pure (formal), as opposed to empirical, concepts. "Substance" and "quality," in Aristotle's theory, are the highest generic terms that apply, respectively, to knives and sounds, so the equivocation in "The knife and musical note are sharp" can be exposed as a confusion of a substance and a quality. In Kant's theory, by contrast, generic terms represent empirical concepts, and an equivocation that confuses genera, as "The knife and musical note are sharp" confuses bodies and sounds, is not a category-mistake but a confusion of empirical concepts. One makes a category-mistake—violates what is essential to Kant's theory—by misapplying a category rather than by mistaking the category in which an entity belongs. The important point is that Kant's categories apply only to phenomena or appearances, not to entities or things in themselves. Every appearance can be judged according to every category and cannot be said to belong properly in one category rather than another. An appearance of red, for example, has extensive magnitude equal to a spatial area and is hence a quantity; it has intensive magnitude as a sensation with a certain degree of intensity and is hence a quality; it is related to further appearances as accident is to substance and effect to cause; and in relation to other appearances it is possible, actual, or necessary.

In Aristotle's theory, on the contrary, a redness is properly an accident in the category of quality; it exists in a substance from which it may be separated in thought but not in being. The extensive magnitude comprising a spatial area is a quantity of the substance and not of the redness; the intensity of the sensation of redness is a quality of the perceiving subject. Questions concerning the cause or the possibility, actuality, and necessity of the redness can be answered only by references to the substance that is said to be red. When the color is separated in thought from the substance the resulting abstract entity, the color red, can be characterized essentially (red, for example, is darker than orange), but to take it as an entity that itself has accidents is to make the category-mistake of confusing a quality with a substance.

To say that the color red is red is, for Kant, to misapply the relational category of substance and accident. Categories can be applied correctly only to phenomena, and in the case of a relational category both terms of the relation must be phenomena. The phrase "the color red" stands for the concept under which appearances of red are subsumed and not for an appearance that may be related to an appearance of red as substance to accident. This sort of category-mistake needs little attention since with Kant's theory there is no compelling tendency of the human mind to confuse a concept with its instances. But there is a natural tendency to make the mistake of applying categories to what are technically, for Kant, ideas and ideals; the former give rise to antinomies of pure reason and the latter to fallacious proofs of God's existence. Platonism in the form that gains a hold on men's minds is the mistake of applying the category of existence to ideals, not the mistake of confusing a concept with its instances. Along with antinomies and fallacious proofs of God, Kant argued for a third kind of category-mistake, a mistake that occurs when categories are misapplied in judgments about a thinking substance; the result is a set of equivocations giving rise to what Kant called "paralogisms of pure reason." These three kinds of category-mistakes are to be exposed not as sound without sense but as illusions to which the human mind is naturally prone.

POST-KANTIAN THEORIES

Although Kant's theory of categories marks the single most important development in the subject since Aristotle, his list of twelve categories never acquired anything like the dominant role once held by Aristotle's list of ten. Kant's influence has been to change the conception of how a list of categories should be formed, rather than to provide the list itself. Instead of looking for the highest genera of being, the most universal kinds of entities, one should look for the most universal forms of understanding presupposed in the formation of judgments. The strong influence of Kant is evident in the theories of categories of such philosophers as G. W. F. Hegel, Edmund Husserl, and Charles Sanders Peirce.

Peirce's theory is closely connected with his contributions to logic, but his conception of what constitutes a category is sufficiently Kantian to distinguish his theory radically from the theory usually associated with the development of modern logic.

THEORY OF TYPES. Bertrand Russell originally devised his theory of types as a means of avoiding a contradiction he had discovered in Gottlob Frege's logic, but the theory has profound implications for philosophy in general, and under its influence "category" has come to be used frequently as a synonym for "logical type."

As the theory of types is presented in *Principia Mathematica,* its cardinal principle (called by Russell the "vicious-circle principle") is that whatever involves all of a collection must not be one of the collection. The class of white objects, for example, includes (and hence involves) all white objects, and to say that this class is itself a white object is to violate the principle and to utter nonsense. The set of entities consisting of all white objects and the class of white objects is for Russell an "illegitimate totality," a set that "has no total" in the sense that no significant statement can be made about all its members. The purpose of the theory of types is to provide a theoretical basis for breaking up such a set into legitimate totalities. A totality is legitimate when and only when all its members belong to the same logical type, and two entities are of different logical types when and only when their inclusion in the same class yields an illegitimate totality. Whenever an entity involves all the members of a given class its logical type is said to be higher than the type of the members of this class. Logical types thus form an infinite hierarchy with individuals at the lowest level, or zero type, classes of individuals at the next level, then classes of classes, and so on. Since to every class there corresponds a defining property of that class, there is an equivalent hierarchy of logical types with individuals again at the lowest level, but with properties of individuals next, then properties of properties of individuals, and so on. "*X* is a member of the class of white objects" is equivalent to "*X* is white," and the two sentences "The class of white objects is a white object" and "The color white is white" are equally expressions of a type-mistake or category-mistake and are equally nonsensical.

The theory of types, if true, gets rid of the contradiction Russell wanted to avoid. This contradiction arises when the class of all classes that are not members of themselves is said to be or not to be a member of itself. According to the theory of types the attempt to make either assertion violates the vicious-circle principle and results in nonsense. But if this way of avoiding the contradiction is to be satisfactory, there must be reasons for accepting the theory of types other than the fact that if it is accepted the contradiction it was designed to avoid is avoided. Efforts to find such reasons have carried investigations concerning the theory of types from the sphere of technical issues in mathematical logic into the sphere of philosophical issues in a theory of categories. Developments in both spheres have often proceeded independently, and even though technical work in mathematical logic has developed alternatives to the theory of types (especially to the theory as first stated by Russell), the fact that the theory is not needed to avoid the original contradiction is not in itself conclusive evidence that the theory has nothing to be said for it as a theory of categories.

Russell offered in support of the theory of types the fact that it outlaws not only conditions giving rise to the paradox concerning class membership but also those giving rise to an indefinite number of other paradoxes of self-reference, including the ancient paradox of the liar. But alternative ways of avoiding these other paradoxes have been developed. More serious than its nonuniqueness as a consistent solution to the problems it was designed to avoid is a difficulty intrinsic to the theory itself. Even if the theory is true, there seems to be no way to state it without contradiction. The word *type* illustrates the point. In stating the theory one uses this word, which is itself a particular entity, with reference to all entities, so one entity is made to involve the collection of all entities. Russell tried to cope with the difficulty by proposing that a difference in logical type be taken as a difference in syntactical function rather than a difference in the totalities to which two entities may be legitimately assigned. Instead of saying that the color white and a table are of different logical types because the latter but not the former can be included in the class of all white objects without forming an illegitimate totality, we may say that the phrases "the color white" and "a table" belong to different logical types because the latter but not the former yields a significant statement when it replaces *X* in the sentence-form "*X* is white."

Reference to linguistic expressions rather than entities avoids a vicious-circle fallacy because the hierarchy of types asserted by the theory then includes only the totality of expressions within a given language, not the totality of all entities. But any given statement of the theory must be in a metalanguage whose expressions are not included in the totality of expressions covered by the statement. While the theory can thus never be applied to the language in which it is itself stated, it can always in principle be restated in a further language (a meta-metalanguage) so that it applies to the language in which it was originally stated as well as the language to which it originally applied. Universal application of the theory is thus possible in principle by proceeding up an infinite hierarchy of languages, while the application of the theory to each particular language asserts the existence of an infinite hierarchy of types of syntactical functions within that language. But in neither case is there the simple assertion that the class of all entities comprises an infinite hierarchy of logical types.

The conception of logical type as syntactical function is much easier to maintain when the expressions typed are those of an artificial language, such as a logical calculus, rather than those of a natural language, such as English. Generalization about the totality of expressions in an artificial language is easy because this totality is generated by the rules one must lay down if one is to construct an artificial language in a clear and definite sense. But such relativity to the rules of an artificial language makes it impossible to maintain all that was originally claimed for the theory of types. Russell was originally understood as claiming to have *discovered* that what appears to be stated by sentences like "The color white is white" and "The class of white objects is a white object" is simply nonsense. But then it seems that the most one can say is that Russell *constructed* an artificial language (a calculus or formalism) in which the translations of these English sentences are not well-formed formulas. The mere construction of such a language is clearly not the same as the discovery that in point of logic certain apparent statements are really nonsense. The case against Russell's original claim is all the more damaging in view of the fact that formalisms have since been constructed in which translations of certain sentences that are nonsense according to the theory of types are well-formed formulas, and the contradiction the theory of types was designed to avoid does not appear. Enlarging the notion of logical type to include semantic as well as syntactical function does not change the picture. Semantic rules for an artificial language are necessary if one is to do certain things with the language, but these rules, like syntactical rules, are stipulated in the construction of the formalism; addition of such rules in no way furthers the claim to having discovered that certain sentences are nonsense rather than having constructed a language in which they become nonsense.

CATEGORIES AS DISCOVERED IN A NATURAL LANGUAGE

The claim to discovery is essential to a theory of categories, and the claim may still be made if types are found among the expressions of a natural language rather than imposed on the expressions of an artificial language. Instead of beginning with the vicious-circle principle as defining a condition we must impose on any language if we want to make sense, we may begin with expressions in the natural language we ordinarily use—expressions with which we assume we make sense, if we make sense at all—and try to determine what differences in type our making sense requires us to recognize in these expressions. This sort of approach is taken by Gilbert Ryle in *The Concept of Mind,* where he considers expressions we use in talking about mental powers and operations and argues that certain of these expressions cannot belong to the same type or category as others. Ryle's test for a category-difference is a case where one of two expressions cannot replace the other without turning the literal meaning of a sentence into an absurdity. To begin with an obvious case, when "the man" in "The man is in bed" is replaced by "Saturday" the result is clearly an absurd sentence if taken literally. Less obvious cases often go undetected by philosophers and remain a source of philosophical confusion. "He scanned the hedgerow carefully" becomes absurd when "saw" replaces "scanned," although the absurdity disappears when the adverb is omitted. Failure to note that "to see" belongs in the category of "achievement" verbs while "to scan" is a "task" or "search" verb has misled philosophers to posit a mental activity corresponding to seeing that is analogous to the genuine activity of scanning.

For Ryle categories are indefinitely numerous and unordered. The totality of categories is not in principle an infinite hierarchy of types; categories provide no architectonic such as Kant's fourfold division of triads; and there is no distinction setting off one category from all the others as basic regardless of their number, as Aristotle's distinction between substance and accident. There are thus no mistakes that are strictly category-mistakes rather than ordinary equivocations or absurdities. Ryle explains in his article "Categories" that he uses "absurdity" rather than "nonsense" because he wants to distinguish a category-mistake from mere sound without sense. According to Ryle, a category-mistake is not a meaningless noise but a remark that is somehow out of place when its literal meaning is taken seriously; many jokes, he observes, are in fact "type-pranks."

WHAT IS A THEORY OF CATEGORIES?

The above observations suggest that Ryle has no *theory* of categories at all—no principles by which categories can be determined and ordered. Yet he seems unwilling to give up all claims to a theory of categories. He is especially concerned with countering the impression that category-differences are on a par with differences created by a particular set of linguistic rules. In his article "Categories" he considers briefly the question What are types of? He suggests that instead of saying absurdities result from an improper coupling of linguistic expressions, it is more correct to say that they result from an improper coupling of what the expressions signify. But one must be wary of saying that types are types of the *significata* of expressions. A phrase like "*significata* of expressions" can never be used univocally, because such use presupposes that all *significata* are of the same type. Ryle claims we can get along without an expression that purports to specify what types are types of, since the functions of such an expression are "purely stenographic"; if we want an expression performing these functions, he suggests "proposition-factor" but cautions that to ask what proposition-factors are like is ridiculous since the phrase "proposition-factor" has all possible type-ambiguities.

Ryle seems hardly to have advanced the question of the status of a theory of categories beyond the point where Russell left it. It appears to be just as difficult to establish category-differences by appeal solely to ordinary language as to establish them by appeal solely to an artificial language. J. J. C. Smart points out, in "A Note on Categories," that with Ryle's test of a category-difference we are led to make very implausible (if not absurd) claims about category-differences. When, for example, "table" replaces "chair" in "The seat of the chair is hard," the result seems clearly an absurd sentence. Yet if "table" and "chair" do not belong in the same category, what words do? If the phrase "category-difference" is to have anything like the force it has had from Aristotle to Russell, the claim to having discovered that "table" and "chair" are expressions in different categories is itself absurd. Though Ryle may not want to make the claim, he cannot avoid it and maintain his test of a category-difference.

Yet Ryle, whatever his intentions, may be said to have established the negative point that absurdity alone is never a sufficient test of a category-mistake. Aristotle, Kant, and Russell each began with metaphysical or logical principles that purport to set limits of literal sense; a violation of these principles results either in sound without sense or in intellectual illusion, and in both cases in more than simple absurdity. Ryle appears to want the advantages of a theory of categories and at the same time to avoid the embarrassment of having to defend its principles. Such a theory promises to rid philosophy of many fallacious arguments and contradictions, but the promise is worthless if the principles of the theory are no more tenable than the arguments and contradictions it sweeps away. Aristotle's metaphysics of substance and accident, Kant's transcendental logic, and Russell's elevation of the vicious-circle principle have proved as philosophically debatable as Platonic forms, proofs for the existence of God, and paradoxes of self-reference. It is comforting to believe that such debatable principles can be discarded and that the forms, proofs, and paradoxes can be exposed as category-mistakes by appeal to nothing more than what a man of common sense will recognize as an absurdity in his own ordinary language. But unfortunately our common use of "absurdity" covers too much. One can hardly hope to rid philosophy of Platonic forms with no more argument than the claim that saying the color white is white is like saying the seat of a table is hard.

Ryle also calls attention to another negative point about a theory of categories. The theory cannot have a subject matter in the usual sense. We cannot generalize about all proposition-factors, all entities, or all of whatever it is types are said to be types of as we generalize about, for example, all bodies or all biological organisms. We may say that every proposition-factor is of some type, but we cannot say what it is like regardless of its type as we can say what every body or biological organism is like regardless of its type. Since everything we can talk about is a proposition-factor, we have nothing with which they can be contrasted; we do, however, have things with which to contrast bodies and biological organisms. Ryle sees this point as forcing us to accept a phrase like "proposition-factor" as merely a kind of dummy expression we may use to preserve the ordinary grammar of "type" and "category," although the important thing is not to preserve the grammar but to avoid the error of thinking we can preserve it with other than a dummy expression. If we take "proposition-factor" as a metalinguistic expression applying to factors in a particular language, we succeed in preserving the grammar without a dummy expression, but only at the price of making categories relative to a particular set of linguistic rules. The use of a dummy expression is at least consistent with the claim (which Ryle seems to want to make) that a recognition of absurdity is not relative to the rules of a particular language. We may be said to recognize, regardless of our language, the absurdity of saying that the seat of a table is hard or that the color white is white, although we are unable to give criteria of absurdity.

Aristotle tried to cope with the subject-matter problem by holding that while we cannot generalize about all entities as we can about all bodies or all biological organisms ("being is not a genus," as he put it), we can have a science of being because there is one primary type of being—substance—and every other type exists, by being an accident of substance. Although we have, then, nothing with which to contrast all beings, we can contrast substances with accidents, and the science of substance is the science of being *qua* being in that conditions for the being of substance are conditions for the being of everything else. A theory of categories may thus be founded on the principle that substances alone can have accidents and all categories other than substance are categories of accidents. For Kant categories do not distinguish beings or entities but a priori forms of understanding, and, unlike Aristotle's beings or Ryle's proposition-factors, these forms comprise not everything we can talk about but only necessary conditions for judgments about objects of experience. The forms stand in sharp contrast with other objects of discourse and constitute a single subject matter belonging to the science of transcendental logic.

Neither Aristotle's nor Kant's theory of categories seems immune to the objection that its subject matter is created rather than discovered. Aristotle's pronouncements about substance and accident and Kant's about forms of understanding each provide principles that yield a scheme of categories, but one may ask whether the pronouncements are anything more than rules for the construction of a certain kind of language—whether the construction of an Aristotelian metaphysics or that of a Kantian transcendental logic provides a theory of categories with anything more than an artificial language within which certain category-differences are established. An answer to this question is proposed by P. F. Strawson in his *Individuals.* Strawson suggests that theories of metaphysics have tended to be either descriptive or revisionary. A metaphysics is descriptive insofar as it yields a scheme of categories that describes the conceptual scheme we actually presuppose in ordinary language. A theory becomes revisionary to the extent that it leads to a departure from our ordinary scheme. Strawson cites the metaphysical theories of Aristotle and Kant as descriptive, those of René Descartes, Gottfried Wilhelm Leibniz, and George Berkeley as revisionary. While all five philosophers construct special languages, only Aristotle and Kant do so in a way that results in a scheme of categories that describes the conceptual scheme of our ordinary language.

But if in this sense Aristotle and Kant in their theories of categories describe rather than create a subject matter, what they describe is not what they claim as their subject matter. Strawson professes in his own theory of categories to describe the conceptual scheme of our ordinary language, but he does not profess to give principles of being *qua* being or a transcendental deduction of pure concepts of the understanding. If Aristotle and Kant to some extent describe the scheme Strawson sets out to describe, this achievement was certainly not their primary objective, and since they differ radically at crucial points, as in their views of alteration and substantial change, they can hardly be said in any case to describe the same scheme. One must say, rather, that each offers metaphysical or transcendental hypotheses that purport to account for and establish the necessity of the conceptual scheme underlying common sense. One may of course accept much of what they say in description of their schemes as true of what one takes to be our commonsense scheme and yet reject their hypotheses. With the rejection there is no need to defend the hypotheses' claims to a metaphysical or transcendental subject matter, but one then needs to explain how our commonsense scheme is subject matter for description. A description of common features in the grammars of Indo-European languages is not exactly what Strawson means by a description of the conceptual scheme of our ordinary language. But it can hardly be said that his efforts to distinguish the two descriptions are entirely successful. In some of his arguments he seems to appeal to metaphysical hypotheses of his own and hence to have a theory accounting for, and not simply a description of, the conceptual scheme he claims as his subject matter. In other arguments he seems, like Ryle, to make an ultimate appeal to our commonsense recognition of absurdity.

The construction of a theory of categories as descriptive metaphysics differs, according to Strawson, from what has come to be called philosophical, or logical, or conceptual analysis. But the difference is not "in kind of intention, but only in scope and generality." Strawson describes philosophical analysis as relying on "a close examination of the actual use of words," and while this is "the best, and indeed the only sure, way in philosophy," what it can yield is not of sufficient scope and generality "to meet the full metaphysical demand for understanding." But Strawson does not elaborate the demand and gives no criterion for deciding when philosophical analysis must give way to descriptive metaphysics. He sometimes implies that we may pass imperceptibly from one to the other, and this may be the case if to do descriptive metaphysics is simply to articulate what is presupposed in a given philosophical analysis. But it can hardly be the case if descriptive metaphysics, unlike philosophical analysis, has its own peculiar subject matter—being *qua* being, pure concepts of the understanding, our commonsense conceptual scheme, or whatever. Philosophical analysis is clarification of thought about a given subject matter, and to articulate the presuppositions of a given analysis is not to analyze a new subject matter but only to push the original analysis as far as we can. In the end we may arrive at distinctions that agree with what philosophers from Aristotle to Strawson have called "category-differences," and there is no harm in using the label if we mean only that the distinctions are ultimate in the analysis we have given and not also that they have to be supported by a hypothesis about a special subject matter. We can hardly make the additional claim without passing beyond the point where we can hope for help from philosophical analysis.

HISTORICAL NOTES

STOICS AND NEOPLATONISTS. In place of Aristotle's ten categories the Greek Stoics substituted four "most generic" notions or concepts: substratum, or subject; quality, or essential attribute; state, or accidental condition; and relation. The Stoic view, as well as the Aristotelian doctrine, was criticized by the Neoplatonist Plotinus. In his *Sixth Ennead* Plotinus argued that the ultimate categories are neither the Aristotelian ten nor the Stoic four but correspond to the five "kinds" listed in Plato's *Sophist*: being, rest, motion, identity, and difference. The central point for Plotinus was that different categories apply to the intelligible and sensible worlds, the ultimate categories applying only to the former. Plotinus's views on categories figured prominently in medieval discussions only as they were considerably modified by his pupil Porphyry. In Porphyry's short commentary on Aristotle's *Categories,* generally known as the *Isagoge* (*Εἰσαγωγή*, "Introduction"), he accepted Aristotle's list of ten but raised Plotinian questions about the way they exist. He noted that categories are genera and asked whether genera and species subsist (exist outside the understanding) or are in the naked understanding alone; whether, if they subsist, they are corporeal or incorporeal; and finally, whether they are separated from sensibles or reside in sensibles. He remarked that these questions are too deep for an introductory treatise, and we have no record of how he thought they should be answered.

BOETHIUS. Boethius translated the *Isagoge* into Latin, along with Aristotle's *Categories* and *On Interpretation.* He also wrote a commentary on the *Isagoge,* offering answers to Porphyry's unanswered questions, and thus began a tradition, which persisted throughout the medieval period, of accepting Porphyry's questions as presenting the fundamental issues for any account of categories. Since genera and species appear most prominently as genera and species of substances, the issues centered first of all in the signification of common nouns taken as names of kinds of substances. The medieval "problem of universals" thus arose from Porphyry's questions about Aristotle's categories, and prominent medieval philosophers, such as Peter Abelard, Thomas Aquinas, John Duns Scotus, and William of Ockham, are known as conceptualists, realists, or nominalists because of their answers to these questions. The important point for a history of theories of categories is that the discussion of the problem of universals by major figures in medieval philosophy occurred within an unquestioned framework provided by Aristotle's theory of categories—in particular, within a framework that presupposed the basic Aristotelian interrelation of substance and accident and essential and accidental predication.

LOCKE AND HUME. The Aristotelian framework broke down in modern pre-Kantian philosophy. Signs of the breakdown were evident in Thomas Hobbes and Descartes, but its full force appeared in John Locke and David Hume. With Locke's account of substance as an "unknown something" underlying appearances, essential predication in the category of substance becomes impossible, and the signification of common nouns supposed to name kinds of substances can be fixed only by "nominal essences," by conventional factors, rather than by Ockham's "natural signs in the soul." Essential predication, and hence necessary truth, remains possible only when the subjects are things of our own creation ("mixed modes") and not when they are substances in the real world.

The full consequences of Locke's departure from an Aristotelian framework were drawn by Hume. If it is impossible to know what something in the real world necessarily (essentially) is, it is also impossible to know that any one thing in the real world is necessarily connected with another or that any state of a thing at one time is necessarily connected with its state at another time. In other words, not only substance but also causality—an equally if not more fundamental notion (though not recognized as a category by Aristotle)—is made a matter of habit and custom. The stage was set for Kant to answer Hume with a radically new theory of categories.

HEGEL. Despite the radical differences between Kantian and Aristotelian categories, two basic points of similarity remain: (1) Categories provide form but not content for cognitive discourse about the world and thus serve to distinguish what we can meaningfully say in such discourse from what we may seem to say when we make category-mistakes or misapply categories. (2) Categories presuppose the substance-accident (subject-predicate) form basic to Aristotelian logic. Hegel's philosophy retains neither of these points of similarity, although he adopted the Kantian view that the clue to a system of categories is to be found in logic. But instead of turning to logic as a study of forms of reasoning without regard for content, Hegel turned to logic as a dialectical process in which form and content are inseparable. The essential nature of this process is seen not in the forms under which subject and predicate are brought together in the premises of reasoning to make affirmative, negative, disjunctive, hypothetical, and other types of judgment but in the basic stages through which the process itself repeatedly moves. These stages Hegel called "thesis," "antithesis," and "synthesis," and he took them as interrelating the basic ideas, notions, or principles of reason, which he also called "categories." This interrelation of categories constitutes both Hegel's system of philosophy and what he held to be the "system of reality." The categories, then, are many, and their exact number cannot be determined until the system of reality is fully articulated. Hegel thus marked the beginning of a tradition in modern philosophy, in which "category" means simply any basic notion, concept, or principle in a system of philosophy.

This use of "category" is standard not only among Hegel's progeny of absolute idealists but also among metaphysicians generally, who dissociate themselves from analytical philosophy. The use remains even when there is no vestige of Hegel's threefold pattern of thesis, antithesis, and synthesis as a means of ordering the principles of speculative philosophy. The categorial scheme in Alfred North Whitehead's *Process and Reality,* for example, is readily understood as dealing with the sort of notions Hegel called "categories" but hardly with categories in the Aristotelian-Kantian sense of setting limits of cognitive meaning, a sense that still survives in analytical philosophy.

PEIRCE. The collapse of Kant's theory of categories is inevitable, according to Peirce, as logic advances beyond the subject-predicate form recognized by Aristotle. So long as statements like "John gave the book to Mary" are not seen as possessing a logical form fundamentally different from and coordinate with the simple subject-predicate form of statements like "John is tall," categories are determined by what may be taken as different forms of this one-subject–one-predicate relation. Aristotle and Kant analyzed the forms differently, but the relation analyzed was the same. With the development of logic beyond Aristotle (a development to which Peirce made significant contributions), statements like "John gave the book to Mary" are recognized as statements with three-place predicates (x gave y to z) and are different in logical form from statements with one-place predicates (x is tall). Peirce claimed to have demonstrated in his "logic of relatives" that although one-place, two-place, and three-place predicates are basically different in logical form, predicates with more than three places have no features of logical form not already found in three-place predicates.

The demonstration remains one of the more questionable parts of his logic, but Peirce accepted it as proof that in formal logic there are but three fundamentally different types of predicates and hence that there are but three categories. He sometimes referred to his categories as the "monad," the "dyad," and the "polyad," but he preferred the more general expressions "firstness," "secondness," and "thirdness." As genera (or modes) of being, the categories are designated as "pure possibility," "actual existence," and "real generality." A pure possibility stands by itself, determined by nothing but conditions of internal consistency; what actually exists stands in relation to other existences and to some extent both determines and is determined by them; a true generalization is a representation related to other representations, to actually existing things, and to pure possibilities. In his philosophical cosmology Peirce had three universes corresponding to the three modes of being, and in his semeiotic theory, or theory of signs, he developed an extensive classification of signs, with the main divisions triadic, each triad comprising a firstness, a secondness, and a thirdness. Although Peirce's categories thus function architectonically somewhat as Hegel's thesis, antithesis, and synthesis, they serve, as Hegel's triad does not, to set limits of cognitive meaning. Though Peirce did not use the phrase "category-mistake," he said repeatedly in his later writings that nominalism, which he regarded as the great error in the history of philosophy, arises from the failure to recognize real generality as a mode of being distinct from actual existence. In arguing that universals have no actual existence, the nominalist has failed to see that to ask in the first place whether they have such existence is a category-mistake. In his final years Peirce labored to show that the pragmatic criterion of meaning, which he propounded early in his career, is not only consistent with but actually necessitated by his theory of categories.

HUSSERL. The role of categories in setting limits of cognitive meaning figures prominently in the philosophy of Husserl. To determine "primitive forms" or "pure categories" of meaning is the first task of a "pure philosophical grammar." The fundamental form is that of propositional meaning, and other primitive forms, such as the nominal and adjectival, are forms of meaning that belong to constituents of a proposition. After determining these pure categories of meaning, pure logical grammar turns to primitive forms or categories of the composition and modification of meaning (forms such as those exhibited by propositional connectives and modal expressions). In addition to a pure logical grammar, Husserl held, there are a pure logic of consistency (noncontradiction) and a pure logic of truth. The picture is further complicated in that pure logic may be taken as giving rise to a formal ontology and, again, developed into a transcendental logic. A full account of categories requires the full development of logic in all its phases, and in this respect Husserl's view of categories seems reminiscent of Hegel. But at no point (even in formal ontology) did categories cease for Husserl to be purely formal and become inseparable from content. Husserl was careful to distinguish the kinds of nonsense precluded by his categories from nonsense of content (*inhaltlich Unsinn*). A phrase like "if-then is round" is nonsense because it violates a category-difference, a condition of meaningfulness established by logic alone; a phrase like "the seat of the table is hard" violates no such condition, and its nonsense arises from a material, not a formal (logical), incompatibility. While at times Husserl's language may suggest what Rudolf Carnap and others have since called "syntactical categories," it should be noted that Husserl had nothing like Carnap's technical distinction between syntax and semantics and that the "syntactical categories" of Husserl's pure logical grammar are in Carnap's sense neither purely syntactical nor semantical.

FREGE AND WITTGENSTEIN. In their philosophies of mathematics and logic both Peirce and Husserl remained close enough to Kant not to accord set theory the fundamental role it has come to play in logic and the foundations of mathematics. Frege, although he did not present any of his views under the heading "a theory of categories," did far more than Peirce or Husserl to shape the discussion of categories in the twentieth century. Frege analyzed sense and reference, concept and object (notions fundamental to Peirce's and Husserl's theories of categories) in a way that permitted him to take set theory as basic in mathematics and to define cardinal numbers as classes of classes. Russell's efforts to cope with the contradictory notion of the class of all classes not members of themselves (a notion one seems forced to admit with Frege's analysis) produced the theory of types.

The conclusion suggested by the difficulties encountered in the theory of types, that categories as setting limits of cognitive meaning are not proper subject matter for a theory, was first advanced by Ludwig Wittgenstein. In his early work, *Tractatus Logico-philosophicus,* Wittgenstein spoke of the limits of cognitive meaning as the ineffable, as what can be shown but not said. In his later writings he repudiated the suggestion that the limits constitute an ineffable subject matter, something to be unveiled but not articulated as a theory by philosophical analysis. Nevertheless, with the assumption of such subject matter philosophical clarity is to be achieved by the construction of an ideal language, a language is stripped of all superfluous symbolism and is hence unable to give the illusion of transcending the ineffable limits of cognitive meaning. But if this assumption is itself an illusion, as Wittgenstein later held, if we can no more show than we can state the limits of *all* language, then philosophical clarity can be achieved only piecemeal, context by context; there is no short cut via an ideal language. And a fortiori there is no universal scheme of categories to be unveiled, let alone to be established by a theory. Wittgenstein's influence may be seen in the hesitation of Ryle, Strawson, and other present-day analytical philosophers to claim that categories should (or can) have the absolute universality claimed in theories of categories from Aristotle's to the theory of types.

See also Aristotle; Berkeley, George; Boethius, Anicius Manlius Severinus; Descartes, René; Frege, Gottlob; Hegel, Georg Wilhelm Friedrich; Hume, David; Husserl, Edmund; Kant, Immanuel; Leibniz, Gottfried Wilhelm; Locke, John; Peirce, Charles Sanders; Platonism and the Platonic Tradition; Plotinus; Porphyry; Russell, Bertrand Arthur William; Ryle, Gilbert; Smart, John Jamieson Carswell; Strawson, Peter Frederick; Type Theory; Whitehead, Alfred North; Wittgenstein, Ludwig Josef Johann.

Bibliography

STANDARD HISTORIES

Ragnisco, P. *Storia critica delle categorie dai primordi della filosofia greca fino al Hegel,* 2 vols. Florence, 1871.

Trendelenburg, A. *Historische Beiträge zur Philosophie, Vol. I, Geschichte der Kategorienlehre.* Berlin: G. Bethge, 1846.

NEWER WORKS

Ackrill, J. L. *Aristotle's Categories and De Interpretatione.* Oxford: Clarendon Press, 1963. A new translation, written for the serious student of philosophy who does not read Greek. Copious notes, constituting over half the volume, provide an excellent scholarly commentary.

Anscombe, G. E. M., and P. T. Geach. *Three Philosophers.* Ithaca, NY: Cornell University Press, 1961. Contains penetrating but difficult discussion applying recent techniques of analysis to problems of categories in Aristotle, Thomas Aquinas, and Frege.

Black, Max. "Russell's Philosophy of Language." In *The Philosophy of Bertrand Russell,* edited by P. A. Schilpp. Evanston, IL: Library of Living Philosophers, 1946, 229–255. Difficulties with the original theory of types as a theory of categories. See also Russell's reply on pp. 691–695.

Cross, R. C. "Category Differences." *PAS* (1958–1959): 255–270.

Hall, Everett W. "Ghosts and Categorical Mistakes." *Philosophical Studies* 7 (1956): 1–6.

Hall, Everett W. *Philosophical Systems: A Categorical Analysis.* Chicago: University of Chicago Press, 1960. Sketchy survey of different philosophical systems as different categorial schemes.

Harrison, Bernard. "Category Mistakes and Rules of Language." *Mind* 74 (1965): 309–325.

Hillman, D. J. "On Grammars and Category Mistakes." *Mind* 72 (1963): 224–234.

Pap, Arthur. "Types and Meaninglessness." *Mind* 69 (1960): 41–54.

Passmore, John. *Philosophical Reasoning.* New York: Scribners, 1961. Difficulties of maintaining a theory of categories are discussed in Ch. 7.

Popper, Karl R. *Conjectures and Refutations.* New York: Basic, 1962. Chs. 11–14 offer criticisms of the view that limits of meaningfulness can be set by discovery of types or categories.

Quine, W. V. *Word and Object.* Cambridge, MA: Technology Press of the Massachusetts Institute of Technology, 1960. Presents a skillful defense of the view that categories are relative to language.

Rorty, Richard. "Pragmatism, Categories, and Language." *Philosophical Review* 70 (1961): 197–223.

Ryle, Gilbert. "Categories." In *Logic and Language,* Second Series, edited by A. G. N. Flew, 65–81. Oxford: Blackwell, 1953.

Ryle, Gilbert. *The Concept of Mind.* London: Hutchinson's University Library, 1949.

Ryle, Gilbert. "Systematically Misleading Expressions." In *Logic and Language,* First Series, edited by A. G. N. Flew. Oxford, 1951. Pp. 11–36.

Shwayder, D. S. *Modes of Referring and the Problem of Universals.* Berkeley: University of California Press, 1961. Technical discussion of points crucial to a theory of categories, especially Strawson's.

Smart, J. J. C. "A Note on Categories." *British Journal for the Philosophy of Science* 4 (1953): 227–228.

Sommers, Fred. "Types and Ontology." *Philosophical Review* 72 (1963): 327–363.

Strawson, P. F. *Individuals.* London: Methuen, 1959.

Thompson, Manley. "On Category Differences." *Philosophical Review* 66 (1957): 468–508.

Warnock, G. J. "Categories and Dilemmas." In *English Philosophy since 1900.* London and New York: Oxford University Press, 1958. Ch. 7.

Manley Thompson (1967)

CATEGORIES, SYNTACTICAL AND SEMANTICAL

See *Syntactical and Semantical Categories*

CATHARSIS

See *Katharsis*

CATTANEO, CARLO

(1801–1869)

Carlo Cattaneo is possibly the most interesting Italian philosopher of the nineteenth century, and was a distinguished scholar in history, economics, linguistics, and geography. Born in Milan, he received a law degree from the University of Pavia, where for some years afterward he taught Latin and the humanities. In 1839 he founded the journal *Il Politecnico,* which he described as "a monthly repertory of studies applied to culture and social prosperity." Cattaneo led the 1848 Milanese insurrection against Austrian rule, the story of which he related in a masterly booklet, *L'insurrezione di Milano nel 1848* (in *Scritti storici e geografici,* Vol. IV, Florence, 1957; first published in French in Paris, 1848). When the first Italian war of independence ended in failure, in 1849, Cattaneo went into exile, first in Paris and then in Lugano, Switzerland, where for several years he taught philosophy in the local lyceum. Although he was appointed a deputy to the Italian parliament in 1860, he refused to enter the parliament house in order not to have to swear allegiance to the king. He continued to spend most of his time at Lugano, where he edited a new series of *Il Politecnico* from 1860 to 1863, the first series having been suspended in 1844.

The main influence on Cattaneo was the Lombard Enlightenment philosophy espoused by his teacher G. D. Romagnosi, which was interested in scientific inquiry as related to the well-being of society and concerned with progressive government—facets visible in the work of Alessandro Volta and Cesare Beccaria. Cattaneo blended this inheritance with reflection on his own research in fields other than philosophy but generally disregarded philosophical tradition. He developed an original though unsystematic body of ideas that can best be described as an empirical, scientifically minded phenomenology of history or a nonidealistic historicism. The contemporary reader may catch a Marxian ring or occasionally find a resemblance to such thinkers as Wilhelm Dilthey, G. H. Mead, and John Dewey.

For Cattaneo the philosopher's task consists in clarifying objective current historical problems rather than subjective difficulties. There is no single problem to be made the center of systematic speculation, nor any logical or genetic "first truth" on which the chain of deductive reasoning may be hung. There is instead a plurality, itself subject to change, of well-determined and interrelated problems. There are no final solutions to problems, but only a body of perfectible solutions, which are discovered not by absolute reason but by general human reasonableness. Logic is the theory of scientific research; in philosophy, too, the experimental method, which unites men, must supersede metaphysics, whose continuous veerings divided men.

We know in order to act. The aim of all intellectual endeavor is to change the face of Earth for the good of humankind: Both nature and society must be "transformed" by man-invented techniques. Insofar as he brings about a knowledge that is public and beneficial, the philosopher is "a craftsman" who works "for the common people"—"we are all workmen if we supply something useful to mankind." To such philosophy Cattaneo contrasted "the philosophy of the schools," whose "ontological hammer" generated "a hidden, priestly wisdom scorning the common people," drawing on "fantastic hypotheses and imaginary intuitions," and "consuming itself in the repetition of empty formulae"—with the result of "throwing wide-open an immeasurable gap between doctrine and fact about man." In saying such things Cattaneo had in mind particularly Antonio Rosmini-Serbati, who was then trying to reconcile philosophical Catholicism with the subjectivism of modern philosophy.

For Cattaneo thought is social action, and it must be studied in the various human activities. There is no essence of thought to be reached directly. To become acquainted with his own nature, man must not recede into himself but rather must go out into the world to collect information. A complete science of thought amounts to knowledge of all that mankind has produced. By "mankind" Cattaneo meant empirical men in their finite world; while professing to be a follower of Giambattista Vico (who was at the time almost unknown), he was highly critical of Vico's oversimplified principles of interpretation, especially of the notion of historical cycles ("Su la *Scienza nova* del Vico," 1839; "Considerazioni sul principio della filosofia," 1844).

Cattaneo intended the phenomenology of history to overcome in a new way the traditional opposition of appearance and reality. What appears to us is what there is—all the reality we can or must cope with—and we cannot reach it outside the social development of humankind (see especially "Un invito alli amatori della filosofia," 1857). This must be construed methodologically, according to what Cattaneo labeled the "psychology of associated minds." The "solitude of the new-born in front of *things*" is a philosophical myth. "Even sensation is from the beginnings a social fact," and "whatever idea one comes to conceive is never the operation of a solitary mind but rather of several associated minds." (*Psicologia delle menti associate,* 1859–1863, unpublished; quotations taken from *Scritti filosofici,* Vol. II, p. 14; Vol. I, p. 448; Vol. II, p. 16). To help us understand the varieties of human history, a social psychology supported by scientific method must replace individual psychology as connected with that "lobby of theology" which was "[René] Descartes' solitude of consciousness."

See also Beccaria, Cesare Bonesana; Descartes, René; Dewey, John; Dilthey, Wilhelm; Historicism; Mead, George Herbert; Romagnosi, Gian Domenico; Vico, Giambattista.

Bibliography

ADDITIONAL WORKS BY CATTANEO

In addition to the essays mentioned in the article, Cattaneo's main philosophical work consists of studies on Romagnosi, Tommaso Campanella, Wilhelm von Humboldt, and others, the forewords to the annual volumes of *Il Politecnico,* and the lectures (*Lezioni*) delivered at the Lugano Lyceum on cosmology, psychology, ideology (see the pages on categories and language), logic, and law and morals. Students of Cattaneo's philosophy, however, should take into account also many of his writings in other fields.

There are several anthologies of Cattaneo's papers, especially the philosophical ones, the best being those edited by Gaetano Salvemini (Milan, 1922) and Franco Alessio (Florence, 1957). A complete edition of Cattaneo's works, divided into five sections according to subject matter, appeared in 1956 in Florence; the philosophical section, edited by N. Bobbio, comprises three volumes.

WORKS ON CATTANEO

On Cattaneo's life, see the Salvemini introduction. On his historical position, see Mario Fubini, *Il romanticismo italiano* (Bari: Laterza, 1953), passim. On his thought, see the introductions by Alessio and Bobbio, and also Bruno Brunello, *Cattaneo* (Turin, 1925); Alessandro Levi, *Il positivismo politico di Carlo Cattaneo* (Bari: G. Laterza & figli, 1928); and Luigi Ambrosoli, *La formazione di Carlo Cattaneo* (Milan: R. Ricciardi, 1959).

OTHER RECOMMENDED WORKS

Scritti filosofici. Edited by Afredo Saloni. Bari: Editori Laterza, 1965.

I problemi dello Stato italiano. Milano: Mondadori, 1966.

Tutte le opere. Edited by Luigi Ambrosoli. Milan: A. Mondadori, 1967.

Scritti letterari, artistici, linguistici e vari. Edited by Agostino Bertani. Firenze, Le Monnier, 1968.

Scritti scientifici e tecnini. Edited by Carlo G. Lacaita. Firenze: Giunti, G. Barbèra, 1969.

Carlo Cattaneo nel primo centenario della morte. Edited by Adriano Soldini. Bellinzona: Dipartimento della pubblica educazione, 1970.

Carlo Cattaneo. (Studio. Con un'appendice di scritti inediti o dimenticati di C. Cattaneo.) Edited by Biancamaria Frabotta. Lugano: Fondazione Ticino nostro, 1971.

Una filosofia militante. Studi su Carlo Cattaneo. Edited by Norberto Bobbio. Torino: G. Einaudi, 1971.

Opere scelte. Edited by Delia Castelnuovo Frigessi. Torino: G. Einaudi, 1972.

L'uomo e la storia. Storiografia, filosofia della storia, antropologia. Edited by Ferruccio Focher. Milano: Mursia, 1973.

L'opera e l'eredità di Carlo Cattaneo. Edited by Carlo G. Lacaita. Bologna: Il mulino, 1975–1976.

Introduzione a Cattaneo. Edited by Umberto Puccio. Torino: G. Einaudi, 1977.

Antologia degli scritti politici. Edited by Giuseppe Galasso. Bologna: Il mulino, 1978.

Elementi di teoria della propagazione ondosa. Edited by S. Pluchino. Bologna: Pitagora, 1981.

Indice dell'edizione nazionale delle opere di Carlo Cattaneo. Edited by Pietro Esposito. Firenze: Le Monnier, 1995.

Filosofia civile e federalismo nel pensiero di Carlo Cattaneo. Scandicci (Firenze): Nuova Italia, 1996.

La linea lombarda del federalismo. Roma: Gangemi: Fondazione nuovo millennio, 1999.

Del pensiero come principio d'economia publica = Intelligence as principle of public economy. Milano: Libri Scheiwiller, 2001.

Carteggi di Carlo Cattaneo. Serie I, Lettere di Cattaneo. Firenze: Felice Le Monnier; Bellinzona: Edizioni Casagrande, 2001.

Carteggi di Carlo Cattaneo. Serie II, Lettere dei corrispondenti. Firenze: Felice Le Monnier; Bellinzona: Edizioni Casagrande, 2001 .

La scienza nuova dell'umanità: scritti vichiani 1836–1861. Edited by Giuseppe Cospito. Genova, 2002.

Ferruccio Rossi-Landi (1967)
Bibliography updated by Michael J. Farmer (2005)

CAUSAL APPROACHES TO THE DIRECTION OF TIME

What account is to be given temporal priority and of the direction of time? One natural view is that no account is needed (Oaklander 2004), a position that can be defended by arguing, first, that one immediately perceives the succession of events (Bergson 1912), and second, that if one can immediately see that events stand in the relation of temporal priority, then the concept of that relation is primitive and unanalyzable.

There are, however, important objections to this view and to the supporting argument. As regards the latter, the question arises whether perception of change does not turn out, on closer scrutiny, to involve not only a momentary visual state but also short-term memories of immediately preceding visual states. If so, then the acquisition of a belief that something is moving or changing will involve inference, and succession will not be something immediately perceived.

As regards the view itself, one problem is that temporal priority is a relation with certain properties: It is impossible for an event to be earlier than itself; if A is earlier than B, B cannot be earlier than A; and if A is earlier than B, and B earlier than C, then A must be earlier than C. If the concept of the earlier than relation is analytically basic, then no account can be given of these necessary truths: they will have to be treated as synthetic *a priori*. By contrast, if the idea of temporal priority is analyzable, then it should be possible to show that these necessary truths are analytic.

One can assume, then, that the concept of temporal priority must be analyzable. What are the possibilities? The answer is that three main types of accounts have been offered. First, philosophers who favor a tensed account of the nature of time often maintain that the tensed properties of pastness, presentness, and future are basic properties and that the tenseless temporal relations of simultaneity and temporal priority are to be analyzed in terms of those tensed properties (e.g., Broad 1933, Sellars 1962, Prior 1967). According to this view, then, the direction of time logically supervenes on the tensed properties of events.

A second approach holds that if events stand in the relation of temporal priority, and if time has a direction, then such facts must be reducible to properties and relations recognized by physics. The idea, accordingly, is to analyze the relation of temporal priority and the direction of time in terms of such things as the direction of increase in entropy, the direction of the expansion of the universe, or the direction of irreversible processes (e.g., Popper 1956; Grünbaum 1971, 1973; Sklar 1974).

A third possibility is a causal approach. Here the idea is, first, that causal processes involve a direction, and, second, that causal facts are more basic than temporal facts, with the result that the direction of time can be analyzed in terms of the direction of causation.

How do these three alternatives fare? As regards the first, there are two crucial objections. First, it is clear that the relation of temporal priority cannot be analyzed in terms of the tensed properties of pastness, presentness, and futurity alone, since one event may be earlier than another, though both have the same tensed property of pastness. One needs, then, to introduce additional tensed concepts, such as those of one event's being more past than, and more future than, another. These latter, however, are not plausible candidates for primitive concepts, since then one would be unable to explain, for example, why event A's being more future than event B entails that A is future and B is future. However, if one attempts to analyze those concepts, the natural way of doing so is in terms of the concept of the past, and the concept of the future, with the concept of temporal priority. Such analyses, however, will make the analysis of temporal priority in terms of tensed concepts implicitly circular.

Second, even the concept of futurity itself is not a plausible candidate for a basic concept, since it is plausible that it is concepts that pick out immediately given properties and relations that are analytically basic, and the concept of the future does not pick out a property of events that can be immediately perceived. However, if the concept of the future must be analyzed, how is this to be done except in terms of the idea of the present with the idea of temporal priority? So, once again, the attempt to analyze the relation of temporal priority in terms of tensed concepts can be seen to be circular.

In the case of the second approach—which involves analyzing temporal priority in terms of specialized scientific concepts, such as those of entropy and the expansion of the universe—there are also two main objections. First, most proposals for a scientific analysis of temporal priority entail that it is possible that the universe might undergo a temporal reversal. For the universe, rather than expanding forever, may stop expanding, and then begin contracting. Moreover, if this were to happen, entropy would at some point stop increasing and begin decreasing. The direction of time cannot be analyzed, therefore, in terms of the direction of increase in entropy or in terms of the direction of the expansion of the universe, since such analyses entail the unacceptable consequence that the resulting contraction of the universe would be earlier than the time at which the universe stopped expanding.

Second, there are logically possible worlds that contain temporally ordered events, but no increase in entropy or expansion of the universe. Consider, for example, two uncharged particles rotating endlessly about one another due to gravitational attraction. Accordingly, the concept of temporal priority cannot be analyzed in terms of such scientific concepts.

The conclusion, therefore, is that the first two approaches to the analysis of the concept of temporal priority appear unsatisfactory. If this is so, one is left with the third alternative—that of analyzing temporal priority in causal terms.

A CAUSAL THEORY OF THE DIRECTION OF TIME AND TEMPORAL PRIORITY

The idea of analyzing the concept of temporal priority in causal terms is not a recent development, since it dates back at least to Gottfried Wilhelm Leibniz (1715/1969) and Immanuel Kant (1781/1961). In more recent years it was advanced by the mathematician Alfred A. Robb (1914, 1921), and by philosophers such as Henryk Mehlberg (1935, 1937), Hans Reichenbach (1956), D. H. Mellor (1981, 1995, 1998), and Michael Tooley (1987, 1997), among others.

Before setting out a causal theory, it will be best to address an initial objection, the thrust of which is that it may well be, as many philosophers and scientists believe (e.g., Lewis 1976), that backward causation is logically possible, and, if this is so, how can the direction of time be defined in terms of the direction of causation?

One response, adopted by some advocates of a causal approach (Mellor 1981, 1995, 1998; Tooley 1987, 1997), is to argue that backward causation is not logically possible. However, a different response is available. For if one considers, for example, Dr. No traveling backward in time, then it is natural to say that the temporal ordering of events inside his time machine is opposite to the temporal ordering of events outside of it. If so, then in a world where there is backward causation, one needs the concept of the local direction of time, which can be defined in terms of the direction of causal processes in that region. One could then go on to introduce the idea of the overall direction of the universe, defined, as David Lewis (1976, 1979) suggests, in terms of the direction of most causal processes.

How can temporal priority be analyzed in causal terms? A natural starting point is the following postulate:

(*P*) If *A* causes *B*, then *A* is earlier than *B*.

This gives one a sufficient condition for one event's being earlier than another, but it does not provide a necessary condition. So how can one arrive at necessary and sufficient conditions for one event's being earlier than another?

To arrive at an answer, consider the following two plausible claims:

(*Q*) If *A* is earlier than *B*, and *B* is simultaneous with *C*, then *A* is earlier than *C*.

(*R*) If *A* is simultaneous with *B*, and *B* is earlier than *C*, then *A* is earlier than *C*.

These two postulates, with (*P*), then entail two further, more comprehensive propositions relating causation to temporal priority:

(*S*) If *A* causes *B*, and *B* is simultaneous with *C*, then *A* is earlier than *C*;

(*T*) If *A* is simultaneous with *B*, and *B* causes *C*, then *A* is earlier than *C*.

However, in addition, these two conditions, in conjunction with the fact that temporal priority is a transitive relation, entail another, much more encompassing condition:

(*U*) If $\{A_1, A_2, \ldots, A_i, \ldots, A_{n-1}, A_n\}$ is a set of n instantaneous events such that, for every $i < n$, either A_i causes A_{i+1}, or A_i is simultaneous with A_{i+1}, and if, in addition, there is some $i < n$ such that A_i causes A_{i+1}, then A_1 is earlier than A_n.

Principle *U*, entailing, as it does, principles *R*, *S*, and *T*, and more as well, is a comprehensive principle relating causation to temporal priority, and that it follows from the conjunction of the noncausal principles *Q* and *R* with the modest claim involved in *P* shows how powerful principle *P* is.

Principle *U*, of course, still gives one only a sufficient condition for one event's being earlier than another. The idea now, however, is that the sufficient condition that is given by *U* is also a necessary condition. If this is right, then the relation of temporal priority can be analyzed as follows:

A is earlier than *B*

means the same as

For some number n, there is a set of n instantaneous events $\{A_1, A_2, \ldots, A_i, \ldots, A_{n-1}, A_n\}$ such that, first, *A* is identical with A_1, and *B* is identical with A_n;

second, for every $i < n$, either A_i causes A_{i+1}, or A_i is simultaneous with A_{i+1}; and,

third, there is some $i < n$ such that A_i causes A_{i+1}.

This proposed analysis does, of course, involve a temporal notion—namely, that of simultaneity. However, that will be an objection to the analysis only if the concept of simultaneity itself has to be analyzed in terms of temporal priority. The latter, however, does not seem likely, since it would seem possible for there to be a world that consists of a single moment, containing states of affairs all of which are simultaneous with each other.

OBJECTIONS TO A CAUSAL ACCOUNT

Causal analyses of temporal priority are exposed to a number of objections, many of them advanced by J. J. C. Smart (1971). Among the most important are the following. First, given that the laws of physics do not, with one possible exception, involve any asymmetry, is it possible to explain causal priority without appealing to temporal priority? Second, it is surely logically possible for there to be events that have temporal location, but that have neither causes nor effects. However, this would seem to be ruled out by a causal analysis of temporal priority. Third, is it not also logically possible for there to be moments of time at which no events take place—perhaps because the world contains gappy causal laws? But then there would be no way of ordering that moment relative to other moments. Finally, and even more dramatically, is it not logically possible for there to be a spatiotemporal world that contains no events at all? But then there would be no causal relations, and so, according to a causal theory of temporal priority, no ordering of times in such a world.

With regard to the first objection, the answer is that most present-day analyses of causation offer accounts of the direction of causation that do not involve any appeal to temporal priority (Lewis 1973; Tooley 1987, 1997; Mellor 1995). As regards the second objection, it does not tell against the account set out earlier, since an event that does not itself enter into any causal relations may have temporal location by being simultaneous with an event that does enter into causal relations.

The third and fourth objections are more threatening. One way of responding to these objections is by appealing to possible events and causal relations. Here the idea is, in the case of the third objection, that if the world had been different at certain times, there would have been events when, as things stand, there are no events, and that it is those possible causal relations that make it the case that the time when no events occur has a temporal location. Similarly, in the case of the totally empty spatiotemporal world, if there had been events at some times, these would have caused events at other times, and it is those possible causal relations that serve to order moments of time.

The problem with this sort of response is that if temporal order is to be analyzed causally, it seems clear, especially in the case of the totally empty world, that there are no truth makers for counterfactuals concerning such possible events. A different response, however, is available (Tooley 1987, 1997). The basic idea is that if one adopts a realist conception of space-time, then the continued existence of space-time is itself something that requires explanation if it is not to be a cosmic accident. However, what sort of explanation is possible, other than one according to which regions of space-time themselves causally give rise to other regions of space-time? If such immanent causal connections between spatiotemporal regions are possible, then the temporal ordering of different moments of time can, on a causal theory, be given by those causal relations, rather than only by causal relations between events in space-time.

See also Physics and the Direction of Time; Time; Time, Being, and Becoming.

Bibliography

Bergson, Henri. *Matter and Memory*. New York: Macmillan, 1912.

Broad, C. D. *Examination of McTaggart's Philosophy*. 2 vols. Cambridge, U.K.: Cambridge University Press, 1933.

Davies, P. C. W. *The Physics of Time Asymmetry*. Berkeley: University of California Press, 1974.

Grünbaum, Adolf. "The Meaning of Time." In *Basic Issues in the Philosophy of Time*, edited by Eugene Freeman and Wilfrid Sellars, 195–228. LaSalle, IL: Open Court, 1971.

Grünbaum, Adolf. *Philosophical Problems of Space and Time*. 2nd ed. Dordrecht, Netherlands: D. Reidel, 1973.

Kant, Immanuel. *Kritik der reinen Vernunft* (1781). Translated as *Critique of Pure Reason*. London: Macmillan, 1961. See book 2, chapter 2, section 3 of the "Transcendental Analytic."

Leibniz, Gottfried Wilhelm. "The Metaphysical Foundations of Mathematics" (1715). In *Philosophical Papers and Letters*. 2nd ed. Translated and edited by Leroy E. Loemker, 666–674. Dordrecht, Netherlands: D. Reidel, 1969.

Lewis, David. "Causation." *Journal of Philosophy* 70 (1973): 556–567.

Lewis, David. "Counterfactual Dependence and Time's Arrow." *Noûs* 13 (1979): 455–476.

Lewis, David. "The Paradoxes of Time Travel." *American Philosophical Quarterly* 13 (1976): 145–152.

Lewis, David. *Philosophical Papers*. Vol. 2. New York: Oxford University Press, 1986.

Malament, David. "Causal Theories of Time and the Conventionality of Simultaneity." *Noûs* 11 (1977): 293–300.

McCall, Storrs. *A Model of the Universe: Space-Time, Probability, and Decision*. Oxford, U.K.: Clarendon Press, 1994.

McCall, Storrs. "Objective Time Flow." *Philosophy of Science* 43 (1976): 337–362.

Mehlberg, Henryk. "Essai sur la théorie causale du temps." *Studia Philosophica* 1 (1935): 119–258; 2 (1937): 111–231.

Mehlberg, Henryk. "Physical Laws and Time's Arrow." In *Current Issues in the Philosophy of Science*, edited by Herbert Feigl and Grover Maxwell, 105–138. New York: Holt, Rinehart, and Winston, 1961.

Mellor, D. H. *The Facts of Causation*. New York: Routledge, 1995.

Mellor, D. H. *Real Time*. New York: Cambridge University Press, 1981.

Mellor, D. H. *Real Time II*. New York: Routledge, 1998.

Oaklander, L. Nathan. *The Ontology of Time*. Amherst, NY: Prometheus, 2004.

Oddie, Graham. "Backwards Causation and the Permanence of the Past." *Synthese* 85 (1990): 71–93.

Popper, Karl. "The Arrow of Time." *Nature* 177 (1956): 538.

Price, Huw. *Time's Arrow and Archimedes' Point: New Directions for the Physics of Time*. New York: Oxford University Press, 1996.

Prior, Arthur N. *Past, Present, and Future*. Oxford, U.K.: Clarendon Press, 1967.

Prior, Arthur N. *Time and Tense*. Oxford, U.K.: Clarendon Press, 1968.

Reichenbach, Hans. *The Direction of Time*. Berkeley: University of California Press, 1956.

Robb, Alfred A. *The Absolute Relations of Time and Space*. Cambridge, U.K.: Cambridge University Press, 1921.

Robb, Alfred A. *A Theory of Time and Space*. Cambridge, U.K.: Cambridge University Press, 1914.

Sellars, Wilfrid. "Time and the World Order." In *Minnesota Studies in the Philosophy of Science*. Vol. 3, edited by Herbert Feigl and Grover Maxwell, 527–616. Minneapolis: University of Minnesota Press, 1962.

Shoemaker, Sydney. "Time without Change." *Journal of Philosophy* 66 (1969): 363–381.

Sklar, Lawrence. *Space, Time, and Spacetime*. Berkeley: University of California Press, 1974.

Smart, J. J. C. "Causal Theories of Time." In *Basic Issues in the Philosophy of Time*, edited by Eugene Freeman and Wilfrid Sellars, 61–77. LaSalle, IL: Open Court, 1971.

Smith, Quentin. *Language and Time*. New York: Oxford University Press, 1993.

Tooley, Michael. *Causation: A Realist Approach*. New York: Oxford University Press, 1987.

Tooley, Michael. *Time, Tense, and Causation*. Oxford, U.K.: Clarendon Press, 1997.

Von Bretzel, Philip. "Concerning a Probabilistic Theory of Causation Adequate for the Causal Theory of Time." *Synthese* 35 (1977): 173–190.

Michael Tooley (2005)

CAUSAL CLOSURE OF THE PHYSICAL DOMAIN

The thesis that physics is causally closed asserts that:

> Every physical effect has a sufficient immediate physical cause, insofar as it has a sufficient immediate cause at all.

If this thesis is true, it distinguishes physics from all other subject domains. The biological realm is not causally closed, for example, because biological effects often have nonbiological causes, as when the impact of a meteorite precipitated the extinction of the dinosaurs. Again, meteorology is not causally closed: The burning of carbon fuels—a nonmeteorological event—is causing global warming. Nor, importantly, is the mental realm causally closed: A mental pain can be caused by sitting on a physical thumbtack, and a train of thought can be interrupted by a loud noise.

Physics, by contrast, does seem to be causally closed. If one considers any physical effect, then there will arguably always be some prior physical cause: People expect to be able to account for physical effects without leaving the physical realm itself. In particular, this seems to hold even for physical effects that take place within the bodies of conscious beings. When the muscle fibers in a person's arm contract, this is presumably due to electrochemical activity in the nerves, which is due to prior physical activity in the person's motor cortex, and so on. In principle, it would seem possible to account for this entire sequence solely in terms of the resources offered by physics itself, and without making any essential appeal to any other subject matter.

At first pass, the causal closure of physics is solely a claim about how things go within physics itself. It does not assert that everything is physical, only that everything physical that has a cause has a physical cause. As such, it does not rule out realms of reality that are distinct from the physical realm. It is entirely consistent with the causal closure of physics itself; there should be nonphysical realms that operate independently. The closure of the physical says only that *within the physical realm* every physical effect has a physical cause.

Even so, the causal closure of the physical does give rise to a powerful argument for reducing many prima facie nonphysical realms to physics: It suggests that *anything that has a causal impact on the physical realm* must itself be physical. The reason is that the causal closure of the physical seems to leave no room for anything nonphysical to make a causal difference to the physical realm, because it specifies that every physical effect already has a physical cause.

Intuitively, of course, people take it that many prima facie nonphysical events, such as biological, meteorological, and mental events, do have physical effects. A burrowing animal can dig a hole in the ground; a hurricane can destroy houses; one's current thoughts can give rise to patterns on a computer screen. However, the causal closure of the physical says that these effects already have physical causes. So it seems that the only way to respect the causal efficacy of realms such as the biological, meteorological, and mental is to conclude that they are not distinct from the physical after all. If one wants to maintain that the animal's burrowing, the hurricane, and a person's thoughts have physical effects, then apparently there is a need to identify these processes with the physical causes that their physical effects are already known to have.

Note that this line of reasoning only argues for a reduction to physics of those realms that *do* have physical effects. The causal closure of the physical provides no argument against the possibility of nonphysical realms that lack any physical effects. For example, it is arguable that mathematical, moral, and modal facts have no physical effects. If this is right, then the causal closure of the physical offers no reason to collapse these realms into the physical. (Of course, there may be other arguments against the possibility of such nonphysical realms of reality, such as their epistemological inaccessibility, but that is a different matter.)

The remainder of this entry contains three sections: First, a discussion of the evidence for the causal closure of physics from a historical perspective; second, a consideration of how the thesis can be made properly precise; and finally, an examination of the details of the argument that causal closure implies physicalism about the mental and similar realms.

A HISTORICAL PERSPECTIVE ON THE EVIDENCE FOR THE CAUSAL CLOSURE OF PHYSICS

Why should one believe the causal closure of physics (which for the moment shall be regarded as the simple claim that every physical effect has a sufficient physical cause)? If this thesis is true, it is not an a priori matter, but something that follows from the findings of science. But exactly which findings? What part of science, if any, argues that physical is causally closed?

At first sight it may seem that causal closure follows from the presence of conservation laws in physics: If there are laws specifying that important physical quantities stay constant over time, does not this show that the later values of physical quantities must be determined by earlier values? However, it depends what conservation laws one has. Not just any set of physical conservation laws rule out the possibility of nonphysical causes for physical effects.

Thus consider Descartes's early seventeenth-century physics. This was based on the conservation of *amount of motion*, which Descartes took to be the product of the masses of all bodies by their scalar *speeds*. (So amount of motion is different from momentum, which is the product of mass by vectorial *velocity*: A car going round a bend at a constant speed conserves amount of motion but not momentum.) As Leibniz observed, Descartes's conservation of amount of motion alone leaves plenty of room for nonphysical causes to intrude on the physical realm. In particular, if mental causes (operating in the pineal gland?) cause particles of matter to change their direction (but not their speed), this would not in any way violate the conservation of amount of motion.

Descartes's physics might allow an independent mind to affect the brain, but Descartes's physics is wrong, as Leibniz further observed. Leibniz himself replaced Descartes's law of the conservation of "motion" with the two modern laws of conservation of (vectorial) momentum and of (scalar) kinetic energy, and thereby arrived at what are now regarded as the correct laws governing impacts. Leibniz's physics, unlike Descartes's, did indeed imply that the later values of all physical quantities are determined by their earlier values, and therewith the causal closure of the physical. However, Leibniz did not draw the modern physicalist conclusion that the mind must therefore be identical to the brain. Because it seemed incontrovertible to him that mind and brain must be ontologically separate, he instead inferred from the causal closure of physical that the mind in fact has no causal impact on the physical world. (It only appears to do so because of the "preestablished harmony" with which God has arranged both the mental and physical worlds.)

Whereas Leibniz's physics implies the causal closure of the physical, this is not true of the Newtonian system of physics that replaced it at the end of the seventeenth century. The crucial difference is that, where Leibniz upheld the central principle of the "mechanical philosophy" and maintained that all changes of velocity are due to impacts between material particles, Newton allowed that accelerations can also be caused by disembodied forces, such as the force of gravity. Moreover, Newton's system was open-ended about the range of different forces that existed. In addition to gravity, Newton and his followers came to recognize magnetic forces, chemical forces, and forces of adhesion—and indeed vital and mental forces, which arose specifically in living bodies and sentient beings. If one counts vital and mental forces as nonphysical (and this point will be revisited in the next section), then the admission of such forces undermines the causal closure of the physical. For it means that physical effects, in the form of accelerations of particles of matter, will sometimes be due to the operation of nonphysical vital or mental causes.

Newtonian physics has its own conservation principles, but unlike Leibniz's they do not uphold the causal closure of the physical. Crucially, Newton's physics differs from Leibniz's in the way the conservation of energy must be understood. The existence of Newtonian forces means that Leibniz's conservation of kinetic energy no longer holds true; for example, two bodies receding from each other will slow down due to their mutual gravitational attraction, and so lose kinetic energy. Newtonian conservation additionally needs the notion of *potential* energy: the latent energy stored when bodies are "in tension" in force fields, as when two receding gravitating bodies cease to move apart and are about to accelerate together again. The notion of potential energy was not prominent in early Newtonian physics, but by the middle of the nineteenth century physicists concluded that all forces operated so as to conserve the *sum* of potential and kinetic energy—any loss of kinetic energy would mean a rise in potential energy, and vice versa.

This emergence of the modern version of the "conservation of energy" placed strong restrictions on what kinds of forces can exist, but it by no means ruled out vital and mental forces. Provided that the fields of these forces stored in latent form any losses of kinetic energy they occasioned (consider by way of comparison the notion of "nervous energy"), their presence would be perfectly consistent with the conservation of kinetic plus potential energy. True, the conservation of kinetic plus potential energy did apparently imply that all forces must be governed by deterministic force laws (otherwise what would ensure that they always paid back any kinetic energy they borrowed?), and this greatly exercised many Victorian thinkers, especially given that nothing in early Newtonian physics had ruled out spontaneously arising mental forces. But, even so, the Newtonian conservation of energy did not stop *deterministic* vital and mental forces affecting the physical realm.

Nevertheless, during the late nineteenth and twentieth centuries an increasing number of scientists have come to doubt the existence of vital and mental forces. The most significant evidence seems to have come from physiology and molecular biology, rather than from physics itself. During this period a great deal has come to be known about the workings of biological systems (including brains), and there has been no indication that anything other than basic physical forces are needed to account for their operation. In particular the twentieth century has seen an explosion of knowledge about processes occurring within cells, and here too there is no evidence that this involves anything other than familiar physical chemistry. The result has been that the overwhelming majority of scientists now reject vital and mental forces, and accept the causal closure of the physical realm.

THE CAUSAL CLOSURE THESIS REFINED

Much recent discussion of the causal closure thesis has revolved around the question of exactly how "physical" should be understood in the claim that every physical effect has a physical cause. As Carl Hempel originally observed, advocates of the causal closure thesis seem to face a dilemma. On the one hand, they can equate "physical" with the category of phenomena recognized by *current* physical theory. But then it seems implausible that "physics" in this sense is closed; past form suggests strongly that physics will in time come to posit various new fundamental causal categories. Alternatively, advocates of causal closure might wish to equate "physical" with the ontology of some ideal *future* physics. But then it is hard to see how the causal closure of the "physical" could have any current philosophical significance, given that people are as yet ignorant of exactly what this "physical" includes.

However, this dilemma is by no means inescapable. True, neither current physics nor ideal future physics gives us a suitable notion of "physics" for framing the causal closure thesis. But this does not mean there are not other suitable notions of "physics." Indeed there are arguably a number of *different* ways of understanding "physics" that will yield a well-evidenced and contentful causal closure thesis.

For a start, one could simply define *physical* as "neither essentially mental nor biological." This understanding of "physical" was in effect assumed at the end of the last section, in the argument that the nonexistence of vital or mental forces establishes the causal closure of physics. Note that nothing in that argument assumed a definitive list of fundamental physical categories; rather the thought was simply that this list would *not* include any sui generis mental or vital entities. This is a relatively inclusive understanding of "physical"; it counts as a "physical" cause anything that is not mental or vital, and to this extent renders the causal closure of the physical a relatively weak thesis. But even so it remains a thesis of much philosophical interest, because it still argues that any mental or vital causes of physical effects must be identical to causes that can be identified without using mental or vital categories.

A rather stronger reading of "physical" would take it to cover any categories of the *same general kind as are recognized by current physical theory*. Now the list of fundamental "physical" categories will be taken to include not just anything nonvital or nonmental, but more specifically only items that display the same kind of spatiotemporal pervasiveness and simple mathematical characterizability as those assumed in contemporary physics. Again, there seems good reason to suppose that "physics" in this sense is casually closed, and therefore that anything that in this sense has "physical" effects must itself be "physical."

Finally, and even more specifically, there is the option of equating "physical" with *microscopic*. Modern physical theory characteristically operates at a level of microscopic spatiotemporal detail. Correspondingly, it is plausible that every microscopic effect can be accounted for by (a combination) of microscopic causes. This version of the causal closure thesis thus argues that anything that has microscopic effects must itself be identical to (a combination) of microscopic causes.

The remainer of this section deals with some complications in the formulation of the causal closure thesis. In the version of the thesis at the beginning of this article, every physical effect was referred to as having a "sufficient immediate physical cause," rather than just having "a physical cause." This was to ensure that the physical realm is genuinely causally closed. The specification that the physical cause be "sufficient" is needed to ensure that it causes the physical effect by itself, and not solely in virtue of its conjunction with some sui generis nonphysical cause—such a mixed cause would obviously violate the causal closure of physics. Again, the requirement that the physical cause be "immediate" is needed to ensure that it not produce the physical effect only via some intermediary nonphysical cause—such nonphysical intermediaries would again violate the causal closure of physics.

The earlier formulation of the causal closure thesis also specifies that every physical effect has a sufficient immediate physical cause "insofar as it has a sufficient immediate cause at all." The reason for this latter qualification is to accommodate the indeterminism of modern quantum mechanics, which states that certain physical effects are random, without any sufficient determining cause. It remains the case, however, that according to quantum mechanics these random physical effects still have their *probabilities* fixed by sufficient immediate physical causes. And this in itself will sustain the argument that anything that affects the physical realm must itself be physical. At first sight it may seem that quantum indeterminism creates room for nonphysical causes (determinations of the will, perhaps) to exert a downward influence on the physical realm, by influencing whether or not certain random physical events occur. But this in itself would violate the causal closure of the physical, understood now as including the claim that the *probabilities* of underdetermined quantum physical events are fixed by sufficient immediate physical causes. For, if a nonphysical cause influences whether or not random physical events occur, it must presumably make a difference to the probabilities of those events, and this itself will contradict the thesis that those probabilities are already fixed by sufficient physical causes.

THE ARGUMENT FROM CAUSAL CLOSURE TO PHYSICALISM

What follows now is a closer look at the argument that moves from the causal closure of the physical to the conclusion that anything with a physical effect must itself be physical. The focus will be on the case of *mental* causes of physical effects, but most of the points made will apply to items with physical effects generally.

Recall the point that the argument gets no grip on realms that have no physical effects. As mentioned earlier, Leibniz used this point to evade physicalism about the mental by holding that the mental and physical realms are causally insulated from each other, albeit unfolding in "preestablished harmony." Contemporary philosophers who share Leibniz's conviction that mental states cannot possibly be physical tend to adopt a somewhat different ploy. Instead of denying any causal contact between conscious mind and brain, they allow that brain processes cause conscious mental effects but deny that these conscious states then have any converse influence on the physical realm. The contemporary philosophers of mind Frank Jackson and David Chalmers have both argued in favor of this "epiphenomenalist" position (Jackson 1982, Chalmers 1996). By viewing conscious states as "causal danglers" that exert no independent influence on the physical realm, they avoid any conflict with the thought that the causal closure leaves no room for anything nonphysical to make a difference to physical effects.

Perhaps there is another loophole in the argument from causal closure. In effect, this argument holds that a nonphysical mind cannot have physical effects because then those effects would have too many sufficient causes—both a nonphysical mental cause and the physical cause guaranteed by causal closure. However, such overdetermination of effects by two sufficient causes is not unknown. Imagine a case of a man who is simultaneously shot and struck by lightning, where either cause would have sufficed for his death on its own. Why should the physical effects of mental causes not similarly be overdetermined by two independent causes?

However, it is not clear that this is a good comparison. Overdetermination by distinct causes occasionally occurs by chance. But if a nonphysical mind has physical effects, then causal closure means that overdetermination of those effects will be routine. This calls for some explanation of why the two independent causes—mental and physical—should always be found together. If the two causes really are distinct, then will not some mechanism be needed to ensure that a sufficient physical cause is in place whenever a mental cause has a physical effect? However, no plausible such mechanism suggests itself.

So the possibility of overdetermination by both physical and mental causes does not support a distinct mental realm in the face of the causal closure of physics. However, there is another sense in which the causal closure of physics does leave it open that all behavioral effects may have both a physical cause and a nonidentical mental cause.

It has been a common theme in much recent physicalist philosophy of mind that mental properties are not *type-identical* to physical properties: many physicalist philosophers of mind are persuaded that, because beings with different physical constitutions can share mental properties such as pain, mental properties must be functional properties that are variably (or multiply) realized by physical properties, or disjunctions of physical properties, or some other kind of property that is metaphysically fixed by (supervenes on) physical properties, but not strictly identifiable with them.

Now, to the extent that causes involve properties, this denial of type-identity for mental and physical properties means that the mental and physical causes of behavioral effects cannot be strictly identical. However, this kind of double causation does not amount to the kind of overdetermination by distinct causes that was argued to be unacceptable above. As long as mental causes supervene metaphysically on physical causes, they are not fully distinct from them, and there is already a built-in explanation for why there should always also be a physical cause (as required by the causal closure of the physical) whenever a mental cause produces a behavioral effect. The denial of type identity creates some space between mental and physical causes, but not so much as to render it mysterious that they are always found hand in hand.

See also Causation: Philosophy of Science; Physicalism.

Bibliography

Chalmers, D. *The Conscious Mind*. Oxford: Oxford University Press, 1996.

Jackson, F. "Epiphenomenal Qualia." *Philosophical Quarterly* 32 (1982): 127–136.

Kim, J. *Mind in a Physical World*. Cambridge, MA: MIT Press, 1998.

Papineau, D. *Thinking about Consciousness*. Oxford: Oxford University Press, 1992.

David Papineau (2005)

CAUSAL OR CONDITIONAL OR EXPLANATORY-RELATION ACCOUNTS

Edmund Gettier attacked the traditional analysis of knowledge by showing that inferring a true belief from a false but justified belief produces a justified true belief that does not qualify as knowledge. Subsequent analyses of knowledge were motivated in large part by the wish to avoid examples of the type Gettier used. One way to do so is to insist that a belief must be connected in some proper way to the fact that makes it true in order for it to count as knowledge. In Gettier's examples beliefs are only accidentally true since there are no proper connections between them and the facts that make them true. Analyses that require such connections may either retain or drop the justification condition from the traditional analysis. Without it they are thoroughly externalist analyses since they require only that a belief be externally connected with the fact that makes it true, not that the subject be able to specify this connection.

One intuitive way to specify the proper connection is to say that it is "causal": The fact that makes a belief true must help cause the belief in the subject if the subject is to have knowledge. When this causal relation holds, the truth of the belief is nonaccidental. The causal analysis of knowledge therefore excludes standard Gettier-type cases, but it seems on reflection to be both too weak and too strong: too strong in that knowledge of universal propositions, mathematical truths, and logical connections seems to be ruled out if these cannot enter into causal relations; too weak in allowing knowledge when a subject cannot distinguish a fact that causes her belief from relevant alternatives. Suppose, for example, that a subject *S* cannot tell red expanses from green ones but believes that there is a red expanse before her whenever either a red or a green expanse is there. Then, on an occasion in which a red expanse is before *S* the usual sort of perceptual causal connection will hold, but knowledge that the expanse is red will be lacking.

A different way to specify the necessary connection that handles the sort of case just cited is provided by the "conditional" account. According to this account, *S* knows that *p* only if *S* would not believe that *p* if *p* were not true. In close possible worlds in which *p* is not true, it must be the case that *S* does not believe it. This rules out the case of the red and green expanses since, in a close world in which the expanse is not red but green, *S* continues to believe it is red. A further condition required by this account is that in close worlds in which *p* continues to be true but other things change, *S* continues to believe that *p*.

The conditional account handles both Gettier's cases and those that require the distinction of relevant alternatives. But once again there are examples that seem to show it both too weak and too strong. That the first condition is too strong can be shown by a variation on the color expanse example. Suppose that *S* cannot tell red from green but is very good at detecting blue. Then, on the basis of seeing a blue expanse *S* can come to know that there is not a green expanse before her. But if this proposition were false (if there were a green expanse before her), she would still believe it true (she would think she was seeing red). That the second condition is too strong seems clear from the case of a very old person whose mental capacities are still intact but soon will fail him. That there are close worlds in which he does not continue to believe as he does now by exercising those capacities does not mean that he cannot know various facts now through their exercise.

That these conditions are too weak can perhaps be shown by cases in which someone intentionally induces a Gettier-type belief in *S*. In this case, if the belief were not true, it would not have been induced in *S*, and yet *S* does not know. Such a case might or might not be ruled out by the second condition, depending on how it is specified and on how the second condition is interpreted. But there are other cases that seem more certainly to indicate that the conditions are too weak. If *S* steadfastly believes every mathematical proposition that she entertains, then the conditions will be met, but she will not know all the true mathematical propositions that she entertains.

An analysis of knowledge should not only accommodate various intuitions regarding examples; it should also be useful to the normative epistemologist in reconstructing the structure of knowledge and addressing skeptical challenges. The conditional account, as interpreted by its main proponent, Robert Nozick (1981), has interesting implications regarding skepticism. According to it, I can know various ordinary perceptual truths, such as that I am seated before a fire, even though I cannot know that there is no Cartesian demon always deceiving me. This is because in the closest possible worlds in which I am not before the fire, I do not believe that I am (I am somewhere else with different perceptual evidence). But in the closest world in which there is a Cartesian demon, I do not believe there is one (since all my perceptual evidence remains the same). These implications are welcome to Nozick but are troubling to other philosophers. My knowledge of being before the fire depends on the demon world not being among the closest in which I am not before the fire. But, according to the conditional account, I cannot know that this last clause is true. Hence, I cannot show that my knowledge that I sit before the fire is actual, as opposed to merely being possible, and it seems that I ultimately lack grounds for being convinced that this is so. Furthermore, implications regarding more specific claims to knowledge and skeptical possibilities are counterintuitive as well. For example, according to this account I cannot know that my son is not a robot brilliantly constructed by aliens, although I can know that I do not have a brilliantly constructed robot son.

A third way of specifying the required connection that makes beliefs true is to describe it as "explanatory." If *S* knows that *p*, then the fact that *p* must help to explain *S*'s belief. To see whether this account handles the sorts of cases cited, we would need to define the notion of explanation being used here. One way to do so is in terms of a certain notion of probability: Roughly, *p* explains *q* if the probability of *q* given *p* is higher than the probability of *q* in the relevant reference class (reflecting relevant alternatives); put another way, if the ratio of (close) possible worlds in which *q* is true is higher in the worlds in which *p* obtains than in the relevant contrasting set of worlds. Given this interpretation, the analysis handles the perceptual discrimination case. In it *S* does not know there is a red expanse before him because its being red does not raise the probability of his belief that it is relative to those possible worlds in which this belief is based on its being green. The analysis also allows knowledge in the variation that defeats the conditional account. In it *S* knows that there is not a green expanse before her since the fact that the expanse is not green (i.e., it is blue) explains her belief that it is not green. Since the account must allow explanatory chains, it can be interpreted so as to include knowledge of mathematical propositions, which do not enter into causal relations. In the usual case in which *S* has mathematical knowledge that *p* her belief must be explanatorily linked to *p* via some proof. The truth of *p* makes a proof possible, and the ratio of close worlds in which *S* believes *p* must be higher in worlds in which there is a proof than in the overall set of worlds.

The explanatory account needs to be filled out further if it is to accommodate cases involving intentionally produced beliefs resembling Gettier's examples since in such cases the fact that *p* helps to explain why the belief that *p* is induced in *S*. As an externalist account, it would also need to provide defense for the claim that *S* can know that *p* even when, from his point of view, he has no good reasons for believing *p*. The analysis does suggest an approach to answering the skeptic different from that suggested by the conditional account. A proponent of this analysis would answer the skeptic by showing that nonskeptical theses provide better explanations of our ordinary beliefs than do skeptical theses.

See also Epistemology; Nozick, Robert.

Bibliography

Goldman, Alan H. *Empirical Knowledge*. Berkeley, CA.: University of California Press, 1988.

Goldman, Alvin I. "A Causal Theory of Knowing." *Journal of Philosophy* 64 (1967): 357–372.

Goldman, Alvin I. "Discrimination and Perceptual Knowledge." *Journal of Philosophy* 73 (1976): 771–791.

Klein, Peter. "Knowledge, Causality, and Defeasibility." *Journal of Philosophy* 73 (1976): 792–812.

Nozick, Robert. *Philosophical Explanations*. Cambridge, MA: Harvard University Press, 1981.

Sainsbury, R. M. "Easy Possibilities." *Philosophy and Phenomenological Research* 57 (4) (1997): 907–919.

Alan H. Goldman (1996)
Bibliography updated by Benjamin Fiedor (2005)

CAUSATION: METAPHYSICAL ISSUES

Causal concepts have surely been present from the time that language began, since the vast majority of action verbs involve the idea of causally affecting something. Thus, in the case of transitive verbs of action, there is the idea of causally affecting something external to one—one finds food, builds a shelter, sows seed, catches fish, and so on—while in the case of intransitive verbs, or at least those describing physical actions, it is very plausible that they involve the idea of causally affecting one's own body —as one walks, runs, jumps, hunts, and so on.

It was not long after the very beginning of philosophy in ancient Greece that serious reflection concerning the nature of causation arose, with Aristotle's famous discussion of causation in Book 2 of his *Physics*. The result was Aristotle's doctrine of four types (or, perhaps, aspects) of causes—material, formal, efficient, and final—an account that was immensely influential for about two thousand years.

What was not realized at any point during this time, however—perhaps because of the sense of familiarity with the idea of causation occasioned by the almost ubiquitous presence of causal concepts in even the most rudimentary parts of language—is that the concept of causation gives rise to very serious, puzzling, and difficult philosophical questions. Thus it was only many centuries after Aristotle, with David Hume and his famous discussions of the relation of cause and effect (1739–1740 and 1748), that philosophers realized that the idea of causation was by no means simple and straightforward.

Why did Hume see what so many thoughtful philosophers before him had not? The reason, it would seem, was that Hume held—as did the other British empiricists, John Locke and Bishop (George) Berkeley—that while some concepts can be analyzed in terms of other concepts, in the end analysis must terminate in ideas that apply to things in virtue of objects' having properties and standing in relations that can be immediately given in experience. Hume therefore asked whether the relation of causation was one that could be given in immediate experience. His conclusion was that it could not. The question for Hume, accordingly, was how the concept of causation could be analyzed in terms of ideas that do pick out properties and relations that are given in experience, and once this question was in view, Hume was able to show that arriving at a satisfactory answer was a very difficult matter.

FUNDAMENTAL ISSUES AND ALTERNATIVE VIEWS

One of the central issues in the philosophy of causation concerns, then, this Humean problem: Is the concept of causation basic and unanalyzable, or, on the contrary, does it stand in need of analysis? If it does need to be analyzed, how can this be done?

Many different answers have been offered to these questions. But the various approaches can be divided up into four general types: direct realism, Humean reductionism, non-Humean reductionism, and indirect, or theoretical-term, realism.

This fourfold division, in turn, rests upon the following three distinctions: first, that between reductionism and realism; second, that between Humean and non-Humean states of affairs; and, third, that between states that are immediately observable and those that are not. Let us, then, consider each of these distinctions in turn, starting with that between reductionism and realism.

REALISM VERSUS REDUCTIONISM. The realism-versus-reductionism distinction in this area arises in connection with both causal laws, and causal relations between states of affairs, and gives rise to a number of related theses. In the case of causal relations between states of affairs, a thesis that is essential to reductionism is this:

Basic Reductionism with respect to causal relations. Any two worlds that agree both with respect to all of the non-causal properties of, and relations between, particulars, and with respect to all causal laws, must also agree with respect to all of the causal relations between states of affairs. Causal relations are, then, logically supervenient upon the totality of instances of non-causal properties and relations, together with causal laws.

But while this thesis is an essential part of a reductionist view of causation, it is not sufficient. The reason is that this thesis can be combined with a view of causal laws according to which they obtain in virtue of atomic, and therefore irreducible, facts. What is needed, then, is a reductionist thesis concerning causal laws, and here there are two important possibilities:

Strong Reductionism with respect to causal laws. Any two worlds that agree with respect to all of the non-causal properties of, and relations between, particulars, must also agree with respect to causal laws. Causal laws are, then, logically supervenient upon the totality of instances of non-causal properties and relations.

Moderate Reductionism with respect to causal laws. Any two worlds that agree both with respect to all of the non-causal properties of, and relations between, particulars, and with respect to all laws of nature, must also agree with respect to causal laws. Causal laws are, then, logically supervenient upon the totality of instances of non-causal properties and relations, together with laws of nature.

What lies behind this strong reductionism versus moderate reductionism distinction? The answer is that while most philosophers who are reductionists with regard to causation tend to identify laws of nature with certain cosmic regularities, it is possible to be a reductionist with regard to causation while holding that laws are more than certain cosmic regularities: One might hold, for example, that laws of nature are second-order relations between universals. Such a reductionist would reject Strong Reductionism with regard to causal laws, while accepting Moderate Reductionism.

Each of these two reductionist theses concerning causal laws then entails, in conjunction with the Basic Reductionist thesis concerning causal relations, a corresponding thesis concerning causal relations between states of affairs:

Strong Reductionism with respect to causal relations. Any two worlds that agree with respect to all of the non-causal properties of, and relations between, particulars, must also agree with respect to all of the causal relations between states of affairs. Causal relations are, in short, logically supervenient upon the totality of instances of non-causal properties and relations.

Moderate Reductionism with respect to causal relations. Any two worlds that agree both with respect to all of the non-causal properties of, and relations between, particulars, and with respect to all laws of nature, must also agree with respect to all of the causal relations between states of affairs. Causal relations are, then, logically supervenient upon the totality of instances of non-causal properties and relations, together with laws of nature.

To be a reductionist with regard to causation, then, is to accept the Basic Reductionist thesis with respect to causal relations, and either the Strong or the Moderate Reductionist thesis with respect to causal laws. This then commits one either to the Strong Reductionist thesis or the Moderate Reductionist thesis with respect to causal relations.

A realist with regard to causation, correspondingly, is one who rejects either the Basic Reductionist thesis concerning causal relations, or else both the Strong and the Moderate Reductionist theses with regard to causal laws, or all of these.

HUMEAN VERSUS NON-HUMEAN REDUCTIONISM. In addition to the gulf between reductionism and realism, there are also very important divides within both reductionism and realism. In the case of reductionism, the crucial division involves a distinction between what may be called Humean and non-Humean states of affairs. So let us now turn to that distinction.

Different authors offer different characterizations of what a Humean state of affairs is. The basic idea, however, is that Humean states of affairs are ones that consist of particulars having properties and standing in relations, where the properties and relations in question are, in some sense, immediately observable. The idea of being immediately observable can then be interpreted in different ways. A very restrictive interpretation would be one where immediate observation is equated with direct acquaintance, so that only properties and relations that are the objects of Hume's simple ideas—that is, properties and relations that can be immediately given in experience—are classified as immediately observable. Alternatively, one could construe the idea of immediate observation more broadly, so that any properties and relations that can be directly or noninferentially perceived would count as immediately observable.

What would be an example of a non-Humean state of affairs? One type would be any state of affairs that involves a dispositional property or power, since even if, for example, one sees something in the process of dissolving in water, an inference is involved if one is to arrive at the conclusion that the object is such that it is disposed to dissolve when it is in water, since its dissolving on the occasion in question could be a pure accident, or could be caused entirely by some external force, rather than being due to an intrinsic property of the object itself. So an inference is involved, and therefore the water-solubility of an object cannot be an object of direct perception.

Some twentieth-century approaches to causation attempt to analyze causation in terms of powers and propensities. Such approaches are reductionist, but not of a Humean sort.

DIRECT VERSUS INDIRECT REALISM WITH REGARD TO CAUSATION. Realists with regard to causation either reject the Basic Reductionist thesis concerning causal relations, or else both the Strong and the Moderate Reductionist theses concerning causal laws. But there is a crucial divide within realist approaches, and it concerns the question of whether causal states of affairs are immediately observable. According to direct realism, some causal states of affairs are immediately observable; according to indirect, or theoretical-term realism, no causal states of affairs are immediately observable.

What causal states of affairs are directly observable, according to a direct realist approach to causation? Since it is not at all plausible that one can be directly acquainted with causal laws, the relevant states of affairs must consist of causal relations between states of affairs. Thus direct realism can be defined as a version of realism that claims that the relation of causation is immediately given in experience.

Indirect, or theoretical-term realism rejects this claim, maintaining either that the relation of causation is itself an irreducible, theoretical relation, or, alternatively, that causal laws are irreducible, theoretical states of affairs, or both. Either way, then, the relation of causation is not directly observable.

DIRECT REALISM

We can now turn to a consideration of the four general types of approaches to causation, beginning with direct realism. This view of causation involves four main theses: first, that the relation of causation is directly observable; second, that that relation is not reducible to non-causal properties and/or relations; third, that the relation of causation is also not reducible to non-causal properties and/or relations together with causal laws—since such a reduction would entail that one could not be directly acquainted with the relation of causation; fourth, that the concept of the relation of causation is analytically basic.

A number of philosophers have claimed that the relation of causation is observable, including David Armstrong (1997), Elizabeth Anscombe (1971), and Evan Fales (1990). Thus Anscombe argues that one acquires observational knowledge of causal states of affairs when one sees, for example, a stone break a window, or a knife cut through butter, while Fales, who offers the most detailed argument in support of the view that causation is observable, appeals especially to the impression of pressure upon one's body, and to one's introspective awareness of willing, together with the accompanying perception of the event whose occurrence one willed.

Suppose that it is granted that in such cases one does, in some straightforward sense, observe that one event causes another. Does this provide one with a reason for thinking that direct realism is true? For it to do so, one would have to be able to move from the claim that the relation of causation is thus observable to the conclusion that it is not necessary to offer any analysis of the concept of causation, that the latter can be taken as analytically basic. But observational knowledge, in this broad, everyday sense, would not seem to provide adequate grounds for concluding that the relevant concepts are analytically basic. One can, for example, quite properly speak of physicists as seeing electrons when they look into cloud chambers, even though the concept of an electron is certainly not analytically basic. Similarly, the fact, for example, that sodium chloride is observable, and that one can tell by simply looking and tasting that a substance is sodium chloride does not mean that the expression 'sodium chloride' does not stand in need of analysis.

But might it not be argued in response, first, that, one can observe that two events are causally related in precisely the same sense in which one can observe that something is red; second, that the concept of being red is analytically basic, in virtue of the observability of redness; and therefore, third, that the concept of causation must, for parallel reasons, also be analytically basic?

This response is open, however, to the following reply. If a concept is analytically basic, then one can acquire the concept in question only by being in perceptual or introspective contact with *an instance* of the property or relation in question that is picked out by the concept. One could, however, acquire the concept of a physical object's being red in a world where there were no red physical objects: It would suffice if things sometimes looked red, or if one had hallucinations of seeing red things, or experienced red after-images. The concept of a physical object's being red must, therefore, be definable, and cannot be analytically basic.

What is required if a concept is to be analytically basic? The answer that is suggested by the case of the concept of redness is that for a concept to be analytically basic, the property or relation in virtue of which the concept applies to a given thing must be such that that property or relation is immediately given in experience, where a property or relation is immediately given in experience only if, for any two qualitatively indistinguishable experiences, the property must either be given in both or given in neither.

Is the relation of causation immediately given in experience? The answer is that it is not. For given any experience *E* whatever—be it a perception of external events, an awareness of pressure upon one's body, or an introspective awareness of some mental occurrence, such as an act of willing, or a process of thinking—it is logically possible that appropriate, direct stimulation of the brain might produce an experience, *E**, that was qualitatively indistinguishable from *E*, but which did not involve any causally related elements. So, for example, it might seem to one that one was engaging in a process of deductive reasoning, when, in fact, there was not really any direct connection at all between the thoughts themselves—since all of them were in fact being caused instead by something outside of oneself. Causal relations cannot, therefore, be immediately given in experience in the sense that is required if the concept of causation is to be unanalyzable.

Let us now turn to objections to direct realism. The first has, in effect, just been set out. For if, for any experience in which one is in perceptual or introspective contact with the relation of causation, there could be a qualitatively indistinguishable, hallucinatory experience in which one was not in contact with the relation of causation, it would be possible to acquire the concept of causation without ever being in contact with an instance of that relation. But such experiences are logically possible. So the concept of causation must be analyzable, rather than being analytically basic.

Second, it seems plausible that there is a basic relation of causation that is necessarily irreflexive and asymmetric, even if this is not true of the ancestral of that relation. If either reductionism or theoretical-term realism is correct, one may very well be able to explain the necessary truths in question, since the fact that causal concepts are, on either of those views, analyzable means that those necessary truths may turn out to be analytic. Direct realism, by contrast, in holding that the concept of causation is analytically basic, is barred from offering such an explanation of the asymmetry and irreflexivity of the basic relation of causation. It therefore has to treat these as a matter of synthetic *a priori* truths.

Third, direct realism encounters epistemological problems. Thus, features such as the direction of increase in entropy, or the direction of the transmission of order in non-entropic, irreversible processes, or the direction of open forks, often provide evidence concerning how events are causally connected. In addition, causal beliefs are often established on the basis of statistical information—using methods that, especially within the social sciences, are often very sophisticated. Given an appropriate analysis of the relation of causation, one can show why such features are epistemologically relevant, and why the statistical methods in question can serve to establish causal hypotheses, whereas if causation is a basic, irreducible relation, it is not at all clear how either of these things can be the case.

HUMEAN REDUCTIONISM

Humean reductionist approaches to causation are of three main types: first, accounts that analyze causation in terms of conditions that in the circumstances are nomologically necessary, sufficient, or both; second, accounts in which counterfactual conditionals play the crucial role; and third, accounts based upon probabilistic relations of a Humean sort.

CAUSES AND NOMOLOGICAL CONDITIONS. This first Humean reductionist approach comes in different forms. According to perhaps the most common version, a cause is a condition that is necessary in the circumstances for its effect. To say that event *c* is necessary in the circumstances for event *e* is roughly to say that there is some law, *l*, and some circumstance, *s*, such that the nonoccurrence of *c*, in circumstance *s*, together with law *l*, logically entails the nonoccurrence of *e*.

It may be held instead that a cause is a condition that is sufficient in the circumstances for its effect. To say that event *c* is sufficient in the circumstances for event *e* is to say that there is some law, *l*, and some circumstance, *s*, such that the occurrence of *c*, in circumstance *s*, together with law *l*, logically entails the occurrence of *e*. Finally, it has also been suggested that for one event to cause another is for its occurrence to be both necessary and sufficient in the circumstances for the occurrence of the other event.

What problems do such approaches encounter? Perhaps the most serious difficulty concerns the direction of causation. Suppose, for example, that our world were a Newtonian one, and thus one where the basic laws were time-symmetric. Then the total state of the universe in 1950 would have been both necessary and sufficient not only for the total state in 2050 but also for the total state in 1850. It would therefore follow that events in 1950 had caused both events in 2050 and events in 1850.

Less general objections are also important. First, if a cause is necessary in the circumstances for its effect, this precludes cases of causal preemption, in which event *d* would have caused event *e* were it not for the presence of event *c*, which both caused *e* and prevented *d* from doing so. In such a case *c* is not necessary for *e* since, if *c* had not occurred, *e* would have been caused by *d*. Second, cases of causal overdetermination are also ruled out. For if both *c* and *d* are causally sufficient to bring about *e*, and both do so, then neither *c* nor *d* was necessary in the circumstances for the occurrence of *e*.

These objections can be avoided if one holds instead that a cause is sufficient in the circumstances for its effect. But then other objections emerge. In particular, it follows that there can be no causal relations if all the laws of nature are probabilistic. This is a serious difficulty, especially given the indeterministic nature of quantum mechanics.

COUNTERFACTUAL CONDITIONAL APPROACHES. A second important reductionist approach attempts to analyze causation using subjunctive conditionals. One way of arriving at this approach is by analyzing causation in terms of necessary or sufficient conditions (or both) but then interpreting the latter, not as nomological connections, as above, but as subjunctive conditionals. Thus one can say that *c* is necessary in the circumstances for *e* if, and only if, had *c* not occurred *e* would not have occurred, and that *c* is sufficient in the circumstances for *e* if, and only if, had *e* not occurred *c* would not have occurred.

John L. Mackie (1965/1993, 1974) took this tack in developing a more sophisticated analysis of causation in terms of necessary and sufficient conditions. Thus, after defining an INUS condition of an event as an insufficient but necessary part of a condition which is itself unnecessary but exclusively sufficient for the event, and then arguing that *c*'s being a cause of *e* can then be analyzed as *c*'s being at least an INUS condition of *e*, Mackie asked how necessary and sufficient conditions should be understood. For general causal statements, Mackie favored a nomological account, but for singular causal statements he argued for an analysis in terms of subjunctive conditionals.

The most fully worked-out subjunctive conditional, or counterfactual approach, however, is that of David Lewis (1973/1986, 1979/1986, 2000). His basic strategy involves analyzing causation using a narrower notion of causal dependence and then analyzing causal dependence counterfactually: (1) an event *c* causes an event *e* if, and only if, there is a chain of causally dependent events linking *e* with *c*; (2) an event *g* is causally dependent upon an event *f* if, and only if, had *f* not occurred *g* would not have occurred.

Causes, so construed, need not be necessary for their effects because counterfactual dependence, and hence causal dependence, are not necessarily transitive. Nevertheless, Lewis's approach is closely related to necessary-condition analyses of causation since the more basic relation of causal dependence is a matter of one event's being counterfactually necessary in the circumstances for another event.

What problems arise for such approaches? One objection involves overdetermination, where two events, *c* and *d*, are followed by an event *e*, and where each of *c* and *d* would have been causally sufficient, on its own, to produce *e*. If it is true, in at least some actual or possible cases of this sort, both that *c* causes *e* and that *d* causes *e*, then one has a counterexample to Lewis's counterfactual analysis.

A second objection involves cases of preemption; that is, cases where there is some event *c* that causes *e*, but where there is also some event *d* that did not cause *e*, but that failed to do so only because the presence of *c* prevented it from doing so.

Until the late twentieth century, the discussion of preemption had focused on cases where one causal process preempts another by blocking the occurrence of some state of affairs in the other process, and a variety of closely related ways of attempting to handle this type of preemption have been advanced, involving such notions as fragility of events, quasi-dependence, continuous processes, minimal-counterfactual sufficiency, and minimal-dependence sets (Lewis 1986, Menzies 1989, McDermott 1995, Ramachandran 1997). But none of these approaches can handle the case of trumping preemption, advanced by Jonathan Schaffer (2000), where one causal process preempts another without preventing the occurrence of any of the states of affairs involved in the other causal process.

Third, there is once again the problem of explaining the direction of causation. One possibility is to define the direction of causation as the direction of time, but neither Mackie nor Lewis favors that approach: both think that backward causation is logically possible. Mackie's main proposal appeals to the direction of irreversible processes involving the transmission of order—such as with outgoing concentric waves produced by a stone hitting a pond—and Lewis advances a somewhat related proposal, in which the direction of counterfactual dependence, and hence causal dependence, is based upon the idea that events in this world have many more effects than they have causes. But the problem with both of these suggestions is that the relevant features are at best contingent ones, and it would seem that, even if the world had neither of these features, it could still contain causally related events.

A final objection, and the most fundamental of all, is concerned with the truth conditions of the counterfactuals that enter into the analysis. One familiar approach to counterfactuals maintains that the truthmakers for counterfactuals concerning events in time involve causal facts (Jackson 1977). Such analyses cannot of course be used in an analysis of causation, on pain of circularity. Accordingly, Lewis formulated his analysis of causation in terms of counterfactuals whose truth conditions are a matter of similarity relations across possible worlds (Stalnaker 1968, Lewis 1973). It can be shown, however, by a variant on an objection advanced by Bennett (1974) and Fine (1975), that this account of counterfactuals does not yield the correct truth-values in all cases (Tooley 2003). Moreover, the same type of counterexample also shows an analysis of causation based on such conditionals will generate the wrong truth-values in the cases in question.

PROBABILISTIC APPROACHES. Among the more significant developments in the philosophy of causation since the time of Hume is the idea, motivated in part by quantum mechanics, that causation is not restricted to deterministic processes. This has led several philosophers to propose that causation itself should be analyzed in probabilistic terms.

The central idea is that causes must make their effects more likely. This idea can, however, be expressed in two rather different ways. The traditional approach, developed by Hans Reichenbach (1956), I. J. Good (1961/1962), and Patrick Suppes (1970), focuses upon types of events and involves the notion of positive statistical relevance. According to this notion, an event of type *C* is positively relevant to an event of type *E* if and only if the conditional probability of an event of type *E*, given an event of type *C*, is greater than the unconditional probability of an event of type *E*. The basic idea, then, is that for events of type *C* to be direct causes of events of type *E*, a necessary condition is that the former be positively relevant to the latter.

But do causes necessarily make their effects more likely? Consider two types of diseases, *A* and *B*, governed by the following laws. First, disease *A* causes death with probability 0.1, while disease *B* causes death with probability 0.8. Second, contracting either disease produces complete immunity to the other. Third, in condition *C*, an individual must contract either disease *A* or disease *B*. (Condition *C* might be a weakening of the immune system.) Finally, assume that individual *m* is in condition *C* and contracts disease *A*, which causes his death. Given these conditions, what if *m*, though in condition *C*, had not contracted disease *A*? Then *m* would have contracted disease *B*. But if so, then *m*'s probability of dying had he not contracted disease *A* would have been 0.8—higher than his probability of dying given that he had contracted disease *A*. So the claim that lies at the heart of probabilistic approaches—that causes necessarily make their effects more likely—cannot be true.

NON-HUMEAN REDUCTIONISM

Traditional probabilistic approaches, in analyzing causation in terms of statistical relations, offered a Humean reductionist account of causation. In the late twentieth century, however, an alternative type of probabilistic approach to causation was suggested, one that involves analyzing causation in terms of propensities, or objective chances. Objective chances, however, do not logically supervene upon the totality of Humean states of affairs, as is shown by the fact, for example, that if atoms of a given type take a certain average time t to undergo radioactive decay, that fact is logically compatible with different objective chances of such atoms' undergoing decay within a given period of time. An analysis of causation that involves objective chances is therefore a reductionist account of a non-Humean sort.

OBJECTIVE CHANCE APPROACHES TO CAUSATION. A number of philosophers —such as Edward Madden and Rom Harré (1975), Nancy Cartwright (1989), and C. B. Martin (1993)—have both advocated an ontology in which irreducible dispositional properties, powers, propensities, chances, and the like, occupy a central place, and maintained that such an ontology is relevant to causation. Often, however, the details have been rather sparse. But a clear account of the basic idea of analyzing causation in terms of objective chances was set out in 1986 both by D. H. Mellor and by David Lewis and then, in the 1990s, Mellor offered a very detailed statement and defense of this general approach in his book *The Facts of Causation* (1995).

Mellor's approach, in brief, is roughly as follows. First, Mellor embraces an ontology involving objective chances, where the latter are ultimate properties of states of affairs, rather than being logically supervenient upon causal laws together with non-dispositional properties, plus relations. Second, Mellor proposes that chances can be defined as properties that satisfy three conditions: (1) The Necessity Condition: if the chance of *P*'s obtaining is equal to one, then *P* is the case; (2) The Evidence Condition: if one's total evidence concerning *P* is that the chance of *P* is equal to *k*, then one's subjective probability that P is the case should be equal to k; (3) The Frequency Condition: the chance that P is the case is related to the corresponding relative frequency in the limit. Third, chances enter into basic laws of nature. Fourth, Mellor holds that even basic laws of nature need not have instances, thereby rejecting reductionist accounts in favor of a realist view. Fifth, any chance that P is the case must be a property of a state of affairs that temporally precedes the time at which P exists, or would exist. Finally, and as a very rough approximation, a state of affairs c causes a state of affairs e if and only if there are numbers x and y such that (1) the total state of affairs that exists at the time of c—including laws of nature—entails that the chance of e is x, (2) the total state of affairs that would exist at the time of c, if c did not exist, entails that the chance of e is y, and (3) x is greater than y.

This approach to causation is open to three main types of objections. First, this account necessarily involves the Stalnaker-Lewis style of counterfactuals, and, as was noted earlier, such a closest-worlds account of counterfactuals is unsound.

Second, there are a number of objections that can be directed against the view that objective chances are ontologically ultimate properties, one of which is as follows. Imagine that the world is deterministic, that every temporal interval is divisible, and that all causation involves continuous processes. Suppose that x at time t has an objective chance equal to 1 of being C at time $(t + \Delta t)$. Then there are an infinite number of moments between t and $(t + \Delta t)$, and for every such moment, t, it must be the case either that x at time t has an objective chance equal to 1 of being C at time t, or that x at time t has an objective chance equal to 1 of not being C at time t. But then, if objective chances are ontologically ultimate, intrinsic properties of things at a time, it follows that x at time t must have an infinite number of intrinsic properties—indeed, a non-denumerably infinite number of properties.

This view of the nature of objective chances involves, accordingly, a very expansive ontology indeed. By contrast, if objective chances, rather than being ontologically basic, supervene on categorical properties plus causal laws, this infinite set of intrinsic properties of x, at time t disappears, and all that one may have is a single, intrinsic, categorical property—or a small number of such properties— together with relevant laws of nature.

Third, there are objections to the effect that, even given this view of objective chances, the resulting account of causation is unsound. Here one of the most important is that, just as in the case of attempts to analyze causation in terms of relative frequencies, it can be shown that the crucial claim that a cause raises the probability of its effect remains unsound when one shifts from relative frequencies to objective chances.

INDIRECT, OR THEORETICAL-TERM, REALISM

Direct realism with regard to causation is, as we saw earlier, deeply problematic. There is, however, a very different form of causal realism, according to which causation is a theoretical relation between events. On this view, all knowledge of causal states of affairs is inferential knowledge, and the concept of causation stands in need of analysis. But unlike reductionist accounts, the relevant analysis does not imply that causal states of affairs are logically supervenient upon non-causal states of affairs.

A THEORETICAL-TERM REALIST ACCOUNT OF CAUSATION. This approach to causation involves finding postulates that serve to define implicitly the relation of causation. One suggestion here (Tooley 1990), for example, starts out with postulates for causal laws that say, very roughly, that the *a posteriori* probabilities of effects are a function of the *a priori* probabilities of their causes, whereas, by contrast, the *a posteriori* probabilities of causes are not a function of the *a priori* probabilities of their effects. Then, when one adds the further postulate that causal laws involve the relation of causation, the result is an implicit definition of the relation of causation. That implicit definition can then be converted into an explicit one by using one's preferred approach to the definition of theoretical terms. So, for example, if one adopts a Ramsey/Lewis approach, the relation of causation can be defined as that unique relation between states of affairs that satisfies the relevant open sentences corresponding to the postulates in question.

REALISM OR REDUCTIONISM?

Reductionist approaches to causation are, as we have seen, exposed to a variety of objections. In addition, however, there are general objections that appear to tell against any reductionist approach. Two especially important ones are, first, that the Basic Reductionist Thesis is unsound, and, second, that reductionism cannot provide a satisfactory account of the direction of causation.

SINGULARISM AND CAUSAL LAWS. According to the Basic Reductionist Thesis, causal relations are logically supervenient upon the totality of instances of non-causal properties and relations, together with causal laws. But this thesis is exposed to a number of objections, such as the following. Assume that indeterministic laws are logically possible and that, in particular, it is a basic law both that an object's acquiring property *P* causes it to acquire either property *Q* or property *R*, but not both, and that an object's acquiring property *S* also causes it to acquire either property *Q* or property *R*, but not both. Suppose now that some object simultaneously acquires both property *P* and property *S* and then immediately acquires both property *Q* and property *R*. The problem now is that, given that the relevant laws are basic, there cannot be any non-causal facts that will determine which causal relations obtain. Did the acquisition of *P* cause the acquisition of *Q*, or did it cause the acquisition of *R*? On a reductionist approach, no answer is possible. Accordingly, causal relations between events cannot be logically supervenient upon causal laws plus non-causal states of affairs.

REDUCTIONISM AND THE DIRECTION OF CAUSATION. What determines the direction of causation? Reductionists have advanced various suggestions, but some arguments seem to show that no reductionist account can work. One such argument appeals to the idea of a very simple world—consisting, say, of a single particle, or of two particles rotating endlessly about one another. Such simple worlds would still involve causation since the identity over time of the particles, for example, requires causal relations between their temporal parts. But since such worlds are time-symmetric, the events in them will not exhibit any non-causal patterns that could provide the basis for a reductionist account of the direction of causation. Accordingly, no reductionist account of the direction of causation can generate the correct answer for all possible worlds. It would seem, then, that only a realist account of causation will do.

See also Anscombe, Gertrude Elizabeth Margaret; A Priori and A Posteriori; Aristotle; Armstrong, David M.; Bennett, Jonathan; Berkeley, George; Cartwright, Nancy; Hume, David; Lewis, David; Locke, John; Mackie, John Leslie; Philosophy of Statistical Mechanics; Reductionism in the Philosophy of Mind; Realism; Reichenbach, Hans; Suppes, Patrick.

Bibliography

Anscombe, G. E. M. *Causality and Determination.* Cambridge, U.K.: Cambridge University Press, 1971.

Aristotle. *Physics.* Book 2.

Armstrong, David M. *A World of States of Affairs.* Cambridge, U.K.: Cambridge University Press, 1997.

Armstrong, David M., and Adrian Heathcote. "Causes and Laws." *Noûs* 25 (1991): 63–73.

Bennett, Jonathan. "Counterfactuals and Possible Worlds." *Canadian Journal of Philosophy* 4 (1974): 381–402.

Cartwright, Nancy. *Nature's Capacities and their Measurement.* Oxford: Clarendon Press, 1989.

Davis, Wayne. "Probabilistic Theories of Causation." In *Probability and Causation: Essays in Honor of Wesley Salmon,* edited by James H. Fetzer, 133–160. Dordrecht: Reidel, 1988.

Dowe, Phil. *Physical Causation.* New York: Cambridge University Press, 2000.

Dowe, Phil, and Paul Noordhof, eds. *Cause and Chance.* London and New York: Routledge, 2004.

Eells, Ellery. *Probabilistic Causality.* Cambridge, U.K.: Cambridge University Press, 1991.

Ehring, Douglas. *Causation and Persistence.* New York: Oxford University Press, 1997.

Fair, David. "Causation and the Flow of Energy." *Erkenntnis* 14 (1979): 219–250.

Fales, Evan. *Causation and Universals.* London and New York: Routledge, 1990.

Fine, Kit. "Critical Notice—*Counterfactuals.*" *Mind* 84 (1975): 451–458.

Good. I. J. "A Causal Calculus." Parts 1 and 2. *British Journal for the Philosophy of Science* 11 (1961): 305–318; 12 (1962): 43–51.

Hausman, Daniel M. *Causal Asymmetries.* Cambridge, U.K.: Cambridge University Press, 1998.

Hesslow, Germund. "Two Notes on the Probabilistic Approach to Causation." *Philosophy of Science* 43 (1976): 290–292.

Hume, David. *An Enquiry concerning Human Understanding.* London: 1748.

Hume, David. *A Treatise of Human Nature.* London: 1739–1740.

Jackson, Frank. "A Causal Theory of Counterfactuals." *Australasian Journal of Philosophy* 55 (1977): 3–21.

Lewis, David. "Causation." *Journal of Philosophy* 70 (1973): 556–567. Reprinted, with postscripts, in *Philosophical Papers.* Vol. 2. Oxford: Oxford University Press, 1986.

Lewis, David. "Causation as Influence." *Journal of Philosophy* 97 (4) (2000): 182–197.

Lewis, David. "Counterfactual Dependence and Time's Arrow." *Noûs* 13 (1979): 455–476. Reprinted, with postscripts, in *Philosophical Papers.* Vol. 2. Oxford: Oxford University Press, 1986.

Lewis, David. *Counterfactuals.* Cambridge, MA: Harvard University Press, 1973.

Lewis, David. "Postscripts to 'Causation.'" In his Philosophical Papers. Vol. 2, 172–213. Oxford: Oxford University Press, 1986.

Mackie, John L. "Causes and Conditions." *American Philosophical Quarterly* 2 (1965): 245–264. Reprinted in *Causation,* edited by Ernest Sosa and Michael Tooley, 33–55. Oxford: Oxford University Press, 1993.

Mackie, John L. *The Cement of the Universe.* Oxford: Oxford University Press, 1974.

Madden, Edward H., and Rom Harré. *Causal Powers.* Oxford: Blackwell, 1975.

Martin, C. B. "Power for Realists." In *Ontology, Causality and Mind,* edited by John Bacon, Keith Campbell, and Lloyd

Reinhardt. Cambridge, U.K.: Cambridge University Press, 1993.
McDermott, Michael. "Redundant Causation." *British Journal for the Philosophy of Science* 40 (1995): 523–544.
Mellor, D. H. *The Facts of Causation*. London: Routledge, 1995.
Mellor, D. H. "Fixed Past, Unfixed Future." In *Contributions to Philosophy: Michael Dummett*, edited by Barry Taylor, 166–186. The Hague: Nijhoff, 1986.
Menzies, Peter. "Probabilistic Causation and Causal Processes: A Critique of Lewis." *Philosophy of Science* 56 (1989): 642–663.
Ramachandran, Murali. "A Counterfactual Analysis of Causation." *Mind* 106 (1997): 263–277.
Reichenbach, Hans. *The Direction of Time*. Berkeley and Los Angeles: University of California Press, 1956.
Salmon, Wesley C. "Probabilistic Causality." *Pacific Philosophical Quarterly* 61 (1980): 50–74.
Salmon, Wesley C. *Scientific Explanation and the Causal Structure of the World*. Princeton, NJ: Princeton University Press, 1984.
Schaffer, Jonathan. "Trumping Preemption." *Journal of Philosophy* 97 (4) (2000): 165–181.
Sosa, Ernest, and Michael Tooley, eds. *Causation*. Oxford: Oxford University Press, 1993.
Stalnaker, Robert C. "A Theory of Conditionals." In *Studies in Logical Theory, American Philosophical Quarterly*, Monograph 2, edited by Nicholas Rescher, 98–112. Oxford: Blackwell, 1968.
Strawson, Galen. *The Secret Connexion: Causation, Realism, and David Hume*. Oxford: Oxford University Press, 1989.
Suppes, Patrick. *A Probabilistic Theory of Causality*. Amsterdam: North-Holland, 1970.
Tooley, Michael. *Causation: A Realist Approach*. Oxford: Oxford University Press, 1987.
Tooley, Michael. "The Nature of Causation: A Singularist Account." *Canadian Philosophers, Canadian Journal of Philosophy* Suppl. 16 (1990): 271–322.
Tooley, Michael. "Probability and Causation." In *Cause and Chance*, edited by Phil Dowe and Paul Noordhof. London and New York: Routledge, 2004.
Tooley, Michael. "The Stalnaker-Lewis Approach to Counterfactuals." *Journal of Philosophy* 100 (7) (2003): 321–327.
Tooley, Michael. *Time, Tense, and Causation*. Oxford: Oxford University Press, 1997.
Von Bretzel, Philip. "Concerning a Probabilistic Theory of Causation Adequate for the Causal Theory of Time." *Synthèse* 35 (1977): 173–190.
Von Wright, Georg Henrik. *Explanation and Understanding*. Ithaca, NY: Cornell University Press, 1971.

Michael Tooley (1996, 2005)

CAUSATION: PHILOSOPHY OF SCIENCE

In *The Critique of Pure Reason* (first published in 1781), the German philosopher Immanuel Kant maintained that causation was one of the fundamental concepts that rendered the empirical world comprehensible to humans. By the beginning of the twenty-first century, psychology was beginning to show just how pervasive human reasoning concerning cause and effect is. Even young children seem to naturally organize their knowledge of the world according to relations of cause and effect.

It is hardly surprising, then, that causation has been a topic of great interest in philosophy, and that many philosophers have attempted to analyze the relationship between cause and effect. Among the more prominent proposals are the following: Causation consists in the instantiation of exceptionless regularities (Hume 1975, 1999; Mill 1856; Hempel 1965; Mackie 1974); causation is to be understood in terms of relations of probabilistic dependence (Reichenbach 1956, Suppes 1970, Cartwright 1983, Eells 1991); causation is the relation that holds between means and ends (Gasking 1955, von Wright 1975, Woodward 2003); causes are events but for which their effects would not have happened (Lewis 1986); causes and effects are connected by physical processes that are capable of transmitting certain types of properties (Salmon 1984, Dowe 2000).

It often happens, however, that advances in science force people to abandon aspects of their common sense picture of the world. For example, Einstein's theories of relativity have forced people to rethink their conceptions of time, space, matter, and energy. What lessons does science teach about the concept of causation?

RUSSELL'S CHALLENGE

In 1912, the eminent British philosopher Bertrand Russell delivered his paper "On the Notion of Cause" before the Aristotelian Society. In this paper, he claimed that the notion of cause had no place in a scientific worldview:

> All philosophers, of every school, imagine that causation is one of the fundamental axioms or postulates of science, yet, oddly enough, in advanced sciences such as gravitational astronomy, the word "cause" never appears … To me, it seems that … the reason why physics has ceased to look for causes is that, in fact, there are no such things. The law of causality, I believe, like much that passes muster among philosophers, is a relic of a bygone age, surviving, like the monarchy, only because it is erroneously supposed to do no harm. (p. 1)

Russell was not alone in this view. Other writers of the period, such as Ernst Mach (the German physicist and philosopher of science), Karl Pearson (the father of modern statistics), and Pierre Duhem (French physicist, as well as historian and philosopher of science), also argued that causation did not belong in the world of science. This view was shared by the logical positivists, a group of philosophers working primarily in Austria and Germany between the World Wars whose ideas shaped much of philosophy of science in the twentieth century. A general suspicion of causal notions also pervaded a number of fields outside of philosophy, such as statistics and psychology.

CAUSATION IN SCIENCE

Despite Russell's remark, it is simply false that the word "cause" (and its cognates) does not appear in the advanced sciences. Russell's claim can be readily refuted by perusing any leading science journal. Admittedly, some uses of the word "cause" and its cognates have specific technical meanings—such as talk of "causal structure" in connection with the general theory of relativity—but frequently enough these words are used in their ordinary English sense. To cite just one example, an issue of *Physical Review Letters* from 2003 contains an article titled "Specific-Heat Anomaly Caused by Ferroelectric Nanoregions in Pb(Mg[sub 1/3]Nb[sub 2/3])O[sub 3] and Pb(Mg[sub 1/3]Ta[sub 2/3])O[sub 3] Relaxors." Moreover, it has become common in physics to classify a variety of phenomena as "effects": there is the "Hall effect," the "Kondo effect," the "Lamb-shift effect," the "Zeeman effect," and so on. But surely "cause and effect" are an inseparable pair: where there are causes, there are effects that are caused by them, and where there are effects, there are causes that cause them.

The person on the street is more likely to encounter causal claims from the medical sciences, such as: "Cholesterol in the bloodstream causes hardened arteries, which in turn causes heart attacks." While the medical sciences may not be as advanced as Russell's example of gravitational astronomy, it is implausible to think that these causal claims are the result of conceptual confusion, or are otherwise scientifically disreputable.

Despite the falsehood of its most provocative claim, however, Russell's paper does succeed in highlighting a number of important and interesting problems about the role of causation in science.

ANTI-FUNDAMENTALISM

Although the advanced sciences have hardly eschewed talk of causation, it is true that the deepest physical principles—such as Newton's three laws of motion, his law of universal gravitation, Maxwell's equations governing the electric and magnetic fields, Schrödinger's equation governing the evolution of quantum systems, and Einstein's field equations relating the distribution of mass-energy in the universe with the structure of space and time—make no mention of causation. All of these principles take the form of mathematical equations and act as constraints on possible states of physical systems (under suitable mathematical characterizations). A given sequence of states may be compatible with, for example, Newton's laws of motion, but nothing in those laws explicitly says that certain states (or aspects of those states) cause others. This suggests that the causal relation is not part of the constitution of the world at the deepest metaphysical level, a view that the historian and philosopher of science John Norton labels "anti-fundamentalism" (Norton 2003). Indeed, the world described by fundamental physics is in many ways at odds with the ordinary picture of a world regimented by cause and effect relationships.

ASYMMETRY

People normally think of causation as both *asymmetric* and *temporally biased*. It is asymmetric in the sense that if *C* is a cause of *E*, then (always? typically?) *E* is not a cause of *C*. This claim must be stated with some care. It may be, for instance, that anxiety is a cause of insomnia, which is in turn a cause of anxiety. But it is one's anxiety on Monday evening that causes insomnia on Monday night, which in turn causes anxiety on Tuesday morning. Monday night's insomnia is not both the cause and the effect of one and the same episode of anxiety. Causation is temporally biased in the sense that causes (always? typically?) occur before their effects in time.

By contrast, the fundamental laws of physics mentioned above are all *time-reversal invariant*. That is, if a particular sequence of states of a physical system is consistent with the laws of physics, then the temporally reversed sequence is also consistent with those laws. The laws of physics do not discriminate between the past and the future in the way that causation does, with two possible exceptions. The first exception involves the statistical laws governing the decay of certain mesons. While these laws exhibit a slight temporal asymmetry, the phenomena in question seem too esoteric to be of much help in understanding the asymmetry of causation.

The second exception is the second law of thermodynamics, which states that the entropy of a closed system can increase but never decrease. Thus a closed system whose entropy is increasing is consistent with the second law, while the temporal reverse of this system is not. The second law of thermodynamics is not, however, a fundamental law. The entropy of a physical system is determined by the physical state of the particles that make up the system, as characterized in terms of ordinary physical parameters such as position and momentum. These particles are in turn governed by the time-reversal invariant laws already mentioned. It is thus something of a mystery how the asymmetric second law of thermodynamics can arise from the underlying symmetric dynamics governing the constituents of thermodynamic systems. One prominent view is that the second law of thermodynamics is the result of de facto temporal asymmetries in the boundary conditions of the universe.

There have been a few attempts to ground the asymmetry of causation in the second law of thermodynamics. The basic idea is that the best characterization of our physical universe will include not only the fundamental laws of physics, but also the statement that in the past our universe was in a state of very low entropy—the so-called "past hypothesis."When entertaining various counterfactual suppositions, one conjoins those suppositions with the laws of physics and the past hypothesis to determine what the world would be like if those suppositions were true. Because people hold fixed features of the past, but not of the future, when entertaining contrary-to-fact suppositions, any changes from the actual world introduced in those suppositions will tend to entail significant changes in the future but only insignificant changes in the past. In this way, macroscopic features of the future will counterfactually depend upon what is true in the present, whereas macroscopic features of the past will not. This asymmetric relation of counterfactual dependence can then serve as the basis of an account of causation (such as that of David Lewis in "Causation" [1986]). If this account is correct, then the existence of an asymmetric causal relation is not guaranteed by the laws of physics but is rather the consequence of contingent asymmetries in the boundary conditions of the world.

The best-known attempt to account for causal asymmetry is the common cause principle, first formulated by the German-American Philosopher Hans Reichenbach and presented in his posthumously published book *The Direction of Time* (1956). For Reichenbach, temporal order and causal order are conceptually intertwined. Reichenbach defines causation in terms of probabilities and temporal order, but temporal order is itself defined in terms of asymmetries in probabilities. Let *A* and *B* be two events that are probabilistically *correlated*; in other words, the probability that *A* and *B* will occur together, $P(A \,\&\, B)$, is greater than the product of the individual probabilities, $P(A)P(B)$. (If the two probabilities are equal, then *A* and *B* are said to be probabilistically *independent*.) An event *C* is said to "screen off" *A* from *B* if it renders them *conditionally* independent; that is, if $P(A \,\&\, B|C) = P(A|C)P(B|C)$. If there is an earlier event *C* that screens off *A* from *B*, but no later event that does so, then the trio *ABC* forms a *conjunctive fork open to the future*. If there is a later screener-off *E*, but no earlier one, then *ABE* is a conjunctive fork open to the *past*. Finally, if there is an earlier and a later screener-off, then that is a *closed* fork. According to Reichenbach, the overwhelming majority of open forks are open to the future, and this probabilistic asymmetry provides the basis for the distinction between the past and the future. Reichenbach further held that if two events *A* and *B* are correlated, and neither is a cause of the other, then there exists a common cause of *A* and *B* in their mutual past that screens *A* off from *B*.

Reichenbach believed that his common cause principle was related to the second law of thermodynamics. Think of $A \,\&\, B$ as one possible state of a physical system, the other possible states being $A \,\&\, {\sim}B$, ${\sim}A \,\&\, B$, and ${\sim}A \,\&\, {\sim}B$. A probability distribution over these states in which *A* and *B* are correlated contains *information*, in a sense that is made precise within the mathematical field of information theory. From a formal perspective, information is inversely related to entropy. Thus a correlation between *A* and *B* is like a low entropy state of a physical system, and it is to be explained in terms of an earlier causal interaction between the system and its external environment.

There are a number of difficulties facing Reichenbach's common cause principle. The principle seems to fail for certain quantum phenomena involving distant correlations, such as the one featured in the famous thought experiment by the physicists Albert Einstein, Boris Podolski, and Nathan Rosen, in their 1935 paper "Can Quantum Mechanical Description of Reality Be Considered Complete?" In a simplified version of this setup, two particles form a single system in which the total spin is zero. If the particles are separated, and the spin of each particle is measured, they will always be found to have opposite spins. There is thus a correlation between the outcome of the two measurements. Neither measurement result can be a cause of the other, for the measurements can be conducted at such a great distance that not even a light signal could connect the two. Yet a series of mathematical and empirical results, beginning with the work of the physicist John Bell in 1964, show that there can be no earlier state of the two-particle system that screens off the measurement outcomes.

A further problem is that it is unclear why Reichenbach's fork asymmetry should hold within the physical framework of classical statistical mechanics. Within this framework, a system possesses a microstate that evolves deterministically according to Newton's laws of motion. An "event" *A* is just a coarse-grained characterization of the state of the system at a particular time, consistent with many different microstates. A probability distribution is defined over the possible states of the system. Suppose that the events *A* and *B* are correlated according to this probability measure, and that there is an earlier event *C* that screens off *A* from *B*. It is possible to take the image of *C* under the deterministic dynamics of the system; that is, one can evolve each microstate in *C* to some point in time after the occurrence of *A* and *B* and collect the resulting set of microstates into a new event *C'*. By construction, *C'* will stand in the same probability relations with *A* and *B* that *C* did. Hence, *C'* will be a later event that screens off *A* from *B*, and *ABCC'* will form a closed fork. Because this procedure is fully general, it is not clear how there can be forks open to the future at all. One possible reply to this worry is that in such a closed fork, the later screener-off C' will just be a heterogeneous collection of microstates, and hence will not qualify as an "event" in the relevant sense. This reply raises two new questions: first, which sets of microstates constitute genuine events? Second, why should we expect that only earlier screeners off will be genuine events?

FURTHER CAUSAL ANOMALIES

There are a number of further respects in which the world described by fundamental physics seems not to be one ruled by relations of cause and effect. It is well known that certain quantum-mechanical phenomena such as radioactive decay appear to be *indeterministic*. For example, even a complete description of the present state of a carbon-14 atom cannot allow one to predict whether or not it will decay during a certain period of time, but will instead yield only a probability that decay will occur. If the atom does eventually decay, can anything be said to cause the decay event? This kind of indeterminism provides part of the motivation for attempts to analyze causation in terms of probabilities. But even probabilistic theories of causation have difficulties when indeterminism is coupled with the sorts of distant correlations described in the previous section.

Moreover, even classical Newtonian physics admits indeterminism. For example, John Norton, in "Causation as Folk Science," describes a system consisting of a point mass sitting at the apex of a bell-shaped dome. Newton's laws of motion permit the point mass to rest there indefinitely, but they also allow it to begin sliding down the side of the dome in an arbitrary direction after an arbitrary finite time. No force is necessary to dislodge the mass: the sudden motion of the mass down the side of the dome is fully consistent with the constraint that at every instant, the force acting on the mass (due to the pull of gravity, and the reactive push of the dome's wall) is proportional to its acceleration. Such a motion thus appears to be entirely uncaused.

Einstein's general theory of relativity also gives rise to causal anomalies. For example, the Austrian-American mathematician Kurt Gödel showed that Einstein's field equations permitted solutions in which there were *closed causal curves*. Thus it may be possible for a billiard ball to get knocked, continue rolling along its new trajectory, and then eventually bump into its earlier self, knocking it into that new trajectory in the first place. Such a scenario appears to be at odds with people's ordinary conception of causation as an asymmetric relation, for the collision between the older and younger billiard ball causes the trajectory of the younger ball, which in turn causes that collision.

CAUSAL INFERENCE

One of Russell's targets in "On the Notion of Cause" was the so-called "law of causality"; indeed, it is this law, rather than the "notion of cause" itself, whose utility is compared to that of the British monarchy. Russell cites a formulation of this principle from the nineteenth-century British philosopher John Stuart Mill: "The Law of Causation, the recognition of which is the main pillar of inductive science, is but the familiar truth, that invariability of succession is found by observation to obtain between every fact in nature and some other fact which has preceded it." (Mill 1856, p. 359.)

According to Mill, science discovers causal relationships by discovering invariable regularities in nature, and the success of science presupposes the pervasiveness of such regularities. Russell was certainly right to challenge the importance of this law to science—not because science is not in the business of discovering causal relationships, but because causal inference in science does not rest upon the discovery of perfect regularities.

Causal inference presents a prima facie difficulty, first articulated by the Scottish philosopher David Hume in 1739. Suppose that one billiard ball collides with a second, causing it to move. One can observe the motion of the first billiard ball; and one can observe the motion of the second billiard ball; but one cannot observe the causation that connects the two together. How, then, is a person to acquire knowledge of causal relationships?

Traditionally there have been two main lines of response to this problem. One line that has already been mentioned is to reject the notion of causation on the grounds that it is inaccessible to empirical investigation. The second line, adopted in different ways by Hume, Mill, and a number of twentieth and twenty-first century philosophers, is to try to spell out systematic connections between causation and observable phenomena such as empirical regularities in order to explain how the former can be inferred from the latter. The "law of causation" championed by Mill and attacked by Russell stems from this second line of response to the problem. (A third possibility, defended in the early part of the twentieth century by the French-American philosopher C. J. Ducasse, and in the middle of the twentieth century by the Belgian psychologist André Michotte, is to reject the claim that causation is not subject to direct perception. Even if this is possible in special cases such as billiard ball collisions, however, this hardly seems to be an adequate explanation for causal knowledge generally.) This problem concerning the empirical accessibility of causation has been a driving force behind attempts to banish causation, and also behind attempts to provide causation with a sound philosophical analysis.

In fact, however, causal inference is neither impossible nor a matter of reading causal relations off universal regularities or correlations. Causal inference, like other forms of scientific inference, is broadly "hypothetico-deductive" in character. A causal hypothesis is formulated, and in conjunction with various background assumptions (often involving causal relationships themselves), it is used to derive predictions about what types of correlations will be observed. These predictions are then compared with observations. In this way, causal hypotheses may be subjected to empirical test without the need for a direct reduction of causal claims to claims about regularities and the like.

EXPERIMENTATION

The most reliable causal knowledge comes not from passive observations, but from controlled experimentation. In the medical sciences, the experiments often take the form of randomized clinical trials. Consider the claim that a particular drug causes lowered blood pressure. How might one test this claim? One possibility would be to make the drug available on the open market and observe hypertension patients who choose to take the drug and those who do not. There is a problem with this methodology. Suppose that the drug is expensive; one might expect that patients who buy the drug will be wealthier on average then those who do not. Wealthier patients might enjoy any number of other benefits—such as access to better healthcare generally, better diets, and so on—that influence whether or not they experience a reduction in hypertension. If one finds that patients who take the drug do in fact experience greater reduction in blood pressure levels than those who do not, it can still not be known whether this reduction is due to the drug or due to one of the other advantages associated with wealth. In a randomized trial, it is determined randomly which patients will receive the drug and which will be given a placebo instead. Randomization helps to ensure that treatment is not correlated with any other causes that might influence recovery.

This example helps to show the importance of the distinction between genuine causal relationships, on the one hand, and mere regularities or correlations on the other. Suppose that the drug is available only to wealthy patients, and that patients who take the drug fare better, on average, than those who do not. If this correlation is due to the wealth of the patients who use the drug, rather than to any effect of the drug itself on hypertension, then one would not expect the correlation to persist under various policy interventions. For example, if the drug were to be covered by insurance, so that less wealthy patients could also afford to take the drug, then the correlation between use of the drug and lowered hypertension would disappear. As the philosopher Nancy Cartwright puts it in her paper "Causal Laws and Effective Strategies" (1983), causal relationships support "effective strategies," while mere correlations or regularities do not. It is for this reason, Cartwright argues, contrary to the opinion of Russell, that the notion of cause cannot be dispensed with. It is also for this reason that one often finds the most self-conscious attention to the specific concerns of causal inference in those branches of science that have a practical dimension, such as medicine and agronomy.

In many areas of science, randomized trials are not feasible. This may be due to the inability to produce the putative cause at will, or it may be due to the lack any analog of a control group that receives placebos. Nonetheless, in the experimental setting, it is often possible to isolate the influence of the cause under investigation by preventing other causes from operating. For example, an experiment might be conducted within a metallic container to eliminate external magnetic influences; or the experimental apparatus may be set afloat in a pool of mercury to prevent vibrations from being transmitted through the floor of the laboratory (as was done in the famous Michelson-Morley experiment of 1887, which failed to detect any effect of the earth's motion on the speed at which light traveled). Sometimes the experimental preparations are more mundane, such as thoroughly dusting the apparatus to eliminate the effects of stray dust particles, or even removing pigeons found nesting in the apparatus (as was required by Arno Penzias and Robert Wilson, who discovered the cosmic microwave background in 1965).

CAUSAL MODELS

In some fields, such as macroeconomics, epidemiology, and sociology, experimental manipulation is simply not feasible, and causal relationships must be inferred from observed correlations. Beginning around 1990 has been an explosion of interest in developing causal modeling techniques to facilitate such nonexperimental causal inferences. Two important works that have garnered a substantial amount of attention from philosophers are *Causation, Prediction and Search* (2000), by the philosophers Peter Spirtes, Clark Glymour, and Richard Scheines, and *Causality: Models, Reasoning, and Inference* (2000) by the computer scientist Judea Pearl. Both frameworks employ graphs to represent causal relationships among sets of causal variables. The variables in a set V form the nodes of a graph, and certain pairs of variables are connected by *edges* in the graph. In a *directed graph*, the edges take the form of arrows, which point from one variable into another. If a graph over the variable set V contains an arrow from the variable X to the variable Y, that indicates that X is a *direct cause* of Y (also called a *parent* of Y): the value of X has an effect on the value of Y that is not mediated by any other variable in the set V.

The causal structure represented by a directed graph is connected to a probability distribution over the values of the variables by the *causal Markov condition*. This condition states that, conditional upon the values of its direct causes, the values of a variable are probabilistically independent of the values of all other variables, except for its effects. In other words, a variable's parents screen off that variable from all other variables, except for its effects. (The causal Markov condition is closely related to Reichenbach's common cause principle, discussed above.)

With the help of the causal Markov condition, as well as other conditions such as the *minimality* and the *faithfulness* conditions, a graph representing causal relationships among a set of variables will serve as a model that makes predictions about probabilistic relationships among the variables. In particular, it predicts that certain variables will be dependent or independent of others, either unconditionally, or conditional upon the values of other variables. These predictions can then be tested using normal statistical means.

The most obvious use of these methods is to test whether a postulated set of causal relationships among the variables in the set V is consistent with the statistical data about the values of those variables. But there are other types of problems where these methods can be applied. Even if one does not begin by hypothesizing a specific causal model, it is possible to determine which sets of causal relations among a variable set are consistent with the statistical data. Typically, the data will not single out one causal model, but will only pick out an equivalence class of statistically indistinguishable models. In this case, background knowledge may help to narrow the set of plausible models. In a different sort of problem, one begins with a qualitative causal model and uses it to make quantitative predictions about the effects of interventions that have not yet been performed.

It is important to note that the causal Markov condition is not an a priori constraint on the relationship between causal structure and probability. It can fail, for instance, if a variable set V omits a variable that is a common cause of two variables included in V. The causal Markov condition is at best an empirical assumption that holds for a wide variety of causal structures, and hence any application of techniques based on the causal Markov condition to infer causal relationships from probabilistic data carries substantive empirical presuppositions. A number of critics have charged that these presuppositions severely limit the utility of the new causal modeling techniques.

CONCLUSIONS

Contrary to Russell's claim, causal notions are as pervasive in science as they are in philosophy and everyday life. New scientific techniques continue to be developed for the discovery of causal relationships. Nonetheless, the world as it is described by the deepest physical principles bears little resemblance to a world that is regimented by asymmetrical causal relationships. Thus there remain a number of deep puzzles about how causal relationships can emerge from physical laws that themselves make no mention of causality.

See also Causation, Metaphysical Issues; Probability and Chance.

Bibliography

Albert, David. *Time and Chance*. Cambridge, MA: Harvard University Press, 2000.

Arntzenius, Frank. "Physics and Common Causes." *Synthese* 82 (1990): 77–96.

Bell, John. "On the Einstein-Podolsky-Rosen Paradox." *Physics* 1 (1964): 195–200.

Cartwright, Nancy. *How the Laws of Physics Lie*. Oxford: Clarendon Press, 1983.

Corry, Richard, and Huw Price, eds. *Causation and the Constitution of Reality*. Oxford: Oxford University Press, 2005.

Dowe, Phil. *Physical Causation*. Cambridge, U.K.: Cambridge University Press, 2000.

Ducasse, Curt J. "On the Nature and Observability of the Causal Relation." *Journal of Philosophy* 23 (1926): 57–68.

Duhem, Pierre. *The Aim and Structure of Physical Theory*. Princeton, NJ: Princeton University Press, 1991.

Earman, John. *A Primer on Determinism*. Dordrecht, Netherlands: Riedel, 1986.

Eells, Ellery. *Probabilistic Causality*. Cambridge, U.K.: Cambridge University Press, 1991.

Einstein, Albert, Boris Podolski, and Natha Rosen. "Can Quantum Mechanical Description of Physical Reality Be Considered Complete?" *Physical Review* 47 (1935): 777–780.

Field, Hartry. "Causation in a Physical World." In *Oxford Handbook of Metaphysics*, edited by Michael Loux and Dean Zimmerman. Oxford: Oxford University Press, 2003.

Gasking, Douglas. "Causation and Recipes." *Mind* 64 (1955): 479–487.

Gopnik, Alison, and Laura Schulz. *Causal Learning: Psychology, Philosophy and Computation*. Oxford: Oxford University Press, 2005.

Hempel, Carl Gustav. "Aspects of Scientific Explanation." In *Aspects of Scientific Explanation and Other Essays in the Philosophy of Science*. New York: Free Press, 1965.

Hume, David. *An Enquiry concerning Human Understanding*. Oxford: Oxford University Press, 1999.

Hume, David. *A Treatise of Human Nature*, 2nd ed. Oxford: Clarendon Press, 1975.

Kant, Immanuel. *A Critique of Pure Reason*. Translated by Paul Guyer and Allen Wood. Cambridge, U.K.: Cambridge University Press, 1998.

Lewis, David. "Causation," with Postscripts. In *Philosophical Papers, Volume II*. Oxford: Oxford University Press, 1986.

Mackie, John. *The Cement of the Universe*. Oxford: Clarendon Press, 1974.

McKim, Vaughn, and Stephen Turner. *Causality in Crisis? Statistical Methods and the Search for Causal Knowledge in the Social Sciences*. Notre Dame, IN: University of Notre Dame Press, 1997.

Michotte, André. *The Perception of Causality*. New York: Basic Books, 1963.

Mill, John Stuart. *A System of Logic: Ratiocinative and Inductive*. 4th edition. London: Parker and Son, 1856.

Moriya, Yosuke, Hitoshi Kawaji, Takeo Tojo, and Tooru Atake. "Specific-Heat Anomaly Caused by Ferroelectric Nanoregions in Pb(Mg(sub 1/3]Nb(sub 2/3])O(sub 3] and Pb(Mg(sub 1/3]Ta(sub 2/3])O(sub 3] Relaxors." *Physical Review Letters* 90 (2003): 205901.

Norton, John. "Causation as Folk Science." *Philosopher's Imprint* 3 (4) (2003). Available from www.philosophersimprint.org/003004/.

Pearl, Judea. *Causality: Models, Reasoning, and Inference*. Cambridge, U.K.: Cambridge University Press, 2000.

Pearson, Karl. *The Grammar of Science*. 3rd ed. reprint. New York: Meridian, 1957.

Price, Huw. *Time's Arrow and Archimedes' Point*. Oxford: Oxford University Press, 1996.

Reichenbach, Hans. *The Direction of Time*. Berkeley: University of California Press, 1956.

Russell, Bertrand. "On the Notion of Cause." Proceedings of the Aristotelian Society 13 (1913): 1–26

Salmon, Wesley. *Scientific Explanation and the Causal Structure of the World*. Princeton, NJ: Princeton University Press, 1984.

Spirtes, Peter, Clark Glymour, and Richard Scheines. *Causation, Prediction, and Search*, 2nd ed. Cambridge, MA: MIT Press, 2000.

Suppes, Patrick. *A Probabilistic Theory of Causality*. Amsterdam: North-Holland, 1970.

van Fraassen, Bas. "The Charybdis of Realism: Epistemological Implications of Bell's Inequality." *Synthese* 52 (1982): 25–38.

von Wright, Georg. *Causality and Determinism*. New York: Columbia University Press, 1975.

Woodward, James. *Making Things Happen: A Theory of Causal Explanation*. Oxford: Oxford University Press, 2003.

Christopher R. Hitchcock (2005)

CAUSATION IN INDIAN PHILOSOPHY

Indian philosophical theories, from their earliest speculative cosmologies and explorations of the nature of human existence—in the Vedas and Upanisads, whose compositions were completed by roughly the first half of the first millennium BCE—emphasized the plight of humans and their struggle towards a soteriological goal. An understanding of the evolution of the world and the place of human beings within it held out the hope of improving their lot, either in some other place after death or in the next life in the round of deaths and rebirths. Or even, as the Upanisads suggested, in the ultimate avoidance of rebirth itself—a theme adopted by much Indian philosophy thereafter.

As in Western metaphysical speculations about the nature of the cosmos and man's place within it, the Indian thinkers made central and vital use of the concept of a cause—*karana* in Sanskrit—and progressively developed a sophisticated understanding of this concept.

VEDAS AND UPANISADS

The earliest Vedic answers to the question of cosmological evolution suggested a god or gods, variously named and described, as creating and ruling over the human world. Such views invoked probably the most obscure and difficult application of the concept of causation—that of creation—but had at least the merit of putting men and gods in a continuing relationship. Men could worship their gods, and indeed could wield a degree of control, through religious ceremonies that aimed to elicit benefits from them.

The Upanisads took a more subtle turn, concentrating on a deeper understanding of the nature of man himself. The "inner self," the *atman*, was distinguished from its physical embodiment and was taken to proceed through a series of rebirths according to a causal law of *karma*—whereby moral merit or demerit dictated the nature of the next rebirth. Ultimately it would hopefully achieve release from rebirths and acquire its final state of bliss (*moksa*).

The period from the fourth to the second century BCE was one of quite subtle developments, with new and deeper ideas of the causal operation of the law of *karma*, of the nature of human existence, and of the nature of and route to the soteriological end for man. The Hindu *Bhagavad Gītā* was composed—a part of the great epic the *Mahabharata* (the actual period of composition is still much disputed)—and two nonorthodox systems of ideas were introduced: Jainism and Buddhism. Interestingly, both Jainism and Buddhism have no place for deities in their systems, human existence and progression to the ultimate state of release from rebirth being said to depend on the efforts of the individual. We will look at these three systems, and at just some of the later developments through the classical period of Indian philosophy.

BHAGAVAD GĪTĀ

The *Bhagavad Gītā* (Song of the Lord) takes the form of a dialogue between the warrior-prince (*ksatriya*) Arjuna and Lord Krishna, who is a human manifestation (*avatara*) of the god Vishnu. Arjuna hesitates to lead his army into battle against his cousins who have usurped control of the state, suffering a confusion about which duty he should follow: fight to rectify the wrong they have done to society or refrain from fighting to protect his family and caste. Krishna argues that Arjuna should fight. The world is in a final epoch of the cycle of evolution and corruption, a process of dissolution that requires his coming to advise mankind on correct behavior. As Vishnu, he has designed the nature of human society with its hierarchy of castes and their associated socioreligious duties. By the law of *karma*, the *ātman* of each individual goes through the process of birth-death-rebirth (*sāmsara*), gaining merit according to good deeds and demerit according to bad. *Karma* in this context therefore has moral, religious, and soteriological dimensions. *Moksa*, final release, is achieved through individual effort. And the central theme of the *Bhagavad Gītā* is the doctrine of *karma-yoga*, a route to salvation that involves acting according to established socioreligious duties, for the sake of maintaining the social fabric and for pleasing god.

Quite apart from the question whether *karma-yoga* actually resolves a conflict of duties such as Arjuna's, there is a further question: whether the *Bhagavad Gītā* really leaves any room for freedom of action for Arjuna, or indeed mankind in general. The text ascribes such enormous powers to Vishnu that individual human effort seems futile. Nature—the world in which the *atman* becomes embodied—is a creation of Vishnu. It involves the interplay between three "strands" (*gunas*), called *sattva*, *rajas*, and *tamas*—which can be translated as "goodness," "passion," and "inertia," respectively. All nature is but the playing out of the interaction between these *gunas* in a mechanistic, deterministic way. The balance of the *gunas* in a particular individual also dictates his character and hence his actions. The *atman* cannot affect the *gunas*, and there seems no chance of choosing to follow the path of *karma-yoga*, much less any other activities.

The *Bhagavad Gītā* adds further worries for its *karma-yoga* theme, for Vishnu has foreknowledge of all that will happen, and retains a tight control over all actions—overt and psychological—of all human beings. "The Lord abides in the hearts of all beings, O Arjuna, causing them to turn round by His power as if they were mounted on a machine," declares Krishna in the final chapter. So the *Bhagavad Gītā* is a brave but flawed attempt to teach an ethics of engagement in traditional socioreligious duties. The law of *karma* was supposed to allow human beings to strive towards *moksa*, the law itself being a creation of Vishnu to ensure a just outcome for our efforts. The text's failure to sustain this account perhaps goes a long way toward explaining why a good deal of later philosophical speculation (if not common religious practices), including much of so-called orthodox or Hindu philosophy, found no room for a deity as originating and controlling human existence.

JAINISM

Jainism was founded in the sixth century BCE by Vardhamana—who became known as Mahavira (Great spiritual hero)—and is named after the Sanskrit word for *conqueror* (*jina*). (Though Vardhamana left no texts, a particularly important text was composed by Umasvati some nine centuries later: *Tattvarthadhigama Sutra*, or *Discourse on the Nature of Things.*) It is system that supposedly commends itself to reason. Rejecting the authority of the Vedas, it nevertheless keeps the idea of a spiritual substance, a *jiva*. Entrapment in the round of births and deaths is seen as a consequence of fine polluting karmic dust that restricts the all-knowing ability of the *jiva*. The route to salvation involves the elimination of this pollution, to achieve the state of perfect knowledge (*kevala*). In contrast to the complex interpretation of the workings of the law of *karma* in the orthodox tradition, the Jain account might appear a straightforward theory of physical causation. Yet the process of karmic improvement nevertheless has a serious moral dimension, for it involves a commitment to five "vows of restraint": nonviolence (*ahimsa*), truthfulness (*satya*), no theft (*asteya*), sexual continence (*brahmacharya*) and nonattachment to worldly pleasures (*apigraha*). By the individual's own efforts, therefore, the desired end of perfect knowledge is achieved.

BUDDHISM

Buddhism was founded, also in the sixth century BCE, by Siddartha Gautama, who became known as the Buddha (the Enlightened One) and spent many years proclaiming his insights into the predicament of the cycle of births and deaths and the route to release into *nirvana*. He left no writings of his own, but his teachings are recorded in the collection known as the *Sutta Pitaka* of the Pali work the *Tripitaka* (Three baskets of tradition). The Buddha taught a system of ideas that was in stark contrast to the earlier orthodox Vedic tradition, rejecting any reliance on those texts, on the priestly caste (the Brahmins), and on the orthodox depiction of salvation. Nothing brings out this contrast more than claim that reality has these three marks: impermanence (*anitya*), no-soul (*anatman*) and suffering (*duhkha*). A standard depiction of reality (*brahman*) by the Hindu tradition is quite the opposite: being as a permanent (*sat*), consciousness (*cit*) and bliss (*ananda*).

The Buddha's system is supposedly based upon observation, both of the world outside him and of the inner workings of his mental world. Crucially, he could not observe an *atman*. Instead, he reports as his fundamental discovery that all the ingredients observed obey a general principle of "dependent origination" (*pratityasamutpada*). Whatever comes into existence is the causal consequence of previous existents. Causal generation has a complex form where a number of such previous existents produce together the new existent. And each and every existent is momentary. Applying this general principle to the specific case of a sentient being, he classified all its momentary causal ingredients into five groups (*skandhas*). These can be rendered as these (following their later interpretation in the work *Milindapanha*, or Questions of King Milinda): thoughts (*vijnana*), feelings (*vedana*), volitions (*samskara*), perceptions (*samjna*) and bodily ingredients (*rupa*). And, most crucially, there being a complex interplay between the ingredients both within and across the groups, he identifies as the *fundamental* causal factor driving them all—through this life and through into rebirths—the thought "I am a permanent entity."

This cognitive error, involved as it is in the Hindu idea of the *ātman*, is the root cause of all grasping—for fame, for power, and for all other worldly goods—and therefore the root cause of suffering and rebirths. Only the correction of this error can lead to salvation. Moreover, this correction leads to a general change in motivations for action, whereby selfish desires are replaced by altruistic ones such as compassion, and the adoption of such altruistic desires in its turn helps to achieve the cognitive correction.

Within this new account of the human predicament is clearly embedded a sophisticated theory of causation. Dependent origination, the momentariness of the ingredients of causal chains, and the necessity linking the steps in causal development, together offer an impressive analysis of *karana*. Later Buddhist thinkers further sophisticated these ideas and indeed developed the theme that each new causal product is *genuinely* new, for the effect is not already existent in the cause. Such is the doctrine of *asatkaryavada*, the nonexistence of the effect in the cause.

SANKHYA

Sankhya is an orthodox school that, in common with Jainism and Buddhism, finds no room for a deity. The earliest authoritative text of the school is the *Sankhyakarika* (Verses on discrimination) of Isvarakrishna. Though this was probably composed in the fifth century CE, it is thought that the system of ideas can be traced back into the Vedic period.

There are, in this system, two kinds of substance: the experiencer and the experienced. The former (comparable to the *atman* of the Upanisads) is *purusa*, an inactive "silent witness" of the latter, *prakrati* or nature. *Purusas* are eternal and numerous, whereas *prakrati* is eternal and singular. The account of *prakrati* in Isvarakrishna's text is a complex story about its evolution out of an original state of equipose between the *gunas.*

Sattva is the strand of nature that is productive of consciousness or intelligence; *rajas* is the strand productive of activity; *tamas* the strand productive of resistance. The original state of equipose is *pradhana*, meaning "the inferred one" because its existence is claimed on the basis of inference by analogy from experience. The first evolute is *Mahat* (the Great One) or *buddhi* (the subtle material that forms the basis of consciousness). Next comes *ahamkara* (the basis of individuation or self-sense), and then evolution takes two directions where either *sattva* or *tamas* predominates. Through the *sattva* route evolve *manas* (mind, of perhaps better brain), the five organs of perception, and the five organs of action. Through the *tamas* route evolve the five subtle elements (essences of sound, touch, taste, smell, and sight), and the five gross elements (ether, air, light, water, and earth) that are the constituents of all gross matter.

At first sight the process seems to be a cosmic evolution, with at least some roots in the early Vedic tradition. Yet it clearly is also designed to explain the nature of *sāmsara* and *moksa* for individual *purusas.* But why does nature evolve in this way? There is no deity to start it and plan its process. A *purusa* becomes entrapped in *samsara* by becoming engrossed in the play of nature before it, and, losing its awareness of its distinction from *prakrati*, it conceives itself as an embodied self, as an actor within the natural world. To achieve *moksa* it needs to regain its awareness of its distinct status as the pure inactive witness of *prakrati.* The Sankhyans indeed identify the following two purposes behind the evolution of *prakrati*: it evolves to provide experience for *puruṣas* yet at the same time to provide the possibility of this ultimate release from *sāmsara.*

SANKARA'S CRITIQUE

Sankara, the eighth-century Hindu philosopher, criticizes the Sankhyan system's explanation of the evolution of *prakrati* as follows: neither *prakrati* nor *puruṣas* can provide the efficient cause (*nimitta karana*) of this evolution, for *prakrati* is insentient—it lacks *cit*, or intelligence—and *purusas* are inactive. Such evolution cannot be spontaneous, for no spontaneous activity is evident in experience. However, the Sānkhyans believe they can find such cases; but the important issue between them and Sankara seems to be more fundamental. The Sānkhyans are working with the idea of the purpose of evolution, as opposed to causation. The evolution of *prakrati* is a natural development that serves the purposes of *puruṣas*, and no intelligent designer is required contrary to Sankara's insistence. We might well compare the Sānkhyan approach to that of Aristotelian teleological explanation.

Sankara's criticism comes in his major text, the *Brahma-sutra-bhasya* (Commentary on the verses concerning reality). He is a major figure in the Vedanta school, which takes its inspiration from the ancient Upanishads. Unlike the Sankhyans, he is unwilling to engage in speculative reasoning beyond the words of those texts and claims to be merely restating their essential message. Other figures in the Vedanta tradition also wrote commentaries on the *Brahma sutra*, and we can judge Sankara's philosophical inventiveness from the quite striking differences in the contents of those commentaries.

Both Sankara and the Sānkhyans adopt a view of causation whereby the effect preexists in the material cause (*upadana karana*)—called *satkaryavada.* They differ, however, in the detail. For the Sankhyans the evolution of *prakrati* is a *real* process of natural unfolding out of the potentialities of the *gunas*—a position known as *parinamavada.* Sankara, however, finds difficulties with the notion of potentiality and argues instead for the more extreme position of the identity of the effect with the cause—there is only a *merely apparent* transformation from cause to effect. Applying this claim—known as *vivartavada*—to the case of the emergence of the experienced world out of the one real thing, *Brahman*, which is undifferentiated consciousness, the implication is that the experienced world is but an illusory appearance of *Brahman.* The route to *moksa* is the realisation of this difficult truth.

NYĀYA

Nyaya is another orthodox school, beginning with the third-century BCE text by Gautama, the *Nyāya Sutras* (Verses on argument). Important commentaries were written by Vatsyayana and Uddyotakara in about the third and sixth centuries CE, respectively, and substantial developments continued with the Navya-nyāya (or "new Nyāya") thinkers of the fourteenth to sixteenth centuries. Since argument or reasoning is often concerned with causal relations in the observed world, the Nyāya philosophers gave considerable attention to an analysis of such relations.

Causation, on their understanding, is the real production of new things out of the parts of matter (ultimately atoms). This is another version of *asatkaryavada*, for the effect is a *new* existent. From threads we can make a cloth, and from clay we can make a pot: The cloth and the pot are new products of the causal process. They do, however, stand in a special relationship to the threads and clay, a relationship called *samavaya* (inherence). The cloth, for example, is said to inhere in the threads as *one in many*, one thing in many things; just as much as the threads are parts of the cloth as *many in one*. The idea of a material cause (*upadanakarana*) is given this new interpretation by this school—the matter or parts out of which something is made is called the "inherent cause"(*samvayikarana*).

Causation also involves an efficient cause (*nimittakarana*) or causes, such as the work of the weaver and the motions of the loom. Any case of causal production is likely to involve a multitude of factors—actions or material ingredients and all their individual qualities—and the Nyāya philosophers duly classify such factors further in terms of their efficacious or peripheral role in the process. A cause, in the final analysis, is the sum of the causal factors that are the invariant and unconditional antecedent of the effect.

The Nyāya account was criticized by both Buddhists and Sankara. For the Buddhists it is in stark contrast to the aggregate (*skandha*) theory, according to which the "new" product is merely the sum of the parts, and they try to fault the special relation of inherence that the Nyāya theory makes central to its account. Sankara, too, finds this relation logically flawed, since it leads to an infinite regress. If the parts and the new object are related by this *samavaya* relation, what relates *it* to the parts and the object? It seems it would have to be another case of *samavaya*, and then the same question arises again—without end.

See also Atomic Theory in Indian Philosophy; Brahman; God in Indian Philosophy; Negation in Indian Philosophy.

Bibliography

Gambhirananda, S., trans. *Brahma-sutra-bhasya of Sri Sankaracarya*. 2nd ed. Calcutta: Advaita Ashrama, 1972.

Hiriyanna, M. *Outlines of Indian Philosophy*. London: George Allen & Unwin, 1932. An established substantial introduction to Indian philosophy.

Jaini, J. L., trans. *Umasvati's Tattvarthadigamasutra*. Arrah, India: The Central Jaina Punlishing House, 1920.

Jha, G. *Nyayasutras of Gautama*. Poona: Oriental Book Agency, 1939.

O'Flaherty, W. D., ed. *The Rig Veda*. Harmondsworth: Penguin Books, 1981.

Radhakrishnan, S., ed. *The Principal Upanisads*. Oxford and New York: Oxford University Press, 1966.

Radhakrishnan, S., and C. A. Moore, eds. *A Sourcebook in Indian Philosophy*. Princeton, NJ: Princeton University Press, 1957. A useful resource containing extracts and sometimes complete translations (including the *Bhagavad Gītā*) of primary source materials.

Sastri, S. S. S., trans. *The Sankhyakarika of Isvara Krishna*. Madras: University of Madras, 1948

Warren, H. C., ed. *Buddhism in Translations*. Cambridge, MA: Harvard University Press, 1915.

Brian Carr (2005)

CAUSATION IN ISLAMIC PHILOSOPHY

According to the Qur'anic position, God is the voluntary creator of the universe. In causal theory, one finds an apparently necessary connection between cause and effect. Islamic philosophy experiences a profound tension between these two ideas—the Qur'anic legacy of God's will and the idea of independent causes leading to effects. From this perspective, one may observe four stages in the concept of causation in Islamic philosophy.

THE FIRST STAGE

The first stage, beginning with the rise of Islam in the seventh century and extending well into the tenth, is dominated by the Qur'anic understanding of cosmos, which assigns God as the fundamental cause of the universe and of the events taking place within it. A cause is thus conceived as a "means" or "way" conditioned or provided by God as a blessing to achieve something, as indicated in the following verses: "Do they not look at the camels how they are created? And at the sky how it is raised? And at the mountains how they are fixed firm? And at the earth how it is spread out?" (Qur'an 88:17–20); "it is God who causes the seed and the date-stone to split and sprout. He brings forth the living from the dead, and brings forth the dead from the living …" (Qur'an 6:95–104; also 67:3–4; 24:39; 2:118). Early philosophers of the Kalām Theology School attempted to express this Qur'anic understanding by their metaphysics of atoms and accidents. They argue that because each atom is created and annihilated at every instance, no being can subsist by itself and have an effect on another body except through the creation of an omnipotent God. In this scheme, causation is conceived as a creation at every instance, including human actions. Abū'l-Ḥasan ʿAlī ibn Ismaʿīl al-Ashʿarī (d. 935) argued that "God wills everything which can be willed" and that every instance of causation is to be conceived within the domain of this all-embracing divine will (1953, p. 33).

THE SECOND STAGE

In the second stage the Muslim Neoplatonic Aristotelians establish a philosophical theory claiming the necessary connection of cause and effect. Abū Yūsuf Ya'qūb ibn Isḥāq al-Kindī (c. 801–866), Abu Naṣr Muḥammad al-Fārābī (870–950), and Abū 'Alī al-Ḥusayn ibn Sīnā (980–1037) are the proponents of this school. Al-Kindī and al-Fārābī thus establish an emanationist system of universe that follows from God necessarily. This world system is decidedly necessitarian, neatly elaborated by Ibn Sīnā in a causally deterministic way. In his scheme, the universe is conceived as a hierarchical order of beings, which offers a cosmic pattern for causation in general and a model for all causal interactions. Each being is connected to the next in a necessarily ordered chain of causation beginning with God through the heavenly spheres down to the remote spheres of dark and primitive matter. The philosophers of the Kalām School vehemently objected to this theory claiming that, if accepted, the Qur'anic understanding of God's absolute will and power becomes vacuous.

THE THIRD STAGE

Three prominent philosophers represent the third stage: Abū Ḥāmid Muḥammad al-Ghazālī (d. 1111), Abū'l-Walīd Muḥammad ibn Rushd, known as Averroes (d. 1198), and Ṣadr al-Dīn Muḥammad ibn Ibrāhīm al-Shirāzī, known as Mullā Ṣadrā, or Ṣadrā (d. 1641). Against the philosophers of the Neoplatonic Aristotelian School, al-Ghazālī argues along Humean lines that people observe in existence not a necessity but two things that are contiguous. The connection, therefore, between a cause and its effect is due to the prior decree of God, who creates them side by side. What does not have a free will cannot enter into a temporal relation. When a piece of cotton burns, it is not the fire that is burning, for fire is inanimate and in itself has no action. What proof can be given that the fire is the agent? The only proof is that people observe an act of burning, not any other mediating factor. Therefore, existing contiguously with a thing does not prove causation between two things. Ghazali denies skepticism by arguing that the repeated occurrence of events fixes unshakably in our minds the belief in their occurrence according to past habit.

Ibn Rushd objected to this theory, arguing that in denying the necessity of a causal link, al-Ghazālī's motive was to defend the exclusive prerogative of God's sovereignty and efficient causal agency in all events. But the denial of this connection involves the rejection of an agent in an act, and hence, the logical ground for the idea of God as an efficient cause is destroyed. Moreover, logic implies the existence of causes and effects, and knowledge of these effects can only be obtained through knowledge of their causes. Hence, denial of causes implies the denial of knowledge, which, in turn, implies that nothing can be really known.

Mullā Ṣadrā developed an existential theory of causation based on the primacy of existence. An abstract notion of existence arises in the mind, but that notion cannot yield true reality. For, in each case, existence is a unique individual in an ongoing process of renewal. Essences arise in the mind as a result of this process when existence becomes further diversified into modes. It is existence that moves within this process; both the cause and the caused are existence; the essence is caused to arise in the mind in connection to particular beings. Causation must be considered within that existential process in which the problem of necessary connection does not arise. In each instance of causality there is a temporal emergence in which the temporal emergent, that is, the cause, is not the true cause but only a preparatory condition for it. The true cause in such an emergence is, therefore, the eternal creative act of God. In that case, this process is continuous, not discrete, involving change in the substance of everything that moves within the process.

THE FOURTH STAGE

In the fourth stage one finds primarily the idea of causal explanation on the basis of the Qur'anic notion that God acts regularly and that there is no change in this regular course of action, called *sunnat Allah*. No thinker in this stage paid more attention to the problem of causation than the twentieth century thinker, Bediüzzaman Said Nursi of Turkey (d. 1960). Nursi uses two arguments to defend al-Ghazālī's theory of causation. The first is the argument from theodicy that establishes that "might and majesty require causes to be veiling occasions of God's omnipotence for the human mind" (Nursi 1996, p. 1278). God creates things for certain good ends. If causes are not seen as veils for God's acts, the human mind will directly infer God in all natural phenomena and attribute the seemingly evil results of these actions to him. This inference harms God's might and glory. Similarly, we may not be able to see good results immediately and thus blame God for evil. The second argument claims that "God's uniqueness and glory require causes to withdraw their interference from the actual efficacy" (Nursi 1996, p. 1278). The nature of an effect exhibits a perfection that is the result of a rational planning and omnipotence. These qualities are not inherent in the causes producing their effect; hence, the true cause is outside the event, deduced by the mind and experienced by the awakened heart. There is thus only one true cause, God, who assures people of the causal nexus through the first argument by theodicy.

See also al-Fārābī; al-Ghazālī, Muhammad; al-Kindī, Abū-Yūsuf Ya'qūb ibn Isḥāq; Aristotelianism; Averroes; Avicenna; Causation: Metaphysical Issues; Islamic Philosophy; Mullā Ṣadrā; Neoplatonism.

Bibliography

al-Ash'arī, Abū'l-Ḥasan 'Alī ibn Isma'īl. *Al-Ibanah 'an Usul al-Diyanah: The Elucidation of Islam's Foundation.* Translated with an introduction and notes by Walter Klein. New Haven, CT: American Oriental Society, 1940. Reprint, New York: Kraus Reprint Corporation, 1967.

al-Ash'arī, Abū'l-Ḥasan 'Alī ibn Isma'īl. *Kitab al-Luma'*. In *The Theology of Al-Ash'ari.* Translated by Richard J. Beyrouth: Imprimerie Catholique, 1953.

Colish, M. L. "Avicenna's Theory of Efficient Causation and its Influence on St. Thomas Aquinas." *Tommaso d'Aquino nel suo Settimo Centenario* 1 (1975): 296–306.

Druart, T-A. "Al-Fārābī's Causation of the Heavenly Bodies." *Islamic Philosophy and Mysticism*, edited by Parviz Morewedge. Delmar, NY: Caravan, 1981.

Fakhri, Majid. *Islamic Occasionalism and its Ctitique by Averroes and Aquinas.* London: George Allen & Unwin Ltd., 1958.

Ivry, A. L. "Averroes on Causation." In *Studies in Jewish Religious and Intellectual History, Presented to Alexander Altmann*, edited by Siegfried Stein and Raphael Loewe. Tuscaloosa: University of Alabama Press, 1979.

Goodman, Lenn Evan. "Did al-Ghazālī Deny Causality?" *Studia Islamica* 47 (1978): 83–120.

Gyekye, K. "Al-Ghazālī on Causation," *Second Order* 2 (1973): 31–39.

Kogan, Barry S. *Averroes and the Metaphysics of Causation.* Albany: State University of New York Press, 1985.

Nursi, Bediüzzaman Said. *Mesnevi-i Nuriye.* Printed in the *Risale-i Nur Külliyati.* 2 vols. Includes the complete works of Nursi. Istanbul: Nesil Publications, 1996.

Shanab, R. E. A. "Ghazālī and Aquinas on Causation." *Monist* 58 (1974): 140–150.

Alparslan Açikgenç (2005)

CAVELL, STANLEY

(1926–)

Stanley Cavell, American philosopher and long-time professor of philosophy at Harvard University, has written on epistemology, philosophy of language, moral philosophy, and aesthetics; on Shakespeare and Romanticism and Samuel Beckett; on modernism in the arts, classic Hollywood film comedies and melodramas of the 1930s and 1940s, and opera; on his most direct influences, J. L. Austin and Ludwig Wittgenstein, especially with reference to their attempts to draw words back to their everyday homes; on Friedrich Nietzsche and Martin Heidegger, who articulate our perhaps inevitable ambivalence toward what the latter calls "average everydayness"; on Kant, who in limiting knowledge to make room for faith makes the conditions and boundaries of human understanding and the recognition of our finitude dominant themes for subsequent thought; and also on the Kantian inheritance in the transcendentalism of Thoreau and Emerson, who conceptualize these issues in terms of lost contact with things themselves and the possibility of an intimacy regained that allows for acceptance of the world's independence from us. Cavell's circle of interests has its unity: his overarching concern is with philosophy's aspirations to self-knowledge and with obstacles the intellect erects to self-knowledge, particularly in the form of distortions of self-expression and loss of voice. Cavell links these threats to skepticism, conceived not just as a general doubt about the extent of our cognitive capacities, but as an expression of a tragic condition of withdrawal haunting the present age. Later, he finds acknowledgment of and response to this condition in images of recovery articulated in the dimension of the moral life he calls "Emersonian perfectionism."

Several essays in *Must We Mean What We Say* (1969) defend the salience of philosophical appeals to ordinary language. In doing so, they prepare for the comprehensive diagnosis of skepticism and the impulses behind it offered in Cavell's central work, *The Claim of Reason: Wittgenstein, Skepticism, Morality, and Tragedy* (1979). Because appeals to "what we say when" draw on knowledge of native tongues, they do not directly refute the skeptic by convicting him of linguistic mistakes. The skeptic, after all, remains a master of language. On the other hand, because skeptical procedures do not fully fit ordinary ways of raising and responding to doubts about particular claims, Cavell interprets skepticism's negative conclusions about the limits of human knowledge not as failures of certainty, but as intellectualized disappointment with the sources of our capacities for making sense of the world.

Accordingly, part one of *The Claim of Reason* offers a reading of the later Wittgenstein's notion of criterion, on which criteria constitute not certainty, but the relevance and applicability of our concepts to worldly circumstances. On this view, our capacity to speak intelligibly is based on nothing deeper (nor less deep) than our agreement in judgment, which agreement is not secured prior to particular judgments. Criteria are thus subject to repudiation, as our agreements may seem to run thin. The skeptic errs in implying that criteria should be grounded in something deeper, lest our whole conception of things be deemed irredeemably subjective. But because the skeptic reminds us of the repudiability of criteria, the skeptic's progress (or lack thereof) conveys an important moral: our sense of things is not a cognitive accomplishment.

Part two elaborates the external world skeptic's failure to live up to his own self-conception as a perfect knower. This skeptic faces a dilemma: either he fails to specify concrete claims about the external world for scrutiny, or his doubts about the claims he does single out do not generalize to all beliefs about external objects. Here Cavell discerns a truth behind the external world skeptic's efforts—that our relation to the external world as a whole is not a matter of knowledge about an, as it were, all-encompassing object, but rather one of acceptance. While such a conclusion may seem to exacerbate the skeptic's sense that we are cut off from the world, Cavell asks whether this discomfort, expressive of disappointment with ordinary modes of inquiry, criteria—even our manner of involvement with things—is self-imposed.

Part three of *The Claim of Reason* explores the nature of practical reasoning and the limits of both morality and traditional moral theorizing. Cavell sets himself against the "moralization of morality": the assumption that if morality is genuinely rational, it must rest on rules grounding its verdicts and rendering it competent to assess the value of every action. Much as the skeptic prescinds from actual practices of evaluating epistemic claims, so the moralist refuses the concept of morality by failing to locate its role in everyday life.

Part four, exploring symmetries and asymmetries between external world and other minds skepticism, argues that in the case of other minds, acknowledgment of others—not certainty about their inner lives—is in question. The tragic fate of the present age is that for the most part, we live our skepticism, tending, as a matter of historical fact, to shirk our responsibilities in knowing others and in making ourselves known to them. At stake is the voice—our expressiveness, and the barriers we erect to it.

Cavell's later writings explore his sense that responding to our tragically skeptical state, working through the issue of the voice, is a crucial task of modernity. Cavell reads romanticism (exemplified in Wordsworth and Coleridge as well as Emerson and Thoreau, thematized most explicitly in *In Quest of the Ordinary: Lines of Skepticism and Romanticism* [1998]) as registering both the success of and dissatisfaction with Kant's settlement with skepticism. Acknowledging that the quest for knowledge, at least as conceived by skepticism, blocks our access to the things themselves, romanticism seeks other routes to their recuperation. These lie in the particulars of our ability to make sense of them, despite the lack of philosophical grounding for our ways of doing so. At the same time, in reading the defining texts of moral perfectionism (especially in *Conditions Handsome and Unhandsome: The Constitution of Emersonian Perfectionism* [1990] and *Cities of Words: Pedagogical Letters on a Register of the Moral Life* [2004]), Cavell finds in this openness the potential for the creation or discovery of a self capable of articulating its own identity, its own ideals and possibilities, again without need of a foundation from outside. In large part, recovery from the threat of skepticism lies in everyday uses of words, not because they express a set of commonly-held beliefs, but insofar as they manifest a responsiveness to ourselves and the world that enables us to find our conditions intelligible.

Bibliography

WORKS BY CAVELL

Must We Mean What We Say. New York: Scribners, 1969.

The World Viewed: Reflections on the Ontology of Film. New York: Viking, 1971.

The Senses of Walden. New York: Viking, 1972.

The Claim of Reason: Wittgenstein, Skepticism, Morality and Tragedy. Oxford: Oxford University Press, 1979.

Pursuits of Happiness: The Hollywood Comedy of Remarriage. Cambridge, MA: Harvard University Press, 1981.

Themes Out of School: Effects and Causes. San Francisco: North Point Press, 1984.

Disowning Knowledge: In Six Plays of Shakespeare. Cambridge, U.K.: Cambridge University Press, 1987.

In Quest of the Ordinary: Lines of Skepticism and Romanticism. Chicago: University of Chicago Press, 1988.

This New Yet Unapproachable America: Lectures after Emerson after Wittgenstein. Chicago: University of Chicago Press, 1988.

Conditions Handsome and Unhandsome: The Constitution of Emersonian Perfectionism. Chicago: University of Chicago Press, 1990.

A Pitch of Philosophy: Autobiographical Exercises. Cambridge, MA: Harvard University Press, 1994.

Philosophical Passages: Wittgenstein, Emerson, Austin, Derrida. Oxford: Basil Blackwell, 1995.

Contesting Tears: The Melodrama of the Unknown Woman. Chicago: University of Chicago Press, 1996.

Emerson's Transcendental Etudes. Stanford, CA: Stanford University Press, 2003.

Cities of Words: Pedagogical Letters on a Register of the Moral Life. Cambridge, MA: Harvard University Press, 2004.

SELECTED SECONDARY WORKS

Eldridge, Richard, ed. *Stanley Cavell.* Cambridge, U.K.: Cambridge University Press, 2003.

Goodman, Russell, ed. *Contending with Stanley Cavell.* Oxford: Oxford University Press, 2004.

Gould, Timothy. *Hearing Things: Voice and Method in the Writings of Stanley Cavell.* Chicago: University of Chicago Press, 1998.

Mulhall, Stephen. *Stanley Cavell: Philosophy's Recounting of the Ordinary.* Oxford: Clarendon Press, 1994.

Edward Minar (2005)

CAVENDISH, MARGARET

(1623?–1673)

Margaret Cavendish was born into the Lucasses, a family of English gentry. She does not seem to have had an education that was in any way remarkable for a young woman of her time. Indeed, she reports that while she had the usual tutors, her mother "cared not so much for our dancing and fidling, singing and prating of several languages" (Cavendish 1667), deeming honesty and civility more important. One consequence is that Cavendish was never able to speak or read any language but her native English. In 1643, when she was about twenty, she became a maid of honor to Charles I's wife, Queen Henrietta Maria, and the next year she followed the queen into exile in Paris.

While at the court in exile, she met and subsequently married William Cavendish, who eventually became the Duke of Newcastle and who was a widower some twenty years her senior. The marriage seems to have been a happy one, and indeed, it is Margaret, a second and childless wife, who lies buried next to William in Westminster Abbey. Margaret Cavendish found a husband who supported her ably in her intellectual endeavors. In marrying into the Cavendish family, she became a member of a family that had been in the forefront of the intellectual life of the time. Newcastle's cousins, the Devonshires, were patrons of Thomas Hobbes, and Newcastle and his brother, Sir Charles Cavendish, had as part of their circle a number of leading thinkers, including Marin Mersenne, Pierre Gassendi, and René Descartes. It is not clear to what extent this wider circle was available to Cavendish, but both her husband and her brother-in-law were prepared to encourage and to instruct her as she developed her intellectual interests. Cavendish published copiously, in a wide variety of genres, throughout her life, both while she and her husband lived in exile in Holland and after they returned to England in 1660, after the restoration of Charles II. The Newcastles lived on their return at the family estate, Welbeck, in Nottinghamshire, but made visits to London. During one of these visits, Cavendish made a ceremonial visit to the Royal Society, unusual in that they did not otherwise admit women to its meetings. Cavendish died in 1673, at the relatively young age of fifty, some three years before her husband.

Cavendish published over a dozen works, including poetry, plays, epistolary treatises, a life of her husband and a shorter one of herself, a novel, and some six works in natural philosophy. Cavendish reworked her ideas about natural philosophy throughout her life, improving them as she enlarged her reading and altered her vocabulary and her grasp on the issues about which she was writing. Among her works in natural philosophy, probably the best and most interesting are her last, *Grounds of Natural Philosophy* (1668/1996), where she lays out her material in its most organized form, and two slightly earlier works, *Philosophical Letters* (1664/1994) and *Observations upon Experimental Philosophy* (1666/2001). These last two are especially interesting because, in them, Cavendish situates her own views against a commentary on several leading thinkers of her day.

From *Grounds of Natural Philosophy* one learns the basic premises of Cavendish's approach to natural philosophy. She tells the reader there can be no substance but body, which exists in degrees of purity. While the less pure parts of matter are inert, the purer parts are self-moving and are endowed with self-knowledge. These come in two sorts, again distinguishable by their degree of purity: a sensitive part, which is living, and a rational part, which understands. Natural phenomena are to be explained in terms of the doings of matter, under the guidance of reason and as carried out by sense. Thus, Cavendish's account of nature is one of a number of accounts that try to explain natural phenomena in terms of the motions that lead to the division and composition of otherwise undifferentiated matter. Cavendish has absorbed and is working within one of the dominant explanatory paradigms of her day.

As *Philosophical Letters* and *Observations upon Experimental Philosophy*make clear, Cavendish developed her own version of this paradigm. *Philosophical Letters* consists of a series of letters to a fictional female correspondent discussing passages of Hobbes, Descartes, Henry More, and Francis Mercury van Helmont, with a final, less focused part answering a number of different questions and mentioning a number of different authors, including Galileo Galilei, Walter Charleton, and Robert Boyle. Unlike Hobbes and Descartes, Cavendish rejects the idea that there can be purely mechanical explanations for such human functions as sensation, insisting on the self-moving, knowledgeable nature of sensation, which she says "patterns out" or imitates objects sensed. She rejects a mechanical or "transfer" theory of motion as unintelligible and provides an alternative, under which all motion is self-generated action on the basis of self-knowledge, rather than a passive reaction to impact. Thus, while a materialist, Cavendish is not a mechanist, but a vitalist. She energetically distinguishes herself, however, from other contemporary vitalists, like More, on the grounds that More's immaterial plastic spirit of nature, as immaterial, is impotent to move matter. Cavendish's vitalism is materialist and not dualist. Cavendish's position can be seen as developing in conversation with a number of related theorists, with whom she shares a number of views, while carving out her own position.

In *Observations upon Experimental Philosophy* Cavendish takes on the experimenters of the Royal Society, in particular Robert Hooke. She criticizes Hooke for supposing that microscopes provide a unique view into the heart of things, on the grounds that adding a dubious instrument to a dubious sense organ does not improve matters. Her overall approach is to urge the claims of reason to give understanding over the deliverances of the senses. Although arguing for the special virtues of reason, Cavendish does not suppose that reason is a source of certainty in natural philosophy. Instead, her approach is probabilistic. Toward the end of *Philosophical Letters* she writes that

> the undoubted truth in Natural Philosophy is, in my opinion, like the Philosophers Stone in Chymistry, which has been sought by many learned and ingenuous Persons and which will be sought as long as the Art of Chymistry doth last; but although they cannot find the Philosophers Stone, yet by the help of this Art they have found out many rare things, both for use and knowledg. (1664/1994, p. 508)

While one cannot attain undoubted truth, to refuse to be guided by it would be like refusing to take medicine on the grounds that one will die eventually.

See also Boyle, Robert; Descartes, René; Galileo Galilei; Gassendi, Pierre; Hobbes, Thomas; Materialism; Mersenne, Marin; More, Henry; Vitalism; Women in the History of Philosophy.

Bibliography

WORKS BY CAVENDISH

Philosophical Fancies. London: N.p., 1653

Philosophical and Physical Opinions. London: Printed for J. Martin and J. Allestrye, 1655.

"Philosophical Letters: or, Modest Reflections upon some Opinions in Natural Philosophy" (1664). In *Women Philosophers of the Early Modern Period*, edited by Margaret Atherton. Indianapolis, IN: Hackett, 1994.

Observations upon Experimental Philosophy (1666). Edited by Eileen O'Neill. New York: Cambridge University Press, 2001.

A True Relation of My Birth, Breeding and Life, as printed in *The Life of William Cavendish, Duke of Newcastle.* London: 1667, 157–158.

Grounds of Natural Philosophy (1668). Introduction by Colette V. Michael. West Cornwall, CT: Locust Hill Press, 1996.

"The Blazing World." In *The Description of a New World, called the Blazing World and Other Writings*, edited by Kate Lilley. New York: New York University Press, 1992.

Political Writings. Edited by Susan James. New York: Cambridge University Press, 2003.

WORKS ABOUT CAVENDISH

Bowerbank, Sylvia, and Sara Mendelson, eds. *Paper Bodies: A Margaret Cavendish Reader.* Orchard Park, NY: Broadview Press, 2000.

Broad, Jacqueline. "Margaret Cavendish." In *Women Philosophers of the Seventeenth Century*, 35–64. New York: Cambridge University Press, 2002.

Hutton, Sarah. "Anne Conway, Margaret Cavendish, and Seventeenth-Century Scientific Thought." In *Women, Science, and Medicine, 1500–1700: Mothers and Sisters of the Royal Society*, edited by Lynette Hunter and Sarah Hutton, 218–234. Stroud, U.K.: Sutton Publishing, 1997.

Hutton, Sarah. "In Dialogue with Thomas Hobbes: Margaret Cavendish's Natural Philosophy." *Women's Writing* 4 (3) (1997): 421–432.

Hutton, Sarah. "Margaret Cavendish and Henry More." In *A Princely Brave Woman: Essays on Margaret Cavendish, Duchess of Newcastle*, edited by Stephen Clucas, 185–198. Aldershot, U.K.: Ashgate, 2003.

Hutton, Sarah. "Science and Satire: The Lucianic Voice of Margaret Cavendish's *Description of a New World called the Blazing World.*" In *Authorial Conquests: Essays on Genre in the Writings of Margaret Cavendish*, edited by Line Lottegnies and Nancy Weitz, 161–178. Madison, NJ: Fairleigh Dickenson University Press, 2003.

James, Susan. "The Innovations of Margaret Cavendish." *British Journal for the History of Philosophy* 7 (2) (1999): 219–244.

Margaret Atherton (2005)

CELSUS

Celsus, a Middle Platonist (Origen wrongly called him an Epicurean) critic of Christianity, wrote the *Alethes Logos*

(True doctrine) about 178 CE. We know the work—whose title derives from a Platonic expression (*Meno* 81a)—only through quotations in Origen's reply, *Contra Celsum,* composed seventy years later. Celsus began his work by assuming the character of a Jew and attacking Christian views from this standpoint. Then he proceeded on his own to demonstrate their inadequacy in relation to the basic axioms of contemporary philosophical theology, especially with regard to the doctrines of God and providence and poetic-philosophical inspiration; as a Platonist he found the Christian idea of the Incarnation both impossible and immoral. At the end of his work he urged the Christians to abandon their irrational faith and join him in upholding the state and its religion. After Christianity was recognized by the Roman government, Celsus's work was destroyed.

The theology of Celsus is based, in his own view, on an ancient tradition handed down, especially among oriental wise men, from remote antiquity. This tradition, the "true doctrine," informed him of the existence of one god known by many names and worshiped by all pious men. Such a "polytheistic monotheism," he believed, had been perverted or misunderstood, first by the Jews and then by the Christians. If they were to return to the tradition, they would abandon their irrational exclusiveness and would recognize the divine right of the one emperor. His work thus culminates in a theology of politics.

Origen's reply is important not only because in it his philosophical theology, developed earlier, is clearly expressed in relation to Celsus's views, but also because it shows the extent to which he agreed with Celsus in opposing more literal religious conceptions. Each held, for example, that his own authoritative traditions are to be understood symbolically, whereas the other's traditions must be meant literally. But Origen finally took his stand on the particularity of the Hebrew-Christian tradition, which Celsus found totally unacceptable.

See also Origen; Platonism and the Platonic Tradition.

Bibliography

Bader, R. *Der 'Αληθηὸ λόγος des Kelsos.* Stuttgart and Berlin, 1940. Critical edition of Greek text.

Chadwick, Henry. *Origen: Contra Celsum.* Cambridge, U.K. Cambridge University Press, 1953. Translation with introduction and very full notes.

Robert M. Grant (1967)

CENSORSHIP

"Censorship" is the suppression of speech or symbolic expression for reason of its message. Liberal Western constitutionalism has traditionally condemned censorship on both instrumental and intrinsic grounds, classically articulated by John Stuart Mill in *On Liberty.* In this traditional liberal view, freedom of speech instrumentally serves the ends of truth and self-government. Censorship, by entrenching orthodoxy and suppressing dissent, impedes the advancement of truth and the processes of democratic change. Freedom of speech is also intrinsically valuable, in this view, as an aspect of human autonomy. Censorship illegitimately interferes with that autonomy, because speech, unlike action, typically causes others no harm. The proper response to bad speech is more speech, not government regulation.

Late-twentieth-century and early-twenty-first-century critics have challenged both the instrumental and the intrinsic justifications for freeing speech from censorship. First, some suggest that the power to speak is so unequally distributed that free competition in the marketplace of ideas is unlikely to produce either truth or democracy. For example, advocates of regulating campaign advertisements argue that wealthy voices dominate and thus distort political debate, and advocates of hate-speech regulation argue that racial epithets and invective perpetuate a form of cultural white supremacy in which minority voices are effectively silenced. These critics would turn the traditional free-speech principle on its head. In their view freedom of speech helps to entrench the existing status quo while government regulation of the speech of powerful groups can level the playing field. Redistribution of speaking power would advance truth and political equality better than a regime of laissez-faire.

Second, some critics argue that the defense of free speech on autonomy grounds undervalues the harms that speech causes. On this view speech regulation ought to be more widely allowed to protect the countervailing autonomy interests of listeners or bystanders. Liberal constitutional democracies generally permit censorship only to avert a narrow range of material harms. For example, incitement to riot may be forbidden, as may publication of the movements of troops at war. But censorship is rarely permitted on the ground that speech will cause disapproval, anger, alarm, resentment, or offense on the part of the audience. American constitutional law categorically forbids such justifications. Legal systems that permit them do so only in exceptional contexts: For example, British law forbids expressions of racial hatred, and some international human rights laws forbid advocacy of genocide.

Free-speech critics argue that such exceptions should be more the rule. First, some argue, government should be free to prevent injury, not only to bodies, but also to hearts and minds, including the injury caused by expressions of caustic opinion. Second, others argue, speech should be regulable for its social impact, even in the absence of immediate physical harm. On this view speech is not self-regarding but rather helps to structure social life. Thus, for example, pornography, hate speech, and graphic television violence inculcate attitudes that make society more immoral, sexist, racist, lawless, or violent than it would be if a different rhetoric prevailed. Speech helps construct society by socializing behavior, and reconstructing society, in this view, requires regulating speech.

At stake in these debates is whether speech will continue to be understood, like religious and reproductive practices, as presumptively a matter for private resolution, or instead will be subject to greater government regulation in the pursuit of social ends, including that of maximizing the quantity or diversity of speech itself.

See also Democracy; Liberty; Mill, John Stuart.

Bibliography

Bork, R. "Neutral Principles and Some First Amendment Problems." *Indiana Law Journal* 49 (1971): 1.

Coetzee, J. M. *Giving Offense: Essays on Censorship.* Chicago: University of Chicago Press, 1996.

Dworkin, R. "The Coming Battles over Free Speech." *New York Review of Books,* 11 June 1992, 55.

Gates, H. L., Jr. "Let Them Talk." *New Republic,* 20 September 1993, 37.

Haworth, Alan. *Free Speech.* New York: Routledge, 1998.

MacKinnon, C. A. *Only Words.* Cambridge, MA: Harvard University Press, 1993.

Matsuda, M. J., et al. *Words that Wound: Critical Race Theory, Assaultive Speech, and the First Amendment.* Boulder, CO: Westview Press, 1993.

Meiklejohn, A. *Free Speech and Its Relation to Self-Government.* New York: Harper, 1948.

Mill, J. S. *On Liberty.* London: J. W. Parker and Son, 1859.

Scanlon, T. "A Theory of Free Expression." *Philosophy and Public Affairs* 1 (1972): 204.

Strossen, N. *Defending Pornography: Free Speech, Sex, and the Fight for Women's Rights.* New York: Scribners, 1995.

Sunstein, C. R. *Democracy and the Problem of Free Speech.* New York: Free Press, 1993.

Kathleen M. Sullivan (1996)
Bibliography updated by Philip Reed (2005)

CHAADAEV, PËTR IAKOVLEVICH

(c. 1794–1856)

Pëtr Iakovlevich Chaadaev was a Russian thinker and writer. He was a member of the old nobility (his mother's father was the celebrated historian Mikhail Mikhailovich Shcherbatov [1733–1790]). He studied at Moscow University and participated in the great war of 1812 and in the subsequent campaign against Napoleon Bonaparte in Europe. In 1816–1817, while an officer in the Hussars, he met and became friends with Aleksandr Sergeevich Pushkin (1799–1837), who in his young years dedicated three letters in verse to Chaadaev. In 1821 Chaadaev resigned from military service, cutting short what had promised to be a brilliant career. From 1823 to 1826 he traveled in Europe (England, France, Italy, Switzerland, and Germany), where he became acquainted with Friedrich Wilhelm Joseph von Schelling and Hugues Félicité Robert de Lamennais, whose religious-philosophical ideas made a profound impression on him. At that time he also became friendly with a number of representatives of certain European religious sects, who were adherents of Catholic socialism. The acquaintance with European culture, social heritage, and ideas precipitated a spiritual crisis in Chaadaev: the transition from Enlightenment deistic beliefs about the universe to a modern version of Christianity, consisting in a syncretic union of religion, philosophy, history, sociology, natural science, art, and literature.

After his return Chaadaev wrote (from 1829 to 1831) his main work: *Lettres philosophiques*. It was written in French and consisted of eight treatises in the form of letters addressed to a lady. This work signified the start of an original Russian philosophy, as well as the formation of a new worldview for Chaadaev. Here, Chaadaev attempted to develop a religious justification for the social process. The establishment of a "perfect order on earth" is possible, in his opinion, only by means of the direct and constant action of "Christian truth," which, through the continuous intellectual interaction of many generations, forms the foundation of "the universal-historical tradition" in the movement of social history and facilitates "the education of the entire human race" (1991 Vol. 1, p. 644). In Chaadaev's view this social idea of Christianity evolved, first, in Catholicism. This idea defined, as Chaadaev points out in the first letter, "the sphere in which Europeans live and in which alone under the influence of religion the human race can fulfill its ultimate purpose" (p. 652).

From this premise Chaadaev infers that European successes in the domains of culture, science, law, and material progress were the fruits of Catholicism as a socially active, political religion; and therefore these successes could serve as the starting point of a higher synthesis. The interpretation of Christianity as a historically progressive social development became for Chaadaev the foundation of a critique of the contemporary Russian situation. In Russia Chaadaev found neither "elements" nor "embryonic indications" of European progress. In his opinion the reason for this was that, when it initially separated from the Catholic West, Russia "erred concerning the true spirit of religion": Russia did not recognize "the purely historical side," that is, the socially transformative principle, to be an inner property of Christianity (658). The consequence of this was that Russia lagged behind Europe and had not gathered "all the fruits" of science, of culture, of civilization, of a well-ordered life. Chaadaev believed that, for Russia to achieve the successes of European society, it was insufficient for it simply to adopt the European forms of development: It had to change everything from the beginning, by repeating, under the flag of the salvific Catholic idea, the entire history of western Europe.

The first "Philosophical Letter" was published in the Moscow journal *Teleskop* (1836). This publication produced in thinking Russia an impression similar to a "rifle shot resounding in a dark night" (in the words of Alexander Ivanovich Herzen, 1954–1965). After its publication the journal was prohibited by the government, and its editor-publisher, N. I. Nadezhdin (1804–1856) was arrested and expelled from Moscow, while Chaadaev himself was declared, "by imperial order," to be insane. This "Philosophical Letter" was the only work of Chaadaev's to be published during his lifetime. Chaadaev's conclusions in this letter provoked a serious critique and disputation in circles of the Russian intelligentsia. Despite the official prohibition of the polemic around the *Philosophical Letters*, there were serious responses to them from Pushkin, P. A. Viazemskii (1792–1878), Aleksandr Ivanovich Turgenev (1784?–1846), Filip Filipovich Vigel (1786–1856), D. P. Tatishchev (1974–), Schelling, and others. By and large, these commentators did not agree with Chaadaev, but they recognized that it was legitimate and timely to formulate philosophical problems connected with solving the riddle of "the sphinx of Russian life" (in Herzen's words). Chaadaev's publication also provoked a serious split in Russian social life, a split that acquired the character of a dispute that, in principle, could never be resolved.

Although Chaadaev was prohibited from publishing his ideas, he continued his philosophical search. To accusations that he was insufficiently patriotic, he responded with the article "L'apologie d'un fou" (The apology of a madman; written in 1837 but first published in Paris in 1862), in which, speaking about Russia, he affirms that "we are called to solve most the problems of the social order, to answer the most important questions which preoccupy mankind" (1991 Vol. 1, p. 675). Here, he admits that the traditions of Orthodox Christianity possess indisputable merits and have played a beneficial role in the formation of the Russian mind. He is prepared to see Russia's calling in the fact that "at the proper time [it] would offer a solution to all the questions provoking disputation in Europe." In the 1840s Chaadaev's house in Moscow became the center of an important literary and philosophical circle.

Following in Chaadaev's footsteps, many Russian writers and philosophers became sufficiently bold to pose and ask into fundamentally important but hitherto systematically unexplored problems of social development. This exploration made it possible to clarify conceptions regarding the historical evolution of Russia, and it had a significant influence on the formation of the two fundamental trends in Russian social thought: the Westernizing orientation (Timofei Nikolaevich Granovskii [1813–1855], Vissarion Grigor'evich Belinski, Herzen, and Konstantin Dmitrievich Kavelin) and the Slavophile orientation (Aleksei Stepanovich Khomiakov, Ivan Vasil'evich Kireevskii, Konstantin Sergeevich Aksakov [1817–1860], and Yu. F. Samarin [1819–1876]. Chaadaev himself found a common language with representatives of both camps, although he also critiqued both; at various times he was invited to contribute to journals that held diametrically opposed positions.

Chaadaev's ideas on the philosophy of history proved to be a stimulus for such different thinkers as Khomiakov, Herzen, Apollon Aleksanrovich Grigor'ev (1822–1864), Konstantin Nikolaevich Leont'ev, Nikolai Iakovlevich Danilevskii (1822–1865), and Vladimir Sergeevich Solov'ëv (Solovyov). In essence, these ideas marked the start of the development of an original Russian philosophy.

Chaadaev's esthetic judgments reflected the influence of his "one idea"; they are subordinate to the moral ideal worked out by him. For Chaadaev, beauty in art is inseparable from truth and goodness. The artist is a guide leading people toward endless perfection; in transient things the artist discerns the milestones on this path. Somewhat paradoxically, Chaadaev condemned the art of antiquity, in which, he believed, "all the moral elements were chaotically confused" (1991 Vol. 1, p. 359). In contrast, Gothic art was, for Chaadaev, "something sacred and heavenly," serving as an expression of moral feelings and compelling man "to lift his gaze toward heaven" (p. 359). In contemporaneous letters Chaadaev valued Nikolai Vasil'evich Gogol's (1809–1852) *Selected Passages from a Correspondence with Friends* (1846), in which "among weak and even sinful pages there are pages of astonishing beauty, full of infinite truth" (1991 Vol. 2, p. 1991). Chaadaev's aesthetic judgment was defined by his moral creed: "[M]oderation, tolerance, and love for all that is good, whatever form it might take" (p. 200).

Chaadaev's legacy was most accurately assessed by Khomiakov, who wrote in 1860:

> An enlightened mind, an artistic feeling, a noble heart—those are the qualities that attracted everyone to him. But at a time when it appeared that Russian thought had become submerged in heavy and involuntary sleep, he was especially valuable to us because he was awake and awakened others, because in the thickening darkness of that time he did not allow the lamp of truth to go out.

See also Aesthetic Judgment; Belinskii, Vissarion Grigor'evich; Enlightenment; Herzen, Aleksandr Ivanovich; Kavelin, Konstantin Dmitrievich; Kireevskii, Ivan Vasil'evich; Lamennais, Hugues Félicité Robert de; Leont'ev, Konstantin Nikolaevich; Russian Philosophy; Schelling, Friedrich Wilhelm Joseph von; Solov'ëv (Solovyov), Vladimir Sergeevich.

Bibliography

WORKS BY CHAADAEV

Russian Philosophy, edited by James M. Edie, James P. Scanlan, and Mary-Barbara Zeldin, with George L. Kline, 101–154. Chicago: Quadrangle Books, 1965.

Philosophical Letters, and Apology of a Madman. Translated by Mary-Barbara Zeldin. Knoxville: University of Tennessee Press, 1969.

Polnoe sobranie sochinenii i izbrannye pis'ma (Collected works and selected letters). 2 vols. Moscow: Izd-vo "Nauka," 1991.

P. Ya. Chaadaev: Pro et contra. Antologiia (P. Ya. Chaadaev: Pro et Contra. An Anthology). St. Petersburg, Russia, 1998.

WORKS ABOUT CHAADAEV

Herzen, A. I. *Sobranie sochinenii v 30—ti tomakh* (Works in 30 volumes). Moscow: USSR Academy of Sciences, 1954–1965.

Khomiakov, A. S. *Polnoe sobranie sochinenii* (Complete works). Moscow: Universitetskaia tipografiia, 1900.

McNally, Raymond T. *Chaadayev and His Friends: An Intellectual History of Peter Chaadayev and His Russian Contemporaries*. Tallahassee, FL: Diplomatic Press, 1971.

Moskoff, Eugene A. *The Russian Philosopher Chaadayev: His Ideas and His Epoch*. New York: N.p., 1937.

Zenkovsky, V. V. *A History of Russian Philosophy*. 2 vols. Translated by George L. Kline. New York: Columbia University Press, 1953. Originally published in two volumes under the title *Istoriia russkoi filosofii* (Paris 1948–1950).

Viacheslav Koshelev (2005)
Translated by Boris Jakim

CHAIN OF BEING

See *Lovejoy, Arthur Oncken*

CHAMBERLAIN, HOUSTON STEWART

(1855–1927)

Houston Stewart Chamberlain, the Anglo-German race theorist and philosophical and historical writer, was born in Southsea, near Portsmouth, England. Despite his English birth and family, his early indifference toward England and all things English developed into a lifelong hatred. Chamberlain was brought up by relatives in France. After being forced to attend schools in England, he returned to England only briefly, in 1873 and 1893. A nervous breakdown determined the course of his physical and mental development. (Frequently ill, hypersensitive, neurotic, he was crippled during the last thirteen years of his life by an incurable paralysis.) He traveled in western and central Europe for nine years seeking a cure. A German tutor inspired him to turn his mind to German literature and philosophy, and eventually he chose Germany as his home. As early as 1876 he wrote, "My belief that the whole future of Europe—that is, of world civilization—is in Germany's hands has become a certainty" (*Lebenswege meines Denkens*, p. 59).

Chamberlain's intellectual development began with the study of botany and other natural sciences; this was soon completely supplanted by a preoccupation with philosophy, literature, theology, art, and history. The turning point of his life was his meeting his future father-in-law, Richard Wagner, "the sun of my life," whom Chamberlain considered the greatest poet and musician of all time. Johann Wolfgang von Goethe inspired the central concept of Chamberlain's picture of the world and his "theory of life," the concept of *Gestalt* (form) as the expression of all that is timeless and unchangeable. The *Gestalt* is encountered as the primary concept in the intuition of everything living (*Anschauung*) and must be grasped and interpreted in thought. It is the key to metaphysics and art, two fields which Chamberlain passionately defended against rationalism and "the coarsely empirical theory of evolution."

RACE

Chamberlain's "Lebenslehre" (Theory of life), which he first drafted in 1896 (it was not published until 1928 and was then titled *Natur und Leben* [Nature and life]), presented the position of most of his later writings, a position to which he frequently sacrificed historical truth in *Die Grundlagen des 19. Jahrhunderts* (*Foundations of the Nineteenth Century*), his weakest but best-known work. Chamberlain upheld "Life," intuition, metaphysics, "holy art" in the Wagnerian sense, and antidemocratic thought against rationalism, biological materialism (of Jewish origin), the superficial belief in progress, and moral decadence. His *Weltanschauung*—a favorite word of Chamberlain's—is closely related to Wagner's theory of decadence and regeneration. It carries with it the urge to improve the world, and Chamberlain felt himself called into the battle for moral renewal not of humanity in general (he spoke derogatorily of "the ghost, humanity"), but of the Teutonic culture and people. To save culture from the threat of materialism was also the declared aim of his books on Immanuel Kant and Goethe.

In the *Grundlagen* Chamberlain represented history as a conflict of opposing philosophies of life, represented by the Jewish race on the one hand and by the Germanic-Aryan race on the other. The application of the biological idea of race to the study of cultural phenomena was widespread around the turn of the twentieth century. Under the influence of Charles Darwin, it was used by anthropologists, ethnologists, religious historians, and others. It could serve both as a basis for scholarly interpretation and as a vehicle for racism, following the example of Comte Joseph Arthur de Gobineau. It was natural for Chamberlain to take over the concept of race from his scientific studies, but the significance he gave to it went beyond what was tenable in the light of the scientific knowledge then available and even denied the relevance of scientific criticism: "Even if it were proved that there had never been an Aryan race in the past, we are determined that there shall be one in the future; this is the decisive point of view for men of action" (*Grundlagen,* 1st ed., Vol. I, p. 270). Intuition and instinct, an overwhelming irrationalism, the capacity to sweep away logical contradictions—these are the major characteristics of this "historical" work.

Without ever giving a precise definition of "race," Chamberlain considered it to be the "*Gestalt* in particular, transparent purity" (*Natur und Leben,* p. 152) "Only thoroughbred 'races,'" he held, "accomplish the extraordinary" (*Rasse und Persönlichkeit,* p. 75). In connection with his race theory, Chamberlain emphasized the significance of nations: "It is almost always the nation as a political entity that creates the conditions for the formation of a race, or at least for the highest expressions of the race" (*Grundlagen,* 1st ed., Vol. I, p. 290). The awareness of racial identity, not physical characteristics, determined a race. Thus Chamberlain could speak of the English or Japanese "races" and also employ the term in a very broad sense, as when he included the Slavs and Celts among the Teutonic peoples.

Race was always dominant in Chamberlain's thought, whether he was describing the "heritage of the old world" as Hellenic art and philosophy, Roman law, and the coming of Christ; the cultureless chaos of peoples which separated the ancient from the modern world; or the role of the Jews and the Teutonic peoples, who entered Western history as "pure" races and whose antagonism shaped the modern world. He recognized the existence of other historical forces, such as religion or the desire for power, but he placed them far below race in importance. He was thus led to the paradox of trying to prove that the historical Jesus, whose birth he regarded as "the most important date in the entire history of humanity," was not a Jew. Chamberlain denied that the Jewish people possessed any metaphysical inclinations or philosophical tendencies. Their outstanding characteristics in his view were materialism and rationalism. They were thus incapable of religion and could not have produced the man Jesus. The Jews served Chamberlain as a dark foil for the image of the Germanic peoples, whom he celebrated as the creators of "all present culture and civilization" and whose standard-bearers were the Germans. Paul Joachimsen, in a memorial article, described the aim of the *Grundlagen* as "to demonstrate the elements of Western cultural development in the light of an Aryan theodicy." But whereas Joachimsen considered Chamberlain's work as a document already belonging to the past, we know today what terrible consequences his ideas had when they were translated into reality after his death. The chief ideologist of National Socialism, Alfred Rosenberg, showed himself to be Chamberlain's disciple in his *Mythus des 20. Jahrhunderts* (Myth of the twentieth century).

GOETHE AND KANT

One must not interpret Chamberlain's personality exclusively by the *Grundlagen.* His philosophical books on Kant and Goethe provide a far more solid basis for judgment and are more representative of his inclination and his intellectual position. His *Goethe* (1912) is a milestone in studies of the poet. Chamberlain was concerned to present "a clear, enthusiastic, and at the same time a critically reflective, grasp of this great personality in its essence and effect." Chamberlain found in Goethe the same polarities which he found in himself: nature and freedom, intuition and concept, poet and scholar, Christian and pagan—in brief, "the juxtaposition of opposed vocations." Jean Réal rightly described *Goethe* as "full of originality, of depth, and of prejudice" ("Houston Stewart Chamberlain et Goethe").

Chamberlain interrupted his studies of Goethe, which he pursued for more than twenty years, in order to write his *Immanuel Kant* (1905). Through Kant's limitation of the possibility of metaphysics Chamberlain came to realize the place of religion in human life. This side of Kant's thought appealed to Chamberlain's antirationalistic, vitalistic tendencies.

During World War I, Chamberlain composed fanatical anti-English propaganda. He was an intimate of Kaiser Wilhelm II from 1901 until well into the kaiser's exile in the Netherlands. He was quite naturally unable to come to terms with the Weimar Republic and turned his sympathies to Adolf Hitler, whom he first met in 1923. *Mensch und Gott* (Man and God), written in Chamberlain's old age, is an impressive attempt at a philosophical synthesis but casts no light on his personality as a whole. One can agree with the judgment of Friedrich Heer in *Europa—Mutter der Revolutionen* (Stuttgart, 1964, p. 6): "H. S. Chamberlain presents himself as a highly significant symbol combining high culture and barbarism."

See also Darwin, Charles Robert; Gobineau, Comte Joseph Arthur de; Goethe, Johann Wolfgang Von; Kant, Immanuel; Racism.

Bibliography

PRIMARY WORKS

Richard Wagner. Translated by G. Ainslie Hight. Munich: Bruckmann, 1897.

Die Grundlagen des 19 (Foundations of the Nineteenth Century), 2 vols. Translated by John Lees. London: Lane, 1911.

Goethe. Munich: Bruckmann, 1912.

Immanuel Kant. Die Persönlichkeit als Einführung in das Werk, 2 vols. Translated by Lord Redesdale. London: Lane, 1914.

Deutsches Wesen. Ausgewählte Aufsätze. Munich: Bruckmann, 1916.

Lebenswege meines Denkens (My thought's path through life). Munich: Bruckmann, 1919.

Mensch und Gott. Betrachtungen über Religion und Christentum. Munich: Bruckmann, 1921.

Rasse und Persönlichkeit. Aufsätze. Munich: Bruckmann, 1925.

Briefe 1882–1924 und Briefwechsel mit Kaiser Wilhelm II. Edited by Paul Pretzsch, 2 vols. Munich: Bruckmann, 1928.

Natur und Leben. Edited by Jakob von Uexkiill. Munich: Bruckmann, 1928.

Foundations of the Nineteenth Century, 2 vols. Translated by John Lees. New York: Fertig, 1968.

SECONDARY WORKS

Baylen, Joseph O., and Rolf F. Munster. "Adolph Hitler as Seen by Houston Stewart Chamberlain: A Forgotten Letter." *Duquesne Review* 12 (2) (1967): 81–88.

Biddiss, Michael D. "History as Destiny: Gobineau, H. S. Chamberlain, and Spengler." *Transactions of the Royal Historical Society* 7 (1997): 73–100.

Chamberlain, Anna. *Meine Erinnerungen an Houston Stewart Chamberlain.* Munich: Beck, 1923.

Field, Geoffrey G. *Evangelist of Race: The Germanic Vision of Houston Stewart Chamberlain.* New York: Columbia University Press, 1981.

Joachimsen, Paul. "Houston Stewart Chamberlain." *Zeitwende* 3 (1927): 347–361, 430–439.

Lindner, Erik. "Houston Stewart Chamberlain: The Abwehrverein and the 'Praeceptor Germaniae,' 1914–1918." *Leo Baeck Institute Year Book* 37 (1992): 213–236.

Réal, Jean. "Houston Stewart Chamberlain et Goethe." *Études germaniques* 5 (1950): 154–166.

Réal, Jean. "La lettre à l'amiral Hollmann (1903) ou Guillaume II à l'école de Houston Stewart Chamberlain." *Études germaniques* 6 (1951): 303–312.

Réal, Jean. "The Religious Conception of Race: Houston Stewart Chamberlain and Germanic Christianity." In *The Third Reich; A Study under the Auspices of the International Council for Philosophy and Humanistic Studies with the assistance of UNESCO.* New York: Praeger, 1955.

Seillière, Ernest. *Houston Stewart Chamberlain, le plus récent philosophe du pangermanisme mystique.* Paris: La Renaissance du livre, 1917.

Stackelberg, Roderick."Houston Stewart Chamberlain and Idealized Racism." In *Idealism Debased.* Kent, OH: Kent State University Press, 1981.

Stolberg-Wernigerode, Otto Graf zu. "Houston Stewart Chamberlain." In *Neue deutsche Biographie,* Vol. 3. Edited by Historische Kommission bei der Bayerischen Akademie der Wissenschaften. Berlin: Duncker and Humblot, 1957.

Ziegenfuss, Werner. "Houston Stewart Chamberlain." In *Philosophen-Lexikon,* Vol. 1. Edited by Werner Ziegenfuss. Berlin: de Gruyter, 1949.

Antonia Ruth Schlette (1967)
Translated by Tessa Byck
Bibliography updated by Philip Reed (2005)

CHANCE

Much is asked of the concept of *chance*. It has been thought to play various roles, some in tension, or even incompatible, with others. Chance has been characterized negatively as the absence of causation; yet also positively—the ancient Greek "tyche" reifies it—as a cause of events not governed by laws of nature, or as a feature of laws of nature. Chance events have been understood epistemically as those whose causes are unknown; yet also objectively as a distinct ontological kind, sometimes called "pure" chance events. Chance gives rise to individual unpredictability and disorder; yet it yields collective predictability and order: stable long-run statistics and, in the limit, aggregate behavior susceptible to precise mathematical theorems. Some authors believe that to posit chances is to abjure explanation; yet others think that chances are themselves explanatory. During the Enlightenment, talk of chance was regarded as unscientific, unphilosophical, the stuff of superstition or ignorance; yet at the beginning of the twenty-first century it is often taken to be a fundamental notion of our most successful scientific theory, quantum mechanics, and a central concept of contemporary metaphysics.

Chance has both negative and positive associations in daily life. The old word in English for it, "hazard," which derives from French and originally from Arabic, still has unwelcome connotations of risk; "chance" evokes uncertainty, uncontrollability, and chaos. Yet chance is also allied with luck, fortune, freedom from constraint, and diversity. And it apparently has various practical uses and benefits. It forms the basis of randomized trials in statistics, and of mixed strategies in decision theory and game theory; it is appealed to in order to resolve problems of fair division and other ethical stalemates; and it is even thought to underpin biological and cultural adaptation. Throughout history, "chance" devices have been a source of entertainment, as well as of scorn.

A BRIEF HISTORY OF THEORIES OF CHANCE

The study of gambling games motivated the first serious mathematical study of chance by Blaise Pascal and Pierre de Fermat in the mid-seventeenth century, culminating in the *Port Royal Logic*. But inchoate ideas about chance date back to antiquity. Epicurus, and later Lucretius, believed that atoms occasionally underwent uncaused, indeterministic swerves—an early doctrine of pure chance. Aristotle, by contrast, believed that all events are necessary and regarded what we call coincidences (as in "We met at the market place by chance") as the intersections of independent deterministic causal chains—a view later shared by Thomas Aquinas, Antoine Augustin Cournot, and John Stuart Mill. Augustine believed that God's will controls everything, and thus that nothing happens by chance. In the middle ages, Averroes had a notion of "equipotency" that arguably resonated with Gottfried Wilhelm Leibniz's and later Pierre Simon de Laplace's ideas about "equipossibility," which undergirded their classical interpretation of probability: The probability of an event is the ratio of the number of equipossible cases in which it occurs to the total number of such cases. Girolamo Cardano, Galileo, Fermat, and Pascal also anticipated this interpretation.

Throughout the development of probability theory during the seventeenth through nineteenth centuries by authors such as Christian Huygens, Jakob Bernoulli, Thomas Bayes, Pierre Simon de Laplace, the Marquis de Condorcet, Abraham de Moivre, and John Venn, the fortunes of chance were at best mixed. De Moivre called chance "a mere word." David Hume captured the attitude of his time when he wrote, "'Tis commonly allowed by philosophers that what the vulgar call chance is nothing but a secret and conceal'd cause" (Hume 1975, p. 130). The triumphs of Newtonian mechanics engendered great confidence in determinism, personified by Laplace's image of an intelligent being (the so-called "Laplacean demon") for whom "nothing would be uncertain and the future, as the past, would be present to its eyes" (Laplace 1951, p. 4). Eliminativism about chance in nature had, moreover, good theological credentials: God's omniscience apparently made the world safe for determinism. But even the atheist Bertrand Russell insisted that a chance event is merely one whose cause is unknown. F. H. Bradley found the very notion of chance unintelligible.

Nonetheless, other intellectual developments set the stage for a revival of chance. With the burgeoning of social statistics in the nineteenth century came a realization that various social phenomena—births, deaths, crime rates, etc.—while unpredictable on an individual basis, conformed to large-scale statistical regularities. A somewhat analogous pattern of collective order from individual chaos appeared in statistical mechanics. The social sciences and then the physical sciences thus admitted statistical laws into their conceptual repertoire. This culminated in the early twentieth century with the advent of quantum mechanics, which appeared to show that chance was irreducible and ineradicable. Andrey Kolmogorov's axiomatization of probability came soon after

Werner Heisenberg and Erwin Schrödinger brought quantum mechanics to its apogee.

Meanwhile, chance was also making a comeback in philosophy. Charles Sanders Peirce defended pure chance on the basis of empirical evidence. William James saw the postulation of chance as a way to resolve the apparent conflict between determinism and free will. To be sure, philosophers such as John Stuart Mill, Moritz Schlick, and C. D. Broad thought that capricious chance could provide no ground for genuine freedom. Nevertheless, chance had regained its respectability. In the 1950s Hans Reichenbach's work on probabilistic causation placed chance in the limelight in the philosophy of science.

THE MATHEMATICS OF CHANCE

The mathematics of chance, unlike its philosophy, is relatively uncontroversial. That mathematics is widely taken to be probability theory. In Kolmogorov's theory (1933/1950), events are assigned numerical values between 0 and 1 inclusive:

$$P(X) \geq 0$$

$$P(\Omega) = 1$$

(Here Ω is the universal set of all possible outcomes.) The probability of one of two mutually exclusive events occurring is the sum of their probabilities:

$$P(X \cup Y) = P(X) + P(Y) \text{ if } X \cap Y = \emptyset$$

(This law has an infinite generalization.) And the conditional probability of A given B is as follows:

$$P(A|B) = P(A \cap B)/P(B) \text{ for } P(B) > 0$$

While Kolmogorov's theory remains the orthodoxy, some philosophers (e.g., James Fetzer, Paul Humphreys, Karl Popper) question its appropriateness for chance.

CHANCE IN SCIENCE

Probability was introduced into physics in the late nineteenth century, when James Clerk Maxwell and Ludwig Boltzmann grounded thermodynamics in statistical mechanics. The status of this probability was an important interpretive issue, but it was not universally regarded as objective chance. Statistical mechanics was based on Newtonian particle mechanics, which was apparently deterministic. There are profound and ongoing controversies over the existence and nature of chance in both statistical mechanics and quantum mechanics.

In nonrelativistic quantum mechanics, according to the canonical Copenhagen interpretation, there are two rules for the evolution of a physical system:

- *Schrödinger's equation* prescribes a deterministic evolution for the state of the system. Typically, the state is a superposition (combined state) of the various definite-property states that the system might possess (e.g., definite position, definite momentum, etc.). While the system is in a superposition, it has no single value for such quantities.
- The *collapse postulate* is where chance enters quantum mechanics. Upon measurement of such a superposition, the state instantaneously collapses to one of the quantity's eigenstates (definite-property states). Which one is a matter of chance, the probability for each being derivable by Born's rule.

Albert Einstein considered this intrusion of chance into microphysics an unacceptable violation of causality and hoped for an underlying deterministic theory, with hidden variables, that explains the apparently chancy behavior of quantum systems. In 1935, Einstein, Boris Podolsky, and Nathan Rosen (EPR) insisted that there must be such an underlying theory, arguing that the quantum-mechanical description of a certain two-particle system is incomplete. Neils Bohr and Werner Heisenberg effectively criticized the EPR argument, and since an experimental test of an EPR pair of particles appeared to be physically unrealizable, most physicists quickly forgot the debate.

In 1952 David Bohm proposed a variant of the EPR setup using two coupled particles with correlated spins. Bohm's variant was both immune to the criticisms of Bohr and Heisenberg and physically realizable. In 1965 John Bell proved a now-legendary theorem stating that no local hidden-variable theory, of the type desired by Einstein, could replicate the statistical predictions of quantum mechanics for the correlated spins. Contrary to what the EPR paper had assumed, an underlying hidden-variable theory that assigned definite local values of spin to individual particles was incompatible with the predictions of quantum mechanics. Physicists then realized that a decisive experimental test was possible, and numerous experiments were performed in the 1970s, culminating in Alain Aspect's 1982 experiments, widely regarded as decisive. Nature sided with Bohr and Heisenberg, not Einstein.

Ironically, however, this confirmation of the predictions of quantum mechanics did not definitively show that God plays dice, to use Einstein's memorable phrase. In 1952 Bohm also formulated a hidden-variable variant of quantum mechanics that ascribes definite positions to all particles at all times, reproduces all the experimental predictions of standard quantum mechanics, and is perfectly deterministic. This is consistent with Bell's theorem. No *local* hidden-variable theory can match the predictions of quantum mechanics for coupled particles, but Bohm's version of quantum mechanics is *nonlocal*: A particle in one place may be affected, instantaneously, by distant events. Einstein would have approved of Bohm's theory for its deterministic microphysics and disapproved of it for violating the even more cherished precept of no nonlocal interactions.

There are other versions of quantum mechanics besides Bohm's that reject chancy collapses. It is thus unclear whether the success of quantum-mechanical theories implies a fundamental indeterminism in nature, and whether future experiments can resolve the issue.

Evolutionary biology is another area of science in which the existence and role of chance has been sharply debated. Evolutionary fitness is held by some philosophers and biologists to be fundamentally chancy, while others disagree.

PHILOSOPHICAL ACCOUNTS OF CHANCE

Now, at the beginning of the twenty-first century, "chance" is typically taken to be synonymous with "objective probability," as distinguished from epistemic or subjective probability. *Frequentists*, originating with Venn, identify chance with relative frequency. For example, the chance that a particular coin lands heads is the frequency of tosses on which it so lands, divided by the total number of tosses. If we restrict ourselves to actual outcomes, then such frequencies will presumably be finite. A concern is that the outcomes may ill-reflect the true chances; a fair coin may land heads nine times out of ten. At the extreme, the *problem of the single case*, various events are unrepeatable, yet arguably have nontrivial chances (e.g., the outcome of the next presidential election). In such cases, mismatch between chance and relative frequency is guaranteed. Sometimes we might include in the reference class for a given event various other events. For example, regarding your chance of getting cancer, the class might include various other people like you. But there may be competing classes that yield different relative frequencies. You may belong both to the class of smokers and the class of those with no family history of cancer. What, then, is the real chance? This is the *problem of the reference class*.

Some frequentists follow Richard von Mises in requiring the sequences of trials that ground chances to be *infinite*, and thus presumably hypothetical. Then the chance of an outcome type is identified with its *limiting* relative frequency. (Further randomness constraints might also be imposed on the sequences.) Counterintuitively, such "chances" are then sensitive to the ordering of the trials (a sequence with infinitely many heads and tails can be rearranged to give whatever limiting relative frequency we like). Moreover, the appeal to hypothetical trials, let alone infinitely many of them, may betray the empiricist and scientific scruples that made frequentism initially appear attractive, for such "chances" are not constrained by anything in our experience.

Historically associated with Peirce and Popper, *propensity* accounts of chance postulate primitive dispositions, or tendencies, possessed by various physical systems. Propensity theories fall into two broad categories. According to *single-case* propensity theories, propensities measure the tendencies of a system to produce given outcomes; according to *long-run* propensity theories, propensities are tendencies to produce long-run outcome frequencies over repeated trials. The former have been advocated by the later Popper, David Miller, and James Fetzer; the latter by the early Popper, Paul Humphreys, and Donald Gillies.

Adopting a long-run view answers a need for testability of propensity attributions, one arguably found wanting for single-case propensity attributions. A long-run attribution may be held falsified if the long-run statistics diverge too much from those expected. However, defining propensities in terms of long-run relative frequencies may render single-case chance attributions problematic. This poses a dilemma for the long-run propensity theorist. If propensities are linked too closely to long-run frequencies, the view risks collapsing into a variant of frequentism. But if the view is cast so as to make single-case chance attributions possible, it risks collapsing into a variant of the single-case propensity view.

Long-run propensity theories may be motivated by the worry that in a single case there can be factors present that are not part of the description of the chance setup but that affect the chances of various outcomes. If the long-run propensity theorist responds by, in effect, falling back on long-run frequentism, the single-case propensity theorist goes the other way, embracing all causally or physically relevant details as part of the chance setup, determining the single-case chance (though we cannot measure it) for any given trial. The chance of each outcome is determined by everything that might influence the evolution of the setup. Propensity theories of this type respect some of our physical and causal intuitions, but pay a price epistemically. Since each single-case setup is presumably unique, we cannot use frequencies to estimate the chances or to falsify hypotheses about them.

A final problem, specifically for *conditional* propensities, is *Humphreys' paradox*. If $\Pr(A|B)$ is a propensity, it seems to have a built-in causal direction, from B to A; the "inverse" conditional probability $\Pr(B|A)$ can often be calculated, but it appears to get the causal direction wrong. Various authors argue that inverse probabilities cannot be considered propensities, earlier events not having propensities to arise from later events. Thus, not all conditional probabilities may be interpretable as propensities.

While frequentist and propensity theories have dominated philosophical accounts of chance, a recent recurring proposal is that "chance" be viewed as a theoretical term similar to others in the sciences, such as "mass" or "fitness." In this post-positivist era, philosophers mostly agree that such terms cannot be reduced to non-theoretical terms. Instead, we may view theoretical terms as implicitly defined by their roles in scientific and philosophical theories. This approach avoids many of the difficulties discussed above, but it may not satisfy philosophers who find something troubling about the very notion of chance (see below). It also renounces giving a philosophical account of chance with *normative* status—claiming, for example, that theorists *should* admit objective chances into quantum mechanics but not into economics.

Pioneering work by David Lewis on the connections between chance and *credence* (subjective probability) has inspired *Humean best-system* theories. They share these tenets:

- Chances are defined so that their distinctive connection with credences is rendered transparent (see "Chance and Credence" below).
- Chances supervene on (are determined by) the entire history of actual events, and not on anything modal that does not itself supervene on the actual.
- Chances are determined by the laws of nature: the regularities of a best system (theory) that optimizes the balance of simplicity, strength (covering as many phenomena as possible), and fit (how typical actual events are, given the chances posited by the system).

Humean best-system accounts aim to be as acceptable to empiricists as finite frequentism, while avoiding the defects of that account.

CHANCE AND CREDENCE

Perhaps the most crucial demand we make of chances is that they guide our bets, expectations, and predictions—that they be guides to life in the face of uncertainty. This role is captured by some chance-credence principle or other, the most common coinage recently being Lewis's Principal Principle (Lewis 1986, p. 83–132):

$$(PP)\ Cr(A|ch(A) = x \,\&\, E) = x$$

Here Cr is one's credence function, A is a proposition, $ch(A)$ is the chance of A (presumably time-indexed), and E is further evidence that one may have. For (PP) to be applicable, E cannot be relevant to whether A is true or false, other than by bearing on the chance of A. (PP) codifies something crucial about chance. A touchstone for any theory of chance is that it should underwrite (PP). There is considerable controversy over which theory (if any) can meet this challenge.

CHANCE AND DETERMINISM

Determinism is the thesis that any complete past or present state of the world, conjoined with the laws of nature, entails all future events. In a deterministic world, some insist, chance has no work left to do, the entire future being already determined by past events. Philosophers are divided over whether determinism rules out (nontrivial) chances. Since the definition of determinism says nothing about chance, more is needed to argue that determinism rules out chances.

D. H. Mellor, Popper, and others who view propensities as fundamental physical loci of indeterminism, see an immediate inference from determinism to the nonexistence of chances. Frequentists such as Venn and Reichenbach see no such inference: intermediate frequencies can exist in both deterministic and indeterministic worlds. The Humean best-system approach leaves open whether a deterministic system of laws can include chance laws (although Lewis rejects this possibility). And on the implicit-definition approach, intermediate chances and determinism coexist just in case our fundamental physical theories are deterministic but some scientific theory postulates objective probabilities. Statistical mechanics uses chances, but its underpinnings are deterministic, and typical uses of chance in biology and the social sciences involve no presumption for or against determinism, as Isaac Levi (1990) and others have argued.

Nor does indeterminism guarantee the existence of chances. Fundamental physical laws may fail to entail a unique future without being probabilistic. However, if these laws are probabilistic, as some interpretations of quantum mechanics contend, then chances are apparently guaranteed on any but a skeptical/subjectivist view.

SUBJECTIVISM, SKEPTICISM ABOUT CHANCE, AND EXCHANGEABILITY

Chance is meant to play a certain theoretical role. It is a further matter what, if anything, actually *plays* this role. According to Bruno de Finetti, nothing does. "Probability does not exist," he said (1990, p. x), meaning that *chance* does not exist and that all probability is subjective. Skepticism about chance is easily assimilated to skepticism about kindred modal notions—possibility, counterfactuals, causation, laws of nature—that seem not to be straightforwardly reducible to nonmodal notions, in particular, notions congenial to an empiricist. And skepticism specifically about chance can be based on further arguments, for one can be skeptical not just about its modality, but also about its putative *degrees*. Subjectivists have also argued that chance is redundant, its alleged role being completely discharged by credences. Richard Jeffrey, Bas van Fraassen, Brian Skyrms, and others have developed subjectivist positions in the spirit of de Finetti.

Moreover, the mathematics of chance (unlike the other modal notions) permits a particular eliminativist gloss. A sequence of trials is said to be *exchangeable* with respect to a probability function if the probabilities of trial outcomes are invariant under finite permutations of trials; probabilities may be sensitive to the numbers of outcomes of each kind, but not to their ordering. De Finetti (1990) showed that when this condition is met, there is a unique representation of the probability distribution over the trials as an expectation of simpler probability distributions according to which the trials are independent and identically distributed. For example, if your credences over the results of repeated coin tossing are exchangeable, then it is as if you treat the trials as tosses of a coin of unknown bias, with credences over the possible biases. Subjectivists have argued that this delivers some of the supposed benefits of chance, without any questionable metaphysics.

CONCLUSION

Many of the perplexities about chance—its controversial metaphysics, its seeming resistance to reduction, its epistemological recalcitrance, etc.—are familiar from other modal notions. But chance has been handled in mathematics and philosophy with more precision than those other notions. In the process, still further perplexities have been born. For the foreseeable future, at least in the writings of philosophers and philosophically minded scientists, chance is probably here to stay.

See also Probability and Chance.

Bibliography

A BRIEF HISTORY OF THEORIES OF CHANCE

David, F. N. *Games, Gods, and Gambling: A History of Probability and Statistical Ideas.* Mineola, NY: Dover, 1962.

Franklin, James. *The Science of Conjecture: Evidence and Probability before Pascal.* Baltimore, MD: Johns Hopkins University Press, 2001.

Hacking, Ian. *The Emergence of Probability.* Cambridge, U.K.: Cambridge University Press, 1975.

Hacking, Ian. *The Taming of Chance.* Cambridge, U.K.: Cambridge University Press, 1990.

Hume, David. *A Treatise of Human Nature*, edited by L. A. Selby-Bigge, 2nd ed. Oxford: Clarendon Press, 1975.

Laplace, Pierre Simon. *A Philosophical Essay on Probabilities.* English edition 1951 (originally published 1814). New York: Dover Publications Inc.

THE MATHEMATICS OF CHANCE

Billingsley, Patrick. *Probability and Measure.* 3rd ed. New York: John Wiley and Sons, 1995.

Kolmogorov, Andrei N. *Grundbegriffe der Wahrscheinlichkeitrechnung.* Berlin: J. Springer, 1933. Translated as *Foundations of Probability.* New York: Chelsea, 1950.

Skyrms, Brian. *Choice and Chance: An Introduction to Inductive Logic.* 4th ed. Belmont, CA: Wadsworth, 1999.

CHANCE IN SCIENCE

Albert, David. *Time and Chance.* Cambridge, MA: Harvard University Press, 2000.

Bell, John S. *Speakable and Unspeakable in Quantum Mechanics.* Cambridge, U.K.: Cambridge University Press, 1987.

Einstein, Albert, Boris Podolsky, and Nathan Rosen. "Can Quantum-Mechanical Description of Physical Reality Be Considered Complete?" *Physical Review* 47 (1935): 777–780.

Sklar, Lawrence. *Physics and Chance.* Cambridge, U.K.: Cambridge University Press, 1993.

Sober, Elliott. *Philosophy of Biology.* 2nd ed. Boulder, CO: Westview Press, 2000.

PHILOSOPHICAL ACCOUNTS OF CHANCE

Fetzer, James H. *Scientific Knowledge: Causation, Explanation, and Corroboration.* Dordrecht, Netherlands: D. Reidel, 1981.

Fine, Terrence. *Theories of Probability.* New York: Academic Press, 1973.

Gillies, Donald. "Varieties of Propensity." *British Journal for the Philosophy of Science* 51 (2000): 807–835

Loewer, Barry. "David Lewis's Humean Theory of Objective Chance." *Philosophy of Science* 71 (2004): 1115–1125.

Mellor, D. H. *The Matter of Chance.* Cambridge, U.K.: Cambridge University Press, 1971.

Miller, David. *Critical Rationalism: A Restatement and Defence.* La Salle, IL: Open Court Press, 1994.

Sober, Elliott. "Evolutionary Theory and the Reality of Macro Probabilities." In *Probability in Science*, edited by Ellery Eells and James H. Fetzer. La Salle, IL: Open Court, 2005.

CHANCE AND CREDENCE

Lewis, David, "A Subjectivist's Guide to Objective Chance." In *Studies in Inductive Logic and Probability*. Vol II., University of California Press, 263-293, 1980; reprinted with postscripts in *Philosophical Papers*, Vol. II. Oxford: Oxford University Press, 83-132, 1986. Lewis, David. "Humean Supervenience Debugged." *Mind* 103 (1994): 473–490.

Popper, Karl. "The Propensity Interpretation of Probability." *British Journal of the Philosophy of Science* 10 (1959): 25-42.

Vranas, Peter. "Who's Afraid of Undermining?" *Erkenntnis* 57 (2002): 151–174.

CHANCE AND DETERMINISM

Levi, Isaac. "Chance." *Philosophical Topics* 18 (2) (1990): 117–148.

Loewer, Barry. "Determinism and Chance." *Studies in History and Philosophy of Modern Physics* 32 (2001): 609–620.

Strevens, Michael. *Bigger than Chaos: Understanding Complexity Through Probability*. Cambridge, MA: Harvard University Press, 2003.

SUBJECTIVISM, SKEPTICISM ABOUT CHANCE, AND EXCHANGEABILITY

de Finetti, Bruno. *Theory of Probability*, Vol. 1. Chichester: Wiley Classics Library, John Wiley & Sons, 1990

Skyrms, Brian. "Bayesian Projectibility." In *Grue: The New Riddle of Induction*, edited by Douglas Stalker, 241–262. Chicago: Open Court, 1994.

WEB RESOURCES

"Chance." The Chance Project, Mathematics Department, Dartmouth College. Available from http://www.dartmouth.edu/~chance/.

Hájek, Alan. "Probability, Interpretations of." In *The Stanford Encyclopedia of Philosophy*, summer 2003 ed., edited by Edward N. Zalta. Available from http://plato.stanford.edu/archives/sum2003/entries/probability-interpret/.

Alan Hájek (2005)
Carl Hoefer (2005)

CHANNING, WILLIAM ELLERY

(1780–1842)

William Ellery Channing, America's most famous Unitarian minister, was described by Ralph Waldo Emerson as "one of those men who vindicate the power of the American race to produce greatness." Channing, born in Newport, Rhode Island, was graduated from Harvard in 1798. The following two years he spent as a tutor in Richmond, Virginia, and in private study. During this period he underwent a profound religious experience, and in 1801 he returned to Harvard for theological study. He was ordained the minister of Boston's Federal Street Congregational Church in 1803 and held this pastorate throughout his life. He died in Bennington, Vermont.

Channing was not an original or profound thinker, a systematic philosopher, or a great writer. His significance in the history of ideas lies in his representative influence, his achievement in expressing and synthesizing the diverse strands of thought that appeared in America at the end of the eighteenth and the beginning of the nineteenth centuries.

Although Channing was celebrated in his own lifetime as a man of letters (his critical essays on John Milton, Napoleon Bonaparte, and François Fénelon were widely read both here and abroad), his lasting reputation stands on his attempt to develop an "enlightened" religious faith for the Americans of his generation. Jonathan Edwards had responded to the spirit of the Enlightenment by employing the ideas of John Locke and Isaac Newton to revitalize Calvinist dogma. Channing employed the liberating spirit of eighteenth-century thought to free Christianity from an outmoded theology. "God has given us a rational nature," he said in his famous sermon "Unitarian Christianity" (1819), "and will call us to account for it." Without denying the authority of Scripture, Channing argued that men should "reason about the Bible precisely as civilians do about the Constitution under which we live." This rational approach to revelation led Channing to reject the "irrational and unscriptural doctrine of the Trinity." Substituting the moral perfection of God for the Calvinist conception of divine sovereignty, Channing also repudiated such doctrines as natural depravity and predestination. "It is not because his will is irresistible but because his will is the perfection of virtue that we pay him allegiance," Channing asserted. "We cannot bow before a being, however great and powerful, who governs tyrannically."

As a religious thinker Channing was liberal but not radical. Eighteenth-century skepticism had no place in his thinking. He was influenced considerably by Scottish "commonsense" philosophers, such as Adam Ferguson and Richard Price, and in his discourse "The Evidences of Revealed Religion" (1821) he relied heavily on the traditional arguments of William Paley in attempting to refute David Hume and assert the validity of miracles.

Channing is also important for his influence on the New England transcendentalists. Like Jean-Jacques Rousseau, whose writings he admired, he was partly an Enlightenment figure and partly a romantic. Channing's romanticism is most apparent in the sermon "Likeness to

God" (1828), in which he asserted that humankind discovers God not only through Scripture and rational inquiry but also through consciousness. Long before Emerson's famous essays were published, Channing was preaching that in all its higher actions the soul had "a character of infinity" and describing sin as "the ruin of God's noblest work." Despite the fact that Channing never professed enthusiasm for the "new views," the similarity between his conception of the divine potential in human nature and the later pronouncements of Emerson and Theodore Parker is unmistakable. The path to transcendentalism lay through Unitarianism, and it was Channing who helped to pave the way.

Finally, Channing is significant for his humanitarian influence. His belief in the parental character of God and the dignity of humanity provided an ideological base for humanitarian efforts, and he spoke out in favor of most of the reform causes of his day. His pamphlet against slavery, written in 1835, attracted wide attention. Although Channing always shied away from radical solutions to social disorder, no one was more influential in articulating the gospel of human dignity that nourished most American reformers before the Civil War.

See also Edwards, Jonathan; Emerson, Ralph Waldo; Enlightenment; Fénelon, François de Salignac de la Mothe; Ferguson, Adam; Hume, David; Locke, John; Milton, John; Newton, Isaac; Paley, William; Parker, Theodore; Price, Richard; Rousseau, Jean-Jacques.

Bibliography

The most usable edition of Channing's works is a one-volume edition (Boston, 1886). There are several full-length studies of Channing, including David Edgell's *William Ellery Channing: An Intellectual Portrait* (Boston: Beacon Press, 1955); Arthur Brown's *Always Young for Liberty* (Syracuse, NY: Syracuse University Press, 1956); and Robert L. Patterson's *The Philosophy of William Ellery Channing* (New York: Bookman Associates, 1952).

Irving H. Bartlett (1967)

CHAOS THEORY

A physical system has chaotic dynamics, according to the dictionary, if its behavior depends sensitively on its initial conditions, that is, if systems of the same type starting out with similar sets of initial conditions can end up in states that are, in some relevant sense, very different. But when science calls a system chaotic, it normally implies two additional claims: That the dynamics of the system is relatively simple, in the sense that it can be expressed in the form of a mathematical expression having relatively few variables, and that the geometry of the system's possible trajectories has a certain aspect, often characterized by a strange attractor.

Chaos theory proper, it should be noted, has its home in classical physics (and other kinds of dynamics that share the relevant properties of classical physics). The extent to which chaotic mathematics is fruitful in understanding the quantum realm is still a matter of debate.

SENSITIVE DEPENDENCE ON INITIAL CONDITIONS

In the popular imagination a chaotic system is one whose future state may be radically altered by the smallest of perturbations—as when the fluttering of a butterfly's wings creates a disturbance whose size is inflated to the point where it tips the meteorological balance on the other side of the globe, creating a tornado where there would otherwise have been none. Though the "butterfly effect" marvelously engages human fear and wonder at the unpredictability of things, it captures rather less completely what is interesting and distinctive about modern chaos theory.

The idea of an inherent unpredictability in human and other affairs due to the inflation of small disturbances is an old one. Swift wrote in *Thoughts on Various Subjects* (1711) that "A Wise man endeavors, by considering all Circumstances, to make Conjectures, and form Conclusions: But the smallest Accident intervening, (and in the Course of Affairs it is impossible to see all) doth often produce such Turns and Changes, that at last he is just as much in doubt of Events, as the most ignorant and unexperienced Person" (p. 415).

Modern mathematics is able to characterize the sensitivity of initial condition dependence in various ways that lie far beyond Swift's means. Notions such as the Liapunov exponent help to quantify the speed at which the trajectories of systems starting out with similar initial conditions will diverge. Measure theory quantifies something like the chance that a small initial difference will lead to a relatively large difference in outcome, in systems where not every small change makes such a difference. There is nothing here, though, that would have astounded Swift.

SIMPLICITY

The central insight of chaos theory is that systems governed by simple equations, that is, systems whose behavior can be characterized by a small number of variables, called low dimensional systems, are often sensitive to initial conditions. At first blush this realization has a pessimistic cast. Most obviously it leads to the conclusion that even a simple dynamics may be unpredictable in the medium to long term, as which of two significantly different outcomes occurs may depend on such first details of the initial conditions as to lie beyond the resolving power any reasonable observational effort.

Somewhat less obviously certain kinds of sensitivity to initial conditions impede systematic dynamical understanding. A famous example closely connected to the origins of chaos theory is the three body problem, the task of elucidating all the properties of the dynamics of a three body system in Newtonian gravitational theory. In 1890 Henri Poincaré showed that three body systems can tend to chaos in the modern sense of the word, and concluded that a systematic treatment of three body dynamics would be difficult if not impossible.

Chaos can be an impediment to prediction and systematic understanding in low dimensional systems then. However, if low dimensional chaos is bad news for the study of systems known to have low-dimensional dynamics, it is good news for the study of systems known only to have chaotic dynamics. Traditionally such systems were modeled by complex equations, if at all; chaos theory introduces the serious possibility that these systems may be governed by equations with very few variables. Underlying the complex appearances may be a simple reality. The prospect of finding a hidden simplicity in such complex phenomena as turbulent flows, the weather, the movements of financial markets, and patterns of extinction is what most excites proponents of chaos theory. (Much the same prospect animates the advocates of catastrophe theory, the study of cellular automata, "complexity theory," and so on.)

To what extent can the nature of this hidden simplicity, if it exists, be divined? Given sensitive dependence on initial conditions, it is difficult to find the simple equation that best predicts the observed phenomena, since small errors in measuring initial conditions can make even the true model look like a bad predictor. More feasible is to infer some of the more interesting properties of the putative underlying law, such as the degree of sensitivity to initial conditions and certain geometrical aspects of the dynamics induced by the law (discussed below).

Under favorable conditions this information can be used to model accurately the behavior of chaotic systems to some extent—or at least that is the hope both of academic chaoticians and of those hoping to use the mathematics of chaos theory to beat the financial markets.

By far the boldest posit made in undertaking such work is the assumption that there is a simple dynamic law lying behind the subject system's complex behavior. For elaborate systems such as ecosystems and economies, the assumption of dynamic simplicity is often no more than a leap of faith; however, Strevens describes some circumstances in which ecosystems and some other complex systems have a low dimensional macrodynamics.

The Geometry of Chaos Trace the trajectory of a paradigmatically chaotic system through the space of possible states and the result is a complicated tangle of looping paths. It is the geometry of this tangle more than anything else—more even than sensitive dependence per se—that is distinctive of chaos (though there is disagreement as to which feature of the geometry is most important).

One especially striking feature of such trajectory tangles is their often-fractal structure: They cut out a shape in the space in which they are embedded so intricate that mathematicians ascribe it a fractional dimension. Such a shape is a strange attractor (strictly speaking an attractor only if it is a set of trajectories that systems starting from some points outside the attractor eventually join).

Many of the more interesting properties of chaotic systems can be understood as arising from the intricate geometry of the trajectory tangle. One well-known example is the appearance of "period-doubling cascades" in systems that are moving from a periodic to a chaotic regime of behavior: As some parameter affecting the system's dynamics is tweaked, the system first oscillates between two states, then between four states, then eight states, and so on, with shorter and shorter times between each successive doubling, until it goes chaotic. What is interesting about this behavior is that it turns up in many physically quite different kinds of systems, and that there are certain aspects of the period doubling, notably the rate at which the doubling increases, that are the same (in the limit) in these otherwise rather different systems. This universality in chaotic systems holds out the promise of understanding the behaviors of a considerable range of systems in terms of a single mathematical—in this case, it turns out, a geometrical—fact. So far however the wider significance of this understanding is unclear.

A more practical part of chaotic geometry is the use of limited data about the behavior of chaotic systems to reconstruct to a certain extent the geometry of the system's trajectory. Suppose that the behavior a chaotic system is characterized by three variables, so that the system's "trajectory tangle" is a subset of three-dimensional space. Suppose also that only a single property of the system's dynamics can be observed, a function of the values of the three variables. In favorable conditions, this single set of observations can be used to recover the geometrical structure of the three-dimensional dynamics. Various predictions, quantitative and qualitative, can then be made from the recovered geometry.

This is a powerful technique, as it assumes no knowledge of the number or even the nature of the underlying variables. However its success does depend on, among other things, the simplicity assumption explained above: The technique supposes that there are no more than a small number of variables.

CHAOS AND PROBABILITY

The disorderly behavior of chaotic systems can be called "random" in a loose and popular sense. Might the behavior of at least some such systems be random in a stronger sense? The suggestion that chaos might provide a foundation for probabilistic theories such as statistical mechanics has been one of the more fruitful contributions of chaos theory to philosophy.

The best scientific theories of certain deterministic or near deterministic systems are probabilistic. Perhaps the most prominent examples are the systems characterized by statistical mechanics and population genetics; the simplest examples are various gambling setups such as a roulette wheel or a thrown die. The probabilistic characterization of these systems is apt because the various events that make up their behavior (die throws or deaths, for example) are patterned in characteristically statistical ways, that is, in ways that are captured directly by one or other of the canonical probability distributions in statistical theory.

The mathematics of chaos offers an explanation of the probabilistic aspect of these patterns, and so offers an explanation of the success of probabilistic theories applied to certain sorts of deterministic systems.

The explanation, or rather the family of explanations, is quite complex, but it can be loosely characterized in the following way. A paradigmatically probabilistic pattern has two aspects: A short term disorder, or randomness, familiar to every gambler, and a long term order that is quantified by the statistics characterizing a probability distribution, such as the one-half frequency of "heads" in a long series of coin tosses.

Chaotic systems are capable of producing probabilistic patterns because they are capable of producing both this short term disorder and the requisite kinds of long-term order. The short-term disorder is due to the sensitive dependence on initial conditions; the long-term order to other aspects of the "geometry of chaos," principally chaotic dynamics' resemblance to a "stretch-and-fold" process.

Nowhere near all chaotic systems, it should be noted, generate probabilistic patterns. Indeed this area of investigation is not, in a certain sense, mainstream chaos theory: There are no strange attractors or period-doubling cascades, though there is a characteristically chaotic geometry to the relevant trajectory tangles. As well as explaining the success of probabilistic theorizing in science, chaos has been put forward—for much the same reasons—as a foundation for the metaphysics of probability, on the principle that what explains the probabilistic pattern is deserving to a considerable extent of the name probability.

PHILOSOPHICAL SIGNIFICANCE

What is the philosophical significance of chaos? With respect to general philosophy of science, opinion is divided. Some philosophers, for example Stephen Kellert, have argued that chaos theory requires the abandoning of prediction as the touchstone of successful science, a new conception of the nature of scientific explanation, and the end of reductionism. Others, for example Peter Smith, have argued that these conclusions are too extreme, and that insofar as they are justified, chaos theory is not necessary for their justification, though it may well have brought to philosophy's attention problems previously wrongly ignored.

With respect to certain foundational questions about science, the significance of chaos is less controversial. The notion of determinism and (in the context of processes that are deterministic deep down) the notions of randomness and probability cannot be discussed without reference to work on dynamical systems since Poincaré that falls within the ambit—broadly conceived—of chaos theory.

See also Geometry; Philosophy of Physics; Poincaré, Jules Henri; Probability and Chance; Swift, Jonathan.

Bibliography

Bass, Thomas. *The Predictors*. New York: Henry Holt, 1999.

Belot, Gordon, and John Earman. "Chaos Out of Order: Quantum Mechanics, The Correspondence Principle and

Chaos." *Studies in History and Philosophy of Modern Physics* 28 (1997): 147–182.

Earman, John. *A Primer on Determinism.* Dordrecht: Reidel, 1986.

Kellert, Stephen H. *In the Wake of Chaos.* Chicago: Chicago University Press, 1993.

Ornstein, Donald, and Benjamin Weiss. "Statistical Properties of Chaotic Systems." *Bulletin of the American Mathematical Society* 24 (1991): 11–116.

Sklar, Lawrence. *Physics and Chance.* Cambridge, U.K.: Cambridge University Press, 1993.

Smith, Peter. *Explaining Chaos.* Cambridge, U.K.: Cambridge University Press, 1998.

Stewart, Ian. *Does God Play Dice? The Mathematics of Chaos.* Oxford, Blackwell, 1989.

Strevens, Michael. *Bigger than Chaos: Understanding Complexity through Probability.* Cambridge, MA: Harvard University Press, 2003.

Suppes, Patrick. "Propensity Representations of Probability." *Erkenntnis* 26 (1987): 335–358.

Michael Strevens (2005)

CHARDIN, PIERRE TEILHARD DE

See *Teilhard de Chardin, Pierre*

CHARRON, PIERRE

(1541–1603)

Pierre Charron, a skeptical philosopher and theologian, was born in Paris in a family of twenty-five children. He studied at the universities of Paris, Bourges, Orléans, and Montpellier and received a law degree from Montpellier in 1571. Sometime during his student years he became a priest. He was a successful preacher and theologian in southern France, serving as preacher in ordinary to Queen Margaret of Navarre and as a theological advisor and teacher in various dioceses in the Midi. In spite of his many worldly successes, he tried to retire to a monastic order in 1589 but was refused admittance because of his age.

During the 1580s Charron met Michel Eyquem de Montaigne in Bordeaux and became his close friend and disciple. Montaigne made Charron his intellectual heir, adopting Charron as his son. After Montaigne's death in 1592 Charron wrote his major works: *Les trois veritez* (Bordeaux, 1593), *Discours chrestiens* (Bordeaux, 1601; Paris, 1604), *De la sagesse* (Bordeaux, 1601), and *Petit traicté de sagesse* (written in 1603, published posthumously in Paris, 1606). These works were popular and were republished often in the seventeenth century, especially the skeptical *De la sagesse*, which was highly influential in disseminating skeptical views and arguments into philosophical and theological discussions and played an important role in the development of modern thought, libertinism, and fideism.

OPPOSITION TO CHARRON

Serious efforts to suppress and reject Charron's skeptical views were made by such figures as the Jesuit Father François Garasse, who in 1623 accused Charron of having supplied *le brèviare des libertins* and of having been a secret atheist trying to destroy religion. His work, which was first condemned in 1605, was seen as more dangerous than Montaigne's, partly because Charron was a professional theologian, partly because he wrote more didactically. Pierre Chanet, a Protestant medical doctor, published *Considerations sur la sagesse de Charon* (1643), an attempted Aristotelian refutation of Charron's skepticism about the possibility of knowledge.

Although Charron, like Montaigne, was attacked on many sides, his views were also defended and advanced by the so-called *libertins érudits*—Gabriel Naudé, Guy Patin, François de La Mothe Le Vayer, and Pierre Gassendi—and were supported in varying degrees as theologically orthodox by various French Counter-Reformation leaders. Pierre Bayle considered Charron an excellent and prime representative of fideistic Christian thought. Interest in and concern with Charron's views diminished in the eighteenth century, and he came to be considered a second-rate and derivative Montaigne whose style lacked the freshness and literary quality of his mentor's. In the light of more recent criticism suggesting that Montaigne was or might have been a sincere believer and that his skepticism was part of a theological movement of the period, Charron, too, has begun to be reexamined and reevaluated.

CHARRON'S VIEWS

The first statement of Charron's views was the *Trois veritez*, a tract against Calvinism and the views of its French leader, Philippe Duplessis-Mornay. The three truths Charron sought to establish were that God exists, that Christianity is the correct view of God, and that Catholicism is the true statement of Christianity. Most of this enormous work deals with the last claim. However, the work begins with a brief discourse on knowledge of God, developing skepticism about the possibility of human knowledge in this area, on the basis of both human rational limitations and the nature of God. One's own capacities are so limited and unreliable that it is doubtful that one could really know anything in either the natural or the supernatural realm. God's nature is infinite and therefore surpasses all attempts to define or limit it. Hence, one cannot know, in rational terms, what God is. Thus, the greatest theologians and philosophers know as much or as little about God as do the humblest artisans. One's knowledge consists only of negative information, what God is not. In fact, Charron announced, "the true knowledge of God is a perfect ignorance about Him" (*Trois vritez*, 1595, p. 26).

Charron combined the skeptic's views about the inadequacy and unreliability of human knowledge with the mystic's and negative theologian's view that God is unknowable because he is infinite and then utilized this combination to attack atheism. The denial that God exists proceeds from some definition of God, from which absurd conclusions are then drawn. Such a definition can only be the result of human presumption, the attempt to measure divinity by human means, and, as such, is worthless, since atheists do not, and cannot, know what they are talking about.

Throughout the *Trois veritez* Charron argued principally in a negative way, trying to show that it is unreasonable not to believe in God, Christianity, and Catholicism and that the evidence adduced by opponents is unreliable or dubious. He often contended that opponents, usually Calvinists, had to base their case on the results obtained by the weak and miserable human capacities, employing these defective results as measures of divine truth.

DE LA SAGESSE

Charron's skeptical defense of the faith was made more explicit in *De la sagesse* and in his defense of that work, *Petit traicté de sagesse*. His major thesis was that since man cannot discover any truth except by revelation, morality should be based on following nature, except when guided by divine light. To support this thesis, Charron first put forth most of Montaigne's skeptical views in an organized fashion. One must first know oneself ("The true science and the true study of man is man," *De la sagesse*, book 1, chapter 1), and this involves knowing the limitations on what one can know. Charron presented the traditional skeptical critique of sense knowledge, questioning whether one possesses the requisite senses for gaining knowledge, whether one can distinguish illusions and dreams from veridical experience, and whether one can, in view of the enormous variability of sense experiences, determine which ones correspond to objective states of affairs. Next, he raised skeptical questions about one's rational abilities, contending that one possesses no adequate or certain criteria that enable one to distinguish truth from falsehood. He pointed out that in fact one believes things mainly as a result of passions and social pressures, not reasons and evidence. One actually functions a as beast and not as a rational being. Hence, one should accept Montaigne's contention that men possess no genuine principles unless God reveals them. Everything else is only dreams and smoke.

The second book of *De la sagesse* presents a discourse on the method for avoiding error and finding truth, in view of the human predicament. Charron's method closely resembles the one René Descartes set forth later: examine all questions freely and dispassionately, keep prejudice and emotions out of all decisions, develop a universality of mind, and reject any decisions that are in the slightest degree dubious. This skeptical method, Charron claimed, is of greater service to religion than any other there may be. It leads one to reject all dubious opinions until one's mind is "blank, naked and ready" to receive the divine revelation on faith alone. The complete skeptic will never be a heretic, since if he or she has no opinions, he or she cannot have the wrong ones. If God pleases to give him or her information, then the skeptic will have true knowledge. Until the skeptic receives the revelation, he or she should live by a *morale provisoire*, following nature. The last book of *De la sagesse* presents this theory of natural morality, showing how one ought to live as a skeptic and noble savage if one has no divine guidance.

De la sagesse was one of the first important philosophical works to be written in a modern language and to present a moral theory apart from religious considerations. Some considered the work a basic didactic statement of Pyrrhonian skepticism, challenging both traditional philosophical claims to knowledge and religious ones and thus preparing the ground for a thoroughly naturalistic view of human nature and conduct. Charron claimed that the argument in *De la sagesse* only represented part of his view, dealing with the human situation apart from divine guidance.

The overall theory stated in his various works, his ecclesiastical career, and the piety expressed in his *Discours chrestiens* suggest that he was a sincere fideist, who saw skepticism as a means of destroying the enemies of the true faith while preparing the soul for salvation.

The problem of interpreting Charron's views involves a larger issue, that of assessing the purport of the revival of skepticism in the Renaissance and the relation of this revival to Reformation and Counter-Reformation thought. Skeptical thought, perhaps, played several different and possibly incompatible roles in the period. Both then and now, skeptics like Charron could provide the "rationale" both for antirational fideism and for irreligious naturalism.

See also Bayle, Pierre; Fideism; Gassendi, Pierre; La Mothe Le Vayer, François de; Montaigne, Michel Eyquem de; Naturalism; Reformation; Renaissance; Skepticism, History of.

Bibliography

WORKS BY CHARRON

Oeuvres (1635). Geneva, Switzerland: Slatkine Reprints, 1970.

WORKS ABOUT CHARRON

Adam, Michel. *Études sur Pierre Charron.* Talence, France: Presses univeritaires de Bordeaux, 1991.

Bayle, Pierre. "Charron (Pierre)." In *Dictionnaire historique et critique.* 2 vols. Rotterdam: Reinier Leers, 1697.

Belin, Christian. *L'oeuvre de Pierre Charron, 1541–1603: Littérature et théologie de Montaigne à Port-Royal.* Paris: Slatkine, 1995.

Bremond, Henri. "La folle 'sagesse' de Pierre Charron." *Le correspondant* 252 (1913): 357–364.

Busson, Henri. *La pensée religieuse francise de Charron à Pascal.* Paris: Librairie philosophique J. Vrin, 1933.

Charron, Jean. "Pierre Charron." In *A Critical Bibliography of French Literature. Vol. 3, The Seventeenth Century*, edited by Nathan Edelman, 476–478. Syracuse, NY: Syracuse University Press, 1961. Annotated bibliography of works about Charron.

Charron, Jean. *The "Wisdom" of Pierre Charron: An Original and Orthodox Code of Morality.* Chapel Hill: University of North Carolina Press, 1961.

Dini, Vittorio, and Domenico Taranto, eds. *La Saggezza moderna: Temi e problemi dell'opera di Pierre Charron.* Naples: Edizioni scientifiche italiane, 1987.

Gray, Floyd. "Reflexions on Charron's Debt to Montaigne." *French Review* 35 (1962): 377–382.

Gregory, Tulio. *Genèse de la raison classique de Charron à Descartes.* Paris: Presses Universitaires de France, 2000.

Horowitz, Maryanne Cline. "The Origin of Pierre Charron's Concept of Natural Law in Man." PhD diss., University of Wisconsin, 1970.

Julien-Eymard d'Angers. *Pascal et ses précurseurs: L'apologétique en France de 1580 à 1670.* Paris: Nouvelles Éditions latines, 1954.

Julien-Eymard d'Angers. "Le stoïcisme en France dans la première moitié du XVIIe siècle. Les origines (1575–1616)." *Études franciscaines* 2 (1951): 389–410.

Maia Neto, José R. "Charron's Construction of *Épochè* as Wisdom." Presented at the annual meeting of the Renaissance Society of America, April 1–3, New York: 2004.

Maia Neto, José R. "Charron's *Epoché* and Descartes' *Cogito*: The Sceptical Base of Descartes' Refutation of Scepticism." In *The Return of Scepticism: From Hobbes and Descartes to Bayle*, edited by Gianni Paganini, 81–113. Dordrecht, Netherlands: Kluwer Academic, 2003.

Paganini, Gianni. *Scepsi Moderna: Interpretazioni dello scetticismo da Charron a Hume.* Cosenza, Italy: Busento, 1991.

Popkin, Richard H. "Charron and Descartes: The Fruits of Systematic Doubt." *Journal of Philosophy* 51 (1954): 831–837.

Popkin, Richard H. *The History of Scepticism: From Savonarola to Bayle.* Rev. ed. New York: Oxford University Press, 2003.

Rice, Eugene F. *The Renaissance Idea of Wisdom.* Cambridge, MA: Harvard University Press, 1958.

Sabrié, Jean B. *De l'humanisme au rationalisme: Pierre Charron (1541–1603), l'homme, l'oeuvre, l'influence.* Geneva, Switzerland: Slatkine Reprints, 1970.

Richard H. Popkin (1967, 2005)

CHARTRES, SCHOOL OF

A cathedral school existed at Chartres as early as the sixth century but did not become famous until the eleventh and twelfth centuries. Under Bishop Fulbert (d. 1028), a pupil of Gerbert of Aurillac, students, among them Berengar of Tours, flocked to Chartres to study the *trivium* and *quadrivium,* medicine and theology. Later, Bishop Ivo brought renown in canon law. The high point was reached in the early twelfth century under Bernard of Chartres and his brother Theodoric (Thierry) and their pupils Gilbert of Poitiers (de la Porrée), William of Conches, and Clarembald of Arras. Also associated with the school in various ways were Bernard of Tours, Adelard of Bath, Alan of Lille, and John of Salisbury. The Chartrains of this period were humanists who loved the literature and philosophy of classical antiquity. The richness of their program of studies is evident in Theodoric's *Heptateuch,* a handbook of the seven liberal arts and a collection of the authors who were read. In the early twelfth century Chartres was the center of Latin Platonism. Plato himself was known only indirectly through a fragment of the *Timaeus* in the translation and commentary of Chalcidius and through Macrobius, Apuleius, Seneca, and Boethius, whose *Opuscula Sacra* and *Consolatio Philosophiae* were much commented on. Devotion to Platonism produced realist interpretations of the problem of universals, speculations about the Ideas, matter and form, cosmological thought, and discussions about the world soul. Aristotle was generally less highly esteemed. The Chartrains knew only his logical writings (the *Organon*), including the *logica nova* (the rediscovered *Prior Analytics, Topics,* and *Sophistic Refutations*), which makes an early appearance in Theodoric's *Heptateuch.* Under the inspiration of Boethius, attempts were made to reconcile Aristotelianism and Platonism. Theology was presented largely in philosophical clothing. Confident of the harmony of faith and learning, the Chartrains attempted to establish the existence of God by numerical speculations, to synthesize Platonic cosmology and biblical revelation, and to compare the Platonic world soul with the Holy Spirit, as in William of Conches. God was considered to be the form of all being, a view that has been called pantheistic by some historians. Greek and Arabian writings on medicine, astronomy, and mathematics, including works by Hippocrates, Galen, Ptolemy, Euclid, al-Khwarizmi, Johannitius, and others were circulated and read in translation. In the early twelfth century Chartres was without a peer as a school of classical and humane learning and of Platonism, and it was rivaled in philosophy only by Paris. The bloom was fading fast by midcentury, but the influence of the school continued to be marked among the disciples of Gilbert of Poitiers, in thirteenth-century writings on natural philosophy, and still later in the works of Nicholas of Cusa.

See also Aristotle; Bernard of Chartres; Bernard of Tours; Boethius, Anicius Manlius Severinus; Galen; Gerbert of Aurillac; Gilbert of Poitiers; Hippocrates and the Hippocratic Corpus; John of Salisbury; Nicholas of Cusa; Plato; Platonism and the Platonic Tradition; Seneca, Lucius Annaeus; Theodoric of Chartres; William of Conches.

Bibliography

Clerval, A. *Les écoles de Chartres au moyen âge.* Paris: A. Picard, 1895.

Geyer, B. *Die patristische und scholastische Philosophie.* Basel, 1927, Pp. 226–252.

Gregory, T. *Anima Mundi. La filosofia di Guglielmo di Conches.* Florence: G.C. Sansoni, 1955.

Parent, J. *La doctrine de la création dans l'école de Chartres.* Paris: J. Vrin, 1938.

Wulf, M. de. *History of Mediaeval Philosophy.* Translated by E. C. Messenger. London: Nelson, 1952. Vol. I, pp. 173–188. Translation of *Histoire de la philosophie médiévale.* Louvain: Institut Supérieur de Philosophie, 1934.

David Luscombe (1967)

CHATEAUBRIAND, FRANÇOIS RENÉ DE
(1768–1848)

François René de Chateaubriand, the French author, was born at Saint-Malo in Brittany and educated at Dol-de-Bretagne and Rennes in preparation for studying for the priesthood at the Collège de Dinan. Finding that he had no vocation, he followed the tradition of his social class and became an army officer instead. In 1788 he joined the order of the Knights of Malta, went to Paris, and began to associate with men of letters. From then on literature was his chief interest in life, though his literary career was paralleled by a career in diplomacy and politics. In 1803 he was appointed an attaché at the French embassy in Rome, and upon the return of Louis XVIII to power he played a role in politics in the Ministry of the Interior. His main diplomatic post was that of French plenipotentiary at the Congress of Verona, an account of which he published in 1838.

Chateaubriand's political as well as his religious views were in a state of constant flux. As a young man he had been favorable to the revolution, but he was soon disillusioned and in 1792 went into voluntary exile in London. There he published his *Essai historique, politique et moral sur les révolutions,* which he later retracted. This work was clearly influenced by the Philosophes, especially Jean-Jacques Rousseau, and, though far from atheistic, was definitely favorable to deism and opposed to Christianity. As Charles-Augustin Sainte-Beuve showed a half-century later in his *Causeries du Lundi,* the printed version of Chateaubriand's views was much less extreme than what he really thought. Having undergone a personal crisis when he learned of the death of his mother, he returned from exile in 1800 and began the preparation of one of his most famous works, *Le génie du Christianisme.* The aim of the volume was to persuade the public that Christianity had as many themes worthy of artistic expression as paganism. It produced, said Sainte-Beuve, "a whole army of parlor Christians." This was precisely the goal of its author, to make Christianity fashionable.

In September 1816, Chateaubriand published his pamphlet *De la monarchie selon la charte,* which preached political liberalism in a constitutional monarchy. This brought on his temporary political ruin, but he soon recovered and was utilized by the government in various diplomatic posts. Toward the close of his life he developed an intimacy with Mme. Récamier and her circle but withdrew from politics and devoted himself to the preparation of his memoirs, the *Mémoires d'outretombe* (published posthumously in 1849).

Chateaubriand's contributions to French philosophy were indirect. The early *Essai sur les révolutions* made it clear that he considered any type of philosophy to be antireligious and religion to be a substitute for philosophy. In it he attempted to show that no philosophy could ever hope to reach the truth, for truth was discovered not by reasoning but by some inner light, a kind of feeling (*sentiment*), perhaps what Blaise Pascal called the heart. It was this belief that appeared in such works as *Atala,* where the theme of the Noble Savage is developed. Though Atala is herself a Christian, she is a Christian by sentiment, not by reason, and her form of Christianity was believed by her inventor to be higher and nobler than that deduced by argument.

Similarly, Chateaubriand anticipated William Wordsworth in maintaining even as a young man that in the contemplation of nature, in the sense of the landscape, there is a spontaneous revelation of the truths of morality and religion. The famous passage "Night among the American Savages," which terminates the *Essai* and was reprinted in part in the *Génie du Christianisme,* is not only a description of a moonlight scene near Niagara Falls but also an evocation of the nobility of soul that belongs only to men who have lived in a state of cultural primitivism far from the contamination of society. Like Rousseau, Chateaubriand pitted nature and society against each other, and it is significant that in this passage the Indians are only two women, two small children at the breast, and two warriors. There is no mention of a tribe or village. The sole contact these people have with anything outside themselves is with the "ocean of trees." But it is to be noted that far from reinforcing the sense of individuality, this contact, on the contrary, induces an absence of all distinct thoughts and feelings, a kind of mystical union with that God who is nature itself.

This type of anti-intellectualism reappeared in the *Génie du Christianisme.* Chateaubriand said in the preface to this work that he turned away from eighteenth-century liberalism when he learned of his mother's death. He was in exile in London at the time. "I wept," he wrote, "and I believed." The evidence of tears was proof of the truths of Catholicism, as in the *Essai* the feelings aroused by natural scenery were proofs of the truth of deism. But Catholicism is hardly a religion spontaneously kindled in the hearts of all people. It is a religion initiated and developed in society. Hence, Chateaubriand found himself aligned with the Traditionalists, a group as far from Rousseauistic sentimentalism as can be imagined. For whereas Joseph Marie de Maistre and the Vicomte de Bonald believed reason was the faculty that united human beings, the sentimentalists believed it was what divided them into conflicting sects.

It was perhaps for this reason that Chateaubriand emphasized the gifts Christianity had made to European culture. He wrote at the height of the Neoclassical movement, when the masters were Jacques Delille in poetry, Antonio Canova in sculpture, and Jacques Louis David in painting. They, of course, found their inspiration in classical mythology and history. Chateaubriand tried to prove that there was more to be found in the Catholic tradition. However true this may have been, the point he was making was that to the extent that any set of beliefs increases the amount of beauty and goodness in the world, that set of beliefs is true. There is a concealed pragmatic test here that is of interest historically and would probably not be able to resist criticism. But at a time when men had lived through a period of horror brought on by the suppression of religion, it was understandable that they should attribute the horrors to the philosophy they believed had generated the antireligious practices. To Chateaubriand at this time the one alternative to philosophy was Catholicism, not that natural religion which he had lauded in the *Essai.* And this belief he never abandoned. He was not the type of writer to set down a body of premises from which he would deduce certain inferences. On the contrary, his hatred of philosophy was such that he simply stated his conclusions as his heart dictated; it remained for others to disentangle the form of his argument. He established a cultural atmosphere rather than a set of doctrines, and his works are more properly viewed as long poems of a purely lyrical nature than as doctrinal treatises.

Bibliography

WORKS BY CHATEAUBRIAND

Essai historique, politique et moral sur les révolutions. London, 1797.

Le génie du Christianisme. Paris, 1802. See especially the preface.

Les martyrs. Paris, 1809.

Oeuvres complètes, 20 vols. Paris, 1858–1861. Introduction by C. A. Sainte-Beuve.

WORKS ON CHATEAUBRIAND

Bertrin, Abbé Georges. *La sincérité religieuse de Chateaubriand.* Paris, 1899.

Blum, Christopher O., ed. and tr. *Critics of the Enlightenment: Readings in the French Counter-Revolutionary Tradition.* Wilmington, DE: ISI, 2004.

Chinard, G. *L'exotisme américain dans l'oeuvre de Chateaubriand.* Paris: Hachette, 1918.

Grimsley, Ronald. *Soren Kierkegaard and French Literature: Eight Comparative Studies.* Cardiff: Wales University Press, 1966.

Hilt, Douglas. *Ten against Napoleon.* Chicago: Nelson-Hall, 1975.

Law, Reed G., and Bobbie W. Law. *From Reason to Romanticism.* Denver: Big Mountain Press, 1966.

Sainte-Beuve, C. A. "Chateaubriand, anniversaire du Génie du Christianisme." In *Causeries du Lundi*. Vol. X, pp. 74–90. Paris: Garnier, 1855.

Sainte-Beuve, C. A. *Chateaubriand et son groupe littéraire sous l'Empire*. Paris, 1869.

George Boas (1967)
Bibliography updated by Tamra Frei (2005)

CHATTON, WALTER

(c. 1285–1343)

Walter Chatton was born in the village of Chatton in Northumbria. He entered the Order of Friars Minor at a young age and pursued the normal course of theological studies. His first lectures on the Sentences of Peter Lombard, called *Reportatio*, were held between 1321 and 1323. At the time Chatton, with William of Ockham and Adam Wodeham, was located in one of the Franciscan studia, probably London or Oxford, where Wodeham was the scribe or *reportator* of Chatton's lectures. A second commentary on the Sentences (incomplete), called *Lectura*, dates from 1328 to 1330. Besides these two Sentence commentaries, a single set of *Quodlibetal Questions* (incomplete) survives. Chatton became the fifty-third regent master for the Franciscans at Oxford in 1330. He went to Avignon in 1333 and was appointed by Popes Benedict XII (d. 1342) and Clement VI (c. 1291–1352) as one of the examiners of the writings of Thomas Waleys (d. 1349) and Durandus of Saint-Pourcain. He was appointed as bishop designate of the diocese of St. Asaph in Wales but died before the see had become vacant.

In virtually every distinction, question, and article of his lectures, Chatton attacks the views of Ockham, who in turn was appraised of these criticisms by Ockham's most noteworthy disciple, Wodeham. Chatton's other favored opponent was Peter Aureol, who had frequently criticized Chatton's favorite philosopher-theologian, John Duns Scotus. It is practically impossible to follow Chatton's train of thought without knowledge of the views of Ockham and Aureol.

One of Chatton's frequently invoked hermeneutical principles was designated as "my proposition" and can be called the antirazor as the foil of Ockham's principle of parsimony. If a situation cannot be adequately described by two propositions, then a third must be invoked, and if this is not adequate a fourth is required and so on.

In the domain of natural philosophy, Chatton was an indivisibilist, who viewed the continua, both permanent and successive, quantitative and temporal, as composed of indivisibles or instants. The argument being that whatever God by his absolute power can do successively, he could do instantaneously, and thus there would be, according to the divisibilists' view, an infinite multitude capable of accretion ad infinitum. Chatton is conscious that he is in the minority and is counter to the views of Aristotle and most philosopher-theologians.

Concerning the ten Categories of Aristotle, Ockham held that only substance and quality enjoyed extramental existence. In contrast, Chatton claimed that all the categories in one way or another were distinct realities and he took every opportunity to attack Ockham's claim that quantity was simply extended substance and not extramentally real.

According to Ockham relations as such are not some *tertia quid*. A white thing A and a white thing B both regarding their fundament whiteness and their distinct termini as things enjoy extramental reality, but this does not mean that their relation of similarity requires extramental status. Naturally, Chatton posits *res respectivae* and counters Ockham's views whenever possible.

Initially, Ockham held that concepts were nothing more than *esse obiectiva* (their being known) and not accidents or qualities of the mind. Because of Chatton's critique, Ockham modified his view and admitted that concepts were qualities of the mind. However, this did not mean that universals qua universals were things outside the mind, such that Ockham is best qualified as a conceptualist (nominalist in the medieval sense), where as Chatton and Scotus are best classified as moderate realists.

Chatton's other principal adversary was Aureol. The latter had criticized Scotus's opinion that a univocal concept of being was absolutely essential in any attempt to prove the existence of God. Aureol noted that the modes "finite" and "infinite" did not come under the purview of "being" as univocal. Chatton admits the objection while claiming that there is a concept of being that includes all its modes, including the ultimate individual difference or individual property (the word *haeceitas* occurs rarely and perhaps only once in Scotus's writings) and is a purely logical concept and not a metaphysical one.

Scotus's view of the principle of individuation as not being a double-negation (Henry of Ghent), a determinate quantity (St. Thomas Aquinas), or a collection of accidents (Porphyry and Anicius Manlius Severinus Boethius), but something positive that Scotus called the ultimate or individual difference or property, came under considerable attack from his successors. Ockham would claim that no such principle was required because God created individuals and not species, genera, or universals. Chatton, however, strove to defend Scotus's view even while cognizant of its difficulties.

Just as Chatton regularly attacked Ockham, so Wodeham frequently criticized Chatton's views, particularly if Chatton was seen as misinterpreting or misunderstanding Ockham's positions.

In the realm of theology Chatton may be read as favoring positive theology, namely, as concerned with what the scriptures and the church fathers had to say. He is less concerned about what God might do or what he might have done by his absolute power (hypothetical theology).

Chatton is thus one of the earliest Scotises and his views attest to the intellectual ferment of his age. He is an interpreter of Scotus and offers alternative approaches in philosophical-theological discourse to his fellow Franciscans, Aureol, Ockham, and Wodeham.

See also Duns Scotus, John; Peter Aureol; William of Ockham; Wodeham, Adam.

Bibliography

WORKS BY CHATTON

Quaestio utrum quantum et continuum componantur ex indivisibilibus sicut ex partibus integralibus, edited by J. E. Murdoch and E. A. Synan. *Franciscan Studies* 26 (1966): 212–288.

Reportatio et Lectura super Sententias: Collatio ad Librum Primum et Prologus, edited by Joseph C. Wey. Toronto, Canada: Pontifical Institute of Mediaeval Studies, 1989, viii + 430 pp.

Reportatio super Sententias. 3 vols., edited by Joseph C. Wey and Girard J. Etzkorn. Toronto, Canada: Pontifical Institute of Mediaeval Studies, 2002–2004.

Reportatio super Sententias. Liber II, dist. 1–20, edited by J. C. Wey and G. J. Etzkorn. Toronto: Pontifical Institute of Mediaeval Studies, 2004, xii + 370 pp.

Reportatio super Sententias. Liber III, dist. 1–33; Liber IV, qq. 1–11, edited by J. C. Wey and G. J. Etzkorn. Toronto: Pontifical Institute of Mediaeval Studies 2005, xiii + 399 pp.

WORKS ABOUT CHATTON

Baudry, L. "Gauthier de Chatton et son Commentaire des Sentences." *Archives d'histoire doctrinale et littéraire du moyen âge* 14 (1943–1945): 337–369.

Brown, Stephen F. "Medieval Supposition Theory in Its Theological Context." *Medieval Philosophy and Theology* 3 (1993): 121–157.

Brown, Stephen F. "Walter Chatton's Lectura and William of Ockham's *Quaestiones in libros Physicorum Aristotelis*." In *Essays Honoring Allan B. Wolter*, edited by William A. Frank and Girard J. Etzkorn, 81–93. St. Bonaventure, NY: Franciscan Institute, 1985.

Fitzpatrick, Noel A. "Walter Chatton on the Univocity of Being: A Reaction to Peter Aureoli and William of Ockham." *Franciscan Studies* 31 (1971): 88–171.

Gál, G. "Gualteri de Chatton et Guillemi de Ockham controversia de natura conceptus universalis." *Franciscan Studies* 27 (1967): 199–212.

Maurer, A. "Ockham's Razor and Chatton's Anti-razor." *Medieval Studies* 46 (1984): 463–475.

Tachau, Katherine H. "The Early Reaction to Aureol and Ockham: The Views of Walter Chatton." In *Vision and Certitude in the Age of Ockham: Optics, Epistemology, and the Foundations of Semantics, 1250–1345*, 180–208. Leiden, Netherlands: E. J. Brill, 1998.

Girard J. Etzkorn (2005)

CHEMISTRY, PHILOSOPHY OF

Ideas about the diversity of matter in terms of elements and compound substances and their transformations have been pivotal to any scientific or prescientific approach to nature. From ancient natural philosophy and alchemy to modern nineteenth-century chemistry, these ideas were made the basis of philosophical systems and became the target of critical reflection. After a temporary interruption when modern philosophy of science focused on mathematical physics, philosophy of chemistry emerged anew in the 1980s and has become a flourishing field in which philosophers, chemists, and historians of chemistry are engaged. While many of the old philosophical issues have been rediscovered and discussed, new issues have also appeared as a result of shifts of general philosophical focus, alliances with historians and sociologists of science, the development of chemistry, and changes in its role in society.

ONTOLOGICAL ISSUES

The objects of chemistry are subject to many ontological debates beyond simple issues of definition, and these debates also have an impact on epistemological and methodological issues. Following the example of microphysics, many philosophers and chemists take atoms and molecules as the basic objects of chemistry. Yet despite the numerous techniques available to visualize molecules, the notion of a molecule is a theoretical concept with many model assumptions that do not apply to nonmolecular substances, such as water, metals, and salts. It is not so much the lack of optional microstructural descriptions for these substances, but the variety of models, which are continuously refined and adapted to certain contexts and problems, that makes such models a weak basis for defining the basic objects of chemistry. Another option is to take material substances, either elementary or compound, as the basic objects. Yet, far from being phenomenologically given entities, pure substances are the final results of infinite purification operations; that is, they are ideal laboratory artifacts. This fact has in turn inspired operational definitions. Whether one takes microstructures or pure substances as basic is not an arbitrary decision, but rather has direct impact on chemical classification and all derived concepts, because there is no simple one-to-one relationship between the two kinds of entities. There are microstructures without corresponding pure substances, and there are substances with many different microstructures.

A second but related ontological issue is about natural kinds in chemistry. Microstructuralists, following Hilary Putnam, have claimed that water is a natural kind because it is determined by a microstructural essence. This claim faces the problems mentioned above. Yet the substance-based approach to natural kinds is confronted not only with a potentially infinite number of possibly essential properties (see below) but also with the artificiality of pure substances. Even if pure substances were stable kinds independent of our conceptualization, they are not independent of laboratory purification. Nonetheless, the experimental reproducibility of sufficiently pure substances provides, within limits, a successful operation to ensure relatively stable kinds.

A third ontological issue is about whether substances (or microstructures) or transformations are the basic objects of chemistry. This issue refers to the general debate between substance and process philosophy. If not closed in bottles, substances continuously undergo chemical reactions and are only intermediate states in an ongoing process. Quantum chemistry describes even these states as processes. Furthermore, traditional chemical characterization of substances goes by chemical properties, that is, by all the dispositions of substances to transform into other substances under certain conditions, including the presence of still other substances as reactants. Substance philosophers define a chemical reaction as the change of certain substances, whereas process philosophers define a substance by its characteristic chemical reactions. A third option, proposed by Joachim Schummer, combines substances and processes in a network of dynamic relations, as the proper object of chemical research. On this view, substances and reactivities mutually define each other. Answering the ontological question has direct consequences on whether chemists can best organize their knowledge in the form of substance databases, reaction databases, or combined substance-reaction databases.

Although all substances and transformations are usually considered objects of chemistry, the metaphysical distinction between natural and synthetic pervades both commonsense and chemical reasoning. Yet the notion of natural substances—substances that can be isolated from natural resources by purification—is questionable. Not only is purification a technical operation; also, most elements would have to count as synthetic when natural resources are lacking. On the other side of the ledger, all substances that can be isolated from natural resources can also be synthesized in the early twenty-first century, which undermines the distinction. Furthermore, we have little evidence to claim that a synthetic substance will never be isolable from natural resources in the entire universe.

EPISTEMOLOGICAL AND METHODOLOGICAL ISSUES

A central epistemological issue is whether chemical knowledge can be complete or not. Microstructural essentialists claim that a perfect microstructural description of any substance yields complete chemical knowledge. However, chemical properties are not manifest properties but dispositional relations (that is, relations of the form "*A* under certain conditions is disposed to react with *B* to form *C* and *D*"). This means that the structure of experimental chemical knowledge is relational, dispositional, and open-ended. Because new properties are defined by new conditions and new potential reactants (currently produced at 15.5 million new chemicals per year), experimental chemical knowledge can increase indefinitely without reaching a state of being complete. It is an open question to what extent theoretical approaches can compensate for the incompleteness on the experimental level.

Chemistry differs from other sciences in that its theoretical concepts need to serve different methodological goals. Besides the traditional goals of accurately describing, explaining, and predicting phenomena, theoretical concepts in chemistry also fulfill purposes of classification and synthesis. By 2004 the chemical classification system had distinguished 78.3 million different substances and ordered them by classes and subclasses. And beyond mere prediction of phenomena, theoretical concepts provide experimental guidelines for producing millions of new substances and reactions per year. For all three methodological goals, the main theoretical approach has been chemical-structure theory, which emerged in mid-nineteenth century and has been influenced and diversified by many different developments since, including quantum chemistry and spectroscopic instrumentation. Apart from this theory, a multitude of other theoretical concepts and models have been developed for particular substance classes and phenomena and for various purposes.

The main methodological issue in current philosophy of chemistry is to bring order to this complex picture without imposing upon chemistry methodologies tailored to other disciplines. Several case studies have shown that received approaches, for instance, Karl Popper's view that science makes progress by falsifying theories, are rather useless in chemistry. There is some agreement that chemists favor methodological pluralism and pragmatic application of models, rather than methodological universalism and the ideal of a single axiomatic theory. A study on scientific realism has suggested that entity realism, rather than theory realism, is a more appropriate methodological ideal in chemistry. The received methodological focus on methods of justification has been widened to include methods for research, that is, for developing new knowledge. Many detailed studies on the different kinds and uses of models in chemistry, from theoretical chemistry to chemical engineering, have been undertaken. Besides the impact of quantum mechanics (see the next section), the impact of spectroscopic instrumentation on theoretical concepts since the mid-twentieth century has received considerable attention, in fact, so much attention that interest in the "instrumental revolution" has replaced the older focus on the eighteenth-century "chemical revolution" by Antoine-Laurent Lavoisier and others. The methodological integration of both chemical analysis and synthesis, which form the major experimental activity of chemists, has overcome received distinctions between science and technology. Studies on the formal sign-language system of chemistry, consisting of structural formulas and reaction mechanisms, have illuminated its multipurpose theoretical capacity, but further studies are required to understand changes stemming from various theoretical and experimental developments.

REDUCIBILITY TO PHYSICS

Whether chemistry is reducible to physics is a question that could come up only in the mid-nineteenth century, when modern physics emerged as its own discipline, because the former meaning of "physics" (natural science or natural philosophy) included chemistry as a branch. Before then, mechanical (physical) approaches were among several competing approaches within theoretical chemistry, though not very successful. The question became meaningful only with the development of quantum mechanics and its application to chemistry since the late 1920s. Following a speech by Paul Dirac in 1929, many quantum physicists and philosophers of physics have taken for granted that the whole of chemistry would be reducible to quantum mechanics, and so would be part of physics.

Wary of making such bold claims, philosophers have carefully distinguished between different meanings of "reduction." An ontological reduction claims that the supposed objects of chemistry are actually nothing other than the objects of quantum mechanics and that quantum-mechanical laws govern their relations. In its strong, eliminative version, an ontological reduction states that there are no chemical objects proper. Antireductionists argue that theoretical entities are determined by their corresponding theories, and that theoretical entities of different theories cannot be identified. For instance, from the different meanings of the term "electron" in quantum electrodynamics and in chemical-reaction mechanisms, they conclude that the term "electron" has different references, which rules out an ontological reduction. An epistemological or theoretical reduction claims that all theories, laws, and fundamental concepts of chemistry can be derived from first-principle quantum mechanics as a more basic and more comprehensive theory. This claim has prompted many detailed studies (see below). Methodological reductionism, while acknowledging the current failure of epistemological reduction, recommends applying quantum-mechanical methods to all chemical problems, because that would be the most successful approach in the long run (approximate reductionism). But the mere promise of future success is not convincing unless accompanied by a comparative assessment of different methods. By modifying the popular notion that the whole is nothing but the sum of its parts, philosophers have developed two further versions of reductionism. Emergentism acknowledges that new properties of wholes (say of water) emerge when the parts (say oxygen and hydrogen) are combined, but it does not deny that the properties of the whole can be explained or derived from the relations between the parts (epistemological reductionism). Supervenience, in a simple version, means that, although epistemological reductionism might be wrong, the properties of a whole asymmetrically depend on the properties of the parts, so that every change of the properties of the whole is based on changes of the properties of the parts or the relations between the parts, but not the other way round.

When these terms are applied to the reduction of chemistry to quantum mechanics, that is, to chemical entities as wholes and quantum-mechanical entities as parts, emergentism and supervenience presuppose elements of epistemological or ontological reductionism. Thus, criticism of these positions applies accordingly. For instance, if one denies that chemical electrons are the same as quantum-electrodynamic electrons or, more generally, that quantum-mechanical entities are proper parts of chemical wholes, one ends up rejecting supervenience altogether.

Recent criticism has focused on epistemological reductionism by pointing out the technical limits of quantum mechanics with regard to particular chemical concepts, laws, and problems. Two quantum chemists, Guy Woolley and Hans Primas, have shown that the concept of molecular structure, which is central to most chemical theories, cannot be derived from first-principle quantum mechanics, because molecular structures cannot be represented by quantum-mechanical observables. Eric Scerri has argued that current quantum-mechanical approaches cannot calculate the exact electronic configuration of atoms, which was formerly considereda successful reduction of the chemical law that underlies the periodic system of elements. Jaap van Brakel has pointed out that successful applications of quantum mechanics to chemical problems frequently include model assumptions and concepts taken from chemistry. Joachim Schummer has argued that quantum-mechanical approaches are nearly absent and useless in areas that chemists are mainly concerned with: chemical reactions, synthesis, and classification.

Criticism of the reduction of chemistry to quantum mechanics, as the lowest level in the standard hierarchy of reductions, also challenges microreductionism as a general position and thus contributes to general philosophy. In the most detailed philosophical study on various forms of reductionism, Jaap van Brakel has used the case of chemistry to argue for a kind of pragmatism in which the "manifest image" of common sense and the empirical sciences is epistemologically primary over the "scientific image" of microphysics. Nikos Psarros presupposes a rejection of reductionism in his extensive project of seeking the cultural foundation of chemical concepts, laws, and theories in prescientific cultural practices, norms, and values. For many others, including Joachim Schummer, rejecting reductionism supports a pragmatist and pluralist position that clearly distinguishes between fields of research where quantum-mechanical approaches are strong and even indispensable and those where they are poor or even useless compared to other approaches. Once reductionism has lost its function of securing the unity of the sciences, new relationships between chemistry and other disciplines could become subject to philosophical and historical investigations, including studies of such multidisciplinary fields as atmospheric science, biomedical science, materials science, and nanotechnology.

FURTHER TOPICS

Current philosophy of chemistry reaches far beyond ontological, epistemological, and methodological issues. On the one hand, there are strong trends in historical research. Pertinent classical works on chemistry by such philosophers as Aristotle, Immanuel Kant, Georg Wilhelm Friedrich Hegel, Pierre Duhem, Ernst Cassirer, and Gaston Bachelard have been rediscovered, and these have allowed reinterpretations of the history of philosophy of science. Philosophical works by chemists of the past, such as Benjamin C. Brodie, Wilhelm Ostwald, Frantisek Wald, Edward F. Caldin, Fritz Paneth, and Michael Polanyi, have also been rediscovered. Historians and philosophers of chemistry have explored the development of many fundamental concepts in chemistry, such as chemical substance, element, atom, the periodic system of elements, molecular structure, chemical bond, chemical reaction, affinity, and aromaticity. In addition, important historical developments in chemistry have been philosophically scrutinized, such as the transitions from alchemy to modern chemistry and from phlogistic to antiphlogistic chemistry; the emergence of physical chemistry, quantum chemistry, and biochemistry; and the development of molecular-model building and instrumentalization.

On the other hand, philosophers of chemistry have also applied theoretical insights to practical problems, discovered a wider spectrum of philosophical perspectives on chemistry, and engaged in contemporary issues. Epistemological and ontological studies have found useful applications in chemistry education and information management. Beyond the traditional scope of philosophy of science, perspectives on chemistry from philosophy of technology, language, culture, and literature, and from metaphysics, aesthetics, ethics, sociology, and public understanding of science have all been exploited. For instance, studies on the role of visualization and aesthetics in chemical research have been undertaken to understand the heuristics and dynamics of research in a broader cultural context beyond traditional epistemic and technological goals. Philosophers and historians have investigated the historical roots and the cultural value conflicts underlying the widespread chemophobic attitude of society and the peculiar opposition of natural versus chemical. In addition to taking up general professional ethics, philosophers have challenged the legitimacy of chemical-weapon research, questioned the alleged moral neutrality of synthesizing new substances for scientific purposes, discussed the scope of moral responsibility of chemists for their synthetic products, and developed moral frameworks for assessing chemical-research practice. Finally, with the rise of nanotechnology, in which chemistry is particularly involved, philosophers of chemistry have taken a leading role in discussing the societal and ethical implications of this nanotechnology of the ultra-small.

Bibliography

Baird, Davis. *Thing Knowledge: A Philosophy of Scientific Instruments*. Berkeley, CA: University of California Press, 2003.

Bensaude-Vincent, Bernadette. *Eloge du mixte: Matériaux nouveaux et philosophie ancienne*. Paris: Hachette, 1998.

Bhushan, Nalini, and Stuart Rosenfeld, eds. *Of Minds and Molecules: New Philosophical Perspectives on Chemistry*. New York: Oxford University Press, 2000.

Burbidge, John W. *Real Process: How Logic and Chemistry Combine in Hegel's Philosophy of Nature*. Toronto: University of Toronto Press, 1996.

Earley, Joseph E., ed. *Chemical Explanation: Characteristics, Development, Autonomy*. New York: New York Academy of Science, 2003.

Foundations of Chemistry. Published since 1999. Includes special issues on "The Periodic System" (2001) and "Explanation and the Chemical Sciences" (2004).

Hoffmann, Roald. *The Same and Not the Same*. New York: Columbia University Press, 1995.

Hyle: International Journal for Philosophy of Chemistry. Published since 1995. Includes special issues on "Models in Chemistry" (1999–2000), "Ethics of Chemistry" (2001–2002), "Aesthetics and Visualization in Chemistry" (2003), and "Nanotech Challenges" (2004). Available from http://www.hyle.org/.

Janich, Peter, and Psarros, Nikos, eds. *The Autonomy of Chemistry*. Würzburg, Germany: Königshausen und Neumann, 1998.

Janich, Peter, and Nikos Psarros, eds. *Die Sprache der Chemie*. Würzburg, Germany: Königshausen und Neumann, 1996.

Klein, Ursula, ed. *Tools and Modes of Representation in the Laboratory Sciences*. Dordrecht, Netherlands: Kluwer, 2001.

Laszlo, Pierre. *La parole des choses, ou Le langage de la chimie*. Paris: Hermann, 1993.

Morris, Peter J. T., ed. *From Classical to Modern Chemistry: The Instrumental Revolution*. Cambridge, U.K.: Royal Society of Chemistry, 2002.

Primas, Hans. *Chemistry, Quantum Mechanics, and Reductionism: Perspectives in Theoretical Chemistry*. Berlin: Springer, 1981.

Psarros, Nikos. *Die Chemie und ihre Methoden: Ein philosophische Betrachtung*. Weinheim, Germany: Wiley-VCH, 1999.

Psarros, Nikos, and Kostas Gavroglu, eds. *Ars mutandi: Issues in Philosophy and History of Chemistry*. Leipzig, Germany: Leipziger Universitätsverlag, 1999.

Psarros, Nikos, Klaus Ruthenberg, and Joachim Schummer, eds. *Philosophie der Chemie*. Würzburg, Germany: Königshausen und Neumann, 1996.

Schummer, Joachim. *Realismus und Chemie: Philosophische Untersuchungen der Wissenschaft von den Stoffen*. Würzburg, Germany: Königshausen und Neumann, 1996.

Sobczynska, Danuta, Pawel Zeidler, and Ewa Zielonacka-Lis, eds. *Chemistry in the Philosophical Melting Pot*. Frankfurt, Germany: Peter Lang, 2004.

Van Brakel, Jaap. *Philosophy of Chemistry: Between the Manifest and the Scientific Image*. Louvain, Belgium: Leuven University Press, 2000.

Joachim Schummer (2005)

CHENG HAO

(1032–1085)

Cheng Hao, also called Cheng Mingdao, was cofounder, with his brother Cheng Yi, of the neo-Confucian school of Nature and Principle (*li*). He held some minor official posts but devoted most of his life to teaching.

By making principle the foundation of his philosophy and identifying it with the nature of man and things, Cheng Hao and his brother set the pattern for the neo-Confucian philosophical movement known since the eleventh century as the school of Nature and Principle. To Cheng Hao principle was the principle of nature (*tian li*), a concept that he evolved himself; it was the natural law. It had all the characteristics of principle as conceived by Cheng Yi, but as the principle of nature it was self-existent and unalterable. Whereas Cheng Yi stressed the doctrine that principle is one but its manifestations are many, Cheng Hao emphasized more strongly the principle of production and reproduction as the chief characteristic of nature. To him the spirit of life was in all things. This creative quality was *ren*, the highest good. In man, *ren* becomes humanity, or love, which makes him the moral being he is. It enables him to embrace all things and heaven and earth as one body.

Whatever is produced in man, that is, whatever is inborn in him, is his nature. In its original, tranquil state, human nature is neither good nor evil. The distinction arises when human nature is aroused and manifested in feelings and actions and when these feelings and actions abide by or deviate from the mean. The chief task of moral and spiritual cultivation is to calm one's nature through absolute impartiality and the identification of internal and external life. To achieve this end Cheng Hao advocated sincerity and seriousness.

There can be no denying that Cheng Hao was the more idealistic and his brother the more rationalistic. Cheng Hao more or less concentrated on self-cultivation, whereas his brother advocated both seriousness and learning. Under the influence of Buddhism Cheng Hao also advocated quietism. The two brothers had vastly different temperaments and therefore showed divergent tendencies, but it is not true, as some scholars claim, that one was monistic and the other dualistic.

See also Buddhism; Cheng Yi; Chinese Philosophy: Overview; Chinese Philosophy: Buddhism.

Bibliography

The works of Cheng Hao and his brother Cheng Yi are in *Er Cheng quan shu* ("The Complete Works of the Two Ch'engs").

Chan, Wing-tsit. *A Source Book in Chinese Philosophy.* Princeton, NJ: Princeton University Press, 1963.

Fung Yu-lan. *A History of Chinese Philosophy.* Translated by Derk Bodde, Vol. II. Princeton, NJ: Princeton University Press, 1953.

Graham, Angus G. *Two Chinese Philosophers, Ch'eng Ming-tao and Ch'eng Yi-ch'uan.* London: Lund Humphries, 1958; LaSalle, IL: Open Court Press, 1992.

Graham, Angus C. "What Was New in the Ch'eng-Chu Theory of Human Nature?" In *Studies in Chinese Philosophy and Philosophical Literature.* Albany: SUNY Press, 1990.

Feng Youlan. "Cheng Hao and Cheng Yi." *Chinese Studies in Philosophy* 13 (Win–Spr 1981–82): 127–182.

Wing-tsit Chan (1967)
Bibliography updated by Huichieh Loy (2005)

CHENG I

See *Cheng Yi*

CH'ENG MING-TAO

See *Cheng Hao*

CHENG YI

(1033–1107)

Cheng Yi, or Cheng Yi-chuan, was the most outstanding Chinese teacher of his time, a lecturer to the emperor on Confucian classics, and cofounder, with his brother Cheng Hao, of the neo-Confucian school of principle (*li*) that dominated Chinese thought for many centuries.

The central concept of the school is principle. The concept, negligible in ancient Confucianism, had been developed by the neo-Daoists and Buddhists, but the Cheng brothers were the first to build their philosophy primarily on it. To them, principle is self-evident and self-sufficient, extending everywhere and governing all things. It is laid before our very eyes. It cannot be augmented or diminished. It is many, but it is essentially one, for "definite principles" are but principle. "Principle is one but its manifestations are many." It is universal truth, universal order, universal law. Most important of all, it is the universal principle of creation. It is dynamic and vital. Man and all things form one body because all of them share this principle. It is identical with the mind and with the nature of man and things. Since principle is principle of creation and since life-giving is good, principle is the source of goodness. To be good is to obey principle. Thus, principle is both natural and moral and both general and specific. It has meaning as an abstract reality, but more so as the moral law of man.

The relation between principle and material force, which actualizes things, is not a dualistic one. Although Cheng Yi said that "material force exists after physical form and is therefore with it whereas the Way [principle] exists before form and is therefore without it," he also said that "what makes yin and yang [material force] is the Way." Material force is the physical aspect of principle. In the process of creation each operation is new, for material force is perpetually generated by Origination. (Origination is comparable to creation, except that it is natural and self-caused and is not an act of any being.)

To understand principle one can study one thing intensively or many things extensively. One can also read books, study history, or handle human affairs, for all things and affairs, including blades of grass, possess principle. This intellectual approach makes Cheng's system strongly rationalistic. The approach, however, is balanced by the moral, for whereas "the pursuit of learning depends on the extension of knowledge," "self-cultivation requires seriousness." This dual emphasis reminds one of the Buddhist twofold formula of meditation (dhyana) and wisdom (prajna).

See also Buddhism; Cheng Hao; Chinese Philosophy: Overview; Chinese Philosophy: Buddhism.

Bibliography

The works of Cheng Hao and his brother Cheng Yi are in *Er Cheng quan shu* ("The Complete Works of the Two Ch'engs").

Chan, Wing-tsit. *A Source Book in Chinese Philosophy.* Princeton, NJ: Princeton University Press, 1963.

Fung Yu-lan. *A History of Chinese Philosophy.* Translated by Derk Bodde, Vol. II. Princeton, NJ: Princeton University Press, 1953.

Graham, Angus G. *Two Chinese Philosophers, Ch'eng Ming-tao and Ch'eng Yi-ch'uan.* London: Lund Humphries, 1958; LaSalle, IL: Open Court Press, 1992.

Graham, Angus C. "What Was New in the Ch'eng-Chu Theory of Human Nature?" In *Studies in Chinese Philosophy and Philosophical Literature.* Albany: SUNY Press, 1990.

Feng Youlan. "Cheng Hao and Cheng Yi." *Chinese Studies in Philosophy* 13 (Win–Spr 1981–82): 127–182.

Wing-tsit Chan (1967)
Bibliography updated by Huichieh Loy (2005)

CH'ENG YI-CH-UAN

See *Cheng Yi*

CHERNYSHEVSKI, NIKOLAI GAVRILOVICH

See *Chernyshevskii, Nikolai Gavrilovich*

CHERNYSHEVSKII, NIKOLAI GAVRILOVICH
(1828–1889)

Nikolai Gavrilovich Chernyshevskii, the Russian literary and social critic, was the guiding spirit of Russian nihilism and a major representative of positivistic materialism in nineteenth-century Russian philosophy.

Chernyshevskii was born in Saratov, Russia. The son of an Orthodox priest, he attended a theological seminary before entering the University of St. Petersburg in 1846. After his graduation in 1850, he taught secondary school in Saratov until 1853, when he returned to St. Petersburg, secured a master's degree in Russian literature, and began writing for leading reviews. He soon became a principal editor of *Sovremennik* (The contemporary), and by the early 1860s was the foremost spokesman of radical socialist thought in Russia. Arrested in 1862, he was banished to Siberia in 1864 and passed the remaining twenty-five years of his life in forced exile. He was permitted to return to Saratov, in failing health, a few months before his death.

In his student days Chernyshevskii was attracted to the writings of the French socialists and of G. W. F. Hegel and the left-wing Hegelians. In 1849 he read Ludwig Feuerbach's *Essence of Christianity* and by 1850 had formed an allegiance to Feuerbach that was decisive in his philosophical development. He was also influenced by the English utilitarians, notably John Stuart Mill, whose *Principles of Political Economy* he translated into Russian in 1860.

Chernyshevskii's master's dissertation and first philosophical work, *Esteticheskie otnosheniia iskusstva k deistvitel'nosti* (The aesthetic relation of art to reality; St. Petersburg, 1855), is a critique of Hegelian aesthetics "deduced" (as Chernyshevskii later expressed it) from Feuerbach's naturalistic principles. Chernyshevskii argued that art is an aesthetically inferior substitute for concrete reality. The essential purpose of art is to reproduce the phenomena of real life that are of interest to man, compensating for his lack of opportunity to experience the reality itself. The derivative purposes of art, which give it a moral dimension, are to explain this reality for the benefit of man and to pass judgment upon it. Chernyshevskii developed his aesthetic views further, emphasizing the social context of art, in his *Ohcerki gogolevskogo perioda russkoi literatury* (St. Petersburg, 1855–1856; translated as *Essays on the Gogol Period of Russian Literature*).

In his chief philosophical work, a long essay titled *Antropologicheskii printsip v filosofii* (The anthropological principle in philosophy; 1860), Chernyshevskii exhibited his acceptance of Feuerbach's anthropologism and adopted the materialistic position he retained throughout his life. By "the anthropological principle" Chernyshevskii meant the conception of man as a unitary organism whose nature is not bifurcated into "spiritual" and "material" elements. He argued that philosophical questions can be resolved only from this point of view and by the methods of the natural sciences. Indeed, in all their essentials such questions had already been resolved by the sciences, according to Chernyshevskii: Man is a complex chemical compound whose behavior is strictly subject to the law of causality, who in every action seeks his own pleasure, and whose character is determined by the features of the environment within which he is obliged to act.

On this basis Chernyshevskii advocated "rational egoism"—an ethical theory of enlightened egoistic utilitarianism—and maintained that radical reconstruction of the social environment is needed to create happy and productive individuals. He portrayed these "new people" and the socialist order of the future in a novel, *Chto delat'?* (*What Is to Be Done?*, St. Petersburg, 1863), which was the principal literary tract of Russian nihilism and was for decades enormously influential in the radical movement. In his socioeconomic thought in general Chernyshevskii emphasized the peasant commune and the artel and is considered an important forerunner of Russian Populism.

Chernyshevskii was a severe critic of neo-Kantian phenomenalism. In a number of letters and in the essay *Kharakter Chelovecheskovo Znaniya* (The character of human knowledge; Moscow, 1885), written in exile, he espoused epistemological realism and condemned the skepticism and "illusionism" (as he called it) of such scientists as Rudolf Virchow and Emil Heinrich Du Bois-Reymond.

Bibliography

WORKS BY CHERNYSHEVSKII

Polnoye Sobraniye Sochineni (Complete works). 16 vols. Moscow, 1939–1953.

Sobranie sochinenii (Works). 5 vols. Moscow: Pravda, 1974.

Selected Philosophical Essays. Westport, CT: Hyperion, 1981.

What Is to Be Done?. Translated by M. R. Katz. Ithaca, NY: Cornell University Press, 1989.

WORKS ON CHERNYSHEVSKI

Paperno, I. *Chernyshevsky and the Age of Realism: A Study in the Semiotics of Behavior*. Stanford, CA: Stanford University Press, 1988.

Randall, F. B. *N. G. Chernyshevskii*. New York: Twayne Publishers, 1967.

Venturi, Franco, *Il populismo russo*. 2 vols. Turin, 1952. Translated by Francis Haskell as *Roots of Revolution*. New York: Knopf, 1960.

Woehrlin, W. F. *Chernyshevskii: The Man and the Journalist*. Cambridge, MA: Harvard University Press, 1971.

Zenkovskii, V. V. *A History of Russian Philosophy*. Translated by G. Kline. New York and London: Routledge, 2003.

James P. Scanlan (1967)

Bibliography updated by Vladimir Marchenkov (2005)

CHICHERIN, BORIS NIKOLAEVICH

(1828–1904)

Boris Nikolaevich Chicherin, a Russian philosopher, was educated at Moscow University, where he studied under both K. D. Kavelin and T. N. Granovskii. Until 1868 he was a professor at Moscow University; he also served briefly as tutor to the royal family and as mayor of Moscow (1881–1883). He was cautiously liberal in politics and, after an early period of agnosticism, devoutly Russian Orthodox in religion.

Chicherin wrote substantial critical studies of Vladimir Solov'ëv (1880) and Auguste Comte (1892), as well as several works on philosophy of law and on the state. His ethical individualism, like that of N. I. Kareev, was close to Immanuel Kant's, but, unlike Kareev, Chicherin was an orthodox Hegelian in logic, ontology, and philosophy of history. This eclecticism generated an unresolved tension in his thought. On the one hand Chicherin asserted that great men are merely "organs and instruments of a universal spirit" and that, under certain conditions, a nationality (*narodnost'*) "may become an individual person." On the other hand he insisted that man as a rational creature and "bearer of the Absolute" is an end in himself and must not be "treated as a mere instrument."

Chicherin asserted, with N. K. Mikhailovskii, that "not society, but individuals, think, feel, and desire"; he opposed the "monstrous notion" that society is a higher organism, an all-devouring Moloch, whose function is "to make mankind happy by putting it in chains." Chicherin was alert to encroachments by the social and political spheres on the private and personal realm; he saw the individual—the "foundation-stone of the entire social edifice"—as a single spiritual substance, possessed of reason and free will, and hence of a moral worth and dignity that demand respect.

Chicherin saw the dialectical movement of both thought and being as a passage from initial unity to final multiplicity, through the two intermediary stages of relation and combination. Thus, more explicitly than G. W. F. Hegel, he converted the dialectical triad into a tetrad.

See also Agnosticism; Comte, Auguste; Hegel, Georg Wilhelm Friedrich; Kant, Immanuel; Kareev, Nikolai Ivanovich; Kavelin, Konstantin Dmitrievich; Philosophy of Law, History of; Mikhailovskii, Nikolai Konstantinovich; Solov'ëv (Solovyov), Vladimir Sergeevich.

Bibliography

Two of Chicherin's works, *Polozhitel' naia filosofiia i edinstvo nauki* (Positive philosophy and the unity of science; Moscow: n.p., 1892) and *Osnovaniia logiki i metafiziki* (Foundations of logic and metaphysics; Moscow: n.p., 1894), have been translated as *Philosophische Forschungen* (Heidelberg, 1899). Chicherin's *Filosofiya prava* (Philosophy of law) was published in Moscow in 1900.

For discussion of Chicherin, see V. V. Zenkovsky, *Istoriia russkoi filosofii,* 2 vols. (Paris, 1948 and 1950), translated by G. L. Kline as *A History of Russian Philosophy,* 2 vols. (New York: Columbia University Press, 1953), pp. 606–620.

George L. Kline (1967)

CHICHERIN, BORIS NIKOLAEVICH [ADDENDUM]

In the last quarter of the twentieth century the reputation of Boris Nikolaevich Chicherin underwent a remarkable revival, both in Russia and the West. Already before the collapse of the Soviet Union Chicherin fascinated those Soviet philosophers of law who sought stealthily to combine civil liberties with state power. That fascination, masked by an accompanying critique of Chicherin's bourgeois liberalism, was expressed in an important 1975 book by Valerii Dimitrievich Zor'kin. The collapse of the Soviet regime in 1991, the unexpected elevation of Zor'kin to the post of chief justice of the Russian Constitutional Court, the broad search by intellectuals for new ways to combine freedom and authority in the post-Soviet era, and a general scholarly reconsideration of the Russian national tradition in philosophy—all these factors contributed indirectly to the new interest in Chicherin's political thinking.

At the beginning of the new millennium Chicherin has found new admirers not among Russian liberals but among moderate conservatives who approve of his doctrine of the state as absolute or undivided sovereign, who applaud his pragmatic recognition that individual liberty must be balanced against the general needs of society, who share his support for capitalism constrained only by the needs of the economically defenseless, and who find his Realpolitik in statecraft wiser than dogmatic nationalism or naive internationalism. In addition to studying his political philosophy, post-Soviet Russian scholars have examined anew Chicherin's philosophy of history, making a much more positive assessment than before of his advocacy of a modified Hegelian approach to understanding the laws or regularities of historical development. The tendency has been to regard him as an important innovator, one of the originators of the influential state school of historical writing.

In the West Chicherin has been interpreted as the most important theoretician of liberalism in Russia, the figure who between 1855 and 1866 systematized hostility toward serfdom and defense of civil rights into a coherent liberal political program favoring the gradual introduction into Russia of the rule of law. Chicherin's program sharply distinguished between civil rights (freedom of conscience and speech) and political rights (freedom of suffrage, constitutional guarantees, and representative government). He argued that Russian political culture at midcentury was not yet mature enough for political rights but that it could responsibly uphold civil rights. This view, based on Baron de Montesquieu's notion that liberty rests on a complex relationship among the geographical, cultural, social, political, and historical institutions prevailing in a given country, made Chicherin unpopular with the radical left and recalcitrant right.

In 1882–1883 Chicherin warned in his two-volume book *Sobstvennost' i gosudarstvo* (Property and the state) that individual liberty in Europe and Russia was being endangered by "a new monster rising above the state: it is called 'society'" (Chicherin 1882, p. xix). His apprehension that social pressure for equality would soon destroy liberty bears strong resemblance to Alexis Tocqueville's (1805–1859) fear of the "tyranny of the majority." Consequently, during the last two decades of his life Chicherin stood as Russia's strongest advocate of individual liberty against society and the state. His program came to approximate what Friedrich Augustus von Hayek would later call "classical liberalism" or what other scholars would name "the old liberalism" in distinction to the new, social liberalism that came to prevail in the West after John Stuart Mill. The philosophical foundations of that program, both Hegelian and Kantian, were elucidated in his remarkable *Filosofiia prava* (Philosophy of law; 1900). In it Chicherin made plain his antipathy to the collectivist idealism of Plato, Johann Gottlieb Fichte, and Karl Christian Friedrich Krause; to Benthamite utilitarianism; to Rudolf von Jhering's (1818–1892) command theory of law; to Russian socialism in all its variants; to Marxism; and to Vladimir Sergeevich Solov'ëv's (Solovyov) mystical fusion of law and morality.

That Chicherin's name has been appropriated both by Russian *étatist* conservatives and Western individualists may point back to the "unresolved tension in his thought" (George Louis Kline's phrase) between Hegelian determinism and Kantian individualism, but may also be an indication of Chicherin's life-long effort to find an appropriate balance between authority and liberty, duty and right, the needs of society and the requirements of the individual. His conviction that it is impossible in politics to realize simultaneously all values in their fullness and that some values (e.g., liberty and equality) are irreconcilable in principle anticipated the value pluralism of Isaiah Berlin.

Bibliography

WORKS BY CHICHERIN

Liberty, Equality, and the Market: Essays. Translated and edited by G. M. Hamburg. New Haven, CT: Yale University Press, 1998.

Sobstvennost' i gosudarstvo, Chast' 1. Moscow: Tipografiia Martynova, 1882.

WORKS ABOUT CHICHERIN

Hamburg, G. M. *Boris Chicherin and Early Russian Liberalism, 1828–1866.* Stanford, CA: Stanford University Press, 1992.

Walicki, Andrzej. "Boris Chicherin: The 'Old Liberal' Philosophy of Law." In *Legal Philosophies of Russian Liberalism*, 105–164. Oxford, U.K.: Clarendon Press, 1987.

Zor'kin, Valerii Dimitrievich. *Is istorii burzhuazno-liberal'noi politicheskoi mysli Rossii vtoroi poloviny XIX–nachala XX v* [From the history of bourgeois liberal political thought in Russia in the late 19th and early 20th century]. Moscow: Izdatel'stvo Moskovskogo Universiteta, 1975.

G. M. Hamburg (2005)

CHINESE PHILOSOPHY

This composite entry is comprised of the following sub-entries:

OVERVIEW
BUDDHISM
CONFUCIANISM
CONTEMPORARY
DAOISM
ETHICS
LANGUAGE AND LOGIC
METAPHYSICS AND EPISTEMOLOGY
RELIGION
SOCIAL AND POLITICAL THOUGHT

OVERVIEW

In its twenty-five hundred years of evolution Chinese philosophy has passed through four periods: the ancient period (until 221 BCE), when the so-called Hundred Schools contended; the middle period (221 BCE–960 CE), when Confucianism emerged supreme in the social and political spheres, only to be overshadowed in philosophy first by Neo-Daoism and then by Buddhism; the modern period (960–1900), when Neo-Confucianism was the uncontested philosophy, although by no means without variety or conflicts of its own; and the contemporary period (from 1912), when Neo-Confucianism, having become decadent and being challenged by Western philosophy, first succumbed to it, then was revived and reconstructed, but at mid century was overwhelmed by Marxism.

ANCIENT PERIOD: HUNDRED SCHOOLS (UNTIL 221 BCE)

The Hundred Schools, which included individual agriculturalists, diplomatists, military strategists, and other independent thinkers, had one thing in common, their primary concern with man both as an individual and as a member of society. This humanistic note was dominant from the earliest times and characterized all schools. The most prominent of the schools were the Confucianists, the Daoists, the Mohists, the Logicians, the Yin Yang school, and the Legalists.

Chinese thought at the dawn of civilization was dominated by the fear of spiritual beings. During the Shang dynasty (1751–1112 BCE) the Chinese would do nothing important without first finding out, through divination, the pleasure of the spirits. But when the Zhou overthrew the Shang, in 1112 BCE, human talent was needed to consolidate the newly established kingdom and to fight the surrounding barbarians. Human skill in irrigation proved to be more effective than praying to the spirits for rain. And the tribal anthropomorphic Lord (*Di*), who controlled human destiny at his whim, was now replaced by impartial and universal Heaven (*Tian*). The Mandate of Heaven (divine election) for the House of Zhou to rule rested on the moral ground that rule belongs to the man of virtue. In the final analysis, it was man's ability and virtue that counted. Humanism had reached a high pitch.

CONFUCIAN SCHOOL. The person who elevated humanism to the highest degree was Confucius (551–479 BCE). His central concerns were the "superior man" and a well-ordered society. Up to his time the ideal man was the aristocrat, the *junzi* (literally, "son of a ruler") a perfectly natural concept in a feudal society. In a radical departure from the past, Confucius formulated an entirely new ideal, the superior man, one who is wise, humane, and courageous, who is motivated by righteousness instead of profit, and who "studies the Way [Dao] and loves men." This conception of the superior man has never changed in the Confucian tradition.

Nature of the individual. Confucius never explained how it is possible for one to become a superior man. He seemed to imply that man is good by nature, but he said only that "by nature men are alike but through practice they have become far apart." It was necessary to explain how we know that man can be good. Mencius (c. 372–c. 298 BCE), one of his two major followers, supplied that explanation. From the facts that all children know how to love their parents and that a man seeing a child about to fall into a well will instinctively try to save him, Mencius concluded that man's nature is originally good, possessing the "Four Beginnings"—humanity (*ren*), righteousness (*yi*), propriety (*li*), and wisdom—and the innate knowledge of the good and the innate ability to do good. Evil is due not to one's nature but to bad environment, lack of education, and "casting oneself away." The superior man is one who "develops his mind to the utmost" and "nourishes his nature."

Xunzi (c. 295–c. 238 BCE), although holding essentially the same idea of the superior man, contended that the original nature of man is evil. He argued that by nature man seeks for gain and is envious. Because conflict and strife inevitably follow, rules of propriety and righteousness have been formulated to control evil and to train men to be good. Propriety and righteousness are not native moral characteristics of man but the artificial efforts of sages. Thus, Xunzi was directly opposed to Mencius. Nevertheless, both were truly Confucian because their central objective was the good man.

Nature of society. Confucius wanted a society governed by men of virtue who, through personal examples and moral persuasion rather than law or punishment, would bring about the people's welfare and social order. Mencius, applying his theory of original goodness, reasoned that if a ruler applies his originally humane mind to the administration of his government, he will have a humane government, and what Confucius desired will naturally ensue. Xunzi, on the other hand, felt that since man's nature is evil, he needs rulers to regulate him by law and teachers to guide him by rules of propriety and righteousness. Once more he and Mencius were opposed, but again they aimed at the same thing—namely, a well-ordered society.

Relation of the individual and society. The Confucian school, then, is devoted to the harmonious development of the individual and society. This theme is systematically presented in the little classic *The Great Learning,* traditionally ascribed to the Confucian pupil Zengzi (505–c. 436 BCE). It consists of eight successive steps: the investigation of things, the extension of knowledge, the sincerity of the will, the rectification of the mind, the cultivation of the personal life, the regulation of the family, national order, and world peace. The goal is a harmonious world in which man and society are well developed and adjusted.

The harmony of the individual and society rests on several basic ideas. Foremost of these is humanity (*ren*). Confucius discussed humanity more than any other subject, and throughout history it has remained one of the key concepts in Confucianism. Previously the term connoted particular virtues, such as kindness, benevolence, and affection. Confucius interpreted it to mean the general virtue, the foundation of all particular virtues. Humanity is the moral character, which enables man to attain true manhood. The moral character is developed in oneself and in one's relations with others. A man of *ren,* "wishing to establish his own character, also establishes the character of others." Thus, *ren* has two aspects, conscientiousness (*zhong*) and altruism (*shu*).

Following Confucius, Mencius stressed humanity. But he almost always mentioned humanity and righteousness (*yi*) together, the first in the Confucian school to do so. By this time a clear distinction between what is good, correct, or proper and what is evil, incorrect, or improper had to be made. He wanted the innate sense of correctness fully exercised. Xunzi felt the same necessity to define correctness, but he sought to achieve this end through the precision of and distinctions made in law, rules of propriety, and music.

Another idea behind the harmony of the individual and society is the rectification of names. For Confucius it meant verifying or implementing an exact correspondence between titles of rank and actual fulfillment of responsibilities. Mencius, however, took "rectification" to mean correcting errors in one's heart (moral errors). Xunzi gave it a logical interpretation. To him rectification was distinguishing the concepts of names and actualities, similarities and differences, and particularity and generality. In doing this he developed the only logical aspect, in the formal sense, of ancient Confucianism. Confucius, Mencius, and Xunzi all believed that when names are rectified the positions of the individual and society will be well adjusted.

The third concept basic to social harmony is the mean (*zhongyong*). By this Confucius chiefly meant moderation as a guide to human action, but he implicitly referred to the ideals of centrality and harmony as well. The reference to centrality and harmony was greatly elaborated in the classic *The Doctrine of the Mean,* traditionally ascribed to Confucius's grandson Tzu-ssu (492–431 BCE). Centrality (*zhong*) consists in not deviating from the mean, and harmony (*yong*) exists in the common, the ordinary, and the universal. Centrality in the individual is the state of equilibrium in one's mind before the feelings are aroused, and harmony is the state after they are aroused. In society centrality and harmony together mean complete concord in human relations. Ultimately, through the moral principle, heaven and earth will attain their proper order and all things will flourish in a harmonious universal operation. At this point the doctrine of the mean assumed metaphysical significance, which made it a profound influence on Neo-Confucianism.

When the individual behaves correctly and society operates in the right manner, the Way is said to prevail. The Way (Dao) is the moral law, or moral order. It is the Way of Heaven. Heaven was no longer conceived of as the anthropomorphic Lord (*Di*), the greatest of all spiritual beings. To Confucius, Heaven was the origin of all things the Supreme Reality, whose purposive character is manifested in the Way. The Supreme Being only reigns, leaving the Way to operate by itself. But no one can be separated from this Way, and for the Way to be meaningful it must be demonstrated by man. "It is man that can make the Way great," Confucius said. The note of humanism was sounded again.

DAOIST SCHOOL. To the Confucian school Dao was a system of moral truth, the expression of Heaven. To the Daoist school, however, it was Nature itself. Laozi (c. sixth century BCE), the founder of the school, equated Dao with Heaven, the "self-so" (*ziran*), and the One. It is eternal, spontaneous, nameless, and indescribable, at once the beginning of all things and the way in which they pursue their course. It is nonbeing, not in the sense of nothingness but in the sense of not being any particular thing. It is absolute and mystical. When it is possessed by an individual thing, it becomes that thing's character or virtue (*de*). The ideal life of the individual, the ideal order of society, and the ideal type of government are all based on it and guided by it. As the way of life it denotes simplicity, spontaneity, tranquility, weakness, and, most important of all, nonaction (*wuwei*), or, rather, letting Nature take its own course. Laozi's concept of Dao was so radically different from those of other schools that his school alone eventually came to be known as the Daoist school (Daojia).

Zhuangzi (born c. 369 BCE), Laozi's chief follower, took a step forward and interpreted Dao as the Way of unceasing transformation. In so doing he gave Dao a dynamic character. In the universal process of constant flux all things are equalized from the point of view of Dao. At the same time, since everything transforms in its own way, its individual nature is to be respected. Thus, in the ideas of Zhuangzi there is a curious combination of universality and particularity, a point that had far-reaching effect on later Daoist developments.

Although the Daoist school was definitely more transcendental than the Confucian, its chief concern, like that of the Confucian school, was man. Laozi discoursed mainly on government, and Zhuangzi discussed at great length the way to find spiritual freedom and peace. There is no desertion of society or the individual in Daoism.

The dominant notes in the Daoist school were, however, oneness and naturalness. It is not surprising that the Daoists strongly attacked other schools, particularly the Confucian, for making distinctions of all kinds. But so far as interest in man and society was concerned, the school agreed with the Confucian and other schools.

MOHIST SCHOOL. The Daoist school in time became strong enough to compete with Confucianism, but in the ancient period it was the Mohist school, founded by Mozi (c. 470–c. 391 BCE), that rivaled Confucianism in prominence. In practically all its major doctrines it stood opposed to Confucianism. The most serious and irreconcilable issue was that between the Mohist doctrine of universal love and the Confucian doctrine of love with distinctions. Mozi wanted people to love other people's parents as they love their own, whereas the Confucianists, especially Mencius, insisted that although one should show love to all, one should show special affection to his own parents. Otherwise there would be no difference between other people's parents and one's own, and family relationships would collapse.

In further opposition Mozi condemned religious rites and musical festivals as economically wasteful; the Confucianists held that ceremonies and music are necessary to provide proper expression and restraint in social behavior. This conflict on the practical level stemmed from the fundamental opposition of utilitarianism and moralism. In this issue, as in the issue of universal versus graded love, Mozi justified his doctrines on the basis of "benefits to Heaven, to spiritual beings, and to all men."

Mozi also attacked the Confucianists' teaching of humanity (*ren*) and righteousness (*yi*), for advocating them but for failing to recognize that humanity and righteousness originated with Heaven. As he repeatedly said, it is the will of Heaven that man should practice humanity and righteousness, be economical, and practice universal love, and it is man's duty to obey the will of Heaven. Of all the ancient schools only the Mohist placed ethics on a religious basis.

LOGICIANS. The Mohist doctrine of universal love was subscribed to by the Logicians. Their main interest, however, lay in a discussion of names and actualities. The school was small and has left little imprint, if any, on subsequent Chinese intellectual history. But it was the only school devoted to such metaphysical problems as existence, relativity, space, time, quality, actuality, and causes. Its most outstanding scholars were Hui Shi (c. 380–c. 305 BCE) and Gongsun Long (born 380 BCE). To Hui Shi things were relative, but to Gongsun Long they were absolute. The former emphasized change, whereas the latter stressed universality and permanence. The Logicians employed metaphysical and epistemological concepts that were primitive and crude, but they were the only group in ancient China interested in these concepts for their own sake.

YIN YANG SCHOOL. While the schools mentioned above were thriving, the Yin Yang school prevailed and influenced all of them. We know nothing about its origin or early representatives, but its ideas are simple and clear. Basically, it conceived of two cosmic forces, one yin, which is negative, passive, weak, and disintegrative, and the other yang, which is positive, active, strong, and integrative. All things are produced through the interaction of the two. Associated with the theory of yin and yang is that of the five agents, or elements (*wuzing*)—metal, wood, water, fire, and earth. According to this theory things succeed one another as the five agents take their turns. Originally the two doctrines were separate. It is generally believed that Zou Yan (305–240 BCE), the representative thinker of the Yin Yang school, was the one who combined the interaction of yin and yang with the rotation of the five agents.

Yin and yang were at first conceived as opposed to each other, succeeding each other, or complementary to each other. The five agents, too, were conceived as overcoming one another or producing one another. Eventually all alternatives were synthesized so that harmony reigns over conflict and unity exists in multiplicity. Yin, yang, and the five agents are forces, powers, and agents rather than material elements. The whole focus is on process, order, and laws of operation. Existence is viewed as a dynamic process of change obeying definite laws, following definite patterns, and based on a preestablished harmony.

One implication of this doctrine is the correspondence and at the same time the unity of man and Nature, for both are governed by the same process. Another is that the universe is a systematic, structural one, determinate, describable, and even predictable. Still another implication is that the universe is a perpetual process of rotation. Just as the five agents rotate, so history proceeds in cycles, and just as yin and yang increase and decrease, so things rise and fall. The Yin Yang school, more than any other, put Chinese ethical and social teachings on a cosmological basis. Generally speaking, its ideas have affected every aspect of Chinese life, be it metaphysics, art, marriage, or even cooking. Wherever harmony is sought or change takes place, the forces of yin and yang are at work.

LEGALIST SCHOOL. Philosophically the Legalist school is the least important because it had no new concept to offer. In fact, it did not concern itself with ethical, metaphysical, or logical concepts, as other schools do. Its chief objective was the concentration of power in the ruler. Within the Legalist school there were three tendencies—the enforcement of law with heavy reward and punishment, the manipulation of statecraft, and the exercise of power. The school, called Fajia (meaning school of law) in Chinese, had many representatives, some of them prime ministers, but the most outstanding was Han Feizi (died 233 BCE), who combined the three tendencies of his school.

The Legalist school assumed the evil nature of man and rejected moral values in favor of concrete results. In insisting that laws be applicable to all, it unwittingly subscribed to the doctrine of the equality of all men, and in insisting that assignments be fulfilled with concrete results, it strengthened the doctrine of the correspondence of names and actualities. There is no doubt that compared to other schools, it looked to circumstances rather than principles and to the present rather than the past. It agreed with them in one respect, that life is in a process of constant change.

The Legalists helped the Qin to liquidate the feudal states and establish a new dynasty in 221 BCE. The Qin enforced the Legalists' totalitarian philosophy, suppressed other schools, and burned their books in 213 BCE. The contest of the Hundred Schools now came to an end.

MIDDLE PERIOD (221 BCE–960 CE)

The Legalists ruled the Qin with absolute power and tolerated no other schools, but other schools were by no means totally absent from the scene. When the dynasty was overthrown by the Han in 206 BCE, some of these schools reemerged, carrying with them a crosscurrent of thought. The result was a syncretic movement.

SYNCRETIC CONFUCIANISM. Confucianism became the state ideology in 136 BCE It was supreme in government, society, education, and literature and remained so until the twentieth century. But philosophically it was almost overwhelmed by the doctrine of yin and yang. This can readily be seen in the philosophies of the *Book of Changes* and Dong Zhongshu.

The *Book of Changes* (*Yijing*) is a Confucian classic, but the Daoists also made much use of it. (Tradition ascribes part of the work to Confucius, but it was most probably composed several centuries later, although portions may have been in existence in Confucius's lifetime.) It shows the strong impact of the Yin Yang school. According to the *Book of Changes* creation of the world begins with the Great Ultimate (*taiji*), which engenders yin and yang. Yin and yang, in their turn, give rise to the four forms of major and minor yin and yang. The four forms produce the eight elements (*bagua*), which, through interaction and multiplication, produce the universe. The cosmogony is naive and elementary, but it introduced into Confucianism the strong features of Daoist naturalism and the interaction of yin and yang. Since then the Confucianists have viewed the universe as a natural and well-coordinated system in which the process of change never ceases.

The syncretic spirit was also strong in Dong Zhongshu (179–104 BCE), the most outstanding Confucian philosopher of the period. He combined the Confucian doctrines of ethics and history with the ideas of yin and yang. Greed and humanity, the two foremost moral qualities, he correlated with yin and yang, respectively. Likewise, he equated human nature and feelings with yang and yin and thereby with good and evil. All things are grouped into pairs or into sets of five to correspond to yin and yang and the five agents. Ultimately they are reduced to numbers. In this arrangement historical periods parallel the succession of the five agents, and man, the microcosm, corresponds to Nature, the macrocosm. But Dong went beyond the idea of mere correspondence. To him, things of the same kind activate each other. There is the universal phenomenon of mutual activation and influence that makes the universe a dynamic, organic whole.

Unfortunately, this doctrine soon degenerated into superstition. Early in the Han dynasty (206 BCE–220 CE) there was a wide belief in prodigies, which were taken to be influences of Nature on man or vice versa. Wang Chong (27 CE–c. 100 CE), an independent thinker, revolted against this. He declared that Heaven (Nature) takes no action and that natural events, including prodigies, occur spontaneously. Man is an insignificant being in the vast universe, and he does not influence Nature or become a ghost at death to influence people. In addition, Wang Chong insisted that any theory must be tested by concrete evidence, and he supported his own theories with numerous facts. Thus, he raised rationalistic naturalism to a height never before reached in Chinese history and prepared for the advent of rationalistic and naturalistic Neo-Daoism, which was to replace Confucian philosophy.

NEO-DAOISM. Under the influence of the doctrine of the correspondence of man and Nature and the belief in prodigies, Han dynasty thinkers were chiefly concerned with phenomena. Thinkers of the Wei-Jin period (220–420), however, went beyond phenomena to find reality behind space and time. They were interested in what is profound and abstruse (*xuan*), and consequently their school is called Xuan Xuanxue ("profound studies") or the Metaphysical school. They developed their doctrines in their commentaries on the *Laozi,* the *Zhuangzi,* and the *Book of Changes,* the "three profound studies." To Wang Bi (226–249), the most brilliant Neo-Daoist, ultimate reality is original nonbeing (*benwu*). It is not nothingness but the pure being, original substance, which transcends all distinctions and descriptions. It is whole and strong. And it is always correct because it is in accord with principle (*li*), the universal rational principle that unites all particular concepts and events. The note of principle was a new one. It anticipated Neo-Confucianism, which is based entirely on it.

Guo Xiang (died 312), another famous Neo-Daoist, developed his theory in his comments on Zhuangzi's doctrine of self-transformation. To Guo Xiang, things transform themselves according to principle, but each and every thing has its own principle. Everything is therefore self-sufficient, and there is no need for an overall original reality to combine or govern them, as Wang Bi believed. Whereas Wang Bi emphasized nonbeing, the one, and transcendence, Guo Xiang emphasized being, the many, and immanence.

As a movement Neo-Daoism did not last long, but its effect on later philosophy was great. It raised the Daoist concepts of being and nonbeing to a higher level and thereby formed the bridge between Chinese and Buddhist philosophies.

BUDDHISM. In the first several centuries Buddhism existed in China as a popular religion rather than as a philosophy. When Buddhists came into contact with the Chinese literati, especially the Neo-Daoists, in the third century, they matched Buddhist concepts with those of Daoism, identifying *Tathatā* (Thusness, *Nirvāṇa*) with the Daoist "original nonbeing," for example. Under Neo-Daoist influence, early Buddhist schools in China all engaged in discussions on being and nonbeing.

Middle Doctrine and Dharma Character. The problems of being and nonbeing largely characterize the two major Buddhist schools that developed in China in the sixth century, the Middle Doctrine (Zhonglun), or Three Treatise (San-lun), school and the Dharma Character (Faxiang), or Consciousness Only (Weishi), school. The Middle Doctrine school, systematized by Jizang (549–623), was based on three Indian scriptures—the *Mādhyamika Śāstra* (Treatise on the Middle Doctrine), by Nāgārjuna (c. 100–200), the *Dvādaśamikāya Śāstra* (Twelve gates treatise), also by Nāgārjuna, and the *Śata Śāstra* (One-hundred verses treatise), by Ārya-deva (exact dates unknown), a pupil of Nāgārjuna. This school regarded both being and nonbeing as extremes whose opposition must be resolved in a synthesis. The synthesis, itself a new extreme with its own antithesis, needs to be synthesized also. In the end all oppositions are dissolved in the True Middle or emptiness. The school was essentially nihilistic and is often called the school of Nonbeing.

In contrast, the Consciousness Only school, which was founded by Zuangzang (596–664), regarded all dharmas (elements of existence) and their characters—that is, the phenomenal world—as real, although only to a certain degree because they are illusory, apparent, and dependent. The school divides the mind into eight consciousnesses, the last of which contains "seeds" or effects of previous deeds and thoughts that affect future deeds and thoughts. Future deeds and thoughts are "transformations" of present ones, and present ones are "transformations" of past ones. When an individual attains perfect wisdom all transformations are transcended. In these transformations dharmas are produced. Some, the products of imagination, have only illusory existence. Others have dependent existence because they depend on causes for their production. But those of the "nature of perfect reality" have true existence. Since the school accepts dharmas and their character as real, it is often called the school of Being.

In spite of the fact that their basic problems of being and nonbeing are Chinese, the two schools were essentially no more than Indian schools transplanted to Chinese soil. They lacked the spirit of synthesis and were too extreme for the Chinese, and they declined after a few centuries, a relatively short time compared to other schools. In the meantime the Chinese spirit of synthesis asserted itself, notably in the Tiantai (Heavenly Terrace) and Huayan (Flower Splendor) schools.

Tiantai. According to the Tiantai school, which was founded by Zhiyi (538–597) in the Tiantai Mountains, dharmas are empty because they have no self-nature and depend on causes for production. This is the Truth of Emptiness. But since they are produced, they do possess temporary and dependent existence. This is the Truth of Temporary Truth. Thus, dharmas are both empty and temporary. This is the Truth of the Mean. Each truth involves the other two so that three are one and one is three. This mutual identification is the true state of all dharmas. In the realm of temporary truth—that is, the phenomenal world—all realms of existence, whether of Buddhas, men, or beasts, and all characters of being, such as cause, effect, and substance, involve one another, so that each element, even an instant of thought, involves the entire universe. This all-is-one-and-one-is-all philosophy is expressed in the famous saying "Every color or fragrance is none other than the Middle Path."

Huayan. In the same spirit of synthesis, the Huayan school, established by Fazang (596–664), propagated the doctrine of the universal causation of the realm of dharmas. This realm is fourfold. It contains the realm of facts, the realm of principle, the realm of principle and facts harmonized, and the realm of all facts interwoven and mutually identified. Principle is emptiness, static, the noumenon, whereas facts are specific characters, dynamic, constituting the phenomenal world. They interact and interpenetrate and in this way form a perfect harmony. This doctrine rests on the theory of the six characters, which states that each dharma possess the six characteristics of universality, speciality, similarity, difference, integration, and disintegration. Thus, each dharma is both one and all. The world is in reality a perfect harmony in all its flowery splendor.

Chan. Whereas Buddhist philosophy in the sixth and seventh centuries came to be more and more Chinese with the Tiantai and Huayan schools, Confucian philosophy remained dormant. In the eighth and ninth centuries its very life was threatened by the growth of Chan, or the Meditation school (Zen in Japan).

The Meditation doctrine, introduced from India by Bodhidharma (fl. 460–534), aimed at the realization of the Ultimate Reality through sitting in meditation. Its emphasis was on concentration to the point of absence of thought in order to get rid of attachments. As the Meditation school developed it conceived of the mind as split into the true mind, which does not have thought or attachments to the characters of dharmas, and the false mind, which has them. Sitting in meditation was the effort to get rid of them.

Hui Neng (638–713), an aboriginal from the south, rose in revolt against the tradition. He and his followers refused to divide the mind but maintained that it is one and originally pure. Erroneous thoughts and erroneous attachments are similar to clouds hiding the sun. When they are removed the original nature will be revealed and great wisdom obtained. The way to discover the original nature is calmness and wisdom. Calmness does not mean not thinking or having nothing to do with the characters of dharmas. Rather, it means not being carried away by thought in the process of thought and being free from characters while in the midst of them. Sitting in meditation is useless, and external effort, such as reciting scriptures or worshiping Buddhas, is futile. When the mind is unperturbed by selfishness or deliberate effort and is left to take its own course, it will reveal its pure nature, and enlightenment will come suddenly. Instead of assuming a dualistic nature of the mind, ignoring the external world, and aiming at uniting with the Infinite, as Indian meditation did, Chinese meditation assumed the original goodness of nature, took place in the midst of daily affairs, and aimed at self-realization.

Chinese influences on Chan are obvious. Buddhism had become characteristically Chinese, with its interest in the here and now. It swept all over China. The Confucian Way was in imminent danger of disappearance. Han Yu (768–824), the greatest Confucianist of the Tang dynasty (618–907), had to defend the Confucian Way and demanded that Buddhist and Daoist books be burned. His contribution to Confucian philosophy is negligible, but he paved the way for Confucian awakening.

MODERN PERIOD: NEO-CONFUCIANISM (960–1912)

The combination of the wide spread of Chan and the attractiveness of the Huayan and Tiantai metaphysics, as well as the Chan psychology, woke the Confucianists from a long slumber. For centuries, within the Confucian school itself, efforts had been confined to textual studies and flowery compositions. Reaction, long overdue, now set in. Consequently in the early years of the Song dynasty (960–1279) Confucianists raised new problems and attempted to find solutions.

Since the *Book of Changes* had exerted tremendous influence throughout the ages, the Confucianists naturally turned to it for inspiration and support. But instead of using it for divination, as the Daoists did, they used it for a study of human nature and destiny on the basis of principle. This new movement eventually came to be known as the school of Nature and Principle (Xingli Xue or, in English, Neo-Confucianism).

The man who opened the vista and determined the direction of Neo-Confucianism was Zhou Dunyi (also called Zhou Lianxi, 1017–1073). Elaborating on the cosmogony of the *Book of Changes,* he held that in the evolution of the universe from the Great Ultimate through the two material forces of yin and yang and the five agents to the myriad things, the five agents are the basis of the differentiation of things, whereas yin and yang constitute their actuality. The two forces are fundamentally one. Consequently the many are ultimately one and the one is actually differentiated in the many. Both the one and the many have their own correct states of being. The nature and destiny of man and things will be correct in their differentiated state if they all follow the same universal principle. This was the central thesis of Neo-Confucianism for the next several centuries. The influence of the Buddhist one-in-all-and-all-in-one philosophy is unmistakable.

RATIONALISTIC NEO-CONFUCIANISM.

Neo-Confucianism developed in two different directions, the rationalistic school of Principle and the idealistic school of Mind.

Cheng–Zhu philosophy. The central figures in the rationalistic movement were Cheng Yi (Cheng Yichuan, 1033–1107), who formulated the major concepts and provided the basic arguments, and Zhu Xi (1130–1200), who supplemented and refined them and brought Neo-Confucianism into a systemic, rationalistic whole. At the center of the school is its concept of principle (*li*); its other major concepts are the Great Ultimate, material force, the nature of man and things, the investigation of things, and the moral quality of humanity, or *ren.*

The idea of principle, virtually absent in ancient Confucianism, probably came from Neo-Daoism and Buddhism. If so, it was employed to oppose them. In the view of the Neo-Confucianists of the Song dynasty both Daoist nonbeing and Buddhist emptiness are too abstract, but their principle is concrete. Cheng Yi repeatedly said that for a thing to exist there must first be its principle, the law according to which it will exist. Principle is definite, correct, self-evident, and self-sufficient. It is in each and every thing. Put differently, the principle for each particular thing is a definite one.

Since the possible number of things in the world is infinite, the number of actual and potential principles is infinite. As new things appear, new principles are realized.

In the production and reproduction in the universe the process of daily renewal never ceases. This is a principle in itself, and there is always a new principle to make a new thing possible. But all principles are at bottom one, called the Great Ultimate. As substance the Great Ultimate is one, but as it functions it is manifested in the many, or the innumerable concrete things. The Great Ultimate is both the sum total of all principles and principle in its oneness.

The manifestations of the Great Ultimate depend on material force, which actualizes things. Operating as yin and yang, material force provides the stuff that makes a thing concrete. Things differ from one another because of their material endowments, and they resemble one another because of principle. Principle as the Great Ultimate exists before physical form (*xing er shang*), whereas material force exists after physical form (*xing er xia*). Logically speaking, principle is prior to material force, but as Zhu Xi emphasized, they are never separate. Without material force principle would be neither concrete nor definite, and without principle there would be no law by which material force could operate. In the universe there has never been any material force without principle or principle without material force.

When principle is endowed in man it becomes his nature. Man's nature is originally good because principle is good, and principle is good because it is the source of all goodness. Evil arises when feelings are aroused and deviate from principle. In this respect Neo-Confucianism retains the traditional Confucian doctrine that Nature is good whereas feelings are sources of evil. The Song Neo-Confucianists made a sharp distinction between the principle of Nature and selfish human desires.

Through moral cultivation selfish desires can be eliminated and the principle of Nature realized. To the rationalistic Neo-Confucianists the first step toward cultivation was the investigation of things (*gewu*). According to Cheng Yi every blade of grass and every tree possesses principle. Therefore, all things should be investigated. One can investigate by studying inductively or deductively, by reading books, or by handling human affairs. When things are investigated, as *The Great Learning* taught, one's knowledge will be extended, one's will sincere, one's feelings correct, and one's personal life cultivated. When this is done one will have fully developed one's nature and fulfilled one's destiny.

The development of human nature, according to the Cheng Yi–Zhu philosophy, does not stop with personal perfection but involves all things. This is where the concept of *ren* comes in. To Cheng Yi and Zhu Xi, as to previous Confucianists, *ren* is humanity, the moral quality that makes man a true man. But under the influence of the century-old Confucian doctrine of the unity of man and Nature and also the cosmological scale of Buddhist ethics, the Neo-Confucianists applied the concept of *ren* to all things and said that through it man can "form one body with heaven, earth, and all things." Furthermore, they added a new note to *ren* by interpreting the word in its other sense, that of seed or growth. *ren* was then understood to be the chief characteristic of heaven and earth, the production and reproduction of things. This life-giving character is the highest good. It is inherent in man's nature. Man's duty is to develop it and put it into practice. Neo-Confucianism returned to the chief topic and fundamental ethical concern of Confucius and gave it new meaning.

As has been indicated, Zhu Xi and Cheng Yi were the chief figures of rationalistic Neo-Confucianism. However, Cheng Yi's older brother Cheng Hao, their uncle Zhang Zai, and Shao Yong, who with Cheng Yi and Zhou Dunyi are called the Five Masters of early Song Neo-Confucianism, also contributed substantially to it.

Cheng Hao. Cheng Hao (Cheng Mingdao, 1032–1085) shared many ideas with his brother. The two were really the twin leaders of the school in its formative stage. Whereas Cheng Yi stressed the idea of principle as one and its manifestations many, Cheng Hao stressed principle as production and reproduction. He saw the spirit of life in everything, which impressed him much more than the rational character of things. Furthermore, to Cheng Hao the highest principle was the principle of Nature, a concept he evolved himself. He believed that principle is more than the rational basis of being. It is the principle of Nature, the self-evident universal truth that carries with it the dictate to distinguish right from wrong and the imperative to do good. Instead of focusing his attention on the investigation of things, he directed it to the calmness of mind. Only when the mind is calm—that is, free from selfishness, cunning, and deliberate effort—can it be peaceful. One can then respond to things as they come and naturally maintain a balance between the internal and the external. Cheng Hao considered understanding the nature of *ren* to be of the greatest importance. The man who has such an understanding will be free from all opposition between the self and the other and will be able to form one body with all things. It can easily be seen that although he differed from his brother on many points, Cheng Hao strengthened Neo-Confucianism by providing it with warmth and spirituality.

Zhang Zai. Unlike the Cheng brothers, Zhang Zai (Zhang Hengqu, 1020–1077) regarded principle not as above or different from material force but as the law according to which material force operates. He identified material force with the Great Ultimate and considered yin and yang as merely the two aspects of material force. As substance, before consolidation takes place, material force is the Great Vacuity (*taixu*). As function, in its activity and tranquility, integration and disintegration, and so forth, it is the Great Harmony. But the two are the same as the Way (Dao). In its ultimate state material force is one, but in its contraction and expansion and the like it is manifested in the many. Similarly, in ethics *ren* is one, but in its application in the various human relations, as filial piety toward parents, brotherly respect toward brothers, and so on, it is many. Zhang Zai's advocacy of the concept of vacuity was too Daoistic to be attractive to his fellow Neo-Confucianists, but in making the doctrine of the one and the many the metaphysical foundation of Confucian ethics, he made "a great contribution to the Confucian school," in Zhu Xi's description.

Shao Yong. Shao Yong (1011–1077) agreed with his contemporaries that there are supreme principles governing the universe, but he added that they can be discerned in terms of numbers. In his cosmology change is due to spirit; spirit gives rise to number, number to form, and form to concrete things. Since the Great Ultimate engenders the four forms of major and minor yin and yang, Shao Yong used the number 4 to classify all phenomena. In his scheme there are the four seasons, the four heavenly bodies, the four kinds of rulers, the four periods of history, and so on. Since the structure of the universe is mathematical, elements of the universe can be calculated and objectively known. The best way to know is to "view things as things." All these are new notes in Neo-Confucianism that set Shao Yong apart from the rest. He was as much interested in the basic problems of principle, nature, and destiny as were other Neo-Confucianists. However, he hardly discussed social and moral problems, and his whole metaphysical outlook was too near Daoist occultism to be considered part of the main current of rationalistic Neo-Confucianism.

IDEALISTIC NEO-CONFUCIANISM. In spite of the fact that the rationalistic Neo-Confucianists tried to maintain a balance between principle and material force in metaphysics and between the investigation of things and moral cultivation in the way of life, they tended to be one-sided in their emphasis on principle and the investigation of things.

Lu Xiangshan. Opposition to these trends arose in Zhu Xi's own time, notably from his friend and chief opponent, Lu Xiangshan (Lu Jiuyuan, 1139–1193). Cheng Yi and Zhu Xi had regarded mind as the function of man's nature, which is identical with principle. To Lu mind *was* principle. It is originally good and endowed with the innate knowledge of the good and the innate ability to do good, as Mencius had taught long before. It is one and indissoluble. There is no such distinction as that between the moral mind, which is good, and the human mind, which is liable to evil, a distinction made by Zhu Xi. Both the principle of Nature and human desires are good, and they should not be contrasted, as they were by Zhu Xi. The mind fills the whole universe. Throughout all ages and in all directions there is the same mind. It is identical with all things, for there is nothing outside the Way and there is no Way outside things. In short, the mind is the universe. To investigate things, then, is to investigate the mind. Since all principles are inherent and complete in the mind, there is no need to look outside, as did Cheng Yi and Zhu Xi.

This thoroughgoing idealism shows not only the influence of Mencius but also the impact of Buddhism. However, Lu was no less a critic of Buddhism than were other Neo-Confucianists. Actually, he criticized Zhu Xi not to promote Buddhism but to uphold Confucianism. In his opinion the way of Zhu Xi led to a divided mind, aimless drifting, and devotion to isolated details that meant little to life. Lu advocated instead a simple, easy, and direct method of recovering one's originally good nature. It consisted in having a firm purpose, "establishing the nobler part of one's nature," and coming to grips with fundamentals. In short, Zhu's way was "following the path of study and inquiry," whereas Lu's way was "honoring the moral nature."

Lu's opposition did not have any immediate effect, for rationalistic Neo-Confucianism was too strong to be checked. It dominated the Chinese intellectual world for several hundred years. By the fifteenth century, however, it had degenerated into concern only with isolated details and had lost touch with the fundamentals of life. There was no longer any intellectual creativity or moral vigor in it.

Wang Yangming. Opposition rose again, this time from Wang Yangming (Wang Shouren, 1472–1529), who pushed the idealistic movement to its highest point in Chinese history. Wang reiterated most of Xiangshan's ideas but carried some of them to new heights. Like Lu, he said that the mind is principle and that things are in the mind, but he emphasized the direction of the mind—that is, the will. To him a thing (or affair) was nothing but the mind determined to realize it. There is no such thing as filial piety, for example, unless one is determined to put it into practice and actually does so. Like Lu, Wang said that the investigation of things is the investigation of the mind; however, he added that since the most important aspect of the mind is the will, the sincerity of the will must precede the investigation of things, an idea diametrically opposed to Zhu Xi's contention that as things are investigated, one's will becomes sincere. Going beyond Mencius's doctrine of the innate knowledge of good, Wang held that because of one's innate ability to do good, one necessarily extends the innate knowledge into action. Knowledge and action are really identical; one is the beginning and the other the completion. Here are two original doctrines, the extension of the innate knowledge and the unity of knowledge and action, both of which represent new steps in Chinese thought.

Wang Fuzhi. For 150 years the idealistic philosophy of Wang Yangming dominated China, putting Zhu Xi's rationalism on the defensive. A number of philosophers attempted compromise, without much success. In the seventeenth century Wang's idealism declined, and Zhu Xi's rationalism reasserted itself. But rationalism enjoyed neither monopoly nor prominence, for revolts arose one after another. From the seventeenth century on, Confucianists regarded both Zhu and Wang as too speculative. The spirit of the time demanded the evident, the concrete, and the practical.

One of the first to rebel was Wang Fuzhi (Wang Chuanshan, 1619–1692). He rejected the central Neo-Confucian thesis that principle is a universal, transcending and prior to material force. Instead, he contended that principle is identical with material force. It is not a separate entity that can be grasped but the order and arrangement of things. The Great Ultimate and the principle of Nature are no transcendent abstractions. They, along with the mind and the nature of things, are all within material force. Wang Fuzhi boldly declared, "The world consists only of concrete things." He also refused to accept either the distinction between the principle of Nature and human desires or the subordination of human desires.

Dai Zhen. In the same spirit, Dai Zhen (Dai Dongyuan, 1723–1777) attacked the Neo-Confucianists, particularly those of the Song dynasty, for their conception of principle. He said that they looked upon principle "as if it were a thing." To him principle was nothing but the order of things, and by things he meant daily affairs, such as drinking and eating. The way to investigate principle, he thought, is not by intellectual speculation or by introspection of the mind but by critical, analytical, minutely detailed, and objective study of things based on concrete evidence. Dai Zhen's conception of principle led him to oppose vigorously the Neo-Confucianists' view of human feelings and desires, which he thought they had undermined. In his belief principle can never prevail when feelings are not satisfied, for principles are merely "feelings that do not err." Dai Zhen perpetuated the Neo-Confucian doctrine that the universe is an unceasing process of production and reproduction, except that to him Nature, like principle, was but an order.

Kang Youwei. By the end of the nineteenth century there was a swing back to the philosophy of Wang Yangming. The sad situation in China called for dynamic and purposive action that only an idealism like Wang's could provide. All of these factors conditioned the thought of Kang Youwei (1858–1927), the greatest Confucianist of the time. In an attempt to translate Confucian philosophy into action he enunciated the extraordinary theory that Confucius was first and last a reformer. Kang himself engineered the abortive political reform of 1898. Obviously influenced by the Christian concepts of utopia and progress, he envisaged the Age of Great Unity. In his theory of historical progress history proceeds from the Age of Chaos to the Small Peace and finally to the Great Unity, when nations, families, classes, and all kinds of distinctions will be totally abolished. The philosophical basis for this utopia is his interpretation of *ren.* He equates it with what Mencius called "the mind that cannot bear" to see the suffering of others. It is compassion. It is also the power of attraction that pulls all peoples together. As such it is ether and electricity, which permeate all things everywhere.

Kang was philosophically superficial but historically important. He showed that at the turn of the twentieth century China was at a philosophical crossroad.

CONTEMPORARY PERIOD (FROM 1912)

Philosophy in twentieth-century China was indeed confusing and chaotic, but certain tendencies could clearly be seen. There was first of all importation from the West. In the first three decades Charles Darwin, Ernst Heinrich Haeckel, Friedrich Nietzsche, Arthur Schopenhauer, Henri Bergson, Immanuel Kant, René Descartes, William James, John Dewey, Karl Marx, and others were introduced, each with his champion. Of these, James and Dewey were the most influential, since pragmatism was advocated by Hu Shih, leader of the intellectual revolution. Only Marxism, however, has remained strong, and it has become the established state philosophy.

Under the stimulation of Western philosophy both Confucianism and Buddhism resurged from a long period of decadence. In the 1920s and early 1930s, Ouyang Jingwu (1871–1943), strongly impressed by Western idealism, sought to revive Buddhist idealism as it was centuries ago, and his opponent, Abbot Taixu (1889–1947), attempted to transform Buddhist idealism in the light of Western philosophy. Since neither knew Western philosophy or was really a philosopher, their movements, though extensive and vigorous, resulted more in religious reform than in intellectual advancement, and in the late 1930s their work quickly disappeared from the philosophical scene.

The renewal of Confucian philosophy, however, was different. Feng Youlan (1895–1990) developed his philosophy on the basis of rationalistic Neo-Confucianism, and Xiong Shili (1885–1968) built his on the foundation of idealistic Neo-Confucianism. Since the 1930s they became the two most prominent philosophical thinkers in China. While importation from the West and reconstruction of traditional philosophy were going on, certain philosophers tried to evolve their own systems out of Western thought. The most successful of these was Zhang Dongsun (1886–1962), who alone produced a comprehensive and mature philosophy.

Feng Youlan. Trained in philosophy at Columbia University, Feng Youlan derived his rationalism from the Neo-Confucianism of Cheng Yi and Zhu Xi and converted Neo-Confucian concepts into formal logical concepts. According to him, his "new rationalistic Confucianism" is based on four main metaphysical concepts—principle, material force, the substance of Dao, and the Great Whole. The concept of principle is derived from the Cheng-Zhu proposition "As there are things, there must be their specific principles." A thing must follow principle, but principle does not have to be actualized in a thing. It belongs to the realm of reality but not actuality and is purely a formal concept. The concept of material force is derived from the Cheng-Zhu proposition "If there is principle, there must be material force" by which a thing can exist. Material force is basic to the concept of existence but does not itself exist in the actual world. It is only a formal logical concept. The concept of Dao means a "universal operation," the universe of "daily renewal" and incessant change. Finally, the Great Whole, in which one is all and all is one, is also a formal concept, being the general name for all, not an assertion about the actual world. It corresponds to the Absolute in Western philosophy.

Basically, Feng's philosophy is a combination of Neo-Confucianism and Western realism and logic. Feng called his own system a "new tradition." It is new not only because it has interpreted Neo-Confucian ideas as formal concepts. In addition, Feng's system has replaced Neo-Confucianism, which is essentially a philosophy of immanence, with a philosophy of transcendence. To Feng the world of actuality is secondary.

In 1950, Feng repudiated his philosophy because it "neglects the concrete and the particular," but in 1957 he still maintained that Confucius was an idealist rather than a materialist. This suggests that he was not entirely Marxian in his interpretation of Chinese thought. He remained the most important Chinese philosopher of the last thirty years—the most original, the most productive, and the most criticized.

Xiong Shili. Xiong Shili called his philosophy the "new doctrine of consciousness-only." According to his main thesis reality is endless transformation of closing and opening, which constitute a process of unceasing production and reproduction. The original substance is in perpetual transition at every instant, continually arising anew and thus resulting in many manifestations. But reality and manifestations, or substance and function, are one. In its closing aspect original substance has the tendency to integrate, resulting in what may temporarily be called matter, whereas in its opening aspect it has the tendency to maintain its own nature and be its own master, resulting in what may temporarily be called mind. This mind itself is one part of the original mind, which in its various aspects is mind, will, and consciousness.

Xiong's terminology comes from the *Book of Changes* and the Buddhist Consciousness Only school, but his basic ideas—the unity of substance and function and the primacy of the original mind—come from Neo-Confucianism, especially that of Wang Yangming. He avoided Zhu Xi's bifurcation of principle and material force and Wang's subordination of material force to the mind and has provided the dynamic idea of change in Neo-Confucianism with a metaphysical foundation.

Zhang Dongsun. The theory of Zhang Dongsun (born 1886) has been variously called revised Kantianism, epistemological pluralism, and panstructuralism. Chiefly formulated between 1929 and 1947, it is derived from Kant but rejects Kant's bifurcation of reality into phenomena and noumena and Kant's division of the nature of knowledge into the a posteriori and the a priori. To Zhang knowledge is a synthesis of sense data, form, and methodological assumptions. Perception, conception, mind, and consciousness are all syntheses, or "constructs," and constructs are products of society and culture. He maintained that although he combined Western logic with modern psychology and sociology, his system was his own. During World War II he shifted more and more from metaphysics to the sociology of knowledge and thus was drawn closer and closer to Marxism.

During the years since World War II neither Xiong's, Feng's nor Zhang's philosophy has become a movement, although Xiong has exercised considerable influence on a number of young philosophers. While Zhang is keeping silent, Xiong maintaining his position, and Feng still reconsidering his philosophy, Marxism has become the triumphant and official system of thought. It demands that philosophy be practical, scientific, democratic, and for the masses. Traditional philosophy is being studied and will survive, but it is being interpreted in a new light.

See also Buddhism; Communism; Mysticism, History of.

Bibliography

Chan, Wing-tsit, ed. *A Source Book in Chinese Philosophy.* Princeton, NJ: Princeton University Press, 1963.

Creel, H. G. *Chinese Thought from Confucius to Mao Tse-tung.* Chicago: University of Chicago Press, 1953.

De Bary, Wm. Theodore, Wing-tsit Chan, and Burton Watson, comps. *Sources of Chinese Tradition,* with contributions by Yi-pao Mei, Leon Hurvitz, T'ung-tsu Ch'u, and John Meskill. 2 vols. New York: Columbia University Press, 1960.

Fung, Yu-lan. *A Short History of Chinese Philosophy.* New York: Macmillan, 1948.

Fung, Yu-lan. *A History of Chinese Philosophy,* trans. Derk Bodde. Vol. 1, The Period of the Philosophers, and vol. 2, The Period of Classical Learning. Princeton, NJ: Princeton University Press, 1937, 1952, 1953.

Graham, A. C. *Disputers of the Tao.* La Salle, IL: Open Court, 1989.

Graham, A. C. *Studies in Chinese Philosophy and Philosophical Literature.* Albany: State University of New York Press, 1990.

Hall, David L., and Roger T. Ames. *Anticipating China: Thinking through the Narratives of Chinese and Western Culture.* Albany: State University of New York Press, 1995.

Hall, David L., and Roger T. Ames. *Thinking from the Han: Self, Truth and Transcendence in China and the West.* Albany: State University of New York Press, 1998.

Hansen, Chad. *A Daoist Theory of Chinese Thought.* New York: Oxford University Press, 1992.

Hsiao, Kung-chuan. *A History of Chinese Political Thought.* Vol. 1, From the Beginnings to the Sixth Century A.D. Translated by F. W. Mote. Princeton, NJ: Princeton University Press, 1979.

Liu, Shu-hsien. *Understanding Confucian Philosophy: Classical and Sung-Ming.* Westport, CT: Greenwood Press, 1998.

Loewe, Michael, ed. *Early Chinese Texts: A Bibliographic Guide.* Berkeley: University of California Press, 1993.

Mote, Frederick W. *Intellectual Foundations of China.* 2nd ed. New York: McGraw-Hill, 1971, 1989.

Munro, Donald J. *The Concept of Man in Early China.* Stanford, CA: Stanford University Press, 1969.

Needham, Joseph. *Science and Civilisation in China.* Vol. 2, History of Scientific Thought. Cambridge, MA: Cambridge University Press, 1956.

Nivison, David S. *The Ways of Confucianism.* Chicago and La Salle, IL: Open Court, 1996.

Roetz, Heiner. *Confucian Ethics of the Axial Age: A Reconstruction under the Aspect of the Breakthrough toward Postconventional Thinking.* Albany: State University of New York Press, 1993.

Schwartz, Benjamin. *The World of Thought in Ancient China.* Cambridge, MA: Belknap Press of Harvard University Press, 1985.

Shun, Kwong-loi. *Mencius and Early Chinese Thought.* Stanford, CA: Stanford University Press, 1997.

Van der Leeuw, Karel L. "The Study of Chinese Philosophy in the West: A Bibliographic Introduction." *China Review International,* 6, (2) (Fall 1999): 332–372.

Vittinghoff, Helmolt. "Recent Bibliography in Classical Chinese Philosophy," *Journal of Chinese Philosophy* 28: 1 & 2 (March/June 2001).

Waley, Arthur. *Three Ways of Thought in Ancient China.* London: Allen and Unwin, 1939.

Wing-Tsit Chan (1967)
Bibliography updated by Huichieh Loy (2005)

BUDDHISM

In India, Buddhism was a heterodox religious movement against the authority of the Vedas, the Bible of orthodox Hinduism. Gautama Buddha (c. 563–c. 483 BCE) dismissed the extreme ascetic way of life often adopted by Indian religious believers and taught the middle way. While Hindu philosophers asserted the existence of atman (I, self, ego, or soul) as the innermost essence of a human being and ontologically identified this essence with Brahma, the absolute reality of the universe, the Buddha repudiated the ideas of atman and Brahma, and proclaimed that everything is causally conditioned and nothing is absolute, permanent, and eternal.

All Buddhists have accepted the Buddha's teaching of anatman (nonself), but have apprehended his philosophical message differently. For the early, conservative Hinayana Buddhists, the Buddha's denial of ātman implies and even entails the existence of dharmas (divine laws), changing realities of the universe, and impermanent constituents of human beings. But later, progressive Mahayana Buddhists contended that the concept of dharma is as unintelligible as that of ātman. Both monistic absolutism and pluralistic realism are extreme views and should be eradicated. The true teaching of the Buddha is that all things are empty (*sunya*).

Both conservative and progressive Buddhist teachings had been introduced to China by the first century

CE. The Chinese preferred Mahayana and revered Nāgārjuna (c. 163–263) as the father of Mahayana Buddhism. The first Mahayana school founded by Nāgārjuna in India was named Mādhyamika, a name derived from the Sanskrit noun *madhyamā*, meaning middle or neutral. The Mahayana philosophy of emptiness as the middle way had laid a fine foundation for the development of Buddhism in China. The creation of new Chinese Buddhist schools—such as Tiantai, Huayan, Chan, and Pure Land—was directly or indirectly related to Nāgārjuna's philosophy.

THE SANLUN PHILOSOPHY OF EMPTINESS

In China, Indian Mādhyamika Buddhism is called the Sanlun (three-treatises) School. Nāgārjuna's *Madhyamakārikā* (Middle way treatise), *Dvādaśanikāyaśāstra* (*Twelve Gate Treatise*), and *Śataśāstra* (Hundred verse treatise), with the main verses by Āryadeva (third cent.), are devoted to the philosophy of emptiness and have been emphasized by Chinese Sanlun Buddhists. For Chinese Sanlun Buddhists, the notions of anatman, the middle way, and emptiness are synonymous in the Buddha's philosophy. Thus, the Sanlun school is also known as the middle-way school (*Zhongdao Zong*) and the emptiness school (*Kong Zong*).

More than any other Chinese philosophers, the Sanlun masters had a great interest in logical analysis and logical argument. They analyzed the dynamic and static worldviews, and they critically examined the nature and function of language and basic linguistic units such as subject, predicate, and predication. They questioned the essence and use of truth, knowledge, and logic, and they investigated various logical concepts and constructs such as right and wrong, negation and affirmation, and the meaning of thesis, antithesis, and synthesis in rational reasoning and conceptual disputes.

Usually people accept motion or change as an undeniable fact of experience. Even the Buddha, as well as the *Yijing* (Book of changes), seems to teach that all things are in a constant state of flux. Laozi's *Daodejing* (Way and power classic) also proclaims that "reversing" is the Dao (Way) of heaven. But under the influence of Indian Mahayana philosophy, Sengzhao (373–414), a brilliant Sanlun philosopher, wrote the famous essay *Wu buqian lun* (Things do not shift), arguing that motion is empty. He analyzed motion and pointed out that so-called motion consists of a part that has already passed (*yiqu*), a part that has yet to pass (*weiqu*), and a part that is passing (*qushi*). Change cannot be found in the part already passed, since it is already gone. Nor can it be found in the part yet to pass, since it is not yet. Nor can it be apprehended in the part that is passing, since passing makes sense if and only if there is an act of passing. But in examining whether there is an act of passing, we cannot use the act of passing to establish an act of passing without begging the question. So motion is impossible.

Zeno, a Greek philosopher, was well known for his argument that motion is impossible. Unlike Zeno, the Chinese Sanlun denial of motion does not entail the affirmation of rest. For Sanlun Mādhyamika, the concept of rest cannot be established either. Rest is the cessation of motion. If it is real, it must happen at some place and time. Does rest occur where something has already past, or where something has yet to pass, or where something is passing? None of these can be established. Therefore there can be no rest, or cessation of motion. For Sanlun masters, motion and rest are both empty, devoid of definite nature or essence, and hence not real. So one cannot maintain that reality is either permanent or impermanent. Therefore, any substantive or dynamic metaphysics must be repudiated.

According to Chinese Sanlun Mādhyamikas, philosophers appear to be very intelligent, but actually have often been fooled by language. Both Hindu and traditional Buddhist metaphysicians have failed to see the emptiness of words and names. Laozi understood the inadequacy of human language, as can be seen in the opening to his *Daodejing*, where he wrote, "The way that can be stated is not the real Way; Names that can be named are not real names." However, Laozi and later Daoists did not logically analyze language and did not present discursive arguments to substantiate their philosophy. Following Nāgārjuna's philosophy, Chinese Sanlun masters did logically analyze language, arguing that language is a conceptual game (*xilun*).

Sanlun masters critically examined the nature and the structure of conceptual and verbal statements, and argued that the relationship between two basic linguistic units, the subject (*kexiang*) and the predicate (*xiang*), cannot be rationally well formed, and that predication in our ordinary use of language is really not intelligible. They studied the precise relationship between the subject and the predicate, examining whether they are identical or different from one another. On the one hand, if two are identical, they are one, and it makes no sense to call one a subject and the other a predicate. Logically, the sentence is then a tautology and does not say anything about the world. Hence, in this case, predication is doing no real work. On the other hand, if the subject and the predicate differ, predication is again unintelligible, since being (the similarity of subject and predicate) and not being (the difference between subject and predicate) cannot be at the same place at the same time. Hence it is absurd to unite what is different to form one sentence describing the same thing. Since every logical or conceptual statement consists of a subject and predicate, reality cannot be intelligently described. Therefore, so-called logic is in essence illogical.

In the view of the Sanlun masters, language and logic are empty. They are conventional and do not have a priori or absolute validity. Words have no definite meaning in themselves. The meaning of a term is not the object for which it stands, but depends on conditions and circumstances. If conditions change, the meaning of the word changes and might even be lost.

For the Sanlun masters, conceptualization, like a fish trap, has no intrinsic value and reality by itself, though it does have a practical use and can be employed to attract unenlightened persons to Buddhism. Yet the true message of the Buddha's teachings can be properly apprehended only if people comprehend the emptiness of words and discard conceptualization. Jizang (549–623), the most eminent Sanlun master, stated, "It is not that language is given in order to have Dharma [the Buddha's truth or teachings], but rather that Dharma is presented in order to eliminate language (Jizang 1854, p. 94c; Cheng 1984, p. 119).

According to Jizang, without practical benefits, truth and logic would lose their meaning. In ordinary life, humans have all sorts of emotional and intellectual attachments; they are attached to some view and stick to some law or principle. To free them from attachment, the Buddha preached a certain truth and followed a certain logic. To avoid the substantive or static view of the universe, he taught that everything is in flux, and to repudiate the dynamic view of the universe, he claimed that existence is real. Actually, terms such as "being" and "nonbeing," "permanent" and "impermanent," "to be" and "not to be," "real" and "unreal" are all empty. The Buddha's message can be regarded as the truth insofar as it helps dispel ignorance and illusion.

Ultimately, all conceptualizations should be discarded, and one should be silent. Such silence is not a form of absolutism or nihilism, but the manifestation of *prajñā* (wisdom). For ordinary people, to know is to know something; epistemology assumes objects to be known, acts of knowing, and a knower. In the ordinary way of thinking, an assertion of knowledge implies an ontological commitment. *Prajñā* is not to know something, but rather to apprehend that reality is empty, and so to be freed from attachments. In his essay *Boruo wuzhi* (*Prajñā* as nonknowing), Sengzhao (384–414) stated, "Real *prajñā* is as pure as empty space, without knowing, without seeing, without acting, and without objects. Thus knowledge is in itself without knowing, and does not depend on anything in order to be without knowing (Sengzhao 1858, p. 153; Cheng 1984a, p. 105).

To apprehend the empty logic of *prajñā*, one should understand, according to Jizang's *Sanlun xuanyi* (Profound meaning of the three treatises), that the refutation of erroneous views is the illumination of the right view (*poxie xianzheng*). In ordinary or even Aristotelian logic, negation and affirmation differ. Negation is usually asserted with the aim of affirming, establishing a thesis: Not *P* implies something other than *P*; the denial of a thesis entails the affirmation of an antithesis. For Chinese Sanlun masters, enlightened persons are empty-minded, free from affirmation and negation. Negation is used merely to repudiate erroneous views or to affirm negation itself. Not *P* means only the absence of *P*. *Prajñā* is the absence of any view, and is not a view in itself. The refutation of erroneous views and the affirmation of right views are not separate acts but the same. If a right view is held in place of an erroneous view, it becomes a new erroneous view and requires refutation. For Jizang, "Originally there was nothing to affirm and now there is nothing to negate (Jizang 1852, p. 6; Cheng 1984a, p. 47). An attachment to some view is a sickness (*bing*), and the logic of emptiness is the medicine (*yao*) to cure this intellectual sickness.

The Buddhist doctrine of emptiness, according to Chinese Sanlun masters, is not a metaphysical view. Rather, it is the doctrine that one should repudiate all metaphysical views, and to do so requires not the presentation of another metaphysical view, but simply the abolition of all metaphysics.

Emptiness (*śūnyatā*) is essentially a soteriological device. It is merely an instrument for eliminating extreme views. If there is no extreme to be removed, there need be no affirmation or negation. The so-called right view is really just as empty as the wrong view, and it is cited as right "only when there is neither affirmation nor negation." If possible, one should not use such terms as "right" and "wrong." For Jizang, "we are forced to use the word 'right' in order to put an end to wrong. Once wrong has been ended, then right no longer remains. Then the mind is attached to nothing." Even emptiness is empty. Jizang contended, "If one still clings to emptiness, then there is no medicine that can eliminate the disease (Jizang 1852, p. 7).

The Sanlun philosophy was brilliant and authentically derived from Indian Mādhyamika thought. But the philosophy was too abstract and too Indian for the Chinese. Consequently, the Sanlun School declined in China after the death of Jizang in 623. However, its teachings inspired various Chinese Buddhists to develop new Buddhist movements in China.

THE ROUND TEACHING OF TIANTAI

Tiantai Buddhism, a sect of Mahayana Buddhism, had no Indian counterpart and was founded in China in the sixth century. It was initiated by Huiwen (550–577) and was well established by Zhiyi, also known as Zhikai (538–597), the greatest Tiantai master. Zhiyi lived and taught in the area of Mt. Tiantai in Zhejiang province, and hence the school came to be called the Tiantai School (Tendai in Japanese). Tiantai masters examined the Buddhist scriptures and held that the text *Saddharmapuṇḍarīka* (Lotus of the wonderful law) contains the best and most perfect doctrinal teaching of the Buddha, and consequently this school is also known as the Lotus (*huafang*) School.

Since ancient times Chinese have tended to think holistically or inclusively. Confucians and Daoists tended to observe things as they are and, with increasing ontological penetration, to see differences. The wonder of the universe, for Confucianism and Daoism, is a harmony among diversities and even opposites. According to the Yin-Yang School, the *Yijing* (Book of changes), and the *Daodejing* (Way and power classic), the universe is a united whole. It is composed of pairs of opposites: yin and yang, positive and negative, male and female, right and wrong. The interaction of yin and yang produces all things and all kinds of movement. Following this vein of thinking, Tiantai masters adopted the *yuanjiao* (round approach, doctrine, or teaching) and developed a philosophy of all in one and one in all.

Tiantai Buddhism disliked the analytic approach. For Tiantai masters, the analytic approach is a deductive and exclusive way of thinking that may reduce a complex world to one single reality, as seen in Hinduism, or a few simple fixed entities, as seen in Theravada Buddhism. Such thinking is one-sided and extreme, and hence should be eradicated. To avoid extremes, Tiantai Buddhists maintained that the Buddha's dharma is the direct observation, and pure and total description, of what is immediately given. Buddhism, for Tiantai masters, seeks to describe or to see things as they present themselves. "What the Buddha has accomplished is the teaching foremost, rare and inconceivable. Only the Buddhas can realize the true nature of all things; that is to say, all things are thus-formed, thus-natured, thus-substantiated, thus-caused, thus-forced, thus-activated, thus-circumstanced, thus-effected, thus-enumerated and thus-beginning-ending-completing (*Saddharma-pundarika* [The wonderful law of lotus], chapter 2).

Tiantai Buddhists held that Hindu and other Buddhist philosophers had distorted the original or true state of the things and polluted our comprehension of the universe. Tiantai philosophy sought to return to things themselves, that is, to penetrate to original, pure phenomena as they present themselves before any conceptualization or analytic judgment. "Thus-formed, thus-natured," in Tiantai teaching, indicates things as they present themselves. The Buddha's dharma, for Tiantai masters, seeks to penetrate to the fundamental or original data, to return to reality (*rushi*), as they appear to us in immediate experience. One should return to things themselves by means of direct awareness. For Tiantai masters, whoever sees things in this way sees what they called the original or true state of things (*zhufa shixiang*).

According to Tiantai masters, secular and even Buddhist philosophers have often ignored the richness of the universe and chopped complex, concrete, living facts into one absolute reality or a few simple elements. Tiantai Buddhists dismissed such philosophies as discriminative doctrines (*biejiao*). They did not divide the harmonious world into noumenon (*li*) and phenomena (*shi*). Nor did they reduce one concrete thing to another or give up any assertion; instead, they attempted to describe each fact in its fullness. They called their attitude and approach to the world the *yuanjiao* (round teaching, doctrine, or approach).

According to the round approach, all things, absolute and relative, are a united whole; noumenon is phenomena, and phenomena are noumenon. The relationship between the one and the many is like that of the ocean and waves. One ocean cannot be an ocean without many waves, and many waves cannot occur outside the one ocean. Thus, all is one, and one is all.

The Tiantai round approach is also used to apprehend Buddhist truth. Nāgārjuna is said to have taught, "Emptiness is called the middle way. For it is a provisionary name for causality (Nāgārjuna, "Zhong Lun" [The middle treatise], 18). For Huiwen and his followers, Nāgārjuna's statement taught that causality (*yinyuan*, dependent coarising) indicates lack of permanence and hence emptiness (*kong*), and thus it can serve as a substitute name (*jiaming*) for the middle way (*zhongdao*). This awakened Huiwen to perceive the triple truth of emptiness, of temporariness, and of the mean. For Tiantai Buddhists, all things are empty because they are causally conditioned and hence are devoid of self-nature, but they do have temporary existence. Things by nature are empty and temporary; this principle constitutes the mean. These three—emptiness, temporariness, and the mean—penetrate one another and are found perfectly harmonized and united. A thing is empty but exists temporarily. It is temporary because it is empty. The fact that everything is empty and at the same time temporary constitutes the middle truth. One should consider the three truths not as separate but as a perfectly harmonious threefold truth.

In reality, the three truths, according to Tiantai Buddhism, are three in one and one in three. The principle is one, but its explanation is threefold, and each of the three truths has the value of all. From the perspective of emptiness, we may deny the existence of the temporary and the middle, for we consider emptiness as transcending all. The three principles would be empty. The same is the case from the perspective of temporariness or the mean. So when one principle is empty, all will be empty; when one is temporary, all will be temporary; when one is middle, all will be middle. These three principles are otherwise called identical emptiness, identical temporariness, and identical mean, and also the absolute threefold truth.

HUAYAN BUDDHISM AND THE MYRIAD MANIFESTATIONS

Huayan Buddhism, another sect of Mahayana Buddhism, was founded in China in the seventh century. It is named after the title of its chief scripture *Huayan jing* (*Avatamsaka sutra*, Flower-wreath sutra). According to this school, the Buddhist dharma is like the seed of a fine plant. It was planted by the Buddha in India; it grew and produced branches and leaves; eventually it blossomed, bearing beautiful flowers. Early Buddhism, various Hinayana and Mahayana schools, are the branches and leaves of the dharma. Huayan Buddhism is the flower of the dharma, the highest and the most splendid outcome of the Buddha's dharma.

The Huayan School was initiated by Dushun, also known as Fashun (557–640), but Fazang (643–712) is usually considered the real founder of the school because he was responsible for the final systematization of its teachings. Like Tiantai Buddhists, Huayan Buddhists developed a philosophy of one in all and all in one, and they also called their way of conceptualizing things *yuanjiao* (round approach, teaching, or doctrine). They wanted to observe and describe all things, phenomenal and noumenal, as purely and as fully as possible. They first rejected ordinary empiricism, which cuts up things into simple sense data, and they questioned Indian scholastic Buddhism, which reduced complex phenomena to simple dharmas. For Huayan masters, genuine phenomena are not the same as sensory phenomena. Alleged empirical facts or sensory appearances are really constituted phenomena and do not represent the true state of things.

The denial that sensory appearances represent the true state of the things does not, however, imply that Huayan masters denied sensory appearance in the world. In his famous *Jin shizi zhang* (Essay on the gold lion), Fazang used a gold lion to illustrate the case. We do perceive sensory phenomena such as a gold lion, but the appearance of the gold lion is not of a real lion. The proper understanding of things is that the true essence of such things is something other than physical form.

Sensory phenomena are empty; they do appear to exist, but their state of existence is not genuine. In the strict sense, sense experience is the manifestation of illusion (*huan*). To understand genuine being or genuine phenomena, one must contemplate things without qualities (*wuxiang*) by suspending one's natural belief in the existence of sense qualities or sense data. For Fazang, "To contemplate the qualityless is [to contemplate] the fact that the qualities of the tiniest part of matter arise out of the evolution of mind … , lacking any inherent nature of their own. This fact is called that of the qualityless" (Fazang, *Huayanjing yihaibaimen* [The hundred gates on the meaning of the flower splendor scripture] 1875, p. 627).

The contemplation of things without qualities, according to Huayan Buddhism, leads one to apprehend *li* (principle, noumenon) and to know the essence of the world. Such contemplation is a kind of empty-minded, disinterested observation of things, both objective and subjective, in their fullest breadth and depth. Thus seeing things as they are and as they are not is a round approach. For Huayan masters, it would empty or open up one's mind to see that being and nonbeing produce each other, to see that qualities and the qualityless complement each other, and thus to be aware of the essential relationship between phenomena and noumenon. Fazang wrote, "Noumenon does not interfere with phenomenon, what is pure is ever mixed. [Likewise] phenomena ever comprise noumenon in its totality, for what is mixed is ever so.… There is no barrier between what is pure and what is mixed" (Fazang, *Huayanjing yihaibaimen* [The hundred gates on the meaning of the flower splendor scripture] 1875, p. 627).

Every event or fact is rich and complex. In describing the complex world, Huayan Buddhists claimed that a tiny particular thing involves and embraces all things in totality. Fazang wrote, "All things of the senses are revealed in their true essence and become merged into one great mass. Great functions arise, every one of which represents the Absolute. The myriad manifestations, despite their variety, harmonize and are not disparate. The all is the one, for all things equally have the nature of non-being. The one is the all, for cause and effect follow in an unbroken sequence. In their power and function, each implies the other and freely rolls up or spreads out. This is called the perfect teaching of the One Vehicle [the highest Buddhist truth]" (Fazang, *Jinshizi Zhang* [Essay on the gold lion], chapter 7).

In Huayan Buddhism, the universe is composed of an infinite number of possible differentiated worlds (*dharmadhātu*). As a whole, the universe is to be regarded as fourfold: the world of phenomena (*shifajie*, the realm of facts), the world of noumenon (*lifajie*, the realm of principle), the world of phenomena and noumenon united (*shiliwuaifajie*), and the world of phenomena united or interwoven with other phenomena (*shishiwuaifajie*). For Huayan masters, the Tiantai round approach is not inclusive or comprehensive enough. It merely touches on the first three realms of the universe but fails to see the world of phenomena united with other phenomena. According to the Huayan School, Huayan Buddhism better and more fully investigates and describes things themselves than other teachings. From its preeminent doctrine of *yuanjiao*, one can see that all things form a harmonious whole by mutually penetrating (*xiangru*) and mutually identifying (*xiangji*), and that phenomena are "the fact and the world of fact perfectly harmonized" (*shishiwuaifajie*) (Cheng 1984b, p. 222).

The distinct feature of Tiantai and Huayan Buddhism is their propagation of *yuanjiao* (round teaching, doctrine, or approach). In many ways, the Chinese round teaching in both Tiantai and Huayan philosophies is similar to Western phenomenology. Phenomenology can be seen as a purely descriptive study of any subject matter in which phenomena are described by means of direct awareness (*Anschauung*). In phenomenology, phenomena are not identified with sense experience or sense data, and the truth and falsity of phenomenological statements do not depend on sensory observation. For phenomenologists, sensory observation is instituted and categorized under certain general concepts, and hence in the strict sense, sensory experience is already constituted or polluted. The ideal of phenomenology is to return "to the things themselves" (*zu den Sachen selbst*). Actually, this is also the ideal of the round teaching that Tiantai and Huayan masters had tried to practice.

The object of phenomenological research includes whatever can conceivably be experienced, even what occurs in wild dreams. Phenomenologists do not neglect any aspect of our experience and seek to describe all things in their full possible concreteness. Tiantai and Huayan Buddhists had a similar objective in their round approach. Like phenomenologists, they aimed to investigate things, both subject and object, in their fullest breadth and depth. This is why Huayan masters taught the fourfold *dharmadhātu* as a way of exploring the infinite number of possible differentiated worlds, and claimed that their philosophy was "more round," "more complete," better, and higher than Tiantai and other Buddhist teachings. This is also why Huayan Buddhism is said to be the most splendid flower of the Buddha's dharma.

The phenomenological approach has negative and positive aspects, involving, as it does, turning away from something and turning toward something else. Negatively, it avoids preconceptions and brackets constituted phenomena. Positively, it turns to the things themselves and describes them as purely and as fully as possible. The negative aspect has a positive function: to facilitate genuine intuition of the given. In a similar way, the Buddhist round approach has a double character: *zhi* (cessation, stoppage, or stillness) and *guan* (observation, contemplation, awareness, or examination). *Zhi* is like Husserl's *epochē*, the suspension of all natural belief in the objects of experience. This is not to deny the world, but to become a disinterested spectator who can rediscover what has previously been lost. By means of *guan*, one can penetrate to the essence of things and obtain the unattached insight of true reality.

The phenomenological method is said to involve a change of attitude. One must look at the world with new eyes. The result is said to be a change in one's experience. The method of *zhiguan* in the Buddhist round approach also involves a change of attitude. One transforms from an attached way of life to an enlightened one, experiencing a sense of peace and transcendence: "How calm, still and pure! How deep, stable, and quiet! How pure and clear the inner silence! It functions without the character of functioning, and acts without the character of acting" (Fazang, *Dasheng Zhiguan Famen* [The Mahayana method of zhiquan], chapter 4.) Through this transformation, the true state of all things is apprehended, and the universe is seen as the manifestation of an absolute mind, known as *zhenru* (true reality) or *rulaizang* (*tathāgatagarbha*).

It is interesting to see that the final outcome of the method of *zhiguan* is similar to that of Husserl's transcendental deduction, namely, the discovery of transcendental consciousness or mind. This is not subjective idealism, because subject and object, as well as the absolute and the relative, are seen to be interdependent, mutually penetrating, and even mutually identifying.

CHAN (ZEN)

Unlike Tiantai and Huayan Buddhism, the Chan School (Zen in Japanese), founded in China in the sixth century, does not aim to establish a round doctrine or to fully describe the universe. Chan Buddhism was claimed not to be a doctrine at all but a way of avoiding systematic views. Chan stories repeatedly teach that Chan Buddhism is not a body of fixed truths; instead, it is the abandonment of all views.

Although Chan masters did not develop theories, Chan Buddhism has some philosophical foundations found in Western philosophy: critical inquiry, autonomy, intellectual freedom, and creativity. Socrates is well known for saying that the unexamined life is not worth living. For him and many others, the philosophical enterprise consisted of inquiry rather than an accumulation of final truths. In the West, philosophy has often been regarded as the highest form of inquiry because, unlike other sciences, it alone does not involve presuppositions. True philosophers take nothing for granted. Similarly, Chan masters took nothing for granted.

Chan Buddhism has been critical of Buddhism viewed as a religion. Often a religion presupposes the authority or divinity of its founder and the infallibility of his words, but Chan Buddhism invoked no such presuppositions. Chan masters often rejected any special status for Gautama Buddha and repudiated the certainty of Buddhist scriptures. When the Buddha was born, he is alleged to have proclaimed, "Above the earth and below the heavens, I alone am the Honored One!" Chan master Yunmen (864–949) commented on this saying, "If I had been with him at the moment of his uttering this, I would surely have struck him dead with one blow and thrown the corpse into the maw of a hungry dog" (Suzuki 1964, p. 40). Chan masters would not subscribe to the views of a religious leader. One must enlighten oneself. Enlightenment (*wu*) must occur within and be done personally. In fact, according to Chan masters, any person who obtains enlightenment is a Buddha.

For Socrates, the autonomous activity of philosophy was integral to being genuinely human. For Chan Buddhism, to live genuinely is to live the life of enlightenment, and to live the life of enlightenment is to live autonomously. Simply following the Buddha faithfully and practicing the dharma diligently does not engender an enlightened outlook. Rather, one must be autonomous (*zizhu*). In the Chan lifestyle, a true Buddhist conducts his life freely and leisurely (*ziyou zizai*).

The main message of Chan Buddhism, believed to have been composed by Bodhidharma (470–543), is succinctly stated thus:

> A special transmission outside scriptures;
>
> No dependence upon words and letters;
>
> Direct pointing at human mind;
>
> Seeing into one's own nature to attain Buddhahood (Dumoulin 1988, p. 85).

Chan masters repudiate any blind acceptance of scriptures, for "the entire scriptures from beginning to end are nothing but deceitful words" (Chung-yuan 1971, p.143). The so-called holy scriptures of Buddhism have often been set aside, thrown away, and even burned by Chan masters.

The radical approach of Chan Buddhism created a refreshing Buddhist epistemology that emphasized opening up the mind to the serious issue of what truth is. For some Buddhists, truth is objective and can be spoken and written about. In this view, the Buddha and the patriarchs transmitted truth, and the scriptures contain their messages, often identified with the dharma. But for Chan Buddhism, truth is not something objective, nor can it be spoken and written about. The Buddhist dharma is not conveyed by ink marks on the pages of scripture. Huineng (638–713), the sixth patriarch, was said to be illiterate, and yet was a Chan master. When Fada, a devout monk, studied the *Lotus Sutra* three thousand times and still could not understand it, he came to ask Huineng for instruction. The master said, "The Dharma is quite clear; it is only your mind that is not clear. Whether Sutra-reciting can enlighten you or not all depends on yourself. … If the mind is deluded, the *Lotus* [*Sutra*] turns you around, if the mind is enlightened, you turn around the *Lotus* [*Sutra*]" (Huineng 1952, p. 24).

Truth, for Chan Buddhism, is something living and personal. To equate truth with a proposition is to objectify and conceptualize it, to make it static and dead. For Chan masters, "The real truth is nothing else but one's own mind. Thus … the real teaching must be transmitted directly from one mind to another" (Chung-yuan 1971, p. 86). Genuine spiritual education occurs in personal communication between Chan master and disciple. This mind-to-mind transmission resembles what Martin Buber, the great twentieth-century thinker, described as an I-thou relationship, rather than an I-it relationship. To see the truth as an object and to conceptualize it is to shift from a personal I-thou point of view to an impersonal I-it understanding.

True meditation, a central Chan practice, does not refer to sitting in a certain posture with legs crossed, but to "the brightening up of the mind-works" (Suzuki 1956, p. 85). Mazu (709–788) used to sit diligently and frequently in meditation. Master Huairang (677–744) asked him, "Virtuous one, why are you sitting in meditation?" Mazu replied, "I want to become a Buddha." Thereupon the master picked up a tile and rubbed it repeatedly in front of the hermitage. Mazu asked, "What is the master doing?" Huairang answered, "I am polishing the tile to make a mirror." Mazu exclaimed, "How can you make a mirror by polishing a tile?" The master responded, "How can you make a Buddha by practicing sitting meditation?" (*Jingde Chuandeng Lu*, Vol. 5). The monk was said to be enlightened immediately, and later became a great Chan master.

The personal experience of the dharma, according to Chan masters, is not remote, abstract, or transcendent. It occurs in one's present daily life. Zhaozhou (778–897) asked Master Nanquan (748–834), "What is the Dao [the Way]?" The master replied, "Everyday-mindedness is Dao." In another instance, after attaining great enlightenment under Mazu, Pangyun stated, "I am an ordinary man who fulfills his daily tasks. How plain are the Buddhist teachings!" According to the Chan School, "In the carrying of water and the chopping of wood—therein lies Dao" (Chung-yuan 1971, p. 145).

An enlightened person does not live outside samsara, or this world of rebirth, and he should not ignore karma, or cause and effect. He should treasure this life and value the virtues of labor in daily affairs. Baizhang (720–814), who founded the Chan monastic order, was said to live by the principle "A day without work—a day without eating" (Dumoulin 1988, p. 103). When he was old and his disciples hid his tools, he refused to eat until he could work again. Chan practitioners do not adhere to rigid moral precepts, but practice a work ethic in daily life.

Chan philosophy has similarities with contemporary ordinary-language philosophy in that both favor the ordinary use of language. For Chan Buddhism, however, any concrete fact or lived experience is rich and complex. Things may appear to be simple and ordinary, yet are really quite complicated and extraordinary. Chan Buddhists have sometimes used metaphysical statements to convey their understanding, and have also expressed themselves through strange words and strange acts (*qiyan qixing*). Consequently, the Chan literature abounds with irrational statements and absurd actions.

The use of strange words and strange acts in Chan Buddhism actually accords with the Mādhyamika practice of revealing the truth of emptiness and the middle way. According to Nāgārjuna, the Buddha's dharma was given, and hence should be understood, by means of twofold truth, a convenient term for the perspectives of conventional and ultimate truth. The former sees things from a viewpoint deluded by attachment, while the latter sees things without attachment.

Following Nāgārjuna's philosophy, Chan masters often expressed themselves through twofold truth, and hence their teachings and practices may be apprehended from two standpoints. Ordinary sentient beings do not see the emptiness of all things. So, to comply with conventional usage, Chan masters may say, "I see" or "you should see" the objects of right knowledge. But from a higher, unattached standpoint, all things are empty, and so the same master may also state, "I do not see" or "one should not see" any right object; on the contrary, one should see the emptiness of all things. For instance, once Shenhui asked Huineng, "Do you see or not?" The master replied, "I both see and also do not see." The puzzled disciple asked, "How can you see and also not see?" The master instructed, "If your mind is attached, you do not see; if your mind is without attachment, you see." The seemingly inconsistent expressions of Chan Buddhism were delivered with twofold truth in mind. Understood in this light, they are not as illogical as they might appear.

Although Chan Buddhism is a Mahayana practice, in many ways it strongly reflects Chinese thinking and feeling. Such Chan ideas as *xing* (nature, essence, own nature), *xin* (mind, human mind), *foxing* (Buddha nature), *foxin* (Buddha mind), and the key message that everyone has a Buddha nature are more like Chinese Confucian thought than Indian Mahayana Buddhism.

The central message that Bodhidharma brought from India to China in the sixth century also differs from the Indian Mahayana philosophy of emptiness. For Nāgārjuna, all things are causally conditioned and hence empty of any nature (*xing*) of their own. So, whereas the Chan masters instruct one to see the nature of things (*jianxing*), the Indian Mahayana scriptures teach the believer to reject this idea. Chan practice has to be regarded as a special transmission outside the scriptures. For Chan masters, one cannot and should not follow the ancient Indian scriptures literally; otherwise one will never be enlightened. Therefore, Chan Buddhism advises, "No dependence on words and letters."

The notion of the nature of things (*xing*) was important in the minds of Chinese thinkers long before Buddhism was introduced to China. Both orthodox and less orthodox Confucianists accepted the view that things had natures. Confucius and Mencius are well known as saying that human nature is good. In their teachings, the mind (*xin*) is the nature of a human. This human nature or mind is more important for its axiological value rather than for its ontological substance, in contrast with such notions as Hindu Brahma and atman, Theravada Buddhist *svabhava* (inborn nature), and Greek substratum. This notion of value makes humans valuable and endows them with a spiritual quality. Without this nature, a person would be merely a beast. With this nature, a person can become a sage. According to Mencius, Confucianism teaches that one should exhaust one's mind and know one's nature (*jinxin zhixing*). One who practices this will be a gentleman and a sage.

Chan masters skillfully assimilated the Confucian sense of nature, mind, and sagehood into Buddhist thought. The result of this skillful measure (*fangbian*, *upaya* in Sanskrit) was the doctrine of "direct pointing at the human mind; seeing into nature to attain Buddhahood" (Dumoulin 1988, p. 85). Huineng opened his famous *Platform Sutra* with the same message: "Virtuous ones! The Bodhi-nature is originally pure. Making use of this mind alone, one can directly become a Buddha" (Huineng 1952, opening statement).

Inspired by Confucian thought, Chan masters transformed the traditional Buddhist doctrine of gradual enlightenment into the teaching and practice of abrupt or sudden enlightenment (*dunwu*). In Indian Buddhist teachings, not everyone has a Buddha nature and can become a Buddha. But according to Confucius and Mencius, all human beings are alike in nature and become different owing to different external environments. In the original state, humans have innocent, fine minds that cannot bear to see the suffering of others. But this mind was lost. The aim of education is to recover what has been lost. Can we find the original mind? Mencius's answer was positive and optimistic. He wrote that the original mind is "all already complete in oneself," and that the truth "is not far to seek, but right by oneself." Following this positive, optimistic philosophy, Chan masters proclaimed that everyone has a Buddha nature, is able to become a Buddha, and can suddenly attain enlightenment.

PURE LAND'S MESSAGE OF HOPE

While most Buddhists took a positive view of human nature, Pure Land Buddhism (Jingtu, Jōdo in Japanese), also founded in China in the sixth century, acknowledged human weakness and was pessimistic about individual efforts to achieve nirvana. Reading scriptures, sitting in meditation, keeping moral precepts, understanding the dharma, and training for enlightenment are all fine, but really too much and too extreme for most. Pure Land Buddhism is a protest against, as well as a step away from, intellectual, scriptural, and disciplinary forms of Buddhism. The main message of Pure Land Buddhism is that one cannot and need not attain nirvana by effort, but may obtain it with the help and compassion of Amitabha Buddha.

The Pure Land message, according to this school, was the Buddha's original teaching, which was rediscovered by Nāgārjuna, later revered as the first patriarch of the Pure Land School. According to Pure Land masters, Nāgārjuna taught, "Although there are innumerable ways in the teachings of the Buddha, they can be classified roughly: the difficult way and the easy way." The difficult way is to approach *Avaivartike* (a state of no return to the world of delusion) by diligently following the eightfold path and practicing the six virtues of perfection (*pāramitās*); the easy way teaches faith in Amitabha Buddha. The Mahayana doctrine of emptiness is the teaching of the easy way, for it teaches the emptiness of all our views and efforts.

Although Indian Mahayana teachings appear to differ from Pure Land Buddhism, Tanluan (476–524), the real founder of Pure Land Buddhism in China, is said to have been inspired by Nāgārjuna's philosophy of emptiness. He drew on Nāgārjuna's *Dasabhumi-vibhastra* (A commentary by Nagarjuna on the ten stages in bodhisattva wisdom) to advocate that, because humans have little spiritual capacity, they should not pursue the difficult path. Traditional religious life represents the difficult way, which, more properly speaking, according to Tanluan, is the teaching of enlightenment through one's own power (*zili*). But the Mahayana way teaches salvation by relying on an external power (*tali*). By relying on the Buddha's help and compassion, one can empty oneself and be awakened and saved by the Buddha's help and compassion.

Pure Land Buddhism shifted the focus of the Buddha's dharma from the discipline of observing moral precepts (*vinaya*) and an emphasis on wisdom (*prajñā*) to the spread of compassion (*karuṇā*). Pure Land Buddhism is a religion of repentance, mercy, forgiveness, and grace. One obtains salvation by faith and devotion rather than by work or learning. Life, according to the Buddha's first noble truth, involves suffering. Yet formal religion has not made our lives more comfortable; on the contrary, it has frustrated and confused the minds of many clerics and laypeople because few can sustain the rigors of mastering Buddhist doctrine, either by practicing monastic discipline or by studying scriptures. An enlightened Buddha would see this state of suffering, have compassion, and be willing to help humans rise from the ocean of sufferings.

Amitabha, a compassionate bodhisattva according to Pure Land Buddhism, saw the miserable condition of sentient beings and determined to extend his great mercy to them, making forty-eight vows to save them. Failing his vows, he would not become a Buddha. Thus, while people may not be smart enough to digest Buddhist scriptures and may not have time to sit in meditation, they may yet hope for salvation by calling on the name of Amitabha Buddha (*Amituofo* in Chinese). The recitation or invocation of Amitabha's name became the trademark of Pure Land Buddhism. This simple act was said to help people enter into the western paradise, or the Pure Land. In fact, it became the most common Buddhist practice in China, Korea, and Japan, and the most popular means for salvation by which millions have sought release from suffering. So Pure Land Buddhism transformed Buddhism into a popular religion by preaching the simple gospel of hope.

Pure Land masters equated chanting "Amituofo" with Buddhism. Daochuo (562–645), the second patriarch of Pure Land Buddhism, was said to repeat the name of Amitabha Buddha seventy thousand times per day. Chanting "Amituofo" was believed to enable a person to be reborn in the Pure Land. Here, religious language does not describe the universe nor analyze truth. Rather, it is a calling for help, a therapy to relieve anxiety, frustration, despair, and other sufferings in life. The sound of "Amituofo" seems to have a power to comfort people and pacify the mind. The ultimate cause of the effectiveness of the invocation, according to Pure Land masters, is Amitabha Buddha himself, who aspired to save all beings. It is really through the power of Amitabha Buddha's vows that mortals, by reciting his name, can be released from the hell fires that a life of sin and evil bring on.

The power of chanting "Amituofo" is good news, because even persons who have committed the most egregious sins can be saved if they recite the name of Amitabha Buddha. According to Shandao (613–681), an eminent Pure Land master, Pure Land Buddhism not only offers salvation to known sinners, but also leads good people to repent and confess their sins. Those who sincerely acknowledge and believe that they are sinful, lowly persons continually involved in error and shut off from salvation are enlightened Buddhists. If one can repent of sin, no matter how small the sin, one will gain a deep sense of release from suffering and can aspire to birth in the Pure Land through Amitabha Buddha's vows. Confession, repentance, humility, and forgiveness, rather than punishment and condemnation, are the virtues promoted and practiced by the Pure Land community.

BUDDHISM IN CHINESE CULTURE

From the sixth century, Indian Buddhism became sinicized. Divergent Chinese Buddhist philosophies and practices were assimilated and fitted into the Chinese tradition, and exercised a lasting influence on almost every aspect of Chinese life. By the eighth century, Chinese Buddhism became firmly established and triumphantly spread throughout China. Chinese culture became an aggregation and synthesis of Confucianism, Daoism, and Buddhism. However, this syncretism did not go easily and smoothly. There were three major persecutions of Buddhists in Chinese history. The most devastating one occurred in 845. After this, most Buddhist schools declined in China. Then the Chan and Pure Land schools became predominant over other Buddhist schools and practices.

From the Song dynasty (960–1279) onward, chanting "Amituofo" has been the major religious practice among devout Buddhists. Chan philosophy was attractive to and popular among Chinese intellectuals, and was a vital cultural force, especially in literature and the arts. In fact, it led Confucian scholars to reexamine classical Confucian philosophy and develop neo-Confucianism, even though neo-Confucian scholars frequently attacked Buddhism when defending their orthodox teachings. Like Chan Buddhists, neo-Confucian scholars cultivated the mind, and even used Buddhist terms, some equating *li* (principle, reason) with the Dao, and others with the mind. Like Tiantai and Huayan Buddhists, many Confucianists adopted the round approach to develop an all-in-one and one-in-all worldview. In many ways what was new in neo-Confucianism was quite Buddhist in spirit.

The influence of Buddhism can also be seen in twentieth-century new Confucianism, as in Feng Youlan's (1895–1988) famous book *Xin lixue* (A new study of principle). Like metaphysically minded Buddhists, Feng investigated the principles in and behind things with the aim of reaching the highest sphere of life, namely "forming one body with all things." Xiong Shili (1885–1968), the founder of twentieth-century new Confucianism, was obviously a Buddhist Confucian. He promoted the Mahayana philosophy of consciousness only (*weishi*) and reinterpreted the Confucian metaphysics found in the *Yijing* (Book of changes) in the light of this doctrine. His eminent disciples, among them Tang Junyi (1909–1978) and Mou Zongsan (1909–1995), examined the round approach (*yuanjiao*), and they debated whether Tiantai or Huayan philosophy represented the highest teaching. Mou Zongsan found the Tiantai School to be the best. To develop his moral metaphysics, he adopted Tiantai philosophy, especially the idea that phenomena are noumenon and noumenon is phenomena. Tang Junyi, Fang Dongmei (1899–1977), and many other twentieth-century Confucian scholars have contended that Huayan philosophy, rather than Tiantai philosophy, represented a fuller development of Buddhist thought.

Fang Dongmei, just before his death, made the following statement:

> From emptiness I came.
>
> To emptiness I return.
>
> Emptying the emptiness without possessing any being
>
> It is in nowhere that my heart will dwell (Shen 2003).

Thus, the latest approaches to Confucianism have been profoundly influenced by Buddhist thought. One cannot properly understand Chinese philosophy or the history of Chinese thought without knowing Buddhist philosophy.

See also Chinese Philosophy: Overview; Chinese Philosophy: Contemporary.

Bibliography

Chen, Kenneth. *Buddhism in China*. Princeton, NJ: Princeton University Press, 1964.

Cheng, Hsueh-li. *Empty Logic: Mādhyamika Buddhism from Chinese Sources*. New York: Philosophical Library, 1984a.

Cheng, Hsueh-li. *Exploring Zen*. New York: Peter Lang, 1996.

Cheng, Hsueh-li. "Phenomenology and T'ien-t'ai and Hua-yen Buddhism." *Analecta Husserliana* XVII (1984b): 222.

Chung-yuan, Chang. *Original Teaching of Ch'an Buddhism*. New York: Vintage Books, 1971.

Cook, Francis H. *Hua-yen Buddhism: The Jewel Net of Indra*. University Park: Pennsylvania State University Press, 1977.

De Bary, William Theodore. *The Buddhist Tradition in India, China, and Japan*. New York: Random House, 1972.

Dumoulin, Heinrich. *Zen Buddhism: A History*, Vol. 1: *India and China*. New York: Macmillan, 1988.

Fazang. *Dasheng Zhiguan Famen* (The Mahayana method of zhiquan). Chapter 4.

Fazang. "Huayanjing yihaibaimen" (The hundred gates on the meaning of the flower spendor scripture). *Taisho* 1875, Chapter I.

Fazang. *Jinshizi Zhang* (Essay on the gold lion). Chapter 7.

Gimello, Robert M., and Peter N. Gregory, eds. *Studies in Ch'an and Hua-yen*. Honolulu: University of Hawaii Press, 1983.

Huineng. *The Sutra of Huineng*. Hong Kong: H.K. Buddhist Distributor Press, 1952.

"Jingde Chuandeng Lu" (Jingde record on the transmission of light). *Taisho* 2076, Vol. 5.

Jizang. "Er Di Yi" (The meaning of twofold truth). *Taisho* 1854, p. 94c.

Jizang. "Sanlun Xuanyi" (The profound meaning of three treatises). *Taisho* 1852, p.6.

Nagarjuna. *Zhong Lun* (The middle treatise), XXIV: 18.

Saddharma-pundarika (The wonderful law of lotus). Chapter 2.

Sengzhao. "Zhao Lun," Part III. *Taisho* 1858, p. 153.

Shen, Vincent. "Fang Dongmei." *Encyclopedia of Chinese Philosophy*. New York: Routledge, 2003.

Suzuki, D. T. *An Introduction to Zen Buddhism*. New York: Grove Press, 1964.

Suzuki, D. T. *Zen Buddhism*. Garden City, New York: Doubleday Anchor Books, 1956.

Swanson, Paul. *Foundations of T'ien-t'ai Philosophy*. Berkeley, CA: Asian Humanities, 1989.

Takakusu, Junjirō. *The Essentials of Buddhist Philosophy*. Honolulu: University of Hawaii Press, 1947.

Wright, Arthur F. *Buddhism in Chinese History*. Stanford, CA: Stanford University Press, 1959.

Hsueh-li Cheng (2005)

CONFUCIANISM

CONFUCIANISM AS AN ETHICAL TRADITION

After the Zhou people conquered the Shang people in the middle of the eleventh century BCE, the early Zhou kings ruled by letting feudal lords govern vassal states. As their powers grew, feudal lords fought one another and resisted the Zhou king until the state of Qin conquered all other states in 221 BCE. A number of ethical and political thinkers lived in the period from the sixth to third century BCE, proposing different ways of restoring order as well as ideal ways of life for human beings. Among them, several thinkers, including Confucius (sixth century BCE), Mencius (fourth century BCE) and Xunzi (third century BCE), as well as their followers, were regarded as belonging to the same movement of thought. This movement of thought was referred to retrospectively in the Han dynasty (206 BCE to 220 CE) as *rujia*, or the school of *ru*. The English term *Confucianism* is now often used as a translation of *rujia* to refer to this school of thought.

Unlike what the term *Confucianim* suggests, the expression *rujia*, or "the school of *ru*," does not bear any special relation to the name of the individual known as Confucius. Instead, *ru* referred to a social group that already existed before the time of Confucius. The group consisted of professional ritualists who performed rituals in such ceremonial contexts as funeral rites, sacrifices to ancestors, and marriage ceremonies. In addition, these ritualists were often professional teachers, not just of rituals but also of other disciplines such as music. Certain individuals who were members of this group in virtue of being professional ritualists and teachers (including Confucius, Mencius, and Xunzi) came to develop concerns that were no longer restricted to rituals or to their own economic sustenance. Instead, they directed their attention to finding a remedy for the chaotic social and political situation of the times and to establishing the ideal way of life for human beings. They believed that the remedy lay with the maintenance and restoration of certain traditional norms and values, including but going beyond rituals, and proposed that, ideally, people should follow a way of life that embodies such norms and values. Unlike what the term *Confucianism* might suggest, these norms and values did not originate with Confucius but date back to a much earlier time.

Still, in referring to this movment of thought as *rujia* or "the school of *ru*," the Chinese did regard Confucius as the first and most important thinker of the movement. Both Mencius and Xunzi, the two other major Confucian thinkers from that period, also regarded themselves as defending Confucius's teachings, and their different developments of Confucius's teachings competed for influence in the Han dynasty. In the Tang dynasty (618–907), the Confucian thinker Han Yu (768–824) regarded Mencius as the true transmitter of Confucius's teachings, and this view was endorsed by Zhu Xi (1130–1200) of the Song dynasty (960–1279). Zhu Xi included the *Analects* (*Lunyu*) of Confucius and the *Mencius* (*Mengzi*), along with the *Great Learning* (*Daxue*) and *Centrality and Commonality* (*Zhongyong*), the latter two texts dating probably to early Han, among the Four Books. These texts eventually became the canons of the Confucian school, and Mencius came to be regarded as second only to Confucius in importance. Different kinds of Confucian teachings continued to evolve after Zhu Xi's times, represented by major figures such as Wang Yangming (1472–1529) of the Ming dynasty (1368–1644) and Dai Zhen (1724–1777) of the Qing dynasty (1644–1912).

Suppose we characterize ethics in terms of a concern with the question how one should live, where the scope of "one" is supposed to extend considerably beyond the person raising the question. Confucian thinkers do share a concern of this kind. Furthermore, they are reflective not just in having a conception of how one should live, but also in being concerned with the proper spirit behind the observance of rituals and other traditional norms, and with the grounds for observing these traditional norms and values. This warrants describing them as ethical thinkers. Also, although there are substantive differences in the views of different Confucian thinkers, these thinkers also share a broad similarity, both in defending certain traditional norms and values and in the use of certain common key terms in elaborating on their thinking. They share the same allegiance to Confucius's teachings and, after the time of Zhu Xi, also share a conception of certain canonical texts that define the Confucian school. These similarities warrant regarding them as belonging to the same tradition of thought and describing Confucianism as an ethical tradition. The rest of the article will elaborate on some of the main characteristics of this ethical tradition.

CONCEPTION OF THE SELF

To start with, let us consider how the Confucians view the self and the human constitution. They use the term *ti*, often translated as "body," to talk about a person's body, and they also have ways of referring to parts of the body, such as the four limbs and the senses. These parts of the body are not regarded as inert; not only do they have certain capacities, such as the eye's capacity of sight, but they also exhibit certain characteristic tendencies. For example, the four limbs are drawn toward rest, while the senses are drawn toward such ideal objects as beautiful colors or pleasurable objects of taste. Such tendencies are referred to as *yu*, a term often translated as "desires" and paired with an opposite term often translated as "aversion." These terms have, respectively, the connotations of being drawn toward and being repelled by certain things. The terms can be used not just for parts of the body but also for the person as a whole to describe how the person is drawn toward things like life and honor and repelled by things like death and disgrace.

That human beings have such tendencies as part of their basic constitution is regarded as a fact about them that is pervasive and difficult to alter. Facts of this kind are referred to as the *qing* of human beings, where *qing* means "facts" and, in this context, the connotation of certain facts about human beings that reveal what they are genuinely like. Later, *qing* comes to refer to what we would describe as emotions, including such things as joy, sorrow, and anger, these also being regarded as parts of the basic constitution of a person.

There is another feature of the Chinese view of the person for which it is difficult to find a Western equivalent. The body of a person is supposed to be filled with *qi*, a kind of energy or force that flows freely in and gives life to the person. *Qi* is responsible for the operation of the senses; for example, it is supposed to make possible speech in the mouth and sight in the eyes. Conversely, it can be affected by what happens to the senses; for example, *qi* can grow when the mouth takes in tastes and the ear takes in sounds. Also, *qi* is linked to the emotions, and what we would describe as a person's physical and psychological well-being is regarded as dependent on a proper balance of *qi*. For example, both illness and such emotional responses as fear are explained in terms of the condition of *qi*.

Among the different parts of the person, special significance is attached to *xin*, the organ of the heart that is viewed as the site of what we would describe as cognitive and affective activities. *Xin*, a term often translated as "heart" or "mind," can have desires (*yu*) and emotions (*qing*) and can take pleasure in or feel displeasure at certain things. It can also deliberate about a situation, direct attention to and ponder about certain things, and keep certain things in mind. One capacity of the heart/mind (*xin*) that is particularly important for Confucian thinkers is its ability to set directions that guide one's life and shape one's person as a whole. Such directions of the heart/mind are referred to as *zhi*, a term sometimes translated as "will."

Zhi can refer to specific intentions such as the intention to stay in or leave a certain place, or to general goals in life such as the goal of learning to be a sage. It is something that can be set up, nourished, and attained; it can also be altered by oneself or swayed under others' influence, and lost through insufficient persistence or preoccupation with other things. Early texts sometimes compare setting one's *zhi* in certain directions to aiming at a target in archery, and *zhi* is sometimes used interchangeably with another character that means "recording something" or "bearing something in mind." Probably, *zhi* has to do with the heart/mind's focusing itself on and constantly bearing in mind certain courses of action or goals in life, in such a way that *zhi* will guide one's action or one's life unless it is changed by oneself or under others' influence or unless one is led to deviate from it by other distractions. *Zhi* (directions of the heart/mind) differs from *yu* (desires) in this respect: although *zhi* pertains to the heart/mind, *yu* can pertain to the heart/mind or to parts of the body such as the senses or the four limbs. Furthermore, whereas *zhi* involves focusing the heart/mind in a way that guides one's actions or one's life in general, *yu* involves tendencies that one may choose to resist rather than act on.

With this survey of the different aspects of the person as background, let us consider the notion of self as it applies to Confucian thought. Now, besides the use of first-person pronouns, the Chinese language has two characters with the meaning of "oneself." *Zi* is used in reflexive binomials referring to one's doing something connected with oneself, such as one's examining oneself or bringing disgrace upon oneself. *Ji* is used to talk about not just one's doing something connected with oneself but also others doing something connected with oneself (such as others appreciating oneself), oneself doing something connected with others (such as oneself causing harm to others), or one's desiring or having something (such as a certain character) in oneself. The two characters differ in that the former emphasizes one's relation to oneself, whereas the latter emphasizes oneself as contrasted with others. In addition, the character *shen*, which is used to refer sometimes to the body and sometimes to the person as a whole, can also be used to refer to oneself or to one's own person when prefixed with the appropriate possessive pronoun.

These linguistic observations show that the Chinese have a conception of the way one relates to oneself. Furthermore, in connection with Confucian thought, the characters just mentioned are often used to talk about one's examining oneself and cultivating oneself on the basis of such self-examination. This further observation shows that Confucian thinkers also work with a conception of one's being related to oneself in a self-reflective manner, with the capacity to reflect on, examine, and bring about changes in oneself. So they have a conception of the self in the sense of a conception of how one relates to oneself in this self-reflective manner.

Confucian thinkers ascribe the capacity of self-reflection just described to the heart/mind, to which they also ascribe a guiding role. They emphasize the importance of self-cultivation—that is, the process of constantly reflecting on and examining oneself, setting one's heart/mind in the proper direction, and bringing about ethical improvements in oneself under the guidance of the heart/mind. There has been extensive disagreement within the Confucian tradition about how the heart/mind can set itself in the proper direction. For example, Mencius and Xunzi disagree about whether a certain ethical direction is already built into the heart/mind and whether one should derive the proper direction by reflecting on the heart/mind or by learning from the outside. Later, Zhu Xi and Wang Yangming disagree in the different emphases they place on learning and on attending to the heart/mind in the process of self-cultivation. Despite such disagreements, they all regard the heart/mind as that which guides the process of self-cultivation.

Furthermore, they also agree on another distinctive feature of the heart/mind—not only can it set directions that guide the person's life and shape the person as a whole, but it is also independent of external control in having the capacity to hold on to the directions it sets without being swayed by external forces. For example, both the *Analects* and the *Mencius* emphasize its guiding role, comparing the directions (*zhi*) of the heart/mind to the commander of an army. In addition, the *Analects* notes one point of dissimilarity—although an army can be deprived of its commander, even a common person cannot be deprived of the directions set by the heart/mind. Such directions can, of course, be influenced by outside factors, but the point is that the heart/mind has the capacity to resist such influences and, for the Confucian thinkers, one should ideally cultivate oneself to attain such a steadfastness of purpose after having set the heart/mind in the proper directions. This independence of the heart/mind from external control is also emphasized by Xunzi, who compares the heart/mind to the position of the ruler and the senses to the offices of government; like the ruler, the heart/mind issues order but does not take order from anything.

Not only is the heart/mind independent of external control, but it also has the capacity to constantly step back to reflect on and improve its own operations. Three early Confucian texts—the *Xunzi*, *Great Learning*, and *Centrality and Commonality*—emphasize the idea that the heart/mind should cautiously watch over its own activities to ensure that all of them, however minute or subtle, are completely oriented in an ethical direction. This idea is presented in terms of watching over *du*, where *du* refers to the minute and subtle workings of the heart/mind that are not yet manifested outwardly and to which one alone has access. The idea is taken up by later Confucian thinkers, who in addition emphasize the importance of watching out for and eliminating what they call "selfish desires," that is, the distortive influences in the heart/mind that might lead one to deviate from the ethical direction. This aspect of Confucian thought shows that the Confucians ascribe to the heart/mind a self-reflexiveness; for any of its own activities, however minute and subtle, it has the capacity to reflect on and reshape such activities to ensure their orientation in an ethical direction. This self-reflexiveness is related to the independence of the heart/mind from external control—even though its activities can be influenced by external circumstances, the heart/mind has the capacity to constantly step back and reshape its own activities under the conception of what is proper, which it forms on the basis of its own reflections.

Given their emphasis on the distinctive role of the heart/mind, did Confucian thinkers believe in some kind of mind-body distinction? In a sense, they do emphasize a distinction between the heart/mind and other aspects of the person. The heart/mind has the distinctive capacity to reflect on these other aspects and on its own activities, to form a conception of what is proper, and to regulate and shape other aspects of the person and its own activities under such a conception. On the other hand, the distinction that the Confucian thinkers emphasize pertains to the distinctive capacities and modes of operation of the heart/mind rather than to the heart/mind as a distinctive kind of entity that occupies a "mental" as opposed to a "physical" realm. The character *xin*, translated here as "heart/mind," refers to the organ of the heart that is a part of the body just as the senses are. And just as the heart/mind can operate in the manner described earlier, the senses also have their own modes of operation, such as distinguishing between and being drawn toward certain sensory objects. What distinguishes the heart/mind from other parts of the body is not that it pertains to a "mental" as opposed to a "physical" realm but that its modes of operation are different from, and enable it to perform a guiding function in relation to, other parts of the body.

Furthermore, there is also a sense in which Confucian thinkers deemphasize the distinction between the heart/mind and other aspects of the person. Earlier, we considered the Confucian emphasis on one's cautiously watching over the minute and subtle activities of the heart/mind, activities that are not yet outwardly manifested. In elaborating on this idea, the relevant texts also emphasize the point that, though initially not discernible from the outside, these activities of the heart/mind will inevitably be manifested outwardly, and so one cannot conceal from others the way one truly is. Indeed, the different aspects of the person described earlier are all interactive. For example, the life forces (*qi*) that fill the body can be affected by what happens to the body, such as the tastes that the mouth takes in and the sounds that the ear hears; conversely, the life forces can generate speech in the mouth and sight in the eyes. Also, the directions (*zhi*) of the heart/mind can guide and shape the life forces while depending on the life forces for their execution; conversely, the directions of the heart/mind can be swayed if the life forces are not adequately nourished.

It follows from the intimate link between the heart/mind and the life forces, and between the life forces and the body, that the heart/mind is also intimately linked to the body. Various Confucian texts observe how the condition of the heart/mind makes a difference to one's bodily appearance. For example, Mencius observes how one's ethical qualities, while being rooted in one's heart/mind, are reflected in one's face, back, and the four limbs, while the *Great Learning* observes how virtue adorns the whole person just as riches adorn a house. Thus, while the heart/mind is distinguished from other aspects of the person by its modes of operation and its guiding role, it is at the same time intimately linked to other aspects of the person. It is not a kind of "private" or "inner" entity that eludes observation by others, but its condition is inevitably reflected in other parts of the person. In their emphasis on self-cultivation, the Confucians have in mind a transformation not just of the heart/mind but of the person as a whole. Accordingly, if the self is viewed as the object as well as the subject of self-reflection and self-cultivation, it would be more appropriate to describe the Confucian conception of the self as comprising not just the heart/mind but the whole person, including various parts of the body.

Indeed, not only does self-cultivation affect one's whole person, but it also has an attractive and transformative power on others, a power that many Confucians regard as the ideal basis for government. For them, the ideal goal of government is to transform people's character, and the way to accomplish this is to first cultivate oneself and to let the transformative power of one's cultivated character take effect. This does not mean that governmental policies are not important. However, proper policies are themselves a manifestation of the cultivated character of those in power, and properly carrying out policies transmitted from the past also requires a cultivated character. So the ultimate basis for order in society lies with cultivating oneself, and there is an intimate link between self-cultivation and transformation of others' character.

ETHICAL IDEAL

Having considered the Confucian conception of the self, let us consider the nature of the ethical ideal that the Confucians espouse. This ideal is presented through several key terms, three of the most important being *li*, *yi*, and *ren*.

Li originally referred to rites of sacrifice and subsequently broadened in scope to include rules governing ceremonial behavior in various social contexts, such as marriages and burials, as well as ways of presenting gifts, receiving guests, asking after the health of parents, or having audience with a prince. Subsequently, its scope broadened further to include rules governing behavior appropriate to one's social position, such as supporting one's parents in their old age. Though the term can be used to include social norms in general, *li* often retains the connotation of ceremonial behaviour. The *Xunzi*, for example, although sometimes using *li* interchangeably with *li yi* ("rites and propriety") to refer to various social norms, more often uses *li* in connection with ceremonial practices and their minute details. Whether it is the ceremonial or nonceremonial that is emphasized, *li* includes only rules that are part of a continuing cultural tradition and that pertain to the relations between people in different social positions or in recurring social contexts; behavior such as saving a drowning person, though proper, is not a matter of *li*. Also, Confucian thinkers emphasize the importance of the proper spirit behind the observance of *li*, which include attitudes such as respectfulness, attentiveness, and seriousness.

From a contemporary perspective, it may appear puzzling how rules as diverse as those ranging from details of rituals to rules governing conduct between people in different social positions could be placed together under one single concept. However, the rules of *li* do exhibit a unity both in the attitude that they are supposed to reflect and in the social functions they perform. A serious and reverential attitude toward others underlies both the observance of the responsibilities one has in virtue of one's social position and the observance of rules governing ceremonial behavior; a breach of *li*, even in ceremonial contexts—such as being dressed improperly when receiving a guest—demonstrates a lack of the proper attitude and constitutes a serious offense. And, just as the rules governing interaction between individuals in different social positions promote order and minimize conflict, the rules governing ceremonial behavior promote harmony and the proper channeling and beautification of one's feelings in those areas of life associated with strong emotions, such as funerals and mourning or marriage ceremonies, during which individuals from different families become united as one family. The common spirit underlying the various rules of *li* and their common social functions show that their being grouped together is not based on a failure to distinguish between categorically different areas of life.

Another point worth noting is that the Confucian attitude toward *li* is not entirely conservative. Although the *Analects* contain only one passage that apparently endorses, on economic grounds, a deviation from an existing *li* practice, the *Mencius* is more explicit in asserting that *li* can be overridden by other considerations in exigencies. The *Xunzi* discusses the importance of adapting *li* to the changing circumstances of life, and later Confucian thinkers such as Wang Yang-ming also observe that what is of importance is to preserve the spirit behind *li* rather than to adhere to its minute details.

The Confucian readiness to deviate from or adopt *li* relates to another key term in Confucian thought, *yi*. *Yi* has the earlier meaning of a proper regard for oneself or a sense of honor, involving one's not brooking an insult, and lack of *yi* is often linked to disgrace in early texts. It is subsequently used to refer to what is proper or fitting to a situation, and is linked to *chi*, a character often translated as "shame."

Chi is a reaction to an occurrence or situation that one regards as beneath oneself and potentially lowering one's standing, and it is like shame in presupposing standards to which one is seriously committed. However, it is unlike shame in that it can be directed not just to past occurrences that fall below such standards but also to future prospects of such occurrences. Although *chi* can be directed to the manner in which one is treated in public, it is not typically associated with the thought of being seen or heard, and the typical reaction associated with it is not hiding or disappearing. Rather, it is associated with the thought of one's being tainted by a certain occurrence, and the typical reaction associated with it is to "wash off" what is tainting by distancing oneself from or remedying the situation. Even when directed to the past, it does not carry the connotation of dwelling on the past occurrence, but instead emphasizes a firm resolution to remedy the situation. It is more like the attitude of regarding something as contemptible or beneath oneself, and is linked to ideas such as disdain or a refusal to do certain things.

Yi, for Confucian thinkers, has to do with a firm commitment to certain ethical standards, involving one's disdaining and regarding as beneath oneself anything that falls below such standards. These standards include not being treated in a disgraceful manner as measured by certain public norms, and so one common example of *yi* behavior is a refusal to accept treatment in violation of *li*. However, they also include other measures that go beyond what is honourable or disgraceful by public standards; the *Xunzi* emphasizes a distinction between social honor and disgrace, as opposed to "propriety" (*yi*) honor, and disgrace. Accordingly, *yi* can also provide a basis for departing from a rule of *li*.

The firm commitment that *yi* involves is also related to a certain attitude toward external goods not within one's control. The Confucians advocate one's not being swayed in one's purpose by such external considerations and one's willingly accepting the consequences. In face of adversities to oneself or the prospect of great profits, one is supposed not just to conform to what is proper in one's behavior but also to be free from any distortive influences that might lead to a deviation from what is proper. One should not be subject to fear or uncertainty in face of adversities, and one should willingly accept such adversities, an attitude conveyed in the use of the the character *ming*.

Though often translated as "fate" or "destiny," *ming* does not refer to some opaque force operative in human events that cannot be thwarted. Instead, it serves primarily to express a certain attitude toward occurrences that go against one's wishes and to which one attaches importance, an attitude that follows upon one's recognition of certain constraints on one's activities. The constraints may be causal in that the occurrences are actually not within one's control, such as the failure of one's political endeavors or unexpected illness or death. The constraints may be normative such that the occurrences are something one could alter even though such alteration would involve improper conduct. Whichever is the case, having done what one could within the limits of what is proper, one should willingly accept the undesirable outcome by not engaging in improper conduct to alter things and not worrying about that outcome. Instead, one should resolve to redirect attention to other pursuits, such as Confucius's turning his attention to teaching after having accepted the failure of his political mission.

Finally, let us turn to the Confucian notion of *ren*. In its earlier use, *ren* refers either to kindness, especially from a ruler to his subjects, or to the qualities distinctive of members of certain aristocratic clans. It is used by Confucian thinkers sometimes in a broader sense to encompass all the ideal ethical attributes for human beings and sometimes to refer to a specific ethical attribute that emphasizes affective concern for others. Even for early Confucians such as Mencius, such affective concern should extend not just to human beings, but also to certain kinds of animals. For later Confucians of the Sung-Ming period, it involves a concern for everything, including plants and what we would describe as inanimate objects. For both early and later Confucians, *ren* involves a gradation. One should have a special concern for parents and family members that one does not have for other people, not just in the sense of a more intense affection but also in the sense of observing certain special obligations to them as defined by *li*. One's relation to other human beings also differs from one's relation to other animals and objects; for example, in the case of animals bred for food, *ren* toward them is primarily a matter of one's being sparing in their use, not using them in excess, and not treating them in an abusive manner.

In later Confucian thought, *ren* is understood in terms of two ideas associated with Heaven (*tian*), which has the connotations of both a supreme diety and the underlying purpose or design of the natural order. In early texts, Heaven, the ideal ruler, and even oneself are often described as forming one body with other people and things. Later Confucian thinkers continue to advocate similar ideas and characterize *ren* in these terms. Heaven and Earth and the ten thousand things originally forming one body with myself, and *ren* involves attaining this state of unity with all things. Though one may have deviated from this state of existence, the task of self-cultivation is to enlarge one's heart/mind until one sees everything as connected to oneself. This idea is sometimes put in terms of a medical analogy. Just as medial texts refer to as a lack of *ren* numbness in one's limbs, an inability to feel for other people is also a lack of *ren*.

In early texts, Heaven is also regarded as what gives birth to things, and its operation is described in terms of a ceaseless life-giving force, an idea highlighted in the early text *Book of Change* (*Yijing*). In later Confucian thought, Heaven's giving birth to and nourishing the ten thousand things is described as its *ren*. The heart/mind of humans should be identical with the heart/mind of Heaven and Earth, which is to give life to things. This is *ren* in the human context, a quality compared to the life-giving power of a seed. This idea of a ceaseless life-giving force is related to the idea of forming one body with the ten thousand things—in giving life to all things, it is as if all things are part of one's own body.

With the above explication of the ethical ideal as background, let us consider the Confucian view of the relation between the self and the social order. As in the case of the relation between the heart/mind and other aspects of the person, there is a sense in which Confucian thinkers emphasize the independence of the self from the social order, and a sense in which they emphasize their intimate relation.

As we have seen, Confucian thinkers emphasize the capacity of the heart/mind to reflect on one's own life, including the activities of the heart/mind itself, as well as its capacity to reshape one's life and its own activities on the basis of such reflection. In virtue of such a capacity, one also has the capacity to step back from one's place in the social order and assess one's relation to it. In the *Analects*, for example, we find passages describing hermitlike individuals who shun the social and political order, at times ridiculing Confucius and his disciples for their persistent and (to these individuals) futile attempts to bring about social and political reform. The Confucian emphasis on the preparedness to deviate from or adapt traditional norms, less explicit in the *Analects* but more conspicuous in the *Mencius* and the *Xunzi*, also presupposes a capacity to step back and reflect on the existing social order.

At the same time, Confucian thinkers also view the self as intimately related to the social roles one occupies. In viewing human beings as a species distinct from other animals, they see the distinction as residing in the capacity of human beings to draw social distinctions and to abide by social norms associated with such distinctions. The point is found explicitly in the *Xunzi*, which states that what makes human beings human beings is not their biological or physiological constitution but their capability of social differentiation and distinction. It also accounts for Mencius's observation that someone who denies social distinctions or fails to make use of this social capacity is, or has become close to, a lower animal. Later Confucians such as Zhu Xi, although acknowledging that certain other animals exhibit something like social relations, also emphasize that human beings are different from other animals in their unique ability to bring to fruition such relations.

Also, as we have seen, Confucian thinkers advocate an ethical ideal that is informed by the traditional social setup that they advocate. The ideal involves a general observance of traditional norms that govern people's behavior either in virtue of the social positions they occupy (such as being a son or an official) or within other kinds of recurring social contexts (such as a host receiving a guest or sacrificial ceremonies); it alsoinvolves the embodiment of certain attitudes (such as reverence) appropriate to such behavior. In addition, it involves the cultivation of desirable qualities within various social contexts, such as filial piety within the family or devotion when serving in government. Confucian thinkers do acknowledge the importance of a preparedness to deviate from or adapt traditional norms, and later Confucians such as Zhu Xi and Wang Yangming explicitly mention that the fine details of the *li* of ancient times are not all applicable to their times. Nevertheless, they see such deviation and adaptation as themselves based on a certain rationale underlying the social order that, although calling for changes in details in response to changing circumstances, is at the same time something that can be realized only in the evolving social order. It is through participating in this social order and letting oneself be shaped by it that one becomes fully human.

SELF-CULTIVATION

Let us now turn to self-cultivation, the process of, shaping one's own character out of a reflexive concern with the kind of person one is. Confucius stressed learning and reflection as part of the process. The former involves drawing moral lessons from the cultural heritage, which includes such elements as poetry, history, rites (*li*), music, and archery, and embodying such lessons in one's life. The latter involves reflecting on what one has learned so as to adapt it to one's present circumstances. Confucian thinkers after Confucius's times developed different views of human nature, different views of what the basic human constitution is like prior to learning and social influence. These different views have led to different conceptions of self-cultivation.

Some Confucian thinkers, such as Xunzi and Dai Zhen, emphasize the basic biological desires of human beings in elaborating on the basic human constitution. For them, living up to the Confucian ideal is instrumental in satisfying these basic human desires. According to Xunzi, when human beings act out of these desires without regulation, strife and disorder follow. The Confucian Way regulates and transforms such basic desires so that people can satisfy them in an orderly fashion. On this view, self-cultivation involves reshaping and transforming basic human desires, something that Xunzi at times compares to straightening a crooked piece of wood. Dai Zhen also emphasizes the basic biological desires and feelings. He sees the Confucian Way as a matter of one's using one's desires and feelings as a way of gauging others' desires and feelings, and one's satisfying others' desires as one would one's own.

Certain Confucian thinkers, such as Mencius, view human nature primarily in terms of ethical predispositions that human beings share. Mencius opposes the biological conceptions of human nature of his contemporaries and argues that the human heart/mind has a sense of propriety (*yi*) and that human beings do give precedence to propriety over biological desires. He believes that human beings already share certain ethical predispositions, such as the sense of commiseration upon suddenly seeing a child on the verge of falling into a well or the sense of shame when a beggar is given food in an abusive manner. For him, self-cultivation is a process of fully developing these ethical predispositions, a process that he compares to the development of a sprout into a full-grown plant. By directing attention to and nourishing these ethical predispositions, everyone is able to attain the ethical ideal.

Sung-Ming Confucians such as Zhu Xi and Wang Yangming, being self-professed Mencians, draw on the Mencian view but develop it in a different direction. Unlike Mencius, who regards human beings as having ethical predispositions that require nourishment to develop into the ideal ethical attributes, they regard these attributes as already present in the heart/mind in a full-blown form. Certain distortive influences, which they call selfish desires and sometimes selfish thoughts, can prevent the ethical attributes from fully manifesting themselves. *Si*, the character translated here as "selfish," has to do with focusing on oneself, or on people and things with which one forms close associations, in a way that inappropriately neglects other people and things. It involves a separation of the self from other people and things, preventing the life-giving force of *ren* from reaching all things and detracting from one's original unity with them. So, for both Zhu Xi and Wang Yangming, self-cultivation involves restoring the original state of the heart/mind, thereby allowing full manifestation of the ethical attributes. This process is illustrated with analogies such as the clear mirror obscured by dust or still water disturbed by sediments; the ethical task is to remove the dust or sediments to restore the original clarity of the mirror and of water. Zhu Xi and Wang Yangming differ on how to implement this task, the former emphasizing learning and the latter recommending focusing on the operations of the heart/mind.

The Confucian emphasis on self-cultivation, the process of one's doing something to shape one's own character out of a reflective concern with the kind of person one is, is arguably one of the more distinctive features of Confucian ethical thought. This emphasis, however, can lead to the worry that it involves a misdirection of one's ethical attention. This worry can take two different forms—that this concern with one's own character is either too other-directed or too self-directed.

First, some may be concerned that this emphasis on self-cultivaiton may involve an excessive concern for others' opinion of oneself, especially if it involves one's thinking in terms of cultivating such attributes as *ren* and *yi*. The thought is that the terms that refer to ethical attributes are typically used in third-person descriptions rather than in the content of the ethical person's deliberations. So it appears that the first-person exercise of cultivating these attributes in oneself involves being concerned primarily with the way others would describe oneself. It seems that, in aiming at *ren* and *yi* or at becoming like the ancient sages, one's primary concern is with one's being describable by others in a certain way or with acquiring the kind of stature that the ancient sages have in others' eyes. If so, this kind of concern does seem other-directed in a disturbing way.

Part of the response to this worry is that, even if we grant that *ren* and *yi* are more often used by others as a third-person description of the ethical person, a concern with these attributes need not be a concern with one's being describable by others in a certain way. Instead, it can be a concern with one's becoming like the kind of person that one would oneself describe in this way. That is, the third-person description in terms of *ren* and *yi* can be a description of others by oneself rather than of oneself by others. Furthermore, in being concerned with becoming like the kind of person that one would oneself describe in this way, one's primary object of concern is not with the description but with having a certain character that can be described in this way. Likewise, a concern to be like the ancient sages can be a concern with one's character being like theirs, rather than with one's having the kind of stature that they have in others' eyes.

Still, even if a concern with *ren* and *yi* need not be a concern with how others view oneself, it is a concern with one's own character, and this can lead to the second worry that such a concern may be too self-directed. This concern can be too self-directed in two ways: One may be concerned with preserving or promoting one's own self-image as a certain kind of person, or one may be making one's own character the most important ethical consideration, more important than other-regarding considerations. These two forms of the worry are different. The first focuses on the way in which one is concerned with one's character, how it can take on a distortive form so that one's object of concern is one's image of oneself rather than one's character as such. The second focuses on the importance one attaches to one's own character, how one puts undue weight on one's character in comparison to other-regarding considerations.

In connection with the first form of the worry, we have seen that a concern with *ren* and *yi* is a concern with improving one's character. Just as such a concern need not be a concern with the way others' view oneself, it need not be a concern with preserving or promoting one's own self-image. However, the worry about a concern with self-image may arise with regard to the particular actions that one performs, in relation to both acts of *ren* and acts of *yi*. Let us therefore consider the two kinds of action in turn.

In the case of *ren*, let us take a helping action as example. Suppose one's thought in helping is that one should be doing what is *ren*. If so, it seems that what one is concerned with is that one gives expression to one's *ren* character, that one does what is *ren*, or that one preserves one's image of oneself as a *ren* person. In any case, it seems that there is indeed a misdirection of one's attention in acting.

It is unclear, though, that the Confucians would advocate performing such acts with thoughts about one's own *ren*. For example, in the case of the child on the verge of falling into a well, one's compassionate response is described as a direct response to the imminent death of the child, unmediated by thoughts about one's own character. It is true that, in cases in which one acts not out a sufficient concern for others but out of a concern that one should become the kind of person who would be so moved, one might act with the thought of doing what is *ren*. Even so, one's acting with such a thought is itself a way of transforming oneself so that one will act out of a more direct concern for others. Although, ideally, one should not need to act with such a thought, one's doing so is instrumental in the attainment of this ideal and so should not itself be problematic.

Yi involves a firm commitment to distancing oneself from certain things that one regards as below oneself. In acting out of such a commitment, it seems, one's primary concern is with avoiding smears on one's own character, which is a self-directed kind of concern. Now, even if this is correct, it seems that this kind of self-directed concern need not be problematic for actions that do not—at least directly—affect the well-being of others. For example, in the case of the beggar's rejecting food given with abuse, there does not seem to be anything problematic with the thought that to submit to such treatment to avoid starvation is beneath one's dignity. If there is something problematic about acting out of this kind of concern, it will have to do with acts that also affect the well-being of others.

Let us therefore consider an act of this kind, such as King Wu's overthrowing the corrupt last king of the Shang dynasty. In the description of this occurrence in the *Mencius*, there is a reference to *chi*, or regarding something as below oneself. Now, although King Wu's attitude was that he regarded it as below him that he, who was in a position to remedy the situation, should allow the people's suffering to continue, there are two ways in which he was also acting out of a concern that is not self-directed. First, what he regarded as below him is also something he would view with aversion if done by someone else in a comparable position. That is, although he reacted with *chi* because of his special relation to the situation, underlying this reaction is the more general attitude of aversion directed to the act, whether by himself or by others, of allowing avoidable suffering to continue. So, in acting out of *chi*, he was in part also acting out of a more general concern that an act of this kind did not take place. Second, his acting out of *chi* is not exclusive of his acting out of a genuine concern for the people. Presumably, it was because he had such concern that he regarded it as below him that the situation be allowed to continue. As long as this other-regarding concern also played a role in his action, his action did not seem to suffer from a misdirection of attention.

This last point assumes that a concern to avoid what is below oneself and a concern for others converge; but what if the two should come into conflict? This takes us to the second form of the worry about an excessive concern with oneself: the worry that one may attach too much weight to one's own character by comparison to other-regarding considerations. Indeed, Mencius himself had been accused of precisely this kind of self-centeredness. The *Mencius* contains several examples of his refusing to see a ruler because he had not been summoned or treated in accordance with certain rules of *li* appropriate to his position. His critics made the point that, if only he had been willing to "bend" himself a little and have audience with the ruler, he might have been able to effect desirable political changes and thereby help the people. By insisting on an adherence to *li*, he was apparently putting more weight on preserving his own sense of honor than on the well-being of the people.

This is a serious charge, and Mencius's response was to draw on the early Confucian view about the transformative power of a cultivated character. The basis of order in society is the cultivated character of those in power, and what Mencius sought to accomplish in the political realm was to "straighten out" those in power. And straightening out others depends on one's being straight oneself; there has never been a case of one's bending oneself while succeeding in straightening others. So, according to Mencius, it is not possible to achieve the desired political changes by bending oneself. And, to the extent that the well-being of the people depends on a reform of the political order, which in turn depends on the transformative effect of a cultivated person, there cannot be a conflict between a concern for one's character and a concern for others. The same point applies to the relation between one's character and the character of others. Given the belief that the transformative effect on others' character is a natural outgrowth of one's cultivating one's own character, there cannot be a conflict between a concern for one's character and a concern for others' character.

See also Chinese Philosophy: Overview; Chinese Philosophy: Contemporary.

Bibliography

PRIMARY SOURCES (IN TRANSLATION)

Theodore de Bary, William, Wing-tsit Chan, and Burton Watson, eds. *Sources of Chinese Tradition*. 2 vols. New York: Columbia University Press, 1960.

Chan, Wing-tsit, trans. *Instructions for Practical Living by Wang Yang-ming*. New York: Columbia University Press, 1963.

Chan, Wing-tsit, trans. *Reflections on Things at Hand: The Neo-Confucian Anthology Compiled by Chu His and Lu Tsu-ch'ien*. New York: Columbia University Press, 1967.

Chan, Wing-tsit, ed. and trans. *A Source Book in Chinese Philosophy*, Princeton, NJ: Princeton University Press, 1963.

Chin, Ann-ping, and Mansfield Freeman, trans. *Tai Chen on Mencius*. New Haven: Yale University Press, 1990.

Lau, D. C., trans. *Confucius: The Analects*. London: Penguin, 1979.

Lau, D. C., trans. *Mencius*. London: Penguin, 1970.

Watson, Burton, trans. *Hsun Tzu: Basic Writings*. New York: Columbia University Press, 1963.

SECONDARY SOURCES

Creel, H. G. *Chinese Thought from Confucius to Mao Tse-tung*. Chicago: University of Chicago Press, 1953.

Fung, Yu-lan. *A History of Chinese Philosophy*. 2 vols. Translated by Derk Bodde. Princeton, NJ: Princeton University Press, 1937, 1952, 1953.

Graham, A. C. *Disputers of the Tao: Philosophical Argument in Ancient China*, La Salle, IL: Open Court, 1989.

Graham, A. C. *Two Chinese Philosophers*. 2nd. ed. La Salle, IL: Open Court, 1992.

Liu, Shu-hsien. *Understanding Confucian Philosophy: Classical and Sung-Ming*. Westport, CT: Greenwood Press, 1998.

Munro, Donald J. *The Concept of Man in Early China*. Palo Alto, CA: Stanford University Press, 1969.

Nivison, David S., *The Ways of Confucianism: Investigations in Chinese Philosophy*. La Salle, IL: Open Court, 1996.

Roetz, Heiner. *Confucian Ethics of the Axial Age: A Reconstruction under the Aspect of the Breakthrough toward Postconventional Thinking.* Albany: State University of New York Press, 1993.

Schwartz, Benjamin. *The World of Thought in Ancient China.* Cambridge, MA: Belknap Press of Harvard University Press, 1985.

Shun, Kwong-loi. *Mencius and Early Chinese Thought.* Palo Alto, CA: Stanford University Press, 1997.

Shun, Kwong-loi, and David Wong, eds. *Confucian Ethics: A Comparative Study of Self, Autonomy, and Community.* Cambridge, U.K.: Cambridge University Press, 2004.

Tu, Wei-ming. *Confucian Thought: Selfhood as Creative Transformation.* Albany: State University of New York Press, 1985.

Tu, Wei-ming. *Humanities and Self-Cultivation: Essays in Confucian Thought.* Berkeley CA: Asian Humanities Press, 1979.

Kwong-loi Shun (2005)

CONTEMPORARY

The People's Republic of China (PRC) was established in 1949 under the leadership of Chairman Mao Zedong (1893–1976). This date marks an important watershed in the development of Chinese philosophy. Since 1949 the official ideology of the communist regime on mainland China has without question been Marxism-Leninism-Maoism, while other thoughts were ruthlessly suppressed—especially during the period of Cultural Revolution from 1966 to 1977. The nationalist regime had been driven to the island of Taiwan, which in the early twenty-first century still carries the banner of the Republic of China (ROC, 1912–). The official ideology of the Republic of China was the Three People's Principles, formulated by Sun Yat-sen (1866–1925).

Yet apart from anticommunist and political struggles, other thoughts were more or less tolerated. In Hong Kong—a British colony not taken back by China until 1997—freedom of speech was protected. Furthermore, refugee scholars were allowed to develop and express their thoughts in borrowed space and time. Additionally, there was the Chinese diaspora overseas. Among the various elements in the development of Chinese philosophy, there are several mainstreams of thought that can be discerned. This entry will examine Maoism, Western liberalism, and contemporary neo-Confucianism.

MAOISM

The success of Maoism has been credited to Mao Zedong's talent to adapt Marxism-Leninism to the Chinese soil. Mao contributed two articles—"On Contradiction" and "On Practice"—to expound the philosophy of dialectical materialism. He believed he had succeeded the orthodox line of Marxism-Leninism after the death of Stalin, and as such battled against Western imperialism on the one hand and soviet revisionism on the other. According to Feng Youlan (Fung Yu-lan), Mao's thought went through three stages (Feng 1992).

In the first stage Mao advocated new democracy; in the second, he promoted socialism; and in the last stage he was obsessed with extreme leftist thought. The first stage was represented by Mao's essay "On New Democracy," published in 1940 (Mao 1967). According to his diagnosis at that time, China was not ready for a socialist revolution and had to go through a transitory stage of new democracy. This new democracy was led by the proletariat, the workers and farmers, in conjunction with the petite bourgeoisie. Together they formed a united front, and even the national capitalists were allowed to play a part. This united front joined forces to deal with the problems of a semicolonial, semifeudal society.

When the PRC was established in 1949, the government policy followed such a guideline. But the stage abruptly ended in 1954 when the constitution was drafted. Mao's thought entered the second stage, composed of big change: The goal for the next five years was to accomplish a socialist revolution. Thus the nature of the revolution determined what should be done at any particular stage in the revolution, regardless of actual societal conditions. The telos was a kind of utopian socialism, which surfaced after Mao took control to become the great helmsman of the new China.

In the final stage of his thought, Mao went against the bureaucracy and his own party organization and initiated the disastrous Cultural Revolution, putting his authority behind the Gang of Four. His intention was to do away with private property and to establish communes, which he believed would allow poor people to eat without pay. The release of the destructive powers of the Red Guards caused damages unprecedented in Chinese history.

Mao died in 1976, and in 1977 the Gang of Four was removed by Deng Xiaoping (1904–1997), who adopted an open policy to bring about the revival of China. Since then, capitalism has been seen as a necessary stage for China to go through before the socialist revolution can be implemented. As the doors of China opened to the outside world, many intellectuals were attracted by thought other than Marxism. One editorial in the *People's Daily News* in the 1980s said that Marx's ideas were the product of the nineteenth century, that they did not provide all the answers, and hence it was desirable to further develop Marxism. Revisionism, therefore, seems to no longer be a crime, and a prevalent view shared by both mainland China and overseas scholars in the late-twentieth and early twenty-first centuries is that a healthy interaction between Marxism, Western liberalism, and Confucianism may find a direction for the future of China.

WESTERN LIBERALISM

Western liberalism was imported to China near the end of Qing dynasty (1644–1912), but somehow it failed to adapt well to the Chinese soil. The most famous liberal in the early Republic of China era was Hu Shih (1891–1962), a disciple of John Dewey, who during the New Culture Movement (c. 1919) promoted the ideals of democracy and science vigorously, urging for wholesale westernization or modernization without reservation (Chow 1960). Yet his approach by gradual reform quickly lost its appeal and radicalism became the vogue. After the communists took over mainland China in 1949, Hu left for the United States, then in 1958 went to Taiwan to serve as the head of Academia Sinica, where he remained until his untimely death in 1962. In his later years he disengaged from political activities and avoided making severe criticisms of the nationalist government under the leadership of Generalissimo Chiang Kai-shek (1887–1975). Instead, he put an emphasis on tolerance.

Among the liberals in Taiwan, one individual who stood out was Yin Haiguang (Yin Hai-kwong, 1919–1969), honored as a spokesman for the democratic movement in Taiwan under the authoritarian rule by the nationalist regime. In 1966 the government (the ministry of education) prevented Yin from teaching his classes at Taiwan University. He would be diagnosed with cancer in 1967 and die two years later.

A follower of logical positivism, Yin was not a deep thinker. His mentors included Bertrand Russell, A. N. Whitehead, Karl Popper, and F. A. Hayek. For Yin, only formal and empirical sciences are cognitively meaningful, yet he was willing to risk his life to fight for the implementation of democratic ideals. In his later years he returned to tradition and lauded Mencius's affirmation of moral courage to defend what is right under adverse environment (Yin 1966). Because he dared to stand up against the mighty powers of an authoritarian regime, eventually Yin was viewed as a martyr and gained respect because he was able to fulfill the duties of an intellectual as he saw it. At the turn of the twenty-first century certain aspects of Western liberalism have held a great attraction for some liberal-minded intellectuals on mainland China since it opened its doors to the outside world.

Both in Hong Kong and Taiwan, the influx of various trends of Western thought has not ceased. In recent years, these trends poured into mainland China with great speed. Although a majority of Chinese intellectuals in the twentieth century criticized Confucianism, that tradition never died. In fact, the most creative talents were found in the contemporary New Confucian movement, which sought to bring about a synthesis between East and West (Bresciani 2001). Despite the prediction of Joseph Levenson in the late 1960s that Confucianism would become something dead that could only be found in museums (Levenson 1968), it appears to be thriving at the present time like a phoenix reborn from the ashes.

CONTEMPORARY NEO-CONFUCIANISM

Confucianism may mean different things to different people, but it is possible to adopt the following threefold division (Liu 1998): (1) spiritual Confucianism, the tradition of the great Confucian thinkers; (2) politicized Confucianism, the tradition of Han Confucianism that served as the official ideology of the dynasties; and (3) popular (or vulgar) Confucianism, belief at the grassroots level that emphasizes family values, diligence, and education—and note that Confucianism in this last stage cannot be separated from beliefs in popular Daoism and Buddhism or various kinds of superstitions. The three forms of Confucianism must be kept distinct on the conceptual level, however, although in reality they are intricately related. Indeed, institutional Confucianism died when the last dynasty was overthrown in 1912, but the other forms of Confucianism survive. For example, some sociologists, such as Peter Berger, believe that vulgar Confucianism has contributed a great deal to the economic miracles accomplished since the 1970s by Japan and the so-called Four Mini-dragons: Taiwan, Hong Kong, Singapore, and Korea (Berger and Hsiao 1988). Politicized Confucianism has also attracted a large number of admirers. The cover of the June 14, 1993, issue of *Time* magazine was a portrait of Confucius; the issue reported that Francis Fukuyama, author of *The End of History*, was of the opinion that the kind of soft authoritarianism practiced in Singapore posed a greater challenge to Western liberalism than did Islam.

Spiritual Confucianism is a vigorous movement of thought. In 1986, mainland China designated Contemporary New Confucianism as a national research program for a period of ten years (Fang 1997). At first its scope was not clearly defined; it included scholars with various backgrounds, such as scholar-thinker Liang Shuming (Liang Sou-ming, 1893–1988), scholar-statesman Zhang Junmai (Carsun Chang, 1887–1969), historian Qian Mu (Ch'ien Mu, 1895–1990), and intellectual historian and political commentator Xu Fuguan (Hsü Fu-kuan, 1903–1982). After broad consultations and extensive discussions under the guidance of Fang Ke-li and Li Jingquan, the directors of the program, ten case studies were completed.

In addition to the above-named scholars, the program also included six philosophers: Xiong Shili (Hsiung Shih-li, 1885–1968), Feng Youlan (1895–1990), He Lin (Ho Lin, 1902–1992), Fang Dongmei (Thomé H. Fang, 1899–1977), Tang Junyi (T'ang Chün-i, 1909–1978), and Mou Zongsan (Mou Tsung-san, 1909–1995). Later, four younger scholars were included: Yu Yingshi (Yü Ying-shih, 1930–), Liu Shuxian (Liu Shu-hsien, 1934–), Cheng Zhongying (Cheng Chung-ying, 1935–), and Du Weiming (Tu Wei-ming, 1940). The addition of Ma Yifu (1883–1967), a noted scholar in classics studies from the older generation, was also added. Eventually, fifteen names were chosen, and these fifteen may be assigned to four groups in three generations (Liu 2003):

The First Generation:

Group I: Liang, Xiong, Ma, and Zhang

Group II: Feng, He, Qian, and Fang

The Second Generation:

Group III: Tang, Mou, and Xu

The Third Generation:

Group IV: Yu, Liu, Cheng, and Du

Liang, Xiong, and Ma have been recognized as the three elders in the first generation, all of whom chose to remain in mainland China. Only Zhang, as the leader of a third force political party, fled overseas. Liang is seen as the person who initiated the movement, but it was Xiong, known only in a small scholarly circle, who became the spiritual leader of contemporary neo-Confucianism in the narrower sense. The three important representatives of the movement, Tang, Mou, and Xu, were disciples of Xiong.

The scholars in Group II were somewhat younger. Feng and He chose to remain in mainland China. Qian Mu fled to Hong Kong, where he and Tang became the cofounders of New Asia College, an undisputed center for contemporary neo-Confucianism. Fang, once a teacher of Tang, fled to Taiwan, where he taught at Taiwan University and had Liu and Cheng among his disciples. Xu and Mou also went to Taiwan, and from 1963 to 1969 made Tunghai University in Taichung a second center for contemporary neo-Confucianism.

THE IMPORTANCE OF THE THREE GENERATIONS. Without question, the mainstay of contemporary neo-Confucianism is represented by the second generation of scholars: Tang, Mou, and Xu. They signed the famous "Manifesto for a Reappraisal of Sinology and Reconstruction of Chinese Culture," drafted by Tang and issued on New Year's Day in 1958. The other signatory was Zhang, of the first generation (Liu 1996). The third generation scholars, disciples of Hong Kong and Taiwan New Confucians, received advanced academic training and had teaching careers in the United States, thereby acquiring an international dimension in their thought (Liu 2003).

For obvious reasons only refugee scholars outside of mainland China were able to make significant contributions to the further development of Confucian thought. Fang, of the older generation, received his academic training in the United States. He had a grand scheme of philosophy of culture with a comparative perspective of a fourfold division: ancient Greek, modern European, Chinese, and Indian. He also strongly criticized the dualism of modern European thought, which was believed to have a hidden nihilistic tendency (Fang 1957). Fang opted for messages of creative creativity and comprehensive harmony of primordial Confucianism (Fang 1981), as well as urging others to overcome the limitations of different cultures in order to bring about a synthesis of East and West.

Tang and Mou were also well versed in Western philosophy. While Tang had a Hegelian bent, Mou showed an unmistakable Kantian temperament. The famous manifesto drafted by Tang urged the sinologists in the West to study the Chinese culture not just through the eyes of the missionaries, the archaeologists, or the political strategists, but with a sense of reverence and sympathetic understanding of that culture. According to the manifesto, the wisdom of Chinese philosophy is crystallized in its philosophy of mind and human nature (*xin* and *xing*), an unmistakable reference to Sung-Ming neo-Confucianism. Although recognizing the need for the Chinese culture to learn from the West by absorbing its achievements in science and democracy, the manifesto claims that there is something invaluable in the Chinese tradition and suggests that the West may learn from Chinese thought in the following five items:

(1) The spirit to assert what is here and now and to let everything go (in order for nature to take its own course);

(2) All-round and all-embracing understanding or wisdom;

(3) A feeling of warmth and compassion;

(4) The wisdom of how to perpetuate the culture;

(5) The attitude that the whole world is like a family.

THE THREE TRADITIONS' DOCTRINE. In his later years Tang devoted himself to tracing the origins of insights in traditional Chinese philosophy. The last work he published was a comprehensive system of philosophy conceived in his lifetime. The book deals with the whole existence of humans and tries to understand the different activities of the mind, distinguishing the following nine worlds:

(1) the world of discrete things;

(2) the world of species and genus in terms of empirical generalization;

(3) the world of functional operation;

(4) the world of perceptions interpenetrating with one another;

(5) the world of contemplation of what is transcendent and vacuous;

(6) the world of moral practice;

(7) the world of aspiration toward God;

(8) the world of emptiness (*śūnyatā*) of both the self (*ātman*) and elements (*dharma*);

(9) the world of the embodiment of heavenly virtues.

Mou, however, was perhaps the most original thinker in his generation. Going further than the manifesto, he formulated the doctrine of three traditions:

(1) The assertion of Daotong (the tradition of the Way): We must assert the value of morality and religion, jealously guarding the fountainhead of the universe and human life as realized by Confucius and Mencius through a revitalization of the learning of the mind and the human nature.

(2) The development of *Xuetong* (the tradition of learning): We must expand our cultural life and further develop the learning subject as to absorb the Western tradition of formal sciences such as logic and mathematics on the one hand and empirical sciences on the other.

(3) The continuation and expansion of *Zhengtong* (the tradition of politics): We must recognize the necessity of adopting the democratic system of government as developed in the West in order to fulfill truly the political ideal of a government of humanity of the sages and worthies in the past.

After Mou dug deeply in the Chinese tradition and devoted himself to scholarly studies of Daoism, Confucianism, and Buddhism, in the latest stage of his thought he brought into focus a comparative perspective. In *Intellectual Intuition and Chinese Philosophy* he pointed out that the major difference between Chinese and Western philosophies lies in the fact that the three major Chinese traditions all believed in the possibility of intellectual intuition, whereas major Western traditions deny that there is such a possibility. Mou used Kant as his point of departure because Kant believed that all human knowledge must depend on sensible intuition, and only God has intellectual intuition. For Kant, freedom of the will, immortality of the soul, and the existence of God can only be postulates of the practical reason, hence Mou was of the opinion that Kant could only develop a metaphysics of morals, not a moral metaphysics. In *Phenomenon and the Thing-in-itself* Mou made a distinction between what he called "ontology with adherence" and "ontology without adherence." The former has been highly developed in the Western traditions, and the latter has been elaborately formulated in the Oriental traditions. When the infinite mind puts restrictions on itself, the knowing subject is formed; this is the result of a dialectical process. The adherence of the knowing mind and the realization of the infinite mind actually share the same origin. It is here that a foundation for the unity of the two perspectives can be found (Liu 1989).

Because the second generation neo-Confucians developed their ideas within a most adverse environment, they tended to stress what is positive in the Confucian tradition. But the third generation neo-Confucians face a very different context—they presuppose the pluralistic framework of the West. For example, Du Weiming feels that there is no need to prove that the Confucian tradition is better than other spiritual traditions, so long as it can be shown that it is one of the worthy spiritual traditions in the world; from modern to postmodern era, the flexible understanding of reason and the emphasis on harmony in the Confucian tradition are to its advantage. Liu Shuxian offers a new interpretation of *liyi fenshu* (one principle, many manifestations) which he inherited from

Sung-Ming neo-Confucian philosophy. He fully realizes that the Confucian tradition certainly does not have a monopoly of one principle, which would find different manifestations in different spiritual traditions. For example, the Golden Rule, credited to Confucius by Hans Küng, has been formulated in different ways in the East and in the West as well as in the ancient and modern times (1993). Thus, Liu vigorously supported the formulation of a global ethic in the awakening of a global consciousness. Because the world has turned into a global village with only limited resources, and because people need to live peacefully together, certainly the Confucians will have something significant to say in the future.

See also Chinese Philosophy: History of.

Bibliography

Berger, Peter L., and Hsin-huang Hsiao, eds. *Search for an East Asian Development Model.* New Brunswick, NJ: Transaction Publishers, 1988.

Bresciani, Umberto. *Reinventing Confucianism: The New Confucian Movement.* Taibei, Taiwan: Ricci Institute, 2001.

Chan, Wing-tsit. *A Source Book in Chinese Philosophy.* Princeton, NJ: Princeton University Press, 1963.

Chow, Tse-tsung. *The May Fourth Movement: Intellectual Revolution in Modern China.* Cambridge, MA: Harvard University Press, 1960.

Fang, Ke-li. *Xiandai xinruxue yu zhongguo xiandaihua* [Contemporary New Confucianism and the modernization of China]. Tianjin, China: Tianjin renmin chubanshe, 1997.

Fang, Thomé H. *Chinese Philosophy: Its Spirit and Its Development.* Taibei, Taiwan: Linking Publishing, 1981.

Fang, Thomé H. *The Chinese View of Life.* Hong Kong: The Union Press, 1957.

Feng Youlan (Fung Yu-lan). *The Hall of Three Pines: An Account of My Life.* Translated by Denis C. Mair. Honululu: University of Hawaii Press, 2000.

Feng Youlan. *Zhongguo xiandai zhexueshi* [A history of modern Chinese philosophy]. Hong Kong: Zhonghua shuju, 1992.

Fukuyama, Francis. *The End of History and the Last Man.* New York: Free Press, 1992.

Furth, Charlotte, ed. *The Limits of Change: Essays on Conservative Alternatives in Republican China.* Cambridge, MA: Harvard University Press, 1976.

Küng, Hans, and Karl-Josef Kuschel, eds. *A Global Ethic: The Declaration of the Parliament of the World's Religions.* London: SCM Press, 1993.

Levenson, Joseph R. *Confucian China and Its Modern Fate.* 3 vols. Berkeley: University of California Press, 1968.

Liu, Shu-hsien (Shuxian). "Postwar Neo-Confucian Philosophy: Its Development and Issues." In *Religious Issues and Interreligious Dialogues*, edited by Charles Wei-hsun Fu and Gerhard E. Spiegler. Westport, CT: Greenwood Press, 1989.

Liu, Shu-hsien. "Confucian Ideals and the Real World: A Critical Review of Contemporary Neo-Confucian Thought." In *Confucian Traditions in East Asian Modernity*, edited by Tu Wei-ming, 92–111. Cambridge, MA: Harvard University Press, 1996.

Liu, Shu-hsien. *Essentials of Contemporary Neo-Confucian Philosophy.* Westport, CT: Praeger Publishers, 2003.

Liu, Shu-hsien. *Understanding Confucian Philosophy: Classical and Sung-Ming.* Westport, CT: Greenwood Press, 1998.

Makeham, John, ed. *New Confucianism: A Critical Examination.* New York: Palgrave Macmillan, 2003.

Mao Zedong (Mao Tse-tung). *Selected Works of Mao Tse-tung.* Vol. 2. Beijing: Foreign Languages Press, 1967.

Mou Zongsan (Mou Tsung-san). *Xianxiang you wuzesheng* [Phenomenon and the thing-in-itself]. Taibei, Taiwan: Xuesheng shuju, 1975.

Tang Junyi (T'ang Chün-i). *Shengming cunzai yu zinlin jingjie* [Human existence and the worlds of the mind]. 2 vols. Taibei, Taiwan: xuesheng shuju, 1977.

Yin, Haiguang (Yin Hai-kwong). *Zhongguo wenhua te changwang* [Reappraisal of cultural change in modern China]. 2 vols. Taibei, China: Book World, 1966.

Shu-hsien Liu (2005)

DAOISM

Philosophical Daoism (also spelled Taoism) dates from the classical period (fifth through third century BC) and conventionally refers to the contents of the *Zhuangzi (Chuang Tzu)* and the *Laozi (Lao Tzu or Daode Jing/Tao-Te Ching)*. Some extend the term to cover less philosophical transitional texts of popularized Daoism of the Han (second century BC)—for example, the *Liezi* and the *Huainanzi*. Another movement, called Neo-Daoism, dates from the end of the Han (200-plus). The term "Daoism" is fundamentally misleading since no group, no leader, and no association linked those thinkers. The Han historians who coined the term centuries later viewed the philosophers as founders of their credulous religion, Huang-Lao, which flourished after classical philosophy was extinguished by Qin despotism (220 BCE). The main basis for the classification was thus: (1) their philosophical interest in the concept of *dao* (way or normative guide); and (2) relatively skeptical, anarchic, antisocial attitudes which contrasted with Confucianism.

PHILOSOPHICAL DAOISM: A QUICK TOUR

The concept of *dao* (tao) was central to ancient Chinese philosophizing. It is essentially a normative, practical concept—a way or guide to action. Almost all ancient Chinese thinkers philosophized about *dao*, about choosing, reforming, following *daos* as well as understanding their relation to "constant" nature (*tian*$^{\text{nature:sky}}$), to human nature (*xing*^{nature}), and to society.

Those subsequently classed as daoist thinkers are distinguished by their more metaethical interest in *dao* in contrast to Confucians and Mohists who mainly advocated a variety of normative *daos*. Daoists discussed mainly three kinds of *dao*: human (or social) *dao*; *tian*^{natural} *dao*; and "Great" *dao*. When I instruct you to cross the road on the green light, I am delivering a bit of human *dao*. Natural *dao* (often translated heavenly *dao*) is akin to what we would consider the constancies of science. Natural *dao* is the way things reliably (constantly) happen. The salient contrast is that Chinese thinkers do not elaborate this idea with the idea of law—universal, modally necessary propositions. Great *Dao* refers to the entire actual history of space and time—whatever has happened, is happening or will eventually happen in the universe is part of Great *Dao*. *Dao* is simply the counterpart of Ludwig Wittgenstein's "All that is the case." What amounts to determinism in Chinese thought is treating *tian dao* and Great *Dao* as identical—the constancies in nature make only one world history possible.

Daoist philosophers typically distance themselves from various human *dao* (paradigmatically Confucian or Mohist *dao*) by contrasting them to natural *dao* and/or Great *Dao* (the actual *dao*). Ancient Chinese moralists had tended to treat *tian*$^{\text{nature:sky}}$ as the authority for their account of the correct human *dao*. "Primitivist" daoism, usually regarded as an earlier form associated with Yang Zhu (sometimes called "Yangism") and the *Laozi* advocates being natural and rejects the social (historical or conventional *daos*). "Mature" Daoist analysis, typified by the inner chapters of the *Zhuangzi* centers on the insight that while human *daos* are normative, neither the natural nor the actual *dao* are, and that the guidance of any human *dao* depends on and presupposes natural *dao*.

Mature Daoism avers that nature does not authorize or endorse any *particular* social *dao*. This claim has two versions: pluralist and primitivist. Denying *one* is compatible with their being either *many* or *none*. The pluralist (relativist) reading of the claim takes it to entail that de facto rival practices are natural *daos* in virtue of their being actual practices. Thus, they are continuous with natural constancies. Great *Dao* versions suggest that all *actual* rival *daos* are part of Great *Dao* simply in virtue of actually being followed—*daos* are made by "walking" them. Pluralist Daoists end up vaguely associated with anarchism because they reject the Confucian-Mohist assumption that political authority exists to bring about a harmony of *daos*—making everyone follow a single *dao*. The social world survives as well (or better) when people follow different ways of life. Focus on either *tian*$^{\text{nature:sky}}$ *dao* or Great *Dao* thus undermines the sense that it is imperative to impose any particular first-order *dao* on all of society.

Primitivist versions of Daoism, however, typically take the form that nature does endorse a particular normative *dao*, though not a human one. That a single, constant, correct way of life cannot be expressed or presented in practices, rules, narratives, maps, examples, songs or any other human or social form of communication and advocacy. Though we usually think in terms of one natural *dao*, there could, in principle, be multiple, equally "primitive" *daos*.

The ambiguity between these two versions is neatly expressed in the opening stanza of the *Daode Jing*: "Any *dao* that can *dao* (guide) is not constant *dao*." Both primitive and mature versions underwrite a shared theme of harmony with nature—the pluralist seeing the point of such harmony as permissive and tolerant and the primitivist seeing it as more intolerant, as rejecting or prohibiting any conventional *dao*.

Metaphysically, Daoism is naturalistic though religious versions of Daoist primitivism evoke mystical and supernaturalist themes that remind interpreters of European, Middle Eastern, and South Asian mystical supernaturalism. The various mystical analyses, following the Indo-European model, are buttressed by an intuitive epistemology. Detaching from social *daos* means eschewing language, words, and norms of use that underwrite public discourse (reasoning) about what to do. The essential form language norms take is learned inclinations to distinguish or discriminate what is "this" from "not this." Intuitionism advocates "recovering" the simple, primitive, pre-social dispositions by forgetting names and the attitudes that linked them to action.

Translated to the language of Indo-European rationalism, this line of reasoning treats the pluralist insight as entailing an irrationalist absolutist conclusion. It endorses the tempting illicit inference from relativism (our distinctions are "socially constructed") to dogmatic, absolutist monism (there are no distinctions in [moral] reality). Religious and other nonphilosophical interpreters view this non-sequitur as the essence of Daoism.

HISTORICAL OUTLINE: THE RANGE OF DAOISM(S)

Moralizing schools proposed rival *dao* (social guiding discourse) for general order. The term "Daoism" was applied to the general reflection on what it was to propose, accept, reject, a *dao*—the epistemology, semantics and metaphysics of *dao*. This meta-focus on *dao* inclined these thinkers to a variety of metaethical positions: skeptical, relativist, and mystical. Their doubt about the goal of unifying society's *dao* and their philosophical "distancing" from direct advocacy of a normative *dao* made them seem ethically amoral and politically liberal, libertarian and even anarchistic. Zhuangzi in particular emphasized his differences with the moralists—the Confucians and Mohists.

Religious Daoism, by contrast, is an extremely broad classification of popular and/or local religions that took many different forms at different times in China are distinguished mainly negatively—by their not identifying primarily with Confucianism or Buddhism. The earliest known example was the "Huang-Lao" sect that flourished at the beginning of China's philosophical dark age induced by Qin repression and Han Confucian orthodoxy. Religious Daoism's relation to philosophical Daoism is both controversial and obscure. Daoism acquired organizational religious trappings from its interactions with Buddhism after the latter arrived in China around the second century AD. Characterizing aspects of Daoism as "religious" prior to that time is simply to draw a distinction between relatively credulous, superstitious, popular readings and more reflective, skeptical, philosophical readings of the same texts.

It is common to trace a Daoist political "ethos" to hermits who lectured Confucius against social involvement. Another way to trace Daoism's origins runs through the shadowy figure of Yang Zhu. He seems to have drawn on something like the romantic conflict between what Yang Zhu thought of as our nature (our natural mode of development) and social-political structures. We know of him mainly through the Mencius's attack on him as an egoist. Mencius reports that Yang Zhu refused to risk a single body hair to "save the empire." The Yangist theme survives in Daoism—where it is also known as "primitivism."

In more orthodox Chinese moralizing, Confucian and Mohist, human nature is "shaped" via our being socialized through following some *dao*—a shared guiding discourse. Primitivists resist this social shaping and seek to "restore" natural and spontaneous patterns of action. Mencius's attack probably distorts primitivism, therefore, since it arguably rejects only social or conventional *daos*, not all guidance.

The picture is further blurred by subsequent history of Daoism. These interpretive tensions became part of the Chinese conception of Daoism in later periods. A philosophical "dark age" prior to the Han followed by the credulous Confucian orthodoxy that emerged as the "spirit" of the Han dynasty, effectively extinguished critical philosophical thought.

The autocratic rulers of the Qin and Han were highly superstitious and the courts tended toward the more authoritarian, dogmatic readings. Such readings sustain their claims of special or esoteric access to knowledge (for example, trance states induced by breathing exercises) that imperiously ignores any demand for deeper justification (for example, intuitionism or mysticism).

The Han eventually enshrined Confucianism as an official orthodoxy and the basis of the examinations that qualify one for political office. This inclined Confucian theorists to view their tradition as embracing and subsuming all other learning and treating Daoism as compatible with Confucianism. This task was made easier by emphasis on the more "religious" texts identified as Daoist. These Han texts borrowed stories, attitudes, and phrases from the two original daoist writings. Hence, the *Liezi*, the *Huainanzi*, and the *Baopuzi* were often included among the classics of Daoism.

The fall of the Han saw the emergence of a "mixed teaching"—Neo-Daoism. Its most influential writers were avowed Confucians motivated by the urge to "harmonize" the two traditions. The first, Wang Bi (c. 300) probably was familiar mainly with the Han religious echoes of Daoist thinking. He interpreted the *Laozi* alongside a cosmological divination manual, *The Book of Changes* (*I Ching* or *Yijing*). He treated *dao* as a term of creationist cosmology. *The Book of Changes* with its *yin-yang* account of change and its generational cosmology thus entered the list of Daoist texts.

Neo-Daoism, in turn, eventually facilitated and informed the assimilation of the newly imported Indian Buddhism which in turn inspired the development of a uniquely Chinese form of Buddhism—Chan (Zen). This blended outlook is one major vehicle by which Daoism survived in Chinese thinking.

One could say that Daoist philosophy, per se, was successfully extinguished by imperial suppression of thought that initiated China's philosophical dark age and the institution of the Han "official Confucian orthodoxy" which cemented it firmly in place. The result is that so many religious forms are regarded as Daoist, the term may have no meaningful value in identifying a unified philosophical trend or movement.

AN "INTERNAL" HISTORY OF PHILOSOPHICAL DAOISM

The *Zhuangzi* contains its own history of thought (Chapter 33) tracing the development of ideas leading up to Zhuangzi's doctrine, which we *could* call "mature" Daoism. The word "Daoism" however, had still not been coined and the *Zhuangzi* history takes itself as simply tracing a movement of thought motivated by progressive attempts to remove bias and replace narrow perspectives with more impartial ones.

This "internal" account of a "Daoist" dialectic starts from a traditional baseline and takes its first step with thinkers like the Mohists (90/33/17). They question the assumption that tradition is right and seek for a neutral standard for deciding which social *dao* to use in the public moral education project. They legitimized their chosen *dao* by appealing to a standard—the intentions of *tian*[nature:sky]. That was equivalent to a *natural* distinction between benefit and harm (the *natural* urge to benefit and aversion to harm). This standard motivates their utilitarianism, which formed such a demanding morality that they "wore out their heels" running from state to state stopping wars, opposing despots, relieving starvation and so forth.

The next phase of the urge to impartiality leads to a version of primitivism—attempting to identify and remove the biases that socialization has instilled in the *xin*[heart:mind]. It is these, they argue that divide men, induce competition, fuel disagreement, and make life miserable by creating desires which can be satisfied for only a few. They targeted the obviously social desires such as status, "cultivated" tastes, honor and so on (other texts attribute related slogans to them; for example, "to be insulted is no disgrace" and "farewell to narrowness.") The natural desires, they argued, are few and more easily satisfied. They are also universal in contrast to the cultivated desires which differ depending on tradition.

The first clear focus on the meta-nature of *daos* is then attributed to Shen Dao, Tian Ping, and Peng Meng. Shen Dao is also famous as a contributor to legalism. They started from the shared early classical assumption that we should follow a natural *dao*[guide]. And, like Mencius, thought of language as the paradigm of what is "unnatural." So impartiality comes from avoiding all language—all judgment about what is *shi-fei*[this-not this]. They motivate this by developing a concept of "Great *Dao*"—Great *Dao* is collection of all things and all events in a kind of everything concept. It is *dao*-like because it is a process, not an object. It is the history of all objects through all time, including the future. It "leaves nothing out."

The various competing normative *dao*[guides] imply that some possible future course of events (a *way* things might go) is the one we should "walk." To *dao*[guide] that *dao*[guide] is to recommend the future histories that result from the selected "walking." To learn one of those *dao*[guides] is to learn how to contribute to bringing about some future history. While there are many such possible future histories, there is only one actual history—one actual past and one actual future. He calls that actual history of the world, that actual course of events that all things will follow, Great *Dao*. The actual is natural so the Great *Dao*, the natural pattern of behaviors, events, and processes, requires no learning, no knowledge, no language or *shi-fei*[this-not this] distinctions.

This conception of the actual *dao* of the past and future has a deterministic flavor. Nothing we do can "miss" the Great *Dao*. Even a clod of earth cannot miss it (HY/92/33/50). From this conception of the world as all that is or will be, Shen Dao draws fatalistic sounding conclusions—"abandon knowledge and discard self" (HY/92/33/45). Flow with the inevitable and be indifferent, make not *shi-fei*[this-not this] judgments. He rejects all moral (and other) teaching and just … lives …

The account is critical of Shen Dao's theory: "Shen Dao's guide does not lead to the conduct of a living man but the tendency of a dead man. It is really very strange. … They made reversing what is human a constant value; didn't take the common view and couldn't avoid inconsistency. That which they called a guide was a non-guide and what they approved could not but be wrong. [They] did not know how to guide. …" (HY 92/33/51-4). Laozi, traditionally regarded as the founder of Daoism slots into the "internal history" at this point. He, like Shen Dao, is attracted to the conception of impartiality that underlies a recommendation that we "abandon knowledge." However, the *Laozi* does not seem to appeal to a Great *Dao* conception to justify it. Its appeal is more to "freedom" than to "determinism." The freedom, however, is relative to society, conventions and language.

The *Daode Jing* contains a classic expression of the ancient Chinese contrast theory of names. Words come in opposites and are learned together. In learning them, we learn to divide things in one of a range of possible ways and become "blind" to alternate ways of doing it. Along with the socially sanctioned distinctions, we learn to desire in socially prescribed ways thus acquiring the society's *dao*. Behavior motivated by this system of names, divisions and desires is called *wei*[deem:do] and the Laozi advocates that we should avoid *wei*-ing (*Wu-wei* = lack deeming-actions).

Thus if we can "forget" what we learn from conventional society, we can return to natural spontaneous action—symbolized by the newborn child. The child does move, but the motions are not motivated by any conception of how to divide the world into socially sanctioned categories or conditioned, socialized desires. We recover a natural freedom that is also a much reduced level of simpler desires that will enable people to live in peace—not necessarily together because the "natural" structure of primitive desires may only support society at the level of Neolithic villages. This idyllic return is sometimes called primitivism and the *Daode Jing* contains a classic depiction of this peaceful world of agrarian villages whose peaceful, contented inhabitants lack any incentive even to visit the next door village—though they can "hear the cocks crow and the dogs bark" (Ch. 81).

This primitivism still countenances a "natural" *dao*—a prescriptive course of action that originates from *tian*$^{\text{nature:sky}}$ and contrasts with the artificial *daos* of moralizing society—the Confucians and the Mohists. The moralists like Mozi would also maintain that their conception of the moral *dao* was the *dao* of *tian*^{nature}. Mencius, similarly, appeals to the normative authority of *tian*^{nature} to justify action according to the "innate" (Confucian) moral tendencies that grow in the *xin*$^{\text{heart-mind}}$. Mencius is critical of Yang Zhu, a figure often treated as a proto-Daoist who, thought he seems to have no meta-theory of Dao, is reputed to espouse a version of primitivism (which some call Yangism). Implicitly that his argument also seems to appeal to the notion of *tian*$^{\text{nature:sky}}$ as an authority—where the command of *tian*$^{\text{nature:sky}}$ is a "simpler" dictate to care for the essentials of life and abandon the dangers of political and social involvement.

In fact, despite leaving behind the deterministic tone of Shen Dao's "Great *Dao*," the *Laozi* is caught in a similar paradox. Shen Dao's reasoning illustrates what is wrong with any *dao* that has blanket anti-language interpretations. His advice to "abandon knowledge" is self-refuting advice since that falls within the range of what it advocates abandoning—prescriptive doctrines. It is a prescriptive paradox—if we obey it, we disobey it. So we can continue to learn *daos* and still be natural. The deep point is that natural *daos* are irrelevant to the issues being debated by the moralists. In being natural they lose their capacity to guide. The could not warrant any particular *shi-fei*$^{\text{this-not this}}$ that was relevant to judging or choosing some human action. Everything that happens must be the same—either all *shi*$^{\text{this:right}}$; all *fei*$^{\text{not-this:wrong}}$, all both or all neither. The crucial implication of his approach is that an injunction like "be natural" has no normative force.

So the trend of thought first recognized as forming the pattern we have come to call Daoism is one that reacts to Confucian conventionalism by trying to find a more universal, impartial point of view. It may include movements such as primitivism that seek to remove all social-conventional influence and those that analyze how conventions shape and induce our attitudes, desires and actions, and to a general interest in natural or transcendent standards or "ways" that undermine dogmatic conventionalism. The hint of paradox in the latter positions may be recognized and embraced or accepted as inescapable. The paradox, particularly of the anti-language implications of these developments led to the mature phase of philosophical daoism.

MATURE PHILOSOPHICAL DAOISM: THE ZHUANGZI

Classical thinkers found names and language relevant to not only Daoism. The *Analects* community of Confucianism became committed to "rectifying" names to make role-based behavior guides prescriptively reliable. Gongsun Long presented himself as defending Confucian practice with his one-name-one-thing rule. Confucians may not have wanted to claim him since he derived from this his notorious commitment to the assertability of "white horse not horse." Mohism produced the most sophisticated of these theories—an early version of semantic realism that may have derived from reflections on Mozi's three *fa*^{standards} (standards) of *yan*^{language} (language).

Mohists argued that name boundaries are determined by objective similarities and differences in things. So, against the name "rectifiers," they maintained that a "reality" can properly be called by several names—at times general or particular. But this position, they discovered, still left many puzzles. One was this: Which similarities count in correct naming or types? The others puzzles concern how to deal with compounding of names and strings. Mohists developed no syntactical theory of word-roles such as adjective and verb. All descriptive terms that picked out parts of reality were called "names." The way the parts combine when the words combine, however, struck them as irregular. Beyond noting and classifying some of the variation, however, Mohists did not seem to propose a systematic solution.

Zhuangzi, traditionally cited as the second daoist philosopher, engaged frequently in discussion with Hui Shi, cited as among the members of the "school of names." Hui Shi however, seems to represents a third posture within the school of names—name relativism. His implicit criticism of the realists emerges when he draws attention to terms that are implicitly comparative; for example, 'large', before, and 'high', and indexicals, for example, 'today' and 'south.' These do not apply in virtue of objective similarity. More theoretically, he averred that any two things, no matter how different, are similar in *some* respect, and no matter how similar, are different in *some* respect. So any two things can be included in the scope of a term in virtue of some similarity or could be placed included in a different range and named by different terms in virtue of *some* difference. Thus placement of things in a named range, even if based on similarity and difference, is not a *constant* or *reliable dao*.

Despite the relativist ground of his linguistic reasoning, Hui Shi seems to have drawn an absolutist conclusion. Since all linguistic divisions are relative, the absolute or language-independent world must be devoid of any distinctions—a mystical, unnamable, one. In effect, distinctions and differences among things are socially constructed. Since naming is based on distinctions and since language is constructed of names, Hui Shi's ending position resembles that of Shen Dao and Laozi—the familiar, anti-language, Daoist, mystical, monism—all is an inexpressible one. From this, Hui Shi then drew a hybrid Mohist-Daoist prescriptive conclusion, "Love all things equally, the cosmos is one body."

The Later Mohists, however, diagnosed the problem in these defeatist, negative conclusions about language and distinction-based judgment. The problem may take different forms and the Mohist diagnosis is repeated in three forms. First, distinctions are manifest in language in *shi-fei*$^{\text{this-not this}}$ indexicals. With a name in view, it does or does not apply to some indexically accessed item—"this" or "not this." To have a distinction is for something to be "not-this." So, to oppose all distinctions is to oppose *fei*-ing. However to oppose *fei*-ing is to *fei fei*-ing. Anyone who does so confronts a pragmatic contradiction. To *fei fei*-ing is to *fei*. Similarly, to *deem* all language as *bei*$^{\text{not-acceptable}}$ (not-acceptable) is *bei*$^{\text{not-acceptable}}$. And since, in the context of primitivism, such views amount to rejecting learning or education in language the third form is to teach that teaching is wrong is wrong. This explains the paradox that plagued Shen Dao and Laozi and any doctrine (for example, some interpretations of Mencius) that denigrate principles or linguistic guides in general in favor of following only "natural" *daos*.

Zhuangzi takes the paradox seriously and responds first by abandoning all such anti-language claims and appeals to *tian*^{nature} as an authority for *dao* while, second, still sustaining his skeptical, relativist distance from Confucian convention. The trick is to note that all (actually existing) language is natural—as natural as such nonhuman sounds as the whistling of wind or twittering of birds. Humans, their societies, and their languages are products of nature as much as are ground squirrels and their high-pitched chirps.

The disagreeing human thinkers—the 10,000 distinctions and differences marked in language—are among the "pipes of *tian*^{nature}." Thus he avoids taking an anti-language stance while still standing as an ironic "Daoist" distance from convention. From that stance he can continue to "poke fun" at the moralists—not for pretending to express "natural" *dao* (they do) but insisting that others, their opponents, *do not*. The sense in which theirs are natural (as indeed they are) is the sense in which their opponents *daos* are natural too.

All the warring discourse *daos* are, by hypothesis, natural. How, Zhuangzi asks, can a language exist without its being acceptable (in that community) to speak it? All *dao* that are actually walked (that generate behavior) are (in virtue of having emerged naturally in a natural world) *natural*. All the *daos* that anyone may *actually* appeal to in condemning rival *daos* must exist—and hence be natural. This does not entail that all *possible daos* are natural, but all existing and, no doubt, *many* that don't exist, are natural in the sense they have or might emerge in nature—for example, without any supernatural intervention.

This allows Zhuangzi to continue Daoism's trend of detachment and ironic neutrality in the fervent debates among the moralists. He also generalizes earlier themes (noted above) of how different *daos* shape our attitudes, our desires, and our descriptive language. This generalization emerges with a hint of mild skepticism. The anti-language position is an error position—all doctrines of morality/reality are false. The Mohist paradox undermines that. We cannot consistently conclude that no claims in language are correct. Neither can we claim that all linguistic utterance is correct since judgments according the standards of one natural language conflict with those of another. Each treats its own use as acceptable and others an unacceptable.

Each position in debate about *dao* depends on presuppositions—a presupposed *dao*. The *dao* is the *way* of speaking that language. An argument for one *dao* over another, also presupposes an implicit *dao*—a *way* of choosing which *dao* to follow in a situation. And even when we have selected which *dao* to follow, we may disagree about now to interpret our agreed *dao*. A way of interpreting *this dao* is still another presupposed *dao*. When we perform any *dao*, we perform an entire hierarchy of *daos*.

Thus, winning an argument doesn't give one assurance of being right *simpliciter*—it presupposes some way of picking a winner. There is no completely *neutral* way of assigning a right and wrong. Zhuangzi's skepticism is not based on contrasting human cognitive weakness with some ideal perspective, but draws on the infinite regress of standards involved in guidance by a way, a *dao*. It is skepticism because it doesn't deny we might have acted rightly, only that we cannot know in ways that we could, correctly show others is correct (that is move as judged from their *daos*). Skepticism in the *Zhuangzi* rests on the observation that we cannot be sure we are using the right standard of "knowing."

Zhuangzi expresses another aspect of the same point. Consider the standard objection to "Ideal Observer" theories of morality (eg. Right = if what some God-like judge would judge to be right). The objection goes that what the Ideal Observer should do is irrelevant to my decision about what I, an ordinary observer, should do. The *Zhuangzi* frequently reflects on the theme of how a perfect perspective is neither useful nor comprehensible to us. What God should do is wildly irrelevant to the real practical questions that confront us. We could neither understand nor use the answer to "What would a perfect person do?"

This leads in two ways back to the naturalism characteristic of Daoism. Not only are *actual* conventions natural, but there is a natural *dao* that both guides the selection (evolution) of conventional *dao* and guides the interpretation of them. Thus, the *Zhuangzi* argues that there is no way to disentangle the realm of *tian*$^{\text{nature:sky}}$ and the realm of *ren*^{human}—no way to ground the claims of moralists or mystics to have found *the* single naturally correct way.

THE FATE OF DAOISM UNDER THE EMPIRE

Philosophy in China suffered a dark age initiated in the third century BC by the emergence of the imperial structure under a totalitarian ideology. Authoritarian misgivings about the tendency of philosophers to cast doubt on conventional ways of making distinctions and the assumed political goal of unifying the social world under one *dao* motivated this political authoritarism. Paradoxically, most would say the Qin favored Daoism since the superstitious rulers sought in it the "secret of long life." This, of course, served rather to replace Daoism's philosophical reflections with credulous religious dogma and the interpretation dominant in "legalist" commentary. The Qin dynastic family and its so-called "legalist" *dao* of governance lasted only one generation. However, the institutional structure survived in the Han which anointed Confucianism as the unifying *dao*.

This totalizing position led Confucianism to an eclecticism which sought to embrace everything from royal superstitions to naturalistic cosmic forces (yin and yang) and ground them in a Confucian *dao* that they could use to manipulate the ruler. Confucians assured us that this moralized cosmology "incorporated Daoism" harmoniously with Confucianism, implying that Daoism entailed the superstitious yin-yong cosmology they had worked out. Several new "Daoist" texts emerged which mixed quotations from the *Zhuangzi* and this moralized yin-yang cosmology. These further tended to shape the accepted interpretation of Daoism to better suit the bureaucracy's purpose.

The stasis of a naturalized Confucianism and a cosmologized Daoism survived with slight variation until the modern period. The main interruption was the importation of Buddhism, which continued the stable institutional model and the tendency to eclectic blending into a single harmonious officially recognized *dao*. Imperial rule tended always to patronize some "approved" eclectic ideology. In such contexts, the critical and skeptical quality of thought of the classical period never reemerged.

The fall of the Han brought with it a crisis in confidence in this cosmic Confucianism. This did little to disrupt the assumption of fundamental compatibility of Daoism and Confucianism, but did lead to greater focus on the classical Daoist philosophical texts. The result has been called Neo-Daoism, though the main thinkers identified themselves as Confucians. They inflated the cosmic interpretation of Daoism into something closer to pure metaphysics (via its explicit interest in the contrast of *being and non-being)*. The result was a holistic "round" metaphysics with *non-being* at the core (basic *non-being*) and "being" as the periphery (functionally oscillating fluctuations in the field of "*non-being*").

The main point of controversy within Neo-Daoism was whether the *non-being* was really nothing or really "something." From there the philosophical level of Daoist discourse declines more than advances. Wang Bi interpreted the *Laozi* in tandem with a cosmological divination manual, the *Yi-Jing*, into what he assumed was a single system. *Non-being* was the basis of everything, the great-ultimate that was also the non-ultimate. Wang Bi explained the dynamic between *non-being* and *being* not as causation, but as the relation of "substance and function."

Guo Xiang interpreted the *Zhuangzi* giving us the received version and conforming to the outlines of Wang Bi's system except for his Parmenidean insistence that *non-being* simply was not. This he coupled with a radically un-Parmenidean view that *being* constantly changed "of itself." The Neo-Daoist systems were the originating models of the puzzling substance-function dualism that re-appeared regularly in most later philosophical systems, both Buddhist and Neo-Confucian, right up through modern times.

Neo-Daoist speculations on *being and non-being* helped facilitate early discussions of Buddhist philosophy—particularly the puzzle of the nature of Nirvana (and thus of the Buddha-Nature). Buddhism, however, brought with it the apparatus of monastic ecclesiastical authority that bequeathed more familiar religious structures to the existing fragments of "Daoist" superstition. The resulting religious movements are what survived the Buddhist period into modern times as what the West came to know as "Daoism."

KEY DAOIST CONCEPTS

This section explores two concepts that play a central role in Daoist philosophy—*dao*[guide] and *de*[virtuosity] (virtuosity). Together the terms have come to mean something like "ethics." We, however, take them to be the basic concepts of a broader notion of normativity. The normativity is broader because there can be a *dao* (and *de*) of language (correct way of use) of knowledge (ways to know) as well as to act.

DAO (WAY, GUIDE, ROAD). The main characteristic that justified Chinese historians in identifying a school to call Daoism is philosophical interest in the concept of *dao*. The almost universally accepted translation is a primitive of English—"way." So it subsumes "manner," "course," "technique," "system," "fashion," "custom," "style," "practice," "tradition," "discipline," "road," "direction," "path," and so forth.

A way is an answer to a "how" or "what-to-do" question. We typically use talk of ways in advising someone. Ways are thus *practical* (prescriptive or normative) concepts. A road, as a concrete (or asphalt!) example guides us and facilitates our arrival somewhere. Ways are prescriptive structures that have physical realizations. We can refer to the physical forms as ways or *daos* without thereby recommending them. The *Zhuangzi* reminds us that thievery has a *dao*. We can use both *dao* and "way" simply to describe—as when a Confucian undertakes to pursue his father's *dao* for three years after his death or we say, "I saw the way you did that."

There are interesting differences between *dao* and "way." Classical Chinese language lacks pluralization; for example, not simply has no plurals, but has no grammatical role for plurals. Most common nouns function like collective nouns, roughly analogous to plurals or mass nouns of English. So *dao* is more like "ways" or "way-stuff" or "the way-part or aspect of things" than it is like "*a* way." Like other common nouns, *dao* has a part-whole structure, that is additive—two parts simply yield a larger part of the same thing. What we describe as one way would function like one part or component of what in Chinese we call *dao*. Multiplicity in common nouns in ancient Chinese emerges via modification. So they might discuss, for example, my-*dao*, Sage-King's-*dao*, natural-*dao*, past-time's-*dao* and so forth. This feature explains why *dao* might appear more *metaphysical* than "way" and helps appreciate familiar Daoist spatial metaphors like "humans encounter each other in *dao* as fish do in water" (*Zhuangzi* Ch. 6). *Dao* is a little like the water—a feature of the realm in which humans live, work, and play. To be human is to be in a framework of ways to act, go, and speak. So-called Daoists are more likely to play with these metaphysical metaphors than Confucians or Mohists—who mainly point to (their favored part of) *dao*.

A second difference is that unlike "way," *dao* may be used as a verb. The best-known example is the famous first line of the *Dao*de Jing. Literally "*dao* can be *dao* not constant *dao*." For the middle *dao*, roughly one out of three translators uses "speak," another third use "tell" and the rest use near synonyms such as "expressed," "defined in words," or "stated." In a famous Confucian example of this use, Confucius criticizes *dao*-ing the people with laws rather than *dao*-ing them with ritual. (This verbal sense is often marked by a graphic variation *dao*[to direct].)

"Speak" is in some ways too narrow and in others too broad as a way translating this verbal use. It is too broad because in Western tradition, speaking is conventionally linked to describing, representing, picturing, expressing, defining, or "capturing" some reality. The Chinese verbal use resembles more what a European would express by "advocate" "acknowledge" or "recommend," for example, to "guide-speak." To *dao* is to put guidance into language. *Dao*-ing is giving advice.

"Speak" is, in other ways, too narrow. One can *dao* in written form or even by example—as when we *dao* with law or with ritual (texts or exemplars). Consider, again, the concrete translation for *dao*: "road" or "path." A woodsman with an ax *daos* when he chops bark from the trees as he enters the forest; He is *dao*-ing when he is "blazing" the trail. As the *Zhuangzi* notes, "A *dao* is made by walking it."

What a road shares with a pattern of blazes in a forest is that both, like maps and verbal instructions, can serve as normative guides. What they also share, is that they require *reading* and *interpretation*. In following any kind of *dao*, we "interpret" it. This might be hard, as when we interpret blazes in bark, or piles of stones left by boy scouts or a Hansel's string of bread crumbs or the two-days-old tracks left by a deer. Or it may be relatively easy, as when I follow the asphalt ribbon between my house and the store. These examples should illustrate the symbolic guiding nature of all "roads." To interpret a road/path/*dao* is to extract guidance in the form of an actual "walking," not to develop a theory or belief. This use of "interpretation" is more familiar in artistic contexts—in music, dance, or drama. The interpretation of a score, line or character in a play consists in a performance of it.

The metaphysics of *dao* should mark this distinction between normative way *types* (treated as guides) and interpretive tokens (the result of practically interpreting a guide). The token is an actual history, a string of actions. The token may itself be *taken as a guide* (that is as an exemplary model), but in that case, it in turn requires interpretation. There are various *ways* to follow the example. We have to extrapolate from the exemplar's situation to our own. So the distinction between type and token ways can be relative; it is actually a distinction between normative and descriptive senses. When we treat a token as subject to evaluation relative to some normative *dao*-type, it is descriptive. When we treat it as a *model* guiding our own performance, it is normative.

This should help us understand the notion of natural *daos*. Roads and ways need not be human constructions. Nature's "engineers," deer or mountain goats, also make paths. Famously animals from ants to pack rats, swallows to dogs make or mark and read their own ways. Other species may read and use these as humans do when lost in the mountains. Other "ways" are pure natural possibilities of sequences that will result in attaining a goal; for example, their being a way through a forest or across a river. That way consists of their being a fallen log or several large stones in a fortuitous configuration—fortuitous, that is, from the point of view of human actors. We discover these structures in nature as we "feel our way" along. We may learn to read natural signs and exact guidance from natural clues better over time.

However, the concept of a naturally constant *dao* threatens to follow the Great *Dao* into losing its normative role. The *Zhuangzi* recognized this danger most clearly in pointing out that all recommendations (all prescribed *dao*) are *natural* in virtue of actually being advanced and promoted. Nature—the structure of natural constancy—does not select any of these. Any selection requires a *dao* interpreter and interpreters select using different standards—higher-level *daos* of selection and interpretation. Thus, while some *daos* are impossible, the appeal to nature does not adjudicate among any actual rival formulations, such as those of Confucians versus Mohists. Nature does not evaluate or prescribe its possibilities. Like the Great *dao*, they just are.

DE (VIRTUOSITY, VIRTUE, POWER). A Daoist formula for *de* is "*dao* within." Translators most commonly use "virtue" as a translation but hurry to remind us that it is "virtue" in the ancient Greek sense of an excellence. "Power" can work as an alternative translation because it reflects the link between *de* and successful action or achievement for its possessor. This author prefers "virtuosity" to capture both the sensitivity to context and *fit* and to remind us of the aesthetic features of these normative concepts. Virtuosity is the capacity of a performer to "interpret" a score-like *dao* into a *superb* performance (in that theater, for that audience, and so forth). Thus *de* is the capacity to perform *dao* correctly—successfully, beautifully, and well.

Daoist reflections on *de* sometimes point to "natural" or prelearned capacities to learn or perform some *dao* with skill. Think of Wittgenstein's talk of the unexplained human ability to catch on and continue the correct grammar of a human language. This stress sometimes suggests the hardwiring or the machine language translation required to implement or interpret other programming. While many Daoist comments may be taken to refer to such "natural" skills, the concept of *de* itself seems to include *de* that is acquired in the process of learning, internalizing, practicing, and fine-tuning our performance of some *dao*.

Natural *dao* is presupposed in learning social *daos* in a number of ways. There is a natural way humans learn to acquire and perform normative *dao* and there are different ways to perform in different natural contexts. There are both natural and social-practice ways to select which *dao*-type to execute and multiple ways to evaluate the performance-generated *dao*-tokens. So, as Zhuangzi observes, we live so pervasively in such a "sea" of *dao* that, like fish in water, we forget that we forget *dao* as we swim around it.

See also Chinese Philosophy: Overview; Chinese Philosophy: Contemporary.

Bibliography

Alt, Wayne. "Logic and Language in the Chuang-tzu." *Asian Philosophy* 1 (1) (1991): 61–76.

Ames, Roger, ed. *Wandering at Ease in the Zhuangzi*. Buffalo, NY: SUNY Press, 1998.

Berling, Judith A. "Paths of Convergence: Interactions of Inner Alchemy, Taoism, and Neo-Confucianism." *Journal of Chinese Philosophy* 6 (1979): 123–.

Blofeld, John. *Taoism: The Quest for Immortality*. London: Mandala Books, 1979.

Carus, Paul. *The Canon of Reason and its Virtue*. Chicago: Open Court, 1913.

Chen, Ellen Marie. "Nothingness and the Mother Principle in Early Chinese Taoism." *International Philosophical Quarterly* 9 (September 1969): 391–405.

Ch'en, Ku-ying. *Lao Tzu: Text, Notes, and Comments*. Translated by Rhett Y. W. Young and Roger T. Ames. San Francisco, CA: Chinese Materials Center, 1977.

Cook, Scott. "Zhuang Zi and His Carving of the Confucian Ox." *Philosophy East and West* 47 (4) (1997): 521–554.

Creel, Hurlee G. *What Is Taoism?* Chicago: University of Chicago Press, 1970.

Cua, Antonio S. "Opposites As Complements: Reflections on the Significance of Tao." *Philosophy East and West* 31 (2) (April 1981): 123–140.

Duyvendak, J. J. L. *Tao Te Ching*. London: John Murray, 1954.

Fu, Charles Wei-hsun. "Creative Hermeneutics: Taoist Metaphysics and Heidegger." *Journal of Chinese Philosophy* 3 (1976): 115–143.

Fung, Yu-lan. *History of Chinese Philosophy*. Princeton, NJ: Princeton University Press, 1952.

Girardot, Norman J. *Myth and Meaning in Early Taoism: The Theme of Chaos (hun-tun)*. Berkeley: University of California Press, 1983.

Graham, Angus, tr. *The Book of Lieh-tzu*. London: John Murray, 1960.

Graham, Angus. *Chuang tzu: The Inner Chapters*. London: Allen & Unwin, 1981.

Graham, Angus. "Chuang-tzu's Essay on Seeing Things as Equal." *History of Religions* 7 (1969): 137–159.

Graham, Angus. "Daoist Spontaneity and the Dichotomy of 'Is' and 'Ought.'" In *Experimental Essays on Chuang-tzu*, edited by Victor Mair, 3–23. Honolulu: University of Hawaii Press, 1983.

Graham, Angus. "The Date and Composition of the Lieh-tzu." *Asia Major* 8 (2) (1961): 139–198.

Graham, Angus. *Disputers of the Tao: Philosophical Argument in Ancient China*. La Salle, IL: Open Court, 1989.

Graham, Angus. "How Much of the Chuang-tzu Did Chuang-tzu Write?" *Journal of the American Academy of Religion* 47 (3) (1979).

Hall, David L. "Process and Anarchy: A Taoist Vision of Creativity." *Philosophy East and West* 28 (3) (July 1978): 271–285.

Hansen, Chad. *A Daoist Theory of Chinese Thought*. New York: Oxford University Press, 1992.

Hansen, Chad. "A Tao of Tao in Chuang Tzu." In *Experimental Essays on Chuang-tzu*, edited by Victor Mair, 24–55. Honolulu: University of Hawaii Press, 1983.

Hansen, Chad. "The Zhuangzi: A Historical Introduction." In *The Dao of Zhuangzi*, edited by Tsai Chih Chung, 9–22. Garden City, NY: Anchor Books, 1997.

Henricks, Robert G. *Lao-tzu: Te-Tao Ching: A New Translation Based on the Recently Discovered Ma-wang-tui Manuscripts*. New York: Ballantine, 1989.

Hsiao, Kung chuan. *A History of Chinese Political Thought*, Vol. 1: *From the Beginnings to the Six Dynasties*. Princeton, NJ: Princeton University Press, 1979.

Hu, Shih. "A Criticism of Some Recent Methods Used in Dating Lao Tzu." *Philosophy East and West* 40 (1) (1989): 17–33.

Kasulis, T. P. "The Absolute and the Relative in Taoist Philosophy." *Journal of Chinese Philosophy* 4 (1977): 383–394.

Kjellberg, Paul, and Philip J. Ivanhoe, ed. *Essays on Skepticism, Relativism, and Ethics in the Zhuangzi*. Buffalo, NY: SUNY Press, 1996.

Kohn, Livia, ed. *Taoist Meditation and Longevity Techniques*. Ann Arbor: Center for Chinese Studies Publications, University of Michigan, 1989.

Kupperman, Joel J. "Not in So Many Words: Chuang Tzu's Strategies of Communication." *Philosophy East and West* 39 (3) (July 1989): 311–317.

Lau, D. C., tr. *Lao Tzu: Tao Te Ching*. Baltimore: Penguin Books, 1963.

Lau, D. C., tr. "The Treatment of Opposites in Lao-tzu." *Bulletin of the Society for Oriental and African Studies* 21 (1958): 344–360.

Liu Xiaogan. *Classifying the Zhuangzi Chapters*. Ann Arbor: Center for Chinese Studies, University of Michigan, 1994.

Mair, Victor, ed. *Experimental Essays on Chuang-tzu*. Honolulu: University of Hawaii Press, 1983.

Mair, Victor, tr. *Tao Te Ching: The Classic Book of Integrity and the Way*. New York: Bantam Books, 1990.

Maspero, Henri, tr. *Taoism and Chinese Religion*. Amherst: University of Massachusetts Press, 1981.

Munro, Donald, J. *The Concept of Man in Early China*. Stanford, CA: Stanford University Press, 1969.

Needham, Joseph. *Science and Civilization in China*. Vol. 2: *History of Scientific Thought*. Cambridge, U.K.: Cambridge University Press, 1962.

Robinet, Isabelle. "Metamorphosis and Deliverance from the Corpse in Taoism." *History of Religions* 19 (1) (1979): 37–70.

Roth, Harold D. *The Textual History of the Huai Nanzi*. Ann Arbor, MI: Association of Asian Studies, 1992.

Roth, Harold D. "Who Compiled the Chuang Tzu?" *Chinese Texts and Philosophical Contexts*, edited by Henry Rosemont, 84–95. La Salle, IL: Open Court, 1991.

Saso, Michael. *Taoism and the Rite of Cosmic Renewal*. Pullman: Washington State University Press, 1972.

Schwartz, Benjamin. *The World of Thought in Ancient China.* Cambridge, MA: Harvard University Press, 1985.

Sivin, N. "On the Word 'Taoist' As a Source of Perplexity, with Special Reference to the Relations of Science and Religion in Traditional China." *History of Religions* 17 (3–4) (February/May 1978): 303–330.

Smullyan, Raymond. *The Tao Is Silent.* New York: Harper and Row, 1977.

T'ang, Chün-i. "Cosmologies in Ancient Chinese Philosophy." *Chinese Studies in Philosophy* 5 (1) (Fall 1973): 4–47.

Van Norden, Bryan V. "Competing Interpretations of the Inner Chapters of the 'Zhuangzi.'" *Philosophy East and West* 46 (2) (1996): 247–269.

Waley, Arthur, tr. *The Way and Its Power: A Study of the Tao Te Ching and its Place in Chinese Thought.* London: Allen & Unwin, 1934.

Watson, Burton. *The Complete Works of Chuang Tzu.* Records of Civilization: Sources and Studies No. LXXX, Columbia College Program of Translations from the Oriental Classics. New York: Columbia University Press, 1968.

Watts, Alan Wilson. "The Philosophy of the Tao." In *The Way of Zen*, 23–48. Harmondsworth: Penguin Books, 1962.

Watts, Alan Wilson. *Tao: The Watercourse Way.* Harmondsworth: Penguin Books, 1975.

Welch, Holmes. *Taoism: The Parting of the Way.* Boston: Beacon Press, 1966.

Welch, Holmes, and Anna Seidel, eds. *Facets of Taoism.* New Haven, CT: Yale University Press, 1979.

Wong, David. "Taoism and the Problem of Equal Respect." *Journal of Chinese Philosophy* 11 (1984): 165–183.

Wu, Kuang-ming. *Chuang Tzu: World Philosopher at Play.* New York: Crossroad Publishing Company, 1982.

Yearley, Lee. "The Perfected Person in the Radical Chuang-tzu." In *Experimental Essays on Chuang-tzu*, edited by Victor Mair. Honolulu: University of Hawaii Press, 1983.

Yearley, Lee. "Zhuangzi's Understanding of Skillfulness and the Ultimate Spiritual State." In *Essays on Skepticism, Relativism, and Ethics in the Zhuangzi*, edited by Paul Kjellberg and Philip J. Ivanhoe, 152–182. Buffalo, NY: SUNY Press, 1996.

Zhuangzi. "The Zhuangzi." Citations (HY) from the Harvard Yenching Institute Sinological Index Series, Supplement no. 20. Cambridge, MA: Harvard University Press, 1956.

Chad Hansen (2005)

ETHICS

The first recorded dynasty in Chinese history is the Shang (1766–1050 BCE). It came to an end when the Zhou family overthrew the Shang and justified its act on the grounds that the Shang kings had become corrupt and forfeited the right to rule conferred by the ruling force of the world, *tian* (which literally means "sky" and is usually translated as "Heaven"). Although the Zhou kings claimed validation by Heaven, their rule declined in the time of Kongzi (551–479 BCE; better known in the West by his Latinized name Confucius), entailing a breakdown of the social, political, and moral order. The dao, the way or path, that the Zhou claimed to possess was lost. As Angus C. Graham (1989) puts it, the primary question of the age was: Where is the dao? Whoever could rediscover it could regain the *de*, the human power and excellence, that enabled the early Zhou kings to create the golden age of harmony and flourishing that was lost. Each philosophy of the ancient period provides its version of the dao.

CONFUCIAN ETHICS

Benjamin Isadore Schwartz (1985) characterizes the Confucian dao as emphasizing respect for rightful authority, where the rightfulness of authority is based on the achievement of ethical excellence. Confucianism is a virtue ethic because of its central focus on three interrelated subjects: character traits identified as the virtues; the good and worthwhile life; and contextualist modes of ethical deliberation. The virtues are traits of character that are necessary for living a good life and that typically involve judging in the context at hand what must be done. The virtues belong to the *junzi* (the noble person, most often translated as "gentleman"), who is living in accord with the dao. Such a person can be said to have realized in a high degree the overall ethical excellence that befits human beings.

Consider the virtue of *ren*. In 12.22 Kongzi identifies *ren* with loving or caring for people. Understood in this way, *ren* is one particular virtue among a number possessed by the *junzi* such as wisdom and courage. Translators such as D. C. Lau (1979) focus on this meaning of *ren* and translate it as "benevolence." However, *ren* has a much broader meaning in the *Analects* (but perhaps not in the *Mengzi*, where it seems restricted to the meaning of a particular virtue). At a number of places, *ren* is associated with an array of different virtues: for example, the observance of ritual in 3.3, and sympathetic understanding of others in 6.30. In fact, *ren* seems so closely associated with the ideal of the *junzi*, or morally noble person, that it seems to stand for complete human excellence.

A virtue distinctive of the Confucian ethic is that of ritual observance or ritual propriety. In the *Analects* the rituals (*li*) include ceremonies of ancestor worship, the burial of parents, and the rules governing respectful and appropriate behavior between parents and children. In general, the *li* in the *Analects* are ceremonies or customary practices that express one or more of several ethically significant attitudes: reverence, respect, care, gratitude, and a feeling of indebtedness. Later, the word came to cover a broad range of customs and practices that spelled out courteous and respectful behavior between people occupying specific social stations. Herbert Fingarette (1972) argues that this emphasis on ritual propriety conveys the profound insight that ceremonies, customs, and conventions constitute much of what is distinctive about human activity. A handshake means nothing unless understood against a background of conventions that establish the relevant physical movements as a way of greeting another person. So too, many of the ways of respecting and expressing care or gratitude toward others are possible only because they have been conventionally established as ways to express those attitudes. This implies that *ren* as complete human excellence cannot be understood as something separate and independent from *li*.

As Kwong-loi Shun (1993) points out, however, this does not mean that *ren* reduces to any given set of practices adopted by a community, since alternative practices in a different community might be devised to express the same ethical attitude or there might be nonconventional means of expressing that attitude. *Li* also are portrayed in the *Analects* as crucial for the project of ethical self-cultivation: dedicated observance of the rites, along with a sincere commitment to have the appropriate attitudes they are conventionally established to express, are crucial for developing and strengthening the dispositions to have those attitudes. Sincerely engaging in a ritual that is conventionally established to express reverence for parents or ancestors makes stronger the disposition to revere. Finally, there is an aesthetic dimension to the ethical importance of *li*. One is more or less graceful and elegant in the performance of *li*. One has made such observance more or less a second nature, from which it flows effortlessly and spontaneously. One who is so accomplished lives a life of beauty, and this is part of the *junzi* ideal.

The concept of *yi* refers both to that which is right or appropriate for the given situation and to the trait of character that consists in reliably identifying and acting on what is right. The *Analects* 4:10 says that the *junzi* is not predisposed to be for or against anything, but goes with what is *yi*. As Antonio Cua (1998) points out, traditional rules of ritual propriety provide one with a sense of what is courteous and respectful action given standard contexts, while the virtue of *yi* allows one to identify when those rules need to be set aside in exigent circumstances. In 4A17 Mengzi (371–289 BCE; better known in the West as Mencius) observes that to save the life of one's drowning sister-in-law one must suspend the customary rule of propriety prohibiting the touching of man and woman when they are giving and receiving. When his interlocutor wants to apply this idea of suspending the usual rules of propriety to save the entire country from drowning, Mengzi replies that one saves one's sister-in-law with one's hand but cannot save the country from drowning in chaos and corruption with one's hand. The country can only be pulled out by the dao.

This passage not only illustrates that one may have to set aside customary rules of propriety in exigent circumstances but also that analogy is a way to judge what is *yi* for the situation at hand. One starts with a case where the judgment seems right (touching the sister-in-law when she is drowning) and attempts to transfer a like judgment to a like situation. One can also criticize an analogy by pointing out a relevant unlikeness between the two cases. One cannot save the country through violations of ritual propriety, but only through setting it back on the dao, which itself may require one to observe propriety on many occasions.

The term *de* is used to refer to the power or excellence that a thing can achieve when it acts according to the dao for things of its kind. One who gets or attains the dao and achieves virtues such as *yi* achieves a power or excellence appropriate to things of one's kind. In the *Analects* the human *de* that is *ren* brings with it a power to influence and attract other people and even the surrounding environment. Human *de* is a kind of moral charisma that comes with the achievement of the virtues just discussed and can be possessed by any good human being, but when it appears in rulers, it allows them to command others without appealing to physical threats (as Edward Slingerland [2003] points out, such an ideal may manifest the theme of *wu-wei*, or effortless action, which is traditionally associated with the daoists). The Confucian prescription for bringing China back to the dao is partly based on this belief in *de* as possessed by rulers and in the strategy of Confucian scholars offering their moral advice to rulers.

Western interest in Confucianism rests on reasons that are similar to those underlying the enduring interest in Western virtue ethics. Those who are skeptical of the modernist ambition to construct ethical theories around general principles of action, seeing them as too vague and abstract to provide much guidance on the one hand, and too reductivist to capture the rich array of ethical considerations on the other hand, turn to the ancient ideals of good character and judgment that are sensitive to context. Virtue ethics also tend to embody the theme that the ethical life of right (and in the case of Chinese and contemporary Western virtue ethics) caring relationship to others is necessary for human flourishing. In the *Mengzi* this theme emerges in identification of the distinctively human potentials with the incipient tendencies to develop the moral virtues.

At the same time, Confucian ethics is distinctive for the centrality it gives to family life in its conception of the good life. Part of the reason for this centrality lies in the Confucian appreciation for the family as the first arena in which care, respect, and deference to legitimate authority is learned (*Analects* 1.2). The way in which particularist reasoning is illustrated in historical stories such as those about Shun is also a distinctive feature of Confucian ethics. These stories present paradigms of good judgment and of good individuals, from which persons engaged in ethical self-cultivation should learn through analogy with relevantly similar situations in their own lives. Those who hold that much moral learning and reflection is accomplished through the telling of and listening to stories and other narratives have reason to study Confucianism. Another distinctive feature of Confucian ethics, as mentioned earlier, is the emphasis it gives to rituals as providing much of the distinctive substance of human life, as a necessary dimension of moral self-cultivation, and as contributing to the aesthetic dimension of the good life.

Mengzi and Xunzi (313–238 BCE) engaged in a vigorous, provocative debate over human nature and whether there are natural tendencies that form the basis for development of a good person. Mengzi holds that there are innate moral concepts that infuse intuitive judgments and feelings (people spontaneously feel compassion for a child about to fall into a well; a beggar knows intuitively to reject food that has been thrown on the ground and trampled on). Xunzi holds that human nature is dominated by the desire for gain and sensual gratification and that rather than having a natural basis, morality is invented to prevent the destructive conflict caused by people acting from their natures.

The contrasting ways in which Mengzi and Xunzi portray moral development raise important issues about the relation between reasoning, feeling, and moral judgment. Mengzi tends to portray moral perception, reasoning, and feeling as working in concert in ways that call into question any strict separation between perception and reasoning on the one hand and feelings such as shame and compassion on the other (Wong 1991, 2002). By contrast, Xunzi holds that the mind has the power to shape and retrain its desires and feelings, but his portrait of moral development seems to presuppose appropriate conative and affective elements that form the base for such reshaping (Van Norden 1992, Wong 1996). Taking all these distinctive features together, it is fair to say that Confucianism offers an especially rich moral psychology that Antonio Cua (1998, 2005), Philip J. Ivanhoe (2000), David S. Nivison (1996), and Shun (1997) illuminate.

Another respect in which Confucianism differs from modern Western moral theories bears especially on the cross-cultural comparison of values. Confucian morality lacks a focus comparable to that found in modern Western moralities on individual rights to liberty and to other goods, where the basis for attributing such rights to persons lies in a moral worth attributed to each individual independently of what conduces to individual's responsibilities to self and others. Confucianism rather assumes that the ethical life of responsibility to others and individual flourishing are inextricably intertwined, and in such a way, Craig Ihara (2004) argues, that the individual's dignity is honored without resort to the concept of rights. A frequent Western interpretation of Confucian ethics is that it subordinates the individual to the group. David L. Hall and Roger T. Ames (1998) respond that this interpretation erroneously presupposes that the individual and community are potentially at odds in ways the Chinese tradition does not conceive them to be. The nature of the individual is conceived relationally, they argue, so that it is just plain wrong to have the Chinese separating the individual from the group in the first place, much less subordinating the individual to the group.

Another frequent criticism from the Western side is that Confucianism fails to provide adequate protection to those legitimate interests an individual has that may conflict with community interests. On the other side, Henry Rosemont (1991) criticizes rights-focused moralities for ignoring the social nature of human beings and of portraying human life in an excessively atomistic fashion. Against those who argue that Confucianism does not sufficiently protect the individual, Rosemont (2004) replies that the Confucian framework of responsibilities to others can afford significant economic and social protections to the individual and arguably addresses the human need for community and belonging better than rights frameworks.

Moreover, it is arguable that rights in some sense can play a role in the Confucian tradition, even if such rights are not grounded in the idea of the independent moral worth of the autonomous individual. Within that tradition, Joseph Chan (1999) argues, rights might function to protect individuals' interests when the right relationships of care irretrievably break down. Furthermore, rights to be protected in one's speech can receive a Confucian justification as conducive to the health of the community. Mengzi advised kings to attach more weight to the opinions of their people than to those of their ministers and officers in making certain crucial decisions. Xunzi recognized the need for subordinates to speak their views freely to their superiors. If one carries the reasoning in Mencius and Xunzi one step further, one sees the need to protect a space in which they may speak freely without fear of suppression, and hence derive a right in the "thin" sense of what one has whenever one has justifiable claims on others to assure one's possession of things or one's exercise of certain capacities (Wong 2004).

That there are developments of each tradition that bring each closer to the other may suggest that each could learn from the other. One might worry about the kind of individualism that prompts citizens in affluent nations such as the United States to tolerate gross inequality of opportunity. One therefore might look to a tradition that appreciates the way people thrive or falter within specific communities that nurture or shut them out. On the other side, a tradition that has tended to value the idea of social harmony at the cost of sufficiently protecting dissenters pointing out abuses of power or just plain bad judgment by authorities would do well to look at enduring traditions that do not value social harmony as highly.

MOHIST ETHICS

Mozi (470–391 BCE) is said to have begun as a student of Confucianism and eventually came to reject it in favor of a consequentialism that in important respects anticipates Western utilitarianism by two millennia. While Confucians saw the problem with China as loss of respect for authority and a related loss of moral basis for authority, Mozi saw the problem as partiality. Heads of families knew only to love their own families and mobilized their families to usurp others. Lords knew only to love their own states and consequently mobilize their own to attack others. Such partiality causes destructive conflict that harms everyone, so the proper conclusion is to override one's own tendencies to partiality and to practice *jianai*, sometimes translated as "universal love" but arguably better translated as "impartial concern."

Schwartz (1985) points out that *ai* in the *Mozi* means neither *Eros* nor *agape* but something closer to a concern for all that is justified on the basis that its practice advances one's own welfare and the welfare of those to whom one is partial. The doctrine of impartial concern, when combined with Mozi's emphasis on evaluating beliefs according to the benefits and harms that result from them, qualifies him as a kind of utilitarian. His is not, however, a hedonistic or welfare utilitarianism of the kind most commonly represented in the Western tradition. His conception of benefit and harm refers to no psychological goods and harms such as pleasure and pain but exclusively to material goods and harms such as enriching the poor, increasing the population, and bringing about order.

Because he advocated impartial concern, Mozi had no use for the Confucian doctrine of graded concern: that the degree of one's concern should depend on the nature of one's relationship to the person in question (one's family being owed the most concern). Because he relied on pragmatic appeals to people's existing interests to justify his moral position and because he took the rationalist position that people should have no trouble doing what they see to be in their interests, he saw no use for Confucian ritual as a mode of moral self-cultivation.

The traditional attitude toward Mozi is that he was a relatively minor philosopher, but that is changing. His criticism of Confucian-graded concern and his advocacy of impartial concern is of broad interest and raises the question of how to fit within a coherent moral framework the special concern parents and children ought to have toward one another with the universal and equal concern one ought to have toward all persons as persons (Wong 1989). Moreover, Chad Hansen (1992) argues persuasively that Mozi's vigorous argumentation against the Confucians constituted a pivotal point, after which subsequent Confucian thinkers such as Mengzi and Xunzi had to defend Confucianism with argument. Mozi was unique in developing explicit standards for argumentation, and his school developed a distinctive focus on questions of logic, argumentation, and philosophy of language.

DAOIST ETHICS

The two great daoist texts of the ancient period are the *Daodejing* (Book of the way and its power; traditionally but dubiously attributed to the historical figure Laozi, c. sixth century BCE), and the *Zhuangzi* (a good part of the first seven chapters, the so-called inner chapters, was probably written by the historical figure Zhuangzi, c. 360 BCE). It may seem paradoxical to write of daoist ethics, but daoism thrives on (apparent?) paradox. On the one hand daoism expresses strong skepticism about distinctions between good and bad, right and wrong. On the other hand it also makes recommendations that add up to putting forward a way of life. Joel J. Kupperman (1999) observes that the *Zhuangzi* commends a way of life that does not take oneself and one's ideas so seriously.

The way of life commended in the *Zhuangzi* also includes openness to what might escape one's current conceptualizations and preconceptions. One is invited to see that one's conceptualizations of the world are inevitably incomplete and distorting. One attempts to order the world by sorting its features under pairs of opposites, but opposites in the real world never match neatly with one's conceptual opposites. Real "opposites" escape one's attempts to cleanly separate them. Despite one's best efforts, they switch places in one's conceptual maps, blur, and merge into one another. That is why chapter 2 of the *Zhuangzi* says that the sage recognizes a *this*, but a *this* that is also *that*, a *that* that is also *this*. In chapter 5, men who have had their feet amputated as criminal punishment are scorned by society, but not by their daoist masters, who see what is of worth in them. In fact, both the *Zhuangzi* and *Daodejing* express an underlying suspicion of the needs that evaluative judgments serve; it is precisely to dominate or to undermine others that one subsumes them under the disfavored halves of one's value dichotomies.

The *Zhuangzi* further emphasizes the need to accept the inevitable in human life, the need to manage one's desires to achieve tranquility in the face of the inevitable, and to identify with the world that makes acceptance and management of desires possible. Both the *Zhuangzi* and *Daodejing* commend *wu-wei*, literally translated as "non-action," but meaning something like unforced acting with the grain of things. It is a style of action that consists in being receptive rather than aggressive, following from behind rather than leading in front, accommodating rather than confrontational, and being flexible and ready to change with the situation rather than rigid and operating from general predetermined principles. Seeing what is of worth in people and getting attuned to the grain of things are themes that stand in tension with the skepticism expressed by both the *Zhuangzi* and *Daodejing*, and one of the central interpretative problems is how to reconcile them (Hansen 1992, Kjellberg and Ivanhoe 1996, Wong 2005).

The *Zhuangzi* addresses such recommendations largely to the private individual who has become disaffected with the popular striving after conventional success and with the earnest moral idealism of the Confucians. By contrast, the *Daodejing* often addresses its recommendations to rulers, and even when it does not it expresses a primitivist social philosophy that holds that humanity was at its best when its desires were the fewest and when it did not guide itself through self-conscious valuing. Chapter 19, for example, says, "Exterminate the sage, discard the wise, and the people will benefit a hundredfold; exterminate benevolence, discard rectitude, and the people again will be filial; exterminate ingenuity, discard profit, and there will be no more thieves and bandits" (Lau 1985, p. 23). The rejection of conventional success and earnest idealism is here paired with the promise that if one stops trying to impose one's will on others (along with the usual value dichotomies) one may actually result in the ends one originally hoped to achieve.

What is interesting about *wu-wei* as applied to political leadership, as Michael Lafargue (1992) points out, is that it implies an organic notion of social harmony that contrasts with the conception of harmony as imposed by a dominating person who stands out from the rest of the group. A leader in an organic social group models the kind of self-effacement and sparseness of desire that all members should have. One suspects that such a leader must do more than model to be effective, but the *Daodejing* does not dispense specific advice or strategies. It rather provides metaphors from nature about the strength to be found in water and in valleys, associated with the female, that can overmatch the strength to be found in rock and in mountains, associated with the male.

In the *Daodejing* both the skepticism about the adequacy of conceptual structures and the confidence in *wu-wei* have traditionally been thought to be rooted in a monistic vision of the universe that is centered on the notion of the dao. Consider chapter 4 of that text where the dao is described as being empty, as seeming something like the ancestor of the myriad of things, as appearing to precede the Lord (*di*). In chapter 1, the constant dao is characterized as nameless, and the nameless is the origin of Heaven and Earth. Insofar as it is named, one could call it the mother of all things. The dao of the *Daodejing* might be the indeterminate ground in which determinate things are incipient, as suggested by Robert Neville (1989). Chung-ying Cheng (1989) suggests that the embrace of an indeterminate ground of the determinate may reflect the decision to give the phenomenon of change a fundamental place in ontology, rather than an absolutely stable being as in Parmenidean ontology and as later reflected in Aristotelian and Cartesian notions of substance. One reason for a continuing Western interest in Chinese metaphysics has partly been fueled by the perception that contemporary physics has undermined the strategy of giving determinate being ontological primacy.

BUDDHIST ETHICS

In Chinese strains of Buddhism, especially Chan Buddhist texts such as the *Liuzu tanjing* (Platform sutra of the sixth patriarch) by Huineng (638–713), there is also a sense that evaluative categories cannot reliably order the world and the confidence that one can become attuned to the world so as to move with its grain. This is not surprising since daoism profoundly influenced Buddhism on its importation into China. However, Buddhist ethics is distinguished by its special emphasis on the elimination of suffering and on the way it explains suffering by referring to the human attachment to the self as a fixed ego entity. The Buddhist scripture, *The Questions of King Milinda* (Conze 1959), articulates a view of the self as based on nothing more than a floating collection of various psychophysical reactions and responses. Contrary to the folk belief, there is no fixed center or relatively unchanging ego entity. One's bodily attributes, various feelings, perceptions, ideas, wishes, dreams, and in general a consciousness of the world display a constant interplay and interconnection that leads one to believe that there is some definite *I* that underlies and is independent of the ever-shifting series, but there is only the interacting and interconnected series.

In Buddhism, this view of the self has deep practical implications. It points toward the answer to human suffering, which ultimately stems from a concern for the existence and pleasures and pains of the kind of self that never existed in the first place. The recognition that none of the "things" of ordinary life are fixed and separate entities, anymore than the self is, leads to recognizing all of life as an interdependent whole and to the practical attitude of compassion for all of life. One can only be struck by the similarity between the Buddhist view of the self and David Hume's doubts in *The Treatise of Human Nature* about the existence of a unitary and stable self. Such a conception of the self may lay claim to one's renewed attention because it fits better with a naturalized conception of human beings as part of this world and not as Cartesian-thinking substances that somehow operate apart from the rest of nature. Consider also Derek Parfit's (1984) argument that acceptance of a Humean or a Buddhist view of the self can lead to sense that one is less separate from other selves and to a wider concern when one's projects seem not so absolutely different from other people's projects. Some might see Buddhist impersonal concern as unreasonably demanding of human beings who are so strongly partial to themselves and their own (a criticism made of utilitarianism also), but as Owen Flanagan (1991) argues, that Buddhism is a vibrant and long-lived tradition with many committed practitioners provides some support for the viability of impersonal concern as an ideal that is capable of claiming allegiance and influencing how people try to live their lives.

Another concern some have about Buddhist ethics is that it appears to advocate a dampening of desire and attachment to things and people. Attachment and clinging to the impermanent is deemed the root of suffering. There is a similar vein of thought in daoism, but combined with a more complex attitude that allows attachments to remain in a transformed state, allowing one to accept the death of a loved one as part of the process of change that one embraces and even celebrates. Chapter 18 of the *Zhuangzi* portrays its namesake as sobbing on the death of his wife, but stopping and even turning to drumming on a pot and singing after he realizes that his wife has gone to become a companion to spring, summer, autumn, and winter. This more complex attitude also surfaces in Buddhism, and not surprisingly in Chinese versions of it such as Chan (later becoming Zen in Japan), where it is stressed that enlightenment is to be found in the ordinary, in one's life here and now, not in a rejection of or escape from this life.

NEO-CONFUCIAN ETHICS

The neo-Confucian Zhuxi (1130–1200) reinterpreted ethical themes inherited from the classical thinkers and grounded them in a cosmology and metaphysics, partly as a response to the growing influence of daoism and Buddhism in his time. The dao or way of Heaven is expressed in principle (*li*, not to be confused with the *li* that means ritual propriety). It is embedded in something like the indeterminate ground of the daoists, but results in the myriad of determinate things when it is sheathed in *qi*, the material energy stuff of the universe. This sheathing, however, also results in base emotions and conflict. The task of human beings is to return to their own original goodness through purification of *qi* so that *li* can be expressed, an idea that is similar to the Buddhist theme that the Buddha nature is present in all things and that enlightenment is attained through purification of that nature. Another great neo-Confucian, Wang Yangming (1472–1529), seems more pragmatic than metaphysical. He taught of the sage who formed one body with Heaven and Earth and the myriad things, but he showed little of Zhu's interest in the *li* or principle of existent things, focusing rather on the rectification of the base thoughts of the mind.

THE LEGALIST CRITIQUE OF AN ETHICS-BASED APPROACH TO GOVERNMENT

Confucian, daoist, and Buddhist ethics recommend in one way or another the project of self-cultivation resulting in significant self-transformation, even if the basis of such transformation is present in human nature. In Confucian ethics and in some versions of daoist and Buddhist ethics, this transformation can result in the ethical transformation of a whole society. The legalist Hanfeizi (281–233 BCE) expresses skepticism about the ambitions of such projects, and in particular the Confucian project of bringing a society back to the dao through the ethical self-cultivation of the ruling elite. Hanfeizi argues that widespread good behavior, never mind the right motivations, is an achievement requiring fortuitous circumstances. He does not dispute the Confucian belief that the sage-kings of ancient times were virtuous and ruled over a harmonious and prosperous society. He does dispute that their virtue was the primary cause. What about, he asks, those kings in more recent times who were *ren* and *yi*, benevolent and righteous, and who got wiped out for their trouble? Virtue is not the explanation of success or failure. The explanation, argues Hanfeizi, has much more to do with the scarcity of goods in relation to the number of people.

Hanfeizi's subsequent emphasis on authority, on clear and consistent law, backed by severe punishment for its violation, is designed not to provide an alternative method of making the people follow the dao, but first and foremost to prevent the worst things from happening, the worst forms of chaos, bloodshed, and human misery. Legalism is commonly regarded as a philosophy of pure Realpolitik, but is perhaps better conceived as an ethic and political philosophy that is shaped by a severe pessimism about human nature and about the practicality of moral idealism.

SOME METHODOLOGICAL ISSUES

A common Western perception of Chinese ethical teaching is that it is "wisdom" literature, composed primarily of stories and sayings designed to move the audience to adopt a way of life or to confirm its adoption of that way of life. By contrast, Western ethical philosophy is systematic argumentation and theory. One reason to think there is such a difference is the fairly widespread wariness in Chinese philosophy of a discursive rationality that operates by deduction of conclusions about the particular from high-level generalizations. Confucians seem more willing than daoists to articulate their teachings in the form of principles, but in accordance with the conception of *yi* as action that is right for the circumstances at hand, such principles seem to function as designators of values or general considerations that ought to be given weight in judgments about what to do. Never lost is recognition of the necessity for the exercise of discretion in judgment according to the particular circumstances at hand. However, such contextualist themes appear in Western philosophical traditions, beginning with Aristotle. Perhaps it is fairest to say that the Chinese and Western traditions have differed over the emphasis and relative dominance accorded to particularism versus top-down normative theorizing.

Arne Naes and Alastair Hanay (1972) characterize Chinese philosophy as invitational in its method of persuasion, meaning that it portrays a way of life in a vivid fashion so as to invite the audience to consider its adoption. The *Analects*, for example, portrays the ideal of the *junzi* as realized by persons of genuine substance who are undisturbed by the failure of others to recognize their merits (1.1: "To be unrecognized by others yet not complain, is this not the mark of the junzi?"). In the *Mengzi* 2A2, such a person possesses a kind of equanimity or heart that is unperturbed by the prospects of fame and success. This unperturbed heart corresponds to the cultivation of one's *qi* (vital energies) by uprightness.

One might be able to see such passages as appealing to experiences the audience might have in its encounters with persons who do seem to possess special strength, substance, and tranquility through identification with and commitment to a cause they perceive to be far greater than themselves. One need not interpret such sayings as attempting to persuade by the pure emotive effect of certain words, as in propaganda. Rather, they may correspond to a way of doing philosophy that attempts to say something about values in life that can be supported by experience, even if not all testimony will agree (Kupperman 1999). The daoists recommend a way of life that they explicitly characterize as one that cannot be argued for, but their recommendation receives some support through commonly shared experience.

Consider again the notion of *wu-wei* and its illustrations in the *Zhuangzi* through stories of exemplary craft. Most famously, Zhungzi's Cook Ding cuts up an ox so smoothly and effortlessly that his knife never dulls, as if he is doing a dance with his knife as it zips through the spaces between the joints. He does this not through "perception and understanding" but through *qi*, the vital energies of the body. Suggested here is a portrait of acting in the world that consists of complete and full attention to present circumstances so that the agent can act with the grain of things (the Cook Ding passage refers to *tianli* or heavenly patterns). Such a portrait does resonate with the actual experience of craftspeople, artists, athletes, musicians, and dancers who have advanced beyond self-conscious technique and rule-following, who become fully absorbed in the experience of working with the material, the instruments, or in the movement of their bodies and who experience their actions as an effortless flow and in fact perform at high levels. In such ways, Chinese thinkers draw a picture of the world that must in the end be evaluated by explanatory power in some broad sense. One must ask whether the picture helps make sense of one's experience of the world (again in a broad sense of experience not limited to quantifiable observations in replicable experiments) and whether it preserves features of that experience that one thinks are *prima facie* genuine.

The contrast between Chinese philosophy as invitational and Western philosophy as argumentative has some truth in it, but the difference is more a matter of degree than an absolute contrast. It was Aristotle in the *Nicomachean Ethics*, after all, who said that discussions about the good in human life cannot be properly assimilated by the young because they do not have enough experience of life. And Plato, despite his insistence on the centrality of argumentation to philosophy, dispatches the short analytical arguments presented in book 1 of the *Republic* in favor of long expository portraits of the ideal city-state and the harmonious soul for the rest of that work, often presenting little or no argument for some of his most crucial claims. Other of his claims, about the divisive effects of family loyalties and the ill effects of democracy, obviously appeal to experience, even if not all testimony will agree. Furthermore, as noted earlier, Mozi's criticism of Confucians required response in kind. Shun (1997) reveals the extensive argumentative context behind Mengzi's response to the Mohists. Methods of argumentation reach their most sophisticated state of development in Xunzi (see Cua 1985), who vigorously criticizes Mozi's, Zhuangzi's, and Mengzi's theory of human nature.

Differences in the way philosophy is done may reflect differences in the interests philosophy is meant to satisfy. Hansen (1992) argues that the classical Chinese thinkers did not conceive of the primary function of language to be descriptive and as attempting to match propositions with states of affairs, but as a pragmatic instrument for guiding behavior. Western interpreters have been unable to see this, argues Hansen, because they have imposed their own concerns with correspondence truth and metaphysics on the Chinese tradition. One result, in his view, is the wrong-headed interpretation of daoism as founded on the mystical doctrine of attunement to a metaphysically absolute dao. Hall and Ames (1987) criticize Fingarette's (1972) influential interpretation of Confucius's dao as an ideal normative order transcending the contingencies of time, place, history, and culture. Hall and Ames argue Confucius's dao was not conceived as a tradition and language-independent reality against which linguistically formulated beliefs were to be measured as reliable or unreliable, but in fact a cumulative creation of individuals working from within a context provided by a society's tradition, consisting of customs, conventions, conceptions of proper behavior and good manners, and conceptions of right conduct and of what is of ultimate value and of what lives are worth living. Such controversies indicate the continuing vibrancy of the Chinese philosophical tradition as it interacts with the West.

See also Chinese Philosophy: Religion; Chinese Philosophy: Social and Political Thought.

Bibliography

Chan, Joseph. "A Confucian Perspective on Human Rights for Contemporary China." In *The East Asian Challenge for Human Rights*, edited by Joanne R. Bauer and Daniel A. Bell. Cambridge, U.K.: Cambridge University Press, 1999.

Cheng, Chung-ying. "Chinese Metaphysics as Non-metaphysics: Confucian and Daoist Insights into the Nature of Reality." In *Understanding the Chinese Mind: The Philosophical Roots*, edited by Robert E. Allinson. Hong Kong: Oxford University Press, 1989.

Conze, Edward, tr. *Buddhist Scriptures*. London: Penguin, 1959.

Cua, Antonio. *Ethical Argumentation: A Study in Hsün Tzu's Moral Epistemology*. Honolulu: University of Hawaii Press, 1985.

Cua, Antonio. *Human Nature, Ritual, and History: Studies in Xunzi and Chinese Philosophy*. Washington, DC: Catholic University of America Press, 2005

Cua, Antonio. *Moral Vision and Tradition: Essays in Chinese Ethics*. Washington, DC: Catholic University of America Press, 1998.

Fingarette, Herbert. *Confucius: The Secular as Sacred*. New York: Harper Torchbooks, 1972.

Flanagan, Owen. *Varieties of Moral Personality*. Cambridge, MA: Harvard University Press, 1991.

Graham, Angus C., tr. *Chuang-Tzu: The Inner Chapters*. Indianapolis, IN: Hackett, 2001.

Graham, Angus C. *Disputers of the Tao: Philosophical Argument in Ancient China*. La Salle, IL: Open Court, 1989.

Hall, David L., and Roger T. Ames. *Thinking from the Han: Self, Truth, and Transcendence in Chinese and Western Culture*. Albany: SUNY Press, 1998.

Hall, David L., and Roger T. Ames. *Thinking through Confucius*. Albany: SUNY Press, 1987.

Hansen, Chad. *A Daoist Theory of Chinese Thought: A Philosophical Interpretation*. New York: Oxford University Press, 1992.

Ihara, Craig. "Are Claim Rights Necessary? A Confucian Perspective." In *Confucian Ethics: A Comparative Study of Self, Autonomy, and Community*, edited by Kwong-loi Shun and David B. Wong. New York: Cambridge University Press, 2004.

Ivanhoe, Philip J. *Confucian Moral Self Cultivation*. 2nd ed. Indianapolis, IN: Hackett, 2000.

Kjellberg, Paul, and Philip J. Ivanhoe. *Essays on Skepticism, Relativism, and Ethics in the Zhuangzi*. Buffalo: SUNY Press, 1996.

Knoblock, John, tr. *Xunzi: A Translation and Study of the Complete Works*. 3 vols. Stanford, CA: Stanford University Press, 1988.

Kupperman, Joel J. *Learning from Asian Philosophy*. New York: Oxford University Press, 1999.

Lafargue, Michael. *The Tao of the Tao Te Ching*. Albany: SUNY Press, 1992.

Lau, D. C., tr. *Confucius: The Analects*. New York: Penguin, 1979.

Lau, D. C., tr. *Tao Te Ching*. New York: Penguin, 1985.

Naes, Arne and Alastair Hanay. *Invitation to Chinese Philosophy: Eight Studies*. Oslo: Universitetsforlaget, 1972.

Neville, Robert. "The Chinese Case in a Philosophy of World Religions." In *Understanding the Chinese Mind: The Philosophical Roots*, edited by Robert E. Allinson. Hong Kong: Oxford University Press, 1989.

Nivison, David S. *The Ways of Confucianism*, edited by Bryan Van Nordan. La Salle, IL: Open Court, 1996.

Parfit, Derek. *Reasons and Persons*. Oxford, U.K.: Clarendon Press, 1984.

Rosemont, Henry. *A Chinese Mirror: Moral Reflections on Political Economy and Society*. La Salle, IL: Open Court, 1991.

Rosemont, Henry. "Whose Democracy? Which Rights? A Confucian Critique of Modern Western Liberalism." In *Confucian Ethics: A Comparative Study of Self, Autonomy, and Community*, edited by Kwong-loi Shun and David B. Wong. New York: Cambridge University Press, 2004.

Schwartz, Benjamin Isadore. *The World of Thought in Ancient China*. Cambridge, MA: Belknap Press, 1985.

Shun, Kwong-loi. "Jen and Li in the Analects." *Philosophy East and West* 43 (1993): 457–479.

Shun, Kwong-loi. *Mencius and Early Chinese Thought*. Stanford, CA: Stanford University Press, 1997.

Slingerland, Edward. *Effortless Action: Wu-Wei as Conceptual Metaphor and Spiritual Ideal in Early China*. New York: Oxford University Press, 2003.

Van Norden, Bryan, "Mengzi and Xunzi: Two Views of Human Agency." *International Philosophical Quarterly* 32 (1992): 161–184.

Watson, Burton, tr. *Basic Writings of Mo Tzu, Hsün Tzu, and Han Fei Tzu*. New York: Columbia University Press, 1967.

Watson, Burton, tr. *The Complete Works of Chuang Tzu*. New York: Columbia University Press, 1968.

Wong, David B. "Is There a Distinction between Reason and Emotion in Mencius?" and a reply to a commentary by Craig Ihara. *Philosophy East and West* 41 (1991): 31–44, 55–58.

Wong, David B. "Reasons and Analogical Reasoning in Mengzi." In *Essays on the Moral Philosophy of Mengzi*, edited by Xiusheng Liu and Philip J. Ivanhoe. Indianapolis, IN: Hackett, 2002.

Wong, David B. "Rights and Community in Confucianism." In *Confucian Ethics: A Comparative Study of Self, Autonomy, and Community*, edited by Kwong-loi Shun and David B. Wong. New York: Cambridge University Press, 2004.

Wong, David B. "Universalism versus Love with Distinctions: An Ancient Debate Revived." *Journal of Chinese Philosophy* 16 (1989): 252–272.

Wong, David B. "Xunzi on Moral Motivation." In *Chinese Language, Thought, and Culture: Nivison and his Critics*, edited by Philip J. Ivanhoe. Chicago: Open Court, 1996.

Wong, David B. "Zhuangzi and the Obsession with Being Right." *History of Philosophy Quarterly* 22 (2005): 91–107.

David B. Wong (2005)

LANGUAGE AND LOGIC

This entry focuses on concepts, issues, and themes of Chinese philosophy that involve language in view of its relation to reality, thought, and logic; the discussion is thus arranged on three central concerns in this regard: the issue of the relation between language and reality; the issue of the relation between language and thought; and the issue of the relation between language and logic. This entry is neither a historical study nor a comprehensive survey of the relevant ideas of thinkers from different historical periods, although there will inevitably be references to them. It is known that the term "logic" has been ambiguously and vaguely used; in this entry on language and logic in Chinese philosophy, first, by "logic" is meant primarily two things: (1) logical *reasoning* as embedded or expressed in natural (Chinese) language; and (2) the syntactic-semantic structure of Chinese language that underlies the surface grammar of Chinese language. The author neither pretend nor plan to discuss them exhaustively but to the extent that the issues to be addressed bear on Chinese philosophy and/or that the issues to be addressed are philosophically interesting. In this sense, this entry is not a discussion of logic or logical thought on their own in the history of Chinese thought, no matter how the term "logic" is understood.

LANGUAGE AND REALITY

The issue of the relation between language and reality has been one classical concern in philosophical study of language concerning what language is about, in Chinese tradition as well as in Western tradition. The classical issue emerged in Chinese tradition in terms of the issue of *ming-shi* (*ming* means "name" while *shi* means "reality") in its broad sense. In this part is discussed how some representative approaches in Chinese tradition explore four aspects of the issue: first, the issue of the issue of *zheng-*

ming (name rectification), the issue of reference, the issue of whether language can capture reality, and the issue of the relation between truth concern and *dao* concern.

NAME AND ACTUALITY: NAME-RECTIFICATION APPROACH. In the pre-*Qin* period three figures put forward their doctrines of name rectification: Confucius (551–479 BCE), Gongsun Long (320–250 BCE), and Xun Zi (298–238 BCE). The points of Confucius' and Gongsun Long's accounts are here rendered more philosophically interesting, though Xun Zi suggested a much more systematical account of names. The focus is on the first two due to space.

It is known that Confucius' major concern is with moral and social issues. His doctrine of name rectification serves his major concern. Nevertheless, the focus here is on those interesting points suggested in this doctrine from the point of view of philosophy of language. The passages in the *Analects* that are directly related to the issue of name rectification are three: 13.3, 12.11, 12.17, of which I make full citation to give a complete account (my translations).

> 13.3: Zi-lu asked, "If the ruler of the *Wei* State has you in charge of the state administration to governing the state and the people, what would be the priority of your administration?" Confucius replied, "It would surely be the rectification of names." Zi-lu wondered, "Is it so? What a pedantic way! Why is there need to bring in the rectification of names?" Confucius said, "You, how unenlightened you are! When a *junzi* (an enlightened gentleman) is ignorant of something, he is not expected to offer any opinion on it. If names are not rectified, then what is said in speech would not be in accord with things as they are (supposed to be); if what is said in speech would not be in accord with things as they are (supposed to be), then what is [supposed] to be done by using words would not be accomplished; if what is [supposed] to be done by using words is not be accomplished, then the [adequate] socially established ritual rules as manifested via ceremonies and music will not implemented; if these [adequate] socially established ritual rules will not implemented, then punishment will not be just; if punishment would not be just, then the people will not know where to move forward. Therefore, a *junzi* should give names only to those that surely can be adequately delivered in speech and deliver in speech only what surely can be adequately carried out in practice."
>
> 12.17: Jikangzi asked Confucius about governing. Confucius replied, "To govern is to rectify. If you lead the people by rectifying yourself, who would dare not to be rectified?"
>
> 12.11: Duke Jing of the Qi State asked Confucius about governing. Confucius replied, "Let the ruler [those that bear the title 'ruler' in the society] be the ruler [become what is prescriptively symbolized by the name 'ruler'], the minister be the minister, the father be the father, and the son be the son." The Duke said, "Excellent! Surely, if a ruler is not the ruler, a minister not the minister, a father not the father, and a son not the son, then, even if there are all the grain, how could I get to eat it?"

Confucius' doctrine of name rectification might as well be another way of presenting his teachings on moral cultivation and adequate governing: the teaching delivered in 12.17 is to rectify yourself to fit what those terms that signify your ranks, duties, functions and moral attributes mean (12:17), which amounts to sageliness within, while the teaching delivered in 12.11 is to participate in rectifying others to fit what those terms that signify their ranks, duties, functions, and moral attributes mean (12:11), which amounts to kingliness without. However, what really interests us here is some, explicitly or implicitly, suggested general point concerning the relation between language and reality. Let us start with an apparent puzzle: There appears to be a tension between the suggested two kinds of rectification approaches. On the one hand, the trademark title of this doctrine is "name rectification," and, as highlighted in 13.3, Confucius emphasizes the significance of name rectification. Nevertheless, on the other hand, 12.17 and 12.11 indicate that what is rectified is actually the persons who bear the (social-title) name. Which one is the primary goal while which serves as means? What is the due relation between the two kinds of rectification? Why doesn't Confucius directly emphasize rectifying the moral agent?

The reason seems to be this. To rectify the person (self and others) for the sake of self cultivation and of social reform, there needs a standard or norm that per se needs language as means or even as medium for the sake of its being carried out, communicated and passed on. Actually this is a two-level rectification process with the goal of rectifying the agent into a certain prescriptively specified person. The first step is to take a semantic accent strategy: instead of directly talking about how to rectify the agent, it is to first rectify her (social-title) name under examination through assigning it a certain due prescriptive content which specifies the standard or norm to be met by any eligible referents of the name and thus gives the primary identity condition of such referents. The second step is to rectify the agent based on the primary identity condition of the expected referents of the name that has been established in the preceding semantic accent strategy.

An interesting point concern the relation between name and actuality, which is implicitly suggested by Confucius' account of name rectification is this. The due identity condition of actuality of a thing (say, a ruler) is not simply its status-quo happening or current appearance (say, the ruler-title-bearing person); rather, it consists in realization of its due place without transgressing its due scope (say, the person who really possesses the moral character that is expected for the ruler); name rectification will play its important or even indispensable role through the name carrying out and delivering the norm which specifies such a due place of the thing that is normatively denoted by the name (say, through rectifying the name "ruler").

If Confucius' account only implicitly suggests the foregoing point concerning social-title names and their due referents, one of Gongsun Long's contributions in this regard lies in his explicitly making the point in more general terms concerning any name and its related actuality and in a more sophisticated way. In this essay "*Ming-Shi-Lun*" (On name and actuality), Gongsun Long explains, "What the heaven and earth produce are things. When a thing goes its own way without transgressing its limit, it achieves its actuality (*shi*); when its actuality goes its own way without being out of its track, it achieves its due place (*wei*). If a thing goes beyond its due place, it is in wrong place; if a thing is in its due place, it is in right place. One is expected to rectify a thing in wrong place into right place; one is not expected to challenge a thing in due place by virtue of it being in wrong place. The rectification of a thing is the rectification of its actuality; the rectification of its actuality is implemented through the rectification of its name. Once its name is rectified, the standards for 'that' and 'this' will be formed up and stabilized" (my translation). Gongsun Long here emphasizes that a thing needs to go its own way without transgressing its limit to achieve its actuality; he further stresses that, once a thing achieves its actuality, there remains an issue of how to keep its actuality in due place; he explicitly points out that the so-called name rectification lies in rectifying the actuality of a thing in its due place through rectifying the due content of its name which identifies such due place and thus gives due identity condition for the thing and its actuality.

THE ISSUE OF REFERENCE: PURPOSE-PERSPECTIVE-SENSITIVITY APPROACH. But the above Confucius' and Gongsun Long's views on the relation of name and actuality via their accounts of name rectification would raise one general question concerning the issue of reference: whether, and in which way, the subject would contribute to the identity of a thing when she refers to the thing. Though with their distinctive backgrounds and concerns, Gongsun Long, the Mohist, and Zhuang Zi are kindred in spirit on this issue, taking essentially the same approach to the effect that an referring agent's referring action, which involves her purpose and focus, assigns a certain identity to the thing referred to, or specifies some aspect(s) of the referent as its identity (or multiple identities) and that, sensitive to one's purpose and focus, one is entitled to make her perspective shift in one's referring practice to focus on some other aspect of the referent as its identity. This approach might as well be called the "purpose-perspective-sensitivity approach." This section will focus on Gongsun Long's account and then briefly present Zhuang Zi's view; the Mohist relevant point will be addressed when the Mohist view on reasoning is discussed in the "Language and Logic" part of this essay.

In his essay "*Zhi-Wu-Lun*" (On referring to things), Gongsun Long emphasizes "No things [that are identified or named as things] are not what are referred to [by linguistic names] … if there is no referring in the world, nothing can be called a 'thing.' If without referring [names], can anything in the world be called 'what is referring to'?" (my translation). Gongsun Long's point here is that the relevant contributing elements involved in the subject's act of referring via a name (such as what is the subject's purpose, which aspect of the referent the subject intends to seek or focus on) make their intrinsic contributions to identity of the referent of the name. This point is also explicitly and emphatically addressed in his essay, "*Bai-Ma-Lun*" (On the white horse), as indicated in the passage "What makes a white horse a horse is their same [common] aspect given that it is what is sought. If what is sought is the common aspect, a white horse would be not distinct from (*bu-yi*) a horse [in regard to the common aspect]. If what is sought is not some distinct but the same aspect, then why is it that yellow and black horses meet what is sought in one case but not in the other? It is evident that the two cases are distinct" (my translation).

This crucial passage gives the fundamental rationale behind a number of Gongsun Long's arguments for the thesis "[the] white horse [is] not [the] horse." The statement "The white horse is not the horse" is just another way to say in our ordinary discourse "The white horse has its distinct aspect which the horse does not [necessarily] have," while the statement "The white horse is the horse" is just another way to say in our ordinary discourse "The white horse has its common aspect which the horse [necessarily] does have." Each of the two can be right, depending on which aspect of the white horse the referring subject is seeking or focusing on and thus refers to concerning the identity of the white horse. In so doing, she alerts us to avoiding the danger of over-assimilating distinctions, especially when the distinctive aspects need to be emphatically focused on.

Zhuang Zi proceeds essentially in the same direction on the issue (*The Zhuang-Zi*, Inner Chapter 3 "*Yong-Sheng-Zhu*"). Given an ox as whole already there, now what is its identity? How should one refer to it in terms of language? How should one identify it? As something exclusively determined by its "essence" or as a pack of flesh and bones? It seems to Zhuang Zi that, based on one's specific purpose, one can legitimately refer an ox as a pack of flesh and bones. One can say that, from the Zhuang Zi style view of the philosophy of language, the relation between language and an object in the world is not one-to-one relation but many-to-one relation: There are multiple referring expressions that refer to various genuine aspects of the same object. Depending on one's purpose, one is entitled to take a certain perspective to focus on one aspect of the object and thus identify the object as what the referring expression capturing that aspect would tell. What is important is that these distinctive referring expressions refer to different aspects of the same object, the ox as a whole, which are metaphysically complementary to each other.

THE *DAO* CONCERN IN CHINESE PHILOSOPHY AND ITS LANGUAGE ENGAGEMENT. A classical issue in Chinese tradition is whether, through language engagement, we can capture and deliver the ultimate reality, which the Chinese term "*dao*" primarily means (that is, the so-called metaphysical *dao*). The term "language engagement (with an ultimate concern)" means any reflective endeavor to capture (reach or characterize) what is ultimately concerned through language. Let us have a case examination of the opening statement, *Dao-ke-dao-fei-chang-Dao*, of Chapter 1, of the daoist classic the *Dao-De-Jing* whose legendary author is Lao Zi. For one thing, this passage has been considered to give a representative or classical presentation of the daoist attitude toward the relation between language and the world; for another thing, many subsequent interpreters in Chinese tradition resorts to this passage to make their points in this regard.

One standard, and also most prevalent, interpretative translation (Creel 1983) of this passage is this: "The *dao* that can be told of [in language] is not the eternal *dao*" (Chan 1963, p.139). According to this interpretation, what the first statement reveals is a fundamental daoist insight that is strikingly similar to that of Wittgenstein's well-known idea about the spoken and the unspoken: Language expressions or formulations cannot really capture what those expressions or formulations aim to say; any language engagement is doomed to fail to capture the genuine *dao*; the genuine *dao* has to be captured in a way that is beyond language; contemplation of the *dao* in silence requires sharply distinguishing the eternal *dao* from what can be formulated or captured in (or by) language, for the two are simply opposed to each other. This standard interpretation is partially correct: The *dao* that has been characterized in terms of language does not exhaust, and is not identical to, the genuine *dao*.

Although this interpretative translation has been circulated for a long time and does deliver part of the daoist message, it has been challenged whether it completely captures and delivers Lao Zi's genuine point as a whole in the context of the *Dao-De-Jing*. It is not merely because this standard interpretative translation neither syntactically nor semantically captures the Chinese original but also because it seems to miss some important point of Daoism in this regard. Another interpretation (Mou 2000) gives the following interpretative translation of the opening statement: "The *Dao* can be reached in language [*Dao-ke-dao*], but the *Dao* that has been characterized in language is not identical with, or does not exhaust, the eternal *Dao* [*fei-chang-Dao*]." Though partially agreeing to the first interpretation, this interpretation differs from the first one in this significant aspect: The *dao* that have been captured in language is not bogus *dao* but still parts of the genuine *dao*; and this understanding of the partial *dao* in terms of language engagement would significantly contribute to our capturing the *dao* as a whole. This is based on one crucial characteristic of the metaphysical *dao*: The metaphysical *dao* as unifying force that runs through the whole universe is not something separate or beyond and above all those finite things in the world that are particular and concrete; particular things in the universe, *wan-wu* (ten-thousand things), which obtain the power from the *dao*, are considered as manifestations of the metaphysical *dao* and individualized-particularized *daos*; the relation between the metaphysical *dao* and its manifestations in *wan-wu* is essentially *yin-yang* complementary; *dao* and *wan-wu* are interdependent, interpenetrating, interactive and correlative.

Epistemologically speaking, and from the point of view of language engagement, the metaphysical *dao* thus can be somehow captured through our language and our understanding of *wan-wu*. In this way, the point of the second interpretation is this: Instead of indiscriminately giving a negative claim against any language engagement with the ultimate concern, in the opening statement, Lao Zi reveals a two-sided transcendental insight which, on the one hand, positively affirms the role of the language-engaged finite point of view in capturing the ultimate concern and, on the other hand, alerts us to the limitation of the finite point of view and emphasizes the transcendental dimension of the *dao*.

It is noted that, in this regard, A. C. Graham's view seems to be much more moderate than the foregoing standard interpretation when he explains why there is the trouble with words: "The trouble with words is not that they do not fit at all but they always fit imperfectly; they can help us towards the Way, but only if each formulation in its inadequacy is balanced by the opposite which diverges in the other direction" (Graham 1989, p. 219). Nevertheless, the above second interpretation is more moderate than Graham's to this extent: It is not the case that the language engagement *always* fits *imperfectly*. That really depends on which part, dimension, or layer of the *dao* is set out to be captured in language engagement and on what kind of language function is at issue.

First, if a language engagement does not pretend to be exhaustive or conclusive regarding the *dao* but rather takes a finite point of view, it is reasonable to say that what has been captured in language in that case does fit adequately. When a language engagement takes a finite point of view, what is needed is not to reject such a finite point of view per se, but to hold the transcendental insight simultaneously, which would alert us to the limitation of the finite point of view and its due scope. Second, capturing something in language does not necessarily mean imposing a definition or formulation with a certain fixed format, meaning or usage. For instance, in contrast to *mere* description and descriptive designation, rigid designation via direct reference is one way to reach the genuine *dao* as a whole, as Lao Zi's own language-engagement practice illustrates (for example, Lao Zi did somehow successfully use the term *dao* to designate the *dao* as a whole).

TRUTH CONCERN AND *DAO* CONCERN. It seems that the truth concern is a dominant concern in Western tradition while the *dao* concern is a dominant concern in Chinese tradition. What is the relation between the truth concern and the *dao* concern? Are they dramatically and totally different reflective concerns in philosophy? (Given that the term "dao" primarily means the metaphysical *dao* concerning the way of the world as it is, especially in Daoism, and that any reflective concern, including the *dao* concern, that is open to criticism and self-criticism needs to be characterized in terms of language, and also given that one important aspect of the truth concern is about the relation between language and reality, this is a significant topic concerning the relation between language and reality at the meta-philosophical level.)

Although, as this author sees it, a silent majority of philosophers who are familiar with Chinese philosophy have considered both concerns essentially in accordance with each other, some scholars argue otherwise. There are two representative views. One takes it that, in contrast to what is called "Western sentential philosophy," the dominant portion of the classical Chinese philosophy is a non-sentential philosophy that is not essentially related to those concepts that are intrinsically connected with sentential philosophy like proposition (or semantic content), truth and belief (Hansen 1985/2003). This argument might as well be called the "no-sentential-concern argument." Another view takes it that the significant part and the primary concern of the classical Chinese philosophy have been considered be its moral concern and its ethical accounts; and the moral concern is not with how to understand impersonal material world but with the ethical constitution in the human society. In this way, it is not the by-default account of truth (the correspondence account) but a pragmatic account of truth that plays the role (Hall 1997, 2001). This argument might as well be called the "pragmatic truth argument."

In contrast to the silent majority's presupposed position, these views have been voiced prominently and loudly especially in West and thus have left on many who are not familiar with Chinese philosophy the impression to the effect that there is no truth concern in Chinese philosophy and that the truth concern in Western tradition and the *dao* concern in Chinese tradition are dramatically different from each other. This impression is incorrect at least to the following extent: First, it is highly controversial; second, to many experts, it is not so. But their views deserve careful examination, and the involved issue deserves a systematic discussion, instead of being silently dismissed. Though it is not a place to give such a detailed discussion here, I intend to use the following strategy to assist the interested reader in examining the issue: this entry briefly addresses a number of basic things, to which one needs to pay due attention when one intends to explore the issue and give adequate evaluation of the competing views, but which might be ignored by some advocates of the above mentioned challenges.

Let us start with our pre-theoretic, or "folk," understanding of truth: A true (linguistic) sentence or statement (or the thought/belief it delivers) describes or characterizes (extra-linguistic) things as they are. When the term "our" is used here, its reference by no means includes only people in West but surely also includes people in Chinese speaking regions, now and in the past, no matter how such a pre-theoretic understanding has been indicated in their natural languages—whether it is expressed by a unified single term in a phonetic language (like "truth" in English), or it is expressed via various multiple-character phrases in the Chinese ideographic language (such as *shi-shi-qiu-shi*, meaning "seeking what things actually are," or *qiu-dao*, meaning "pursuing the *dao*/way of the world"). For convenience, this pre-theoretic understanding of truth is sometimes called our pre-theoretical "correspondence" understanding to highlight the accordance relation of our thought or our language with (the *dao*/way of) the world (including the human society) in which truth under such an understanding consists. Now the reader can think about this: Given that those approaches in Chinese philosophy as discussed in the preceding sections of this part are all distinctive illustrations of the *dao*-concern on several significant fronts and thus that all of them are thus intended to capture and deliver extra-linguistic things as they are, are those approaches dramatically separate and different from the reflective truth concern that is based on the foregoing pre-theoretic understanding of truth?

At this point three notes are due. First, the metaphysical commitment of our pre-theoretic understanding of truth per se as presented above is minimal: It does not commit to any ad hoc metaphysical criterion for what counts as reality, and it is compatible with a variety of ontological accounts of extra-linguistic things (say, snow's being white). For example, a *realist* pre-theoretic "correspondence" understanding of truth is actually a *combination* of our pre-theoretic understanding *of truth and a realist* ontological understanding or explanation of what counts as, say, snow's being white. (In this way, any argument that resorts either to the fact that some specific version of the truth concern in West is combined with some unfavorable metaphysical explanation or to the fact that a certain metaphysical account of the *dao* is so different from some representative metaphysical understanding of what counts as reality cannot automatically imply that the *dao* concern in Chinese tradition and the truth concern in Western tradition are dramatically different.)

Second, it is arguably right that our pre-theoretical "correspondence" understanding of truth plays its important and enormous explanatory role both in our daily lives and in our reflective lives (including philosophical inquiries). In most cases, whether for the sake of psychological satisfaction, intellectual enjoyment, scientific honesty, legal obligation or success of our actions or even for its own sake, we intend to understand what really happen(ed) around us rather than illusions, we hope that others tell us truths instead of lies or mere wishful thinking, we want to know those beliefs, thoughts or statements that are true. Moreover, in almost all of cases, we (even for those who advocate some understandings of truth that clearly revise or go against our pre-theoretic understanding of truth) seriously intend that the genuine contents of our own thoughts and claims to be delivered (or represented) to, and understood by, others "correspondently"—or without distorting or losing their original contents; we intend to behave in a way that does not go against the laws or *dao*/way of the world. In this sense and to this extent, it is not merely the case that, in many situations, with such a pre-theoretic understanding of truth, we consciously pursue truths; rather, it is a stronger case: whether consciously or unconsciously, we unavoidably presuppose our pre-theoretic "correspondence" understanding of truth both in our ordinary folk talks and in our reflective talks including philosophical discourses, either as one central explanatory norm to regulate and explain the purpose of our thoughts and actions or as one important explanatory basis to explain some other significant things in our folk and reflective lives.

Third, there is the distinction between truth nature and truth criterion: The former is examined by asking what truth is, what truth consist in or what it is for a statement (or belief) to be true, while the latter is examined by asking what is the criterion by which one can identify, judge and distinguish true statements from false ones. Our pre-theoretic understanding of truth is about the truth nature instead of truth criterion. Actually, the foregoing three notes indicate three significant respects, among others, in which one can critically examine the relation between the truth concern and the *dao* concern in Chinese tradition as well as the nature and due functions of major competing theoretic accounts of truth in the Western tradition. (For further discussion of the issue, see Mou 2006.)

LANGUAGE AND THOUGHT

Besides the issue of the relation between language and reality, another important concern of philosophical reflection on language is the issue of the relation between language and thought. This entry will discuss this issue as explored in Chinese tradition in two fronts: (1) the issue of the relation between speech and ideas in mind in regard to whether and to what extent the former can capture and deliver the latter; (2) a reflective concern with how the structure of Chinese language bear on the orientation of philosophical thought in Chinese tradition.

SPEECH AND IDEAS: FOUR APPROACHES. The relation between speech and ideas in mind is one central concern in the so-called *yan-yi-zhi-bian*, that is, the debate on the relation between speech (*yan*) and meaning (*yi*, in the sense to be explained), which originated in the *Wei-Jin* period; but the following discussion will not limited to a number of representative approaches in this debate during that time but incorporates some other representative approach in Chinese tradition. (Note that, though using the ready-made translation "speech and meaning" of *yan-yi* here for the sake of convenience, and though *yi* in this debate also means *dao*-like principles in its metaphysical sense and the human understanding of them, by *yan-yi* is meant "speech and ideas in mind" in this context.) In the following, four representative approaches are focused on: (1) the "meaning-delivery-beyond-speech-capacity" approach; (2) "forgetting-speech-once-achieving-meaning" approach; (3) the "meaning-delivery-within-speech-capacity" approach; (4) the context-sensitivity approach. The first three approaches are three representative approaches in the *yan-yi-zhi-bian*during the *Wei-Jin* period, though the first two are actually kindred in spirit (see Chen 2004 for a recent discussion; my interpretation of the third approach is somewhat different than his), while the fourth one is my interpretative elaboration of the relevant points of Ji Zang's Buddhist Middle-Way doctrine of double truth.

The "meaning-delivery-beyond-speech-capacity" approach was advocated by Ji Kan (223–262). This approach's main arguments are these. First, some of our ideas in mind are so delicate and sophisticated that speech simply cannot capture them. Second, our ideas in mind are dynastic while speech is static, and therefore speech cannot fully capture ideas in mind. The "forgetting-speech-once-achieving-meaning" approach was advocated by Wang Bi (226–249). This approach acknowledges a certain important role played by speech as a means to achieve meaning. For example, when one intends to understand some other's ideas or when one intends to have one's own ideas to be understood by some other, one has to rely on speech to understand them or express them.

But this approach still takes it that eventually speech would hinder one's understanding ideas per se and so that one should forget speech once achieving the ideas. This line of thought sounds like a Wittgenstein's well-known metaphor to the effect that, once one climbs up on the building by means of a ladder, one needs to discard the ladder to keep oneself in the high position. It is noted that, though the first and second approaches have their differences in emphasis and focus, they share the basic positions concerning the relation between speech and ideas. Both think that ideas are primary while speech is only secondary, that ideas and speech can, and should, be separate and that at most speech serves merely as a means and makes no contribution to the constitution of thought and ideas.

The "meaning-delivery-within-speech-capacity" approach is suggested by Ouyang Jian (?–300). This view has been ignored for a long time and not a strong voice in the traditional Chinese philosophy in contrast to the mainstream approach on this issue; but some of the points of this approach deserve a close examination. Ouyang argues that:

> Surely one can achieve a principle in the form of ideas in one's mind; however, without language [as media and as means], those ideas cannot exist in a smooth and coherent way. Given that a thing has been stabilized in a certain definite aspect, without language [in terms of name], one cannot identify and thus distinguish the thing [in view of the stabilized definite aspect] from the others. If one's ideas cannot exist in a smooth and coherent way through the role of language, they cannot hold tight in connection with each other; if the thing cannot be identified and distinguished in terms of name, the distinctive ideas and insights cannot be shown evidently. But, as a matter of fact, the distinctive ideas can be shown evidently in terms of distinctive names, and speech holds ideas tight in connection and in a smooth and coherent way. Let us see why it is so. It is not because a thing has its ready-made fixed name; it is not because a principle has its fixed unchangeable language

> expression. The reason is this. When people intend to capture things as they are in a distinguishing way, they give them distinctive names. When people intend to declare their distinctive ideas, they employ distinctive language expressions that fit distinctive ideas. Names [and/or their meanings] change in accordance with the transformation of their named things; while speeches [and/or their meanings] change in accordance with the change of the contents of ideas. It is just like echo responds to sound, shadows attaches to body; they do not exist as two separate things. If they are not separate things, then speech can fully capture ideas; this is why I hold on my position.
>
> (*YI-WEN-LEI-JU*, VOL.19)
> (MY TRANSLATION)

There are two interesting points that seem to really engage with the two preceding views. First, speech is not merely a means but also a medium of ideas at least in regard to its contribution to their internal coherent construction. Second, as far as speech as means is concerned, though speech is relatively static and stable, that certainly does not mean that language is just as static as a dead thing; language itself also keep changing responding to the change of what it is to express. This is true as evidenced by the history of the development of natural languages. Although Ouyang's first point is still quite vaguely made and expressed, his position makes distinct contribution on the issue.

The fourth approach, the context-sensitivity approach, suggested by Ji Zang (540–623), a significant figure of Chinese Buddhism who elaborated and systematized *Mahayana* doctrine of Buddhism. Ji Zang's doctrine of double truth has interesting implications from the point of view of philosophy of language. First, a brief outline of the major ideas of his double-truth account. It seems to Ji Zang that there are two kinds of truth, truth in the common sense and truth in the higher sense, on each of three varying levels; what is the truth in the higher sense at a lower level becomes merely truth in the common sense at the higher level. At the first level, the common people take all things as really being and know nothing about their non-being, while the Buddhas have told them that actually all things are non-being and empty. At the second level, to say that all things are being is one-sided, but to say that all things are non-being is also one-sided; at this level, the Buddhas would say that what is being is simultaneously what is non-being. At the third level, saying that the middle truth consists in what is not one-sided means to make distinctions, and so this is merely a common sense truth; the higher truth consists in saying that all distinctions are themselves one-sided, and the middle path is neither one-sided nor not-one-sided. That amounts to denying the adequacy of any speech to capture the truth in the higher sense at this highest level, that is, the highest truth, which needs to be contemplated in silence.

Although Ji Zang as a Buddhist thinker still maintains that the highest truth cannot be captured and delivered via language but has to be contemplated in silence, but he emphasizes that all those truths, both in the common sense and in the higher sense and both at the first level and at the second level, can be captured and delivered in terms of language that involves relatively stabilized and fixed conceptual distinctions. With his explicitly distinguishing truths in distinct senses and at distinctive levels and acknowledging important role played by language at the first and second levels, Ji Zang's general point is philosophically interesting: we need to have it sensitive to the context whether speech can effectively capture and deliver the truths, that is, our understandings and comprehensions of the world.

There are two notes concerning evaluation of the foregoing views. First, to evaluate the ancient thinkers' views here, we indeed need to pay attention to those still valuable thoughts; on the other hand, we also need to note that one of the reasons why those ancient thinkers held that speech is not able to fully capture meaning is this: some conceptual and explanatory resources in contemporary philosophy that are available to us to capture and deliver some sophisticated ideas and thoughts were simply unavailable to those ancient thinkers; so there is no wonder why they felt the linguistic means then available to them were not sufficient to capture some complicated thoughts and ideas. Second, as emphasized at the outset, the term *yi* in the *yan-yi-zhi-bian* (the debate on the relation between speech and meaning) has its much wider coverage than what the term "thought" in the contemporary debate on the relation between language and thought is to cover: the latter primarily mean propositional thoughts while the former's coverage includes non-propositional ideas, emotions and some characteristic existential experience; a claim putting into doubt or denying the capacity of speech to capture such non-propositional mental things could be compatible with the positions by those whose primary concern is with the relation between language and propositional thoughts.

THE ISSUE OF THE STRUCTURE OF CHINESE LANGUAGE AND REFLECTIVE WAY OF THINKING IN CHINESE PHILOSOPHY. It seems that certain characteristic features of Chinese language influence or encourage some orientations in the Chinese (folk and reflective) way of thinking. Due to the topic, the focus will be on such influence on reflective inquiry in Chinese philosophy. Nevertheless, the reflective way of thinking is not separate from, but largely in accordance with the folk way of thinking via some reasonable pre-theoretic intuitive understanding on those issues that deserve further reflection.

We start with some known facts about certain characteristic features of Chinese ideographic language and Western phonetic language (say, English) in comparison that might, to some extent and in a certain scope, reflect some distinctive orientations or tendencies in the ways of thinking of the two linguistic communities. We know how we as English speakers give our names and addresses: We first give our given names (thus being called "first name") and last give our family names (thus being called "last name"). However, in Chinese, the family name goes first (thus the family name is really the first name in Chinese way) and then the given name (for example, the real order of my whole name in Chinese is "Mou Bo" instead of "Bo Mou"). For, in philosophical terms, the family (name) is both metaphysically and logically prior to the individual (name), and the former provides a necessary holistic background for understanding the latter. By the same token, in contrast to its way in English, a mailing address (taking mine as an example) should go this way when delivered in Chinese: "USA, California, San Jose, San Jose State University, Department of Philosophy, Mou Bo"; that is, the larger thing goes first while the smaller thing next. It is arguably right that the structure of Chinese language in this respect to some extent bears on the orientation of the way of thinking of the Chinese people as a whole.

(There are two notes. First, when the word "bear on" is used instead of "influence" alone, what is meant is that the relation between the former and the latter is bi-directional instead of one-directional. The actual situation might be this: When the way of the Chinese language originally formed up, it was influenced by the way of thinking of the people around that time; on the other hand, when such a way has become relatively stable and been followed and passed on generation by generation, it has conversely influences the way of thinking of the future Chinese language speakers to some extent. Second, the foregoing influence certainly implies neither that the people speaking in Chinese tend to put the family/the collective interest first nor that, say, English speakers tend to do otherwise. Even if such a distinctive order of which one is mentioned first, next, and last indeed influence which one would first go in mind at some level, surely one can say that, though saying things in a certain order, I actually think about all the involved things once for all simultaneously. Exactly how it would happen if any has yet to be carefully examined.)

Now, through a representative case analysis, we examine how the structure of Chinese language bears on the orientation of reflective inquiries in Chinese philosophy through one case analysis. The Platonic one-many problem has been a long-term issue in the Western philosophical tradition. The problem begins with the following observation: objects around us share features with other objects; and many particular individuals, say, horses bear the same name "horse." The Platonic one-many problem presupposes that there is one single universal entity which is common or strictly identical across all those particular concrete horses and by virtue of which many individual horses bear the same name "horse"; the single universal entity is labeled "horseness." The Platonic one-many problem is how to characterize the status of universals and the ways by which particulars share universals. However, there seems to be one puzzle: why the classical Platonic one-many problem in the Western philosophical tradition has not been consciously posed in the Chinese philosophical tradition and why, generally speaking, classical Chinese philosophers seem less interested in debating the relevant ontological issues. One suspects that the structures (the surface and deep ones together) and uses of different languages might play their roles in pushing philosophical theorization in different directions; the ways of speaking and writing of the Chinese language might somehow reveal and reflect Chinese folk ideology and then influence the ways in which certain philosophical questions are posed and certain ontological insights are formed.

The problem of relating Chinese thought to the structure and functions of the Chinese language has for generations tantalized sinologists and those philosophers who are concerned with the problem. Nevertheless, in the last two decade, some significant progress has been made in this regard. Chad Hansen (1983) advances a novel and provocative theory about the nature of the classical Chinese language. The central thesis of Hansen's theory is his mass-noun hypothesis. Its main ideas are these: (1) the (folk) semantics of Chinese nouns are like those of mass-nouns (i.e., those nouns referring to the so-called interpenetrating stuffs, like the nouns "water" and "snow"), and naming in Chinese is not grounded on the existence of, or roles for, abstract entities (either on the ontic level or on the conceptual level) but rather on finding "boundaries" between things; (2) influenced by the mass-noun semantics, the classical Chinese semantic theorists and ontological theorists ew words in ways that are natural to view mass nouns rather than count nouns, and Chinese theorists tend to organize the objects in the world in a mereological stuff-whole model of reality (the term "mereology," in its technical sense, means the (mathematical) theory of the relation of parts to whole).

In this way, according to Hansen, the language theory of classical Chinese philosophers differs fundamentally from the language theory of Western philosophy. This hypothesis has been challenged mainly in three ways. One way is to challenge the mass-stuff model from the perspective of a holographic process ontology (Cheng 1987, Hall and Ames, 1987).

Although some scholars also emphasize the implicit ontology of Chinese language, they focus on the case analysis of the typical philosophical nouns or terms, such as *tai-ji*, *wu*, *yin-yang*, *wu-xing*, which constitute the basic lexico (vocabulary) of Chinese metaphysical systems as found in the writings of the early Confucianists, the early daoist, and Neo-Confucianists. They argue that those nouns stand for interpenetrating wholes and parts in a quite different sense from Hansen's: the individual things behave in the on-going patterns and in the events or processes of interaction among them, and the universe behaves as an organic whole with parts exemplifying the structure of the whole; they claim that Chinese words in general share this ontological feature of combining universality and particularity, abstractness and concreteness, activity and the result of activity. In this way, some writers (Hall and Ames, 1987) prefer to consider the relations of "parts" and "wholes" in terms of the model of "focus" and "field" and take Chinese ontological views as holographic rather than mereological.

Another way is to directly challenge Hansen's mass noun hypothesis, arguing that there is a clear grammatical distinction in classical Chinese between count nouns and other nouns (Harbsmeier 1989, 1991). Claiming that there is a clear grammatical distinction in classical Chinese between count nouns and other nouns (generic nouns and mass nouns), Harbsmeier (1991) insists that the mass-noun hypothesis is "historically implausible and grammatically quite wrong-headed." However, as Hansen himself emphasizes (1992), his mass-noun hypothesis is not a syntactic claim that classical Chinese nouns have mass-noun grammar but a semantic interpretive hypothesis that the semantics of Chinese nouns may be like those of mass nouns, and classical Chinese theorists view words in ways that are natural to view mass nouns. So it seems to Hansen that Harbsmeier systematically confuses syntax and semantics and misinterprets his semantic hypothesis. Although one can agree with Hansen at this point, Harbsmeier's criticism is not irrelevant in the following sense. It seems that Harbsmeier insists that his alleged distinction between count nouns and other nouns is not merely grammatical but also semantic (or takes the grammatical difference in question to have semantic implications); Hansen thus needs to deal with the linguistic (semantic) evidence against his hypothesis that the semantics of classical Chinese nouns may be like those of mass-nouns.

The foregoing first challenge from the point of view of a holographic process ontology could be compatible with Hansen's approach; for the process ontology is essentially compatible with the ontological position, a kind of nominalism, presupposed or implied by Hansen's mereological mass-stuff hypothesis. Hansen's view is given in a semantic perspective that can be compatible with a pragmatic perspective with its focus-field orientation. I have responded to Hansen's view in a similar semantic perspective and within the same mereological-analysis track. But, disagreeing with Hansen's mass-noun hypothesis, I suggest and argue for a collective-noun hypothesis (Mou 1999). Its main ideas are these: (1) Chinese common nouns typically function, semantically and syntactically, in the way collective-nouns (that is, those nouns that denote collections of individual things, like the English nouns "people" or "cattle") function, and the folk semantics of Chinese nouns are like those of collective-nouns; (2) their implicit ontology is a mereological ontology of collection-of-individuals both with the part-whole structure and with the member-class structure, which does justice to the role of abstraction at the conceptual level; and (3) encouraged and shaped by the folk semantics of Chinese nouns, the classical Chinese theorists of language take this kind of mereological nominalism for granted; as a result, the classical Platonic one-many problem in the Western philosophical tradition has not been consciously posed in the Chinese philosophical tradition, and classical Chinese philosophers seem less interested in debating the relevant ontological issues. This mereological collection-of-individuals model of reality would provide a more reasonable interpretation of the semantics of classical Chinese nouns and the classical Chinese ontological theory. The collective-noun hypothesis makes a stronger claim that Chinese nouns do not function as count nouns but typically function, both syntactically and semantically, as collective-nouns.

LANGUAGE AND LOGIC

As indicated at the outset, the term "logic" in this essay on language and logic in Chinese philosophy means two related things: first, logical reasoning as embedded or expressed in natural (Chinese) language; second, the syntactic-semantic structure of Chinese language that underlies the surface grammar of Chinese language. The two are related in this way: The reasoning as embedded in a language is intrinsically connected with the syntactic structure of such a language and makes sense in view of its semantic structure which per se is related to its syntactic structure; thus, to understand the reasoning as embedded in natural (Chinese) language, one needs to understand its syntactic-semantic structure. Actually, in the discussions of the previous two parts, the second issue has already been addressed in view of its relations with the central concerns there. In this part, we focus on the first issue. With space limitation, the strategy is this: we will start with an examination of some reasoning patterns in the Mohist discourse and then raise a general issue about the due relation between two modes of reasoning; that is, deductive reasoning versus evocative reasoning, in view of Chinese philosophical practice.

REASONING PATTERNS IN THE MOHIST DISCOURSE. The two trademark basic principles for deductive reasoning are the principle of non-contradiction and the law of identity, both of which are expected to be observed for the sake of good deductive reasoning. The principle of noncontradiction states that it is not the case that both that p and not p (where p is any proposition). The law of identity states that everything is identical with itself (for everything x, $x = x$). We begin with an example of reasoning via Aristotelian deductive logic:

Pr.1 If x is y, then to do something to x is to do it to y.

Pr.2 Robbers are people.

Therefore, killing robbers is killing people.

Pr.3 It is wrong to kill people.

Therefore, it is wrong to kill robbers.

However, the Mohist disagrees to this reasoning, arguing that killing robbers is not killing people. Their reason is this. In our ordinary language use, we often shift our attention from what is shared between them to what is distinct between them, depending on the nature of context and concrete situation. The Mohist distinguishes three sorts of contexts and considered the case of "killing robbers/killing people" as one case of the second kind (Graham 1989).

(1) The involved context would typically call our attention to what is shared between involved parties: In such a kind of contexts, for example, we say "Black horses are horses" or "Riding black horses is riding horses." (Typically, for the purpose of riding a horse, the color of the horse does not matter.) One example given in the Mohist text is this: "Huo is a person; to be concerned for Huo is to be concerned for persons." In the context of the Mohist text, Huo is a slave who is too humble for one to be concerned for anything about them except that he is a person; someone concerned for him is concerned for anyone as a person. Also note that the Mohist held the view of universal concern for anyone.

(2) The involved context would typically call our attention to what is distinct between involved parties. Consider three sentences in such a kind of contexts. First, "A carriage is wood; but riding a carriage is not riding wood": Typically, what is concerned with in the context of talking on riding something is whether or not the thing has the riding-function. Second, "Her younger brother is a handsome man; but loving her younger brother is not loving a handsome man": Typically, in this context, loving him is not for his looks. Third, "Robbers are people; abounding in robbers is not abounding in people, being without robbers is not being without people: Typically, in this context, what is called attention to is something distinct with robbers.

(3) The involved context would typically call our attention to both what is common and what is distinct between involved parties. One might say both "The white horse is not the horse" (in so saying, as analyzed before in view of Gongsun Long's approach, one pays attention to the distinct aspect of the white horse from the horse) and "Riding the white horse is riding the horse" (for the sake of riding a horse, the color of the horse does not matter).

What the Mohist calls our attention to is a variety of reasoning patterns embedded in our linguistic practice and the context in which reasoning utterances are made. In contrast, deductive reasoning focuses on logical necessity and logical entailment that seems to be concerned about only in the context (1) among the foregoing three kinds of contexts as the Mohist identifies. It is noted that such a focus-shift is not supposed to make at random but has its due metaphysical foundation: an object of study really possesses its multiple aspects/layers/dimensions. When saying "robbers are people," one focuses on the aspect of robbers, A, that makes them being people; nevertheless, when saying "killing robbers is not killing people," one's focus shifts to some other aspect of robbers, A*, which is possessed by robbers rather than by the other people and which makes robbers deserve being killed (from the Mohist point of view): killing robbers for the sake of A*; that does not amount to killing people for the sake of A* because people generally speaking do not possess A*. Note that this challenge is rather to the indiscriminate applicability of deductive reasoning at the surface level than to its applicability to various extents in different linguistic contexts. That constitutes a deep reason why the Mohist view, as A. C. Graham points out, has its "Wittgensteinian look," which emphasizes the language use and claims that meaning consists in use.

LOGICAL VERSUS EVOCATIVE ARGUMENTATIONS IN CHINESE PHILOSOPHY. It is known that any philosophical inquiry needs to base its conclusion on justification or argumentation rather than simply dogmatically taking something for granted. There are two basic modes of argumentations in philosophy, one is logical (in its narrow sense) and the other evocative, though sometimes only the former is highlighted and celebrated. The two modes of argumentations are sometimes contrasted as "logical versus rhetoric," "inferential versus preferential" or "probative versus prohairetic." A logical argument is a set of statements in which one or more of the statements, the premises, purports to provide a reason or evidence for the truth of another statement, the conclusion, either in deductive way or in inductive way. When it does, we say that the premises entail or support the conclusion, or that the conclusion "follows from" the premises. We traditionally divide logical arguments into deductive and inductive arguments. The term "evocative" is used in contrast to the term "logical" used in the narrow sense; it means producing or suggesting or triggering (generally speaking, evoking) some subsequent thought or conclusion primarily in some non-"logical" way, neither deductively nor inductively as specified above. Among a variety of evocative argumentations, what have been often addresses especially in humanities are argument by (relevant) analogy [drawing its conclusion by evoking a similarity between some particular aspect of two things from, or on the basis of, their similarity in some other particular aspect(s) or in some other general aspect], argument by appealing to value [drawing its conclusion by appealing to one's value which is appreciated through one's life-experience and understanding of the world (and/or the human society)], and argument by appealing to (credible) authority [draws its conclusion by appealing to trustworthy and knowledgeable authority on the issue under examination].

Both modes of argumentations are widely used in the classical Chinese philosophy. Let us consider some examples in Confucius' *Analects* to illustrate the point. Contrary to some unjustified impression, this classical text is not lack of deductive reasoning; though some of the deductive-reasoning cases need one to be careful enough to identify between lines, some other are quite evident—for example, the reasoning given in the previous citation where Confucius' doctrine of name rectification is discussed. On the other hand, the argumentation implicit in Confucius' version of the Golden Rule as delivered in 6.28 of the *Analects* illustrate both argument by analogy and argument by appealing to value. Its conclusion is that one should treat others in a certain moral way; which way? One is expected to identity the way partially based on how one would like to be treated: Due to the common human-being identity among human beings that result in similarities in many relevant aspects between human moral beings, [Confucius' version of] the Golden Rule guides the moral agent to "draw the analogy from oneself [the way one would desire to be treated]" to how to treat others in a moral way (that is, to evoke the similarity in regard to what would be desired and what would be rendered moral, by both the moral agent and the moral recipient). Furthermore, the moral agent is not expected to start from nowhere but to be a moral agent with (a certain degree of) moral sensibility; that is, the virtue of *ren*; this initial moral sensibility serves as the internal starting point of how the moral agent is to adequately draw the analogy. This moral value, according to Confucius, is commonly, more or less, shared by all human moral agents; this moral value would thus contribute to what would be rendered moral by both the moral agent and the moral recipient (the similarity in this regard). In this way, Confucius' version of the Golden Rule appeals to the moral value to justify a reasonable version of the Golden Rule. Through this example, one can see how argument by analogy and argument by appealing to value interplay in the argumentation in Confucius' version of the Golden rule.

Indeed, when appealing to value and appealing to authority, one should be careful; otherwise, one might fall into fallacies. But, what is at issue is not whether people and philosophers have ever made adequate argument by appealing to value or to authority in their reflective practice. Philosophers do it, more or less, directly or indirectly, and explicitly or implicitly, in their argumentations and explanations, and both in the Chinese tradition and in the Western tradition. What is really philosophically interesting is how to do it in some adequate way to avoid fallacies. In this connection, unlike deductive reasoning, there is no formal rule manual available but some general guidelines. Those general guidelines, largely, present themselves as explanations of what constitute fallacies in reasoning or argumentation. One case is the fallacy of dubious authority regarding current situation: An argument commits this fallacy when it mistakes some person as a trustworthy and knowledgeable authority about the current situation. Another case is the fallacy of relevance: mistaking relevant dissimilarities as irrelevant: An argument (typically, an argument by analogy) commits this fallacy when it mistakes relevant differences between two (kinds of) things as irrelevant to the issue under examination. For example, to illustrate the fallacy of relevance, let us consider how Mencius criticizes an argument by analogy made by Gao Zi, his contemporary in regard to the original human (moral) nature:

> Gao Zi said, "[Original] Human [moral] nature is like the willow tree, and righteousness is like making a drinking cup. To turn human nature into humanity and righteousness is like turning the willow tree into cups." Mencius responded, "Could you make the cups out of the willow tree without violating its nature, or do you have to violate the nature of the willow tree before you can make the cups? If you have to violate the nature of the willow tree in order to make cups, then [based on your analogy] do you have to also violate human nature in order to make it into humanity and righteousness? Your analogy would lead all people in the world to consider humanity and righteousness as the source of disaster [because they required the violation of human nature]!" (*Mencius* 6A:1. My modification of the translation in Chan 1963, p. 51)

Mencius here criticizes Gao Zi for his inadequately paying attention only to some superficial similarity between making a cup and building character but ignoring a crucial difference between making a cup out of the willow tree (injuring the willow) and building human moral character from the human original moral nature (without involving violence and injury); in this way, in our terminology here, Mencius actually criticizes Gao Zi for his mistaking one significantly relevant dissimilarity between both as irrelevant in his argument by analogy.

The relation of the two modes of argumentations together with their respective nature and status in philosophical inquiry has been under reflective examination. We can think about a number of questions in view of the cited cases above in the traditional Chinese philosophy and through examining our own reflective practice in argumentation: When carrying out deductive (or evocative) argumentation, could one's argumentation be totally immune from evocative (or deductive) argumentation? (Think about where premises in many deductive arguments come from; also think about whether one still needs to rely on a certain standard and resort to the two basic principles of deductive reasoning mentioned above in some way when carrying out evocative argumentation.) One strategic methodological point in regard to the relation between the two modes of argumentation is that they come into "mutually supportive overall harmonization" (Rescher 1994, p. 58). That is especially true in view of Chinese philosophical practice. For this orientation is kindred in spirit with the *yin-yang* way of thinking which emphasizes the complementary nature between seemingly competing approaches. Indeed, the *yin-yang* way of thinking has fundamentally influenced the orientation of mentality, and the way of carrying out reflective argumentation, of subsequent Chinese thinkers in various schools or movements.

See also Chinese Philosophy: Metaphysics and Epistemology.

Bibliography

Ames, Roger, and David Hall. *Thinking through Confucius.* Albany, NY: SUNY Press, 1987.

Analetcs. Translated by D. C. Lau as *Confucius: The Analects* (Harmondsworth, Middlesex: Penguin Classics, 1979).

Chan, Wing-tsit. *A Source Book in Chinese Philosophy.* Princeton, NJ: Princeton University Press, 1963.

Chao, Y. R. "Notes on Chinese Grammar and Logic." *Philosophy East and West* 5 (1955): 31–41.

Chen, Bo. "Debate on Language-Meaning and the Skeptic Argument about Meaning," Presented at the ISCWP international conference "Davidson's Philosophy and Chinese Philosophy" (June 8 and 9, 2004; Beijing, China). Chinese abstract in *World Philosophy* 5 (2004): 26–28.

Cheng, Chung-ying. "Inquiries into Classical Chinese Logic." *Philosophy East and West* 15 (1965) (3–4): 195–216.

Cheng, Chung-ying. "Logic and Language in Chinese Philosophy." *Journal of Chinese Philosophy* 14 (1987): 285–307.

Chmielewski, Janusz. "Notes on Early Chinese Logic (I)." *Rocznik Orientalistyczny* 26 (1) (1962): 7–21.

Creel, Herrlee. "On the Opening Words of the Lao-Tzu." *Journal of Chinese Philosophy* 10 (1983): 299–329>

Dao-De-Jing (Lao-Zi) (in Chinese). *Lao Tzu, Tao te ching.* Translated by D. C. Lau. Harmondsworth, Middlesex: Penguin Classics, 1979.

Fung, Yiu-ming. *On Gong-Sun-Long-Zi.* Taipei: Dongda Publishing House, 2000 (in Chinese).

Fung, Yu-lan. *A History of Chinese Philosophy*, 2vols. Translated by Derk Bodde. Princeton, NJ: Princeton University Press, 1952–1953.

Gong-Sun-Long-Zi (in Chinese).

Graham, Angus C. *Disputers of the Tao*. La Salle, IL: Open Court, 1989.

Graham, Angus C. *Studies in Chinese Philosophy and Philosophical Literature*. Albany: SUNY Press, 1990.

Graham, Angus C. *Yin-Yang and the Nature of Correlative Thinking*. Singapore: Institute of East Asian Philosophies, 1986.

Hall, David. "The Import of Analysis in Classical China—A Pragmatic Appraisal." In *Two Roads to Wisdom?—Chinese and Analytic Philosophical Traditions*, edited by Bo Mou, 153–167. Chicago: Open Court, 2001.

Hall, David. "The Way and the Truth." In *A Companion to World Philosophies*, edited by in Eliot Deutsch and Ron Bontekoe, 214–224. Oxford: Blackwell, 1997.

Hansen, Chad. "Chinese Language, Chinese Philosophy, and 'Truth.'" *Journal of Asian Studies* 44 (3) (1985): 491–519.

Hansen, Chad. *A Daoist Theory of Chinese Thought*. New York: Oxford University Press, 1992.

Hansen, Chad. *Language and Thought in Ancient China*. Ann Arbor: University of Michigan Press, 1983.

Hansen, Chad. "The Metaphysics of *Dao*." In *Comparative Approaches to Chinese Philosophy*, edited by Bo Mou, 205–224. Aldershot, U.K.: Ashgate, 2003.

Harbsmeier, Christoph. "Marginalia Sino-logica." In *Understanding the Chinese Mind: The Philosophical Roots*, edited by Robert E. Allinson, 125–166. New York: Oxford University Press, 1989.

Harbsmeier, Christoph. "The Mass Noun Hypothesis and the Part-Whole Analysis of the White Horse Dialogue." In Chinese Texts and Philosophical Contexts, edited by Henry Rosemont, Jr., 49–66. La Salle, IL: Open Court, 1991.

Hu, Shih. *The Development of the Logical Method in Ancient China*. Shanghai: Commercial Press, 1922.

Mei, Tsu-lin. "Chinese Grammar and the Linguistic Movement in Philosophy." *Review of Metaphysics* 14 (1961): 463–492.

Mei, Tsu-lin. "Subject and Predicate: A Grammatical Preliminary." *Philosophical Review* 70 (1961): 153–175.

Mencius. Translated by D. C. Lau. Hammondsworth, Middlesex: Penguin, 1970.

Mou, Bo. "Truth Pursuit and Dao Pursuit." In *Davidson's Philosophy and Chinese Philosophy*, edited by Bo Mou. Leiden, The Netherlands: Brill Academic Publishers, 2006.

Mou, Bo. "The Structure of the Chinese Language and Ontological Insights: A Collective-Noun Hypothesis." *Philosophy East and West* 49 (1999): 45–62.

Mou, Bo. "Ultimate Concerns and Language Engagement: A Re-Examination of the Opening Message of the *Dao-De-Jing*." *Journal of Chinese Philosophy* 27 (4) (2000): 429–439.

Reding, Jean-Paul. "Analogical Reasoning in Early Chinese Philosophy." *Asiatische Studies* 40 (1986).

Rescher, Nicholas. *Metaphilosophical Inquiries*. Princeton, NJ: Princeton University Press, 1994,

Rosemont, Henry Jr. "On Representing Abstractions in Archaic Chinese." *Philosophy East and West* 24 (1974).

Schwartz, Benjamin I. *The World of Thought in Ancient China*. Cambridge, MA: Harvard University Press, 1985.

Wu, Kuang-ming. "Counterfactuals, Universals and Chinese Thinking." *Philosophy East and West* 37 (1987): 84–94.

Yi-Jing (I Ching). Translated by Cary F. Beynes as *The Book of Changes*. London: Routledge & Kegan Paul, 1968.

Zhuang-Zi. Translated by Burton Watson as *Chuang Tzu: Basic Writings*. New York: Columbia University Press, 1996.

Bo Mou (2005)

METAPHYSICS AND EPISTEMOLOGY

In traditional Chinese philosophy, epistemology was not an explicitly developed discipline, even if Chinese philosophers since ancient times were interested in problems related to human knowledge and developed some implicit theories of knowledge. Traditionally, there was no technical Chinese term equivalent to "epistemology" in Western philosophy, for which Chinese now use the terms "zhishilun" and "renshilun" as modern translations. In contrast, metaphysics has been a central interest of Chinese philosophy, traceable back to its origin in the *Yijing* or *Zhouyi* (The [Zhou] book of changes, c. 6th –5th century BCE). The discourse on the Way (*daolun*), in various forms, has always been an essential constituent of traditional Chinese philosophy. The term "xingershangxue," or simply "xingshangxue," now serving as the Chinese translation of the term "metaphysics" in Western philosophy, comes from the great appendix of the *Zhouyi*, where we read, "What is above forms [*xing er shang*] is the Way [*dao*]; what is under forms [*xing er xia*] is concrete things [*qi*]" (Kong, juan, p. 158). Knowledge of metaphysical reality, essential to Chinese philosophy, is also a fundamental concern of Chinese theory of knowledge.

The following discussion will first deal with Chinese theories of knowledge, ascending from ordinary knowledge to science to wisdom. All three moments have their metaphysical presuppositions, especially wisdom, which is in essence the knowledge of ultimate reality and thus leads to metaphysics properly speaking.

KNOWLEDGE

It is easy to identify some texts in which traditional Chinese philosophers discussed the subject-object structure of knowledge or the knower-known relation in the process of knowing. For example, Xunzi (298–238 BCE) said, "That by which one can know is human nature; that which can be known are the principles of things" (p. 523). Mo Di (fl. 400 BCE) said, "Wisdom (*zhi*) is the capacity

… by which, when one knows, one necessarily knows (as with eyesight)" (p. 212), and "Wisdom, by means of the capacity to know when in contact with things, enables one to describe it, like the seen" (p. 212). Unlike in Western epistemology, where the relation between subject and object or knower and known plays an essential role, in Chinese philosophy, this is only instrumental to a deeper dynamic process in which the individual attains knowledge of external things and cognitively appropriates objects in the world for building a meaningful life.

Chinese philosophers distinguished different types of knowledge, such as the Mohists' distinction between knowledge by hearsay, knowledge by explanation, and knowledge by personal experience, and Mencius's distinction between knowledge by the senses and knowledge by thinking. But more important is the Chinese concern with how to prepare the mind to know external things as they are, without bias. This can be seen in the Huanglao Daoist ideas of emptying (*xu*), unifying (*yi*), and quieting (*jing*) the mind. These notions were later developed by Xunzi as a way to attain the great clear enlightened state of mind (*da qingming*). Xunzi can be seen as the greatest theorist of knowledge in Chinese philosophy. The last master thinker in the Jixia Academy (374–221 BCE), Xunzi developed his epistemological thinking as theoretical support for scholarly argumentation in the academy, which consisted of different competing schools.

In the manner of an intellectualist, Xunzi emphasized humans' cognitive ability to discern right and wrong, which he termed "discernment" (*bian*). When expressed in discourse, this ability is displayed in what he called "discerning discourse" or "argumentation" (*bianshuo*). Xunzi conceived of the Way as the ultimate standard for discerning right and wrong, which included classes (*lei*), coherence (*tong*), and distinctions (*fen*) as subcriteria. Since things exist in different classes or categories (*lei*), their corresponding names should also be divided similarly or differently, as the case may be. The function of discourse is to make proper distinctions and classifications (*fen*) among things and names. Finally, all classifications and distinctions in discourse should be composed into a coherent system (*tong*).

To judge right from wrong well, one has to keep one's mind in a great clear enlightened state, attained by making one's mind empty, one, and still (*xu, yi er jing*), ideas that Xunzi received and developed from the Daoists, especially (370–290 BCE). Xunzi understood that when the mind is empty, "what has already been stored [in the mind] does not hinder the reception of new knowledge," that when the mind is one, "the knowledge of particular things does not hinder their unity," and that when the mind is still, "dreams and noisy fancies do not disorder one's knowing mind" (Xunzi, p. 510).

According to Xunzi, in the process of knowing and arguing for one's knowledge, one must, negatively, discard all obscuring factors and, positively, be alert to other, easily neglected aspects of an issue in dispute. Human knowledge is expressed by concepts, which, for Xunzi, are names (*ming*). Names can be analyzed according to the concepts of intentions and extensions of Western formal logic. With respect to intentions, Xunzi distinguished between names discerning superiority/inferiority and names discerning identity/difference, representing concepts respectively indicating values and facts, for him the former being higher than the latter. With respect to extensions, Xunzi made the distinction between generic names (*gongming*) and specific names (*bieming*), analyzable by reference to the relations of "inclusion" and "belonging to" between classes and subclasses. Classes can be seen as the basis of all deductive and inductive reasoning. Since the Way, as the ultimate standard for judging right from wrong, can be classified into different classes (*lei*), *lei* is imbued with both logical and ontological meanings.

SCIENCE

Before modern European science emerged in the sixteenth century, Chinese science was much more advanced than European science, as shown by Joseph Needham in *Science and Civilization in China*. Chinese philosophers were often enthusiastic about and full of scientific knowledge. For example, Zhu Xi (1130–1200), though living in the twelfth century, was well acquainted with different kinds of scientific knowledge, and is therefore a good example to showcase the philosophical import of Chinese science. Zhu Xi can be seen as the great synthesizer of medieval Chinese scientific knowledge and its philosophical foundation, even if he lived earlier than such Western medieval thinkers as Robert Grosseteste (1175–1253), Roger Bacon (1210–1292), Albert the Great (1200–1280), St. Bonaventura (1217–1274), and St. Thomas Aquinas (1225–1274). Zhu Xi's *Wenji* (Collected writings) and *Yulei* (Classified conversations) display his rich knowledge in the domains of calendrical astronomy, botany, music and harmonics, geomancy, medicine, etc. Also, he frequently discussed matters of science with his disciples, sometimes for the sake of scientific knowledge, sometimes to illustrate Chinese classical texts.

Some of Zhu Xi' observations on natural phenomena are quite interesting and true. For example, he said, "Mountains were formed by the elevation of sea bottom."

He then proceeded to prove it by pointing to the presence of seashells on top of mountains, saying, "On high mountains there are often seen shells of oyster and shellfish in the rocks. These rocks must have been earth in ancient times, and those shells from oysters and shellfish in the water. The lower becomes the higher, the soft becomes hard. This phenomenon is worthy of pondering upon, for these facts can be verified" (1999, bk. 5, p. 19). In this particular case, Joseph Needham admires Zhu Xi, writing, "Zhu Xi recognized the fact that the mountains had been elevated since the day when the shells of the living animals had been buried in the silt mud of the sea-bottom" (1959, p. 598). Note that Zhu Xi's remarks here concern mountain formation as well as fossils of sea animals. In other areas of science, Zhu Xi also correctly observed that the source of moonlight was the sun, and he correctly explained such phenomena as tides and eclipses of sun and moon.

Even if Zhu Xi was full of natural knowledge and was rational in attitude, he was not satisfied with the technical dimension of scientific knowledge and sought deeper understanding by exhausting the principles of all things and developing a holistic vision of reality. In fact, his interest in knowledge of nature should be understood in his philosophical concepts of *gewu zhizhi* (investigating things to extend knowledge). For Zhu Xi, *li*, meaning principle, reason, or order, could be found in everything and was worthy of investigation. He said, "As high as the Ultimate Infinite, the Great Ultimate, and as low as one herb, one tree, as tiny as one insect, each has its principle. … If we leave one thing uninvestigated, then we lack one principle" (1999, bk. 1, p. 295). The object of Zhu Xi's investigation was the order existing in other things, which presupposed that things and their principles possessed a certain otherness. The attainment of knowledge would include knowledge of other things and knowledge of self, or better said, a detour through the other that leads to a return to oneself, as when one finally achieves sudden penetration into the nature of things and attains transparent self-knowledge. Thus, the investigation of things is a detour in which one first goes outside one's self to the other and by knowing the other, one can finally come back to knowing one's own self.

So much for the Zhu Xi example. What is to be said about the epistemological specificity of Chinese science in comparison with European modern science? Generally speaking, Western modern science was historically grounded in the Greek heritage of *theōria*, the disinterested pursuit of truth and sheer intellectual curiosity. Aristotle said in his *Metaphysics* that science began in a way of life that included leisure (*rhaistōnē*) and recreation (*diagōgē*), such as the Egyptian priests enjoyed who discovered geometry. They did not need to care about daily necessities of life and could wonder about the causes of things and seek knowledge for its own sake. The result of their wonder was theories, whose meaning, according to Aristotle, was determined, in one sense, by practice, "not in virtue of being able to act, but of having the theory for themselves and knowing the causes" (*Metaphysics* 981b 6–7), and, in another sense, with respect to universal objects, seen by Aristotle as the first characteristic of science (*Metaphysics*, 982a 3–10, 20–23).

In contrast, Chinese science in general began as a concern leading not to universal theorization but to universal praxis. It was because of his concern with the destiny of the individual and society that Chinese began to philosophize. The great appendix of the *Zhouyi* asserts that the study of changes began with concern and anxiety over natural calamity, not in leisure and recreation. It also suggests that the practical intention of Chinese science was to serve as guidance for a universal praxis. Nevertheless, both modern European science and traditional Chinese science are concerned with the universal, or better, the universalizable, character of science, the one more with universal theories, the other more with universal praxis, yet both of them criticize and seek to transcend particular interests, with a view to attaining universality.

Because of its pragmatic concern, Chinese traditional science, in thinking about the secrets of nature, tends to use concrete images and construct concrete models for understanding natural phenomena. These images or models came directly from an intuitive or speculative vision of reality. Models in traditional Chinese science were based on analogies, that is, they were concrete models of images or small-scale models that combined the functions of explanation and pragmatic operation. For example, the construction of astronomic clepsydras (water clocks), very important in Chinese astronomy and hydraulics, expressed the genius of traditional Chinese science. Here were models that linked the movements of the heavens with the more visible movement of water or other fluid to create a visible image. In modern terms, the Chinese way of thinking in science is more analogous in form, giving birth to images and icons, which provide a more intuitive grasp of a situation in action. By contrast, the construction of models in modern European science is guided by theories presentable in mathematic form. Such models serve to mediate between mathematical theories and concrete empirical data. Modern European science, as exemplified by Newton's physics and Leibniz's *mathesis universalis* (a universal science modeled on mathematics), is akin to the digital way of thinking and provides a more structured and lucidly conceptualizable understanding.

The special features of traditional Chinese science in comparison with modern European science concerning the epistemic structures involved in the process of constructing scientific knowledge are these: First, on the rational side, modern European science, in constructing theories, uses logically and mathematically structured languages to formulate theories of local validity, that is, with explanatory and predictive power in a particular domain of phenomena. In comparison, Chinese traditional science did not utilize logico-mathematical structures in its theory formation. Chinese never pondered about the structure of language to the point of elaborating a logic system for the formulation and control of scientific discourse. Mathematics, although highly developed, was used only for describing and organizing data, not for formulating theories. Chinese quasi-scientific theories, lacking logical and mathematical structure, were principally presented through intuition and speculative imagination. They might have the advantage of offering insight into the totality of life and environment and giving a reasonable interpretation of them, but these "theories" somehow lacked the rigor of structural organization and logical formulation.

Second, on the empirical side, modern European science is characterized by well-controlled systematic experimentation, which, by elaborating on the sensible data and our perception of them, keeps in touch with the real world, but in an artificial, technically controlled way. In contrast, the empirical data in traditional Chinese sciences were gathered through detailed but passive observations, with or without the assistance of instruments. Traditional Chinese science seldom tried any systematically organized experimentation to exercise active artificial control over human perception of natural objects.

Third, in modern European science, there is conscious checking of the correspondence between the rational side and the empirical side to combine them into a coherent whole so as to serve the objective of explaining and controlling the world. The rational side of science builds up a theoretical vision of the world, while the empirical side relates this vision to the scientist's sensible construction and controlled experience of the world. Philosophical reflection, in checking the correspondence between these two aspects, assures us of their coherence and unity. In contrast, traditional Chinese science did not conceive of any interactive relation such as deduction/falsification or induction/verification or tests/confirmation to relate empirical knowledge and its intelligible ground of unity. Although Chinese traditional science did have its visions of proper science and knowledge in general, it did not have modern European science's epistemological reflection and philosophy of science—disciplines that check the nature of and correspondence between empirical and rational constructs.

Still, there is unity in traditional Chinese science. Confucius (551–479 BCE) said that there is a unity binding, or a guiding thread penetrating, all his knowledge. Confucius thus seemed to affirm the complementary interaction between empirical data and thinking. He said, "He who learns without thought is confused. He who thinks without learning is in danger" (*Analects* 2.15). These words remind one of Kant's proposition that sensibility without concepts is blind, whereas concepts without sensibility are void. But we should be clear that the mode of unity in traditional Chinese science was a kind of mental integration with ultimate reality through ethical praxis. Here praxis or practical action was not the technical application of theories to control concrete natural or social phenomena. Rather, it was an active process of realizing what is proper in the life of the individual and society. Science and technology are not to be ignored, but must be reconsidered in the context of this ethical praxis.

From the analysis above, it becomes clear that traditional Chinese science should be characterized as reasonable, and not rational in the sense of modern Western science. To be rational, one has to control the gathering of empirical data through systematic experimentation, to formulate theories in logico-mathematical language, and to check the relation of empirical data and theories through philosophical reflection. By contrast, to be reasonable, one has to find meaning for human life with reference to the totality of existence. Chinese philosophy, in its quest for what is reasonable, was caught in the tension between reference to the totality of human existence and reference to the totality of all existence. Confucianism insists on referring to the totality of human existence, whereas Daoism seeks to escape from the all too human tendencies of humanist philosophy and to refer rather to the totality of all existence, as expressed by the concept of the Way (*dao*). Daoist philosophy, as a philosophy anchored in the Way and the totality of all existence, and Confucianism, as a philosophy anchored in the totality of human existence, exemplify two complementary aspects of Chinese reasonableness.

WISDOM

Wisdom is the common concern of Chinese epistemology and metaphysics. Ultimately speaking, in all Chinese philosophical traditions, wisdom is what one's knowledge should finally achieve, and wisdom in some sense always refers to what is really real, to ultimate reality. In ancient China, the same ideogram (*zhi*) was used for both knowledge and wisdom, but later a radical was added to the character to differentiate wisdom (*zhi*) from knowledge (also *zhi*). The modern term for wisdom is *zhihui.* Chinese Mahayana Buddhism, while using *zhihui*, prefers the term *banruo*, a Chinese phonetic translation of the Sanskrit *prajñā*. When Xuanzang (596–664) set up a system of regulations for his translation project, he showed a particular respect for the term *banruo* in his "five categories of terms not to be translated" (*wu bu fan*), while the Chinese term *zhihui* appeared for him to be superficial. Nevertheless, the term *zhihui* was also often used in Chinese Buddhism to express the idea of wisdom.

In Confucianism, wisdom means three things. First, wisdom means accumulating knowledge under a unifying thread or penetrating unity, as Confucius said. In this sense, knowledge comes from investigating the natures or principles of things so as to be able to unfold them according to their natures, instead of imposing theories upon them or exploiting their energy for human short-term interests. Second, wisdom means achieving total self-understanding. For Wang Yangming (1472–1529), this entails achieving one's inborn knowledge, completely developing one's true nature, and arriving at one's full potential of the moral knowledge proper to humans. Finally, wisdom means awareness of one's own destiny or heavenly mandate. Confucius took his understanding of his heavenly mandate, at age fifty, as a crucial point of his life. Also, the *Doctrine of the Mean* (c. 5th century BCE) says, "Wishing to know man, he must not fail to know Heaven" (Chan, p. 105).

In Daoism, *Laozi*, despite its critical and negative attitude toward instrumental knowledge and calculation, as shown in its negative use of the term "knowledge," nevertheless uses the term *ming*, defined as enlightened knowledge of the constant law of nature: "To know harmony is to accord with the constant; to know the constant is wisdom" (chap. 55). According to Daoism, to be wise, which is more than possessing mere intellectual knowledge, is to know the constant laws of nature, and from there, to be one with the Way and thereby to live a life of freedom, understood not as merely making free choices or arriving at autonomous decisions, but rather as complying with the spontaneous rhythms of nature.

In Chinese Mahayana Buddhism, the Chinese term *banruo* is taken to mean only perfect wisdom. This is a development of the Indian tradition, where the term *prajñā* means knowledge as well as wisdom, perfect wisdom as well as imperfect wisdom. In Chinese Buddhism, wisdom means attaining enlightenment, a state in which one understands that all is empty and thus seeks to rid oneself of original ignorance. The term *zhihui* (wisdom) was used to translate *prajñā*, especially in Weishi's (for example, in Xuanzang's Cheng Weishi Lun, 659 CE) concept of transforming consciousness into wisdom (*zhuan shi de zhi* or *zhuan shi cheng zhi*). For the Weishi School, more Indian than Chinese, wisdom arises from Alaya consciousness (Alya vijñāna). But for the Sanlun School, wisdom means realizing the ultimate emptiness of the world. In Chan (Zen) Buddhism, wisdom is the immediate self-realization of Buddhahood in the details of everyday life.

In his *Banruo wuzhi lun* (Wisdom as nonknowing), Sengzhao (383–414) distinguished wisdom from common knowledge. For him, knowledge is epistemologically structured by the relation of the knowing subject and known object, and therefore is relative and limited to a particular object. The content of knowledge is expressed in logical propositions that should be free of logical contradiction. In contrast, wisdom is all-knowing and comprehends all things, including itself. Therefore, it lacks subject-object structure and is not limited and relative to any particular object. Its self-awareness results from its own crystal-clear mirroring and not from any self-reflection or intuition. For Sengzhao, wisdom was a mysterious function of a mind characterized by emptiness, and emptiness he identified with ultimate reality, which belongs to the ontology and therefore is beyond all logical considerations, including the principle of noncontradiction. For Sengzhao, wisdom was absolutely pure and was beyond all sorts of delusions arising from relative knowledge.

Jizang (549–623) developed a typology of three types of wisdom. First was ultimate wisdom (*shixiang banruo*), which penetrates into ultimate reality, or the emptiness of all things. This is the ultimate ground of the other types of wisdom. Second was illumining wisdom (*zhengguan banruo*), which throws light upon the ultimate reality in all its different facets and manifestations. In this application of ultimate wisdom in meditating on the essence of each and every thing, one comes to see that each of them is empty. Third was linguistic wisdom (*wenzi banruo*), which enables one to give powerful linguistic expression to the perfect congruence between ultimate reality and its manifestations.

METAPHYSICS AS KNOWLEDGE OF ULTIMATE REALITY

Metaphysics concerns knowledge of ultimate reality. Even if all the schools of Chinese philosophy used "dao" (the Way) as a common term to refer to ultimate reality, there were other terms used in different schools, even different terms used by different philosophers within one school. For example, in Confucianism, different Confucians took the concepts of heaven, humanness, sincerity, and principle or reason as ultimate reality. In the following sections, we will see what different schools took as ultimate reality: heaven, humanness, sincerity, and principle in Confucianism, the Way in Daoism, and emptiness in Buddhism.

ULTIMATE REALITY IN CONFUCIANISM. Generally, the concept of ultimate reality in Confucianism moves from heaven (*tian*), a residue from ancient Chinese religious beliefs; to humanness (*ren*) in Confucius himself; then to sincerity (*cheng*) in Zisi, Confucius's grandson; and to mind (*xin*) or principle (*li*) in neo-Confucianism. In the prephilosophical tradition, the *Shijing* (Book of odes) and the *Shangshu* (Book of documents) used the concept of heaven, imbued with a religious sense, to represent God on High. A residue of this notion could still be found in Confucius when he said, "If heaven wished to destroy this legacy, we latecomers would not have access to it. Since heaven is not going to destroy this culture of ours, what can the people of Kuang do to me?" (*Analects* 9.7). Confucius also said that he prayed to heaven, yet heaven, though manifesting itself through regular cosmic movement, remained silent, thus maintaining a certain unfathomability. Confucius said, "Does heaven speak? And yet the four seasons turn, and the myriad things are born and grow within it" (*Analects* 17.19).

Confucius's proper contribution consisted in proposing the concept of humanness (*ren*) as a transcendental foundation for ritual (*li*). Humanness, a transcendental capacity in each person, had an ontological dimension in that it presupposed that all beings are interconnected, and this allows humans to be affected and respond to other people and things. Confucius considered this transcendental capacity of each person to affect and respond to others as the transcendental foundation of ritual. Sometimes humanness was combined with the Way to specify the way of humanness. With this metaphysical move, the concept of *ren* achieved metaphysical status in neo-Confucians such as Zhou Dunyi (1017–1073) and Zhang Zai (1020–1077), who extended humanness to the whole cosmos (a cosmic humanness), surely a metaphysical concept. Also, Zisi (493–406 BEC), Confucius's grandson, developed Confucius's idea of ultimate reality in *Zhongyong* (*Doctrine of the Mean*) with the concept of sincerity (*cheng*), which had two levels of meaning: On the psychological level, *cheng* meant being true to one's own self; on the metaphysical level, *cheng* meant the really real, truth, or reality itself.

Under the influence of Tiantai Buddhism and Chan Buddhism, idealist neo-Confucians such as Lu Xiangsan (1139–1193) and Wang Yangming took mind imbued with moral values to be ultimate reality. Such a mind was attainable through moral practice and moral effort. They thereby laid the foundation for a kind of moral metaphysics. In affirming that the Great Ultimate is principle or reason (*li*), the realist neo-Confucian Zhu Xi took principle or reason to be ultimate reality. For Zhu Xi, even if everything has its own principle, by way of metaphysical participation they share their reality with the cosmic principle that ultimately governs the whole world.

ULTIMATE REALITY IN DAOISM. Daoism coherently used "Way" (*dao*) as a metaphysical concept to denote various levels of metaphysical reality and ultimate reality itself. Etymologically, the ideogram for *dao* is composed of two elements, the head and the act of walking on a way. Together they mean a way on which one could find direction and a way to some point. Though *dao* was never limited to the idea of a physical way, this image of a way suggests the meaning of *dao*: The *dao* puts everything on its way. In common use, *dao* also means "to say," "to speak," or "to discourse," such as the second "dao" in the opening of *Laozi*, which says, "The way that can be spoken of is not the constant Way" (chap. 1). In Daoism, the function of discourse is always negative. Discourse, once said, must be hushed; words, once written, must be erased. One can never discourse about ultimate reality in any human language. This is quite different from Western philosophy, from the beginning of which emphasis has been on the function of language, of logos, to express reality. Apart from these two levels of meaning, *dao* in Daoism has three other uses that are more philosophical:

First, it refers to laws of becoming or laws of nature, especially in the term *tiandao* (the Way of heaven) or *tiandi zhi dao* (the Way of heaven and earth). In Daoism, the laws of nature have two aspects: (1) The structural law says that all things are structurally constituted of different yet complementary elements, such as being and nonbeing, yin and yang, movement and rest, weak and strong, and so on. (2) The dynamic law says that once a state of affairs has developed to the extreme in a process of change, it will naturally move to its opposite state of affairs.

Second, it refers to the origin giving birth to all things. If all things are regulated by laws of nature, there must be an origin that gave birth to all things, there must be a cosmic law. Normally, the origin gives birth to all things in a process of differentiation and complexification, as indicated by these words in *Laozi*: "The Way gave birth to one. One gave birth to two. Two gave birth to three. Three gave birth to all things" (chap. 42).

Finally, it refers to ultimate reality. The Way ultimately represents the ever self-manifesting act of existence. If there is an origin giving birth to all things, then before the origin, there must be a self-manifesting act of existence, defined in relation to all things. The self-manifesting act of existence is reality itself, whereas everything we say about the Way is but a constructed reality, which can never be reality itself. One can mention the Way to express something about it, but what is said becomes a constructed reality and not reality itself. To keep one's mind open to reality itself, all human constructions stand in need of further deconstruction.

Most of the time in traditional Daoism, these three levels of the Way were closely related one another, so closely that they were often mixed up and seldom clearly distinguished in the texts. It is with philosophical effort that they can be analyzed into clearly distinguished aspects of a well-connected whole. This is to say, in traditional Daoism, ultimate reality and its multifaceted manifestations can be logically distinguished but are not ontologically distinct.

ULTIMATE REALITY IN BUDDHISM. Chinese Mahayana Buddhism, like Indian Buddhism, takes emptiness as ultimate reality. Although the Sanskrit term *śūnyatā* has many meanings in the Indian tradition, its Chinese equivalent *kong* has three major philosophical meanings, each with its own focus: First, on the ontological level, emptiness means that all things come and go through interdependent causation and therefore lack any self-nature or substance of their own. Second, on the spiritual level, it means that the spiritual achievement of the sage consists in total freedom, attaching himself neither to being nor to nonbeing, neither to dualism nor to nondualism, not even to any form of spiritual achievement, no matter how high or deep it is. To keep one's spirit totally free, one must even empty the emptiness. Third, on the linguistic level, emptiness means that all the words we use are artificially constructed, without any fixed correspondence or reference to reality.

Although Indian Buddhism put more emphasis on the ontological and the linguistic senses of emptiness, Chinese Mahayana Buddhism, generally speaking, emphasized mostly the spiritual sense of emptiness. For example, in the *Buzhen kong lun* (On the emptiness of the unreal), Sengzhao, appropriating Daoist philosophy, interpreted emptiness as the spiritual achievement of a sage (though he also gave other meanings to the term "emptiness"). For example, we read, "The sage moves within the thousand transformations but does not change, and travels on ten thousand paths of delusion but always goes through. This is so because he leaves the empty self-nature of things as it is and does not employ the term 'emptiness' to make things empty" (Chan 1963, p. 356, with corrections).

The spiritual achievement of a sage, who has no attachment to the realm of either being or nonbeing, not even any attachment to his own spiritual achievement, results from a mysterious function of his mind, which on the one hand is nonsubstantial and empty, yet on the other hand is mysterious in function and self-transcending. Because of this, the Way (emptiness as the ultimate reality) and sagehood are not far away from us and can be realized at the moment of enlightenment. "Things when touched become real. … Man when enlightened becomes mysterious" (Sengzhao, vol. 45, pp. 152–153). The idea of a mysteriously enlightened mind rendering real all things touched by it significantly influenced other Chinese Mahayana schools, especially Tiantai and Chan. In Tiantai and Chan Buddhism, the mind was taken to be ultimate reality.

INBORN KNOWLEDGE AND MORAL METAPHYSICS

Idealist neo-Confucianists, such as Lu Xiangsan and Wang Yangming, considered moral knowledge as inborn and the realization of moral knowledge to be the only access to the really real. They were idealists in the sense that they took mind as the ultimate reality, identifying the human mind and the cosmic mind, which they saw as the ontological source of all values and moral knowledge. For them, knowledge meant mainly moral knowledge and was therefore value-laden. Since moral knowledge comes from the mind, humans must be capable of knowing it before all empirical knowledge. As a kind of innate knowledge, it is to be realized through human moral effort and moral practice, called "realization of innate knowledge" by Wang Yangming. Innate moral knowledge is like a permanent light within everyone, arising before the emotions. The individual realizes it by overcoming selfish tendencies, and thereby arrives at ultimate reality. Morality was thus considered a pragmatic way to access ultimate reality, and thus had metaphysical import.

Inheriting this line of thought, Mou Zongsan (1909–1995), a well-known figure in modern Confucianism, proposed the idea of moral metaphysics (*daode de xingshangxue*). He distinguished between moral metaphysics and the metaphysics of morals, the latter being a metaphysical study of morality and therefore moral philosophy rather than metaphysics. His idea of moral metaphysics represented an effort to emphasize the role of Confucianism and moral actions in Chinese metaphysical thinking. He also distinguished between the moral metaphysics of Confucianism and the liberation metaphysics (*jietuo de xingshangxue*) of Daoism and Buddhism. Even for Mou, these three traditions of Chinese philosophy saw the human mind as capable of intellectual intuition (*zhi de zhijue*), yet he preferred the Confucian way of attaining ultimate reality through moral practice and moral self-awareness. He thought that humans could achieve intellectual intuition through moral action and realize the noumenon of humanness (*ren*), which represented for him the ultimate reality or the thing in itself. Sometimes Mou named it "the free infinite mind/heart," or "the true self," that, as noumenon, possessed universality, infinity, and creativity, and through a process of self-negation similar to Johann Gottlieb Fichte's "I" positing a "non-I," it could unfold itself into a world of phenomena. In Mou's philosophy, intellectual intuition is an act of self-awareness of the free infinite mind, which replaced the concept of a personal God in Christianity, Islam, and Judaism.

Mou's moral metaphysics, by making Confucianism a kind of metaphysics, and thus making Confucian moral praxis an instrument for attaining ultimate reality, neglected the proper value and practical methods of Confucian moral praxis. Also, he considered morality a matter of finding one's true self, without relation to others, and thus without a proper ethical dimension. In this way, Confucianism lends its own weak points to a grand metaphysical system modeled after European philosophy. Also, by positing such an exclusively moral metaphysics, Mou neglected other metaphysical experiences, such as those in encounters with nature, in artistic creativity, in religious piety, and in historical encounters—all so rich in metaphysical implications in traditional Chinese culture. In his absolute idealism, Mou blurred and even confused the distinction between reality itself and constructed reality.

METAPHORICAL METAPHYSICS

Chinese philosophical traditions such as Confucianism, Daoism, and Buddhism all hold that ultimate reality, whatever its name, always has an unfathomable dimension and therefore is hidden from all human constructions and human languages. For this reason, the terms Chinese philosophers use to indicate ultimate reality—terms such as *tian* (heaven), *ren* (humanness), *cheng* (sincerity), *dao* (the Way), the mind, principles, emptiness, etc.—are used metaphorically rather than descriptively or ostensively. They express ideas about ultimate reality with a certain tangible image of it, which is to say that they are in some sense image-ideas, instead of pure ideas. Chinese philosophers, when grasping ultimate reality with enlightening insight, tend to form original image-ideas, something between a pure idea and an iconic image, thereby retaining the holistic character of the manifestation and the intuitive nature of the perception. This idea-image evokes the richness of ultimate reality without exhausting it, and therefore has the status of a metaphor.

This basic characteristic of Chinese metaphysics provides foundations for Chinese artistic, moral, and scientific practices and historical actions. Artistic creativity, by imagination and poetic transformation, renders this idea-image into a concrete iconic image and thereby materializes it. In moral and ethical reasoning, practical reason brings the idea-image to bear on an ethical situation, leading one to intervene and thereby take moral responsibility. In science, natural philosophers built models with reference to image-ideas, creating analogical images of reality so as to grasp natural processes in an organic and holistic way. In the historical arena, one can discern, by referring to idea-images, traces of notions of ultimate reality in the historical events and actions taken by historical agents. In this sense, Chinese art, ethics, science, and history are imbued with metaphysical significance.

Generally speaking, metaphor allows us to see one thing as something else. In other words, metaphor has an "as-structure," a term first used by Martin Heidegger to characterize interpretation. In the Chinese tradition, metaphysics or discourse on the Way is already a metaphorical interpretation of ultimate reality. Compared with the original manifestation of ultimate reality, various ways of realizing idea-images also possess an as-structure, in the sense that they allow us to see ultimate reality as idea-images, the later thereby serving a certain metaphorical function. In this sense, Chinese metaphysics can be characterized as a kind of metaphorical metaphysics. Viewing it in this way, one can achieve a true understanding of the spirit of Chinese philosophy.

See also Chinese Philosophy: Language and Logic; Chinese Philosophy: Religion.

Bibliography

Aristotle. *Metaphysics*. In *The Complete Works of Aristotle*, Vol. 2, edited by Jonathan Barnes. Princeton, NJ: Princeton University Press, 1984.

Chan, Wing-tsit, trans. and ed. *A Source Book in Chinese Philosophy*. Princeton, NJ: Princeton University Press, 1963.

Fang, Thomé. *Chinese Philosophy: Its Spirit and Its Development*. Taipei: Linking, 1981.

I Ching, or Book of Changes. 2 vols. Translated by Cary F. Baynes from the German version of Richard Wilhelm. New York: Pantheon Books, 1950.

Kong Yingda. *Zhouyi zhengyi*. In *Shisanjing zhushu* (Commentary on the thirteen Confucian classics), Vol. 1. Taipei: Yiwen yinshuguan, 1985.

Lau, D. C., trans. *Confucius: the Analects*. London: Penguin, 1979.

Lau, D. C., trans. *Lao Tzu: Tao Te Ching* London: Penguin, 1963.

Mo Di. *Mozi*. Taipei: Guanwen shuju, 1965.

Mou Zongsan. *Zhi di zhixue yu Zhongguo zhexue* (Intellectual intuition and Chinese philosophy). Taipei: Taiwan shangwuyin shuguan, 1971.

Mou Zongsan. *Xinti yu xingti* (The substance of mind and the substance of nature). Taipei: Zhengzhong shuju, 1978.

Mou Zongsan. *Yuanshan lun* (On supreme good). Taipei: Taiwan xuesheng shuju, 1985.

Needham, Joseph. *Science and Civilization in China*, Vol. 3. Cambridge, U.K.: Cambridge University Press, 1959.

Robinson, H. Richard. *Early Mādhyamika in India and China*. Delhi: Motilal Banarsidass, 1976.

Shen, Vincent (Shen Tsingsong). "Laozi de xingshang sixiang" (Laozi's metaphysics). *Zhexue yu wenhua* 15 (12) (1988): 814–822.

Shen, Vincent (Shen Tsingsong). "Zhuangzi de daolun: Dui dangdai xingshang kunhuo de yige jieda" (Zhuangzi's discourse on the Way: Answers to contemporary metaphysical questions). *Guoli zhengzhi daxue zhexue xuebao* 1 (1994): 19–34.

Shen, Vincent (Shen Tsingsong). *Wuli zhihou: Xingshangxue de fazhan* (After physics: The development of metaphysics). Taipei: Niudun, 1987.

Sengzhao. *Zhaolun* (Treatises of Zhao). In *Taishō shinshū daizōkyō*, edited by Takakusu Junjirō and Watanabe Kaigyoku, Vol. 45. Tokyo: Taishō Issaikyō Kankōkai, 1924–1932.

Tang Junyi. *Zhongguo zhexue yuanlun: Yuandao pian* (Inquiry on Chinese Philosophy: Inquiry on the Dao). 3 vols. Hong Kong: New Asia Institute, 1973.

Xunzi. *Xunzi*. In *Er shi er zi* (Works of twenty-two masters), Vol. 4. Taipei: Prophet Press, 1976.

Zhang Dainian. *Key Concepts in Chinese Philosophy*. Translated by Edmund Ryden. New Haven, CT: Yale University Press, 2002.

Zhu Xi. *Zhuzi yulei* (Classified conversations of Master Zhu). Books 1 and 5. Beijing: Zhonghua shuju, 1999.

Vincent Shen (2005)

RELIGION

The subject of the religious dimensions of Chinese philosophy covers both a vast time period—at least two and a half millennia—and a vast array of religious traditions, including theistic religions like Islam and Christianity. This entry, however, will focus on only a few topics and on two indigenous traditions—Confucianism and Daoism—and those streams of Buddhism often, if controversially, said to be most characteristically Chinese, such as the Chan (Japanese Zen) tradition. These traditions not only share features but adherents of each, even fierce adherents, often adopted ideas and practices from the other traditions in ways that can seem disconcerting to people familiar with only Western religions. (Thus, the truth in the clichés that a person can be a Confucian at work and a Daoist at home or that Chinese Buddhists often employ Confucian ethical ideas.) This phenomenon raises interesting philosophical questions about the meaning, in China, of a religious tradition as well as about the character of an adherent's structure of beliefs, but this entry will treat them only obliquely in what follows.

Another, perhaps more vexing concern is the nature of the relationship between religion and philosophy in China. This subject has often been examined, in both China and the West, in a way that basically reflects the desire to guarantee that Chinese philosophy has none of the baleful qualities that characterize religion (religion in this context usually means folk religion, or put more baldly, superstition and magic). The relationship is, however, complicated, and one can best approach it by discussing the notion of religion as it affects this subject.

THE NOTIONS OF RELIGION AND RELIGIOUS THOUGHT

The attempt to define the phenomenon of religion and religious thought (and thereby also specify the forms of various religions and their processes of thinking) is a modern Western project—and one with many critics. It often combines attempts to map out a sphere of human life in a reasonably objective fashion with a desire to improve human life, which usually means to make human affairs more rational. The treatment of Chinese religion, a notoriously messy phenomenon or set of phenomena, exemplifies most that is bad and good in the project.

One is, however, interested in only one facet of that treatment, and one can begin this investigation by turning to Clifford Geertz's (1973) sophisticated and immensely influential account (or definition) of religion. For him a religion is: "(1) a system of symbols which acts to (2) establish powerful, pervasive, and long-lasting moods and motivations in men [an ethos] by (3) formulating conceptions of a general order of existence [a worldview] and (4) clothing these conceptions with such an aura of factuality that (5) the moods and motivations seem uniquely realistic." Geertz comments at length on this definition, but of special importance is his claim that "a group's ethos is rendered intellectually reasonable by being … adapted to the … world view … while the world view is rendered emotionally convincing by being presented as an image of [the ethos]" (pp. 89–90).

This account seems to fit much Chinese religious thought, even to pinpoint crucial features of it. This is especially true if one focuses both on how Geertz exhibits the porous boundaries between elite and popular attitudes and, especially, on how he develops the ways his five elements interact with each other to create a closed perspective, a seamless web of reflection and reinforcement, in which ethos and worldview interact. Daoism is replete with stunning examples of these processes, but they also appear prominently in other traditions.

Moreover, and of special significance for this entry, the religious thought that results is detailed and can even count as rigorous, given its premises and notions of entailment. Furthermore, it often involves cosmological or cosmogonic subjects, many of which include science-like accounts of both natural and human phenomenon. (Correlative thinking, which finds homologies between the natural and human to control the latter through aligning it with the former, is only one of the most prominent and famous instances.) Finally, much of this thinking depicts a universe that is well, even fabulously, endowed with a great variety of beings (e.g., see Wang Bi 1994; Ko Hung 1966; Robinet, 1997, pp. 115–148, 195–256.).

Such thinking shares, however, few of the assumptions and notions that would make it credible to one's common contemporary experience, much less to one's understanding of philosophy. That is, this thinking cannot be formulated in a way that meets the conditions of plausibility found in an experience informed by, for instance, modern scientific explanation, historical consciousness, and ideas about the rights of all humans. Moreover, it makes difficult any understanding both of changes within a tradition, even if such changes were not always clearly recognized by participants, and of reasoned conversations among adherents of different traditions.

A focus on these kinds of Chinese religious thought, a common focus among scholars today, surely can be justified as a valuable and integral kind of historical inquiry. Nevertheless, this kind of focus also underlies the common perception that almost all Chinese philosophy lacks real analytical rigor, sophisticated modes of inquiry, and evident ways in which to attend to significant alternative views and therefore to reflect critically on given social forms.

The aim here, in contrast to the kind of historical inquiry just noted, is to show the ways in which many religious dimensions in Chinese thought are imperfectly captured by such criticisms and therefore have a claim on one's philosophical attention. Indeed, by examining three topics at length, and mentioning several others, this entry will illustrate how one can enrich an understanding of both philosophy and religion that, understandably, arises mainly from Western examples. One can, that is, be involved in the distinctive sort of intellectual exercise in which one tries to place oneself within a world that is much larger than the world one normally inhabits, a world the modern situation has, thankfully, forced on one. Before beginning that, however, one needs briefly to examine a different approach to the idea of religion.

The word *religious* refers of course to many phenomena, but most important in this case is the reference to an orientation that differs from and judges many features of the ordinary world, even if it also underlies other features of that world. (It is the latter feature that Geertz's [1973] examination usually emphasizes.) The religious, in this sense, rejects commonplace approaches to human fulfillment because normal life contains too many apparently insurmountable difficulties and because a marvelous spiritual actualization is possible.

The dialectic of great need and grand fulfillment means this orientation fits within what can be called a discontinuous or nonameliorative type of religion. This type of religion is, in many ways, fundamentally discontinuous with the activities and expectations of normal life; it seeks far more than just to ameliorate the problems ordinary life produces, and therefore it makes a substantial break with normal life rejecting attempts to build on what is already present. In contrast, in an continuous or ameliorative religion people work within the framework normal life provides. Their aim is to deepen and extend the best ideas and practices people have. The latter applies bandages to what are perceived as minor wounds, while the former calls for major surgery. The latter, of course, labels that kind of major surgery mutilation, while the former labels the mere application of bandages malpractice.

The distinction between discontinuous and continuous religion is not a simple binary one. Rather, the two types define the ends of a continuum and specific features of a religious tradition will fit at places within the continuum. Significant features of Confucianism, for example, fit on the continuous end and significant features of early Daoism and Chan Buddhism on the discontinuous end. (Moreover, many of the most substantial debates among and within these traditions are illuminated by understanding where on the continuum a disputed feature, such as meditational activity, fits.) Nevertheless, all of them have pronounced discontinuous elements, and they appear prominently in their most able philosophical thinkers (e.g., see Mencius 1970, Book 2A; Chuang-Tzu 2001, pp. 76–93; Hui-neng 1967, #28–#47, #149–#174; Graham 1958, pp. 67–91).

These traditions may lack many of the discontinuous qualities that characterize theistic religious, but they also share other features, if often manifesting them in a distinctive way. Put schematically, three discontinuous religious elements are especially important in these traditions. One is a focus on a sacred realm that is related to but differs dramatically from the human realm. This realm provides thinkers with a perspective from which they can evaluate ordinary activities in ways that most people find perplexing at best and insulting at worst. Another is a belief that kinds of empowerment occur that exceed what appears in ordinary life, are crucial to people attaining any true flourishing, and can produce people who transcend the limits of ordinary understanding. Specifying exactly how this empowerment operates and how sacred and human realms interact, even how independent they are, is difficult enough, however, to demand special uses of language. (As it will be seen, despite its theoretical imprecision the needed language aids rather than impedes the fundamental spiritual discipline of self-cultivation.)

A final discontinuous element is the distinctive quality of members' adherence to the traditions of which they are a part. These thinkers recognize that traditions contain regenerative powers individuals alone could not produce and yet also can be a source of debilitating false fixities. This recognition leads them both to treasure their traditions and to be extremely sensitive to the dangers present in false teachings, misleading authorities, and the communities that gather around them.

TOPICS IN CHINESE RELIGIOUS THOUGHT

One can now turn to three subjects that illustrate the distinctive contribution to philosophy that religious elements in Chinese philosophy can provide. One is the subject of ritual, a second the differences and similarities between normal and religious excellences, and a third the need to employ various genres to present religious realities persuasively, a topic that helps one understand some distinctive, formal features of Chinese philosophy. Before beginning that examination, however, one should briefly note six other topics that illustrate the range of pertinent material that could be examined. This entry will, if telegraphically, describe each of the six; provide one paradigmatic, and accessible, instance from early Chinese thought; and then note resemblances to Western materials, thereby risking the embarrassment brief generalizations can produce.

(1) In each tradition one finds the belief that skillful people, and thus the idea of skillfulness, manifests a religious excellence that tells one much about the character of perfected action, thought, and selfhood. Little that resembles this focus, and the understanding that results from it, has ever appeared in Western philosophical discussions (Chuang-Tzu 2001, pp. 62–65, 135–142).

(2) Each tradition treats, if often with different results, the question of participation in or retreat from social or political involvement, seeing it as a choice that can be understood philosophically only if one grasps the religious dimensions of each alternative. A version of the question has, of course, been central in the West, but its religious dimensions—and what arises from considering them—has been far less central (Mencius 1970, Books 4A, 5B).

(3) Each tradition sees the purported religious excellence of aimless wandering (*you*), powerfully presented in early Daoism, as an ideal that raises the deepest philosophical questions about ordinary ideas of intention and responsibility. The absence of a similar ideal, and thus of the resulting questions, means certain religious challenges to basic ideas about human purposes and obligations are never fully engaged in the West (Chuang-Tzu 2001, pp. 43–47, 66–75).

(4) An agnostic posture toward many central religious notions is understood by many thinkers in these traditions to be a mark of true spiritual achievement. Neither the implications nor the gen-

eral importance of this posture are probed in the Western as they are in China, although the attitude surely is not absent (Xunzi 1994, pp. 3–32. 88–112).

(5) Humor is a crucial religious excellence in early Daoism (as well as in the Chan tradition) and the philosophical import of the perspective humor generates is illustrated constantly and occasionally even analyzed at length. With some notable exceptions, humor is rarely a central subject in especially Western theistic traditions (Chuang-Tzu 2001, pp. 122–125, 207–210).

(6) All these traditions provide myriad illustrations of the ways in which commentaries on texts thought to be religiously authoritative constitute a, perhaps the, major way in which philosophical thinking is both motivated and constrained. The resemblance to traditional practices in the West is close here, but both the elusive character of the Chinese texts commented on and the character of the constraints on inquiry provide illuminating insights (Confucius 2003, Books 4–7).

Any of these six topics could productively be examined at length, but now the focus of this entry will shift to three topics that are especially illuminating for one's inquiry: ritual, the relationship between normal and religious virtues, and the genres needed to present religious realities persuasively.

RITUAL

Ritual, probably the most adequate of the multitudinous translations of the character *li*, is surely among the most distinctive and complex of all Chinese notions. Put simply, the single notion covers two activities that most contemporary Westerners think are quite different. One activity is solemn, explicit religious activities such as marriage or internment services. The other activity, however, is what can be called etiquette or, more accurately, those reasonable and humane learned conventions that make up the ethos of a culture (e.g., see Xunzi 1994, pp. 49–73; Chuang-Tzu 2001, pp. 87–93; Robinet 1997, pp. 166–183; Gregory 1991, pp. 41–43, 274–285; Ching 2000, pp. 72–90).

Ritual covers, then, everything from the solemn performance of an elaborate ceremony to the "excuse me" after a sneeze. Explicit religious activities and social activities are, that is, part of one continuum, although there are, of course, notable differences. In specifically religious rituals, for example, the focus is on humans facing thresholds, situations where people move to a new state or respond to what lies beyond their ordinary routines.

The combining of these two senses of ritual is open to the criticism that it displays an unsophisticated kind of thinking that fails to differentiate what can and should be separated. The defense of the combination, one most evident in Confucianism but present in the other two traditions, rests on the notion that social rituals are more than just pedestrian social facts. Social and religious rituals resemble each other, that is, because both are sacred ceremonies that express and foster a spontaneous coordination that is rooted in reverence. Moreover, both exemplify learned, conventional behavior that manifests distinctly human rather than simply animal-like actions. Both therefore promote crucial human qualities and respond to central human needs.

Ritual is, then, a notion of overarching significance in Chinese religious thought and contests about its character and value are frequent. In fact, debates about ritual often served to focus debates among competing visions of life. Seeing, therefore, the various views of ritual (social and religious) that continually appear, if in somewhat different forms in different times and traditions, can help one understand the philosophical import of the idea.

Especially prominent in these debates are three kinds of attacks on ritual and three defenses of it. Put telegraphically, the different positions are as follows. One group attacks rituals as a wasteful, even unjust, use of scarce natural and human resources. Another group attacks them as a social artifice that distorts significant human capacities and reinforces destructive social organizations. A third group sees them as an inadequate form of social control that is best replaced by clear rewards and punishments.

One defense of ritual sees in it a process that activates transhuman forces and uses those forces to help humans. Another justifies ritual in terms of the innate human capacities for it or even inertial tendencies toward it; human beings, that is, need ritual if they are to be actualized. A last defense believes rituals are sanctified by tradition; they therefore need no real justification and must always be meticulously followed no matter what the apparent price.

Many, although surely not all, of the most sophisticated thinkers from these traditions think each of these approaches is flawed, and they therefore reinterpret religious rituals both to win outsiders' assent and to deepen their own and other adherents' assent. They usually proceed, to focus just on religious rituals, by distinguishing among three different kinds. First are rituals that are useless or even harmful; sacrificing a pig to cure an illness falls in this class. Second are rituals that adorn life in important but not critical ways; rituals to produce rain fall in this class. Third are rituals that provide a crucial service to human life; death or internment rituals fall in this class.

Such reformulations manifest a set of common characteristics, and they are worth noting because of what they tell one about attitudes to religion. Most generally, the overarching goal of all these reformulations is the protection and encouragement of fully flourishing human activity. That goal provides the criterion both for dividing necessary from unnecessary religious ideas and actions and for reforming the meaning of the necessary ones. Second, these reformulations critically examine all simple anthropomorphic descriptions of the transhuman realm and replace them with designations that are symbolic or stress the mysterious. Third, if closely related to the second, they criticize depictions of activities that describe a manipulative relationship between the human and the transhuman. In fact, they often redescribe those activities in terms of how feelings are rearranged and spiritual attitudes are generated.

The grounds these thinkers use to defend ritual tell one much about the role of religion in Chinese philosophy. They usually, that is, presume that one is frail in ways that often are difficult for one to accept. Not only does one live between origins and terminations one cannot control but one also constantly faces the numinous. Moreover, one is prone to primordial reactions, and one must treat them in a fashion that both controls their destructive side and nurtures their constructive side. Stringent limits, then, define what people can do; they cannot immediately form themselves into what simple rational judgment might commend them to be. Ritual roles present, for instance, roles that people have no real choice but to assume, with the role of the mourner, however defined, being perhaps the clearest instance.

Underlying this perspective is a negative judgment about a philosophical approach that rejects ritual because it desires to produce a rigorous and coherent picture of the world that will provide simple, reasonable grounds for ideas and actions. Proponents of this approach reject internment rituals, for example, because to them the principle of noncontradiction is crucial; a person is either dead or not dead. They want to face life and death directly and they put everything into clear-cut categories.

Against such an approach, it is argued that when life is seen clearly, and in the death of others one sees it especially clearly, one can neither make it into a coherent understandable whole, nor respond adequately to it by focusing on simple practical expedients. Human life is too fragile and delicate, too complex and contradictory to capture in simple rational systems. One touches life as it actually is, then, only through the complex pathos, the human contradictions, the struggle to find peace, and the openness to the numinous that rituals exemplify. A related but different kind of judgment on some kinds of ordinary philosophical attitudes underlies the second subject, and to that one may now turn.

RELIGIOUS AND ORDINARY VIRTUES

To distinguish between religious and ordinary virtues (or excellences) in Chinese thought might seem to be problematic or even just wrong-headed, but investigating the subject can illustrate, among other things, the usefulness of examining apparently inapplicable Western ideas in the Chinese context. The relevant Chinese thinkers never, of course, make any formal distinction between normal and religious virtues, except when discussing those virtues that bind only those adepts who adopt monastic rules. Moreover, their general conceptual framework does not lead them (and probably literally could not allow them) to distinguish between what, say, Catholic Christianity calls natural and supernatural virtues. They surely would, that is, reject any distinction that rests on a clear-cut differentiation between what humans cause and what a deity, distinguished by the quality of aseity or being unmoved, causes.

Nevertheless, a crucial feature of much Chinese philosophy is the conviction that some virtues (or unnamed features of some virtues) have a special character. They produce actions and attitudes that both differ from normal virtues and change a range of normal actions in profoundly important ways. In fact, a number of traditional Western ways of theoretically distinguishing religious and normal virtues seem to be implied. Examples include sharp distinctions made among the kinds of objects pursued, among the goals of the intentions manifested, among the precise forms of behavior produced, and among the kinds of empowerment displayed. Moreover, and perhaps even more striking, many think humans are susceptible to transformations so total as to make some individuals fundamentally different from the rest, to make them, for example, the possessors of truly extraordinary abilities to affect the natural and human world (e.g., see Chuang-Tzu 2001, pp. 96–99, 143–150; Yearley 1990, pp. 144–168; Gregory 1991, pp. 255–274; Graham 1958, pp. 96–118).

A simpler example of such transformations concerns the role of distinctive kinds of belief in adherents' lives, a role that both resembles and differs from the role of faith in some theistic traditions. These beliefs go considerably beyond the evidence that would, and should, compel assent in normal affairs, and they often play a prominent role in guiding action. They include beliefs about the significance of certain books and historical figures, but most revealing may be beliefs about the role of some virtues and perspectives.

Two straightforward but illuminating examples of these latter beliefs come from what is probably the earliest part of the earliest (and arguably most important) book in Chinese thought, Confucius's *Analects* (Lunyu): "Virtue (*de*) never dwells in solitude; it will always bring neighbors" (4, 25), and "The Master said 'In the morning hear the Way (*Dao*); in the evening, die content'" (4, 8). Each passage represents a dramatic enough claim to be considered religious, as well as, of course, a claim that can be, and was, probed philosophically.

Indeed, beliefs like these are often at the center of debates with those people who lack them because they find them either unintelligible or unjustified. The religious perspectives that define each of these traditions, that is, are far from self evident to everyone. They include attitudes and confident judgments about many matters that seem problematic or even bizarre to many people outside the tradition. Moreover, adherents within a tradition also entertain questions about their own beliefs; they are not inoculated against the queries and doubts that other people manifest. One crucial spiritual dynamic in all these traditions, then, is to see obvious problems in their own position, if one uses either ordinary standards or another tradition's standards, and yet continually to reaffirm specific, central beliefs.

These Chinese ideas on religious beliefs, as well as on other virtues, reflect an ontological perspective in which the sacred realm and the ordinary realm are closely intertwined, in which an organismic, an interrelated and interdependent, cosmology operates. Indeed, Chinese religious thought manifests in its own fashion the ontological principle that guides the analysis of this topic in, say, Aristotelian Christianity: The sacred does not destroy but presupposes and perfects the normal. Unlike many traditions the ordinary is not, that is, eradicated by the religious and replaced by something fundamentally different. (This feature probably most clearly distinguishes discontinuous Chinese religious traditions from most other discontinuous traditions.) Rather, the ordinary provides the basis that is developed into a more actualized form. In fact, one can even argue that Chinese thinkers are able to develop this principle more fully than could Aristotelian Christians because they lack those theological ideas that impede a full development, notably the notion of a natural order created by a God distinguished from it by aseity.

These ideas lead Chinese philosophers to understand (perhaps even more clearly than do their counterparts in other traditions) that treating religious virtue well involves a kind of balancing of opposing demands. On the one hand, religious virtues are virtues where one cannot draw on too many normal presumptions and arguments to defend, or even to make plausible, the virtue else it ceases to be a religious virtue. On the other hand, however, one cannot simply disregard normal presumptions and arguments else the virtue ceases to be a plausible option for most people. This activity involves balancing on a tightrope, a posture that recalls Ludwig Wittgenstein's comment that an "honest religious thinker is like a tightrope walker … [who] almost looks as though he were walking on nothing but air … [because his] support is the slenderest imaginable … [and] yet it really is possible to walk on it" (1984, p. 73e).

The balancing act involves not falling into either of two dangerous alternatives. On the one hand, the religious virtue must not rely on notions that no reasonable person can really entertain seriously. The claim that only through sacrificial rituals is one able to appease a spirit's anger or a dead person's perturbation is an example of such a notion. The virtues cannot rest, then, on what seems to sensible people to be implausible ideas. On the other hand, if the virtue is truly a religious one, it must not rely on such common and sensible notions that most people would, with little thought, accept it. The idea that one should help others if the help causes neither pain nor dislocation would be an example. The virtue cannot, then, simply repeat the conventional wisdom of the day. The need for this kind of distinctive balancing when presenting religious materials leads one to the genres such an approach demands.

GENRE AND THE PERSUASIVE PRESENTATION OF RELIGIOUS REALITIES

The delicate kind of balancing we see in the presentation of religious virtues leads directly to the subject of the ways in which religious features affect the genres, the modes of presentation, manifest in much Chinese philosophy. (These choices about genre are, moreover, especially significant because a number of these philosophers were capable of, and well trained in, more rigorous forms of theoretical analysis.) Indeed, the rationale for presenting religious features in different genres provides an excellent way to examine the widespread perception that Chinese philosophy often does not seem to operate as philosophy ought to operate (e.g., see Mencius 1970, Book 6A; Chuang-Tzu 2001, pp. 48–61, 106–107; Hui-neng 1967, #1–#10; Wang Yang-Ming 1963, # 139, #168–#171, #226–231).

It is said, that is, that Chinese thought (as noted earlier) lacks sustained formal argumentation, sophisticated forms of analytic inquiry, and evident ways in which to reflect critically on presuppositions. These criticisms can witness to the kind of disabling parochialism (and circularity) that allows for little discussion, but their more powerful forms focus well the subject of how presentation and persuasion operate in Chinese religious philosophy.

The best way to approach this subject is to look at responses to a simple, deceptively simple, question: How can one persuasively represent a world, a world the understanding of which is crucial to any true human fulfillment, that far exceeds one's normal understanding? Representing that world persuasively is critical because only through such representation can one keep before people realities central to any religious vision but discontinuous with ordinary understandings. Representing that world is exceedingly difficult because it involves presenting realities that differ from, and even challenge, people's ordinary perspectives. The needed kinds of language must therefore persuade people in ways that differ from the kinds of persuasion either logical argument or even ordinary language utilize.

One illuminating instance of such a mode, and one much favored in China, is the use of concise, compelling, and often elusive locutions, such as the two from Confucius noted earlier about virtue always bringing neighbors and about the Way and death. These expressions provide one with a great deal of textured material in a terse, striking form. Indeed, they both arrest and often stay with one because they give one something intriguing and rewarding to which one can return. These statements can, then, embed themselves in one's mind and lead one to mull them over, searching out their various implications and applications to one's own life. Such statements become meditational objects that work on one, as do all meditational objects, in both evident and mysterious ways. A specific literary device like this aims, then, to produce in the reader fascination, sympathetic identification, attentive perplexity, and other even more complex emotional states, such as pretending. All are states that can produce significant personal changes.

Put another way, two features of religious perspectives make necessary forms like these: First, simple rational arguments about such perspectives will only rarely affect those people who most need help, a group that includes most of everyone at different points in their lives. Second, those arguments, or even the appropriate principles they produce, will often not fundamentally affect most people in those situations where they most need help.

Especially important, therefore, is persuading people that ideas, actions, and perspectives they find odd, perplexing, or simply wrong are worth considering, even worth adopting. And that task's difficulty is heightened by the relative absence, in comparison to theistic traditions, either of limpid theological propositions about the sacred's character or of graphic accounts in authoritative texts of the actions of the highest sacred beings.

The problem, then, is how to employ language that is odd, often very odd, and yet still have it be persuasive. (It resembles, therefore, the balancing needed in presenting ordinary and religious virtues, but the scope of operations is much wider.) To attain the needed representation one must stretch language beyond its evident limits and recognizable shapes while one also understands that such stretching seems to violate those forms and expectations that allow language to convey meaning. How can one, that is, represent a world that transcends one's ordinary categories and even reference points in a way that is both realistic and persuasive? The Chinese responses to these interrelated questions, evident more in their practices than in their theories, rest on three ideas, or more accurately claims, that are implicit in their practice.

The first and most obvious involves distinguishing the persuasively presented from the well argued and emphasizing the former. Presentations may, then, fail to fit well the criteria for good argument, indeed may even be instances of reasoned attempts to doubt the value, when the subject is religious, of many kinds of reasoned arguments. (*Persuasively presented* is, of course, a considerably wider category than is *well argued*, and utilizing it necessarily involves one, as it will be seen, in the treatment of issues about the character of rhetorical presentation and those subjects that follow in its wake.)

Second is a general characteristic of much Chinese religious thought: the judgment that considerations about the deepest religious matters best manifest their distinctive subject matter when understood as treating irresolvable but illuminating and productive tensions. These tensions arise from the presence of apparently conflicting ideas and experiences each of which is irreducible; any resolution, therefore, that even diminishes the tensions must be rejected. Indeed, a resolution need not even be sought because keeping the tension's irresolvability in mind both enables people to understand better the character of religious reflection and presentation and clarifies their relationship to religious realities.

The third notion or claim is a direct corollary of the preceding two: the idea that literalism is the most dangerous of all human deformations at least when religion is the subject, and probably even when life itself is the subject. Literalism can take different forms but at one end of the spectrum is an unwillingness (or perhaps inability) to read beyond a surface meaning—literalism in its most evident sense. At the other end, however, is an unwillingness (or perhaps inability) to do anything but read beyond the most evident sense; the wooden pursuit of allegorical readings displays another, more abstract kind of literalism. The first fails to grasp the import of the representation; the second's easy movement beyond the surface overlooks all the surface's rich texture.

Chinese religious thinkers, then, usually focus less on straightforward conceptual analysis or argument and more on persuasive presentations that work with irresolvable but revelatory and productive tensions, aim to change people's understanding and action, and nurture the avoidance of literalism. That focus helps to explain their use of genres that are, to employ Western categories, more often literary than theoretical.

The use of these genres, genres that aim to present realities that can be made evident or compelling in no other way, means rhetoric is crucial. And that means that one does not simply face passages that are the shadowgraphs of ideas, passages that can be put into propositional forms that leave no remainder. The language used is not the mere adornment of an idea; it is constitutive of the idea. The language used is not just a device to persuade the recalcitrant or intellectually inept. Rather, it is what makes possible any appropriation of the proper perspective.

Processes of persuasion like these can be thought to be problematic for many reasons. For example, the process seems to disregard too many significant, if ordinary, kinds of thinking; the process will often fail to provide warrants for adjudicating differences; and the process is not attentive enough to the need for the theoretical analysis and justification of at least many rhetorical statements.

Chinese thinkers are aware of these problems. They understand they must evaluate rhetoric and that such an evaluation involves both a detailed understanding of how rhetoric works and a grasp of the character and appropriate roles of logical argument. (In fact, they often display a remarkable grasp of different rhetorical modes and therefore also of the ways in which such modes may obfuscate.) Probably most important, however, is a recognition that rhetorical presentations are part of a more general process of self-cultivation that involves teachers, various spiritual disciplines, and participation in a tradition. This remains true despite the difficulties they often see in the ordinary understandings of self-cultivation and of traditions that dominate most communities.

Nevertheless, it remains true that they often gravitate to distinctive genres when presenting religious perspectives because only those genres can produce what must be produced. They accept, that is, a version of the "good person criterion," a criterion also evident in the Aristotelian tradition (Yearley 1990, pp. 62–72). They believe that a person's character determines what can be perceived and understood, and therefore that the ultimate measure of a person or an action's excellence, or even meaning, is the excellence of the person who makes the judgment. Most important here, they recognize that this criterion has dramatic implications for both presentation and persuasion, and they are more than willing to live with the consequences.

See also Buddhism; Chinese Philosophy: Daoism; Chinese Philosophy: Ethics; Chinese Philosophy: Metaphysics and Epistemology; Confucius.

Bibliography

Ching, Julia. *The Religious Thought of Chu Hsi.* New York: Oxford University Press, 2000.

Chuang-Tzu. *Chuang-tzu: The Inner Chapters.* Translated by Angus Graham. Indianapolis, IN: Hackett, 2001.

Confucius. *Confucius Analects, with Selections from Traditional Commentaries.* Translated by Edward Slingerland. Indianapolis, IN: Hackett, 2003.

Geertz, Clifford. *The Interpretation of Cultures: Selected Essays.* New York: Basic, 1973.

Graham, Angus. *Two Chinese Philosophers: Ch'eng Ming-tao and Ch'eng Yi-Yuan.* London: Lund Humphries, 1958.

Gregory, Peter. *Tsung-mi and the Sinification of Buddhism.* Princeton, NJ: Princeton University Press, 1991.

Hui-neng. *The Platform Sutra of the Sixth Patriarch: The Text of the Tun-Huang Manuscript.* Translated by Philip Yampolsky. New York: Columbia University Press, 1967.

Ko Hung. *Alchemy, Medicine, and Religion in the China of A.D. 320: The Nei P'ien of Ko Hung (Pao-p'u tzu).* Translated by James R. Ware. Cambridge, MA: MIT Press, 1966.

Mencius. *Mencius.* Translated by D. C. Lau. Baltimore, MD: Penguin, 1970.

Robinet, Isabelle. *Taoism: Growth of a Religion.* Translated by Phyllis Brooks. Stanford, CA: Stanford University Press, 1997. [op. 1992]

Wang Bi. *The Classic of Changes: A New Translation of the I Ching as Interpreted by Wang Bi.* Translated by Richard Lynn. New York: Columbia University Press, 1994.

Wang Yang-Ming. *Instructions for Practical Living and Other Neo-Confucian Writings by Wang Yang-Ming.* Translated by Wing-tsit Chan. New York: Columbia University Press, 1963.

Wittgenstein, Ludwig. *Culture and Value*, edited by G. H. Von Wright. Chicago: University of Chicago Press, 1984.

Xunzi. *Xunzi: A Translation and Study of the Complete Works.* Vol. 3. Translated by John Knoblock. Stanford, CA: Stanford University Press, 1994.

Yearley, Lee H. *Mencius and Aquinas: Theories of Virtue and Conceptions of Courage.* Albany: SUNY Press, 1990.

Lee H. Yearley (2005)

SOCIAL AND POLITICAL THOUGHT

Chinese philosophy began in the sixth century BCE with social and political philosophy as a response to the collapse of traditional bronze-age feudal society (Shang and Zhou dynasties). As the loyalty of the nobility to the Zhou kings began to give way to the realpolitik of sheer military might, dozens of small kingdoms vied with one another for imperial domination in what became known appropriately as the Warring States period (475–221 BCE). This strife ended when the kingdom of Qin finally conquered the last of its competitors to unite, for the first time, the many warring states into a single military, imperial empire.

The problem was how to unify and rule such a heterogeneous collection of different ethnic groups. Into this breach came China's first philosophers. In the feudal period, social custom was maintained by etiquette as practiced and maintained by the aristocrats and by punishments applied to ordinary people. People did the morally right thing not out of an inner sense of obligation but simply because this was the prescribed behavior for anyone born into a particular class. As the feudal order broke up, Confucians attempted to convert the customary etiquette of the hereditary nobility into an internally felt and inwardly directed moral imperative for everyone. The Daoists advocated a back-to-nature simplification in which government does little and simply lets the people pursue their own affairs, as they traditionally did for centuries. The Mohists tried to break down ethnic and tribal boundaries through the practice of impartial universal love. And the legalists tried to extend the role of punishment more broadly to everyone: aristocrats and educated elite, as well as peasants. There were thus four recommended replacements for the dying feudal social order: develop a universal personal morality (Confucians); return to a nearly anarchic state of nature (Daoists); embrace a policy of universal impartial love (Mohists); establish and universally enforce applicable law (legalists).

CONFUCIUS

Confucius (551–479 BCE) was the first thinker to offer new methods for the postfeudal period. Philosophers in the early Warring States period tended to be either conservatives who wanted to preserve the old values of the dying feudal system or revolutionaries who wanted to start afresh with new ideas and a new set of values. Confucius was one of the conservatives. He sought to revive on a new foundation the values of the Zhou dynasty, the last of the feudal regimes. Confucius claimed not to be an original thinker; he always said he was just preserving the past. But since the feudal order had virtually disappeared by the time Confucius was born, he realized that these values could only be preserved by restructuring them so as to meet the new conditions. In this effort he was certainly original. In the past, aristocratic feudal values were informally handed down from parents to children in elite noble families. Confucius was the first Chinese thinker to advocate that these values be systematized, logically defended, universalized, and formally taught to everyone. If everyone would learn and practice the ancient virtues of loyalty to elders and rulers (*cheng*), moral righteousness (*yi*), and compassion for others (*ren*), the country would be well run, contented, and prosperous. Indeed, Confucius insisted that if people would simply fulfill the roles assigned to them, all would behave virtuously. For example, if the ruler would act like a ruler (that is, protect and care for his people), the country would be well taken care of. The ruler who takes advantage of his subjects to enrich himself is not a true ruler and should not be called a ruler (*wang*). This is what Confucius called the "rectification of names": Things should be called by their right names, and people should live up to the roles assigned them by their designated titles.

Beyond assuming a universal basis for such an extension of the old feudal values, Confucius did not develop a theory of universal human nature. This he left to his followers. When the Daoists and other competing schools of philosophy criticized Confucius for foolishly trying to revive the old values of the nobility of a then defunct feudal era, Confucius's followers responded by arguing that all people have the same basic nature, that to be happy and successful, people must fulfill this nature, and that this required developing and following the traditional Chinese virtues of the ancient feudal nobility.

Soon after Confucius's death there arose many competing schools of philosophy in China and many competing varieties of Confucianism itself, reflecting serious disagreements among the followers of Confucius, especially Mencius and Xunzi. When the small warring states were finally united for the first time under the military dictatorship of Ying Zheng (259–210 BCE), China's first imperial emperor, the legalist philosophers (*fajia*) convinced the emperor that the only way to truly unite the country was to eliminate all the argumentative and therefore divisive schools of philosophy (except legalism). In 213 BCE all the philosophy books the government could find were burned, and some Confucians and other philosophers who refused to abandon their philosophical practice were buried alive. Shortly afterwards, during the Han dynasty (206 BCE–220 CE), the legalist position was reversed, an attempt was made to revive the ancient schools of philosophy, and after a prolonged debate, Confucianism was adopted over Daoism and Mohism as the official philosophy of the state. The only other philosophical school besides Confucianism to survive was Daoism, which then became a private philosophy of the educated elite, whose public lives were primarily Confucian. Confucianism thereby became China's official legitimizing discourse justifying imperial rule, although quietly and behind the scenes legalism continued to provide the practical basis for actual rule.

Confucius did not develop the systematic ethical theory we know today as Confucianism. This was left to his followers: Mencius, Xunzi, and Dong Zhongshu. Confucius himself sought to return to traditional feudal values (such as filial piety) of the Zhou dynasty. Confucius's critics, especially the Daoists, attacked this attempt to rehabilitate the traditional virtues. Just because such virtues may have worked in the past, what reason was there to suppose that these rules were applicable to the new circumstances? A theory of ethics should be based on something more permanent in nature and reality, not the historical conventions of a particular society at a particular time and place. In response to this criticism, the followers of Confucius developed the idea that the traditional Chinese virtues could be defended as based on an unchanging and eternal human nature shared by people of all classes, at all times, and at all places.

But *is* there a common human nature, and if so, what is that nature? Here the followers of Confucius could not reach agreement. Mencius held that human nature is essentially good, while Xunzi argued that it is essentially evil, to which Dong Zhongshu argued that it is both, that human nature comprised two opposing elements, one good and the other evil.

MENCIUS

In many ways Mencius (c. 376–c. 292 BCE) followed the example of Confucius. Like Confucius, he divided his time between offering (mostly unwanted) advice to the rulers of his day and teaching students in a private capacity. Also like Confucius, Mencius sought to rectify names. Things should be called by their correct names, and things (people) that did not live up to their names (titles) should not be called by those names. For example, when Mencius was asked whether it was morally permissible to kill a king, Mencius replied in effect that if this so-called king is a true king, then of course it is wrong to kill him, but if this so-called king is not a true king but only a tyrant, then killing him is not killing a king but only a tyrant, and so is morally permissible.

But in other ways Mencius deviated from the path followed by Confucius and most other Confucians before and after him. More than any other Confucian, including Confucius himself, Mencius emphasized the morality of following nature, human nature, as opposed to social convention. In this respect Mencius comes close to the Daoists. In one episode recorded in his book, Mencius tells the story of the man from Song who helped his rice plants grow taller by pulling on them, which of course caused them to wither and die. Mencius's point is that the farmer should have let nature take its course. Of course, the rice has to be planted and then transplanted and weeded and watered and protected from birds and other animals, but beyond that the rice plants should be left to grow and develop all by themselves without further human interference. By analogy, we should not impose alien social practices on children but should help them cultivate their innate human nature.

By the time of Mencius there were many competing schools of philosophy. Mencius often bemoaned the enormous popularity of what he regarded as two extremist schools of thought, the followers of Mozi (c. 468–c. 376 BCE) and Yang Zhu (440–360 BCE), Mozi arguing that we should love all people equally and Yang Zhu that we should not lift a finger to help anyone but ourselves. Like Confucius, Mencius followed a middle path between these two extremes, emphasizing the traditional Chinese virtue of filial piety, that is, loyalty to members of one's own family and obligation to those immediately above and below in the social hierarchy of one's particular community.

According to Mencius, all people are born with the potential and tendency to be kind-hearted and virtuous, though this potential can either be nourished and developed, so that the individual becomes good, or else neglected, thwarted, and perverted, so that the individual becomes bad. Mencius was not saying that children are moral from birth. He realized that they must be trained and taught, and that they learn by practice and experience. He also realized that neglected or mistreated children will usually become bad. Nonetheless, his theory is that in either case there is an innate tendency or disposition to be good.

In his most famous example, Mencius asked what is the immediate and spontaneous response of any person upon seeing a child about to fall into a well. Mencius said that everyone naturally and spontaneously wants to rush to help the child. This does not mean that everyone is a morally good person. It only means that everyone is born with the germ of the Confucian virtue of compassion (*ren*), along with the germ of the other traditional Chinese virtues of righteousness (*yi*), propriety (*li*), and wisdom (*zhi*).

Mencius valued this distinctively human capacity for virtue above all other parts of a person and urged readers to honor, preserve, and develop that part of themselves above all else. "To know one's nature is to know heaven [*tian*]" (*The Mencius*). That is, humans alone have the capacity to realize what their nature is and to choose to follow it and in this way to consciously align themselves with heaven. Mencius saw this human capacity as a bodily part (the benevolent mind that cannot bear to see others suffer), though the highest part, coming from heaven, in contrast with the rest of the human body, which people share with the lower animals and which comes from earth.

Although Mencius did not stress rationality as what is distinctively human, as Western philosophers do, he did stress the capacity of the mind (*xin*) to think. In *Mencius* (the book), Mencius argued that some people become better than others (even though they all have the same human nature) because they realize the value of this small but superior part of themselves.

Finally, Mencius is often called the most democratic of Chinese philosophers. Although Mencius, like Confucius before him, defended the ancient feudal traditions, especially of the Zhou dynasty, he radically reinterpreted them to conform to his own political ideas of equality. For example, in feudal times, society was arranged for the benefit of the aristocracy and defended as being mandated by Heaven (*tian ming*). Of course, it is hard to tell who has the mandate of heaven, except in a circular way by who actually rules. The ruler in power can claim to enjoy the mandate of heaven, and the only argument against this claim by those who oppose him is their ability to oust him from power and take over themselves. Mencius offers an independent, noncircular criterion for who has and does not have the mandate of heaven: that the ordinary people support and are happy with the government. The only justification for government and economic policy is that it serve the people. To give another example, in feudal times the division of political and economic duties was hereditary, whereas for Mencius this division of labor can only be justified on grounds of merit. Let each person serve according to his innate ability, whether as farmers, teachers, or government officials.

XUNZI

In the third century BCE the most prominent Confucian and one of the most important philosophers in China was Xunzi (340–245 BCE). Xunzi argued, against Mencius, that human nature is essentially evil, that is, selfish and aggressively antisocial. It is only through education, training, discipline, and the threat of punishment, Xunzi argued, that people become socially cooperative. Xunzi speculated that originally men were free to follow their own selfish bent without fear of recrimination or punishment. But when they realized that they were as often the victims of aggressive abuse as its perpetrators, that they were getting robbed as often as they were robbing from others, they willingly accepted the authority of a ruler capable of maintaining order and punishing transgressions. Like the social-contract philosopher Thomas Hobbes, Xunzi argued from people's evil nature to the need for a strong central government to control human behavior by education and a system of rewards and punishments. If strong governmental authority were removed, Xunzi speculated, chaos would result as the strong rode rough shod over the weak, with no law enforcement to prevent or punish them.

One major difference between Mencius's and Xunzi's theories of human nature is that Mencius defined human nature as what is uniquely and distinctively human, whereas Xunzi defined human nature as what all people are born with, even if this allotment is also shared with lower animals. Relating his theory to ancient, prephilosophical Chinese traditions, Xunzi said that human nature is the product of two factors. One, the contribution of heaven (*tian*), gives human beings the rational and intelligent capacity to be civilized, cultured, and virtuous, and the other, the contribution of earth (*di*), is our animal nature, which we are conscious of as feeling and emotion. Whereas Mencius said that we receive from heaven the germ of moral virtue, Xunzi maintained that we receive from heaven only the capacity or potential for virtue and civilized life.

Thus, for Xunzi, a person at birth is just like one of the lower animals except for possessing the capacity of becoming civilized and virtuous. If we define human nature as Xunzi did (as what all people are born with), then we will point to the tendencies people actually have to be greedy, selfish, and aggressive, but if we define human nature as Mencius did (as what is unique to people), then we will tend to discount greedy behavior, since it is shared with lower animals, and to emphasize instead the capacity of humans to develop virtuous behavior, to become moral creatures. As Mencius says, "Slight is the difference between man and the brutes. The ordinary person loses this distinguishing feature, while the true human being retains it" (*The Mencius*).

In a sense, the difference between Mencius and Xunzi is very small. Both acknowledged that we have natural desires for food and sex, and both acknowledged that we have the capacity to resist such desires when it is dangerous or inappropriate to indulge them. The difference is largely a matter of the relative weight placed on nature and nurture. Xunzi thought that because human beings are intelligent, when they realize the difficulties that uncontrolled indulgence in the desire for food and sex can lead to, they seek to set limits on those desires. Like Mencius, Xunzi acknowledged that the ordinary person can become a sage.

According to Xunzi, human goodness comes from development of human culture. Culture is uniquely human. "Heaven has its seasons, Earth has its resources, man has his culture" (*The Xunzi*). Humans should properly take what comes from heaven and earth and create a distinctly human culture. Just as Mencius held there were the four germs of human goodness, so Xunzi held there are the four germs of evil, all of which spring from the innate desire for profit and sensual pleasure. How, then, do humans become good? And what motivates them to become good if they are inherently evil? Xunzi developed two lines of argument.

First, humans need (and know they need) some kind of social organization, cooperation, and mutual support. To secure the required social organization, they need rules of conduct, ceremonial rites (*li*). (Ceremonial rites were of greater importance to Xunzi than to Confucius, who stressed compassion for others, *ren*.) We need rules of conduct to set limits on the satisfaction of desires.

Second, we need morality (*li*), culture, civilization to complete our humanity. The rules of conduct cultivate and refine our humanity. Unlike the Daoists, who rejected what comes from humans to return to nature, Xunzi advocated the way of humanity.

Xunzi further developed Confucius's sophisticated view of the utility of elaborate ceremonies, without the need for belief in conscious humanlike deities. For Xunzi, this involved a kind of aesthetic distance. We have both intellect and emotion. We intellectually know that death is the end of everything (and that gods cannot help improve the weather through prayers), but we emotionally need to hold on to some hope of something better to follow death (and the possibility of some help from a benevolent heaven). So we create in our rituals a kind of poetic imagination in which we believe and disbelieve all at the same time. Ordinary people can believe literally, while educated people can appreciate the same ceremonies aesthetically and symbolically. For civility, human emotions must have a physical embodiment, which distances the emotion from its natural expression. Thus, art and music become a way of inculcating proper social attitudes in the educational process and avoiding natural, animalistic expressions of such attitudes as aggression, for example.

Xunzi regarded dispute and argumentation as a sign of political disorder, and so encouraged the idea that a return of political order (at the end of the feudal period) would lead to the end of philosophical disputes and argumentation among the many different contending schools of philosophy. Unfortunately, through Xunzi's influence on the legalists Li Si and Han Fei, this contributed to the famous book burning of 213 BCE.

In some ways Xunzi resembled the Daoists, especially in his rationalist, scientific attitude toward nature or heaven (*tian*). In other ways, however, Xunzi followed Confucius in arguing that we ought nonetheless to keep up all the state ceremonies, even sacrifices to ancestors and gods, though they have no real causal effect. Why? Because these practices were socially beneficial; the emperor publicly praying for a good harvest did not make the crops grow any better, but it did help unify the people and organize their efforts toward a common goal.

DONG ZHONGSHU

Is there a human nature shared by all people, and if so what is it like? As discussed above, the followers of Confucius could not agree. Mencius held that it was essentially good, while Xunzi argued that it was essentially evil, to which Dong Zhongshu (179–104 BCE) argued that it was both, that human nature was composed of two opposing elements, one good and the other evil. Dong, in other words, found a middle ground between the views of Mencius and Xunzi (though probably closer to Xunzi). He agreed with Mencius that in a sense human nature contains the germ of goodness, but he disagreed with Mencius that this is enough to say that humans are by nature good. The germ of goodness is not actually good any more than a tomato seed is a tomato or an egg is a chicken. To become good, that germ must be nurtured and cultivated. He thus agreed more with Xunzi's emphasis on the need for government to educate and train people to become good citizens. Whereas Mencius said that goodness is a natural "tendency" of people, Dong claimed it is a mere "potential."

Dong also developed the theory that human nature must compete with people's innate tendencies toward greed and selfishness. In Dong's human psychology, the opposing forces of yin (emotion and feeling) and yang (our distinctively human nature) are in constant conflict with one another. If both these tendencies are innate, one may ask, are they both not parts of human nature? The answer here can be related to the idea that human nature is a normative concept. Like Mencius, Dong would like to say that human nature is the higher, better part of humans, the morally good part (derived from the positive yang aspect of heaven), which humans alone are capable of. The instinctive, emotional part (derived from the negative yin aspect of heaven), which all humans possess but also share with lower animals, is just as innate, but lacks the normative quality of the morally good potential of human nature.

The main difference between Mencius and Dong lies in their views of the role of government in fostering moral goodness. Mencius would have government take a far less intrusive role, merely encouraging and cultivating the germ of moral goodness already there. In contrast, Dong, like Xunzi, thinking of the enormous challenge of the Qin and Han dynasties in unifying the many previously warring states, held that government must mold and shape humans, who have the capacity for goodness but cannot become good without the intervention of the state. Lurking in the background of this Confucian debate lay the worry that moral cultivation, however noble an ideal, would not politically unify the vast military empire without strong state coercion.

MOZI

Mozi, or Mo Di as he is also known (c. 468–c. 376 BCE), was China's second philosopher, after Confucius. In his own lifetime and for two hundred years following his death, Mohism was at least as influential as Confucianism or any other early Chinese school of philosophy. But by the time of the Han dynasty (206 BCE–220 CE), Confucianism and Daoism had absorbed all the other schools of philosophy, and from then on, Mozi exercised little influence.

Philosophy arose in China at the end of the feudal period, and many scholars believe that the Confucians emerged from the ritual advisors (the *ru*) to the early feudal lords, while the Mohists emerged from the feudal warrior class. Certainly, Mozi's philosophy is much more down to earth, practical, and less elitist than Confucianism. Mozi opposed Confucius on several grounds, but four stand out as most important: that right action is determined by its practical results and consequences and not, as Confucius had urged, because duty required it, regardless of the consequences; that one should not privilege members of one's own family, especially one's parents, siblings, and children, but should love everyone equally; that morality should be based not on an unchanging human nature, which may or may not exist, but on our ability to transform people into morally better individuals through education and law; and that we should honor and obey a personal God, who rules heaven and earth, rewarding the faithful and punishing all others.

Mozi argued that the cause of the world's ills was the fact that people loved each other partially, that you love your mother and your clansmen more than you love my mother and my clansmen, for example, and that the cure for the world's ills is therefore to embrace universal, impartial love, in which everyone loves everyone else equally. Where there is competition, partial love leads "us" to hate and want to destroy "them." And so we have discrimination, ethnic cleansing, genocide, and warfare. How does one overcome these tendencies? According to Mozi, "Partial love should be replaced by universal, impartial love" (*The Mozi.*

Mozi realized (with the help of his Confucian critics) that impartial love is contrary to our ordinary feelings; you will tend to favor your relatives over mine. The Confucians were naturally appalled at Mozi's rejection of the traditional Chinese virtue of filial piety, that one's primary responsibility in life is to one's own parents and children. The Confucians therefore vigorously argued against Mozi's views on impartial love, arguing that since this is contrary to nature, no one could or would follow Mozi's advice (even if he were right). Nonetheless, Mozi argued that a system of rewards and punishments can induce and socially condition people to practice universal love (if not actually to *feel* love equally toward everyone).

Specifically, he argued that if the ruler urges people to love one another impartially, they would strive to do so; that since God created humans and loves them all impartially, God wants us to love each other impartially and rewards us when we do and punishes us when we do not; and that this too encourages people to embrace impartial love. Mozi did not think or argue that we are born with a sense of universal love of humanity in our hearts, only that we can be trained to adopt such an attitude. In this regard, Mozi argued that humans are infinitely pliable and can be molded into any form desired by the government (either to love partially or to love impartially).

Contrary to Confucius, Mozi argued that we should do the right thing to receive the rewards (*li*) we will receive by doing the right thing and to avoid the punishment we will suffer in this life and the next if we do the wrong thing. Sometimes Mozi argued that we should do what will produce the best results for everyone, not just for ourselves, and here he sounds like the nineteenth-century British utilitarians (Jeremy Bentham, James Mill, and John Stuart Mill), who argued that we should always do what will produce the greatest happiness for the greatest number of people.

Like Confucius, Mozi took his political theories to government leaders, offering his advice on how to improve government performance and social conditions, and like Confucius, his advice was largely ignored. Mozi was utilitarian in the sense that his standard for judging a philosophical position was whether it will benefit the people. Like John Stuart Mill, Mozi produced a theory that is more social and political than moral. That is, he was less interested in describing why individuals should love their neighbors as much as themselves than in telling government leaders how ordinary people can be motivated to practice universal, impartial love and how this will benefit the country as a whole.

Mozi explicitly criticized Confucius and the Confucians for preaching atheism (since this makes the gods angry, and the gods will then take it out on the people, making their lives miserable). He also criticized the Confucians for extravagance in spending on lavish state ceremonies (including musical ceremonies) and funerals (including three years of mourning), for proposing a complex educational system (it is simply too much to master all the old Zhou-dynasty ritual and history classics), and finally for relying too much on fate (*ming*). Like Xunzi, Mozi argued that without government there would be chaos and hardship, with constant disagreements over what should be done, and that the people thus decided that it is better to have an absolute dictator to decide disputes for all.

DAOISM

Like Confucians and Mohists, Daoists also tried to influence government, and very nearly succeeded in convincing the Han emperor Wu Di (r. 141–87 BCE) to choose Daoism over Confucianism as the official philosophy of the state. Only the extraordinary influence of Dong Zhongshu led the emperor to give the nod in the end to Confucianism.

The Daoists favored the natural over the artificial and mercilessly criticized the Confucians for their emphasis on the humanly created civilized culture of art and literature, ritual and custom, which children must learn through an elaborate process of socialization and acculturation. The Daoists were especially critical of the Confucians' attempts actively to foster and promote morality. Sometimes the Daoists expressed themselves by saying that one should practice "nonaction" (*wu wei*), which, the context makes clear, does not mean doing nothing, which is impossible, but rather not acting too deliberately, purposefully, or self-consciously, that is, not trying so hard, just letting events take their natural course.

Trying too hard to do anything, the Daoists thought, only proves how lacking one is in that regard. Also, generally speaking, the harder we try, the less we succeed, the Daoists argued. Morality, like humor and lightheartedness, cannot be learned by rote, by mechanically following some set of rules, the Daoists insisted, but must spring from the heart spontaneously. Since morality is generally pitted against natural impulses, the Daoists were firmly opposed to morality as it is generally understood, that is, as a set of socially approved guidelines or rules to which all are expected to conform.

The Daoists also found themselves at the opposite extreme from the Confucian moral theory of government. The Daoists advocated just letting events take their natural course, leaving well enough alone. According to the Daoists, events happen naturally, spontaneously (*ziran*), of their own accord. The principle that directs the growth and development of creatures and other things in the world is not some cause from outside, but a guiding force stemming from within those creatures. This is the natural and therefore preferred order of things. The worst thing one can do, especially rulers, is to try to improve on this natural order by enacting and enforcing laws.

It seems perfectly natural for rulers to feel that affairs are not going as well as they might and therefore to try to figure out what would make them better and to enact laws to bring about those changes. But for the Daoists, it is better for governments to let the people alone. Ordinary people have been managing their affairs from time immemorial, not by following formally enacted laws, but simply by following time-honored traditions and customs, which generally work just fine. By trying to improve the situation, the ruler may upset these established customs, confuse people, and make the situation worse.

Before governments found it necessary to introduce harsh laws to regulate behavior and punishments to enforce those laws, people lived simply without the need for laws. The ruler should keep government at this simple, primitive level. It is better not to give the ordinary people fancy ideas or encourage them to improve their lot. Keep them ignorant and simple. The Confucians were wrong to encourage knowledge and virtue. By insisting on learning and moral training, they made people feel ignorant and immoral, sense a need to study and learn what they did not know, and want to reform their ordinary ways of behaving.

Thus, even moral education is bad, according to the Daoists, because it tries to force on people overly sophisticated and difficult culture that goes against their nature. In direct opposition to the Confucians, the Daoists therefore rejected indoctrination in the traditional virtues: compassion, righteousness, propriety, and wisdom. If you have to teach morality, that is a sure sign that the situation has been allowed seriously to deteriorate. When affairs are running smoothly, the people naturally and spontaneously know what to do and how to behave—without thinking about it and without the need of books and formal instruction. Just like children, people are happier this way, not feeling inadequate and unhappy because they are constantly told how ignorant or sinful or uneducated or uncultivated they are.

It is also a mistake, the Daoists argued, to encourage the acquisition of expensive goods and higher standards of living. This just makes people envious of their richer neighbors and leads them to lie and steal and even kill to enrich themselves. The wise ruler will keep the people ignorant of fancy, expensive goods. If they never see such goods, they will never want them and never be tempted to stray from their simple everyday lives to get goods they cannot afford. Once the ruler allows inflated desires and competition among the people, the ruler must promulgate and enforce laws to prevent people from stealing and taking advantage of one another. But the more laws are passed and enforced, the more people see the laws and the government as their enemy, and therefore the more they will try to break the laws and overthrow the government. And this requires still more laws and severer punishments, in a vicious upward spiral.

LEGALISM

The legalist theory was best expressed by Han Fei, also known as Han Feizi (c. 280–233 BCE), at the end of the Warring States period. The legalists thought that it was not enough just to leave the people to their traditional customs, as the Daoists recommended, but that it was too much to transform everyone into a moral agent, as the Confucians and Mohists proposed. Neither sort of advice really takes into account what rulers themselves want. Rulers are generally not interested in being morally good, nor are they satisfied in just keeping the people quiet and docile. They usually have their own agendas: to gain fame by conquering neighboring kingdoms, to enrich themselves and their families, or perhaps both. Since most of the early Chinese philosophers were trying to persuade rulers of the time how best to govern, the legalists thought it better to advise rulers on how to achieve what rulers themselves wanted than to try to get them to accept the moralistic goals of the philosophers (who had no experience in ruling). The problem that Confucius faced in training kings to be philosophers was that the kings did not want to be philosophers—they wanted lives of action, wealth, and power. The legalists (ever political realists) accordingly dropped the more ambitious normative project of formulating the ends that governments should strive for and opted instead for a more instrumental approach to how to achieve the goals rulers already had.

To accomplish these political goals, the legalists advised the rulers to adopt a law-and-order administration supported by a strict system of rewards and punishments. Like their Western counterparts, the legalists were realists, arguing that it is not necessary for the king to be morally virtuous or for the bulk of the population to practice moral behavior. All the king needs to do, the legalists maintained, is to decide what he wants and then to insure compliance by formulating clear laws with absolutely certain rewards (for obeying these laws) and punishments (for disobeying them), and the people will do whatever the king wants. After all, he is the king. He does not have to follow the moral principles of someone else—certainly not those of a philosopher! The king can propose whatever he wants and call this "justice" and make others call it "justice" as well, however inherently unjust his proposals may in fact be. And since he has the army to back him up, he cannot be seriously challenged.

Most Chinese philosophers were conservatives, revering and urging a return to a halcyon past, as Confucius thought the Zhou dynasty had been. Han Fei, on the other hand, as a legal and historical realist, argued that different historical eras face different problems requiring different solutions, and that the solutions of the past are not necessarily appropriate for the present. The story he offered is of a farmer who, seeing a hare kill itself by running into a tree stump, abandons farming to sit and wait by the tree stump for another hare. In the new expansionist military dictatorships following the end of the feudal period, a strict system of rewards and punishments for clearly formulated and promulgated laws is a much surer way of ensuring compliance than moral education, the legalists felt. Even if the ruler enacts a system of universal moral education, how many people are actually going to become moral agents, always doing the right thing simply because it is the morally right thing to do?

The ruler also needs statecraft (*shu*). He need not do the work himself; he need simply hold people to their job descriptions (the rectification of names). As a pragmatist, the ruler is concerned not with the methods needed to achieve results but only with the results. If the minister lives up to his job description, he is rewarded; otherwise, punished. After a while, incompetents do not apply.

In a sense, the legalist ruler follows the Daoist injunction of nonaction: "doing nothing, yet there is nothing that is not done" (*Daodejing*). And all this rests securely on the simple but basic foundation of human self-interest. Like his teacher Xunzi, Han Fei thought that human nature was evil, but unlike Xunzi, he sought not change human nature through education and training but only to establish a workable system of government built on this self-interested human nature. The legalists were strangely like the Daoists: Do not fight human nature; work with it. Even the Daoist Zhuangzi (c. 369–c. 286 BCE), seems to agree with the legalist principles of management: "The superior must have no activity, so as thus to have control of events; but the subordinates must have activity, so as thus to be controlled by events. This is the invariable way" (*The Zhuangzi*). The tax collector, for example, knows that he must collect taxes. If at the end of the year he has collected his allotted quota, the ruler rewards him; if not, the ruler punishes (and replaces) him. He may fail because of drought and famine, in which case, but, whether fair or unfair, he will lose his job—if not his head. In this way, the job gets done. The subordinates are controlled by events, and yet the ruler has done nothing except employ the right statecraft.

In another way, however, the legalists advocated the complete opposite of what the Daoists advocated. The Daoists held that human beings were completely innocent; the legalists that they were completely self-interested. The Daoists upheld individual freedom; the legalists, absolute social control. The Daoists regarded the legalists as shallow pragmatists—they knew that certain methods worked, but they had no idea *why* they worked.

CONCLUSION

In a way, the Daoists agreed with Confucius and Mencius that the ruler needs to have fundamental knowledge of human nature. Like the Confucians but unlike the Daoists, the legalists developed a social and moral philosophy in tune with the breakdown of feudal class distinctions. The Confucians and Mohists were revolutionary and idealistic—they sought to transform human nature (or, in the case of the Mohists, at least human behavior) by developing an inner sense of right and wrong through education. In contrast, the more realistic and pragmatic legalists developed methods for controlling people with their self-interested natures.

For two millennia China's political philosophy has been a combination of openly espousing legitimizing Confucian discourse while silently employing the more pragmatic legalist methods to achieve the ruler's objectives, along with Daoist principles of not interfering in the day-to-day affairs of the vast majority of the peasant population where their affairs did not conflict with the ruler's personal objectives.

See also Chinese Philosophy: Ethics.

Bibliography

Chan, Wing-tsit. *A Source Book in Chinese Philosophy.* Princeton, NJ: Princeton University Press, 1963.

Creel, Herrlee G. *Confucius and the Chinese Way.* New York: Harper Torchbooks, 1960.

Fung, Yu-lan. *A History of Chinese Philosophy.* 2 vols. Translated by Derk Bodde. Princeton, NJ: Princeton University Press, 1983.

Fung, Yu-lan. *A Short History of Chinese Philosophy.* New York: Macmillan, 1966.

Graham, Angus C. *Disputers of the Dao*. La Salle, IL: Open Court, 1989.

Graham, Angus C. *Studies in Chinese Philosophy and Philosophical Literature*. Albany, NY: SUNY Press, 1990.

Hanson, Chad. *A Daoist Theory of Chinese Thought*. Oxford, U.K.: Oxford University Press, 1992.

Ivanhoe, Philip J., and Bryan W. Van Norden, eds. *Readings in Classical Chinese Philosophy*. New York: Seven Bridges Press, 2000.

Knoblock, John. *Xunzi*. 3 vols. Stanford, CA: Stanford University Press, 1988–1994.

Lao-tzu (Laozi). *Tao Te Ching: The Classic Book of Integrity and the Way*. Translated by Victor Mair. New York: Bantam Books, 1990.

Lau, D. C. *Confucius: The Analects*. New York: Penguin Books, 1979.

Lau, D. C. *Mencius*. New York: Penguin Books, 1970.

Lowe, Scott. *Mo Tzu's Religious Blueprint for a Chinese Utopia*. Lewiston, U.K.: Edwin Mellen Press, 1992.

Rosemont, Henry, ed. *Chinese Texts and Philosophical Contexts*. La Salle, IL: Open Court, 1991.

Schwartz, Benjamin. *The World of Thought in Ancient China*. Cambridge, MA: Harvard University Press, 1985.

H. Gene Blocker (2005)

CHINESE ROOM ARGUMENT

In 1980 the philosopher John R. Searle published in the journal *Behavioral and Brain Sciences* a simple thought experiment that he called the "Chinese Room Argument" against "Strong Artificial Intelligence (AI)." The thesis of Strong AI has since come to be called "computationalism," according to which cognition is just computation, hence mental states are just computational states:

COMPUTATIONALISM

According to computationalism, to explain how the mind works, cognitive science needs to find out what the right computations are—the ones that the brain performs to generate the mind and its capacities. Once we know that, then every system that performs those computations will have those mental states: Every computer that runs the mind's program will have a mind, because computation is hardware-independent: Any hardware that is running the right program has the right computational states.

THE TURING TEST

How do we know which program is the right program? Although it is not strictly a tenet of computationalism, an answer that many computationalists will agree to is that the right program will be the one that can pass the Turing Test (TT), which is to be a system that is able to interact by e-mail with real people exactly the way real people do—so exactly that no person can ever tell that the computer program is not another real person. Alan M. Turing (1950) had suggested that once a computer can do everything a real person can do so well that we cannot even tell them apart, it would be arbitrary to deny that that computer has a mind, that it is intelligent, that it can understand just as a real person can.

This, then, is the thesis that Searle set out to show was wrong: (1) mental states are just computational states, (2) the right computational states are the ones that can pass the TT, and (3) any and every hardware on which you run those computational states will have those mental states too.

HARDWARE-INDEPENDENCE

Searle's thought experiment was extremely simple. Normally, there is no way I can tell whether anyone or anything other than myself has mental states. The only mental states we can be sure about are our own. We cannot be someone else, to check whether they have mental states too. But computationalism has an important vulnerability in this regard: hardware-independence. Because any and every dynamical system (i.e., any physical hardware) that is executing the right computer program would have to have the right mental states, Searle himself can execute the computer program, thereby himself becoming the hardware, and then check whether he has the right mental states. In particular, Searle asks whether the computer that passes the TT really understands the e-mails it is receiving and sending.

THE CHINESE ROOM

To test this, Searle obviously cannot conduct the TT in English, for he already understands English. So in his thought-experiment the TT is conducted in Chinese: The (hypothetical) computer program he is testing in his thought-experiment is able to pass the TT in Chinese. That means it is able to receive and send e-mail in Chinese in such a way that none of its (real) Chinese pen-pals would ever suspect that they were not communicating with a real Chinese-speaking and Chinese-understanding person. (We are to imagine the e-mail exchanges going on as frequently we like, with as many people as we like, as long as we like, even for an entire lifetime. The TT is not just a short-term trick.)

SYMBOL MANIPULATION

In the original version of Searle's Chinese Room Argument he imagined himself in the Chinese Room, receiving the Chinese e-mails (a long string of Chinese symbols, completely unintelligible to Searle). He would then consult the TT-passing computer program, in the form of rules written (in English) on the wall of the room, explaining to Searle exactly how he should manipulate the symbols, based on the incoming e-mail, to generate the outgoing e-mail. It is important to understand that computation is just rule-based symbol manipulation and that the manipulation and matching is done purely on the basis of the shape of the symbols, not on the basis of their meaning.

Now the gist of Searle's argument is very simple: In doing all that, he would be doing exactly the same thing any other piece of hardware executing that TT-passing program was doing: rule-fully manipulating the input symbols on the basis of their shapes and generating output symbols that make sense to a Chinese pen-pal—the kind of e-mail reply a real pen-pal would send, a pen-pal that had understood the e-mail received, as well as the e-mail sent.

UNDERSTANDING

But Searle goes on to point out that in executing the program he himself would not be understanding the e-mails at all! He would just be manipulating meaningless symbols, on the basis of their shapes, according to the rules on the wall. Therefore, because of the hardware-independence of computation, if Searle would not be understanding Chinese under those conditions, neither would any other piece of hardware executing that Chinese TT-passing program. So much for computationalism and the theory that cognition is just computation.

THE SYSTEM REPLY

Searle correctly anticipated that his computationalist critics would not be happy with the handwriting on the wall: Their "System Reply" would be that Searle was only *part* of the TT-passing system. That whereas Searle would not be understanding Chinese under those conditions, the *system as a whole* would be!

Searle rightly replied that he found it hard to believe that he plus the walls together could constitute a mental state, but, playing the game, he added: Then forget about the walls and the room. Imagine that I have memorized all the symbol manipulation rules and can conduct them from memory. Then the whole system is me: Where's the understanding?

Desperate computationalists were still ready to argue that somewhere in there, inside Searle, under those conditions, there would lurk a Chinese understanding of which Searle himself was unaware, as in multiple personality disorder—but this seems even more far-fetched than the idea that a person plus walls has a joint mental state of which the person is unaware.

BRAIN POWER

So the Chinese Room Argument is right, such as it is, and computationalism is wrong. But if cognition is not just computation, what is it then? Here, Searle is not much help, for he first overstates what his argument has shown, concluding that it has shown (1) that cognition is not computation at all—whereas all it has shown is that cognition is not all computation. Searle also concludes that his argument has shown (2) that the Turing Test is invalid, whereas all it has shown is that the TT would be invalid if it could be passed by a purely computational system. His only positive recommendation is to turn brain-ward, trying to understand the causal powers of the brain instead of the computational powers of computers.

But it is not yet apparent what the relevant causal powers of the brain are, nor how to discover them. The TT itself is a potential guide: Surely the relevant causal power of the brain is its power to pass the TT! We know now (thanks to the Chinese Room Argument) that if a system could pass the TT via computation alone, that would not be enough. What would be missing?

THE ROBOT REPLY

One of the attempted refutations of the Chinese Room Argument—the "Robot Reply"—contained the seeds of an answer, but they were sown in the wrong soil. A robot's sensors and effectors were invoked to strengthen the System Reply: It is not Searle plus the walls of the Chinese Room that constitutes the Chinese-understanding system, it is Searle plus a robot's sensors and effectors. Searle rightly points out that it would still be him doing all the computations, and it was the computations that were on trial in the Chinese Room. But perhaps the TT itself needs to be looked at more closely here:

BEHAVIORAL CAPACITY

Turing's original Test was indeed the e-mail version of the TT. But there is nothing in Turing's paper or his arguments on behalf of the TT to suggest that it should be restricted to candidates that are just computers, or even that it should be restricted to e-mail! The power of the TT is the argument that if the candidate can do everything a real person can do—and do it indistinguishably from the way real people do it, as judged by real people—then it would be mere prejudice to conclude that it lacked mental states when we were told it was a machine. We don't even really know what a machine is, or isn't!

But we do know that real people can do a lot more than just send e-mail to one another. They can see, touch, name, manipulate, and describe most of the things they talk about in their e-mail. Indeed, it is hard to imagine how either a real pen-pal or any designer of a TT-passing computer program could deal intelligibly with all the symbols in an e-mail message without also being able to do at least some of the things we can all do with the objects and events in the world that those symbols stand for.

SENSORIMOTOR GROUNDING OF SYMBOLS

Computation, as noted, is symbol manipulation, by rules based on the symbols' shapes, not their meanings. Computation, like language itself, is universal, and perhaps all-powerful (in that it can encode just about anything). But surely if we want the ability to understand the symbols' meanings to be among the mental states of the TT-passing system, this calls for more than just the symbols and the ability to manipulate them. Some, at least, of those symbols must be grounded in something other than just more meaningless symbols and symbol manipulations—otherwise the system is in the same situation as someone trying to look up the meaning of a word in a language—let us say, Chinese—that he does not understand … in a Chinese-Chinese dictionary! E-mailing the definitions of the words would be intelligible enough to a pen-pal who already understood Chinese, but they would be of no use to anyone or anything that did not understand Chinese. Some of the symbols must be grounded in the capacity to recognize and manipulate the things in the world that the symbols refer to.

MIND READING

So the TT candidate must be a robot, able to interact with the world that the symbols are about—including us—directly, not just via e-mail. And it must be able to do so indistinguishably from the way any of the rest of us interact with the world or with one another. That is the gist of the TT. The reason Turing originally formulated his test in its pen-pal form was so that we would not be biased by the candidate's appearance. But in today's cinematic sci-fi world we have, if anything, been primed to be overcredulous about robots, so much more capable are our familiar fictional on-screen cyborgs than any TT candidate yet designed in a cog-sci lab. In real life our subtle and biologically based "mind reading" skills (Frith and Frith 1999) will be all we need once cognitive science starts to catch up with science fiction and we can begin T-Testing in earnest.

THE OTHER-MINDS PROBLEM

Could the Chinese Room Argument be resurrected to debunk a TT-passing robot? Certainly not. For Searle's argument depended crucially on the hardware-independence of computation. That was what allowed Searle to "become" the candidate and then report back to us (truthfully) that we were mistaken if we thought he understood Chinese. But we cannot become the TT-passing robot, to check whether it really understands, any more than we can become another person. It is this parity (between other people and other robots) that is at the heart of the TT. And anyone who thinks this is not an exacting enough test of having a mind need only remind himself that the Blind Watchmaker (Darwinian evolution), our "natural designer," is no more capable of mind reading than any of the rest of us is. That leaves only the robot to know for sure whether or not it really understands.

See also Artificial Intelligence; Computationalism; Functionalism; Machine Intelligence.

Bibliography

Anderson, David, and B. Jack Copeland. "Artificial Life and the Chinese Room Argument." *Artificial Life* 8 (4) (2002): 371–378

Brown, Steven. "Peirce, Searle, and the Chinese Room Argument." *Cybernetics and Human Knowing* 9 (1) (2002): 23–38

Dyer, Michael G. "Intentionality and Computationalism: Minds, Machines, Searle, and Harnad." *Journal of Experimental and Theoretical Artificial Intelligence* 2 (4) (1990): 303–319.

French, Robert. "The Turing Test: The First Fifty Years." *Trends in Cognitive Sciences* 4 (3) (2000): 115–121.

Frith, Christopher D., and Uta Frith. "Interacting Minds—A Biological Basis." *Science* 286 (1999): 1692–1695.

Harnad, Stevan. "The Annotation Game: On Turing (1950) on Computing, Machinery and Intelligence." In *The Turing Test Sourcebook: Philosophical and Methodological Issues in the Quest for the Thinking Computer*, edited by Robert Epstein and Grace Peters. Amsterdam: Kluwer Academic, 2004. http://cogprints.org/3322.

Harnad, Stevan. "Can a Machine Be Conscious? How?" *Journal of Consciousness Studies* 10 (4–5) (2003): 69–75, http://cogprints.org/2460/.

Harnad, Stevan. "Minds, Machines, and Searle." *Journal of Theoretical and Experimental Artificial Intelligence* 1 (1989): 5–25, http://cogprints.org/1573/.

Harnad, Stevan. "On Searle on the Failures of Computationalism." *Psycoloquy* 12 (61) (2001), http://psycprints.ecs.soton.ac.uk/archive/00000190/.

Harnad, Stevan. "The Symbol Grounding Problem." *Physica D* 42 (1990): 335–346, http://cogprints.org/3106/.

Harnad, Stevan. "Symbol-Grounding Problem." In *Encyclopedia of Cognitive Science*. London: Nature Publishing Group, 2003, http://cogprints.org/3018/.

Harnad, Stevan. "What's Wrong and Right about Searle's Chinese Room Argument?" In *Essays on Searle's Chinese Room Argument*, edited by M. Bishop and J. Preston. New York: Oxford University Press, 2001, http://cogprints.org/4023/.

Overill, Richard E. "Views into the Chinese Room: New Essays on Searle and Artificial Intelligence." *Journal of Logic and Computation*14 (2) (2004): 325–326.

Pylyshyn, Zenon W. *Computation and Cognition: Toward a Foundation for Cognitive Science*. Cambridge, MA: MIT Press, 1984.

Searle, John R. "Explanatory Inversion and Cognitive Science." *Behavioral and Brain Sciences* 13 (1990): 585–595.

Searle, John R. "The Failures of Computationalism: I." *Psycoloquy* 12 (62) (2001), http://psycprints.ecs.soton.ac.uk/archive/00000189/.

Searle, John. R. "Is the Brain's Mind a Computer Program?" *Scientific American* 262 (1) (January 1990): 26–31.

Searle, John. R. "Minds and Brains without Programs." In *Mindwaves: Thoughts on Intelligence, Identity, and Consciousness*, edited by Colin Blakemore and Susan Greenfield. Oxford, U.K.: Blackwell, 1987.

Searle, John. R. "Minds, Brains, and Programs." *Behavioral and Brain Sciences* 3 (3) (1980): 417–457, http://www.bbsonline.org/documents/a/00/00/04/84/index.html.

Searle, John R. *Minds, Brains, and Science*. Cambridge, MA: Harvard University Press, 1984.

Souder, Lawrence. "What Are We to Think about Thought Experiments?" *Argumentation* 17 (2) (2003): 203–217.

Turing, Alan M. "Computing Machinery and Intelligence." *Mind* 59 (236) (1950): 433–460, http://cogprints.org/499/.

Wakefield, Jerome C. "The Chinese Room Argument Reconsidered: Essentialism, Indeterminacy, and Strong AI." *Minds and Machines* 13 (2) (2003): 285–319.

Stevan Harnad (2005)

CHISHOLM, RODERICK

(1916–1999)

Roderick Chisholm was a twentieth-century American philosopher who made major contributions in almost every area of philosophy, but most notably in epistemology and metaphysics. Chisolm was an undergraduate at Brown University from 1934 to 1938 and a graduate student at Harvard from 1938 to 1942. He served in the military from 1942 to 1946, and then, after briefly holding a teaching post with the Barnes Foundation and the University of Pennsylvania, he returned in 1947 to Brown University, where he remained until his death.

EPISTEMOLOGY

In epistemology Chisholm was a defender of foundationalism. He asserted that any proposition that it is justified for a person to believe gets at least part of its justification from basic propositions, which are themselves justified but not by anything else. Contingent propositions are basic insofar as they correspond to self-presenting states of the person, which for Chisholm are states such that whenever one is in the state and believes that one is in it, one's belief is maximally justified. There are two types of self-presenting states: intentional states (ways of thinking, hoping, fearing, desiring, wondering, intending, etc.) and sensory states (ways of being appeared to by the various senses). A noncontingent proposition is basic if understanding it is sufficient for understanding that it is true and also sufficient for making it justified. "2 + 3 = 5" and "If Jones is ill and Smith is away, then Jones is ill" are examples of such propositions, says Chisholm.

Self-presentation and understanding are among the basic sources of epistemic justification, but according to Chisholm there are other sources as well. The most important of these other sources are perception, memory, belief coupled with a lack of negative coherence (e.g., no inconsistencies among the propositions believed), and belief coupled with positive coherence (i.e., mutual support among the proposition believed). For each of these sources, Chisholm forwards an epistemic principle that describes the conditions under which the source generates justification.

Despite his thinking that there are many sources of epistemic justification, Chisholm is rightly regarded as a foundationalist because all the sources are such that they can produce justified beliefs only because some propositions are justified basically. For example, Chisholm's principles concerning perception and memory make reference to propositions that are justified because they correspond to self-presenting states. In the case of perception, the relevant states are sensings, and for memory the relevant states are beliefs, in particular, beliefs to the effect that one remembers something. In a similar spirit, Chisholm says that coherence relations among propositions are not capable of generating justification for propositions that have nothing else to recommend them; their role instead is to increase the degree of justification that propositions have by virtue of being supported by basic propositions.

Chisholm is also a proponent of internalism in epistemology, in two senses of the term. First, he thinks that epistemic justification supervenes on human conscious states; thus, whether one's beliefs are justified is determined by one's own internal states rather than by conditions obtaining in one's external environment. Second, he thinks that the conditions, if any, that justify one's beliefs are accessible to one; thus, one is always able to determine if one reflects carefully enough, whether one's beliefs are justified.

Chisholm's epistemology is resolutely antiskeptical. Indeed, he says that the proper way to begin doing epistemology is by presupposing that some human beliefs are justified and that indeed some constitute knowledge. Epistemology, so conceived, becomes primarily a search for the conditions that account for these beliefs being justified. A second task is to define the conditions that turn a true belief into knowledge. Chisholm's approach to this latter task is to defend a nondefeasibility account of knowledge. One knows a proposition *p*, he says, whenever one believes *p*, *p* is true, and *p* is nondefectively evident for that person, where *p* is nondefectively evident that person (some details aside) just in case there is a set of basic propositions that justify *p* and that justify nothing false.

METAPHYSICS

Chisholm also had well-worked-out views on almost every major issue in metaphysics, but his most influential views were concerned with thought and language, ontology, action, and material bodies.

With respect to thought and language, Chisholm was a defender of the primacy of thought; the intentionality of language is to be understood in terms of the intentionality of thought, he says, rather than conversely. He develops this idea in his direct attribution theory of reference. At the heart of the theory is a proposal that people are able to refer to things other than themselves by directly attributing properties to them and that people indirectly attribute properties to things by directly attributing properties to themselves. For example, if John is the only person in a room with Sally and John is wearing a blue sweater, then by directly attributing to herself the property of being a person *x* such that the only other person in the room with *x* is wearing a blue sweater, Sally indirectly attributes to John the property of wearing a blue sweater and thereby refers to John. Using these notions of direct and indirect attribution, Chisholm provides an account of various semantic notions including sense and reference.

In ontology, Chisholm's view is that there are only two kinds of entities: attributes and the individual things that have these attributes. Everything else, including propositions, states of affairs, possible worlds, and sets, can be understood in terms of these two categories. Attributes are possible objects of thought—more specifically, what people are able to attribute, either directly (to themselves) or indirectly (both to themselves and other things). Thus in ontology, Chisholm once again is a defender of the primacy of thought in that he uses the phenomenon of intentionality to identify and understand what kinds of entities there are.

His theory of action is an indeterministic one. The fundamental notions are those of undertaking and causing, and with respect to the latter notion he carefully distinguishes among necessary causal conditions for an event, sufficient causal conditions, and causal contributions. With these notions in hand, he opposes compatibilist attempts to understand what it is for a person to be free to undertake something, insisting that one has undertaken to do something freely only if there was no sufficient causal condition for one to undertake it (although there may have been extensive causal contributions to the undertaking).

Much of Chisholm's work on bodies is concerned with puzzles about the persistence of physical bodies through time, and most of these puzzles, in turn, are concerned with apparent violations of Leibniz's principle of the indiscernibility of identicals. According to this principle, if *X* and *Y* are identical, then whatever is true of *X* is also true of *Y*. One famous puzzle, for example, is the ship of Theseus. Even if one plank of the ship is replaced at a time *t*, it is the same ship—namely Theseus's—that exists before *t* and after *t*, and yet the ship might appear to have different properties before *t* and after *t*. Chisholm attempts to solve this and other puzzles about the identity of physical bodies through time by using his fundamental ontological categories, attributes, and individual things, to make precise the seventeenth-century distinction between substances and their modes.

See also Classical Foundationalism; Internalism and Externalism in Ethics; Persistence; Reference.

Bibliography

Bogdan, R., ed. *Roderick M. Chisholm.* Dordrecht, Netherlands: D. Reidel, 1986. Critical essays on Chisholm and a helpful self-profile.

Chisholm, R. *The First Person: An Essay on Reference and Intentionality.* Minneapolis: University of Minnesota Press, 1981. A detailed defense of the direct attribution theory of reference.

Chisholm, R. *Human Freedom and the Self.* Lawrence, KS: University of Kansas Press, 1964. A defense of his indeterministic account of human freedom.

Chisholm, R. *Perceiving: A Philosophical Study.* Ithaca, NY: Cornell University Press, 1957. His first major work on epistemology.

Chisholm, R. *Person and Object: A Metaphysical Study.* London: Open Court Publishing Company. 1976. Most of his metaphysical positions are defended in this volume.

Chisholm, R. *Theory of Knowledge.* 3rd edition. Englewood Cliffs, NJ: Prentice-Hall, 1987. His most influential work in epistemology; the later editions contain important modifications of his earlier views.

Lehrer, K., ed. *Analysis and Metaphysics: Essays in Honor of R. M. Chisholm.* Dordrecht, Netherlands: D. Reidel, 1975. Critical essays on Chisholm's metaphysics and epistemology.

Richard Foley (1996, 2005)

CHOICE, AXIOM OF

See *Set Theory*

CHOMSKY, NOAM

(1928–)

Noam Chomsky is the foremost linguistic theorist of the post–World War II era, an important contributor to philosophical debates, and a notable radical activist. His influence is felt in many other fields, however, most notably, perhaps, in the area of cognitive studies.

Chomsky's main achievement was to distinguish linguistic competence from its manifestations in performance and to characterize competence as a system of explicit rules for the construction and interpretation of sentences. Indeed, this achievement provided a model for investigations, in this and other cognitive domains, that replaced then-dominant models based on the notion of analogy and oriented to the causal explanation of behavior.

The competence of individuals to use their language is constituted, on Chomsky's account, by their (tacit) knowledge of a formal grammar (or system of rules); their linguistic performance, involving the deployment of such knowledge, may be influenced by a host of extraneous factors that need not be accounted for by the grammar itself but, instead and if possible, by subsidiary theories (e.g., of perceptual processing, etc.). Furthermore, knowledge of such a system of rules permits a kind of creativity in performance that exhibits itself in the novelty, in relation to speakers' prior linguistic experiences, of (many of) the sentences they actually produce. (Crudely put, they can understand and produce sentences they have never before encountered.)

The competence/performance distinction reflects Chomsky's preference for "Galilean" theorizing (i.e., for a "modular" approach), and its introduction was tremendously liberating. A direct attack on performance, under broadly behavioristic auspices, had proved barren, for reasons Chomsky identified with devastating clarity in his review of B. F. Skinner's *Verbal Behavior.* Also pertinent was Chomsky's analysis of linguistic creativity in a second, distinct sense: the appropriateness and yet stimulus-independence (and therefore causal inexplicability) of much of what a speaker says in concrete circumstances. Shifting the linguist's problematic from behavior to the system underlying behavior was probably Chomsky's most important contribution to the development of "scientific" studies of social phenomena. (Of course, the competence/performance distinction owes much to Ferdinand de Saussure's earlier distinction between *langue* and *parole.* But Saussure did not think of the system underlying behavior as primarily rule-based, and so his distinction proved less fertile than Chomsky's.)

In a series of works beginning with *Cartesian Linguistics,* Chomsky took up what he came to call "Plato's problem"—that of explaining how the gap is bridged between individuals' limited opportunities, as children, for acquiring knowledge of their (native) language(s) and the competence to make many subtle and complex discriminations that, as mature speakers, they do indeed possess. He solved this problem, siding with classical rationalists such as Gottfried Wilhelm Leibniz, by assuming the existence, as an innate species-wide attribute, of a "universal grammar." During the course of language acquisition, limited data fixes the values of free "parameters" associated with this grammar, thus providing a basis for full-blown knowledge of the language that far exceeds the ordinary "inductive" implications of these data.

Chomsky has also been a notable advocate, very significantly in a discipline previously marked by instrumentalist assumptions about theorizing, of a realist perspective on theoretical entities and processes. In early work deep structures were postulated as sources, via transformations, of familiar superficial structures of sentences. So, for instance, a superficially passive sentence was said to be derived from the same deep structure as its active counterpart. And while it might have been more in line with then-contemporary practice to treat these so-called deep structures as pure postulates, useful in simplifying the description and taxonomization of the superficial sentences of our "experience," Chomsky advocated, instead, that they be treated as having psychological reality and thereby fostered many profound psycholinguistic studies intended to bear out or refute this contention. A topic of continuing importance is whether it is only structures or, instead, derivational processes as well that are to be treated as "real."

Less noticed by commentators is Chomsky's profoundly individualistic approach to linguistic phenomena. For him, language itself is a secondary phenomena; primacy is accorded to an individual's competence, a purely psychological phenomenon. Indeed, Chomsky explains the coordination of linguistic interaction, not by reference to any transpersonal system of conventions (as might be thought appropriate in relation to other social phenomena), but, instead, to a harmony—between the competence of the speaker and the marginally different competence of the hearer—that depends largely on the innate constraints on their (typically) quite separate episodes of language acquisition. Even if each learns in isolation from the other, and has quite (though not "too") different experiential bases for learning, each will acquire an "idiolect" that is accessible to the other: Otherwise rather different data-sets fix the free parameters of the universal grammar in sufficiently similar ways to permit mutual intelligibility.

Other philosophically important themes in Chomsky's work include: (1) his identification of the ideological interests that are served by certain allegedly "scientific" approaches to the study of human behavior; (2) his argument for treating the capacity for language as species-specific and thus as an aspect of the human "essence"; (3) his speculations about the possibility that there are innate limitations on the human capacity for knowledge of the world; and (4) his continued defense, in the face of broadly "postmodernist" opposition, of the role of reason in understanding and improving the human condition and of the viability of the notion of "progress" in relation to these projects.

See also Behaviorism; Cognitive Science; Leibniz, Gottfried Wilhelm; Modernism and Postmodernism; Postmodernism.

Bibliography

WORKS BY CHOMSKY

Syntactic Structures. The Hague: Mouton, 1957.

"A Review of B. F. Skinner's *Verbal Behavior.*" In *The Structure of Language,* edited by J. A. Fodor and J. J. Katz. Englewood Cliffs, NJ: Prentice-Hall, 1964.

Cartesian Linguistics. New York: Harper, 1966.

Language and Mind. New York: Harcourt Brace, 1972.

For Reasons of State. London: Fontana, 1973.

Language and Problems of Knowledge. Cambridge, MA: MIT Press, 1988.

WORKS ON CHOMSKY

D'Agostino, F. *Chomsky's System of Ideas.* Oxford: Clarendon Press, 1986.

Harman, G., ed. *On Noam Chomsky.* New York: Anchor Press, 1974.

Kasher, A., ed. *The Chomskyan Turn.* Oxford: Blackwell, 1991.

Sampson, G. *Liberty and Language.* Oxford: Oxford University Press, 1979.

Fred D'Agostino (1996)

CHRISTIANITY

The present entry is restricted to Christian belief and scarcely touches on the origins of "Christianity" or its history and institutional forms. Among Christian beliefs only a few can be treated; certain others, such as the existence and attributes of God, are discussed in other entries.

CHRISTIAN BELIEF

Perhaps the first thing that should be said about Christian belief is that it does not constitute a philosophy. That is to say, it is not a metaphysical system comparable, for example, to Platonism or the systems of Aristotle and Benedict de Spinoza. Although the body of Christian doctrine does consist largely of metaphysical beliefs, in the sense that they are beliefs whose scope transcends the empirical world, it differs from what are usually identified as philosophical systems by its essential relation to and dependence on particular historical events and experiences. Such systems as Platonism begin with philosophical concepts and principles and seek by means of these to construct a comprehensive mental picture of the universe. Christianity, on the other hand, begins with particular, nonrecurrent historical events that are regarded as revelatory and on the basis of which Christian faith makes certain limited statements about the ultimate nature and structure of reality.

The relationship between experience and discursive reflection in Christianity can be brought out by distinguishing two orders of Christian belief. There is a primary level, consisting of direct reports of experience, secular and religious, and a secondary level, consisting of theological theories constructed on the basis of these reports.

At the primary level Christian literature affirms a number of both publicly verifiable historical facts and "religious facts," or "facts of faith." The latter consist of incidents in the history of Israel as understood and participated in by the prophets and in the life of Jesus as he was responded to by the apostles, these events being seen by faith as revelatory of God. The resulting testimonies of the prophets and apostles are not formulations of theological doctrine but direct expressions of moments of intense religious experience. The four New Testament gospels are writings on this primary level, recording events that occurred either within the purview of secular history or within the religious experience of the early Christian community.

Within this primary stratum of Christian belief certain facts of faith have always stood out as being preeminently important. By means of these Christianity has defined itself in distinction to other religions. Among the total body of those who have called themselves Christians there is no universally agreed-on list of these defining facts of faith, except insofar as such lists have been adopted, locally or more widely, by particular Christian communions, sects, or movements. However, it is safe to say that the main streams of contemporary Christianity, claiming continuity of faith with the first Christian generation, affirm at least the following: the reality of God and the propriety of speaking of him in a threefold manner, as Father, Son, and Spirit; the divine creation of the universe; human sinfulness; divine incarnation in the person of Jesus, the Christ; his reconciliation of man to God; his founding of the Christian church and the continuing operation of his Spirit within it; and an eventual end to human history and the fulfillment of God's purpose for his creation. Stated in this general form these are facts of faith that cumulatively define Christianity. Many further tenets are regarded as essential by different subgroups within Christianity, but the above probably constitute the permanent core that is acknowledged by virtually the whole of Christendom, past and present.

The second order of Christian belief consists in theological theories or doctrines that seek to explain these facts of faith and to relate them to one another and/or to human knowledge in general. The formulation of doctrines is essentially a discursive and speculative activity, differing from theory construction in secular philosophy only in that the theologian includes in his data, and indeed accords a central and determinative importance to, the special facts of Christian faith.

This distinction can now be illustrated by reference to some of the central Christian themes, noting both the relevant facts of faith and the theological theories that have been developed about them.

CREATION. The doctrine of creation (which Christianity holds in common with Judaism) stands somewhat apart from the other doctrines to be described below. The others have arisen out of reflection on specific historical phenomena, but belief in the divine creation of the universe, although connected with the religious experience of absolute dependence on God, has presumably been arrived at primarily as an implicate of the monotheistic understanding of God as the sole ultimate reality.

The doctrine of the divine creation of the universe out of nothing stands in contrast to other conceptions of its origin. This doctrine denies that the universe is eternal, although the denial does not entail the belief that it was created at some moment in time—Augustine, for example, taught that time is itself an aspect of the created world. The doctrine also excludes the Platonic notion of a Demiurge fashioning the world out of a formless matter and the Neoplatonic notion of the physical universe's coming to be by emanation from the Absolute. In distinction to these ideas the doctrine of *creatio ex nihilo* asserts that the universe has been summoned into existence out of nothing (that is, not out of anything) by the creative will and purpose of God.

INCARNATION. Jesus was born about 5 BCE in Palestine and was executed by crucifixion at Jerusalem probably in 29 or 30 CE. There immediately arose a conviction among his disciples, reflected in all the New Testament documents, that he had been raised by God from the dead, and under the compulsion of this conviction the Christian church came into existence, witnessing to both the divine status and the saving power of Jesus, now proclaimed as the Christ.

The beliefs of Jesus' disciples about him are reflected in the four memoirs, or gospels, which were produced in different centers of the apostolic church during the second half of the first century. On the one hand, these depict him as fully and authentically human, subject, like other men, to temptation, hunger, pain, fatigue, ignorance, and sorrow. But at the same time they affirm that he is Lord, Messiah (*Christos*), the Son of God. This extremely exalted view reaches its highest expression in the Fourth Gospel, which claims in its prologue to Jesus' life that the Word (Logos), which was in the beginning with God, and was God, and through which all things were made, "became flesh, and dwelt among us, full of grace and truth; and we have beheld his glory, glory as of the only Son from the Father" (John 1:14; the conception of the Logos in the Fourth Gospel derives both from the Word and the wisdom of God in the Old Testament and from the Logos as the universal principle of reason in Greek philosophy). The faith that Jesus was the Christ apparently arose out of a practical acceptance of his status as one who had authority to forgive sins, to declare God's mind toward man, to reveal the true meaning of the divine Law, to heal diseases, and to assume that men's eternal destiny and welfare was bound up with their responses to him. This practical acknowledgment of his unique authority probably crystallized into conscious conviction as to his deity under the impact of the resurrection events.

In the gospels these two beliefs, identifying Jesus both as a son of man and as the Son of God, occur together without any attempt to theorize about the relationship between them. Thus, this primary stratum of Christian literature contains, as data for theological reflection, reports of (*a*) the publicly observable fact that Jesus was a man, and (*b*) the fact of faith that he was divine, in that "in him all the fullness of God was pleased to dwell" (Colossians 1:19).

During its first four centuries of life these data provided the church with its chief intellectual task. The eventual outcome of the Christological debates, formalized by the Council of Chalcedon (451), was not to propound any definitive theory concerning the relationship between Jesus' humanity and his divinity but simply to reaffirm, in the philosophical language of that day, the original facts of faith. The various views that were from time to time branded as heretical came under this condemnation because directly or by implication they denied one or the other of the two fixed points of Christian thought in this field, the human and divine natures of Christ.

The first of the Christological heresies, the Docetism of some of the Gnostics in the first and second centuries, denied the real humanity of Christ, suggesting that he was a human being in appearance only. The motive behind this theory was to exalt his divine status, but the effect was to deny one of the foundation facts of Christianity as historically based faith. The next great heresy, Arianism, in the fourth century, went to the opposite extreme, denying continuity of being or nature between the Godhead and Christ and regarding him as a created being, so that "there was a time when he was not" (*ἦν ὅτε οὐκ ἦν*). It was in the controversy with Arianism that the notion of substance (*οὐσία, substantia*) became a key category in the Christological debates. Arius declared that the Son was *ὁμοιούσιον τῷ πατρί* (of *like* substance with the Father), whereas the Council of Nicaea (325), excluding Arianism as a heresy, insisted that the Son was *ὁμοούσιον τῷ πατρί* (of the *same* substance as the Father). It was made clear by Athanasius, the champion of orthodoxy, that the iota's difference between these formulations involved an immense religious difference, for only a savior who came from the Godward side of creation could offer man an ultimate salvation. This Homousian Christology was reaffirmed by the Council of Chalcedon and has ever since been the position of the main streams of historic Christianity.

Since the mid-nineteenth century a number of theologians (for example, the Ritschlian school and H. R. Mackintosh) who accept the Nicene and Chalcedonian affirmations of the full humanity and real deity of Christ have questioned the adequacy of the category of substance in terms of which that affirmation was made. They have pointed out that it belongs to the thought-worlds of Plato and Aristotle and that it is a static notion, contrasting in this respect with such characteristically dynamic biblical categories as purpose and action. Accordingly there is now a fairly widespread tendency to describe the incarnation as a complex event constituting God's self-revealing action in man's history. In the New Testament records we see God at work in and through a human life, dealing with human beings in a way that makes plain the divine nature in its relation to man. The acts and attitudes of Jesus toward the men and women with whom he had to do were God's acts and attitudes in relation to those particular individuals, expressed in the finitude of a human life. Along these and other lines Christological discussion continues.

THE TRINITY. The Trinitarian doctrine is a second-order Christian belief. It was gradually developed within the church both to take account of certain data at the experiential level and to aid the development of the general system of Christian doctrine, some of the key points of which are related by the Trinitarian framework.

The New Testament basis for this doctrine was the Christian community's threefold awareness of God, first as the transcendent moral creator witnessed to in the prophetic tradition received from Judaism; second, as having been at work among them on earth in the person of Christ; and third, as the Holy Spirit, which was referred to apparently indiscriminately as the Spirit of God and the Spirit of Christ, inspiring and guiding both individuals and the Christian community.

The doctrine of the Trinity developed in close conjunction with Christology and made possible the completion of the church's thought concerning the person of Christ. For it had never been the accepted Christian conception that God, simply as such and in his totality, became man in the incarnation. The belief that "God was in Christ" (2 Corinthians 5:19) was held in conjunction with the belief that God was also and at the same time sustaining and governing the universe. The God who was incarnate in Christ was the God who had created heaven and earth. This was expressed by the affirmation that God is both Father and Son; and the reality of the Spirit, operating in the world both before and after the thirty or so years of the incarnation, required the further expansion into a Trinitarian formulation. Thus, the doctrine of the Trinity (*a*) asserts the full deity of Christ as the second person of the Trinity; (*b*) prohibits a too simple conception of incarnation (as one branch of the theological tradition has put it, Christ is *totus deus,* wholly God, but not *totum dei,* the whole of God); and (*c*) recognizes the universal presence and activity of God in the world as the divine Spirit. This latter point is of great practical importance because it entails a Christian message not only about God's actions in the past but also about a divine activity in the present that can directly affect the individual today.

In the Trinitarian discussions that accompanied the Christological debates one of the main questions concerned the issue of equality versus subordination within the Trinity. Is the Son subordinate to the Father, or the Spirit to both? The answer that was eventually embodied in the *Quicunque vult,* or "Athanasian" Creed, of the sixth century was that the members of the Trinity are coeternal and have an equal divine status; the Son is eternally begotten by the Father, and the Spirit eternally proceeds from the Father and the Son. (The latter point was the occasion of the rift in the sixth century between the Eastern church, with its center at Constantinople, and the Western church, with its center at Rome. In its original form the Nicene Creed described the Spirit as proceeding (only) from the Father. Later the Western church added the famous *filioque*—"and the Son"—an insertion that Eastern Christianity rejected as an unwarrantable tampering with the creed.)

In the accepted Trinitarian language the Father, the Son, and the Holy Spirit are spoken of as three "Persons," the Latin *persona* having been used to translate the Greek ὑπόστασις (which had displaced πρόσωπον—literally, "face"—in this context). *Persona* is not, of course, the equivalent of "person" in the modern sense of an individual center of consciousness and purpose. Originally a persona was the mask worn by an actor, then his part in the play, and then by further extension any part a person might play in life. Thus, whereas τρεῖς ὑπόστασεις suggests three divine entities, *tres personae* suggests three roles or functions of the deity. These two different conceptions have each been developed in Christian thought, leading to what have been called respectively "immanent," or "ontological," and "economic" theories of the Trinity.

According to the ontological theories the doctrine of the Trinity is an affirmation about the transcendent metaphysical structure of the Godhead. It asserts that God in his inner being consists of three divine realities that are individually distinct and yet bound together in a mysterious unity—"three in one and one in three." The extreme form of this view is the "social" conception of the Trinity as comprising three consciousnesses. According to the economic theories, on the other hand, the doctrine is about God specifically in his relation to the world. It asserts that the one God has acted toward humankind in three distinguishable ways—in creation and providence, in redemption, and in inner guidance and sanctification. God must indeed, in his inner being, be such as to become related in these ways to his creation, but this does not necessarily require the postulation of three distinct and yet intimately related divine realities.

REDEMPTION. That human beings are sinful is a theological statement of the observable fact that men and women are persistently self-centered and that even their highest moral achievements are quickly corrupted by selfishness. Yet although we thus fail, exhibiting a chronic moral weakness and poverty, our failure is not inevitable; we are ourselves, at least in part, responsible for it. The biblical story of the fall of man depicts this situation by means of the myth that man was originally created perfect but fell by his own fault into his present state, in which he is divided both in himself and from his fellows and God.

At its primary level of belief Christianity claims that by responding to God's free forgiveness, offered by Christ, men are released from the guilt of their moral failure (justification) and are drawn into a realm of grace in which they are gradually re-created in character (sanctification). The basis of this claim is the Christian experience of reconciliation with God and, as a consequence, with other human beings, with life's circumstances and demands, and with oneself. The "justification by faith" of which Paul spoke, and which represented the main religious emphasis of the Reformation of the sixteenth century, means that men are freely accepted by God's gracious love, which they have only to receive in faith. In Paul Tillich's contemporary restatement, a man has only to accept the fact that although unacceptable even to himself, he is accepted by God.

In this case, work at the secondary level of theological reflection did not begin seriously until the church had been preaching the fact of divine reconciliation and atonement for about a thousand years. Anselm, in the eleventh century, taught that the death of Christ constituted a satisfaction to the divine honor for the stain cast upon it by man's disobedience, and this remains the core of Catholic atonement doctrine. Martin Luther and John Calvin, in the sixteenth century, spoke of Christ's death as a substitutionary sacrifice by which Christ suffered in his own person the punishment that was justly due humankind, and this remains the core of official Protestant atonement doctrine. In the nineteenth century, however, the thought was developed (going back to Anselm's contemporary Peter Abelard) that God's forgiveness does not need to be purchased by Christ's death, but that this brings home to the human heart both man's need for divine forgiveness and the reality of that forgiveness. There were in the twentieth century and on into the twenty-first century continuing efforts to understand Christ's redeeming work in a way that would bring together the valid insights in these and other traditional views, each of which by itself has seemed one-sided.

HEAVEN, HELL, AND JUDGMENT. Jesus impressed upon his hearers in the strongest possible terms the absolute importance of decisions made and deeds performed in this present life. He regarded men and women as free and responsible persons on whose daily choices depended their own final good and happiness or irretrievable loss and failure. In doing this he used the traditional language of heaven and hell, which were understood until comparatively recently in terms of a prescientific cosmology, with heaven located in the sky above our heads and hell in the ground beneath our feet. Heaven is now generally conceived of as the enjoyment of the full consciousness of God's presence and participation in the divine "kingdom," which represents the final fulfillment of God's purpose for his creation; and hell is viewed as self-exclusion from this.

There are many perennially debated questions in this area. Are men divinely predestined, some to eternal salvation and others to eternal damnation ("double predestination"), as Augustine and Calvin taught? Does "hell" signify an eternal state, or is it a temporally bounded purgatorial experience that might lead to eventual salvation? (The adjective *αἰώνιος*, which is used in the New Testament, can mean either "eternal" or "for the aeon, or age"). Or does "hell" perhaps signify sheer annihilation? Can the final frustration of God's purpose by the loss of part of his human creation be reconciled with his ultimate sovereignty, and does the idea of never-ending torment, as a form of suffering out of which no good is finally brought, rule out the possibility of a Christian theodicy? Are all men to be finally saved ("universalism"), or only some?

In relation to such questions it is perhaps useful to distinguish between two standpoints from which eschatological statements may be made. There is the existential standpoint of "real life," in which we exercise a fateful responsibility in our moral choices and are confronted with the tremendous alternatives of spiritual life and death, symbolized by heaven and hell. There is also the detached standpoint of theological reflection, in which it seems possible to deduce from the two premises of the sovereignty and the love of God that although damnation is abstractly conceivable and is known in existential experience as a dread possibility, God's saving purpose in relation to his creatures will nevertheless in the end be triumphant, and eternal loss will remain an unrealized possibility.

THE CHURCH. Although Christianity as historically institutionalized lies outside the narrow scope of this entry, it must be added that Christian faith has always drawn people together into a community of faith, or church. The largest Christian institution, the Roman Catholic Church, holds that the authentic Christian community is defined by its visible continuity, manifested in a succession of bishops and popes, with the earliest church. Protestantism holds that the Christian community is defined by a different continuity, that of faith, and affirms that the external institutions associated with Christian faith are continually in need of reformation in the light of the original Christian data embodied in the scriptures.

See also Abelard, Peter; Anselm, St.; Arius and Arianism; Aristotle; Calvin, John; Gnosticism; God, Concepts of; Heaven and Hell, Doctrines of; Luther, Martin; Neoplatonism; Platonism and the Platonic Tradition; Ritschl, Albrecht Benjamin; Spinoza, Benedict (Baruch) de.

Bibliography

THE BIBLE

Old Testament. 7th ed. Edited by R. Kittel. Stuttgart, 1951. Hebrew text.

New Testament. 2nd ed. Edited by G. D. Kilpatrick. London, 1958. Greek text.

American Revised Standard Version. New York, 1952–1957. Old and New Testaments and Apocrypha in translation.

New English Bible. Vol. 1: New Testament. London, 1961. Translation.

COLLECTIONS OF CHRISTIAN LITERATURE

Baillie, John, John T. McNeill, and Henry P. Van Dusen, eds. *Library of Christian Classics,* 26 vols. London and Philadelphia, 1954–.

Migne, J. P., ed. *Patrologia Graeca.* 162 vols. Paris, 1857–1866.

Migne, J. P., ed. *Patrologia Latina.* 221 vols. Paris, 1844–1864.

Roberts, Alexander, and James Donaldson, eds. *The Ante-Nicene Fathers.* 10 vols. Grand Rapids, MI, 1951.

Schaff, Philip et al., eds. *Nicene and Post-Nicene Fathers of the Christian Church.* Grand Rapids, MI, 1952–1956. Two series, each in 14 vols.

ENCYCLOPEDIAS

Campenhausen, H. F. von et al., eds. *Die Religion in Geschichte und Gegenwart.* 3rd ed. 7 vols. Tübingen: Mohr, 1957–1965.

Hastings, James, ed. *Encyclopedia of Religion and Ethics,* 13 vols. Edinburgh, 1908–1926.

Vacant, A. et al., eds. *Dictionnaire de Théologie catholique.* 3rd ed. 15 vols. Paris, 1923–1950.

HISTORY OF CHRISTIANITY

Latourette, K. S. *A History of the Expansion of Christianity.* 7 vols. New York and London: Harper, 1937–1945.

HISTORY OF CHRISTIAN THOUGHT

Harnack, Adolf von. *Lehrbuch der Dogmengeschichte.* 4th ed. 3 vols. Tübingen, 1909–1910. Third ed. translated by Neil Buchanan as *History of Dogma.* 7 vols. London, 1894–1899; New York: Russell and Russell, 1958.

Kelly, J. N. D. *Early Christian Doctrines.* London: A. and C. Black, 1958.

Seeberg, Reinhold. *Lehrbuch der Dogmengeschichte.* 4th ed. 4 vols. Basel, 1953–1954. Translated by C. E. Hay as *Textbook of the History of Doctrines.* Grand Rapids, MI, 1952.

Wolfson, H. A. *The Philosophy of the Church Fathers.* Cambridge, MA: Harvard University Press, 1956–.

ROMAN CATHOLICISM

Denzinger, H. J. D. *Enchiridion Symbolorum Definitionum et Declarationum de Rebus Fidei et Morum,* 29th ed. Freiburg, Germany, 1952. Translated by R. J. Defarrari as *The Sources of Catholic Dogma.* St. Louis, MO: Herder, 1957.

Schmaus, Michael. *Katholische Dogmatik.* 5 vols. Munich, 1948–1958.

Smith, G. D., ed. *The Teaching of the Catholic Church.* 2 vols. London: Burns, Oates and Washburne, 1948; New York: Macmillan, 1949.

Thomas Aquinas. *Summa Contra Gentiles.* Editio Leonina Manualis. Rome, 1934. Translated by A. C. Pegis, J. F. Anderson, V. J. Bourke, and C. J. O'Neil as *On the Truth of the Catholic Faith.* 4 vols. New York, 1955–1957.

Thomas Aquinas. *Summa Theologiae.* 6 vols. Editio altera Romana. Rome, 1894. Translated by the English Dominican Fathers. London, 1911–1922; New York, 1947–1948.

PROTESTANTISM

Barth, Karl. *Kirchliche Dogmatik.* Munich: Kaiser, 1932–. Translated as *Church Dogmatics,* edited by G. W. Bromiley and T. F. Torrance. Edinburgh: Clark, 1936–.

Calvin, John. *Institutio Christianae Religionis.* Basel, 1536. Critical ed. by P. Barth and W. Niesel. Munich, 1926. Translated by F. L. Battles as *Institutes of the Christian Religion,* edited by J. T. McNeill. 2 vols. Philadelphia: Westminster Press, 1961.

Luther, Martin. *A Commentary on St. Paul's Epistle to the Galatians.* Edited and translated by Philip Watson. London, 1953.

Luther, Martin. *Lectures on Romans.* Translated by W. Pauck. London and Philadelphia, 1961.

Luther, Martin. *Werke.* 58 vols. Weimar, 1883–1948.

Schleiermacher, Friedrich. *Der Christliche Glaube.* Critical ed. by M. Redeker. Berlin, 1960. Translated as *The Christian Faith,* edited by H. R. Mackintosh and J. S. Stewart. Edinburgh, 1928; New York: Harper and Row, 1963.

Tillich, Paul. *Systematic Theology.* 3 vols. Chicago: University of Chicago Press, 1951–1964.

EASTERN ORTHODOXY

Bulgakov, Sergei N. *L'Orthodoxie.* Paris, 1932. Translated by E. S. Cram as *The Orthodox Church.* London: Centenary Press, 1935.

Tsankov, Stefan. *Das orthodoxe Christentum des Ostens.* Berlin, 1928. Translated by D. A. Lowrie as *The Eastern Orthodox Church.* London, 1929.

Zernov, Nicholas. *Eastern Christendom.* New York: Putnam, 1961.

CONTEMPORARY ECUMENICAL MOVEMENT

Bell, G. K. A., ed. *Documents on Christian Unity.* 4 vols. London, 1924–1958.

Neill, Stephen C., and R. Rouse, eds. *A History of the Ecumenical Movement, 1517–1948.* Philadelphia: Westminster Press, 1954.

CREATION

Gilkey, Langdon B. *Maker of Heaven and Earth.* Garden City, NY: Doubleday, 1959.

THE PERSON OF CHRIST

Baillie, D. M. *God Was in Christ.* London and New York: Scribners, 1948.

Hendry, G. S. *The Gospel of the Incarnation.* Philadelphia: Westminster Press, 1958.

Knox, John. *Jesus: Lord and Christ.* New York: Harper, 1958.

Mackintosh, H. R. *The Doctrine of the Person of Jesus Christ.* London and New York: Scribners, 1912.

Pittenger, W. Norman. *The Word Incarnate.* New York: Harper, 1959.

ATONEMENT

Anselm. *Cur Deus Homo?,* edited by F. S. Schmitt. Bonn, 1929. Also in *Opera Omnia,* edited by F. S. Schmitt, Vol. II. Anonymous translation in Ancient and Modern Library of Theological Literature. London, 1889. "Satisfaction" theory.

Aulen, Gustaf. *Christus Victor.* Translated by A. G. Hebert. London: Society for Promoting Christian Knowledge, 1931. "Christus Victor" theory.

Denney, James. *The Christian Doctrine of Reconciliation.* London: George H. Doran, 1918. "Penal-substitutionary" theory.

Mozley, J. K. *The Doctrine of the Atonement.* New York: Scribners, 1916. Historical.

Rashdall, Hastings. *The Idea of Atonement in Christian Theology.* London: Macmillan, 1919. "Moral influence" theory.

TRINITY

Franks, R. S. *The Doctrine of the Trinity.* London: Duckworth, 1953. Historical.

Hodgson, Leonard. *The Doctrine of the Trinity.* London: Nisbet, 1943.

Welch, Claude. *In His Name.* New York, 1952. Welch and Hodgson represent the two types of theory described in this entry.

ESCHATOLOGY

Althaus, Paul. *Die letzten Dinge.* 4th ed. Gütersloh, 1933.

Cullmann, Oscar. *Christus und die Zeit.* Zürich, 1946. Translated by F. V. Filson as *Christ and Time.* Philadelphia, 1950; rev. ed., London, 1962.

Hügel, F. von. *Eternal Life.* Edinburgh: T. and T. Clark, 1912.

CHRISTIANITY AND OTHER RELIGIONS

Farmer, H. H. *Revelation and Religion.* London: Nisbet, 1954.

Kraemer, H. *Religion and the Christian Faith.* London: Lutterworth Press, 1956.

OTHER RECOMMENDED TITLES

Beaty, Michael, ed. *Christian Theism and the Problems of Philosophy.* Notre Dame, IN: University of Notre Dame Press, 1990.

Feenstra, Ronald, and Cornelius Plantinga Jr., eds. *Trinity, Incarnation, and Atonement.* Notre Dame: University of Notre Dame Press, 1989.

Flint, Thomas, ed. *Christian Philosophy.* Notre Dame, IN: University of Notre Dame Press, 1990.

Morris, Thomas. *The Logic of God Incarnate.* Ithaca, NY: Cornell University Press, 1986.

Murray, Michael, ed. *Reason for the Hope Within.* Grand Rapids, MI: Eerdmans, 1999.

Padgett, Alan, ed. *Reason and the Christian Religion: Essays in Honour of Richard Swinburne.* Oxford: Oxford University Press, 1994.

Plantinga, Alvin. *Warranted Christian Belief.* Oxford: Oxford University Press, 2000.

Swinburne, Richard. *The Christian God.* Oxford: Clarendon Press, 1994.

Swinburne, Richard. *Responsibility and Atonement.* Oxford: Clarendon Press, 1989.

Swinburne, Richard. *The Resurrection of God Incarnate.* Oxford: Clarendon Press, 2003.

Van Inwagen, Peter. *God, Knowledge and Mystery: Essays in Philosophical Theology.* Ithaca, NY: Cornell University Press, 1995.

Vesey, Godfrey, ed. *The Philosophy in Christianity.* Cambridge, U.K.: Cambridge University Press, 1990.

White, Vernon. *Atonement and Incarnation: An Essay in Universalism and Particularity.* Cambridge, U.K.: Cambridge University Press, 1991.

John Hick (1967)
Bibliography updated by Christian B. Miller (2005)

CHRYSIPPUS

(c. 279–206 BCE)

Chrysippus, the Stoic philosopher born at Soli, in Cilicia, became the third leader of the Stoa at Athens upon the death of Cleanthes, in 232 BCE. This post he held until his own death. Because of his defense of the Stoa against the attacks of Arcesilaus and the skeptical Academy, and undoubtedly also on the basis of his voluminous writings, it was said in antiquity "if there had been no Chrysippus, there would be no Stoa." He wrote 705 books, about half of which, judging from the catalog preserved by Diogenes Laertius, dealt with logic and language. None of his works is extant, though quotations from his books and assessments of some of his views have survived in the works of other ancient authors.

Chrysippus's epistemology is empirical. Presentations of objects are produced in the ruling part of the soul by movements engendered in the sense organs of the percipient. Illusory presentations can be distinguished from those that are veridical by deliberation, which consists in checking any given presentation against a fund of common notions, that is, families of remembered similar presentations; if the presentation is found to be sufficiently like some common notion, one may assent to it, thus acknowledging its veridical character.

Propositions are either simple or nonsimple. The truth condition of a simple proposition is the occurrence of the fact it conveys. The truth conditions of nonsimple propositions are functions of the truth-values of their ingredient propositions.

Chrysippus formulated five undemonstrated argument forms whose variables are to be specified by propositions. Among them are forms of the *modus ponens* and the *modus tollens* arguments. Arguments of varying complexity can be constructed by combining two or more of these basic forms. Chrysippus enjoyed a particular renown for his competence as a dialectician.

The moral philosophy of Chrysippus is concerned primarily with a statement of the final end of life and the relation of other things to it and with a consideration of the emotions and therapy for those enslaved by them. The final good is "to live in accordance with one's experience of the things which come about by nature." This is equivalent to living in accordance with reason, which in man supervenes upon instinct as a guide in life. The excellence of reason is wisdom, or knowledge of what is really good and what is really bad. Chrysippus's view in regard to the source of this knowledge is ambivalent. On the one hand—and this is obviously the doctrine that coheres best with his epistemology—it derives from generalizations made upon particular experiences. On the other hand, there are fragments implying that his knowledge is innate.

Emotions are great obstacles to happiness and are to be totally eradicated. In keeping with his monistic psychology, which rejects the Platonic doctrine of a tripartite soul, Chrysippus conceived of an emotion as a recently formed false judgment about the goodness or badness of something; such a judgment causes "a forceful and excessive impulse." Therapy for the emotions consists in persuading their victims that the judgments constituting the emotions are false.

The dominant motifs of the natural philosophy of Chrysippus are monism and determinism. The one substance that converts periodically into an elaborately structured universe has two constant aspects, a passive one and an active one. The passive is matter; the active is identified variously as reason, pneuma (spirit or breath), and God. Chrysippus regards so-called individual substances not as discrete units of matter but rather as "parts" of one primary substance. Everything that occurs is controlled unexceptionably by fate, which is "the continuous causal chain of the things that exist." Nothing comes about except in accordance with antecedent causes. Even in the case of states of affairs that might seem to be of a spontaneous or uncaused nature, "obscure causes are working under the surface." Chrysippus believed that humans were responsible for their conduct, and he sought in several ways to show that such a belief was not undermined by the rigorously deterministic view he espoused.

__See also__ Arcesilaus; Cleanthes; Determinism, A Historical Survey; Dialectic; Diogenes Laertius; Greek Academy; Platonism and the Platonic Tradition; Stoicism.

Bibliography

Arnim, Hans V. *Stoicorum Veterum Fragmenta*. Leipzig: Teubner, 1903.

Bréhier, E. *Chrysippe et l'ancienne Stoïcisme*. Paris, 1951.

Mates, B. *Stoic Logic*. Berkeley: University of California Press, 1953.

Pohlenz, M. *Die Stoa*. Göttingen: Vandenhoeck and Ruprecht, 1948.

Josiah B. Gould Jr. (2005)

CHUANG TZU

See *Zhuangzi*

CHUBB, THOMAS

(1679–1747)

Thomas Chubb, the English Arian and deist, was born at East Harnham, near Salisbury, the son of a maltster. Receiving little formal education, he read widely in geography, mathematics, and theology while working as apprentice to a glovemaker and, later, as a tallow chandler. At one time he lived in the house of Sir Joseph Jekyll, master of the rolls, in the capacity, it is alleged, of a sort of superior servant. Through the kindness of friends (one of whom was the celebrated surgeon William Cheselden) and the sales of his candles, his last years, spent at Salisbury, were largely devoted to study and to the presidency of a debating society. Chubb's importance, frequently overlooked, lies in the fact that a self-educated and humble artisan developed a good style of writing and mastered the prevalent rationalistic thinking sufficiently well to compete on equal terms with highly educated upper-class scholars and divines. He was the first, and one of the few, leading English deists of poor circumstances (only Peter Annet and Thomas Morgan shared this humble background). With Chubb it was apparent that deism had filtered down to the level of the common people and had become widespread.

Chubb's first publication was an Arian tract, *The Supremacy of the Father Asserted,* inspired by William Whiston's *Primitive Christianity Revived* of 1711 and published in 1715 upon the recommendation of Whiston.

Although Chubb went through an early phase of Arminianism and was always hard pressed to reconcile Jehovah with the rationalistic concept of a Supreme Being, he nevertheless became and remained a "Christian deist." Skeptical of the Jewish revelation, he was less so of the Islamic and openly accepted the Christian, at least as he understood it. In *The True Gospel of Jesus Christ asserted* (1732) and *The True Gospel of Jesus Christ Vindicated* (1739) he identified the essence of Christianity with the few simple principles of natural religion as found, for example, in Lord Herbert of Cherbury. He openly compared the propagation of primitive Christianity with the then current spread of Methodism and thereby rejected the claims of supernatural power associated with the early church. He defended his sort of rationalistic Christianity against some of the aspersions of that formidable deist Matthew Tindal. Although Voltaire had some kind words to say about Chubb, it is unlikely that he had read many of Chubb's tracts and certainly did not accept the concept of "Christian deism."

Chubb, like the general run of deists, found reason sufficient to guide humankind to God's favor and the happiness of another world; he was suspicious of mystery and of miracles and critical of some passages in the Scriptures; he regarded revelation not as divine but as the work of honest men who gave a fair and faithful account of matters of fact; he was dubious about a particular providence and, therefore, of prayer; he argued against prophecy and miracle and believed in the dignity of human nature and in free will. Among the multitudinous answers to Chubb from the more orthodox, the foremost came in 1754 from Jonathan Edwards of Massachusetts. *A Careful and Strict Enquiry into The modern prevailing Notions of the Freedom of Will, Which is supposed to be essential To Moral Agency, Vertue and Vice, Reward and Punishment, Praise and Blame,* Edwards's chief claim to philosophical fame, devotes no fewer than nineteen pages to the refutation of Chubb on free will. Chubb, it may reasonably be inferred, was widely read in America.

In fine, though adding little constructive thought to the deistic movement, this humble and least formally educated of the English deists was definitely one of its most valuable and popular spokesmen. In the nonpejorative sense of the term he was a candid freethinker.

See also Deism.

Bibliography

Chubb was prolific in publication, and his ardent deism was expressed in the titles of a few of his chief works: *The Comparative Excellence and Obligation of Moral and Positive Duties* (1730); *A Discourse concerning Reason, With regard to Religion and Divine Revelation* (1731); *The Sufficiency of Reason in Matters of Religion Farther Considered* (1732); *The Equity and Reasonableness of the Divine Conduct, In Pardoning Sinners upon Their Repentence Exemplified* (1737), which was directed against Bishop Butler's famous *Analogy of Religion* of the previous year; *An Enquiry into the Ground and Foundation of Religion. Wherein Is shewn, that Religion Is founded in Nature* (1740); and *A Discourse on Miracles, Considered as Evidence to Prove the Divine Original of a Revelation* (1741).

Other works by Chubb include *Four Tracts* (1734) and *Some Observations Offered to Publick Consideration.... In which the Credit of the History of the Old Testament Is Particularly Considered* (1735). The posthumous *Works of Mr. Thomas Chubb*, 2 vols. (London, 1748) contains the valuable "Author's Farewell to his readers."

See also Sir Leslie Stephen's *History of English Thought in the Eighteenth Century* (London: Smith Elder, 1876; the paperback, 2 vols., New York: Harcourt Brace, 1963, follows the revised edition of 1902) and the general bibliography under the "Deism" entry.

OTHER RECOMMENDED TITLE

Bushell, Thomas L. *The Sage of Salisbury: Thomas Chubb, 1679–1747.* New York: Philosophical Library, 1967.

Ernest Campbell Mossner (1967)
Bibliography updated by Tamra Frei (2005)

CHU HSI

See *Zhu Xi*

CHURCH, ALONZO

(1903–1995)

Alonzo Church, an American logician and philosopher, was born in Washington, D.C. He received his PhD from Princeton in 1927, having written his dissertation under Oswald Veblen on alternatives to the axiom of choice. He spent a year at Harvard and then a year in Europe, studying first at Göttingen and then at Amsterdam with L.E.J. Brouwer. He returned to Princeton where he was professor of mathematics from 1929 to 1967, after which he moved to UCLA to become professor of mathematics and philosophy. He retired from teaching at UCLA in 1990. Church's most important contributions to logic were his analysis of the concept of effective computability and his proof of the undecidability of first-order logic (Church's theorem).

A function of natural number is effectively computable if there is an algorithm—a surefire method requiring no ingenuity to follow—that will yield the value of the function for any given natural number as input. Church devised a formal system, the lambda calculus (which subsequently became an important tool in computer science), and proposed that a function of natural numbers be taken to be computable if it is *lambda definable*—definable by way of a formula in the calculus. The analysis has little to recommend it initially, but experience with intuitively computable functions led Church to conjecture that every such function is lambda definable—a conjecture now known as *Church's thesis.* Alan Turing gave a more compelling analysis of computability in terms of abstract computing machines (Turing machines) and it was subsequently shown that lambda definability is equivalent to this notion of *Turing computability*. Various other analyses have been proposed and all have turned out to be equivalent to Church's definition. This is often regarded by logicians as evidence for the correctness of the conjecture. Church's thesis is now almost universally accepted.

Say, for instance, that a property of an expression is (effectively) decidable if there is an algorithm for deciding whether or not any given expression has the property. This notion can be identified with a certain sort of effective computability by supposing that all expressions have been assigned numbers (in some effectively determinate way) and then saying that a property of an expression is *effectively decidable* if there is an algorithm that will yield 0 (*no*) when applied to the number for the expression if the expression does not have the property and will yield 1 (*yes*) if the expression does have the property. If one then identifies the existence of such an algorithm with the lambda definability (or Turing computability) of that function, as Church's (or the Church-Turing) thesis proposes, one has a precise definition of effective decidability. Church's theorem shows that the property of being a valid formula of first-order predicate logic is not decidable in this sense. Thus, unlike the propositional calculus for which truth tables yield an effective procedure for deciding tautologousness, the validity of a first-order formula can not be decided, yea or nay, by any uniform algorithmic procedure.

Church's most important philosophical contributions involve the realism-nominalism controversy in the philosophy of mathematics and logic and problems and theories about meaning. He was a realist or Platonist about abstract entities and provided powerful arguments against various attempts to explain away such entities.

Rudolf Carnap and others associated with logical positivism displayed a general animosity toward such abstracta as numbers, functions, properties, and propositions. Carnap attempted to analyze sentences ostensibly ascribing belief in a proposition to someone in terms of sentences and a relation of "intensional isomorphism" between sentences. Roughly, the relation holds when the sentences in question are made up of necessarily equivalent parts, arranged in the same order. Church objected that a sentence ascribing a belief to someone does not mention a sentence of a particular language. He goes on to give a detailed and compelling refutation of Carnap's specific proposal. The method used, what is now called the "translation argument," appears to be of general applicability and makes it seem implausible that any replacement of propositions by more concrete things such as sentences will be successful. Church also raised powerful objections to nominalist maneuvers by A. J. Ayer and Israel Scheffler. Problems about the notion of synonymy were raised by Nelson Goodman and Benson Mates. Church answered these decisively.

Church's work on the logic of sense and denotation, a formal intensional logic incorporating some of Gottlob Frege's ideas about meaning, was one of his most important projects for philosophy, but it remains unfinished. The basic new idea is the "delta-relation"—the relation that holds between the sense of an expression and the denotation of that expression in some possible (N.B.) language. This is taken to be a logical relation and it is said that the sense is a *concept of* the denotation. It is postulated that a concept (the sense of some expression in some possible language) is a concept of at most one thing. And if F is a concept of a function f and X is a concept of an object x, then $F[X]$ is a concept of $f(x)$. Church assumes that one can construe concepts of functions as certain functions on concepts, so that $F[X]$, plausibly taken to be a certain complex entity, is just construed as application of the function F to an argument X.

Various difficulties were encountered in working out this last idea, as well as in developing an axiomatic treatment of a *criterion of identity* for concepts that would render them suitable for the analysis and logic of the propositional attitudes—belief, knowledge, and the like. Modifying Carnap's notion of intensional isomorphism, Church proposed that two sentences (or other complex expressions) express the same proposition (or concept) if they are *synonymously isomorphic*—roughly, that they consist of synonymous expressions arranged in the same order. The development of axioms for the logic of sense and denotation that this idea suggests Church calls "Alternative (0)." Church was unable to complete an adequate formalization of this important conception.

See also Ayer, Alfred Jules; Brouwer, Luitzen Egbertus Jan; Carnap, Rudolf; Computability Theory; First-Order Logic; Frege, Gottlob; Goodman, Nelson; Logic, History of; Mathematics, Foundations of; Meaning; Realism; Turing, Alan M.

Bibliography

PRIMARY WORKS

"A Formulation of the Logic of Sense and Denotation." In *Structure, Method, and Meaning: Essays in Honor of Henry M. Sheffer*, edited by Paul Henle. New York: Liberal Arts Press, 1951.

"Logic and Analysis." *Atti del XII Congresso Internazionale de Filosofia* Venezia, 12–18 settembre, 1958.

"On Carnap's Analysis of Statements of Assertion and Belief." *Analysis* 10 (1950): 97–99.

"Outline of a Revised Formulation of the Logic of Sense and Denotation," pt. 1. *Noûs* 7 (1973): 24–33.

"Outline of a Revised Formulation of the Logic of Sense and Denotation," pt 2. *Noûs* 8 (1974): 135–156.

"Propositions and Sentences." In *The Problem of Universals—A Symposium*, 1–12. Notre Dame, IN: University of Notre Dame Press 1956.

SECONDARY WORKS

Anderson, C. Anthony. "Alonzo Church's Contributions to Philosophy and Intensional Logic." *The Bulletin of Symbolic Logic* 4 (1998): 129–171.

C. Anthony Anderson (2005)

CHURCH FATHERS

See *Patristic Philosophy*

CHURCH'S THESIS

See *Computability Theory*

CHWISTEK, LEON

(1884–1944)

Leon Chwistek, a Polish mathematical logician, philosopher, aesthetician, essayist, and painter, was a lecturer at the University of Kraków and from 1930 a professor of mathematical logic at the University of Lvov.

THEORY OF REALITIES

The central problem of Chwistek's philosophy was a criticism of the idea of a uniform reality. It had been shown by Bertrand Russell that in logic admission of the totality of all functions of x produces contradictions; Chwistek claimed that in philosophy, likewise, many obscure and misleading thoughts result from the assumption of a single all-inclusive reality.

The results of this criticism led Chwistek to the thesis of a plurality of realities. Out of many possible realities four are particularly important to philosophy. The first, the reality of natural objects, is assumed by common sense; natural objects are of a given form regardless of our perception. Chwistek's defense of natural reality and our knowledge of it is reminiscent of the British common-sense philosophy of the nineteenth century. The objects studied in physics are not natural; the telescopic and microscopic worlds, matter, and the particles upon which the forces are supposed to act form a second reality. They are constructions, not something naturally given. The third reality, that of impressions, the elements of sensation, as studied by David Hume or Ernst Mach, forms the world of appearances. The fourth reality is that of images, produced by us and dependent on our will, fantasy, and creative processes.

All four of these realities are necessary to account for our knowledge. In addition, when we reflect that we speak about a reality, we cannot include ourselves or our reflection in this reality. Such a reflection must be a part of a higher reality. Otherwise confusions and contradictions arise. The act of discourse cannot be a part of the universe of discourse.

AESTHETICS

Chwistek applied the doctrine of plurality of realities to investigations in many areas—aesthetics, for example. Natural reality is dealt with by primitive art. In primitive art each object is given one color only, and perspective is not obeyed. The primitivist paints not as he sees but as things are supposed to be by themselves. He uses his vision, but mainly he uses his knowledge about the world. Realism in art depicts the physical reality as it is conceived at a given time. Impressionism is the art of the reality of impressions; it flourished in a society that had developed psychological research and made psychologism its fundamental scientific method. Futurism is the art of free images, of an actively created reality of fantasy and mental constructions.

In each style of art the artist tries to give a perfect form to his creation independent of the kind of reality he is working with. The form is the common feature of all works of art. Thus, Chwistek justified all styles by relating them to different realities, and he advocated formism: evaluation of form, not of reality, is the proper aesthetic evaluation.

MATHEMATICS AND SEMANTICS

Chwistek extended his pluralism to mathematics. There is no one system of mathematics, but there are many mutually exclusive systems. Various geometries coincide only in part. When we build analysis based on logic, we can accept, reject, or accept the negations of some extralogical existence axioms, such as the axiom of choice, the axiom of infinity, and the assumption of the existence of transfinite cardinal numbers. Logic itself should not decide any existence problem.

This restrained program for logic was paired with the requirement that logic be understandable in a nominalistic manner and deal with expressions in a constructive, mechanically computable way. Among principles often accepted as logical are some propositions questionable from the constructivist point of view—for example, the axiom of reducibility and the axiom of extensionality. The axiom of reducibility has to do with the distinction between predicative and impredicative concepts. An impredicative concept is a concept definable only by a definiens containing a quantifier that accepts as one of its values the very concept being defined. Russell and Chwistek ruled out such definitions as involving a vicious circle.

As was incisively pointed out by Kurt Gödel (in *The Philosophy of Bertrand Russell,* P. A. Schilpp, ed. [Evanston, IL, 1946], pp. 135–138), impredicative definitions involve a vicious circle only if one takes, as Chwistek did and Russell did not, a nominalistic attitude toward logic. Only if the quantifier is understood as a summary reference (infinite conjunction) to all of its values that are expressions and if one of the values of a quantifier that occurs in the definiens is the expression that is the definiendum do we presuppose what we want to define. Russell was not a nominalist. His exclusion of impredicative definitions was a way of avoiding antinomies. By differentiating between ranges of values of variables according to the way the quantifier binding a variable occurs, Russell constructed the ramified theory of logical types. This is a somewhat awkward theory. In analysis we want to speak about, for example, the real number that is the least upper bound of a set of real numbers that has a bound. To introduce this concept we must quantify over real numbers greater than all real numbers of a class that includes the least of them. Russell's theory avoids this impredicativeness by setting the least upper bound in a different logical type from the starting real numbers. But then the least upper bound and the real numbers involved cannot be values of the same variables, and several statements about particular sets of real numbers (for example, that a given function is continuous) are impossible.

To overcome this difficulty Russell accepted the axiom of reducibility, which says that every propositional function is coextensive with a predicative one. In many cases we cannot construct such a predicative function, and therefore constructivists, such as Chwistek, cannot accept this axiom. Moreover, for a nominalist, that two propositional functions are coextensive is not a sufficient guarantee of their identity. Thus, Chwistek attempted the task, which Russell called "heroic," of forming a purely constructivist system of the foundations of mathematics without impredicative definitions, the axiom of reducibility, or the axiom of extensionality. He observed, as F. P. Ramsey did, that results similar to Russell's can be obtained by the simple theory of types (where one distinguishes only between variables ranging over individuals, properties of individuals, properties of such properties, etc.) instead of the more complicated ramified theory. But simple type theory is inconsistent with the axiom of intensionality, which Chwistek wanted to be free to accept and which asserts the nonidentity of the concepts defined by two different propositional functions (even if they are coextensive).

The systems Chwistek constructed for the foundations of mathematics were such that they answered the philosophical needs of their author. They were admittedly more complicated than Russell's. "But it may be erroneous to think that clear ideas are never complicated; while we must agree that many simple ideas are, as a matter of fact, very obscure." Chwistek presented several formulations of his attempts at a constructivist theory, all of them too sketchy to be judged definitive. The relation to other constructivist systems is hard to establish. The last few versions were called "rational metamathematics." This theory deals with expressions, some of which are theorems.

A principal part of rational metamathematics, the fundamental system of semantics, uses two specific primitive signs, *c* and *, about which we stipulate that *c* is an expression and that if *E* and *F* are expressions, then **EF* is an expression. These formation rules assign a definite tree (or grouping) structure to each finite expression as well as to any two expressions written one after the other. Some of the allowed combinations of *c* and * may have no meaning—in this Chwistek was a formalist. To some other expressions we assign meaning, and in accordance with this assignment we accept proper axioms. We take 0 to be an abbreviation of **cc.* The fundamental substitution pattern (*EFGH*)—which is read "*H* is the result of substituting *G* for every occurrence of *F* in *E*"—is taken to be an abbreviation of ****EE*FF*GG*HH.* The Sheffer stroke function, |*EF,* is regarded as an abbreviation of ***EE**EE*EE***FF**FE*FF. Identity = *EF* stands for (*EOOF*).

See also Aesthetics, History of; Aesthetics, Problems of; Gödel, Kurt; Russell, Bertrand Arthur William; Semantics.

Bibliography

SELECTED WORKS BY CHWISTEK

Wielość Rzeczywistości (Plurality of realities). Kraków, 1921.

"The Theory of Constructive Types." *Annales de la Société Polonaise de Mathématique* 2 (1924, for 1923): 9–48, and 3 (1925, for 1924): 91–141.

"Fondements de la métamathématique rationnelle." *Bulletin de l'Académie Polonaise des Sciences et des Lettres,* Series A (1933): 253–264. Written with W. Hetper and J. Herzberg.

"Remarques sur la méthode de la construction des notions fondamentales de la métamathématique rationnelle." *Bulletin de l'Académie Polonaise des Sciences et des Lettres,* Series A (1933): 265–275. Written with W. Hetper and J. Herzberg.

Granice Nauki. Lvov and Warsaw, 1935. Rev. ed. translated by H. C. Brodie and A. P. Coleman as *The Limits of Science.* London: K. Paul, Trench, Trubner, 1948.

Wielość Rzeczywistości w Sztuce (Plurality of realities in art). Edited by K. Estreicher. Warsaw, 1960.

Pisma Filozoficzne i Logiczne (Philosophical and logical writings). Edited by K. Pasenkiewicz, 2 vols. Warsaw: Naukwoe, 1961–1963.

A reformulation of Chwistek's system of semantics by John Myhill appears in the *Journal of Symbolic Logic* 14 (1949): 119–125, and 16 (1951): 35–42.

Palace Boga. Próba rekonstrukcji. Warsaw: Panstwowy Instytut Wydawniczy, 1968.

Niejedna rzeczywistosc: racjonalizm krytyczny Leon Chwistka. Sens i rzeczywistosc. Crakow: Inter esse, 2004.

H. Hiż (1967)

CICERO, MARCUS TULLIUS
(106–43 BCE)

The Roman orator and statesman Marcus Tullius Cicero, of Arpinum, had a lifelong interest in philosophy and wrote a number of philosophical works during periods of forced retirement from public life. He was well acquainted with the four main Greek schools of his time and counted among his friends and teachers the Epicureans Phaedrus and Zeno, the Stoic Posidonius, the Peripatetic Staseas, the Academics Philo and Antiochus, and many others. He identified himself primarily with the Academy, though he found much to admire also in the Stoa and Lyceum. He rejected Epicureanism.

In a famous passage in a letter to Atticus (xii, 52, May 21, 45 BCE), with reference to some of his books on philosophy, Cicero calls them copies ("apographa"), written with little effort; he supplied only the words ("Verba tantum adfero, quibus abundo"). A week earlier he had written: "It is incredible how much I write, even at night; for I cannot sleep" (*Ad Atticum* xiii, 26). Modern scholars have found in such passages support for the view that these writings are chiefly valuable for the reconstruction of lost Greek originals, which Cicero in his haste sometimes misunderstood or jumbled together. The search for sources has been a major preoccupation of Ciceronian scholars for almost a century.

A more generous view is that in spite of his own statements Cicero's philosophical writings are more than hasty copies of Greek originals; they present a fairly coherent and modestly original system of thought. At a minimum Cicero took from the Academy a framework for his views. The Platonism of the New Academy had abandoned the search for truth and was occupied, rather, with the confrontation of conflicting opinions. Carneades, its leading spokesman, had even devised criteria for preferring one opinion to another. Within such a framework Cicero examines alternative views and makes his selection (though not necessarily in terms of Carneades' criteria). The views examined extend to all three commonly accepted branches of philosophy—logic, physics, ethics—and the presentation follows an orderly plan. Within this broad coverage, however, are many unresolved conflicts; clearly, Cicero's primary purpose was to offer to his Roman readers a wide range of philosophical opinions rather than to construct a well-integrated system.

PHILOSOPHY AND RHETORIC

Whatever originality Cicero's views possess is not in their components (he believed that the Greeks had already exhausted the varieties of possible opinions) but in their combination. The most conspicuous feature of his thought is the union of philosophy with rhetoric. This union carries with it some criticism of Socrates, who was blamed for their separation (see *De Oratore* iii, 61), and appears to align Cicero with Isocrates rather than Plato; yet he does not consider the union incompatible with Platonism. Carneades had prepared the way for a reconciliation between rhetoric and the Academy when he made philosophy a contest between opinions, and Greek theoretical rhetoricians had long since sought to implement Plato's prescription in the *Phaedrus* for a scientific rhetoric. Cicero could also point to the literary excellence of the dialogues as evidence that Plato was a master of the rhetorical art (ibid. i, 47).

The union of rhetoric and philosophy gave Cicero the materials for construction of his humanistic ideal.

The highest human achievement lies in the effective use of knowledge for the guidance of human affairs. Philosophy and the specialized disciplines supply the knowledge, and rhetorical persuasion makes it effective. Each is useless without the other, and the great man is master of both. Cicero associates this ideal with a free society—that is, a constitutional republic in which persuasion rather than violence is the instrument of political power. He believes that Rome has the essential features of such a state but that unless a great man is found to guide it, its freedom is in jeopardy.

Commitment to the union of eloquence and knowledge led Cicero to the view that if the statesman-philosopher is to speak persuasively on all subjects, he must have knowledge of all subjects. But recognizing the impossibility of such a requirement, Cicero advocated liberal education as the best approximation. An important part of liberal education is the study of philosophy, and Cicero's philosophical works provided materials for this study. Thus, in his philosophical writings no less than in his great public orations, he was combining wisdom and eloquence in the service of the Roman people.

PHILOSOPHICAL WORKS

The literary form that Cicero used emphasizes his didactic intent. Most of the philosophical works are dialogues, preceded by an introduction in defense of philosophical studies. The speakers are distinguished Romans, including Cicero himself, and frequently the listeners are young men just beginning their political careers. Conflicting views are presented in long speeches, with few interruptions. Sometimes the clash of opinions leads to insult and denunciation, especially when Epicureans are involved, but personal abuse of one speaker by another is avoided. There is hardly a vestige of dramatic conflict in such dialogues as *Tusculanae Disputationes,* where the conversation is between a young man and his preceptor. In two late works, *De Officiis* (*On Duties,* addressed to Cicero's son) and *Topica* (addressed to a young lawyer, Trebatius), the dialogue form is discarded.

In logic Cicero wrote *Academica,* in two versions (45 BCE), on the dispute between dogmatists and Academic skeptics about the criterion of truth; only portions of these are extant. *Topica* (44 BCE), though usually grouped with the rhetorical works, is also on logic. The title is from Aristotle, but the treatment is not. Cicero compiles a single exhaustive list of kinds of argument without distinction between the philosophical and the rhetorical.

There are three works, planned as a unit, on physics: (1) *De Natura Deorum,* (2) *De Divinatione,* and (3) *De Fato* (45–44 BCE). They present Epicurean, Stoic, and Academic arguments and counterarguments about religion and cosmology. Cicero himself was inclined to accept the Stoic arguments for a divine providence, but he rejected the Stoic doctrine of fate.

The major ethical writings are *De Finibus Bonorum et Malorum* (45 BCE), in which Epicurean, Stoic, and Peripatetic ethical views are examined; *Tusculanae Disputationes* (45 BCE), on fear of death, on pain, on distress of mind, and on other matters; and *De Officiis* (44 BCE), a practical ethics based on Stoic principles.

On political theory Cicero wrote two dialogues with titles taken from Plato. There is *De Re Publica* (51 BCE), from which the famous "Dream of Scipio" is an excerpt. The subject matter of the "Dream" ensured its preservation; it portrays the virtuous soul enjoying a more perfect existence after death in the region above the moon. The rest of the work is fragmentary. The other political dialogue, *De Legibus* (date uncertain), depicts Roman law as a very nearly perfect realization of Greek (chiefly Stoic) theory.

Some of the rhetorical works, especially the first book of *De Oratore* (55 BCE), discuss the relation of philosophy to rhetoric and present the ideal of the great man in whom both are united.

Minor works on philosophical themes include *Paradoxa Stoicorum, De Senectute, De Amicitia,* and the lost *Consolatio* and *Hortensius.* Cicero also translated two Platonic dialogues, *Protagoras* (lost) and *Timaeus* (W. Ax, ed., Leipzig, 1938).

See also Ancient Skepticism; Antiochus of Ascalon; Carneades; Greek Academy; Hellenistic Thought; Philo of Larissa; Stoicism.

Bibliography

TEXTS AND TRANSLATIONS

The standard Latin editions for most of Cicero's works are published by Teubner (various editors). New critical editions of the philosophical works are being published by Oxford University Press; two have appeared (more are imminent): *De Finibus,* edited by L. D. Reynolds (1998), and *De Officiis,* edited by Michael Winterbottom (1994). Texts and facing translations of the entire corpus, including all philosophical works except a partial Latin translation of Plato's *Timaeus,* are published by the *Loeb Classical Library,* various editor-translators (Cambridge, MA: Harvard University Press, 1914–1949). Superior translations of philosophical works include:

Academica: Brittain, Charles. *Cicero: On Academic Scepticism.* Indianapolis, IN: Hackett, 2005.

De Amicitia: Powell, Jonathan G. F. *Cicero: On Friendship and The Dream of Scipio.* Warminster: Aris and Phillips, 1990.

De Fato: Sharples, Robert W. *Cicero: On Fate, and Boethius: The Consolation of Philosophy IV.5–7, V.* Warminster: Aris and Phillips, 1991.

De Finibus Bonorum et Malorum: Annas, Julia, and Raphael Woolf. *Cicero: On Moral Ends.* Cambridge, U.K.: Cambridge University Press, 2001.

De Legibus: Zetzel, James E. G. *Cicero: On the Commonwealth and On the Laws.* Cambridge, U.K.: Cambridge University Press, 1999.

De Natura Deorum: Walsh, Patrick G. *Cicero: The Nature of the Gods.* Oxford: Oxford University Press, 1997.

De Officiis: Atkins, E. Margaret, and Miriam T. Griffin. *Cicero: On Duties.* Cambridge, U.K.: Cambridge University Press, 1991.

De Oratore: May, James M., and Jakob Wisse. *Cicero: On the Ideal Orator.* New York: Oxford University Press, 2001.

De Re Publica: Zetzel, James E. G. *Cicero: On the Commonwealth and On the Laws.* Cambridge, U.K.: Cambridge University Press, 1999.

Topica: Reinhardt, Tobias. *Cicero: Topica.* Oxford: Oxford University Press, 2003.

Tusculanae Disputationes: Graver, Margaret. *Cicero on the Emotions: Tusculan Disputations 3 and 4.* Chicago: University of Chicago Press, 2002.

Dyck, Andrew R. *A Commentary on Cicero, De Legibus.* Ann Arbor: University of Michigan Press, 2004.

Dyck, Andrew R. *A Commentary on Cicero, De Officiis.* Ann Arbor: University of Michigan Press, 1996.

Gawlick, Gunther, and Woldemar Görler. "Cicero." In *Die Philosophie der Antike,* Vol. 4, edited by Helmut Flashar. Basel: Schwabe, 1994. A comprehensive survey of his philosophical work and thought, with extensive, analytical bibliographies.

Inwood, Brad, and Jaap Mansfeld, eds. *Assent and Argument: Studies in Cicero's Academic Books.* Leiden: Brill, 1997.

MacKendrick, Paul. *The Philosophical Books of Cicero.* London: Duckworth, 1989. Useful synopses of each work.

Powell, Jonathan G. F., ed. *Cicero the Philosopher.* Oxford: Oxford University Press, 1995. Articles on diverse aspects of his thought.

Powell, Jonathan G. F., and John A.North, eds. *Cicero's Republic = Bulletin of the Institute of Classical Studies,* suppl. 76. London: University of London, 2001. Articles on his political thought.

Rawson, Elizabeth. *Cicero: A Portrait.* Ithaca, NY: Cornell University Press, 1983. A thoughtful and engaging biography emphasizing his intellectual life.

P. H. DeLacy (1967)

Bibliography updated by Stephen A. White (2005)

CIRCULARITY IN EPISTEMOLOGY

See *Epistemology, Circularity in*

CIVIL DISOBEDIENCE

The idea of civil disobedience comes out of the tradition of social and political protest whose best known advocates are the nineteenth-century American transcendentalist Henry David Thoreau, the Indian reformer Mohandas Gandhi, and the American civil rights leader, Martin Luther King, Jr. While the idea of civil disobedience has diverse roots, the views of these activist/thinkers set the stage for academic and popular discussion.

Philosophical discussions of civil disobedience generally focus on two questions. First, what is civil disobedience? Second, can acts of civil disobedience be morally justified?

DEFINING "CIVIL DISOBEDIENCE"

The definition of civil disobedience that best accords with the tradition of Thoreau, Gandhi, and King categorizes acts as civil disobedience if they have four features. They must be: (1) illegal; (2) nonviolent; (3) public; and (4) done to protest a governmental law or policy.

Thoreau's refusal to pay his taxes has all these features. It was illegal, nonviolent, and public. (Unlike a tax evader, Thoreau did not hide his not paying.) And, it was done to protest policies of the United States government that Thoreau thought were seriously unjust—support of slavery and an aggressive war against Mexico.

Actions such as Thoreau's are sometimes described as "conscientious refusal," refusing to obey a law that requires one to act immorally. While conscientious refusal is not identical with publicly protesting a policy, the two usually go together. Generally, people who refuse to obey unjust laws hope that their act will stimulate others to see that the law is wrong and to work for change. Thoreau spoke publicly about the reasons for his act, and his lecture became the classic essay "Civil Disobedience."

Gandhi and King went beyond individual conscientious refusal and organized large numbers of people to disobey the law as a means of protest. These illegal acts were intended to publicize serious injustices and to rally support for change. If enough people were to disobey an unjust law, it might be impossible for a government to enforce it.

Acts of civil disobedience cover a spectrum ranging from: (a) conscientious refusal by individuals; to (b) symbolic disobedience that is meant to convey a message about the wrongness of government policy; to (c) large-scale acts of disobedience that aim to render a government unable to carry out its policies.

Not everyone would accept the definition given above. Some argue that civil disobedients must accept the punishment, but this does not seem necessary. For example, someone who publicly burns a draft card might flee the country if the punishment were extremely severe; yet the original act would still be civil disobedience, even if the act of fleeing is not. John Rawls (1999) has argued that civil disobedience addresses a community's sense of justice, but this overlooks the fact that a community can have mistaken or conflicting conceptions of justice. Finally, some argue that civil disobedience can be violent, but this overlooks the connotations of the word "civil" and violates the tradition of Gandhi and King, who were explicitly committed to nonviolent strategies of resistance. Moreover, because violent acts require stronger types of justification, including them in the definition complicates the evaluation of civil disobedience. Violent acts will have to be distinguished from nonviolent ones when people try to see if civil disobedience can be morally justified. In the end, the test of definitions is that they help to clarify matters, and lumping together violent and nonviolent acts in this case does not seem helpful.

Using the definition above, the question "Is civil disobedience ever morally justified?" can be understood to mean "Is it ever morally permissible to engage in nonviolent, public violations of the law in order to protest a governmental law or policy?"

THE DUTY TO OBEY THE LAW

Asking whether civil disobedience can be morally justified presupposes that there is a moral duty to obey the law. If there were no such moral duty, then breaking the law would not need a special justification. In addition, people who think that civil disobedience can never be justified must believe that the moral duty to obey the law is absolute and can never be overridden by other moral concerns.

Socrates' arguments in the *Crito* are often taken as a source of the view that people must always obey the law. Socrates appears to argue that people must always obey the law because the state is like a parent and one must obey one's parents, that the state has benefited him and therefore should be obeyed, and that he has made a tacit agreement to obey the laws by living in Athens all his life. In the *Apology*, however, Socrates states that he will disobey the law if it requires him to violate the commands of the gods. Socrates, then, is a source of both the individualist tradition that approves civil disobedience and the authoritarian, statist tradition that condemns it.

In his *Leviathan*, Thomas Hobbes provides a famous argument for the duty of obedience to law. He argued that recognition of government's authority is justified because it is the only way for people to avoid a state of nature in which everyone is a threat to everyone else. If all people followed their own judgment and recognized no legal authority, this would lead to a situation of unlimited conflict in which life is "nasty, brutish, and short" (*Leviathan*, Ch. XIII). Hobbes thought that peace could be achieved only if people agree to obey a sovereign who enforces the laws. If everyone claims a right to act according to their own judgment and to disregard the law, then government would be undermined, and there would be a return to anarchy and a state of war by "every man, against every man" (*Leviathan*, Ch. XIII). In short, individuals must trade away their personal autonomy if peace and security are to be possible.

In a much discussed argument from the 1960s, Robert Paul Wolff turned Hobbes's argument on its head in order to defend a version of philosophical anarchism. Wolff agrees with Hobbes that governments claim authority over what citizens should do and thus take away personal autonomy. But, Wolff claimed, personal autonomy—deciding what is right and wrong for oneself and acting on those decisions—can never legitimately be traded away (Wolff 1976). Therefore, governmental authority can never be morally legitimate. From Wolff's anarchist perspective, it is obedience to law rather than disobedience that is morally questionable.

There is also a cynical tradition that sees laws as devices for protecting the interests of the rich and powerful. Thrasymachus, a character in Plato's *Republic*, defined justice as whatever is in the interests of the stronger. This idea is echoed in the Marxist view that the legal system is a device whose real purpose is to protect the property and power of the wealthy. This cynical perspective suggests that it is foolish to believe in a moral obligation to obey the law.

JUSTIFYING CIVIL DISOBEDIENCE

Debates about civil disobedience are often conducted in all-or-nothing terms. They presuppose either (a) that there is an absolute obligation to obey the law no matter what, or (b) that there is no obligation to obey the law at all. From this perspective, support for civil disobedience leads to anarchism, whereas opposition to it requires mindless conformity to governmental authority.

A different tradition emerges from John Locke's *Second Treatise on Civil Government*. While Locke argued that governments and laws could be legitimate and should be taken seriously, he also defended a right of revolution in cases where the government violates the rights that it is supposed to defend. According to Locke, the duty to obey is conditional on the nature of the government. There is no duty to obey a tyrannical government. This Lockean view acknowledges a general moral duty to obey the law while recognizing that there are circumstances in which disobedience—and even revolution—might be justified. Locke's view is echoed in the American *Declaration of Independence*, which affirms a right to "alter or abolish" a government that violates its people's rights.

Defenders of civil disobedience, then, need not be anarchists. They can recognize the moral force of the law while at the same time believe that the moral force of the law is conditional. When the right conditions do not exist, various forms of disobedience—including civil disobedience—may be justified. If the conditions that warrant obedience to law do exist, then people who violate the law are acting wrongly. Just as obedience to law can be morally required in some cases and morally forbidden in others, so likewise civil disobedience can be justified in some cases and not in others.

The argument for civil disobedience is strongest when a specific law requires people to act immorally. A broader justification for disobedience arises when a government lacks legitimacy. Gandhi's campaign for Indian independence, for example, challenged the legitimacy of British colonial rule. If British rule was illegitimate, then there was no moral duty to obey British laws. Still, for both moral and tactical reasons, Gandhi used civil disobedience selectively.

KING'S DEFENSE OF SELECTIVE OBEDIENCE

While there are plausible justifications for disobedience to some laws and some governments, a serious problem faces people who engage in civil disobedience but nonetheless appeal to others to obey the law. Martin Luther King Jr.'s classic "Letter from a Birmingham Jail" discusses just this problem. Critics charged that King was inconsistent because he urged segregationists to obey laws that enforced racial equality at the same time that King and his followers stated their willingness to violate other laws. If selective obedience was permissible for King, why was it not permissible for his opponents?

King defended himself by providing criteria for justified disobedience. He argued that it is morally permissible to disobey the law: (a) when the law itself is unjust because it "degrades human personality" rather than respecting people; (b) when the laws are binding on a minority group but do not bind the majority that imposes it; (c) when those who are mistreated are deprived of rights of democratic participation in the process of enacting the law; or (d) when a proper law is unjustly applied so as to deprive people of their rights of protest. These conditions, he argued, were met by those campaigning for racial equality but not by those who supported segregation.

King's argument shows how one can consistently defend the right to disobey the law and also take obedience to law seriously. He recognizes a strong presumption in favor of obedience but argues that the presumption is overridden in the kinds of circumstances he describes.

UNJUSTIFIED CIVIL DISOBEDIENCE

Acts of civil disobedience are not as difficult to justify as forms of protest that use violence. Nonetheless, acts of civil disobedience can be morally wrong. For example, they can be committed on behalf of an unjust cause. Thoreau, Gandhi, and King all protested serious evils, but if a person mistakenly believes that a law or policy is unjust, then an act of disobedience against it will not be morally justified. Moreover, even if a law or policy is bad, its defects may not be serious enough to justify violating the law. If obedience to law is something people expect of others when they disagree with a law, then those same people are not justified if they disobey laws simply because they disagree with them. Disobedience must be reserved for serious cases, and even then, it may not be justified if legal means are available for effectively promoting change. It is only when effective, legal means are unavailable that civil disobedience is permissible. Finally, such acts can be wrong if they undermine just and valuable institutions.

A strong case, then, can be made for the view that civil disobedience can be morally justified under certain conditions. Whether specific acts of civil disobedience are justified, however, is often controversial. This is because people often disagree about the seriousness of the evils being opposed, the availability of other effective means of protest, and the long-term effects on valuable institutions and practices. People who agree that civil disobedience can be justified in theory can still disagree about whether it is justified in practice.

See also Hobbes, Thomas; King, Martin Luther; Locke, John; Thoreau, Henry David.

Bibliography

Bedau, Hugo Adam, ed. *Civil Disobedience in Focus.* London: Routledge, 1991.

Gandhi, M. K. *Non-violent Resistance.* New York: Schocken Books, 1961.

Hobbes, Thomas. *Leviathan.* Many editions.

King, Martin Luther, Jr. "Letter from a Birmingham Jail." In *Why We Can't Wait.* New York: Signet Books, 1964.

Locke, John. *Second Treatise on Civil Government.* Many editions.

Nathanson, Stephen. *Should We Consent to Be Governed?.* 2nd ed. Belmont, CA: Wadsworth, 2001.

Plato, *Apology, Crito,* and the *Republic.* Many editions.

Rawls, John. "The Justification of Civil Disobedience." In *John Rawls: Collected Papers,* edited by Samuel Freedman. Cambridge, MA: Harvard University Press, 1999.

Thoreau, Henry David. "Civil Disobedience" and "A Plea for Captain John Brown." In *Walden and Other Writings of Henry David Thoreau,* edited by Brooks Atkinson. New York: Modern Library, 1950.

Wolff, Robert Paul. *In Defense of Anarchism.* 2nd ed. New York: Harper and Row, 1976.

Zinn, Howard. *Disobedience and Democracy: Nine Fallacies on Law and Order.* New York: Vintage Books, 1968.

Stephen Nathanson (2005)

CIXOUS, HÉLÈNE
(1937–)

Hélène Cixous was born in Oran, Algeria, on June 5, 1937. Her father was of French-colonial and Jewish descent and her mother was Austro-German. Cixous grew up in Algeria, although she studied in France and began her academic career there. Her first text, *Le prénom de Dieu* (God's first name), was published in 1967. Since 1968, she has been a professor of English literature at Université de Paris VIII–Vincennes, a university considered "revolutionary" for its opposition to traditional institutional structures, which she helped found. Cixous also established the first women's studies center in Europe at Université de Paris VIII.

Cixous has been consistently concerned with the repressive and exclusionary consequences of institutional and systemic forms of power. She has been interested in both individual and collective liberation struggles, such as the liberation of the self from the impact of psychoanalysis, the liberation of women, and Third World struggles. She has published approximately fifty novels, plays, and theoretical essays. Within the United States, the best known of her writings have been "The Laugh of the Medusa" (1976) and *The Newly Born Woman* (1986). Much of her work has been originally published in French and has not been translated into English.

Cixous is well known for her notion of *écriture feminine.* In "The Laugh of the Medusa," Cixous maintains that to define a feminine practice of writing, or écriture feminine, is not possible since "it will always surpass the discourse that regulates the phallocentric system" that aims to theorize or enclose it (1976, p. 883). Cixous discusses her wariness of reductive language that would simplify or capture her practice of écriture feminine. Nonetheless, her basic attempt is to free language and to offer new ways of writing and speaking. To do so, she emphasizes the fictional and poetic elements in her writing. In questioning structures of power, Cixous advocates the freeing of self through writing. In turn, freeing the self (or the subject) means rethinking traditionally repressed categories; for example, woman, the body, and writing. Cixous argues against the association of the phallic subject with narcissism and death, which simultaneously equates women with death. In contrast to an emphasis on narcissism and death, Cixous suggests an economy of the gift—an economy that is based on giving and receiving. The exchange represented by an economy of the gift would mark a new mode of exchange, for Cixous, and would arise through linguistic changes. In turn, in Cixous's view, it is only through linguistic changes that social changes are possible. Thus, Cixous encourages women to "write themselves"; that is, women should write their bodies and their desires, which have always and only been written and discussed by men.

The transformation of the relationship between self and other is central to Cixous's writing and constitutes its political dimension. While Cixous wrote her dissertation on Irish author James Joyce, her emphasis on life over death separated her from him. Although Cixous recognized Joyce for his emphasis on transforming linguistic structures as a means of changing mental structures, Joyce ultimately maintained that one must lose (kill the other) in order to have (live). Despite Cixous's recognition of loss and death as inevitable for life, her aim is to emphasize life over death (thereby reversing the emphasis of many male authors). One way in which Cixous highlights life, and the economy of the gift, is through a focus on the mother and child relationship; specifically, the mother and daughter relationship. Cixous suggests that the woman/mother gives insofar as she nourishes the child. Woman is both the container and the contained. Woman's relationship to the Other, or to otherness, thus differs from the relationship between man and the Other since things happen to him from the outside. Cixous uses the metaphor of "white ink," or of writing in breast milk, to convey the idea of reuniting with the maternal body. She also argues for a bisexuality that would extend subjectivity beyond dualisms to configure a multiple, rather than a fixed and static, subject.

In addition to Joyce, Cixous's work has been informed by several German and French philosophers, including Martin Heidegger and Jacques Derrida. In *La Venue à l'écriture* (1977), a strongly Derridean work, Cixous advances the position that écriture feminine is not necessarily writing by a woman; instead, it is writing likewise practiced by certain male authors (such as Joyce and Jean Genet). Cixous has furthered the work of psychoanalyst Jacques Lacan, though amidst controversy, by pointing out that women and men enter into the symbolic order (the structure of language) differently. She critiques Lacan's naming of the phallus as the center of the symbolic and suggests that this view marks language as "phallocentric" (the idea that the structure of language is centered by the phallus). In this regard, she both echoes and presses Derrida's insight that the Western privileging of spoken words over written words renders the structure of language as "logocentric." Like Derrida, she interrogates the binary structure of language in the West and exposes its role in maintaining oppressive structures of thought.

Often Cixous is placed alongside Luce Irigaray, Julia Kristeva, and Catherine Clément as being one of the French or continental feminists. However, the use of the phrase, "the French feminists," is problematic here in that it tends to conceal from consideration other feminists who are French. Moreover, the phrase overlooks the more complicated backgrounds of the so-called "French" feminists themselves. Not unlike these other thinkers however, and most notably Irigaray, Cixous has been charged with essentialism. That is, she has been criticized for engaging with an essential, identifiable, and named femininity within the texts she examines. Cixous's response to such accusations, not unlike Irigaray's, would be to claim that she does not intend to engage with a biological category "woman"; rather, she aims to interrogate the cultural position held by such categories within discourse and systems of language.

See also Feminism and Continental Philosophy.

Bibliography

WORKS BY HÉLÈNE CIXOUS

"The Laugh of the Medusa." Translated by Keith Cohen and Paula Cohen. *Signs* 1 (Summer 1976): 875–893.

The Newly Born Woman. With Catherine Clément. Edited by Betsy Wing. Minneapolis: University of Minnesota Press, 1986.

"Coming to Writing" and Other Essays. Edited by Deborah Jenson. Translated by Sarah Cornell, Deborah Jensen, Ann Liddle, and Susan Sellers. Cambridge, MA: Harvard University Press, 1992.

Hélène Cixous, Rootprints: Memory and Life Writing. With Mireille Calle-Gruber. New York: Routledge, 1997.

WORKS ABOUT HÉLÈNE CIXOUS

Conley, Verena Andermatt. *Hélène Cixous: Writing the Feminine*. Lincoln: University of Nebraska Press, 1991.

Sellers, Susan, ed. *The Hélène Cixous Reader*. New York: Routledge, 1994.

Wilcox, Helen, ed. *The Body and the Text: Hélène Cixous Reading and Teaching*. New York: Palgrave Macmillan, 1991.

Mary K. Bloodsworth-Lugo (2005)

CLANDESTINE PHILOSOPHICAL LITERATURE IN FRANCE

The body of clandestine literature in France that deals with philosophy, religion, ethics, and social problems is impressive. It can be traced back to the sixteenth century, and the diffusion, particularly wide between 1714 and 1740, of the allegedly atheistic treatise *La béatitude des Chrétiens ou le fléau de la foy,* published by Geoffroy Vallée in 1572, and of other tracts of early date bears witness to the continuity and vitality of the tradition of free thought in France. The term "Clandestine philosophical literature" usually refers to works known to have circulated in manuscript form during the first half of the eighteenth century and the importance of the subject lies in the fact that the circulation of these works provided one of the sources of the French encyclopedic movement and a solid foundation for liberalism. For the period between 1700 and 1750, I. O. Wade has listed 392 extant manuscripts of 102 different treatises, including 15 translations from other languages. Many more are known to have been in circulation.

The technique of the clandestine manuscript essay was used to circumvent the severe censorship and was most common between 1710 and 1740, when the activities of copyists, colporteurs, and the police were particularly vigorous. Works that found their way into print were often impounded, but they were copied and distributed until the French Revolution. Occasionally authors whose identities could be established were incarcerated. This happened to de Bonaventure de Fourcroy in 1698 for his

Doutes sur la religion proposées à Mss. les Docteurs de Sorbonne, but he soon secured his release from the Bastille. Most often the police found it futile to make arrests and concentrated on preventing the diffusion of the tracts. Public burning, usually in effigy, of works condemned by the Parlement of Paris did not prevent reprints and manuscript copies from being made in the Low Countries, one of the centers of the clandestine trade. After 1750, however, covert circulation became increasingly unnecessary, owing to the breakdown of the censorship, and a number of the more important treatises were printed, many with the indication of a false place of publication.

Voltaire, Henri-Joseph Dulaurens, Baron d'Holbach, and Jacques-André Naigeon, in their desire to foster deism or atheism, prolonged the life of the anonymous tracts by including them in collective volumes, such as *Nouvelles Libertés de penser* (Amsterdam, 1743, 1770), *Recueil nécessaire* (by Voltaire; Geneva, 1765, 1766, 1768, 1776), *L'évangile de la raison* (by Voltaire; Geneva, 1764, 1765, 1767, 1768), *Recueil philosophique* (by Naigeon; "Londres," 1770), and *Bibliothèque du bon sens portatif* (by Holbach; "Londres," 1773). The treatises constituted one of the main sources from which the *philosophes* drew their polemics.

Through the records preserved in the Archives de la Bastille and from statements appearing in manuscripts and letters by Dubuisson, Nicolas Fréret, G. de Bure, and Charles-Marie de la Condamine, we know something of the organization and diffusion of these manuscripts. Le Coulteux, Charles Bonnet, Lépiné, and a certain Mathieu or Morléon (who was incarcerated in 1729) are known to have specialized in the works of Henri de Boulainvilliers and his friends. These works were distributed often in the vicinity of the Procope and other cafés to listed patrons and initiates, including members of the clergy and the Parlement. Copies such as those of Jean Meslier's *Testament* were made by professionals, occasionally the personal secretaries of men like the Comte de Boulainvilliers, the Comte d'Argenson, and Chrétien-Guillaume de Lamoignon de Malesherbes, and the practice of employing copyists was continued throughout the century. The price of such copies varied greatly. A sum as prohibitively high as twenty pistoles is known to have been asked for Jean-Baptiste de Mirabaud's *Examen critique du Nouveau Testament.*

The clandestine movement, fed by new discoveries in science, reflected the climate of world opinion, an attitude to life and society, man and his welfare, God and the universe which, although not new, was reinforced by new arguments and gained an ever-increasing audience. Although the tracts appeared sporadically and were mostly anonymous, they share a few common characteristics and must be judged as a stage in the history of free thought, which goes back to the Renaissance in France and has its deepest roots in the works of Epicurus and Lucretius.

THEOPHRASTUS REDIVIVUS

The *Theophrastus Redivivus* (1659) is significant in that it establishes a link between the atheism of men of the Renaissance and that of men of the seventeenth century (it refers, for example, to Lucilio Vanini and Cyrano de Bergerac) and also of the eighteenth century, when it was secretly circulated. The author, possibly a regent in one of the Parisian colleges, wrote in Latin a 2,000-folio-page compendium of historical references. He developed the arguments that if God exists he is the Sun and that the world is eternal. For the author all religions are false, and miracles, oracles, prophecies, and revelations are man-made. The resurrection of the dead and the immortality of the soul are absurdities; happiness is to be found only in living according to nature, which is revealed to us through experience; there is no absolute good or evil, as we may deduce from the multiplicity of customs and laws; man is a species of animal endowed with speech and reason. Animals, however, are not totally devoid of these faculties. The author referred neither to Pierre Gassendi nor to René Descartes, but he did mention the treatise *De Tribus Impostoribus,* attributing to Frederick II the proposition that Moses, Christ, and Muḥammad were three remarkable impostors.

BACKGROUND

Throughout the seventeenth century the *libertins* in the wake of François Rabelais and Michel Eyquem de Montaigne became erudite skeptics, radical naturalists, associating freedom of morals and freedom of belief. As freethinkers they were prompted more by a feeling of revolt against asceticism and scholasticism than by any convincing argument. Gassendi contributed to the rehabilitation of Epicurus and Lucretius. Emmanuel Maignan, too, in his *Cursus,* evolved a philosophy that bridged Aristotle and Epicurus, linking matter and thought, sensationism and the spiritual world, and developing the idea of a scale of being. But it was from Descartes that the movement of free thought gained its greatest impetus. Cartesian rationalism and mechanism provided freethinkers with a new certainty and their systems with a new coherence. Long after his philosophy had been adopted by the Jesuits and had consequently grown unpopular, Descartes continued to exercise a determining influence on free thought through the method he advocated. His philosophy, however, was commonly misunderstood by freethinkers and with Julien Offray de La Mettrie it culminated in an extreme mechanistic materialism that Descartes would have decried.

Benedict de Spinoza's influence on the clandestine literature was considerable but rather indirect. His work was largely known through the writings of other thinkers, like Pierre Bayle and Boulainvilliers, and his philosophy was commonly distorted by Cartesian misrepresentation. The *Ethics* was little known, and frequently its views were reconstituted through refutations. The *Tractatus Theologico-Politicus* was of interest on account of its biblical criticism, and in Holland, Jean Le Clerc, professor of philosophy and Hebrew at the University of Amsterdam, was allowed to carry on this critical work. In France, however, the uncompromising attitude of Jacques Bénigne Bossuet stifled biblical criticism. Richard Simon, a well-known teacher at the Oratorian school at Juilly who had admitted in his *Histoire critique du Vieux Testament* (1678) the truth of much of Spinoza's exegesis while recognizing the authority of the Bible, succeeded in offending both Catholics and Protestants and was expelled from the Oratorian congregation in 1678. He retired to continue his rational critique in two *instructions pastorales* (1702, 1703), *Histoire critique du texte du Nouveau Testament* (1683), *Histoire critique des versions du Nouveau Testament* (1690), and *Histoire critique des principaux commentateurs du Nouveau Testament* (1692).

Disputes that reached the general public—such as those over the authorship of the Pentateuch, in which Isaac La Peyrère, Thomas Hobbes, Spinoza, Simon, Le Clerc, and others held different views—led to much perplexity. The body of anonymous treatises that continued such discussions and in many cases rejected revelation is naturally large. These include the *Examen de la religion,* the *Analyse de la religion* (written after 1739), and the *Militaire philosophe* (composed between 1706 and 1711).

Hobbes's *Leviathan* (1651) seems to have been little known in France. Bayle's *Dictionnaire,* however, enjoyed great authority, and his *Lettre sur la comète de 1680* popularized the ideas that the conception of Providence did not rest on rational premises and that atheists could be good men. Bayle's views were those of a protestant, but his argument was such that his articles could easily be used to develop anti-Christian ideas. The anonymous writers also read Bernard Le Bovier de Fontenelle and knew something of the English deists whose thought developed along parallel lines. There were translations of works by Bernard Mandeville, Lord Bolingbroke, John Toland, Anthony Collins, and Thomas Woolston, but it was only after the publication of Voltaire's *Lettres anglaises* (1734), which discussed Newtonian physics and philosophy and the ideas of John Locke, that the English influence became significant. Gottfried Wilhelm Leibniz's influence, too, was felt only at a late stage, partly because he was known primarily through Bayle and also through Pierre-Louis Moreau de Maupertuis, whose ideas served to link the *Monadology* with Denis Diderot and materialism.

THE COTERIE OF BOULAINVILLIERS

The only group of writers known to have been involved in concerted action was that centered in the Comte de Boulainvilliers and closely linked with d'Argenson, the duc de Noailles, and the Académie des Inscriptions. This coterie included Nicolas Fréret, Mirabaud, César Dumarsais, and J.-B. Le Mascrier. Voltaire, in his *Dîner du comte de Boulainvilliers* (1767), attested to the important influence of this group, which was especially responsible for the diffusion of Boulainvilliers's *Esprit de Spinoza* (known to have existed by 1706 and first published in 1719 in Holland).

FRÉRET. Nicolas Fréret (1688–1761), a student of law, joined the coterie of Boulainvilliers at the age of nineteen. Fréret appended to copies of the *Histoire ancienne* an account of Boulainvilliers's life and works. In 1714 he was admitted to the Académie des Inscriptions; in 1715 he was imprisoned for some months in the Bastille, where he read Bayle's *Dictionnaire* and wrote a Chinese grammar. From 1720 to 1721 he was preceptor of the duc de Noailles.

The *Lettre de Thrasibule à Leucippe* (written c. 1722 and published in London, probably in 1768; also published in *Oeuvres de Fréret,* Vol. IV, London, 1775) is generally attributed to him. Systematic and Cartesian in its presentation, this treatise combines sensationist psychology and naturalist ethics. Thrasibule, a Roman, describes the early Christians as combining Jewish beliefs with Stoicism and as influenced by both monotheist and polytheist currents. He argues that knowledge is acquired through our senses and has only relative validity. Only the truths of mathematics and reason are universal. Religious beliefs however, do not spring from reason; it is reason alone that should guide man in regulating his life, establishing society and laws, and achieving happiness. This work can be seen as an early essay in comparative religion, and it sharply reflects the growing interest in the science of law and social philosophy. It perhaps influenced Baron de Montesquieu, and Jean-Jacques Rousseau annotated it while engaged in writing the *Discours sur l'inégalité.*

Fréret is also reputed to be the author of an *Examen critique des apologistes de la religion chrétienne* (composed after 1733), which introduces the historical method adopted by Voltaire in, for example, the *Essai sur les moeurs* and the *Dictionnaire philosophique,* in which Voltaire acknowledged his debt. Fréret was held in high esteem as a savant. He was a chronologist, a geographer, an orientalist, and a philologist as well as a philosopher, and he delivered papers on a wide variety of subjects to the Académie des Inscriptions, becoming its permanent secretary in 1743. These *Mémoires de l'Académie* outline new methods for the study of prehistory and geography as well as history. Fréret specialized in mythology, opposing the *évhéméristes,* who believed that all myths had a basis in historical fact. A pioneer in comparative philology, he made known the Chinese linguistic system. His *Oeuvres complètes* were published by Leclerc de Septchênes in Paris, 1796–1799, but about half his works were omitted (many of his manuscripts bequeathed to the Académie des Inscriptions have never been published), and a few of the treatises included cannot be attributed to him.

MIRABAUD. Jean-Baptiste de Mirabaud (1675–1760) was educated by the Oratorian congregation and entered a military career. He then became secretary to the duchess of Orléans and preceptor of her two youngest daughters. In 1724 he translated *Gerusalemme liberata* by Torquato Tasso. He was elected to the Académie Française in 1726, becoming its secretary in 1742. Mirabaud read his manuscripts to select groups of friends. He was probably the author of four essays (described below), often to be found together, that threw new doubts on biblical chronology and promoted Fontenelle's method of oblique attack on miracles. Many of Mirabaud's notes recall ideas expressed in *La religion chrétienne analysée* (a popular post-1742 tract attributed by Voltaire and Claude François Nonnotte to Dumarsais). The *Opinion des anciens sur le monde* (c. 1706–1722) challenges the story of Genesis. In the *Opinions des anciens sur la nature de l'âme* (composed before 1728, published in *Nouvelles Libertés de penser*) Mirabaud pointed out that the Jews, the Greeks, and the Romans envisaged the soul as material and that the Egyptians introduced the belief in the immortality of the soul as a restraining influence on public morals. The *Opinion des anciens sur les Juifs* (c. 1706–1722), based on Jacques Basnage's *Histoire des Juifs* (1706), tries to prove that the Jews had no right to claim to be a "chosen" people. The *Examen critique du Nouveau Testament* (c. 1706–1722), which deals with the canonical and the noncanonical gospels, stresses that neither Philo nor Josephus mentioned Christ and that Christian morality conflicts with natural morality. Much of our information on Mirabaud is derived from the *Notice sur Jean-Baptiste de Mirabaud* (Paris, 1895), by Paul Mirabaud.

DUMARSAIS. César Chesneau Dumarsais (1676–1756), a grammarian, was personally known to Fontenelle and Voltaire and was associated with the *Encyclopédie* until his death. For a time he was preceptor in the family of John Law. Dumarsais edited, with Le Mascrier, some of the deistic works of Mirabaud and wrote a defense of Fontenelle's *Histoire des oracles* and probably the deterministic essay *Le philosophe* (written before 1728); edited by Herbert Dieckmann in 1948). He was probably responsible for *La religion chrétienne analysée* (also known as *Examen de la religion* and *Doutes,* in which inconsistencies in the Bible are shown up, the doctrine of original sin is attacked, and the doctrine of the Trinity is stated to be contrary to reason. It is argued that God should be worshiped without ceremony and that man must follow his reason, which is his *lumière naturelle,* and adopt a social morality incompatible with Christian dogma.

MESLIER. The most interesting of the clandestine authors was no doubt Jean Meslier (1664–1729), a priest who was directly or indirectly influenced by Spinoza. (Reading François de Salignad de La Mothe Fénelon's *Démonstration de l'existence de Dieu* and R.-J. de Tournemine's *Réflexions sur l'athéisme* helped Meslier clarify his ideas.) He identified nature with matter, which he saw as eternal and as endowed with movement. He favored a mechanical interpretation of nature, rejecting the arguments of those who believed in chance and in a divine design. In his 1,200-page *Testament,* Meslier listed the errors, illusions, and impostures of Christianity. His attack on Christianity is one of the most detailed and comprehensive ever written, and his materialistic system is particularly interesting in that it foreshadows many aspects of Diderot's thought.

Voltaire is known to have acquired a copy of the *Testament* and to have made extracts, which he dated 1742 and published in 1761 or 1762 under the title *Extrait.* The first edition sold out immediately and was followed in the same year by an edition of 5,000 copies. In 1772 Holbach published extracts under the title *Le bon sens du curé*

Meslier, and in 1789 Sylvain Maréchal published *Le Cathéchisme du curé Meslier.*

Meslier's social ideas were remarkable for the time. He claimed in very general terms that all men are equal and have the right to live, to be free, and to share in the fruits of the earth. He divided humankind into workers and parasites and saw in revolt the best hope of better conditions. He dreamed of a class struggle, not reconciliation.

OTHER WORKS

Among other anonymous works that cast doubts on the proofs of the truth of Christianity and allege contradictions in the Bible are five manuscript volumes of the *Examen de la Genèse* and the *Examen du Nouveau Testament* (probably written in the late 1730s or early 1740s), which are attributed to Mme. du Châtelet, Voltaire's mistress. She purports to have proved that the stories of the Bible relate barbarous and cruel events and cannot have been inspired by God. No doubt she received some help from Voltaire, but she relied chiefly on the work of Meslier and Woolston and especially on the *Commentaire littéral sur tous les livres de l'Ancien et du Nouveau Testament* (23 vols., Paris, 1707–1716) by Augustin Dom Calmet.

Among other manuscripts whose authorship is now known is *Le ciel ouvert à tous les hommes* (also titled *Le paradis ouvert* and *Nouveau Système de la religion chrétienne*), by the priest Pierre Cuppé, which must have been in draft in 1716. The tract never assails orthodoxy, but Cuppé submitted the Scriptures to scrutiny and preached toleration and brotherly love, concluding that all men are saved by God's love. Cuppé's stress on his respect for reason, as well as his deistic beliefs, led to his being considered a forerunner of French deism.

The author of *Le militaire philosophe* (1706–1711; published in London by Naigeon in 1768) is unknown. It is first a commentary of Nicolas Malebranche's views on religion. It gives a frank exposition of deism, which won Voltaire's commendation. After a strongly worded criticism of the Old and the New Testaments, the work rejects Christianity and develops the doctrine of natural religion, stressing the roles of reason and instinct. Man, who is both body and soul, is free and immortal, and his behavior should be governed by reason and by conscience. Man must worship God and abide by the golden rule. The author foreshadowed Montesquieu in his insistence on the absolute character of justice and the relative nature of civil laws and in his treatment of chance, which he rejected as an explanation of events. He anticipated Voltaire in his use of the figure of a watchmaker to explain the function of God. His idea that truth is to be found in the individual soul was later developed by Rousseau.

A widely disseminated treatise was *Israël vengé,* by Isaac Orobio, a Spanish Jew who escaped from the Inquisition to France and then to Holland and died in 1687 or 1688. His originally unpublished critical attack on the Christian religion was translated by A. Henriquez and published in London in 1770. It was circulated by Jean Lévesque de Burigny.

The *Jordanus Brunus Redivivus* is a materialistic compilation. The author believed in the Copernican system (and the existence of other solar systems with living beings) and in the eternity of matter. There are no innate ideas, no objective good or evil. Man is motivated by pain and by pleasure. Experience can deceive us. Reason alone is valid but must not be thought infallible. The laws of nature are eternal, but everything is in a state of flux. Certain passages of this work bring to mind Diderot's *Rêve de d'Alembert.* Other manuscripts whose authorship is uncertain include *Lettre d'Hypocrate à Damagette* (1700 at latest), *Recherches curieuses de philosophie* (1713), *Suite des Purrhoniens: qu'on peut douter si les religions viennent immédiatement de Dieu ou de l'invention des politiques pour faire craindre et garder les préceptes de l'homme* (c. 1723), *Traité de la liberté* (a determinist and materialist tract, probably by Fontenelle, c. 1700), *Essai sur la recherche de la vérité,* and *Dissertation sur la formation du monde* (1738), which was inspired by Lucretius and formulates transformist theories while upholding the conception of fixed species.

INFLUENCE

It will be seen that the clandestine tracts fall into two main categories, those written from the standpoint of critical deism and those that are atheistic, deterministic and materialistic. The outstanding eighteenth-century literary works based on this movement can be similarly characterized. Montesquieu's adoption of the letter form for *Les lettres persanes* (1731) may owe something to the *Lettre à Damagette,* and the views expressed in *Lettre persane 46* reflect those expressed in *La religion chrétienne analysée.* Voltaire, who adopted the form for his *Lettres philosophiques,* published anonymously in 1734, wrote in the same year a *Traité de métaphysique* (which Mme. du Châtelet kept under lock and key), which embodied his own deism as well as many of the ideas expressed in the clandestine literature.

Toward the middle of the century atheism gained ground, no doubt encouraged by such treatises as *Lettre sur la religion, sur l'âme et sur l'existence de Dieu.* Diderot's *Pensées philosophiques,* published anonymously in 1746, allegedly at the Hague but actually in Paris, and condemned to be burned by the Parlement of Paris, is characteristic of this tendency. Although based on a translation of the Earl of Shaftesbury, the work succeeds in presenting an original and vividly expressed atheism side by side with more commonplace arguments in favor of natural religion. In particular it challenges Christian belief in miracles, outlining the principles of the new biblical criticism. In the eighteenth century alone the *Pensées philosophiques* ran to twenty editions (some with crude interpolations) and reprints. It was translated into German, Italian, and English and was the subject of long and heated controversy. Twelve signed or anonymous refutations by Protestants, Catholics, parliamentarians, and others were published, some of them, together with Diderot's text, being circulated in manuscript form.

As government policy wavered and censorship grew slack, an increasing number of the manuscripts of earlier date were published, and anonymity became a thin veil, if not a mere convention. The main current of what has become known as clandestine literature, which many have identified with the tradition of free thought, came to an end with the advent of Montesquieu, Voltaire, Rousseau, and Diderot. In their works it found its finest literary expression, and thanks to them it became integrated into coherent patterns that have won it a place in the history of ideas.

See also Boulainvilliers, Henri, Comte de; Meslier, Jean.

Bibliography

The most important reference works in the field are I. O. Wade, *Philosophical Ideas in France from 1700 to 1750* (Princeton, NJ, 1938), and J. S. Spink, *French Free-Thought from Gassendi to Voltaire* (London: University of London, Athlone Press, 1960). The following works are also very important: W. H. Barber, *Leibniz in France* (Oxford: Clarendon Press, 1955); A. Vartanian, *Diderot and Descartes* (Princeton, NJ: Princeton University Press, 1953); and P. Vernière, *Spinoza et la pensée française avant la Révolution* (Paris, 1954).

The reader should also consult E. R. Briggs, "L'Incrédulité et la pensée anglaise en France au début de XVIIIe siècle," in *Revue d'histoire littéraire de la France* 41 (1934): 497–538; E. R. Briggs, "Pierre Cuppé's Debts to England and Holland," in *Studies on Voltaire and the XVIII Century,* edited by Theodore Besterman, Vol. VI (Geneva: Institut et Musée Voltaire, 1958), pp. 37–66; Pierre Brochon, *Le livre de colportage en France depuis le XVIe siècle, sa littérature, ses lecteurs* (Paris: Librairie Gründ, 1954); Herbert Dieckmann, ed., *Le Philosophe: Texts and Interpretation,* Washington University Studies, New Series, Language and Literature, No. 18 (St. Louis, MO, 1948); Herbert Dieckmann, "The Abbé Jean Meslier and Diderot's *Eleuthéromanes,*" in *Harvard Library Bulletin* 7 (Spring 1953): 231–235; J. P. Free, *Rousseau's Use of the Examen de la religion and of La Lettre de Thrasibule à Leucippe,* unpublished doctoral dissertation (Princeton, NJ, 1935); A. D. Hole, *Mirabaud's Contribution to the Deistic Movement and His Relation to Voltaire,* Princeton doctoral dissertation *Abstracts* (Princeton, NJ, 1952); G. Lanson, "Questions diverses sur l'histoire de l'esprit philosophique en France avant 1750," in *Revue d'histoire littéraire de la France* 19 (1912): 1–29, 293–317; A. R. Morehouse, *Voltaire and Jean Meslier* (New Haven, CT: Yale University Press, 1936); R. R. Palmer, *Catholics and Unbelievers in Eighteenth Century France* (Princeton, NJ: Princeton University Press, 1939); Renée Simon, "Nicolas Fréret, académicien," in *Studies on Voltaire and the XVIII Century,* edited by Theodore Besterman, Vol. XVII (Geneva: Institut et Musée Voltaire, 1961); J. S. Spink, "La Diffusion des idées matérialistes et anti-religieuses au début de XVIIIe siècle: Le *Theophrastus Redivivus,*" in *Revue d'histoire littéraire de la France* 44 (1937): 248–255. See also Diderot's *Pensées philosophiques,* edited by Robert Niklaus (Geneva: Droz, 1950).

OTHER RECOMMENDED TITLES

Darnton, Robert. *The Corpus of Clandestine Literature in France, 1769–1789.* New York: Norton, 1995.

Sutcliffe, Adam. "Judaism in the Anti-Religious Thought of the Clandestine French Early Enlightenment." *Journal of the History of Ideas* 64 (1) (2003): 97–117.

Robert Niklaus (1967)
Bibliography updated by Tamra Frei (2005)

CLARKE, SAMUEL

(1675–1729)

Samuel Clarke, the most important British philosopher and theologian of his generation, was born in Norwich, England, on October 11, 1675. He took his BA degree at Cambridge in 1695, defending Isaac Newton's views. In 1697 he provided a new annotated Latin translation of Jacques Rohault's *Treatise of Physics*, and in his notes criticized René Descartes's physics in favor of Newton's. In that same year he was introduced into the Newtonian circle, probably by William Whiston (1667–1752), whom he had befriended. In 1704 he delivered his first set of Boyle Lectures, *A Demonstration of the Being and Attributes of God: More Particularly in Answer to Mr. Hobbes, Spinoza, and Their Followers*. They were so successful that he was asked to deliver the 1705 lectures as well under the title *A Discourse concerning the Unchangeable Obligations of Natural Religion and the Truth and Certainty of Christian Revelation*. His connection with Newton became official in 1706, when he translated the *Opticks* into Latin. In the same year Anthony Collins, a materialist follower of John

Locke's, engaged Clarke in a long and famous exchange on whether matter can think.

After becoming one of Queen Anne's (1665–1714) chaplains, Clarke was elevated in 1709 to the rectory of St. James's, Westminster. In 1712 Clarke published *The Scripture Doctrine of the Trinity*, which was accused of Arianism, the view that Christ is divine but created. The ensuing theological controversy culminated two years later in his humiliating promise to the Upper House of Convocation not to preach or write on the trinity any longer. However, suspicions of crypto-Arianism remained. François-Marie Arouet de Voltaire reports that Bishop Edmund Gibson (1669–1748) effectively prevented Clarke's elevation to the see of Canterbury by pointing out that Clarke was indeed the most learned and honest man in the kingdom, but had one defect: He was not a Christian.

After the Hanoverian accession Clarke developed a close relationship with Caroline of Anspach (1683–1737), the Princess of Wales, and through her mediation he engaged Gottfried Wilhelm Leibniz in the most famous philosophical correspondence of the eighteenth century. The exchange dealt with many of the issues that had occupied Clarke in his Boyle Lectures, such as divine immensity and eternity, the relation of God to the world, the soul and its relation to the body, free will, space and time, and the nature of miracles. It also discussed more strictly scientific topics, such as the nature of matter, the existence of atoms and the void, the size of the universe, and the nature of motive force, which were then often given both a philosophical and a scientific treatment. In 1717 Clarke published his translation of the correspondence with Leibniz together with an attack on a work by Collins denying the existence of free will. This was his last significant philosophical work, although in 1728 he wrote a short essay for the *Philosophical Transactions* trying to show, against the Leibnizians, that the proper measure of force is not mv^2 but mv. He died in 1729 after a short illness and was survived by his wife, Katherine, and five of his seven children.

Clarke was a polite and courtly man who, however, was vivacious with his friends and seems to have been fond of playing cards. He was also a classicist of repute, and seems to have held Marcus Tullius Cicero's views in high esteem. Voltaire, who met him, was impressed by his piety and admired his logical skills so much that he called him "a veritable thinking machine." Indeed, his reputation was such that in 1710 George Berkeley sent him the first edition of his *A Treatise concerning the Principles of Human Knowledge* (Clarke declined to comment on it).

THE ATTACK AGAINST NATURALISM AND THE DEFENSE OF NATURAL RELIGION

Clarke's primary philosophical interests lay in theology, metaphysics, and, to a lesser degree, ethics. His philosophical vocabulary and some of his metaphysical ideas were influenced by Descartes, whom he followed in holding that the world contains two types of substance, mind and matter, the combination of which constitutes humans. However, he sided with Nicolas Malebranche and Locke in denying that introspection lets one reach the substance of the soul. Indeed, like Locke and Newton, he held that one just does not know the substance of things. Furthermore, Clarke's overall judgment of Descartes was critical. He shared the view expressed by Henry More, Blaise Pascal, Pierre Bayle, and Leibniz that Descartes's system could be, and had been, used to further irreligion and had naturally developed into Spinozism. In particular, he believed that Descartes's identification of matter with extension, and therefore space, entails making it eternal and infinite. He defended natural religion from naturalism (the view that nature constitutes a self-sufficient system of which humans are but a part) and revealed religion from deism.

Clarke's attack against naturalism revolved around five connected points. First, God is a necessarily existent omnipotent, omniscient, eternal, omnipresent, and supremely benevolent person. Second, nature and its laws are radically contingent. God, endowed with a libertarian will, chose to create the world and to operate in it by a reasonable but uncaused fiat. Third, although space and time are infinite, matter is spatiotemporally finite, and being endowed only with *vis inertiae* it has no power of self-motion. Fourth, God is substantially present in nature (or better, nature is literally in God, since space and time are divine attributes) and constantly exercises his power by applying attractive and repulsive forces to bodies. Except for the law of inertia, which describes the essentially passive nature of matter, strictly speaking, the laws of nature do not describe the behavior of matter, which is just dead mass constantly pushed around, but the modalities of the ordinary operation of the divine power. As for occasionalism, natural laws prescribe the actions of the divine will rather than describe those of bodies.

Fifth, although the soul is extended and interacts with the body, it is necessarily immaterial because matter, being constituted of merely juxtaposed parts, cannot possibly think even by divine intervention; moreover, the soul has been endowed by God with a libertarian will.

The first four points guarantee that nature is not a self-sufficient system, so much so that without direct and constant divine physical intervention planets would fly away from their orbits, atoms would break into their components, and the machinery of the world would literally grind to a halt; the fifth guarantees that the soul is not a part of nature. In the remainder of this entry, it will be seen that these points emerge from a consideration of Clarke's views on God, free will, matter and the laws of nature, space and time, and the soul.

GOD

The proof of the necessary existence and attributes of God occupies most of *A Demonstration of the Being and Attributes of God*. The main lines of Clarke's argument are as follows. Since something exists now, something has always existed because nothing comes from nothing. What has existed from eternity is either an independent being (one having in itself the reason of its existence), or an infinite series of dependent beings. However, such a series cannot be the being that has existed from eternity because by hypothesis it can have no external cause, and no internal cause (no dependent being in it) can cause the whole series. Hence, an independent being exists. As a separate argument, Clarke also reasoned that since space and time cannot be thought of as nonexistent and they are obviously not self-subsistent, the substance on which they depend, God, must exist necessarily as well. Finally, teleological considerations show that God is necessarily endowed with intelligence and wisdom. In addition, God has, though not with metaphysical necessity, all the moral perfections, whose nature is the same in the divine being as in humans.

Clarke rejected the view of God as substantially removed from space and time. Divine eternity involves both necessary existence and infinite duration. Rather traditionally, the former consists in the fact that God contains the reason (but not the cause) of his own existence. The latter, however, cannot be identified with the traditional view that God exists in an unchanging permanent present without any succession since, like Newton, he considered such a position unintelligible. Consequently, Clarke attributed distinct and successive thoughts to God, as he perceived these as preconditions of the will. Hence, God is immutable with respect to his will and his general and particular decrees only in the sense that the divine being does not change his mind. However, as Clarke also made clear in his exchanges with Joseph Butler, God is not in space and time.

Clarke's criticism of the Scholastic view of divine immensity or omnipresence was analogous to that concerning eternity: the claim that the immensity of God is a point, as his eternity is an instant is, he held, unintelligible. However, while for Clarke God's temporal presence is analogous to humans' at least in involving temporal succession, his views about God's spatial presence were somewhat less clear because he did not explicitly state whether he adopted holenmerism (the view that the divine substance is whole in the whole of space and whole in each and every part) or the view that God is dimensionally extended. Nevertheless, there is evidence that he held the latter view. For Clarke vigorously denied Leibniz's charge that extension is incompatible with divine simplicity, because it introduces parts in God, without making any reference to holenmerism, and in addition he did not defend holenmerism from More's famous critique. Finally, Collins mentions him with Thomas Turner (1645–1714) and More as supporters of the dimensional extension of God.

For Clarke, divine eternity and immensity are to be identified with space and time. Usually, he held that space and time are just divine properties. However, in his fourth letter he also told Leibniz that, in addition, they are necessary effects of God's existence and necessary requirements for divine eternity and ubiquity, without supplying any argument to show that these different accounts are equivalent or even compatible. At other times, as in the letter to Daniel Waterland (1683–1740) and in the *Avertissement* to Pierre Des Maizeaux (1673–1745), in the latter of which Newton had more than a hand, he held that they are not, strictly speaking, properties.

As Leibniz and an anonymous correspondent (almost certainly Waterland) readily noted, echoing Bayle's critique of Newton and Malebranche, the identification of divine immensity with space endangers the simplicity of the divine being because space has parts, albeit not separable ones. Clarke's solution was to claim parity between spatial and temporal extendedness: Since the former is compatible with the simplicity of what "stretches" temporally, the latter is compatible with the simplicity of what stretches spatially. In addition, from the fact that the divine consciousness is extended, one should not infer that it is proper to talk about it in terms of spatial parts any more than it is to talk of the spatial parts of an instant of time although, as Newton had noted in the General Scholium to book 3 of *Principia*, an instant is the same everywhere.

FREE WILL

Clarke attached great importance to the issue of free will. He held that the highest form of freedom involves willing as one should, namely, having one's will in step with one's right values. He also believed that freedom of the will, or liberty, entails a libertarian power of self-determination (a point he emphasized against Leibniz's compatibilist views) and that it is a necessary condition both for that higher form of freedom and for religion. Thomas Hobbes's and Benedict (Baruch) de Spinoza's views—which in Clarke's mind Leibniz had de facto adopted—that everything happens deterministically or necessarily destroys liberty. Against them he held that the causal version of the principle of sufficient reason in the cosmological argument shows that the necessary being on which the contingent world depends must have a libertarian will. For the notion of a necessary agent is contradictory, as agency involves the libertarian capacity of suspending action. Moreover, if God operated necessarily, things could not be different from how they are. But the number of planets, their orbits, indeed, the law of gravitation itself could have been different, as any reasonable person (but not Spinoza) could plainly see. Furthermore, the obvious presence of final causes indicates that divine activity follows not necessary but architectonic patterns.

Besides attacking necessitarianism and determinism with arguments drawn from general metaphysical considerations, Clarke criticized the Hobbesian view that volition is caused by one's last evaluative judgment and the Spinozistic position that the two are identical. He was ready to grant that the understanding is fully determined to assent to a proposition perceived as true in the same way in which an open eye is fully determined to see objects. In this sense the assent is necessary. However, he held, the necessity of the last evaluative judgment is totally immaterial to the issue of freedom. In his judgment, his opponents were guilty of basic philosophical errors. On the one hand, if they maintained that the content of the evaluation, the evaluative proposition, is identical with the volition or causes it, they were confusing reasons with causes. As he explained to Collins, the proposition "doing X is better than doing Y" can provide a reason for action but cannot cause anything because it is an abstract entity. On the other hand, if Clarke's opponents maintained that not the evaluative proposition but one's perceiving or believing it is identical with, or a partial cause of, volition, then they were falling foul of a basic causal principle. Against Descartes, Clarke insisted that judging (assenting to what appears true and dissenting from what appears false) is not an action but a passion. But what is passive cannot cause anything active. So, there is no causal link between evaluation and volition. What causes the volition is the principle of action itself, which Clarke identified with the agent, that is, the spiritual substance.

Having shown that God is endowed with liberty, Clarke argued that humans are as well. Not involving qualities such as complete causal independence and self-existence, liberty is a power God can transfer to one. Furthermore, experience assures one that one has been granted liberty, since one's actions seem to one to be free, exactly as they would do on the supposition that one is really a free agent. Of course, he conceded, this does not amount to a strict demonstration; but denying that one has free will is on a par with denying the existence of the external world, a coherent but unreasonable option. The burden of proof, he felt, is not on the supporter of liberty, but on its denier.

MATTER AND THE LAWS OF NATURE

Clarke's views on matter are best seen in connection with his ideas about miracles. Like Joseph Glanville (1636–1680), Thomas Sprat (1635–1713), Robert Boyle, and Locke, he belonged to that group of English intellectuals associated with the Royal Society, who thought that miracles could be used as evidence for the claim that Christianity is the true religion. According to Clarke a miracle is a work effected in an unusual manner (by which he seems to have meant in a way not subsumable under the laws of nature) by God himself or some intelligent agent superior to man for the proof or evidence of some doctrine, or the attestation of the authority of some person. However, he claimed, "modern deists," noticing that nature is regular, have concluded that there are in matter certain absolutely inalterable laws or powers that render the course of nature unchangeable and therefore miracles impossible.

The deistic view, Clarke argued, is completely wrong. Everything that is done in the world is done either immediately by God himself or by sentient beings; matter is not capable of any laws or powers whatsoever, except for the negative power of inertia. Consequently, the apparent effects of the natural powers of matter—the laws of motion, gravitation, or attraction—are but the effects of God's acting on matter continually, either directly or through intelligent creatures. The course of nature, then, is just the divine will operating continuously and uniformly. This mode of operation is perfectly free and as easily altered as preserved at any time. Of course, Clarke admitted, the divine will infallibly follows necessarily correct judgments, and consequently God always acts on the basis of rules of "uniformity and proportion." However, given that the will, in God as in humans, is not causally determined by the understanding, the rules governing the ordinary power of God, a subset of which are the laws of nature, are freely self-imposed, and not the unavoidable result of the necessarily correct divine understanding. They are a manifestation of God's moral, and therefore free, attributes, not God's metaphysical, and therefore necessary, ones.

Clarke steadfastly maintained that matter has neither an essential nor an accidental power of self-motion. The first claim was common among early modern philosophers and held not only by the occasionalists but also by thinkers of different persuasions like Descartes, Locke, and Boyle. In fact, even Pierre Gassendi, who had upheld the notion of an active matter by claiming that atoms have an internal corporeal principle of action, had fallen short of claiming that they possess it essentially. Clarke's second claim, however, was more controversial. For although mechanists programmatically tried to substitute a nature made of inert particles for the living nature of Renaissance philosophy, the attempt soon ran into great difficulties. Strict mechanism proved inadequate to explain phenomena like exothermic reactions or the spring of the air, which causes a deflated closed balloon in a vacuum tube to expand. Consequently, mechanism was altered to include particles variously endowed with powers of motion, attraction, and repulsion.

Clarke's position on the activity of matter was radical: The various nonmechanical powers of particles are the result of direct divine or spiritual activity. He could not bring himself to accept active matter because he thought it a prelude to atheism. For, as noted earlier, he believed that denying divine continuous, direct intervention in nature in effect amounts to eliminating God, as John Toland had by endowing matter with essential self-motive powers. Clarke's views, however, had serious drawbacks. A God who is actually extended and constantly operates physically on matter looks suspiciously like the soul of the world, as Leibniz charged using Newton's identification in the *Opticks* of space as the *sensorium* of God. Similarly, the placement of gravitational forces within the purview of ordinary divine activity drew from Leibniz the accusation of obscurantism, a throwback to the quaint idea of angels causing the rotation of the spheres.

SPACE AND TIME

According to Clarke the ideas of space and time are the two first and most obvious simple ideas that exist. Like many of the philosophers who investigated the nature of space and time, he tended to produce arguments with regard to space, presumably leaving the reader to infer that parallel arguments could be drawn with respect to time. With Newton, he argued that while matter can be thought of as nonexisting, space exists necessarily because to suppose any part or the whole of space removed is to suppose it removed from and out of itself, namely taken away while it still remains, which is contradictory. Although space is not sensible, it is not nothingness, mere absence of matter, as it has properties such as quantity and dimensions. One might add other properties Clarke attributed to it, such as homogeneity, immutability, continuity, and, probably, impenetrability since bodies do not penetrate space but space penetrates them. For Clarke, space is also not an aggregate of its parts but presumably an essential whole preceding all it parts, a position motivated at least in part by the view that space is a divine property. As for Newton, space is necessarily infinite because limiting it is supposing it is bounded by something that itself takes up space or supposing it is bounded by other space, and both suppositions are contradictory.

Since absolute space has an essential and invariable structure independent of the bodies in it and is not altered by their presence, any possible world must conform to it, as creatures must be in space and God, whose power is limited to the metaphysically possible, cannot alter the essence of things. The same is true of time, which flows equably independently of anything in it. In short, in contrast to God all creatures occupy an absolute position in space and time that one may or may not be able to determine.

The introduction of absolute space, allegedly demanded by Newtonian physics, offered Clarke an immediate philosophical advantage in the fight against Spinoza. For it showed that the Cartesian identification of extension with matter, which had made possible Spinoza's excesses, was wrong—a consequence that was not lost on Bayle and was insisted on by Colin Maclaurin (1698–1746). Of course, the existence of absolute space introduced a new difficulty, that of its relation to God, but Clarke thought he had solved it by claiming that space and time are attributes of God or the result of divine existence.

THE SOUL

In 1706 Henry Dodwell (1641–1711) published a book in which he defended conditional immortality: One's soul is naturally mortal and following the death of the body can be kept in existence only by divine supernatural intervention. Clarke wrote an open letter to Dodwell complaining that he had opened the floodgates to libertinism by providing an excuse for the wicked not to fear eternal punishment. He then argued that the soul, being immaterial, is naturally immortal and gave his own version of the traditional argument for the immateriality of the soul from the alleged unity of consciousness, insisting that not even God could make matter conscious. Clarke's argument failed to convince Collins, who made no bones about his materialist leanings and intervened in defense of Dodwell. Clarke told Collins that if thinking in humans were a mode of matter, it would be natural to conceive that it may be the same in other beings. Then, Clarke continued, every thinking being, including God, would be ruled by the same absolute necessity governing the motion of a clock. The result would be the destruction of every possibility of self-determination and the undermining of the very foundations of religion.

Clarke's argument for the immateriality of the soul revolved around three basic claims. First, necessarily consciousness is an individual power, that is, each consciousness is one undivided entity, not a multitude of distinct consciousnesses added together. Second, an individual power cannot result from, or inhere in, a divisible substance; or, alternatively, an individual power can only be produced by, or inhere in, an individual being. Third, matter is not, and cannot possibly be, an individual being. The conclusion is that consciousness cannot possibly be the product of, or inhere in, matter.

For Clarke, although the soul is necessarily immaterial, it can causally affect the body because material qualities such as figure and mobility are deficiencies or imperfections that can be brought about by consciousness, which is a positive quality; moreover, one experiences the causal power by which one moves one's body. However, his position on whether the body causally affects the soul was less than clear. At times he leaned toward the view that it does, and at other times that it does not.

According to Clarke the soul is in space and is extended. As he eventually told Leibniz, the soul is in a particular place, the *sensorium*, which a part of the brain occupies. Clarke inferred the presence of the soul in the *sensorium* through an argument employing two independent premises: first, that something can act only where it is substantially, and second, that the soul interacts with the body. The conclusion is that the soul is substantially present where (at least) a part of the body is.

Saying that the soul must be substantially present where a part of the brain is does not fully determine how the soul is present. It rules out mere Cartesian operational presence, but it fails to determine whether the soul's presence is to be understood in terms of holenmerism or in terms of dimensional extension. However, there is cumulative evidence that for Clarke the soul is merely coextended with a part of the brain. Clarke used an analogy with space, which he took to be both extended and indivisible, to explain how the soul could be extended and indivisible; but holenmerism does not apply to space. He did not address Leibniz's accusation that the extension of the soul destroys its unity by appealing to holenmerism; rather, he defended the claim that the soul "fills" the *sensorium*. In sum, Clarke's views on freedom, with their ties to morality and religion, together with his views on causality, pushed him toward the thesis that the soul is extended.

ETHICS AND REVEALED RELIGION

Although some of his sermons contain interesting analyses of individual Christian virtues, the most sustained exposition of Clarke's ethics is contained in *A Discourse concerning the Unalterable Obligations of Natural Religion and the Truth and Certainty of the Christian Revelation*, his second set of Boyle Lectures. Clarke started by stating that clearly there are different relations among persons and that from these relations there arises a "fitness" or "unfitness" of behavior among persons. So, for example, given the relation of infinite disproportion between humans and God, it is fit that one honors, worships, and imitates the Lord. In other words, from certain eternal and immutable factual relations among persons there arise certain eternal and immutable obligations, which in their broad features can be rationally apprehended by anyone with a sound mind, although in some particularly complex cases one may be at a loss in clearly demarcating right from wrong. For Clarke, being grounded in necessary relations, morality, like geometry, is universal and necessary. As such, it is independent of any will, be it divine or human, and of any consideration of punishment or reward as anyone, but not Hobbes, can plainly see. So, Clarke's view thus far can be characterized as a variety of rationalist deontology.

For Clarke, morality has three main branches: dealing with duties toward God, other humans, and oneself—all grounded in the notion of fitness. Duties toward others are governed by equity, which demands that one deals with other persons as one can reasonably expect others to deal with oneself, and by love, which demands that one furthers the happiness of all persons. Duties toward oneself demand that one preserves one's life and spiritual well-being so as to be able to perform one's duties. Suicide, then, is wrong.

Since God's will is uncorrupted by self-interest or passion, divine volitions and moral commands are extensionally equivalent. Hence, God wants one to follow morality, and such a desire is manifested in laws God has set up. But since laws require sanctions, and since such sanctions are not uniformly present in this life, moral laws are associated with reward and punishment in the next life. Moreover, human depravity makes the prospect of future sanctions a necessary incentive for proper behavior.

However, Clarke seemed prepared to go further, claiming against the Stoics and his beloved Cicero that in one's present state virtue is not the highest good (this being happiness) and that consequently it would be unreasonable, not just psychologically difficult, to lay down one's life for the sake of duty. Virtue, Clarke claimed, is not happiness but only a means to it, as in a race running is not itself the prize but the way to obtain it. The present sorry state of humankind, beset by ignorance, prejudice, and corrupt passions, renders divine revelation necessary, contrary to what deists think, and therefore the remaining lectures are mainly devoted to establishing the reliability of the Gospels.

Clarke's theory was criticized on several grounds. He never quite explained the nature of the relations among persons that ground morality, leaving both his followers and detractors to argue inconclusively about it. Hume famously charged Clarke's theory with motivational impotence because the intellectual perception of fitness cannot, alone, move the will. Matthew Tindal, who devoted chapter fourteen of his *Christianity as Old as the Creation* to an analysis of Clarke's ethics, noted that Clarke's rationalist strand hardly fits with his insistence on the need for Christian revelation, since his arguments establishing the reliability of scripture seem to require much more intellectual effort than the apprehension of one's moral duties. Even more pointedly, Tindal, who approved Leibniz's claim that the Chinese should send missionaries in natural theology and its subsequent morality to Europe, noted that revelation is neither necessary nor sufficient for proper moral behavior even for common people.

See also Arius and Arianism; Bayle, Pierre; Berkeley, George; Boyle, Robert; Butler, Joseph; Cicero, Marcus Tullius; Collins, Anthony; Deism; Descartes, René; Determinism and Freedom; Gassendi, Pierre; Hume, David; Laws of Nature; Leibniz, Gottfried Wilhelm; Locke, John; Malebranche, Nicolas; Matter; Miracles; More, Henry; Newton, Isaac; Pascal, Blaise; Renaissance; Rohault, Jacques; Space; Spinoza, Benedict (Baruch) de; Stoicism; Time; Tindal, Matthew; Toland, John; Voltaire, François-Marie Arouet de.

Bibliography

WORKS BY CLARKE

Works of Samuel Clarke (1738). 4 vols. New York: Garland, 1978. This contains all of Clarke's published works.

A Demonstration of the Being and Attributes of God and Other Writings, edited by Ezio Vailati. New York: Cambridge University Press, 1998. This offers a selection of passages relevant to Clarke's first Boyle Lecture besides the lecture itself.

WORKS ABOUT CLARKE

Ariew, Roger, ed. *Correspondence: G. W. Leibniz and Samuel Clarke*. Indianapolis, IN: Hackett, 2000. This contains Clarke's famous exchange with Leibniz.

Attfield, Robin. "Clarke, Collins, and Compounds." *Journal of the History of Philosophy* 15 (1977): 45–54.

Attfield, Robin. "Clarke, Independence, and Necessity." *British Journal for the History of Philosophy* 1 (2) (1993): 67–82.

Ducharme, Howard. "Personal Identity in Samuel Clarke." *Journal of the History of Philosophy* 24 (1986): 359–383.

Ferguson, James P. *Dr. Samuel Clarke: An Eighteenth Century Heretic*. Kineton, U.K.: Roundwood Press, 1976.

Ferguson, James P. *The Philosophy of Dr. Samuel Clarke and Its Critics*. New York: Vantage Press, 1974.

Force, James. "Samuel Clarke's Four Categories of Deism, Isaac Newton, and the Bible." In *Scepticism in the History of Philosophy: A Pan-American Dialogue*, edited by Richard H. Popkin, 53–74. Dordrecht, Netherlands: Kluwer Academic, 1996.

Gay, John. "Matter and Freedom in the Thought of Samuel Clarke." *Journal of the History of Ideas* 24 (1963): 85–105.

Hoskin, Michael "Causality and Free Will in the Controversy between Collins and Clarke." *Journal of the History of Philosophy* 25 (1987): 51–67.

Hoskin, Michael "Mining All Within: Clarke's Notes to Rohault's *Traite de Physique*." *The Thomist* 24 (1961): 253–263.

Le Rossignol, James E. *The Ethical Philosophy of Samuel Clarke*. Leipzig, Germany: n.p., 1892.

Rowe, William L. *The Cosmological Argument*. Princeton, NJ: Princeton University Press, 1975.

Stewart, Larry. "Samuel Clarke, Newtonianism, and the Factions of Post-revolutionary England." *Journal of the History of Ideas* 42 (1981): 53–71.

Vailati, Ezio. *Leibniz and Clarke: A Study of Their Correspondence*. New York: Oxford University Press, 1997.

Whiston, William. *Historical Memoirs of the Life of Dr. Samuel Clarke*. London: N.p., 1730.

Yolton, John W. *Thinking Matter: Materialism in Eighteenth-Century Britain*. Minneapolis: University of Minnesota Press, 1983.

Ezio Vailati (2005)

CLASSICAL FOUNDATIONALISM

Classical foundationalism maintains that all knowledge and justified belief rest ultimately on a *foundation* of knowledge and justified belief that has not been inferred from other knowledge or belief. Because the classical foundationalist typically assumes an account of knowledge in terms of justified or rational true belief, it might be best to focus on the distinction invoked between inferentially and noninferentially justified beliefs. What is written in this entry will apply mutatis mutandis to the distinction between inferential and noninferential knowledge.

THE PRINCIPLE OF INFERENTIAL JUSTIFICATION

If one thinks about most of the beliefs one takes to be justified and asks what justifies them, it seems natural to answer in terms of other justified beliefs. A person's justification for believing that it will rain, for example, may consist in part of that person's justifiably believing that the barometer is dropping rapidly. But under what conditions can one justifiably infer the truth of one proposition *P* from another *E*? The classic foundationalist typically insists that to be justified in believing *P* on the basis of *E* one must be justified in believing *E*. So, for example, one cannot be justified in believing that the world will end tomorrow by basing that belief on an unsupported hunch that the earth will be hit by a giant meteor. More controversially, many classic foundationalists—at least implicitly—also seemed to presuppose that to be justified in believing *P* by inferring it from *E* one must also be justified in believing that *E* confirms (makes probable) *P* (where *E*'s entailing *P* is the upper limit of *E*'s making probable *P*). Thus, one cannot justifiably infer the arrival of Armageddon from a fortune-teller's prediction that the world will end tomorrow unless one has some good reason to believe that the fortune-teller's predictions make probable the occurrence of the events predicted. Call the principle stating both of the above requirements for justification the principle of inferential justification (PIJ):

> To be justified in believing *P* on the basis of *E* one must be: (1) justified in believing *E*; and (2) justified in believing that *E* makes probable *P*.

The principle of inferential justification is a crucial premise in the famous regress argument for foundationalism. If the principle is correct, then to be justified in believing some proposition *P* on the basis of some other evidence, *E1*, one would need to be justified in believing *E1*. But if all justification were inferential, then to be justified in believing *E1* one would need to infer it from something else *E2*, which one justifiably believes, and so on ad infinitum. This first regress is generated invoking only clause (1) of the principle of inferential justification. If the second clause is correct, the potential regresses proliferate endlessly. To be justified in inferring *P* from *E1* one must justifiably believe not only *E1* but also that *E1* makes likely *P*, and one must infer this from something else *F1*, which one must justifiably infer from some other proposition *F2*, which one justifiably infers .... And so on.

But one must also justifiably believe that *F1* makes likely that *E1* makes likely *P*, so one must justifiably infer *that* from some other proposition *G1*, which one justifiably infers .... And so on. If all justification were inferential then to justifiably believe any proposition *P* a person would need to complete not just one but an infinite number of infinitely long chains of reasoning. However, the human mind is finite and cannot complete infinitely long chains of reasoning. To avoid the absurd conclusion that people cannot ever be justified in believing anything whatsoever, we must suppose that some beliefs are justified without inference and that these noninferentially justified beliefs ground the justification of all other justified beliefs.

The principle of inferential justification is also often a critical assumption of classic skeptical arguments, most of which presuppose a strong form of foundationalism. So, for example, Hume seemed to conclude that we have no reason for believing any description of an external world when ultimately all we have to rely on as evidence is our knowledge of fleeting and subjective experience. The problem, Hume argued, is that we have no way of establishing sensations as reliable indicators of the existence of external objects that they take to be their cause. Indeed, the difficulty of avoiding a fairly radical skepticism within the constraints of classical foundationalism is one reason so many philosophers became disillusioned with the view.

NONINFERENTIAL JUSTIFICATION

Classical foundationalists refer to the foundations of knowledge and justified belief in a variety of ways—for example: noninferentially justified beliefs, self-evident truths, directly evident truths, incorrigible beliefs, infallible beliefs, and so on—but there is no consensus on what confers foundational status on a belief. Some, following Descartes, seek foundations in beliefs that do not admit of the possibility of error. As will be seen, the possibility in question may be interpreted in a number of different ways, but classical foundationalists usually invoked a very strong concept of possibility: If a belief is foundational it must be inconceivable that the belief be false. The having of the belief must somehow entail its truth. Thus Descartes famously purported to find an ideal foundation for knowledge in one's belief that one existed. It seems trivially true that if someone *S* really does believe that he or she exists, that belief couldn't possibly be false. *S* has to exist in order to believe that *S* exists (or to be in any other conscious state).

Still other foundationalists sought to identify noninferential justification with whatever fact is the truth-maker for the alleged noninferentially justified belief. So, for example, some foundationalists would claim that my justification for believing I am in pain—when I am—is the pain itself. Of course, such a view hardly qualifies as a philosophical theory until its proponent gives a principled account of how some truth-makers justify us in believing the claims they make true, whereas others do not.

Although it was not always spelled out, many other classical foundationalists sought the source of foundational knowledge in some relation (other than belief) obtaining between a believer and the truth conditions of what is believed. One metaphor often invoked is the concept of acquaintance. When one believes that one is in pain when one is in pain, for example, one is directly acquainted or confronted with the pain itself (the very state that makes true the proposition believed). It is the knower's direct confrontation with the relevant aspect of reality to which the truth in question corresponds that obviates the need for any inference. Another variation on the view might insist that noninferential justification consists not just in acquaintance with the fact that is the truth-maker for one's belief but also acquaintance with the correspondence between the truth bearer (sometimes taken to be a thought or "picture" of reality) and the truth-maker.

In addition to direct acquaintance with contingent facts that can yield noninferentially justified beliefs in empirical propositions, there may also be direct acquaintance with logical relations holding between propositions, states of affairs, or properties that yields direct knowledge of necessary truths. So, for example, one might claim that one's noninferential justification for believing that squares have four sides is constituted in part by one's acquaintance with the properties of being a square and having four sides and the way in which the former contains the latter. Or one might hold that one's noninferential justification for believing that nothing can be both red all over and blue all over at the same time is constituted in part by one's acquaintance with the way in which being red excludes being blue.

On the above view, one might locate the source of both a priori and a posteriori foundational knowledge in the same relation of acquaintance. Traditionally, philosophers have made a great deal of the distinction between a priori knowledge (knowledge of necessary truths that is in some sense independent of sense experience) and a posteriori knowledge (knowledge of contingent truth that somehow relies on sense experience). But it is hard to see in what sense knowledge of one's own beliefs, for example, fits neatly into this traditional way of making the distinction. That one believes that it will rain tomorrow is a contingent truth that one knows, but it doesn't seem that one's knowledge of that truth depends on sense experience. On the acquaintance theory, the difference between a priori and a posteriori knowledge might better be thought of as lying more on the side of the relata of the acquaintance relation than on the source of the knowledge.

CRITICISMS

Classical foundationalism has come under considerable attack from many different directions. The second clause of the principle of inferential justification is particularly controversial. A worry exists that it is far too strong a requirement for inferential justification and may simply invite a vicious regress. In assessing the claim that inferential justification requires access to a probability connection between one's premises and one's conclusion, it is important to make sure that the arguments one considers are not enthymematic. as we ordinarily talk, it is natural to describe the dark clouds overhead as evidence of an approaching storm. But it is doubtful that the the presence of the clouds by itself constitutes the entire body of evidence from which people predict the storm; it is the dark clouds together with one's knowledge of a past association between dark clouds and storms. One might argue that when one considers genuinely non-enthymematic reasoning it is less plausible to suppose that one needs knowledge of connections between premises and conclusion in order to legitimately infer one's conclusion.

Still, even in the case of deductively valid arguments there is a great deal of plausibility to the claim that one cannot get justification for believing the conclusion of the argument unless one not only has reason to believe the premises but also sees the connection between premises and conclusion. To avoid regress, people need noninferential knowledge of connections between premises and conclusions; and whereas it may not be that hard to convince oneself that one can discover without inference that one proposition entails another, it is much harder to convince oneself that one can just "see" probability connections (connections that are lower than entailment).

Without noninferential awareness of probability, however, skepticism looms on the horizon. Of course, in deciding what one can or cannot be noninferentially justified in believing, the question of just what might constitute noninferential justification needs to be addressed.

WHAT CONSTITUTES NONINFERENTIAL JUSTIFICATION? Some would argue that the search for infallible beliefs as the foundations of knowledge is both fruitless and misguided—at least if infallibility is understood in terms of a belief's entailing the truth of what is believed. As has been shown, there are trivial examples of beliefs that do entail the truth of what is believed. My beliefs that "I exist; that I am conscious; that I have beliefs" are all trivially infallible in the sense defined. Critics have pointed out, however, that if one believes a necessary truth, one's belief will also trivially entail the truth of what is believed. If one says that *P* entails *Q* when it is impossible for *P* to be true while *Q* is false, then every proposition will entail a necessary truth—necessary truths cannot be false.

But surely belief in a necessary truth does not constitute knowledge if the person holds the belief as a matter of pure whimsy. If one becomes irrationally convinced that every third sentence of a book expresses a truth, and by employing this decision procedure for belief ends up, by a remarkable coincidence, believing an extraordinarily complex necessary truth (far too complex for one to even recognize as a necessary truth) it hardly seems right to suppose that one would have any justification whatsoever for believing that truth. Once one sees that the entailment relation between belief and the truth of what one believes is not sufficient for knowledge or justified belief, one might begin to wonder whether it is ever getting at the heart of any interesting *epistemic* concept.

Still other philosophers have pointed out that beliefs that entail their truth are few and far between, and that if knowledge rests on a foundation of these, then that foundation is precarious indeed. Consider a favorite example of a foundational belief offered by classical foundationalists: the belief one has that one is in pain. Believing that one is in pain seems to be a state logically distinct from the pain. As such it seems always at least conceivable that the belief could occur—perhaps produced by some evil demon—without the pain. for all we know, the brain state causally responsible for one's believing that one is in pain is a distinct brain state from the one causally responsible for the pain. If so, then one could presumably induce belief in pain without producing the pain. Yet if one cannot get foundational justification or knowledge for accepting descriptions of one's own psychological states, then an impoverished foundation indeed exists upon which to attempt to build an edifice of knowledge.

EXTERNALIST APPROACHES TO INFALLIBILITY. Some contemporary philosophers are sympathetic to the idea of direct knowledge understood in terms of beliefs that cannot be false, but have understood the relevant possibility in causal or nomological terms. Thus the circumstances that produce the belief that *P* may be *causally* sufficient for the truth of *P*. It is not easy to spell out in an interesting way how one might specify the relevant circumstances causally responsible for a belief, but this approach does succeed in raising an alternative to the classical foundationalists' emphasis on conceivability or logical possibility as the relevant concept to employ in defining epistemically interesting concepts of infallibility. It also raises the prospects of a much richer array of propositions being contained in the foundations. Such externalist approaches to understanding infallibility, however, are probably anathema to classical foundationalists, who typically wanted the conditions that constitute foundational knowledge or justification to be conditions to which people have a kind of unproblematic direct access (a desire that might itself raise again the specter of vicious regress).

It was pointed out earlier that one cannot very well identify truth-makers as the source of noninferential justification without giving a plausible account of just what gives some truth-makers a critical epistemic role that most others fail to have. But reliance on the concept of acquaintance to define the concept of foundational knowledge has not fared much better when it comes to contemporary philosophical fashion. The standard line most often taken is that there is no such relation and, even if there were, it would be of no epistemic interest. Foundational knowledge must be knowledge of *propositions* if it is to yield the premises from which people can infer the rest of what they justifiably believe. But acquaintance with a fact seems to be a relation that has nothing to do with anything that has a truth value. Facts are not the kinds of things that can be true or false. How does acquaintance with a fact yield access to truth? Indeed, can one even make sense of reference to facts independently of truth? Some philosophers would argue that to refer to a fact is just another way of referring to a proposition's being true. If facts are reducible to truths, it would clearly be uninformative to locate the source of noninferential knowledge of truths in terms of acquaintance with facts to which truths correspond.

The claim that acquaintance with facts is not by itself constitutive of noninferential knowledge of truths is one that an acquaintance theorist might grant, however. As was noted earlier, one might introduce a critical role for truth-bearers to play in one's acquaintance theory. To be noniferentially justified in believing some proposition *P*, one might argue, one must be acquainted not only with the fact that *P* but the truth-making relation of correspondence between the thought that *P* and the fact that *P*. When one has acquaintance with the truth-bearer, the truth-maker, and the truth-making relation that holds between them, one is in a complex state that does just constitute the most fundamental kind of propositional knowledge.

NONINFERENTIAL JUSTIFICATION. To attack various versions of foundationalism is not, of course, to respond to the regress argument for foundationalism. It has already been noted that some contemporary foundationalists accept the fundamental idea that there are foundations to knowledge but reject classical accounts of what those foundations consist in. As was seen in considering alternative conceptions of infallibility, many externalists identify justificatory conditions for belief with the circumstances producing the belief. Reliabilists, for example, count a belief as justified if it is reliably produced and they allow that a belief might be reliably produced even if the input producing the belief involves no other beliefs. Such reliable "belief-independent" processes can end a regress of beliefs justified by reference to other beliefs. Reliabilist conceptions of noninferential justification also divorce noninferential justification from infallible justification. According to some reliabilists, a justified belief might result from nondoxastic input and be just barely more likely to be true than not.

As was true of those who seek foundations in the causal impossibility of mistake, reliabilists offer the prospect of a greatly expanded class of propositions that might be noninferentially justified. Like other versions of externalism, however, it is not clear that reliabilism succeeds in capturing a concept of justification that would interest the classical foundationalist. The classical foundationalist sought justification that would provide a kind of assurance of truth, and it is not clear how the causal origin of a belief by itself (when one has no access to that origin) could satisfy one's intellectual curiosity.

THE COHERENCE THEORY OF JUSTIFICATION

Historically, the other main alternative to classical foundationalism was the coherence theory of justification. The coherentist rejects the classical foundationalist's assumption that justification is linear in structure. According to the coherentist, there is no escape from the circle of one's beliefs—nothing can justify a belief but other beliefs. But one doesn't justify a belief by reference to other prior justified beliefs. Rather, each belief is justified by reference to its fit in an entire system of beliefs. When each belief does its part in contributing to a clear, coherent picture of the world, each belief is justified. The coherentist, however, faces a serious dilemma. The coherentist must choose between the view that coherence by itself confers positive epistemic status on the beliefs that cohere, and the view that it is one's awareness of the coherence between one's beliefs that confers such status. If the coherentists embrace the first horn of the dilemma, they are left with a view that seems vulnerable to counterexample. Does one really want to allow that if one consults one's astrologer and comes to believe a set of complex propositions that coincidentally cohere beautifully—even though due to their complexity one could never discover that coherence—the beliefs in question are all justified?

However, if one requires that one must be aware of the coherence among one's beliefs in order to acquire justification for those beliefs, one faces once again the regress that drove so many to foundationalism. To be aware of coherence one must be aware of the fact—that is, have a justified belief—that one has the beliefs one has and that they stand in various logical and probabilistic connections. But how does one come to know what one believes? If one answers in terms of coherence to which one has access the problem just arises again. If one gives oneself unproblematic direct access to one's beliefs and the connections that hold between them, one has simply returned to classical foundationalism.

See also Analysis, Philosophical; A Priori and A Posteriori; Coherentism; Correspondence Theory of Truth; Descartes, René; Epistemology; Evidentialism; Hume, David; Knowledge, A Priori; Propositions.

Bibliography

Armstrong, David. "Is Introspective Knowledge Incorrigible?" Philosophical Review 72, (1963): 427–32.

Audi, Robert. *The Structure of Justification*. Cambridge, U.K.: Cambridge University Press, 1993.

Ayer, A. J. *The Foundations of Empirical Knowledge*. New York: St. Martin's Press. 1955.

BonJour, Laurence, and Sosa, Ernest. *Epistemic Justification*. Oxford: Blackwell, 2003.

Butchvarov, Panayot. *The Concept of Knowledge*. Evanston, IL: Northwestern University Press, 1970.

Chisholm, Roderick. *The Foundations of Knowing*. Minneapolois, MN: University of Minnestoa Press, 1982.

Conee, Earl, and Feldman, Richard. *Evidentialism*. Oxford: Oxford University Press, 2004.

De Paul, Michael, ed. *Resurrecting Old-Fashioned Foundationalism*. Totowa, NJ: Rowman and Littlefield, 2001.

Descartes, Rene. *Discourse on Method and Meditations*, trans. Laurence LaFleur. Indianapolis: Bobbs-Merrill, 1960.

Fales, Evan. *A Defense of the Given*. Lanham, MD.: Rowman and Littlefield, 1986.

Foley, Richard. *The Theory of Epistemic Rationality*. Cambridge, MA: Harvard University Press, 1987.

Fumerton, Richard. *Metaepisptemology and Skepticism*. Lanham, MD: Rowman and Littlefield, 1996.

Klein, Peter. "Human Knowledge and the Infinite Regress of Reasons." *Philosophical Perspectives* 13 (1999): 297–325.

McGrew, Timothy. *The Foundations of Knowledge*. Lanham, MD: Littlefield Adams. 1995.

Plantinga, Alvin. "Justification in the 20th Century." In *Philosophical Issues 2: Rationality in Epistemology*, edited by Enrique Villanueva, 43–78. Atascadero, CA: Ridgeview Publishing Co., 1992.

Price, H. H. *Perception*. London: Methuen, 1950.

Russell, Bertrand. "Knowledge by Acquaintance and Knowledge by Description." *Proceedings of the Aristotelian Society*, 11, 108–128. Reprinted in Russell, Bertrand, *Mysticism and Logic*, London: Allen and Unwin, 1963, 152–167.

Sellars, Wilfred. *Science, Perception and Reality*. London: Routledge and Kegan Paul, 1963.

Richard Fumerton (1996, 2005)

CLASSICAL MECHANICS, PHILOSOPHY OF

Classical physics is the research tradition beginning with Isaac Newton's *Mathematical Principles of Natural Philosophy* (often called simply the *Principia*) of 1687, which was overtaken by relativity theory and quantum mechanics in the early twentieth century and is still undergoing lively development in such areas as chaos and catastrophe theory. The "Newtonian" physics canonized in textbooks includes many elements added long after Newton, such as vector notation, the analytical mechanics that Joseph-Louis Lagrange and William Hamilton developed in the late eighteenth and early nineteenth centuries, and the laws of energy conservation and of electromagnetic phenomena formulated in the mid-nineteenth century. Indeed, Leonhard Euler in 1749 was the first to express Newton's second law as the familiar relation between a body's instantaneous acceleration and the momentary force that the body experiences; Newton's own version of the law set the body's change in momentum during a finite period of time equal to the impulse on the body (the force times the period's length, for constant force over the period). However, the subject of this entry is the anachronistic classical mechanics found in textbooks.

Though classical mechanics is false, as relativity and quantum mechanics reveal, there are many reasons for philosophers to continue investigating its proper interpretation (i.e., what the world would be like if classical mechanics were true). Many of the difficulties encountered in trying to interpret modern physics also arise in connection with classical physics, but in a simpler context. Moreover, many of the venerable metaphysical and epistemological ideas vigorously developed by modern philosophers such as George Berkeley, David Hume, and Immanuel Kant are best understood in connection with the classical physics that originally prompted them. Furthermore, one should not wait to deploy one's interpretive faculties only after physics has secured the final theory of everything; if one did, progress in both physics and philosophy would suffer. Finally, although classical physics lacks some of the provocative features exhibited by relativity and quantum mechanics, it has long served philosophers as the exemplar of what genuine scientific understanding would be. By studying it, one can learn about the concepts, logic, and limits of science. This entry touches on only a few of the metaphysical and epistemological questions that classical physics provokes.

BASIC ONTOLOGY: MASS AND MATTER

Philosophers have worked to identify the ontologically fundamental objects, properties, and relations that classical mechanics posits. Among the candidates proposed have been distance, time interval, velocity, force, matter, mass, electric charge, and inertial reference frame. All raise difficult questions.

Mass is the single parameter relating a body's motion to the force on the body. Remarkably, that relation in classical mechanics is the same for macroscopic bodies as for their constituents; classical mechanics "scales up." Newton defined mass as measuring the amount of matter composing a body, though he did not define *matter* itself. In contrast, the nineteenth-century Scots physicist James Clerk Maxwell (1952), who formulated the laws of electromagnetism, defined mass in terms of momentum and energy, which he believed more fundamental. An alternative approach later pursued by Ernst Mach (1960), the Moravian physicist and philosopher, characterizes mass operationally: The masses of two bodies are related as the inverse ratio of their mutually induced accelerations when isolated from other bodies. If mass is not defined operationally, but instead is an intrinsic property responsible for resistance to force, then according to many philosophers, one knows the effects for which mass is responsible, but one cannot know what mass is in itself. Similar considerations apply to electric charge.

Classical mechanics is sometimes interpreted as deeming a macroscopic body to be a swarm of point bodies in a void. In an alternative interpretation classical mechanics takes bulk matter to be continuous space-filling stuff, or instead to be composed of many bodies of a small but finite dimension made of continuous media, having no internal structure, and separated by empty space. Newton's laws and Charles-Augustin de Coulomb's electrostatic force law are often codified in terms of pointlike bodies, whereas the basic equations of hydrodynamics and the theory of elastic solids are typically expressed in terms of continua. Mass points present obvious difficulties; when two collide, they must be inside each other and the gravitational force between them becomes infinite. Continuous media avoid the latter problem, since at a point, there is no finite quantity of mass; there is only mass density, defined as the limit of mass per volume as the volume becomes arbitrarily small. But collisions still present a problem: When two bodies collide, do they occupy a common point? Or is there simply no finite volume between them? (If a point separates them, then how are they in contact?)

BASIC ONTOLOGY: MOTION AND FORCE

A body's velocity is its position's instantaneous rate of change, and its acceleration is its velocity's instantaneous rate of change. As ordinarily defined, a quantity's rate of change at an instant is its average rate of change during a finite interval around that instant, in the limit of an arbitrarily short interval. Hence, a body's velocity at time t is just a mathematical property of the body's trajectory in a neighborhood of t, which includes some of the body's trajectory after t. But its velocity at t is supposed to be an initial condition in the causal explanation of its subsequent trajectory. That would apparently require points in that subsequent trajectory to help causally explain themselves. This is puzzling. Furthermore, consider a body moving uniformly across the surface of a smooth horizontal table and then falling off the edge. At the final moment that the body is on the table (assuming that the table includes its edge), its trajectory's second derivative is undefined; taken from the left it is zero, but taken from the right it is equal to the gravitational acceleration. Presumably, though, a body has a well-defined acceleration at all times.

Force is characterized by William Thomson and Peter Guthrie Tait in their canonical mid-nineteenth-century physics text as "a direct object of sense" (1895–1896, p. 220). However, other natural philosophers regarded forces as redundant in classical mechanics once fields are admitted as local causes or remote charges and masses are acknowledged as acting at a distance. The late nineteenth-century German physicist Heinrich Hertz regarded forces as mere calculational devices between cause and effect, "simply sleeping partners, which keep out of the business altogether when actual facts have to be represented" (1956, p. 11).

FUNDAMENTAL LAWS

Newton's three laws of motion, with his inverse-square law of gravity, are commonly regarded as the fundamental laws of classical physics. In the nineteenth century the laws of electromagnetism were added to them. The status of the conservation laws and the variational principles of classical physics remains more controversial, as will be seen.

Newton's second law is sometimes taken to be "The net force on a body, divided by its mass, equals its acceleration in any inertial frame of reference." But how is *inertial frame* defined? Mach suggested that inertial frames are frames where the universe's average matter is not accelerating. But this definition leads to predictions that depart from those made by Newtonian mechanics regarding, say, a body in otherwise empty space or in a universe where (according to Newton) all other matter is accelerating. Sometimes *inertial frame* is taken to be defined by Newton's first law: a frame is inertial exactly when a body feeling no forces remains at rest or in uniform rectilinear motion in that frame. But then Newton's first law is true by definition.

The chief alternative is to presuppose points of absolute space, as Newton did, and to define an *inertial frame* as a rigid Euclidean frame at rest or in uniform rectilinear motion with respect to those points. However, even disregarding objections to absolute space as either empirically inaccessible or in contravention of metaphysical scruples, Newton's approach contains surplus ontological structure. A particular frame need not be privileged as at rest. Rectilinear uniform motion need only be distinguished from other paths; the frames pursuing such trajectories are inertial. *Inertial frame* is thereby defined independent of Newton's first law, which is not tautologous but just a consequence of Newton's second law. (Newton's first law is never instantiated, since every body feels some component gravitational forces.)

In this "neo-Newtonian" space-time, there is no fact of the matter regarding a body's velocity. (But there is a fact regarding its acceleration and its velocity relative to another body.) There is also no fact regarding the distance between two nonsimultaneous events, unlike in Newton's absolute space and time. All inertial frames are equal in neo-Newtonian space-time.

However, absolute velocity figures in the classical laws of electromagnetism. Absolute space is then no longer superfluous. This fact opened one of Albert Einstein's paths to relativity theory.

HOW MUCH DOES CLASSICAL PHYSICS SAY?

Thomson and Tait interpret Newton's second law as requiring every acceleration to be caused by some force (1895–1896, p. 223). But simply as an equation, Newton's laws make no explicit mention of causes and effects; they merely relate a perpetually isolated system's past and future states to its current state. Accordingly, Bertrand Arthur William Russell concludes that the notion of a causal relation (insofar as it goes beyond a correlation demanded by the laws) has no place in physics, but is "a relic of a bygone age" (1929, p. 247). David Lewis (1983–1986) draws a different moral, arguing instead that since classical physics reveals causal relations, those relations must supervene on the laws and the actual course of events.

There are many similar questions about how richly or austerely classical physics describes the world. For instance, the law of energy conservation might be interpreted as specifying that the universe's total quantity of energy is fixed. But it might instead be taken as saying more: That for any volume over any temporal interval, the change in energy within must equal the energy that has flowed across its boundary. Alternatively, the conservation laws (of mass, energy, linear momentum, and angular momentum) might not be understood as laws of classical physics at all. They do not follow immediately from Newton's laws of motion and gravity.

TIME-REVERSAL INVARIANCE

Newton's laws are time-reversal invariant. Roughly speaking, if a sequence of events is permitted by the laws, then the laws also permit those events to occur in reverse order. The laws recognize no difference between past and future just as they fail to discriminate among spatial directions. However, certain macroscopic processes are never observed to occur in reverse. For example, when two bodies of unequal temperature touch, heat flows from the warmer to the cooler body. Although there are configurations of the bodies' molecules that would lead by Newton's laws to the warmer body's becoming still warmer, many more configurations would produce the result one sees. So irreversibility can be reconciled with Newton's laws if, roughly speaking, all the possible microrealizations of a system's macrostate are equally likely.

But this equiprobability is not required by Newton's laws. Its origin remains puzzling. Furthermore, even if a closed system far from equilibrium (e.g., with an unequal distribution of heat) were much more likely to head toward equilibrium (i.e., to increase its entropy) than away from equilibrium, entropy's increase in the space-time region one observes would remain unexplained. It would still be mysterious why one's space-time region is so far from equilibrium in the first place.

MECHANISM AND DETERMINISM

Classical mechanics suggests that the universe is like a majestic clockwork, the laws fully determining the universe's past and future states given its present state, and a body changing its motion only because another body touches it. But gravity and electromagnetism apparently operate by action at a distance. Newton famously offered no hypotheses (*hypotheses non fingo*) regarding the means by which gravity operates. Accordingly, some natural philosophers ceased to seek local causes for all effects. In contrast, Michael Faraday and Maxwell regarded fields of force as existing on a par with bodies. The field at a given location would cause a body there to feel a force. The field picture avoids positing action at a distance but departs significantly from the picture of material particles in the void: Fields occupy all locations, even where there is no ordinary matter.

In 1814 Pierre Simon de Laplace invoked his famous "demon" to explain the determinism of the clockwork universe:

> Given for one instant an intelligence which could comprehend all the forces by which nature is animated and the respective situation of the beings who compose it—an intelligence sufficiently vast to submit these data to analysis—it would embrace in the same formula the movements of the greatest bodies of the universe and those of the lightest atom; for it, nothing would be uncertain and the future, as the past, would be present to its eyes. (1951, p. 4)

Twentieth-century research revealed that Laplace may have overstated the determinism of a universe governed by classical physics (although there is no obvious way in which the indeterminism of classical physics supports the freedom of the will). When two point bodies collide, their mutual gravitational interaction becomes infinite, yet the laws of energy and momentum conservation nevertheless allow an analytic solution to the classical equations of motion to be extended uniquely through the collision singularity. However, this extension is generally impossible when three bodies collide. Furthermore, Newton's laws enable a closed system of point bodies to undergo an infinite number of triple near collisions in a finite time (as the sequence of encounter times converges to some particular moment). By the slingshot effect resulting from these close approaches, certain bodies attain infinite acceleration in finite time and so afterward are absent from any finite region of the universe. They are literally nowhere to be found. Since Newton's laws are time-reversal invariant, they permit this sequence of events to proceed in reverse, so that "space invaders" suddenly appear in the system from nowhere. Determinism is thereby violated without a collision occurring. Of course, the invaders' unanticipated appearance violates mass, energy, and momentum conservation, illustrating that these principles fail to follow from Newton's laws alone.

ANALYTICAL MECHANICS

In 1661 Pierre de Fermat derived the law of refraction from the postulate that in traveling from one location to another, a ray of light takes the path that minimizes the travel time. To some (such as the eighteenth-century French mathematician Pierre-Louis Moreau de Maupertuis), Fermat's principle suggested that nature produces effects with the greatest economy, efficiency, or ease—demonstrating God's wisdom. However, this metaphysical moral was undermined somewhat by the discovery that light may also take the path of greatest travel time. For example, consider a point light source at the center of an ellipsoidal mirror. The points around the mirror's margin that can reflect light back to the center are exactly the two points along the mirror's minor axis (i.e., where the edge is closest to the center) and the two points along the mirror's major axis (i.e., where the edge is farthest from the center).

Fermat's principle was generalized by Euler, Lagrange, and Hamilton into the variational principles of analytical mechanics. Given the system's initial configuration (the initial positions and velocities of its particles) and final configuration, there are various paths (through configuration space) by which the system may get from one to the other. These paths may differ, for instance, in the time it takes the system to arrive at its final configuration and in the configurations through which the system passes along the way. Roughly speaking, the Euler-Lagrange "principle of least action" states that the time integral of the system's total kinetic energy is "stationary" along the actual path as compared to all sufficiently close possible paths. That is, roughly speaking, the sum of the kinetic energies at all the points along the path actually taken is a minimum, maximum, or saddle point as compared to the sums for similar paths that are not taken. (So "the principle of least action" does not demand that the action be "least.")

Similarly, Hamilton's principle states roughly that of all the possible paths by which the system may proceed from one specified configuration to another in a specified time, the actual path as compared to other possible, slightly different paths makes stationary the time integral of the system's Lagrangian (i.e., the difference between the system's total kinetic and potential energies). A possible path may violate energy conservation and other laws; Hamilton's principle picks out the path demanded by the laws. So to apply Hamilton's principle, scientists must contemplate counterlegals: what would have been the case, had the system violated natural laws in certain ways. But a possible path must respect the constraints on the system, which may include a body's having to remain rigid or in contact with a certain surface.

These constraints may be plugged into the variational principles without the forces that constrain the system having to be specified. This gives variational principles a practical advantage over Newton's laws, since the forces of constraint may be unknown, and emphasizes the style of explanation that variational principles supply. Newton's laws are differential equations; they determine the instantaneous rates of change of the system's properties from the system's conditions at that moment, such as the forces on it. The system's trajectory over a finite time interval is then built up, point by point, and the forces are efficient causes of the system's acceleration. In contrast, variational principles make no mention of forces; instead, they invoke the system's energy. The explanations they supply specify no efficient causes. Variational principles involve integral equations; they determine the system's trajectory as a whole, rather than point by point.

TELEOLOGY

Explanations that use variational principles sound teleological; the system appears to aim at making a certain integral stationary. But then the system's final configuration apparently helps to explain the path that the system takes to that destination; later events help to explain earlier ones. That is puzzling. How does a light ray "know," at the start of its journey, which path will take less time? How can the light adjust the earlier part of its route to minimize its later path through optically dense regions (where it cannot travel as fast) unless it knows about those distant regions before it sets off?

Some natural philosophers (such as Max Planck) suggested that variational principles are more basic laws than Newtonian differential equations, especially considering that unlike Newton's laws, variational equations of the same form apply to any set of variables sufficient to specify the system's configuration. Other natural philosophers (notably Gottfried Wilhelm Leibniz) embraced both mechanical and teleological explanations as equally fundamental. Leibniz declared that there are

> two kingdoms even in corporeal nature, which interpenetrate without confusing or interfering with each other—the realm of power, according to which everything can be explained mechanically by efficient causes when we have sufficiently penetrated into its interior, and the realm of wisdom, according to which everything can be explained architectonically, so to speak, or by final causes when we understand its ways sufficiently. (1969, pp. 478–479)

Other natural philosophers (such as Mach) denied final causes but also denied efficient causes as well (allowing only the relations specified by natural laws). The most common view, however, has been to reject teleological explanations as a relic of anthropomorphic characterizations of nature and to regard variational principles as logical consequences of more fundamental, mechanical laws. The variational principles follow from the Newtonian differential equations roughly because the entire path can minimize the integral only if each infinitesimal part does (since otherwise, by replacing that part with another, one would create a new path with a smaller integral), and the minimum for each infinitesimal part reflects the gradient of the potential there, which is the force. The variational principle thus arises as a byproduct of the relation between the force and an infinitesimal section of the path.

See also Berkeley, George; Chaos Theory; Determinism, A Historical Survey; Faraday, Michael; Hamilton, William; Hertz, Heinrich Rudolf; Hume, David; Kant, Immanuel; Laplace, Pierre Simon de; Laws, Scientific; Leibniz, Gottfried Wilhelm; Lewis, David; Logic, History of: Precursors of Modern Logic; Mach, Ernst; Maxwell, James Clerk; Newton, Isaac; Philosophy of Physics; Planck, Max; Quantum Mechanics; Relativity Theory; Russell, Bertrand Arthur William.

Bibliography

Diacu, Florin, and Philip Holmes. *Celestial Encounters: The Origins of Chaos and Stability.* Princeton, NJ: Princeton University Press, 1996.

Earman, John. *A Primer on Determinism.* Dordrecht, Netherlands: Reidel, 1986.

Earman, John. *World Enough and Space-Time: Absolute versus Relational Theories of Space and Time.* Cambridge, MA: MIT Press, 1989.

Feynman, Richard, Robert B. Leighton, and Matthew Sands. *The Feynman Lectures on Physics.* 3 vols. Reading, MA: Addison-Wesley, 1963–1965.

Hertz, Heinrich. *The Principles of Mechanics.* Translated by D. E. Jones and J. T. Walley. New York: Dover, 1956.

Lange, Marc. *An Introduction to the Philosophy of Physics: Locality, Fields, Energy, and Mass.* Oxford, U.K.: Blackwell, 2002.

Laplace, Pierre Simon de. *A Philosophical Essay on Probabilities.* Translated by Frederick Wilson Truscott and Frederick Lincoln Emory. New York: Dover, 1951.

Leibniz, Gottfried Wilhelm. *Philosophical Papers and Letters.* 2nd ed. Translated and edited by Leroy E. Loemker. Dordrecht, Netherlands: Reidel, 1969.

Lewis, David. *Philosophical Papers*. 2 vols. New York: Cambridge University Press, 1983–1986.

Lindsay, Robert Bruce, and Henry Margenau. *Foundations of Physics*. New York: Wiley, 1936.

Mach, Ernst. *The Science of Mechanics: A Critical and Historical Account of Its Development*. 6th ed. Translated by Thomas J. McCormack. LaSalle, IL: Open Court, 1960.

Maxwell, James Clerk. *Matter and Motion*. New York: Dover, 1952.

Newton, Isaac. *Sir Isaac Newton's Mathematical Principles of Natural Philosophy and His System of the World*. 2 vols. Translated by Andrew Motte and revised by Florian Cajori. Berkeley: University of California Press, 1962.

Russell, Bertrand. "On the Notion of Cause." In *Our Knowledge of the External World*. London: Norton, 1929.

Sklar, Lawrence. *Philosophy of Physics*. Boulder, CO: Westview Press, 1992.

Thomson, William, and Peter Guthrie Tait. *Treatise on Natural Philosophy*. 2 vols. Cambridge, U.K.: Cambridge University Press, 1895–1896.

Yourgrau, Wolfgang, and Stanley Mandelstam. *Variational Principles in Dynamics and Quantum Theory*. 3rd ed. London: Pitman, 1968.

Marc Lange (2005)

CLASSIFICATION

See *Definition; Logical Terms, Glossary of*

CLAUBERG, JOHANNES

(1622–1665)

Johannes Clauberg, a German Cartesian philosopher, was born in Soligen, February 24, 1622, and died in Duisburg, January 31, 1665. Though he lived a short life, his philosophical output was considerable; his name became almost synonymous with that of René Descartes in Germany. Clauberg studied in Cologne and Bremen, where he came under the influence of reformed scholasticism and the pedagogical and methodological ideals of Jan Amos Comenius. At Bremen he also met Tobias Andreae, whom he later joined in Groningen in 1644 after Andreae was appointed professor of History and Greek. He disputed some theses in 1646 and published his first independent treatise, *Ontosophia*, in 1647. Clauberg's initial works, including *Ontosophia*, do not display the influence of Descartes's philosophy, though Clauberg rewrote the book along Cartesian lines in later editions. After travels to France, to the Protestant Academy in Saumur and Paris (where he seems to have met some early Cartesians), and to England, Clauberg attended the lectures of the Cartesian Johannes de Raey in Leiden in 1648. It is clear that by 1648 Clauberg had become interested in Descartes's philosophy. Clauberg made his official entrance into the Cartesian world as a result of his participation in what is sometimes called the "Conversation with Burman." The latter is a manuscript of the University of Göttingen reporting a lengthy discussion between Descartes and (presumably) Frans Burman, a young theology student at Leiden. The discussion, conducted in Latin, apparently occurred on April 16, 1648, at Descartes's retreat in Egmont. According to the manuscript, Burman dictated his impressions of the meeting to Clauberg on April 20. Clauberg evidently kept a copy and had a second one made by some unknown scribe some months later; this is the surviving copy.

In that period Clauberg was approached about becoming a professor of theology in Herborn; he began his duties the following year, in 1649, as professor of philosophy instead, with occasional teaching in theology. However, he was not happy with his position; his teaching load was heavy and he probably resented the combination of theology and philosophy, protesting as well that the professor of theology had some teaching duties in philosophy. A conflict with his more conservative colleagues developed. On November 1, 1651, Clauberg's employer, the Count of Nassau, officially decreed that the only philosophy allowed in Herborn was Aristotelico-Ramist philosophy, either separately or jointly. As a result, Clauberg and his friend and fellow Cartesian Christoph Wittich, who had been appointed professor of mathematics, left Herborn in December 1651 and accepted posts in Duisburg, a town that fell under the jurisdiction of the Elector of Brandenburg. In Duisburg, Clauberg's position was initially Rector of the town's Gymnasium; when the Academy of Duisburg was opened in 1655 he and Wittich became doctors of theology. Clauberg married Catharina Mercator in 1652; they had one son and five daughters. For the rest of his life, the now-settled Clauberg lived the life of a professor in a small German town; he was even rector of the Academy in 1655 and 1659. He attracted many students to Duisburg, several of whom became professors themselves.

WORKS

Clauberg must have already started on his second book, *Defensio cartesiana*, when still in Leiden, though it was published only in 1652. It is primarily a reply to *Consideratio theologica* (1648), a detailed commentary on Descartes's *Discourse on Method* from an orthodox theological point of view, by the Leiden Professor Jacobus Revius. Clauberg also added materials attacking his erstwhile colleague Cyrianus Lentulus (or Lentz), Professor of Practical Philosophy at Hernborn. The *Defensio Cartesiana* provoked a reply from Revius, which Clauberg answered with *Initiatio Philosophi sive dubitatio cartesiana* (1655). The conflict also involved Andreae, who published a two-volume response to Revius in 1653–1654, triggering yet another treatise from Revius in 1654. In his defense of Cartesianism, Clauberg distinguished between Descartes's popular and his esoteric works; according to Clauberg, the *Discourse on Method* belongs to the first category, whereas the *Meditations* and *Principles of Philosophy* belong to the second.

The promulgation of Cartesianism required Clauberg to write a number of other works explaining Descartes's physics and metaphysics, such as *Paraphrasis in Renati Descartes Meditationes*, *Differentia inter Cartesianam et alias*, and *Physica*. Clauberg also published some volumes of disputations. But doubtless his most influential books were *Logica vetus et nova*, first published by Elzevier in 1654, and the smaller *Logica contracta*. After Clauberg's death, the Amsterdam professor of philosophy Johann Theodor Schallbruch provided an edition of his works, *Opera omnia philosophica*, partly based on unpublished material in the possession of Clauberg's son, Johann Christopher; the added material included Clauberg's notes on Descartes's *Principles of Philosophy*, his correspondence with Andreae, a biography of Clauberg, and a general index to all of Clauberg's treatises.

CARTESIANISM

Clauberg's work is a paradigm of what first-generation Cartesian scholastics needed to accomplish. Clauberg made progress elaborating Cartesian themes, such as espousing occasionalism for the relation between mind and body, and created texts to fill the gaps in the collegiate curriculum as it would be taught by a Cartesian. With the *Principles of Philosophy*, Descartes began the process of producing textbooks from which to teach Cartesian philosophy. However, scholastic textbooks usually had quadripartite arrangements mirroring the structure of the collegiate curriculum: logic, ethics, physics, and metaphysics. And Descartes produced at best only a partial physics and what could be called a general metaphysics; he did not finish his physics—he did not produce the expected final two parts of the *Principles of Philosophy* on animals and on man—and did not write a particular metaphysics. He did not produce a logic or ethics for his followers to use or to teach from. These things must have been perceived as glaring deficiencies in the Cartesian program and in the aspiration to replace Aristotelian philosophy in the schools.

So the Cartesians rushed in to fill the voids. One can understand Louis de la Forge's additions to the *Traité de l'homme*, for example, as an attempt to complete the physics, and Clauberg's later editions of *Ontosophia* or Baruch Spinoza's *Cogitata metaphysica*, for instance, as endeavors to produce a more conventional-looking metaphysics. Descartes, of course, saw himself as presenting Cartesian metaphysics as well as physics, both the roots and trunk of his tree of philosophy. But from the point of view of schools texts, the metaphysical elements of physics (general metaphysics) that needed to be discussed by Descartes—such as the principles of bodies: matter, form, and privation; causation; motion: generation and corruption, growth, and diminution; place, void, infinity, and time—were expected to be taught in a course on physics. The scholastic course on metaphysics (particular metaphysics) dealt with other topics, not discussed directly in the *Principles of Philosophy*, such as being, existence, and essence; unity, quantity, and individuation; truth and falsity; good and evil. Such courses usually also ended up with questions about knowledge of God, names or attributes of God, God's will and power, and God's goodness. The *Principles of Philosophy* by itself was not sufficient as a text for the standard course in metaphysics.

Clauberg's *Ontosophia*, however, discussed being in general, dividing it into its general and primary sense of "intelligible" being, a secondary and lesser sense of "something" to be distinguished from "nothing," and a third, particular sense of "real" being, being outside the intellect, or substance, contrasting it with accident and mode. Clauberg went on to talk about essence, existence, and duration. His remaining chapters concerned pairs of concepts such as one and many; true and false; good and evil; perfect and imperfect; distinct and opposite; the same and another; exemplar and image.

CARTESIAN LOGIC

Beyond completing Cartesian physics and metaphysics, there were even attempts at producing Cartesian ethics; a Latin-language manual called *Ethica*, printed in 1685, was said to have been authored by Descartes. Descartes never wrote such a work, but a translator was able to put together a tripartite treatise out of Descartes's own words: (1) on the greatest good, happiness, and free will; (2) on passions; and (3) on love. There were numerous stabs at creating Cartesian-style logic texts as well, Clauberg's *Logica vetus et nova* being first of its kind, together with the *Logique* of Jacques Du Roure. The attempt to publish a Cartesian textbook that would mirror what was taught in the schools culminated in the famous multivolume works of Pierre-Sylvain Régis and of Antoine Le Grand, which included expanded versions of Cartesian physics and metaphysics, together with treatises on ethics and logic.

Scholastic logic, as taught in the seventeenth century, typically followed an order of topics dictated by the various books of Aristotle's *Organon: Categories, On Interpretation, Prior Analytics, Posterior Analytics, Topics, and Sophistical Refutations.* For example, after some preliminary questions on the usefulness of logic, whether logic can be called science or art, and the definition and divisions of logic, Scipion Dupleix wrote a six-part logic, corresponding to Aristotle's six logical works: (1) categories—that is, substance, quantity, quality, relations, and so forth; (2) nouns, verbs, and statements; (3) syllogism; (4) science and demonstration; (5) topics; and (6) paralogisms. One can say similar things about the logic textbooks of other early seventeenth-century scholastics, such as Eustachius a Sancto Paulo and Pierre du Moulin. Clauberg's *Logica contracta* followed a similar pattern, starting with the categories and continuing with attribute and accident, cause and effect, subject and adjunct, relation, whole and part, the same and other, universal and singular, definition, and division. His second part of logic began with the grades of judgment, qualitative statement, truth and falsity, opposition, conversion and equivalence, and composite statement, and continued with argument and syllogism, both perfect and imperfect, and true and false. Clauberg's third part of logic dealt with the grades of memory and his fourth part concerned teaching and dialectics, order, and fallacy. Very little of this was Cartesian.

A major problem to resolve in producing a Cartesian logic was that Descartes, in keeping with a standard Renaissance view, was extremely negative about the subject. According to Descartes in the *Discourse on Method* (repeating views he had previously elaborated in the unfinished *Rules*), syllogisms are useless: they serve to explain things one already knows, or even to speak without judgment on matters of which one is ignorant, rather than to learn them; although logic might contain true and good precepts, nevertheless there are so many other precepts mixed up with them, that are either harmful or superfluous, that it is practically impossible to separate them from one another. Descartes proposed instead his four rules of method—the rules of evidence, of the division of difficulties, of the order of inquiry, and of the completeness of enumerations—as a method of discovery exempt from the faults of formal logic.

However, Descartes also called his rules of method the principal rules of logic. According to Descartes, before applying himself to true philosophy a person who has only common and imperfect knowledge should study "logic," but not the logic of the Schools: Such logic corrupts good sense rather than increasing it. Descartes's logic instead teaches people to direct their reason with a view to discovering the truths of which they are ignorant. The more moderate late Cartesian views about logic were reinforced in a text familiar to Clauberg. Commenting to Burman on the *Discourse* passage about the harmful role of logic, Descartes supposedly asserted that his statements did not apply so much to logic, which provides demonstrative proof on all subjects, but to dialectic, which teaches how to hold forth on all subjects. Descartes's subtle shift in position allowed Clauberg to reinterpret Descartes's rules of method as part of logic, now integrated into a legitimate branch of learning that even included syllogisms.

Clauberg's *Logica vetus et nova* begins with a Prolegomena arguing, along Descartes's line from the end *of Principles of Philosophy*, Part 1, that the principal origin of error is to be found in the prejudices of childhood. Logic is the corrective for these mental imperfections; thus, in the first book of his logic, Clauberg devises a scheme that involves Descartes's rules of method and traditional logic, following the pattern of his *logica contracta*, as three "grades" or levels of logic. The first level has to do with accepting clear and distinct perceptions; it includes the rule of evidence and ends up with the rule about the division of difficulties, but it also discusses traditional topics such as: substance, attribute, and mode; essence and existence; universal and singular; definition; and division. The second level concerns right judgment and involves the rule about the order of inquiry, ending with the rule of the completeness of enumerations; it also discusses induction and syllogism. Clauberg's third level concerns memory.

Clauberg provided the initial pattern for Cartesian logic, though other Cartesians found it more expedient to follow more closely the scholastic order in logic, grafting on a section about method at the end of their treatises. Later Cartesian logics, such as the Port-Royal Logic and Le Grand's *Logick* are divided into four parts: (1) Ideas, including Aristotle's categories, universals, and names; (2) Propositions (or Judgments), truth and falsehood; (3) Reasoning (or Discourse), including syllogisms, topics, and sophisms; and (4) Method. By method, however, these writers meant analysis and synthesis, which does not have to be anything particularly Cartesian, though we do find Descartes's rules of method enumerated in the chapters on analysis. The Port-Royal Logic supplanted Clauberg's logic and was ultimately adopted and abbreviated by Régis as his logic in his *General System of Cartesian Philosophy*. One can legitimately think, however, that Clauberg understood Descartes's views on logic better than subsequent Cartesians.

See also Cartesianism.

Bibliography

WORKS BY CLAUBERG

Tessarakas thesium philosophicarum, de logicae ab aliis disciplinis quibus cum vulgo confundi assolet distinctione … moderatore Tobias Andreae. Groningen, Netherlands: J. Nicolai, 1646.

Disputatio theologico-practica de conscientia … sub praesidio Matthiae Pasoris.… Groningen, Netherlands: Eissens, 1646.

Elementa philosophiae sive Ontosophia. Scientia prima, de iis quae Deo creaturisque suo modo communiter attribuuntur. Groningen, Netherlands: Nicolai, 1647. With editions in 1660 and 1664.

Defensio cartesiana adversus Iacobum Revium Theologum Leidensen, et Cyriacum Lentulum, professorum Herbornensem: pars prior exoterica, in qua Renati Cartesii Dissertatio de Methodo vindicatur, simul illustria Cartesianae logicae et philosophiae specimina exhibentur. Amsterdam: Elsevier, 1652.

Logica vetus et nova, modum inveniendae ac tradendae veritatis, in Genesi simul et analysi facili methodo exhibens. Amsterdam: Elzevier, 1654. With editions in 1656, 1658, 1683, 1685, and 1692.

Initiatio philosophi, sive dubitatio Cartesiana, ad metaphysicam certitudinem viam aperiens. Leiden, Netherlands: Wyngaerden, 1655.

De Cognitione Dei et nostri, quatenus naturali rationis lumine, secundum veram philosophiam, potest comparari, exercitationes centum. Duisburg, Germany: Wyngaerden, 1656, with another edition in 1685.

Logica contracta. 3rd ed. Duisburg, Germany: Cunradi, 1670. With editions in 1683, 1701, 1702, 1711, 1737, and 1721. There might have been a first edition plus a second edition in 1659. The *Logica contracta* is also printed with adaptations of Clauberg's works, such as *Ontosophia, quae vulgo metaphysica vocatur, notis perpetuis in philosophiae et theologiae studiosorum usum illustrata, a Joh. Henrico Suicero. In calce annexa est Claubergii logica contracta* (Zurich: Gessner, 1694).

Unterschied zwischen der cartesianischen und der sonst in den Schulen gebraüchlichen Philosophie. Duisburg, Germany: Wyngaerden, 1658. Dutch translation, Nijmegen: Van Hervelt, 1658. The work is best known in a Latin version, *Differentia inter Cartesianam et alias in Scholis usitatam Philosophiam conscripta.…* (Groningen, Netherlands: Edzardi, 1680) with another edition in 1681.

Paraphrasis in Renati Descartes meditationes de prima Philosophia. In quibus Dei existentia, et Animae humanae à Corpore distinctio demonstrantur. Duisburg, Germany: Wyngaerden, 1658, with another edition in 1668. Dutch translation, 1683.

Ars etymologica Teutonem e philosophiae fontibus derivata; id est, via Germanicarum vocum & origines & praestantiam detegendi, cum plurium, tum harum Vernunft, Suchen, Außspruch exemplis. Duisburg, Germany: Asendorf, 1663.

Physica, quibus rerum corporearum vis & natura … explicantur. Amsterdam: Elzevier, 1664.

Theologorum academiae Duisbergensis Johannis Claubergii et Martini Hundii disputationes selectae, quibus controversiae fidei adversus omnis generis adversarios. Duisburg, Germany: Haius, 1665.

Chilias thesium ad philosophiam naturalem pertinentium … disputanda in Academia Duisburgensi. Groningen, Netherlands: Cöllen, 1668.

Dictata physica privata, id est physica contracta seu theses physicae, commentario perpetuo explicatae. Frankfurt: Ilsner, 1681. With another edition in 1689.

Opera omnia philosophica. Edited by Johannes Theodor Schalbruch. 2 vols. Amsterdam: Blaeu, 1691. With another edition in 1710. Reprint, Hildesheim: Olms, 1968. (Contains *Physica Contracta; Disputationes Physicae; Theoria Corporum Viventium; Metaphysica de Ente, cum Notis; Paraphrasis in Meditationes Cartesii; Notae breves in Cartesii Principia Philosophiae: nunc primum editae; Exercitationes Centum de Cognitione Dei et Nostri; Logica vetus et nova; Logica contracta; Defensio Cartesiana; Dubitatio Cartesiana; Differentia Cartesianam inter & Vulgarem Philosophiam; Exercitationes & Epistolae Joh. Claubergii & Tob. Andreae varii argumentis, nunc primum editae;* plus an *Index locupletissimus* and a *Vita* of Clauberg by Henricus Christianus Henninus.)

WORKS ABOUT CLAUBERG

Balz, Albert G. A. *Cartesian Studies.* New York: Columbia University Press, 1951.

Bohatec, Joseph. *Die Cartesianische Scholastik in der Philosophie und Theologie der reformierten Dogmatik des 17. Jahrhunderts.* Leipzig, Germany: A. Deichert, 1912.

Brosch, Pius. *Die Ontologie des Johannes Clauberg. Eine historische Würdigung und eine Analyse Ihrer Probleme.* Greifswald, Germany: E. Hartmann, 1926.

Dibon, Paul. *L'enseignement philosophique dans les universités néerlandaises à l'époque pré-cartésienne.* Leiden, Netherlands: s.n., 1954.

Dibon, Paul. *Regards sur la Hollande du Siècle d'Or.* Naples: Vivarium, 1990.

Müller, Hermann. *Johannes Clauberg und seine Stellung im Cartesianismus.* Jena, Germany: H. Pohle, 1891.

Thijssen-Schoute, C. Louise. *Nederlands Cartesianisme.* Amsterdam: Noord-Hollandse Uitgeversmaatschappij, 1954.

Verbeek, Theo. *Descartes and the Dutch: Early Reactions to Cartesian Philosophy, 1637–1650.* Carbondale: Southern Illinois University Press, 1992.

Verbeek, Theo, ed. *Johannes Clauberg (1622–1665) and Cartesian Philosophy in the Seventeenth Century.* Dordrecht, Netherlands: Kluwer, 1999.

Weier, Winfried. *Die Stellung des Johannes Clauberg in der Philosophie*. Mainz, Germany: Johannes Gutenberg-Universität, 1960.

Wundt, Max. *Die deutsche Schulmetaphysik des 17. Jahrhunderts*. Tübingen, Germany: Mohr (Siebeck), 1939.

Roger Ariew (2005)

CLEANTHES

(c. 331–330 BCE–c. 230–229 BCE)

Cleanthes (sometimes referred to as Cleanthes of Assos) was the second head of the Stoic school. Ancient biographical information is found in Diogenes Laërtius's *Lives of the Philosophers* (7. 168-176) and in Philodemus's history of Stoicism (columns 18-19). Born in 331–330 BCE, in Asia Minor, he came to Athens in 281–280. He took over leadership of the school on the death of its founder, Zeno of Citium, in 262–261 and held that position until his own death in 230–229. The most important contemporary Stoic was Ariston of Chios, against whom Cleanthes defended the version of Zeno's legacy that became standard, insisting on the vital importance of logic and physics as well as ethics. His own student and successor, Chrysippus, maintained this integrated system. Cleanthes also defended Stoic epistemology against the skepticism of the academic Arcesilaus.

Cleanthes was a prolific author in every area of philosophy. He wrote four books of interpretation of Heraclitus, a defense of Zeno's natural philosophy, and works on the interpretation of poetry and myth, which probably aimed to show that ancient wisdom supported Stoicism. He is now better known for the surviving portions of his philosophical poetry, which includes thirty-nine lines of his *Hymn to Zeus* and four lines on the topic of fate. In physics he wrote on the basic principles (active and passive, God and matter), on cosmogony (a cyclical recreation of the cosmos punctuated by recurring conflagrations of all matter), and on cosmology (with a particular emphasis on the role of the sun as the organizing principle). In theology he is important for his theory about the origins of the conception of God reported in book two of Cicero's *On the Nature of the Gods* and other more dialectical arguments reported by Sextus Empiricus.

Cleanthes' response to the Master Argument of Diodorus Cronus was to hold (1) that there are possibilities which neither are nor will be true and (2) that the impossible does not follow from the possible; but (3) to deny that every past truth is necessary, thereby perhaps avoiding an excessively necessitarian version of his determinism. He was a materialist, holding that anything that causes or is caused must be material, but followed Zeno in invoking incorporeal predicates as necessary features of a causal account of material interaction. He may have been the first to use the term *lekton* ("sayable") for such items. He wrote several works on dialectic, logic, and epistemology, but ultimately his contribution in this area was eclipsed by that of his brilliant successor Chrysippus.

Like all Stoics he held that the soul is a material stuff, a warm, breathy substance capable of perception and intelligence; he invoked the authority of Heraclitus particularly for his psychology. One argument for the physical nature of the soul was the heritability of psychological traits as well as corporeal characteristics. Cleanthes held that the soul survived the death of the person but only until the next conflagration; postmortem survival of personal traits seems not to have been envisaged.

In ethics he held that living according to nature is equivalent to living virtuously and took a particularly strong anti-hedonistic stance, using parables and images to dramatize the starkness of the choices one must make in planning one's life. He held the controversial view that in planning one's life one must look only to cosmic nature rather than to any more limited nature (such as that of the species or the individual), a position that coheres with his theological and cosmological views. He wrote extensively on practical ethics, but held that the norms applicable specifically to individuals in their social roles must be based on general philosophical principles. He held a strong version of the unity of virtues, maintaining that it is a single disposition (called "strength" and "power" rather than "health") manifested as different virtues (such as courage and justice) according to the circumstances where it is applied. Virtue is a cognitive state consisting of the secure and irreversible knowledge of doctrines and factors relevant to decision making. Hence it is a permanent trait once achieved.

His psychology is often thought to have had a dualistic character because Galen, perhaps following Posidonius, exploited Cleanthes' writings when arguing against the monistic views of Chrysippus. It would, however, be a mistake to infer dualistic psychology from the fact that Cleanthes dramatized a debate between reason and emotion in a poem, no doubt for protreptic purposes. In all areas of his philosophy Cleanthes was committed to the main lines of Stoic orthodoxy as set down by his master Zeno.

See also Arcesilaus; Aristo of Chios; Chrysippus; Stoicism; Zeno of Citium.

Bibliography

H. Dörrie. *"Kleanthes" Real-Enzyklopedie der Altertumswissenschaft.* Suppl.-Bd. 1970 XII : Nachtr. 1705–1709.

Dorandi, T., ed. *Filodemo Storia dei filosofi: La stoà da Zenone a Panezio.* Leiden: Brill, 1994.

Guérard, C. "Cléanthe d'Assos." In *Dictionnaire des Philosophes Antiques.* Vol. 2, ed. R. Goulet. Paris: Éditions du Centre national de la recherche scientifique, 1989–2003.

Brad Inwood (2005)

CLEMENT OF ALEXANDRIA

(c. 150–c. 213)

Clement of Alexandria (full Latin name, Titus Flavius Clemens), the Christian theologian of the Alexandrian school, was born of pagan parents, probably in Athens. Clement learned from several teachers in the Mediterranean world before he came to Alexandria, where he studied under the Christian philosopher Pantaenus, a converted Stoic who was the head of the catechetical school. Clement remained in Alexandria from 175 to 202, writing and teaching, until he fled during the persecution of the emperor Septimius Severus. He died in Palestine.

Alexandria's heritage of learning, culture, syncretism, and religious mystery may be seen in his writing. His three major works form a trilogy that leads from paganism to mature Christianity. In the *Protrepticus* (Exhortation) he attacks the absurdities of pagan deities and exhorts his readers to turn to Christianity. In the *Paedagogus* (Tutor) he instructs Christians in the good life. In his chief work, the unfinished *Stromateis* (Patchwork), he sets down his philosophical opinions in unsystematic notes—"Gnostic notes concerning the true philosophy." This work, which represents the final stage of instruction, includes much material that he had learned from his teachers but hesitated to write about because of its difficult and sacred nature. He regards obscurity, compression of style, and haphazard arrangement as safeguards against the abuse of sophistry. Clement used the word *gnostic* because he wanted to show that there was a true Christian *gnosis,* or knowledge, which developed out of faith and which was better than the boasted knowledge of the heretical Gnostics. Gnosticism was especially strong in Alexandria. Clement put forward an attractive alternative to it and attacked what he considered to be its peculiar tenets of esoteric knowledge, dualism, and ethical determinism. Knowledge, he said, grows out of faith and is not distinct from it. There is one God who made all things. Men are free to choose the way they will go.

Clement wrote against the background of Middle Platonism, of Antiochus of Ascalon, Maximus of Tyre, Albinus, and Numenius, whose thought was governed by the problem of defining the relation between the one and the one-many, and of deriving the latter from the former. The difference between a one and a one-many, or between simple and complex unity, is like the difference between the unity of a pinpoint and the unity of a spider's web. In Middle Platonism these two unities were developed into divine entities. Simple unity is divine and transcendent, while complex unity is divine and immanent. Clement was influenced by the Alexandrian Jewish Platonist Philo, for whom God is a simple, bare unity and the Logos an all-embracing cosmic whole. Clement's thought is governed by the pattern of simple and complex unity; and his accounts of God, goodness, and truth are expressed in these terms.

God is the transcendent one, a simple unity, the ultimate first principle and cause of all things. The categories of logic cannot be applied to him. "Nor are any parts to be ascribed to him, for the one is indivisible." God cannot properly be named. The good names we give him are supports to our minds to stop us from erring. Taken separately, these names do not say what God is like, but together they show his power. While God cannot be known, the Son, or the Logos, is wisdom, knowledge, and truth. He unites in himself the world of Platonic forms, or "powers," as they are also called in later Platonism. "The Son is not simply one thing as one thing nor many things as parts, but one thing as all things. All things come from him. For he is the circle of all the powers rolled into one and united." Within this unity of the Son the individual believer is saved. Faith is union in him, while disbelief is separation, estrangement, and division. Paganism is wrong because it multiplies the nature of divinity, and Marcion, the Christian heretic, is wrong because he divides the supreme God from the Creator of the world, making two Gods instead of one.

God's goodness is perfect and unique. God does not prevent evil and suffering from taking place, but when they do, he turns them to good account. He may use suffering as a form of correction for sinners. After death, imperfect souls may be sanctified by an intelligent non-material fire. The complex goodness of men is always assimilation to God—growing like him by participation in his goodness. Clement constantly refers to Plato's statement in the *Theaetetus* concerning assimilation to God. All men, says Clement, receive the image of God at their birth and all may then, as they choose, become assimilated to him and receive his likeness. In the *Paedagogus,*

Clement gives detailed instruction for Christian behavior. From Plato came the emphasis on self-knowledge, and the conception of evil as ignorance and virtue as knowledge. Virtue comes through discipline and the pursuit of goodness, without thought of ulterior gain. The harmony of the soul is aided by the harmony of the body. From Aristotle, Clement draws the notion of virtue as the fulfillment of man's function and the achievement of his end. This fulfillment is found in pursuing the mean between extremes and in possessing right reason. Clement draws heavily on Stoic ethics, commending what is in accord with nature and in harmony with reason. There is a class of things intermediate between good and evil. One should recognize the things that are in one's power and the things which are not, and avoid being dominated by one's irrational passions.

Clement speaks of truth in two ways. The simple elements of Christianity are true, and heresy is to be rejected as false. Truth is one and unique, powerful and strong in delivering men from error. It comes from God and is preserved within the tradition of the church. Second, Clement speaks of truth as including all that is consistent with basic Christian truth. This truth is a whole composed of many parts. It is one body from which each of the philosophical sects has torn a limb, or part, falsely imagining it to be the whole of truth. The many parts must be brought together, so that the perfect Logos, the truth, may be known. The truth of philosophy was partial, but real. It was for the Greeks, as the Law was for the Jews, a schoolmaster to bring them to Christ. Clement shared with others the quaint notion that the Greeks stole their ideas from the Hebrews.

Faith is an act not a process. Faith is the acceptance from God of an indemonstrable first principle from which all other truth may be deduced. It is a judgment of the soul, an Epicurean preconception, and a Stoic assent. Knowledge (*gnosis*) is both logical and spiritual, joining things together either by logical reasoning or by spiritual vision. The eighth book of the *Stromateis* is a notebook of logic composed of materials from various sources. It deals with demonstration and definition in an Aristotelian way, gives a Stoic refutation of the skeptical suspension of judgment (that is, if one must suspend judgment, then one should suspend judgment concerning suspense of judgment), and treats of cause, using both Stoic and Aristotelian terms. Causes may be original, sufficient, cooperating, and necessary. Spiritual knowledge is growth in Christ, awareness of God's universal presence, and union with him in love. Symbolism reveals hidden connections and points to unity. Knowledge is always a complex unity, while faith is a simple unity.

Clement achieved the first real synthesis of classical philosophy and Christianity. The Apologists had used particular ideas to bridge the gap between philosophy and Christianity. In Justin's writings, for example, God is described in terms of the Platonic ineffable being, and the divine reason implanted in men is expounded along Stoic lines; but there is no comprehensive conceptual framework that enables these and other ideas to modify one another. Clement's synthesis was developed by Origen, and the result was the theology of the fourth-century Greek Fathers and of Augustine.

See also Patristic Philosophy; Platonism and the Platonic Tradition.

Bibliography

TEXTS AND TRANSLATIONS

Stählin, Otto, ed. *Clemens Alexandrinus. Die griechischen christlichen Schriftsteller der ersten drei Jahrhunderte.* Vol. 39.2. Leipzig: Hinrichs, 1936. Vols. 12, 15, 17, 39.1, revised by Ludwig Früchtel and Ursula Treu. Berlin: Akademie-Verlag, 1970–1985.

By various hands, with parallel French translation: *Sources Chrétiennes,* Vols. 2b (*Protrepticus*), 23 (extracts from Theodotus), 30, 38 (*Stromata* 1–2), 70, 108, 158 (*Pedagogue*), 278–279, 428, 446, 463 (*Stromata* 4–7). Paris: Éditions du Cerf, 1965–2004.

Wilson, William. In *The Ante-Nicene Fathers: Translations of the Writings of the Fathers down to A.D. 325,* Vol. 2, edited by Alexander Roberts and James Donaldson, revised by A. Cleveland Coxe. Grand Rapids, MI: Eerdmans, 1951.

FURTHER READING

Behr, John. *Asceticism and Anthropology in Irenaeus and Clement of Alexandria.* Oxford: Oxford University Press, 2000.

Clark, Elizabeth A. *Clement's Use of Aristotle. The Aristotelian Contribution to Clement of Alexandria's Refutation of Gnosticism = Texts and Studies in Religion* 1. New York and Toronto: Edwin Mellen, 1977.

Lilla, Salvatore R. C. *Clement of Alexandria: A Study in Christian Platonism and Gnosticism.* London: Oxford University Press, 1971.

Osborn, Eric F. *The Philosophy of Clement of Alexandria.* Cambridge, U.K.: Cambridge University Press, 1957.

E. F. Osborn (1967)

Bibliography updated by G. R. Boys-Stones (2005)

CLIFFORD, WILLIAM KINGDON

(1845–1879)

A English mathematician and philosopher, William Kingdon Clifford was born in Exeter, the son of a justice of the peace. At the age of fifteen he went to Kings College, London. There he gained a minor scholarship to Trinity College, Cambridge, to which he went in 1863. He began to exhibit powers of originality in mathematics, publishing a number of mathematical papers during the year in which he first entered Cambridge.

At the university Clifford distinguished himself not only by his intellect but also by his singular character. As one of the most prominent undergraduates, he was soon invited to join the Apostles, an exclusive Cambridge club made up of the twelve most distinguished undergraduates of the time. Here he exhibited some of that breadth of learning and clarity of mind for which he was to be noted all his life. It appears that he was highly concerned about religious questions because he studied Thomas Aquinas and learnedly supported the Catholic position. Later, however, he became an agnostic and turned against religion; Herbert Spencer and Charles Darwin became the most important influences upon his thinking in many areas.

Clifford was elected a fellow of Trinity in 1868. In that year he began the practice of giving public lectures, a source from which most of his published work stems. He participated in a scientific expedition, which was wrecked off the coast of Catania, Sicily. In 1870 he was appointed professor of applied mathematics at University College, London. Soon after, he became a member of the most distinguished intellectual society of the day, the Metaphysical Society, as well as of the London Mathematical Society. Tragically, his life was drawing to a close, for he had contracted tuberculosis. His condition worsened, until by 1878 it was evident that the disease was far advanced. In 1879 he traveled south to try to counteract the disease, but he died on March 3 of that year.

During Clifford's lifetime he published only a textbook on dynamics and some scattered technical and nontechnical papers based on his lectures. It remained for a number of his friends to gather together his work. H. J. S. Smith edited the mathematical papers, F. Pollock the philosophical ones. The young Karl Pearson edited and completed his popular work on science, *The Common Sense of the Exact Sciences.*

SCIENTIFIC EPISTEMOLOGY

Clifford's philosophical views must be placed within the context of several major influences upon his thought: the Kantian frame in epistemology, the Riemannian frame in geometry, and the Darwinian frame in biology. On the basis of these and other influences, Clifford constructed a scientific epistemology and attempted to construct a scientific metaphysic. A discussion of his epistemology is first in order, since out of it grew his metaphysics. Clifford conceived of knowledge as a biological response to the world. Its structure, therefore, is determined by that adjustment. Nevertheless, any analysis of knowledge as such reveals that within it the form and the content of knowledge are distinguishable from each other. Immanuel Kant believed that he had determined a method to make this distinction in all cases. Clifford, taking his cue from Kant, believed that he too could make this distinction, but in a way that took into account the ultimately biological character of knowledge. He thought that an analysis of the foundations of science, and in particular of the axioms of geometry, would reveal that these axioms are forms of experience in the life of any particular individual. Thus, since the biological adaptation of the race has crystallized three-dimensional Euclidean space, this spatial framework has become the one in which individuals see spatially locatable objects. Clifford went even further in this direction by claiming that such a construction is ultimately a growth of experience which has been transformed into neural capacities. Thus, Clifford conceived of the form-content distinction of knowledge as one relative to the biological development of the race. What is at one time the content of experience is later, through a biological process, transformed into a form of experience.

The principles of geometry and arithmetic serve, for individuals, to structure their experience. They are or correspond to ways in which our sense data are "spatially" or "numerically" organized. Their logical status is therefore closely akin to the one that Kant assigned to them. They are a priori, for no experience is capable of verifying or falsifying them, whereas at the same time they are synthetic, since the predicate term is not contained in the subject term.

Within this framework of thought it is intelligible to discuss Clifford's concrete epistemological ideas. He offered analyses of what might be called (1) perceptual statements, (2) geometric, arithmetical, and even physical principles, and (3) belief statements in general.

PERCEPTUAL STATEMENTS. In various essays Clifford offered an analysis of perceptual statements concerning objects, persons, and the spatial aspects of objects and persons. In general, he refused to admit a phenomenalist analysis of such statements. In all cases some ideal conception, be it of "an eject" (a technical term that will be explained later) or of "a form of experience"—in other words, a conception which is not itself definable in terms of a set of sense experiences—enters into the meaning of the statement, either explicitly or implicitly. This is true with the qualification that Clifford sometimes suggested that statements about physical objects are reducible to statements about sense experiences.

GEOMETRIC, ARITHMETICAL, AND PHYSICAL PRINCIPLES. The analysis that Clifford provided of the several kinds of statements differed somewhat from one another, and it would be wise to examine them in sequence. As has already been indicated, the statements of geometry and arithmetic state universal and therefore formal characteristics of experience. In the case of geometric statements, Clifford asserted that they are universally true about the objects of our perceptions, in the sense that all perceptions of spatial relationships must conform to them. Furthermore, they are necessary, since the perceptions compatible with the negations of such statements are impossible. Clifford contended that Kant had established the necessary properties of space by a subjective method, a method of introspection, whereas Clifford attempted to demonstrate such properties by a consideration of the neurological bases of perception. The limits of what is perceptible, given man's neurological structure, were, for Clifford, what is known a priori to the individual, while those perceptions whose contradictions are not imperceivable, again given man's neurological structure, are known a posteriori. Clifford proceeded to demonstrate, to his satisfaction, that at this level of analysis both Euclidean and non-Euclidean space are compatible with the neurological structure of perception, and that it is a matter of the general explicatory value of a geometric theory as to which of the various geometries is to be accepted. Of course, man's neurological structure evolves over time, so that what is necessary at one time is not necessary at another—this indicates that Clifford used the term *necessary,* in this context, in a relative sense.

Clifford's analysis of arithmetical statements differs somewhat from his analysis of geometric statements. He thought that their validity depended upon several factors: (1) the tautological character of certain parts of language, (2) the acceptance of a general principle of the uniformity of nature of the kind that J. S. Mill suggested, and (3) the acceptance of an analysis of arithmetical operations in terms of the physical operation of counting. Numerals are assigned in a one-to-one correspondence with standard sets of objects, each set containing one member more than the preceding set. The operations of addition, multiplication, and, by implication, subtraction and division are next defined in terms of the physical operations of juxtaposition of sets of objects. Clifford then claimed that if the meaning of "distinct objects" were granted, along with the assumption that all objects maintain their identity through space and time (the uniformity of nature), then the laws of arithmetic can be seen to hold for all objects. On the basis of the natural numbers, he sketched the development of the more complex number systems.

Clifford did not have much to say about the status of physical laws and theories, except to suggest that there are some principles of physics that are, like the principles of geometry and arithmetic, rules for the ordering of sense impressions.

BELIEF STATEMENTS. Clifford's examination of the basis of belief in the natural sciences led him to a more general analysis of belief. Indeed, it was this general analysis of belief and the agnostic and antireligious conclusion to which it led that occasioned great opposition on the part of William James and others. Clifford claimed that no statement is worthy of belief unless all the possible evidence points to the truth of the statement. He recognized that in practice it is impossible to have available all the possible evidence about the truth or falsity of a proposition. Failure of memory, the expenses of collecting information, and a host of other factors contribute to this impossibility. But he claimed that an acceptance of the principle that similar causes have similar effects (another version of the principle of the uniformity of nature) permits our acceptance of many beliefs in cases where the standard of all possible evidence is not met. Such a principle permits an inductive inference from known facts to unknown ones, and thus permits us to make up for evidence we do not possess. These ideas are contained in his essay "The Ethics of Belief," to which James's famous essay "The Will to Believe" is a reply. In that essay James claimed that a belief is worthy of acceptance in some cases where there is no empirical evidence either for or against the content of the belief. And this criterion permitted James to believe in the existence of God.

SCIENTIFIC METAPHYSICS

Clifford's epistemological views were the occasion for his speculative metaphysical ideas. He had been wrestling with the problem of whether the existent world is wholly phenomenal in character or whether there are entities of a nonphenomenal character which go to make it up. In earlier essays—for example, "The Philosophy of Pure Sciences"—he inclined toward a purely phenomenalist view, but in his more mature and well-known essay "On the Nature of Things-in-Themselves" he reversed his former stand. Not all existence is phenomenal in character. He was clear, for example, that the ego cannot be analyzed in purely phenomenal terms. Clifford thus postulated the existence of what he termed "ejects" as well as of phenomenal "objects." An eject is distinguished from an object in the following way: An object can be an object of *my* consciousness, an eject is something *outside* my consciousness. Thus, another's ego (and this holds for all persons) is an eject; it is never in my consciousness. Clifford postulated that there are nonpersonal as well as personal entities that are ejects. The elements of ejects are themselves what Clifford called feelings. They are constituents of everything, he claimed, since the fact that there is a continuity of forms in nature gives assurance that, at least to some degree, any entity in nature possesses the same qualities that all others have. Since feelings are elements of consciousness, all entities therefore have this aspect of consciousness to a certain extent, although it is only to more complex entities that we ascribe consciousness. The elementary entities that are called "feelings" were considered by Clifford to be absolute existents and therefore things-in-themselves. Clifford then named these elementary entities mind-stuff, since they participate somehow in the character of the mental. Their necessarily incomplete representation in the mind of man is what is known as the material world. There exists a complex mirroring relation—indeed, Clifford used the image of two reflecting mirrors—between the external world and its representation in knowledge. Thus, Clifford's speculative metaphysic ultimately postulated a Spinozistic world in which the mental and physical are really two different ways of looking at the same world. Another possible interpretation of his thought is that all existence is ultimately infused with a psychic aspect, that is, that panpsychism is the most correct view of reality.

In conclusion, it is worthwhile mentioning several areas of thought in which Clifford was ahead of his time:

(1) Clifford recognized the fact that scientific laws are always "practically inexact." By this notion he wished to point out that a scientific law is never exactly confirmed by the evidence for it but rather is confirmed within the limits of experimental error. A law is accepted on the basis of experimental evidence even if that experimental evidence does not exactly coincide with what, on the basis of deductions from the law, one might expect to be confirming evidence. This is so simply because all measurement of evidence in modern scientific practice involves taking into account errors of measurement, and such errors of measurement must be "factored out" before a definite conclusion is reached as to the relevance of the evidence.

(2) Clifford, in the brief note "On the Space-Theory of Matter," declared himself to be in the geometric tradition that holds that the determination of the truth or falsity of geometrical axioms is empirical. Clifford saw that through a change in the basic assumptions of microgeometry (geometry of the infinitesimally small) he could work out a system of geometry and physics that would clear up the anomalies in physical theory that existed in his day. He saw that a reformulation of microgeometry in non-Euclidean terms could achieve this result, and in this respect he anticipated, at least in part, Albert Einstein's program. He never, however, carried through this program on his own; he merely suggested that such a program was feasible.

(3) Clifford showed the possibility, at least in principle, of constructing a wholly empirical geometry in the following special sense: Geometry is considered to be a set of statements about the relations between geometrical objects such as points, lines, planes, and volumes. These geometrical objects and relations, however, are themselves characterized in a completely empirical way, not as ideal objects, as they are usually characterized in most treatments of geometry. That is, they are identified with the physical objects or aspects of physical objects. The principles of geometry are then empirical statements whose truth or falsity is a matter of observation. This point of view is close to a geometric operationalism. Clifford's account of it is found in his book *The Common Sense of the Exact Sciences.*

See also Darwin, Charles Robert; Einstein, Albert; Epistemology; Geometry; James, William; Kant, Immanuel; Mill, John Stuart; Pearson, Karl; Perception; Thomas Aquinas, St.

Bibliography

For works by Clifford, see *The Common Sense of the Exact Sciences,* edited by Karl Pearson (New York: Appleton, 1885), reissued with a preface by Bertrand Russell and a new introduction by James R. Newman (New York: Dover, 1955);

Lectures and Essays, edited by F. Pollock, 2 vols. (London: Macmillan, 1879); and *Mathematical Papers,* edited by H. J. Smith (London: Macmillan, 1882).

For literature on Clifford, see George S. Fullerton, *A System of Metaphysics* (New York: Macmillan, 1904), which contains a criticism of Clifford's theory of mind-stuff; and A. S. Eddington, *The Nature of the Physical World* (Cambridge, U.K.: Cambridge University Press, 1929).

Howard E. Smokler (1967)

COCKBURN, CATHARINE TROTTER

(1679?–1749)

Catharine Trotter, according to her editor and biographer, was born on August 16, 1679, the younger of two daughters of David Trotter, a captain in the Royal Navy and his wife, Sarah Ballenden, of a well-connected Scottish family. Trotter's father died of the plague while on a voyage that was to have made his fortune. Instead, his family was forced to survive on an irregularly disbursed pension from the reigning monarch. Trotter was educated at home, and perhaps largely self-educated, although she seems to have taught herself French and Latin. She was a precocious writer, publishing a novella at a young age, followed by poems, and ultimately five plays, four appearing between 1695 and 1701 and the last in 1706, all of which achieved a certain renown.

In 1701 Trotter began to live with her married sister in Salisbury, where she remained until her own marriage in 1708. In Salisbury Trotter joined the circle surrounding Gilbert Burnet (1643–1715), the bishop of Salisbury, which included his wife, the devotional writer Elizabeth Burnet (1661–1709), and his cousin, Thomas Burnet of Kemnay (1656–1729), a lively correspondent of Trotter's. It was during her time in Salisbury that Trotter's theological and philosophical interests began to manifest themselves. In 1702 she published *A Defense of Mr. Locke's Essay*, a reply to criticisms of John Locke by yet another Thomas Burnet (c. 1635–1715), and in 1707 *A Discourse concerning a Guide in Controversies*, the fruits of her struggles with Roman Catholicism, justifying her decision to return to the Church of England.

In 1708, she married the clergyman Patrick Cockburn (1678–1749), and her scholarly interests were for some time suspended while she struggled to raise a family of four in somewhat reduced circumstances, brought on when her husband lost his curacy, on finding himself unable to swear the oath of abjuration on the ascension of George I (1660–1727) to the throne. In 1726 Cockburn was able to reconcile himself with this oath and became first the rector at Aberdeen and then the vicar of Long Worsley in Northumberland, where the family was still living at the time of Catherine's death in 1749.

With the restoration of the family fortunes, Cockburn's philosophical interests also revived, and in 1726 she published *A Letter to Dr. Holdsworth.* While she did not resume publishing until close to the end of her life, first bringing out *Remarks upon Some Writers in the Controversy concerning the Foundation of Moral Virtue and Moral Obligation* in 1743 and then *Remarks upon the Principles and Reasonings of Dr. Rutherforth's Essay* in 1747, it is clear from letters written throughout this period, particularly those to a niece, Anne Arbuthnot, that Cockburn maintained a lively reading program and developed her intellectual interests in correspondence.

Cockburn's works were collected by Thomas Birch and published after her death, and include, in addition to her published philosophical work, several hitherto unpublished pieces, a play, and a fascinating collection of letters. Some doubts have been raised about the dates of Cockburn's life supplied by Birch, stimulated by a letter to G. Burnet written in 1707, in which she reports the marriage of a son and the birth of a grandchild. Since, according to Birch's reckoning, this would make Trotter a mere twenty-seven, it has been suggested that her birth date should be pushed back to accommodate the birth of a son and grandson. There are some limits, however, on the extent to which Trotter's age in 1706 can be adjusted, since according to Birch's account, she was seventy-one at the time or her death and was publishing close to that time. An alternative possibility is that Trotter was not in fact the birthmother of the son she mentions casually to Birch.

Each of Cockburn's works takes roughly the same form, that of a loosely organized commentary on some other work, often itself critical in nature. Her earlier work defends Locke against various attacks, and her later work is written in defense of Samuel Clarke.

Her presentation then can appear somewhat diffuse and disorganized. In her early defense of Locke against Thomas Burnet, for example, she considers three different criticisms: that Locke's rejection of innate moral principles leaves him with no resources on which to ground one's knowledge of moral principles, that Locke provides no way in which he can establish God's veracity, and, finally, that an account of personal identity based like Locke's on consciousness instead of substance does not provide grounds for personal immortality.

There are, however, some common threads that tend to reappear in much of her work. In particular, Cockburn is very much embroiled in eighteenth-century attempts to walk a middle ground between deism and voluntarism. Her concern is to argue that human beings can, by means of their intellectual resources, derive an understanding of moral concepts based on their nature as sensitive, rational, and social beings. It is through this complex understanding of ourselves that we are able to work out what is suitable or fit for us. Cockburn argues that the complexity of our nature does not limit our grasp of what is fit for us simply to what is pleasant or what is in our self-interest, but that we can derive a full sense of our moral obligation from our nature as rational, social beings. Therefore, there is no need to turn to an otherwise unmotivated appeal to God's decrees to account for the full range of our moral obligations. Cockburn also wants to maintain that, while our understanding of the nature of these obligations rests on our understanding of ourselves, it is nevertheless God's decrees that give these principles the force of law. But since we know that God is good, and we understand, from our own case, what it is to be good, we also know that God would not require of us actions that are, as we understand it, irrational. Her position is designed to guard against both the view that human morality is entirely independent of religion and against the view that our obligations have only a religious and no rational support.

See also Locke, John.

Bibliography

WORKS BY COCKBURN

The Works of Mrs. Catharine Cockburn, Theological, Moral, Dramatic and Poetical. Several of Them Now First Printed. Revised and Published, with an Account of the Life of the Author. 2 vols. Compiled by Thomas Birch. London: J. and P. Knapton, 1751.

WORKS ABOUT COCKBURN

Atherton, Margaret. "Women Philosophers in Early Modern England." In *A Companion to Early Modern Philosophy*, edited by Steven Nadler, 404–422. Malden, MA: Blackwell, 2002

Bolton, Martha Brandt. "Some Aspects of the Philosophical Work of Catharine Trotter." *Journal of the History of Philosophy* 31 (4) (October 1993): 565–578.

Broad, Jacqueline. "Catharine Trotter Cockburn." In *Women Philosophers of the Seventeenth Century*, 141–165. New York: Cambridge University Press, 2002.

Nuovo, Victor. "Catharine Cockburn." In *The Dictionary of Seventeenth-Century British Philosophers*, edited by Andrew Pyle. Bristol, U.K.: Thoemmes Press, 2000.

Waite, Mary Ellen. "Catharine Trotter Cockburn." In *A History of Women Philosophers. Vol. 3, Modern Women Philosophers, 1600–1900*, edited by Mary Ellen Waite, 101–125. Dordrecht, Netherlands: Kluwer Academic, 1991.

Margaret Atherton (2005)

CODE, LORRAINE

(1937–)

Lorraine Code is a Canadian philosopher with interests in epistemology, feminist epistemology, and the politics of knowledge. She is Distinguished Research Professor of Philosophy at York University, where she is also appointed to the Graduate Programs in Women's Studies and Social and Political Thought. Code has authored five books and numerous articles, and has edited five collections. From 1999 to 2001, she served as a Canadian Council Research Fellow.

Code describes her work as an interrogation of local and global politics of knowledge that harm people and nature. She argues, for example, that traditional philosophical epistemologies foster the exploitation of people and nature by Western sciences and institutions because they include tenets that obscure the role of social and political relations in the formation of knowledge. Recently Code has undertaken the constructive project of developing an alternative, "ecologically modeled" epistemology that, she maintains, avoids the failings of traditional epistemologies.

Code's critical and constructive projects consistently focus on the ethical dimensions of knowledge making and epistemological accounts of it. In *Epistemic Responsibility* (1987) she argues that epistemic responsibility is not exhausted by "purely epistemological" standards. Code contends that an emphasis in epistemology on virtue and responsibility would result in attention to the social contexts of knowing, including the relevance of social relations and social roles to what is recognized as knowledge. Such analyses would, in turn lead, to more robust notions of epistemic responsibility.

A concern with the ethical implications of epistemology is also central in *What Can She Know?* (1991). Here Code focuses on the "alignments" in "mainstream epistemology": on one hand, characteristics its values (for example, objectivity and rationality) and, on the other hand, shifting conceptions of masculinity. Code argues that these alignments contribute to institutional knowledge (for example, in the sciences and law) and to social institutions that undermine women's abilities to act as knowers while rendering invisible the politics of gender at work. She uses these alignments in a more general argument that subjective factors inform all knowledge claims and epistemic ideals. From this perspective, theories of knowledge that obscure the role of such factors are not just factually flawed, but they are also ethically flawed because they underwrite the continuation of a form of subjectivity that, although changing overtime, has consistently put women at a disadvantage. Not surprisingly, when Code poses the question in this work of whether a distinctly feminist epistemology is desirable, she is not enthusiastic. She holds that efforts to achieve universality, which she here attributes to epistemology in general, are at odds with the attention to particularity, context, and other aspects of subjectivity that her arguments call for.

In *Rhetorical Spaces: Essays on Gendered Locations* (1995), Code undertakes the kind of fine-grained studies she recommends. Her essays explore cases in which specific and rhetorically and socially constructed locations—including those of marginalization and power—have an impact on who is deemed credible and what counts as knowledge. In one, a victim of sexual harassment seeks to reconcile her memories with conflicting accounts and to understand how trusting herself relies in part on her credibility in the eyes of others. Other essays, focusing on institutionalized knowledge such as health care, explore ways in which everyday knowledge practices are sites of social interactions that contribute to or deny credibility to various subjects and groups.

In *Ecological Thinking* (2005) and elsewhere, Code builds from her earlier work to advance a sustained argument for what she calls "an ecologically modeled" theory of knowledge. Code maintains that explanatory models in ecology are promising for a theory of knowledge precisely because they assume a mutual dependency of organisms, an interrelatedness between their well-being and features of their environment, including features that are cruel. Code argues that such models contrast sharply with the individualism and instrumentalist conceptions of rationality that characterize traditional epistemology and obscure the ethics and politics of knowledge-making practices. Incorporating these noninstrumentalist ideas into epistemology, she maintains, would result in a model that could accommodate the insights of feminist, multicultural, and postcolonial studies into precisely those dimensions of knowledge making that have been obscured by traditional epistemology.

See also Epistemology; Feminist Philosophy; Feminist Epistemology.

Bibliography

BOOKS BY CODE

Epistemic Responsibility, Dartmouth: University Press of New England, 1987.

What Can She Know: Feminist Theory and the Construction of Knowledge. Ithaca, NY: Cornell University Press, 1991.

Rhetorical Spaces: Essays on Gendered Locations. New York and London: Routledge, 1995.

Ecological Thinking. Oxford: Oxford University Press, 2005.

Feminist Philosophy: Routledge Contemporary Introductions to Philosophy. New York and London, Routledge, 2005.

EDITED COLLECTIONS

Feminist Perspectives: Philosophical Essays on Method and Morals (with Sheila Mullett et al). Toronto: University of Toronto Press, 1988.

Changing Methods: Feminists Transforming Practices (with Sandra D. Burt). Orchard Park: Broadview Press, 1995.

Encyclopedia of Feminist Theories. New York and London: Routledge, 2000.

Feminist Interpretations of Hans-Georg Gadamer. University Park: Penn State University Press, 2002.

The Sex of Knowing (with Michelle DeDoeuff et al). New York and London: Routledge, 2003.

OTHER WORKS BY CODE

"What Is Natural about Epistemology Naturalized?" *American Philosophical Quarterly* 1 (1996): 1–22.

"Feminists and Pragmatists: A Radical Future?" *Radical Philosophy* 87 (1998): 22–30.

"How to Think Globally: Stretching the Limits of Imagination." *Hypatia: A Journal of Feminist Philosophy* 2 (1998): 73–85.

"Flourishing." *Ethics and the Environment* 1 (1999): 63–72.

Lynn Hankinson Nelson (2005)

COGNITIVE SCIENCE

Cognitive science is the interdisciplinary study of mind, in which the concepts and methods of artificial intelligence (AI) are central (Boden forthcoming). The most prominent disciplines within the field are AI, artificial life (A-life), psychology, linguistics, computational neuroscience, and philosophy—especially the philosophy of mind and language. Cognitive anthropology is included too, though often goes unseen under the label of evolutionary psychology.

The many relevant subfields include robotics, whether classical, situated, or evolutionary; studies of enactive vision, where the organism's own movements (of eyes and/or body) provide crucial information for acting in the world; the psychology of human-computer interaction, including various aspects of virtual reality such as avatars; and computational theories of literature, art, music, and scientific discovery. Nonhuman minds are studied by computational ethology and neuroethology, and by A-life.

WHO IS A COGNITIVE SCIENTIST?

Not everyone working in the key disciplines is a cognitive scientist. Only those taking a computational approach to questions about mind are considered cognitive scientists.

Some AI workers, for example, are not cognitive scientists because they have no theoretical interest in human thought. Their aim is to challenge their ingenuity as computer engineers by getting a program or robot to do a task that people either cannot do or do not want to do. If hunches, or experimental evidence, about human psychology can help them achieve that goal, that is fine. But if nonhuman tricks are available, such as looking ahead in a chess game to consider all the legal possibilities for several moves, they will use them. These computer scientists are engaged in technological AI, not psychological AI. Only the latter is a proper part of cognitive science.

Even someone who does have a professional interest in human minds need not be a cognitive scientist. For instance, many social psychologists study patterns of interpersonal behavior without asking about the information processes that underlie them and make them possible. Even some cognitive psychologists insist that they are not cognitive scientists, because they follow James Gibson's (1979) affordance theory of perception—which allows for information pickup but not for information processing. (Their self-description is based on an overly narrow view of what cognitive science covers: Gibsonian insights have become prominent in various areas of cognitive science, such as enactive vision.)

Similarly, many linguists—sociolinguists and historical philologists, for instance—are not primarily concerned with just how language is generated and/or understood. But even those who do focus on these computational matters do not all agree. Chomskian linguistics, for example, was crucial in the rise of cognitive science and has deeply influenced the philosophy of mind; but non-Chomskian accounts of syntax have been developed since. In addition, theories of pragmatics have become at least as prominent as theories of syntax—and pragmatics is an aspect of situatedness, a concept of growing importance within cognitive science as a whole. As for anthropology, most anthropologists see their field as a hermeneutic enterprise, not a scientific one. They reject psychological explanations of culture in general, and computational accounts in particular.

COGNITIVE SCIENCE IS ABOUT MORE THAN COGNITION

It includes cognitive psychology, of course: the study of language, memory, perception, problem solving, and creative thinking. What is more, most research has focused on individual human adult cognition. However, other aspects of mind are studied too: motivation, emotion, choice (Dennett 1984), development, psychopathology, interpersonal phenomena, motor control, and animal psychology.

Consider emotion, for example. The role of emotion in problem solving, attitude formation, and neurosis were topics of research in AI and computational psychology in the early 1960s. But the problems were too difficult, and were largely dropped. Interest revived later, partly because of neuroscientific work on emotional intelligence and partly because of advances in the computational theory of scheduling in multigoal systems (Sloman 1993). Interdisciplinary conferences on the psychology, neuroscience, computer modeling, and philosophy of emotion blossomed at the turn of the century, when the topic became a prominent aspect of research.

Whether the focus of attention is on development or psychopathology, emotion or motor control, the prime interest for cognitive science is in the abstractly defined computational functions that generate the behavior concerned. But the neural mechanisms that implement them are often studied too. Despite the functionalist doctrine of multiple realizability, many cognitive scientists want to know how psychological functions are actually implemented in the brain. When functionalism began in the 1960s, little attention was paid to the nervous system by philosophers or AI scientists. Since the 1980s, that has been less true.

Indeed, neuroscience as such has become increasingly concerned with computational questions. On the one hand, there are theories (and computer models) of specific neural circuits doing closely specified things. For instance, cells in the retina and/or visual cortex that compute particular visual features, such as light gradients or surface textures; or cells in the female cricket's brain that enable her to discriminate the song of male crickets of the same species, and to move accordingly. On the other hand, there are broad-brush theories about the computational functions carried out by large areas of the brain, where the focus is less on specific individual cells than on general neuroanatomy: the different cell types, locations, and connections of the neurons.

DEVELOPMENTAL ISSUES

Most cognitive scientists study already established phenomena, although many include learning in their subject matter. Some, however, study—and model—mental development. And some do this because they believe that adult psychology cannot be properly understood without knowing how it developed. In short, they see the mind as an epigenetic system, deeply informed by its developmental history.

Epigenesis was stressed long ago by Conrad Waddington in biology and Jean Piaget in psychology. It is self-organized development, grounded in innate predispositions in continual dialectic interaction with the (internal and external) environment. For example, there are inborn dispositions to attend to broadly facelike stimuli, or to human speech-sounds. Once the attention is caught, learning can help develop the infant's pattern recognition and discriminatory powers. In some cases, such as face recognition, the neural mechanisms relevant at different stages have been largely identified.

An epigenetic view is not strictly environmentalist, nor strictly nativist either. Rather, it stresses the dialectical interplay between the two. Late twentieth-century work in developmental neuroscience and developmental psychology has therefore led to a radical reconceptualization of nativism (Elman et al. 1996). Some philosophers of biology have defined new accounts of self-organization and dynamical development accordingly (Oyama 1985).

WHAT IT MEANS TO SAY THAT COGNITIVE SCIENCE IS COMPUTATIONAL

Cognitive science employs computational models of mind in two senses.

First, the substantive concepts in its theories are computational. The mind is seen as some sort of computational system (just what sort is hotly disputed), and mental structure and mental processes are described accordingly (Haugeland 1997). So whereas many psychologists (and other scientists) use computers to express/clarify their theories, and especially to manipulate their experimental data, only cognitive scientists import computational ideas into their theories.

Second, computer modeling is often used to clarify and test computational theories of mind. Often, but not always, some work in cognitive science (in AI and psychology, not just in philosophy) employs computational concepts and insights, but with insufficient detail to allow programs to be written. When programming is possible, it provides several advantages. Even program failures can be scientifically illuminating, pointing out lacunae or mistakes in the theory, or fundamental limitations of the methodology being used. However, successes may be even more instructive. For if a program—or a robot—produces a given performance, one knows that it suffices to do so.

Whether real minds (or brains) use similar processes to produce equivalent performance is another matter: just because a program does something in a certain way, it does not follow that people do too. This question can be answered only by empirical evidence. Sometimes, a programmed theory models not only psychological phenomena at various levels, but also the details of their underlying neural base. In such cases, validation requires both psychological and neuroscientific evidence.

The references to computational ideas in the previous two paragraphs cover concepts rooted in two different intellectual traditions, namely, cybernetics and Turing computation. These were closely linked in the years when cognitive science began.

A seminal paper by Warren McCulloch and Walter Pitts (1943) prompted early work both in neural nets and in what is sometimes called GOFAI, or "Good Old-Fashioned AI." (It also influenced the design of the von Neumann computer.) McCulloch and Pitts integrated three key ideas of the early twentieth century: propositional logic, neuron theory, and Turing computation. They proved that anything expressible in the propositional calculus is computable, and can be mapped onto some specifiable neural net. In addition, they suggested that a fourth key idea—feedback, the core concept of cybernetics—could be defined in terms of these networks, in which case purpose and learning could be embodied in them too.

A few years later they published another paper, in which they argued that probabilistic networks are more like brains and can do things naturally that logic-based systems cannot (Pitts and McCulloch 1947). They still insisted, nevertheless, that their original, logical, account was correct in principle.

In short, the concept of computational systems is normally used within the field to cover both GOFAI and connectionism. (Some philosophers, however, restrict it to the former.) Cognitive science includes both.

Sometimes, the reason why a computational theory is not actually modeled is that suitable computer technology does not yet exist. By the same token, many advances in cognitive science have depended partly upon advances in computing technology. These include both increases in size (computing power) and new types of virtual machine, embodying forms of computation that were not possible previously.

In some cases, the core ideas had already been defined long before the technology was available to test/explore them. Parallel distributed processing, for instance, was envisaged over twenty years before computers became powerful enough for it to be implemented in interesting ways. Similarly form-generating interactive diffusion equations and cellular automata were both first defined in the 1950s, but not extensively studied until the advent of large machines and computer graphics in the late 1980s. And genetic algorithms, glimpsed in the 1950s and defined in the late 1960s, were first implemented in the 1980s. Once the technology was available, further questions arose that had not been posed before.

SOME PHILOSOPHICAL PROBLEMS

Many philosophical disputes arise within cognitive science. One dispute concerns the relative merits of the two AI approaches mentioned above: classical (symbolic) AI and connectionism, or neural networks. The latter is broadly inspired by the basic structure of the brain. (Some recent work in artificial neural networks tries to take more account of the subtleties of real neurons; even so, these models are hugely oversimplified in comparison with the real thing.) There are several types of neural networks, but the one most widely used within cognitive science—and the one of greatest interest to philosophers—is parallel distributed processing, or PDP.

Some researchers champion only one of these AI approaches, whereas others admit both because of their complementary strengths and weaknesses. Symbolic AI, or GOFAI, is better for modeling behaviors that involve hierarchical structure, advance planning, deliberation, and/or strict sequential order. The conscious, deliberative aspects of the mind are best suited to this approach. Connectionism, by contrast, is better for modeling the tacit learning and knowledge involved in pattern recognition, including the fuzzy family resemblances between instances of one and the same concept.

It does not follow that all unconscious mental processes are best modeled by PDP systems. Some psychoneural theories of action errors, including various clinical syndromes, employ hybrid (mixed) models in which the hierarchical aspects represent both conscious and unconscious processing.

INTERNAL REPRESENTATION. Another debate concerns the nature and importance of various kinds of internal representation. Connectionist representations are different from GOFAI ones, and several philosophers have argued that they are closer to the neural representations that embody concepts (Churchland 1989; Clark 1989, 1993; Cussins 1990). Computational neuroscience has described further types of representation. One example is emulator systems, which are neural mechanisms whose physical dynamics mimic the temporal changes being represented. Another, based on the anatomy of the cerebellum, is a way of representing motor behavior that is based neither on logic (GOFAI) nor on statistics (PDP), but on noneuclidean tensor geometry.

Some philosophers follow the AI community and/or the neuroscientists, in accepting that representations may take many different guises, depending on the role they have evolved to play. Others, however, argue that only formal-symbolic structures, expressed in a *language of thought*, are properly termed representations, and that only these can generate human conceptual/linguistic thought (Fodor 2000).

NATURE OF COMPUTATION. The nature of computation is a third topic of controversy (Scheutz 2002). Most philosophers define it as Alan Turing did in the 1930s—and his is still the only really clear definition. However, practicing AI scientists think of computation in a number of different ways, based on virtual machines whose properties are different from those of a Turing machine. Moreover, some people are trying to go beyond Turing computation by defining new forms of computers (hypercomputers), some—but not all—of which involve quantum computing. Some of these may turn out to be relevant to human brains, but others will not.

MEANING IN THE REAL WORLD. A fourth area of philosophical discussion focuses on whether—and if so, how—meaning (intentionality) can be grounded in the real world—and whether it can properly be attributed to programs and/or robots. Evolutionary theories of intentionality rule out GOFAI programs (as do many philosophers), but—arguably—allow meaning to be ascribed to some evolved robots. The grounding problem, on this view, is solved by the way in which the relevant mechanism has evolved in situated, embodied systems.

Empirical work that is closely related to the problem of intentionality includes research on *theory of mind.* Very young children are unable to grasp that each person is an agent with their own set of beliefs and interests, which may differ from those of the child. So although the child realizes that adults (and even other children) know many things that they do not, the child does not appreciate that someone else may believe something to be true that the child knows to be false. (This is why infants do not lie: they cannot conceive of doing so.) Normally, theory of mind develops spontaneously at around ages four or five, although in autistic children it apparently does not. In other words, inbuilt predispositions have evolved that lead the young child first to engage with other humans (maintaining eye contact, pointing to direct attention, turn-taking in communication, etc.), and eventually to attribute intentional states to them. Philosophers have asked (for instance) whether they do this by theorizing about other people's minds or by simulating, or empathizing with, them (Davies and Stone 1995).

CONSCIOUSNESS IN COMPUTATIONAL TERMS. A fifth philosophical puzzle concerns whether consciousness could be explained in computational terms—or in any other scientific, naturalistic, manner (Heil 2004, Newell 1980, Searle 1993). Research in various disciplines within cognitive science has shown that there is no such thing as the problem of consciousness; rather, there are many problems of consciousness, because the term is used to make many different distinctions. Some of these are much better understood than they were twenty years ago, thanks to computational work in AI, psychology, and neuroscience. Reflective self-consciousness, for example, and the bizarre dissociations of consciousness typical of multiple personality, are intelligible in terms of recursive processing, guiding procedures, and access limitations within complex hierarchical structures for perception, memory, and action.

Considerable controversy, however, still attends the problem of qualia. Some cognitive scientists argue that *qualia* can be analyzed in terms of complex dispositions for making discriminatory computations (Dennett 1991). Others see them as aspects of an irreducible informational feature of the universe, applying not only to human brains but to atoms as well (Chalmers 1996). Still others make further suggestions, including several based on quantum physics. In short, there are many theories of *qualia*, and no agreement about what a successful theory might look like.

OPPOSITION TO ORTHODOX COGNITIVE SCIENCE. A sixth controversy—or rather, batch of controversies—arises from recent work that opposes orthodox (neo-Cartesian) cognitive science (Cliff, Harvey, and Husbands 1993; Port and van Gelder 1995; Wheeler 2005). This involves both empirical theory/modeling and philosophical discussion. In general, it draws on the traditions of phenomenological philosophy and/or autopoietic biology, rather than Cartesianism. It rejects both symbolic and connectionist AI, and the concept of representation. It highlights embodied systems (not abstract simulations), embedded in their environment and responding directly to it. Examples include situated robotics in AI, dynamical systems theory, ecological psychology, and A-life studies of evolution and coevolution.

Philosophies inspired by these empirical researches include the theory of extended mind (Clark 1997). This starts from the position that minds must necessarily be embodied and that memory storage lies largely outside the skull (ideas familiar within phenomenology and GOFAI, respectively) and goes on to argue that an individual person's mind is extended over the surrounding cultural artifacts: language, customs, and material objects—from palaces to pencils. The claim is that mind is not merely deeply influenced by these things, but it is largely constituted by them.

Philosophical questions associated with A-life include whether evolution is a necessary characteristic of life, and whether the concept of autopoiesis captures the essence of life (Bedau 1996; Maturana and Varela 1987). If living things are defined as autopoietic systems—whose physical unity, boundaries, and self-maintenance are attained by self-organized metabolic processes—then questions about the origins of life take on a different color, as do questions about the possibility of strong A-life (life in computer memory)—so called by analogy to strong AI.

Philosophers of A-life consider not only the nature of life as such, but how and why it is related to mind. Must all minds be evolved, for example? Autopoietic theorists define all life as involving cognition, while insisting that only linguistic life (i.e., adult humans) involves representations. But questions remain about whether, and if so why, life really is essential for mind. By the same token, questions remain about whether the study of A-life is essentially unrelated to cognitive science or fundamental to it.

CULTURE AND COGNITIVE SCIENCE. Finally, culture-directed research in cognitive science raises philosophical questions too. One concerns the nature of group mind, or as it is more commonly called, distributed cognition (Hutchins 1995). Can one identify aspects of cognition that cannot be attributed to any single individual, but only to a team of enculturated persons acting in concert—and if so, can one model such phenomena in computers? Two more such questions concern the evolution of information-processing mechanisms that underlie important cultural phenomena—religion or aesthetic appreciation, for example—and the evolution of culture as such.

See also Computationalism; Neuroscience; Psychology.

Bibliography

Boden, Margaret A. *The Creative Mind: Myths and Mechanisms.* 2nd ed. London: Routledge, 2004.

Boden, Margaret A. *Mind as Machine: A History of Cognitive Science.* Oxford: Oxford University Press, forthcoming.

Bedau, Mark A. "The Nature of Life." In *The Philosophy of Artificial Life,* edited by Margaret A. Boden. Oxford: Oxford University Press, 1996.

Chalmers, David J. *The Conscious Mind: In Search of a Fundamental Theory.* Oxford: Oxford University Press, 1996.

Churchland, Paul M. *A Neurocomputational Perspective: The Nature of Mind and the Structure of Science.* Cambridge, MA: MIT Press, 1989.

Clark, Andy J. *Associative Engines: Connectionism, Concepts, and Representational Change.* Cambridge, MA: MIT Press, 1993.

Clark, Andy J. *Being There: Putting Brain, Body, and World Together Again.* Cambridge, MA: MIT Press, 1997.

Clark, Andy J. *Microcognition: Philosophy, Cognitive Science, and Parallel Distributed Processing.* Cambridge, MA: MIT Press, 1989.

Cliff, David; Harvey, Inman; and Husbands, Philip. "Explorations in Evolutionary Robotics." *Adaptive Behavior* 2 (1993), 73–110.

Cussins, Adrian. "The Connectionist Construction of Concepts." In *The Philosophy of Artificial Intelligence,* edited by Margaret A. Boden. Oxford: Oxford University Press, 1990.

Davies, Martin, and Tony Stone, eds. *Folk Psychology: The Theory of Mind Debate.* Oxford: Blackwell, 1995.

Dennett, Daniel C. *Consciousness Explained.* Boston: Little Brown, 1991.

Dennett, Daniel C. *Elbow Room: The Varieties of Free Will Worth Wanting.* Cambridge, MA: MIT Press, 1984.

Dennett, Daniel C. *The Intentional Stance.* Cambridge, MA: MIT Press, 1987.

Elman, Jeffrey L., Elizabeth A. Bates, Mark H. Johnson, et al. *Rethinking Innateness: A Connectionist Perspective on Development.* Cambridge, MA: MIT Press, 1996.

Fodor, Jerry A. *The Mind Doesn't Work That Way: The Scope and Limits of Computational Psychology.* Cambridge, MA: MIT Press, 2000.

Gibson, James J. *The Ecological Approach to Visual Perception.* Boston: Houghton Mifflin, 1979.

Haugeland, John, ed. *Mind Design II: Philosophy, Psychology, Artificical Intelligence.* 2nd ed. Cambridge, MA.: MIT Press, 1997.

Heil, John, ed. *Philosophy of Mind: A Guide and Anthology.* Oxford: Oxford University Press, 2004. See especially 3–6, and 9–10.

Hutchins, Edwin L. *Cognition in the Wild.* Cambridge, MA: MIT Press, 1995.

McCulloch, Warren S., and Walter H. Pitts. "A Logical Calculus of the Ideas Immanent in Nervous Activity." In *The Philosophy of Artificial Intelligence,* edited by Margaret A. Boden. Oxford: Oxford University Press, 1990. Essay first published in 1943.

Maturana, Humberto R., and Francisco J. Varela. *The Tree of Knowledge: The Biological Roots of Human Understanding.* Boston: New Science Library, 1987.

Newell, Allen. "Physical Symbol Systems." Cognitive Science 4 (1980): 135–183.

Oyama, Susan. *The Ontogeny of Information: Developmental Systems and Evolution.* Cambridge, U.K.: Cambridge University Press, 1985.

Pitts, Walter H., and Warren S. McCulloch. "How We Know Universals: The Perception of Auditory and Visual Forms." In *Embodiments of Mind,* edited by Seymour Papert. Cambridge, MA: MIT Press, 1965. Essay first published in 1947.

Port, Robert F., and Timothy J. van Gelder, eds. *Mind as Motion: Explorations in the Dynamics of Cognition.* Cambridge, MA: MIT Press, 1995.

Scheutz, Matthias, ed. *Computationalism: New Directions.* Cambridge, MA: MIT Press, 2002.

Searle, John R. *The Rediscovery of the Mind.* Cambridge, MA: MIT Press, 1993.

Sloman, Aaron. "The Mind as a Control System." In *Philosophy and the Cognitive Sciences,* edited by Christopher Hookway and Donald Peterson. Cambridge, U.K.: Cambridge University Press, 1993.

Wheeler, Michael W. *Reconstructing the Cognitive World: The Next Step.* Cambridge, MA: MIT Press, 2005.

Margaret A. Boden (1996, 2005)

COHEN, HERMANN

(1842–1918)

Hermann Cohen, a neo-Kantian philosopher, was born at Coswig, Anhalt, Germany. His father, Gerson Cohen, was a teacher and precentor at the synagogue; his mother was Friederike née Salomon. In 1878 Hermann married Martha Lewandowski, the daughter of Professor Louis Lewandowski, who was also a precentor at the synagogue and a composer of Jewish ritual songs. In 1853 Hermann went to the gymnasium of Dessau, which he attended for some years. He left there prematurely and went to the Jewish Theological Seminary at Breslau. Later, as a student at the University of Breslau, he wrote the essay "Über die Psychologie des Platon und Aristoteles," which won the prize of the philosophical faculty in August 1863. On August 5, 1864, he took the bachelor's examination as an extramural pupil at the Breslau Matthias Gymnasium. In the fall of the same year he went for further university studies to Berlin. He wrote an essay, "Philosophorum de Antinomia Necessitatis et Contigentiae Doctrinae" and entered it for a university prize. Since the prize was not awarded to him, he submitted the work (somewhat altered) to the philosophical faculty at Halle. On the basis of this work he was awarded the doctorate of philosophy by this faculty on October 27, 1865.

On his return to Berlin he published several studies, some of them in *Zeitschrift für Völkerpsychologie und Sprachwissenschaft.* Heymann Steinthal, the coeditor of this periodical, who was warmly interested in the very gifted young man, had stimulated his interest in social psychology. It was not until 1870 that his publications disclosed a special interest of their author in Kantian philosophy. In that year Cohen intervened in the Homeric struggle that had broken out between Adolf Trendelenburg and Kuno Fischer over Trendelenburg's criticism of the Kantian transcendental aesthetic. Trendelenburg agreed with Immanuel Kant that the concepts of space and time are a priori, but he denied their exclusion from things-in-themselves, which was, in Kant's opinion, an unavoidable consequence of their intuitive apriority. According to Trendelenburg, a third possibility was left, namely the validity of space and time with regard to all existing objects *in spite of* the apriority of their *concepts.* Fischer, defending Kant against the charge of leaving this "gap," insisted that Kant's assignment of both space and time to human sensibility, in the transcendental aesthetic, was irrefutable. Cohen, a pupil of Trendelenburg, but not a favorite one, in an essay published in the above periodical (7 [3]: 239–296) gave the Solomonic judgment. Trendelenburg was right in criticizing Fischer, but wrong in criticizing Kant.

PHILOSOPHICAL TEACHING

This judgment already contained in germ the whole of Cohen's future philosophical achievement. In the following year his first philosophical book, *Kants Theorie der Erfahrung* (Berlin, 1871) made it clear why, in his opinion, both Trendelenburg and Fischer were wrong. The teaching of the transcendental aesthetic, which showed space and time to be forms of our sensibility, had to be complemented by the teaching of the transcendental logic, where these forms are shown to be a priori conditions of possible experience. Possible experience, as Kant said throughout the *Critique,* is the only object of a priori knowledge. Therefore, the exclusive subjectivity of space and time, assumed by both parties to be Kant's complete view, disappears entirely if one takes into account the methodological difference between a psychological classification of space and time among native ideas and the Kantian transcendental theory of their being the a priori conditions of the possibility of experience.

By thus extending the matter in question to the whole of Kant's theory of a priori knowledge, Cohen gave evidence of the philosophical turn of his gifts. In 1873 he presented to the philosophical faculty of Marburg a treatise titled *Die systematischen Begriffe in Kants vorkritischen Schriften* (Berlin, 1873) with an application for the *venia legendi* (lectureship). On the recommendation of F. A. Lange, Cohen's application was accepted. Lange died two years later, and in January 1876 Cohen, proposed by the faculty, was appointed to the vacant chair. He devoted his work to the fortification and extension of his new interpretation of Kant, which from the beginning had aroused admiration for the author's energy and devotion, though many doubted the compatibility of Cohen's interpretation with Kant's real opinion.

In any case, Cohen found himself confronted with a serious problem. If the objectivity of space and time consisted in their being a priori conditions of the possibility of experience, the question remained from what principle experience itself derived its validity. There was no identity between the conditions of experience and the conditions of things-in-themselves. This was unquestionably Kant's teaching. But, as Cohen observed, Kant had a new concept of experience. Actually, the innovation—if there was one—was David Hume's, not Kant's. Experience, according to Hume, is a statement on matters of fact presupposing some connection of these matters by general rules. The difference between Kant and Hume is not in the concept of experience but in the question of whether it is possible to justify the universality of that intellectual presupposition with regard to the objects of sense perception. Hume claimed it is not possible; those a priori assumptions are not a matter of intelligence at all. Man is driven to them by the laws of nature, which make him believe automatically in the possibility of experience.

This might not be a satisfactory answer. But Cohen's solution to the question—to derive the objectivity of those presuppositions (including space and time) from their being a priori conditions of experience—was not only not satisfactory—it was no answer at all. It was an answer that answered by what was the subject of the question. If, therefore, Cohen wished neither to accept the unconditioned subjectivity of Kant's possibility of experience nor to fall back on Hume's skepticism—which way was left to him?

It was the way of a cryptopositivism. The objectivity of doubtful a priori assumptions, such as space, time, and the categories, was demonstrable, according to Cohen, by means of the "fact of science" (*das Faktum der Wissenschaft*). Surely it was a historical fact that Isaac Newton had used these assumptions as principles in establishing his mathematical theory of the phenomena of nature. It was also a fact that Newton was far from justifying the assumption of these principles by deriving them from experience. But this by no means made the fact of their use as nonempirical principles of natural science equivalent to the fact of an existing a priori knowledge of nature. It was, on the contrary, evident that none of Newton's mathematical laws of natural phenomena, formulated in differential equations, could be called a knowledge of those phenomena if it was not verifiable by experience. How, then, could those principles presupposed by Newton's physics assume the character of a priori requirements for the cognition of nature by the mere fact of being presupposed by Newton, if the cognitive character of these presuppositions with regard to natural phenomena was demonstrable only by experience?

Despite this unanswerable question, Cohen boldly proclaimed that Newtonian science demonstrated by its own historical facticity the possibility of an a priori knowledge of nature by means of the concepts of space, time, and the Kantian categories. He called the manner of this demonstration the "transcendental method." It proved to be an enormous success. Cohen's pupils vied with each other in showing that modern science would not have been possible if its promoters had not presupposed what they actually had—that is, space, time, and the principles assigned by Kant to pure understanding. This, if it was meant to be a legitimation of a priori knowledge of natural phenomena by means of those principles, was clearly a vicious circle.

The desire to escape this consequence determined Cohen's philosophical development and the fate of neo-Kantianism in general. Cohen realized eventually that his transcendental method, if it were to prove effective with regard to a priori knowledge of nature, required the tearing down of the insurmountable barrier Kant had fixed between a priori and empirical knowledge by means of his distinction between sensibility as receptivity and understanding as spontaneity. Therefore Cohen posited a kind of thinking that originated by its own act the whole field of principles of our knowledge ("Denken des Ursprungs"). Thus, all human knowledge must be in principle a priori knowledge.

In *Die Logik der reinen Erkenntnis* (Berlin, 1902) Cohen elaborated this puzzling idea. He explained by abundant historical comments that the real task of metaphysics was the thinking of the origin. If this is to be regarded as more than an utter triviality, it testifies that the author, in order to escape the deadly embrace of Hume, fled into the arms of Johann Gottlieb Fichte and G. W. F. Hegel. Once more he fell victim to the ancient illusion of being able to understand Kant better than Kant himself by dropping the conditions essential to the very problem of transcendental philosophy. Thus Cohen, however unintentionally, encouraged a new movement from Kant to Hegel in German neo-Kantianism. Even Heideggerian existentialism claimed some kinship with the critique of pure reason by proclaiming the search for the "common root" of sensibility and intelligibility, necessarily problematical with Kant, as a way of salvation from all possible transcendental problems.

PRACTICAL PHILOSOPHY

Cohen similarly interpreted Kant's moral philosophy according to the maxim that to interpret Kant one must go beyond him in his *Kants Begründung der Ethik* (Berlin, 1877). He inherited from Trendelenburg's Aristotelianism the idea of virtue as the supreme problem of moral philosophy. Combined with the Kantian assumption of an a priori principle of morals, this idea generated the problem of ethics as the problem of an a priori science of virtue. Here again Aristotle intervened by his teaching that all other virtues are implied in justice. Thus, the problem of morals presented itself to Cohen as the problem of an a priori knowledge of justice. All a priori knowledge, according to Cohen's transcendental method, required some factual science to justify it. Kant did not presuppose any such factual science in his *Critique of Practical Reason.* In this Cohen believed Kant to be mistaken. According to him, morals does have a basic science, jurisprudence, because the idea of justice is the constitutional law of this science. If there were no a priori law of justice, the sort of systematic knowledge of the laws that the Romans assigned to *iurisprudentia* would not be possible. In identifying *iurisprudentia* with *scientia iusti,* Cohen found that the a priori character of Kant's categorical imperative was justified by the factual existence of jurisprudence.

POLITICS

It is easy to observe that autonomy as conditioned by the categorical imperative is by no means the principle of a society that, like the state, is realizable under the conditions of experience. And it is no less easy to see that the positive laws of a given state, the objects of jurisprudence, in spite of the possibility of their being systematically treated by jurisprudence, do not necessarily agree with some a priori idea of justice. Nevertheless, the idea of a human society constituted by the law of autonomy meant a quite personal engagement to Cohen, above and beyond all philosophical subtleties concerning its meaning or its justification. This engagement drove him from the field of transcendental deductions into politics. It made him a public champion of those whose personal dignity granted by the law of autonomy was infringed upon by society. He eventually found himself among them. Some years after he settled at Marburg, anti-Semitism appeared on the German political stage. The famous historian Heinrich von Treitschke published in his *Preussische Jahrbücher* (Vol. 1879, No. 11) an article in which he called attention to an attitude allegedly adopted by a good many Jewish writers, whom he accused of being antinational and anti-Christian. He held that they should respect the feelings of the majority. The weak point in Treitschke's pleas was the authority that he assigned to what in his romanticism he called Christian German culture.

Cohen in his *Eine Bekenntnis in der Judenfrage* (Berlin, 1880), without attacking Treitschke's romantic idea of a law given by Germano-Christian feeling, boldly announced that the Jews already belonged to the German nation—not *in spite of* their being Jews, but *because* they were Jews. This, of course, was too much for both parties. But to Cohen the philosopher and learned Jewish theologian it seemed quite simple to demonstrate. The Germans, he argued, are the nation of Kant. The Jews are a nation whose creed has been purified by the prophets. The teachings of the prophets, as Cohen's learnedness interpreted them, were identical with Kant's ethical idealism. Therefore, whoever tells a Jew that he can belong to the German nation only at the cost of his religion denounces him as having no true morality of his own. From that time on, Cohen continued as a collaborator in the interpretation of Jewish tradition by adapting it to his philosophy. His writings in this field were edited by Bruno Strauss and published with an introduction by Cohen's admirer Franz Rosenzweig as *Hermann Cohens jüdische Schriften* (3 vols., Berlin, 1924).

Besides the startling historical and ideological identifications of his Germano-Jewish patriotism, there was yet another reason for Cohen's reputation as a political outsider. It was not unusual to support the workingman's longing for a decent living according to the law of humanity. All the so-called *Katheder-Sozialisten,* among them some of the most influential professors of the German Empire, did it. But the mixture of philanthropy and justice that Cohen considered the supreme principle of his moral philosophy made him believe in a basic accordance between the doctrine of Karl Marx and his own. Thus, he became responsible for the legend of a kinship between Kant and Marx. This was enough to color the politician Cohen with a red tinge—and if his true patriotic German feeling separated him from Jewish orthodoxy and Zionism, his rather innocent socialism did not make him a favorite with either his government or his faculty.

Hence, his retirement in 1912 brought a great disappointment with it. The faculty, not very fond of intricate transcendental deductions that were admired by students but doubted by philosophers, refused to give his chair to the man of his choice, Ernst Cassirer. The choice of his colleagues, Paul Natorp dissenting, was a young experimental psychologist.

LATER RELIGIOUS VIEWS

Deeply hurt, Cohen left Marburg and retired to Berlin. There he devoted himself to a lectureship at the Lehranstalt für Wissenschaft des Judentums, of which he was already a member of the board of trustees. Thus, he was again a theologian. Meanwhile, his philosophy had dissolved theology into a transcendental deduction of the eternity of cultural progress governed by the "social ideal"; namely, the community of autonomous beings. But in actual fact there was no solid deduction even of this eternity. The question of whether religion had any meaning at all arose again. Cohen answered it in two books, *Der Begriff der Religion im System der Philosophie* (Giessen, 1915) and *Die Religion aus den Quellen des Judentums* (Leipzig, 1919). In both of these works the point of departure lies in the observation that the belief in the eternity of cultural progress is of little comfort to the individual in his personal sufferings. Therefore, an empty space has been left by philosophy. This space may be filled by God as a savior bringing personal consolation to all people. Cohen found this idea of the Divine Being splendidly expressed by the prophets and the Psalmist. But the mere idea of a powerful personal Helper does not cause that Helper to exist; and since this idea, according to Cohen himself, could not be justified by his philosophical system, the question of a savior's existence was left entirely to personal conviction. To the great satisfaction of his religious friends, Cohen, when he died, seemed to be in full possession of this conviction.

AESTHETICS

The manner in which Cohen addressed religious problems in his last writings was prepared by his aesthetics. Aesthetics had been treated by Kant within the frame of what he called the critique of judgment. Cohen's comment, published under the title *Kants Begründung der Ästhetik* (Berlin, 1889), once again disclosed the author's difficulty in harmonizing his own ideas in this field with the peculiar but at bottom simple Kantian theory of aesthetic pleasure.

In spite of the stock of questions left unanswered by Cohen's principles, he continues to live in the memory of philosophers as a Kantian who dominated to a great extent the philosophical discussions of his time. But if Cohen's own interpretation was attractive, it did not make Kant attractive; and his school of neo-Kantianism eventually expired. The unbearable viciousness of the famous gnosiological circle, wrongly imputed to Kant himself but inextricably woven into Cohen's own omnipresent transcendental method, drove the younger generation to the worship of new gods. But even so, Cohen has left a stimulus to study "that Kant" whom, as one of his pupils is reputed to have said, "nobody ever knew." The feeling expressed by these words was precisely Cohen's own feeling when he began his work.

See also Aesthetics, History of; Aesthetics, Problems of; Aristotle; Ethics, History of; Fichte, Johann Gottlieb; Fischer, Kuno; Hegel, Georg Wilhelm Friedrich; Hume, David; Kant, Immanuel; Lange, Friedrich Albert; Marx, Karl; Neo-Kantianism; Newton, Isaac; Rosenzweig, Franz.

Bibliography

WORKS ON COHEN

Cassirer, Ernst. "Hermann Cohen." *Social Research* 10 (2) (1943): 219–232.

Kinkel, Walter. *Hermann Cohen, Einführung in sein Werk.* Stuttgart, Strecker and Schröder, 1924.

Natorp, Paul. *Hermann Cohen als Mensch, Lehrer, und Forscher.* Marburg, Germany, 1918.

Rosmarin, T. W. *Religion of Reason, Hermann Cohen's System of Religious Philosophy.* New York: Bloch, 1936.

Vuillemin, J. *L'héritage kantien et la révolution copernicienne.* Paris: Presses universitaires de France, 1954.

Julius Ebbinghaus (1967)

COHEN, HERMANN [ADDENDUM]

Philosophical research between 1960 and 2004 looked at Cohen's thought from both a historical and a theoretical viewpoint. In the age of the integration of German Jews into German society, he was the foremost advocate of the need for a meeting between the Enlightenment and Judaism.

Cohen had an important influence on various philosophical fields. Ernst Cassirer's neo-Kantian approach to human culture (1943) and J. B. Soloveitchik's neo-Kantian attitude to religion, particularly Judaism (1986), owe their method to his work. Both Husserl's and Heidegger's interpretations of Kant's transcendental philosophy, and therefore the phenomenological or existentialist concept of the *self*, derive from Cohen's theory of knowledge (Dussort 1963, Vuillemin 1954). Hans Kelsen's juridical positivism was inspired by Cohen's idea of "natural right" (Winter 1980). Franz Rosenzweig's philosophy of divine revelation—as a bond between a human being and God through "religious love"—stems from Cohen (Altmann 1970). Lastly, Cohen's essays on the history of philosophy influenced Leo Strauss's interpretations of Spinoza, Maimonides, and the relation between "Jerusalem" and "Athens" (Kajon 2002).

Cohen's logic has inspired examinations into the fundamental principles of mathematics and physics (Holzhey 1986). Unlike Hegelianism on the one hand and postmodernism on the other, Cohen's ethics sought the relation between reason and the facts of law, state, and history (Gigliotti 1989). His aesthetics invites a criticism of *art for art's sake* (Poma 1997). His philosophy of religion expresses the need for a "religion of reason" which keeps the profundity of religious life (Zac 1984).

Cohen's thought stems from both Jewish tradition and European idealism, hence its fertile, albeit problematic, character.

Bibliography

COHEN'S WORKS

Werke "Hermann-Cohen-Archiv am Philosophischem Seminar Zürich" under the direction of Helmut Holzhey. Hildesheim, Germany: Olms, 1977–.

WORKS ON COHEN

Altmann, Alexander. "Hermann Cohens Begriff der Korrelation." In *Von der mittelalterlichen zur modernen Aufklärung: Studien zur jüdischen Geistesgeschichte*, 300–317. Tübingen, Germany: Mohr, 1970.

Cassirer, Ernst. "Hermann Cohen." *Social Research* 10 (2) (1943): 219–232.

Dussort, Henry. *L'école de Marbourg.* Paris: PUF, 1963.

Gigliotti, Gianna. *"Avventure e disavventure del trascendentale." Studio su Cohen e Natorp.* Napoli, Italy: Guida, 1989.

Holzhey, Helmut. *Cohen und Natorp.* Basel-Stuttgart, Germany: Schwabe, 1986.

Kajon, Irene. *Il pensiero ebraico del Novecento: Una introduzione*. Roma, Italy: Donzelli, 2002. (English edition: *Contemporary Jewish Philosophy: An Introduction*. London: RoutledgeCurzon, 2005.)

Kinkel, Walter. *Hermann Cohen: Einführung in sein Werk*. Stuttgart, Germany: Strecken und Schröder, 1924.

Natorp, Paul. *Hermann Cohen als Mensch, Lehrer, und Forscher*. Marburg, Elwert: 1918.

Poma, Andrea. *The Critical Philosophy of Hermann Cohen*. Translated by John Denton. Albany: State University of New York Press, 1997.

Rosmarin, T. W. *Religion of Reason: Hermann Cohen's System of Religious Philosophy*. New York: Bloch, 1936.

Soloveitchik J. B. *The Halakhic Mind*. New York: Seth Press, 1986.

Vuillemin, J. *L'héritage kantien et la révolution copernicienne*. Paris: Presses Universitaires de France, 1954.

Winter E. *Ethik und Rechtswissenschaft: Eine historisch-systematische Untersuchung zur Ethik-Konzeption des Marburger Neukantianismus im Werke Hermann Cohens*. Berlin: Duncker & Humblot, 1980.

Zac, Sylvain. *La philosophie religieuse de Hermann Cohen*. Paris: Vrin, 1984.

Irene Kajon (2005)

COHEN, MORRIS RAPHAEL

(1880–1947)

Morris Raphael Cohen, the American naturalistic philosopher, was born in Minsk, Russia. When twelve years old, he was brought to New York City by his parents, who immigrated to America in search of greater opportunity and freedom. In his early youth he came under the influence of the Scottish freelance scholar Thomas Davidson. Cohen was graduated from the College of the City of New York (City College) in 1900 and received his PhD in philosophy from Harvard University in 1906. At Harvard he studied under Josiah Royce, William James, and Hugo Münsterberg.

From 1912 to 1938, Cohen taught philosophy at City College. He was an outstanding teacher, and some of his students became eminent teachers, philosophers, and lawyers. He was a visiting lecturer in philosophy at Johns Hopkins, Yale, Stanford, and Harvard and from 1938 through 1941 was a professor at the University of Chicago. For years he gave courses at the New School for Social Research. He was also a lecturer at the law schools of St. John's University, Columbia, Yale, Harvard, Cornell, the University of Buffalo, and New York University. Although an agnostic, he had been a dedicated Jew. His wit, his critical spirit, his erudition, and his interest in a wide range of friends made him a colorful and animating person.

Cohen's philosophic interests included the philosophy of science, metaphysics, logic, social philosophy, legal philosophy, and the philosophy of history. His contribution to legal philosophy has been especially widely recognized.

METAPHYSICAL AND LOGICAL PRINCIPLES

Cohen's general philosophic outlook is naturalistic. There is no place in his philosophy for the extranatural and no place for extrascientific methods to attain knowledge. His outlook is also rationalistic, for he assumed that rationality is inherent in nature. His philosophy is based on three principles: rationality, invariance, and polarity. These three principles, coherently interwoven, provide his view of reality.

RATIONALITY. In its long history the concept of rationality has acquired a variety of meanings. It has meant logical order, inductive generalization, and wisdom. Each of these meanings has been significant. Cohen did not offer an inclusive definition of rationality, but in his philosophy of nature the first meaning is dominant and in his ethical and legal philosophies the third meaning is central.

Rationality as logical order may be considered methodologically or ontologically. Methodologically, it is a procedure to order our objects of thought in a logical way. Most philosophers, except for mystics and irrationalists, feel the necessity of such a procedure. Yet Cohen went beyond the methodological use of rationality and insisted on its ontological status. The rules of logic and pure mathematics "may be viewed not only as the principle of inference applicable to all systems but also as descriptive of certain abstract invariant relations which constitute an objective order characteristic of any subject matter" (*Reason and Nature*, p. 142).

For Cohen, as a logical realist, the formal aspects of logic apply to everything. As against idealists, positivists, and pragmatists, he was firm in insisting that the rational order is independent of human or superhuman mind. Idealists, according to him, deny the objectivity of logical order by giving it only a psychological status, but the psychological description of reasoning as a mental event cannot determine, according to him, whether a given logical argument is valid. Positivists, his arch philosophic enemies, fall short in a similar way. As sensations are considered the only deliverance of the external world, for positivists logical connections are mere fictions. Pragmatists, he argued, similarly depreciate the status of rational order. In their attempt to interpret the truth of judgment in terms of practical consequences, they consider logical relations as merely practical tools of thought without any ontological standing.

However, Cohen admitted an element of contingency in nature. "By no amount of reasoning," he wrote, "can we altogether eliminate all contingency from our world" (ibid., p. 82). The universe is ultimately what it is, and contingency cannot be eliminated. And by contingency Cohen meant that the world contains an irrational element in the sense that "all form is the form of something which cannot be reduced to form alone" (*Studies in Philosophy and Science*, p. 11).

INVARIANCE. Science is not, as Cohen rightly pointed out, a mere observation of particular facts; it is never satisfied with stating only what has occurred. The aim of science is to determine the universal, invariant relations of particular events. To say that sulfur has melted at 125°C. is a mere statement of fact similar to the statement that Russians for generations have used the Cyrillic alphabet, but to say that sulfur always melts at 125°C. means that if ever anything conforms to the category of sulfur, it melts at this temperature. The second statement expresses not only a historical event but also an invariant relation that belongs to "the eternal present."

Although the essence of particular things is their invariant relations, our knowledge of these is only probable. Only in logic or in mathematics can we attain certainty; in the world of facts our knowledge is only probable, for we cannot prove that the opposite of a given factual statement is absolutely impossible.

POLARITY. According to the principle of polarity, opposites involve each other. As Cohen expressed it in *Reason and Nature*, "Opposites such as immediacy and mediation, unity and plurality, the fixed and the flux, substance and function, ideal and real, actual and possible, and so on, like the north (positive) and the south (negative) poles of a magnet, all involve each other when applied to any significant entity" (p. 165).

In addition to its methodological value as a guide to the clarification of ideas, the principle of polarity, like the principle of rationality, has ontological status. Empirical facts, such as the existence of the north and south poles, are said to be resultants of opposing tendencies. Cohen generalized this alleged fact as the principle of "the necessary copresence and mutual dependence of opposite determinations."

ETHICS

Historically, there have been two major opposing theories of morality—the absolutist and the relativist. Cohen examined both of these theories and found them unsatisfactory. The absolutist is too rigid and uncritical; the relativist is too chaotic, without guiding principles. Cohen thought the principle of polarity could reconcile the two opposing views. Actually, these two views provide a vantage point for arriving at the truth. Concretely, every issue of life involves choice. The absolutist is right "in insisting that every such choice logically involves a principle of decision," and the relativist is right "in insisting on the primacy of the feeling or perception of the demands in the actual case before us" (ibid., p. 438). We may thus have an ethical system that is rigorously logical and at the same time richly empirical. Such an ethics must be grounded in what human beings desire and believe, and yet its primary condition must be the logical analysis of judgment as to what constitutes right and wrong, good and evil—an ethic that is the rational formulation of our ends.

LAW

Cohen was a pioneer in introducing legal philosophy as a significant study to universities and law schools. As Leonora Cohen Rosenfield wrote, "His philosophical treatment of the law in relation to man and the social order may prove in time to be his foremost influence."

For Cohen law is essentially a system for the orderly regulation of social action. Jurisprudence must avoid the extremes of positivism and formalism. "Law without concepts or rational ideas, law that is not logical is like prescientific medicine—a hodge-podge of sense and superstition," yet law without reference to the actual facts of human conduct would be empty. A law is both stable and dynamic; it is a balance between prevailing customs and the emerging demands of society. Cohen was especially critical of what he called the "phonograph theory of law," the theory that the judge arrives at his decision in a mechanical way, according to unchanging laws. Cohen effectively argued that the judge's opinions on social and economic questions deeply influence his decisions. One of the chief merits of his analysis of law is his insistence on the interdependence of the factual and the normative. As he maintained, "Justice and the law, the ideal and the actual are inseparable, yet identifiable."

See also Idealism; James, William; Philosophy of Law, History of; Positivism; Pragmatism; Rationalism; Realism; Royce, Josiah.

Bibliography

WORKS BY COHEN

Reason and Nature: An Essay on the Meaning of Scientific Method. New York: Harcourt Brace, 1931. Cohen's major work.

Law and the Social Order: Essays in Legal Philosophy. New York: Harcourt Brace, 1933. Important work.

An Introduction to Logic and Scientific Method. New York: Harcourt Brace, 1934. Written with Ernest Nagel.

A Preface to Logic. New York: Holt, 1945. Important work.

The Meaning of Human History. La Salle, IL: Open Court, 1947. Important work.

A Dreamer's Journey. Boston: Beacon Press, 1949. Autobiography.

Studies in Philosophy and Science. New York: Holt, 1949.

Reason and Law: Studies in Juristic Philosophy. Glencoe, IL: Free Press, 1950.

The Faith of a Liberal: Selected Essays Freeport, NY: Books for Libraries Press, 1970.

WORKS ON COHEN

Baron, Salo W., Ernest Nagel, and Koppel S. Pinson, eds. *Freedom and Reason: Studies in Philosophy and Jewish Culture in Memory of Morris Raphael Cohen.* Glencoe, IL: Free Press, 1951. See Part I.

Cairns, Huntington. "The Legal Philosophy of Morris R. Cohen." *Vanderbilt Law Review* 14 (1960).

Kuhn, M. A. *Morris Raphael Cohen: A Bibliography.* New York: City College of New York Library, 1957. Available in the City College library.

Rosenfield, Leonora Cohen. *A Portrait of a Philosopher: Morris R. Cohen.* New York: Harcourt Brace, 1962.

Yervant H. Krikorian (1967)
Bibliography updated by Michael Farmer (2005)

COHERENCE THEORY OF TRUTH

The coherence theory is one of the two traditional theories of truth, the other being the correspondence theory. The coherence theory is characteristic of the great rationalist system-building metaphysicians Gottfried Wilhelm Leibniz, Benedict (Baruch) de Spinoza, G. W. F. Hegel, and Francis Herbert Bradley; but it has also had a vogue with several members of the logical positivist school, notably Otto Neurath and Carl Gustav Hempel, who were much influenced by the systems of pure mathematics and theoretical physics. According to the coherence theory, to say that a statement (usually called a judgment) is true or false is to say that it coheres or fails to cohere with a system of other statements; that it is a member of a system whose elements are related to each other by ties of logical implication as the elements in a system of pure mathematics are related. Many proponents of the theory hold, indeed, that each member of the system implies every other member. To test whether a statement is true is to test it for coherence with a system of statements. The system with which all true statements must cohere is said by its logical positivist supporters to be that accepted by the scientists of the contemporary culture. The metaphysical supporters of coherence, on the other hand, insist that a statement cannot properly be called true unless it fits into the one comprehensive account of the universe or reality, which itself forms a coherent system. In either case, no statement can be known to be true until it is known to cohere with every other statement of the system; where the system consists of all true statements, such knowledge is unattainable.

It is not altogether possible to give a plausible exposition of the theory independently of its close historical links with rationalist and idealist metaphysics, but the account might go something like this.

In practice, we sometimes reject as false an ordinary person's assertions—for instance, that he saw a ghost—or even a scientist's results—for instance, in experiments on extrasensory perception—on the ground that they do not cohere with the other commonsense or scientific views that we also hold as true.

MEANING OF TRUTH

In the exact and reputable science of pure mathematics, the logical test for the truth or acceptability of any proposition is whether it coheres with some of the other propositions, and ultimately with the axioms, of its system. In this test, which is not merely a practical one, for a proposition to cohere with other propositions is for it to be logically deducible from them. Further, this coherence is what we mean by calling such a proposition true.

INTERNAL RELATIONS. It is characteristic of the parts of a logical system like that of pure mathematics that no part would be what it is if its relations to the other parts were different from what they are. Thus, 2 would not be the number we associate with the numeral 2 if it were the third of 4 instead of the half of 4 or the cube root of 27 instead of the cube root of 8. Hence, it is said, the meaning and the truth of, for instance, "2 + 2 = 4" are bound up with the meaning and the truth of all the other statements in the arithmetical system; and our knowledge of its meaning and its truth is bound up with our knowledge of their meaning and their truth. This principle that nothing would be what it is if its relations to other things were different—which is called the doctrine of internal relations—holds, say the metaphysical supporters of coherence, for every element, whether in thought or in reality. For example, they argue that we would not even understand, much less know the truth or falsity of, a statement about something blue if blue were "divorced in our thought from all the colours in the spectrum to which it is related by likeness and difference, all the shades within its own range, and all the definition it possesses in virtue of being thought as a quality rather than as a substance or a relation" (Brand Blanshard, *The Nature of Thought*, Vol. II, p. 316). Further, not only would we not know the meaning or truth of such a statement, but it also cannot properly be said to have its meaning or truth-value independently of its relations to other statements. The statement "Caesar crossed the Rubicon in 49 BCE" is said to be pregnant with a meaning "owing to the concrete political situation within which it took place" that it would not otherwise have.

DEGREES OF TRUTH. A corollary of the principle of internal relations and of the coherence theory in general is the doctrine of degrees of truth. If the truth of any given statement is bound up with, and can only be seen with, the truth of all the statements of the system and thus is bound up with the whole system, it is argued that individual statements as such are only partly true—and, therefore, partly false—while only the whole system is wholly true. "Truth," said Bradley, "must exhibit the mark of expansion and all-inclusiveness."

CRITERION OF TRUTH

Coherence theorists might admit that their arguments hitherto have been drawn from the nature of the a priori reasoning typical of mathematics and metaphysics; but some have also claimed that an examination of the a posteriori reasoning of the empirical sciences and ordinary life also supports the theory, not only as giving the meaning of "truth" but also as giving the test of truth (ibid., pp. 226–237). In testing for truth it is obvious, runs the claim, that coherence is our only criterion when dealing with statements about the past. No one can now compare the statement that the battle of Hastings was fought in 1066 with anything else than other statements, such as those that occur in documents, history books, or works of art. However, we can contrast with this a statement about something present, such as "There is a cat on the mat." If asked how you would test this, your reply might be "I would look and see. If what I saw corresponded to what was asserted, I would call the judgment true." However, you are assuming that "there is some solid chunk of fact, directly presented to sense and beyond all question, to which thought must adjust itself" (ibid., p. 228). What you take and use as a fact is really "another judgement or set of judgements, and what provides the verification is the coherence between the initial judgement and these" (ibid.). Consider how much of your previous experience and education, how great an exercise of your powers of conceptualization, has gone into your perception of the cat on the mat; how much, in a word, your supposed perception of fact is really a judgment, since, without a stock of judgments, what is seen could never be identified as a cat and a mat, respectively. Your test of the truth of the judgment that there is a cat on the mat or your comparison with what was there turns out to be a comparison of the original judgment with another judgment. This example, in addition, shows not only that coherence is the test or criterion of truth, but also that it gives the meaning of "truth," for it shows that the truth of the tested judgment consists in its coherence with other judgments and not with something other than a judgment.

ASSUMPTIONS OF THE THEORY

The arguments used by supporters of the coherence theory rest on various assumptions about meaning, fact, thought, and judgment that are linked partly with the impression made on them by the a priori reasoning of mathematics and logic and partly with their theory of knowledge.

A PRIORI AS PARADIGM OF TRUTH. Metaphysics is traditionally nonempirical; its conclusions are a priori deductions from certain tenets, such as George Berkeley's "To be is to be perceived" or Zeno's analysis of infinity. The conceptual statements typical of philosophy—such as that no one can know what is false, that no one can know what has not yet been proved, or that no one can know what is going to be—are true or false because of logical relations between such concepts as knowledge, truth, proof, and the future. Further, ever since Plato, mathematics has been the metaphysician's ideal; Leibniz's system was based on certain principles that he held to characterize logic and mathematics, and Spinoza's famous book on ethics is subtitled "proved in geometrical order." Some of the logical positivists, because of their training in mathematics and theoretical physics, sought to establish all knowledge as a vast system of logically interrelated statements expressed in the language of physics. In such systems, the criterion of truth is indeed the coherence of the statement under consideration with at least some other members of the system.

Criticism. Coherence of a statement with other members of the system is not sufficient to prove the coherence theory of truth. First, the a priori statements typical of pure mathematics, unlike the empirical statements of science and everyday life, serve not to give information about characteristics of objects in the world but to show the various conclusions that can be derived from a given set of axioms and a given set of rules for operating on them. It is no objection to the truth of a given mathematical statement that there are or may be other systems with whose members it does not cohere or that it is a member of a system with no application to the world.

However, it is an objection to coherence as the meaning of "truth" or as the only criterion of truth that it is logically possible to have two different but equally comprehensive sets of coherent statements between which there would be, in the coherence theory, no way to decide which was the set of true statements. To reject a particular empirical statement like "He saw a ghost" because it conflicts with the body of our beliefs is not to assimilate the judgments of everyday life to those of mathematics, since this rejection, unlike the analogous one in mathematics, is made only because we think the body of our everyday beliefs has already been shown to be true of the world. Coherence of one judgment with another is accepted as a practical test of truth only because the second judgment is independently accepted as true.

Metaphysical supporters of the coherence theory distinguish their comprehensive system from particular systems such as those of mathematics by linking it to experience by means of their theory of knowledge, which assimilates what is thought, what is experienced, and what is. This appeal to experience and reality is indeed an inconsistency in the metaphysical version of the coherence theory, but it is more sensible than the position of the logical positivist supporters of the theory, who, in the name of consistency, allow that mutually incompatible but internally coherent systems of statements differ not in truth but only in the historical fact that our contemporaries have adopted one of the systems.

Second, there is in the a priori statements typical of mathematics and philosophy a close connection between meaning and truth. Such statements as "Twice two is half of eight" or "What is known cannot be false" are true in virtue of the meanings of the words that express them; it is because the meanings of the words are internally related as they are that these statements are true. It is not because of the relations between the meanings of "knowledge" and "breakfast," however, that it is true that no one knows what Pompey had for breakfast on the day he was murdered, nor is it because of the relations between the meanings of "two" and "four" that it is true that I made two mistakes on page four of my typescript.

Third, even within mathematics coherence gives the criterion, not the meaning, of truth. Mathematical statements are true in virtue of the criterion of coherence with each other, whereas it would seem that empirical statements are true in virtue of the criterion of correspondence with the nature of the world. However, to say that either kind of statement is true is to say that what it asserts is a fact. Whether "*X* is *Y*" is a mathematical or an empirical statement, if "*X* is *Y*" is true, then it is a fact that *X* is *Y*.

Fourth, even when confined to mathematics, the coherence doctrine of degrees of truth does not seem tenable. The fact that a given statement in mathematics is not true unless it coheres with some (or even all) other statements in the system does not imply that it is not itself wholly true; it could at most imply that it does not give the whole truth.

Ambiguities in degrees of truth. It is worth pointing out here how the theory of degrees of truth depends for its plausibility and its air of paradox on various ambiguities. There are at least three different ways in which we may qualify truth. First, we commonly ask how true something is, meaning how much truth is there in it, and commonly reply that it is partly, entirely, or perfectly true. For example, [in 1967] the report that African-Americans in the southern U.S. have been deprived of their right to vote might be said to be not quite true, either on the supposed grounds that they have been denied the opportunity to exercise their right rather than been deprived of it or that, although there has been a deprivation of the right, it is women who have been deprived.

Second, instead of asking how much truth there is in something, we may quite differently ask how much of *the* truth there is in it. To ask how much truth there is in something is to ask how much of what is not true is included; to ask how much of *the* truth there is in something is to ask how much of what is true is not included. A particular statement could be perfectly true without containing more than a minute proportion of the whole truth. Being wholly true is not the same as being the whole truth, nor is being partly true the same as being part of the truth. What is only partly true is necessarily partly false, but what is part of the truth may be entirely true.

Third, we can, in the case of general statements like "Water boils at 100° C," ask how far or under what conditions is it true. It may, for example, be true of water at sea level but not at high altitudes.

When coherence theorists say that every statement is only partly true, they usually seem to mean that every statement is only part of the truth, since nothing but the whole system of statements can give the whole of the truth. What they mean, therefore, is quite correct but wrongly expressed, because they have confused the first and the second of the above qualifications of truth. A typically ambiguous assertion is Blanshard's remark that "the trueness of a proposition is indistinguishable from the amount of truth it contains." At other times, as in their discussion of mathematical statements, by "degrees of truth" they mean "true in certain conditions." Thus, the statement "2 + 2 = 4" is said to be only partly true, as it is true in pure mathematics but not necessarily in all applied fields. Here again, what is meant is correct enough—not that such statements are not perfectly true, but that they are not universally true. The main reason, however, for the coherence theorists' belief in degrees of truth is based on a mistaken deduction from their doctrine of internal relations. Because each statement is, according to this doctrine, logically connected with other statements, it follows both that the truth of each statement is dependent on the truth of other statements and that our knowledge of its truth depends on our knowledge of the truth of these other statements. What appears to be true might turn out to be false when its further connections become known. Hence, it is said, "a given judgement is true in the degree to which its content could maintain itself in the light of a completed system of knowledge." This conclusion, however, is mistaken. A statement can be perfectly true in itself even though it would not have been true unless it had been connected in certain ways with other true statements; and it can be perfectly true whether we know this or not.

EPISTEMOLOGICAL ASSUMPTIONS. The second main influence in the usual defense of the coherence theory—that of a particular theory of knowledge—can be seen most prominently in the argument for transforming the commonsense belief that a statement (or judgment) is true if and only if it corresponds to facts into the doctrine that the judgment is true if and only if it coheres with another judgment or set of judgments. The first move in this transformation is from (*a*) "'There is a cat on the mat' is true if and only if it corresponds to the fact that there is a cat on the mat" to (*b*) "'There is a cat on the mat' is true if and only if it corresponds to the situation described as 'There is a cat on the mat.'" This is an illegitimate move, however, since a fact is not a situation, an event, or an object; otherwise we would have to postulate negative and conditional situations, events, and objects, to be described by such statements as "It is a fact that no one has yet succeeded in doing this" and "It is a fact that anyone who did succeed would be munificently rewarded." Hence, even if the moves designed to show that the situations, events, and objects we discover are not independent of our method of discovering them were valid, they would not show that facts are not independent of our methods of discovering them.

The second move in the transformation is from (*b*) "'There is a cat on the mat' is true if and only if it corresponds to the situation, event, or object describable as 'There is a cat on the mat'" to (*c*) "'There is a cat on the mat' is true if and only if it corresponds to what is verified to be a cat on the mat." This is illegitimate, however, since (*b*) is an explanation, although a false one, of the meaning of "true," whereas (*c*) contains the reason why someone might hold that there is a cat on the mat. Something can be true without anyone's knowing it to be true, although, of course, no one would sincerely say it was true unless he thought he knew it was. Idealist supporters of the coherence theory, like Bradley, move easily from (*b*) to (*c*) because they tend to identify reality with experience and knowledge, what is with what is experienced or with what is known. Further, they move distractingly to and fro between assertions about truth and assertions about *the* truth (the whole truth, the ultimate truth, a part of the truth), from assertions about the notion of truth to assertions about that which actually happens to be true. Thus, they speak of the identity of reality and truth when they mean the identity of reality and *the* truth, that is, what is true.

The third move in the transformation is from (*c*) "'There is a cat on the mat' is true if and only if it corresponds to what is verified to be a cat on the mat" to (*d*) "'There is a cat on the mat' is true if and only if it corresponds to a verification, or an experience, that would be expressed in the judgment (or, in logical positivist language, "the observation statement") 'I see (or there is) a cat on the mat.'" Because of this move they rule out the correspondence theory as a test of the truth of statements about the past, since there can be no verifying experience about what happened in the past. This move, too, is illegitimate because it assimilates what is verified, or experienced, to the verification, or experience, of it—the cat on the mat that I perceive to my perception of the cat on the mat. Such an assimilation is a standard part of the theory of knowledge of the Idealist metaphysicians, but an analogous assimilation is made by some logical positivists who, in their talk about observation statements, do not carefully distinguish between the report of what is discovered and that of which it is a report. Having reached (*d*), the coherence theorist then emphasizes how much our previously acquired powers of judgment are exercised in this experience. He concludes that the second term with which our original judgment that there is a cat on the mat corresponds is not, as we thought, a fact; it is really another judgment or set of judgments.

Whether the whole argument is designed to show that correspondence is really coherence when the correspondence is put forward as giving the nature of truth or only when it is put forward as giving the criterion of truth, it seems equally invalid.

What the coherence theory really does is to give the criteria for the truth and falsity of a priori, or analytic, statements. Any attempt to change the meaning of "coherence" from coherence with other statements to coherence with fact (or reality of experience) is to abandon the theory. A merit of the theory is that it sees that the reasons for calling an analytic statement true or false are not those which some correspondence theorists, primarily thinking of empirical statements, try to fasten on all statements. When it sets itself up as the theory of truth, its mistake is twofold. First, it suggests that the criteria appropriate to a priori, or analytic, statements apply to every kind of statement; what the metaphysicians really did was to suppose all statements to be a priori.

Second, it confuses the reasons, or criteria, for calling a statement true or false with the meaning of "truth" or "falsity." As far as the criteria of truth are concerned, we can say only of a priori, or analytic, statements that they are true because they cohere with each other, and only of empirical statements that they are true because of what the world is like; however, as far as the meaning of truth is concerned, we can say of any kind of statement that it is true if it corresponds to the facts. Thus, as well as saying that a true a priori statement coheres with other statements in the system, we can also say that it corresponds to the a priori facts. It may be a fact that the sum of the angles of a Lobachevskian triangle is less than two right angles and also that the field of Waterloo is a mile square. What we must remember is that although both sorts of statements, if true, state the facts—tell us how things are—this amounts to something different in the two cases; the size of the angles of a Lobachevskian triangle is not something in the world in the way that the size of the field of Waterloo is.

See also Analytic and Synthetic Statements; Blanshard, Brand; Bradley, Francis Herbert; Coherentism; Correspondence Theory of Truth; Fallacies; Hegel, Georg Wilhelm Friedrich; Hempel, Carl Gustav; Idealism; Leibniz, Gottfried Wilhelm; Logical Positivism; Neurath, Otto; Rationalism; Spinoza, Benedict (Baruch) de; Truth.

Bibliography

Ayer, A. J. "The Criterion of Truth." *Analysis* 3 (1935–1936): 28–32. Reprinted in *Philosophy and Analysis*, edited by M. Macdonald. Oxford: Blackwell, 1954. Attacks the coherence theory as put forward by the logical positivists.

Bender, John W., ed. *The Current State of the Coherence Theory*. Boston: Kluwer, 1989.

Blanshard, Brand. *The Nature of Thought*. London: Allen and Unwin, 1939. Vol. II, Chs. 25–27.

BonJour, Laurence. *The Structure of Empirical Knowledge*. Cambridge, MA: Harvard University Press, 1985.

Bradley, F. H. *Appearance and Reality*. Oxford, 1893. Chs. 15 and 24.

Bradley, F. H. *Essays on Truth and Reality*. Oxford: Clarendon Press, 1914. Chs. 7 and 11.

Dancy, Jonathan. "On Coherence Theories of Justification: Can an Empiricist Be a Coherentist?" *American Philosophical Quarterly* 21 (1984): 359–365.

Davidson, Donald. "A Coherence Theory of Truth and Knowledge." In *Reading Rorty*, edited by Alan R. Malachowski. Cambridge, MA: Blackwell, 1991.

Devitt, Michael. *Realism and Truth*. Oxford: Blackwell, 1984.

Ewing, A. C. *Idealism: A Critical Survey*. London: Methuen, 1934. Ch. 5.

Hempel, C. G. "On the Logical Positivists' Theory of Truth." *Analysis* 2 (4) (1935): 49–59.

Joachim, H. H. *The Nature of Truth*. Oxford: Clarendon Press, 1906.

Khatchadourian, Haig. *The Coherence Theory of Truth: A Critical Evaluation*. Beirut: American University, 1961.

Kirkham, R. L. *Theories of Truth: A Critical Introduction*. Cambridge, MA: MIT Press, 1992.

Putnam, Hilary. *Reason, Truth, and History*. Cambridge, U.K.: Cambridge University Press, 1981.

Quine, W. V., and J. S. Ullian. *The Web of Belief*, 2nd ed. New York: Random House, 1978.

Rescher, Nicholas. *The Coherence Theory of Truth*. Oxford: Clarendon Press, 1973.

Russell, Bertrand. *An Inquiry into Meaning and Truth*. London, 1940. Ch. 10.

Schlick, Moritz. "Facts and Propositions." *Analysis* 2 (5) (1935), 65–70. Reprinted in M. Macdonald, ed. *Philosophy and Analysis*. Oxford, 1954. Attacks the coherence theory as put forward by the logical positivists.

Sellars, Wilfrid. *Science, Perception, and Reality*. Atascadero, CA: Ridgeview Press, 1991.

Sosa, Ernest. *Knowledge in Perspective: Selected Essays in Epistemology*. Cambridge, U.K.: Cambridge University Press, 1991.

Sosa, Ernest. "Reflective Knowledge in the Best Circles." *Journal of Philosophy* 94 (1997).

Sylvan, Richard. "On Making a Coherence Theory of Truth True." *Philosophica* (1990): 77–105.

Walker, Ralph. *The Coherence Theory of Truth: Realism, Anti-Realism, Idealism.* London: Routledge, 1989.

Woozley, A. D. *Theory of Knowledge.* London: Hutchinson, 1949. Pp. 146–169.

Alan R. White (1967)
Bibliography updated by Benjamin Fiedor (2005)

COHERENTISM

One of the three major views of the nature of epistemic justification, the coherence theory (or "coherentism") experienced a revival during the 1970s and 1980s after its near total eclipse earlier in the twentieth century. Although its origins can be traced to idealists, including Francis Bradley, Bernard Bosanquet, and Brand Blanshard, the coherence theory has more recently been espoused by empiricist-minded contemporary philosophers such as Wilfrid Sellars, Nicholas Rescher, Keith Lehrer, Gilbert Harman, and Laurence Bonjour. The coherence theory of justification stands as an alternative to both the more traditional foundations theory and the view called reliabilism. It should not be confused with a coherence theory of truth. A coherence theorist about justification can acknowledge a fact that cripples the coherence theory of truth, namely, that there are instances of coherent, hence justified, beliefs in falsehoods.

Although the details of different versions of the coherence theory vary widely, all versions share a positive thesis and a resulting negative claim. The coherence theory's positive thesis is that a belief is justified or warranted for a person to the degree that that belief coheres with the rest of that person's belief system. As a fabric derives its strength from the reciprocal ties and interconnections among its constitutive threads, so, for the coherentist, beliefs derive their justification from their interconnectedness with one's other beliefs. The negative claim endorsed by all coherentists is that foundationalism is in error when it asserts that some of our justified beliefs are privileged or basic—that is, their justification is at least partly independent of their connectedness with other held beliefs.

The coherentist's picture of mutual support or fit among our beliefs departs (to varying degrees) from the strictly linear image of justification that classical foundationalism endorses. For the foundationalist epistemic justification is transmitted to nonbasic beliefs, from those that are basic or foundational, along lines of inference and explanation. Inferred beliefs are justified by those from which they are inferred. For the coherentist the belief's justificatory status has less to do with the grounds on which a belief is based and more to do with the whole cluster of relations (of consistency, implication, probability, explanation, and the like) that more or less strongly fix that belief within the network of other held beliefs.

The exact nature of epistemic coherence, however, is very difficult to clarify, and disagreements occur even among coherentists. Some have argued that coherence is always and ultimately explanatory coherence, a question of whether a belief is a member of the best overall explanatory account accessible to an individual. Others claim that there are justificatory relations of comparative reasonableness of competing beliefs that reflect concerns wider than explanation alone, including measures of subjective probability and the relative informativeness of the proposition believed. Logical consistency seems to be a minimal necessary condition for maximal coherence, but some have argued that at least certain inconsistencies are unavoidable but do not so undermine coherence as to prevent beliefs from being justified. Speaking generally, coherence is a property of a belief system that is determined by the (various) connections of intelligibility among the elements of the system. Most agree that these include deductive, inductive, and abductive relations, as well as other explanatory and probabilistic connections. Some writers, especially pragmatists, are prepared to add relations such as the relative simplicity or the power of the explanations contained in one's belief system as contributors to overall coherence.

Motivation for the coherence theory comes most directly from finding foundationalism unworkable and believing as a consequence that some version of coherence must be correct. Another motivation comes from the observation that it seems apt and possible to ask about any belief what a person's reasons are for holding it. The theory also appears particularly compatible with the realization that all instances of epistemic justification are defeasible—that is, the justification of a given belief is always liable to undermining by other held beliefs, no matter how strong the initial grounds or evidential basis of the belief might be. Since undermining can come from any element of one's system that might be negatively relevant to a specific belief, it appears that complete epistemic justification, the kind necessary to support claims of knowledge, is sensitive to all of the connections among our beliefs, precisely as the coherence theorist urges. This argument for the coherence theory is not decisive, however, since foundationalists can freely admit that warrant is undermined by a lack of coherence while still rejecting the coherentist's positive claim that coherence is the source of all epistemic justification.

In addition to the unclarities surrounding measuring degrees of coherence, numerous objections have been offered to coherentism. Four have been particularly prominent.

THE CIRCULARITY OBJECTION

If there are no foundational beliefs that act as the ultimate source of epistemic justification, and if the lines of justification transmission are not infinitely long (which appears absurd given the finitude of our mental capacities), then the coherence theory seems forced to claim that justification can be ultimately but not viciously circular. It is not immediately clear how circularity of this sort is anything but vicious, no matter how wide the circle may be, even though some have argued that wideness of a justificatory circle immunizes against viciousness. But if *A* is the source of justification for *B,* how can *B* be the source of justification for *A*? The coherentist can reply that the "source" of justification is the entire belief system. The linear model of justification on which the circularity objection is based may not be forceful against a more holistic construal of the relation. Taken as a holistic and higher-order relation constituted by lower-order reciprocal relations (at least some of which are asymmetric, such as "explaining" and "being explained by"), coherence might be able to avoid the problem of vicious circularity.

THE PROBLEM OF PERCEPTUAL BELIEFS

Certain simple and apparently immediate perceptual beliefs seem to be justified for us on the basis of the perceptual experience we currently are having rather than on any considerations about how that belief coheres with the rest of our belief system. Experience often seems to warrant beliefs that are anomalous—that is, do not cohere with already-held beliefs. In such cases we do not think that we are justified in rejecting the new belief on grounds of incoherence but often concede that revision of some previously held beliefs is appropriate. Coherentists have replied to this objection by arguing that the justification of even the most immediate perceptual belief requires that that belief cohere with our metabeliefs regarding how reliable or trustworthy we take our perceptual processes to be in the particular conditions. It is such metabeliefs that make it more reasonable to accept the anomalous perceptual experience than it is for us to conclude that we are hallucinating or have been deceived in some fashion. The introduction of metabeliefs into the explanation why immediate perceptual beliefs are often justified for us has struck many, however, as overintellectualizing our epistemic situation, as well as possibly reintroducing foundational principles into the theory of justification.

THE ISOLATION OBJECTION

This objection, closely related to the problem of perceptual beliefs, begins with the observation that coherence is a cognitively internal relation, relating belief to belief. But might not a thoroughly coherent system of beliefs nonetheless fail to be justified because they are not properly linked to the external perceptual circumstances? Would acceptance of a coherent fiction be justified if it were entirely the product of wishful thinking? The continual perceptual input we receive from the world must be assimilated into our belief system or else the justification for those beliefs will often suffer from undermining. The coherence theory seems too internalist to be a complete theory of epistemic justification, the objection concludes. Since coherence does not necessarily serve the epistemic goals of pursuing truth and avoiding error in our belief system, further constraints seem necessary if our notion of justification is to relate appropriately to knowledge. Coherentists respond in a number of ways to the isolation objection.

One alternative is to admit the objection's force and add a requirement that all justified systems include the belief that certain kinds of spontaneously occurring beliefs such as perceptual and memory beliefs are reliable or likely to be true. Demonstrating that this constraint is not an ad hoc amendment to coherentism is a difficult matter. A similar requirement applied to acceptances based on spontaneous wishful thinking would be obviously ad hoc and unacceptable. Some have suggested that metabeliefs about the trustworthiness of our perceptual beliefs in certain circumstances are not ad hoc and are important and legitimate members of our belief system, justified, as all beliefs are, through their coherence with our other beliefs. Whether such beliefs can be noncircularly defended, whether they constitute a sort of foundational belief, and whether they are realistically necessary for epistemic justification are each open matters.

THE INFERENTIAL-STRUCTURE OBJECTION

The foundationalist's traditional view—that whether one is epistemically justified in believing some proposition depends crucially upon the actual course of inference taken in arriving at a belief—is not easily relinquished. Coherence, however, is a relation determined only by the contents of beliefs and not by the order in which they have been inferred. Consequently, it appears possible that a series of beliefs inferred one from the other in a wholly fallacious manner might nevertheless cohere maximally with a background system of beliefs as long as there is another valid (but unused) course of inference that does connect them. This leads to the conclusion that, even if the coherence theory adequately captures the concept of epistemically justifiable beliefs relative to a system, it fails to explicate the notion of being justified in believing a proposition. Coherentists have responded to this challenge by relying once more on metabeliefs, claiming that when we infer *A* from *B* and *B* from *C* we also accept or believe that *A* follows from *B*, and not, for example, that *C* follows from *A*. Incorrect metabeliefs will, on some versions of coherentism, cause incoherence and loss of justification, keeping blatantly fallacious reasoning from ending in justified beliefs. This response, however, may generate an infinite regress of metabeliefs. Not all uses of inference schemes contain premises stating that the scheme is valid. One can infer *B* from *A* without first having to infer that *B* follows from *A*. Some coherentists answer this and other objections by admitting that their proposed conditions for coherence constitute ideals to which human knowers should aspire but seldom in actuality achieve. Debate over the merits of the coherence theory promises to continue unabated.

See also Blanshard, Brand; Bosanquet, Bernard; Bradley, Francis Herbert; Classical Foundationalism; Coherence Theory of Truth; Epistemology; Epistemology, History of; Harman, Gilbert; Lehrer, Keith; Reliabilism; Rescher, Nicholas; Sellars, Wilfrid.

Bibliography

Audi, R. "Foundationalism, Coherentism, and Epistemological Dogmatism." In *Philosophical Perspectives,* edited by J. Tomberlin, Vol. 2. Atascadero, CA: Ridgeview, 1988.

Bender, J. W., ed. *The Current State of the Coherence Theory.* Philosophical Studies, Vol. 44. Dordrecht: Kluwer Academic, 1989.

Bonjour, L. *The Structure of Empirical Knowledge.* Cambridge, MA: Harvard University Press, 1985.

Lehrer, K. *Theory of Knowledge.* Boulder, CO: Westview Press, 1990.

Plantinga, A. *Warrant: The Current Debate.* Oxford: Oxford University Press, 1993.

Pollock, J. *Contemporary Theories of Knowledge.* Totowa, NJ: Rowman and Littlefield, 1986.

John W. Bender (1996)

COLERIDGE, SAMUEL TAYLOR

(1772–1834)

Samuel Taylor Coleridge, the critic, romantic poet and philosopher, was born four years before the publication of Jeremy Bentham's *Fragment on Government,* and died only two years before the death of Bentham's most influential disciple, James Mill, at a time when the young John Stuart Mill was making a brilliant success in political journalism. The striking fact about Coleridge's place in English intellectual history, however, is that he developed a form of idealism in virtual isolation from the mainstream of empirical philosophy. In developing his own philosophical insights, Coleridge turned to Immanuel Kant. He had two reasons for doing this. First, he was deeply dissatisfied with the mechanistic theory of mind still flourishing in English philosophy, since he was unable to formulate within its terms certain views about poetic imagination; while Kant's *Critique of Judgment* (1790) had, however, set out with great rigor, and within a much more tractable conceptual framework, views essentially similar to Coleridge's own.

Second, Coleridge thought he saw in Kant's Transcendental Dialectic a way of combating the chronic latitudinarianism in English theology that had predominated throughout the eighteenth century and continued until the time of the Oxford Movement. But it must be remembered that although Coleridge was a serious student of Kant and one of Kant's earliest and ablest English interpreters, he was not a systematic or academic philosopher. His philosophical writings are always disorganized, eclectic, aphoristic. Philosophy became for him what poetry had always been: a necessary means for self-analysis, for the objectification of his personal engagement with life.

PHILOSOPHICAL DEVELOPMENT

What can be very schematically called the first stage in Coleridge's philosophical development was a highly enthusiastic acceptance in 1794 of David Hartley's theory of association and the "necessitarianism" which that doctrine seemed to imply. Also at this time, after an intense study of John Locke and of William Godwin's *Inquiry concerning Political Justice* (1793), Coleridge became strongly inspired by the Enlightenment ideal of social perfectibility. So inspired was he that in December of that year, having had these enthusiasms reciprocated by Robert Southey, he left Cambridge without taking his degree. In January 1795 he lectured at Bristol on religion and politics and became preoccupied with Southey on the project of a pantisocracy, an ideal socialist community consisting of twelve young men and their wives, which was to be established on the banks of the Susquehanna. This project never really got under way; but its rather serious practical outcome for Coleridge was his marriage on October 4, 1795, to the uncomplicated Sara Fricker, sister of Southey's pantisocratic fiancée. Coleridge's early marriage was unfortunate because it prevented his developing what would have been in every way a more compatible relationship with Sara Hutchinson, whom he met through the Wordsworths in 1799 and whose inaccessibility he spent the greater part of his life lamenting. (Thus the celebrated *Dejection: An Ode,* written in 1802, should be considered more as a crescendo in this lament than as a statement of any alleged conflict between imagination and metaphysics.)

Despite his temporary acquiescence in Hartley's psychology, it was in fact Hartley's theology that most of all appealed to Coleridge. In particular, Hartley's idea of an ascending scale of affections, from primary sensations of pleasure and pain through new complexes of association to self-interest and eventually to sympathy, moral sense, and theophany (*Religious Musing,* 1794–1796) made a lasting impression on him. To this idea, conceived of mechanistically by Hartley, Coleridge later found an organically conceived analogue in Friedrich von Schelling's *Naturphilosophie.* Possibly in 1795, and certainly in 1796, Coleridge read George Berkeley. The next important stage of his philosophical development consisted in the replacement of Hartley's passive concept of mind by Berkeley's never consistently expressed notion of finite mind being actually creative in perception and imagination when it is considered as participating in the infinite, all-productive mind of God. Once more it was the place of God in the philosophy of Berkeley that most concerned Coleridge; and Berkeley's view of nature as purposive, as divine language, found expression in a number of poems written between 1796 and 1800 (for instance, *Destiny of Nations,* ll. 18–20; *Frost at Midnight,* ll. 59–62; *Apologia pro Vita Sua*).

By 1797 the Godwin-Hartley-necessity phase was over. It is probably significant that Coleridge emancipated himself from the mechanical theory of mind at the same time that he lost his once firmly held belief in the ideals of the French Revolution (*France: An Ode,* 1798). In September 1798, Coleridge accompanied the Wordsworths to Germany. After a short meeting in Hamburg with the poet F. G. Klopstock, Coleridge left the Wordsworths to see the countryside and settled himself at the University of Göttingen in order to improve his German and to collect material for a biography of Gotthold Ephraim Lessing. At Göttingen he attended the biological lectures of J. F. Blumenbach and had theological arguments with disciples of the rationalist J. G. Eichhorn. He returned to England in July 1799, transporting £30 worth of German philosophy books "with a view to the one work, to which I hope to dedicate in silence the prime of my life." This work was his never-completed *Opus Maximum.* Thus, the third period of Coleridge's philosophical development was a long assimilation of Kant and the German romantic philosophers, particularly Schelling, which he began in earnest in 1801 and continued well beyond 1816, when he was settled in the London house of James Gillman and able to write his most important philosophical works.

PHILOSOPHY AND FAITH

That "seminal" quality of mind that J. S. Mill detected in Coleridge and praised so highly needs, as we shall see, slight reevaluation. Mill was perhaps right in claiming that the "Germano-Coleridgean" school had done more for the philosophy of human culture than any of their predecessors could have done. Yet, in stressing the great contributions made to social theory by a series of Continental thinkers from Johann Gottfried Herder to Jules Michelet and in attributing to Coleridge simply a share in those contributions, Mill tended to ignore the less philanthropic and more personalistic aspects of European romanticism. For Coleridge was a post-Kantian "philosopher of life" in the tradition of Heinrich Heine's *Die romantische Schule.* For example, the closeness in particular doctrines and virtual identity in general philosophical orientation between Coleridge and Friedrich von Schlegel is remarkable. Both thinkers are essentially religious critics of the Enlightenment's secular anthropology. That man is a "fallen creature … diseased in his will" is a principle as axiomatic to Coleridge and Schlegel as it is self-dramatizing and even morally pernicious to the philosophical radicals.

Where Bentham and his followers write primarily as social reformers seeking, in the manner of David Hume and Claude-Adrien Helvétius, a means of harmonizing individual egoism with the general good of society, the "Germano-Coleridgeans" take man's tragic alienation from God to be the fundamental datum not only of religion but also of philosophy. For the Benthamites the area of moral significance is in socioeconomic relationships, the external actions of everyday public association. For Coleridge, on the other hand, almost as much as for Søren Kierkegaard, the locus of reality is in the individual's experience of God. Thus, with thinkers like Coleridge philosophy inevitably becomes a form of theosophy. Religion is the highest exercise of the human spirit, and philosophy is a kind of rational prolegomenon that prepares the way for man's fuller appreciation of his relationship with God. Philosophy does this by trying to ascertain "the origin and primary laws (or efficient causes) either of the world man included (which is Natural Philosophy)—or of Human Nature exclusively, and as far as it is human (which is Moral Philosophy)." The remaining branch of philosophy, according to Coleridge, is epistemology, which deals with "the question concerning the sufficiency of the human reason to arrive at the solution of both or either of the two former problems.

REASON AND UNDERSTANDING

The core of Coleridge's epistemology is contained in his distinction between Reason and Understanding and his insistence that these differ not in degree but in kind. Although the terminology Coleridge uses here is decidedly Kantian, Kant's distinction between understanding (*Verstand*) and reason in the narrow sense (*Vernunft*) is only superficially similar to Coleridge's. Like his parallel distinctions between Imagination and Fancy, Genius and Talent, Symbol and Allegory, Coleridge's contrast between Reason and Understanding is more evaluative than descriptive and well illustrates his characteristic attempt to keep empiricist and associationist concepts in a subordinate position within a larger idealist framework. Understanding is "the faculty of judging according to sense … the faculty by which we reflect and generalize," which roughly corresponds to Locke's definition of it as "the power of perception." In other words, it is what Coleridge takes to be the pragmatic reasoning faculty of the empiricists.

The Coleridgean Reason, however, is a higher and more esoteric faculty that has at least three not very clearly differentiated functions. In its "speculative" aspect, Reason (1) provides us with basic logical rules of discourse, the so-called laws of thought; (2) is the origin of synthetic a priori truths in mathematics and science; and, in its most important "practical" aspect (3) is "the source of ideas, which … in their conversion to the responsible will, become ultimate ends." Reason produces Ideas or ideals that, although not capable of demonstration, are nevertheless not self-contradictory and may have a clear and distinct form. But they can also, says Coleridge, be more like an instinct or longing: "a vague appetency towards something which the Mind incessantly hunts for … or the impulse which fills the young Poet's eye with tears, he knows not why."

What Coleridge's distinction amounts to is this: "Understanding" is a pejorative blanket term for the negative aspects of eighteenth-century logic and science, while "Reason" is an approbatory label for those personal ideals and religious beliefs that are psychologically foreign to, or at least not logically entailed by, scientific empiricism. "Reason" thus is clearly allied with Christian faith. Coleridge is not, then, doing a piece of straight conceptual analysis in making this distinction, even though he often writes as if he thinks he is. Instead, he is persuasively psychologizing in an attempt to reorient contemporary philosophical attitudes into unison with contemporary Christian ideals. The barely disguised function of Coleridge's distinction is to give metaphysical respectability to those Ideas of God, freedom, and immortality that Kant had rightly regarded as merely regulative rather than constitutive elements of knowledge.

MIND AND NATURE

Philosophy must begin, says Coleridge, with a primary intuition that can be neither merely speculative nor merely practical, but both in one. Here Coleridge significantly modifies the views of Schelling. If the existence of external nature is taken to be the primary intuition, as in natural philosophy, then it becomes necessary to explain how mind or consciousness can be related to it. If, conversely, mind is taken to be primary, as in the Cartesian *Cogito,* we must account for the existence and significance of nature. The only satisfactory way to do either of these things is to suppose that there is in fact no dualism between nature and mind. Nature appears as extrinsic, alien, and in antithesis to mind. The difference is not absolute, however, but merely one of degree of consciousness and, consequently, of freedom.

Nature is mind or spirit slumbering, unconscious of itself. It is representable under the forms of space and time, subject to the relations of cause and effect, and requires an antecedent explanation. Mind, however, originates in its own (that is, God's) acts and exists in a realm of freedom. But if in its turn this qualitative difference between nature and mind is to be accounted for, a first cause must be postulated that is itself neither exclusively mind nor exclusively nature, subject or object, but the identity of both. Such a first cause or unconditional principle could not be a natural thing or object because each thing is what it is in consequence of some other thing. Nor can this principle be mind as such, because mind exists only in antithesis to nature. (Rather than indulging in tautology here, Coleridge seems to be making the phenomenologist's point that consciousness is always intentional; i.e., is consciousness *of* something.) The unconditioned must be conceived, apparently, as a primeval synthesis of subject and object, consciousness and nature, in the self-consciousness of God. In God or Spirit lies the identity of the two, of being and knowing in the "absolute I AM."

Thus nature and mind seem to be conceived by Coleridge as two dialectical opposites resulting from God's free act of self-alienation in becoming self-conscious. On this last point, however, he is in his published works particularly (and perhaps necessarily) obscure. Unlike Johann Gottlieb Fichte and Schelling, Coleridge wishes to combine the dialectics of the Identity-Philosophy with the traditional Christian concept of dualism between creature and creator. In the unpublished *Opus Maximum* and other manuscripts, he elaborates this point of divergence from the Germans by distinguishing the "personeity" of God from the "personality" of man and goes to great lengths in accounting for the problem of evil. What is important and seminal in Coleridge's metaphysics, however, is not its details or conclusions, but the rich suggestiveness of its basic categories applied to certain problems in aesthetics and social theory.

IMAGINATION AND FANCY

From the formal dialectics of his idealism Coleridge drew a living description of how the artist's mind works. Since conscious life exists only through contradiction, or doubleness, the whole of nature out of which conscious life develops must exhibit opposing forces in the reconciling and recurrence of which "consists the process and mystery of production." Art is produced through that same dialectical struggle for the reconciliation of opposites that takes place between mind and nature. Art is not, then, merely imitative, but symbolic of reality. Like all symbols (as Coleridge defines them), it is consequently an inherent part of the process it represents; and the artist as creator, his consciousness being the focus of nature and Idea, matter and form, becomes symbolic of God. So, like God, the artist or Genius must suffer alienation in order to create. He needs to be in a special sense disinterested, emotionally aloof for a while from his subject matter and from himself. For in the joy of creation "individuality is lost." He must first "eloign himself from nature in order to return to her with full effect." Just as in the cosmic struggle for synthesis, so in the microcosm of art and the individual artist's mind, there is an attempted fusion of conscious and unconscious forces.

The artist (Coleridge usually considers the case of the poet) achieves such fusions in virtue of his special psychological makeup; that is, through his having the power of Imagination. Coleridge's theory of Imagination, however, does not neatly reflect any of the everyday uses of "imagination" distinguished by modern linguistic analysts. His poet does not create through merely imaginary (unreal) fantasy, nor does he imagine in the sense of making to himself or his reader a kind of supposal, veridical or false. And although it is of course true that the poet is imaginative in being creative or inventive, it is not the case, according to Coleridge, that it is in this fact alone that the poet's Imagination consists.

Nor is Imagination "invention" in the sense that it adds to the real, as common usage might suggest. Instead, as we have seen, Coleridge's view is that the poem and the poet are microcosmic analogues, indeed symbolic parts, of reality. His theory is not concerned, then, with an elucidation of ordinary senses of "in imagination" or even with ordinary senses of "with imagination." It is, typically, a piece of speculative (though not therefore unempirical) psychology that is the rather overweighted vehicle for a value judgment. In this and certain other respects, Coleridge's theory of Imagination has interesting affinities with Jean-Paul Sartre's theory in which imagination is related to the notion of nihilation of consciousness. Needless to say, Sartre is borrowing from a later development of the same German tradition to which Coleridge was indebted.

Coleridge considers three things: primary Imagination, secondary Imagination, and Fancy. The power of primary Imagination is not peculiar to poets, but is standard psychological equipment for all men. It is Coleridge's term for what he considers to be finite mind's repetition in perception of God's creative act. His view seems to be that by synthetically perceiving and categorizing things that are not me, I become conscious of myself, and that this state of human self-consciousness is analogous to God's own creative schizophrenia. Secondary Imagination is the specialized poetic faculty. Differing only in degree and in its mode of operation from primary Imagination, it is the poet's power of unifying chaotic experience into the significant form of art. Thus, secondary or poetic Imagination "dissolves, diffuses, dissipates, in order to recreate … it struggles to idealize and to unify. It is essentially *vital,* even as all objects (*as* objects) are essentially fixed and dead."

Fancy, on the other hand, differs in kind from Imagination. While poetic Imagination is organic in its operation, producing true analogues of God's creation, Fancy is merely mechanical, aggregative; it is at best imitative rather than symbolic and the instrument of Talent, as opposed to Genius. Fancy is in fact that lower-grade imagination that Locke and Hume set beside sense and memory as a third, nonreferential, source of ideas. Thus Fancy is allied to Understanding, while Imagination, in its ability to transcend and transform the phenomenal, is allied to Reason. It embodies in works of art that inner struggle between nature and mind within which art and Genius are temporary points of resolution.

Despite Coleridge's unhelpful talk about Imagination and Fancy being mental faculties, there is no doubt that the concrete application of these essentially evaluative concepts leads to a highly practical literary criticism. To mention only one instance, Coleridge's conception of the work of art as in some degree analogous to a biological organism and his distinction between mechanical regularity and organic form in poetry has had the greatest possible influence on modern criticism. Largely through the far-reaching implications of his distinction between Imagination and Fancy, Coleridge became the first English writer on poetry since the Renaissance to embody the highest powers of critical response within a framework of philosophical concepts that seemed to explain and reinforce that response rather than to inhibit or destroy it.

MORALS AND POLITICS

Although Coleridge was in his ethical theory a follower and acute critic of Kant, he is interesting today not so much for his own positive views as for his attack upon utilitarianism. Coleridge launches this attack in two ways. First, he tries to demonstrate the logical absurdity of the greatest happiness principle by reductio ad absurdum techniques; second, he "postulates the Will," which involves the claim that the utilitarian notion of personality is psychologically inadequate. On the logical side, Coleridge opens fire with the surprisingly modern assertion that the whole of moral philosophy is contained in one question: "Is *Good* a superfluous word … for the pleasurable and its causes—at most a mere modification to express degree and comparative duration of pleasure?" His reply is that the meaning of *good* can be decided only by an appeal to universal usage, for the distinction between *good* and *pleasurable,* which, he holds, is common to all languages of the civilized world, must "be the consequent of a common consciousness of man as man."

Then, avoiding the error J. S. Mill was soon to make, Coleridge distinguishes between things that are good because they are desired, and things that are or ought to be desired because they are good. This leads him to conclude that *good* cannot be defined simply in terms of pleasure or happiness. Against the Benthamite view that the agent's motive has nothing to do with the morality of his action, Coleridge makes two points, partly logical and partly psychological. The utilitarian position cannot generally hold, he says, because it follows from it that I could do a morally right act by sheer chance. But such complete lack of inward, conscious participation on my part could never be a sufficient criterion for my acting morally. The utilitarian principle therefore confounds morality with law. Moreover, it is no defense here to say that the principle was put forward as a criterion for judging the morality of the action and not that of the agent, because this last distinction is "merely logical, not real and vital." Acts cannot be dissociated from an agent any more than ideas from a mind.

In his social philosophy, Coleridge writes in the tradition of Edmund Burke. His mature views are contained in *On the Constitution of the Church and State,* which was begun as an attempt to formulate objections to various bills for Catholic emancipation and finished as an idealist treatise containing the whole logomachy of organism and the reconciliation of opposites. In any society there are always two antithetical forces at work. Since, dialectically speaking, "opposite powers are always of the same kind, and tend to union," Coleridge's idea of a well-functioning society is the nonrevolutionary reconciliation of forces working for permanence with forces working for progression. These he identifies with, respectively, the aristocratic, landed interest and the bourgeois, commercial interest of early Victorian England; a monarch also being required to maintain cohesion.

Coleridge's habit of generalizing from the history and the contemporary pattern of British political institutions rather than, as he alleges, drawing a description of the idea of a state, should at least make suspect his application of these largely a priori principles. This habit leaves Coleridge, like G. W. F. Hegel, wide open to the charge of surrounding the constitution of his own country with an aura of metaphysical sanctity to which it has no claim. Despite such ruinous methodology, however, what Coleridge has to say about the intelligentsia and the part it has to play in the dissemination of culture has been influential.

Coleridge contrasts *cultivation* with *civilization.* Civilization he takes to denote external, material social progress, while cultivation is more inward and personal: the "harmonious development of these qualities and faculties that characterize our humanity." So that cultivation can take place, Coleridge proposes the formation of a state-endowed class, the "clerisy" or "national church," which would effectively consist of professors of liberal arts officially established throughout the country. The national church would, however, be in no sense identical with the Church of England or with any purely religious organization. Its purpose would be to preserve the results of learning, to "bind the present with the past" and to give every member of the community an understanding of his social rights and duties. The almost limitless possibilities for authoritarianism in such an arrangement are, again, obvious. Nevertheless, in Coleridge's *Church and State* the idea of culture as something independent of material progress was first systematically introduced into English thinking, and was from then onward available in various forms, not merely to influence society but also to judge it.

CONCLUSION

Though it is no doubt true that Coleridge was, with Bentham, one of the great seminal minds of England in his age, it is not true without qualification that the cultural powers wielded by Bentham and Coleridge were "opposite poles of one great force of progression." Here Mill was surely indulging in public-spirited wish fulfillment rather than relating the facts. Coleridge and his German contemporaries undoubtedly brought to social consciousness those deeper insights into the nature of the individual and the organic complexities of human associations that were classically synthesized by Hegel in the *Philosophy of Right* (1821). Yet the inherent ambiguity of these insights has today become a disturbing commonplace. Mill inevitably overlooked the darker side of romanticism. For once the romantic artist or philosopher ceases to believe in God, he tends either to find a new object of veneration in history or hero worship or, more recently, to relinquish his very inwardness and imagination in solipsistic nausea. It was Coleridge's curious fortune that he never lost his belief in God.

See also Aesthetics, History of; Bentham, Jeremy; Berkeley, George; Burke, Edmund; Cartesianism; Enlightenment; Fichte, Johann Gottlieb; Godwin, William; Hartley, David; Hegel, Georg Wilhelm Friedrich; Helvétius, Claude-Adrien; Herder, Johann Gottfried; Hume, David; Idealism; Imagination; Kant, Immanuel; Kierkegaard, Søren Aabye; Lessing, Gotthold Ephraim; Locke, John; Mill, James; Mill, John Stuart; Romanticism; Schelling, Friedrich Wilhelm Joseph von; Schlegel, Friedrich von.

Bibliography

The Complete Works of S. T. Coleridge, edited by W. G. T. Shedd, 7 vols. (New York: Harper, 1853 and 1884), was very far from complete. Fortunately, Professor Kathleen Coburn is now in the process of preparing the first scholarly and really comprehensive edition of practically everything Coleridge wrote, apart from the *Collected Letters,* edited by E. L. Griggs, 6 vols. (Oxford: Clarendon Press, 1956–1971). Coburn has already brought out two volumes of Coleridge's *Notebooks* (London and New York, 1957 and 1962) and his *Philosophical Lectures* (London: Pilot Press, 1949). Coburn's *Inquiring Spirit: A New Presentation of Coleridge from His Published and Unpublished Prose Writings* (New York: Pantheon, 1951) gives an exciting foretaste of what is to come.

Among the prose works essential for a study of Coleridge as a thinker, note particularly the following: *Biographia Literaria* (New York: Kirk and Merein, 1817), edited by John Shawcross, 2 vols. (Oxford: Clarendon Press, 1907); *The Friend,* 3 vols. (London: Fenner, 1818); *Aids to Reflection* (London: Taylor and Hessey, 1825); *On the Constitution of the Church and State, According to the Idea of Each* (London, 1830); *Coleridge on Logic and Learning,* edited by A. D. Snyder (London, 1929); *S. T. Coleridge's Treatise on Method,* edited by A. D. Snyder (London: Constable, 1934); *Coleridge's Shakespearean Criticism,* edited by T. M. Raynor (London: Constable, 1930); *Specimens of the Table Talk of the late S. T. Coleridge,* edited by H. N. Coleridge, 2 vols. (London: Murray, 1835).

On Coleridge's general philosophical position, see especially John H. Muirhead, *Coleridge as Philosopher* (London: Allen and Unwin, 1930) and Elizabeth Winkelmann, *Coleridge und die Kantische Philosophie* (Leipzig: Mayer and Müller, 1933). Both these works are reliable but philosophically very old-fashioned. Among the very large number of articles on Coleridge's thought, A. O. Lovejoy, "Coleridge and Kant's Two Worlds," reprinted in *Essays in the History of Ideas* (Baltimore: Johns Hopkins Press, 1948) deserves special attention. James D. Boulger, *Coleridge as Religious Thinker* (New Haven, CT: Yale University Press, 1961) gives a good account of the later Coleridge.

On the theory of imagination, see especially James V. Baker, *The Sacred River* (Baton Rouge: Louisiana State University Press, 1957); I. A. Richards, *Coleridge on Imagination* (2nd ed., New York: Norton, 1950); René Wellek, *A History of Modern Criticism* (London, 1965), Vol. 2, Ch. 6; J. M. Cameron, "Poetic Imagination," in *Proceedings of the Aristotelian Society,* n.s. 62 (1961–1962): 219–240. The best short work in this field is Gordon McKenzie, *Organic Unity in Coleridge,* University of California Publications in English, Vol. 7, No. 1 (Berkeley: University of California Press, 1939), 1–108. R. H. Fogle, *The Idea of Coleridge's*

Criticism (Berkeley: University of California Press, 1962) is suggestive if not always epistemologically acute.

A reliable account of Coleridge's political thought is given in John Colmer, *Coleridge: Critic of Society* (Oxford: Clarendon Press, 1959). J. S. Mill, "Bentham" and "Coleridge," in *London and Westminster Review* (1838 and 1840) will always remain great classics. Also see F. R. Leavis, *Mill on Bentham and Coleridge* (London: Chatto and Windus, 1950) and Raymond Williams, *Culture and Society, 1780–1950* (New York: Columbia University Press, 1958), Part II, Ch. 3. Justus Buchler, *The Concept of Method* (New York: Columbia University Press, 1961) contains an interesting analysis of the *Treatise on Method* and compares Coleridge's views with those of other thinkers, including Bentham.

OTHER RECOMMENDED WORKS

Appleyard, J. A. *Coleridge's Philosophy of Literature: The Development of a Concept of Poetry, 1791–1819*. Cambridge, MA: Harvard University Press, 1965.

Barfield, Owen. *What Coleridge Thought*. Middletown: Wesleyan University Press, 1971.

Coleridge, Samuel Taylor. *The Friend: A Series of Essays to Aid in the Formation of Fixed Principles in Politics, Morals, and Religion with Literary Amusements Interspersed*. London: W. Pickering, 1844.

Coleridge, Samuel Taylor. *The Relation of Philosophy to Theology, and of Theology to Religion*. London: Ward, 1851.

Gallant, Christine, ed. *Coleridge's Theory of Imagination Today*. New York: AMS Press, 1989.

Hamilton, Paul, D. Phil. *Coleridge's Poetics*. Oxford: Basil Blackwell, 1983.

Haney, David P. *The Challenge of Coleridge: Ethics and Interpretation in Romanticism and Modern Philosophy*. University Park: Pennsylvania State University Press, 2001.

Haney, John Louis. *The German Influence on Samuel Taylor Coleridge*. New York: Haskell House, 1966.

Hedley, Douglas. *Coleridge, Philosophy and Religion: Aids to Reflection and the Mirror of the Spirit*. Cambridge, U.K.: Cambridge University Press, 2000.

Hodgson, John A. *Coleridge, Shelley, and Transcendental Inquiry: Rhetoric, Argument, Metapsychology*. Lincoln: University of Nebraska Press, 1989.

Lockridge, Laurence S. *Coleridge the Moralist*. Ithaca: Cornell University Press, 1977.

Marks, Emerson R. *Coleridge on the Language of Verse*. Princeton, NJ: Princeton University Press, 1981.

McKusick, James C. *Coleridge's Philosophy of Language*. New Haven, CT: Yale University Press, 1986.

McNiece, Gerald. *The Knowledge that Endures: Coleridge, German Philosophy and the Logic of Romantic Thought*. London: Macmillan, 1992.

Modiano, Raimonda. *Coleridge and the Concept of Nature*. Tallahassee: Florida State University Press, 1985.

Newlyn, Lucy. *The Cambridge Companion to Coleridge*. Cambridge, U.K.; New York: Cambridge University Press, 2002.

Orsini, Gian Napoleone Giordano. *Coleridge and German Idealism: A Study in the History of Philosophy with Unpublished Materials from Coleridge's Manuscripts*. Carbondale: Southern Illinois University Press, 1969.

Perkins, Mary Anne. *Coleridge's Philosophy: The Logos as Unifying Principle*. Oxford: Clarendon Press; New York: Oxford University Press, 1994.

Perry, Seamus. *Coleridge and the Uses of Division*. Oxford: Clarendon Press; New York: Oxford University Press, 1999.

Swinden, Patrick. "Coleridge and Kant." In *Literature and the Philosophy of Intention*. Basingstoke, Hampshire: Macmillan; New York: St. Martin's Press, 1999.

Taylor, Anya. *Coleridge's Defense of the Human*. Columbus: Ohio State University Press, 1986.

Wheeler, Kathleen M. "Coleridge's Attack on Dualism." In *Romanticism, Pragmatism, and Deconstruction*. Oxford, U.K.; Cambridge, MA: Blackwell, 1993.

Wylie, Ian. *Young Coleridge and the Philosophers of Nature*. Oxford; New York: Oxford University Press, 1989.

Michael Moran (1967)

Bibliography updated by Desiree Matherly Martin

COLET, JOHN

(1466–1519)

John Colet, the Christian humanist and English educator, was the founder of St. Paul's School for Boys, leader of the "Oxford Reformers" Sir Thomas More and Desiderius Erasmus, and chief transmitter of Florentine Platonism from Italy to such English Renaissance figures as Edmund Spenser, John Donne, and John Milton. The son of a London lord mayor, Colet took a master's degree from Oxford (1490) and then explored Plato, Plotinus, and Origen in Latin translation. From 1493 to 1496, he traveled in France and Italy. The appealing tradition that he studied in Florence under Marsilio Ficino was shattered in 1958 when Sears Jayne discovered correspondence between Colet and Ficino in a copy of Ficino's *Epistolae* (1495) at All Soul's College, Oxford. This correspondence shows that Colet never visited Florence or met Ficino.

Upon his return to Oxford in 1496, Colet delivered Latin lectures on St. Paul's Epistles to the Romans and Corinthians. The visiting Erasmus and others applauded as Colet, frequently quoting the Florentine Platonists, propounded a new "historical approach" to the study of Scripture. In 1504 Colet was appointed dean of St. Paul's Cathedral, where, contrary to custom he preached frequently and in English. His congregation included the young lawyer Thomas More.

Colet's penchant for controversy is illustrated by his *Convocation Sermon* (1512), in which he wrathfully condemned his own bishops for their moral laxness. Charges of heresy provoked by this sermon were dismissed by his friend Archbishop Warham, but Colet was soon again involved in controversy. He attacked the war policy of

Henry VIII and was summoned to court; but Henry, after hearing Colet's arguments, was so dazzled that he made the dean a royal chaplain.

Colet's chief contribution to philosophy was his remarkably successful attempt to blend pagan and Christian thought. In practice Colet followed the approach of St. Augustine, who argued that pagan philosophy, when properly controlled, is a useful handmaiden for Christianity. By pagan philosophy, Colet understood especially Florentine Platonism, a weird conglomeration of original Platonism, later Neoplatonism, and private Florentine speculation on man, love, beauty, and mystical union. Much of this speculation came to Colet through Ficino's *Theologia Platonica* (1482) and Giovanni Pico della Mirandola's *Heptaplus* (1489), both of which he admiringly quoted or paraphrased in his scriptural treatises.

Despite his debt to the Florentines, Colet avoided the heretical Florentine approach which proclaimed that pagan philosophy and Christianity are equal and even identical. Instead, Colet was careful, as was his model Augustine, to purge pagan views of heretical "errors" before merging them with Christian doctrine. For example, Colet favored the Platonic soul-body terminology over Paul's spirit-flesh, but rejected Plato's dictum that the soul alone comprises the total personality. Again, Colet accepted the Neoplatonic view that Creation was a merging of form and matter, yet he was careful to emphasize that this form is not an emanationist overflow from God's essence, but rather an entity created by God outside himself. In the realm of redemption, Colet accepted Plato's position that only a harmonized soul can govern the body, but he deviated from Plato in insisting that such harmonization can come only from the Holy Spirit's infusion of sanctifying grace. Even in the delicate area of mysticism, Colet borrowed from the *Symposium* the view that love transforms the lover into the object loved.

Whether Colet was as successful in adhering to Catholic as to generally Christian doctrine is a controversial issue. A doctrinal cleavage between Colet and More would seem to be reflected in the *Dialogue on Tyndale* (1529), where More strongly rebuts a form of religion (described in words almost identical to Colet's *Exposition of Romans*), which condemns, as mere shadows, all types of external religion such as sacraments, vestments, and ritual. A comparative study of Colet and More suggests that Colet might have found himself in grave difficulty with Catholic authorities had he lived until the doctrinal reformation of 1534.

Bibliography

During the period 1867–1876, Joseph Hirst Lupton issued five volumes in which he edited Colet's *Treatise on Sacraments* and translated the remainder of Colet's extant Latin works: two treatises on the Hierarchies of the pseudo-Dionysius (c. 490–550); the lectures on St. Paul's First Epistle to the Corinthians; a similar series on the Epistle to the Romans; a Genesis commentary in the form of *Letters to Radulphus*; an exposition (never given as lectures) on the first five chapters of Romans; and *On Christ's Mystical Body, the Church.* Lupton's translations have been out of print since 1893, but Bernard O'Kelly began modern translations with *John Colet's Enarratio Primum S. Pauli Epistolam ad Corinthios* (Oxford, 1963). Colet's only English works, the *Convocation Sermon* and the *Right Fruitful Monition* pamphlet, are printed in the appendix to Lupton's *A Life of John Colet* (London: Bell, 1887), still the indispensable biography. Another biographical classic is Frederic Seebohm's *The Oxford Reformers* (London: Longmans Green, 1867). Colet's influence as educator is detailed in M. F. McDonnell's *The History of St. Paul's School for Boys* (London, 1909).

Since World War II there has been a revival of interest in Colet's thought, as evidenced by Eugene Rice Jr., "John Colet and the Annihilation of the Natural," in *Harvard Theological Review* 45 (July 1952): 141–163; Albert Duhamel, "The Oxford Lectures of John Colet," in *Journal of the History of Ideas* 14 (October 1953): 493–510; Ernest William Hunt, *Dean Colet and His Theology* (London: Church Historical Society, 1956); Leland Miles, *John Colet and the Platonic Tradition* (La Salle, IL: Open Court, 1961; London, 1962), and Sears Jayne, *John Colet and Marsilio Ficino* (London: Oxford University Press, 1963).

OTHER RECOMMENDED TITLES

Gleason, John B. *John Colet.* Berkeley: University of California Press, 1989.

Kaufman, Peter I. *Augustinian Piety and Catholic Reform: Augustine, Colet, and Erasmus.* Macon, GA: Mercer University Press, 1982.

Miles, Leland. "Platonism and Christian Doctrine: The Revival of Interest in John Colet." *Philosophical Forum* 21 (1963–1964): 87–103.

Leland Miles (1967)

Bibliography updated by Tamra Frei (2005)

COLLIER, ARTHUR

(1680–1732)

Arthur Collier, an English idealist philosopher, was born at Langford Magna, Wiltshire, where his father was rector. In 1697 he entered Pembroke College, Oxford, but transferred in 1698 to Balliol. He took orders and in 1704 succeeded to the family living at Langford Magna. Such events as mark his life were of a private character. He was in constant financial difficulties, arising, it is said, from his own impracticality and the extravagance of his wife; his writings did nothing to bring him into contact with a wider world since scarcely anybody read them. He was buried at Langford on September 9, 1732.

Collier makes no mention of John Locke. He read George Berkeley (with whose views his own partly coincide), but only after the publication of Collier's major work, *Clavis Universalis* (1713). René Descartes, Nicolas Malebranche, and Collier's neighbor John Norris were the philosophers who particularly interested Collier, although he was also considerably influenced by Francisco Suárez and other late scholastic philosophers.

Malebranche and John Norris had argued that perception provides us with no direct evidence for the existence of an external world. They did not deny, however, the existence of such a world, even though it is an embarrassment to their metaphysics. They retain it for theological reasons. Collier agreed with them in rejecting the view that perception reveals an external world to us but went on to argue that the very conception of an external world is self-contradictory.

PHILOSOPHICAL VIEWS

In the Introduction to *Clavis Universalis* Collier begins by explaining just what he wishes to assert and what to deny. His starting point is that what we perceive is "in the mind"; the objects of perception, that is, depend upon the mind for their existence. In denying their externality Collier is denying their independence or self-subsistence; he is not at all denying that they exist. "It is with me a first principle," he writes, "that whatsoever is seen, is." Indeed, even what is imagined must exist, since it is an actual object of mind. Collier does not deny, either, that what we perceive seems to us to be independent of our minds. But, he suggests, this "quasi-externeity" also characterizes what we imagine as much as what we see. The difference between types of objects of perception lies only in the degree of vividness with which they are perceived.

Collier is not, of course, alleging that our mind causes the ideas which it has. Ideas, he says, exist in the mind qua perceiver, not qua voluntary agent. Nor is he asserting that the ideas which other people perceive are internal to my mind. "The world which John sees is external to Peter, and the world which Peter sees is external to John." Peter's world and John's world may be similar, but they are numerically different. The crucial point for Collier is that every object must be "in-existent" to some mind; every object has existence, but no object has "extra-existence."

To establish his main conclusions, Collier makes use of two main lines of argument, to each of which a book of the *Clavis Universalis* is devoted. In the first book he sets out to show that we have no good reason for believing that objects exist externally to mind. It is generally supposed that we directly perceive them to be external, but the "quasi-externeity" of objects is no proof, he argues, that they are really external. Everybody admits that in hallucinations, for example, we can suppose objects to be external which are not in fact external. As for the Cartesian argument that there must be an external world because otherwise God would have deceived us when he implanted in us so strong an inclination to believe that there is, Collier points out that according to Descartes himself we are constantly mistaken about what is and what is not a property of the external world. If we can be mistaken about the externality of colors, for example, without God's veracity being impugned, why not about the existence of objects?

Thus far, Collier's argument has been in some measure an *argumentum ad hominem*; he has supposed it to be an intelligible hypothesis that there is an external world and has argued only that there is no good reason for accepting that hypothesis. In the second book he goes further. The concept of an external world is, he says, riddled with contradictions. To establish this point, he calls upon the commonplace skeptical arguments of his time, which had ordinarily been used, however, to demonstrate that the concept of the physical world is as full of mysteries and obscurities as are the concepts of theology rather than to show that it does not exist. Philosophers have demonstrated, Collier argues, that an external world must be finite and that it must be infinite, that it must be infinitely divisible and that it cannot be infinitely divisible, that it is capable of motion and that it cannot be capable of motion. Faced with this situation, we have no alternative but to declare that the very concept of an external world is self-contradictory. Finally, he argues, no intelligible account can be given of the relation between an external world and God. Stress its dependence on God's will, and its externality vanishes; stress its externality, and it takes on the attributes of God.

In a letter to the publisher Nathaniel Mist, Collier pushes his argument slightly further. The subtitle of *Clavis Universalis* was, he now says, misleading insofar as in it he professed to provide "a demonstration of the non-existence or impossibility of an external world." This suggests that the existence of an external world is a possibly true, even if in fact a false, hypothesis. The correct account of the matter is that the doctrine that an external world exists is "neither true nor false"; it is "all-over nonsense and contradiction in terms," the very concept of an external world being self-contradictory.

RELIGIOUS VIEWS

Collier's other publications consist of *A Specimen of True Philosophy, in a Discourse on Genesis* (1730), which is designed as a preliminary essay to a complete commentary on the Bible, and a series of seven sermons published as *Logology* (1732). These works are primarily theological. Collier's metaphysical views are more clearly formulated in the brief "Confession" he wrote in 1709 but did not publish. There is, he says, one substance, God, which is "being itself, all being, universal being." The existence of everything else is dependent upon the existence of God not only causally but also in the sense that particular things have no substance of their own. However, although everything but God is ultimately dependent on him, everything except Christ is also relatively dependent on something else; qualities "in-exist" in objects, objects in the mind, and the mind in Christ, through whom God made the transition from universality to particularity. Not unnaturally, Collier was accused of Arianism. He thought of himself, however, as reconciling the Arians and the orthodox by admitting Christ's dependence on God but asserting his priority to all created things and even to time, Christ's begetting being "the first pulse of time."

In Great Britain attention was first drawn to Collier's work by Thomas Reid and Dugald Stewart, but he has never exerted any real influence, being overshadowed by Berkeley. In Germany he attracted some attention as a result of an abstract of the *Clavis Universalis* published in the *Acta Eruditorum* (1717) and a German translation by John Christopher Eschenbach in 1756. He is quoted by Christian Wolff, and it is sometimes supposed, without any real evidence, that the Kantian antinomies derive from his work.

See also Arius and Arianism; Berkeley, George; Descartes, René; Idealism; Locke, John; Malebranche, Nicolas; Norris, John; Reid, Thomas; Stewart, Dugald; Suárez, Francisco; Wolff, Christian.

Bibliography

For *Clavis Universalis* see Ethel Bowman's edition (Chicago: Open Court, 1909) or Samuel Parr, *Metaphysical Tracts of the Eighteenth Century* (London: E. Lumley, 1837), which also includes *A Specimen* and a brief précis of *Logology.* Antonio Casiglio has translated *Clavis Universalis* into Italian, with notes (Padua, 1953), and has included as an appendix to an article on Collier's *True System* an Italian translation of that work in *Sophia* 23 (3–4) (1955): 302–321. Collier's "Confession" is in Robert Benson, *Memoirs of the Life and Writings of the Rev. Arthur Collier* (London: E. Lumley, 1837).

See also John Henry Muirhead, *The Platonic Tradition in Anglo-Saxon Philosophy* (London and New York: n.p., 1931); Georges Lyon, *L'idéalisme en Angleterre au XVIIIe siècle* (Paris: F. Alcan, 1888). On Collier and Berkeley see George Alexander Johnston, *The Development of Berkeley's Philosophy* (London: Macmillan, 1923), Appendix I; for Collier and Immanuel Kant see A. O. Lovejoy, "Kant and the English Platonists," in *Essays Philosophical and Psychological in Honor of William James … by His Colleagues at Columbia University* (New York: Longmans, Green, 1908), and H. J. de Vleeschauwer, "Les antinomies kantiennes et la *Clavis Universalis* d'Arthur Collier," in *Mind* 47 (187) (1938): 303–320.

John Passmore (1967)

COLLINGWOOD, ROBIN GEORGE

(1889–1943)

Robin George Collingwood, the English philosopher and historian, was born in Coniston, Lancashire. His father, W. G. Collingwood, friend and biographer of John Ruskin, educated him at home until he was old enough to enter Rugby and imbued him with a Ruskinian devotion to craftsmanship and art and an adult attitude toward scholarship. Although Collingwood later wrote contemptuously of most of his teachers at Rugby and praised Oxford chiefly for leaving him to himself, his undergraduate work in Greek and Latin was excellent and in *literae humaniores* (philosophy and history from Greek and Latin texts), brilliant. He was elected to a fellowship at Pembroke College in 1912, and to the Waynflete professorship in 1934. Except for a period of service with the admiralty intelligence during World War I, he remained at Oxford throughout his career, until in 1941 illness compelled him to retire.

Although he always considered philosophy his chief vocation, Collingwood was a pupil of the great Romano-British archaeologist F. J. Haverfield. Since he alone of Haverfield's pupils both survived the war and remained at Oxford, Collingwood considered it his duty to transmit Haverfield's teachings to others. Although he was a competent excavator, most of Collingwood's work was theoretical. Both in suggesting questions that excavation might answer and in drawing together and interpreting the results of others' excavations, he was brilliant. The final monuments to his historical labors are his sections on Roman Britain in the first volume of the *Oxford History of England* (1936; 2nd ed., 1937) and in Tenney Frank's *An Economic Survey of Ancient Rome* (5 vols., New York, 1933–1940). To these must be added his extensive contributions to the revised edition of the British section of Theodor Mommsen's *Corpus Inscriptionum Latinarum*, begun by Haverfield, for which Collingwood drew each inscription from his own accurate rubbings.

The consensus of present-day archaeologists appears to be that Collingwood's "imperishably accurate" work on inscriptions will prove more valuable than his works of synthesis and interpretation. Collingwood himself expected that his interpretations would be superseded, but he was convinced that first-rate thinking in history, as in natural science, remains valuable even if further evidence requires that its conclusions be revised. In most of his work his willingness to propose hypotheses was fruitful. He knew something that cautious historians often forget—that nothing is evidence except for or against some hypothesis.

Collingwood's philosophical work falls roughly into three periods: (1) 1912–1927, his acceptance of idealism; (2) 1927–1937, his mature philosophy of the special sciences, conceived as resting on an idealist foundation; and (3) 1937–1943, his rejection of idealism. His ethical and political views will be discussed separately.

ACCEPTANCE OF IDEALISM

In his first book, *Religion and Philosophy* (London, 1916), Collingwood maintained three doctrines familiar to readers of his later work: (1) that creations of the human mind, no matter how primitive, must be studied historically, not psychologically; (2) that historical knowledge is attainable; and (3) that history and philosophy are identical. What he meant by this third doctrine depends on what he meant by "history" and by "philosophy"; in subsequent years he changed his mind about both.

In his *Autobiography* (London, 1939) Collingwood related that in 1917 a publisher rejected a manuscript, *Truth and Contradiction*, in which he had reached conclusions about truth and about the relation between history and philosophy that are characteristic of his thought at a much later period. Those conclusions are that truth or falsity does not belong to propositions but to complexes of questions and answers; that all such complexes rest on "absolute presuppositions" that are neither true nor false; and that since the business of philosophy is to elicit the absolute presuppositions held by different people at different times, philosophy is really a branch of history.

Since Collingwood destroyed the manuscript of *Truth and Contradiction* after writing his *Autobiography*, it is impossible to ascertain how closely the earlier work anticipated the later. However, in *Ruskin's Philosophy* (London, 1920), a lecture delivered in 1919, he asserted that a man's philosophy is "the [set of] principles which … he assumes in all his thinking and acting"; and he went on to maintain that since most men do not know what their philosophy is, "it is the attempt to discover what people's philosophy is that marks the philosopher." At least until 1919, therefore, Collingwood conceived of philosophy as a historical investigation of humankind's ultimate and largely unacknowledged principles, but it may be doubted whether Collingwood at that time denied that ultimate principles are either true or false. In *Ruskin's Philosophy* he sympathized with G. W. F. Hegel's refusal to accept as ultimate any dualism, whether of reason and understanding or of theory and practice. And two years later, in an essay, "Croce's Philosophy of History" (*Hibbert Journal* 19 [1921]: 263–278), he attacked Benedetto Croce for holding that philosophy was being "absorbed" into history, so that it is "cancelled out entirely as already provided for" by history. Collingwood did not then think that either history or philosophy in the ordinary sense could absorb the other but rather that each, if seriously pursued, leads to the other. He agreed with the "idealistic" Giovanni Gentile that they are "poised in equilibrium."

PUBLICATION OF *SPECULUM MENTIS*.

Speculum Mentis (Oxford, 1924) was Collingwood's first attempt to construct a philosophical system. In it he critically reviewed five "forms of experience," ordered according to the degree of truth each attains.

Art. Art, the lowest form of experience, Collingwood defined after Croce as pure imagination, which he distinguished from sensation, on the one hand, assertion, on the other. Unlike sensation, imagination is active and has its own guiding principle, Beauty. "Beauty," however, must be defined in terms of imagination and not vice versa. As a form of experience, the deficiency of art is that while in itself a work of art is neither true nor false, it inevitably suggests assertions: It is expressive. Despite Croce's definition, then, imagination in art is in conflict with expression in art, and their conflict shows that art alone cannot satisfy the human spirit.

Religion. Art gives rise to religion, in which something imagined is affirmed as real. Like art, religion has its own guiding principle, holiness. The artistic consciousness does not affirm that what it imagines is real; but religion, even Christianity, which Collingwood considered its highest form, affirms something imagined—a Father in heaven, the Real Presence in the sacrament, the resurrection of the dead—as real. These affirmations, Collingwood held, symbolize something true; but religion requires that they be affirmed in their symbolic form: "A philosopher would not be regarded as a Christian for subscribing to a statement which he declared to be a mere paraphrase of the Apostles' Creed in philosophic terms."

Christianity, by affirming the incarnation and atoning death of God, symbolizes the overcoming of the opposition between man and God. This unity of man with God symbolizes man's capacity to attain nonsymbolic, direct knowledge.

Science. Theoretical science is the first form of experience in which man tries by reason to grasp truth. But theoretical science, whether a priori as in mathematics or empirical as in natural science, is abstract. Natural science is the application of mathematics to the empirical world, conceived as subject to laws (mechanism) and composed of an ultimate undifferentiated stuff (materialism). But the world, as we experience it, is not merely mathematical, mechanical, and material. Theoretical science is therefore only supposition: Its truths are hypothetical. It can say truly, "If there were an *S*, there would be *P*," where *S* and *P* are events in a material world specified in mechanistic terms; but mechanistic terms are not unconditionally applicable to the world of experience. They are abstract; and to abstract is to falsify.

History. History appears to offer a way of escape from the abstractness of theoretical science; for it treats of the world of experience as a concrete temporal process. In their highest development, all theoretical sciences—physics and biology no less than the social sciences—assume a historical form. But history, too, has its characteristic deficiency. At bottom it is an extension of the historian's perception; and a perceived world is alien to its perceiver: a spectacle. Perception can never be knowledge because it can never grasp the whole historical process, and what is beyond the perceiver's ken may have implications for what is within it. Every specialist in a period is ignorant of a large part of what came before it, and his ignorance "introduces a coefficient of error into his work of whose magnitude he can never be aware." Even if this were not true, he could not escape the limitation of all attempts at knowledge in which subject and object are distinct. Since what is merely object is alien, it is falsified by the very process of appropriating it.

Philosophy. But one form of experience, philosophy, yields truth. Philosophy is self-knowledge. In it the distinction between knowing subject and known object vanishes. The self that is known is that which has attained all the subordinate forms of experience—art, religion, science, and history—and corrected their distortions. Philosophy has no positive content of its own: It is the awareness of what is true in those subordinate forms. In knowing their limitations it transcends them. Hence the absolute mind exists in the life of each individual mind to the extent that the individual mind raises and solves problems in any form of experience; as long as this process goes on, each mind is infinite. "The truth is not some perfect system of philosophy: It is simply the way in which all systems, however perfect, collapse into nothingness on the discovery that they are only systems."

MATURE PHILOSOPHY

PHILOSOPHY OF RELIGION. From 1924 to 1930, Collingwood further explored the positions of *Speculum Mentis*, especially those in aesthetics and religion. For the most part he remained content with his earlier theory of art, but in an essay, "Reason Is Faith Cultivating Itself" (*Hibbert Journal* 26 [1927]: 3–14), and a pamphlet, *Faith and Reason* (London, 1928), he abandoned the doctrine of *Speculum Mentis* that religion is essentially symbolic. Religion, he argued, can rid itself of superstition. Christianity correctly insists that there is a sphere of faith that transcends reason and is its basis. Neither the belief that the universe is rational nor that life is worth living can be established by scientific or ethical inquiry, yet they underlie natural science and rational ethics. Popular Christianity expresses those beliefs symbolically; but symbolizations are not essential to it. The ignorant believer who denounces philosophical or scientific paraphrases of Christian dogmas has no right to speak for Christianity.

PHILOSOPHY OF HISTORY. In his *Autobiography* Collingwood recorded that during the summer of 1928 he finally perceived the flaw that had vitiated his philosophy of history in *Speculum Mentis*. He presented his revised views in a pamphlet, *The Philosophy of History* (London, 1930). In 1936 he wrote the lectures that are the fullest statement of these views and that make up the greater part of his *Idea of History* (Oxford, 1946). The error he detected in *Speculum Mentis* was that the historical past is a spectacle, an object alien to the historian's mind. It has two roots: the realist error that knowing is fundamentally like perceiving; and the idealist error that the same thought cannot exist in different contexts. Against the realists, Collingwood maintained that every thought is an act that may be performed at different times and by different minds. A historian can know that Caesar enacted a certain thought if he can reconstruct that thought in his own mind (so reenacting it) and demonstrate by evidence that his reconstruction is true of Caesar. Against the idealists, he maintained that, while some contexts change the character of a thought, others do not. The fact that, with my knowledge of modern geometry, I rethink one of Euclid's thoughts, for instance, the forty-fifth proposition of his first book, does not entail that my thought is different from Euclid's.

The key to Collingwood's conception of historical verification is his repeated declaration that historical method is "Baconian," a matter of putting evidence to the question. Given any piece of evidence, more than one reconstruction can be made of the action of which it is a relic. But each reconstruction, taken together with other knowledge, will entail consequences different from those of its fellows. A given reconstruction is established if no consequence that can be drawn from it conflicts with the evidence and if every other reconstruction has some consequence that does conflict with it. If a historian cannot show that one reconstruction, and only one, can be reconciled with the evidence, he must suspend judgment.

Historians must not only show what happened but also explain it. Collingwood proved that the two tasks are accomplished together. The past happenings that historians are concerned to discover are acts; and an act is a physical event that expresses a thought. To discover that an act took place includes discovering the thought expressed in it; and discovering that thought explains the act.

NATURAL SCIENCE. Just as in *The Idea of History* and in the writings that preceded it Collingwood had demolished the historical skepticism of *Speculum Mentis,* so in a set of lectures written in 1933–1934, which became *The Idea of Nature* (Oxford, 1945), he renounced his earlier skepticism about natural science and confessed that since "the knowledge acquired for mankind by Galileo and Newton and their successors … is genuine knowledge," philosophy must ask "not whether this quantitative material world can be known but why it can be known." His answer to that question, however, was equivocal. Collingwood named three constructive periods in European cosmological thought: the Greek, the Renaissance, and the modern, each with its characteristic view of nature. But he said curiously little about the question, "Why is one view of nature replaced by another?" In his introduction to *The Idea of Nature* he declared that "natural science must come first in order that philosophy may have something to reflect on," which suggests that views of nature change only as scientific thought changes; but in his exposition of the change from the Renaissance to the modern view of nature and in his criticisms of modern views, he often wrote as though philosophy might decide what is or is not a tenable view of nature without referring to natural science at all.

METAPHYSICS. Abandoning his earlier view that philosophy is no more than awareness of the limitations of subordinate forms of experience, Collingwood, in his *Essay on Philosophical Method* (Oxford, 1933), assigned philosophy the task of "thinking out the idea of an object that shall completely satisfy the demands of reason." He no longer rejected natural science and history as offering false accounts of such an object. Instead, he described each as limited in its aims. Natural science attempts to find true universal hypothetical propositions; history seeks true categorical propositions, but only about individuals in the world. The propositions of philosophy must be both categorical (about something existent) and universal (about everything existent). Hence, its object can only be the *ens realissimum,* the being that comprehends all being, of which all finite beings are appearances.

Although distinct from history, philosophy is nevertheless closely allied to it. Just as the various definitions that have been proposed for any philosophical concept constitute a scale of forms, of which the lower are appearances of the higher, so do the various metaphysical systems that purport to give an account of the *ens realissimum.* The way to knowledge in metaphysics is through critical reflection on its history.

REJECTION OF IDEALISM

AESTHETICS AS THEORY OF LANGUAGE. In 1937 Collingwood was invited to revise or to replace his *Outlines of Philosophy of Art* (London, 1925), in which he had largely followed the theory of art in *Speculum Mentis.* He chose to replace it; and his new book, *The Principles of Art* (Oxford, 1938), moved closer to Croce, whose article "Aesthetic" Collingwood had translated for the 1929 edition of the *Encyclopaedia Britannica.* Collingwood began by assuming that an aesthetic usage of the word *art* has been established in the modern European critical tradition and that it is the business of aesthetics to define what *art* so used means. The classical definition of art as representation (*mimesis*), in all its varieties, confounded art with craft (*techne, ars*), that is, with the production of something preconceived. Analysis shows that none of the classical definitions state either a necessary or a sufficient condition of art. Works of art may be, and commonly are, also works of craft. But what makes something a work of art and determines whether it is a good or a bad one is not what makes it a work of craft.

A work of art is an imaginative creation; the function of imagination is to raise what is preconscious (for instance, mere feeling) to consciousness by giving it definite form. Since this activity is expression, Collingwood repudiated his earlier stand and accepted Croce's doctrine that imagination and expression are identical. He also accepted Croce's view that all expression, in any medium, is linguistic; for any form by which the preconscious is raised to consciousness is linguistic. Language thus begins in the cradle. Children speak before they learn their mother tongues.

The primitive language of the cradle is too narrow in range to serve the purposes of any but infants; it must be enriched by "intellectualizing" it so that it can express thoughts as well as feelings. An intellectualized language is one containing "conceptual" terms, and all conceptual thinking is abstract.

An intellectualized language does not cease to be expressive; rather its range of expressiveness is increased. Art is, therefore, not an activity cut off from, say, science. Every fresh linguistic utterance is imaginative and can be considered a work of art. Hence Croce was right when he said that there is poetry without prose, but no prose without poetry. And since it is the nature of art to be expressive, good art is successful expression. Bad art is the malperformance of the act of bringing preconscious thoughts and feelings to consciousness, a malperformance that misrepresents what is thought and felt. It can arise only in a corrupt consciousness. Critics can detect bad art, works of corrupt consciousness, by comparing them with successful works.

PHILOSOPHY OF MIND. In his last book, *The New Leviathan* (Oxford, 1942), Collingwood amplified and corrected the philosophy of mind he had outlined in *The Principles of Art*. Mind is consciousness, and while every act of consciousness has an object, no act of consciousness involves consciousness of itself. The various functions of consciousness are stratified into orders. The most primitive of them is consciousness of feeling. An act involving consciousness of a primitive act belongs to a higher order. Collingwood distinguished five such orders: primitive consciousness, appetite, desire, free choice, and reason. In principle, there is no upper limit to the orders of consciousness; for in reasoning about an act of reason a higher-order act is brought into being.

Holding that feeling (that is, sensation with its emotional charge) is not an act of consciousness, Collingwood denied that one can become conscious of an act of consciousness by introspection or inner sense. All acts of consciousness are linguistic; mind is the child of language. In analyzing the various forms of language, Collingwood reiterated his conclusion in *The Principles of Art* that conceptual thinking is abstract, and he expressly repudiated the idealist doctrine that to abstract is to falsify.

All theories of the relation between body and mind betray a philosophical misconception. Body and mind are not two related substances: They are man as investigated in two different ways, physiologically and historically. There is no conflict between physiology and history. To hold that Brutus's movement in stabbing Caesar can be investigated and explained physiologically does not imply that Brutus's act cannot be investigated historically nor does it detract from the value of a historical explanation of that act. Here Collingwood strikingly anticipated Gilbert Ryle's view as expressed in *The Concept of Mind* (New York, 1950).

LATER METAPHYSICS. In his *Autobiography* Collingwood reaffirmed his adherence to the conception of metaphysics as a historical science of absolute presuppositions which he claimed to have reached in *Truth and Contradiction*. In the *Essay on Metaphysics* (Oxford, 1940) he amplified this position. Every science, whether theoretical or practical, consists in asking and answering questions; and every sequence of questions rests ultimately on absolute presuppositions that are not answers to questions. Since truth or falsity belongs only to answers to questions, absolute presuppositions are neither true nor false. The task of metaphysics is to ascertain what is absolutely presupposed in a given society and how one set of absolute presuppositions has come to be replaced by another. Metaphysicians, however, must not criticize the absolute presuppositions they discover; for criticism presupposes that they are either true or false. A society does not consciously change its absolute presuppositions. Since most men are quite unconscious of their absolute presuppositions, any change in them is unconscious too and comes about because of internal strains.

Collingwood did not acknowledge what must have been obvious to his readers, that in the *Autobiography* and in the *Essay on Metaphysics* he had jettisoned the metaphysics of the *Essay on Philosophical Method*. His views in the *Essay on Metaphysics* are so incoherent that some sympathetic critics have ascribed his change of mind to illness. (Both the *Autobiography* and the *Essay on Metaphysics* were written while he was recovering from a series of strokes.) However, his conception of metaphysics in the *Essay on Philosophical Method*, no less than his earlier conception in *Speculum Mentis*, rested on idealist doctrines from which he had been gradually freeing himself. He still believed that philosophical concepts are not abstract. The doctrine that philosophical propositions are both categorical and universal cannot be detached from the idealist theory of the concrete universal. But both in *The Principles of Art* (written before his illness) and in *The New Leviathan* Collingwood explicitly declared that all concepts are abstract.

Although in his *Autobiography* Collingwood repudiated his earlier idealist conception of philosophy, his views about religion, natural science, and history remained virtually intact. Nor were his views on art altered by his later historicism in metaphysics. This suggests that his change of mind in 1938 may be less fundamental than has been thought. After 1924 the main direction of Collingwood's thought was opposed to skepticism in the special sciences. His earlier skepticism had sprung from his idealistic rejection of abstract thinking and his conviction that philosophical thought is not abstract. By 1938 his work on the philosophy of art and the special sciences had overthrown both these errors, and it became clear that he could no longer hold the idealistic metaphysics of the *Essay on Philosophical Method.* It is natural that in seeking something to put in its place he reverted to his youthful historicism, and that it in turn proved inadequate. His inability to find a substitute for idealism does not show that he was mistaken in rejecting it; nor does it prejudice his achievements in aesthetics, philosophy of history, and philosophy of mind.

ETHICS AND POLITICS

In *Speculum Mentis* Collingwood recognized three forms of ethics: utilitarian, in which action is conceived as a means to an end; duty or concrete ethics, in which action is conceived as determined by the will to act in accordance with the moral order of the objective world; and absolute ethics, in which the distinction between the individual and society, and with it the sense of abstract law, disappears. The first form was held to be characteristic of science, the second of history, and the third of philosophy. Both in *Speculum Mentis* and in the *Essay on Philosophical Method* he represented the forms of ethics on a scale in which the higher forms complete and correct the lower.

Collingwood never renounced this triadic scheme, although in *The New Leviathan* he proposed a new view of the connection between morality and theoretical science, namely, that theoretical science reflects moral practice. Teleological science reflects utilitarian morality; "regularian" science reflects a morality of law; and history reflects the concrete morality of "duty."

In *The New Leviathan* Collingwood set out to bring the "classical politics" of Thomas Hobbes and John Locke up to date. He accepted the classical conception of politics as bringing men out of a state of nature into a state of civil society. Essentially, political life is a process in which a nonsocial community (i.e., the state of nature) is transformed into a social one. This cannot happen unless the rulers understand that social life is a life in which people freely engage in joint enterprises. Civilization is "a process whereby a community undergoes a change from a condition of relative *barbarity* to one of *civility*." Barbarism is hostility to civilization; but although barbarous communities always strive to destroy civilized ones, in the long run the defeat of barbarism is certain.

See also Aesthetics, History of; Art, Expression in; Croce, Benedetto; Determinism in History; Galileo Galilei; Gentile, Giovanni; Hegel, Georg Wilhelm Friedrich; Historicism; Hobbes, Thomas; Idealism; Imagination; Locke, John; Newton, Isaac; Philosophy of History; Presupposing; Renaissance; Ruskin, John; Utilitarianism.

Bibliography

The obituary essays by R. B. McCallum, T. M. Knox, and I. A. Richmond in *Proceedings of the British Academy* 29 (1943): 463–480, together with T. M. Knox's editorial preface to Collingwood's *The Idea of History*, are indispensable and contain full bibliographies. E. W. F. Tomlin, *R. G. Collingwood* (London: Longmans Green, 1953) is useful but elementary. Alan Donagan, *The Later Philosophy of R. G. Collingwood* (Oxford: Clarendon Press, 1962) treats of Collingwood's work after 1933.

OTHER RECOMMEDED WORKS

Collingwood, R. G. *Roman Britain*. Rev. ed. Oxford: Clarendon, 1966.

Collingwood, R. G. *Essays in the Philosophy of Art*. Bloomington, Indiana University Press, 1966.

Collingwood, R. G. *Faith & Reason; Essays in the Philosophy of Religion*. Edited by Lionel Rubinoff. Chicago, Quadrangle Books, 1968.

Collingwood, R. G. *Essays in Political Philosophy*. Edited by David Boucher. Oxford: Clarendon, 1989.

Alan Donagan (1967)

Bibliography updated by Michael J. Farmer (2005)

COLLINS, ANTHONY
(1676–1729)

Anthony Collins, the English deist, freethinker, theologian, and philosopher, was born at Hounslow, near London, the son of Henry Collins, a well-to-do gentleman. Anthony Collins was educated at Eton and at King's College, Cambridge, and for a while was a student in the Temple. This training in the law later enabled him to maintain an excellent reputation for many years as justice of the peace and deputy lieutenant in Middlesex and in Essex. He was married twice to daughters of the landed gentry. A devoted admirer of John Locke both as philosopher and as writer on religion, Collins, aged twenty-seven, made the pilgrimage to Oates early in 1703 to meet the master, then aged seventy. They were strongly attracted to one another. Later that year Locke wrote poignantly to Collins: "You complain of a great many defects [in yourself] and that complaint is the highest recommendation I could desire to make me love and esteem you and desire your friendship. And if I were now setting out in the world, I should think it my great happiness to have such a companion as you, who had a true relish of truth … and, if I mistake not you have as much of it as I ever met with in anybody." In his will Locke left Collins a legacy of £110 and some books and maps, and named him one of three trustees of his estate. Collins arranged tributes to the master that appeared in 1708 as *Some Familiar Letters between Mr. Locke and several of his friends* and in 1720 as *A Collection of Several Pieces of Mr John Locke, published by M. Des Maizeaux under the direction of Mr Anthony Collins.*

By that time Collins had made a lasting, if at the time a notorious, name for himself through a series of outspoken yet restrained publications, all of which were anonymous (although most sophisticated readers were aware of the author's identity). The more important include *An Essay concerning the Use of Reason in Propositions, the Evidence wherof depends upon Human Testimony* (1707); *Priestcraft in Perfection: Or, A Detection of the Fraud of Inserting and Continuing this Clause (The Church hath Power to Decree Rites and Ceremonys, and Authority in Controversys in Faith) In the Twentieth Article of the Articles of the Church of England* (1710); *A Discourse of Free-Thinking, Occasion'd by the Rise and Growth of a Sect call'd Free-Thinkers* (1713; actually published late in 1712); *A Philosophical Inquiry concerning Human Liberty* (1715).

In 1711 Collins made the first of many visits to Holland, where he met numerous men of intellect. Soon after the appearance of the *Discourse of Free-Thinking*, with accompanying public uproar, Collins visited Holland briefly, possibly for reasons of prudence. His later major works include *A Discourse of the Grounds and Reasons of the Christian Religion* (1724), which elicited thirty-five replies within two years and which Bishop Warburton later named one of the most plausible books ever written against Christianity, admitting that the replies might have been left to confute one another; *The Scheme of Literal Prophecy Considered* (The Hague, 1725; London, 1726), a sequel to the *Discourse; A Discourse concerning Ridicule and Irony in Writing* (1727); and the *Dissertation on Liberty and Necessity* (1729). This last, together with the earlier *Philosophical Inquiry concerning Human Liberty*, constitutes a powerful statement of the doctrine of necessitarianism. By and large, it is to be noted, the English deists upheld the freedom of the will.

During all this time Collins carried on vigorous, frequently witty, controversies with—to name but a few—Henry Dodwell the elder, famous nonjurist; and such clerical antagonists as Richard Bentley, the classical scholar; Samuel Clarke, the rationalist; and William Whiston, the biblical literalist. His health weakened by repeated attacks of the stone, Collins died late in 1729 and was buried in Oxford chapel. It is said that despite a lifetime of controversy, he was never attacked on the basis of his character. Collins represents the philosophical skeptic in the true sense of the word.

FREETHINKING

The right and the necessity to inquire freely and fearlessly into all subjects, especially religion, was Collins's constant and fundamental thesis. Its master statement is the *Discourse of Free-Thinking*, but it was adumbrated in two earlier works. The *Essay concerning the Use of Reason* makes the point that reason is "that faculty of the Mind whereby it perceives the Truth, Falsehood, Probability or Improbability of Propositions." Truth and falsehood are known rationalistically and are certain. Probability may take the form of opinion when discovered by reason or of faith when perceived by testimony. Testimony is the foundation of much of our knowledge but can never impugn the natural (rationalistic) notions implanted in the mind of man. The Bible, consequently, is not to be taken seriously when it portrays God in human terms; certain parts of the Bible are to be accepted, while others are to be rejected. Thus, Collins combined Locke's arguments for the reasonableness of Christianity and morality and religious principles with the rationalistic Common Notions of Lord Herbert of Cherbury. *Priestcraft in Perfection* carried the attack, common to most deists of the eighteenth century, against the dogmas of established churches. Such dogmas, Collins argued, must be viewed as fraudulent when contrary to reason. The appeal to mystery and to things above reason simply will not do.

The title page of the *Discourse of Free-Thinking* is embellished with several quotations: one from the Old Testament, one from the New Testament, one from Cicero, and one from the earl of Shaftesbury. The influence of Shaftesbury is apparent throughout, but Collins was less hesitant to employ the method of ridicule (as is fully attested in the *Discourse concerning Ridicule and Irony in Writing*). The general definition of the right to think freely was applied mainly to religion. Collins pointed out that the new science and the new philosophy had exposed many errors of the past; the Reformation was the result of fearless thinking on the part of a few leaders; the abundant literature of travel exposed the superstitions of peoples throughout the world and also the infinite numbers of pretenders to divine revelation. Freedom had exorcised the witches that so plagued James I and Charles I: "great numbers of witches have been almost annually executed in England, from the remotest antiquity to the late Revolution; when the liberty given and taken to think freely, the Devil's power visibly declin'd, and England as well as the United Provinces ceas'd to be any part of his Christian territories." (The "Witches Act" of 1603 was to be repealed in 1736.)

With tongue in cheek, Collins suggested that the Society for Propagating the Gospel in Foreign Parts was really a freethinking organization because infidels must be asked to examine and to reject their native traditional religions in order to accept true religion. He further suggested that such zealous divines as Francis Atterbury, George Smalridge, and Jonathan Swift be drafted annually for this enterprise in the same manner as "military missionarys." The argument then turned against the priests of all ages who are responsible for quibbling about biblical interpretations and end up calling one another atheists. The Bible, Collins continued, is clearly replete with corrupted texts—30,000 in the New Testament alone, according to one authority. Its text, therefore, is to be examined in the same scholarly and critical manner as the texts of all ancient books. The *Discourse* concluded with a refutation of the standard objections to freethinking. Atheism is not, after all, the worst of all evils; enthusiasm and superstition hold that title, according to Francis Bacon. Cicero was quoted to confute the claim that some false ideas are necessary for the good of society (an early version of the Marxian notion of religion as the opiate of the people). A long list of freethinkers was given, including Socrates, Plato, Aristotle, Epicurus, Plutarch, Cicero, and Seneca among the ancient pagans; Solomon and the prophets of the Old Testament; Josephus, the Pharisee; Origen, the Church Father; and, among the moderns, Bacon, Thomas Hobbes, and Archbishop Tillotson ("whom all English free-thinkers own as their head"). Collins then asserted that he might well have added other names, such as Michel Eyquem de Montaigne, René Descartes, Hugo Grotius, Richard Hooker, Lord Falkland, Lord Herbert of Cherbury, John Milton, Ralph Cudworth, Sir William Temple, and the master, Locke. All enemies of freethinking were branded crack-brained and enthusiastical, malicious, ambitious, inhumane, ignorant, or brutal—or courters of priests, women, and the mob.

BIBLICAL CRITICISM

The Discourse of the Grounds and Reasons of the Christian Religion and the *Scheme of Literal Prophecy Considered* follow the rational, scholarly methods for biblical criticism described earlier, but concentrate on the question of the fulfillment of Old Testament prophecies in the New Testament. The most cogent attacks are on the virgin prophecy in the book of Isaiah and the unusually specific prophecies in the book of Daniel. In both works Collins pursued the theme of the necessity of thinking freely and went out of his way to defend the right of Whiston, one of his chief adversaries, to think freely—although wrongly, as he saw it—about prophecy. Whiston was a literalist, and Collins had no great difficulty and no little sport in pointing out the absurdities to which Whiston was driven. Collins himself had promised to investigate the miracles of the New Testament but was unable to do so before his final illness and death, and the task fell to Thomas Woolston.

Like John Toland before them, Collins and Woolston forced the issue of the scriptural canon upon the orthodox and opened the way in England for historical criticism.

See also Deism; Woolston, Thomas.

Bibliography

Attfield, Robin. "Clarke, Collins and Compounds." *Journal of the History of Philosophy* 15 (1977): 45–54.

Berman, David. "Anthony Collins: His Thought and Writings." *Hermathena* (1975): 49–70.

Bibliotheca Anthony Collins. London, 1732.

Broome, J. H. "Une Collaboration: Anthony Collins et Desmaizeaux." *Revue de littérature comparée* 30 (1956): 161–179.

Cranston, Maurice. *John Locke, A Biography*, 460–477. London: Longmans Green, 1957. The Collins-Locke friendship.

Disraeli, Isaac. *Curiosities of Literature*. Vol. III, 333–343. Boston: Veazie, 1860.

Dybikowski, James. "Anthony Collins (1676–1729)." In *British Philosophers, 1500–1799 (Dictionary of Literary Biography, Vol. 252)*, edited by Peter Fosl. Farmington Hills, MI: Thomson Gale, 2002.

Dybikowski, James. "Anthony Collins' Defense of Free-Thinking." In *Scepticism, Clandestinity and Free-Thinking*, edited by Gianni Paganini. Paris: Champion, 2002.

Hahn, Joseph. *Voltaires Stellung sur Frage der menschlichen Freiheit in ihrem Verhältnis sur Locke und Collins*. Borna and Leipzig, 1905.

Nichols, John. *Illustrations of the Literary History of the Eighteenth Century*. Vol. II, 148–150. London: Nichols and Bentley, 1817.

Snobelen, Stephen. "The Argument over Prophecy: An Eighteenth-Century Debate between William Whiston and Anthony Collins." *Lumen* 15 (1996): 195–213.

Thorschmid, Urban G. *Critische Lebensgeschichte Anton Collins*. Dresden and Leipzig, 1755.

Torrey, Norman L. *Voltaire and the English Deists*. New Haven, CT: Yale University Press, 1930. Ch. 3, "Voltaire and Anthony Collins: Metaphysics and Prophecies."

See also the general bibliography to the *Deism* entry.

Ernest Campbell Mossner (1967)
Bibliography updated by Tamra Frei (2005)

COLORS

The phenomena of "color" pose a special puzzle to philosophers characterizing the mind, the world, and the interaction of the two. In various ways, both subjective and objective, both appearance and reality, color has been the subject of wide disagreement. Besides the extreme view that colors are literally sensations—which would imply that they are not in the category of properties and that they last precisely as long as sensations—the main views are these.

PHYSICALISM

D. M. Armstrong, J. J. C. Smart, and others have suggested that red (or being red), for example, is a physical property—perhaps a surface physical characteristic (like Robert Boyle's "textures")—or a propensity to reflect some kinds of light more than others. The threat that physical science might be unable to find a predicate coextensive with "red" seems small; but there are challenges to the idea that any such property can be identified with red. First, will a physical property have the same higher-level properties as red does? Red is a "unique" color—there is a "pure" shade of red with no hint of any other color (unlike orange, every shade of which evidently contains red and yellow); however, it seems nonsense to say that some reflectance characteristic is "unique." The physicalist may perhaps reply: A reflectance characteristic can indeed have the property of "uniqueness"—if that is understood as the property of *suggesting to a normal observer no hint of any other color.* (That higher-level property will no doubt be the subject of a later reduction.) A second challenge is this: Ordinary people surely know, for example, that red is more similar to orange than to blue, but if colors are properties whose true nature is revealed only in science, then (until they know more science) they should be in no position to know this. The physicalist may have a reply: This kind of knowledge is of phenomenal similarity, not physical similarity—and on that ordinary perceivers are authoritative. Both challenges suggest an important point, however—that physicalism can at best be a theory about properties that we think of initially without any thought of physical science.

DISPOSITIONAL VIEWS

The view that colors are dispositions to produce experiences has long been nearly an orthodoxy in the field. Proposed by Boyle and John Locke it has seemed a perfect way to capture the connections between color concepts and color experience. You cannot, it seems, grasp the idea of red unless things sometimes look red to you. And you cannot have a full grasp of the idea unless you realize that your color judgments will be defeasible if it turns out that either you or the conditions are abnormal. The proposal may be strengthened by adding an actuality operator: To be red, an object needs to look red to such observers and in such conditions as *actually* count as normal. This last phrase shall be abbreviated as "to look red [etc.]."

A preliminary worry can perhaps be met. Are there any such things as "normal conditions" and "normal observers"? Normal conditions vary hugely with the nature of the object and with our interests; in some cases (e.g., bioluminescent fish) there may be no clear answer to the question what normal conditions are. "Normal observers" pose a further problem: Even when we rule out "color-blind" people, there is surprising disagreement among the remainder (e.g., over which shade of green is "unique"). These problems may not be fatal. If there is indeterminacy in the truth of "*x* is disposed to look red to normal observers under normal conditions," there may be an exactly corresponding indeterminacy in the truth of "*x* is red"—the moral may be that some things have no determinate color, not that color is mischaracterized by the dispositional thesis.

Dispositional views vary according to whether they take the experience of a thing's looking red to be a sensation or a representation. The sensationalist version faces the suspicion that the required "sensations of red" (or the "red' regions of the visual field" in C. Peacocke's language) are mythical creatures of a modern-day sense-datum theory. The view also implies that when an object looks red, it looks disposed to produce red' regions in the visual field. And that seems excessively sophisticated.

The representational version has a related problem: if "red" literally means "disposed to look red [etc.]," then "looks red" will have to mean "looks disposed to look red [etc.]"—which is surely false. This—like related objections about circularity—shows that "red" cannot mean "disposed to look red [etc.]"; but it may not rule out a nonobvious identity of redness and the disposition to look red [etc.], or an a priori necessary coextensiveness.

A final challenge—for both versions of the dispositional view—is more serious. Imagine a yellow object that also emits death rays, so that anyone who looks at it is killed before he can see its color. The object will be yellow but have no disposition to produce experiences as of yellow in normal observers. (The example is due to Saul Kripke.) One can indeed insist that the object would look yellow to normal observers if only we masked the death rays. But we need to mask the death rays without masking or changing the color. And there is no knowledge of what that amounts to, independent of a substantial conception of what color is. We may believe, for example, that the color of a surface is a matter of the way it reflects incident light; so we can change and mask anything that leaves intact the object's *way of changing incident light.* But if we have that belief, it is no thanks to the definition of yellow as simply "the disposition to look yellow [etc.]." Our prime conception of color must have a different source.

VIEWS AVAILABLE

If the physicalist and dispositional views can at best be true with respect to properties first identified by some other route, then we need a new account of our thought about color and of the object of that thought. If color thinking contains an error, the options are projectivism and eliminativism; more easily overlooked is the possibility that color thinking may contain no error and a nonreductive simple realism be the appropriate view.

PROJECTIVISM

Galileo Galilei and (at times) René Descartes and Locke are the first of many to treat colors as properties of experiences, which we wrongly "project" onto external objects. Attractive though the view is, it faces two tasks. It must establish its right to a sensational conception of color vision; and it must clarify what exactly is meant by "projecting" a sensation. The difficulty is to find a precise account of projection that does not make the process so absurd that humans could not commit it or so innocent that it is not actually a mistake.

REPRESENTATIONAL ERROR THEORY AND ELIMINATIVISM

Some have suggested that color vision is representational—color vision involves the apparent representation of properties of external objects, but there is in fact no suitable external referent. C. L. Hardin has a related view: colors are properties neither of external objects nor of experiences. Colors are to be "eliminated," though there remain "chromatic perceptual states," which are to be reduced to neural states.

The strengths of these views must lie in the careful analysis of what is involved in naive thought about color. If naive thought makes fundamental assumptions that are false, then error theory must be the right conclusion. But an everyday commitment to the notions of normal observers and normal conditions may (as we have seen) not be disastrous. Incoherence in everyday color thought may have to be sought elsewhere.

AUTONOMY VIEWS

If color experience apparently represents features of physical objects, what is to prevent us from saying that (in ordinary cases) it correctly represents features of those things, namely colors? These colors would need to be supervenient upon physical properties, though they might or might not be reducible to them. (The model might be Davidson's or Jerry Fodor's view of mental properties.) Colors would have their place in a scheme of explanation that was autonomous with respect to physics, in that its legitimacy was not dependent upon ratification by physics. And that explanatory scheme would no doubt make connections between the colors we see and the contingencies of our perceptual system—thus making those colors not only genuine features of external objects but also in a certain way subjective and relative.

The view needs to overcome the suspicions that the only genuine properties are those recognized in physics, or those intelligible from an "absolute" point of view. A defense is needed of the idea that the world (and not just the mind) can contain subjective items, and an account of the mind's thought about such items. Until these tasks are achieved the autonomy view will at best be programmatic. If they cannot be achieved, the option seems to be an error theory. They are large tasks, central in the philosophy of mind and metaphysics, and it is a measure of the difficulty of the topic that they have taken so long to come clearly to light.

See also Armstrong, David M.; Boyle, Robert; Davidson, Donald; Descartes, René; Eliminative Materialism, Eliminativism; Galileo Galilei; Kripke, Saul; Locke, John; Metaphysics; Philosophy of Mind; Physicalism; Projectivism; Qualia; Smart, John Jamieson Carswell.

Bibliography

Armstrong, D. M. *A Materialist Theory of the Mind.* London: Routledge and Kegan Paul, 1968. Chap. 12.

Boghossian, P., and J. D. Velleman. "Colour as a Secondary Quality." *Mind* (1989): 81–103.

Hardin, C. L. *Color for Philosophers: Unweaving the Rainbow.* Indianapolis: Hackett, 1988.

Hilbert, D. R. *Color and Color Perception: A Study in Anthropocentric Realism.* Stanford, CA: Center for the Study of Language and Information, 1987.

Peacocke, C. *Sense and Content.* Oxford: Clarendon Press, 1983. Chap. 2.

Westphal, J. *Colour.* Oxford: Blackwell, 1987; 2nd ed., 1991.

Justin Broackes (1996)

COMBINATORY LOGIC

Combinatory logic is a branch of mathematical logic that analyzes certain processes, such as substitution, which are associated with variables. These processes are taken for granted in most formulations of logic, but they are complex, and since a fundamental part of the resulting theory is recursively undecidable the analysis is not trivial. Combinatory logic contributes to simplifying the ultimate foundations of mathematical logic and to explaining the paradoxes; it contains an arithmetic in which exactly those numerical functions that are partial recursive are representable; and it has potential applications to the deeper study of such areas as logical calculuses of higher order, computer programming, and linguistics.

Before one can define combinatory logic precisely, it is necessary to explain some notions concerning formal systems. This will be done in the next section. In the following section the definition will be given and a plan presented according to which the later sections of this article will develop the subject. Each technical term is defined by the context in which it appears in italics.

FORMAL SYSTEMS

Consider a formal system of the following type: There is a class of formal objects, or *obs,* constructed from certain primitive obs, or *atoms,* by certain *operations*; each ob has a unique such construction. Among these operations a binary one, called *application,* is singled out. If this is the only operation, the system is called *applicative*; otherwise it is *quasi-applicative.* There is a unique unary predicate, symbolized by the sign "⊢" used as prefix; the *elementary statements* are then of the form

(1) $$\vdash X,$$

where X is an ob. The *elementary theorems* form an inductive subclass of the elementary statements; they are generated from certain initial ones, the *axioms,* by *deductive rules.* The atoms, obs, elementary statements, and axioms are definite classes—that is, it can be effectively ascertained whether a proposed member of one of them is actually a member—but concerning the elementary theorems it is required only that the correctness of a derivation by the deductive rules can be effectively checked. Combinatory logic takes such a system as basis. Other sorts of system exist, but all those ordinarily used in mathematical logic can be reduced to the above type.

Assuming such a system, we observe the following conventions: The application of X to Y is symbolized as (XY). Parentheses are omitted according to the rule of association to the left and also to the rule that outside parentheses are superfluous, so that $XY_1Y_2Y_3$ is the same ob as $(((XY_1)Y_2)Y_3)$. A *combination* of given obs is an ob formed from some or all of them by application alone. The sign "≡" stands for definitional identity; "→" and "⇄" for metatheoretic implication and equivalence, respectively. Finally, "=" is defined, say, by

(2) $$X = Y \rightleftarrows \vdash \mathbf{Q}XY,$$

where $\mathbf{Q}$ is a specific ob, the axioms and rules being such that equality has the appropriate properties.

With such a formal system one associates two sorts of ontology. On the one hand, some persons insist on describing more definitely what the obs are; on the other hand, one may give a description of the meaning one intends for the elementary statements. The first description will be called a *representation*; the second description will be called an *interpretation.*

For a representation it is customary to state that the obs are words in an object language. We will not do that here—all symbols belong to the *U-language* (metalanguage)—but it can be done quite easily for any given object language with two or more symbols. This permits a certain freedom in regard to use and mention.

An interpretation for combinatory logic may be described as follows (this is for motivation only and does not imply a commitment to any special type of metaphysics): One associates with certain obs *contensive* (known from prior experience) notions called *interpretants.* The fact that Y is the interpretant of X will be expressed simply as X means Y. Then if X means a function and Y means a possible value for the first assignment of that function, XY will mean the result of assigning the intepretant of Y as value to the first argument of X. Thus, if X means the addition function of natural numbers and Y means the number 1, then XY will mean a form of the successor function, and if Z means the number 2, then XYZ will mean the number 3. This device reduces many-place functions to unary ones without postulating ordered pairs. An elementary statement (1) will mean that X means an asserted statement; the interpretation is a valid one when every asserted statement is true.

DEFINITION AND DIVISIONS OF COMBINATORY LOGIC

The usual formal systems contain a special class of obs, usually atoms, called (*formal*) *variables.* These are so named in the formalization and play a special role, such that arbitrary obs can be substituted for them (perhaps under restrictions). Variables do not have interpretants; obs containing them mean functions in which they stand for arguments. Thus, the elementary statements of *Principia Mathematica,* Sec. 1A, are not about p, q, r but about negation (~) and alternation ∨); the interpretants of its elementary theorems state rather complex relationships, indicated by the variables, between these functions.

Let $\mathcal{H}$ be a system as defined earlier, and let $\mathcal{H}(x_1, \cdots, x_m)$ be the system formed by adjoining $x_1, \cdots, x_m$ as variables—that is, as new atoms—without further changes. As stated above, the natural interpretant of an ob M of $\mathcal{H}(x_1, \cdots, x_m)$ is that function over $\mathcal{H}$ whose value for arguments $a_1, \cdots, a_m$) is the result of substituting $a_1, \cdots, a_m$ for $x_1, \cdots, x_m$, respectively, in M. Let us say that an ob X of $\mathcal{H}$ designates M when and only when

$$Xx_1x_2 \cdots x_m = M \tag{3}$$

is derivable in $\mathcal{H}(x_1, \cdots, x_m)$. The system $\mathcal{H}$ is called *combinatorially complete* when and only when such an X exists for every M. A *constant* (that is, an ob of an $\mathcal{H}$ containing no variables) X is called a *proper combinator* when and only when it designates a combination of variables alone; a *combinator* is any combination of proper combinators.

Combinatory logic may now be defined as that branch of logic which studies combinators. This is tantamount, at least for applicative systems, to studying combinatorial completeness.

There are two methods of achieving combinatorial completeness. The first is to postulate a designator for every M. This idea leads to the *theory of λ-conversion,* which is discussed in the next section. It is a quasi-applicative system with bound variables. The other method is to exhibit all combinators as combinations of certain atomic ones, after which we can get along with an applicative system. This leads to *synthetic combinatory logic,* to which the rest of the article is devoted. The two approaches have been shown to be equivalent.

The subject of combinatory logic divides itself into two parts in another way. In the first part, called *pure combinatory logic,* one introduces no constant atoms except combinators and those atoms necessary to define equality and pays no attention to whether the obs have interpretants. In the second part, called *illative combinatory logic,* one introduces atoms meaning other logical notions, such as implication, quantification, and semantical categories. The question whether an ob has an interpretant, and if so, what sort of interpretant, belongs to the illative theory.

THEORY OF Λ-CONVERSION. In the theory of λ-conversion we postulate that given $M, x_1, \cdots, x_m$, there is an X in $\mathcal{H}$ such that (3) holds. This X, in Alonzo Church's notation, is $\lambda x_1 \cdots x_m M$. It suffices to postulate this for $m = 1$, for we can define

$$\lambda x_1 \cdots x_m x_{m+1} M \equiv \lambda x_1 \cdots x_m (\lambda x_{m+1} M).$$

Thus, we need only a binary operation forming λxM from x and M. This operation is the only primitive operation besides application. Thus, x is a variable and is bound (in a natural extension of the usual sense) in λxM. One must distinguish, just as in predicate calculus, free and bound occurrences of variables. One understands "ob of $\mathcal{H}$" to include any ob formed from atoms of $\mathcal{H}$ and variables without free occurrences of variables not in $\mathcal{H}$. Further, given an ob M, a variable x, and an ob N, we define $[N/x]M$ (subject to restrictions to prevent confusion of bound variables) as the ob obtained by the substitution of N for x in M.

In view of the intended interpretation, the following are acceptable (subject to the stated restrictions) as axiom schemes:

$$(\alpha) \qquad \lambda xM = \lambda y[y/x]M,$$

$$(\beta) \qquad (\lambda xM)N = [N/x]M.$$

Along with this one has the rules for equality, which give as a special case

$$(\xi) \qquad M = N \rightarrow \lambda xM = \lambda xN.$$

The equality relation is called *convertibility,* and "cnv" is often used instead of "=." We call (β) (as well as η and δ below) a *replacement scheme.* The definition is equivalent to saying that X cnv Y when and only when X can be converted to Y by zero or more successive applications of replacement schemes in either direction. There is also defined a relation of *reducibility,* indicated by "red," in which the replacement schemes can be used from left to right only. An ob is said to be in *normal form* when and only when no replacement scheme can be so applied to it.

There are various modifications of this system. In λI-*conversion* (the original λ-conversion), λxM is defined only when M contains a free occurrence of x; in λK-*conversion* this restriction is dropped. Again the additional axiom scheme (for x not free in U)

$$(\eta) \qquad \lambda x(Ux) = U$$

is acceptable from interpretations which maintain a strong extensionality principle. If it is adopted, the theory is here called $\lambda\eta$-*conversion,* in contrast to the original $\lambda\beta$-*conversion.* Finally one may introduce axiom schemes (δ) which single out special constants δ_1, δ_2, · · · and allow constants of the form $\delta_k U_1 U_2 \cdots U_{nk}$, where n_k is fixed by δ_k and the U_j are in normal form, to be replaced by other constants determined in some uniform manner. Note that (δ) is, in principle, illative.

The various forms of λ-conversion have differences in interpretation. In λI-reduction no component is dropped; hence, if X has a normal form, so does every part of X. This is not true for λK-reduction, a disadvantage if one identifies possession of an interpretant with having a normal form. Again, if one accepts (η), every ob means a function (in some sense), and sometimes this is unacceptable. However, one may prefer to make such distinctions in the illative theory.

The principal result concerning λ-conversion is the Church–Rosser theorem. This states that if X cnv Y, then one can find effectively a Z such that X red Z and Y red Z. Thus, two different combinations of variables are never interconvertible; this establishes consistency. In 1936, Alonzo Church and J. B. Rosser ("Some Properties of Conversion," in *Transactions of the American Mathematical Society* 39, pp. 472–482) proved the theorem for $\lambda I\beta$-conversion; it has since been extended to all forms of λ-conversion.

The decision problem for all equations $X = Y$ was shown by Church in 1936 ("An Unsolvable Problem of Elementary Number Theory," in *American Journal of Mathematics* 58, pp. 345–363) to be recursively unsolvable, as was the problem of determining whether X has a normal form. This result was the basis of Church's later proof of the recursive unsolvability of the decision problem for predicate calculus.

Since every kind of λ-conversion is equivalent to a synthetic theory and vice versa, the results described below for the synthetic theory are also results of λ-conversion and in some cases were first so obtained.

FOUNDATIONS OF PURE SYNTHETIC THEORY. Table 1 contains a list of special combinators. The names assigned to the combinators are in the first (X) column and the values of m and M to be used in equation (3) are in the second and third columns. The other columns will be explained later. In the various formulations certain of the combinators will be atomic; the corresponding equations (3) will then be assumed as axiom schemes in which 'x_1', · · ·, 'x_m' stand for arbitrary obs.

We seek to define, for arbitrary M, x_1, · · ·, x_m, an X such that (3) holds. The X so defined will be $[x_1, \cdots, x_m]M$; this means the same thing as $\lambda x_1 \cdots x_m M$ but is a defined, not a postulated, concept. One way of defining it is to use an induction on m, as above, and then, for $m = 1$, an induction on the structure of M. The latter can be obtained, for instance, by defining X to be **K**M when M does not contain x, to be **I** when M is x, and to be $\mathbf{S}X_1X_2$ when $M \equiv M_1M_2$ and we have already defined $X_1 \equiv [x]M_1$, $X_2 \equiv [x]M_2$. Such an algorithm defines all combinators in terms of **I**, **K**, **S** as atoms; the definitions are very long, but suitable modifications improve matters. The fourth column of the table gives some definitions obtained by suitably modified algorithms. Other modifications give definitions in terms of **I**, **B**, **C**, **S** for all cases where M actually contains x; these are suitable for an analogue of λI-conversion.

Thus, we get a definition for $[x]M$ compatible with any of the forms of λ-conversion if we postulate schemes (3) as stated, together with the properties of equality. The analogues (with $[x]M$ in place of λxM) of (α) and (β) will then hold. But we do not have the analogue of (ξ), nor do we have an extensionality principle

$$(\zeta) \qquad U_1x = U_2x \rightarrow U_1 = U_2$$

even under the restrictions that are appropriate for $\lambda\beta$-conversion. One can obtain these properties by adjoining a finite number of *combinatory axioms*. Examples of these axioms are

(4) $\qquad\qquad \mathbf{SK} = \mathbf{KI},$

(5) $\qquad\qquad \Psi\mathbf{SK} = \mathbf{BK}.$

Given a form of λ-conversion, we can choose these axioms so that there is a many–one mapping of the resulting system into the λ-conversion and another one vice versa, such that an equation in either system is a theorem exactly when its image is in the other. Thus, λ-conversion and the synthetic theory are equivalent. Bruce Lercher, in 1963, extended these considerations to include (δ).

It is possible to define, in several ways, a combinator **Y** such that for any X, $\mathbf{Y}X = X(\mathbf{Y}X)$. If Γ means negation, then $\mathbf{Y}\Gamma$ means the same as its own negation. For $\mathbf{Y} \equiv \mathbf{WS}(\mathbf{BWB})$, this is the notion at the root of the Russell paradox. Thus, in a combinatorially complete system one cannot exclude the paradoxes; one must explain them in the illative theory.

In the foregoing, equality can be taken as primitive. Then the axioms consist of the combinatory axioms, all instances of the reflexive law, and (3) (for atomic combinators); the rules are the usual rules for equality. When we press the analysis deeper so as to define equality by (2), the schemes (3) become rules; for example, that for **S** gives the pair of rules (one in each sense)

(6) $\qquad\qquad \vdash U(\mathbf{S}XYZ) \rightleftarrows \vdash U(XZ(YZ)),$

whereas reflexivity can come from an axiom. The result is a system with a finite number of axioms (no axiom schemes) and about a dozen rules, each with one or two premises and otherwise no more complex than (6) and such that the premises uniquely determine the conclusion. There are also only a finite number of atoms—variables are used only in the metatheory—and the single operation of application. The structure is therefore very simple. But all functions of variables can be performed therein, and with suitable illative additions it can form a basis for almost any logical system.

COMBINATORY ARITHMETIC. From the formal standpoint the natural numbers are constructions from a single atom, 0, by a single unary operation, σ. On this basis one can develop the usual recursive arithmetic, and one can explain how to count. Assume that such a system is given, represented, say, in the words in some alphabet

TABLE 1

X	m	M	Definition	FX
B	3	$x_1(x_2x_3)$	**S(KS)K**	$\mathbf{F}(\mathbf{F}\beta\gamma)\mathbf{F}(\mathbf{F}\alpha\beta)(\mathbf{F}\alpha\gamma))$
C	3	$x_1x_3x_2$	**S(BBS)(KK)**	$\mathbf{F}(\mathbf{F}\beta(\mathbf{F}\alpha\gamma))(\mathbf{F}\alpha(\mathbf{F}\beta\gamma))$
I	1		———	$\mathbf{F}\alpha\alpha$
K	2		———	$\mathbf{F}\alpha(\mathbf{F}\beta\alpha)$
S	3	$x_1x_3(x_2x_3)$	———	$\mathbf{F}(\mathbf{F}\alpha(\mathbf{F}\beta\gamma))(\mathbf{F}(\mathbf{F}\alpha\beta)(\mathbf{F}\alpha\gamma))$
W	2	$x_1x_2x_2$	**SS(KI)**	$\mathbf{F}(\mathbf{F}\alpha(\mathbf{F}\alpha\beta))(\mathbf{F}\alpha\beta)$
ϕ	4	$x_1(x_2x_4)(x_3x_4)$	**B(BS)B**	
ψ	4	$x_1(x_2x_3)(x_2x_4)$	———	

with only one letter. These words we shall call the *natural numbers*. Further, let σ be the successor function, δ the predecessor function, τ the ordered-pair function, and μ the operation such that for any numerical function f, μf is the least n for which $f(n) = 0$ and is undefined if there is no such n.

One can find a representation of the natural numbers as combinators; indeed, there are many choices. For any such choice let angle brackets "$\langle\ \rangle$" symbolize the combinatory analogues of the arithmetic notions indicated within them. Thus, $\langle n\rangle$ is, for any numeral n, the *combinatory numeral*which represents it, $\langle +\rangle$ the analogue of addition, etc. The analogues are often not uniquely determined.

The first representation, by Church in 1933, chose $\langle n\rangle$ so that $\langle n\rangle f$ is the nth iterate of f (the first iterate being f itself). If one has **K**, then $\langle 0\rangle$ is **KI** and $\langle\sigma\rangle$ is **SB**. Then $\langle n\rangle$ is the $\mathbf{Z}_n$ of H. B. Curry and Robert Feys (*Combinatory Logic*). Further, $\langle +\rangle$, $\langle\cdot\rangle$, and $\langle e\rangle$>, where $e(x,y) = x^y$, have simple definitions (for example, $\phi\mathbf{B}$, **B**, and **CI**, respectively) from which their arithmetical properties follow. There are other proposals for combinatory numerals; one, made by Dana Scott in 1963, has a simple $\langle\delta\rangle$. For the sake of generality, $\langle n\rangle$ is here unspecified, but a **Z** is postulated such that $\mathbf{Z}\langle n\rangle = \mathbf{Z}_n$. If $\langle n\rangle \equiv \mathbf{Z}_n$, then $\mathbf{Z} \equiv \mathbf{I}$.

Next one can define combinators $\mathbf{D}$ ($\equiv \langle\tau\rangle$), $\mathbf{D}_1$, $\mathbf{D}_2$ such that

$$\mathbf{D}_1(\mathbf{D}xy) = x,\ \mathbf{D}_2(\mathbf{D}xy) = y.$$

For instance (as Paul Bernays suggested in 1936),

$$\mathbf{D} = [x,y,z].\mathbf{Z}z(\mathbf{K}y)x.$$

For this

(7) $\qquad\qquad \mathbf{D}xy\langle 0\rangle = x,\ \mathbf{D}xy\langle\sigma n\rangle = y,$

so that $\mathbf{D}_1$ and $\mathbf{D}_2$ can be $[x]x\langle 0\rangle$ and $[x]x\langle 1\langle$, respectively. One can also define $\mathbf{D}$ in terms of $\langle\delta\rangle$ rather than $\mathbf{Z}$.

Next a combinator $\mathbf{R}$ can be defined such that

$$\textbf{(8)}\qquad \mathbf{R}xy\langle 0\rangle = x,\ \mathbf{R}xy\langle\sigma\rangle = y\langle n\rangle(\mathbf{R}xy\langle n\rangle).$$

If $x = \langle g\rangle$ and $y = \langle h\rangle$, where g and h are, respectively, k-place and $(k + 2)$-place numerical functions, $\mathbf{R}xy$ can be taken as $\langle f\rangle$, where f is the $(k + 1)$-place numerical function defined by the "primitive recursion scheme" from g and h. Since the other processes of forming primitive recursive functions have combinatory analogues, definition of $\mathbf{R}$ will ensure that $\langle f\rangle$ is defined for any primitive recursive f.

Several definitions of $\mathbf{R}$ exist. The first (given by Bernays in 1936) depends on the fact that $f(n)$ can be obtained (for $k = 0$, as an example) by iterating n times, starting with $\tau(0,g)$, the function ϕ such that $\phi(\tau(x,y)) = t(\sigma x,h(x,y))$ and taking the second member. This leads to the definition (in two stages)

$$Y \equiv [u]\mathbf{D}(\langle\sigma\rangle(\mathbf{D}_2u))\ (y(\mathbf{D}_1u)\ (\mathbf{D}_2u)),$$

$$\mathbf{R} \equiv [x,y,z](\mathbf{D}_2(\mathbf{Z}zY(\mathbf{D}\langle 0\rangle x))).$$

Another possibility is to define a combinator Ω such that for given obs p, q, r, the ob $t = \Omega pqr$ satisfies the conditions

$$\textbf{(9)}\qquad t\langle n\rangle = \begin{cases} p\langle n\rangle & \text{if } r\langle n\rangle = \langle 0\rangle, \\ qf\langle n\rangle & \text{if } r\langle n\rangle = \langle 1\rangle, \end{cases}$$

thus:

$$Y \equiv \mathbf{D}(\mathbf{K}p)([u](q([z](u(rz)uz)))),$$

$$\mathbf{\Omega} \equiv [p,q,r,x](Y(rx)Yx).$$

For $p \equiv \mathbf{K}x$, $q \equiv [u,z](y(\langle\delta\rangle z)(u(\langle\delta\rangle z)))$, $r = \mathbf{I}$, the ob $[x,y]\Omega pqr$ is an $\mathbf{R}$, different from the foregoing, satisfying (8). There are still other ways of defining $\mathbf{R}$. Since $\langle\delta\rangle$ can be defined as $\mathbf{R}\langle 0\rangle\mathbf{K}$ and $\mathbf{Z}$ as $\mathbf{R}\ (\mathbf{KI})(\mathbf{K}(\mathbf{SB}))$, we have any primitive recursive function as soon as we have either $\mathbf{Z}$ or $\langle\delta\rangle$ and a discrimination for $\langle 0\rangle$.

We can go further. If we take $p \equiv \mathbf{I}$, $q \equiv [u,z]\ (u(\langle\sigma\rangle z))$, while r is a given function $\langle g\rangle$, then Ωpqr is an $\langle f\rangle$ such that $f(n) = n$ if $g(n) = 0$ and otherwise $f(n) = f(\sigma n)$. This shows that we can define $\langle\mu\rangle$ in terms of the above q as $[x](\Omega\mathrm{I}qx\langle 0\rangle)$. Consequently, every partial recursive numerical function is definable by combinators. The converse of this thesis follows by the usual arguments involving Gödel numeration.

These conclusions are not greatly affected if one restricts the system to correspond with restricted forms of λ-conversion. The passage from η-conversion to β-conversion hardly makes any difference. The omission of $\mathbf{K}$ complicates things somewhat—one needs ordered triples instead of ordered pairs. But the main conclusion, that every partial recursive function is definable by combinators and vice versa, stands.

Some generalizations are known. One can define by combinators certain transformations between obs and their Gödel numbers. An extension to recursive functionals of certain types can be obtained by using an analogue of (δ). There is also an extension to certain transfinite ordinal numbers.

ILLATIVE THEORY. By definition illative combinatory logic includes all considerations where there are atoms which neither are combinators nor are necessary to express equality. We consider here those cases in which the new atoms mean ordinary logical notions—for example, II (absolute universality), $\mathbf{P}$ (implication), Ξ (relative universality or formal implication), $\mathbf{F}$ (functionality—$\mathbf{F}XYZ$ means that Z is a function from X into Y), Σ (instantiality), Λ (conjunction), Γ (negation), Θ (descriptive quantifier), etc. In addition, we need obs meaning semantical categories, such as $\mathbf{E}$ (the category of all obs—$\mathbf{E}$ is definable, for example, as $\mathbf{WQ}$), $\mathbf{H}$ (propositions), $\mathbf{J}$ (individuals), $\mathbf{M}$ (sets), $\mathbf{N}$ (numbers), etc.

The meaning of these obs is expressed more precisely by the rules associated with them. For the first four obs these are

RULE Π: $\quad\vdash \Pi X \ \&\ \vdash \mathrm{E}U \rightarrow\ \vdash XU.$

RULE $\mathbf{P}$: $\quad\vdash \mathbf{P}XY \ \&\ \vdash X \rightarrow\ \vdash Y.$

RULE $\mathbf{\Xi}$: $\quad\vdash \mathbf{\Xi}XY \ \&\ \vdash XU \rightarrow\ \vdash YU.$

RULE $\mathbf{F}$: $\quad\vdash \mathbf{F}XYZ \ \&\ \vdash XU \rightarrow\ \vdash Y(ZU).$

These rules, when relevant, are to be postulated in addition to the combinatory rules given earlier; the latter can be summarized as

RULE Eq: $\quad\vdash X \ \&\ X = Y \rightarrow\ \vdash Y.$

These notions are, of course, interdefinable; in fact, one can take as atoms either $\mathbf{F}$, Ξ, or Π and $\mathbf{P}$ and define the others as follows (there are two possible definitions for Ξ in terms of $\mathbf{F}$):

$$\mathbf{F} \equiv [x,y,z](\Xi x(\mathbf{B}yz)),$$

$$\Xi \equiv [x,y](\Pi([z](\mathbf{P}(xz)(yz)))),$$

$$\Pi \equiv \Xi\mathbf{E},$$

$$\mathbf{P} \equiv \Psi\Xi\mathbf{K} = [x,y](\Xi(\mathbf{K}x)(\mathbf{K}y)),$$

$$\Xi'' \equiv [x,y](\mathbf{F}xy\mathbf{I}),\ \Xi'' \equiv [x,y](\mathbf{F}x\mathbf{I}y).$$

The system based on **F** as primitive is called $\mathscr{F}_1$, or the theory of *functionality*; that on Ξ as $\mathscr{F}_2$, or the theory of *restricted generality*; and that on Π and **P** as $\mathscr{F}_3$. With reasonable axioms, these are listed in order of increasing strength.

Although the Church–Rosser theorem shows that pure combinatory logic is consistent, in the illative theory one easily runs into contradictions. Thus, if one were to assume

(10) $\vdash \mathbf{P}(\mathbf{P}\alpha(\mathbf{P}\alpha\beta))(\mathbf{P}\alpha\beta)$

as an axiom scheme, with the Greek letters standing for arbitrary obs, the theory would be inconsistent in the sense that (1) would hold for any X. But (10) is a thesis of the *absolute* (that is, positive intuitionistic) *propositional algebra.* Thus, it is necessary, if the theory is to contain this algebra, that (10) be a theorem scheme with a restricted range for the Greek letters. In its early stages illative combinatory logic will have axiom schemes with such restrictions. Later, perhaps, these schemes will be reduced to axioms by quantifying over a suitable category.

This requires some sort of machinery of categories or types. Such machinery is taken for granted in the usual systems of mathematical logic. It consists of four items: (*a*) a list of primitive categories (such as those listed above), (*b*) devices for forming derived categories, (*c*) assignments of the primitive notions to categories, (*d*) means for determining the categories of composite notions. Of these items (*a*) and (*c*) are special to the theory considered, but (*b*) and (*d*) are general processes which are appropriate for study in combinatory logic. Since composite obs are formed by application alone, one would expect a means of assigning a category to XY when those for X and Y are known; the general principle is that if X is a function from α to β and Y belongs to α, then XY belongs to β. This principle is expressed by Rule **F**, so the basis for this generalized theory of types is $\mathscr{F}_1$.

From the illative standpoint one would expect that each combinator would be assigned a category depending on parameters expressing that it is a function transforming from certain sorts of categories to categories of certain other sorts. Such *functional characters* for some basic combinators of the table are listed there in the fifth column. Assignments of these characters to the atomic combinators would then be axiom (or at least theorem) schemes of $\mathscr{F}_1$. However, these schemes cannot be accepted with the Greek letters standing for arbitrary obs, for if one so accepts **FW**, the theory is again inconsistent. Even $\mathscr{F}_1$ has to be formulated with restrictions on the Greek letters.

The most radical restriction is the requirement that the Greek letters range over an inductive class of F-obs generated from certain otherwise unspecified atoms θ_1, $\theta_2, \cdots$ by the operation of forming $\mathbf{F}\alpha\beta$ from α and β. One further restricts Rule Eq thus:

RULE **Eq'**: $\vdash \xi X \ \&\ X = Y \rightarrow \vdash \xi Y.$

The resulting theory is called the *basic theory of functionality.* In this theory every elementary statement will be of the form

(11) $\vdash \xi X,$

where ξ is an F-ob and X is a combinator. The theory is demonstrably consistent. If X is a *stratified* combinator—that is, if X satisfies (3) and one can derive $\vdash \eta M$ by Rule **F** alone from the axiom schemes and assignments of categories to the variables—then one can derive a statement of the form (11) stating that X has the appropriate functional character. There is a converse to this which is somewhat difficult to state, but it shows that the X's for which (11) can be derived are greatly restricted; in particular, they have a normal form.

There are several "stronger" theories of functionality with less drastic restrictions. A theory in which one uses only combinators that do not repeat variables can be constructively proved consistent without restrictions on the Greek letters. Constructive consistency proofs have been obtained for some other theories of $\mathscr{F}_1$.

All these systems of $\mathscr{F}_1$ are extremely weak. To obtain stronger and natural theories one proceeds to $\mathscr{F}_2$ (or adds assumptions to $\mathscr{F}_1$ which are equivalent to this). In $\mathscr{F}_2$ reasonable schemes **ΞI**, **ΞK**, etc., with Greek letters restricted to a class of "canonical obs," can be formulated from which the corresponding **FI**, **FK**, $\cdots$ can be derived. Thus, $\mathscr{F}_2$ has a deduction theorem; it also includes the absolute propositional calculus of pure implication. There is a Gentzen-like theory of "verifiability" from which it follows that certain weak forms of the illative theory are consistent.

The study of illative combinatory logic is still in its preliminary stages. Little is known, for example, about $\mathscr{F}_3$. It is clear that ordinary logical systems can be founded on a combinatory basis, but little has been published along this line. On such a basis E. J. Cogan, in 1955, analyzed the foundations of Gödel's set theory and also the predicate calculus and some other calculuses; owing to an unfortunate oversight in the definition of "class," the system was inconsistent, as Rainer Titgemeyer showed in 1961, but the necessary changes are rather minor. Other investigations of this sort are in the process of development or publication. Some authors, such as F. B. Fitch, go in a somewhat different direction.

In illative combinatory logic we are dealing with concepts of such generality that we have little intuition in regard to them. This explains why proposals by competent logicians beginning with Gottlob Frege (not all combinatory, but the principle applies) have later proved inconsistent. We must, indeed, proceed by trial and error. No doubt we shall continue to find both inconsistencies in weaker systems and consistency proofs of stronger systems. In due course nonfinitary methods will be used, and much is to be expected of them. But the possibility remains that we may always be interested in systems for which neither consistency nor inconsistency is known.

Combinatory logic was inaugurated by Moses Schönfinkel in 1924. He introduced the notion of application, the combinators **B, C, I, K, S** (his *Z, T, I, C, S*), and an illative notion *U*. He showed how statements of logic could be expressed in terms of these notions, but he gave no deductive theory of them. He became ill shortly after writing the paper and was unable to do anything further in the subject. Curry, beginning in 1929, produced the first deductive synthetic theory and introduced the terminology used here. The theory of λ-conversion was developed by Church from 1932. Subsequent improvements were made by these authors and by Rosser, S. C. Kleene, Bernays, Fitch, and Paul Rosenbloom. The present state of the subject is the result of an interaction of the work of these authors and their students.

See also Church, Alonzo; Frege, Gottlob; Logical Paradoxes; Logic, History of; Quantifiers in Formal Logic.

Bibliography

Items listed here either are of broad scope or treat aspects of the subject not included in the text. For sources, details, etc., see the bibliographies in the works cited.

Church, Alonzo. *The Calculi of Lambda-Conversion.* Princeton, NJ: Princeton University Press, 1941; 2nd ed., 1951. The standard work on λ-conversion, with references.

Church, Alonzo. "The Richard Paradox." *American Mathematical Monthly* 41 (1934): 356–361. Expounds a system modeling illative notions on the pure theory.

Cogan, E. J. "A Formalization of the Theory of Sets from the Point of View of Combinatory Logic." *Zeitschrift für mathematische Logik und Grundlagen der Mathematik* 1 (1955): 198–240. Contains a readable introduction and some information on illative theory going beyond Curry and Feys (below). For an inconsistency, see text, section on illative theory.

Curry, H. B. "The Elimination of Variables by Regular Combinators." In *The Critical Approach to Science and Philosophy,* in honor of Karl R. Popper, edited by Mario Bunge, pp. 127–143. New York: Free Press of Glencoe, 1964. Contains, on pp. 128–131, a discussion of the "ontology" of combinatory logic, partly in answer to Quine (below).

Curry, H. B., and Robert Feys. *Combinatory Logic,* Vol. I. Amsterdam: North-Holland, 1958. A monograph, with full bibliography, historical sketch, etc.

Fitch, F. B. "The System CΔ of Combinatory Logic." *Journal of Symbolic Logic* 28 (1963): 87–97. A nonfinitary system with consistency proof. Refers to Fitch's other papers.

Quine, W. V. "Variables Explained Away." *Proceedings of the American Philosophical Society* 104 (1960): 343–347. An alternative formulation of combinatory logic, to be used in combination with first-order predicate calculus, which, Quine claims, involves fewer ontological presuppositions.

Rosenbloom, Paul. *The Elements of Mathematical Logic.* New York: Dover, 1950. Very compact. Departures from standard notations hinder reading.

Rosser, J. B. *Deux Esquisses de logique.* Paris: Gauthier-Villars, 1955. A masterly exposition of certain parts of the pure theory.

Schönfinkel, Moses. "Über die Bausteine der mathematischen Logik." *Mathematische Annalen* 92 (1924): 305–316. Still readable and interesting for motivation. The statement in the postscript (by Heinrich Behmann) to the effect that parentheses can be eliminated by **Z** (that is, **B**) alone is erroneous.

Haskell B. Curry (1967)

COMEDY

See *Humor*

COMENIUS, JOHN AMOS

(1592–1670)

John Amos Comenius, also called Komensky, the Czech philosopher of education and theologian, was born in Uhersky Brod. Comenius was a member of the Community of the Moravian Brethren (*Unitas Fratrum*) and studied Protestant theology at the universities of Herborn and Heidelberg. Shortly after his return to Moravia, the Thirty Years' War broke out. The Protestant Czechs were defeated by the Catholic Hapsburg monarchy, and Comenius became a permanent exile. Elected bishop of the *Unitas* in 1632, he considered it his main mission as a pastor and as a theological writer to preserve the faith and unity of the dispersed Moravian brethren.

In his writings, which range from such topics as theology, politics, philosophy, and science (as he understood science) to linguistics and education, as well as in his personal life, he combined such contradictory strands of thought as world immanence and world transcendence, interest in science and dependence on false prophets, progressivism, and apocalyptic expectations. In order to understand this mingling of ideas, we must project ourselves into the baroque age, when so many illustrious minds were wandering from one extreme to another. Thus, despite scholastic and Calvinist influences during his years of study, Comenius's concept of the divine regime contained a notable admixture of Neoplatonic, evolutionary, mystical, and pantheistic ideas. God was for him the God of Nature as well as the God of Heaven. However, all these pantheistic leanings did not shake the foundations of Comenius's faith, and throughout his life he clung to the fundamentals of the Christian dogma. Nevertheless, it was the cosmic curiosity in Comenius's religion that opened his mind to the unfolding of the natural and humanistic sciences. Yet Comenius lacked any real understanding of science in the Newtonian sense. The generic concept under which he subsumed the new scientific pursuits was that of "Light," to be understood as both the "Light of God" and the light of reason that God has kindled in man in order to guide him on his way toward eternal truth.

No doubt a certain utopian chiliasm inspired Comenius, but he also shared with the greatest minds of his time the enthusiasm about a new discovery, the discovery of "method," understood as a form of systematic and empirical inquiry which would guarantee the harmonization between man's reason and the natural—and perhaps even the supernatural—universe. The man who impressed Comenius most of all was Francis Bacon. Through Bacon, he became convinced that the new inductive method would shed light not only on the *arcana naturae* but also on the mysteries of the human mind and of human learning. The long title of Comenius's *Great Didactic* (*Didactica Magna*) tells the reader that the author believes he has found a system to teach "all things to all men." Comenius was one of the first to grasp the significance of a methodical procedure in schooling, to project a plan of universal education, and to see the significance of education as an agency of international understanding. Often quoted are the eight principles of teaching that Comenius expounds in Chapter 9 of the *Great Didactic,* in strange analogy to what he supposes to be the economy and order of the sun's functioning in the universe. Still valid in these principles is the emphasis on the interrelation between mental maturity and learning, on the participation of the student, and on the logical interconnection of the subjects in the curriculum.

Education—to be extended to both sexes, all men, and all peoples—should be crowned by a *pansophia* (encyclopedic synthesis of universal knowledge), with the aim of a *dilucidatio* (systematic interpretation) of the order of all things within the cosmic order. For the promotion of the great and worldwide mission of education, Comenius recommended a "Universal College" of the great and wise men of the whole world, and an easily constructed international language for the peace and "for the reform of the whole world" and as an "antidote to the confusion of thought."

In 1668 he dedicated a treatise, *The Way of Light* (*Via Lucis*), "to the torch bearers of this enlightened age, members of the Royal Society of London, now bringing real philosophy to a happy birth." He expressed the "confident hope" that through their endeavors "philosophy brought to perfection" would "exhibit the true and distinctive qualities of things … for the constantly progressive increase of all that makes for good to mind, body, and estate."

Bibliography

WORKS BY COMENIUS

The Great Didactic. Translated by M. W. Keatinge. London: A. and C. Black, 1923.

The Way of Light. Translated by E. T. Campagnac. Liverpool: Liverpool University Press, 1938.

The Labyrinth of the World and the Paradise of the Heart. Translated by Matthew Spinka. Chicago: National Union of Czechoslovak Protestants in America, 1942.

John Amos Comenius, Selections, edited by Jean Piaget. New York, 1957. Contains references to more-recent Czech literature.

WORKS ON COMENIUS

Bušek, Vratislav, ed. *Comenius.* Translated by Káca Polácková. New York: Czechoslovak Society of Arts and Sciences in America, 1972.

Kozik, František. *The Sorrowful and Heroic Life of John Amos Comenius.* Prague: State Educational Publishing House, 1958.

Kvacala, J. *J. A. Comenius.* Berlin, 1914. Contains a large bibliography.

Laurie, S. S. *John Amos Comenius.* Boston, 1885.

Petru, Eduard. "The Harmonizing Influence of God in the Understanding of J. A. Comenius." *Ultimate Reality and Meaning* 20 (2 and 3) (1997): 99–106.

Sadler, John E. *J. A. Comenius and the Concept of Universal Education.* London: Allen and Unwin, 1966.
Ulich, Robert. *History of Educational Thought.* New York: American Book, 1950.
Ulich, Robert. *Three Thousand Years of Educational Wisdom.* 2nd ed. Cambridge, MA: Harvard University Press, 1954.

Robert Ulich (1967)
Bibliography updated by Tamra Frei (2005)

COMMON CAUSE PRINCIPLE

No correlation without causation. This is the most compact formulation of Reichenbach's Common Cause Principle (RCCP). More explicitly RCCP is the claim that if two events A and B are correlated, then either A and B stand in a causal relation, $R_{cause}(A, B)$, or, if A and B are causally independent, $R_{ind}(A, B)$, then there is a third event C, a so-called Reichenbachian common cause that brings about the correlation by being related to A and B in a specific manner spelled out in the following definition, first given by Reichenbach (1956): Event C is called a (Reichenbachian) common cause of the correlation

(1) $$p(A \wedge B) - p(A)p(B) > 0$$

if the following conditions hold:

(2) $$p(A \wedge B|C) = p(A|C)p(B|C)$$

(3) $$p(A \wedge B|C^{\perp}) = p(A|C^{\perp})p(B|C^{\perp})$$

(4) $$p(A|C) > p(A|C^{\perp})$$

(5) $$p(B|C) > p(B|C^{\perp})$$

Here A, B, and C are assumed to be elements in a Boolean algebra $\mathcal{S}$ and they are to be interpreted as representatives of random events. $p(A|C) = p(A \wedge C)/p(C)$ and so on denote the conditional probability of A on condition C, $C^{\perp}$ denotes the complement of C, and it is assumed that none of the probabilities involved is equal to zero.

RCCP is a metaphysical claim about the causal structure of the world, and it has been debated extensively in the philosophical literature whether RCCP is a valid principle. How could RCCP fail? The first step in any attempt to falsify RCCP is to display common cause incomplete probability spaces, that is, probability spaces that contain at least one correlation that does not have a common cause in the given probability space. Common cause incomplete probability spaces exist; however, the mere existence of such probability spaces does not entail that RCCP is not valid because RCCP is not the claim that given a correlated pair (A, B) of events in $\mathcal{S}$ there has to exist a common cause C that belongs to $\mathcal{S}$: RCCP is a pure existence claim, not requiring the common cause to belong to the specific set of events $\mathcal{S}$. If, however, one wishes to maintain the validity of RCCP against the threat posed by the existence of common cause incomplete probability spaces, one has to be able to claim that the probability space $(\mathcal{S}, p)$ is consistently extendable into a larger probability space $(\mathcal{S}', p')$ that does contain a common cause of the given correlation. If this can be done, one calls $(\mathcal{S}, p)$ "common cause completable" (with respect to the given correlation). It can be shown that every common cause incomplete probability space is common cause completable with respect to any finite set of correlations in it. (It is an open problem whether common cause extendability with respect to an infinite number of correlated events also holds.)

In view of common cause completability of probability spaces, one can always defend RCCP against attempts of falsification by referring to "hidden" common causes—"hidden" in the sense of not being accounted for in the set of events $\mathcal{S}$. Thus any successful falsification of RCCP must require some properties of the common cause in addition to those required by Reichenbach. One such possible requirement is that different correlations have a *common* common cause. One can show that different correlations cannot in general have a common common cause—not even in case of two correlations.

Assuming that RCCP is valid, one is led to the question of whether our theories predicting probabilistic correlations can be causally rich enough to contain also the causes of the correlations. According to RCCP, causal richness of a theory $(\mathcal{S}, p)$ would manifest in the theory's being causally closed: $(\mathcal{S}, p)$ is called *common cause closed with respect to* R_{ind}, if for every pair (A, B) of correlated events such that $R_{ind}(A, B)$ holds, there exists a common cause C in $\mathcal{S}$ of the correlation.

Whether a probabilistic theory is common cause closed with respect to the causal independence relation R_{ind} depends on how R_{ind} is specified. The weaker R_{ind} (i.e., the more pairs of random events are causally independent) the stronger the notion of common cause closedness with respect to R_{ind} and the more difficult it is for $\mathcal{S}$ to be common cause closed with respect to R_{ind}. For instance no probability space with a finite set of random events can be common cause closed with respect to the weakest R_{ind} (i.e., if $R_{ind}(A, B)$ holds for all A and B). However if $R_{ind}(A, B)$ is strong enough to imply that the presence of A implies neither the presence of B nor the presence of $B^{\perp}$

(and conversely, replacing *A* with *B*) then finite probability spaces can be common cause closed (with respect to R_{ind})—though they are not necessarily so. EPR correlations predicted by quantum mechanics are generally viewed as ones that might not admit a common cause type explanation—if the common causes are required also to conform to relativistic causality (such common causes are called "local").

Proving the impossibility of local common causes of EPR correlations involves two difficulties: First one has to link RCCP to quantum mechanics, which is non-trivial task since Reichenbach's notion of common cause was defined in terms of classical probability theory, not in terms of quantum mechanics. Second one has to formulate "locality" of common causes. One can approach the first problem in two ways: (i) reformulating Reichenbach's notion of common cause in terms of non-classical (quantum) probability spaces; (ii) representing quantum probabilities and quantum correlations in terms of classical probability theory.

Reichenbach's notion of common cause can be reformulated in terms of non-classical probability theory, where $\mathcal{S}$ is replaced by the lattice of projections of a von Neumann algebra and *p* by a state on the von Neumann algebra. The notions of common cause and of common cause completability can be adapted to the non-commutative case, and it can be shown that every non-commutative probability space also is common cause completable. Relativistic causality can also be formulated in terms of non-commutative probability spaces—the resulting theory is known as local algebraic quantum field theory. Locality of common causes of EPR correlations predicted by local quantum field theory can be defined by requiring the common causes to belong to a spacetime region located within the intersection of backward light cones of the spacelike separated regions containing the correlated observables. Whether such localized common causes exist in quantum field theory is an open problem, only partial results are known.

One can also take approach (ii) and formulate locality conditions for the hypothetical common causes of EPR correlations predicted by non-local, non-relativistic quantum mechanics—now represented in classical probability theory. These locality conditions express two sorts of independence: (i) the statistical independence of the random events of choosing measurements in the two wings of a typical correlation experiment and (ii) the statistical independence between choosing measurements in any wing and presence of any combination of the hypothetical common causes of spin correlations in different directions. Again it is an open question whether common causes satisfying these locality conditions can exist. It is known however that the EPR correlations between outcomes of spin measurements in different directions cannot have a common common cause because the assumption of common common causes of EPR correlations in different directions implies Bell's inequality.

See also Bell, John, and Bell's Theorem; Causation: Philosophy of Science; Neumann, John von; Reichenbach, Hans.

Bibliography

Arntzenius, Frank. "The Common Cause Principle." *PSA* 2 (1992): 227–237.

Cartwright, Nancy. "How to Tell a Common Cause: Generalization of the Conjunctive Fork Criterion." In *Probability and Causality*, edited by James H. Fetzer, 181–188. Boston: Reidel, 1988.

Fetzer, James H. Fetzer *Probability and Causality*. Boston: Reidel, 1988.

Hofer-Szabó, Gabor, Miklos Rédei, and Laszlo Szabó. "Common-Causes Are Not Common Common-Causes." *Philosophy of Science* 69 (2002): 623–636.

Hofer-Szabó, Gabor, Miklos Rédei, and Laszlo Szabó. "On Reichenbach's Common Cause Principle and Reichenbach's Notion of Common Cause." *The British Journal for the Philosophy of Science* 50 (1999): 377–398.

Hofer-Szabó, Gabor, Miklos Rédei, and Laszlo Szabó. "Reichenbach's Common Cause Principle: Recent Results and Open Questions." *Reports on Philosophy* 20 (2000): 85–107.

Placek, Tomasz. *Is Nature Deterministic?* Cracow: Jagellonian University Press, 2000.

Rédei, Miklos, and Stephen Summers. "Local Primitive Causality and the Common Cause Principle in Quantum Field Theory." *Foundations of Physics* 32 (2002): 335–355.

Rédei, Miklos. "Reichenbach's Common Cause Principle and Quantum Correlations." In *Modality, Probability and Bell's Theorems*, NATO Science Series, II. Vol. 64, edited by Tomasz Placek and Jeremy Butterfield, 259–270. Boston: Kluwer Academic, 2002.

Rédei, Miklos. "Reichenbach's Common Cause Principle and Quantum Field Theory." *Foundations of Physics*, 27 (1997): 1309–1321.

Reichenbach, Hans. *The Direction of Time*. Los Angeles: University of California Press, 1956.

Salmon, Wesley. "Why Ask 'Why?'?" In *Proceedings and Addresses of the American Philosophical Association* 51 (1978): 683–705.

Salmon, Wesley. "Probabilistic Causality." *Pacific Philosophical Quarterly* 61 (1980): 50–74.

Salmon, Wesley. *Scientific Explanation and the Causal Structure of the World*. Princeton, NJ: Princeton University Press, 1984.

Sober, Elliott. "Common Cause Explanation." *Philosophy of Science* 51 (1984): 212–241.

Sober, Elliott. "The Principle of the Common Cause." In *Probability and Causality*, edited by James H. Fetzer, 211–228. Boston: Reidel, 1988.

Sober, Elliott. "Venetian Sea Levels, British Bread Prices, and the Principle of Common Cause." *The British Journal for the Philosophy of Science* 52 (2001): 331–346.

Spohn, Wolfgang. "On Reichenbach's Principle of the Common Cause." In *Logic, Language and the Structure of Scientific Theories*, edited by Wesley Salmon and Gereon Wolters, 211–235. Pittsburgh: University of Pittsburgh Press, 1991.

Suppes, Patrick. *A Probabilistic Theory of Causality*. Amsterdam: North-Holland, 1970.

Suppes, Patrick, and Mario Zanotti. "When Are Probabilistic Explanations Possible?" *Synthese* 48 (1981): 191–199.

Uffink, Jos. "The Principle of the Common Cause Faces the Bernstein Paradox." *Philosophy of Science*, Supplement, 66 (1999): 512–525.

Van Fraassen, Bas. "The Charybdis of Realism: Epistemological Implications of Bell's Inequality." In *Philosophical Consequences of Quantum Theory*, edited by Jamers Cushing and Ernan McMullin, 97–113. Notre Dame: University of Notre Dame Press, 1989.

Van Fraassen, Bas. "The Pragmatics of Explanation." *American Philosophical Quarterly* 14 (1977): 143–150.

Van Frassen, Bas. "Rational Belief and the Common Cause Principle." In *What? Where? When? Why?*, edited by Robert McLaughlin, 193–209. Boston: D. Reidel, 1982.

Miklós Rédei (2005)

COMMON CONSENT ARGUMENTS FOR THE EXISTENCE OF GOD

Numerous philosophers and theologians have appealed to the "common consent" of humankind (the *consensus gentium*) as support for certain doctrines. Richard Hooker, for example, in his *Treatise on the Laws of Ecclesiastical Polity* appeals to this common agreement of humankind in justifying his view that the obligatory character of certain moral principles is immediately evident. Most frequently the conclusions supported in this way were those asserting the existence of God and the immortality of the human soul. In the present entry we shall confine ourselves to common consent arguments for the existence of God.

Among those who favored arguments of this kind were Cicero, Seneca, Clement of Alexandria, Herbert of Cherbury, the Cambridge Platonists, Pierre Gassendi, and Hugo Grotius. In more recent times these arguments were supported by numerous distinguished Protestant and Catholic theologians. G. W. F. Hegel did not accept the argument, but he thought that it contained a kernel of truth. Rudolf Eisler, in his *Wörterbuch der philosophischen Begriffe*, ranks the argument fifth in importance among so-called proofs of the existence of God, and this seems an accurate estimate of its place in the history of philosophy. At the same time, J. S. Mill was probably right when he observed that, as far as the "bulk of mankind" is concerned, the argument has exercised greater influence than others that are logically less vulnerable. Although there are hardly any professional philosophers at the present time who attribute any logical force to reasoning of this kind, it is still widely employed by popular apologists for religion.

Some supporters claim relatively little. "In no form," wrote the nineteenth-century theologian Robert Flint, "ought the argument from general consent to be regarded as a primary argument. It is evidence that there are direct evidences—and when kept in its proper place it has no inconsiderable value—but it cannot be urged as a direct and independent argument" (*Theism*, p. 349). Cardinal Mercier similarly regarded the argument as "indirect or extrinsic." It does not by itself prove the existence of God, but it is a "morally certain indication that there are proofs warranting the assertion that God exists" (*A Manual of Modern Scholastic Philosophy*, Vol. II, p. 55). Father Bernard Boedder and G. H. Joyce claim a great deal more. Boedder (*Natural Theology*, p. 63) regards it as an "argument of absolute value in itself." The universal consent "of nations in the recognition of God must be deemed the voice of universal reason yielding to the compelling evidence of truth." Later, however, he admits that it is not "absolutely conclusive, except when taken in conjunction with the argument of the First Cause" (ibid., p. 75). Joyce, a twentieth-century writer to whom we owe one of the fullest and clearest statements of one version of the argument, is far more sanguine. He calls it without any qualification a "valid proof of the existence of God" and seems to regard the conclusion as established with "perfect certainty."

The argument has rarely been stated by any philosopher in the form of a simple appeal to the universality of belief in God. In this form it is patently invalid and invites Pierre Bayle's comment that "neither general tradition nor the unanimous consent of all men can place any injunction upon truth." There is, on the face of it, no reason why the whole of humankind should not have been as wrong on a speculative topic as it has been on some more empirical questions on which, history teaches, it has been mistaken. The actual versions of the argument advanced by philosophers are more complicated and can be conveniently grouped into two classes. In the first we have arguments in which the universality of belief, for reasons peculiar to this particular case, is taken as evidence either that the belief itself is instinctive or that it is due to longings or needs which are instinctive. It is then concluded, for a variety of reasons, that the belief must be true. In the second group we have arguments according to which the universality of the belief, in conjunction with the claim that believers used reason in arriving at their position, is treated as evidence for the existence of God. We shall refer to arguments of the first kind as "biological" versions and to those of the second kind as the "antiskeptical dilemma." Whatever the shortcomings of these arguments may be, they cannot be dismissed simply on the ground that the whole of humankind may well be mistaken.

Although no doubt some of the disputes in which philosophers and others have engaged in this connection are antiquated and sometimes have a slightly preposterous ring to modern ears, other related issues are still very much with us. For example, it is still maintained by a number of influential philosophers and psychologists that people are "by nature" religious, so that the spread of skepticism and atheism is likely to lead to highly undesirable results. "It is safe to say," writes Carl Jung about his patients, "that every one of them fell ill because he had lost that which the living religions of every age have given their followers" (*Modern Man in Search of a Soul,* p. 254). Nor are attempts lacking even in our own day to show that everybody "really" believes in God, no matter what they may say or think. In the course of evaluating various forms of the Argument from Common Consent, we shall have occasion to say something about these more contemporary issues as well.

BIOLOGICAL FORMS OF THE ARGUMENT

INSTINCTIVE BELIEF IN GOD. A familiar version of the biological form of the Argument from Common Consent is found in Seneca's *Epistulae Morales* (Letter 117):

> We are accustomed to attach great importance to the universal belief of mankind. It is accepted by us as a convincing argument. That there are gods we infer from the sentiment engrafted in the human mind; nor has any nation ever been found, so far beyond the pale of law and civilization as to deny their existence.

Seneca did not elaborate on the nature of the "sentiment" that is "engrafted in the human mind," but later writers did, especially when replying to criticisms such as John Locke's. In the course of his polemic against the theory of innate ideas, Locke had rejected the initial premise of the argument as plainly false. His reasons were twofold. First, he noted with regret that there were atheists among the ancients, and also, more recently, "navigation discovered whole nations among whom there was to be found no notion of a God" (*Essay concerning Human Understanding,* Book I, Sec. IV). Aside from questioning the prevalence or even the existence of unbelief, the usual reply to this kind of criticism has been to make a distinction between two senses in which an idea or a belief may be said to be innate or instinctive. Such an assertion may mean that the idea or the belief is present in the human mind at birth as an image or some other actual "content," or it may amount to the much milder claim that it is present as a disposition to arrive at the belief when noticing certain things in the world or in oneself (usually this is stated very strongly to the effect that, when noticing the things in question, the person cannot help coming to believe in God). It is then explained that belief in God is instinctive in the latter or dispositional sense only. To avoid the charge of triviality, the defenders of the argument usually insist that because of this disposition, teaching or indoctrination is not required. Thus Charles Hodge, who makes it clear that he advocates a doctrine of the innateness of belief in God in the dispositional sense, adds that "men no more need to be taught that there is a God, than they need to be taught that there is such a thing as sin" (*Systematic Theology,* Vol. I, p. 199). "Adam," he also writes, "believed in God the moment he was created, for the same reason that he believed in the external world. His religious nature, unclouded and undefiled, apprehended the one with the same confidence that his senses apprehended the other" (ibid., pp. 200–201).

Several comments are in order here. To begin with, the theory that belief in God is innate does not become vacuous when it is stated in this way, so long as we are told what the facts are in the presence of which a human being cannot help coming to believe in the existence of God. However, when these facts are specified as the adjustments of organisms to their environment or as our experiences of duty and obligation (and these are the ones most frequently mentioned), Locke's objection seems to be fundamentally intact. For, apart from the question of primitive tribes, a great many of the unbelievers in Western culture appear to have been fully exposed to these facts. But this does not usually move the proponents of the argument. Aside from certain rejoinders that will be discussed later, their formulations usually contain highly elastic words that make possible a speedy disposition of apparent negative instances. The unbeliever may have been exposed to the relevant facts but not "adequately"; or he may have been exposed to them adequately, but his religious nature may have been "clouded" or "defiled"; or, contrary to outward appearances, the unbeliever may really believe, but the belief may be so faint as to be barely perceptible. This last method was adopted by Hodge when faced with the negative evidence drawn from the observations of blind deaf-mutes. Unbelievers like Ludwig Büchner had pointed to several famous cases, including that of Laura Bridgman, who either could not be brought to form an idea of God at all or who reported that, prior to instruction, no such idea had entered their minds. As far as is known, Hodge never made any empirical studies of blind deaf-mutes, but this did not prevent him from replying with full confidence. "The knowledge obtained by Christian instruction so much surpasses that given by intuition," he assures us, that the purely intuitive knowledge of the blind deaf-mute "seems as nothing" (ibid., p. 197).

At this stage one must raise the following questions: Under what circumstances would a human being *not* possess an innate belief in God? More specifically, let us suppose that a person observes the facts of organic adjustment and experiences a sense of duty and obligation but nevertheless maintains, with all appearance of sincerity, that he does not believe in God. Under what circumstances would it be true to say that he had observed the facts adequately, that his religious nature was not clouded or defiled, but that he nevertheless had no belief in God? Unless these questions are satisfactorily answered, the argument does not really get off the ground. For it is meant to be based on an empirical premise, and the premise will not be empirical if it is retained no matter how human beings may respond to the stimuli that are supposed to activate the innate disposition to believe in God.

Waiving this difficulty, and granting that the distinction between the two senses in which a belief may be instinctive circumvents the first of Locke's objections, the argument would still be open to his second criticism, namely, that the universality of an idea or a belief does not establish its innateness. It may well be possible, Locke argued, to account in other ways for the universal occurrence of an idea or the general agreement on a topic. The ideas of the sun and heat, he wrote, are also universal without being "natural impressions on the mind" (op. cit., Book I, Sec. 2). Locke, who was primarily concerned with the origin of the *idea* of God rather than with any question of the universality of belief in God, claimed that he could give an adequate account of how this idea arose in the human mind without an appeal to innate ideas, and John Stuart Mill later offered a detailed account of how belief in God might be universal without being instinctive. Reasons for rejecting such accounts would have to be offered before one could infer the innateness of belief in God from its universality.

Mill, one of the few great philosophers of recent times to discuss this argument in detail, objected to it on several other grounds as well. Assuming a belief to be innate or instinctive, he asked why this should be any reason whatsoever for regarding it as true. The only justification for this transition that Mill could think of he dismissed as begging the question. This is "the belief that the human mind was made by a God, who would not deceive his creatures" (*Three Essays on Religion,* p. 156), which of course presupposes what is to be proved. Whether this is in fact the only possible justification of the inference from the innateness of a belief to its truth, Mill's observation that the former does not by itself afford evidence for the latter seems to be very well taken. The force of his point, however, may be obscured because instinctive beliefs are frequently referred to as a priori and because this and related expressions are ambiguous. In this present context, calling a proposition a priori simply means that it was not affirmed as the result of instruction. In other contexts, and more commonly, to say that a proposition is a priori logically implies that it is a necessary truth and hence requires no empirical confirmation. It should be clear that if a proposition is a priori in the former sense, it does *not* automatically follow that it is a necessary truth or a truth at all. If an empirical or, more generally, a nonnecessary proposition were instinctively entertained, it would stand just as much in need of proof or confirmation as any other; and, except for a few defenders of the Ontological Argument, believers and unbelievers alike are satisfied that "God exists" does not express a necessary proposition.

Flint and others complained that Mill was unfair because there are versions of the argument that cannot be accused of circular reasoning. It will become clear in the next section that the antiskeptical form of the argument is in fact immune from such a criticism (and Mill was probably not familiar with it). However, it is difficult to see how the version of the biological argument which we have been discussing can bridge the transition from the instinctiveness of belief to its truth without introducing God as guarantor of the instinct's trustworthiness.

INNATE YEARNING FOR GOD. There is, however, another version of the biological argument which can perhaps be stated in such a way as to avoid the charge of circular reasoning. This version, moreover, has certain additional advantages over the one considered previously. "All the faculties and feelings of our minds and bodies," writes Hodge, "have their appropriate objects; and the possession of the faculties supposes the existence of those objects." Thus the eye, "in its very structure, supposes" that there is light to be seen, and the ear would be "unaccountable and inconceivable" without the existence of sound. "In like manner" our religious feelings and aspirations "necessitate" the existence of God (op. cit., p. 200). "The yearning for some kind of God," in the words of Chad Walsh, a contemporary defender of the argument, "does point toward an in-built hunger in each of us—a hunger for something greater than we are." But every other hunger has its normal gratification. This is true of physical hunger, of love and sex, and of our craving for beauty. If, similarly, our religious hunger did not have its proper gratification, it would be difficult to see "how it got built into our natures in the first place. What is it doing there?" (*Atheism Doesn't Make Sense*, p. 10).

This version of the argument escapes one of the difficulties of the version considered earlier. It can very plausibly be argued that absence of belief in God does not prove absence of a yearning for God; and in fact there are undoubtedly unbelievers who wish they could believe. But, granting that the existence of unbelievers does not prove that the wish for God's reality is not universal, this version of the argument nevertheless appears to be open to a number of fatal or near-fatal objections. To begin with, there seem to be exceptions here also. There seem to be people who not only do not believe in God but who are also devoid of any hunger for God. Furthermore, even if this hunger were universal, it might, as before, be possible to explain it on some basis other than that it is innate; or, putting the point differently, one would have to be satisfied that all such explanations are inadequate before one could conclude that it is innate. More seriously and waiving such objections as that the analogy between "religious hunger" and either physical hunger or having organs like eyes and ears is more than dubious, statements to the effect that we have eyes because there is light are objectionable on several grounds. Neither the observed facts nor contemporary biological theory warrants any such assertion. We are entitled to say that we have eyes and that there is light and that the eyes are useful because there is light, so that, other things being equal, organisms with eyes are likely to win out in the struggle for survival against organisms without eyes. Many kinds of biological variations are not similarly useful, but these are rarely noticed by proponents of the argument. When reading the teleological formulations of these writers—Walsh's question "How did the longing get *built into* [italics added] our nature in the first place?" or Hodge's remark that "possession of the faculties *supposes* [italics added] the existence of the appropriate objects"—one can hardly avoid the suspicion that although God is not explicitly brought into the premise of the argument, these authors surreptitiously introduce a designer who supplied organisms with their native equipment in order to fit them to their environment. It might indeed be possible to establish the existence of a designer on other grounds, but in the present context the defender of the argument is guilty of circular reasoning and thus would not escape Mill's stricture. No such circularity is involved if the instinctive desire is made the basis of an argument for *immortality* after the existence of a beneficent deity has been independently established. Dugald Stewart, in his *Philosophy of the Active and Moral Powers of Man* (Edinburgh, 1828, Book III, Ch. 4), offered such an argument, observing, "whatever desires are evidently implanted in our minds by nature, … we may reasonably conclude, will in due time be gratified under the government of a Being infinite both in power and goodness." Stewart was not guilty of circular reasoning, since he thought that he had previously proved the existence of God by means of the Design Argument.

THE ANTISKEPTICAL DILEMMA

JOYCE'S ARGUMENT. One of the most carefully developed statements of the second main form of the Common Consent Argument is found in G. H. Joyce's *The Principles of Natural Theology.* There are three stages to this form of the argument. (1) As in the biological versions, it is contended that practically all human beings, past and present, can be counted as believers in God. Here, however, it is not maintained that there are innate tendencies in human beings to believe in God. If anything, the opposite is true: people crave liberty of action and resent any being with superior authority. If, nevertheless, nearly all human beings are "perfectly certain" of the existence of their "absolute Master," this can be so only because "the voice of reason" is so clear and emphatic: "All races, civilized and uncivilized alike, are at one in holding that the facts of nature and the voice of conscience compel us to affirm this [the existence of God] as certain truth" (op. cit., p. 179). (2) If the whole of humankind were mistaken in a conclusion of this kind, it would follow that something is amiss with man's intellect, that "it is idle for man to search for truth." In that event, pure skepticism would be the only alternative. (3) However, all of us, unless we wish to be perverse, realize that "man's intellect is fundamentally trustworthy—that, though frequently misled in this or that particular case through accidental causes, yet the instrument itself is sound" (ibid.). Since reason is fundamentally trustworthy, universal skepticism is not a serious alternative to the acceptance of humankind's conclusion that God exists.

Some writers, though not Joyce, are concerned to add that on this topic great men are at one with the masses of believers. "Even for the independent thinker," writes John Haynes Holmes, "there is such a thing as a consensus of best opinions which cannot be defied without the weightiest of reasons" ("Ten Reasons for Believing in Immortality," in *A Modern Introduction to Philosophy*, edited by Paul Edwards and Arthur Pap, New York, 1965, p. 241). If there were no God and no afterlife, the deceived would include, in the words of James Martineau, "the great and holy whom all men revere." Whom are we to reverence, he goes on, "if the inspirations of the highest nature are but cunningly-devised fables?" (ibid.).

Joyce is aware that the "common consent" of the human race on this subject has been challenged from two sides. To the criticism that there are unbelievers at the present time and that the history of Western countries records instances of other unbelievers, he replies that these are so few in comparison with the number of believers that they do not affect the "moral unanimity of the race," and he adds that he never meant to claim that literally everybody who ever lived has affirmed the existence of God. To the criticism that there are primitive peoples without a belief in God or at least in one God, Joyce replies that there is in fact no race without religion and that even where there is belief in a plurality of gods, it is invariably found that "the religion recognizes a supreme deity, the ruler of gods and men" (p. 182). Joyce concedes that the supreme deity of primitive religions often lacks some of the characteristics attributed to God by Christian and Jewish monotheists. But this does not affect the argument, since "an idea of God does not cease to deserve that name because it is inadequate" (p. 181). A person may be said to believe in God if he believes in a "Supreme Being, personal and intelligent, to whom man owes honor and reverence" (ibid.), regardless of what else he also believes or fails to believe.

OBJECTIONS TO JOYCE'S ARGUMENT. The claim that belief in God is practically, if not indeed strictly, universal in the human race is shared by defenders of both forms of the Common Consent Argument. We shall discuss the difficulties of such a position in some detail in the next section. Meanwhile, it should be pointed out that even if the moral unanimity of humankind on this subject is not questioned, the argument, as presented by Joyce, appears to be open to two powerful objections.

To begin with, it presupposes that all or most believers in God arrive at their belief by means of reason or the intellect. If this is not the case, then the argument clearly fails, since nothing derogatory about reason would follow if it was not the source of the mistaken conclusion. In actual fact, it seems more than doubtful that the majority of men use reason in any significant sense in arriving at belief in God or even in fortifying their belief after their original acceptance of it. In making this observation, "reason" is not used in any specially narrow sense. A person may, in a perfectly familiar and proper sense, be said to have arrived at a conclusion by means of reason without having set out any formal arguments. However, there seems to be a good deal of evidence that the majority of human beings came to their belief in God by traditional indoctrination. Nor is it particularly plausible to maintain that originally this belief was the product of reason. If reason had anything to do with it, its role, in the opinion of most contemporary psychologists, was probably quite subsidiary. Joyce's view that man's natural inclinations would lead to denial rather than to belief in God seems highly doubtful. There is a good deal of disagreement about the exact psychological mechanisms involved, but the majority of psychologists seem to think that man's loneliness and helplessness, as well as his animistic propensities, incline him to belief in protective (and also hostile) cosmic powers. This does not, of course, mean that such beliefs cannot also be adequately supported by rational considerations, but it does undermine Joyce's argument.

It should be emphasized that the view just outlined is by no means confined to antireligious psychologists. Fideistic theists would most certainly endorse these observations, as would many believers who have stressed the evil and suffering in the observable world. Indeed, most of the defenders of the biological form of the Common Consent Argument would be opposed to Joyce's account. "Our own consciousness," in the words of Charles Hodge (op. cit., pp. 199–200), "teaches us that this is not the ground of our own faith. We do not reason ourselves into the belief that there is a God; and it is very obvious that it is not by … a process of ratiocination, that the mass of the people are brought to this conclusion."

Even if this difficulty could be overcome, however, and if it were granted that human beings arrive at their belief in God by reason, Joyce's argument would still be in trouble. If "universal skepticism" stands for the view that human beings can never find the true answer to *any* question, then it is not implied by the rejection of the universal belief of humankind in God. All kinds of other explanations of the "universal error," short of "the radical untrustworthiness" of human reason, seem possible and cannot be ruled out without further ado. It has, for example, been widely held by Kantians, nineteenth-century positivists, and fideists that human reason, while trustworthy as long as it deals with empirical and purely formal issues, is not fit to handle questions transcending experience.

As for the observations of Martineau and Holmes, several points are in order. To begin with, "appeals to the best opinion" are of logical force only in areas in which there are experts, as there are in physics or dentistry, for example. In this sense there is no such thing, either for the independent thinker or for anybody else, as a "consensus of best opinion" when we come to such questions as the existence of God or the immortality of the soul. Furthermore, just as there have been great men and great philosophers who believed in God, so there have also been great men and great philosophers who did not. Since presumably both groups cannot be right, we will be left with the conclusion that men who deserve to be "reverenced" are occasionally mistaken—no matter which view is taken on this subject. Finally, there is nothing about the loftiness of an "inspiration" that guarantees its truth. People whose loftiness makes them believe the best about their neighbors are probably as often mistaken as those whose lack of loftiness makes them believe the worst.

IS BELIEF IN GOD UNIVERSAL?

Let us now turn to a discussion of the detailed objections to the premise which all forms of the Common Consent Argument share, namely, that all or practically all human beings are believers in God.

ANTHROPOLOGICAL OBJECTIONS. To begin with, there is a series of objections based on what is known or allegedly known about primitive tribes and about religions which are not monotheistic. We have already seen that Locke believed, on the basis of the reports of travelers, that there were whole nations without the notion of God. This view was widely advocated by anthropologists and sociologists in the nineteenth century, many of whom did not rely on the reports of others but spent long periods studying the beliefs and habits of primitive peoples at first hand. It was developed in considerable detail by Sir John Lubbock in his pioneering work, *Prehistoric Times,* and it had the unqualified endorsement of Charles Darwin, who, in *The Descent of Man* (Ch. 3), reported confirmations in his own experience with the Fuegians. The denial that belief in God is universal was an essential part of the position of the so-called evolutionary anthropologists. They maintained that there was a gradual transition from animism, via fetishism, to a belief, first, in many gods and then, finally, in a single God. Several of these writers, however, used the word *religion* very broadly to include belief in any unseen spiritual agencies, and in this sense both E. B. Tylor (the eminent evolutionary anthropologist) and Darwin were ready to admit that *religious* belief appeared to be universal among the less civilized tribes. The philosopher Fritz Mauthner, who followed this tradition, expressed himself very strongly on the subject. In *Der Atheismus und seine Geschichte im Abendlande* (Vol. IV, Ch. 10) he accused Christian missionaries of "translation impertinence" in dragging out of aborigines the confession that they believed in a heavenly Father, when more careful investigation revealed that they did not mean anything of the kind. He also protested against the trick, as he called it, by advocates of the *consensus gentium,* of using the word *religion* ambiguously—at first in the broad sense of Tylor and Darwin, in which it may be plausible to maintain the universality of religion, and then shifting to the narrower sense, required by their argument, in which it implies belief in God or gods.

Critics of the argument have also pointed out that there are numerous tribes believing in polytheism without having in their theology one supreme deity. Hence, even if the argument were otherwise sound, it could not prove the existence of a single Supreme Being.

Finally, it has been maintained that there are religions, of which Buddhism is the most notable instance, which have no belief in God at all.

To the last of these criticisms, the customary answer is that, while the founder of such a religion may indeed not have believed in God or gods, once these religions spread, they acquired theologies—and sometimes exceedingly extravagant ones at that. Joyce, who was familiar with this objection, regarded the example of Buddhism as highly favorable to his argument. It was his contention that no religion or philosophical system which rules out belief in God "has ever succeeded in maintaining a prominent hold on any people" (p. 197). In China, Buddhism flourished, but there it became a polytheistic religion. In India, on the other hand, where the original agnostic teachings were not substantially changed, the Buddhist creed could not hold its own and had to give way to modern Hinduism.

The existence of polytheistic religions is not, of course, questioned by defenders of the Common Consent Argument. Some, indeed, like Flint and Mercier, are willing to concede that the argument, by itself, does not favor a stronger conclusion than that God *or* gods exist. This, however, is not the usual reaction. Recent advocates of the argument have commonly challenged the entire scheme of the evolutionary anthropologists. Basing their argument largely on the work of the Austrian anthropologist Father Wilhelm Schmidt (1868–1954) and others belonging to the "theological school," they deny that polytheism antedates monotheism and insist, furthermore, that in every polytheistic religion there is one supreme deity. According to Schmidt, the simplest peoples are also the oldest, and they are believers in a very pure monotheism. Their God possesses all the main attributes of the God of Christianity and Judaism: he is the creator of reality, he supplies the foundation of morality, and he is also omnipotent, omniscient, and supremely good. As societies became more complex, this monotheism became transformed into various kinds of animism, polytheism, and ancestor worship. Even among these later cultures, Schmidt finds "a clear acknowledgment and worship of a supreme being," while all other "supernormal beings" are regarded as far inferior and subject to him.

It would be idle to get involved here in the controversies between Schmidt's school and other schools of anthropology, especially since there are objections to the Argument from Common Consent which can be evaluated without taking sides on anthropological issues. Perhaps the only comment worth making is that while contemporary anthropologists are willing to credit Schmidt and other members of the theological school with some sound criticisms of the evolutionary anthropologists and with a good deal of impressive field work, the great majority of them regard his basic theories as quite unsupported by the available evidence.

UNBELIEVERS IN THE WESTERN WORLD. The other main challenge to the claim that belief in God is universal consists in pointing to the unbelievers in Western culture. It is admitted that unbelievers are a minority, but it is argued that they are and have for some time been too significant a minority not to affect the "moral unanimity of mankind" on this subject. This challenge and the various attempted rebuttals deserve, but have very rarely received, extended discussion.

"Belief" redefined. One way in which the significance of individual unbelievers may be discounted is apparent in the tendency of some Protestant writers to define "belief in God" or "religion" or both so broadly as to make it virtually impossible for a human being not to be a believer or to be religious. In our own day such writers frequently follow Paul Tillich's definition of an atheist as someone who believes that "life is shallow" and of an irreligious person as someone who has "no object of ultimate concern." However, the use of such definitions to do away with unbelievers achieves a victory which is purely illusory. It will now indeed be possible to call a man like Denis Diderot a believer and religious. But in the sense in which there was a dispute about the existence of unbelievers, namely, whether there are people who do not believe in the existence of what is usually understood by "God," Diderot and countless other people will still have to be classified as unbelievers. Moreover, if the premise of the Common Consent Argument is now a true proposition, with "believer" used in the *new* sense, the conclusion established, if any, would not be the one originally aimed at. It would not show that God exists but rather, using Tillich's redefinitions, that life is not shallow and that there are objects of ultimate concern.

Unbelievers discounted as abnormal. One of the favorite devices used to defend the *consensus gentium* against irritating exceptions has been the charge that unbelievers are in effect too morally or mentally defective to count as representative of human opinion. Strangely enough, this tactic was used by Pierre Gassendi, who was highly critical of Herbert of Cherbury's argument and from whom, in view of his own independence of thought, one might have expected something better. In the course of expounding his version of the argument, Gassendi minimized the number and importance of atheists, declaring that they are either "intellectual monstrosities" or "freaks of nature." More recently this defense was adopted by some eminent nineteenth-century Protestant theologians. Thus A. H. Strong, in a text that was widely used in Protestant seminaries, observed that just as the oak must not be judged by the "stunted, the flowerless specimens on the edge of the Arctic Circle," so we must not take account of unbelievers in judging the nature of man (*Systematic Theology,* Vol. I, p. 56). One of the rivals of Strong's book was Hodge's *Systematic Theology.* Hodge was not to be outdone. A man's hand, he reminds us, may be so hardened as to lose the sense of touch, but this does not prove that the hand is not "normally the great organ of touch." Similarly, it is possible that "the moral nature of a man may be so disorganized by vice or by a false philosophy as to have its testimony for the existence of God effectually silenced" (op. cit., p. 198). Human beings cannot abandon belief in God "without derationalizing and demoralizing their whole being" (p. 201); and the belief, or rather lack of belief, of such a "derationalized" and "demoralized" individual does not count.

Perhaps two brief comments will be sufficient here. First, Hodge at least is begging the question when he refers to the "false philosophy" that silences the testimony for the existence of God. The question is precisely whether this is a false philosophy. If this were already known, there would be no need for the Argument from Common Consent. Second, and more important, anybody having the slightest familiarity with the history of unbelief must surely protest that many of the outstanding thinkers of the last two centuries were avowed unbelievers. Like other mortals, they may have been frequently in error, but to dismiss them as freaks, to compare them to stunted, flowerless oaks, or to regard their moral nature as disorganized by vice is surely outrageous nonsense.

Unbelief discounted as an illusion. Some of those who regard the unbeliever as "unnatural" or "monstrous" do not, perhaps, wish to refer to any actual human being. This may be so because some of them also maintain that *really* everybody is a believer in God even though he may say the opposite and believe that he believes the opposite. (The strategy here is rather different from the redefinitional maneuver described above.) Hodge, for example, offers two reasons in support of such a position. First, unbelief is such an unnatural state that it cannot last. "Whatever rouses the moral nature, whether it be danger, or suffering, or the approach of death, banishes unbelief in a moment (ibid., p. 198). There seems to be an obvious answer to this. It is true that unbelievers have become converted or reconverted on occasions, but it is equally true that others have remained unbelievers right to the end of their lives. Furthermore, those who became converted must *really* have been unbelievers before their change of position, or else there would have been no conversion. To this it must be added that there are also shifts in the opposite direction, and if a person does not count as an unbeliever *at all* because he ultimately becomes a believer, then those who change from belief to unbelief will have to be counted as unbelievers exclusively.

Hodge's second reason would probably have a much wider appeal. "It is hardly conceivable," he writes, "that a human soul should exist in any state of development, without a sense of responsibility, and this involves the idea of God. For the responsibility is felt to be not to self, nor to men, but to an invisible Being, higher than self and higher than man" (ibid., p. 197). Hodge is certainly not alone in taking the line that if a person is a moral creature and not lacking in sensibility, then he must be a believer in God. Even at the present time there are many people who seem to rule out a priori the possibility that a good person can be an unbeliever. To give just one illustration, Justice William O. Douglas wrote a highly laudatory preface to a recent collection of the court pleas of Clarence Darrow (*Attorney for the Damned*). Darrow had repeatedly stated and defended his agnosticism, and he never once retracted this position. Nevertheless, seeing that Darrow was such a kind and compassionate man, Douglas remarks: "Darrow met religious bigotry head-on … but he obviously believed in an infinite God who was the Maker of all humanity."

There are several confusions in reasoning of this kind. To begin with, the criteria which all of us employ to determine that a man is kind, that he does not lack sensibility, that he shows responsibility in his relations with other human beings—that, in short, he is a "moral person" or a good man—are quite distinct from those which we employ when determining that he is a believer in God. This at any rate must be so if the statement that all believers in God and only believers in God are good is to be, as it is usually taken to be (both by those who accept it and by those who deny it), a factual claim and not a tautology.

Second, the claim that responsibility is invariably felt not to oneself or to other men but to an invisible Being is unwarranted. Assuming that some people do on occasions feel responsibility to an invisible Being, this is certainly not true of all. If people who assure us that they feel responsible, but not to an invisible Being, are to be discounted or disbelieved, why should we count and accept the assurances of those who say that they feel responsible to the invisible Being? Moreover, it appears that the attitude, even of religious believers, is not generally in accord with Hodge's account. If a believer borrows money and considers himself obligated to return it, he surely, like an unbeliever, regards himself as obligated to the person who lent him the money and not to anybody else. Suppose believers were asked the following question in such a situation: "If an atheistic philosopher persuaded you that God does not exist, but if otherwise the situation remained exactly the same—you needed the money badly, your friend helped you without hesitation, you promised to repay him as soon as possible, and so on—would you still consider yourself obligated to repay the loan?" It seems very doubtful that more than a handful of believers would reply that they no longer regarded themselves as obligated.

Questions about whether a person who says that he believes or disbelieves a proposition and who is apparently not lying, does really believe or disbelieve it, are complicated by the fact that "belief" is an ambiguous word. Without entering into any subtleties or attempting an elaborate analysis, it may be granted that there is nothing absurd in the suggestion that a person may sincerely regard himself as an unbeliever when in fact he is a believer, or vice versa. It is helpful in this connection to distinguish belief in terms of verbal responses and positions adopted in purely theoretical contexts from belief insofar as it is exhibited in actions and in involuntary responses, especially to critical situations.

Bertrand Russell discusses this question in a little-known essay titled "Stoicism and Mental Health." He points out that people who say, with all appearance of sincerity, that they believe in an afterlife seem to fear their own death or regret the death of their friends as much as those who say that they do not believe in an afterlife. He explains this "apparent inconsistency" by remarking that the belief in the afterlife is in most people "only in the region of conscious thought and has not succeeded in modifying unconscious mechanisms" (*In Praise of Idleness,* paperback ed., London, 1960, pp. 133–134). Many of us, like Russell, are inclined to regard the latter, the sense in which belief is expressed in involuntary responses and not merely in theoretical contexts, as the "deeper" sense. We say that a man has reached and avows a certain conclusion, but "deep down" he really believes the opposite. It must be conceded to the defender of the Argument from Common Consent that there are people who are unbelievers in the verbal and theoretical sense but who in a deeper sense do believe in God. This is notoriously true of some who are brought up in a religious home and much later come under the influence of skeptical thinkers.

Nevertheless, the Common Consent Argument is not really helped by this admission. For, in the first place, there can be no reasonable doubt that a good many people are unbelievers in both senses; and second, not a few cases are known of believers, that is, people who sincerely believe in God in terms of their verbal and theoretical responses whose actions show them to be unbelievers "deep down." This fact has been repeatedly stressed by religious writers when castigating some of the members of their own groups as "practical atheists."

Unbelief seen as a negligible influence. Some defenders of the argument are quite ready to admit the existence of highly educated unbelievers. In other words, they question neither the genuineness of the lack of belief nor the intellectual standing of unbelievers. However, they add to this the fact that unbelievers have failed and are bound to fail to make any major inroads on humankind at large. "We find a disposition on the part of some few philosophers to dispute the validity of the belief," writes Boedder (op. cit., p. 68), "but nevertheless the belief has proved to be persistent and indestructible in the mass of humankind. It is this persistency among the mass of men, retained even in the teeth of skeptical opposition, on which our argument is based."

Sometimes a comparison is made between the unbelievers and the philosophers who deny the existence of an external world or the reality of space and time but are rightly laughed off by ordinary people whose common sense is intact. Granting that the ordinary person is in some sense right as against the philosopher who denies the reality of time, to confine ourselves to one such case, the comparison seems to be very weak in more ways than one. For one thing, unbelief in matters of religion is not at all confined to professional philosophers or to people who are naturally referred to as intellectuals. Furthermore, as G. E. Moore has pointed out, the philosophers who *say* such things as "time is unreal" and who presumably in some sense also believe this, also say things and cannot help saying things which indicate that *they also do not believe it.* The very philosophers who say that time is unreal nevertheless use clocks, complain when their students are late, plan for the future, and engage in the same activities that the ordinary man regards as presupposing the reality of time. Nothing even remotely comparable can be found in the case of unbelievers as a class.

However, returning to the original question, it is not at all certain that unbelieving philosophers and other critics of belief in God have not significantly affected the masses. There seems to be a good deal of evidence to the contrary; but even if it were true and the impact has in fact been negligible, this could be explained quite plausibly without supposing either that belief in God is inherent or, as Boedder claims, that reason, properly used, is certain to lead to a theological conclusion.

ARE MEN BY NATURE "GOD-SEEKERS"?

There are philosophers and psychologists of influence who either do not believe in God at all or who, at any rate, do not favor the enterprise of buttressing belief in God by means of "proofs" but are nevertheless concerned to maintain that human beings are by nature religious—that they are, in Max Scheler's phrase, "God-seekers." They would point out that it is this question of "philosophical anthropology," and not any question about the validity of the Common Consent Argument, which is of real interest and human importance. Though perhaps invalid as a proof of the *existence of God,* the Common Consent Argument does embody an important insight about the *nature of man.*

These writers are a great deal more sophisticated than most of the traditional defenders of the argument, whose views we considered in preceding sections. They do not at all deny that, in the most obvious sense, the world is full of unbelievers, but they would add that a great many of these unbelievers feel a strong urge to worship something or somebody and therefore invent all kinds of surrogate deities. Man's "gods and demons," writes Jung, "have not disappeared at all; they have merely got new names." Those, in the words of Miguel de Unamuno, "who do not believe in God or who believe that they do not believe in Him, believe nevertheless in some little pocket god or even devil of their own." "Religious agnosticism," writes Scheler, "is not a psychological fact, but a self-deception … it is an essential law [*ein Wesensgesetz*] that every finite spirit believes either in God or in an idol. These idols may vary greatly. So-called unbelievers may treat the state or a woman or art or knowledge or any number of other things as if they were God" (*Gesammelte Werke,* Vol. V, pp. 261–262). Scheler adds that what needs explanation is not belief in God, which is original and natural, but unbelief or, rather, belief in an idol. The situation is not infrequently compared with the sexual instinct and what we know about the consequences of its suppression. If the sexual instinct does not find natural gratification, it does not cease to be operative but becomes diverted into other and less wholesome channels. The worship of institutions and human deities is said to be a similarly pathological phenomenon.

An evaluation of this position, which amounts in effect to an endorsement of the theory of the religious instinct without inferring the existence of God from it, is not possible here because it would involve elaborate discussions of child psychology and the causation of neurosis and "alienation." Here we can only observe that in the opinion of many contemporary thinkers there is no reason whatever to suppose that human beings are "by nature" religious. In their opinion the "hunger for God," in its orthodox no less than in its newer "substitute" expressions, is invariably the result of certain deprivations and traumatic experiences. People who suffer from insufficient contact with other human beings and who do not find the natural world satisfying will tend to experience longings for something supernatural or feel a need to endow human beings with supernatural attributes. Some of these writers would go further and maintain that traditional religion, through its life-denying morality and irrational taboos, is itself in no small measure responsible for the existence of the type of personality that displays the hunger for God. Sigmund Freud, who took this position, conceded that those in whom the "sweet—or bittersweet—poison," as he called religion, had been instilled early in life were unable to dispense with it later on. The same, he added, is not true of others who have been brought up more soberly. "Not suffering from neurosis," they will "need no intoxicant to deaden it."

See also Cambridge Platonists; Cicero, Marcus Tullius; Clement of Alexandria; Cosmological Argument for the Existence of God; Darwin, Charles Robert; Degrees of Perfection, Argument for the Existence of God; Freud, Sigmund; Gassendi, Pierre; Grotius, Hugo; Hegel, Georg Wilhelm Friedrich; Herbert of Cherbury; Hooker, Richard; Locke, John; Martineau, James; Mercier, Désiré Joseph; Mill, John Stuart; Moore, George Edward; Moral Arguments for the Existence of God; Ontological Argument for the Existence of God; Russell, Bertrand Arthur William; Scheler, Max; Seneca, Lucius Annaeus; Stewart, Dugald; Teleological Argument for the Existence of God; Tillich, Paul; Unamuno y Jugo, Miguel de.

Bibliography

There is no full-length study in any language of the different forms of the Common Consent Argument. The major reference works contain either no entries or else very brief and unhelpful ones. Even Rudolf Eisler's "Consensus Gentium," in *Wörterbuch der philosophischen Begriffe,* 3 vols., 4th ed. (Berlin: E.S. Mittler, 1930), devotes less than a page to this subject.

The fullest defenses of the argument are found in Charles Hodge, *Systematic Theology,* 3 vols. (New York: Scribners, 1871–1873), Vol. I; Bernard Boedder, *Natural Theology* (London, 1896); and G. H. Joyce, *The Principles of Natural Theology* (London: Longmans, Green, 1923). Briefer discussions also favoring the argument are contained in A. H. Strong, *Systematic Theology,* 3 vols. (Philadelphia: Griffith and Rowland, 1907), Vol. I; Robert Flint, *Theism* (London: Blackwood, 1877); Hermann Ulrici, *Gott und die Natur,* 3 vols., 3rd ed. (Leipzig: T.O. Weigel, 1875), Vol. I; and Cardinal Mercier, *A Manual of Modern Scholastic Philosophy,* translated by T. L. and S. A. Parker, 2 vols., 3rd ed. (London: K. Paul, Trench, Trubner, 1928), Vol. II. The famous nineteenth-century biologist G. J. Romanes, in "The Influence of Science upon Religion," which forms Part I of his *Thoughts on Religion* (Chicago: Open Court, 1895), defends the biological form of the argument as proving not that there is a God but that *if* "the general order of nature is due to Mind," then the character of that Mind is "such as it is conceived to be by the most highly developed form of religion."

A popular contemporary statement of the biological version of the argument is advanced in Chad Walsh, *Atheism Doesn't Make Sense* (Cincinnati, n.d.). Among earlier writers, Cicero defended the argument in *De Natura Deorum,* Book II, Sec. II, translated by C. D. Yonge as *The Nature of the Gods* (London, 1892); by Herbert of Cherbury in *De Veritate,* translated by M. H. Carré (Bristol, U.K.: University of Bristol, 1937); and by Pierre Gassendi in *Syntagma Philosophicum,* in his *Opera Omnia,* edited by H. L. H. de Montmorency and F. Henri, Vol. I (Lyons: Lavrentii Anisson and Ioan, 1658).

One of the earliest criticisms of the argument was by Locke, in *Essay concerning Human Understanding* (London: Thomas Bassett, 1690), Book I. There are brief and unsystematic critical discussions in several of the works of the freethinkers of the seventeenth, eighteenth, and nineteenth centuries, including Bayle, Paul-Henri Holbach, and Büchner, but the first detailed and systematic critique is found in J. S. Mill, *Three Essays on Religion* (New York: Henry Holt, 1874). More recently, the argument has been attacked in John Caird, *Introduction to the Philosophy of Religion* (Glasgow: J. Madehose, 1880); Fritz Mauthner, *Der Atheismus und seine Geschichte in Abendlande,* Vol. IV (Stuttgart, 1923); and in two books by Josef Popper-Lynkeus: *Das Individuum und die Bewertung menschlicher Existenz* (Dresden: C. Reissner, 1910) and *Über Religion* (Vienna: R. Löwit, 1924). Popper-Lynkeus' criticisms are, for the most part, an elaboration of David Hume's remark that "the conviction of the religionists, in all ages, is more affected than real." Hume's discussion of this topic occurs in Sec. XII of *The Natural History of Religion* (London, 1757; critical ed. with introduction by H. E. Root, London: A. and C. Black, 1956), a work which also anticipates many of the conclusions of the evolutionary anthropologists of the nineteenth century. There is a discussion, at once critical and sympathetic, in Miguel de Unamuno, *The Tragic Sense of Life in Men and in Peoples,* translated by J. E. Crawford Flitch (New York, 1921).

Two more recent works surveying the evidence concerning the religious beliefs of primitive tribes are Guy E. Swanson, *The Birth of the Gods* (Ann Arbor: University of Michigan Press, 1960), and W. J. Goode, *Religion among the Primitives* (Glencoe, IL: Free Press, 1951). Wilhelm Schmidt's theory is stated in his *The Origin and Growth of Religion,* translated by H. J. Rose (London; Methuen, 1931). A view similar to Schmidt's was expressed by Andrew Lang in various works, including *The Making of Religion* (London: Longmans, Green, 1898) and *Magic and Religion* (London: Longmans, Green, 1901). The *Anthropological Review* 2 (1864): 217–222, contains an interesting summary of an address by the Reverend F. W. Farrar, "On the Universality of Belief in God and in the Future State," in which a great deal of evidence is presented to the effect that neither belief in God nor belief in an afterlife is universal. The discussion following Farrar's address is also reported, and most of the participants, including W. R. Wallace, fully supported Farrar's negative conclusion.

J.-H. Leuba, *The Belief in God and Immortality* (Boston: Sherman, French, 1916), presents evidence concerning belief and unbelief among academic groups in the United States in the early years of the twentieth century. Unfortunately, there has been virtually no study in depth of religious belief and unbelief in the general population of any country.

Jung's views on the natural religious needs of human beings and the sickness of modern men who have lost their religion are stated in *Psychology and Religion* (New Haven, CT: Yale University Press, 1938) and *Modern Man in Search of a Soul,* translated by W. S. Dell and C. F. Baynes (New York: Harcourt Brace, 1933). Scheler's similar views are found in his *Vom Ewigen im Menschen,* in *Gesammelte Werke,* 4th rev. ed., Vol. V (Bern: Francke, 1954). The opposite position is defended by Sigmund Freud in *The Future of an Illusion,* translated by W. D. Robson-Scott (New York: H. Liveright, 1928), and Wilhelm Reich, in *The Mass Psychology of Fascism,* translated by T. P. Wolfe (New York: Orgone Institute Press, 1946). The views of Freud and Reich are foreshadowed in Ludwig Feuerbach, *The Essence of Christianity,* translated by George Eliot (London, 1853).

Paul Edwards (1967)

COMMON SENSE

Several things can be learned about common sense from Dr. Johnson's attempt to refute George Berkeley by kicking the stone. Its philosophical incompetence is not one of them. Dr. Johnson of course misunderstood Berkeley, and his misunderstanding was not a collapse of common sense. He thought that if stones had, as Berkeley said, no "material substance" and were collections of "ideas," a boot ought to go through them without resistance. And if Berkeley had been maintaining that solid objects were only apparently solid and were really collections of what we would ordinarily call ideas, the refutation would have been an appropriate reaction of common sense.

THE NOTION OF COMMON SENSE

Whatever other aspects of meaning the word *sense* may retain in the compound "common sense," it has prominently the force of sense as opposed to nonsense. In what is contrary to common sense there is always something more or less—but obviously—nonsensical. It produces the feeling, varying in strength according to circumstances, that argument is only precariously in place in dealing with it. For to deploy arguments at all *directly* against the manifestly absurd is to invest it with some intellectual dignity and to muffle its self-annihilating character. It is, moreover, to invite the suspicion that one has failed to recognize absurdity, and such failure has a very foolish look. As a man of redoubtable common sense, Dr. Johnson kept dialectic for the right occasion. He did not kick the stone formally in the name of common sense, but his action has traditionally been praised and condemned as a piece of commonsense behavior. Yet he was demonstrating against a philosopher who was also determined to be on the side of common sense.

BERKELEY. Berkeley's notebooks contain the reminder to himself: "To be eternally banishing Metaphisics &c & recalling Men to Common Sense" (*Philosophical Commentaries*, No. 751). Confident that he could always secure the neutrality of common sense when he could not have its assistance, Berkeley went about his own metaphysical enterprise, which was to exhibit the dependence of physical objects on their being perceived. His *Three Dialogues* (1713) is studded with references to common sense: to opinions that are "repugnant" or "shocking" to it, to its "dictates," to the judgment of men of "plain common sense." The objections that have to be most carefully answered are those which appear to proceed from common sense. Since the issues concern mainly the world of perception, the man of common sense in the *Dialogues* is eminently the man who "trusts his senses," who will not tolerate the suggestion that the things he sees and handles are not real things but their mere representations.

The eighteenth century also brought into existence, in France and Scotland, philosophies of common sense—philosophies, to a greater or lesser degree, centered on this notion. They safeguarded what they held to be the beliefs (or "truths") of common sense by defending its authority and—in the Scottish philosophy—by exposing contraries of these beliefs to its blunt rejection.

COMMON-SENSE BELIEFS. It may be asked whether common sense had beliefs until philosophers engaged in its defense ascribed them to it. The *Oxford English Dictionary* lists a variety of meanings for the expression. Three of these, referring to a mental endowment, might be taken together: ordinary understanding—without which a man is out of his mind, or feeble-minded (an early meaning); ordinary, practical, good sense in everyday affairs; and the "faculty of primary truths." Ordinary understanding is not obviously, and practical, good sense is obviously not, the sort of thing that could stamp a set of beliefs with a special character. The third of these meanings is marked "philosophical." A further meaning must be noticed: "the general sense, feeling, or judgement of mankind." Here common sense seems to be a cluster of beliefs or persuasions, somehow "felt" to be true by most people. An argument drawn from common sense, in this case, would amount to an appeal to an ancient tribunal of opinion, common consent. (The most absolute modern proponent of this tribunal has probably been Lamennais, in his *Essai sur l'indifférence*, Paris, 1817–1823.)

Philosophers have frequently meant by common sense an intuitively based common consent. And the philosophers, during and after the eighteenth century, who have argued from common sense and for its beliefs have often thought of common sense in this way. They have, however, as often thought of it in a more ordinary way, as the common sense that is opposed—always at first sight, sometimes irreconcilably—to high and obvious paradox.

Can the common sense that is opposed to gross paradox properly be thought of as having beliefs, however strong? If there is some artificiality in saying that common sense has beliefs, there is none in speaking of its rejection of an opinion; the reason—it might be suggested—is that common sense does not declare itself in advance of attack upon it. The man of plain, ordinary common sense cannot readily be said, for instance, to believe that the things around him continue to exist in his absence—the idea of their not doing so does not cross his mind. But when he encounters the contrary opinion, his common sense asserts itself. On the supposition that the declarations of common sense are essentially reactive, to ascribe to it beliefs specified by what it rejects—and this the philosophers who have maintained its beliefs seem often to have intended—would be a minor linguistic innovation, justified in that it makes its commitments explicit. The supposition would have to be modified in some cases. It does not come naturally to us to speak of a *belief* in our personal identity through time, because this identity is something of which we are aware. Nevertheless, it can be argued that here also common sense has commitments which are not apparent before its reaction to various assertions.

REACTION TO SKEPTICISM. A philosophy of common sense is a natural reaction to the fact, or to the threat, of philosophical paradox or skepticism. The French Jesuit Claude Buffier (1661–1737) saw us as threatened, since René Descartes, with skepticism about all matters of fact beyond the range of our consciousness, the states of which cannot be doubted. What we need is unimpeachable authority for the fundamental convictions shared by all normal men about matters of fact with respect to which consciousness can give no guarantees. Common sense supplies it. It puts us into assured possession of such "first truths" as that there is an external world, that our minds are incorporeal, that we are capable of free agency. First truths have characteristic marks: No attack upon them, and no attempt to prove them, can operate from premises that surpass them in clarity or evidence. They are, and always have been, acknowledged by the vast majority of humankind. Those who imagine they reject them act like others in conformity with them.

HUME. David Hume's work *A Treatise of Human Nature* (1739–1740) produced by reaction a more important philosophy of common sense than Buffier's. In parts of the *Treatise*—to isolate what gave the book its most generally "shocking" aspect—things were reduced to the contents of the mind and the mind to its contents. While many of Hume's conclusions are capable of a milder interpretation than they were given by his readers, Hume himself did not pretend that a number of them were anything but profoundly disturbing to our natural beliefs. At the same time he thought these beliefs had us too tightly in their grip for reasoning to be able to pry us loose. In the *Treatise* "nature" has the last word, but its meaning is left uncertain. We must submit, but whether in submitting to nature we are also submitting to truth is quite another matter. In Hume's later *An Enquiry concerning Human Understanding*, "common sense and reflection" are mentioned as correcting, in some degree, the indiscriminate doubt of an extreme skepticism, but nature and reasoning are still seen as coming into conflict. However, it should be remarked that there is another side to Hume in which these skeptical tendencies are in abeyance.

THE "SCOTTISH SCHOOL"

REID. A central purpose of Thomas Reid's *An Inquiry into the Human Mind on the Principles of Common Sense* (1764), and of his two later books, was, with Hume kept steady in view, to defend common sense against philosophical paradox and skepticism. It was for Reid a doubly difficult undertaking; if, as he held, the truths of common sense were self-evident, how could they be denied? And again, if they were self-evident, how could they be made evident when denied?

The great source of paradoxical or skeptical repudiations of common sense, Reid thought, was an innocent-looking theory that he believed philosophers had very generally adopted in order to explain the possibility of our awareness of anything beyond the present contents of our minds. According to this theory, such awareness is secondhand, necessarily mediated by "ideas" within our minds that are representative substitutes for external things. As its implications were drawn out, the theory, Reid maintained, committed philosophers to a steadily increasing range of conflict with common sense, with no stopping before "ideas," losing their representative character, monopolize existence. The "theory of ideas" is to be found in John Locke, needing only, Reid believed, an unsparing logic such as Hume's to produce Hume's world. (Locke's *An Essay concerning Human Understanding* [1690], has a deceptively commonsense air; its tone is down-to-earth, and experience is set up as the source of knowledge. Locke wanted no paradoxes, and when they were approached by what he said, he was not very efficient at drawing conclusions.)

The truths of common sense cannot be made evident by deductive proofs, but, Reid maintained, there is always absurdity in opinions contrary to its dictates. His most general procedure in defending common sense was to remind us of its command over us. Common sense has so fundamentally determined the scaffolding of ordinary language that the philosopher, in trying to word an opinion which is against common sense, is liable to need another language; and his utterance is continually threatened with incoherence between its structure and its content. The beliefs of common sense govern the behavior even of those who repudiate them in opinion, and they are only fitfully repudiated even in opinion; the paradoxical or skeptical philosopher is no sooner off his guard than he is believing with, as well as acting like, other men. Reid stressed a truism about matters of common sense: They lie within "the reach of common understanding." If this were not so, the judgment of the great bulk of humankind would carry no weight against a philosopher's superior competence. But in "a matter of common sense, every man is no less a competent judge than a mathematician is in a mathematical demonstration" (*Intellectual Powers*, Essay VI, Ch. 4). Whether or not something is a matter of common sense may well have to be investigated—prejudices shamming common sense must be exposed; what Reid denied is that the philosopher is in a better position than anyone else to pronounce on the truth of what really comes from common sense.

Many of the opinions that Reid rejected as contrary to common sense do not appear to be in conflict with the necessities of action he held common sense to impose. Thus, he attacked Berkeley as having denied the existence of a material world, but Berkeley denied that the truth of his opinion would make any changes in our experience; stones, for instance, would remain the solid objects we find them to be. Reid's limited success in vindicating the beliefs of common sense by pointing to inconsistencies between the profession and the practice of dissenters was connected with his interpretation of many of these beliefs; they presented themselves to him as containing an element that lies beyond verification by experience and that might therefore be called metaphysical. He construed, for example, our belief in the existence of a material world as disallowing any phenomenalistic account of the nature of material things, our belief in personal identity as involving a reference of all our experience to its (immaterial) subject, our belief in the freedom of our will as involving indeterminacy of choice.

REID'S FOLLOWERS. The notion of an appeal to common sense in great matters of philosophical dispute was crudely taken up by two of Reid's contemporaries, James Beattie (the poet) and James Oswald. When they were regarded as its representatives, the school that became associated with Reid's name could easily be spoken of as appealing to "the judgment of the crowd." Dugald Stewart (1753–1828), teaching and writing with Reid's moderation, though without his penetrating simplicity, consolidated the school's position in Scotland, and his books helped to make the influence of the ideas he shared with Reid strongly felt in France and America.

SIR WILLIAM HAMILTON. Sir William Hamilton (1788–1856) produced a philosophy in which doctrines of Reid and Immanuel Kant were fused into an unstable compound. It proclaimed the sovereignty of common sense and compromised its deliverances, which for Reid were necessarily objective, with an ambiguous assertion of the "relativity" of knowledge. According to Hamilton, the convictions of common sense come to us with the backing of our entire cognitive nature. They are tests of other truth; their own must be presumed, for they are too elementary to have antecedents from which they could be derived. The only possible falsification of common sense would be demonstrated inconsistency in its deliverances, and this would bring in epistemological chaos. J. S. Mill's *An Examination of Sir William Hamilton's Philosophy* (1865) gave a reactionary, obscurantist look to the authority that Reid and Hamilton claimed for common sense. The "psychological" method, which Mill opposed to their "introspective method," was damagingly designed to show how a belief—such as everyone's belief in an external world—had grown up, taking on in the process the appearance of obviousness; the psychological method would undermine the doctrine that a belief is a dictate of nature by exhibiting its natural history.

CRITICAL COMMON SENSE

Reid and Hamilton both thought that criticism is or may be necessary in order to determine whether a belief is in fact a belief of common sense. They also held, however, that once this fact is established, it follows that the belief is true. The label "critical common sense" might be used, not too misleadingly, to distinguish from this position those philosophical views which combine the greatest respect for common sense with the insistence or admission that at least some of its beliefs are open to critical revision.

ARISTOTLE. If common sense is identified with what is commonly believed and its criticism is thought of as designed to elicit and defend the truth in common beliefs, then Aristotle may be called the first common-sense philosopher. "We must," Aristotle said, "as in all other cases, set the observed facts before us and, after first discussing the difficulties, go on to prove, if possible, the truth of all the common opinions about these affections of the mind, or, failing this, of the greater number and the most authoritative; for if we both refute the objections and leave the common opinions undisturbed, we shall have proved the case sufficiently" (*Nicomachean Ethics*, 1145b2–7; cf. 1172b35–1173a2, *Eudemian Ethics* [attributed to Aristotle], 1216b26–35).

C. S. PEIRCE. The "Critical Common-sensism" argued for by the American philosopher Charles Sanders Peirce (1839–1914) was largely defined in relation to the views held by the Scottish school. It saw the beliefs of common sense, Peirce said, as changeless, the same for all men at all times. It rightly thought of them as having a kind of instinctive character—but instincts can undergo modification. Peirce was sure that these beliefs show some modification as people become civilized and civilization develops. They are not, as ordinarily held, beliefs that have been up for acceptance or rejection; they exist as lifelong "belief-habits." And they possess a logical feature in virtue of which they are doubt-resistant when criticized: They have an essential vagueness. Peirce illustrated this with "our belief in the Order of Nature." Let an attempt be made to give this belief precision, and what results will be found disputable. "But who can think that there is *no* order in nature?" (*Collected Papers*, Vol. V, p. 359).

The "Critical Common-sensist," Peirce said, tries to "bring all his very general first premisses to recognition" and to develop "every suspicion of doubt of their truth" (ibid., p. 363). But the doubt he is looking for must be the real thing, not "paper" doubt; we can no more induce genuine doubt by an act of will than we can give ourselves a surprise by deciding to. "Strong thinkers" are "apt to be great breath-holders," but holding one's breath against belief is not doubting. In claiming "indubitability" for a belief of common sense, Peirce was not declaring its truth—"propositions that really are indubitable, for the time being" may "nevertheless be false" (ibid., p. 347). The future holds possibilities of surprise for all our beliefs. Yet

Peirce seems to have held that though any one of our indubitable beliefs might turn out to be false, they could not all do so.

HENRY SIDGWICK. "Common sense organised into Science," Henry Sidgwick (1838–1900) remarked, "continually at once corrects and confirms crude Common Sense" (*Lectures on the Philosophy of Kant*, p. 425). Sidgwick saw common sense as a great mass of ore, rich in valuable metals, that needs philosophical smelting. It must have removed "inadvertencies, confusions, and contradictions" (ibid., p. 428). However, the procedures by which this is done—rigorous reflection, the adjustment of its beliefs to the assured results of science—are not alien to it. Sidgwick's *Methods of Ethics* (1874) contains a detailed examination of the "morality of common sense," directed toward showing its frequent vagueness, its areas of indecision, its compromises between conflicting ideas, and also toward showing how its fundamental convictions can be taken up into a form of utilitarianism that can reasonably claim the acquiescence of common sense.

G. F. STOUT. For G. F. Stout (1860–1944), common sense has been self-correcting in its evolution and it is still to some extent modifiable. The man in the street is not to be taken as its representative; the common sense of philosophical importance resides in the consensus of ignorant and educated belief. This unanimity is the result of a long development, during which idiosyncrasies of opinion have been worn down by mutual attrition, and mistakes—which common sense itself can see to be such—have been corrected. Common sense is less a matter of particular beliefs than "the persistence of plastic tendencies to certain most general and comprehensive views" (*Mind and Matter*, p. 11). These include such strongly metaphysical dispositions as "the tendency to find Mind in Nature generally" (ibid., p. 14). When a conflict arises between common sense and some scientific or philosophical opinion, the final decision, Stout maintained, rests with common sense, "however indirectly"; for common sense must either be provided with reconciliatory explanations or be brought to see that the considerations in favor of the opinion more than cancel the presumption against it.

RUSSELL AND BROAD. It is convenient to mention here two contemporary philosophers who have thought that there are philosophical opinions which can be described as common sense but who have thought that some of these opinions are quite radically mistaken. Science takes common sense as its starting point, Bertrand Russell says; it has arrived at results with regard to the nature of physical things and their relation to perception that are incompatible with parts of the "metaphysic" of common sense. One does what one can for common sense, but, according to C. D. Broad, sometimes not much is possible; nor should a philosopher feel disturbed at a break with common sense that results from seeing together facts that average people notice only separately and from taking into account other facts of which they are altogether ignorant.

COMMON SENSE AND ORDINARY LANGUAGE

G. E. MOORE. G. E. Moore (1873–1958) did not think that common sense never errs. He seems often to have treated universal, or very general, acceptance as the identifying mark of a commonsense belief, and, as he mentions, things that everybody once believed have turned out to be false. He was prepared to allow that, for all he knew to the contrary, there might be many false propositions included within the vague boundaries of "the Common Sense view of the world." Moore had no special interest in critically sifting the beliefs of common sense for truth and falsity. He was primarily interested in its massive certainties.

Moore's paper "A Defence of Common Sense" (1925) lists sets of propositions that are as obviously true as almost any imaginable: for instance (with considerable paraphrase for the sake of brevity), propositions stating that the earth has existed for many years; that its inhabitants have been variously in contact with, or at different distances from, one another and other things; and that these facts are matters of common knowledge. According to Moore, these "truisms," taken together, imply the truth of the commonsense view of the world in certain of its "fundamental features," for they imply that there are material things, space, time, and other minds besides one's own—in a clear meaning of each of the expressions "material thing," "space," "time," and so on. The abstract words contain ambiguities that are absent from, for example, "The earth has existed for many years," but Moore thought that some philosophers who have denied the existence of material things, of space, of time, or of other minds besides their own are to be understood as having expressed views incompatible with such banally obvious truths. He thus regarded them as paradoxically uttering opinions inconsistent with what they themselves know to be true. They constantly reveal this knowledge in its incompatibility with their opinions; a solipsistic philosopher, for example, sets himself to persuade others that he alone exists.

There is very great doubt, Moore thought, about the correct "analysis," in some important respects, of propositions of common sense that are quite certainly true. (Roughly, for Moore, the analysis of a concept or a proposition lays bare its structure by indicating the concepts it implicitly contains and the way they are combined.) Moore did not think that a phenomenalistic analysis of the concept of a material thing could be ruled out as absolutely impossible. It follows that, in his judgment, a philosopher who was using the sentence "Material things do not exist" simply to word a phenomenalistic doctrine and to repudiate its alternatives would not be repudiating a conviction of common sense that is manifestly true. And if this is so, it is hard to see what a philosopher could have in mind in using the words that would constitute such repudiation. By contrast, denials of the "reality" of space and time on the ground that their concepts are self-contradictory do appear to be in irreconcilable conflict with the most commonplace facts about position and distance, and about past, present, and future.

NORMAN MALCOLM. The philosophical paradoxes that Moore attacked on many different occasions are construed in Norman Malcolm's essay "Moore and Ordinary Language" as disguised, variously motivated rejections of common language, and Moore's defense of common sense is construed as its vindication. A philosopher declares, for instance, "We can never know for certain the truth of any empirical statement." As interpreted by Malcolm, he is saying that it is never right to say "I know for certain" when it is *logically* possible that one is mistaken, that the words are always improperly used in this situation. Moore's reply, characteristically translating from the abstract to the concrete, pointed out the absurdity of anyone's suggesting, when he is sitting on a chair, that he believes he is, that he very probably is, but that he does not know it for certain. What Moore's reply did, on Malcolm's interpretation, was "to appeal to our language-sense," "to make us feel how queer and wrong" it would be to speak here in the way the philosopher proposes and substitute "believe" for "know for certain" or to turn to such words as "probable" ("Moore and Ordinary Language," p. 354).

"A philosophical paradox," Malcolm says (pp. 359–360), "asserts that, whenever a person uses a certain expression, what he says is false." However, from the fact that the expression has a use in ordinary language, it follows, Malcolm argues, that it is free from self-contradiction (since a self-contradictory expression necessarily has no use) and therefore that it *can* be employed to make true statements. And this is enough to refute the paradox. Whether or not people always say something false when using these expressions becomes a matter to be settled by matter-of-fact evidence, and the paradoxical philosopher does not deal in evidence of this sort.

In Malcolm's essay a stronger claim is made in effect for Moore's refutations: They produce indisputably true statements employing the expressions that the paradoxes reject, for they present *paradigms* of the correct application of these expressions. And it is maintained that we could not learn the meaning of some expressions without such paradigms or standard cases; that we could not learn, for example, the meaning of "material thing" without being shown examples of material things, or the meaning of spatial and temporal expressions without acquaintance with spatial and temporal relations, or the meaning of "certain," "probable," "doubtful" without being introduced to the contrasted situations to which they apply. Thus, a statement denying that there is anything answering to one of these expressions must be false. Scrutiny of "the argument from paradigm cases" has been an incident in the recent shift of philosophical interest from common sense (at least under that name) to ordinary language.

LUDWIG WITTGENSTEIN. The way to philosophical paradox is opened, according to Ludwig Wittgenstein (1889–1951), when some feature of ordinary language is misconstrued as only philosophers are likely to misconstrue it. This disorder, along with such other characteristic philosophical aberrations as directionless bafflement, is to be got rid of by bringing words back from their alienation in metaphysical discourse to the familiar surroundings from which they have been abstracted and watching them at work there. Philosophers have not carelessly misunderstood ordinary language; it is waiting for them with "bewitchment" and "illusion." In the emancipation that is achieved when one is able to "command a clear view" of the functioning of language, everything is left, but seen to be, "as it is." Wittgenstein rarely mentioned common sense. He referred in *The Blue Book* (Oxford, 1958, p. 48) to the "common-sense philosopher" (such as Moore or Reid) who, "*n.b.*, is not the common-sense man." The commonsense man, Wittgenstein may be taken to suggest, is man before the philosophical Fall.

See also Paradigm-Case Argument.

Bibliography

THE NOTION OF COMMON SENSE

Berkeley, George. *Three Dialogues between Hylas and Philonous*. London, 1713.

Buffier, Claude. *First Truths*. Translated anonymously. London: J. Johnston, 1780.

Isaacs, Nathan. *The Foundations of Common Sense*. London: Routledge and Paul, 1949.

Lewis, C. S. "Sense." In *Studies in Words*. Cambridge, U.K.: Cambridge University Press, 1960.

Also see the works listed below by Grave, Reid, Stewart, Peirce, Stout (*Mind and Matter*), Malcolm, Moore (*Philosophical Papers*, Ch. 2), and Woozley.

THE "SCOTTISH SCHOOL"

Beattie, James. *An Essay on the Nature and Immutability of Truth*. Edinburgh: A. Kincaid and J. Bell, 1770.

Chastaing, Maxime. "Reid, la philosophie du sens commun." *Revue philosophique de la France et de l'étranger* 144 (1954): 352–399.

Grave, S. A. *The Scottish Philosophy of Common Sense*. Oxford: Clarendon Press, 1960.

Mill, John Stuart. *An Examination of Sir William Hamilton's Philosophy*. London: Longman, Green, Longman, Roberts and Green, 1865. Chs. 3, 8–14.

Reid, Thomas. *Works*. 2 vols, edited by Sir William Hamilton. Edinburgh, 1846–1863. Hamilton's appendices include a long historical and expository dissertation on the notion of common sense.

Stewart, Dugald. *Works*. 2 vols, edited by Sir William Hamilton. Edinburgh, 1854–1860. Vol. III, Ch. 1.

"CRITICAL COMMON SENSE"

Broad, C. D. *The Mind and Its Place in Nature*. New York: Harcourt, Brace, 1925. Chs. 2–4.

Broad, C. D. "A Reply to My Critics." In *The Philosophy of C. D. Broad*, edited by P. A. Schilpp, 803–805. New York: Tudor, 1959.

Peirce, C. S. *Collected Papers*. 6 vols, edited by Charles Hartshorne and Paul Weiss. Cambridge, MA: Belknap Press of Harvard University Press, 1931–1935. Vol. V, pp. 293–313, 346–375.

Russell, Bertrand. "Reply to Criticisms." In *The Philosophy of Bertrand Russell*. 2nd ed., edited by P. A. Schilpp, 700–705. Evanston, IL: Library of Living Philosophers, 1946.

Russell, Bertrand. *Human Knowledge*. London, 1948. Part III; Part IV, Ch. 10.

Sidgwick, Henry. *The Methods of Ethics*. 6th ed. London: Macmillan, 1901.

Sidgwick, Henry. "The Philosophy of Common Sense." In *Lectures on the Philosophy of Kant*, edited by J. Ward, 406–429. London: Macmillan, 1905.

Stout, G. F. *Studies in Philosophy and Psychology*. London: Macmillan, 1930. Ch. 6.

Stout, G. F. *Mind and Matter*. Cambridge, U.K.: Cambridge University Press, 1931.

COMMON SENSE AND ORDINARY LANGUAGE

Campbell, C. A. "Common-sense Propositions and Philosophical Paradoxes." *PAS* 45 (1944–1945): 1–25.

Chappell, V. C. "Malcolm on Moore." *Mind* 70 (279) (July 1961): 417–425.

Chisholm, R. M. "Philosophers and Ordinary Language." *Philosophical Review* 60 (1951): 317–328. Malcolm's reply follows immediately.

Duncan-Jones, A. E., and A. J. Ayer. "Does Philosophy Analyse Common Sense?" *PAS*, Supp. 16 (1937): 139–176. Symposium.

Flew, A. G. N., ed. *Essays in Conceptual Analysis*. London: Macmillan, 1956. Chs. 1 and 6. Discusses paradigm cases.

Malcolm, Norman. "Moore and Ordinary Language." In *The Philosophy of G. E. Moore*, edited by P. A. Schilpp, 345–368. Evanston and Chicago: Northwestern University, 1942.

Malcolm, Norman. "Defending Common Sense." *Philosophical Review* 58 (1949): 201–220.

Moore, G. E. "A Reply to My Critics." In *The Philosophy of G. E. Moore*, edited by P. A. Schilpp, 660–675. Evanston and Chicago: Northwestern University, 1942.

Moore, G. E. *Some Main Problems of Philosophy*. London: Allen and Unwin, 1953. Chs. 1, 5–7, 11.

Moore, G. E. *Philosophical Papers*. London: Allen and Unwin, 1959. Ch. 2, "A Defence of Common Sense," and Ch. 7, "Proof of an External World."

Passmore, J. A. *Philosophical Reasoning*. London: Duckworth, 1961. Ch. 6. Discusses paradigm cases.

Wittgenstein, Ludwig. *Philosophical Investigations*. Oxford: Blackwell, 1953.

Woozley, A. D. "Ordinary Language and Common Sense." *Mind* 62 (247) (July 1953): 301–312.

OTHER RECOMMENDED TITLES

Audi, Robert. *The Architecture of Reason: The Structure and Substance of Rationality*. New York: Oxford University Press, 2001.

Barker, S. F., and T. C. Beauchamp, eds. *Thomas Reid: Critical Interpretations*. Philadelphia: Monograph Series, 1976.

Chisholm, Roderick. *Theory of Knowledge*. Englewood Cliffs, NJ: Prentice-Hall, 1966; 2nd ed., 1977; 3rd ed., 1989.

Cornman, James W. *Perception, Common Sense, and Science*. New Haven, CT: Yale University Press, 1975.

Foley, Richard. *Intellectual Trust in Oneself and Others*. New York: Cambridge University Press, 2001.

Goldman, Alan H. "Epistemic Foundationalism and the Replaceability of Ordinary Language." *Journal of Philosophy* 79 (1982): 136–154.

Guyer, Paul. "Kant on Common Sense and Scepticism." *Kantian Review* 7 (2003): 1–37.

Lehrer, Keith. *Thomas Reid*. London: Routledge, 1989.

Lemos, Noah. "Common Sense and 'A Priori' Epistemology." *Monist* 81 (3) (1998): 473–487.

Lycan, William. "Moore against the New Skeptics." *Philosophical Studies* 103 (2001): 35–53.

Moore, G. E. *Philosophical Studies*. London: Routledge and Kegan Paul, 1922.

Moser, Paul K. "A Defense of Epistemic Intuitionism." *Metaphilosophy* 15 (1984): 196–209.

Moser, Paul K. "Epistemology (1900–Present)." In *Routledge History of Philosophy*, Vol. 10: *Philosophy of the English Speaking World in the 20th Century*, edited by John Canfield. London: Routledge, 1996.

Reid, Thomas. *Essays on the Active Powers of the Human Mind,* edited by B. Brody. Cambridge, MA: MIT Press, 1969.

Reid, Thomas. *Essays on the Intellectual Powers of Man,* edited by B. Brody. Cambridge, MA: MIT Press, 1969.

Schneewind, J. B. "Scottish Common Sense Philosophy." In *The Cambridge Dictionary of Philosophy,* edited by Robert Audi. Cambridge, U.K.: Cambridge University Press, 1995; 2nd ed., 1999.

Wolterstorff, Nicholas. "Reid on Common Sense." In *The Cambridge Companion to Thomas Reid,* edited by Terence Cuneo. Cambridge, U.K.: Cambridge University Press, 2004.

S. A. Grave (1967)
Bibliography updated by Benjamin Fiedor (2005)

COMMUNISM

The voluntary disbanding of the communist state of the Soviet Union in 1991 was the practical defeat of a certain theory of communism as the economic, social, and political antithesis and opponent of the liberal democratic capitalist state that first emerged in the developed Western societies. According to Francis Fukuyama (1992), citing Georg Wilhelm Friedrich Hegel's theory of history, the "death of communism" marks the triumph of liberal democratic states as the paramount achievement of human history. Any further opposition to the extension of the liberal democratic model could only come in the form of regressive social movements seeking to avoid the trauma of inevitable change by clinging to ancient dogmas.

Still, as capitalism becomes the unrivaled global economic system, spilling over the bounds of the nation-state, the social and political achievements and perspectives of the liberal democracies are increasingly being jeopardized by the economic logic of capitalism itself. That the economic power of global corporations imposes demands that most nation-states ignore at their peril necessitates a reappraisal of a complacent triumphalism. In historical retrospect and freed from much of the ideological partisanship of the cold war period, it becomes clear that the challenge of communist claims of social egalitarianism and economic efficiency did much to stimulate progressive social and democratic changes in Western societies throughout the nineteenth and twentieth centuries (Hobsbawn 1994). Rather than a choice between two distinct models, it appears that the thesis of capitalism and the antithesis of communism produced in the West an evolving mixture of elements from both ideal models (Lawler 2001).

MARX'S CONCEPTION OF THE STAGES OF COMMUNISM

Indeed, the perspective of communism as an aspect or dimension of the internal evolution of Western society was the view recommended by the foremost exponent of communism, Karl Marx, who argues that the working people "have no ideals to realize, but to set free elements of the new society with which old collapsing bourgeois society itself is pregnant" (1987, p. 355). In criticizing the conception of communism as an ideal to be realized in the future by contrast to the existing and undesirable state of affairs of the present, Marx distinguishes his "dialectical" understanding of communism from that of rival "nihilistic" theories of communism (Lawler 1994).

NIHILISTIC AND DIALECTICAL COMMUNISMS. The most prominent exponent of the nihilistic conception of communism, and Marx's opponent at the time of the *Communist Manifesto* (1848), was the Russian communist Nikolai Bakunin (1814–1876). In his "Appeal to the Slavs" written in 1848 while he was fleeing arrest in Germany, Bakunin writes:

> Look! The Revolution is all around. It alone is powerful. The new spirit with its ability to dissolve has irrevocably penetrated humanity; it is burrowing into and overturning the deepest and darkest layers of European society. And the Revolution will not rest until it has completely destroyed the old dislocated world and created in its place a new and better world. Thus all the vigour and strength, all the certainty of triumph is in it and only in it. In it alone is life; outside it is death. (Pirumova, Itenberg, and Antonov 1990, pp. 85–86)

Marx and his partner, Friedrich Engels, rejected this utopian and nihilistic vision of creating an alternative society, however egalitarian and committed to social justice, out of the destruction of the old world. Evoking the realist historical perspective of Hegel that "[w]hat is rational is actual and what is actual is rational" (1991, p. 20), Marx argues that only by studying the real world and its actual movement is it possible to discern the internal forces and trends that bring about change, development, and transformation. Communism, he then argues, is a real movement that is actually taking place within the present capitalist society.

TEN HOURS BILL. For example, one of the major social events of the first half of the nineteenth century in England was the passage of a series of factory acts, including the Ten Hours Bill, which limited the workday for women and children to ten hours. Marx describes this modest achievement as of historic significance, "It was the first time that in broad daylight the political economy of the middle class succumbed to the political economy of the working class" (1987, "Inaugural Address of the Working Men's International Association, September 28, 1864"). In Marx's conception the political economy of the middle class, or capitalism, is the pure, unfettered rule of private property and production for the market. Therefore, in limiting the operation of the free market for the sake of the well-being of working people, the factory acts evinced the partial triumph of communism over capitalism taking place within capitalism itself. Other such elements of communism that emerged in the industrial capitalism of the West during the nineteenth and especially the twentieth centuries included free public education, national health care plans (such as, in the United States, Medicare and Medicaid), and national pension or social security plans, as well as laws further limiting the time of the working day and establishing legal conditions for the self-organization of labor through trade unions.

From Marx's perspective the history of Western capitalism presents evidence for the growing emergence within the evolution of capitalism of embryonic elements of an alternative society whose basic characteristics are already discernable, not from the constructions of ideal theory, but from the requirements of actual historical development. A detailed study of Marx's thought on the nature of communism reveals six stages or phases of communist development, beginning with the factory acts and similar infusions of social consciousness into the operation of the capitalist market economy: two phases of communism within capitalism, two phases of the transition between capitalism and communism, and two phases of communism *per se* (Lawler 1998).

DEFINITION OF COMMUNISM. In the *Communist Manifesto*, when Marx projects the final outcome of this evolution, he formally defines communism as "an association, in which the free development of each is the condition for the free development of all" (Marx and Engels 1976, p. 506). The core idea of communism is the all-round freedom of the individual to develop latent abilities without the age-old restrictions that come from the necessities of mere physical survival. Such free development of each is the foundation of an integrally free society. When he further elaborates on this definition in his *Critique of the Gotha Program* (1875), he writes of the highest stage of the evolutionary process, the second phase of communism *per se*:

> In a higher phase of communist society, after the enslaving subordination of the individual to the division of labor, and therewith also the antithesis between mental and physical labor, has vanished; after labor has become not only a means of life but life's prime want; after the productive forces have also increased with the all-round development of the individual, and all the springs of cooperative wealth flow more abundantly—only then can the narrow horizon of bourgeois right be crossed in its entirety and society inscribe on its banners: from each according to his ability, to each according to his needs! (1989, p. 87)

The dramatic final maxim of communism, "from each according to his ability, to each according to his needs," cited out of context as the sum and substance of Marx's conception, appears as an unrealizable, utopian ideal. However, this definition must be comprehended as the outcome of previous stages of historical development. Distribution according to need is only possible at a certain stage or phase of historical evolution when "all the springs of cooperative wealth flow more abundantly." And this abundance of social wealth presupposes both the alienation of labor and the alienation of this alienation—that is, the progressive emergence of creative human labor, labor that has become "not only a means of life but life's prime want" (1989, p. 87). These conditions of a fully developed communism emerge within the previous history of market-oriented society.

LOWER STAGE OF COMMUNISM OR SOCIALISM. For Marx production for the market, although further limited by laws aimed at individual and social well-being, continues well past the communist revolution (initiating the transition between capitalism and communism) and into the lower phase of communism *per se*. In the lower phase of communism, often called socialism, distribution or the individual's income is geared to the quantity and quality of the work that the individual performs. This is the principle of "bourgeois right" that arises out of the requirements of market exchange in which qualitatively different products are equalized by their economic value. Because individuals differ in terms of their needs—for example, one person is single, the other has children to support—the principle of fairness, right, or law according to which each is paid according to work performed results in inequality in real conditions of life.

In this lower phase of communism, however, bourgeois "principle and practice are no longer at loggerheads" (1989, p. 86), as is the case in capitalism. In capitalism the principle of justice calling for "an honest day's pay for an honest day's work" is systematically violated by the fact that individuals do not receive according to their actual labor, but according to the value of their labor power or ability to work. While it is asserted that workers are generally paid according to the work they perform, their wages in fact tend to reflect merely the value of goods and services needed to reproduce them as workers. The difference between the wage thus determined and the value of the goods actually produced is surplus value, the basis of capitalist profit. Paying workers according to the work they actually perform, the principle of the first phase of communism, overcomes the contradiction in capitalism between abstract principle and real practice. But if bourgeois right is finally realized only in this lower phase of communism, both practical inequity and the alienation of labor nevertheless continue.

ALIENATION OF LABOR. The alienation of labor, first described by Marx in his early *Economic and Philosophic Manuscripts of 1844*, consists in the individual's having to work to live, to subsist (1975). When people work only for the sake physical survival, they are subverting their essential human powers. Labor, for Marx, is the defining feature of human beings, distinguishing "the worst architect from the best of bees" (1996, p. 189)—the ability to creatively transform and channel the forces of nature to achieve distinctively human goals. The capacity for creative activity or labor arises out of the nature of the human being as a species being, that is, as a being who is directly concerned with the species as a whole. It is this connection of the individual with the human species, as epitomized in the use of language, that raises consciousness beyond the animal level of concern for (mostly) individual needs to the level of universality that constitutes reflective thought itself. Thus, while the animal is satisfied when its present hunger (and that of its immediate family) is appeased, the human individual is not content until the threat of hunger is banished in general, in terms of the future of the group and ultimately of the species as a whole.

Hence, when people survive only by selling their labor, working not to express their creative ability but to prolong their biological existence, they are alienating this distinctive feature of their humanity. Creative, essentially human, activity is barely possible where the necessities of survival force individuals to engage in repetitive physical work for up to sixteen hours per day. The distinctive human gift is squandered when children are forced into mindless labor from an early age. So when Marx examines the Ten Hours Bill, he recognizes the essential core of communist humanism: restricting the amount of time individuals are forced to work to survive and thereby freeing them, however minimally, to develop their own creative powers. Hence, one of the essential demands of the *Communist Manifesto* is free education for children and the elimination of child labor.

That much of the political platform set forth in the *Communist Manifesto* has in fact been realized in the course of the later evolution of the Western capitalist societies is therefore evidence, from Marx's point of view, not of the triumph of capitalism, but of the incipient emergence, taking place already within capitalism itself, of what he projects as the outcome of this process, the free development of each of communist society. Only when the prime need of the majority of people is to engage in creative activity is the alienation of labor fully overcome. But the seeds of this development and its embryonic growth begin within capitalism. The historic advances of social democracies face new challenges in the early twenty-first century as an unrivaled capitalism emerges on a global scale beyond the controls of the nation-state. Capitalist economic logic implicitly pits workers of advanced countries against those of newly developing nations without centuries of struggle for the rights of the free development of each. Marx's ringing conclusion to the *Communist Manifesto* has therefore become even more relevant: Working people of all countries, unite! (Marx and Engels 1976, p. 519)

COMMUNISM IN THE HISTORY OF WESTERN PHILOSOPHY

ASIATIC COMMUNISM. Viewed in this way, communism is not an alien social theory inserted abruptly at one juncture into Western philosophy by Marx, and then given a more hospitable reception in non-Western states such as Russia and China. The communism of the Soviet Union and China reflects an altogether different historical dynamic rising out of what Marx called, in his characterization of the socioeconomic structure of this part of the world, the "Asiatic mode of production" (1989, p. 263). In this mode of production the ruler, the tsar of Russia or the emperor of China, centralizes both political and economic power in his own hands. The dynamics of Western capitalism involves, on the contrary, the relative separation of political power from economic evolution—a separation that continues, for Marx, until, with the full development of communism, "the public power will lose its political [i.e., repressive] character" (Marx and Engels 1976, p. 505). From this point of view the "cult of personality" of Joseph Stalin (1879–1953) in Russia and Mao Zedong (1893–1976) in China, with state centralization and command of the economy, reflects a kind of Asiatic communism, or a communism developing within the Asiatic mode of production, rather than the communism that Marx discerned as emerging within the womb of Western capitalism. Marx's conception that communism and the market coexist and interpenetrate well after the communist revolution, allowing for a distinct phase of "market socialism," diverges sharply from this "Eastern" approach to communism (Lawler 1998).

POSSESSIVE INDIVIDUALISM. If in terms of content Marx's theory of communism is based on a study of Western society, in terms of philosophical form it is the outcome primarily of one of two major streams in early modern Western philosophy (Lawler 2006). One stream regards the individual as a self-interested being, urged on deterministically by desires arising out of nature, environment, and upbringing, and using reason as a means to achieve maximum individual satisfactions and advantages. The "possessive individualism" (Macpherson 1975) of the modern world sets it apart from the ancient Greco-Roman and medieval views of the individual as constituted by birth or nature for various relatively fixed social functions regarded as necessary for the good of the hierarchically ordered social whole. For the self-interested individual of modern times, the good of the social whole is a means to the individual's own well-being. The classical expression of this trend is the *Leviathan* of Thomas Hobbes, for whom the equal restrictions imposed by the laws of the state (i.e., bourgeois right) establish the civil liberties of capitalist society, including "the liberty to buy, and sell, and otherwise contract with one another; to choose their own abode, their own diet, their own trade of life, and institute [instruct] their children as they themselves think fit; and the like" (1952, p. 113).

Adam Smith's *Wealth of Nations* propounds an economic justification of this perspective, in which the social good or wealth of nations is the largely unintended outcome of individualistic endeavors of production for the market. But in contrast to Hobbes's emphasis on the laws of the state, for Smith the economy is the base of the social order and the state and its laws of formally equal freedoms constitute a secondary framework. In his conception of the primacy of the economic base in relation to the political superstructure, Marx continues such economic materialism (Marx writes: "The totality of these relations of production constitutes the economic structure of society, the real foundation, on which arises a legal and political superstructure and to which correspond definite forms of social consciousness" [1989, p. 263]). However, as seen earlier, the "political economy of the working class" or communism enters this picture when the free operation of buying and selling, and production for the market, are restricted by laws directly aimed at promoting the social good. A radically different understanding of the relation between the individual and the community is implied in the emergence of such communist laws.

PLATO'S HIERARCHICAL COMMUNISM. The second line of thought is continuous with the traditional ancient and medieval view that sees the deliberate promotion of the social good as the highest aim of individual flourishing. In the classical formulation of Plato the public good demands communist or communal ownership of property on the part of the ruling guardians of society to prevent them from using their positions of power for private gain. Such public good also requires the perpetuation of what Plato calls a shameful lie, that is, that the souls of individuals are composed of finer or baser metals, from gold and silver for the rulers and their children to brass and iron for the farmers and artisans and their offspring. This is a lie for Plato, because the souls of human beings are not material, and their destinies, evolving over many lifetimes, are ultimately subject to their own choices (1952, book 10, pp. 437–441). Nevertheless, for the peace and order of society it is necessary that

> none of [the rulers] should have any property of his own beyond what is absolutely necessary.... Gold and silver we will tell them that they have from God; the diviner metal is within them, and they have therefore no need of the dross which is current among men, and ought not to pollute the divine by any such earthly admixture. (1952, book 3, 341)

The modern proponents of the social good are not ashamed to propagate openly their Platonic spiritualism. However, like their counterparts in the stream of possessive individualism, they reject the fixed hierarchies of the past and adopt the standpoint of free and equal individuals. But such equality they ground on the freedom of consciousness or spirit.

DESCARTES'S EGALITARIAN COMMUNISM. Modern egalitarian communism replaces ancient hierarchical communism by stressing the primacy of the free, self-conscious individual, whose awareness that "I think" is, for René Descartes, the foundation of modern scientific method. The self-conscious individual in the modern idealist or spiritualist tradition achieves full self-development only by working directly for the good of others, the good of society as a whole, in such a way that each associates with the other cooperatively in rewarding activities of mutual and common endeavor. Thus, for Descartes the highest activity for the individual is the pursuit of scientific truth, and the motive of this activity is the practical application of scientific knowledge for the well-being of all. Descartes continues the medieval view of the primacy of the social whole, but abandons its aristocratic foundations in a hierarchy of social classes. Nothing is so equally distributed as reason or good sense (Descartes 1952, p. 69), and this common reason is the foundation of all science and the quest for those truths that will liberate humankind from the immense suffering that is due to ignorance and error. Each individual is capable of joining in the step-by-step ascent to truth that science elaborates as it progressively gains access to the laws of the natural and human orders. Thus, recognizing the limitations of his own individual accomplishments, Descartes begs

> all well-inclined persons to proceed further by contributing, each one according to his own inclination and ability, to the experiments which must be made, and then to communicate to the public all the things which they might discover, in order that the last should commence where the preceding had left off; and thus, by joining together the lives and labours of many, we should collectively proceed much further than any one in particular could succeed in doing. (p. 69)

METAPHYSICAL BASIS OF COMMUNISM: MATERIALISM OR SPIRITUALISM? Descartes's metaphysical conception of the human individual as a spiritual being occupying a physical body contrasts with Hobbes's materialist view of the human being as primarily a physical being capable somehow of mental *phantasmata.* Both founders of modern philosophy appeal to the requirements of modern science. But whereas Hobbes regards the new physics of Galileo Galilei as demanding a starting point in the inertial straight-line motion of externally moved matter, Descartes sees the ultimate foundation of science in thinking itself, in the self-conscious "I" that is free to depart from the illusions of sensory perception so as to reconstruct a true picture of the world according to a step-by-step method of thought. While the possessive individualism of Adam Smith's justification of the free market correlates with this first metaphysical option, a fundamentally social orientation, anticipating Marx's theory of species being, follows from the second. It may seem paradoxical to locate Marx's philosophical ancestry in the spiritualism of Plato and Descartes rather than the materialism of Hobbes, but Marx's materialism is a dialectical materialism that is opposed to the mechanistic materialism of Hobbes that was also influential for Smith.

Descartes's metaphysical hierarchy of spirit or consciousness over matter and the body is expressed in practical, ethical, and social requirements. The pursuit of objects that diminish when they are shared with others should be subordinated to the pursuit of objects that are not so diminished. External material wealth diminishes when shared with others, and so one tends to separate oneself from others when one pursues them. However, because one recognizes the good in others, one should freely focus one's mind on the pursuit of those goods that do not diminish when shared, such as knowledge, health, and virtue. So, in a manner reminiscent of Plato's communism, Descartes establishes the community of shared goods as taking precedence over the pursuit of material wealth:

> But I distinguish between those of our goods which can be lessened through others possessing the like, and those which cannot be so lessened. ... But virtue, knowledge, health, and in general all other goods considered in themselves without regard to glory are not in any way lessened in us through being found in many others; and so we have no grounds for being distressed because they are shared by others. (1991, pp. 321–322)

When one shares one's ideas with others, one loses nothing, but enriches both oneself and others. It is a win-win situation. When, however, one pursues limited material goods, then what one person gains the other loses. Therefore, scientific philosophy prescribes a social ethics in which the pursuit of goods of the first type has precedence over pursuit of goods of the second type. So Descartes prescribes the basic maxim of a reasonable and good society: from each according to ability, in cooperation with others, and for the good of all. Therefore, a good society is one in which the creative development of each individual is freely associated with that of other individuals, and working together they promote the full development of society as a whole. But that is just Marx's definition of communism in the *Communist Manifesto*.

LEIBNIZ'S REPUBLIC OF SPIRITS. Similarly, Gottfried Wilhelm Leibniz's monadic human "spirits" achieve their highest development when they are aware of their harmony with one another and actively promote that harmony. So Leibniz writes that "[s]pirits are of all substances the most capable of perfection and their perfections are different in this that they interfere with one another the least, or rather they aid one another the most, for only the most virtuous can be the most perfect friends" (1951a, p. 342). The outcome of such universal social friendship Leibniz calls, variously, the moral world, the city of God, the republic of spirits (p. 343), and "the kingdom of final causes" (1951b, p. 132).

ROUSSEAU'S SOCIAL CONTRACT OF THE POOR. Reflecting this latter term of Leibniz in his *Groundwork of the Metaphysics of Morals*, Immanuel Kant calls the pursuit of the "kingdom of ends" the culminating formulation of the categorical imperative. It was not primarily to Leibniz that Kant turned for his moral theory, however, but to Jean-Jacques Rousseau, whom Kant regarded as the Isaac Newton of moral science (Meld Shell 1996, 81–82). Rousseau heightens the critique of the philosophy of individual self-interest with his analysis of the Hobbsean social contract as a deceptive strategy on the part of the rich to mobilize the poor in defense of their property, for the meager concession of gaining formal political rights. He describes with sarcasm the real essence of this social contract of the rich, "You need me, for I am rich and you are poor. Let us come to an agreement between ourselves. I will permit you to have the honor of serving me, provided you give me what little you have for the trouble I will be taking to command you" (1976, p. 186). Rousseau would have appreciated the sardonic remark of the communist writer Anatole France that "[t]he law, in its majestic equality, forbids the rich as well as the poor to sleep under bridges, to beg in the streets, and to steal bread" (1894/1992, p. 550).

If the materialist philosophy of self-interest underlies this deception, Rousseau finds an alternative basis of community in the heart-felt promptings of the human soul, which the wise educator of *Émile* must nourish by turning the sympathies of youth toward the common human being, those poor and oppressed victims of the fraudulent social contract. Thus, the tutor of Émile counsels:

> To excite and nourish this nascent sensitivity, to guide it or follow it in its natural inclination, what is there to do other than to offer the young man objects on which the expansive force of his heart can act—objects which swell the heart, which extend it to other beings, which make it find itself everywhere outside of itself—and carefully to keep away those which contract and concentrate the heart and tighten the spring of the human *I*? (Rousseau 1979, pp. 222–223)

On such a basis an authentic social contract can be established in which what is emphasized is not the equality of formal legal and political rights (bourgeois right) but relative equality of the conditions of existence. Against the contracted "I" of the philosophy of self-interest, Rousseau emphasizes the expansive "I" that identifies with "the general will." What distinguishes the general will from the particular will is

> not so much the number of votes as the common interest that unites [the citizens], for in this institution each person necessarily submits himself to the conditions he imposes on others. … And asking how far the respective rights of the sovereign and the citizens extend is asking how far the latter can commit themselves to one another, each to all and all to each. (1976, p. 34)

What is crucial is the prevention of the extremes of wealth and poverty, not a mathematical or formal equality, and the means for doing this involve manifold rectifications of the existent inequalities of conditions of life, involving the use of a progressive income tax and universal public education. A society based on the principle of "each to all and all to each" is just Marx's definition of communism in the *Communist Manifesto*.

KANT'S KINGDOM OF ENDS. Kant takes up Rousseau's general will in his formulations of the categorical imperative, culminating in the conception of a "kingdom of ends," according to which one can "abstract from the personal differences between rational beings, and also from the content of their private ends—to conceive a whole of all ends in systematic conjunction" (1956, pp. 100–101). Making it clear that he does not primarily have in mind the establishment of formal legal and political rights, Kant stresses economic relations of production and exchange of goods as an integral part of such systematic conjunction of ends or goals united under the moral consciousness. The kingdom of ends formulation of the categorical imperative asserts a systematic hierarchy of ends as follows:

> What is relative to universal human inclinations and needs has a *market price*; what, even without presupposing a need, accords with a certain taste—that is, with satisfaction in the mere purposeless play of our mental powers—has a *fancy price*; but that which constitutes the sole condition under which anything can be an end in itself has not merely a relative value—that is, a

price—but has an intrinsic value—that is, dignity (p. 102).

Universal respect for the dignity of the human being establishes a community based on common humanity that economic goals must not violate and to which they should be subordinated. Kant repudiates Adam Smith's idea that if everyone pursues their individual interests, the good of all, defined in terms of quantity of goods, will take care of itself. Smith is also far from Descartes's cooperative search for truth, Leibniz's republic of spirits who "aid one another the most," or Rousseau's heart-based community whose maxim is "each to all and all to each," when he writes of the principle of the modern economy:

> It is not from the benevolence of the butcher, the brewer, or the baker, that we expect our dinner, but from their regard to their own interest. We address ourselves, not to their humanity but to their self-love, and never talk to them of our own necessities but of their advantages. Nobody but a beggar chooses to depend chiefly upon the benevolence of his fellow-citizens (1952, p. 7).

In another formulation of the moral society, Kant, referring with Leibniz to the Gospels, calls the goal toward which all morality ultimately points "the highest good (the Kingdom of God)" (1993, p. 135). Leibniz and Kant interpret the Gospels as promoting a *this-worldly* kingdom based on spiritual truth, as Jesus said, "The Kingdom of God is within you" (Luke 17:21). The highest good is a unity of virtue and happiness in which happiness is "in exact proportion to morality" (Kant 1993, p. 117). That is, it is a society in which people who perform their moral duties are happy—meaning, that they have their legitimate needs and wants satisfied. Marx merely reformulates this principle for the highest stage of communism: from each according to ability; to each according to need. That is, with the realization of a society whose governing principle is the highest good, people will perform their duties as creative individuals, working in accord with the good of all, and their needs and wants will be satisfied, from the goods and services provided by society, independently of any strict measurement of their contributions. People who contribute less, materially speaking, but still perform their duty according to their ability, are able to satisfy their particular needs just as freely as those who contribute more. They do not, however, work for the sake of satisfying their needs—which for Kant constitutes heteronomy and for Marx is the general characteristic of the alienation of labor.

IDEAL OF THE HIGHEST GOOD: A FANTASY OR AN EMERGING REALITY? The problem with this ultimate goal of morality, Kant says, is that it seems unrealizable in the real world that one observes around oneself, that is, the world that is governed by the laws enunciated by Adam Smith and that Marx calls the "political economy of the middle class." In this empirical reality the satisfaction of needs is not based on the performance of moral duty, but on market-based laws of supply and demand that can bring misery and death to whole portions of the population as a result of changes in fashion and fad. Writing about the same time as Adam Smith, and well before the Ten Hours Bill of the next century, Kant sees no clear expressions of a countervailing "communist" tendency in the real world capable of counteracting the actual operation of the economy based on self-interest. But unless the moral principle is capable of being realized, he says, it must be "fantastic, directed to empty imaginary ends, and consequently inherently false" (Kant 1993, p. 120). The whole of Kant's moral theory as he understands it thus hangs on the empirical possibility of its being realizable. The apparent contradiction between moral ideal and empirical reality constitutes what Kant calls "the antinomy of practical reason" (pp. 199–126).

Marx again reformulates Kant when he rejects the pursuit of communism as an abstract ideal raised against the real world, as well as Hegel, who opposes the "empty ideal" of a better society and insists that "[w]hat is rational is actual and what is actual is rational" (Hegel 1991, p. 20). Kant's own solution to the problem hinges primarily on the recognition that history does in fact move in the direction of a society based on the moral ideal (Van der Linden 1988). But to justify this conception he must establish the validity of a teleological view of history. His third *Critique of Judgment*, as well as many of his historical essays, argues for this perspective. In this way Kant paves the way for the historical approach of Hegel, who sees all of human history as the expression of the dynamic of "spirit," which he defines as "'I' that is 'We,' and 'We' that is 'I'" (Hegel 1977, p. 110). Therefore, what is both actual and rational in the course of history, according to Hegel, is what Marx later calls communism (MacGregor 1984).

See also Bakunin, Mikhail Aleksandrovich; Descartes, René; Dialectical Materialism; Engels, Friedrich; Galileo Galilei; Hegel, Georg Wilhelm Friedrich; Historical Materialism; Hobbes, Thomas; Kant, Immanuel; Leibniz, Gottfried Wilhelm; Marxist Philosophy; Marx, Karl; Materialism; Newton, Isaac; Nihilism; Plato;

Rousseau, Jean-Jacques; Smith, Adam; Social Contract; Socialism.

Bibliography

Descartes, René. *Great Books of the Western World. Vol. 31, Discourse on Method*, edited by Robert Maynard Hutchins. Chicago: Encyclopaedia Britannica, 1952.

Descartes, René. "To Chanut, 6 June 1647." In *The Philosophical Writings of Descartes. Vol. 3, The Correspondence*. Translated by John Cottingham, Robert Stoothoff, and Dugald Murdoch. New York: Cambridge University Press, 1991.

France, Anatole. *The Red Lily* (1894). In *Bartlett's Familiar Quotations*, edited by John Bartlett. 16th ed. Boston: Little, Brown, 1992.

Fukuyama, Francis. *The End of History and the Last Man*. New York: Free Press, 1992.

Hegel, Georg Wilhelm Friedrich. *Elements of the Philosophy of Right*. Translated by H. B. Nisbet; edited by Allen W. Wood. New York: Cambridge University Press, 1991.

Hegel, Georg Wilhelm Friedrich. *The Phenomenology of Spirit*. Translated by A. V. Miller. Oxford, U.K.: Clarendon Press, 1977.

Hobbes, Thomas. *Great Books of the Western World. Vol. 23, Leviathan*, Part 2. Edited by Robert Maynard Hutchins. Chicago: Encyclopaedia Britannica, 1952.

Hobsbawm, Eric. *Age of Extremes: The Short Twentieth Century, 1914–1991*. New York: Viking Penguin, 1994.

Kant, Immanuel. *Critique of Practical Reason*. 3rd ed., edited and translated by Lewis White Beck. New York: Macmillan, 1993.

Kant, Immanuel. *Groundwork of the Metaphysics of Morals*. New York: Harper and Row, 1956.

Lawler, James. Forward to *Socially Mixed Economies: How Social Gains Develop in Opposed Systems*, by John Weber. Lanham, MD: Lexington Books, 2001.

Lawler, James. "Marx as Market Socialist." In *Market Socialism: The Debate among Socialists*, edited by Bertell Ollman, 23–52. New York: Routledge, 1998.

Lawler, James. "Marx's Theory of Socialisms: Nihilistic and Dialectical." In *Debating Marx*, edited by Louis Patsouras, 173–209. Lewiston, NY: EmText, 1994.

Lawler, James. *Matter and Spirit: The Battle of Metaphysics in Early Modern Philosophy before Kant*. Rochester, NY: University of Rochester Press, 2006.

Leibniz, Gottfried Wilhelm. "Essay on Dynamics." In *Selections*, edited by Philip P. Wiener. New York: Scribner, 1951b

Leibniz, Gottfried Wilhelm. *Selections. Vol. 36, Discourse on Metaphysics*, edited by Philip P. Wiener. New York: Scribner, 1951a.

MacGregor, David. *The Communist Ideal in Hegel and Marx*. Toronto, Canada: University of Toronto Press, 1984.

Macpherson, C. B. *The Political Theory of Possessive Individualism: Hobbes to Locke*. New York: Oxford University Press, 1975.

Marx, Karl. *Karl Marx, Frederick Engels: Collected Works. Vol. 3, Economic and Philosophic Manuscripts of 1844*. Translated by Richard Dixon et al. New York: International Publishers, 1975.

Marx, Karl, and Frederick Engels. *Karl Marx, Frederick Engels: Collected Works. Vol. 6, The Manifesto of the Communist Party*. Translated by Richard Dixon et al. New York: International Publishers, 1976.

Marx, Karl. *Karl Marx, Frederick Engels: Collected Works. Vol. 22, July 1870–October 1871*. Translated by Richard Dixon et al. New York: International Publishers, 1987.

Marx, Karl. *Karl Marx, Frederick Engels: Collected Works. Vol. 24, Critique of the Gotha Program*. Translated by Richard Dixon et al. New York: International Publishers, 1989.

Marx, Karl. *Karl Marx, Frederick Engels: Collected Works. Vol. 29, Contribution to the Critique of Political Economy*. Translated by Richard Dixon et al. New York: International Publishers, 1989.

Marx, Karl. *Karl Marx, Frederick Engels: Collected Works. Vol. 35, Capital*, Vol. 1. Translated by Richard Dixon et al. New York: International Publishers, 1996.

Meld Shell, Susan. *The Embodiment of Reason: Kant on Spirit, Generation, and Community*. Chicago: University of Chicago Press, 1996.

Pirumova, N., B. Itenberg, and V. Antonov. *Russia and the West: Nineteenth Century*. Translated by Vitaly Baskakov, Patricia Beryozkina, and Maureen Ryley. Moscow: Progress Publishers, 1990.

Plato. *Great Books of the Western World. Vol. 7, Republic*, edited by Robert Maynard Hutchins. Chicago: Encyclopaedia Britannica, 1952.

Rousseau, Jean-Jacques. *Discourse on the Origin of Inequality*. In *On the Social Contract, Discourse on the Origin of Inequality, Discourse on Political Economy*. Translated and edited by Donald A. Cress. Indianapolis, IN: Hackett, 1983.

Rousseau, Jean-Jacques. *Émile: or, On Education*, edited by Allan Bloom. New York: Basic Books, 1979.

Smith, Adam. *Great Books of the Western World. Vol. 39, The Wealth of Nations*, edited by Robert Maynard Hutchins. Chicago: Encyclopaedia Britannica, 1952.

Van der Linden, Harry. *Kantian Ethics and Socialism*. Indianapolis, IN: Hackett, 1988.

James M. Lawler (2005)

COMMUNITARIANISM

In the 1980s communitarians displaced Marxists as the most prominent critics of liberal political theory. Communitarians share a belief that liberalism is excessively individualistic or atomistic, ignoring people's dependence on communal relationships. They differ in where they locate this flaw. Some criticize the liberal ideal of freedom of choice, arguing that people's ends in life are defined by their communal ties, not freely chosen (Sandel 1984). Others accept the ideal of freedom of choice, but criticize liberalism for ignoring its social and cultural preconditions (Taylor 1989). Still, others argue that moral reasoning is dependent on communal traditions, so that liberal claims to universal validity are illegitimate (Walzer 1983, MacIntyre 1981).

Commentators sometimes distinguish between backward-looking and forward-looking versions of communitarianism (Phillips 1993). The former asserts that healthy communal bonds existed in the past, lament the decline of community as a result of the increasing emphasis on individual choice and diverse ways of life (the "permissive society"), and seek to retrieve a conception of the common good. This sort of communitarianism is difficult to distinguish from traditional conservatism and is widely criticized for ignoring the ways that most communities historically excluded women, gays, or racial and religious minorities (Frazer 1999). By contrast, forward-looking communitarians disavow nostalgia for the past, accept that individual choice and cultural diversity are now permanent features of modern life, and acknowledge that earlier forms of community were too narrow and exclusive to be retrievable today. Hence, they seek to build new bonds of community that integrate diverse groups and lifestyles, for example, by promoting forms of patriotism, democratic citizenship, or civil society that encourage people from different backgrounds to work together. A more complex version of communitarianism is backward-looking at the local level, allowing ethnic or religious communities to uphold a traditional way of life even if it requires restricting individual freedom, while adopting a forward-looking model at the national level, where the multiplicity of different groups in society must cooperate.

In response to the communitarian critique many liberals attempt to show that they, too, are sensitive to the importance of community and culture and that they can accommodate at least the forward-looking dimensions of communitarianism. Hence, a proliferation of theories of liberal republicanism, liberal patriotism, liberal multiculturalism, and liberal civil society have been witnessed. All these are intended to show that a liberal society is not exclusively individualistic and can accommodate and support a rich array of collective identities and associations, without compromising the basic liberal commitment to the protection of individual civil and political rights.

Given these developments, the original liberal-communitarian debate of the 1980s has given way to a number of new, more differentiated positions and issues. Instead of a stark choice between individualism and communitarianism, one now faces a range of debates about how to sustain bonds of moral solidarity and political community in an era of individual rights and cultural diversity: How to build a common national identity without suppressing ethnic and religious diversity? How to nurture feelings of trust and solidarity in mass societies where people share little in common? How to foster a vibrant public sphere that encourages civic participation and democratic dialogue? How to support family life without imposing traditional gender roles? How to educate children to be public-spirited citizens without inculcating a narrow chauvinism? Communitarianism does not provide a single perspective or framework for answering these questions, and there is a growing sense that the communitarian label obscures as much as it reveals about someone's position on them. Indeed, virtually all the major writers associated with the original communitarian critique express reservations about the label. Nonetheless, these are all questions that have been put on the agenda of political philosophy by the communitarian critique of liberalism. Communitarianism may be fading as a recognizable school of political philosophy, but communitarian concerns have come to dominate political philosophy at the start of the twenty-first century.

See also Liberalism.

Bibliography

Avineri, Shlomo, and Avner de-Shalit, ed. *Communitarianism and Individualism.* New York: Oxford University Press, 1992.

Frazer, Elizabeth. *The Problems of Communitarian Politics: Unity and Conflict.* New York: Oxford University Press, 1999.

Lehman, Edward W., ed. *Autonomy and Order: A Communitarian Anthology.* Lanham, MD: Rowman & Littlefield, 2000.

MacIntyre, Alisdair. *After Virtue: A Study in Moral Theory.* London: Duckwork, 1981.

Mulhall, Stephen, and Adam Swift. *Liberals and Communitarians.* 2nd ed. Oxford, U.K.: Blackwell, 1996.

Phillips, Derek L. *Looking Backward: A Critical Appraisal of Communitarian Thought.* Princeton, NJ: Princeton University Press, 1993.

Sandel, Michael J., ed. *Liberalism and Its Critics.* New York: New York University Press, 1984.

Taylor, Charles. "Cross-Purposes: The Liberal-Communitarian Debate." In *Liberalism and the Moral Life*, edited by Nancy L. Rosenblum, 64–87. Cambridge, MA: Harvard University Press, 1989.

Walzer, Michael. *Spheres of Justice: A Defence of Pluralism and Equality.* Oxford: Blackwell, 1983.

Will Kymlicka (1996, 2005)

COMPOSITIONALITY

The principle of compositionality is the claim that the meaning of a complex expression is determined by its structure and the meanings of its constituents. Normally the thesis is taken to be about some particular language; questions of structure and constituency are then settled by the syntax of that language. By extension, we can talk about compositionality in other representational systems—thoughts, traffic signs, musical notation, and so on—as long as they have their own syntax.

VARIETIES OF COMPOSITIONALITY

The principle is not committed to a specific conception of syntax and semantics, which is why it can be employed in debates between proponents of different conceptions (see, by way of comparison, Partee 1984). Still, if we reject all constraints on either structure or meaning, compositionality becomes trivial. As T. M. V. Janssen (1986) has shown, we can turn any meaning function on a recursively enumerable set of expressions into a compositional one, as long as we can replace the syntactic operations with different ones. And as W. Zadrozny (1994) has shown, we can turn an arbitrary meaning function into a compositional one, as long as we replace the old meanings with new ones from which they are uniformly recoverable. But because the task of semantics is to identify a meaning assignment that respects both what our best syntax tells us about structure and what our best intuitions tell us about synonymy, these results do not show compositionality to be empirically empty (compare Kazmi and Pelletier 1998; Westerståhl 1998; Dever 1999).

Although hardly trivial, the principle as stated is rather weak. For example, consider a view, according to which the meaning of a declarative sentence *s* is the set of possible worlds where *s* is true. According to such a view, tautologies are synonymous, even though (because Rudolf presumably has some tautological beliefs and lacks others) sentences resulting from embedding tautologies in the context of "Rudolf believes that … " are not. Intuitively, this is a violation of compositionality (compare Carnap 1947, sec. 14). Still, the semantics is *not* in conflict with compositionality as stated, because tautologies might differ structurally or in the meaning of their constituents, which could explain how embedding them may yield nonsynonymous sentences. The strengthening of the principle that *is* incompatible with this view requires that the meaning of a complex expression be determined by the meanings of its *immediate* constituents and the syntactic way these constituents are combined. (*e* is an immediate constituent of *e'* if *e* is a constituent of *e'* and *e'* has no constituent of which *e* is a constituent.) Call the strengthened principle *local compositionality* and the original one *global compositionality.*

Compositionality rules out the existence of a pair of nonsynonymous complex expressions built up from synonymous constituents through identical syntactic operations within the same language. As the principle is usually construed, it says nothing about the possibility of such pair of complex expressions existing in *distinct* languages. Still, intuitively, if the Estonian sentence s_1 and the Aramaic sentence s_2 mean different things despite having identical syntactic structure and pairwise synonymous constituents, we should conclude that either Estonian or Aramaic is not compositional. (The same structure and the same meanings of constituents cannot *determine* more than one meaning.) If we want our principle of compositionality to yield this result, we need to strengthen it: we could demand, for example, that there be a single function for all possible human languages that maps the structure of a complex expression and the meanings of its constituents to the meaning of that complex expression (compare Szabó 2000, p. 500). Call this principle *cross-linguistic compositionality* and the original one *language-bound compositionality.*

So, there are at least four versions of the principle of compositionality: language-bound global, language-bound local, cross-linguistic global, and cross-linguistic local. The first is the weakest and it corresponds to how the principle is officially announced; the last is the strongest and it better captures what is typically taken for granted.

There are three well-known claims that are also occasionally referred to as compositionality principles. The first is the *building principle*, which states that the meaning of a complex expression is built up from the meanings of its constituents. This is a fairly strong claim, at least if we take the building metaphor seriously. For then the meanings of complex expressions must themselves be complex entities whose structure mirrors that of the sentence (compare Frege 1984 [1892], p. 193; Frege 1979 [1919], p. 255). The second is the *rule-to-rule principle*, according to which every syntactic rule corresponds to a semantic one that assigns meanings to the output of the syntactic rule on the basis of the meanings of its inputs. If we assume that an arbitrary function deserves to be called a rule, this is equivalent to language-bound local compositionality. The third is the *principle of substitutivity*, according to which if two expressions have the same meaning, then substitution of one for the other in a third expression does not change the meaning of the third expression. Assuming that the semantics is *Husserlian*—that substitution of synonyms at a single syntactic position within a larger expression never changes the meaningfulness of the larger expression (compare Husserl 1913, p. 318)—this is also equivalent to language-bound local compositionality. (For the equivalence results, see Hodges 2001, theorem 4. If we want to insist—plausibly—that semantic rules must be at least computable, the rule-to-rule principle is stronger than language-bound local compositionality. The assumption that the semantics is Husserlian is far from trivial—it entails, for example, that because "Jacques is likely to leave" is meaningful and "Jacques is probable to leave" is not; "likely" and "probable" are not synonyms [compare Gazdar et al. 1985, p. 32].)

FORMAL EXPRESSION

Since R. Montague (1974), it has been customary to capture compositionality formally as the existence of a homomorphism between a syntactic and a semantic algebra. Let the syntactic algebra be a partial algebra $\mathbf{E}=\langle E, (F\gamma)_{\gamma\in\Gamma}\rangle$, where E is the set of (simple and complex) expressions and every $F\gamma$ is a syntactic operation on E with a fixed arity. Let m be a meaning assignment function from E to M, the set of meanings. Let F be a k-ary syntactic operation on E; then m is F-compositional if there is a k-ary partial function G on M such that whenever $F(e_1, \ldots, e_k)$ is defined,

$$m(F(e_1, \ldots, e_k))=G(m(e_1), \ldots, m(e_k)).$$

Finally, let m be compositional just in case m is F compositional for every operation of the syntactic algebra. Whenever m is compositional, it induces the semantic algebra $\mathbf{M}=\langle M, (G\gamma)_{\gamma\in\Gamma}\rangle$ on M and it is a homomorphism between **E** and **M** (compare Westerståhl 1998). (For details and formal results, see Janssen 1986, 1997; Hodges 2001.) As stated, this captures language-bound local compositionality.

ARGUMENTS FOR COMPOSITIONALITY

The argument most frequently used to support the compositionality of natural languages is the *argument from productivity*. It goes back (at least) to Frege, who claimed that "the possibility of our understanding sentences which we have never heard before rests evidently on this, that we can construct the sense of a sentence out of parts that correspond to words" (Frege 1980 [1914?], p. 79). The argument is an inference to the best explanation, which can be expanded and rephrased without assuming that meanings are Fregean senses as follows. Because speakers of a language can understand a complex expression e that they have not previously encountered, it must be that they (perhaps tacitly) know something on the basis of which they can figure out, without any additional information, what e means. If this is so, something they already know must determine what e means. But this knowledge cannot plausibly be in general anything but knowledge of the structure of e and knowledge of the meanings of the primitive constituents of e.

If successful, the argument from productivity establishes global language-bound compositionality. To show that a language is locally and/or cross-linguistically compositional requires detailed empirical investigation. As an argument for global language-bound compositionality, it can be criticized on the ground that although we clearly do understand some complex expressions we have never heard before, it is not self-evident that we could *in principle* understand *all* complex expressions in this manner. In fact, it is hard to see how the sort of general considerations mentioned by the argument from productivity could rule out the existence of isolated *exceptions* to compositionality. (Isolated putative exceptions are often declared to be idioms. Criteria for being an idiom are controversial [compare Nunberg, Sag, and Wasow 1994].)

Besides productivity, two other features of our language comprehension are cited in support of compositionality. One is *unboundedness*: although we are finite beings, we have the capacity to understand each of an infinitely large set of complex expressions. (An example from Platts 1979, p. 47: "The horse behind Pegasus is bald," "The horse behind the horse behind Pegasus is bald," "The horse behind the horse behind the horse behind Pegasus is bald," and so on.) 47. From unboundedeness, productivity follows (assuming that finite beings cannot encounter infinitely many expressions), and thus this is not really an independent consideration. The other feature of language comprehension that supports compositionality is *systematicity*: that there are definite and predictable patterns among the sentences we understand. (For example, anyone who understands "The rug is under the chair" can understand "The chair is under the rug" and vice versa.) Because productivity does not follow from systematicity the argument from systematicity provides independent support for compositionality.

In fact, systematicity supports a stronger principle. The standard explanation for why understanding "black dog" and "white cat" is sufficient for understanding "black cat" and "white dog" is that we can *decompose* the meanings of complex expressions into the meanings of their constituents and then *compose* these into meanings of other complex expressions. The best explanation for the possibility of our ability to compose the meanings of complex expressions from the meanings of their constituents is supposed to be compositionality. By parity of reasoning, the best explanation for the possibility to decompose the meanings of complex expressions into the meanings of their constituents is *inverse compositionality*: that the meaning of any complex expression determines the meanings of its lexical constituents (as well as its syntactic structure) (compare Fodor and Lepore 2002, p. 59; Pagin 2003, p. 292). Compositionality and its inverse yield the view that the meanings of complex expressions can be viewed as having a structure isomorphic to the syntactic structures of those expressions, which in turn, may capture the idea behind the metaphor of the building principle.

See also Meaning; Syntax.

Bibliography

Carnap, R. *Meaning and Necessity: A Study in Semantics and Modal Logic.* Chicago: University of Chicago Press, 1947.

Dever, J. "Compositionality as Methodology." *Linguistics and Philosophy* 22 (1999): 311–326.

Evans, G. *The Varieties of Reference.* Oxford, U.K.: Clarendon Press, 1982.

Fodor, J., and E. Lepore. "Why Compositionality Won't Go Away: Reflections on Horwich's 'Deflationary' Theory." In *The Compositionality Papers.* Oxford, U.K.: Clarendon Press, 2002.

Frege, G. "Letter to Jourdain." 1914? In *Philosophical and Mathematical Correspondence*, edited by G. Gabriel et al., 78–80. Chicago: University of Chicago Press, 1980.

Frege, G. "Letter to Ludwig Darmstaester." 1919. In *Posthumous Writings*, edited by H. Hermes et al., 253–257. Chicago: University of Chicago Press, 1979.

Frege, G. "On Concept and Object." 1892. In *Collected Papers on Mathematics, Logic, and Philosophy*, edited by B. McGuinness, 182–194. Oxford, U.K.: Blackwell, 1984.

Gazdar, G., E. Klein, G. Pullum, and I. Sag. *Generalized Phrase Structure Grammar.* Cambridge, MA: Harvard University Press, 1985.

Hodges, W. "Formal Features of Compositionality." *Journal of Logic, Language, and Information* 10 (2001): 7–28.

Husserl, E. *Logische Untersuchungen II/1.* Tübingen, Germany: Max Niemeyer, 1913.

Janssen, T. M. V. "Compositionality." In *Handbook of Logic and Language*, edited by J. van Benthem and A. ter Meulen, 417–473. Amsterdam: Elsevier, 1997.

Janssen, T. M. V. *Foundations and Applications of Montague Grammar.* Amsterdam: Mathematisch Centrum, 1986.

Kazmi, A., and F. J. Pelletier. "Is Compositionality Formally Vacuous?" *Linguistics and Philosophy* 21 (1998): 629–633.

Montague, R. "Universal Grammar." In *Formal Philosophy: Selected Papers of Richard Montague*, edited by R. Thomason, 222–246. New Haven, CT: Yale University Press, 1974.

Nunberg G., I. Sag, and T. Wasow. "Idioms." *Language* 70 (1994): 491–538.

Pagin, P. "Communication and Strong Compositionality." *Journal of Philosophical Logic* 32 (2003): 287–322.

Partee, B. "Compositionality." In *Varieties of Formal Semantics: Proceedings of the Fourth Amsterdam Colloquium, September 1982*, edited by F. Landman and F. Veltman, 281–312. Dordrecht, Netherlands: Foris, 1984.

Platts, M. *Ways of Meaning: An Introduction to the Philosophy of Language.* London: Routledge, 1979.

Szabó, Z. G. "Compositionality as Supervenience." *Linguistics and Philosophy* 23 (2000): 475–505.

Westerståhl, D. "On Mathematical Proofs of the Vacuity of Compositionality." *Linguistics and Philosophy* 21 (1998): 635–643.

Zadrozny, W. "From Compositional to Systematic Semantics." *Linguistics and Philosophy* 17 (1994): 329–342.

Zoltán Gendler Szabó (2005)

COMPUTABILITY THEORY

0. THE INFORMAL CONCEPT

Computability theory is the area of mathematics dealing with the concept of an effective procedure—a procedure that can be carried out by following specific rules. For example, one might ask whether there is some effective procedure—some algorithm—that, given a sentence about the positive integers, will decide whether that sentence is true or false. In other words, is the set of true sentences about the positive integers decidable? Or for a much simpler example, the set of prime numbers is certainly a decidable set. That is, there are mechanical procedures, that are taught in the schools, for deciding of any given positive integer whether or not it is a prime number.

More generally, consider a set S, which can be either a set of natural numbers (the natural numbers are 0, 1, 2, …), or a set of strings of letters from a finite alphabet. (These two situations are entirely interchangeable. A set of natural numbers is much like a set of base-10 numerals, which are strings of digits. And in the other direction, a string of letters can be coded by a natural number in a variety of ways. The best way is, where the alphabet has k symbols, to utilize k-adic notation, which is like base-k numerals except that the k digits represent 1, 2, … , k, without a 0 digit.) One can say that S is a decidable set if there exists an effective procedure that, given any natural number (in the first case) or string of letters (in the second case), will eventually end by supplying the answer: "Yes" if the given object is a member of S and "No" if it is not a member of S.

And by an effective procedure here is meant a procedure for which one can give exact instructions—a program—for carrying out the procedure. Following these instructions should not demand brilliant insights on the part of the agent (human or machine) following them. It must be possible, at least in principle, to make the instructions so explicit that they can be executed by a diligent clerk (who is good at following directions but is not too clever) or even a machine (which does not think at all).

Although these instructions must of course be finite in length, no upper bound on their possible length is imposed. It is not ruled out that the instructions might even be absurdly long. Similarly, to obtain the most comprehensive concepts, no bounds are imposed on the time that the procedure might consume before it supplies the answer. Nor is a bound imposed on the amount of storage space (scratch paper) that the procedure might need to use. One merely insists that the procedure give an answer eventually, in some finite length of time.

Later, in section 7, more restrictive concepts will be considered, where the amount of time is limited in some way, so as to exclude the possibility of ridiculously long execution times. Initially, however, one wants to avoid such restrictions, to obtain the limiting case where practical limitations on execution time or memory space are removed.

This description of effective procedures, vague as it is, already shows how limiting the concept of decidability is. It is not hard to see that there are only countably many possible instructions of finite length that one can write out (using a standard keyboard, say). There are, however, uncountably many sets of natural numbers (by Cantor's diagonal argument). It follows that almost all sets, in a sense, are undecidable.

The following section will look at how the foregoing vague description of effective procedures can be made more precise—how it can be made into a mathematical concept. Nonetheless, the informal idea of what can be done by effective procedure, that is, what is calculable, can be useful.

For another example, consider what is required for a string of symbols to constitute an acceptable mathematical proof. Before one accepts a proof and adds the result being proved to the storehouse of mathematical knowledge, one insists that the proof be verifiable. That is, it should be possible for another mathematician, such as the referee of the paper containing the proof, to check, step by step, the correctness of the proof. Eventually, the referee concludes either that the proof is indeed correct or that the proof contains a gap or an error and is not yet acceptable. That is, the set of acceptable mathematical proofs should be decidable. This fact will be seen (in section 4) to have significant consequences for what can and cannot be proved. The conclusion follows that computability theory is relevant to the foundations of mathematics.

Before going on, one should broaden the canvas from considering decidable and undecidable sets to considering the more general situation of partial functions. Let U be either the set $\mathbb{N} = \{0,1,2, \ldots\}$ of natural numbers or the set Σ^* of all strings of letters—all words—from a finite alphabet Σ. Then a k-place partial function on U is a function whose domain is included in $U^k = U \times U \times \ldots \times U$ and whose range is included in U. And one can say that such a function is total if its domain is all of U^k.

For a k-place partial function f, one can say that f is an effectively calculable partial function if there exists an effective procedure with the following property:

- Given a k-tuple x in the domain of f, the procedure eventually halts and returns the correct value for $f(x)$
- Given a k-tuple x *not* in the domain of f, the procedure does not halt and return a value

(Strictly speaking, when U is $\mathbb{N}$, the procedure cannot be given numbers, it must be given numerals. Numerals are bits of language, which can be communicated. Numbers are not. Thus, the difference between $U = \mathbb{N}$ and $U = \Sigma^*$ is even less than previously indicated.)

For example, the partial function for subtraction

$$f(m,n) = \begin{cases} m - n & \text{if } m \geq n \\ \uparrow & \text{otherwise} \end{cases}$$

(where $\uparrow$ indicates that the function is undefined) is effectively calculable, and procedures for calculating it, using base-10 numerals, are taught in the elementary schools.

The concept of decidability can then be described in terms of functions: For a subset S of U^k, one can say that S is decidable if its characteristic function

$$C_S(x) = \begin{cases} \text{Yes} & \text{if } x \in S \\ \text{No} & \text{if } x \notin S \end{cases}$$

(which is always total) is effectively calculable. Here, "Yes" and "No" are some fixed members of U, such as 1 and 0 in the case of $\mathbb{N}$.

Here, if $k = 1$, then S is a set of numbers or a set of words. If $k = 2$, then one has the concept of a decidable binary relation on numbers or words, and so forth.

And it is natural to extend this concept to the situation where one has half of decidability: Say that S is semidecidable if its partial characteristic function

$$c_S(x) = \begin{cases} \text{Yes} & \text{if } x \in S \\ \uparrow & \text{if } x \notin S \end{cases}$$

is an effectively calculable partial function. Thus, a set S of words—a language—is semidecidable if there is an effective procedure for recognizing members of S. One can think of S as the language that the procedure accepts.

The following is another example of a calculable partial function:

$F(n)$ = the smallest $p > n$ such that both p and $p + 2$ are prime

Here, it is to be understood that $F(n)$ is undefined if there is no number p as described; thus F might not be total. For example, $F(9) = 11$. It is not known whether or not F is total. Nonetheless, one can be certain that F is effectively calculable. One procedure for calculating $F(n)$ proceeds as follows. "Given n, first put $p = n + 1$. Then check whether or not p and $p + 2$ are both prime. If they are, then stop and give output p. If not, increment p and continue." What if $n = 10^{1000}$? On the one hand, if there is a larger prime pair, then this procedure will find the first one, and halt with the correct output. On the other hand, if there is no larger prime pair, then the procedure never halts, so it never gives an answer. That is all right, because $F(n)$ is undefined—the procedure should not give any answer. (Of course, F is total if and only if (iff) the twin prime conjecture is true.)

Now suppose one modifies this example. Consider the total function:

$$G(n) = \begin{cases} F(n) & \text{if } F(n) \downarrow \\ 0 & \text{otherwise} \end{cases}$$

Here, $F(n)\downarrow$ means that $F(n)$ is defined so that n belongs to the domain of F. Then the function G is also effectively calculable. That is, there exists a program that calculates G correctly. That is not the same as saying that one knows that program. This example indicates the difference between knowing that a certain effective procedure exists and having the effective procedure in one's hands.

One person's program is another person's data. This is the principle behind operating systems (and behind the idea of a stored-program computer). One's favorite program is, to the operating system, another piece of data to be received as input and processed. The operating system is calculating the values of a two-place "universal" function, as in the following example.

Suppose one adopts a fixed method of encoding any set of instructions by a single natural number. (First, one converts the instructions to a string of 0s and 1s—one always does this with computer programs—and then one regards that string as naming a natural number under a suitable base-2 notation.) Then, the universal function

$\Phi(x, y)$ = the result of applying the instructions coded by y to the input x

is an effectively calculable partial function (where it is understood that $\Phi(x, y)$ is undefined whenever applying the instructions coded by y to the input x fails to halt and return an output). Here are the instructions for Φ: "Given x and y, decode y to see what it says to do with x, and then do it." Of course, the function Φ is not total.

Using this universal partial function, one can construct an undecidable binary relation, the halting relation H:

$$\begin{aligned}(x, y) \in H &\Leftrightarrow \Phi(x, y)\downarrow \\ &\Leftrightarrow \text{applying the instructions coded by } y \text{ to input } x \text{ halts}\end{aligned}$$

To see that H is undecidable, one can argue as follows. Suppose that, to the contrary, H is decidable. Then the following function would be effectively calculable:

$$f(x) = \begin{cases} \text{Yes} & \text{if } \Phi(x, x)\uparrow \\ \uparrow & \text{if } \Phi(x, x)\downarrow \end{cases}$$

(Notice the use of the classical diagonal construction.) (To compute $f(x)$, one first would decide if $(x, x) \in H$. If not, then $f(x)$ = Yes. If $(x, x) \in H$, however, then the procedure for finding $f(x)$ should throw itself into an infinite loop, because $f(x)$ is undefined.) The function f cannot possibly be effectively calculable, however. Consider any set of instructions that might compute f. Those instructions have some code number k, but f has been constructed in such a way that $f(k)$ differs from the output from the result of applying instructions coded by k to the input k. (They differ because one is defined and one is not.) So these instructions cannot correctly compute f; they produce the wrong result at the input k. And so one has a contradiction. That the previous relation H is undecidable is usually expressed by saying that "the halting problem is unsolvable"; that is, one cannot effectively determine, given x and y, whether applying the instructions coded by y to the input x will eventually terminate or will go on forever.

While the concept of effective calculability has been described in somewhat vague terms here, the following section will give a precise (mathematical) concept of a computable partial function. And then it will be argued that the mathematical concept of a computable partial function is the correct formalization of the informal concept of an effectively calculable partial function. This claim is known as Church's thesis or the Church-Turing thesis. Church's thesis, which relates an informal idea to a formal idea, is not itself a mathematical statement, capable of being given a proof, but one can look for evidence for or against Church's thesis; it all turns out to be evidence in favor.

One piece of evidence is the absence of counterexamples. That is, any function examined thus far that mathematicians have felt was effectively calculable, has been found to be computable.

Stronger evidence stems from the various attempts that different people made independently, trying to formalize the idea of effective calculability. Alonzo Church used λ-calculus, Alan M. Turing used an idealized computing agent (later called a Turing machine), and Emil Post developed a similar approach. Remarkably, all these attempts turned out to be equivalent, in that they all defined exactly the same class of functions, namely, the computable partial functions!

The study of effective calculability originated in the 1930s with work in mathematical logic. As noted earlier, the subject is related to the concept on an acceptable proof. Since the development of modern computers the study of effective calculability has formed an essential part of theoretical computer science. A prudent computer scientist would surely want to know that, apart from the difficulties the real world presents, there is a purely theoretical limit to calculability.

1. FORMALIZATIONS

In the preceding section, the concept of effective calculability was described only informally. Now, these ideas will be made more precise (i.e., will be made part of mathematics). In fact, several approaches to doing this will be described: idealized computing devices, generative definitions (i.e., the least class containing certain initial functions and closed under certain constructions), programming languages, and definability in formal languages. It is a significant fact that these different approaches all yield exactly equivalent concepts.

TURING MACHINES. In early 1935 Alan M. Turing was a twenty-two-year-old graduate student at King's College in Cambridge. Under the guidance of Max Newman, he was working on the problem of formalizing the concept of effective calculability. In 1936 he learned of the work of Alonzo Church at Princeton University. Church had also been working on this problem, and in his 1936 paper "An Unsolvable Problem of Elementary Number Theory" he presented a definite conclusion: that the class of effectively calculable functions should be identified with the class of functions definable in the λ-calculus, a formal language for specifying the construction of functions. Moreover, he showed that exactly the same class of functions could be characterized in terms of formal derivability from equations.

Turing then promptly completed writing his paper, in which he presented a different approach to characterizing the effectively calculable functions, but one that—as he proved—yielded once again the same class of functions as Church had proposed. With Newman's encouragement, Turing then went to Princeton for two years, where he wrote a doctoral dissertation under Church.

Turing's paper remains a readable introduction to his ideas. How might a diligent clerk carry out a calculation, following instructions? He might organize his work in a notebook. At any given moment his attention is focused on a particular page. Following his instructions, he might alter that page, and then he might turn to another page. And the notebook is large enough that he never comes to the last page.

The alphabet of symbols available to the clerk must be finite; if there were infinitely many symbols, then there would be two that were arbitrarily similar and so might be confused. One can then without loss of generality regard what can be written on one page of notebook as a single symbol. And one can envision the notebook pages as being placed side by side, forming a paper tape, consisting of squares, each square being either blank or printed with a symbol. At each stage of his work, the clerk—or the mechanical machine—can alter the square under examination, can turn attention to the next square or the previous one, and can look to the instructions to see what part of them to follow next. Turing described the latter part as a "change of state of mind."

Turing wrote, "We may now construct a machine to do the work" (1936–1937, p. 251). Of course, such a machine is now called a Turing machine, a phrase first used by Church in his review of Turing's paper in *The Journal of Symbolic Logic*. The machine has a potentially infinite tape, marked into squares. Initially, the given input numeral or word is written on the tape, but it is otherwise blank. The machine is capable of being in any one of finitely many states (the phrase "of mind" being inappropriate for a machine). At each step of calculation, depending on its state at the time, the machine can change the symbol in the square under examination at that time, can turn its attention to the square to the left or to the right, and can then change its state to another state.

The program for this Turing machine can be given by a table. Where the possible states of the machine are q_1, …, q_r, each line of the table is a quintuple $\langle q_i, S_j, S_k, D, q_m \rangle$, which is to be interpreted as directing that whenever the machine is in state q_i and the square under examination contains the symbol S_j, then that symbol should be altered to S_k and the machine should shift its attention to the square on the left (if $D = L$) or on the right (if $D = R$), and should change its state to q_m. For the program to be unambiguous, it should have no two different quintuples with the same first two components. (By relaxing this requirement regarding absence of ambiguity, one obtains the concept of a nondeterministic Turing machine, which will be useful later, in the discussion of feasible computability.) One of the states, say q_1, is designated as the initial state—the state in which the machine begins its calculation. If one starts the machine running in this state and examining the first square of its input, it might (or might not), after some number of steps, reach a state and a symbol for which its table lacks a quintuple having that state and symbol for its first two components. At that point the machine halts, and one can look at the tape (starting with the square then under examination) to see what the output numeral or word is.

Now suppose that Σ is a finite alphabet and that f is a k-place partial function on the set Σ^* of words. One says that f is Turing computable if there exists a Turing machine M that, when started in its initial state scanning the first symbol of a k-tuple $\vec{w}$ of words (written on the tape, with a blank square between words, and with everything to the right of $\vec{w}$ blank), behaves as follows:

- If $f(\vec{w})\downarrow$ (i.e., if $\vec{w} \in \text{dom } f$), then M eventually halts, and at that time it is scanning the leftmost symbol of the word $f(\vec{w})$ (which is followed by a blank square).
- If $f(\vec{w})\uparrow$ (i.e., if $\vec{w} \notin \text{dom } f$), then M never halts.

This definition can be readily adapted to apply to k-place partial functions on $\mathbb{N}$.

Then Church's thesis, also called—particularly in the context of Turing machines—the Church-Turing thesis, is the claim that this concept of Turing computability is the correct formalization of the informal concept of effective calculability. Certainly, the definition reflects the ideas of following predetermined instructions, without limitation of the amount of time that might be required. (The name *Church-Turing thesis* obscures the fact that Church and Turing followed different paths in reaching equivalent conclusions.)

As will be explained shortly, Church's thesis has by now achieved universal acceptance. Kurt Gödel, writing in 1964 about the concept of a formal system in logic, involving the idea that the set of correct deductions must be a decidable set, said that "due to A. M. Turing's work, a precise and unquestionably adequate definition of the general concept of formal system can now be given" (Davis 1965, p. 71).

The robustness of the concept of Turing computability is evidenced by the fact that it is insensitive to certain modifications to the definition of a Turing machine. For example, one can impose limitations on the size of the alphabet, or one can insist that the machine never move to the left of its initial starting point. None of this will affect that class of Turing computable partial functions.

Turing developed these ideas before the introduction of modern digital computers. After World War II he played an active role in the development of early computers and in the emerging field of artificial intelligence. (During the war, he worked on deciphering the German battlefield code Enigma, work that remained classified until after Turing's death.) One can speculate whether Turing might have formulated his ideas somewhat differently, if his work had come after the introduction of digital computers.

PRIMITIVE RECURSIVENESS AND MINIMALIZATION. For a second formalization of the calculability concept, a certain class of partial functions on $\mathbb{N}$ will now be defined as the smallest class that contains certain initial function and is closed under certain constructions.

For the initial functions, one can take the following simple total functions:

- The zero functions, that is, the constant functions f defined by the equation:

$$f(x_1, \ldots, x_k) = 0$$

- The successor function S, defined by the equation:

$$S(x) = x + 1$$

- The projection functions I^k_n from k-dimensions onto the nth coordinate,

$$I^k_n(x_1,\ldots,x_k) = x_n$$

where $1 \leq n \leq k$.

One can form the closure of the class of initial functions under three constructions: composition, primitive recursion, and minimalization.

A k-place function h is said to be obtained by composition from the n-place function f and the k-place functions $g_1, \ldots, g_n$ if the equation

$$h(\vec{x}) = f(g_1(\vec{x}), \ldots, g_n(\vec{x}))$$

holds for all $\vec{x}$. In the case of partial functions, it is to be understood here that $h(\vec{x})$ is undefined unless $g_1(\vec{x}), \ldots, g_n(\vec{x})$ are all defined and $\langle g_1(\vec{x}), \ldots, g_n(\vec{x})\rangle$ belongs to the domain of f.

A $(k + 1)$-place function h is said to be obtained by primitive recursion from the k-place function f and the $(k + 2)$-place function g (where $k > 0$) if the pair of equations

$$h(\vec{x},0) = f(\vec{x})$$
$$h(\vec{x},t+1) = g(t,h(\vec{x},t),\vec{x})$$

holds for all $\vec{x}$ and t.

Again, in the case of partial functions, it is to be understood that $h(\vec{x}, t + 1)$ is undefined unless $h(\vec{x}, t)$ is defined and $\langle t, h(\vec{x}, t), \vec{x}\rangle$ is in the domain of g.

For the $k = 0$ case, the one-place function h is obtained by primitive recursion from the two-place function g with the number m if the pair of equations

$$h(0) = m$$

$$h(t + 1) = g(t, h(t))$$

holds for all t.

Postponing the matter of minimalization, one can define a function to be primitive recursive if it can be built up from zero, successor, and projection functions by use of composition and primitive recursion. In other words, the class of primitive recursive functions is the smallest class that includes the initial functions and is closed under composition and primitive recursion.

Clearly, all the primitive recursive functions are total. One can say that a k-ary relation R on $\mathbb{N}$ is primitive recursive if its characteristic function is primitive recursive.

One can then show that a great many of the common functions on $\mathbb{N}$ are primitive recursive: addition, multiplication, … , the function whose value at m is the $(m + 1)$st prime, …

On the one hand, it is clear that every primitive recursive function should be regarded as being effectively calculable. On the other hand, the class of primitive recursive functions cannot possibly comprehend all total calculable functions, because one can easily "diagonalize out" of the class. That is, by suitably indexing the "family tree" of the primitive recursive functions, one can make a list $f_0, f_1, f_2, \ldots$ of all the one-place primitive recursive functions. One can then consider the diagonal function $d(x) = f_x(x) + 1$. Then d cannot be primitive recursive; it differs from each f_x at x. Nonetheless, if one makes the list tidely, the function d is effectively calculable. The conclusion is the class of primitive recursive functions is an extensive but proper subset of the total calculable functions.

Next, one can say that a k-place function h is obtained from the $k + 1$-place function g by minimalization and one writes

$$h(\vec{x}) = \mu y[g(\vec{x}, y) = 0]$$

if for each $\vec{x}$, the value $h(\vec{x})$ either is the number y such that $g(\vec{x}, y) = 0$ and $g(\vec{x}, s)$ is defined and is nonzero for every $s < y$, if such a number y exists, or else is undefined, if no such number y exists. The idea behind this μ-operator is the idea of searching for the least number y that is the solution to an equation, by testing successively $y = 0, 1, \ldots$

One can obtain the general recursive functions by adding minimalization to the closure methods. That is, a partial function is general recursive if it can be built up from the initial zero, successor, and projection functions by use of composition, primitive recursion, and minimalization.

The class of general recursive functions is (as Turing proved) exactly the same as the class of Turing computable functions. And Church's thesis therefore has the equivalent formulation that the concept of a general recursive function is the correct formalization of the informal concept of effective calculability.

What if one tries to diagonalize out of the class of general recursive functions, as one did for the primitive recursive functions? As will be argued later, one can again make a tidy list $\varphi_0, \varphi_1, \varphi_2, \ldots$ of all the one-place general recursive partial functions. And one can define the diagonal function $d(x) = \varphi_x(x) + 1$. In this equation, $d(x)$ is undefined unless $\varphi_x(x)$ is defined. The diagonal function d is indeed among the general recursive partial functions, and hence is φ_k for some k, but $d(k)$ must be undefined. No contradiction results.

The class of primitive recursive functions was defined by Gödel, in his 1931 paper on the incompleteness theorems. Of course, the idea of defining functions on ℕ by recursion is much older and reflects the idea that the natural numbers are built up from the number 0 by repeated application of the successor function. The theory of the general recursive functions was worked out primarily by Stephen Cole Kleene, a student of Church.

The use of the word *recursive* in the context of the primitive recursive functions is entirely reasonable. Gödel, writing in German, had used simply *rekursiv* for the primitive recursive functions. Retaining the word *recursive* for the general recursive functions was a, however, historical accident. The class of general recursive functions—as this section shows—has several characterizations in which *recursion* (i.e., defining a function in terms of its other values, or using routines that call themselves) plays no role at all.

Nonetheless, the terminology became standard. What are here called the computable partial functions were until the late 1990s standardly called the partial recursive functions. And for that matter, computability theory was called recursive function theory for many years, and then recursion theory. And relations on ℕ were said to be recursive if their characteristic functions were general recursive functions.

An effort is now being made, however, to change what had been the standard terminology. Accordingly, this entry speaks of computable partial functions. And it will call a relation computable if its characteristic function is a computable function. Thus, the concept of a computable relation corresponds to the informal notion of a decidable relation. In any case, there is definitely a need to have separate adjectives for the informal concept (here, *calculable* is used for functions, and *decidable* for relations) and the formally defined concept (here, *computable*).

LOOP AND WHILE PROGRAMS. The idea behind the concept of effective calculable functions is that one should be able to give explicit instructions—a program—for calculating such a function. What programming language would be adequate here? Actually, any of the commonly used programming languages would suffice, if freed from certain practical limitations, such as the size of the number denoted by a variable. One can give here a simple programming language with the property that the programmable functions are exactly the computable partial functions on ℕ.

The variables of the language are $X_0, X_1, X_2, \ldots$ Although there are infinitely many variables in the language, any one program, being a finite string of commands, can have only finitely many of these variables. If one wants the language to consist of words over a finite alphabet, one can replace X_3, say, by X'''.

In running a program, each variable in the program gets assigned a natural number. There is no limit on how large this number can be. Initially, some of the variables will contain the input to the function; the language has no input commands. Similarly, the language has no output commands; when (and if) the program halts, the value of X_0 is to be the function value.

The commands of the language come in five kinds:

(1) $X_n \leftarrow 0$. This is the clear command; its effect is to assign the value 0 to X_n.

(2) $X_n \leftarrow X_n + 1$. This is the increment command; its effect is to increase the value assigned to X_n by one.

(3) $X_n \leftarrow X_m$. This is the copy command; its effect is just what the name suggests; in particular it leaves the value of X_m unchanged.

(4) Loop X_n and endloop X_n. These are the loop commands, and they must be used in pairs. That is, if $\mathcal{P}$ is a program—a syntactically correct string of commands—then so is the string:

loop X_n

$\mathcal{P}$

endloop X_n

What this program means is that $\mathcal{P}$ is to be executed a certain number k of times. And that number k is the initial value of X_n, the value assigned to X_n before one starts executing $\mathcal{P}$. Possibly, $\mathcal{P}$ will change the value of X_n; this has no effect at all on k.

(5) While $X_n \neq 0$ and endwhile $X_n \neq 0$. These are the while commands; again, they must be used in pairs, like the loop commands, but there is a difference. The program

while $X_n \neq 0$

$\mathcal{P}$

endwhile $X_n \neq 0$

also executes the program $\mathcal{P}$ some number k of times. Now, however, k is not determined in advance; it matters very much how $\mathcal{P}$ changes the value of X_n. The number k is the least number (if any) such that executing $\mathcal{P}$ that many times causes X_n to be assigned the value 0. The program will run forever if there is no such k.

And those are the only commands. A while program is a sequence of commands, subject only to the requirement that the loop and while commands are used in pairs, as illustrated. Clearly, this programming language is simple enough to be simulated by any of the common programming language, if one ignores overflow problems.

A loop program is a while program with no while commands; that is, it has only clear, increment, copy, and loop commands. Note the important property: A loop program always halts, no matter what. It is easy, however, to make a while program that never halts.

One can say that a k-place partial function f on $\mathbb{N}$ is while-computable if there exists a while program $\mathcal{P}$ that, whenever started with a k-tuple $\vec{x}$ assigned to the variables $X_1, \ldots, X_k$ and 0 assigned to the other variables, behaves as follows:

- If $f(\vec{x})$ is defined, then the program eventually halts, with X_0 assigned the value $f(\vec{x})$.
- If $f(\vec{x})$ is undefined, then the program never halts.

The loop-computable functions are defined in the analogous way. There is the difference, however, that any loop-computable function is total.

Theorem. (a) A function on $\mathbb{N}$ is loop-computable iff it is primitive recursive.

(b) A partial function on $\mathbb{N}$ is while-computable iff it is general recursive.

The proof in one direction, to show that every primitive recursive functions is loop-computable, involves a series of programming exercises. The proof in the other direction involves coding the status of a program $\mathcal{P}$ on input $\vec{x}$ after t steps, and showing that there are primitive recursive functions enabling one to determine the status after $t + 1$ steps, and the terminal status. Because the class of general recursive partial functions coincides with the class of Turing computable partial functions, one can conclude from the previous theorem that while-computability coincides with Turing computability.

DEFINABILITY IN FORMAL LANGUAGES. In his 1936 paper in which he presented what is now known as Church's thesis, Church utilized a formal system, the λ-calculus. Church had developed this system as part of his study of the foundations of logic. In particular, for each natural number n there is a formula $\mathbf{n}$ of the system denoting n, that is, a numeral for n. More important, formulas could be used to represent the construction of functions. He defined a two-place function F to be λ-definable if there existed a formula $\mathbf{F}$ of the λ-calculus such wherever $F(m, n) = r$ then the formula $\{\mathbf{F}\}(\mathbf{m}, \mathbf{n})$ was convertible, following the rules of the system, to the formula $\mathbf{r}$, and only then. An analogous definition applied to k-place functions.

Church's student, Stephen Cole Kleene, showed that a function was λ-definable iff it was general recursive. (Church and his student, J. B. Rosser, were also involved in the development of this result.) Church wrote in his paper, "The fact … that two such widely different and (in the opinion of the author) equally natural definitions of effective calculability turn out to be equivalent adds to the strength of reasons … for believing that they constitute as general a characterization of this notion as is consistent with the usual intuitive understanding of it" (Alonzo 1936, p. 346).

Earlier, in 1934, Gödel, in his lectures at Princeton, formulated a concept now referred to as Gödel-Herbrand computability. He did not, however, at the time propose the concept as a formalization of the concept of effective calculability. The concept involved a formal calculus of equations between terms built up from variables and function symbols. The calculus permitted the passage from an equation $A = B$ to another equation obtained by substituting for a part C of A or B another term D where the equation $C = D$ had been derived. If a set $\mathcal{E}$ of equations allowed the derivation, in a suitable sense, of exactly the right values for a function f on $\mathbb{N}$, then $\mathcal{E}$ was said to be a set of recursion equations for f. Once again, it turned out that a set of recursion equations existed for f iff f was a general recursive function.

A rather different approach to characterizing the effectively calculable functions involved definability in first-order logic over the structure of the natural numbers with addition and multiplication. Say that a k-place partial function f on $\mathbb{N}$ is a Σ_1-function if the graph of f (i.e., the $(k + 1)$-ary relation $\{\langle x_1, \ldots, x_k, y\rangle \mid f(x_1, \ldots, x_k) = y\}$) is definable in the structure with universe $\mathbb{N}$ and with the operations of addition, multiplication, and exponentiation, by an existential formula (i.e., a formula consisting of a string of existential quantifiers, followed by a quantifier-free part). Then the class of partial Σ_1-functions coincides exactly with the class of partial functions given by the other formalizations of calculability described here. Moreover, Yuri Matijasevič showed in 1970 that the operation of exponentiation was not needed here.

Finally, say that a k-place partial function f on $\mathbb{N}$ is representable if there exists some finitely axiomatizable theory T in a language having a suitable numerals $\boldsymbol{n}$ for each natural number n, and there exists a formula φ of that language such that (for any natural numbers) $f(x_1, \ldots, x_k) = y$ iff $\varphi(\boldsymbol{x}_1, \ldots, \boldsymbol{x}_k, \boldsymbol{y})$ is a sentence deducible in the theory T. Then once again the class of representable partial functions coincides exactly with the class of partial functions given by the other formalizations of calculability described here.

2. BASIC RESULTS

First, one has the remarkable fact that all the formalizations of the preceding section yield exactly the same class of partial functions on $\mathbb{N}$. And this fact is not only remarkable, it is also reassuring, indicating that the concept captured by the formalizations—the concept of a computable partial function—is natural and significant. Moreover, it gives evidence that the concept captured by the formalizations is actually the correct formalization of the informal concept of effective calculability. That is, it gives evidence for Church's thesis (or the Church-Turing thesis). This thesis was first set forth by Church in a 1935 abstract, and then published in full in his 1936 paper. (At the time, Church was unaware of Turing's approach, but he knew of several of the other formalizations described in the preceding section.) This assertion, that computability is the precise counterpart to effective calculability, is not really a mathematical statement susceptible of proof or disproof; rather, it is a judgment that one has found the correct formalization of the one's informal concept.

The situation can be compared to one encountered in calculus. An intuitively continuous function (defined on an interval) is one whose graph one can draw without lifting the pencil off the paper. To prove theorems, however, some formal counterpart of this notion is needed. And so one gives the usual definition of ε-δ-continuity. One should ask if the precise notion of ε-δ-continuity is an accurate formalization of intuitive continuity. If anything, the class of ε-δ-continuous functions is too broad. It includes nowhere differentiable functions, whose graphs cannot be drawn without lifting the pencil—there is no way to impart a velocity vector to the pencil. Nonetheless, the class of ε-δ-continuous functions has been found to be a natural and important class in mathematical analysis.

In a similar spirit, one can ask how accurately the formal concept of computability captures the informal concept of effective calculability. As with continuous functions, the precisely defined class (of computable functions) appears to be, if anything, too broad. It includes functions for which any procedure will, for large inputs, require so much computing time and memory (scratch paper) space as to make implementation absurd. Computability corresponds to calculability in an idealized world, where length of computation and amount of memory are disregarded. (This will be discussed further in section 7.) In any case, however, the class of computable partial functions has been found to be a natural and important class in mathematical logic.

Empirical evidence that the class of computable functions is not too narrow is provided both by the fact that the attempted formalizations (as described in section 1) have all yielded the equivalent concepts, and by the fact that no counterexample have arisen—the functions considered thus far that mathematicians have felt were effectively calculable have turned out to be computable. In the decades since 1936, Church's thesis has gained universal acceptance.

NORMAL FORM. In each of the formalizations described in the preceding section, one can in a straightforward way code the instructions for any computable partial function by a natural number e. In the case of Turing machines, e encodes the set of quintuples that determine the machine's operation. In the case of a function built up from the zero, successor, and projection functions by primitive recursion and minimalization, e encodes the ancestral tree describing exactly how the function is built up. In the case of while programs, e encodes the program.

Normal form theorem. There is a ternary computable relation T and a total computable function U with the following property: For each 1-place computable partial function f on $\mathbb{N}$, there is a natural number e such that

$$f(x) = U(\mu y T(e, x, y))$$

for every number x.

Here (as elsewhere), equality has the natural meaning: Either both sides of the equation are defined and are the same, or else both sides are undefined.

One can construct the relation T (called the Kleene T-predicate) so that $T(e, x, y)$ expresses the idea that e encodes the instructions for f, and y encodes the entire history of the step-by-step computation of f with input x, from the beginning through the final step at which the computational procedure comes to a halt. Then the function U (the upshot function) extracts from y what the answer or output is.

The normal form theorem can be extended to k-place functions. One can make a $(k + 2)$-ary computable relation T_k such that for each k-place computable partial function f, there is a number e such that

$$f(x_1, \dots, x_k) = U(\mu y T_k(e, x_1, \dots, x_k, y))$$

for every $x_1, \dots, x_k$. Moreover, one can construct T_k and U so that they are even primitive recursive.

The significance of the normal form theorem is that it allows one to form a universal partial computable function. One can define

$$\varphi_e(x) = U(\mu y T(e, x, y))$$

(where, of course, $\varphi_e(x) \uparrow$ if the right side of the equation is undefined, which happens if there does not exist a y such that $T(e, x, y)$). Then on the one hand, $\varphi_e(x)$ is a computable partial 2-place function of x and e. And on the other hand, each 1-place computable partial function equals φ_e for some e. That is,

$$\varphi_0, \varphi_1, \varphi_2, \dots$$

is a complete list of all the computable partial 1-place functions.

Similarly, one can extend these ideas to k-place partial functions:

$$\varphi_e^k(x_1, \dots, x_k) = U(\mu y T_k(e, x_1, \dots, x_k, y))$$

Then

$$\varphi_0^k, \varphi_1^k, \varphi_2^k, \dots$$

is a complete list of all the computable partial k-place functions.

Whenever one has such a list, one can diagonalize out of it. One can define the set K by the condition

$$x \in K \Leftrightarrow \varphi_x(x) \downarrow$$

so that a number x (thought of as encoding a program for computing a partial function) belongs to K iff that program, given x itself as input, halts and returns a value.

Then the diagonal function

$$d(x) = \begin{cases} \varphi_x(x) + 1 & \text{if } x \in K \\ 0 & \text{otherwise} \end{cases}$$

is a total function, but it cannot equal φ_e for any e, because it differs from φ_e at e. So d is not a computable function. If K were computable, however, then d would be computable, because the partial function $\varphi_x(x) + 1$ is computable.

One can conclude that K is not a computable set; its characteristic function C_K is not a computable function. But the partial characteristic function

$$c_k(x) = \begin{cases} 1 & \text{if } x \in K \\ \uparrow & \text{otherwise} \end{cases}$$

is a computable partial function; $c_k(x) = 1 + 0 \cdot \varphi_x(x)$.

Theorem. For a set A of numbers, the following are equivalent:

(1) The partial characteristic function of A is a computable partial function

(2) A is the domain of some computable partial function

(3) For some computable binary relation R,

$$x \in A \Leftrightarrow R(x, y) \text{ for some } y$$

(Here (2) $\Rightarrow$ (3) because $x \in \text{dom } \varphi_e \Leftrightarrow T(e, x, y)$ for some y. And (3) $\Rightarrow$ (1) because one can use the function $1 + 0 \cdot \mu y R(x, y)$.)

A set A with the properties of this theorem is said to be computably enumerable (c.e.). The concept of a c.e. set is the formalization of the informal concept of a semidecidable set, discussed in section 0. And Church's thesis assures one that it is the correct formalization.

In the previously standard terminology mentioned earlier, a set A with the properties of the theorem was said to be recursively enumerable (r.e.). In fact, this terminology—especially the abbreviation—has become so well established that the prospects for reform are uncertain.

The theorem extends to the case where A is a k-ary relation on $\mathbb{N}$; now in part (3) the relation R is $k + 1$-ary. Thus, one may speak of c.e. (or r.e.) relations on $\mathbb{N}$.

Unsolvability of the halting problem. The binary relation $\{\langle x, y\rangle \mid \varphi_y(x)\downarrow\}$ is c.e. but not computable.

This relation—the halting relation—cannot be computable lest the previous diagonal function d be computable. It is c.e., because $\varphi_y(x)\downarrow \Leftrightarrow \exists z T(y, x, z)$.

If one defines $W_e = \text{dom}\varphi_e$, then as a consequence of the normal form theorem, one has a complete list

$$W_0, W_1, W_2, \ldots$$

of all the c.e. sets. The set K can be described simply as $\{x \mid x \in W_x\}$.

The following is not hard to see:

Kleene's theorem. A set is computable iff both it and its complement are c.e.

For example, the complement $\overline{K}$ is not only noncomputable, it is not even c.e.

For another example of an undecidable set, take the set of programs that compute total functions:

$$\text{Tot} = \{e \mid \varphi_e \text{ is total}\}$$

The same argument used for K shows that Tot is not computable. Moreover, Tot is not c.e. In fact, a slightly stronger statement holds: There is no c.e. set P such that $\{\varphi_e \mid e \in P\}$ coincides with the class of total computable functions. Thus, if P is a c.e. set of programs that compute only total functions, then there must be some total computable function with no program in P.

Rice's theorem. Suppose that C is a collection of computable partial 1-place functions, and let I be $\{e \mid \varphi_e \in C\}$. Then I is computable only in two trivial cases: when C is empty and when C is the collection of all computable partial functions.

For example, suppose one focuses attention on a particular computable partial function f. Rice's theorem asserts that one cannot always decide of a given program whether or not that program correctly computes f.

The name *computably enumerable* corresponds to yet another characterization: A set is c.e. iff there is a Turing machine (augmented with a suitable output tape) that can generate, in some order, the members of that set, one after another. More formally, a set S of natural numbers is c.e. iff it is either empty or is the range of some total computable function f, that is, $S = \{f(0), f(1), \ldots\}$. In fact, one can even insist that f be primitive recursive. In general the function f will not enumerate the members of S in numerical order, however (i.e., f will not in general be an increasing function). The range of an increasing function (or even of a nondecreasing function) will always be a computable set.

It is easy to see that if f is a two-place computable partial function, then the result of holding one variable fixed (as a parameter)

$$g(x) = f(36, x)$$

is a one-place computable partial function g. Often, one needs the more subtle fact: A program for g can be effectively found from the program for f and the value of the parameter.

Parameter theorem. There is a total computable function ρ such that

$$\varphi_e(t, x) = \varphi_{\rho(e, t)}(x)$$

for all e, t, and x.

The analogous statement holds for more variables, that is, for an m-tuple $\vec{t}$ and an n-tuple $\vec{x}$ in place of t and x. The parameter theorem commonly goes by the cryptic name of the S-m-n theorem.

A deeper result is the following theorem, which is due to Kleene.

Recursion theorem. For any computable partial function g, one can find an e such that

$$\varphi_e(x) = g(e, x)$$

for all x.

Again, x can be replaced by an n-tuple $\vec{x}$. The proof of the recursion theorem is similar to the argument used to produce self-referential sentences in number theory, such as those used in proving Gödel's incompleteness theorem.

3. AXIOMATIZABLE THEORIES

The connection between computability theory and logic hinges on the fact that proofs must be effectively recognizable.

The concept of a proof is basic to logic. What exactly is a proof? As indicated in section 0, for a proof to be acceptable, it must be possible—in principle—to fill in enough steps that a hard-working graduate student (or a referee) can verify its correctness. One cannot demand that this student have the same brilliant insight that the proof's discoverer had. Nor can one demand that the student spend an infinite amount of time checking an infinite number of cases. What one can insist is that, given a correct proof (with all the steps filled in), the student will eventually complete the verification and stand up and say, "Yes, this proof is correct."

This is just to say, however, that the set of correct proofs must be at least semidecidable. And typically one expects that the set will even be decidable, lest the student work forever attempting to verify an incorrect proof. In an axiomatic theory, one expects to be able to tell (effectively) an axiom from a nonaxiom, and one expects to be able to determine (effectively) whether or not a rule of inference is being correctly applied.

Even with the weaker property of semidecidability, it follows that the set of theorems—the set of sentences that have proofs—is semidecidable. (Given a sentence, one could employ the brute-force procedure of going through all strings of symbols in a systematic way, spending more and more time on each, attempting to verify that it is a proof of that sentence.) That is, the set of theorems must be c.e.

More formally, assume one has a first-order language, such as the language for set theory. Formulas are (or can be made to be) strings over a finite alphabet, so the concepts of computability theory are applicable. (It is being assumed here that the language has a reasonably simple array of nonlogical symbols.) One can define a theory to be a set of sentences closed under logical consequence. In particular, for a set A of formulas adopted as axioms, one can obtain the theory T_A consisting of all sentences that are logical consequences of A.

Theorem. (a) If A is a computable set or a c.e. set of axioms, then the set T_A of logical consequences of A is c.e.

(b) (Craig's theorem.) Conversely, if a theory T is c.e., then there is a computable set A of axioms such that T is the set of logical consequences of A.

Part (a) follows from the Gödel completeness theorem for first-order logic. The set of logical consequences of A is the same as the set of sentences derivable from A in the predicate calculus. If one has a machine that can generate the axioms, then one can organize a machine to generate the theorems.

Part (b) utilizes the simple fact that if one can generate the members of T in some order,

$$T = \{\tau_0, \tau_1, \tau_2, \dots\}$$

then one can generate a suitable set of axioms in increasing order:

$$A = \{\tau_0, \tau_0 \wedge \tau_1, \tau_0 \wedge \tau_1 \wedge \tau_2, \dots\}$$

So A is computable.

If one defines a theory T to be axiomatizable if there exists a computable set of axioms for it (or equivalently, if there exists a c.e. set of axioms for it), then there is the conclusion: A theory is axiomatizable iff it is c.e.

For example, the usual ZFC axioms for set theory form a computable set of axioms, so the set of theorems of ZFC is a c.e. set. At the other extreme, taking the set of axioms to be empty, one can conclude that the set of valid sentences is c.e. The set of valid sentences is, however, undecidable:

Church's theorem. Assume the language has at least one two-place predicate symbol. Then the set of valid sentences is not computable.

4. GÖDEL INCOMPLETENESS THEOREM

This section examines Gödel's first incompleteness theorem, from the point of view of computability theory. As the context, first-order theories of arithmetic, that is, theories dealing with the natural numbers with the operations of addition and multiplication, will be considered. Certainly, the study of the natural numbers with addition and multiplication is a basic part of mathematics, in the real sense that it is the topic in mathematics that school children study first.

The structure that is focused on here

$$\mathfrak{N} = (\mathbb{N}; 0, S, +, \times)$$

consists of the set $\mathbb{N}$ of natural numbers with the distinguished element 0 and the operations of successor (S), addition (+), and multiplication (×). The first-order language corresponding to this structure has quantifiers $\forall$ and $\exists$ ranging over $\mathbb{N}$, a constant symbol **0** for the number 0, and function symbols **S**, +, and × for successor, addition, and multiplication.

The set of all sentences of this language that are true in standard structure $\mathfrak{N}$ will be called the theory of true arithmetic. Although this theory deals with basic topics, it is by no means trivial. For example, it is not hard to see that the set of prime numbers is definable in $\mathfrak{N}$, that is, one can write down a formula $\pi(x)$ of the language that is satisfied in $\mathfrak{N}$ when the number n is assigned to x iff n is prime:

$$\begin{aligned} n \text{ is prime} &\Leftrightarrow \models_{\mathfrak{N}} \pi[n] \\ &\Leftrightarrow \models_{\mathfrak{N}} \pi(\boldsymbol{n}) \end{aligned}$$

where one substitutes for x the numeral $\boldsymbol{n}$ for n, that is the numeral **SS⋯S0**. Using this formula π one can then write down a sentence in the language that expresses the twin prime conjecture, or a sentence that expresses Goldbach's conjecture. But the truth or falsity of these conjectures remains unknown.

What can one say quantitatively about the complexity of the theory of true arithmetic? It will be seen in this section that the theory is not c.e. and hence is not an axiomatizable theory. One connection between $\mathfrak{N}$ and computability is expressed by the result:

Theorem. Every computable relation over $\mathbb{N}$ is definable in the structure $\mathfrak{N}$. That is, for each computable k-ary relation $R \subseteq \mathbb{N}^k$ there is a formula $_\rho$ defining R in $\mathfrak{N}$:

$$\langle n_1, \dots, n_k\rangle \in R \Leftrightarrow \vDash_{\mathfrak{N}} \rho[n_1, \dots, n_k]$$

As an immediate consequence of this theorem, one can conclude that c.e. relations are also definable in $\mathfrak{N}$. This is because any c.e. relation Q is the domain of some computable relation R:

$$m \in Q \Leftrightarrow \langle m, n\rangle \in R, \text{ for some } n$$

Thus, if $\rho(x, y)$ defines R in $\mathfrak{N}$, then $\exists y\rho(x, y)$ defines Q. Moreover, $\neg\exists y\rho(x, y)$ defines the complement $\overline{Q}$ of Q. And by repeating the previous argument, the domain of $\overline{Q}$ is definable.

The conclusion is that any relation over $\mathbb{N}$ that is obtainable from the computable relations by the operations of forming the domain (i.e., projection) and forming the complement, iterated any number of times, will be definable in the structure $\mathfrak{N}$. (The converse is also true; these are exactly the definable relations; see section 6.)

In particular, the set $\overline{K}$ is definable in $\mathfrak{N}$, where K is the c.e. but noncomputable set constructed earlier. That is, there is some formula $\kappa(x)$ that defines K, so that $\neg\kappa(x)$ defines $\overline{K}$ and

$$n \in \overline{K} \Leftrightarrow \neg\kappa(\boldsymbol{n}) \text{ is true in } \mathfrak{N}.$$

It follows from this, however, that the set of sentences (of the language) true in $\mathfrak{N}$ cannot be semidecidable, lest equivalence yield an effective procedure for recognizing membership in this. Thus, one comes to the conclusion that truth in arithmetic is not a c.e. concept:

Theorem. The set of sentences true in $\mathfrak{N}$ is not c.e.

(An elaboration of this argument would give Tarski's theorem: The set of sentences true in $\mathfrak{N}$, when converted to a set of natural numbers, is not definable in $\mathfrak{N}$.)

This theorem, with the previous section, asserts that the theory of true arithmetic is not axiomatizable. So any axiomatizable subtheory fails to give all of true arithmetic.

Gödel's incompleteness theorem. For any axiomatizable subtheory T of true arithmetic, one can find a true sentence that is not derivable in T.

In fact, here is how one can find that true, underivable sentence. Let

$$J = \{n \mid T \vdash \neg\kappa(\boldsymbol{n})\},$$

the set of numbers that T "knows" are in $\overline{K}$. Because T is axiomatizable (and hence c.e.), the set J is c.e., and so $J = W_j$ for some number j. Moreover, J is a subset of $\overline{K}$ so it cannot be all of that set; there is a number in $\overline{K}$ that is not in J. In fact, j is such a number.

That is, the sentence $\neg\kappa(\boldsymbol{j})$ is a true sentence (j is really in $\overline{K}$) that T does not prove (T does not know that $j \in \overline{K}$). Thus, the sentence $\neg\kappa(\boldsymbol{j})$ is a specific witness to T's incompleteness.

And what might this sentence $\neg\kappa(\boldsymbol{j})$ say? Interpreted in $\mathfrak{N}$ it speaks of numbers and their sums and products. One can give it a more interesting translation, however:

$$\begin{aligned} \neg\kappa(\boldsymbol{j}) \text{ says } & j \in \overline{K} \\ \text{i.e., } & j \notin W_j \\ \text{i.e., } & j \notin J \\ \text{i.e., } & T \nvdash \neg\kappa(\boldsymbol{j}) \end{aligned}$$

That is, the witness (the true unprovable sentence) asserts, in a sense, its own unprovability!

The conclusion is that the computability theory approach to Gödel's incompleteness theorem, based on c.e. sets, is not so different from the more traditional approach, which uses a diagonal construction to produce a sentence asserting, in a sense, its own unprovability.

5. DEGREES OF UNSOLVABILITY

Some unsolvable problems are more unsolvable than others. To make sense of this idea, one can employ the concept of relative computability.

Consider a fixed set B of natural numbers. Then a partial function f should be considered effectively calculable relative to B if there is a procedure that computes f and is effective except that it is allowed to appeal to an "oracle" for B. An oracle for B can be thought of as a device that, given a number x, responds by saying whether or not x is in B.

Any of the formalizations of calculability given in section 1 can be augmented to incorporate such an oracle. For example, in the case of primitive recursive functions, one can simply add the characteristic function of B

as a new initial function. As before, the various formalizations give exactly the same class of partial functions. Thus, one may speak unambiguously of computability relative to a set B.

Of course, if B is a computable set, however, the computability relative to B is simply equivalent to computability. For a noncomputable set, however, some noncomputable functions will become computable relative to B (the characteristic function of B, for one).

The concept of relative computability was introduced by Turing in a 1939 paper. At first glance, it seems an odd concept, combining as it does the most constructive approach to functions (that of computability) with the least constructive approach (that of a magical oracle). It is to Turing's credit that he perceived the value of the concept.

For sets A and B of natural numbers, one can say that A is computable *in* B, or that A is Turing reducible to B (written $A \leq_T B$) if the characteristic function of A is computable relative to B. That is, saying that $A \leq_T B$ implies that membership in A is no harder to decide than is membership in B. The $\leq_T$ relation is transitive and is reflexive on $\mathcal{P}\mathbb{N}$ (i.e., it is a preordering). Informally, transitivity of $\leq_T$ corresponds to connecting machines in series. Consequently, the symmetric version

$$A \equiv_T B \Leftrightarrow A \leq_T B \text{ and } B \leq_T A$$

is an equivalence relation on $\mathcal{P}\mathbb{N}$, and $\leq_T$ gives a partial ordering of the equivalence classes. These equivalence classes are called degrees of unsolvability, or simply degrees.

There is a least degree **0**, the class of the computable sets. Each degree must be a countable collection of sets (because there are only countably many programs), and so there are $2^{\aleph_0}$ equivalence classes altogether. Any two degrees have a least upper bound. The earlier construction of a noncomputable set K can be relativized:

$$x \in B' \Leftrightarrow \varphi_x^B(x)\downarrow$$

(where φ_e^B is the partial function computed, relative to B, by the program e). Then the degree of B' is strictly larger (under $\leq_T$) than the degree of B; thus, there is no largest degree.

The set B' is called the jump of B. Thus, the jump operation can be applied to a set to obtain a set of higher degree, and this operation can be iterated:

$$B <_T B' <_T B'' <_T B''' <_T \ldots$$

The degrees are not linearly ordered. It is possible to construct simultaneously sets A and B in such a way as to sabotage each machine that might reduce one set to the other. In fact, much more is true; one can construct $2^{\aleph_0}$ degrees that are all incomparable to each other under the ordering.

One can define a degree to be c.e. if it contains a c.e. set. These degrees are of particular interest because they are the degrees of axiomatizable theories. The least degree **0** is the degree of the decidable theories. Earlier, a noncomputable c.e. set $K = \{x \mid \varphi_x(x)\downarrow\}$ was constructed. So the degree of K, denoted $\mathbf{0}'$, is a c.e. degree greater than **0**. The halting problem for Turing machines (regarded as a set of integers) also has degree $\mathbf{0}'$. It is not hard to show that $\mathbf{0}'$ is the largest c.e. degree: for every c.e. degree $\boldsymbol{a}$ one has $\boldsymbol{a} \leq_T \mathbf{0}'$. (Thus, any c.e. set of degree $\mathbf{0}'$ is $\leq_T$-complete for c.e. sets, in the sense that every other c.e. set is computable in it.)

A number of undecidable axiomatizable theories turn out to have degree $\mathbf{0}'$: the validities of predicate calculus (with at least a binary predicate symbol), first-order Peano arithmetic, ZF set theory (if consistent), and others.

In 1944 Emil Post raised the question whether there were any c.e. degrees other than **0** and $\mathbf{0}'$. This question, which became known as Post's problem, was finally answered in 1956 (two years after Post's death), independently by Richard Friedberg (in his Harvard senior thesis) and by A. A. Mučnik (in the Soviet Union). They showed that intermediate c.e. degrees do indeed exist, and in great profusion. Gerald Sacks later showed that any countable partial ordering can be embedded—as a partial ordering—in the partial ordering of c.e. degrees.

Although the natural axiomatizable theories have turned out to have either degree **0** or degree $\mathbf{0}'$, Solomon Feferman showed that every c.e. degree contains some axiomatizable theory.

There is a simpler way in which questions about membership in one set might be effectively reducible to questions about another set. One can define A to be many-one reducible to B (written $A \leq_m B$) if there is a total computable function f such that

$$x \in A \Leftrightarrow f(x) \in B$$

for all natural numbers x. The idea is that each question "$x \in A$?" about A is reduced by f to one question about B. Moreover, if there is such a reduction function f that is one to one, then one can say that A is one-one reducible to B (written $A \leq_1 B$). Clearly,

$$A \leq_1 B \Rightarrow A \leq_m B \Rightarrow A \leq_T B$$

and in general neither arrow can be reversed. Again, both $\leq_1$ and $\leq_m$ are preorders, so the corresponding symmetric relations

$$A \equiv_1 B \Leftrightarrow A \leq_1 B \;\&\; B \leq_1 A \text{ and } A \equiv_m B \Leftrightarrow A \leq_m B \;\&\; B \leq_m A$$

are equivalence relations on $\mathcal{P}\mathbb{N}$, and the equivalence classes (the one-one degrees and the many-one degrees) are partially ordered. John Myhill showed that if $A \equiv_1 B$, then there is a total computable permutation of $\mathbb{N}$ taking A onto B.

It is not hard to make a c.e. set that is $\leq_1$-complete for c.e. sets, that is, every c.e. set is one-one reducible to it. In fact, K is such a set.

6. DEFINABILITY IN ARITHMETIC

As in section 4, let

$$\mathfrak{N} = (\mathbb{N}; 0, S, +, \times)$$

be the standard structure for arithmetic, consisting of the set $\mathbb{N}$ of natural numbers with the distinguished element 0 and the operations of successor, addition, and multiplication. In this structure, what sets (or relations or functions) are definable by first-order formulas? In section 4 it was noted that every computable relation is definable in arithmetic, and section 5 used the fact that some noncomputable sets (such as $\overline{K}$) are also definable. Now, one can approach the matter more systematically.

Say that a relation (on $\mathbb{N}$) is arithmetical if it is definable in $\mathfrak{N}$. Of course, only countably many relations can be arithmetical, because there are only countably many formulas. One wants to classify these relations, according to the quantifier depth of the defining formulas.

From section 2 it is known that a relation A is c.e. iff it is the domain of some computable relation R:

$$\vec{m} \in A \Leftrightarrow R(\vec{m}, n) \text{ for some } n.$$

If $\rho(x_1, \ldots, x_k, y)$ defines R, then the formula $\exists y \rho(x_1, \ldots, x_k, y)$ defines A, so that A is "one quantifier away" from being computable. One can say that such relations A are Σ_1. (Yuri Matijacevič showed in 1970 that in fact every c.e. relation is definable by an existential formula, that is, one of the form

$$\exists y_1 \cdots \exists y_l \, \rho(x_1, \ldots, x_k, y_1, \ldots, y_l)$$

where ρ is quantifier-free, but that fact is not needed here.)

Next, call a relation Σ_2 if it is definable by a formula

$$\exists y_1 \forall y_2 \, \rho(x_1, \ldots, x_k, y_1, y_2)$$

where ρ defines a computable relation. Call a reaction Σ_3 if it is definable by a formula

$$\exists y_1 \forall y_2 \exists y_3 \, \rho(x_1, \ldots, x_k, y_1, y_2, y_3)$$

where ρ defines a computable relation), and so forth.

The dual concept, where one reverses existential and universal quantifiers, gives the Π_k relations. That is, call a relation Π_1 if it is definable by a formula

$$\forall y \, \rho(x_1, \ldots, x_k, y)$$

call it Π_2 if it is definable by a formula

$$\forall y_1 \exists y_2 \, \rho(x_1, \ldots, x_k, y_1, y_2),$$

call it Π_3 if it is definable by a formula

$$\forall y_1 \exists y_2 \forall y_3 \, \rho(x_1, \ldots, x_k, y_1, y_2, y_3),$$

and so forth, where in each case ρ defines a computable relation.

Then the Π_k relations are exactly the complements of the Σ_k relations. In effect, one is measuring how far away a relation is from decidability.

By adding vacuous quantifiers, one sees that any Σ_k relation is both Σ_{k+1} and Π_{k+1}. And every definable relation appears somewhere in this hierarchy, because it will be definable by a prenex formula, the quantifier-free part of which always defines a computable (in fact primitive recursive) relation.

For example, the set $\{e \mid \varphi_e \text{ is total}\}$ of programs of total functions is Π_2, because φ_e is total iff $\forall m \, \exists n \, T(e, m, n)$. By Kleene's theorem, a relation is computable iff it is both Σ_1 and Π_1. The set K is Σ_1 but not Π_1. And in analogy to this fact,one can, for each k, construct a set that is Σ_k but not Π_k. Thus, letting the noun Σ_k denote the collection of all Σ_k relations, one has proper inclusion in both of the chains

$$\Sigma_1 \subset \Sigma_2 \subset \Sigma_3 \subset \cdots$$

$$\Pi_1 \subset \Pi_2 \subset \Pi_3 \subset \cdots$$

and in both cases the union of the chains is exactly the class of arithmetical relations. One can say that these chains define the arithmetical hierarchy.

From the point of view of the arithmetical hierarchy, one can obtain Tarski's theorem that the theory of true arithmetic is not arithmetical:

Tarski's theorem. The set of sentences true in $\mathfrak{N}$, regarded as a set of numbers, is not definable in $\mathfrak{N}$.

Let T be the set of true sentences. It suffices to show, for each k, that T cannot be Σ_k. Let A be a set that is arithmetical but not Σ_k (as indicated, there is such a set, and one can even make it Π_k). Then A is definable by some formula $\alpha(x)$ and

$$n \in A \Leftrightarrow \alpha(\mathbf{n}) \in T$$

which shows that $A \leq_m T$ (where T has been identified with the corresponding set of numbers). That is, for some total computable function f (which substitutes numerals into α),

$$n \in A \Leftrightarrow f(n) \in T.$$

If, contrary to one's hopes, T were Σ_k, then the previous line would let one conclude that A is also Σ_k, which it is not.

There is also a connection between the arithmetical hierarchy and relative computability, as in section 5. The following result extends the fact that a relation is Σ_1 iff it is c.e.

Post's theorem. (a) A relation is Σ_2 iff it is c.e. in $\emptyset'$, the jump of the empty set.

(b) More generally, a relation is Σ_{k+1} iff it is c.e. in $\emptyset^{(k)}$, the kth jump of the empty set.

7. FEASIBLE COMPUTABILITY

Up to now, this entry has approached computability from the point of view that there should be no constraints on the time required for a particular computation, or on the amount of memory space that might be required. The result is that some total computable functions will take a long time to compute. If a function f grows rapidly, then for large x it will take a long time simply to generate the output $f(x)$. There are also, however, bounded functions that require a large amount of time.

To be more precise, suppose one adopts one of the formalizations from section 1 (any one will do), and one defines in a reasonable way the "number of steps" or the "time required" in a computation. (Manuel Blum converted the term *reasonable* into axioms for what a *complexity measure* should be.) Then Michael Rabin showed that for any total computable function h, no matter how fast it grows, one can find another total computable function f with range $\{0, 1\}$ such that for any program e for f (i.e., $f = \varphi_e$), the time required for e to compute $f(x)$ exceeds $h(x)$ for all but finitely many values of x. (The function f is constructed in stages, in such a way as to sabotage any fast program that might try to compute f.)

Is there a more restricted concept of "feasibly computable function" where the amount of time required does not grow beyond all reason, where the amount of time required is an amount that might actually be practical, at least when the input to the function is not absurdly large? To this vague question, an exact answer has been proposed.

Once can call a function f polynomial-time computable (or for short, P-time computable) if there is a program e for f and a polynomial p such that for every x, the program e computes $f(x)$ in no more than $p(|x|)$ steps, where $|x|$ is the length of x.

This definition requires some explanation and support. If f is a function over Σ^*, the set of words over a finite alphabet Σ, then of course $|x|$ is just the number of symbols in the word x. If f is a function over $\mathbb{N}$, then $|x|$ is the length of the numeral for x. (Here, one comes again to the fact that effective procedures work with numerals, not numbers.) So if one uses base-2 numerals for $\mathbb{N}$, then $|x|$ is about $\log_2 x$.

Moreover, there was vagueness about exactly how the number of steps in a computation was to be determined. Here the situation is encouraging: The class of P-time computable functions is the same, under the different reasonable ways of counting steps.

Back in sections 0 and 1 there was the encouraging fact that many different ways of formalizing the concept of effective calculability yielded exactly the same class of functions. As remarkable as that fact is, even more is true. The number of steps required by one formalization is bounded by a polynomial in the number of steps required by another. For example, there exists a polynomial p (of moderate degree) such that a computation by a Turing machine that requires n steps can be simulated by a loop-while program that requires no more than $p(n)$ steps. Consequently, the concept of a P-time computable function is robust: One can get the same class of functions, regardless of which formalization from section 1 is employed. To be sure, the degrees of the polynomials will vary somewhat, but the class of P-time functions is unchanged.

Encouraged by this result, and inspired in particular by 1971 work of Stephen Cook, people since the 1970s have come to regard the class of P-time functions as the correct formalization of the idea of functions for which computations are feasible, without totally impractical running times.

By analogy to Church's thesis, the statement that P-time computability corresponds to feasibly practical computability has come to be known as Cook's thesis or the Cook-Karp thesis. (The concept of P-time computability appeared as early as 1964 in work of Alan Cobham. Jack Edmunds in 1965 pointed out the good features of P-time algorithms. Richard Karp in 1972 extended Cook's work.)

So what are the P-time computable functions? They form a subclass of the primitive recursive functions. All the polynomial functions are P-time computable, as are some functions that grow faster than any polynomial. There is, however, a limit to the growth rate of P-time computable functions, imposed by the fact that printing an output symbol takes a step. That is, there is the following growth limitation property: If f is computable in time bounded by the polynomial p, then $|f(x)| \leq |x| + p(|x|)$. This prevents exponential functions from being P-time computable; there is not enough time to write down the result.

Often, P-time computability is presented in terms of acceptance of languages (i.e., sets of words). Where Σ is the finite alphabet in question, consider a language $L \subseteq \Sigma^*$. One can say that $L \in$ P if there is a program and a polynomial p such that whenever a word w is in L, then the program halts on input w (i.e., it "accepts" w) in no more than $p(|w|)$ steps, and whenever a word w is not in L, then the program never halts on input w (i.e., the program does not accept w). This is equivalent to saying that the characteristic function of L is P-time computable, because one can add to the program an alarm clock that rings after time $p(|w|)$. For example, it is now known that the set of prime numbers (as a set of words written in the usual base-10 notation) belongs to P.

Of course, if the characteristic function of L is P-time computable, then so is the characteristic function of its complement, $\overline{L}$. That is, P = co-P, where co-P is the collection of complements of languages in P.

Informally, L is in P if L is not only a decidable set of words, but moreover there is a fast decision procedure for P—one that can actually be implemented in a practical way. For example, finite graphs can be coded by words over a suitable finite alphabet. The set of two-colorable graphs (i.e., the set of graphs that can be properly colored with two colors) is in P, because it is fast to check that the graph has no cycles of odd length. The set of graphs with an Euler cycle is in P, because it is fast to check that the graph is connected and that every vertex has even degree.

What about three-colorable graphs or graphs with Hamiltonian cycles? Here, there are no known fast decision procedures, but there are weaker facts: Given a proper coloring with three colors, it is fast to verify that it is indeed a proper coloring. Given a Hamiltonian cycle, it is fast to verify that it is indeed Hamiltonian. Both three-colorable graphs and Hamiltonian graphs are examples of languages that belong to a class known as NP.

One way to define NP is to use nondeterministic Turing machines. (The acronym NP stands for *nondeterministic polynomial time.*) Back in section 1 the definition of a Turing machine demanded that a machine's table of quintuples be unambiguous, that is, that no two different quintuples have the same first two components. By simply omitting that demand, one can obtain the concept of a nondeterministic Turing machine. A computation of such a machine, at each step, is allowed to execute any quintuple that begins with its present state and the symbol being scanned. Then, one can say that $L \in$ NP if there is a nondeterministic Turing machine M and a polynomial p such that whenever a word w is in L, then *some* computation of M starting from input w halts in no more than $p(|w|)$ steps, and whenever a word w is not in L, then no computation of M starting from input w *ever* halts. (An accepting computation can be thought of as having made a number of lucky guesses.)

There is an equivalent, and somewhat more workable, characterization along the lines of Σ_1 definability: $L \in$ NP iff there is binary relation $R \in$ P and a polynomial p such that for every word w,

$$w \in L \Leftrightarrow \exists y[|y| \leq p(|w|) \text{ and } R(w, y)].$$

Another example of a language in NP is SAT, the set of satisfiable formulas of sentential logic. The truth-table method for determining whether a formula with n sentence symbols is satisfiable involves forming all 2^n lines of the formula's truth table and looking to see if there is a line making the formula true. This is not, however, a feasible algorithm, because 2^{80} microseconds greatly exceeds the age of the universe. If one (nondeterministically) guesses the correct line of the table, however, then one can quickly verify that the formula is true under that line.

There is a clear analogy between computable and c.e. sets on the one hand, and P and NP on the other hand. The computable sets are decidable; the sets in P are decidable by fast algorithms. And c.e. sets are one existential quantifier away from being computable; sets in NP are one existential quantifier away from being in P. Moreover, there are c.e. sets that are complete with respect to $\leq_m$; there are NP sets with a similar property. One can say that

L_1 is P-time reducible to L_2 if there is a P-time computable (total) function f that many-one reduces L_1 to L_2. The following result was proved independently by Cook (1971) and Leonid Levin (1973):

Cook-Levin theorem. SAT is in NP, and every NP language is P-time reducible to SAT.

In other words, SAT is NP-complete. Karp showed that many other NP languages (three-colorable graphs, Hamiltonian graphs, and others) are NP-complete.

P VERSUS NP. How far does the analogy between NP and c.e. go? It is known that there are noncomputable c.e. sets, and a set is computable iff both it and its complement are c.e. While it is clear that P $\subseteq$ NP $\cap$ co-NP (i.e., every language in P is in NP, as is its complement), it is not known whether P = NP, or if NP is closed under complement.

The diagonalization that produces a noncomputable c.e. set can be relativized in a straightforward way to show that for any fixed oracle B, there is a set B' that is c.e. in B but not computable in B. Might some diagonal argument produce a set in NP that was not in P? Would that argument then relativize? The definitions of P and NP extend easily to P^B and NP^B, where the computations can query the oracle B (in one step).

In a 1975 paper, Theodore Baker, John Gill, and Robert Solovay showed that there are oracles B and C such that on the one hand $P^B = NP^B$ and on the other hand $P^C \neq NP^C$. This result suggests that the P versus NP question is difficult, because whatever argument might settle the question cannot relativize in a straightforward way. It has also been shown that if one chooses the oracle B at random (with respect to the natural probability measure on $\mathcal{P}\mathbb{N}$), then $P^B \neq NP^B$ with probability 1.

The P versus NP question remains the outstanding problem in theoretical computer science. In recognition of this fact, the Clay Mathematics Institute is offering a million-dollar prize for its solution.

8. ANALYTICAL HIERARCHY

The ideas in section 5 can be utilized to consider partial functions that take as input not only numbers (or words over a finite alphabet), but sets of numbers or, more generally, functions from $\mathbb{N}$ to $\mathbb{N}$. One can think of the computational procedure as being given a set or a function if it is given an oracle for it.

Let $\mathbb{N}^\mathbb{N}$ be the set of all total functions from $\mathbb{N}$ to $\mathbb{N}$. For a function α in $\mathbb{N}^\mathbb{N}$, a calculation can query an oracle for α by giving it a number n. The oracle then supplies (in one step) the number $\alpha(n)$. For example, the partial function whose value at α is the least n, if any, for which $\alpha(n) = 0$ is a computable partial function on $\mathbb{N}^\mathbb{N}$. One can broaden the concept of computability to include partial functions that take as inputs k numbers and l members of $\mathbb{N}^\mathbb{N}$, and produce numbers as outputs.

For definiteness, suppose that f is a partial function on $\mathbb{N} \times \mathbb{N}^\mathbb{N}$. Informally, f is effectively calculable if there exists an effective procedure that, when given a number x and an oracle for an α in $\mathbb{N}^\mathbb{N}$, eventually halts and returns the correct value $f(x, \alpha)$ if this is defined, and never halts if $f(x, \alpha)$ is undefined. As before, the various formalizations in section 1 all can be adapted to incorporate inputs from $\mathbb{N}^\mathbb{N}$. One can thereby obtain the concept of a computable partial function on $\mathbb{N} \times \mathbb{N}^\mathbb{N}$.

The basic results of section 2 can be adapted to this broader situation. An essential point is that any one computation takes finitely many steps before producing its output and so can make use of only finitely many values from the given oracles. To obtain a normal form theorem, one again needs to adopt a way of encoding an entire step-by-step history of a computation when a program e is given an input number x and an oracle α. It is natural to do this in such a way that, where y is the number encoding the history, the oracle is asked for values $\alpha(t)$ only for $t < y$. Let $\overline{\alpha}(y)$ be a number encoding the finite sequence $\alpha(0), \alpha(1), \ldots, \alpha(y-1)$ consisting of the first y values of α.

For the Kleene T-predicate, one now needs for $T(e, x, s, y)$ to say that e encodes a program, and y encodes the step-by-step history of the computation that program produces on input x, where the oracle supplies values according to the sequences coded by s. This is a decidable property of e, x, s, and y.

Normal form theorem. There is a 4-ary computable relation T on $\mathbb{N}$ and a total computable function U with the following property: For each computable partial function on $\mathbb{N} \times \mathbb{N}^\mathbb{N}$, there is a natural number e such that

$$f(x, \alpha) = U(\mu y T(e, x, \overline{\alpha}(y), y))$$

for every x and α.

Analogous results hold for partial computable functions with more arguments. It is interesting to note that because U and T have only natural numbers as arguments, computability on $\mathbb{N} \times \mathbb{N}^\mathbb{N}$ can be characterized in terms of computability on $\mathbb{N}$.

As before, one can define a subset of $\mathbb{N} \times \mathbb{N}^\mathbb{N}$ to be computable if its characteristic function is computable. Informally, this means that one has an effective decision procedure that, given $\langle x, \alpha \rangle$, decides whether or not it is in the set. Of course, the decision procedure will be able to utilize only finitely much information about α before rendering a verdict. Because of this fact, any computable set will be both open and closed in the natural topology on $\mathbb{N} \times \mathbb{N}^{\mathbb{N}}$ (where $\mathbb{N}$ has the discrete topology and $\mathbb{N}^{\mathbb{N}}$ has the product topology).

Moreover, one can define the c.e. sets to be the ones whose partial characteristic function is a computable partial function. From the normal form theorem, it follows that if Q is c.e., then there is a computable ternary relation R on $\mathbb{N}$ such that

$$Q(x, \alpha) \Leftrightarrow \exists y R(x, \overline{\alpha}(y), y)$$

for every x and α. Any such set Q will be open in the natural topology.

In section 6 the connection between computability and definability in arithmetic was examined. The definable relations formed a hierarchy, where the place of relation in the hierarchy (Σ_k or Π_k) depended, roughly, on how many quantifiers away from being computable it was.

Now, one can extend those ideas to second-order definability in arithmetic, where besides quantifiers over $\mathbb{N}$, quantifiers over $\mathbb{N}^{\mathbb{N}}$ can be used. One can start with

$$\Sigma_0^1 = \Pi_0^1 = \text{the class of arithemetical relations.}$$

Furthermore, one can define Σ_{k+1}^1 to consist of relations definable from Π_k^1 relations by prefixing existential quantifiers over $\mathbb{N}^{\mathbb{N}}$. Similarly, one can define Π_{k+1}^1 to consist of relations definable from Σ_k^1 relations by prefixing universal quantifiers over $\mathbb{N}^{\mathbb{N}}$. Finally, one can define Δ_k^1 to be $\Sigma_k^1 \cap \Pi_k^1$.

As with the arithmetical hierarchy, one has proper inclusion in both of the chains

$$\Sigma_1^1 \subset \Sigma_2^1 \subset \Sigma_3^1 \subset \cdots$$

$$\Pi_1^1 \subset \Pi_2^1 \subset \Pi_3^1 \subset \cdots$$

and in both cases the union of the chains is exactly the class of relations that are second-order definable in $\mathfrak{N}$. One can say that these chains define the analytical hierarchy.

See also Cantor, Georg; Church, Alonzo; Computationalism; Computing Machines; First-Order Logic; Gödel, Kurt; Gödel's Theorem; Logic, History of; Machine Intelligence; Mathematics, Foundations of; Modern Logic; Peano, Giuseppe; Tarski, Alfred; Turing, Alan M.

Bibliography

Barwise, Jon, ed. *Handbook of Mathematical Logic.* Amsterdam, Netherlands: North-Holland, 1977. Part C, "Recursion Theory," comprises eight papers on computability theory.

Church, Alonzo. "An Unsolvable Problem of Elementary Number Theory." *American Journal of Mathematics* 58 (1936): 345–363.

Davis, Martin, ed. *The Undecidable: Basic Papers on Undecidable Propositions, Unsolvable Problems, and Computable Functions.* Hewlett, NY: Raven Press, 1965. A collection of fundamental papers by Kurt Gödel, Alonzo Church, Alan M. Turing, J. B. Rosser, Stephen Cole Kleene, and Emil Post.

Griffor, Edward R., ed. *Handbook of Computability Theory.* Amsterdam, Netherlands: Elsevier, 1999. A collection of eighteen papers exploring topics in computability theory.

Herken, Rolf, ed. *The Universal Turing Machine: A Half-Century Survey.* New York: Oxford University Press, 1988.

Kleene, Stephen Cole. *Introduction to Metamathematics.* Amsterdam, Netherlands: North-Holland, 1952.

Rogers, Hartley. *Theory of Recursive Functions and Effective Computability.* New York: McGraw-Hill, 1967.

Soare, Robert I. *Recursively Enumerable Sets and Degrees: A Study of Computable Functions and Computably Generated Sets.* Berlin: Springer-Verlag, 1987.

Turning, A.M. "On Computable Numbers, with an Application to the Entscheidungsproblem." *Proceedings of the London Mathematical Society* 42 (1936–1937): 230–265. A correction, 43 (1937): 544–546.

Herbert B. Enderton (2005)

COMPUTATIONALISM

Computer science has been notably successful in building devices capable of performing sophisticated intellectual tasks. Impressed by these successes, many philosophers of mind have embraced a computational account of the mind. *Computationalism*, as this view is called, is committed to the literal truth of the claim that the mind is a computer: Mental states, processes, and events are computational states, processes, and events.

THE BASIC IDEA

What exactly are computational states, processes, and events? Most generally, a physical system, such as the human brain, implements a computation if the causal structure of the system—at a suitable level of description—mirrors the formal structure of the computation. This requires a one to one mapping of formal states of the computation to physical state-types of the system. The mapping from formal state-types to physical state types can be called an *interpretation function I. I* allows a sequence of physical state-transitions to be seen as a computation.

An example should make the central idea clear. A physical system computes the addition function if there exists a one-to-one mapping from numbers to physical state types of the system such that any numbers n, m, and $n+m$ related as addends and sums are mapped to physical state types related by a causal state-transition relation. In other words, whenever the system goes into the physical state specified under the mapping as n, and then goes into the physical state specified under the mapping as m, it is caused to go into the physical state specified under the mapping as $n+m$.

Traditionally, computational processes have been understood as rule-governed manipulations of internal symbols or representations—what computer scientists call *data structures*. Though these representations typically have meaning or semantic content, the rules apply to them solely in virtue of their structural properties, in the same way that the truth-preserving rules of formal logic apply to the syntax or formal character of natural language sentences, irrespective of their semantic content. Computationalism thus construes thinking as a type of mechanical theorem-proving.

Computationalism has been the predominant paradigm in cognitive psychology since the demise of behaviorism in the early 1960s. The failure of behaviorism can be traced in no small part to its refusal to consider the inner causes of behavior—in particular, the capacity of intelligent organisms to represent their environment and use their representations in controlling and modulating their interactions with the environment. Computationalism avoids this failing, explaining intelligent behavior as the product of internal computational processes that manipulate (construct, store, retrieve, and so on) symbolic representations of the organism's environment.

Many philosophers of mind find computationalism attractive for two reasons. First, it promises a physicalistic account of mind; specifically, it promises to explain mental phenomena without positing any mysterious nonphysical substances, properties, or events. Computational states are physically realized in the computer; they are just the physical states specified by the mapping I. Computational operations, as noted, are purely mechanical, applying to the objects in their domain—typically, symbols—in virtue of their structural properties. Moreover, computationalism, if true, would show how it is possible for mental states to have both causal and representational properties—to function as the causes of behavior, and to be about things other than themselves. Mental states, on this view, are relations to internal symbols, and symbols have a dual character: They are both physically constituted, hence causally efficacious, and bearers of meaning.

A second reason why philosophers of mind find computationalism attractive is that it promises a nonreductive account of the mind. A serious problem with reductive physicalist programs—such as central state identity theory—is that they are overly chauvinistic; they seek to identify mental state-types, such as pain, with their specific physical (i.e. neural) realization in humans, thus denying mentality to systems that lack human physiology. Functionalists, by contrast, take it to be a contingent fact about mental states and processes that they are realized in neural matter; these same mental processes may, in other creatures or devices, be realized in other ways (e.g., in a silicon-based circuitry). According to functionalism, it is the causal organization of a system—rather than its intrinsic physical makeup—that is crucial to its mentality. Computationalism endorses—and affords a precise specification of—the basic idea of functionalism. The computational characterization given by I provides an abstract characterization of that causal organization for a given system. Computational explanation is itself a species of functional explanation; it provides an analysis of a cognitive capacity in terms of the organized interaction of distinct components of the system, which are themselves functionally characterized—that is, described abstractly in terms of what they do rather than what they are made of.

A commitment to computationalism by philosophers of mind has frequently taken the form of a commitment to a computational construal of the *Representational Theory of Mind* (hereafter, RTM-C), which is an account of propositional attitudes, such states as beliefs, desires, hopes, fears, and so on. According to RTM-C, propositional attitudes are relations to internal representations—for example, to believe that P is to bear a certain relation to a token of an internal representation that means that P. Each attitude type is construed as a distinct computationally characterizable relation to an internal representation; thus, believing is one type of computational relation, and desiring another. The RTM-C has been advertised, by, for example, Jerry Fodor in *Psychosemantics* (1987), as a scientific vindication of the commonsense practice of explaining a subject's behavior by appealing to his or her propositional attitudes. If true, it would underwrite the practice of individuating propositional attitudes along two distinct dimensions, by *attitude* and by *content*. Subjects can hold various attitudes toward a single proposition; they may believe, doubt, or fear that the conflict in the Middle East will never by resolved. And subjects bear the same relation—belief, say—to many different propositions. On the RTM-C, the various attitudes correspond to distinct computational operations, and distinct data structure-types over which these operations are defined have distinct contents. The transparency of the relation between the commonsense explanatory scheme and the underlying computational realization of human psychology is an attractive feature of the view. However, it may also seem rather surprising that the two explanatory structures are virtually isomorphic. (Imagine if commonsense physics had anticipated the basic explanatory structure of quantum physics.)

The RTM-C is a heavily committed empirical hypothesis about the nature of the mind. Unlike computationalism, which claims simply that the mind is a computer, RTM-C purports to specify in broad outline the computational architecture of the mental processes that produce behavior. Computationalism is therefore compatible with the falsity of RTM-C. Is there any reason to believe RTM-C? It has been claimed that existing work in computational cognitive science provides empirical support for the RTM-C. Fodor (1987) points out that computational models of human cognitive capacities construe such capacities as involving the manipulation of internal representations. Psycholinguistic theories, for example, explain linguistic processing as the construction and transformation of structural descriptions, or *parse trees*, of the public language sentence being processed. It should be noted, however, that in order for a psychological theory to provide support for the RTM-C—for the claim that to have an attitude A toward a proposition P is to bear a computational relation R to a internal structure that means that P—it is not sufficient that the theory posits computational operations defined over internal representations. The posited representations must have appropriate contents—in particular, they must be interpreted in the theory as the contents of attitudes that one is prepared to ascribe to subjects independently of any commitment to the RTM.

For example, consider a psycholinguistic theory that explains a subject's understanding of the sentence "the dog bit the boy" as involving the construction of a parse tree exhibiting the constituent structure of the sentence. The theory supports the RTM only if there are independent grounds for attributing to the subject the content ascribed to the parse tree. There may be grounds for attributing to the subject a belief in a certain distal state of affairs—that a specific dog bit a specific boy—but this is not the content ascribed to the parse tree by the psycholinguistic theory. The parse tree's content is not even of the right sort. It does not represent a distal state of affairs; it represents the constituent structure of the sentence comprehended. The psycholinguistic theory supports the RTM only if the subject has propositional attitudes about the grammatical constituents of the sentence, such things as noun phrases and determiners. Such attitudes may be attributed to subjects as a consequence of the acceptance of the RTM-C, but these attitudes would not provide independent empirical support for the view.

SOME GENERAL ISSUES

Developments in computer science in the 1980s, in particular, the construction of *connectionist* machines—devices capable of performing cognitive tasks but without fixed symbols over which their operations are defined—have necessitated a broadened understanding of computation. Connectionist processes are not naturally interpretable as manipulations of internal symbols or data structures. Rather, connectionist networks consist of units or nodes whose activation increases or decreases the activation of other units to which they are connected until the ensemble settles into a stable configuration. Because connectionist networks lack symbols, they lack the convenient "hooks" to which, in the more traditional *classical* models, semantic interpretations or meanings are attached. Semantic interpretations, in connectionist models, are assigned either to individual units (in localist networks), or, more commonly, to patterns of activation over an ensemble of units (in distributed networks). Therefore, representation in connectionist devices is, in one respect, not as straightforward as it is in classical devices, because it is not as transparent which states or structures of the device count as *representations*. But issues concerning how the interpreted internal states or structures acquire their meaning—in other words, how a given semantic interpretation is justified—are fundamentally the same for the two kinds of machines.

Connectionist networks have had some success modeling various learning tasks—most notably, pattern-recognition tasks. There is continuing discussion within cognitive science about whether connectionist models will succeed in providing adequate explanations of more complex human cognitive capacities without simply implementing a classical or symbol-based architecture. One issue, originally raised by Jerry Fodor and Zenon Pylyshyn (1988), has turned on whether connectionist networks have the resources to explain a putative property of thought—that cognitive capacities are systematically related. For example, subjects can think the thought *the dog bit the boy* only if they can think the thought *the boy bit the dog.* A classical explanation of *systematicity* would appeal to the constituent structure of representations over which the operations involved in these capacities are defined—these representations contain the same constituents, just differently arranged. Connectionists, of course, cannot provide this sort of explanation—their models do not contain structured representations of the sort that the explanation requires.

Whether systematicity constitutes a decisive reason to prefer classical over connectionist cognitive models depends on several unresolved issues: (1) how pervasive the phenomena really is. It is certainly not true generally that if one can entertain a proposition of the form aRb, then one can entertain bRa. One can think the thought *the boy parsed the sentence* but not *the sentence parsed the boy*; (2) whether classical cognitive models are in fact able to provide real explanations of the systematic relations holding among cognitive capacities, rather than simply a sketch of the form such explanations would take in classical models. A real explanation of the phenomena would require, at least, the specification of a compositional syntax for the internal system of representation, something that classicists have so far been unable to provide; and (3) whether connectionist models are in fact unable to explain the systematic relations that do hold among cognitive capacities.

While strong claims have been made on both sides of this dispute, the question remains open. If it turns out that the mind has a connectionist architecture, then it would be expected that a perspicuous account of this architecture would reveal many cognitive capacities to be systematically related. For example, a characterization of the state of the network that consists in an English speaker's understanding of the sentence "the dog bit the boy" would cite the activation levels of various nodes of the network. The subject's understanding of the sentence "the boy bit the dog" would, presumably, activate many of the same nodes, and the explanation for the systematic relation between these two states would appeal to a dynamical account of the network's state transitions. These nodes would not be *constituents* of the subject's thought(s), in the sense required by classical models. And yet the relation between the two thoughts would not be merely accidental but instead would be a lawful consequence of general features of the network's architecture.

Questions such as whether connectionist devices will prove capable of modeling a wide range of complex cognitive capacities, and whether the best explanation of human cognitive capacities will advert to connectionist or classical computational processes, are properly understood as issues within computationalism. It should be noted, however, that the majority of philosophers committed to computationalism tend to interpret computation in classical terms, claiming that mental processes are manipulations of symbols in an internal code or language of thought. (See Jerry Fodor's *The Language of Thought* [1975] for the most explicit account of this view.) For this reason, and for ease of exposition, this entry will continue to refer to computational processes as manipulations of internal representations.

Computationalism requires a *psychosemantics*—that is, an account of how the postulated internal representations (or, in connectionist devices, states of the network) acquire their meaning. In virtue of what fact does a particular data structure mean *snow is white* rather than *2+2=4*? The meanings of natural language sentences are fixed by public agreement, but internal symbols must acquire their meanings in some other way. Philosophers committed to computationalism (and, hence, typically to physicalism) have assumed that an appropriate semantics for the language of thought must respect a "naturalistic constraint," the requirement that the conditions for a mental representation's having a particular meaning must be specifiable in nonintentional and nonsemantic terms. There have been various proposals for a naturalistic semantics. *Information-based* theories identify the meaning of a mental representation with the cause of its tokening in certain specifiable circumstances. *Teleological* theories hold that the meaning of a mental representation is determined by its biological function, what it was selected for.

No proposal is without serious problems, and the difficulty of accounting for the possibility that thoughts can *misrepresent* is the most widely discussed. But the difficulty of specifying naturalistic conditions for mental representation does not undermine computationalism itself. Cognitive scientists engaged in the business of developing computational models of cognitive capacities seem little concerned with the naturalistic constraint, and their specifications of semantic interpretations for these models do not obviously respect it. (See Frances Egan [1995] for argument.) There is no reason to think that the physicalistic bona fides of computational models are thereby impugned.

SUCCESSES AND OBSTACLES

As a hypothesis about the nature of mind, computationalism is not uncontentious. Important aspects of the mental have so far resisted computational analysis, and computational theorists have had little to say about the nature of conscious experience. While computers perform many intellectual tasks impressively, no one has succeeded in building a computer that can plausibly be said to feel pain or experience joy. It is possible that consciousness requires an explanation in terms of the biochemistry of the brain. In other words, the computational strategy of prescinding from the neural details of mental processes may mean that conscious phenomena will escape its explanatory net.

If conscious mental phenomena resist computational analysis, then the computational model of mind cannot be said to provide a general account of the human mind; however, the model may still provide the basis for a theory of those cognitive capacities that do not involve consciousness in any essential way. Cognitive psychologists have applied the computational model to the study of language processing, memory, vision, and motor activity, often with impressive results. Domain-specific processes—such as syntactic processing and early vision—have proved most amenable to computational analysis. It is likely that the information available to these processes is tightly constrained. So-called *modular* processes lend themselves to computational treatment precisely because they can be studied independently of the rest of the cognitive system. One does not need to know how the whole mind works to characterize the relatively simple interactions involved in these processes. The idea that perceptual processes are modular, at least up to a certain point, is well supported. Modular processes tend to be more reliable—they take account of information in the input before being influenced by the system's beliefs and expectations. This is especially important for the perception of novel input. And modular processes are faster—the process does not have to find and retrieve relevant information from memory for the processing to proceed. Ultimately, of course, perceptual processes will have to be integrated with the rest of the system if they are to provide a basis for reasoning, belief formation, and action.

Perceptual mechanisms, as characterized by computational accounts, typically rely on physical constraints—that is, on general information true of the subject's environment—to aid the recovery of perceptible properties of that environment. This information is assumed to be available only to the process in question—not stored in memory, and hence not available to the system for reasoning tasks. For example, the *structure from motion* visual mechanism, characterized by Shimon Ullman in *The Interpretation of Visual Motion* (1979), computes the structure of objects in the scene from information obtained from relative motion. The mechanism computes the unique rigid structure compatible with relatively minimal input data (three distinct views of four non-coplanar points in the object), in effect making use of the fact that objects are rigid in translation. Without the assumption of rigidity, more data is required to compute an object's shape. Whether or not Ullman's model accurately describes the human visual system, the general strategy of positing innate assumptions about the environment that simplify the processing is methodologically sound, given that perceptual mechanisms may be assumed to be adaptations to that environment.

Domain-general processes—such as decision making and rational revision of belief in response to new information—have so far resisted computational treatment. Their intractability is due in part to the fact that general constraints on the information that may be relevant to solutions are difficult, if not impossible, to specify. A system capable of passing the *Turing test*—the requirement that it convince an interlocutor that it is a person for a short period of time—must have access to a vast store of information about the world, about how agents typically interact with that world, and about the conventions governing conversation among agents in the world. All this information must be stored in the system's memory. At any point in the conversation, the system must be capable of bringing that information to bear on the selection of an appropriate response from the vast number of meaningful responses available to it. Human agents, of course, have no trouble doing this. The relevant information is somehow just there when it is needed. The task for the computational theorist is to characterize how this vast store of information is represented in the system's memory in such a way that relevant information can be accessed efficiently when needed. This formidable technical problem is known in the field of Artificial Intelligence (AI) as the *knowledge representation problem*.

A related problem, known in AI circles as the *frame problem*, concerns how a system is able to continuously update its knowledge store as the world around it changes. Every change has a large number of consequences. For example, the typing of the previous sentence on this author's computer requires the provision of a plausible example of the generalization just typed. It also changes the arrangement of subatomic particles in the room, yet it doesn't affect the Dow Jones industrial average or the price of crude oil. The author needs to keep track of some of these consequences, but most can and should be ignored. How, then, does the author update her knowledge store to take account of just those changes that are relevant (for her) while ignoring the vast number that are not? Unless the frame problem can be solved, or otherwise sidestepped, computationalism has a slim chance of providing a general account of human cognitive capacities.

GENERAL OBJECTIONS

Opponents of computationalism have offered arguments purporting to show that the human mind cannot be a computer. One class of objection, typified by Roger Penrose's *The Emperor's New Mind* (1989), takes as its starting point Kurt Gödel's result that any formal system powerful enough to do arithmetic can yield a sentence that is undecidable—that is, a sentence such that neither it nor its negation is provable within the system. A human observer, the argument continues, can see that the undecidable sentence is true; therefore, the human's cognitive abilities outstrip that of the machine. For the argument to establish that human minds are not machines it would have to demonstrate that human cognitive abilities simultaneously transcend the limits of all machines. No version of the argument has succeeded in establishing this strong claim.

A second objection claims that any physical system, including a rock or a piece of cheese, may be described as computing any function, thus computationalism's claim that the human mind is a computer is utterly trivial. If everything is a computer, then computationalism reveals nothing interesting about the nature of mind. The following is John Searle's version of the argument in *The Rediscovery of the Mind* (1992). Recall that to characterize a physical system as a computer is to specify a mapping from formal states of a computation to physical state-types of the system. Take some arbitrary function, say the addition function, and some physical system, say a particular wall. Though the wall appears to be in a constant state, it is known that the wall is made up of atoms in continuous motion. Its physical state is constantly changing. The microphysical state of the wall at time t1 can be interpreted as *two* and its microphysical state at time t2 as *three*, and its microphysical state at time t3 as *five*. And similarly for other combinations of addends and sums. Under this interpretation the physical state transitions of the wall implement the addition function. The wall is an adder!

It is possible, in the above sense, to describe any physical system as computing any function. This does nothing, however, to damage computationalism's claim that the mind is a computer. There are significant differences between the interpretation function under which the wall is an adder, and the interpretation function under which a hand calculator is an adder. One important difference is that in order to know how to interpret the wall's states as sums one has to compute the addition function oneself. The triviality argument does point to an important task for theorists concerned with the foundations of computational cognitive science—namely, specifying the adequacy conditions on interpretation that allow a computational characterization of a physical system to be predictive and explanatory of the systems's behavioral capacities.

A third objection to computationalism has been made by John Searle in his 1980 article "Minds, Brains, and Programs." According to Searle's *Chinese Room* argument, genuine understanding cannot be a computational process. The manipulation of symbols according to rules that operate only on their structural properties is, according to Searle, a fundamentally unintelligent process. The argument, which many have found unconvincing, is formulated explicitly for classical computational models—yet if Searle is right it would apply to any mechanical model of the mind, and hence to connectionist models as well.

It is unlikely that a philosophical argument of the sort discussed in this section will prove computationalism false. Computationalism is a bold empirical hypothesis about the nature of mind that will be evaluated by the explanatory fruit it bears. There is reason for cautious optimism, though substantial progress needs to be made on some formidable technical issues before theorists of mind can be confident that computationalism is true.

See also Artificial Intelligence; Chinese Room Argument; Cognitive Science; Machine Intelligence; Psychology.

Bibliography

Copeland, Jack. *Artificial Intelligence: A Philosophical Introduction*. Oxford: Blackwells, 1993.

Cummins, Robert. *Meaning and Mental Representation*. Cambridge, MA: MIT Press, 1989.

Egan, Frances. "Computation and Content." *The Philosophical Review* 104 (1995): 443–459.

Fodor, Jerry. *The Language of Thought*. New York: Thomas Y. Crowell, 1975.

Fodor, Jerry. *Psychosemantics: The Problem of Meaning in the Philosophy of Mind*. Cambridge, MA: MIT Press, 1987.

Fodor, Jerry, and Zenon Pylyshyn. "Connectionism and Cognitive Architecture: A Critical Analysis." *Cognition* 28 (1988): 3–71.

Penrose, Roger. *The Emperor's New Mind: Concerning Computers, Minds, and the Laws of Physics*. Oxford: Oxford University Press, 1989.

Searle, John. "Minds, Brains, and Programs." *Behavioral and Brain Sciences* 3 (1980): 417–424.

Searle, John. *The Rediscovery of the Mind*. Cambridge, MA: MIT Press, 1992.

Sterelny, Kim. *The Representational Theory of Mind: An Introduction*. Oxford: Blackwells, 1990.

Ullman, Shimon. *The Interpretation of Visual Motion*. Cambridge, MA: MIT Press, 1979.

Frances Egan (2005)

COMPUTATIONAL MODEL OF MIND

See *Computationalism*

COMPUTER ETHICS

Computer ethics is a branch of applied ethics that considers ethical issues raised or significantly amplified by computer technology. The field is sometimes referred to by other terms such as "cyberethics," "information ethics," "information communications technology ethics," "global information ethics," and "Internet ethics." But, whatever the field is called, the computer remains the essential technological feature. Although some computing technology, for example the abacus, is centuries old, computer ethics has developed as a philosophical field with the advent of modern, digital, electronic computing. Modern computing technology, which includes hardware, software, and networks, is highly flexible and powerful. Computers can be programmed and in some cases trained to perform a wide range of functions. Because of this logical malleability computers carry out numerous and diverse applications in society. Computer chips are ubiquitous. They are embedded in everyday items such as cars and clothing, toys and tools, and pets and people.

Communication that depends upon computer technology has grown dramatically through widespread use of the cell phones, global positioning systems, and the Internet. In the early twenty-first century, people in developed countries live in computationally revolutionized and informationally enriched environments. Because computing has become so integrated in society, computer ethics has expanded dramatically to issues involving most activities within society including education, law, business, government, and the military. Through its extensive growth computer ethics is a field of applied ethics that intersects and affects virtually all other branches of applied ethics.

Computer ethics is interesting philosophically, not merely because computing technology is widely used, but because the application of computing technology raises intriguing conceptual issues and serious ethical problems for society. This happens frequently because computers are logically malleable and can be configured to perform old tasks in new ways and to accomplish strikingly new tasks. When computing technology is deployed in novel ways, ethical guidelines for its use are frequently unclear or nonexistent. This creates policy vacuums that may be accompanied by conceptual confusions about how to understand the computerized situation adequately. Hence, computer ethics typically demands doing more than routinely applying ethical principles to ethical issues in computing. Rather computer ethics requires an analysis of the nature and impact of the computing technology and the corresponding formulation and justification of policies for the ethical use of such technology. Listing all of the subject matter of computer ethics would be difficult as the field continues to expand as the application of computing grows, but broadly speaking traditional areas of investigation and analysis include privacy, property, power, security, and professionalism.

Because computers rapidly store and search vast amounts of information, privacy has been an ongoing concern of computer ethics. Personal information in medical documents, criminal records, and credit histories is easily retrieved and transmitted to others electronically, and as a result individuals are vulnerable to the improper disclosure of sensitive information and to the introduction of unknown errors into their records. The threat to privacy has been increasing in part because computing technology enables an enormous amount of information gathering to occur in subtle and undetectable ways. Internet stores track purchases of individuals and place cookies on personal computers inconspicuously. Computerized cameras in satellites, public places, private establishments, and personal cell phones record without notice. Computers utilizing global-positioning satellites routinely track locations of vehicles. Spyware installed on computers surreptitiously surveils the computing activities of unsuspecting users. In general, personal information can be collected from many sources and potentially assembled in databases that can be further merged, matched, and mined to construct profiles of the lives of individuals. Many fear that the widespread use of computers to collect information is creating a panopticon society in which too many details of individual lives are known by others, leaving people with dramatically reduced levels of privacy. Philosophical analyses of the nature of privacy, the policies to protect privacy, and the justifications for privacy are more important than ever.

Property is also a major issue within computer ethics. This has become increasingly important because of the significant growth in hardware and software and the computerization of many popular products including art, photos, music, movies, and games that are produced, transmitted, and portrayed using a digital format. Because digital information can be copied so easily and accurately, the extent to which digital products should be owned and protected is heavily debated. Some libertarians on this issue argue that "information wants to be free" and that traditional intellectual property restrictions should not apply. For instance, those in the open source software movement advocate licensing that permits the free redistribution of software and requires accessibility to a program's source code so that it can be tested and improved by others. Those who advocate the ownership of intellectual digital property argue that with ownership comes pride and profit incentive that will generate digital products that otherwise would never be produced.

Debates over the rights of ownership raise many difficult philosophical issues. What is it that is owned and how should it be protected? A computer disk itself does not have much value; it is the information on the disk that matters. Information seems to be nothing more than an idea and ideas are not normally given intellectual property protection. As an example, consider again computer programs. Computer programs are algorithmic and hence mathematical in nature. This suggests that computer programs, like the Pythagorean theorem, should not be owned at all. However, computer programs generally are fixed in a tangible medium and are lengthy, original human expressions. As such they are appropriately covered by copyright protection. Yet, in their operation on machines computer programs are often novel, useful, nonobvious processes and hence are properly patentable. How, or even whether, computer programs should be protected depends largely on one's philosophical analysis of the nature of computer programs and on a justification of protecting intellectual property.

The basic philosophical issues of computerized property extend well beyond computer programs to every product in digital form. A movie that costs millions of dollars to make can be copied at no significant cost. If a movie is copied illegally using the Internet, to what extent should various contributors be held accountable—the person downloading the copy, the person who maintains a directory on the Internet informing people where copies are located, the person who makes a digital version available for others to copy, the company that makes the software specifically designed to copy movies easily over the Internet, or the Internet service provider?

Computers can create and shift relationships of power. Because computers allow individuals to perform tasks more easily and to accomplish some activities that they could never do without them, those who have access to computers have access to power. As a consequence, an obvious social concern is the disparity in advantage of those who have access to computing, for example in school, over those who do not. Unequal distribution of power may require ethical countermeasures to ensure fairness. To what extent, for example, should disabled citizens be assured of equal access to computing technology? To some degree the Internet has helped to correct this imbalance of power and even shift power toward the individual. For a modest fee individuals can advertise personal items for sale on the Web to a large audience. Politicians who are not well connected to an established political group can run an Internet campaign to express their ideas and to solicit funds. Independent hotel operators can unite through an Internet reservation service to compete with the larger hotel chains.

But the Internet's ability to shift power to the individual allows one person to solicit children to arrange illicit sexual encounters, to send spam e-mails to millions of people, and to spread viruses and worms. Moreover, Internet power shifts can sometimes result in making the strong even stronger. Large corporations can outsource jobs to cheaper labor markets and dominant militaries can enhance their capabilities with computerized communication and weapons. These power shifts raise philosophical questions about what the new relationships should be One of the most important power questions is who should govern the Internet itself.

The issue of rights and responsibilities of individuals on the Internet is complex because the Internet that supports the Web is worldwide. Different countries have different laws and customs and therefore have different concerns about the Web. Any given country may have great difficulty enforcing its concerns with information coming and going beyond its borders. Consider differences with regard to free speech as just one example. France and Germany have been concerned about prohibiting hate speech. China has targeted political speech. In the United States the focus has been largely on controlling pornography over the Internet. Even within a country's borders free speech often raises perplexing conceptual issues. For instance, should pornography that utilizes virtual children be regulated differently than pornography displaying actual children? But, even assuming agreement on the law, how does a country stop or punish a violator of free speech on the Internet who is located in some remote location in the world? Should the law be change to accommodate the realities of the Internet?

Not surprisingly security is as a fundamental problem on the Internet. Computer users can act from a distance over networks and thereby can accomplish goals without being observed. Hackers can break into computers and remove or alter data without being detected. Ordinary citizens can use tools on the Web to gather information from public documents in order to steal the identities of others. Terrorists can disrupt entire networks that control vital resources such as the electric power grid. The lack of security on the Internet is reminiscent of Plato's story of the ring of Gyges that allowed a shepherd to act invisibly. Plato posed the question, Why should someone be just if he can get away with being unjust? Plato's question is not just an abstract theoretical issue given the availability of current computer technology. If an Internet user can act unjustly and get away with it, why should he or she not do it?

Many people who design and operate computing systems regard themselves as computing professionals. But, given that anyone, regardless of educational background, can be hired to do computing, what does it mean to claim that someone is a computing professional? To what standards, including ethical standards, should computing professionals adhere? Although several codes of ethics have been offered to clarify what duties and responsibilities computer professionals have, professional responsibility has been difficult to establish for at least two reasons. First, unlike medicine and law, the field does not have a tradition of professional qualifying examinations and licensing, and therefore enforcement of any code of ethics is difficult. Second, the nature of computing itself makes the assessment of responsibility difficult. Computer programs are often enormously complex, written by dozens of people, and incomprehensible to any one person. Moreover, such large computer programs are brittle in that a tiny, obscure error can shatter the performance of the entire system under certain conditions. To what extent should computing professionals be regarded as liable when such difficult to predict errors lead to major failures or even catastrophic results?

Although traditionally computer ethics has focused on the ethics of computing situations, a philosophically rich part of the field is computational ethics that considers the impact computing has or theoretically may have on ethics itself. Philosophical issues in this area include questions such as: In what ways can ethical decision making be properly assisted by computational methods? In principle, could a computer ever make appropriate ethical decisions? Could computer implants in humans enhance and possibly alter human values? And, could a computer, or perhaps a robot, ever have rights or moral responsibilities?

See also Applied Ethics; Power; Property; Rights.

Bibliography

Bynum, T. W., and S. Rogerson, eds. *Computer Ethics and Professional Responsibility*. Oxford: Basil Blackwell, 2004.

Johnson, D. G. *Computer Ethics*. 3rd ed. Englewood Cliffs, NJ: Prentice-Hall, 2000.

Johnson, D. G., and H. Nissenbaum, eds. *Computers, Ethics, and Social Value*. Englewood Cliffs, NJ: Prentice-Hall, 1995.

Moor, J. H. "What Is Computer Ethics?" *Metaphilosophy* 16 (4) (1985): 266–275.

Spinello, R. A. *CyberEthics: Morality and Law in Cyberspace*. 2nd ed. Sudbury, MA: Jones and Bartlett, 2003.

Spinello, R. A., and H. T. Tavani, eds. *Readings in Cyberethics*. 2nd ed. Sudbury, MA: Jones and Bartlett, 2004.

Tavani, H. T. *Ethics and Technology: Ethical Issues in an Age of Information and Communication Technology*. Hoboken, NJ: John Wiley, 2004.

James H. Moor (1996, 2005)

COMPUTING MACHINES

Any thorough discussion of computing machines requires the examination of rigorous concepts of computation and is facilitated by the distinction between mathematical, symbolical, and physical computations. The delicate connection between the three kinds of computations and the underlying questions "What are machines?" and "When are they computing?" motivate an extensive theoretical and historical discussion. The relevant outcome of this discussion is formulated at the beginning of section 3.

The paradigm of the first kind of computation is given when a human calculator determines, by finitely many and mathematically meaningful steps, the values of number-theoretic functions for particular arguments. The informal concept of such effectively calculable functions is thought to be captured by Kurt Gödel's concept of general recursive functions. The latter notion was introduced in 1934 and arose in an intellectual context that includes the contemporaneous development of David Hilbert's program as well as earlier steps toward modern logic and abstract mathematics.

Alan M. Turing and Emil Post initiated in 1936 a shift from mathematically meaningful steps to basic, not further analyzable ones that underlie mathematical computations. They investigated symbolic processes carried out by human calculators and proposed essentially the same model of symbolic computation that is mathematically presented now by a Turing machine. Turing took, however, an additional, most significant step: He devised a universal machine that can execute the program of any Turing machine, and he had it carry out the necessary symbolic operations. This construction allowed him to prove the effective unsolvability of the halting and decision problems.

The physical details of how a universal machine could actually be constructed did not matter for Turing's theoretical investigations in 1936, but obviously did when he was involved in designing and building an Automatic Computing Engine (ACE). In modern digital computers controlled physical processes are used to realize, efficiently, the stepwise operations of a universal machine. That seems to be true even for quantum computing. In analog computing physical processes are used in a different way. However, independently of the mode of the physical computation, the question can be raised, whether there are physical processes that are carried out by a computing machine, but do not fall under Turing computations.

1. MATHEMATICAL COMPUTATIONS

Human calculating provides a rich prehistory for the development of machines that can take over routine computational tasks. This prehistory points to the pervasive impact computing machines will develop: from the broadly intellectual and socioeconomic to the highly focused scientific. Before coming to the technological challenge of building machines that mimic processes on symbolic configurations, one has to address the problem of determining the nature of such processes and those aspects that are crucial for their machine implementation. After all, physical representations of the symbolic configurations are needed, and machines have to perform on them physical operations that correspond to the symbolic ones.

1.1. PREHISTORY. In the sixteenth and seventeenth centuries Wilhelm Schickard, Blaise Pascal, Gottfried Wilhelm Leibniz, and others constructed mechanical calculators to carry out basic arithmetical operations. The calculatory roots go back, however, not just to ancient Greece but also to Egypt and Mesopotamia; important developments took place also in China, India, and in many different parts of the world under Arab influence. It is no accident for the evolution of computing that algebra and algorithm etymologically come from the same Arab source: the title of a widely used book and the agnomen of its author (Muhammed ibn Musa al-Kwarizmi).

The construction of mechanical calculators is prima facie narrower than the development of other scientific tools and yet it was pursued as having, potentially, a much broader impact through the intimate connection of computing with mathematics and logic. That was clearly sensed and expressed with great expectations by Leibniz. Of course, there had been aids to computation in the form of neatly arranged configurations of pebbles, for example. Another efficient aid had been the Chinese abacus that allows, via a good representation of natural numbers, the human calculator to add, subtract, multiply, and divide through strictly local manipulations of beads. The configurations of the abacus serve as the representation of input, intermediate results, and output of the calculation; they are essentially aids to memory.

The difference between abacus-like devices and mechanical calculators (as developed by Schickard, Pascal, and Leibniz) is formulated in an illuminating way by Charles Babbage:

> Calculating machines comprise various pieces of mechanism for assisting the human mind in executing the operations of arithmetic. Some few of these perform the whole operation without any mental attention when once the given numbers have been put into the machine.
>
> Others require a moderate portion of mental attention: these latter are generally of much simpler construction than the former, and it may also be added, are less useful. (1864/1994, p. 30)

The abacus certainly requires a moderate portion of mental attention, whereas Babbage's difference engine is perfectly in line with the development of automatic computing machines. The difference engine was intended to determine the values of polynomials for given arguments by the method of finite differences; the results were to be printed by the machine and to create reliable tables useful for astronomy and navigation. The evolution of the difference engine brought to light the economic importance of computing and the consequent governmental support of related research. (The British government sponsored Babbage's work; the Swedish government supported the work of Georg Edward Scheutz, who was inspired by a description of Babbage's machine and constructed a difference engine in 1834; an improved version was built between 1851 and 1853 with funds from the Swedish Academy.)

Babbage took later another important conceptual step when developing his analytical engine. He followed the lead of Joseph Marie Jacquard, who had used "cards with holes" as a means of programming a loom to weave intricate patterns. Babbage devised, but never fully constructed, a programmable computing machine with a rather modern organization. In chapter 8 of *Passages from the Life of a Philosopher*, Babbage writes after having described the process of the Jacquard loom:

> The analogy of the Analytical Engine with this well-known process is nearly perfect. The Analytical Engine consists of two parts:
>
> 1. The store in which all the variables to be operated upon, as well as all those quantities which have arisen from the result of other operations, are placed.
>
> 2. The mill into which the quantities about to be operated upon are always brought.Every formula which the Analytical Engine can be required to compute consists of certain algebraical operations to be performed upon given letters, and of certain other modifications depending on the numerical value assigned to those letters. (1864/1994, p. 89)

Evidently, *store* corresponds to the memory and *mill* to the central processing unit of a contemporary computer. The programming constructs in Babbage's design are of such a general character that, Robin Gandy (1980) asserts, the number theoretic functions that are Babbage calculable are precisely those that are Turing computable.

The generality of computational issues, beyond their connection with arithmetic and analysis, is emphasized through the algebraic treatment of logic in the hands of George Boole, Augustus De Morgan, Charles Sanders Peirce, and Ernst Schröder, among others. In this line of research the decision problem was formulated and considered as a central issue. Even in the traditional Aristotelian presentation of logic computational features were considered to be significant by Raymundus Lullus and, importantly, by Leibniz in his project of constructing a universal language and an appropriate calculus ratiocinator. A logical machine in that tradition was built by William Stanley Jevons and described in the *Proceedings of the Royal Society* for January 20, 1870. Finally, it should be mentioned that Gottlob Frege claimed in *Grundgesetze der Arithmetik* (1893) that in his logical system "inference is conducted like a calculation," but continued, "I do not mean this in a narrow sense, as if it were subject to an algorithm the same as … ordinary addition and multiplication, but only in the sense that there is an algorithm at all, i.e., a totality of rules which governs the transition from one sentence or from two sentences to a new one in such a way that nothing happens except in conformity with these rules."

Within mathematics at that time, Leopold Kronecker insisted on the decidability of mathematical notions and the calculability of functions. These logical and mathematical developments were joined in formal mathematics, when Hilbert exploited the effective metamathematical description of formal theories (in his consistency program) and shifted effectiveness requirements from mathematics to metamathematics. It is here that modern computability theory found its ultimate motivation through the emphasis of the decision problem (*Entscheidungsproblem*) in the Hilbert School and the systematic articulation of the significance of Gödel's incompleteness theorems; both issues required a rigorous mathematical concept of effective method or mechanical procedure. Though these issues could have been addressed in their formulation for symbolic configurations, it took a detour through the calculability of number theoretic functions to arrive at sharp mathematical notions.

1.2. UNIFORM CALCULABILITY. Richard Dedekind formulated in his 1888 essay "Was sind und was sollen die Zahlen?" the general concept of a primitive recursive function and proved that all these calculable functions can be made explicit in his logicist framework. Dedekind's idea for the proof was very abstract, namely, to show the existence of unique solutions for functional equations of the form

$$\psi(0) = \omega,$$

$$\psi(\varphi(n)) = \theta(\psi(n)),$$

where ω ?is an element of N, φ is the successor function, and θ an arbitrary given function from N to N. This general point recurs in the early 1920s, for example, in the work of Hilbert, Thoralf Skolem, and Jacques Herbrand. However, the existence of solutions is no longer to be guaranteed by abstract logicist or set theoretic considerations, but by the availability of suitable calculation procedures. Implicit in these discussions is the specification of the class PR of primitive recursive functions. Hilbert's 1925 essay, "On the Infinite," defines this class inductively, in almost the standard contemporary form, by specifying initial functions and closing under the definitional schemas of composition and primitive recursion. One shows by an easy inductive argument that the values of primitive recursive functions can be determined by an effective procedure for any given argument. All primitive recursive functions are in this sense calculable, but there are calculable functions that are not primitive recursive. Hilbert discussed an example due to Wilhelm Ackermann prominently already in 1925.

Herbrand viewed the Ackermann function in 1931 as finitistically calculable. In his systems of arithmetic he considered different classes F of finitist functions for which recursion equations were available. The defining axioms for the elements in F had to satisfy in particular this calculability condition, which had to be proved by finitist means, "We must be able to show, by means of intuitionistic [i.e., finitist] proofs, that with these [defining] axioms it is possible to compute the value of the functions univocally for each specified system of values of their arguments" (letter to Gödel in *Gödel's Collected Works V*, p. 15). The issue of characterizing classes of finitistically calculable functions was crucial for Herbrand's reflections on Gödel's second incompleteness theorem and its impact on Hilbert's program. Inspired by Herbrand's formulation, Gödel defined in his Princeton lectures of 1934 the class of general recursive functions; its definition no longer depends on the problematic concept of finitist provability.

Gödel's class of functions includes all primitive recursive functions and those of the Ackermann type. Assume, Gödel suggests, you are given a finite sequence $\psi_1, \ldots, \psi_k$ of known functions and a symbol ϕ for an unknown one. Then substitute these symbols "in one another in the most general fashions" *Gödel's Collected Works I*, p. 368) and equate certain pairs of the resulting expressions. If the selected set of functional equations has exactly one solution, consider ϕ as denoting a "recursive" function; the definition of general recursive functions is obtained by insisting on two restrictive conditions. The first stipulates a standard form of certain terms, whereas the second condition demands that for every 1-tuple $k_1, \ldots, k_l$ there is exactly one m such that $\phi(k_1, \ldots, k_l) = m$ is a derived equation. The set of derived equations is specified inductively. The basic clauses guarantee that all numerical instances of a given equation as well as all true equalities $\psi_{ij}(x_1, \ldots, x_n) = m$ are derived equations. The rules that allow steps from already obtained equations to additional ones are formulated as follows:

(**R.1**) Replace occurrences of $\psi_{ij}(x_1, \ldots, x_n)$ by m, if $\psi_{ij}(x_1, \ldots, x_n) = m$ is a derived equation;

(**R.2**) Replace occurrences of $\phi(x_1, \ldots, x_l)$ on the right-hand side of a derived equation by m, if $\phi(x_1, \ldots, xl) = m$ is a derived equation.

Gödel emphasized two central features in his definition when comparing it to Herbrand's: first, the precise specification of mechanical rules for carrying out numerical computations in a uniform way; second, the formulation of the regularity condition requiring calculable functions to be total, but without insisting on a finitist proof of that fact.

1.3. NORMAL FORM AND THE μ-OPERATOR. Using Gödel's arithmetization technique to describe provability in the equational calculus Stephen Cole Kleene analyzed the class of general recursive functions in 1936. The uniform and effective generation of the derived equations allowed him to establish an important theorem that is called now Kleene's normal form theorem: *for every recursive function* φ *there are primitive recursive functions* ψ *and* ρ *such that* $\varphi(x_1, \ldots, x_n)$ *equals* $\psi(\varepsilon y.\rho(x_1, \ldots, x_n, y) = 0)$, *where for every n-tuple* $x_1, \ldots, x_n$ *there is a y such that* $\rho(x_1, \ldots, x_n, y) = 0$. The latter equation expresses that y is (the code of) a computation from the equations that define φ for the arguments $x_1, \ldots, x_n$; $\varepsilon y.\rho(x_1, \ldots, x_n, y) = 0$ provides the smallest y, such that $\rho(x_1, \ldots, x_n, y) = 0$, if there is a y for the given arguments (it yields 0 otherwise). Finally, the function ψ considers the last equation in the given computation and determines the numerical value of the term on the r.h.s of that equation, which is a numeral and represents the value of φ for the given arguments $x_1, \ldots, x_n$. This theorem, or rather its proof, is remarkable: it allows to establish equivalences of different formulations with great ease; what is needed for the proof is only that the inference or computation steps are all primitive recursive.

Hilbert and Paul Bernays had introduced in the first volume of their *Grundlagen der Mathematik* (1934) a μ-operator that functioned in just the way the ε-operator did for Kleene. The μ notation was adopted later by Kleene and is still being used in computability theory. Indeed, the μ-operator is at the heart of the definition of a new class of number theoretic functions, the so-called *μ-recursive functions*, and the normal form theorem is the crucial stepping stone in proving that this class of functions is co-extensional with that of Gödel's general recursive ones. The μ-recursive functions are specified inductively in the same way as the primitive recursive ones, except that a third closure condition is formulated:

if $\rho(x_1, \dots, x_n, y)$ is μ-recursive and for every n-tuple $x_1, \dots, x_n$ there is a y such that $\rho(x_1, \dots, x_n, y) = 0$, then the function $\theta(x_1, \dots, x_n)$ given by $\mu y.\rho(x_1, \dots, x_n, y) = 0$ is also μ-recursive.

Gödel's concept characterized a class of calculable functions that contained all known effectively calculable functions. Footnote 3 of the Princeton lectures seems to express a form of Alonzo Church's thesis. In a letter to Martin Davis of February 15, 1965, Gödel rejected that interpretation, "The conjecture stated there only refers to the equivalence of 'finite (computation) procedure' and 'recursive procedure.' However, I was, at the time of these lectures, not at all convinced that my concept of recursion comprises all possible recursions; and in fact the equivalence between my definition and Kleene's … is not quite trivial" (Davis 1982, p. 8). At that time in early 1934 Gödel was equally unconvinced by Church's proposal that effective calculability should be identified with λ-definability; he called the proposal "thoroughly unsatisfactory." That was reported by Church to Kleene on November 29, 1935. In the following year Gödel observed the absoluteness of general recursive functions: If the value of a general recursive function can be computed in a finite or even transfinite type extension of arithmetic, then it can be computed already in arithmetic. Gödel added this important observation to his 1936 paper *On the Length of Proofs* and viewed it as providing evidence that an important and stable class of functions had been isolated. The next section presents considerations of some of the pioneers, obviously including Gödel, as to their reasons why the mathematically rigorous notion of machine computation introduced by Turing, and not general recursiveness, was ultimately viewed as providing the correct concept of mechanical procedure.

2. CONCEPTUAL ANALYSIS

Returning to the beginning, one notices a shift from effective mathematical calculations to mechanical operations of a machine. Church maintained in 1935 that the former are properly captured by the calculations involving general recursive functions. Clearly, if one has appropriate machines that allow the calculation of the base functions and mimic composition, recursion, and minimization, then all recursive functions and thus all effectively calculable ones are seen to be machine computable. Gödel argued in exactly that way in his 193? paper and drew broader conclusions. He asserted that the characteristics of his equational calculus "are exactly those that give the correct definition of a computable function." He expanded that assertion by, "That this really is the correct definition of mechanical computability was established beyond any doubt by Turing" (*Gödel's Collected Works III*, p. 168). The equivalence between general recursiveness and Turing computability is taken to support this claim.

2.1. CHURCH'S THESIS.

Almost a year after his conversation with Gödel, Church came back to his proposal in a letter to Bernays dated January 23, 1935; he conjectured that the λ-calculus may be a system that allows the representability of all constructively defined functions. When Church wrote this letter, he knew that all general recursive functions are λ-definable; the converse was established in collaboration with Kleene by March 1935. This mathematical equivalence and the quasi-empirical adequacy of λ-definability provided the background for the public articulation of Church's thesis. Church announced it in a talk contributed to the meeting of the American Mathematical Society in New York City on April 19, 1935, but formulated it with general recursiveness, not λ-definability as the mathematically rigorous notion.

In his 1936 paper Church restated his proposal for identifying the class of effectively calculable functions with a precisely defined class. To give a deeper analysis Church discussed, in section 7 of his paper, two methods of characterizing the effective calculability of number-theoretic functions. The first of these methods uses the notion of algorithm, and the second employs the notion of calculability in a logic. He argues that neither method leads to a definition that is more general than recursiveness. These arguments have a parallel structure, and this entry discusses only the one pertaining to the second method. Church considers a logic **L**, that is a system of symbolic logic whose language contains the equality symbol =, a symbol { }( ) for the application of a unary function symbol to its argument, and numerals for the positive integers. He defines, "F is *effectively calculable* if and only if there is an expression f in the logic **L** such that: $\{f\}(\mu) = \nu$ is a theorem of **L** iff F(m) = n; here, μ and ν are expressions that stand for the positive integers m and n." Church claims that F is recursive, assuming that **L** satisfies a certain step condition that amounts to requiring the theorem predicate of **L** to be recursively enumerable. The claim follows immediately by an application of the μ-operator; the argument parallels that for Kleene's normal form theorem.

The general concept of calculability is thus explicated by that of derivability in a logic, and Church uses the step condition to sharpen the idea that within such a logical formalism one operates with an effective notion of immediate consequence. The thesis is thus appealed to only in a special case. Given the crucial role this condition plays, it is appropriate to view it as a normative requirement: The steps of any effective procedure (governing derivations of a symbolic logic) must be recursive. If this requirement is accepted and a function is defined to be effectively calculable as above, then Church's step-by-step argument proves that all effectively calculable functions are recursive.

Church gave two reasons for the thesis, namely, (1) the quasi-empirical observation that all known calculable functions are general recursive and (2) the mathematical fact of the equivalence of two differently motivated notions. A third reason comes directly from the 1936 paper, the step-by-step argument from a core conception. However, Church and Gödel found in the end Turing's machine model of computation much more convincing. Church's 1937 review of Turing's paper for the *Journal of Symbolic Logic* asserts that Turing computability has the advantage over general recursiveness and λ-definability of "making the identification with effectiveness in the ordinary (not explicitly defined) sense evident immediately" (pp. 42–43)

2.2. FINITE MACHINES. Church's more detailed argument for the immediate evidence starts out as follows:

> The author [Turing] proposes as a criterion that an infinite sequence of digits 0 and 1 be "computable" that it shall be possible to devise a computing machine, occupying a finite space and with working parts of finite size, which will write down the sequence to any desired number of terms if allowed to run for a sufficiently long time. As a matter of convenience, certain further restrictions are imposed on the character of the machine, but these are of such a nature as obviously to cause no loss of generality—in particular, a human calculator, provided with pencil and paper and explicit instructions, can be regarded as a kind of Turing machine.

He then draws the conclusion, "It is thus immediately clear that computability, so defined, can be identified with … the notion of effectiveness as it appears in certain mathematical problems" (pp. 42–43). Why Turing's notion should convey this immediate conviction Church does not explain; the step from a computing machine "occupying a finite space and with working parts of finite size" to Turing machines is not deepened.

Gödel commented on Turing's notion in his 1951 Gibbs lecture publicly for the first time and made remarks similar to Church's. He explores there the implications of the incompleteness theorems, not in their original formulation, but in a "much more satisfactory form" that is "due to the work of various mathematicians." He stresses, "The greatest improvement was made possible through the precise definition of the concept of finite procedure, which plays such a decisive role in these results" (*Gödel's Collected Works III*, p. 304). There are, Gödel points out, different ways of arriving at a precise definition of finite procedure, which all lead to exactly the same concept.

However, and here is Gödel's substantive remark on Turing, "The most satisfactory way … [of arriving at such a definition] is that of reducing the concept of finite procedure to that of a machine with a finite number of parts, as has been done by the British mathematician Turing" (*Gödel's Collected Works*, pp. 304–305). Gödel does not expand on this brief remark. In particular, he gives no hint of how reduction is to be understood or why the concept of such a restricted machine is equivalent to that of a Turing machine. At this point, it seems, the ultimate justification lies in the pure and perhaps rather crude fact that finite procedures can be reduced to computations of finite machines.

In a deep sense, neither Church nor Gödel seem to have recognized the distinctive character of Turing's analysis, that is, the move from arithmetically motivated calculations to general symbolic processes that underlie them. Most importantly in the given intellectual context, these processes have to be carried out programmatically by human beings: the *Entscheidungsproblem* had to be solved by humans in a mechanical way; it was the normative demand of radical intersubjectivity between humans that motivated the step from axiomatic to formal systems. For this reason Turing brings in human computers and exploits the limitations of their processing capacities, when proceeding mechanically. The Turing machine is in the end nothing but, as Gandy (1980) puts it, a codification of the human computer.

2.3. COMPUTORS. One can call a human computing agent who proceeds mechanically a *computor*; such a computor operates on finite configurations of symbols and, for Turing, deterministically so. At issue is then, how does one step from calculations of computors to computations of Turing machines? Turing explores, as he put it, the extent of the computable numbers (or, equivalently, of the effectively calculable functions) by considering two-dimensional calculations in a child's arithmetic book. Such calculations are reduced to symbolic steps on linear configurations of such a simple character that a

Turing machine operating on strings (instead of letters) can carry them out. Turing's argument concludes, "We may now construct a machine to do the work of the computer. … The machines just described [string machines] do not differ very essentially from computing machines as defined in §2 [letter machines], and corresponding to any machine of this type a computing machine can be constructed to compute the same sequence, that is to say the sequence computed by the computer" (*The Undecidable*, p. 138).

It is important to recall Turing's goal of isolating the basic steps of computations, that is, steps that need not be further subdivided. This leads to the demand that the configurations, which are operated on, must be immediately recognizable by the computor. Combined with the evident limitation of the computor's sensory apparatus, this demand motivates convincingly two restrictive conditions:

(**B**) (*Boundedeness*) There is a fixed finite bound on the number of configurations a computor can immediately recognize

(**L**) (*Locality*) A computor can change only immediately recognizable (sub-) configurations

Turing's considerations, sketched earlier, lead rigorously from operations of a computor on linear configurations to operations of a letter machine and can be generalized to other syntactic or graphic configurations. It should be noted that these constraints apply to Turing machines, but are violated by Gödel's equational calculus, as the replacement operations naturally involve terms of arbitrary complexity.

Turing's analysis secures the generality of mathematical results (e.g., of the incompleteness theorems) and their conclusiveness (e.g., of the undecidability of predicate logic) by respecting the intellectual context that appealed to effective operations carried out by humans without invoking higher mental capacities. It was after all the decision problem, the *Entscheidungsproblem* in the title of Turing's 1936 article, that motivated Turing's work. Its positive solution required "a procedure … that permits—for a given logical expression—to decide the validity, respectively satisfiability, by finitely many operations." Hilbert and Ackermann gave that formulation (pp. 72–73) in their book *Grundzüge der theoretischen Logik* (1928) and considered the decision problem as the main problem of mathematical logic. Why that problem should be considered as the main problem of mathematical logic is stated clearly in their remark, "The solution of this general decision problem would allow us to decide, at least in principle, the provability or unprovability of an arbitrary mathematical statement" (p. 86). Taking for granted the finite axiomatizability of set theory or some other fundamental theory in first-order logic, the general decision problem is solved when that for first-order logic has been solved.

A negative solution of the decision problem required, however, a rigorous characterization of finite procedures and a proof that none of them answers Hilbert and Ackermann's demand. Turing did both, as he gave a convincing conceptual analysis, established the effective unsolvability of the halting problem (or rather of the equivalent printing problem), and showed how to reduce it to the decision problem. Thus, if the latter were effectively solvable, then the halting problem would be; but as it is not, one has a contradiction. The proof of the unsolvability of the halting problem makes crucial use of a particular Turing machine, the universal machine U that, when presented on its tape with the program of a Turing machine M and an input, executes M's program for that input. This particular machine will play a special role in the next section.

3. PHYSICAL REALIZATION

For the further considerations, the most significant outcome of the previous historical and conceptual examination can be restated sharply as follows: Turing's notion of machine computation is obtained by an analysis of symbolic calculations carried out by computors. To put it negatively, Turing's notion is not obtained by an independent analysis of physical devices with the goal of, first, defining a general notion of machine and, second, introducing an appropriate concept of computation for such machines. It was only in 1980 that Gandy gave an analysis of machines and the deterministic computations they can carry out. This is presented in the second subsection below and will be followed, in the last subsection, by a description of the special features of quantum computers. However, what amounts to the physical implementation of Turing's universal machine U is discussed first. That is an absolutely central step in the development of modern computing machines and was taken in intricately intertwined ways, it seems, by Turing and John von Neumann; their work shaped the architecture of modern computers.

3.1. IMPLEMENTING U. In the years following World War II Turing worked on various aspects of the design and the actual building of a practical version of his universal machine U. During the last three months of 1945

he wrote a remarkable document titled *Proposal for Development … of an Automatic Computing Engine (ACE)* and connected, in a lecture to the London Mathematical Society of February 20, 1947, the work on the ACE explicitly with his early theoretical work:

> Some years ago I was researching on what might now be described as an investigation of the theoretical possibilities and limitations of digital computing machines. I considered a type of machine which had a central mechanism, and an infinite memory which was contained on an infinite tape. … It was essential in these theoretical arguments that the memory should be infinite. It can easily be shown that otherwise the machine can only execute periodic operations. Machines such as the ACE may be regarded as practical versions of this same type of machine. (Turing 1947, pp. 106–107)

Turing characterized the ACE in his lecture as a typical large-scale electronic digital computing machine. From a mathematical perspective, Turing viewed being digital as the most relevant property of the ACE, since digital machines can work to any desired degree of accuracy and are not restricted, as analog machines are, to a particular type of computational problem.

From a practical point of view, the property of the ACE to be an electronic machine Turing considered as extremely important: it was to guarantee high speed and thus make it possible to execute complex procedures. The latter possibility requires, beyond the speed of basic operations, an appropriate organization of the machine, so that it can proceed fully automatically—without having to interact with a human operator—while executing a procedure. Turing emphasized, alluding to his universal machine:

> It is intended that the setting up of the machine for new problems shall be virtually only a matter of paper work. Besides the paper work nothing will have to be done except to prepare a pack of Hollerith cards in accordance with this paper work, and to pass them through a card reader connected with the machine. There will positively be no internal alterations to be made even if we wish suddenly to switch from calculating the energy levels of the neon atom to the enumeration of groups of order 720. It may appear somewhat puzzling that this can be done. How can one expect a machine to do all this multitudinous variety of things? The answer is that we should consider the machine as doing something quite simple, namely carrying out orders given to it in a standard form which it is able to understand. (Turing 1946, p. 21)

In the 1947 lecture he made the connection to the universal machine explicit; after discussing memory extensively, he claims that digital computing machines such as the ACE are just "practical versions of the universal machine." He continues, "There is a certain pool of electronic equipment, and a large memory. When any particular problem has to be handled the appropriate instructions for the computing process involved are stored in the memory of the ACE and it is then 'set up' for carrying out that process."

The requirements for building a universal machine can in the end only be satisfied, if the machine is not only digital and electronic but also large scale, as it involves demands for "storage of information or mechanical memory." Indeed, Turing pointed out already in the ACE Report that "the memory needs to be very large indeed." The principled as well as the practical issues of implementation overlapped at this point with developments in the United States. Indeed, Turing recommended reading his report "in conjunction with J. von Neumann's *Report on the EDVAC*." (Herman H. Goldstine [1972] and Andrew Hodges [1983] present complementary views on the tenuous connection between the two projects; a balanced perspective is given by Hodges [1983, pp. 555–556, note 5.26.)

von Neumann completed a first draft of his report on June 30, 1945; the report emerged out of work with the group of J. Presper Eckert and John Mauchly at the Moore School of Electrical Engineering (University of Pennsylvania, Philadelphia). The group had built one of the first electronic calculators, the Electronic Numerical Integrator and Computer (ENIAC) and was evaluating a new memory system for a second, more sophisticated calculator, the Electronic Discrete Variable Calculator (EDVAC). The demand for a large, readily accessible memory emerged out of computational practice, namely, the need to have fast access to instructions, but also to fixed constant parameters and statistical data. That was to be achieved by storing them in the machine; von Neumann writes, "The device requires a considerable memory. While it appeared, that various parts of this memory have to perform functions which differ somewhat in their nature and considerably in their purpose, it is nevertheless tempting to treat the entire memory as one organ" (Goldstine 1972, p. 194).

von Neumann shifted the attention from the technological problems of having a larger memory to logical ones concerning the basic structure of machines with a central control mechanism and extensive memory. This structure is discussed in detail by Goldstine (1972, pp. 204–210).

A higher level of generality was attained in the Electronic Computer Project at the Institute for Advanced Study at Princeton University; this project was begun in March 1946 and directed by von Neumann. The resulting IAS Computer can be viewed as a prototype of all modern computers (the "von Neumann machine"). Its basic architecture, however, is similar to that of the ACE; it is the balance between arithmetical and fundamental logical operations that is distinctive. Goldstine describes the issue as follows:

> The work of Post and Turing made it very clear that from the point of view of formal logics there was no problem to devise codes which were "in abstracto adequate to control and cause the execution of any sequence of operations which are individually available in the machine and which are, in their entirety, conceivable by the problem planner." The problem is of a practical nature and is closely allied to that connected with the choice of elementary operations in the arithmetic organ. (1972, p. 258)

Turing and von Neumann made different compromises between simplicity of basic machine operations and complexity of programs needed to execute mathematical or symbolic procedures. These choices were obviously informed not only by their different computational experience and goals but also by their broader philosophical outlook. (That is movingly described by Hodges [1983, pp. 320–333].)

3.2. DISCRETE MACHINES. Turing's U can be realized within practical limits by physical devices, and one can raise the question whether these devices are just doing things faster than humans can do, or whether they are in a principled way computationally more powerful. Church, as recalled earlier, asserted in 1937 that finite machines are essentially Turing machines; in Gödel's remarks (from 193? and 1951) that assertion is taken for granted. The claim seems to be plausible, but it does require an argument. On the one hand, there may be physical systems that do not obey the same restrictions as computors and consequently may be able to carry out computations not possible for a computor. On the other hand, there may be physically grounded limits for machines in the same way that there are psychologically based constraints for computors.

The character of individual computational steps was at the heart of the conceptual analysis. Because of physical constraints, such steps cannot be accelerated unboundedly or be made arbitrarily complex (Mundici and Sieg 1995, §3). However, there seems to be the possibility of sidestepping these constraints by usingwith massively parallel operations. Cellular automata, introduced by Stanislaw Ulam and von Neumann, operate in parallel; they do not satisfy the boundedness condition (**B**), as the configurations affected in a single computation step are potentially unbounded. They can simulate universal Turing machines and yield discrete simulations of complex physical processes. Konrad Zuse, for example, reflected on digital formulations of physics in his essay *Rechnender Raum* (1967). Edward Fredkin advocated the use of (reversible) cellular automata in physics and conjectured in his *Digital Mechanics* "that there will be found a single cellular automaton rule that models all of microscopic physics; and models it exactly" (1990, p. 254). The interested reader should consult Rolf Herken (1988), Tommaso Toffoli and Norman Margoulis (1987), and, of course, Stephen Wolfram (2002).

Gandy addresses the issue of parallel machine computations in his essay "Church's Thesis and Principles for Mechanisms" (1980), where he proposes a particular mathematical description of discrete mechanical devices and their computations. He then follows Turing's three steps of pertinent analysis, articulation of constraints, and proof of a reduction theorem. The central and novel aspect of Gandy's formulation lies in the fact that it incorporates parallelism in complete generality. Cellular automata fall directly under Gandy's formulation. And yet, the reduction theorem shows that everything calculable by a device satisfying the constraints, a Gandy machine, is already computable by a Turing machine. Here is a sketch of the main considerations.

Gandy (1980) introduces the term *discrete mechanical device* to make it vivid that his analysis is not at all concerned with analog devices, but rather with machines that are discrete and proceed step-by-step by step from one state to the next. Gandy considers two physical constraints as fundamental for such devices: (1) a lower bound on the size of atomic components and (2) an upper bound on the speed of signal propagation. Together, these constraints guarantee what the sensory limitations guarantee for computors, namely that in a given unit of time there is a bound on the number of different observable configurations and of possible actions on them. However, the incorporation of massive parallelism into the mathematical description takes in Gandy's essay a substantial amount of complex mathematical work. In Wilfried Sieg's "Calculations by Man and Machine: Conceptual Analysis" (2002), Gandy machines are axiomatized as special discrete dynamical systems, and this presentation makes clear that they are radical generalizations of Turing machines: the latter modify one bounded part of a state, whereas the former operate in parallel on arbitrarily many bounded parts to arrive at the next state of the system.

Discrete computing machines in the broadest sense, when only constrained by physically motivated boundedness and locality conditions, do not reach beyond the computational power of Turing machines; that is the general moral. Every mathematical model of physical processes faces at least two questions: How accurately does the model capture physical reality, and how efficiently can the model be used to make predictions? It is distinctive for modern developments that, on the one hand, computer simulations have led to an emphasis of algorithmic aspects of scientific laws and that, on the other hand, many physical systems are being considered as computational devices, but under what conditions can a physical system really be viewed in that way? To have one important data point for reflections on this question, this entry will now look at the case of particular quantum systems.

3.3. QUANTUM COMPUTERS. Suppose one has a photon that impinges on a beam splitter and then propagates via two different paths. Quantum theory describes the photon as going partly into each of these two components. The state of the photon is given by the superposition of the two states associated with the two components of the original beam. Any observation of the photon, however, results in either the whole photon or nothing at all. This implies that after a measurement (1) the photon changes its state from being partly in one beam and partly in the other to being entirely in one of the beams, and (2) any interference effect is lost since one of the beams no longer enters into the description of the photon. If a second beam splitter combines the two beams, then the photon will be observed with probability one in a single beam. This certainty is because of quantum interference. Quantum computation arises from the possibility of exploiting a multiplicity of parallel computational paths in superposition as well as quantum interference to amplify the probability of correct outcomes of computations.

As the photon can be in a coherent superposition of being in two beams, the basic unit of quantum information, a *qubit* (from quantum bit), is a two-state system that can be prepared in a superposition of the two logical states 0 and 1. If a computational state can be reached through several alternative paths, then its probability is the squared modulus of the sum of all the probability amplitudes for the constituent paths. (Probability amplitudes determine probabilities and these have to add up to one for any quantum computational state.) Since the probability amplitudes are complex numbers, they may cancel each other and produce destructive interference or enhance each other and produce constructive interference.

Imagine a computation that starts in the input state 0 and reaches the output state in two steps. Suppose a computational step can mimic the action of a beam splitter and generate a superposition of two intermediate output states, 0 and 1 with probability amplitudes $c_0 = i/\sqrt{2}$ and $c_1 = 1/\sqrt{2}$. Then the probability of each output is the same: $|c_0|^2 = |c_1|^2 = 1/2$. However, if the output state is measured after two computational steps, then the probability of the output 1 is one: The action of a beam splitter can be perfectly simulated by quantum computing operations that have no classical analogs. One of these is the $\sqrt{NOT}$, which when applied twice results in the logical operation *NOT*.

Since quantum mechanics describes a state transformation by means of a unitary operator, any quantum computing operation is a unitary transformation on qubits. The description of a quantum Turing machine (*QTM*) is derived from a Turing machine, but using quantum theory to define the operations carried out by the computer, which is now a physical system. Quantum interference allows a *QTM* to act on coherent superpositions of a given state and evolves them via unitary operators into other superpositions, from which the next state results with a certain probability. Any unitary operation on n qubits can be decomposed into simple operations on one or two qubits.

A collection of n qubits constitutes a quantum register of size n (the analogue of a Turing machine tape). A quantum register of two qubits can store all four numbers $|00\rangle$, $|01\rangle$, $|10\rangle$, $|11\rangle$ in superposition. Adding qubits increases the storage capacity of the register exponentially: given a quantum register of size L, a *QTM* can in one computational step perform the same mathematical operation on 2^L numbers; a classical machine has to repeat the same computation 2^L times or has to use 2^L different processors working in parallel. However, if one tries to read a number out of a superposition of the 2^L output states, then one sees just one randomly chosen number. Only after an appropriate number of computational steps can one obtain a single final result that depends—in constructive ways—on all 2^L intermediate results.

This is how quantum algorithms work. Grover's algorithm, as an example, can determine an element from an unsorted list of N items in approximately $\sqrt{N}$ steps. A classical algorithm that scans the entries one by one requires on average $N/2$ steps. Another quantum algorithm, due to Peter Shor, can factorize large integers efficiently. Here, the difference in performance between the quantum and classical algorithms seems exponential. Quantum algorithms solve some important problems more efficiently than classical ones, but they do not increase the class of computable functions.

If, using Ludwig Wittgenstein words, Turing machines are humans who calculate, then quantum Turing machines are physical systems that calculate. What made this shift possible was Deutsch's analysis leading to the assertion, "Every finitely realizable physical system can be perfectly simulated by a universal Turing computing machine operating by finite means" (Deutsch 1985, p. 99). Following David Deutsch (1985), a computing machine operates by finite means if: (1) only a finite subsystem is in motion during anyone step; (2) the motion depends only on the state of a finite subsystem; and (3) the rules that specify the motion can be given finitely in the mathematical sense (e.g., by an integer). "Turing machines," Deutsch asserts, "satisfy these conditions, and so does the universal quantum computer" (p. 100). Thus, boundedness conditions also play a significant role in characterizing the computation of a quantum system.

4. CONCLUDING REMARKS

Computing machines have taken over the tasks of computors and transcend in important ways (e.g., of power and efficiency) human computational capacities. The takeover has two bases: (1) aspects of physical or intellectual reality have a finite symbolic representation, and (2) machines can take on (part of) the effective manipulation of the physical tokens involved in a representation. The latter may consist of just simulating the mechanical steps in human operations, as Turing machines do, or it may involve complex physical processes that are used in a different way, as in the case of quantum computers, when a suitable theoretical description allows them to perform a massively parallel calculation, so to speak, in a single step.

The concrete technological and scientific challenges of building a quantum computer seem enormous. Broad issues surrounding computing machines in general are multifarious and reach from the mathematically fundamental to the methodologically problematic. Can representations, for example, contain infinite components? Are there physical processes that can be viewed as computations, but do not fall within the Turing limits? What is the conceptual nature of analogue computations? Do they have to have a mathematical description that allows a calculable determination? What are the critical physical issues concerning measurement?

The ultimate challenge, articulated by Turing, is to have machines exhibit intelligence. Implementing the universal machine U meant for Turing to build a machine with discipline; producing intelligence required in addition initiative. Here, then, is the core of Turing's challenge, "Our task is to discover the nature of this residue as it occurs in man, and to try and copy it in machines" (*Gödel's Collected Works*, p. 125). Computing machines have become in their modern form scientific tools to explore, in particular, one's own intellectual nature.

See also Boole, George; Church, Alonzo; Computability Theory; Computationalism; De Morgan, Augustus; First-Order Logic; Frege, Gottlob; Gödel, Kurt; Gödel's Theorem; Hilbert, David; Jevons, William Stanley; Leibniz, Gottfried Wilhelm; Logic, History of: Modern Logic; Logic Machines; Machine Intelligence; Mathematics, Foundations of; Neumann, John Von; Pascal, Blaise; Peirce, Charles Sanders; Quantum Mechanics; Turing, Alan M.

Bibliography

The classical 1936 papers by Church, Kleene, Post, and Turing are all reprinted in *The Undecidable: Basic Papers on Undecidable Propositions, Unsolvable Problems, and Computable Functions*, edited by Martin Davis (Hewlett, NY: Raven Press, 1965). Gödel's papers are all available in his *Collected Works*. 5 vols. (New York: Oxford University Press, 1986–2003. Turing's papers from the late 1940s are collected in *Mechanical Intelligence*, edited by D. C. Ince (Amsterdam, Netherlands: North-Holland, 1992). The classical textbook presenting the Turing-Post development of computability theory is Martin Davis's *Computability and Unsolvability* (New York: McGraw-Hill, 1958). Finally, the references to von Neumann's papers and reports are all in Goldstine (1972).

Babbage, Charles. *Passages from the Life of a Philosopher* (1864). New Brunswick, NJ: Rutgers University Press, 1994.

Davis, Martin. "Why Gödel Didn't Have Church's Thesis." *Information and Control*, 54 (1/2) (1982): 3–24.

Deutsch, David. "Quantum Theory: The Church-Turing Principle and the Universal Quantum Computer." *Proceedings of the Royal Society*, A 400 (1985).

Gandy, Robin. "Church's Thesis and Principles for Mechanisms." In *The Kleene Symposium*, edited by Jon Barwise, H. Jerome Keisler, and Kenneth Kunen. Amsterdam, Netherlands: North-Holland, 1980.

Goldstine, Herman H. *The Computer from Pascal to von Neumann*. Princeton, NJ: Princeton University Press, 1972.

Herken, Rolf, ed. *The Universal Turing Machine. A Half-Century Survey*. New York: Oxford University Press, 1988.

Hodges, Andrew. *Alan Turing: The Enigma*. New York: Simon and Schuster, 1983.

Mundici, Daniele, and Wilfried Sieg. "Paper Machines." *Philosophia Mathematica* 3 (1995).

Sieg, Wilfried. "Calculations by Man and Machine: Conceptual Analysis." In *Reflections on the Foundations of Mathematics: Essays in Honor of Solomon Feferman*, edited by Wilfried Sieg, Richard Sommer, and Carolyn Talcott. Urbana, IL: Association for Symbolic Logic, 2002.

Toffoli, Tommaso, and Norman Margoulis. *Cellular Automata Machines: A New Environment for Modeling*. Cambridge, MA: MIT Press, 1987.

Wolfram, Stephen. *A New Kind of Science*. Champaign, IL: Wolfram Media, 2002.

Wilfried Sieg (2005)
Rossella Lupacchini (2005)

COMTE, AUGUSTE

(1798–1857)

Auguste Comte was a French positivist philosopher. Positivism may be viewed as either a philosophical system and method or as a philosophy of history. In the latter aspect, Comte's work was almost an early history of science. He has a good claim to having originated the new science of sociology; certainly, he coined the term. His political philosophy, elaborated on the basis of his positive sociology, was a noteworthy attempt to reconcile science with religion, and the ideals of the Revolution of 1789 with the doctrine of the counterrevolution of his own time. His influence on nineteenth-century thought was strong, he had numerous disciples, such as Émile Littré, and sympathetic supporters, such as John Stuart Mill. His ideas still have important meaning and interest.

LIFE

Comte was born in Montpellier, France. Although his family were ardent Catholics, he announced at the age of fourteen that he had "naturally ceased believing in God." At this time he also seems to have abandoned his family's royalism and to have become a republican.

Comte's relations with his family were strained throughout his life. His mother, twelve years older than her husband, clutched at the son. She once wrote asking for word from him "the way a beggar asks for bread to sustain life" threatening that he would know what he had lost only when she was dead. His father and sister constantly complained of ill health; the latter appears to have suffered from hysteria. Comte portrayed them all as covetous and hypocritical and accused them of keeping him in financial distress. The facts, however, suggest that they did what they could for the son and brother whom they loved and admired but found so strange. It is necessary, in order to understand Comte's philosophy and polity, to comprehend his family's compelling influence on him. Although he rejected the ties to his parents and sister (he also had a brother), with their Catholic royalism and their strong emotional demands, these ties reasserted themselves in altered form in his later life and thought. These same family bonds also become important in understanding his nervous breakdown.

EDUCATION. Two events are outstanding in Comte's early life: his attendance at the École Polytechnique and his service as secretary to Claude-Henri de Rouvroy, Comte de Saint-Simon. The École Polytechnique, founded in 1794 to train military engineers and rapidly transformed into a general school for advanced sciences, was the product of both the French Revolution and the rise of modern science and technology, and it became the model for Comte's conception of a society ordered by a new elite. Although he was there for only a short period, from 1814 to 1816, he immersed himself in the scientific work and thought of such men as Lazare Carnot, Joseph Lagrange, and Pierre Simon de Laplace. Indeed, it was Lagrange's *Analytical Mechanics* that inspired Comte to expound, by means of a historical account, the principles animating each of the sciences.

Expelled from the École at the time of its royalist reorganization, Comte remained in Paris instead of returning home, as his parents desired. He came under the influence of the *idéologues* (Comte de Volney, Pierre-Jean Georges Cabanis, and Comte Destutt de Tracy) and, through his wide reading, of the political economists Adam Smith and J. B. Say, as well as of such historians as David Hume and William Robertson. Of major importance was the Marquis de Condorcet, whom Comte called "my immediate predecessor," and whose *Sketch for a Historical Picture of the Progress of the Human Mind* provided an outline of history in which developments in science and technology played a prominent role in humankind's rise through various stages to a period of enlightened social and political order. Then, in August 1817, he became secretary to Saint-Simon. This crucial relationship lasted seven years, until it dissolved in acrimony.

COMTE AND SAINT-SIMON. The question of what Comte owed his patron, and what he added to the latter's ideas, is vexed. Both men were responding to the same intertwined challenges of the French, scientific, and industrial revolutions. Both sought a science of human behavior, called social physiology by Saint-Simon, and both wished to use this new science in the effort to reconstruct society. Saint-Simon, the older man, had priority in some of the ideas: He was first to announce the law of the three stages, talked of organic and critical periods, and called for a new industrial-scientific elite. Moreover, Comte's early work, including the fundamental opuscule, "Prospectus des travaux scientifiques nécessaires pour réorganiser la société," appeared as the last part of a work that also included two of Saint-Simon's writings.

However, Comte's development of the ideas—for example, the encyclopedic range of data with which he supported the idea of the three stages—went far beyond Saint-Simon and ultimately established a qualitative difference in their systems. Further, where Saint-Simon hoped to deduce his new social science from existing knowledge, such as the law of gravitation, Comte saw each science as having to develop its own method. Comte also perceived that such a development came historically; that is, only in the course of the progress of the human mind. And whereas Saint-Simonianism evolved toward a vague socialism, Comte's thought emerged as a philosophical or scientific position.

LATER LIFE. After the angry break with Saint-Simon, Comte, who could never obtain a satisfactory university post, supported himself primarily by tutoring in mathematics. Gradually, beginning in 1826, he also lectured on his new philosophy to a private audience composed of many of the outstanding thinkers of his time: Henri Marie de Blainville the physiologist, Jean Étienne Esquirol the psychologist, Jean Baptiste Joseph Fourier the mathematician, and others. From these lectures came Comte's major work, the six-volume *Cours de philosophie positive* (1830–1842).

Meanwhile, Comte entered into connubial arrangements, which were only later formalized in a macabre religious ceremony (Comte was then in the midst of his nervous breakdown) insisted upon by his mother. Although Comte was nursed back to health by his wife, the marriage was unhappy and was finally dissolved in 1842. Two years later, Comte met Mme. Clothilde de Vaux and fell deeply in love, and from this love may have come his new emphasis on a universal religion of humanity. In any case, after the *Cours,* which forms the core of Comte's positivism—the part that had the most influence on subsequent philosophers—came such various attempts to set up the religion of humanity as the *Système de politique positive* (1851–1854), and the *Catéchisme positiviste* (1852). In 1857, worn out from his labors, Comte died in wretchedness and isolation. Behind him he left only his monumental attempts at synthesis of many of the most important intellectual strands of his period.

POSITIVE PHILOSOPHY

Comte's positive philosophy emerged from his historical study of the progress of the human mind—the western European mind. India and China, he claimed, had not contributed to the development of the human mind. Indeed, by mind he really meant the sciences: astronomy, physics, chemistry, and physiology (biology). Mathematics, for Comte, was a logical tool and not a science.

THE THREE STAGES. The history of the sciences shows that each goes through three stages: the theological, the metaphysical, and the positive. The progress of each field through the three stages is not only inevitable but also irreversible; it is, in addition, asymptotic—that is, we always approach, but never obtain, perfect positive knowledge.

Briefly, Comte's view of each of the three stages is as follows: In the theological stage, man views everything as animated by a will and a life similar to his own. This general view itself goes through three phases; animism, or fetishism, which views each object as having its own will; polytheism, which believes that many divine wills impose themselves on objects; and monotheism, which conceives the will of one God as imposing itself on objects. Metaphysical thought substitutes abstractions for a personal will: Causes and forces replace desires, and one great entity, Nature, prevails. Only in the positive stage is the vain search for absolute knowledge—a knowledge of a final will or first cause—abandoned and the study of laws "of relations of succession and resemblance" seen as the correct object of man's research.

Each stage not only exhibits a particular form of mental development, but also has a corresponding material development. In the theological state, military life predominates; in the metaphysical state, legal forms achieve dominance; and the positive stage is the stage of industrial society. Thus, Comte held, as did G. W. F.

Hegel, that historical development shows a matching movement of ideas and institutions.

According to Comte, the first science to have gone through the triadic movement was astronomy, whose phenomena are most general and simple, and that affects all other sciences without itself being affected. (For instance, chemical changes on Earth, while they affect physiological phenomena, do not affect astronomical or physical phenomena.)

METHODOLOGY. In the *Cours,* Comte attempted to demonstrate, by a mass of detail, that each science is dependent on the previous science. Thus, there can be no effective physics before astronomy, or biology before chemistry. Further, the history of the sciences reveals the law that as the phenomena become more complex (as biological phenomena are more complex than astronomical), so do the available methods by which those phenomena may be treated—for example, the use of comparative anatomy in contrast to simple observation of planetary movement.

In this part of his work, Comte demonstrated the real power and flexibility of his approach. In contrast to René Descartes, who saw only one right method of conducting the reason—the geometrical method—Comte believed that each science develops by a logic proper to itself, a logic that is revealed only by the historical study of that science. He explicitly named Descartes as his predecessor and claimed to have fulfilled Descartes's work by studying the mind historically instead of merely abstractly. In Comte's view, the logic of the mind cannot be explained in a priori fashion, but only in terms of what it has actually done in the past. In this respect, Comte's position implies a fundamental revolution in philosophy.

Himself a mathematician, Comte objected to the overextended use of mathematics. In his view, mathematics was simply one tool among many. He admitted that while in principle all phenomena might be subject to mathematical treatment, in practice those phenomena far up the scale in complexity, such as biology or his hoped-for new science of sociology, were not amenable to such an approach. On the other hand, Comte sharply dissociated the positive method from the inquiry into first causes; as we have seen, this would be metaphysical, not positive, knowledge.

Observation. The first means of scientific investigation, according to Comte, is observation. We observe facts, and Comte would agree with the logical positivists of our day that a sentence that is not either a tautology or an assertion of empirical facts can have no intelligible sense. However, by the observation of a fact, Comte—perhaps more sophisticated than many of his latter-day followers—did not mean having a Humean sensation or a complex of such sensations. He meant an act of sensing that was connected, at least hypothetically, with some scientific law. Comte admitted that the simultaneous creation of observations and laws was a "sort of vicious circle" and warned against the perverting of observations in order to suit a preconceived theory. However, he insisted that the task of the scientist was to set up hypotheses about invariable relations of phenomena, concomitantly with their verification by observation.

Experimentation. After observation, understood in this sense, experimentation is the next available method. Since it can be resorted to only when the regular course of a phenomenon can be interfered with in an artificial and determinate manner, the method is best suited to physics and chemistry. In biology, interestingly enough, Comte suggested that disease—the pathological case—while not determined beforehand, could serve as a substitute for experimentation.

Comparison. For the more complex phenomena of biology and sociology, the best available means of investigation is comparison. In biology this might be comparative anatomy. In social science, the method might take the form of comparing either coexisting states or consecutive states: The first method anticipated anthropology; the latter comprised historical sociology.

SOCIOLOGY. Comte described the study of consecutive social states as a "new department of the comparative method." This "new department" was the final science to be developed by man, and the only one that had not yet entered the positive stage: sociology. As the last phenomena to be considered as falling under invariant laws, social phenomena were the ones that would give meaning to all the rest. Only by perceiving through the new science of sociology that man is a developing creature who moves through the three stages in each of his sciences could we understand the true logic of his mind.

Comte acknowledged both Baron de Montesquieu and Condorcet as his predecessors in the science of sociology, for they, too, had perceived that social phenomena appear to obey laws when correctly considered. However, the task of bringing sociology into the positive stage, or at least up to its threshold, was performed by Comte alone. He officially announced the advent of the new science in the fourth volume of the *Cours,* 47th lesson, when he proposed the word *sociologie* for what Lambert Adolphe Jacques Quételet had named *physique sociale.*

Statics and dynamics. Comte divided sociology into two parts: statics and dynamics. Social statics is the study of political-social systems relative to their existing level of civilization; that is, as functioning cultural wholes. Social dynamics is the study of the changing levels of civilization; that is, the three stages. The division into statics and dynamics is merely for analytic purposes: The distinction is one between two different ways of organizing the same set of social facts (just as, for example, in biology students of comparative anatomy and of evolution classify the same facts in different ways).

Order and progress. Statics and dynamics, then, are branches of the science of sociology. To this classification, Comte added a division between order and progress, which he conceived as abstractions about the nature of the society studied by sociology. (He further complicated the matter by using the terms *organic* and *critical* or *negative* to describe various periods.) Thus, order exists in society when there is stability in fundamental principles and when almost all members of the society hold similar opinions. Such a situation prevailed, Comte believed, in the Catholic feudal period, and he devoted numerous pages to analyzing the ideas and institutions of medieval social structure.

In contrast to the concept of order, and using images that remind one of the Hegelian dialectic, Comte posited what he called the idea of progress. He identified this progress with the period bounded by the rise of Protestantism and the French Revolution. What was now needed, Comte told his readers, was the reconciliation or synthesis of order and progress in a scientific form. Once a science of society had been developed, opinions would once again be shared and society would be stable. According to Comte, people did not argue over astronomical knowledge, and, once there was true social knowledge, they would not fight over religious or political views. Liberty of conscience, Comte declared, is as out of place in social thought as in physics, and true freedom in both areas lies in the rational submission to scientific laws.

The gradual becoming aware of and understanding of these invariable laws was what Comte meant by progress. (One of these invariable laws, incidentally, was that society must develop in a positive direction.) Thus, in the Middle Ages, when society found its order in terms of shared religious ideas, sociology was in the theological stage, and the French Revolutionary period witnessed the emergence of the metaphysical stage. As has been explained, Comte denigrated the period of progress, from the rise of Protestantism to the French Revolution, while from the point of view of social dynamics, he had to praise the progressive movement toward positivism that took place during this "negative" period. Comte's classification was neither always clear nor consistent.

POLITICAL PHILOSOPHY. Comte's sociology was overly intertwined with his conception of the right polity. In Comte's view, society had broken down with the French Revolution. The Revolution had been necessary because the old order, based on outdated "theological"—Catholic—knowledge, no longer served as a respectable basis for shared opinions; it had been undermined by the progress of the sciences. The Revolution itself offered no grounds for the reorganization of society because it was "negative" and metaphysical in its assumptions. The task, therefore, was to provide a new religion, and a new clergy, that could once again unify society. Comte's solution was a science on which all could agree. In place of the Catholic priesthood, Comte proposed a scientific-industrial elite that would announce the "invariable laws" to society. It was a bold effort to synthesize the old regime (as conceived by Comte) and the Revolution, and to meet the problems of a modern industrial society with the insights about the need for order and shared certainty that were revealed in the theological-feudal period. These insights, religious in nature and intuitive in form, were now to be reformulated by Comte and his followers in terms of positive science.

POSITIVE RELIGION. Comte, in responding to the actual problems of his time, was also working out a synthesis of two bodies of thought. Montesquieu and Condorcet have already been mentioned as the sources of Comte's conception of social statics and social dynamics. Comte's views on organic and critical periods, and his dislike of Protestantism as negative and productive only of intellectual anarchy, were undoubtedly derived from the Catholic counterrevolutionary thinkers Vicomte de Bonald and Comte Joseph de Maistre, whom he began to read around 1821. It was Bonald, in fact, who first announced that one did not argue over social truths any more than one argued over the fact that 2 plus 2 equals 4, and de Maistre stated that Protestantism is a negative ideology. Comte rewarded de Maistre by putting his name in the calendar of positivist saints.

Now the positivist calendar was a product of Comte's increasing turn from his earlier mainly philosophical and scientific interests to a form of mysticism. Comte appointed himself the high priest of a new religion of humanity. The new "religion"—based on Comte's positive science—had its holy days, its calendar of saints (which included de Maistre, Adam Smith, Frederick the

Great, Dante Alighieri, and William Shakespeare), and its positive catechism. It was nontheistic, for Comte never reverted to a belief in God or in Catholic dogma. As an effort to replace the Catholic religion with a new version of the cult of reason of 1793, it is of great interest, but it was not this aspect of Comte's work that influenced such important figures as Littré and J. S. Mill and it is not what is generally meant when one speaks of Comte's Positivism.

EDUCATIONAL THEORY. It was on the basis of the earlier, rather than the later, parts of his work that Comte sought to regenerate education. To know a given science, Comte believed, one must know the sciences anterior to it. According to this scheme, the sociologist must first be trained in all the natural sciences, whose knowledge has already gone through the three stages and become positive. (A by-product of this approach to education was Comte's conviction that the proposed method of studying would aid each science by suggesting answers to its problems from other fields.) Positive education was a necessary foundation for the positive polity, as well as for the positive sociology.

COMTE AND SOCIALISM. To round off this presentation of Comte's thought, a brief word is in order on the relationship of his views to the emerging proletarian movement. The goal of Comte's polity was never the affluent society, although he believed that every social measure ought to be judged in terms of its effect on the poorest and most numerous class. He sought, instead, a moral order, with the positive religion enjoining everyone "to live for others." The two classes from which Comte expected the greatest moral influence were women and proletarians, and he relied on their respective charms and numbers to soften the selfish character of the capitalists. In this way, class conflict would be abolished, and the owners of industry would be moralized instead of eliminated. Comte was against the abolition of private property; on the other hand, he joined Karl Marx in attacking the individualist attitudes and behavior of the property-owning classes. In this context, it is interesting to note that Marx, who claimed not to have read Comte until 1866, when he judged his work "trashy," had as a friend the Comtian Professor E. S. Beesly, who chaired the 1864 meeting establishing the International Workingmen's Association.

CRITICISM AND ASSESSMENT

Against Comte's entire system, various criticisms may be lodged. J. S. Mill took Comte to task for not giving a place in his series of sciences to psychology (instead, Comte concentrated on phrenology) and commented that this was "not a mere hiatus in M. Comte's system, but the parent of serious errors in his attempt to create a Social Science."

Perhaps there is a connection between Comte's disregard of introspective psychology and his unquestioned faith in the possibility of an ultimate positive stage of society and knowledge. For example, Comte did not even consider the question of how we can be sure that the positive stage is the last one. Since the human mind and its logical procedures, in Comte's own view, can be known only in terms of experience, it is at least theoretically possible that another stage might be reached. And how can we be sure that, although the positive method has been extended to all natural phenomena, it can be extended to human phenomena? Even if we grant this—and admittedly it is an appealing and useful assumption—does the discovery of laws regulating human phenomena put us in possession of a final science of humanity? At this point, are we not still without a science of ethics, a science that will tell us with complete positive certainty what end to pursue? Comte considered none of these questions, nor, with his neglect of introspective psychology, the further question of whether man's moral disposition is necessarily improved by the pursuit of science.

On another level, both Comte's sociology and his political philosophy can be criticized as embodying a wrong view of scientific procedure. In his best moments, he knew that science proceeds by free inquiry and constant redefinition of its "laws." However, in setting up a scientific elite, who were to announce fixed and stable laws to society, he betrayed his own insight. The polemic needs of his polity—ordered, organic, and positive—triumphed over the philosophic and scientific method he had so painstakingly elaborated in the *Cours*.

Along this same line of criticism, Comte can be charged with serious errors of fact. His anti-Protestant, pro-Catholic feelings led him to make sweeping and unexamined statements, such as that Protestantism was "anti-scientific" (a conclusion supported, perhaps, by Martin Luther's views, but undermined, for example, by the Puritan involvement in the Royal Society) and that Catholicism was a nonaggressive religion. Thus, speaking of the Crusades, Comte asserted, as a matter of fact: "All great expeditions common to the Catholic nations were in fact of a defensive character." Throughout his work, especially in the last three volumes of the *Cours*, which are devoted to his sociology rather than to the natural sciences, similar remarks are to be found.

Yet, with all the criticisms of either a conceptual or factual nature that can be leveled against Comte's position, one must not lose sight of his essential contributions. He did grasp the notion that knowledge in the various sciences is unified and related. His law of the three stages, while too rigid and schematized, did point to the different ways of viewing the world and to the fact that men at different stages of history have emphasized one way of ordering society more than another. And, most important, Comte did prepare the way for a new science, sociology, that would help study the interrelations of men in society and how these interrelations change in the course of history.

See also Bonald, Louis Gabriel Ambroise, Vicomte de; Cabanis, Pierre-Jean Georges; Condorcet, Marquis de; Dante Alighieri; Descartes, René; Destutt de Tracy, Antoine Louis Claude, Comte; Hegel, Georg Wilhelm Friedrich; Hume, David; Laplace, Pierre Simon de; Littré, Émile; Maistre, Comte Joseph de; Marx, Karl; Mill, John Stuart; Montesquieu, Baron de; Positivism; Saint-Simon, Claude-Henri de Rouvroy, Comte de; Smith, Adam; Volney, Constantin-François de Chasseboeuf, Comte de.

Bibliography

There is no critical edition of Comte's works. His most important writings, all published in Paris unless otherwise stated, are as follows: *Opuscules de philosophie sociale 1819–1828* (1883), which includes the 1822 "Plan des travaux scientifiques nécessaires pour réorganiser la société"; *Cours de philosophie positive,* 6 vols. (1830–1842), and Harriet Martineau's English condensation of *Cours, The Positive Philosophy of Auguste Comte,* 2 vols. (London: John Chapman, 1853), which was personally approved by Comte; *Discours sur l'esprit positif,* prefixed to the *Traité philosophique d'astronomie populaire* (1844); *Discours sur l'ensemble du positivisme* (1848); *Calendrier positiviste* (1849); *Système de politique positive,* 4 vols. (1851–1854), translated by J. H. Bridges, Frederic Harrison, et al. as *The System of Positive Polity,* 4 vols. (London: Longmans, 1875–1877); *Catéchisme positiviste* (1852), translated by Richard Congreve as *The Catechism of Positive Religion* (London: John Chapman, 1858); *Appel aux conservateurs* (1855); and *La synthèse subjective* (1856).

In addition, see P. Valat, ed., *Lettres d'Auguste Comte à M. Valat* (1870); *Lettres d'Auguste Comte à John Stuart Mill, 1841–1846* (1877); *Testament d'Auguste Comte* (1884); *Lettres à des positivistes anglais* (London: Church of Humanity, 1889); *Correspondance inédite d'Auguste Comte,* 4 vols. (1903–1904); and *Nouvelles Lettres inédites. Textes présentés par Paulo E. de Berredo-Carneiro* (1939).

The most important work on Comte, essential to a study of his intellectual development, is Henri Gouhier, *La jeunesse d'Auguste Comte et la formation du positivisme,* 3 vols. (Paris: Vrin, 1933–1941). The same author's *La vie d'Auguste Comte* (Paris: Gallimard, 1931) is the best biography. For an analysis of Comte's philosophical ideas, J. S. Mill, *Auguste Comte and Positivism* (London: Trubner, 1865) is still obligatory. See also Thomas Whittaker, *Comte and Mill* (London: A. Constable, 1908); Lucien Lévy-Bruhl, *La philosophie d'Auguste Comte* (Paris: Alcan, 1900), translated by Kathleen de Beaumont-Klein as *The Philosophy of Auguste Comte* (New York: Putnam, 1903); Émile Littré, *Auguste Comte et la philosophie positive* (2nd ed., Paris: Hachette, 1864); J. Delvolvé, *Reflexions sur la pensée comtienne* (Paris: Alcan, 1908); and Pierre Ducassé, *Méthode et intuition chez Auguste Comte* (Paris: Alcan, 1939).

On Comte's religious attitudes, see George Dumas, *Psychologie de deux Messies positivistes: Saint Simon et Auguste Comte* (Paris: Alcan, 1905).

Jean Lacroix, *La sociologie d'Auguste Comte* (Paris: Presses Universitaires de France, 1956) is one of the most interesting books on Comte. For a critical view of Comte's sociology in relation to morality, H. B. Acton, "Comte's Positivism and the Science of Society," in *Philosophy* 26 (October 1951) is valuable.

Treating Comte as a historian of science are Paul Tannery, "Comte et l'histoire des sciences," in *Revue générale des sciences* 16 (1905), and George Sarton, "Auguste Comte, Historian of Science," in *Osiris* 10 (1952). In this connection, John C. Greene, "Biology and Social Theory in the Nineteenth Century: Auguste Comte and Herbert Spencer," in *Critical Problems in the History of Science,* edited by Marshall Clagett (Madison: University of Wisconsin Press, 1959) is interesting. Frank Manuel, *The Prophets of Paris* (Cambridge, MA: Harvard University Press, 1962), Ch. 6, and F. A. Hayek, "Comte and Hegel," in *Measure* 2 (1951), are rewarding; the Hayek article treats Comte as a historicist.

Bruce Mazlish (1967)

CONCEPTS

Concepts are customarily regarded as intermediaries between mind and world. They are the basic elements of thoughts and the tools by which one classifies things. Concepts are central to the philosophy of mind, and they are often implicated in theories of meaning. There are also some who think that philosophical method is largely a matter of conceptual analysis. There is considerable consensus on the importance of concepts, and, to a lesser extent, on the roles that concepts play, but beyond that there is rampant disagreement. For example, philosophers disagree about the ontology of concepts, the acquisition of concepts, and the content of concepts. In the twentieth century, psychologists began to weigh into these debates, and since the 1970's, much theorizing about concepts has been informed by interdisciplinary dialogue. This entry surveys dominant theories.

WHAT ARE CONCEPTS FOR?

Within philosophy concepts are most often defined as the elements or ingredients of thoughts. Concepts are for thinking. When one ascribes a thought, such as "aardvarks are nocturnal," one typically assumes that the bearer of that thought has a concept of aardvarks and a concept corresponding to the property of being nocturnal. It is sometimes said that a concept is to a thought as a word is to a sentence, but this formula can mislead, because some philosophers do not believe that thought is language-like. However, even those who resist the view that thought is language-like may be attracted to one crucial point of analogy: concepts are believed to be combinable. Those who possess a concept of aardvarks can form the thought that aardvarks are nocturnal, the thought that aardvarks are quadrupeds, or the thought that aardvarks are insectivores, assuming possession of these other concepts. Gareth Evans (1982) suggests that it is a condition on concept possession ("the generality constraint") that, if a person can have the thought that a is F, then that person should also be able to form every other thought of the form a is X, where X ranges over the concepts in that person's conceptual repertoire. Some philosophers think there may be restrictions (e.g., of intelligibility) on combination, but most agree that thought formation through conceptual combination is a central function of concepts.

A second function of concepts is categorization. Many philosophers think that concepts are the primary tools by which one determines that something falls into a category. One knows that two things are both turtles in virtue of having a turtle concept. Historically, some philosophers have reserved the word *concept* and closely related words for general kinds. On this usage there can be a concept of turtles, in general, but not a concept of a particular turtle, say Yertle. Other philosophers tend to say that there can be concepts of individuals and that concepts can be singular as well as general. When one identifies an individual, one can think of that as an act of categorization, broadly construed: One categorizes that individual as belonging to a class with one member. Concepts are implicated in the categorization of kinds and individuals.

Concepts are sometimes said to have a function in inference. This third function often works in concert with the second. One uses concepts to draw inferences about the things that one categorizes. If one encounters a shovel, one can infer that it is used for digging. The knowledge that shovels are used for digging is said, by many, to be contained in one's concept of shovels. Thus, when one applies the concept to some thing, one can use the concept to infer facts about that object.

Concepts are also widely presumed to play a role in linguistic meaning. For some, concepts simply are the meanings of words or components of meanings. On this view concepts are expressed when one uses words. Some philosophers' (especially those who favor reference-based semantic theories) concepts are not meanings. But these authors usually concede that concepts play a central role in the epistemology of language. One comes to understand a word by associating it with a concept. On either approach concepts and language will be closely related.

A fifth function of concepts is related to the other three, but is potentially dissociable. Concepts are said to be representations; they refer to things. Some theories of concepts encompass theories of reference. In this sense, concepts are intermediaries between mind and world.

There is controversy about what concepts are for, but the items on the preceding list are widely accepted. Concepts are usually postulated to play all or some of the preceding roles.

SOME ISSUES OF CONTROVERSY

In describing some of the functions of concepts, a few places of controversy have already been indicated. There are a number of other controversies that deserve special mention.

One issue concerns ontology. It is widely agreed that concepts are intermediaries between mind and world, but where do they reside? One possibility is that they are timeless *abstracta*. This view has been especially popular among those who identify concepts with word meanings. Many semantic theorists believe that meaning enjoy some autonomy from psychology. On this view the meaning of a word does not depend on the images or ideas any individual happens to possess. Others are attracted to this view because they regard concepts as a specification of the essential properties of the things to which they refer.

The concept of a triangle, on this view, might be a geometric definition. Triangles had that definition before anyone discovered it. In contrast, there are philosophers who locate concepts inside the head. On this approach a concept is a mental representation, which plays a causal role in information processing. Others regard concepts as psychological, but eschew talk of mental representations. For example, one might say that a concept is a skill or ability or an operation on mental representations. Immanuel Kant (1997) says concepts are rules for constructing or organizing images. In between those who say that concepts are abstract and those who say they are psychological, there are social theories of concepts, according to which concepts supervene on human practices. What matters is not the contents of any individual's mind, but socially distributed patterns of deference, normative demands, and reason-giving behavior. There is room for uniting all these ontological perspectives into a single theory. For example, one could say that individuals have mental representations (psychological concepts) of community-enforced rules (social concepts) that dictate which timeless, essential properties their thoughts denote (abstract concepts).

Among those who think that concepts are mental representations, there are significant disagreements about representational format. Some think concepts are words in language-like mental code ("the language of thought hypothesis"), others claim they are mental images ("imagism"), and still others say they are weighted connections or patterns of activation in neural networks ("connectionism").

Those who think that concepts are mental representations also disagree about how concepts are attained. Some think that many concepts are innate, and some think that few or none are innate. There are controversies about how learned concepts are acquired. Concepts might be copied from experience, they might be abstracted, they might be learned by strengthening associations, or they might be acquired using a more deliberative procedure, such as the formation and testing of hypotheses. The innateness question is sometimes posed as a question of which concepts are primitive. Many philosophers believe that some concepts are primitive and others are assemblies or inferential networks built up from these. (When two concepts are combined to form a third, they are said to be "features" of that third concept.) Primitive concepts are often thought to be innate, so debates about this issue can sometimes be characterized as debates about how many primitives one has. Historically, however, some philosophers have assumed that many complex concepts are innate as well (such as the concept of God or of identity).

Those who think that concepts are abstract or otherwise external to individual minds sometimes talk about concepts using a definite article, "The concept of X." Those who think that concepts are mental representations are less likely to talk this way, leaving open room that different people may have different concepts of the same thing. There may be exceptions to this rule. It is natural to speak of technical concepts with a definite article ("The concept of natural selection") because there is sometimes just one correct formulation. In addition, some philosophers think concepts are individuated by their referents. On this view any concepts of the same thing will count as being the same concept. Hence, it would always make sense to talk about concepts using the definite article.

Another controversy surrounds the relationship between concepts and language. Besides the question of whether concepts are meanings (hence, whether language depends on concepts), there is a question of whether concepts depend on language. This conclusion has been defended by Ludwig Josef Johann Wittgenstein, Michael Anthony Eardley Dummett, and Donald Davidson. The arguments often turn on the claim that having concepts requires recognizing that thoughts and inferences can be mistaken, which depends in turn on belonging to a language community whose members give and demand reasons for utterances. In contrast, many think that concepts can be possessed without language, and, indeed, Jerry A. Fodor (1975) argues that language learning would be impossible without prior possession of concepts.

All these controversies are significant, but the main issue dividing competing theories of concepts has to do with content. Philosophers disagree about what information one knows in virtue of possessing concepts. One knows a great deal about many categories, but many philosophers believe that only some of this knowledge is conceptually constitutive. Some of this knowledge belongs to one's concepts, and the rest merely belongs to one's conceptions, where conceptions are thought to be more ephemeral and idiosyncratic than concepts. Theories of concepts can be distinguished by where they draw the concept-conception divide.

THE CLASSICAL THEORY

One theory of concepts has been so dominant in the history of philosophy that it has been dubbed "the classical theory." The name is apt, because the theory is championed by Plato. In classical theory, concepts are definitions: They specify conditions that are individually necessary and jointly sufficient for the categories they designate. In his dialogues Plato tries to uncover definitions of concepts such as justice, knowledge, piety, and love. On this approach specifying a concept of justice is a matter of specifying what it is to be just. It is unclear whether Plato thinks concepts are abstract entities or mental entities. He claims that people categorize things by recalling a life in a world of ideal forms, which they inhabited before life in the terrestrial world. Possessing a concept is a matter of intuiting, through memory and reflection, the essence of these ideal forms.

Many philosophers have assumed that some version of the classical theory is correct. Kant (1997) says that concepts are rules that determine the conditions of category membership. He also suggests that many concepts contain other concepts, like houses made from bricks, and in the *Prolegomena to Any Future Metaphysics That Will Be Able to Come Forward as Science, with Selections from the Critique of Pure Reason* (1997) he introduces the term *analytic* to refer to judgments whose predicate concepts are contained in their subject concepts. These judgments are, in effect, true by definition, as opposed to synthetic judgments, which are not true by definition, but must be discovered.

Gottlob Frege (1960) uses the term *concept* (*Begriff*) to refer, narrowly, to the concepts expressed by predicates, but he uses a more encompassing term *sense* (*Sinn*) to refer to the components of thoughts, and each of these, he suggests, can be identified with a descriptive content that determines reference. Frege insists that senses are abstract entities; if they were in the head, he thought they could not serve as the shared meanings of words. Inspired by Frege, Christopher Peacocke (1992) claims that concept possession involves the mastery of inferences, which play a central role in determining reference.

Rudolf Carnap (1956) claims that the concepts used in ordinary thought and talk are riddled with imprecision and that they need to be replaced by concepts that are explicitly defined. Analytic truths are stipulated, and hence immune from empirical refutation.

Defenders of the classical theory disagree about how concepts are attained. Plato obviously thinks concepts are innate, and Carnap thinks explicated concepts must be learned. For many classical theorists, some are innate and others are learned.

The classical theory has been criticized in various ways. Willard Van Orman Quine (1981) argues that the distinction between analytic and synthetic truths is unprincipled, because any putatively analytic claim could be revised under empirical pressure, if, for example, such a revision would be the most conservative way to alter a prevailing theory to accommodate new evidence. Hilary Putnam (1975) argues that definitions are not essential for reference; one can think about natural kinds (e.g., tigers, gold, and water) even if no one grasps the conditions that are necessary and sufficient for falling in the categories. Ludwig Wittgenstein (1953) argues that concepts often lack catchall definitions; instead, concepts group things together on the basis of family resemblances (games are his famous example). Psychologists support Putnam and Wittgenstein by showing that people rarely know the defining features of a category. Georges Rey (1983) counters that the psychological objections presuppose that concepts are in the head and readily available to consciousness—some classical theorists are willing to deny both assumptions.

CONCEPT EMPIRICISM

Plato does not say much about how concepts are mentally represented. Aristotle has more to say. He says that every concept is accompanied by an image. This idea inspired subsequent empiricist philosophers to propose that concepts are perceptual in nature. This basic claim is the essence of concept empiricism. Scholastic philosophers say that nothing is in the intellect that is not first in the senses. The British empiricists, such as John Locke (1979) and David Hume (1978), say that concepts are derived from percepts. Hume says concepts are simply copies of percepts or combinations of copied percepts, and Locke proposes that many concepts are acquired through abstraction from percepts (though there is some disagreement about what he and his scholastic predecessors meant by abstraction).

Concept empiricists differ in several ways from typical classical theorists. First, many concept empiricists are imagists, whereas many classical theorists are not. Concept empiricists usually say that concepts are mental representations (the British empiricists use the term *ideas*), whereas classical theorists often say they are abstracta. Concept empiricists emphasize learning, whereas traditional classical theorists assume that many concepts are innate. Concept empiricists claim that concepts refer either by resemblance or by causal relations to their referents, whereas classical theorists usually assume that concepts refer by satisfying lists of defining conditions.

Nevertheless, there are theories that straddle the border between the classical theory and concept empiricism. The verificationist theories of concepts advanced by Carnap (1956) and other logical positivists are a case in point. For a verificationist, concepts consist in conditions that are necessary and sufficient for reference, but these conditions are specified in observational vocabulary; a concept refers to that which satisfies perceivable conditions of verification.

Concept empiricism is widely believed to face serious objections. One has to do with the concepts of abstract categories. There seem to be concepts of virtue, truth, substance, cause, and being, yet none of these things has any characteristic appearances. If concepts were all derived from perception, it would be hard to explain how people think about these things. Concept empiricists reply by either arguing that people do not have concepts of these things, or by reducing these concepts to perceptual features. Both strategies are hard to pull off.

Another objection is put forward by Kant (1997). He argues that one's capacity to perceive presupposes the possession of certain concepts (including concepts of time and space), which could not be derived from experience. Contemporary psychologists also argue that there is empirical evidence for innate concepts, which are evidently in place before experience, such as the concept of physical object or of number.

PROTOTYPE THEORY

When the classical theory came under attack in the middle of the twentieth century, new alternatives were sought. One alternative, already mentioned, was Wittgenstein's (1953) family resemblance account, according to which one comprehends categories by means overlapping features rather than a catchall definition. This suggestion spawned the emergence of the cluster theory, which identified concepts with features that are not individually necessary for category membership but sufficient when a sufficient number are in place. No one feature may suffice for being a game, and no one feature is necessary, but bring a few features together and one has a game. In effect, the cluster theory is a similarity theory of concepts; it says that one categorizes by looking for similarities with familiar instances.

In psychology, dissatisfaction with the classical theory and inspiration from Wittgenstein (1953) gave rise to the prototype theory. On this approach categorization is also a matter of assessing similarity to a set of features that are not individually necessary for category membership. Prototype theorists do not construe concepts as unwieldy clusters, but as summary representations capturing just those features that are most typical of the category. A prototype is a representation of features that are highly frequent, salient, and diagnostic for category membership. The prototype for the category bird might include features such as flies, has feathers, has a beak, and sings. Following Putnam (1975), philosophers sometimes use the term *stereotypes* for much the same thing. Psychologists, notably Eleanor Rosch and Carolyn Mervis (1975), support the postulation of prototypes by showing that people categorize prototypical category members faster, learn to recognize them earlier, and list prototypical features first when asked to describe a category.

Prototype theorists usually assume that concepts are mental representations, but they diverge on the format of these mental representations. Some say they are made up of images, some say they are patterns in connectionist networks, and some say they are lists of features coded in a language of thought. Like some concept empiricists, prototype theorists argue that concepts are often learned by abstracting from particular category instances, but prototype theorists do not always assume that concepts are grounded in perceptual experience. There can be prototypes for categories that are difficult to discern perceptually, such as a prototypical analytic philosophy paper, a prototypical democracy, or a prototypical lie.

Prototypes are often used in categorization, but some psychologists and philosophers argue that they should not be equated with concepts. One objection is that similarity to a prototype is not necessary for categorization and reference; a shaved, mute, tailless, three-legged dog is completely unlike the dog prototype but still falls under the category. Similarity to a prototype is also not sufficient for categorization and reference: a duck decoy is no duck. Another objection is that prototypes do not combine together compositionally: the prototype for a compound concept is often unlike the prototype for its parts. Pet fish prototypically live in bowls, but neither pets nor fish prototypically live in bowls. Fodor (1998) argues that concepts must combine compositionally to explain that one can generate an unbounded number of novel thoughts from a finite stock of concepts. For similar reasons, prototypes may violate Evans's Generality Constraint (1982), which implies that concepts can be freely recombined; someone might know the prototypes for red fruit and long hair without knowing the prototypes for red hair and long fruit.

THE THEORY THEORY AND HOLISM

Unconvinced by prototype theory, some psychologists developed an alternative, which is associated with the following basic tenets. First, not all concepts are alike; one must distinguish animal concepts, artifact concepts, psychological concepts, mathematical concepts, concepts of physical objects, and so on. Each of these classes is governed by different "folk theories" that comprise small collections of basic principle; for example, folk biology explains that animals have hidden genetic essences, and folk physics explains that solid objects cannot pass through each other. Second, some folk theories lead one to postulate defining essences (as in the case of folk biology), but, unlike classical theorists, psychologists do not assume that these essences are known to those who postulate them; this is called psychological essentialism. Third, each of the concepts within one of these classes may contain causal and explanatory features besides prototypical features; for example, a concept of birds may contain the belief that wings enable flight. Together, these tenets suggest that concepts are like scientific theories: they divide into domains, they postulate hidden features, and they play a role in explanation. The approach has been dubbed the *theory theory*.

Most theory theorists assume that some rudimentary folk theories are innate, but they disagree about which ones. They also disagree about whether one's innate theories remain intact over development, or whether they undergo significant transformations, akin to conceptual revolutions in science. On the latter view adult concepts may be incommensurable with the concepts of children and infants.

The theory theory has been primarily developed by psychologists, but related ideas can be found in philosophy. Quine's (1981) critique of the analytic-synthetic distinction has led some to believe that the basic units for understanding any given category is an entire theory. Quine differs from most psychologists in three respects: He does not claim that theories are insulated from each other (perturbations in one may have ripple effects); he does not claim that theories are mentally represented in the head (Quine is a behaviorist); and he assumes that theories are learned (one's initial sorting behavior is driven by superficial similarities). Still, one might appropriate Quine's ideas into a psychological theory by proposing that each concept is a mental representation individuated by its place in a complete network of mental representations. This would be a holistic theory of concepts.

Critics of the theory theory and holism worry that these approaches entail that concepts are rarely shared. If two people have different theories, then they have different concepts, and their ability to communicate and to obey the same psychological laws becomes difficult to explain. It is also unclear whether these approaches can explain how concepts are combined to form thoughts, because theories are too cumbersome to easily combine together.

INFORMATIONAL ATOMISM

The theory theory and holism pack a lot of information into concepts. Some philosophers prefer the opposite strategy. Fodor (1998) argues that just about every lexical concept (a concept expressed by a single word) is primitive: a primitive concept is one that is not individuated by its relation to any other. This is called atomism. Instead, concepts are individuated by their referents, and concepts refer by falling under the nomic control of properties; roughly, a cow concept refers to cows because it is a law that encounters with cows and causes cow concepts to be tokened. This is called informational semantics.

Informational atomism is unlike all the theories considered so far, because all the others assume that most lexical concepts are complex. A primary advantage of informational atomism is that it can explain how concepts are recombined compositionally. If concepts are primitive symbols, then they can retain their identity when combined, just as words retain their shape when placed into sentences. Concepts can also be easily shared on this view: Two people have the same concept if they have symbols that are under nomic control of the same properties regardless of any difference in their beliefs.

These advantages come at cost. If lexical concepts are primitive, then they cannot be used to explain the inferences one draws or the way one categorizes. For a thoroughgoing atomist, someone could possess a concept of bachelors without knowing that they are male or unmarried. Atomism has also been associated with radical concept nativism. Many philosophers assume that primitive concepts are innate and that complex concepts are learned; if all lexical concepts are primitive, then all are innate. Fodor (1981) used to embrace this consequence, and Fodor (1998) now argues that primitive concepts can be learned.

PHILOSOPHY AS CONCEPTUAL ANALYSIS

Beginning with Plato, one of the dominant methods for doing philosophy has been philosophical analysis. Practitioners begin with a specific concept and reflect on its content. In so doing, they hope to reveal not only how one thinks about the referent of that concept but also what the essence of that referent is. By reflecting on the concept of virtue, for example, one might reveal what it is to be virtuous. The viability of this method depends on which theory of concept is correct. If concepts are definitions, conceptual analysis can reveal the essence of things. But if concepts are merely assemblies of typical features, incomplete and revisable theories, or semantically primitive symbols, then conceptual analysis cannot reveal the essence of things. There is as yet no consensus on which theory of concepts is right, but at stake is the methodology of philosophy itself.

See also Content, Mental.

Bibliography

Carey, Susan. *Conceptual Change in Childhood.* Cambridge, MA: MIT Press, 1985.

Carnap, Rudolf. "Empiricism, Semantics, and Ontology." In *Meaning and Necessity: A Study in Semantics and Modal Logic.* 2nd ed. Chicago: University of Chicago Press, 1956.

Davidson, Donald. "Thought and Talk." In *Mind and Language*, edited by Samuel Guttenplan, 7–23. Oxford, U.K.: Clarendon Press, 1975.

Dummett, Michael. *The Interpretation of Frege's Philosophy.* Cambridge, MA: Harvard University Press, 1981.

Evans, Gareth. *Varieties of Reference* edited by John McDowell. New York: Oxford University Press, 1982.

Fodor, Jerry A. *Concepts: Where Cognitive Science Went Wrong.* New York: Oxford University Press, 1998.

Fodor, Jerry A. *The Language of Thought.* Cambridge, MA: Harvard University Press, 1975.

Fodor, Jerry A. "The Present Status of the Innateness Controversy." In *Representations: Philosophical Essays on the Foundations of Cognitive Science.* Cambridge, MA: MIT Press, 1981.

Frege, Gottlob. "On Sense and Reference." In *Translations from the Philosophical Writings of Gottlob Frege*, edited by Peter Geach and Max Black.bOxford, U.K.: Blackwell, 1960.

Hume, David. *A Treatise of Human Nature*, edited by Peter H. Nidditch. New York: Oxford University Press, 1978.

Kant, Immanuel. *Prolegomena to Any Future Metaphysics That Will Be Able to Come Forward as Science, with Selections from the Critique of Pure Reason*, edited and translated by Gary Hatfield. New York: Cambridge University Press, 1997.

Keil, Frank C. *Concepts, Kinds, and Cognitive Development.* Cambridge, MA: MIT Press, 1989.

Locke, John. *An Essay concerning Human Understanding*, edited by Peter H. Nidditch. New York: Oxford University Press, 1979.

Margolis, Eric, and Stephen Laurence, eds. *Concepts: Core Readings.* Cambridge, MA: MIT Press, 1999.

Medin, Douglas, and Anthony Ortony. "Psychological Essentialism." In *Similarity and Analogical Reasoning*, edited by Stella Vosniadou and Anthony Ortony. New York: Cambridge University Press, 1989.

Murphy, Gregory, and Douglas Medin. "The Role of Theories in Conceptual Coherence." *Psychological Review* 92 (1985): 289–316.

Peacocke, Christopher. *A Study of Concepts.* Cambridge, MA: MIT Press, 1992.

Prinz, Jesse J. *Furnishing the Mind: Concepts and Their Perceptual Basis.* Cambridge, MA: MIT Press, 2002.

Putnam, Hilary. "The Meaning of 'Meaning.'" In *Language, Mind, and Knowledge*, edited by Keith Gunderson. Minneapolis: University of Minnesota Press, 1975.

Quine, Willard Van Orman. "Two Dogmas of Empiricism." In *From a Logical Point of View: Nine Logico-philosophical Essays.* 2nd ed. Cambridge, MA: Harvard University Press, 1981.

Rey, Georges. "Concepts and Stereotypes." *Cognition* 15 (1983): 237–262.

Rosch, Eleanor, and Carolyn Mervis. "Family Resemblances: Studies in the Internal Structure of Categories." *Cognitive Psychology* 7 (1975): 573–605.

Smith, Edward E., and Douglas L. Medin. *Categories and Concepts.* Cambridge, MA: Harvard University Press, 1981.

Spelke, Elizabeth. "Initial Knowledge: Six Suggestions." *Cognition* 50 (1994): 431–445.

Wittgenstein, Ludwig. *Philosophical Investigations.* Translated by G. E. M. Anscombe. Oxford: Basil Blackwell, 1953.

Jesse Prinz (2005)

CONDILLAC, ÉTIENNE BONNOT DE

(1714–1780)

Étienne Bonnot de Condillac was one of the French *philosophes*, known primarily for his development of the doctrine of "sensationism." According to this doctrine, not only all of one's thoughts but even the basic operations on these thoughts derive from sensation.

Condillac was born on September 30, 1714, in Grenoble, one of five children of Gabriel Bonnot, vicomte de Mably, and Catherine de la Coste. He took the name of Condillac after his father purchased an estate of that same name in 1720. Condillac was born with poor eyesight that prevented him from reading before the age of twelve, and he was considered in his childhood to possess only limited intellectual abilities. However, in 1730 he took up residence with his brother, the abbé de Mably, in Lyon to attend the Jesuit college there, and in 1733 he went to Paris to study at the Sorbonne, where he later became a seminarian at Saint-Suplice. Condillac defended his thesis in theology in 1739, and he took holy orders around 1741, though he subsequently devoted himself more to study than to pastoral work. Indeed, he was said to have celebrated Mass only once in his life. While in Paris Condillac frequented the salons and was exposed to the views of John Locke and Isaac Newton. He was influenced in particular by Locke's critique of innatism and Newton's method of explaining phenomena in terms of simple general principles drawn from experience.

Condillac was well connected in French Enlightenment circles. His cousin was Jean Le Rond d'Alembert, coauthor of the *Encyclopédie, ou Dictionnaire raisonné des sciences, des arts et des métiers* (1751–1765), and he was a friend of the other coauthor, Denis Diderot, as well as of Jean-Jacques Rousseau. The entries of the *Encyclopédie* on "Mémoire (*Métaphysiq*)," "Réflexion (*Logique*)," and "Signe (*Métaphysiq*)" reflect the influence of Condillac's views on these topics. The first of his philosophical writings was the *Essai sur l'origine des connaissances humaines* (Essay on the Origin of Human Knowledge), which was published anonymously in 1746, after Diderot had helped him find a publisher. Around this time Condillac corresponded with the French scientist Pierre-Louis Moreau de Maupertuis, who was then the president of the Royal Prussian Academy in Berlin.

In 1746 Condillac submitted an essay on Gottfried Wilhelm Leibniz's theory of monads to a competition sponsored by the academy (it was not selected for the prize), and he was elected to this organization in 1749. Also in 1749 Condillac published his *Traité des systèmes* (Treatise on Systems), a critique of the metaphysics and methodologies of philosophers such as René Descartes, Nicolas Malebranche, Benedict (Baruch) de Spinoza, and Leibniz. He published his second main philosophical work, *Traité des sensations* (Treatise on Sensations), in 1754. The following year he published *Traité des animaux* (Treatise on Animals), a work that emphasizes the differences between human and animal souls, and "Extrait raisonné" of the *Traité des sensations.* In 1755 he also produced a "Dissertation sur la liberté" (Dissertation on Liberty), appended to the *Traité des sensations*, that addresses the issue of human freedom.

In 1758 Condillac became tutor to the young Prince of Parma, grandson of Louis XV. He spent nine years in Parma, during which time he wrote with the help of his brother the multivolume *Cours d'Etudes* (Course of Study), which was published in 1775. He returned to Paris in 1768, when he became a member of the Académie française, but left Paris again in 1773 to take up residence at the chateau de Flux, near Beaugency, which his niece had purchased for him. After that time he published a work on commerce in 1776 and a textbook on logic, which the comte Stanislas Félix Potocki had requested for his Polish schools in 1780. On August 3, 1780, Condillac died at his chateau after a return from a trip to Paris. He left behind an unfinished manuscript, *La langue des calculs* (The Language of Calculation), which was first published in 1798.

MIND AND SENSATIONS

RELATION TO LOCKE. In his *Essai* Condillac acknowledged his great debt to Locke's *Essay concerning Human Understanding*, and in particular to the attack there on innate ideas and to Locke's empirical investigation of the origin of human thought. This debt is reflected in the subtitle of the English translation of the *Essai*: "A Supplement to Mr. Locke's Essay." Even so, Condillac argued explicitly against Locke that one can know with certainty that the mind that is the subject of thought is an indivisible and immaterial substance wholly distinct from body (2001, I.i.§6, pp. 12f). In later years Condillac was especially concerned to distance himself from the materialism of more radical French Enlightenment figures such as Julien Offray de La Mettrie and Paul-Henri Thiry, Baron d'Holbach. In the *Essai* Condillac also distinguished himself from Locke by emphasizing the possibility that when separated from the body one's mind can derive knowledge independently of the senses. However, he noted that in one's present condition, that is, after the fall from the biblical state of innocence that the first humans experienced, the human mind is wholly dependent on the body, to the extent that one can have no thought that does not have a sensory origin. In Condillac's terms, all of one's thoughts are simply "*sensations transformées.*"

Condillac's dualism informs his conclusion that sensations are modification of an immaterial mind. In his *Essai* he also claimed to follow Locke in holding that there are no sensory impressions in one's mind of which one is not conscious. Indeed, at one point he used this same point against the account in Locke's *Essay* of shape perception. This account addresses the speculation of Locke's friend, William Molyneux, that a man born blind would on recovering sight not be able to immediately distinguish a cube from a sphere by vision alone, without the aid of touch. Locke accepted this conclusion and claimed on the basis of this hypothetical case that one's perception of three-dimensional shapes involves not only sensations of light and color but also judgments that alter these sensations "without our taking notice of it." Condillac objected that the phenomenology of shape perception belies this account. One's sensations of light and colors render one immediately conscious of a three-dimensional world. Condillac did mention the 1729 report to the Royal Society in London by the English surgeon William Chesselden that subjects who had blinding cataracts removed could not recognize shapes. But he proposed that this result was due simply to the fact that the subjects were overwhelmed by the new sensory information and thus were unable to focus properly on the shapes (2001, I.vi.§16, p. 110).

RELATION TO BERKELEY. In a 1749 *Lettre sur les aveugles* (Letter on the Blind) Diderot charged that Condillac's *Essai* had failed to respond adequately to an idealism in George Berkeley that precludes any awareness of an external material world. Condillac in effect responded to this charge by attempting in his *Traité des sensations* to give an account of one's perception of the extended world that does not simply assume from the start that such a world exists. He introduced the example of a slowly animated statue to illustrate the manner in which one comes to perceive the external world. This statue is supposed to possess initially only the sense of smell and to perceive this smell merely as an aspect of itself, and not as part of an external world (*Traité des sensations* I.i.2). Even when the statue comes to sense colors, the colors themselves are not considered as constituting distinct shapes. It is only with the sense of touch that the statue acquires an awareness of objects in space and attributes various sensible qualities to such objects (III.iii.§2). Here, Condillac abandoned his view in the *Essai* that one senses shapes by means of the sensations of light and color alone. He also granted in the *Traité*, in effect, that one is not immediately aware of everything in one's sensations. Even though sensations of color are shaped, one cannot recognize the shapes until one comes to associate colors with various tactile sensations.

In a supplement to his 1756 *Lettres à un Américan*, Joseph Adrien Lelarge de Lignac objected that, by allowing in the *Traité* that one has color sensations that are themselves extended, Condillac illicitly attributed to spirits a quality that pertains to bodies alone. In his "Lettre de M. l'abbé de Condillace à l'auteur des Lettres à un Américan," first published the same year, Condillac responded that colors are considered as manners of being of the mind only with respect to their chromatic features, and not with respect to their extension or shape. On the view in the *Traité*, one can recognize the colors as marking out shapes only when one associates them with tactile sensations and, on that basis, attributes the shapes to external objects. But there is still the question whether the color sensations themselves are extended, however one might consider them. Here, Condillac could perhaps draw on Berkeley's view in his *Principles of Human Knowledge* (1710) that extension exists in the mind not "by way of mode or attribute" but "by way of idea." There is still Berkeley's challenge that the extension that exists by way of idea can in no way "resemble" any purported extramental extension. But it is not clear that Condillac was too concerned to respond to this sort of challenge given the skeptical suggestion in his writings that one cannot know for certain whether any object exists external to mind and, if any does, what the nature of such an object is (*Traité des sensations* IV.v).

MENTAL OPERATIONS AND SIGNS

In his introductory remarks in the *Essai* Condillac claimed to have found a "fundamental fact of experience" that explains all operations involved in human knowledge, a fact that consists in "the connection of ideas, either with signs or among themselves" (2001, p. 5). An important part of Condillac's sensationism is his claim that not only the ideas but even their connections with signs or among themselves derive from sensation. He focused in particular on the initial connections forged through imagination, memory, and reminiscence. Imagination occurs when a perception is recalled at the sight of an object. This operation is possible because of an association between the object and perception set up by attention to their conjunction in experience. The attention is itself developed by associations of perceptions with sensations of pleasure and pain. Memory is a more developed operation that involves the recall not of the perception itself, but only of certain signs or circumstances associated with the object. Thus, memory is an imagination of these signs. Finally, reminiscence is the most developed of the operations, which involves not merely the formation of previously experienced perceptions, as in imagination, or previously experienced signs, as in memory, but also the recognition that the recalled perceptions or signs were experienced in the past. The ability so to recognize itself depends on the previous exercise of the imagination and memory.

In the *Essai* Condillac distinguished among three kinds of signs involved in the development of memory and reminiscence. The first two, accidental and natural signs, are not initially recognized as signs. Accidental signs are simply objects that have been experienced with certain circumstances, whereas natural signs are merely one's instinctual reactions to certain experiences. These two become signs only when they are actually associated with the circumstances or experiences. Instituted signs are those that one has chosen to induce thoughts. Though not required for the exercise of imagination and memory, the use of instituted signs allows one to have control over these operations. Such control in turn allows for the development of further rational operations such as abstraction and judgment that according to Condillac are not present in brute animals but are unique to humans.

In a 1752 letter to Maupertuis Condillac wrote that though he had tried to show in the *Essai* how the progress of the mind depends on language, "I was mistaken and gave too much to signs" (1947–1951, vol. 2, p. 536). The mistake here is indicated by Condillac's comment in a 1747 letter to Gabriel Cramer that his work was "not clear enough" on the point that natural and arbitrary signs "are the first principles of the development and progress of the operations of mind" (1953, p. 86). Condillac had of course indicated the importance of these kinds of signs in the *Essai*, but his mistake seems to have consisted in distinguishing them too greatly from instituted signs involved in language. This would explain why he chose to focus in his *Traité* on the nature of sensation and mental operations before the start of language. There, even a statue without language is held to be capable of constructing a rich awareness of a spatially extended world on the basis of primitive sensory experience.

LANGUAGE AND ACTION

In the *Essai* Condillac criticized Locke for addressing the topic of words only after he had provided an account of ideas and mental operations. He insisted that the use of words is in fact "the principle that develops the seed of all our ideas" (2001, p. 8). Though the discussion in the *Traité* indicates that Condillac came to have a greater appreciation of one's prelinguistic abilities, he never relinquished the view that language is crucial for the development of mind. Whereas Descartes and Locke both suggested that thoughts or ideas are prior to and condition the use of language, Condillac insisted that it is the use of language that makes higher-order thoughts and mental operations possible. Here, one has a historical precedent for the "linguistic turn" in twentieth-century analytic philosophy.

Among the higher-order operations that require the use of language, Condillac singled out in particular a reflection that allows the mind to detach itself from current perceptions and apply itself to different objects. The *Essai* introduces the objection that the claim that this operation depends on language seems to be circular, since the use of instituted signs itself requires the abilities involved in reflection. Condillac responded to this objection that the nonlinguistic use of signs prepares the way for the mental operations required for the use of language and that these operations in turn make possible the development of reflection. He compared this relation between reflection and language to the discovery of algebraic signs by means of mental operations that had sufficient exercise to prepare the way for this discovery, but that were more primitive than the sort of mathematical thought that could not have occurred without this discovery (2001, II.i.§4, p. 115).

In the *Essai* Condillac claimed that spoken language derives from a "language of action" that involves voluntary control over nonlinguistic signs. He took the fact that such control develops over time to show that even the will derives from sensation. Still, he also seems to have indicated in the "Dissertation sur la liberté" that the freedom to direct attention is an original mental ability (1947–1951, vol. 1, p. 316). His sensationism thus appears to entail not that the will itself as a capacity derives from sensation, but that the employment of the capacity so derives. The employment of the will is made possible in particular by the habits that the instinctual use of natural and artificial signs produces.

Noam Chomsky claims to find in Antoine Arnauld and Claude Lancelot's *Grammaire générale et raisonnée, ou La grammaire de Port-Royal* a doctrine that posits innate "universal grammar" responsible for language (compare Arnauld and Lancelot 1966 and Chomsky 1966). The historical accuracy of this characterization is a matter of dispute (e.g., see the critical review of Chomsky in Aarsleff 1982, pp. 101–119), but what is undeniable is that Condillac offered an alternative to this sort of linguistics that attempts to explain language in terms of prelinguistic instincts and habits. This alternative was a particularly important influence for one of the classic texts in the field, Johann Gottfried Herder's *Abhandlung Über den Ursprung der Sprache* (1772).

See also Alembert, Jean Le Rond d'; Animal Mind; Arnauld, Antoine; Berkeley, George; Chomsky, Noam; Descartes, René; Diderot, Denis; Encyclopédie; Enlightenment; Experience; Holbach, Paul-Henri Thiry, Baron d'; La Mettrie, Julien Offray de; Leibniz, Gottfried Wilhelm; Locke, John; Malebranche, Nicolas; Maupertuis, Pierre-Louis Moreau de; Newton, Isaac; Rousseau, Jean-Jacques; Sensationalism; Spinoza, Benedict (Baruch) de; Touch.

Bibliography

WORKS BY CONDILLAC

Oeuvres philosophiques. 3 vols., edited by Georges Le Roy. Paris: Presses Universitaires de France, 1947–1951.

Lettres inédites à Gabriel Cramer, edited by Georges Le Roy. Paris: Presses Universitaires de France, 1953.

Condillacou la joie de vivre, edited by Roger Lefévre. Paris: Seghers, 1966.

La logique/Logic, edited by W. R. Albury. New York: Abaris, 1980.

Les monades, edited by Laurence L. Bongie. Oxford, U.K.: Voltaire Foundation at the Taylor Institution, 1980.

Philosophical Writings of Étienne Bonnot, Abbé de Condillac. 2 vols. Translated by Franklin Philip. Hillsdale, NJ: Lawrence Erlbaum Associates, 1982.

Essay on the Origin of Human Knowledge. Translated by Hans Aarsleff. New York: Cambridge University Press, 2001.

HISTORICAL WORKS

Arnauld, Antoine, and Claude Lancelot. *Grammaire générale et raisonnée, ou La grammaire de Port-Royal*, edited by Herbert E. Brekle. Studtgart-Bad: Frommann, 1966.

Chesselden, W. "An Account of Some Observations Made by a Young Gentleman Who Was Born Blind ... and Was Couch'd between 13 and 14 Years of Age." In Royal Society of London, *Philosophical Transactions* 35 (402) (April 1728): 447–450.

Diderot, Denis. "Letter on the Blind for the Use of Those Who See." In *Diderot's Early Philosophical Works*. Translated by Margaret Jourdain. New York: AMS Press, 1973.

Encyclopédie, ou Dictionnaire raisonné des sciences, des arts et des métiers. 17 vols. Paris and Neufchâtel, Switzerland: Briasson et al, 1751–1765.

Lignac, Joseph Adrien Lelarge de. *Suite des "Lettres à un Américan" sur les IV et V Volumes de l'Histoire Naturelle" de M. de Buffon et sur le "Traité des Animaux" de M. l'abbé de Condillac*. 4 vols. Hamburg, Germany, 1756.

CONTEMPORARY WORKS

Aarsleff, Hans. *From Locke to Saussure: Essays on the Study of Language and Intellectual History*. Minneapolis: University of Minnesota Press, 1982.

Chomsky, Noam. *Cartesian Linguistics: A Chapter in the History of Rationalist Thought*. New York: Harper and Row, 1966.

Derrida, Jacques. *The Archeology of the Frivolous: Reading Condillac*. Translated by John P. Leavy Jr. Lincoln: University of Nebraska Press, 1987.

Falkenstein, Lorne. "Étienne Bonnot de Condillac." In *The Stanford Encyclopedia of Philosophy*, edited by Edward N. Zalta. Stanford, CA: Metaphysics Research Lab, Center for the Study of Language and Information, Stanford University, 1995–.

Knight, Isabel F. *The Geometric Spirit: The Abbé de Condillac and the French Enlightenment*. New Haven, CT: Yale University Press, 1968.

Lenois, Raymond. *Condillac*. Paris: F. Alcan, 1924.

Rousseau, Nicolas. *Connaissance et langage chez Condillac*. Geneva: Droz, 1986.

Sgard, Jean, ed. *Condillac et les problèmes du langage*. Geneva: Slatkine, 1982.

Sgard, Jean, ed. *Corpus Condillac, 1714–1780*. Geneva: Slatkine, 1981.

Tad M. Schmaltz (2005)

CONDITIONALS

Conditionals are sentences like the following:

(1) If Oswald did not kill Kennedy, then someone else did

(2) We will not go on the trip if it rains tomorrow

(3) If Oswald had not killed Kennedy, then someone else would have

(4) We would be playing tennis if it were not raining

Conditionals are often believed to be analyzable into a two-place sentence connective and two constituent sentences, the antecedent (the sentence introduced by "if") and the consequent. (Thus, [3] may be analyzed into a binary connective ["If it had been the case that … , then it would have been the case that …"] and the constituent sentences "Oswald did not kill Kennedy" and "someone else did [kill Kennedy].")

Many philosophers believe that there is an important difference between conditionals like (1) and (2) (which are commonly called "indicative conditionals"), and those like (3) and (4) (called "subjunctive" or "counterfactual"). Following Ernest W. Adams (1970), one can motivate this idea by considering (1) and (3). Suppose that you think that Oswald killed Kennedy, acting alone, and that no one else ever thought of committing this crime. You reject (3). But you accept (1): If you are wrong in thinking that Oswald did it, then someone else must be the culprit. Thus, it can be perfectly reasonable to assign different truth-values to the two conditionals. This indicates that an indicative conditional cannot in general have the same meaning as the corresponding counterfactual. Now suppose that this observation is combined with the suggested analysis of conditionals into two constituent sentences and a binary connective. Since (1) and (3) have the same constituent sentences, it is natural to conclude that their difference in meaning must result from a difference in meaning between the conditional connectives contained in the two sentences. The connective occurring in indicative conditionals, it seems, must differ semantically from the one found in counterfactuals.

This line of reasoning can be resisted in a number of ways. In particular, even if (1) and (3) belong to semantically different kinds of conditional, it is not obvious that the line between the two kinds coincides with that between indicative conditionals and counterfactuals. For all the argument shows, some indicative conditionals might have to be classified with (3) or some counterfactuals with (1), and under the influence of Vic H. Dudman (1984) some philosophers argue that indicative conditionals like (2) belong to the same class as (3).

Nonetheless, the standard view has it that conditionals are to be classified into indicatives and counterfactuals, and this entry will focus on theories that rest on this classification. The symbol "→" will be used for the indicative and "□ →" for the counterfactual conditional connective.

INDICATIVE CONDITIONALS

Two of the main approaches to indicative conditionals will be considered.

THE EQUIVALENCE THESIS. Consider the mode of inference

(5) either B or not-A; therefore, if A, then B,

which is instantiated by the argument "Either the butler is guilty, or Fred lied about the ice pick. Therefore, if Fred said the truth, then the butler is guilty." This form of inference might appear to be valid. If it is, then an indicative conditional must be true whenever its antecedent is false and whenever its consequent is true. Moreover, it seems plausible that these are the only cases in which the conditional is true. It cannot be true if it has a true antecedent but a false consequent. (If someone says, "If it rains, she won't come," and it rains but she does come, then the utterance is not true.) This suggests that "$A \rightarrow C$" is true if and only if either A is false or C is true. In other words, "$A \rightarrow C$" has the same truth-conditions as the so-called material conditional, "$A \supset C$." This claim is sometimes called the "equivalence thesis."

It is well known that the equivalence thesis yields many seemingly absurd consequences. For instance, it makes (6) come out true, since (6) has a false antecedent and a true consequent:

(6) If Kennedy survived Oswald's assassination attempt, then he died in the assassination attempt.

Yet (6) does not seem to be assertable.

One strategy for dealing with such apparent counterexamples originates in work by Paul Grice (1991): According to the equivalence thesis, knowledge that A is false or that C is true is sufficient for knowing that "$A \rightarrow C$" is true. But if one's belief in the truth of a conditional rests solely on one's knowledge of the truth-values of its constituents (as in the case of [6]), then there is little point in asserting the conditional. For one could convey more information with fewer words by simply uttering the consequent, or the negation of the antecedent (as the case may be). If one utters the conditional anyway, then the audience, trusting the speaker not to do something pointless, will conclude that the speaker has reasons for believing the conditional that go beyond knowledge of the truth-values of its constituents. The utterance of the conditional would therefore be misleading, and the conditional, although true, is unassertable. When confronted with (6), one notes that it would be a mistake to assert it. This accounts for the feeling that there is something wrong with uttering the conditional. This impression can thus be explained without denying that the conditional is true.

The Gricean account has come in for criticism, but even if it is correct and apparent counterexamples to the equivalence thesis can be explained away, one may wonder whether the thesis is sufficiently well motivated. The previous argument for it rests on the assumption that the inference schema (5) is valid. But this premise has been questioned, because of apparent counterexamples to (5), such as "You will meet nobody, or at least not many people. Therefore, if you meet many people, then you will meet nobody."

The equivalence thesis can be supported in other ways, however: It is the simplest of all candidate truth-conditional theories of indicative conditionals. And Frank Jackson (1987, chapter 2) argues that, although the equivalence theorist must concede that an indicative conditional's degree of assertability can differ from its probability of truth, the equivalence thesis can be used to explain the assertability-conditions and can be supported by appeal to this explanatory power.

THE RAMSEY TEST. Another approach to the semantics of indicative conditionals originates in a footnote in a paper by Frank P. Ramsey (1990, p. 155, n. 1) and has been developed in detail by Adams (1975). It starts from the idea, which is sometimes called the "Ramsey test," that the degree to which a speaker ought to accept "$A \rightarrow C$" equals the person's subjective conditional probability $P(C|A)$ (i.e., $P(A \text{ and } C) / P(A)$), provided that $P(A)$ is not zero so that $P(C|A)$ is defined. (On other versions of this account, $P[C|A]$ measures the degree to which the speaker should regard the conditional as assertable. The discussion below will focus on the acceptability-conditional version of the thesis.) This hypothesis is strongly supported by its ability to predict pre-theoretical intuitions about individual conditionals. Suppose that I am about to cast a fair die. My probability that I will throw a six given that I will throw an even number is one-third, and this is also the degree to which I accept, "I will throw a six if I throw an even number."

One might be tempted to try to explain why the degree of acceptability of "$A \rightarrow C$" equals $P(C|A)$ by the assumption that

(7) a conditional "$A \rightarrow C$" expresses a proposition, and the probability that this proposition is true equals $P(C|A)$ in all probability distributions for which $P(C|A)$ is defined.

However, David K. Lewis shows that (7) is false (he proves this and some stronger results in his 1991a and 1991b). Instead of stating the proof, this entry will point in a nonrigorous and informal way in the direction of the reason why (7) is false (this seems more intuitively helpful than a formal proof):

Let each point of the rectangle in Figure 1 stand for a possible world, and let the rectangle as a whole represent

FIGURE 1

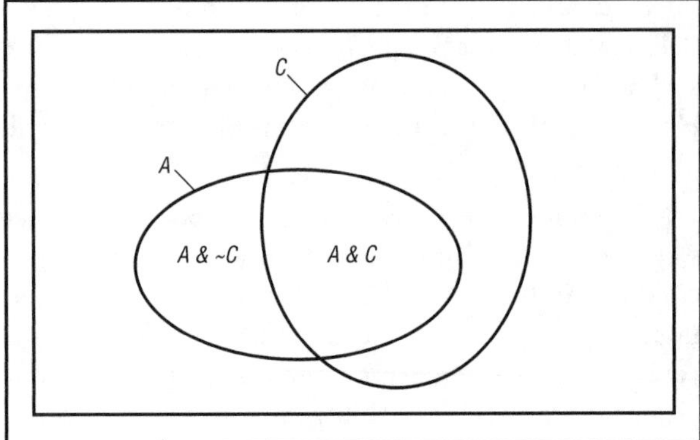

the totality of possible worlds. Propositions can be represented by the regions containing all and only the points that stand for worlds in which these propositions are true. One can model a belief system by distributing one kilogram of mud over the rectangle: If P(*X*) equals *p* in the belief system one intends to represent, then one places *p* kilograms of mud on the region representing the proposition *X*. Every possible way of distributing the mud corresponds to some probability distribution. If (7) were true, then there would have to be some region, namely the one representing the proposition expressed by "*A* → *C*," that bears an amount of mud equal to P(*C*|*A*), that is, to the ratio of the amount on the *A* & *C* region and that on the *A* region, whenever P(*A*) is not zero. However, it is easy to make it plausible that there is no such region. Assume that P(*C*|*A*) equals one-half, which is to say that there is the same (nonzero) amount of mud on the *A* & *C* region as on the *A* & ~*C* region. This is information about the relative amounts of mud on the two regions, and as such it tells one next to nothing about the absolute amount on any specific region. In particular, it seems intuitively plausible that, contrary to (7), there is no region that must be loaded with exactly half a kilogram of mud whenever the *A* & *C* region and the *A* & ~*C* region bear the same (nonzero) amount of mud.

These considerations suggest that there is no one region whose amount of mud equals the ratio of the amount of *A* & *C* mud and the amount of *A* mud whenever this ratio is defined. However, it might be that, whenever the mud is distributed in such a way that the ratio is defined, there is some region whose amount of mud equals the ratio, though it is a different region in different cases. (Note the difference in the scopes of the quantifiers.) Hence, as Bas van Fraassen (1976) points out, for all the argument of the last paragraph shows, it could be that an indicative conditional "*A* → *C*" expresses a proposition and that its probability of truth equals P(*C*|*A*) whenever this conditional probability is defined, but that the proposition expressed by the conditional varies systematically with the speaker's belief system. Philosophers have attempted to extend Lewis's proof so as to rule out this possibility.

As an alternative to finding truth-conditions that fit the Ramsey test, one might give up the idea that indicative conditionals express propositions and make the Ramsey test itself the centerpiece of one's semantic account. Such a theory raises two questions: (1) What account can be given of the meanings of compound sentences that embed indicative conditionals, such as "Either Fred will give you the money if you ask him, or he is more avaricious than Susie"? If indicative conditionals lack truth-values, then one cannot assign a meaning to this sentence using the usual truth-functional construal of the disjunction operator. However, as Allan Gibbard (1981, pp. 234–236) argues, that a nonpropositional account of indicative conditionals does not assign meanings to all compounds of conditionals might be a good thing. For many such compounds are so hard to understand that one may doubt that they have any clear meanings. (Consider "If Fred arrived yesterday if it rains tomorrow, then Susie was in Paris last week.") The thesis that indicative conditionals lack truth-conditions may explain such difficulties of interpretation. (2) The usual criterion for the acceptability of an inference form relates to whether it preserves truth, that is, to whether the conclusion of an instance of it must be true if the premises are true. If indicative conditionals cannot be true or false, then this criterion cannot be applied to inferences involving such conditionals. Adams (1975, chapter 2) tackles this problem by defining a new and independently motivated criterion of acceptability that is more widely applicable. According to this criterion, an inference must preserve probability, in a sense that Adams makes precise as follows: Call 1–P(*A*) the "uncertainty" of the proposition *A*; the uncertainty of a conditional "*A* → *C*" equals 1–P(*C*|*A*). An inference preserves probability just in case there is no probability distribution in which the uncertainty of the conclusion exceeds the sum of the uncertainties of the premises. Classically valid arguments satisfy this condition, as do intuitively acceptable inferences involving indicative conditionals.

COUNTERFACTUALS

Counterfactuals are used to analyze a wide range of philosophically important concepts, such as dispositions, causation, laws of nature, knowledge, practical rationality (counterfactuals are used in decision theory), and freedom of action ("She would have acted differently if she had chosen to do so"). Theories of counterfactuals are of interest in part because they may make it easier to understand and evaluate counterfactual accounts of other notions.

GOODMAN'S ACCOUNT. In the seminal paper "The Problem of the Counterfactual Conditional" (1991) Nelson Goodman proposes an account of roughly the following form for a certain important class of counterfactuals:

> (8) "$A \Box\!\!\rightarrow C$" is true just in case C follows from A, the laws of nature, and suitable true supplementary premises.

This account fits the ordinary-life practice of evaluating counterfactuals well. In determining what would have happened to a certain match if it had been struck on a specific occasion, one needs to draw on knowledge of the particular circumstances, such as the knowledge that (D) the match was dry and (O) oxygen was present, and of the law that (L) dry matches start to burn when struck in the presence of oxygen. These items of knowledge, when combined with the assumption that the match was struck, entail that (B) it burned. This justifies the conclusion that the match would have burned if it had been struck.

Which truths count as "suitable supplementary premises" in the sense of (8)? Clearly, not every truth does. When evaluating the counterfactual "If the match had been struck … ," one cannot regard the truth that it was never struck as a suitable ancillary premise. More generally, if the antecedent is both self-consistent and consistent with the laws, then the suitable auxiliary premises must be consistent with the antecedent plus laws. Otherwise, the antecedent combined with the laws and the supplementary premises would entail everything, so that every counterfactual with the relevant antecedent would come out true—an unwelcome result if the antecedent is consistent.

This condition of consistency does not suffice as a criterion for the suitability of a truth as ancillary premise. For there are different sets of truths that meet the consistency constraint, and depending on which of them one regards as the set of suitable auxiliary premises, different counterfactuals come out true. If one uses (D) and (O) as supplementary premises in evaluating the conditional about the match, one can draw on one's knowledge that (L) is a law to conclude that the match would have burned if it had been struck. Availing oneself instead of (O) and (~B) as auxiliary premises, one can (again using [L]) establish that the match would not have been dry if it had been struck.

The task of stating conditions for a truth's suitability as supplementary premise is central to Goodman's project. After discussing the issue at length, he ends up proposing that a truth *P* is suitable only if *P* is cotenable with the antecedent of the conditional, where this means: It is not the case that *P* would have been false if the antecedent had been true. (For instance, [~B] is not cotenable with "the match was struck," since if the latter sentence had been true, (~B) would have been false. But [D] and [O] would still have been true and are therefore cotenable.) Since this criterion is formulated in counterfactual terms, it renders Goodman's theory circular—a problem of which Goodman is vividly aware. As will become clear below, more recent work on counterfactuals promises to deliver a solution.

THE POSSIBLE-WORLD ACCOUNT. In the late 1960s and early 1970s another account of counterfactual conditionals was developed by Robert C. Stalnaker (1991b) and Lewis (1973). Lewis neatly expresses the core idea: "'*If kangaroos had no tails, they would topple over*' seems to me to mean something like this: in any possible state of affairs in which kangaroos have no tails, and which resembles our actual state of affairs as much as kangaroos having no tails permits it to, the kangaroos topple over" (1973, p. 1).

More formally, the theory is formulated in terms of possible worlds. A possible world in which the antecedent of a counterfactual is true is called an "antecedent-world." One can state the theory (in a somewhat simplified form) by saying that a counterfactual is true just in case its consequent is true in those antecedent-worlds that are most similar to the actual world.

Stalnaker's and Lewis's accounts differ in a number of ways. First, Stalnaker intends his theory to cover both indicative conditionals and counterfactuals, whereas the scope of Lewis's account is restricted to counterfactuals. Second, according to Stalnaker's truth-conditions, but not according to Lewis's, there is always one most similar possible antecedent-world. In consequence, Stalnaker's theory validates the principle of conditional excluded middle, $(A \Box\!\!\rightarrow C)$ or $(A \Box\!\!\rightarrow \sim C)$, whereas Lewis's account does not.

It is an advantage of the possible-world account that it can explain some noteworthy logical features of counterfactuals, namely the failure of a number of inference

FIGURE 2

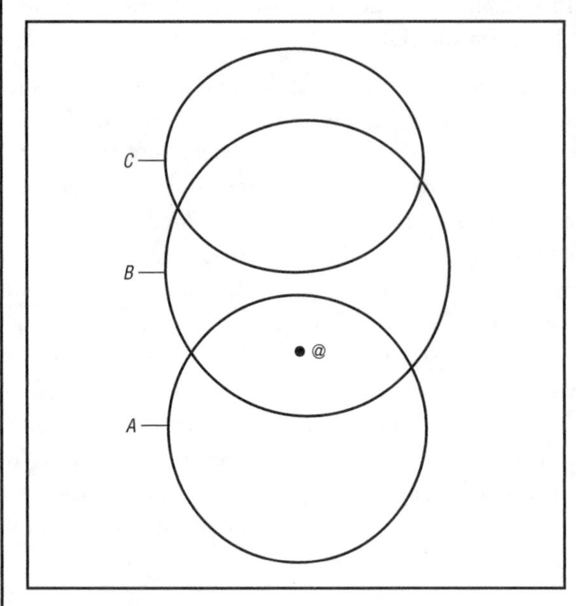

schemata that are valid for the material and strict conditionals, such as the following:

$A \Box\!\!\rightarrow B \therefore \sim B \Box\!\!\rightarrow \sim A$	(Contraposition)
$C \Box\!\!\rightarrow B, B \Box\!\!\rightarrow A \therefore C \Box\!\!\rightarrow A$	(Hypothetical syllogism)
$B \Box\!\!\rightarrow A \therefore (B \,\&\, C) \Box\!\!\rightarrow A$	(Strengthening the antecedent)

To see that these modes of inference are invalid, consider the following counterexamples:

- (Even) if Mary had qualified for the tournament, she (still) would not have won it. Therefore, if she had won the tournament, she (still) would not have qualified for it.
- If Hoover had been born a Russian, he would have been a communist. If Hoover had been a communist, he would have been a traitor. Therefore, if Hoover had been born a Russian, he would have been a traitor (Stalnaker 1991b).
- If we had told them about our plan, they would have been delighted. Therefore, if we had told them about our plan and its likely result, they would have been delighted.

The possible-world account explains the failure of these inference rules, as Figure 2 will render clear. Let the dot labeled "@" stand for the actual world, let the other points in the rectangle represent the other possible worlds, and let the smaller and greater spatial distances between the points represent smaller and greater degrees of similarity between the corresponding worlds. As before, propositions can be represented by regions within the rectangle. In the situation depicted, B is true in the possible A-worlds most similar to the actual world; but $\sim A$ is not true in the most similar possible $\sim B$-worlds. Hence, while "$A \Box\!\!\rightarrow B$" is true, "$\sim B \Box\!\!\rightarrow \sim A$" is false. This shows that contraposition is invalid. Moreover, "$C \Box\!\!\rightarrow B$" and "$B \Box\!\!\rightarrow A$" are true while "$C \Box\!\!\rightarrow A$" is false, and "$B \Box\!\!\rightarrow A$" is true while "$(B \,\&\, C) \Box\!\!\rightarrow A$" is false, so that the diagram also represents counterexamples to hypothetical syllogism and strengthening the antecedent.

If the antecedent of a counterfactual is impossible, then there are no possible antecedent-worlds, so that it is vacuously true that the consequent is true in all the most similar possible antecedent-worlds. The possible-world account therefore entails that all counterfactuals with impossible antecedents are true. But that is implausible: Most philosophers would agree that Willard Van Orman Quine could not have been a hippopotamus, but it does not seem right to say that, if Quine had been a hippopotamus, he would have been a reptile. According to Daniel Nolan (1997) and others, this problem can be remedied if impossible worlds are allowed to figure in the account alongside possible worlds. On this view, impossible worlds are ordered by their comparative similarity to the actual world, just as possible worlds are. A counterfactual "$A \Box\!\!\rightarrow C$" with impossible antecedent is true just in case C is true in the most similar impossible A-worlds. Such an account, however, requires an ontology of impossible worlds, which not all philosophers are happy to accept.

SIMILARITY BETWEEN WORLDS. The notion of similarity between worlds that is used in the analysis of counterfactuals cannot be the one that governs ordinary offhand judgments about overall similarity. This was shown by Kit Fine (1975) among others. Fine used (9) as his example:

> (9) If Nixon had pressed the button, there would have been a nuclear catastrophe.

(9) sounds correct. But offhand it may seem that an antecedent-world devastated by a nuclear explosion is much less similar to the actual world than an antecedent-world in which the signal disappears in the wire after the button-pressing, so that no harm is done. If the notion of offhand similarity were used in analyzing counterfactuals, the account would yield the incorrect verdict that (9) is false and that everything would have been fine if Nixon had pressed the button.

What are the standards of similarity that govern counterfactuals? Many philosophers who address this question assume that different standards are relevant in different contexts of utterance. This assumption is motivated by examples like the following (which is taken from Jackson 1977, p. 9): Frank is in a room on the tenth floor of a building. There is nothing that could break the fall of someone jumping out of the window. It seems safe to say that Frank would get badly hurt if he were to jump. But suppose that Frank says: "I would never jump from a tenth-floor window, unless I had made sure that there was a safety net. So, if I were to jump, a net would be in place, and I would be fine." Frank's reasoning might convince his audience that his counterfactual is true. And yet his conditional seems to be incompatible with the one stated before. The most obvious diagnosis is that the truth-conditions of counterfactuals are context-dependent. In some contexts worlds in which Frank jumps despite the absence of a net count as more similar than those in which he places a net below the window before jumping. In other contexts it is the other way around.

Some of those who take the truth-conditions of counterfactuals to be context-dependent (notably Lewis 1979), believe that there is such a thing as a default assignment of truth-conditions to them, an assignment that hearers choose when interpreting the utterance of a counterfactual unless their presumption in favor of it is removed by distinctive features of the context. That seems plausible enough in the example of the last paragraph: If presented with the case out of the blue and asked for a judgment, one would say that Frank would get badly hurt if he were to jump. It requires some stage-setting (like that provided by Frank's utterance) to create a context in which it seems right to say that he would be fine.

Attempts to describe the default truth-conditions of counterfactuals often start from a special case: counterfactuals whose antecedents are false and describe nomically possible matters of particular local fact. (9) can serve as an example. Pre-theoretical intuitions about this conditional seem to furnish two data points:

(1) *Counterfactual dependence is temporally asymmetrical.* If Nixon had pressed the button, then later on things would have been different from what they were actually like; but matters until shortly before the button-pressing would have been just as they actually were. The most similar antecedent-worlds must therefore be just like the actual world until a short time before the button-pressing, but might be different afterward.

(2) *Laws support counterfactuals.* If Nixon had pressed the button, then events would still have conformed to the actual laws of nature. The most similar antecedent-worlds must therefore be ones that evolve in accordance with the laws of the actual world. In particular, if the missile system is set up in such a way that the actual laws guarantee that button-pressing leads to a nuclear explosion, then there is a nuclear catastrophe in the most similar antecedent-worlds.

Suppose that determinism is true. In that case at least one of the principles (1) and (2) stands in need of some qualification. For determinism entails that every initial segment of the history of the actual world, together with the laws, determines the entire rest of history, and thus determines that Nixon does not press the button. This implies that no antecedent-world can both perfectly conform to the actual laws and be like the actual world throughout some initial segment of its history. Some philosophers (e.g., Lewis 1979) choose to solve this problem by allowing that the most similar antecedent-worlds contain violations of the actual laws, while others allow for backward counterfactual dependence over arbitrarily long periods of time (e.g. Bennett 1984; but see Bennett 2003, §80).

Note that Goodman's problem of specifying which truths are suitable supplementary premises resurfaces on the possible-world theory, in the shape of the question: Which of the actual matters of particular fact must obtain in an antecedent-world for it to count among the most similar? An account of the similarity relation will address this question and, if successful, will at last provide a non-circular solution to Goodman's problem.

See also Entailment, Presupposition, Implicature; Modal Logic; Paraconsistent Logics; Relevance (Relevant) Logics.

Bibliography

Adams, Ernest W. *The Logic of Conditionals: An Application of Probability to Deductive Logic.* Dordrecht, Netherlands: D. Reidel, 1975.

Adams, Ernest W. "Subjunctive and Indicative Conditionals." *Foundations of Language* 6 (2) (1970): 89–94.

Bennett, Jonathan. "Classifying Conditionals: The Traditional Way Is Right." *Mind* 104 (414) (1995): 331–354.

Bennett, Jonathan. "Counterfactuals and Temporal Direction." *Philosophical Review* 93 (1) (1984): 57–91.

Bennett, Jonathan. "Farewell to the Phlogiston Theory of Conditionals." *Mind* 97 (388) (1988): 509–527.

Bennett, Jonathan. *A Philosophical Guide to Conditionals.* New York: Oxford University Press, 2003.

Dudman, Vic H. "Parsing 'If'-Sentences." *Analysis* 44 (1984): 145–153.

Edgington, Dorothy. "On Conditionals." *Mind* 104 (414) (1995): 235–329.

Fine, Kit. "Review of Lewis's *Counterfactuals*." *Mind* 84 (335) (1975): 451–458.

Gibbard, Allan. "Two Recent Theories of Conditionals." In *Ifs: Conditionals, Belief, Decision, Chance, and Time*, edited by William L. Harper, Robert C. Stalnaker, and Glenn Pearce, 211–247. Dordrecht, Netherlands: D. Reidel, 1981.

Goodman, Nelson. "The Problem of the Counterfactual Conditional." In *Conditionals*, edited by Frank Jackson, 9–27. New York: Oxford University Press, 1991.

Grice, Herbert Paul. "Logic and Conversation." In *Conditionals*, edited by Frank Jackson, 155–176. New York: Oxford University Press, 1991.

Harper, William L., Robert C. Stalnaker, and Glenn Pearce, eds. *Ifs: Conditionals, Belief, Decision, Chance, and Time.* Dordrecht, Netherlands: D. Reidel, 1981.

Jackson, Frank. "A Causal Theory of Counterfactuals." *Australasian Journal of Philosophy* 55 (1977): 3–21.

Jackson, Frank. "Classifying Conditionals." *Analysis* 50 (1990): 134–147.

Jackson, Frank. *Conditionals.* Oxford, U.K.: Basil Blackwell, 1987.

Jackson, Frank, ed. *Conditionals.* New York: Oxford University Press, 1991.

Lewis, David K. "Counterfactual Dependence and Time's Arrow." *Nous* 13 (1979): 32–66.

Lewis, David K. *Counterfactuals.* Cambridge, MA: Harvard University Press, 1973.

Lewis, David K. "Probabilities of Conditionals and Conditional Probabilities." In *Conditionals*, edited by Frank Jackson, 76–101. New York: Oxford University Press, 1991a.

Lewis, David K. "Probabilities of Conditionals and Conditional Probabilities II." In *Conditionals*, edited by Frank Jackson, 102–110. New York: Oxford University Press, 1991b.

Nolan, Daniel. "Impossible Worlds: A Modest Approach." *Notre Dame Journal of Formal Logic* 38 (4) (1997): 535–572.

Ramsey, Frank P. "Law and Causality" (1929). In his *Philosophical Papers*, edited by D. H. Mellor. Cambridge, U.K.: Cambridge University Press, 1990.

Stalnaker, Robert C. "A Defense of Conditional Excluded Middle." In *Ifs: Conditionals, Belief, Decision, Chance, and Time*, edited by William L. Harper, Robert C. Stalnaker, and Glenn Pearce, 87–104. Dordrecht, Netherlands: D. Reidel, 1981.

Stalnaker, Robert C. "Indicative Conditionals." In *Conditionals*, edited by Frank Jackson, 136–154. New York: Oxford University Press, 1991a.

Stalnaker, Robert C. "Letter to van Fraassen." In *Foundations of Probability Theory, Statistical Inference, and Statistical Theories of Science*, Vol. 1, *Foundations and Philosophy of Epistemic Applications of Probability Theory*, edited by William L. Harper and Clifford A. Hooker. Dordrecht, Netherlands: D. Reidel, 1976.

Stalnaker, Robert C. "A Theory of Conditionals." In *Conditionals*, edited by Frank Jackson, 28–45. New York: Oxford University Press, 1991b.

Van Fraassen, Bas. "Probabilities of Conditionals." In *Foundations of Probability Theory, Statistical Inference, and Statistical Theories of Science.* Vol. 1, *Foundations and Philosophy of Epistemic Applications of Probability Theory*, edited by William L. Harper and Clifford A. Hooker. Dordrecht, Netherlands: D. Reidel, 1976.

Boris C. A. Kment (2005)

CONDORCET, MARQUIS DE

(1743–1794)

Marie-Jean-Antoine-Nicolas Caritat, Marquis de Condorcet, the French mathematician, historian of the sciences, political theorist, and social reformer, was one of the youngest of the Encyclopedists and the only prominent one to participate actively in the French Revolution. He was born in Ribemont in Picardy and was educated by the Jesuits at the Collège de Navarre. Admitted to the Académie des Sciences in 1769 on the basis of his early mathematical writings, he was elected its perpetual secretary in 1776 and ably depicted the progress of the sciences to a wide public in the customary eulogies (*Éloges*) of deceased academicians, which he presented in this position.

A protégé of Jean Le Rond d'Alembert, for whom Condorcet's election to the Académie Française in 1782 was regarded as a personal triumph, and of Baron de l'Aulne Turgot, who called him to the directorship of the mint during his abortive reforming ministry, Condorcet was active in the prerevolutionary campaigns for economic freedom, religious toleration, legal reform and the abolition of slavery. After his marriage to Sophie de Grouchy in 1786 their salon became one of the most brilliant and influential of the prerevolutionary period. He took part in the opening debates of the French Revolution as a member of the municipal council of Paris and was a convinced republican by the time he was elected to the Legislative Assembly in 1791. Prominent in this assembly, he directed his most sustained efforts toward the elaboration of a project for public education that had great influence on the eventual establishment of the French educational system.

In the National Convention, Condorcet's opposition to the death penalty led him to cast his vote against the execution of Louis XVI (he voted for the supreme penalty short of death). He then undertook the task of drawing up a draft constitution for the new republic, but although accepted by the committee on the constitution, his liberal constitutional scheme—commonly known as the Girondin constitution of 1793—shared the unfortunate fate of the group with which it was associated. In July 1793, Condorcet's indignant defense of his constitution against that prepared by the Jacobins led to his denunciation and flight into hiding. He spent his remaining months of life secluded in Paris, working on the *Sketch for a Historical Picture of the Progress of the Human Mind* (*Esquisse d'un tableau historique des progrès de l'esprit humain*), published posthumously in 1795. He left his asylum in March 1794 and was arrested and imprisoned at Bourg-la-Reine, near Paris. He died during the first night of his imprisonment, either from exhaustion or from a self-administered poison.

PROBABILITY AND SOCIAL SCIENCE

It has often been assumed that Condorcet's increasing preoccupation with social and political affairs, if not the result of a sense of frustration with his mathematical investigations, was at least accompanied by a waning interest in them. Quite the reverse is true. Condorcet's experience at the Académie des Sciences fostered a sense of the power of science to elucidate even the realm of social behavior. His mathematical endeavors were intimately bound up with his fundamental intellectual concern. He aimed to bring to social questions the attitudes and methods of the physical sciences, thereby welding the broken elements of the moral and political sciences into a new social science, which he regarded as the necessary condition of a rational political and social order.

Condorcet seized upon the calculus of probabilities as the essential epistemological connection between the physical sciences and the science of man. All the truths of experience are merely probable, he argued. In the social sciences the observation of facts may be more difficult and their order less constant. The results of the social sciences may therefore be less probable than those of the physical sciences. But Condorcet maintained that the probability of all statements of experience can be expressed and evaluated mathematically within probability theory. Thus, while the statements attained by the social sciences may on occasions be less probable than those of the physical sciences, in Condorcet's view the mathematical estimate of their respective probabilities is equally certain. The meteorologist cannot be certain that it will rain tomorrow, for example, but if on the basis of his observations he can estimate the probability of its doing so as x:1, then he can be certain that there is a probability of x:1 that it will rain tomorrow. Similarly, the economist, who cannot be certain that the standard of living will continue to rise, can in theory arrive at a certain mathematical estimate of the probability of its doing so.

The significance of this argument can be best assessed in terms of the earlier epistemological claims to certainty made by René Descartes on behalf of the mathematical and physical sciences. Condorcet accepted the skeptic's evaluation of the physical sciences as being merely probable. But in arguing that probabilities in the physical sciences (like those in the social sciences) can be evaluated with mathematical certainty, he remained in a sense fundamentally Cartesian. Not only did he hold to the idea of certainty as the criterion of acceptable knowledge, but he also accepted mathematics as the paradigm of certain knowledge (although even this certainty is based in the last analysis, he was occasionally prepared to argue, on the observed constancy of the operation of the human mind). Condorcet's argument in this respect ranks with that of Giambattista Vico as one of the major eighteenth-century attempts to establish the validity of social science. But whereas Vico turned away from the mathematical and physical sciences in search of a historical and organic conception of his new science, Condorcet's probabilistic evaluation of the physical sciences served to integrate them with the science of man in an essentially mathematical conception of science. For Condorcet, the mathematician was able, by using the calculus of probabilities, to subject to the certain evaluation of mathematics even those areas of knowledge condemned by Descartes as untrustworthy. The calculus of probabilities provided a sure means of estimating the validity of our opinions and the probability of our expectations; it bound the moral and physical sciences together on a sliding scale of probabilities which could at all stages be evaluated with mathematical certainty.

Condorcet developed this conception in two very different works. In the first, the *Essay on the Application of Analysis to the Probability of Majority Decisions* (*Essai sur l'application de l'analyse à la probabilité des décisions rendues à la pluralité des voix*, 1785), he set out to discover by means of the calculus of probabilities under what conditions there will be an adequate guarantee that the majority decision of an assembly or tribunal is true. In one of its applications he envisaged such an analysis as the means of solving a perennial problem of liberal thought, that of reconciling the claims of an elite to exercise special responsibilities in the process of decision making with the general principle of universal or majority consent. But the obscure mathematics of the essay and its inevitable reliance on unverifiable assumptions as to the probable truth or error of the opinions of individuals composing social bodies have left it largely ignored by those interested in Condorcet's political theory. More recently, social mathematicians interested in elucidating the relationship between individual and collective choice (whether political or economic) have been able to disengage from the probabilistic framework of this work a theoretical model of collective decision making that is remarkably modern in its implications and approach. (See Black [1958] and Granger [1954]).

The *Essai sur l'application de l'analyse* was intended to convince academicians of the validity of Condorcet's contention that the moral and political sciences can be treated mathematically. The unfinished "Tableau général de la science, qui a pour objet l'application du calcul aux sciences morales et politiques" (General View of the Science Comprising the Mathematical Treatment of the Moral and Political Sciences) was meant for a different audience. It appeared in 1793 in a popular journal that sought to initiate citizens of the new French republic into the social science, or the art of the rational conduct of politics. Condorcet saw the new social mathematics (*mathématique sociale*) as a common, everyday science of conduct ("une science usuelle et commune," *Oeuvres*, Vol. I, p. 550) that would provide the essential foundation of a democratic, but rational, politics. He viewed man in all his conduct as a gambler. Each individual automatically and instinctively balances the probability of one opinion against that of another, the desired goal of a proposed action against its probable results. The mathematical science of man was intended not only as an objective description of social behavior but also as a scientific basis for individual conduct that would enable people to substitute for habitual and instinctive modes of thought and action the precise evaluation of reason and calculation. Social mathematics, coupled with an exact language based on precise philosophical analysis of our ideas, would free human beings from instinct and passion and restore the empire of reason in social affairs. It formed the essential link between scientific advance and moral progress, for evil, as Condorcet remarked, was far more often the result of an erroneous calculation of interest than the product of violent passion.

IDEA OF PROGRESS

In the *Sketch for a Historical Picture of the Progress of the Human Mind*, Condorcet turned to history for a demonstration of the power of reason and calculation in social affairs. The *Sketch* was only the hastily written introduction to a larger work on the history of science and its impact upon society which Condorcet had been contemplating for many years. Some of the fragments of this unfinished work are of considerable philosophical interest. One outlined a project for a universal, symbolic language of the sciences; another elaborated a decimal system of classification addressed to the much-debated problem of scientific classification. But it is with the *Sketch* itself that Condorcet's name and influence have been chiefly associated, and it is with that work—often regarded as the philosophical testament of the eighteenth century—that Condorcet bequeathed to the nineteenth century the fundamental idiom of its social thought, the idea of progress.

The aim of the *Sketch* was to demonstrate man's progressive emancipation, first from the arbitrary domination of his physical environment and then from the historical bondage of his own making. Condorcet shared with other eighteenth-century theorists a view of progress that depended ultimately upon man's cumulative ability to combine sensations and ideas (in the manner revealed by sensationalist psychology) to his own satisfaction or advantage. This Promethean psychological capacity functioned in the same manner in the human race as in the individual; it proceeded by way of a natural, self-revealing logic or "method," from the fundamental data of sense experience to the most general principles of the moral and physical sciences. Condorcet's main concern, therefore, was less to explain the growth of reason in itself—this growth was posited as natural—than to point to the destruction of the obstacles that had inhibited that growth or diverted the historical development of the mind from the natural logic of ideas.

Condorcet's hopes for future progress rested on two conclusions. First, he was convinced that the obstacles which had in the past threatened the advance and dissemination of reason—elitism and tyranny on the one hand; popular prejudice, ignorance, and social and political subjection, on the other—were finally being destroyed under the joint impact of scientific, technological, and political revolution. Second, he believed that the discoveries of sensationalist psychology had made it possible to articulate the natural and fundamental principles of the social art, or science, and he drew from the doctrine of the rights of man—grounded upon the "facts" of man's sensate nature—a comprehensive outline of the principles of liberal democracy that it would be the purpose of the social art to implement.

Although this belief in indefinite future progress was based on the general assertion that observation of past events warrants extrapolation as to the probable future,

Condorcet was not a strict historical determinist. Humans are subject to the general laws of physical nature, he maintained in an unpublished introduction to the *Sketch*, but they have the power to modify these laws and turn them to their own advantage. Although this power is feeble in the individual, when exercised by humankind collectively and over a long period, it can balance the forces of nature and can even be regarded as the work of nature itself. For if nature has endowed humankind collectively with the capacity to learn from experience, to understand its laws, and to modify their effects, the progressive emancipation of humans from nature is itself natural, and the growth of freedom is a natural law. The *Sketch* not only demonstrated the power of the social art but also made clear that it could succeed only as a communal and democratic art. It is this emphasis upon the collective experience and achievements of humankind, this concern with the "most obscure and neglected chapter of the history of the human race" (*Sketch*, Barraclough translation, p. 171)—namely, the progress of the mass of the people in society—that links Condorcet's view of history with his conception of social science.

See also Alembert, Jean Le Rond d'; Descartes, René; Encyclopédie; Mathematics, Foundations of; Philosophy of History; Progress, The Idea of; Turgot, Anne Robert Jacques, Baron de L'Aulne; Vico, Giambattista.

Bibliography

The standard edition of Condorcet's works is A. Condorcet-O'Connor and F. Arago, eds., *Oeuvres de Condorcet.* 12 vols. (Paris, 1847–1849). The *Essai sur l'application de l'analyse à la probabilité des décisions rendues à la pluralité des voix* (Paris: De l'Imprimerie Royale, 1785) and Condorcet's many other mathematical writings are not included in this edition. For a bibliography of these mathematical works see Charles Henry, "Sur la Vie et les écrits mathématiques de Jean-Antoine-Nicolas Caritat marquis de Condorcet." In *Bulletino di bibliografica e di storia delle scienze matematiche e fisiche* 16 (1883): 271–324. See also Charles Henry, ed., *Correspondance inédite de Condorcet et de Turgot (1770–79)* (Paris: Charavay Frères, 1883); Léon Cahen, "Condorcet inédit: Notes pour le Tableau des progrès de l'esprit humain," in *La révolution française* 75 (1922): 193–212; Gilles-Gaston Granger, "Langue universelle et formalisation des sciences: Un Fragment inédit de Condorcet," in *Revue d'histoire des sciences* 7 (1954): 197–219; Alberto Cento, "Dei manoscritti del 'Tableau' di Condorcet," in *Rendiconto del Istituto Lombardo di Scienze e Lettere: Classe di Lettere e Scienze Morali e Storiche* 88 (1955): 311–324; K. M. Baker, "An Unpublished Essay of Condorcet on Technical Methods of Classification," in *Annals of Science* 18 (1962): 99–123. For a modern translation of the *Esquisse*, see *Sketch for a Historical Picture of the Progress of the Human Mind*, translated by June Barraclough, with an introduction by Stuart Hampshire (London: Weidenfeld and Nicolson, 1955).

For reference see Franck Alengry, *Condorcet, guide de la Révolution française, théoricien du droit constitutionnel et précurseur de la science sociale* (Paris: V. Giard and E. Brière, 1903); Duncan Black, *The Theory of Committees and Elections* (Cambridge, U.K.: Cambridge University Press, 1958); Janine Bouissounouse, *Condorcet, le Philosophe dans la Révolution* (Paris: Hachette, 1962); Léon Cahen, *Condorcet et la Révolution française* (Paris: Alcan, 1904); Alberto Cento, *Condorcet e l'idea di progresso* (Florence: Parenti, 1956); Gilles-Gaston Granger, *La mathématique sociale du marquis de Condorcet* (Paris, 1956); Frank E. Manuel, *The Prophets of Paris* (Cambridge, MA: Harvard University Press, 1962); and J. Salwyn Schapiro, *Condorcet and the Rise of Liberalism* (New York: Harcourt Brace, 1934).

See also Keith M. Baker, *Condorcet, From Natural Philosophy to Social Mathematics* (Chicago: University of Chicago Press, 1975); and Edward Goodell, *The Noble Philosopher: Condorcet and the Enlightenment* (Buffalo, NY: Prometheus, 1994).

Keith Michael Baker (1967)
Bibliography updated by Tamra Frei (2005)

CONFIRMATION THEORY

Predictions about the future and unrestricted universal generalizations are never logically implied by our observational evidence, which is limited to particular facts in the present and past. Nevertheless propositions of these and other kinds are often said to be confirmed by observational evidence. A natural place to begin the study of confirmation theory is to consider what it means to say that some evidence *E* confirms a hypothesis *H*.

INCREMENTAL AND ABSOLUTE CONFIRMATION

Let us say that *E* raises the probability of *H* if the probability of *H* given *E* is higher than the probability of *H* not given *E*. According to many confirmation theorists, "*E* confirms *H*" means that *E* raises the probability of *H*. This conception of confirmation will be called incremental confirmation.

Let us say that *H* is probable given *E* if the probability of *H* given *E* is above some threshold. (This threshold remains to be specified but is assumed to be at least one half.) According to some confirmation theorists, "*E* confirms *H*" means that *H* is probable given *E*. This conception of confirmation will be called absolute confirmation.

Confirmation theorists have sometimes failed to distinguish these two concepts. For example, Carl Hempel

(1945/1965) in his classic "Studies in the Logic of Confirmation" endorsed the following principles:

(1) A generalization of the form "All *F* are *G*" is confirmed by the evidence that there is an individual that is both *F* and *G*.

(2) A generalization of that form is also confirmed by the evidence that there is an individual that is neither *F* nor *G*.

(3) The hypotheses confirmed by a piece of evidence are consistent with one another.

(4) If *E* confirms *H* then *E* confirms every logical consequence of *H*.

Principles (1) and (2) are not true of absolute confirmation. Observation of a single thing that is *F* and *G* cannot in general make it probable that all *F* are G; likewise for an individual that is neither *F* nor *G*. On the other hand there is some plausibility to the idea that an observation of something that is both *F* and *G* would raise the probability that all *F* are *G*. Hempel argued that the same is true of an individual that is neither *F* nor *G*. Thus Hempel apparently had incremental confirmation in mind when he endorsed (1) and (2).

Principle (3) is true of absolute confirmation but not of incremental confirmation. It is true of absolute confirmation because if one hypothesis has a probability greater than ½ then any hypothesis inconsistent with it has a probability less than ½. To see that (3) is not true of incremental confirmation, suppose that a fair coin will be tossed twice, let H_1 be that the first toss lands heads and the second toss lands tails, and let H_2 be that both tosses land heads. Then H_1 and H_2 each have an initial probability of ¼. If *E* is the evidence that the first toss landed heads, the probability of both H_1 and H_2 given *E* is ½, and so both hypotheses are incrementally confirmed, though they are inconsistent with each other.

Principle (4) is also true of absolute confirmation but not of incremental confirmation. It is true of absolute confirmation because any logical consequence of *H* is at least as probable as *H* itself. One way to see that (4) is not true of incremental confirmation is to note that any tautology is a logical consequence of any *H* but a tautology cannot be incrementally confirmed by any evidence, since the probability of a tautology is always one. Thus Hempel was apparently thinking of absolute confirmation, not incremental confirmation, when he endorsed (3) and (4).

Since even eminent confirmation theorists like Hempel have failed to distinguish these two concepts of confirmation, we need to make a conscious effort not to make the same mistake.

CONFIRMATION IN ORDINARY LANGUAGE

When we say in ordinary language that some evidence confirms a hypothesis, does the word "confirms" mean incremental or absolute confirmation?

Since the probability of a tautology is always one, a tautology is absolutely confirmed by any evidence whatever. For example, evidence that it is raining absolutely confirms that all triangles have three sides. Since we would ordinarily say that there is no confirmation in this case, the concept of confirmation in ordinary language is not absolute confirmation.

If *E* reduces the probability of *H* then we would ordinarily say that *E* does not confirm *H*. However, in such a case it is possible for *H* to still be probable given *E* and hence for *E* to absolutely confirm *H*. This shows again that the concept of confirmation in ordinary language is not absolute confirmation.

A hypothesis *H* that is incrementally confirmed by evidence *E* may still be probably false; for example, the hypothesis that a fair coin will land "heads" every time in 1000 tosses is incrementally confirmed by the evidence that it landed "heads" on the first toss, but the hypothesis is still extremely improbable given this evidence. In a case like this nobody would ordinarily say that the hypothesis was confirmed. Thus it appears that the concept of confirmation in ordinary language is not incremental confirmation either.

A few confirmation theorists have attempted to formulate concepts of confirmation that would agree better with the ordinary concept. One such theorist is Nelson Goodman. He noted that if *E* incrementally confirms *H*, and *X* is an irrelevant proposition, then *E* incrementally confirms the conjunction of *H* and *X*. Goodman (1979) thought that in a case like this we would not say that *E* confirms the conjunction. He proposed that "*E* confirms *H*" means that *E* increases the probability of every component of *H*. One difficulty with this is to say what counts as a component of a hypothesis; if any logical consequence of *H* counts as a component of *H* then no hypothesis can ever be confirmed in Goodman's sense. In addition Goodman's proposal is open to the same objection as incremental confirmation: It allows that a hypothesis *H* can be confirmed by evidence *E* and yet *H* be probably false given *E*, which is not what people would ordinarily say.

Peter Achinstein (2001) speaks of "evidence" rather than "confirmation" but he can be regarded as proposing an account of the ordinary concept of confirmation. His account is complex but the leading idea is roughly that "*E* confirms *H*" means that (i) *H* is probable given *E* and (ii) it is probable that there is an explanatory connection between *H* and *E*, given that *H* and *E* are true. The explanatory connection may be that *H* explains *E*, *E* explains *H*, or *H* and *E* have a common explanation. Achinstein's proposal is open to one of the same objections as absolute confirmation: It allows evidence *E* to confirm *H* in cases in which *E* reduces the probability of *H*. Achinstein has argued that this implication is in agreement with the ordinary concept, but his reasoning has been criticized, for example, by Sherrilyn Roush (2004).

It appears that none of the concepts of confirmation discussed by confirmation theorists is the same as the ordinary concept of evidence confirming a hypothesis. Nevertheless, some of these concepts are worthy of study in their own right. In particular, the concepts of incremental and absolute confirmation are simple concepts that are of obvious importance and they are probably components in the more complex ordinary language concept of confirmation.

PROBABILITY

All the concepts of confirmation that we have discussed involve probability. However, the word "probability" is ambiguous. For example, suppose you have been told that a coin either has heads on both sides or else has tails on both sides and that it is about to be tossed. What is the probability that it will land heads? There are two natural answers: (i) ½; (ii) either 0 or 1 but I do not know which. These answers correspond to different meanings of the word "probability." The sense of the word "probability" in which (i) is the natural answer will here be called inductive probability. The sense in which (ii) is the natural answer will be called physical probability.

Physical probability depends on empirical facts in a way that inductive probability does not. We can see this from the preceding example; here the physical probability is unknown because it depends on the nature of the coin, which is unknown; by contrast the inductive probability is known even though the nature of the coin is unknown, showing that the inductive probability does not depend on the nature of the coin.

There are two main theories about the nature of physical probability. One is the frequency theory, according to which the physical probability of an event is the relative frequency with which the event happens in the long run. The other is the propensity theory, according to which the physical probability of an event is the propensity of the circumstances or experimental arrangement to produce that event.

It is widely agreed that the concept of probability involved in confirmation is not physical probability. One reason is that physical probabilities seem not to exist in many contexts in which we talk about confirmation. For example, we often take evidence as confirming a scientific theory but it does not seem that there is a physical probability of a particular scientific theory being true. (The theory is either true or false; there is no long run frequency with which it is true, nor does the evidence have a propensity to make the theory true.) Another reason is that physical probabilities depend on the facts in a way that confirmation relations do not. Inductive probability does not have either of these shortcomings and so it is natural to identify the concept of probability involved in confirmation with inductive probability. Therefore we will now discuss inductive probability in more detail.

Some contemporary writers appear to believe that the inductive probability of a proposition is some person's degree of belief in the proposition. Degree of belief is also called subjective probability, so on this view, inductive probability is the same as subjective probability. However, this is not correct. Suppose, for example, that I claim that scientific theory *H* is probable in view of the available evidence. This is a statement of inductive probability. If my claim is challenged, it would not be a relevant response for me to prove that I have a high degree of belief in *H*, though this would be relevant if inductive probability were subjective probability. To give a relevant defense of my claim I need to cite features of the available evidence that support *H*.

In saying that inductive probabilities are not subjective probabilities, we are not denying that when people make assertions about inductive probabilities they are expressing their degrees of belief. Every sincere and intentional assertion expresses the speaker's beliefs but not every assertion is about the speaker's beliefs.

We will now consider the concept of logical probability and, in particular, whether inductive probability is a kind of logical probability. This depends on what is meant by "logical probability."

Many writers define the "logical probability" of *H* given *E* as the degree of belief in *H* that would be rational for a person whose total evidence is *E*. However, the term "rational degree of belief" is far from clear. On some natural ways of understanding it, the degree of belief in *H* that is rational for a person could be high even when *H* has a low inductive probability given the person's evidence. This might happen because belief in *H* helps the person succeed in some task, or makes the person feel happy, or will be rewarded by someone who can read the person's mind. Even if it is specified that we are talking about rationality with respect to epistemic goals, the rational degree of belief can differ from the inductive probability given the person's evidence, since the rewards just mentioned may be epistemic. Alternatively, one might take "the rational degree of belief in *H* for a person whose total evidence is *E*" to be just another name for the inductive probability of *H* given *E*, in which case these concepts are trivially equivalent. Thus if one takes "logical probability" to be rational degree of belief then, depending on what one means by "rational degree of belief," it is either wrong or trivial to say that inductive probability is logical.

A more useful conception of logical probability can be defined as follows. Let an "elementary probability sentence" be a sentence that asserts that a specific hypothesis has a specific probability. Let a "logically determinate sentence" be a sentence whose truth or falsity is determined by meanings alone, independently of empirical facts. Let us say that a probability concept is "logical in Carnap's sense" if all elementary probability sentences for it are logically determinate. (This terminology is motivated by some of the characterizations of logical probability in Carnap's *Logical Foundations of Probability*.) Since inductive probability is not subjective probability, the truth of an elementary statement of inductive probability does not depend on some person's psychological state. It also does not depend on facts about the world in the way that statements of physical probability do. It thus appears the truth of an elementary statement of inductive probability does not depend on empirical facts at all and hence that inductive probability is logical in Carnap's sense.

It has often been said that logical probabilities do not exist. If this were right then it would follow that inductive probabilities are either not logical or else do not exist. So we will now consider arguments against the existence of logical probabilities.

John Maynard Keynes in 1921 published a theory of what we call inductive probability and he claimed that these are logical. Frank Ramsey (1926/1980) criticizing Keynes's theory, claimed that "there really do not seem to be any such things as the probability relations he describes." The main consideration that Ramsey offered in support of this was that there is little agreement on the values of probabilities in the simplest cases and these are just the cases where logical relations should be most clear. Ramsey's argument has been cited approvingly by several later authors.

However, Ramsey's claim that there is little agreement on the values of probabilities in the simplest cases seems not to be true. For example, almost everyone agrees with the following:

> (5) The probability that a ball is white, given only that it is either white or black, is ½.

Ramsey cited examples such as the probability of one thing being red given that another thing is red; he noted that nobody can state a precise numerical value for this probability. But that is an example of *agreement* about the value of an inductive probability, since *nobody* pretends to know a precise numerical value for the probability. What examples like this show is merely that inductive probabilities do not always have numerically precise values.

Furthermore, if inductive probabilities are logical (i.e., non-descriptive), it does not follow that their values should be clearest in the simplest cases, as Ramsey claimed. Like other concepts of ordinary language, the concept of inductive probability is learned largely from examples of its application in ordinary life and many of these examples will be complex. Hence, like other concepts of ordinary language, its application may sometimes be clearer in realistic complex situations than in simple situations that never arise in ordinary life.

So much for Ramsey's argument. Another popular argument against the existence of logical probabilities is based on the "paradoxes of indifference." The argument is this: Judgments of logical probability are said to presuppose a general principle, called the Principle of Indifference, which says that if evidence does not favor one hypothesis over another then those hypotheses are equally probable on this evidence. This principle can lead to different values for a probability, depending on what one takes the alternative hypotheses to be. In some cases the different choices seem equally natural. These "paradoxes of indifference," as they are called, are taken by many authors to be fatal to logical probability.

But even if we agree (as Keynes did) that quantitative inductive probabilities can only be determined via the Principle of Indifference, we can also hold (as Keynes did) that inductive probabilities do not always have quantitative values. Thus if there are cases where contradictory applications of the principle are equally natural, we may take this to show that these are cases where inductive probabilities lack quantitative values. It does not follow that quantitative inductive probabilities never exist, or that qualitative inductive probabilities do not exist. The paradoxes of indifference are thus consistent with the view that inductive probabilities exist and are logical.

How can we have knowledge of inductive probabilities, if this does not come from an exceptionless general principle? The answer is that the concept of inductive probability, like most concepts of ordinary language, is learned from examples, not by general principles. Hence we can have knowledge about particular inductive probabilities (and hence logical probabilities) without being able to state a general principle that covers these cases.

A positive argument for the existence of inductive probabilities is the following: We have seen reason to believe that a statement of inductive probability, such as (5), is either logically true or logically false. Which of these it is will be determined by the concepts involved, which are concepts of ordinary language. So, since competent speakers of a language normally use the language correctly, the wide endorsement of (5) is good reason to believe that (5) is a true sentence of English. And it follows from (5) that at least one inductive probability exists. Parallel arguments would establish the existence of many other inductive probabilities.

The concept of probability that is involved in confirmation can appropriately be taken to be inductive probability. Unlike physical probability, the concept of inductive probability applies to scientific theories. And unlike both physical and subjective probability, the concept of inductive probability agrees with the fact that confirmation relations are not discovered empirically but by examination of the relation between the hypothesis and the evidence.

EXPLICATION OF INDUCTIVE PROBABILITY

Inductive probability is a concept of ordinary language and, like many such concepts, it is vague. This is reflected in the fact that inductive probabilities often have no precise numerical value.

A useful way to theorize about vague concepts is to define a precise concept that is similar to the vague concept. This methodology is called explication, the vague concept is called the explicandum, and the precise concept that is meant to be similar to it is called the explicatum. Although the explicatum is intended to be similar to the explicandum, there must be differences, since the explicatum is precise and the explicandum is vague. Other desiderata for an explicatum, besides similarity with the explicandum, are theoretical fruitfulness and simplicity.

Inductive probability can be explicated by defining, for selected pairs of sentences E and H, a number that will be the explicatum for the inductive probability of H given E; let us denote this number by "$p(H|E)$." The set of sentences for which $p(H|E)$ is defined will depend on our purposes.

Quantitative inductive probabilities, where they exist, satisfy the mathematical laws of probability. Since a good explicatum is similar to the explicandum, theoretically fruitful, and simple, the numbers $p(H|E)$ will also be required to satisfy these laws.

In works written from the 1940s to his death in 1970, Carnap proposed a series of increasingly sophisticated explications of this kind, culminating in his *Basic System of Inductive Logic* published posthumously in 1971 and 1980. Other authors have proposed other explicata, some of which will be mentioned below.

Since the value of $p(H|E)$ is specified by definition, a statement of the form "$p(H|E) = r$" is either true by definition or false by definition, and hence is logically determinate. Since we require these values to satisfy the laws of probability, the function p is also a probability function. So we may say that the function p is a logical probability in Carnap's sense.

Thus there are two different kinds of probability, both of which are logical in Carnap's sense: Inductive probability and functions that are proposed as explicata for inductive probability. Since the values of the explicata are specified by definition, it is undeniable that logical probabilities of this second kind exist.

EXPLICATION OF INCREMENTAL CONFIRMATION

Since inductive probability is vague, and E incrementally confirms H if and only if E raises the inductive probability of H, the concept of incremental confirmation is also vague. We will now consider how to explicate incremental confirmation.

First, we note that the judgment that E confirms H is often made on the assumption that some other information D is given; this information is called background evidence. So we will take the form of a fully explicit judgment of incremental confirmation to be "E incrementally confirms H given D." For example, a coin landing heads on the first toss incrementally confirms that the coin has heads on both sides, given that both sides of the coin are the same; there would be no confirmation if the background evidence was that the coin is normal with heads on one side only.

The judgment that E incrementally confirms H given D means that the inductive probability of H given both E and D is greater than the inductive probability of H given only D. Suppose we have a function p that is an explicatum for inductive probability and is defined for the relevant statements. Let "$E.D$" represent the conjunction of E and D (so the dot here functions like "and"). Then the explicatum for "E incrementally confirms H given D" will be $p(H|E.D) > p(H|D)$. We will use the notation "$C(H, E, D)$" as an abbreviation for this explicatum.

The concept of incremental confirmation, like all the concepts of confirmation discussed so far, is a qualitative concept. For each of these qualitative concepts there is a corresponding comparative concept, which compares the amount of confirmation in different cases. We will focus here on the judgment that E_1 incrementally confirms H more than E_2 does, given D. The corresponding statement in terms of our explicata is that the increase from $p(H|D)$ to $p(H|E_1.D)$ is larger than the increase from $p(H|D)$ to $p(H|E_2.D)$. This is true if and only if $p(H|E_1.D) > p(H|E_2D)$, so the explicatum for "E_1 confirms H more than E_2 does, given D" will be $p(H|E_1.D) > p(H|E_2.D)$. We will use the notation "$M(H,E_1,E_2,D)$" as an abbreviation for this explicatum.

Confirmation theorists have also discussed quantitative concepts of confirmation, which involve assigning numerical "degrees of confirmation" to hypotheses. In earlier literature the term "degree of confirmation" usually meant degree of absolute confirmation. The degree to which E absolutely confirms H is the same as the inductive probability of H given E and hence is explicated by $p(H|E)$.

In later literature, the term "degree of confirmation" is more likely to mean degree of incremental confirmation. An explicatum for the degree to which E incrementally confirms H given D is a measure of how much $p(H|E.D)$ is greater than $p(H|D)$. Many different explicata of this kind have been proposed; they include the following. (Here "$\sim H$" means the negation of H.)

Difference measure: $p(H|E.D) - p(H|D)$

Ratio measure: $p(H|E.D) / p(H|D)$

Likelihood ratio: $p(E|H.D) / p(E|{\sim}H.D)$

Confirmation theorists continue to debate the merits of these and other measures of degree of incremental confirmation.

VERIFIED CONSEQUENCES

The remainder of this entry will consider various properties of incremental confirmation and how well these are captured by the explicata C and M that were defined above. We begin with the idea that hypotheses are confirmed by verifying their logical consequences.

If H logically implies E given background evidence D, we usually suppose that observation of E would incrementally confirm H given D. For example, Einstein's general theory of relativity, together with other known facts, implied that the orbit of Mercury precesses at a certain rate; hence the observation that it did precess at this rate incrementally confirmed Einstein's theory, given the other known facts.

The corresponding explicatum statement is: If $H.D$ implies E then $C(H,E,D)$. Assuming that p satisfies the laws of mathematical probability, this explicatum statement can be proved true provided that $0 > p(H|D) > 1$ and $p(E|D) < 1$.

We can see intuitively why the provisos are needed. If $p(H|D) = 1$ then H is certainly true given D and so no evidence can incrementally confirm it. If $p(H|D) = 0$ then H is certainly false given D and the observation that one of its consequences is true need not alter this situation. If $p(E|D) = 1$ then E was certainly true given D and so the observation that it is true cannot provide new evidence for H.

If H and D imply both E_1 and E_2, and if E_1 is less probable than E_2 given D, then we usually suppose that H would be better confirmed by E_1 than by E_2, given D. The corresponding explicatum statement is: If $H.D$ implies E_1 and E_2, and $p(E_1|D) < p(E_2|D)$, then $M(H, E_1, E_2, D)$. Assuming that p satisfies the laws of probability, this can be proved true provided that $0 < p(H|D) < 1$. The proviso makes sense intuitively for the same reasons as before.

If H and D imply both E_1 and E_2 then we usually suppose that E_1 and E_2 together would confirm H more than E_1 alone, given D. The corresponding explicatum statement is that if $H.D$ implies E_1 and E_2 then $M(H, E_1.E_2, E_1, D)$. It follows from the result in the previous paragraph that this is true, provided that $p(E_1.E_2|D) < p(E_1|D)$ and $0 < p(H|D) < 1$. The provisos are needed for the same reasons as before.

These results show that, if we require p to satisfy the laws of probability, then C and M will be similar to their explicanda with respect to verified consequences and, to that extent at least, C and M will be good explicata. In addition these results illustrate in a small way the value of explication. Although the provisos that we added make sense when one thinks about them, the need for them is likely to be overlooked if one thinks only in terms of the vague explicanda and does not attempt to prove a precise corresponding result in terms of the explicata. Thus explication can give a deeper and more accurate understanding of the explicandum. We will see more examples of this.

REASONING BY ANALOGY

If two individuals are known to be alike in certain respects, and one is found to have a particular property, we often infer that, since the individuals are similar, the other individual probably also has that property. This is a simple example of reasoning by analogy, and it is a kind of reasoning that we use every day.

In order to explicate this kind of reasoning, we will use "*a*" and "*b*" to stand for individual things and "*F*" and "*G*" for logically independent properties that an individual may have (for example, being tall and blond). We will use "*Fa*" to mean that the individual *a* has the property *F*; similarly for other properties and individuals.

It is generally accepted that reasoning by analogy is stronger the more properties that the individuals are known to have in common. So for *C* to be a good explicatum it must satisfy the following condition:

(6) *C (Gb, Fa.Fb, Ga).*

Here we are considering the situation in which the background evidence is that *a* has *G*. The probability that *b* also has *G* is increased by finding that *a* and *b* also share the property *F*.

In the case just considered, *a* and *b* are not known to differ in any way. When we reason by analogy in real life we normally do know some respects in which the individuals differ, but this does not alter the fact that the reasoning is stronger the more alike *a* and *b* are known to be. So for *C* to be a good explicatum it must also satisfy the following condition. (Here *F'* is a property that is logically independent of both *F* and *G*.)

(7) *C (Gb, Fa.Fb, Ga.F'a.~F'b).*

Here the background evidence is that *a* has *G* and that *a* and *b* differ in regard to *F'*. The probability that *b* has *G* is increased by finding that *a* and *b* are alike in having *F*.

Another condition that *C* should satisfy is:

(8) *C (Gb, Ga, F'a. ~F'b).*

Here the background evidence is merely that *a* and *b* differ regarding *F'*. For all we know, whether or not something has *F'* might be unrelated to whether it has *G*, so the fact that *a* has *G* is still some reason to think that *b* has *G*.

In *Logical Foundations of Probability* Carnap proposed a particular explicatum for inductive probability that he called *c**. In *The Continuum of Inductive Methods* he described an infinite class of possible explicata. The function *c**, and all the functions in Carnap's continuum, satisfy (6) but not (7) or (8). Hence none of these functions provides a fully satisfactory explicatum for situations that involve more than one logically independent property.

Carnap recognized this failure early in the 1950s and worked to find explicata that would handle reasoning by analogy more adequately. He first found a class of possible explicata for the case where there are two logically independent properties; the functions in this class satisfy (6) and (8). Subsequently, with the help of John Kemeny, Carnap generalized his proposal to the case where there are any finite number of logically independent properties, though he never published this. A simpler and less adequate generalization was published by Mary Hesse in 1964. Both these generalizations satisfy all of (6)-(8).

Carnap had no justification for the functions he proposed except that they seemed to agree with intuitive principles of reasoning by analogy. Later he found that they actually violate one of the principles he had taken to be intuitive. In his last work Carnap expressed indecision about how to proceed.

For the case where there are just two properties, Maher (2000) has shown that certain foundational assumptions pick out a class of probability functions, called P_I, that includes the functions that Carnap proposed for this case. Maher argued that the probability functions in P_I handle reasoning by analogy adequately and Carnap's doubts were misplaced.

For the case where there are more than two properties, Maher (2001) has shown that the proposals of Hesse, and Carnap and Kemeny, correspond to implausible foundational assumptions and violate intuitive principles of reasoning by analogy. Further research is needed to find an explicatum for inductive probability that is adequate for situations involving more than two properties.

NICOD'S CONDITION

We are often interested in universal generalizations of the form "All *F* are *G*," for example, "All ravens are black," or "All metals conduct electricity." Nicod's condition, named after the French philosopher Jean Nicod, says that generalizations of this form are confirmed by finding an individual that is both *F* and *G*. (Here and in the remainder of this entry, "confirmed" means incrementally confirmed.)

Nicod (1970) did not mention background evidence. It is now well known that Nicod's condition is not true when there is background evidence of certain kinds. For example, suppose the background evidence is that, if there are any ravens, then there is a non-black raven. Relative to this background evidence, observation of a black raven would refute, not confirm, that all ravens are black.

Hempel claimed that Nicod's condition is true when there is no background evidence but I. J. Good argued that this is also wrong. Good's argument was essentially this: Given no evidence whatever, it is improbable that there are any ravens, and if there are no ravens then, according to standard logic, "All ravens are black" is true. Hence, given no evidence, "All ravens are black" is probably true. However, if ravens do exist, they are probably a variety of colors, so finding a black raven would increase the probability that there is a non-black raven and hence disconfirm that all ravens are black, contrary to Nicod's condition.

Hempel was relying on intuition, and Good's counterargument is intuitive rather than rigorous. A different way to investigate the question is to use precise explicata. The situation of "no background evidence" can be explicated by taking the background evidence to be any logically true sentence; let *T* be such a sentence. Letting A be "all *F* are *G*," the claim that Nicod's condition holds when there is no background evidence may be expressed in explicatum terms as

(9) $C(A, Fa.Ga, T)$.

Maher has shown that this can fail when the explicatum p is a function in P_I and that the reason for the failure is the one identified in Good's argument. This confirms that Nicod's condition is false even when there is no background evidence.

Why then has Nicod's condition seemed plausible? One reason may be that people sometimes do not clearly distinguish between Nicod's condition and the following statement: Given that an object is F, the evidence that it is *G* confirms that all *F* are *G*. The latter statement may be expressed in explicatum terms as:

(10) $C(A, Ga, Fa)$.

This is true provided only that *p* satisfies the laws of probability, $0 < p(A|Fa) < 1$, and $p(Ga|Fa) < 1$. (This follows from the first of the results stated earlier for verified consequences.) If people do not clearly distinguish between the ordinary language statements that correspond to (9) and (10), the truth of the latter could make it seem that Nicod's condition is true.

THE RAVENS PARADOX

The following three principles about confirmation have seemed plausible to many people.

(11) Nicod's condition holds when there is no background evidence.

(12) Confirmation relations are unchanged by substitution of logically equivalent sentences.

(13) In the absence of background evidence, the evidence that some individual is a non-black non-raven does not confirm that all ravens are black.

However, these three principles are inconsistent. That is because (11) implies that a non-black non-raven confirms "all non-black things are non-ravens," and the latter is logically equivalent to "all ravens are black," so by (12) a non-black non-raven confirms "all ravens are black," contrary to (13).

Hempel was the first to discuss this paradox. His initial statement of the paradox did not explicitly include the condition of no background evidence but he stated later in his article that this was to be understood. The subsequent literature on this paradox is enormous but most discussions have not respected the condition of no background evidence. Here we will follow Hempel in respecting that condition.

The contradiction shows that at least one of (11)-(13) is false. Hempel claimed that (11) and (12) are true and (13) is false but his judgments were based on informal intuitions, not on any precise explicatum or use of probability theory.

Our preceding discussion of Nicod's condition shows that (11) is false, contrary to what Hempel thought. On the other hand, our explicata support Hempel's view that (12) is true and (13) is false, as we will now show.

In explicatum terms, what (12) says is: If H', E', and D' are logically equivalent to *H*, *E*, and *D* respectively, then $C(H, E, D)$ if and only if $C(H', E', D')$. The truth of this follows from the assumption that *p* satisfies the laws of probability.

Now let "*F*" mean "raven" and "*G*" mean "black." Then (13), expressed in explicatum terms, is the claim $\sim C(A, \sim Fa.\sim Ga, T)$. Maher has shown that this need not be true when p is a function in P_I; we can instead have *C (A, ~Fa. ~Ga, T)*. This happens for two reasons:

(a) The evidence *~Fa.~Ga* reduces the probability of *Fb.~Gb*, where *b* is any individual other than *a*. Thus *~Fa.~Ga* reduces the probability that another individual *b* is a counterexample to *A*.

(b) The evidence *~Fa.~Ga* tells us that *a* is not a counterexample to *A*, which a priori it could have been.

Both of these reasons make sense intuitively.

We conclude that, of the three principles (11)-(13), only (12) is true.

PROJECTABILITY

A predicate is said to be "projectable" if the evidence that the predicate applies to some objects confirms that it also applies to other objects. The standard example of a predicate that is not projectable is "grue," which was introduced by Goodman (1979). According to Goodman's defnition, something is grue if either (i) it is observed before time *t* and is green or (ii) it is not observed before time *t* and is blue. The usual argument that "grue" is not projectable goes something like this: A grue emerald observed before *t* is green, and observation of such an emerald confirms that emeralds not observed before *t* are also green. Since a green emerald not observed before *t* is not grue, it follows that a grue emerald observed before *t* confirms that emeralds not observed before *t* are not grue; hence "grue" is not projectable.

The preceding account of the meaning of "projectable" was the usual one but it is imprecise because it fails to specify background evidence. Let us say that a predicate ϕ is absolutely projectable if $C(\phi b, \phi a, T)$ for any distinct individuals *a* and *b* and logical truth *T*. This concept of absolute projectability is one possible explicatum for the usual imprecise concept of projectability. Let "*Fa*" mean that *a* is observed before *t* and let "*Ga*" mean that *a* is green. Let "*G'a*" mean that either *Fa.Ga* or *~Fa.~ Ga*. Thus "*G'*" has a meaning similar to "grue." (The difference is just that *G* uses "not green" instead of "blue" and so avoids introducing a third property.) Maher has proved that if p is any function in P_I then "*F*", "*G*", and "*G'* " are all absolutely projectable. It may seem unintuitive that "*G'* " is absolutely projectable. However, this result corresponds to the following statement of ordinary language: The probability that *b* is grue is higher given that *a* is grue than if one was not given any evidence whatever. If we keep in mind that we do not know whether *a* or *b* was observed before *t*, this should be intuitively acceptable. So philosophers who say that "grue" is not projectable are wrong if, by "projectable," they mean absolute projectability.

Let us say that a predicate ϕ is projectable across another predicate ψ if $C(\phi b, \phi a, \psi a.\sim\psi b)$ for any distinct individuals *a* and *b*. This concept of projectability across another predicate is a second possible explicatum for the usual imprecise concept of projectability.

It can be shown that if p is any function in P_I then "*G*" is, and "*G'* " is not, projectable across "*F*." So philosophers who say that "grue" is not projectable are right if, by "projectable," they mean projectability across the predicate "observed before *t*."

Now suppose we change the definition of "*Ga*" to be that *a* is (i) observed before *t* and green or (ii) not observed before *t* and not green. Thus "*G*" now means what "*G'* " used to mean. Keeping the definitions of "*F*" and "*G'* " unchanged, "*G'a*" now means that *a* is green. The results reported in the preceding paragraph will still hold but now they are the opposite of the usual views about what is projectable. This shows that, when we are constructing explicata for inductive probability and confirmation, the meanings assigned to the basic predicates (here "*F*" and "*G*") need to be intuitively simple ones rather than intuitively complex concepts like "grue."

See also Carnap, Rudolf; Einstein, Albert; Goodman, Nelson; Hempel, Carl Gustav; Induction; Keynes, John Maynard; Probability and Chance; Ramsey, Frank Plumpton; Relativity Theory.

Bibliography

Achinstein, Peter. *The Book of Evidence*. New York: Oxford University Press, 2001.

Carnap, Rudolf. "A Basic System of Inductive Logic, Part I." In *Studies in Inductive Logic and Probability*. Vol. 1, edited by Rudolf Carnap and Richard C. Jeffrey. Berkeley: University of California Press, 1971.

Carnap, Rudolf. "A Basic System of Inductive Logic, Part II." In *Studies in Inductive Logic and Probability*. Vol. 2, edited by Richard C. Jeffrey. Berkeley: University of California Press, 1980.

Carnap, Rudolf. *The Continuum of Inductive Methods*. Chicago: University of Chicago Press, 1952.

Carnap, Rudolf. *Logical Foundations of Probability*. Chicago: University of Chicago Press, 1950. Second edition 1962.

Earman, John. *Bayes or Bust? A Critical Examination of Bayesian Confirmation Theory*. Cambridge, MA: MIT Press, 1992.

Festa, Roberto. "Bayesian Confirmation." In *Experience, Reality, and Scientific Explanation*, edited by Maria Carla Galavotti and Alessandro Pagnini. Dordrecht: Kluwer, 1999.

Fitelson, Branden. "The Plurality of Bayesian Measures of Confirmation and the Problem of Measure Sensitivity." *Philosophy of Science* 66 (1999): S362–S378.

Gillies, Donald. *Philosophical Theories of Probability*. London: Routledge, 2000.

Good, I. J. "The White Shoe *qua* Herring Is Pink." *British Journal for the Philosophy of Science* 19 (1968): 156–157.

Goodman, Nelson. *Fact, Fiction, and Forecast*. 3rd ed. Indianapolis, IN: Hackett, 1979.

Hempel, Carl G. "Studies in the Logic of Confirmation." *Mind* 54 (1945): 1–26 and 97–121. Reprinted with some changes in Carl G. Hempel. *Aspects of Scientific Explanation*. New York: The Free Press, 1965.

Hesse, Mary. "Analogy and Confirmation Theory." *Philosophy of Science* 31 (1964): 319–327.

Howson, Colin, and Peter Urbach. *Scientific Reasoning: The Bayesian Approach*. 2nd ed. Chicago: Open Court, 1993.

Keynes, John Maynard. *A Treatise on Probability*. London: Macmillan, 1921. Reprinted with corrections, 1948.

Maher, Patrick. "Probabilities for Two Properties." *Erkenntnis* 52 (2000): 63–91.

Maher, Patrick. "Probabilities for Multiple Properties: The Models of Hesse and Carnap and Kemeny." *Erkenntnis* 55 (2001): 183–216.

Maher, Patrick. "Probability Captures the Logic of Scientific Confirmation." In *Contemporary Debates in Philosophy of Science*, edited by Christopher R. Hitchcock. Oxford: Blackwell, 2004.

Nicod, Jean. *Geometry and Induction*. Berkeley and Los Angeles: University of California Press, 1970. English translation of works originally published in French in 1923 and 1924.

Ramsey, Frank P. "Truth and Probability." Article written in 1926 and published in many places, including *Studies in Subjective Probability*, 2nd ed., edited by Henry E. Kyburg, Jr. and Howard E. Smokler. Huntington, New York: Krieger, 1980.

Roush, Sherrilyn. "Positive Relevance Defended." *Philosophy of Science* 71 (2004):110–116.

Salmon, Wesley C. "Confirmation and Relevance." In *Minnesota Studies in the Philosophy of Science*. Vol. VI: *Induction, Probability, and Confirmation*, ed. Grover Maxwell and Robert M. Anderson Jr. Minneapolis: University of Minnesota Press, 1975.

Skyrms, Brian. *Choice and Chance*. 4th ed. Belmont, CA: Wadsworth, 2000.

Stalker, Douglas, ed. *Grue: Essays on the New Riddle of Induction*. Chicago: Open Court, 1994.

Patrick Maher (2005)

CONFUCIUS

(551–479 BCE)

Confucius (Kong Qiu) is one of the early Chinese philosophers and the founder of the ethical teaching known as Confucianism. He was born in a time of political, social, and spiritual crisis that had shattered the traditional way of life as well as the view of a world based on the conventions of ritual propriety (*li*) and the religion of Heaven (*tian*). The hierarchies of the patriarchal feudal system of the Zhou had fallen into decay, giving way to a new social mobility, and because of this, a small but influential middle class emerged. Its members became the clients of private teachers who imparted the knowledge needed in a society that ascribed increasing importance to individual capability instead of descent.

Confucius (a transcription of Kong fuzi—teacher Kong) was one of these teachers. He probably taught the practical "six arts" (writing, mathematics, ritual propriety, music, charioteering, and archery) and dealt with the texts handed down from the past that he is said to have edited and that constitute the core of the later Confucian classics. However, as documented by his "Collected Words" (*Lunyu*, a later compilation), the main focus of his teaching is morality. Confucius dedicates himself to an ideal of education that transcends the social boundaries and roles the disciples would possibly play in their present and later life—the ideal of becoming a gentleman (*junzi*), a truly moral person in solidarity with the community and rooted in self-respect. This endeavor is again embedded in the quest for a still higher goal: To rescue "this culture" from the flood in which it was drowning, and to "change the world" that had lost the dao, the right way (*LY* 9.5, 18.6).

To find a solution for the world in a time when tradition was in crisis enforced a reflection on the established norms in order to reconstruct and rescue their true meaning (*zheng ming*). This gives a philosophical ring to Confucius's ethics. He finds one of the paradigmatic answers to the challenge China's intellectuals were facing: How to redefine humankind's position in a world that had lost its foundation, without the possibility for reiterating the past. His answer is the internalization of ethics as a new basis for the ethical life, which entails both constant self-reference of the individual and norm reflexivity. It has always remained a Confucian conviction that there must be ethical rather than legal or organizational solutions to the basic problems of human existence; that morality must have primacy over all other concerns, also over politics; and that the human being as its agent is capable of moral cultivation. This makes the Confucian position distinct both from the Daoist return to nature and the legalist social engineering.

The general structure of ethics of the *Lunyu* may be described as comprising three steps: (1) In view of the sobering conditions of the time, the "gentleman" *turns away* from society; he no longer trusts public reputation

(*LY* 12.20) and the opinions of the majority (13.24, 15.28); and he is constantly prepared to be misjudged and not acknowledged by others (1.1, 1.16, 14.30, 15.19). He then (2) *turns into his inner self* where in private seclusion he develops self-respect (5.16, 13.19) as the basis for autonomous action and, given the absence of a strong religious backing of ethics, the ultimate reason for being moral. Through regular self-reflection and critical self-examination (1.4, 5.27, 12.4, 15.21) he safeguards the purity of his intentions, which, if necessary, will enable him to, as Confucius is quoted in the *Mengzi*, "withstand thousands or tens of thousands" (2a:2). However, in a final step, the moral actor (3) consciously "overcomes himself" and *returns* to society (*ke ji fu li*) (*LY* 12.1). He thus accepts his responsibility as a moral authority in the interest of the common good, rather than simply trying to stay "clean" in a world where "the *dao* does not prevail" (18.7), far away from the ideal of the "great community" (*da tong*, attributed to Confucius in *Liji* 9).

Return to society implies the critical acknowledgement of the given ethos of a hierarchical world dominated by the principle of male seniority. Without the handed-down rules of propriety (*li*) the human being would be without a firm "standing" (*lì*) (*LY* 8.8, 16.13, 20.3). However, the traditional canon of normative orientations is reconsidered and realigned to a new organizing center—humaneness (*ren*). Humaneness has "to start from oneself" rather than from external guidance (12.1); it is ideally followed for its own sake rather than for reasons of utility (4.2); and it is universally valid, even when one is among barbarian tribes (13.19).

Humaneness is explicated differently, however, in the *Lunyu*, the most conspicuous variants being its affective reading as love (12.22) and its cognitive reading as the golden rule (5.12, 6.30, 12.2, 15.23), the maxim that "consists of one word and can be practiced through all one's life" (15.24) and the "one that goes through all" (4.15). By humaneness in terms of the golden rule, the direct reciprocal relationship with the generalized "other" becomes one of the two complementary dimensions of ethics along with the concrete role orientation.

Confucius's ethics thus promises a "mean" comprising personal integrity and social integration, allowing one to keep faith with the conventional ethos while not surrendering to it. The "gentleman" as its protagonist will fulfill the duties owed to family and society and at the same time, "harmonious, but not conformist" (13.23), maintain a moral watchfulness and inner independence.

It was possible, however, to adopt this ethics with different accents, also because of the vagueness of many *Lunyu* passages and the opacity of its structure. The conflict of opinions about the true teaching of the master, the attempts to regain the original spirit lost in the course of its effective history, as well as Confucius's critique as a rebel, a ritualist, and a moralist out of touch with reality, apparently started shortly after his death. The debate still continues in the twenty-first century, with deontological, pragmatist, aestheticist, communitarian, and religious interpretations competing with each other.

See also Chinese Philosophy: Confucianism.

Bibliography

Creel, Herrlee G. *Confucius and the Chinese Way*. New York: Harper, 1960.

Lau, D. C. *Confucius: The Analects (Lun Yü)*. 2nd ed. Hong Kong: Chinese University Press, 1993.

Roetz, Heiner. *Confucian Ethics of the Axial Age*. Albany: SUNY Press, 1993.

Roetz, Heiner. *Konfuzius*. Munich: Beck, 1998.

Schaberg, David. "Sell it! Sell it! Recent Translations of Lunyu." *Chinese Literature: Essays, Articles, Reviews* 23 (2001): 115–139.

Van Norden, Bryan W., ed. *Confucius and the Analects: New Essays*. New York: Oxford University Press, 2002. Contains a comprehensive bibliography.

Heiner Roetz (2005)

CONNECTIONISM

"Connectionism" is an approach within cognitive science that employs neural networks, rather than computer programs, as the basis for modeling mentality. A connectionist system, or neural network, is a structure of simple neuronlike processors called nodes or units. Each node has directed connections to other nodes, so that the nodes send and receive excitatory and inhibitory signals to and from one another. The total input to a node determines its state of activation. When a node is on, it sends out signals to the nodes to which it has output connections, with the intensity of a signal depending upon both (1) the activation level of the sending node and (2) the strength or "weight" of the connection between it and the receiving node. Typically at each moment during processing, many nodes are simultaneously sending signals to others.

When neural networks are employed for information processing, certain nodes are designated "input" units and others as "output" units, and potential patterns of activation across them are assigned interpretations. (The remaining nodes are called "hidden units.") Typically a "problem" is posed to a network by activating a pattern in the input nodes; then the various nodes in the system simultaneously send and receive signals repeatedly until the system settles into a stable configuration; the semantic interpretation of the resulting pattern in the output nodes is what the system currently represents, hence its "answer" to the problem. Connectionist systems are capable of "learning" from "experience" by having their weights changed systematically in a way that depends upon how well the network has performed in generating solutions to problems posed to it as a training regimen. (Typically the device employed is not an actual neural network but a simulation of one on a standard digital computer.)

The most striking difference between such networks and conventional computers is the lack of an executive component. In a conventional computer the behavior of the whole system is controlled at the central processing unit (CPU) by a stored program. A connectionist system lacks both a CPU and a stored program. Nevertheless, often in a connectionist system certain activation patterns over sets of hidden units can be interpreted as internal representations with interesting content, and often the system also can be interpreted as embodying, in its weighted connections, information that gets automatically accommodated during processing without getting explicitly represented via activation patterns.

Connectionist models have yielded particularly encouraging results for cognitive processes such as learning, pattern recognition, and so-called multiple-soft-constraint satisfaction (i.e., solving a problem governed by several constraints, where an optimal solution may require violating some constraints in order to satisfy others). For example, Terry Sejnowski and Charles Rosenberg trained a network they called NETtalk to convert inputs that represent a sequence of letters, spaces, and punctuation constituting written English into outputs that represent the audible sounds constituting the corresponding spoken English. (The phonetic output code then can be fed into a speech synthesizer, a device that actually produces the sounds.)

Philosophical discussion of connectionism has largely centered on whether connectionism yields or suggests a conception of mentality that is importantly different from the conception of mind-as-computer at the core of classical cognitive science. Several different nonclassical alternatives have been suggested; each has been alleged to fit well with connectionism, and each has been a locus of debate between fans and foes of connectionism. Three proposed interpretations of connectionism deserve specific mention.

On one view, the key difference between classical models of mental processes and connectionist models is that the former assume the existence of languagelike mental representations that constitute a so-called language of thought (LOT), whereas the latter supposedly favor representations that are alleged to be inherently non-languagelike in structure: namely, activation patterns distributed over several nodes of a network, so-called activation vectors. On this interpretation connectionism shares with classicism the assumption that cognition is computation over mental representations—that cognitive transitions conform to rules for transforming representations on the basis of their formal structure, rules that could be formulated as an explicit computer program. (In connectionist systems the rules are wired into the weights and connections rather than being explicitly represented. In classical systems some rules must be hard wired; and there may be—but need not be—other rules that are explicitly represented as stored data structures.) The key difference allegedly turns on the languagelike or non-languagelike structure of mental representations.

This construal of connectionism fits naturally with the idea that human cognition involves state transitions that are all essentially associative—in the sense that they reflect statistical correlations among items the system can represent and can be analyzed as the drawing of statistical inferences. Many fans of connectionism, including Patricia Churchland and Paul Churchland, evidently see things this way and tend to regard connectionism as breathing new life into associationism. Prominent foes of connectionism, notably Jerry Fodor and Zenon Pylyshyn, also see things this way; but they regard the link with associationism as grounds for maintaining that connectionism is bound to founder on the same general problem that plagued traditional associationism in psychology: namely, inability to account for the rich semantic coherence of much human thought. To overcome this problem, Fodor and Pylyshyn maintain, cognitive science must continue to posit both (1) mental representations that encode propositional information via languagelike syntactic structure and (2) modes of processing that are suitably sensitive to syntactic structure and are thereby sensitive to propositional content.

A second interpretation of connectionism claims that connectionist models do not really employ internal representations at all in their hidden units (and, a fortiori, do not employ internal representations with languagelike structure). This view has been defended—by Rodney Brooks, for example—on the grounds that putative representations in connectionist systems play no genuine explanatory role. It has also been defended—for instance, by Hubert Dreyfus and Stuart Dreyfus—on the basis of a Heideggerian critique of the notion of mental representation itself. The approach goes contrary to the views of most (but not all) practicing connectionists, who typically posit internal representations in connectionist models and assign them a central explanatory role.

A third interpretation assumes the existence of internal mental representations; and it does not deny—indeed, the version defended by Terence Horgan and John Tienson resolutely affirms—that mental representations often have languagelike structure. It focuses instead on the classical assumption that cognition is computation (see above). This third approach maintains (1) that much of human cognition is too rich and too subtle to conform to programmable rules and (2) that connectionism has theoretical resources for potentially explaining such nonalgorithmic cognitive processing. The approach stresses that there is a powerful branch of mathematics that applies naturally to neural networks: dynamical systems theory. According to this anticomputational construal of connectionism, there can be cognitive systems—subservable mathematically by dynamical systems, which in turn are subservable physically by neural networks—whose cognitive state transitions are not tractably computable. In other words, mental activity in these systems is too refined and too supple to conform to programmable rules. Humans are alleged to be such cognitive systems, and connectionism (so interpreted) is held to yield a more adequate picture of the mind than the classical computational picture.

One objection to this third interpretation of connectionism alleges that cognitive state transitions in a connectionist system must inevitably conform to programmable rules, especially since neural networks are simulable on standard computers. Another objection, directed specifically at the version that retains languagelike representations, alleges that the LOT hypothesis is intelligible only on the assumption that cognition is computation.

In much of the early philosophical debate between proponents and opponents of connectionism, the first interpretation was largely taken for granted. But as competing interpretations get articulated, defended, and acknowledged, philosophical discussion of connectionism and its potential implications becomes richer.

See also Cognitive Science; Fodor, Jerry A.; Language of Thought; Philosophy of Mind.

Bibliography

Aizawa, K. "Explaining Systematicity." *Mind and Language* 12 (1997): 115–136.

Bechtel, W., and A. Abrahamsen. *Connectionism and the Mind: Parallel Processing, Dynamics, and Evolution in Networks.* 2nd ed. Oxford: Blackwell, 2001.

Churchland, P. M. "Conceptual Similarity across Sensory and Neural Diversity: The Fodor/Lepore Challenge Answered." *Journal of Philosophy* 95 (1998): 5–32.

Clark, A., and P. Millican, eds. *Connectionism, Concepts, and Folk Psychology.* Oxford: Oxford University Press, 1996.

Cummins, R. "Systematicity." *Journal of Philosophy* 93 (1996): 561–614

Dawson, M. *Minds and Machines: Connectionism and Psychological Modeling.* Oxford: Blackwell, 2004.

Horgan, T., and J. Tienson. *Connectionism and the Philosophy of Psychology.* Cambridge, MA.: MIT Press, 1996.

Macdonald, C., ed. *Connectionism: Debates on Psychological Explanation.* Oxford: Blackwell, 1995.

Marcus, G. *The Algebraic Mind.* Cambridge, MA: MIT Press, 2001.

McLeod, P., K. Plunkett, and E. T. Rolls. *Introduction to Connectionist Modelling of Cognitive Processes.* Oxford: Oxford University Press, 1998.

Tomberlin, J., ed. *Philosophical Perspectives 9: AI, Connectionism and Philosophical Psychology.* Atascadero: Ridgeview Press, 1995.

Tuescher, C. *Turing's Connectionism. An Investigation of Neural Network Architectures.* London: Springer-Verlag, 2002.

Terence E. Horgan (1996)
Bibliography updated by Alyssa Ney (2005)

CONSCIENCE

Doubtless from the earliest times in which groups established social customs, or mores, and enforced them, members of such groups who were tempted to violate these mores could almost feel the disapproval of their fellows and hear in their own minds a protesting outcry, perhaps some primitive equivalent of "No!" or "Don't!" In the early eighteenth century such inner voices or feelings were described as edicts of one's moral sense or of one's "conscience." This kind of account of these restraining influences became explicit with the development of faculty psychology, which involved the view that there are different faculties of the human mind responsible for different capacities or abilities which the mind seems to exhibit. Reason was thought of as the rational faculty, emotion as a passional one, and volition as a faculty that enables us to reach decisions and make choices. The moral faculty was thought by some, the earl of Shaftesbury and Francis Hutcheson, for example, to operate through feelings. For instance, a feeling of repugnance would tend to be aroused by the thought of doing anything immoral—anything in violation of the mores—and a feeling of approval by the thought of acting virtuously.

In contrast with this moral-sense type of theory, Samuel Clarke and Richard Price, among others, thought that it must be something akin to reason or the understanding which enabled us to distinguish right from wrong. Joseph Butler termed this faculty of the mind "conscience," and in more recent times this term has become the common one.

Modern behaviorists, to be sure, would not write of conscience as a mental faculty; they refer instead to "learned modes of reaction to stimuli." When one has been conditioned to respond in certain standard ways which are widely and strongly approved, one tends to find that one can break with such approved behavioral norms only after a genuine struggle and a stiff volitional conflict. In any case, whether we speak of the voice of conscience or of the voice of our group or of learned blockage and interference patterns, we often find that there are inhibitions to be overcome before we can break with the mores of our peers.

It has been suggested that a policeman, upholding the law, functions as a kind of government-supported externalized conscience. His mere presence in uniform suffices to warn us not to break, for example, the speed law that we are already bending a bit. Even animals below the human level can be trained to feel the force of such an externalized conscience. Cats, for example, can be trained not to sleep on the couch when humans are in the room. But it is difficult, to say the least, to teach them not to do so when no human observer is present to their senses. With human children and adults, by contrast, it is possible to develop an internalized conscience, which, even in the absence of all enforcers, will remind them, and even stimulate them strongly, not to do certain prohibited actions and to do certain required ones. The driver who stops his car at red traffic lights only when he sees or suspects that an officer is nearby has, like the cat, only an externalized conscience about this type of act, whereas one who habitually stops is, as we say, acting conscientiously—obeying, perhaps unconsciously, his internalized conscience.

That "the voice of conscience" is often effective seems clear, but it is also clear that it can and often does lose its effectiveness. A dutiful son may well adopt many of the mores of his father for a time and then gradually abandon them. If a person persists in violating his conscience, it will grow decrepit, bother him less and less effectively, and it may soon cease to deter him at all.

CONSCIENCE AS A RELIABLE GUIDE

As children many of us were taught that the voice of conscience is the voice of God and, hence, completely reliable. Some would claim, in more sophisticated terms, that although God gave us free will and does not infringe upon our freedom of choice, he nevertheless continues to lend us moral support. He gives us, through conscience, a means for distinguishing right from wrong. If we follow the guidance of conscience, we shall do our duty and act rightly. If we act contrary to its deliverances, we shall surely act wrongly.

There are, however, many difficulties with this kind of account and, indeed, with any other which claims that conscience is a sufficient guide to moral conduct.

First, the consciences of different people, whether members of the same or of different societies, often differ radically. Conscientious objectors to war and volunteers for wartime service usually disagree strongly as to the rightness of a given war. Cannibals do not share the conscientious objections to eating human flesh that vegetarians do, and both these groups differ from those who feel it is morally permissible to eat animal but not human flesh.

Second, there seem to be exceptions to all the edicts of conscience. Even within groups whose members share, say, a conscientious prescription against deliberately taking a human life, the exceptions that the various consciences allow to individuals vary greatly from one person to another. Lev Tolstoy, and presumably some Quakers, would insist that his conscience forbids the taking of a human life under any conditions. By contrast, although many of us verbally would fully accept the commandment not to kill, we would be likely in practice to find ourselves approving some acts of killing, for example in self-defense or in defense of others, and disapproving of some avoidances of killing, for example in a very deserving mercy case.

Third, conscience fails to provide guidance for many important and even some crucial moral questions. Many problems that we confront are so complex that we frankly have very little idea, and certainly no confirmed judgment or deliverance of conscience, as to which alternative is most worthy of being chosen. In many such cases, where getting adequate knowledge in the time available before a decision must be reached is impossible, we know in advance that we would be only too happy to do what is right if we could identify, with some reasonable degree of probability, the right alternative. A situation of this sort must frequently arise for people who cannot pass the decision on to someone else. The president of the United States, for example, cannot avoid the responsibility for important decisions that must be made—very often on vastly less evidence than he would like to have. Similarly, there are many difficult problems to be decided by those of us who are less highly placed, problems where the decision will not indeed be world-shaking but where it will affect a number of lives in important ways. We often sweat with the desire to solve a difficult problem in the right way but are unable, in the time available before a decision must be taken, to find out which way is the right way. In complicated cases the relatively simple prescriptions of conscience tend to prove quite inadequate.

It is not that the prescriptions of our conscience are worthless; they are often of value in reminding us of the moral views which have been taken by other members of our peer group. Awareness also of the edicts that spring from the consciences of others with different backgrounds not infrequently throws light on our own problem. But in complicated and novel cases, the edict of another's conscience cannot provide us with certain knowledge as to what ought to be done.

SOURCES OF DELIVERANCES OF CONSCIENCE

Psychologists, anthropologists, and other social scientists have gathered empirical evidence as to various sources of the deliverances of conscience. Many of the edicts of our conscience seem to have come to us while we still rested at our mother's knee. These were usually simple in form but quite effective for many years. Others came from our fathers, from teachers, from preachers, from lecturers and writers, from friends whom we respected. This wide variety of the sources of the edicts that now emanate apparently from our own consciences explains many things about them: their vagueness, their variability, their changing authority over us. As suggested by behaviorists, at least some of them rest on conditioned responses instilled in us at an early age by repetitions we no longer remember.

Examination of a particular edict of conscience throws significant light on "our inner voices." Suppose we warn our sons, ages four and six, to stay off a railway trestle near our home. We say with great emphasis, "*Never* go out on that trestle, no matter what." One day the younger boy pursues his gay red ball onto the trestle. The older boy rushes to him and pulls him off the trestle just before a train crosses it. Will we punish him for breaking our "absolute" rule? Obviously not. Our consciously instilled rule, now a command of conscience, has its values, positive and negative. It needs supplementation as soon as increasing maturity permits rational consideration. And to this phase anyone who has attained knowledge and discretion should surely move on.

UNIVERSALIZABILITY OF MORAL PRESCRIPTIONS

Since the edicts of conscience have pedestrian empirical sources and are subject to exceptions, it was natural for Immanuel Kant to insist, through his categorical imperative, that every valid moral principle must hold universally: "So act that you can will the maxim or principle of your action to be a universal law, binding on the will of every rational being." This requirement has two facets. First, for an act to be moral it must be done not on whim or impulse or as a mere reflex response to stimuli, but in accordance with some moral principle or maxim. Second, this principle must be one that the agent is willing to have universally adopted. This requirement that a person should act only on a principle that he is willing to have universally adopted seems to introduce undesirable psychological factors that might tend to vary radically from one person to the next. Thus, a pessimist like Arthur Schopenhauer might approve of universal suicide and be willing to have everyone else do so, whereas an optimist might be willing to have everyone work toward increasing the population. Such a formulation of the universalizability principle would thus lead to incompatible moral edicts.

To eliminate such psychological factors and to state the principle in a way closer to Kant's intent, Richard M. Hare urges that a moral principle, to be applicable to a person *A*, must also be applicable in like circumstances to any similar person *B*. Although Hare's intent seems clear, he does not specify the degree of similarity required. Complete identity would make the principle useless. On the other hand, it seems clear that Hare was not suggesting, for example, that because it is right for *A* to make love to his wife, it is also proper that *B*, who is like *A* in various respects, should also make love to Mrs. *A*. Perhaps the universalizability thesis is best stated as follows: If it is right for *A* to do an act of kind *X* in a set of circumstances *C*, then it is right for any *B* who is like *A* in all relevant respects to do an act of kind *X* in circumstances like *C* in all relevant respects. So stated, the principle is analytically and thus necessarily true. But whether we can ever know in practice that both sets of circumstances and both agents are alike in all relevant respects is highly doubtful. It would be difficult, if not impossible, even to specify these respects. But we do know what is meant by this prescription, and we sometimes know with a fair degree of probability that the required likenesses are present.

Because the universalizability principle is analytic, it is necessarily true. But it is an "If … then …" statement: If *A* should do *X* in *C*, then *B* should do *Y* in *D*, where the similarities between *A* and *B*, *C* and *D*, and *X* and *Y* meet the requirements previously mentioned. Quite aside from the difficulties of knowing whether or not these requirements are met, the statement tells us only that if its antecedent is true, its consequent is also true. But to know the antecedent to be true—that *A* ought to do *X* in *C*—we must turn to experience for an answer. To know anything to be good on the whole, we must know if its existence (or occurrence) is preferable to its nonexistence. To know any act to be right, we must know that no possible alternative is preferable to it. Such preferability presupposes empirical knowledge of values. The possibility of such knowledge is a matter of controversy, but many, including the present writer, believe it to be attainable.

See also Behaviorism; Butler, Joseph; Clarke, Samuel; Emotion; Hare, Richard M.; Hutcheson, Francis; Kant, Immanuel; Moral Motivation; Moral Rules and Principles; Price, Richard; Reason; Schopenhauer, Arthur; Shaftesbury, Third Earl of (Anthony Ashley Cooper); Tolstoy, Lev (Leo) Nikolaevich; Volition.

Bibliography

WORKS OF HISTORICAL INTEREST

Aquinas, Thomas, Saint. "Conscience, Question 17, Articles 1–5," and "Synderesis, Question 16, Articles 1–3." In *Truth (Quaestiones Disputate de Veritate)*, translated by J. V. McGlynn. Chicago: H. Regnery, 1952–1954.

Balguy, John. *The Foundation of Moral Goodness.* London: John Pemberton, Part I, 1728; Part II, 1729.

Baylor, Michael G. *Action and Person: Conscience in Late Scholasticism and the Young Luther.* (Studies in Medieval and Reformation Thought, 20) Leiden: E. J. Brill, 1977.

Butler, Joseph. *Five Sermons Preached at the Rolls Chapel and a Dissertation upon the Nature of Virtue.* Indianapolis: Hackett, 1983.

Cicero. *De Finibus.* Translated by H. Rackham. Cambridge, MA: Harvard University Press, 1914.

Cicero. *De Natura Deorum.* Translated by H. McGregor. Hammondsworth, UK: Penguin, 1972.

Clarke, Samuel. *A Discourse concerning the Unchangeable Obligations of Natural Religion and the Truth and Certainty of the Christian Revelation,* 2nd corrected ed. London: Knapton, 1706.

Hutcheson, Francis. *An Inquiry into the Original of Our Ideas of Beauty and Virtue.* London, 1725.

Jonsen, Albert, and Stephen Toulmin. *The Abuse of Casuistry: A History of Moral Reasoning.* Berkeley: University of California Press, 1988.

Kant, Immanuel. *The Moral Law, or Kant's Groundwork of the Metaphysics of Morals.* Translated with analysis and notes by H. J. Paton. London: Hutchinson, 1948.

Potts, Timothy C. *Conscience in Medieval Philosophy.* Cambridge, U.K.: Cambridge University Press, 1980.

Price, Richard. *A Review of the Principal Questions and Difficulties in Morals.* London, 1758.

Shaftesbury, 3d Earl of (Anthony Ashley Cooper). *An Inquiry concerning Virtue or Merit.* London: Bell, Castle, and Buckley, 1699.

MORE RECENT WORKS

Andrew, Edward G. *Conscience and Its Critics. Protestant Conscience, Enlightenment Reason, and Modern Subjectivity.* Toronto: University of Toronto Press, 2001.

Broad, C. D. "Some Reflections on Moral-Sense Theories in Ethics." *PAS* 45 (1944–1945): 131–186.

Fingarette, Herbert. *Self-Deception.* London: Routledge & Keegan Paul, 1969.

Hoose, Jayne, editor. *Conscience in World Religions.* Notre Dame IN: University of Notre Dame Press, 1999.

Hursthouse, Rosalindk Gavin Lawrence, and Warren Quinn, editors. *Virtues and Reasons: Philippa Foot and Moral Theory: Essays in Honour of Philippa Foot.* Oxford: Clarendon Press, 1995.

Jacobs, Jonathan. *Choosing Character. Responsibility for Vice and Virtue.* Ithaca: Cornell University Press, 2001.

Kohlberg, Lawrence. "Conscience as Principled Responsibility: On the Philosophy of Stage Six." In *Conscience: An Interdisciplinary View*, edited by Gerhard Zecha and Paul Weingartner. Dordrecht: D. Reidel, 1987.

Kohlberg, Lawrence. *Essays on Moral Development*, Vol. 1: *The Philosophy of Moral Development.* San Francisco: Harper & Row, 1981.

Langston, Douglas C. *Conscience and Other Virtues.* University Park: Pennsylvania State University Press, 2001.

Nussbaum, Martha. *The Fragility of Goodness.* Cambridge, U.K.: Cambridge University Press, 1986.

Raphael, D. Daiches. *The Moral Sense.* London: Oxford University Press, 1947.

Ross, W. David. *Foundations of Ethics.* Oxford: Clarendon Press, 1939.

Ross, W. David. *The Right and the Good.* Oxford: Clarendon Press, 1930.

Ryle, Gilbert. "Conscience and Moral Convictions." In *Conscience*, edited by John Donnelly and Leonard Lyons. Staten Island NY: Alba House, 1973.

Slote, Michael. *From Morality to Virtue.* New York: Oxford University Press, 1992.

Smith, T. V. *Beyond Conscience. A Critical Examination of Various Doctrines of Conscience.* New York: McGraw-Hill, 1934.

Charles A. Baylis (1967)

Bibliography updated by William O'Neill (2005)

CONSCIOUSNESS

The term *consciousness* refers to several distinct, but related phenomena that figure in the mental functioning of people and other creatures.

KINDS OF CONSCIOUSNESS

One of these phenomena is closely tied to simply being awake. An individual is conscious if it is awake and responsive to sensory stimulation; a person or other creature that is asleep, in a coma, or knocked out is not conscious.

There are also other phenomena we refer to as consciousness. One is conscious *of* something if one senses or perceives the thing or has some suitable thought about it; being conscious of something is being aware of that thing. Because we use a grammatical object to specify what somebody is conscious of, it is convenient to call this phenomenon *transitive consciousness*, as against an individual's being awake and responsive to sensory input, which we can call *creature consciousness* (Rosenthal 1990).

We sometimes describe the states one is aware of as constituting one's current mental life as a stream of consciousness. But there are, in addition, thoughts, desires, feelings, and perceptions that occur outside that stream of consciousness, of which one is wholly unaware. Even though one is unaware of these states, they are nonetheless part of one's mental functioning. We call the states that occur in somebody's stream of consciousness *conscious*, in contrast with those of which that individual is wholly unaware. This is a third use of the term *conscious*. Because consciousness of this sort is a property of mental states, such as thoughts, desires, feelings, and perceptions, we can call it *state consciousness*.

Sometimes we focus deliberately and attentively on some feeling or perception we have; such focused awareness of our mental states is called *reflective*, or *introspective consciousness*. And we call the explicit consciousness of the self to which these states belong *self-consciousness*.

There is disagreement about what connections hold among these several kinds of consciousness. Some theorists hold that an individual cannot be creature conscious—that is, awake and responsive to sensory stimulation—unless at least some of its mental states are conscious. Doubtless that is true for ordinary humans; people are never conscious without being in some conscious states. But, if perceptions and feelings can occur without being conscious, there is in principle no reason why some creatures might be awake and responsive to sensory stimulation even though none of their feelings, perceptions, or other mental states are conscious states.

Not all theorists, however, accept that feelings, perceptions, thoughts, and desires can occur without being conscious. Even Sigmund Freud (1961), who championed the idea of unconscious desires and thoughts, drew the line at qualitative states, such as sensations and feelings. All feelings, he held, are conscious, though we can loosely characterize feelings as unconscious when one is unclear or mistaken about what they are about.

Others, such as Thomas Nagel (1974) and John R. Searle (1990, 1992), accept that nonconscious states occur that function in ways similar to conscious feelings, perceptions, and thoughts, but deny that those nonconscious states are full-fledged feelings, perceptions, or thoughts.

It is also a matter of some controversy whether mental states are conscious in virtue of one's being conscious *of* those states. Earlier writers, such as René Descartes (1984–1991) and John Locke (1975), always described the states we now call conscious as states that one is conscious of. But, because they also held that we are conscious of all our mental states, they saw no need to use the term *conscious* to mark a distinction between those mental states we are conscious of and those we aren't. When, in the late nineteenth century, it became widely accepted that individuals are in some mental states of which they are wholly unaware, the term *conscious* came to mark the contrast between those mental states one is conscious of and those one is not.

Though not all theorists agree that a mental state's being conscious involves one's being conscious of that state, that has long been the dominant view.

QUALITATIVE CONSCIOUSNESS

Mental states fall into three broad groups. Some, such as beliefs, thoughts, desires, hopes, and expectations, have intentional content that can be described by a sentential clause. Thinking is always thinking *that* something is the case; the clause beginning with *that* specifies what it is that one thinks. Similarly with one's desires, hopes, and expectations. The intentional content, described by a *that* clause, specifies what it is that one desires, hopes, or expects.

Pains and other sensations, by contrast, have no intentional content, but instead exhibit some qualitative character, such as the quality of painfulness or the color qualities of visual sensations. A third group of states includes emotions and perceptions, which exhibit both qualitative character and intentional content.

Many theorists hold that the consciousness of qualitative states is something different from the consciousness of other mental states, and that it demands special treatment. Giving an informative theoretical account of qualitative consciousness, on their view, faces special difficulties.

Thus Ned Block (1995) has urged that qualitative states exhibit a special kind of consciousness, which he calls *phenomenal consciousness*, or *phenomenality*. A state has phenomenal consciousness, according to Block, if there is something it is like to be in that state, which happens only when the state has some qualitative character. There is nothing it is like simply to think or believe something, even when one's thought or belief is conscious. Phenomenal consciousness occurs only with states that have qualitative character.

Block (1995) distinguishes a state's having phenomenal consciousness from its having what he calls *access consciousness*. A state is access conscious if its content is poised to figure in reasoning and in the rational control of action and speech. Some qualitative states, which exhibit phenomenal consciousness, also exhibit access consciousness; intuitively, they are the qualitative states one is conscious of. By contrast, when a state is phenomenally conscious but not access conscious, one is wholly unaware of the state. And there is often compelling empirical or theoretical reason to think that qualitative states of which one is unaware do occur (see the next section in this entry).

Block's notion of access consciousness echoes Daniel C. Dennett's (1993) idea that a state's being conscious consists in its having "cerebral celebrity," that is, if it has a widespread effect on memory and on the control of behavior. It also accords with the cognitive theory of consciousness advanced by the psychologist Bernard J. Baars (1988), on which a state is conscious if it occurs in a global workspace that maximizes its connections with other states and behavior.

PROBLEMS ABOUT QUALITATIVE CONSCIOUSNESS

A state's being access conscious consists in its having suitable connections with other states and with behavior. So the notion of access consciousness invites a functionalist account (Lewis 1972, Putnam 1975), on which a state's mental properties are a matter of such connections. Many theorists, however, deny that any such an account can work for qualitative consciousness. They insist that, because conscious qualitative character is an intrinsic property of sensations, it cannot be understood in terms of connections that sensations have with other things.

EXPLAINING CONSCIOUS QUALITIES. The new physics pioneered in the seventeenth century by Galileo Galilei, Descartes, and Isaac Newton holds that we can explain the nature and behavior of physical objects only insofar as we can describe them in mathematical terms. Since commonsense physical qualities, such as color and sound, seem to resist mathematical description, some have followed Locke in construing such properties as powers to cause the corresponding mental qualities. But conscious mental qualities also resist mathematical description, and it may seem that no parallel move is possible for them. Many conclude that conscious mental qualities lie outside the reach of physical explanation, and possibly, therefore, any informative explanation. Thus, Locke argued that sensations either are nonphysical states or, if they are states of material bodies, they must be "superadded" to those bodies by God.

In a somewhat similar spirit, Joseph Levine (2000) has argued that there is an "explanatory gap" that blocks any intelligible explanation of conscious qualitative states in terms of physical processes. Similarly, Nagel (1974) has argued that none of the available naturalist theories of mind can explain what it's like for one to be in a mental state. And David Chalmers (1996) has described as the "hard problem" of consciousness the question why relevant brain processes are accompanied by qualitative consciousness at all, and why particular brain events are accompanied by specific types of mental quality.

Levine has urged that, though we cannot explain qualitative consciousness in physical terms, qualitative consciousness might nonetheless be physical in nature. Others conclude instead that qualitative consciousness cannot have a physical nature, arguing that any such physical nature would make possible a physical explanation of qualitative consciousness. And Colin McGinn (1991) has argued that, though consciousness is physical in nature, we lack the cognitive capacity to understand how that is possible.

It is unclear, however, that the considerations used to support these views are compelling. We rely on well-developed theories to draw systematic connections among things in nature. Even the most ordinary connections among natural processes seem surprising and unintelligible without any commonsense theory to provide context, and come to seem rational only when subsumed by some suitable theory. So it may be that the ties between conscious mental qualities and brain processes now seem unintelligible only because we still have no well-developed theory that links them. But by itself, that current lack gives us no reason to doubt that we will some day have such a theory. And coming to have one would likely overcome any prior intuitive concerns about explaining qualitative consciousness, just as physics and chemistry have made intuitively acceptable various explanations of our commonsense world that would previously have seemed outlandish.

Introspection may also seem to support intuitive doubts about whether rational explanation of conscious qualitative character is possible, since introspection provides no clue about how such an explanation might proceed. But we have no reason to think that introspection would help here; introspection can at most tell us about the qualities themselves, not how they connect with other things.

THE KNOWLEDGE ARGUMENT. Frank Jackson (1982, 1986) has argued that conscious qualitative states are not physical because, even if one knew everything physical there is to know about our psychological and neural functioning, one would not thereby know what it's like for one to be in particular qualitative states. Jackson imagines a neuroscientist who knows everything physical about visual functioning but has never seen anything except in black, white, and gray. Still, Jackson argues, this neuroscientist, on consciously seeing red for the first time, would learn something new, namely, what it's like for one to see red. Since the neuroscientist already knew everything physical about seeing red, the new knowledge of it what it's like for one to see red cannot be knowledge of something physical.

Jackson (2003) has since repudiated this argument, maintaining now that what it's like for one to see red is purely a matter of intentional content. This view is a version of representationalism, which is discussed later in this entry. Others have responded differently to Jackson's original argument, urging that what one would learn on first consciously seeing red is not factual knowledge, but only a kind of acquaintance (Churchland 1985) or an ability to recognize the quality in question (Lewis 1990; cf. Loar 1997).

QUALITIES AND CONSCIOUSNESS. Some theorists contend that qualitative states of which we are in no way conscious cannot occur. Indeed, the very term *qualia* (singular *quale*) is often applied to mental qualities with the implication that such qualities cannot occur without being conscious. But there is compelling reason to holdthat mental qualities do occur outside our stream of consciousness.

Individuals sometimes perceive things without being at all aware that they are doing so. In so-called masked priming experiments (Marcel 1983), subjects briefly exposed first to one visual stimulus and then to another may consciously see only the second. Nonetheless, it is plain that subjects do see the first stimulus, since it affects subsequent behavior in ways characteristic of seeing those stimuli. Thus, subjects who report seeing only the second stimulus can nonetheless make strikingly accurate guesses about the first.

There are other such cases. Individuals with lesions in the cortical area primarily responsible for vision may be wholly unaware of seeing a stimulus and yet guess about its visible character, again with great accuracy, exhibiting what Lawrence Weiskrantz (1997) has called blindsight. These individuals see stimuli, but are not in any way conscious of seeing them. And subliminal perceiving, of which one is wholly unaware, sometimes occurs even in everyday situations.

Not only do qualitative states sometimes occur without being conscious; there are circumstances in which we are conscious of ourselves as being in qualitative states that are different from those we are actually in. John Grimes (1996) reported that subjects will continue to see a highly salient object as unchanged in color or other respects if the relevant changes occur during a saccade, since no visual input reaches the brain during saccades. A subject may thus attentively look at something red but be conscious instead of seeing green. Such a subject would presumably have a sensation of red, despite being conscious of having a sensation of green. Our consciousness of our qualitative states can sometimes be strikingly inaccurate.

According to Block (1995), cases of qualitative states that occur outside our stream of consciousness are phenomenally conscious states that lack access consciousness. Access consciousness makes the difference, he urges, between qualitative states of which we are intuitively aware and those of which we are not. But it's likely that even qualitative states that intuitively occur in one's stream of consciousness sometimes lack access consciousness, on Block's official definition. Visual states near the periphery of our visual field are conscious but are not, without some shift in attention, poised to figure in any general way in reasoning and the rational control of action and speech. Similarly with other perceptual states that lie outside our focus of attention but are nonetheless part of our stream of consciousness. It is likely that access consciousness has more to do with attention than with consciousness.

QUALITY INVERSION Qualitative states figure in perceiving. There is a distinctive mental quality that occurs when one sees something red and a different quality when one sees something green; similarly for perceptible properties accessible by modalities other than vision. That raises the question whether particular mental qualities might play different perceptual roles from one individual to another, or even different roles in the same individual at different times. The question is not about the slight variations in the way people see things, which are detectable in standard ways, but about whether particular mental qualities could play different perceptual roles in ways undetectable by others.

Locke held that such inversion of mental qualities is at least conceivable, and many contemporary theorists share that view. This idea very likely reflects a conviction that mental qualities are individuated solely by the way one is conscious of them, that is, by how they appear to consciousness. If any other factors do figure in the individuation of mental qualities, those factors would enable the detection in others of inversion in the perceptual roles of their mental qualities.

But if mental qualities were individuated only by how we are conscious of them, they would differ only in the way they appear to consciousness. And then mental qualities could not occur without being conscious. Indeed, the evidence that mental qualities do occur without being conscious provides ways of determining their occurrence independent of consciousness. So, that evidence also suggests that any conceivable quality inversion would have to be detectable. It is therefore likely that any satisfactory way of individuating mental qualities will rely on their role in perceiving, independent of whether that perceiving occurs consciously (Rosenthal 2005).

CONSCIOUSNESS AND INTENTIONALITY

As noted earlier, intentional states, such as thoughts, desires, doubts, and expectations, occur both consciously and not consciously.

Freud posited intentional states that are not conscious as the best explanation of various otherwise inexplicable conscious thoughts and desires and various bits of behavior. Thus, a person may do just those things and have just those conscious thoughts and desires that we would expect if the person also had certain other thoughts and desires. And, if the person is unaware of being in those other thoughts and desires, we can best explain the behavior and conscious states by supposing that the person has those thoughts and desires, but they are simply not conscious. Such reasoning again invites a functionalist account of intentional states, on which the intentional properties of a state is a matter of its connections with other states, behavior, and sensory stimulation. But even apart from a functionalist account, it is widely accepted that intentional states with particular contents have characteristic causal connections with other intentional states and with behavior, and that is all Freud's argument requires. Such reasoning is compelling, moreover, independent of the special kinds of case that interested Freud.

Experimental work in social psychology shows that subjects sometimes report having beliefs or desires that would make sense of a situation or conform to social expectations, despite compelling evidence that these subjects do not actually have those beliefs and desires (Nisbett and Wilson 1977). Not only are we sometimes unaware of our thoughts and desires; in such confabulatory cases we are conscious of ourselves as having thoughts and desires that we do not have.

Searle (1990) has argued that intentional states, properly so called, cannot occur without being conscious. As he notes, one's thoughts and desires always represent things in terms of some aspects and not others; Oedipus had a desire to marry a particular woman, but his desire did not represent that woman as his mother. And, as Oedipus's case illustrates, how one's intentional states represent the things they are about makes a difference both to one's mental life and one's behavior.

According to Searle, the way one's intentional states represent things cannot make a difference to one unless those states are conscious. He concludes that genuine thoughts and desires cannot occur without being conscious. But the way one's thoughts and desires represent things can make a difference to one even if those states are not conscious. A thought or desire need not be conscious to affect one's other intentional states and one's behavior, and it will affect those things differently depending on the way it represents things. Genuine intentional states can occur without being conscious.

THEORIES OF CONSCIOUSNESS I

Theories of consciousness often rely on the traditional idea that a state's being conscious involves one's being conscious in some way *of* that state. States of which one is in no way conscious are not conscious states. When we are conscious of something, moreover, we can tell others about it. So a standard test for whether somebody is in a conscious state is whether that person can report being in the state. If somebody can report having a particular thought, feeling, or perception, that state is conscious; if the person cannot report being in the state, it is not. This rule of thumb underlies typical methodology in experimental psychology no less than everyday practice.

But the commonsense observation that mental states are states of which we are conscious goes only so far. A theory of consciousness must also specify how it is that we are conscious of those states. One important feature of our consciousness of those states was highlighted by Descartes, who insisted that we are immediately conscious of our mental states. When we are conscious of a mental state, it seems that nothing mediates between that state and our awareness of it. A theory of consciousness must explain this sense of immediacy in the way we are aware of our conscious states.

INNER SENSE. We also seem to be immediately conscious of things when we perceive them; nothing seems to mediate between the things we perceive and our perceptions of them. This encourages the hypothesis, advanced by Locke, Immanuel Kant (1998), and others, that mental states are conscious because we sense or perceive them. A thought, feeling, or perception is conscious because one is aware of that state by way of some faculty of inner sense, or some internal monitoring mechanism that involves the higher-order perceiving of that state. This theory has traditionally been the most widely held explanation of consciousness; contemporary advocates include David M. Armstrong (1978) and William G. Lycan (1996).

But there are difficulties with this theory. Sensations and perceptions always exhibit some qualitative character; sensing a red object, for example, involves a sensation's having a mental quality of red, as against a mental quality of blue, green, and so forth. Our consciousness of our mental states, however, does not involve any qualitative character. This is obvious when the state we are are conscious of is a thought or desire, which itself has no qualitative character; plainly, no mental quality figures in the way we are conscious of those intentional states.

Qualitative character does figure when we are conscious of sensations and perceptions. But these mental qualities are just the qualities we are conscious of our sensations and perceptions as having. As Aristotle (1993) noted, there are no higher-order qualities in virtue of which we are conscious of our qualitative mental states, in the way the mental quality of red enables us to see red objects. Our higher-order awareness of our conscious states may resemble perceiving in other ways, but qualitative character is so central to perceiving that no form of awareness that fails to involve mental qualities can count as perceiving.

Inner-sense theorists often urge that the higher-order sensing or perceiving they posit serves the function of monitoring our mental states, much as perceiving monitors external objects and bodily conditions. But perceiving is not the only way that the mind might monitor itself. And cases of confabulatory awareness, which Richard E. Nisbett and Timothy DeCamp Wilson have demonstrated, do not in any case fit neatly with a model based on monitoring.

INTRINSIC THEORIES. But we need not appeal to inner sense to capture the apparent immediacy of our consciousness of many mental states. If our awareness of our conscious states were internal to those states themselves, nothing could mediate between a state and one's awareness of it; such consciousness would be intrinsic to each conscious state. This theory, advanced by Franz Brentano (1973) and possibly Aristotle, also has a number of contemporary advocates.

But the intrinsic theory also faces difficulties. There are thoughts and desires that we sometimes have consciously and other times not. A sensation that results from a particular stimulus may be conscious if that stimulus occurs alone, but not conscious if the very same stimulus is followed in a suitable way by a second, masking stimulus (Marcel 1983). It is unclear how we can explain such variation if consciousness is literally built into our mental states.

The problem is particularly pressing when one particular state passes between being conscious and not being conscious. Some perceptual or bodily sensations that are not very intense may be conscious or not depending on where one focuses one's attention. But, since shifts in attention are extrinsic to particular sensations, such shifts should leave consciousness unaffected if consciousness is indeed an intrinsic aspect of mental states.

Brentano held that consciously hearing something makes us conscious of two things: the sound one hears and the hearing itself. And he maintained that we are conscious of the hearing in the way that having a thought about something makes us conscious of that thing, even when we don't perceive it. The intentional content of hearing something, according to Brentano, makes us conscious both of the thing heard and the hearing itself.

Perhaps hearing can have two intentional objects in this way. But there are other cases for which Brentano's model does not work. Doubting something does not make one conscious of the thing one's doubt is about. Consider, then, a case of doubting that it is raining. Even if one's doubt is about both the rain and the state of doubting itself, that will not make one conscious of the doubting. A mental affirmation that one has that doubt would make one conscious of the doubting. But that mental affirmation could not be intrinsic to the doubting, since no mental state involves more than one mental attitude. Similar considerations apply to wondering about something, and many other mental attitudes.

Inner sense and Brentano's intrinsic theory both sought to explain the way our awareness of our conscious states is immediate. But all we really need to explain is why such awareness appears to be immediate, since we do not know that it actually is. Indeed, perceiving is also subjectively unmediated, but we know that there is much that actually mediates between our perceptions and the things we perceive. So the same may well be so with the way we are aware of our conscious states. Despite the subjective impression of immediacy, there may well be mediation we are not subjectively aware of. All we need to explain is the subjective sense of immediacy, and neither the analogy with perceiving nor the intrinsic theory is required for that.

HIGHER-ORDER THOUGHTS. On Brentano's intrinsic theory, every conscious state makes us conscious of itself, in much the way that having a thought about something makes one conscious of that thing. This theory cannot work, at least for cases like doubting and wondering. Inner sense, by contrast, faces the difficulty that, because the awareness of our conscious states does not involve higher-order mental qualities, that awareness cannot be sensing or perceiving. This suggests combining features of the two theories so as to avoid the difficulties of each. Perhaps we are aware of our conscious states by having thoughts about them, as Brentano urged, but those thoughts are distinct from the states we are conscious of, as inner sense maintains about the higher-order perceptions it posits.

This appeal to higher-order thoughts that are distinct from the mental states they make us conscious of avoids the foregoing difficulties that face inner sense and Brentano's theory. The higher-order-thought theory, advanced by David M. Rosenthal (1986, 1990, 2005) and others, also allows for an explanation of the subjective immediacy of our awareness of our conscious states; the theory can require that these higher-order thoughts are independent of any conscious inference. If we are unaware of any inference on which a higher-order thought relies, we will be unaware of any mediation between the states we are aware of and our awareness of them. So, such awareness will be subjectively unmediated. Indeed, we would seldom be aware of these higher-order thoughts, since a third-order thought would be needed for any second-order thought to be conscious. And our typically being unaware of our higher-order thoughts would enhance the subjective sense that our consciousness of our mental states is immediate.

Critics have urged two major difficulties for this theory. One involves the possibility that higher-order thoughts will sometimes misrepresent what mental states we are in. But it is arguable that consciousness does sometimes misrepresent things, as in the confabulatory cases noted earlier. And there are very likely psychological pressures that prevent such misrepresentation from becoming too extreme.

Nonetheless, some have insisted that such misrepresentation cannot occur, in effect relying on the traditional idea, advanced by Descartes, Locke, and others, that the mind is transparent to itself. But there is compelling reason to reject that transparency claim. Confabulatory consciousness and other phenomena show that consciousness does occasionally mislead us; moreover, others sometimes know what we are thinking and feeling better than we ourselves do. Consciousness is neither infallible nor exhaustive.

Another challenge to the higher-order-thought theory pertains specifically to conscious qualitative states. How can higher-order thoughts, which themselves lack qualitative character, result in qualitative states' being conscious? How can simply having a thought result in there being something it is like for one to be in a qualitative state?

This challenge echoes the concern that an explanatory gap may make it impossible to understand how conscious mental qualities could arise as a result of particular neural events. Put most generally, the concern is how conscious qualities can result from anything else. But as noted earlier, connections among things in nature seem intelligible only when we have a well-established theory that subsumes those connections. Since higher-order thoughts are seldom conscious, introspection cannot tell us whether they result in conscious qualities. But it may be that the connections higher-order thoughts have with the thoughts we have about the things we perceive result in our being conscious of the mental qualities that figure in such perceiving.

In any case, no alternative theory has a response to this challenge that is at all satisfactory. By itself, simply positing that our awareness of qualitative states is intrinsic to those states does nothing to explain why there is something it is like for one to be in those states. And inner sense faces a regress, since it could help only if the higher-order perceptions themselves had conscious mental qualities, and we would then need to explain what gives rise to those higher-order conscious qualities.

THEORIES OF CONSCIOUSNESS II

The foregoing theories differ about whether our awareness of our conscious states is intrinsic to those states or external to them, and about whether that awareness is due to our perceiving those states or to our having thoughts about them. But there are other issues about which theories differ as well.

DISPOSITIONAL THEORIES. Peter Carruthers (2000) has argued that a state's being conscious does not require the actual occurrence of a higher-order thought, but only a disposition for such a higher-order thought to occur. Carruthers urges that having an actual higher-order thought for each conscious state would result in cognitive overload, unlike one's merely being disposed to have higher-order thoughts.

But there is no reason to think that our cortical resources cannot accommodate actual higher-order thoughts, and dispositions would themselves make substantial cortical demands. Nor is it obvious that dispositions will do. Since being disposed to have a thought about something does not make one conscious of anything, merely being disposed to have a higher-order thought would not make one aware of one's mental states. Carruthers seeks to meet this difficulty by endorsing the view that the intentional content a state has is partly a matter of what other states it is disposed to cause. So, when a state is disposed to cause a higher-order thought, that very state has higher-order content, which makes one conscious of that state. But, since the state itself has the higher-order content, this view faces the same difficulties that tell against Brentano's theory.

REPRESENTATIONALISM. Some have sought to meet the challenge about conscious mental qualities by denying that there are any. According to representationalism, we are never conscious of any mental qualities, but only the perceptible properties of physical objects, and the states in virtue of which we are conscious of them are purely intentional states. When we see something red, on this view, the only quality we are aware of is the redness of the thing seen; we are not in addition aware of some mental red. Advocates of this view, such as Gilbert Harman (1990), Dennett (1991), Fred Dretske (2000), Armstrong, and Lycan, point out that we never seem to be conscious of two distinct qualities of red, nor to switch from being conscious of the redness of physical objects to being conscious of a mental quality of the seeing itself. Descartes also espoused a form of representationalism, since he regarded all mental phenomena as having only intentional properties, and construed sensations either as purely intentional states or as nonmental bodily states.

But, as Wilfrid Sellars (1963), Sydney Shoemaker (1996), and Rosenthal (2005) have argued, perceptual sensations resemble and differ in ways that reflect the similarities and differences among perceived physical properties. And it is natural to construe the properties in virtue of which those sensations resemble and differ as mental qualities. When we introspectively attend to our qualitative states, moreover, we sometimes become conscious of the relevant qualities *as* qualities of our experiences. So it may well be that we are, after all, often aware of mental qualities that our qualitative states exhibit.

Some theorists, such as Dretske (1993) and Searle (1992), reject the idea that a mental state's being conscious is a matter of one's being conscious of that state. A state's being conscious, on their view, does not involve some higher-order awareness of that state. Rather, according to Dretske (1993), a state is conscious if, in virtue of one's being in that state, one is conscious of something. This is sometimes called a first-order theory of consciousness, in contrast to theories that posit some higher-order awareness.

This account faces a difficulty, however. Perceptions sometimes occur without being conscious. But it is arguable that even those perceptions make us conscious of things. If perceiving something primes one for some conscious state or some behavior, then one was conscious of the thing one perceived even if it did not seem to one that one perceived it. On Dretske's (1993, 2000) view, however, any state in virtue of which one is conscious of something is conscious. And that has the unwelcome result that even the perceptions we seem subjectively not to have are conscious.

Searle (1992) holds that we can subjectively draw no distinction between a conscious state and one's consciousness of it. He concludes that no higher-order awareness figures in a state's being conscious. But when we focus introspectively on our conscious states, we are often aware both of the state thus scrutinized and of the scrutinizing itself. And even if we could not draw that distinction subjectively, we might still have sound theoretical reasons to insist on it.

DENNETT'S THEORY. Dennett (1991) has developed an important theory of consciousness, which emphasizes cases in which consciousness misrepresents what mental states we are in. Visual information that is not central to our focus of attention can be highly degraded, but still we seem subjectively to see things in sharp detail throughout our field of vision. Dennett argues that consciousness extrapolates from available visual information to create a full picture of the environment, in effect filling in missing visual information and providing missing details.

In thus distinguishing the way consciousness represents things from our actual visual states, Dennett's (1991) view resembles higher-order theories, on which our higher-order awareness of mental states is distinct from the states themselves, and so can misrepresent them. But Dennett rejects such higher-order views, arguing that there is no distinction between the way things appear and our awareness of how they appear. So, he construes the divergence between consciousness and visual states not in terms of two mental levels—perceiving and our consciousness of perceiving—but rather as the difference between the way things consciously appear and the subpersonal neural events in virtue of which things appear that way.

Dennett shares with the higher-order-thought theory a view of consciousness as a kind of self-interpretation. On both views we interpret ourselves as being in various commonsense psychological states. But, unlike higher-order-thought theorists, Dennett denies that we are actually in any of the commonsense psychological states we interpret ourselves as being in. The only states that figure in psychological functioning are subpersonal neural events of content fixation, complex patterns of which subserve such functioning.

Searle (1992) and Dennett (1991, 1993) both reject any distinction between the mental states one is in and one's awareness of those states, but they do so for different reasons. Searle rejects that distinction because he holds that we cannot draw it subjectively. Dennett, by contrast, maintains that the psychological states we are conscious of ourselves as being in do not actually occur. But it is arguable that suitable patterns of the subpersonal events of content fixation Dennett countenances actually constitute the mental states of commonsense psychology. If so, we can distinguish between those commonsense mental states and our higher-order awareness of them.

NEURAL CORRELATES, FUNCTION, AND THE SELF

Whether or not conscious qualitative states are physical in nature, few doubt that something specific in brain functioning correlates with qualitative consciousness. This has led to speculation about what that neural correlate of consciousness (NCC) is.

According to Francis Crick and Christoph Koch (1990) the NCC involves the occurrence of synchronized neural oscillation of 35 to 75 hertz in sensory cortex, a synchrony sufficient for a vigorous coalition of neurons firing together. One thing that favors this hypothesis is that such synchronized neural oscillation seems to figure in the way different qualitative properties are bound together in conscious experience. As Anne Treisman (1986) has shown, visual qualities pertaining to color, shape, motion, and orientation occur independently in the early stages of visual processing; so there is a *binding problem* of explaining how they come together in conscious experience. But these qualities are bound together even when qualitative states are not conscious. So, the neural factors operative in such binding may not be the same as those responsible for qualitative consciousness, and synchronized oscillation may subserve only binding, independent of consciousness.

Mental functioning plays a variety of roles, allowing animals to negotiate their way in the world and to satisfy various needs and desires. What, then, is the specific function of consciousness? The answer depends on which kind of consciousness is at issue. Creature consciousness, which consists in an animal's being awake and responsive to sensory stimulation, plainly functions to enable an animal to satisfy needs and avoid danger. Similarly with transitive consciousness, which consists in a creature's being conscious *of* various things.

State consciousness, by contrast, consists in a state's occurring in a creature's stream of consciousness, and it is somewhat less clear what function this has. A mental state's function depends on its causal connections with other states and with behavior and sensory stimuli, and the causal properties of thoughts and desires are mainly a matter of their intentional content, whether or not they are conscious. Similarly, the causal properties of qualitative states depend on their mental qualities; visual sensations of red interact causally in ways suitably different from visual sensations of green, again whether or not they are conscious. So it is unclear what additional function might result from these states' being conscious.

One standard answer is that such consciousness functions to enhance reasoning and planning; perhaps decisions and thinking will be more rational if one is conscious of one's thoughts and desires. This idea underlies Block's (1995) claim that a state is access conscious if its content is poised to figure in the rational control of action and speech, Baars's (1988) related suggestion that conscious states occur in a global workspace, and Dennett's (1993) that consciousness is cerebral celebrity.

But many thoughts and desires have global effects on other states and on behavior even when they are not conscious. And even when planning and thinking is not conscious, it often is rational, as when we solve problems by sleeping on them. Indeed, this is just what we should expect if the causal potential of thoughts and desires depends mainly on their intentional content. There is, moreover, compelling evidence that we are conscious of our decisions only after those decisions have been made (Libet 1985), so that being conscious of those decisions cannot affect whether we make them.

According to Dretske (1993), any state in virtue of which one is transitively conscious of something is a conscious state. So on that view, the function of state consciousness coincides with that of transitive consciousness. But if, instead, a state is conscious just in case one is in some suitable way conscious of that state, the function of state consciousness will rather be whatever function is added by one's being thus conscious of the state. And that may be relatively marginal.

When we introspect our mental states by deliberately and attentively focusing on them, we are conscious of the states we introspect as states of ourselves, and we are in that way conscious of ourselves as centers of consciousness. There are several questions about the nature of such self-consciousness. David Hume (1978) urged that, though we are aware of many of our mental states, we are not aware of anything in addition to those states which we might call a self. Hume was operating with a perceptual model of awareness, and it is plain that we do not perceive such a self. But we are sometimes conscious of things not only by perceiving them, but also by having thoughts about them as being present. So having higher-order thoughts to the effect that one is in various mental states will make one conscious of oneself as being in those states, and hence conscious of the self to which those states belong.

As Descartes and Kant stressed, our mental states are conscious in a way that seems to involve an important unity; we are conscious of them as all being states of a single unitary self or center of consciousness. It is not obvious whether some actual unity underlies this appearance of conscious unity (see Marcel 1993, Rosenthal 2005). But even explaining that subjective appearance requires more than simply explaining the consciousness of the relevant mental states.

See also Knowledge Argument; Qualia; Subjectivity.

Bibliography

Aristotle. *De Anima: Books II, III* (with passages from Book I). 2nd ed. Translated by D. W. Hamlyn, with added material by Christopher Shields. Oxford, U.K.: Clarendon Press, 1993.

Armstrong, D. M. "What Is Consciousness?" *Proceedings of the Russellian Society* 3 (1978): 65–76. Reprinted in expanded form in *The Nature of Mind*, by D. M. Armstrong (St. Lucia, Queensland: University of Queensland Press, 1980, pp. 55–67).

Baars, Bernard J. *A Cognitive Theory of Consciousness*. New York: Cambridge University Press, 1988.

Baars, Bernard J., William P. Banks, and James B. Newman, eds. *Essential Sources in the Scientific Study of Consciousness*. Cambridge, MA: MIT Press/Bradford Books, 2003.

Block, Ned. "On a Confusion about a Function of Consciousness." *The Behavioral and Brain Sciences* 18 (2) (June 1995): 227–247.

Block, Ned, Owen Flanagan, and Güven Güzeldere, eds. *The Nature of Consciousness: Philosophical Debates*. Cambridge, MA: MIT Press/Bradford Books, 1997.

Brentano, Franz. *Psychology from an Empirical Standpoint* [1874]. Translated by Antos C. Rancurello, D. B. Terrell, and Linda L. McAlister; edited by Linda L. McAlister. London: Routledge & Kegan Paul, 1973.

Carruthers, Peter. *Phenomenal Consciousness: A Naturalistic Theory*. New York: Cambridge University Press, 2000.

Chalmers, David J. *The Conscious Mind: In Search of a Fundamental Theory*. New York: Oxford University Press, 1996.

Churchland, Paul M. "Reduction, Qualia, and the Direct Introspection of Brain States." *The Journal of Philosophy* 82 (1) (January 1985): 8–28.

Clark, Austen. *Sensory Qualities*. Oxford, U.K.: Clarendon Press, 1993.

Crick, Francis, and Christoph Koch. "Towards a Neurobiological Theory of Consciousness." *Seminars in the Neurosciences* 2 (1990): 263–275.

Dennett, Daniel C. *Consciousness Explained*. Boston: Little, Brown, 1991.

Dennett, Daniel C. "The Message Is: There Is No *Medium*." *Philosophy and Phenomenological Research* 52 (4) (December 1993): 919–931.

Descartes, René. *The Philosophical Writings of Descartes*, 3 vols. Translated by John Cottingham, Robert Stoothoff, and Dugald Murdoch (vol. III with Anthony Kenny). New York: Cambridge University Press, 1984–1991.

Dretske, Fred. "Conscious Experience." *Mind* 102 (406) (April 1993): 263–283. Reprinted in *Perception, Knowledge, and Belief*, by Fred Dretske, pp. 113–137.

Dretske, Fred. *Perception, Knowledge, and Belief: Selected Essays*. New York: Cambridge University Press, 2000.

Freud, Sigmund. *The Standard Edition of the Complete Psychological Works of Sigmund Freud, Vol. 19, The Ego and the Id*. Translated and edited by James Strachey. London: Hogarth Press, 1961.

Gennaro, Rocco J., ed. *Higher-Order Theories of Consciousness: An Anthology*. Philadelphia, PA: John Benjamins, 2004.

Grimes, John. "On the Failure to Detect Changes in Scenes across Saccades." In *Perception*, edited by Kathleen Akins, 89–110. New York: Oxford University Press, 1996, pp. 89–110.

Harman, Gilbert. "The Intrinsic Quality of Experience." In *Philosophical Perspectives. Vol. 4, Action Theory and Philosophy of Mind*, edited by James E. Tomberlin. Atascadero, CA: Ridgeview, 1990, pp. 31–52.

Hume, David. *A Treatise of Human Nature* [1739]. 2nd ed., edited by L. A. Selby-Bigge. Text revisions and variant readings by Peter H. Nidditch. Oxford, U.K.: Clarendon Press, 1978.

Jackson, Frank. "Epiphenomenal Qualia." *Philosohical Quarterly*. XXXII, 127 (April 1982): 127–136.

Jackson, Frank. "Mind and Illusion." In *Minds and Persons*, edited by Anthony O'Hear. New York: Cambridge University Press, 2003, pp. 251–71. Reprinted in *There's Something about Mary: Essays on Phenomenal Consciousness and Frank Jackson's Knowledge Argument*, edited by Peter Ludlow, Yujin Nagasawa, and Daniel Stoljar (Cambridge, MA: MIT Press/Bradford Books, 2004, pp. 421–442).

Jackson, Frank. "What Mary Didn't Know." *The Journal of Philosophy* 83 (5) (May 1986): 291–295.

Kant, Immanuel. *Critique of Pure Reason* [1787]. Translated and edited by Paul Guyer and Allen W. Wood. New York: Cambridge University Press, 1998.

Levine, Joseph. *Purple Haze: The Puzzle of Consciousness*. New York: Oxford University Press, 2000.

Lewis, David. "Psychophysical and Theoretical Identifications." *Australasian Journal of Philosophy* 50 (3) (December 1972): 249–258.

Lewis, David. "What Experience Teaches." In *Mind and Cognition: A Reader*, edited by William G. Lycan. Cambridge, MA: Basil Blackwell, 1990.

Libet, Benjamin. "Unconscious Cerebral Initiative and the Role of Conscious Will in Voluntary Action." *The Behavioral and Brain Sciences* 8 (4) (December 1985): 529–539.

Loar, Brian. "Phenomenal States." In *The Nature of Consciousness: Philosophical Debates*, edited by Ned Block, Owen Flanagan, and Güven Güzeldere. Cambridge, MA: MIT Press/Bradford Books, 1997, pp. 597–616.

Locke, John. *An Essay concerning Human Understanding*. Edited from the fourth (1700) edition by Peter H. Nidditch. Oxford, U.K.: Clarendon Press, 1975.

Lycan, William G. *Consciousness and Experience*. Cambridge, MA: MIT Press/Bradford Books, 1996.

Marcel, Anthony J. "Conscious and Unconscious Perception: Experiments on Visual Masking and Word Recognition." *Cognitive Psychology* 15 (1983): 197–237.

Marcel, Anthony J. "Slippage in the Unity of Consciousness." In *Experimental and Theoretical Studies of Consciousness*, edited by Gregory R. Bock and Joan Marsh. Chichester, NY: Wiley, 1993, pp. 168–186.

McGinn, Colin. *The Problem of Consciousness: Essays towards a Resolution*. Oxford, U.K.: Basil Blackwell, 1991.

Nagel, Thomas. *The View from Nowhere*. New York: Oxford University Press, 1986.

Nagel, Thomas. "What Is It Like to Be a Bat?" *The Philosophical Review* 83 (4) (October 1974): pp. 435–450. Reprinted in *Mortal Questions*, by Thomas Nagel (Cambridge, U.K.: Cambridge University Press, 1979, 165–179).

Nisbett, Richard E., and Timothy DeCamp Wilson. "Telling More Than We Can Know: Verbal Reports on Mental Processes." *Psychological Review* LXXXIV (3) (May 1977): 231–259.

Putnam, Hilary. "The Nature of Mental States." In *Mind, Language, and Reality: Philosophical Papers, Volume 2*. New York: Cambridge University Press, 1975, pp. 429–440. Originally published as "Psychological Predicates," in *Art, Mind, and Religion*, edited by W. H. Capitan and D. D. Merrill (Pittsburgh: University of Pittsburgh Press, 1967, pp. 37–48).

Rosenthal, David M. *Consciousness and Mind*. Oxford, U.K.: Clarendon Press, 2005.

Rosenthal, David M. "A Theory of Consciousness." Report 40/1990, Center for Interdisciplinary Research (ZiF), University of Bielefeld. Reprinted in *The Nature of Consciousness: Philosophical Debates*, edited by Ned Block, Owen Flanagan, and Güven Güzeldere (Cambridge, MA: MIT Press/Bradford Books, 1997, pp. 729–753).

Rosenthal, David M. "Two Concepts of Consciousness." *Philosophical Studies* 49 (3) (May 1986): 329–359. Reprinted in *Consciousness and Mind*, by David M. Rosenthal.

Seager, William. *Theories of Consciousness: An Introduction and Assessment*. New York: Routledge, 1999.

Searle, John R. "Consciousness, Explanatory Inversion, and Cognitive Science." *The Behavioral and Brain Sciences* 13 (4) (December 1990): 585–696.

Searle, John R. *The Rediscovery of the Mind*. Cambridge, MA: MIT Press/Bradford Books, 1992.

Sellars, Wilfrid. "Empiricism and the Philosophy of Mind." In *Science, Perception, and Reality*. New York: Humanities Press, 1963; Atascadero, CA: Ridgeview Publishing Company, 1991.

Shoemaker, Sydney. *The First-Person Perspective and Other Essays*. New York: Cambridge University Press, 1996.

Siewert, Charles P. *The Significance of Consciousness*. Princeton, NJ: Princeton University Press, 1998.

Simons, Daniel J., and Ronald A. Rensink, "Change Blindness: Past, Present, and Future." *Trends in Cognitive Sciences* 9 (1) (January 2005): 16–20.

Treisman, Anne. "Features and Objects in Visual Processing." *Scientific American* 255 (5) (November 1986): 114–125.

Weiskrantz, Lawrence. *Consciousness Lost and Found: A Neuropsychological Exploration*. New York: Oxford University Press, 1997.

David M. Rosenthal (2005)

CONSCIOUSNESS IN PHENOMENOLOGY

For Edmund Husserl, the two basic features of consciousness are intentionality and temporality. Intentionality means that all consciousness is directed to some object. The thesis that consciousness is temporal means not only that all conscious states have a temporal location but that each of them has within itself a temporal structure and that the temporal structure of consciousness is the basis for all other determinations of consciousness and its objects.

Husserl's philosophical method proceeds through an analysis of conscious life. However, because all consciousness is intentional, the analysis of the forms and structures of various kinds of consciousness (including volitional, emotional, and evaluative, as well as theoretical) is also the appropriate way to analyze the essential forms and structures of various kinds of objects. Because Husserl also believes that consciousness involves at least implicit self-consciousness of one's own mental states, the focus on consciousness shifts the analysis to a sphere that is immediately and directly given in reflection and is therefore the source of apodictic certainty, the transcendental ego. In later works Husserl qualifies this assertion by pointing out that self-givenness even for ideal objects never necessarily involves absolute certainty, so that all purported givenness requires reconfirmation. He also turns his attention to the sphere of passive synthesis, whose results may be directly given to us, while the operations that originally generate them are not, so that a phenomenological reconstruction or intentional analysis is necessary to reveal sedimented or initially hidden and prepredicative elements of consciousness.

Jean-Paul Sartre considered himself a philosopher of consciousness during the first half of his career. He subscribed to the Cartesian ideal of the cogito as the starting point of philosophy and placed a premium on the apodictic evidence it yielded. But he valued consciousness as much for its freedom and spontaneity as for its epistemological translucency. In fact, it was the relevance of translucency to moral responsibility that led him to deny both a transcendental ego and the Freudian unconscious and to posit a "prereflective *Cogito*."

In his *The Imaginary* Sartre describes imaging consciousness as the locus of "negativity, possibility, and lack." Because we are able to "hold the world at bay" and "derealize" perceptual objects imagistically, he argues, we are free. Imaging consciousness becomes paradigmatic of consciousness in general (being-for-itself) in *Being and Nothingness*. Adopting Husserl's thesis that all consciousness is intentional, he insists that this intentionality is primarily practical, articulating a fundamental project that gives meaning/direction (*sens*) to our existence.

Sartre makes much of the prereflective self-awareness that accompanies our explicit awareness of any object, including our egos as reflective objects. Because we are always implicitly self-aware, it is unnecessary to seek self-consciousness in an endless infinity of reflections on reflections or to chase after a subject that cannot be an object (the transcendental ego). The unblinking eye of prereflective consciousness makes possible both bad faith and its overcoming through what he calls "purifying reflection," the authentic "choice" to live at a creative distance from one's ego.

Husserl's students such as Aron Gurwitsch and Ludwig Landgrebe and most of the subsequent figures within the phenomenological tradition such as Martin Heidegger and Maurice Merleau-Ponty built upon Husserl's and Sartre's insights into the importance of self-awareness, intentionality, and temporality—often under other names—but they also stress the prepredicative and the practical nature of this awareness as well as its limitations. Hence they avoid the term "consciousness" for the most part because of its association with Cartesian aspirations to complete self-transparency and absolute autonomy in human knowledge and action that they reject.

See also Authenticity; Descartes, René; Time, Consciousness of.

Bibliography

Husserl, E. *Cartesianische Meditationen*. Husserliana 1, edited by S. Strasser. The Hauge: M. Nijhoff, 1950. Translated by D. Cairns as *Cartesian Meditations: An Introduction to Phenomenology*. The Hauge: M. Nijhoff, 1960. See especially secs. 6–22 regarding intentionality and reflection. See secs. 30–41 regarding the temporal nature of consciousness and passive genesis.

Husserl, E. *Formale und transzendentale Logik*. Husserliana 17 edited by P. Janssen. The Hauge: M. Nijhoff, 1974. Translated by D. Cairns as *Formal and Transcendental Logic*. The Hauge: M. Nijhoff, 1969. Sec. 58 distinguishes between self-givenness and infallibility.

Husserl, E. *Ideen zu einer reinen Phänomenologie und phänomenologischen Philosophie*. Husserliana 3. The Hauge: M. Nijhoff, 1976. Translated by F. Kersten as *Ideas Pertaining to a Pure Phenomenology and Phenomenological Philosophy. First Book*. The Hauge: M. Nijhoff, 1982. See especially secs. 34–62 regarding the intentionality of consciousness and its accessibility to pure reflection.

Nenon, Thomas. "Freedom, Responsibility, and Self-Awareness in Husserl." *New Yearbook for Phenomenology and Phenomenological Philosophy* 2 (2002): 1–21.

Sartre, J.-P. *L'etre et le néant*. Paris: Gallimard, 1943. Translated by H. E. Barnes as *Being and Nothingness*. New York: Philosophical Library, 1956.

Sartre, J.-P. *L'imaginaire*. Paris, 1940. Translated by Jonathan Webber as *The Imaginary*. London: Routledge, 2004.

Sartre, J.-P. *La transcendence de l'ego*. Paris, 1937. Translated by R. Kirkpatrick and F. Williams as *The Transcendence of the Ego: An Existentialist Theory of Consciousness*. New York: Noonday, 1957.

Thomas Flynn (2005)
Thomas Nenon (2005)

CONSENSUS GENTIUM

See *Common Consent Arguments for the Existence of God*

CONSEQUENTIALISM

As a name for any ethical theory or for the class of ethical theories that evaluate actions by the value of the consequences of the actions, "consequentialism" thus refers to classical utilitarianism and other theories that share this characteristic.

Classical utilitarianism, in the philosophies of Jeremy Bentham, John Stuart Mill, and Henry Sidgwick, was consequentialist, judging actions right in proportion as they tended to produce happiness, wrong as they tended to produce pain. In the nineteenth and early twentieth centuries much of the criticism of utilitarianism was directed at the hedonistic value theory on which the ethical theory was founded. Some philosophers, such as G. E. Moore, agreed with the claim of utilitarianism that acts are right insofar as they produce good consequences, wrong as they produce bad consequences, but put forward a richer theory of value, claiming that other things besides pleasure and pain are of intrinsic value and disvalue. Such theories were sometimes labeled ideal utilitarianism. The term *consequentialism* is now used in a generic sense to include both hedonistic and nonhedonistic theories.

The term was probably introduced into usage by Elizabeth Anscombe in "Modern Moral Philosophy" (1958), an essay in which she claims that there is little difference between strictly consequentialist theories and other moral theories from Sidgwick on that permit forbidden acts to be overridden by consequentialist considerations. For example, W. D. Ross, who was an intuitionist in opposition to utilitarianism, even "ideal" utilitarianism, believed that a prima facie wrong action, such as the deliberately unjust punishment of an innocent person, could be outweighed by some consequentialist consideration such as the national interest. One contrast with consequentialism, then, is absolutism, the claim that there are some actions that are never right, whatever the consequences.

In the most usual usage of *consequentialism* as a term for ethical theories, however, it is contrasted, not only to absolutism, but to any theory, such as Kantianism, intuitionism, virtue ethics, rights theories, and so on, that does not in some way make consequences the determinant of right and wrong. The consequences may be considered indirectly. Distinctions have been made between act utilitarianism, which judges acts right or wrong according to the consequences of the particular act, case by case, rule utilitarianism, which judges acts right or wrong according to whether the acts are in accord with or in violation of a useful rule—that is, a rule whose general practice would have good consequences (or better consequences than any feasible alternative rule)—and motive utilitarianism, which judges acts right or wrong if stemming from a motive that, as a motive for action, generally has good consequences. These distinctions carry over to consequentialism as a generic category of ethical theories, and one can speak of act consequentialism, rule consequentialism, and so on. Consequentialist theories can also have a place for virtues and for rights, if the inculcation of certain virtues or the respect for certain rights has good consequences. But for the consequentialist the virtues or rights are not ultimate. Their value is dependent upon their contribution to good consequences.

Abstracting from the alternative theories of value, there are still important controversies regarding consequentialist theories. Some are problems of measuring consequences or making interpersonal comparisons, whatever the theory of value, but these cannot be addressed in the abstract. Another is the theory of responsibility. One prominent criticism of consequentialism, stated, for example, by Bernard Williams (1973), is that it does not adequately distinguish between positive and negative responsibility. The claim is that consequentialism is indifferent between states of affairs that are produced by what an agent does and those that occur because of what someone else would do that the agent could prevent. It becomes an agent's responsibility to prevent someone else from doing harm as well as not to do harm oneself. Related to this is the claim that consequentialism undermines agent integrity. For example, someone opposed to research in chemical and biological warfare might be required to engage in such research to prevent someone else from doing it more zealously. Another criticism is that if it is formulated as a "maximizing" theory, requiring the maximization of best consequences, consequentialism goes beyond the limits of obligation. For example, one would be morally obligated to spend one's wealth and income on others as long as there is anyone who could benefit more than oneself.

There are four basic kinds of responses that the consequentialist can make to these criticisms. One is to stick to the theory, saying that these things are morally demanded, even if not generally recognized in our selfish and self-centered society, as Peter Singer (1971–1972) argues concerning famine relief. Another is to challenge the implications of the examples, claiming that for moral agents to focus energy and attention on their own lives with integrity to their own principles has better consequences than doing otherwise. A third strategy for a nonhedonist is to attempt to avoid some of these objections by enriching the theory of value, such as to claim that integrity is something that is intrinsically valuable. A fourth strategy is to modify the structure of the theory. Michael Slote (1984) has argued in favor of a "satisficing" rather than a maximizing theory. Samuel Scheffler (1982) has proposed a "hybrid" theory that permits an agent either to maximize best consequences or to pursue the "agent-centered prerogative" of not always doing so.

See also Anscombe, Gertrude Elizabeth Margaret; Bentham, Jeremy; Deontological Ethics; Hedonism; Metaethics; Mill, John Stuart; Moore, George Edward; Rights; Ross, William David; Sidgwick, Henry; Utilitarianism; Virtue Ethics.

Bibliography

Anscombe, G. E. M. "Modern Moral Philosophy." *Philosophy* 33 (1958): 1–19.

Bennett, J. "Whatever the Consequences." *Analysis* 26 (1965–1966): 83–102.

Brandt, R. B. "Utilitarianism and Moral Rights." *Canadian Journal of Philosophy* 14 (1984): 1–19.

Crisp, R. "Utilitarianism and the Life of Virtue." *Philosophical Quarterly* 42 (1992): 139–160.

Darwall, Stephen, ed. *Consequentialism*. Oxford: Blackwell, 2003.

Feldman, Fred. "On the Consistency of Act- and Motive-Utilitarianism: A Reply to Robert Adams." *Philosophical Studies* 70 (1993): 201–211.

Feldman Fred. *Pleasure and The Good Life*. Oxford: Oxford University Press, 2004.

Feldman, Fred. *Utilitarianism, Hedonism, and Desert*. New York: Cambridge University Press, 1997.

Hooker, B. *Ideal Code, Real World*. Oxford: Clarendon Press, 2000.

Hooker, B., E. Mason, and D. E. Miller. *Morality, Rules, and Consequences*. Edinburgh: Edinburgh University Press, 2000.

Jackson, Frank. "Decision-Theoretic Consequentialism and the Nearest and Dearest Objection." *Ethics* 101 (1991): 461–482.

Kagan, S. "Does Consequentialism Demand Too Much? Recent Work on the Limits of Obligation." *Philosophy and Public Affairs* 13 (1983–1984): 239–254.

Mulgan, Tim. *The Demands of Consequentialism*. Oxford: Clarendon Press, 2001.

Norcross, Alasdair. "Consequentialism and Commitment." *The Pacific Philosophical Quarterly* 78 (1997): 380–403.

Parfit, Derek. *Reasons and Persons*. Oxford: Clarendon Press, 1984.

Pettit, Philip, ed. *Consequentialism*. Aldershot: Dartmouth, 1993.

Pettit, Philip. "The Consequentialist Perspective." In *Three Methods of Ethics*, by M. Baron, P. Pettit, and M. Slote, Oxford: Blackwell, 1997.

Railton, Peter. "Alienation, Consequentialism and the Demands of Morality." *Philosophy and Public Affairs* 13 (1984): 134–171, reprinted in Scheffler, ed. *Consequentialism and Its Critics*, 93–133.

Scarre, Geoffrey. *Utilitarianism*. London: Routledge, 1996.

Scheffler, Samuel, ed. *Consequentialism and Its Critics*. Oxford: Oxford University Press, 1988.

Scheffler, Samuel. *The Rejection of Consequentialism*. Oxford: Clarendon Press, 1982.

Shaw, William. *Contemporary Ethics: Taking Account of Utilitarianism*. Cambridge, MA: Blackwell, 1999.

Singer, P. "Famine, Affluence, and Morality." *Philosophy and Public Affairs* 1 (1971–1972): 229–243.

Slote, M. "Satisficing Consequentialism." *Aristotelian Society* suppl. 43 (1984): 139–163.

Smart, J. J. C. "An Outline of a System of Utilitarian Ethics." In *Utilitarianism: For and Against*, edited by J. J. C. Smart and B. Williams. Cambridge, U.K.: Cambridge University Press, 1973.

Williams, B. "A Critique of Utilitarianism." In *Utilitarianism: For and Against*, edited by J. J. C. Smart and B. Williams. Cambridge, U.K.: Cambridge University Press, 1973.

Henry R. West (1996)

Bibliography updated by Michael J. Farmer (2005)

CONSERVATION PRINCIPLE

Conservation principles tell us that some quantity, quality, or aspect remains constant through change. Such principles already appear in ancient and medieval natural philosophy. In one important strand of Greek cosmology, the rotation of the celestial orbs is eternal and immutable. In optics at least from the time of Euclid (fl. c. 300 BCE), when a ray of light is reflected, the angle of reflection is equal to the angle of incidence. According to some versions of the medieval impetus theory of motion, impetus permanently remains in a projected body (and the associated motion persists) unless the body is subject to outside interference. Such examples abound.

In the seventeenth century, conservation principles began to play a central role in scientific theories. Galileo Galilei, René Descartes, Christian Huygens, Gottfried Leibniz, and Isaac Newton founded their approaches to physics on the principle of inertia—the principle that a body will undergo uniform rectilinear motion unless interfered with. A multitude of other conservation principles gained currency during the seventeenth century—some still with us, some long ago left behind.

Descartes is an interesting example of an author who attempted to derive all of his physical principles from conservation laws (1991 [1644], esp. pt. 2, secs. 36–42). Descartes believed that the principles of his physics could be derived from the God's immutability, supplemented only by very weak assumptions about the existence of change in the world. He claimed, in fact, that we ought to postulate the strongest conservation laws consistent with such change. These laws were that God preserves at all times the total quantity of motion in the world (the quantity of motion of a body being the product of its volume and its speed), that each thing remains in the same state in every respect unless interfered with, and that in collisions the quantity of motion gained by one body is balanced by the quantity of motion lost by the other. The rest of his physics was supposed to follow from these principles alone.

The most remarkable of seventeenth-century analyses of conservation principles is contained in Huygens's essay on elastic collisions (1977). Huygens began by assuming that if two collinearly moving bodies of equal size move toward one another with equal speeds, in the resulting collision they simply exchange velocities. He then showed that it follows from the principle of Galileian relativity—that an experiment has the same outcome whether performed in a laboratory at rest or in a laboratory in uniform rectilinear motion—that whatever the initial velocity of such bodies, the result of a collision is always that velocities are simply exchanged. Huygens went on to analyze collisions between bodies of unequal size, again relying heavily on Galileian relativity. Among the consequences of his analysis were a number of conservation laws for systems of particles interacting only via elastic collisions: that the center of gravity of such a system undergoes uniform rectilinear motion, that the total kinetic energy of such a system is constant in time, and that the relative velocities (mv) of a pair of colliding particles is unchanged by a collision.

In a sense that will be spelled out below, the principle of Galileian relativity is a symmetry principle. So one of the things that Huygens accomplished was to show that from a symmetry principle one could deduce conservation principles. For an extensive class of physical theories—essentially, all of classical (or nonquantum) physics—it is now possible to establish a deep connection between symmetry principles and conservation laws. The balance of the discussion here provides an elementary introduction to the ideas relevant to understanding this connection.

SYMMETRY

At the most abstract level, a structure is a set of objects instantiating some set of properties and relations. A symmetry of a given structure is a permutation of the set of objects of the structure that leaves invariant all the properties and relations involved in the structure. For any structure, the identity map on its set of objects is, trivially, a symmetry.

For example, suppose that three points have relative pair-wise distances of three, four, and five units. Then there is no nontrivial symmetry that preserves these distances. But if the points instead form the vertices of an equilateral triangle, there will be several nontrivial symmetries, such as any transformation that interchanges two vertices while leaving the third fixed. We will be interested here in dynamic symmetries. As an intuitively plausible example, ordinary translation and rotation in space should be symmetries of any decent physical theory set in Euclidean space. Note that this does not mean that every translation or rotation will be a symmetry of the states allowed by the theory: The theory might treat the behavior of a finite number of point masses, in which case no configuration of the material points could be invariant under any nontrivial translation or under more than finitely many rotations. Rather, in such a case the invariance of the theory amounts to this: The dynamics of the theory is indifferent to the location or orientation of the system in Euclidean space, in that a translation or rotation of any state allowed by the theory will not change the dynamic evolution predicted by the theory, so long as the evolution of the new state is described relative to coordinate axes that have also been translated or rotated.

Its necessary to make all of this a bit more precise. Specifying a physical theory typically involves specifying a set of physically possible states and a dynamics defined on this space of states. Most often, the states involved will be possible instantaneous states of the system, such as the instantaneous positions and momenta of a set of particles, or the values of some field and of its time derivative at each point of space. These states will be collected together to form a space with some interesting mathematical structure (there is no need to be very specific about this structure at this stage). For convenience, a strict form of determinism will be assumed, under which the dynamics is given by the rule that if the state of the system at a given time is a, then its state t units of time later will be b, which we write as $a \underset{t}{\rightarrow} b$. A symmetry of this dynamics, S, will be a one-to-one mapping from the state space onto itself that leaves invariant all of the structure defined on this space, including the arrow relation. So $a \underset{t}{\rightarrow} b$ if and only if $S(a) \underset{t}{\rightarrow} S(b)$.

THE HAMILTONIAN APPROACH

Remarkably, almost all the equations of motion that arise in classical physics can be derived within the mathematical framework of Hamiltonian mechanics.

Consider the Newtonian n-body problem (n point masses interacting according to Newton's law of gravitation). We construct the phase space for this problem, the space of dynamically possible states of the particles. Choosing a point in this $6n$-dimensional abstract space amounts to specifying the position and momentum of each of the n particles (collision states with two or more particles coinciding in position are ruled out a priori, since the expression for the force of gravitational attraction between coincident particles is ill defined). Now, by the nature of the Newtonian equation of motion ($F = ma$), specifying the positions and momenta of the particles at some initial time suffices to determine their positions and momenta at other times (indeed, at all other times, unless a collision or other singularity occurs). So the dynamic content of the theory takes this form: Specifying a point in the phase space determines a curve in the phase space through that point—the idea being that if the given point represents the state of the system of n particles at time $t = 0$, then the curve tells us which points of the phase space represent states of the system at earlier and later times. These curves have the following nice feature: They partition the phase space, in the sense that exactly one curve passes through each point of the phase space (that at least one curve passes through each point follows from the dynamic content of the theory; that no more than one does so is a reflection, roughly speaking, of the determinism of this theory).

At the heart of the Hamiltonian approach lie three insights: (1) The phase space of the system, just in virtue of being a space of possible positions and momenta, carries a natural mathematical structure called a "symplectic form" (a closed nondegenerate two-form). (2) This structure allows the association to each nice real-valued function on the phase space of a family of curves that partitions the phase space. (3) The curves encoding the dynamics of the theory are thus associated with the Hamiltonian for the theory—the function that assigns to each point in phase space the total energy of the corresponding physical state (here the total energy is the sum of the kinetic energy and the gravitational potential energy).

These insights carry over to underwrite a Hamiltonian treatment of a vast assortment of classical (or nonquantum) physical theories. To develop a Hamiltonian treatment, consider the space of initial data for the equations of motion, and take this as the phase space of one's theory, showing that it comes equipped with a natural symplectic form (or generalization thereof) that allows one, in general, to pass from a function on the phase space to a set of curves partitioning the phase space—and in particular to pass from the Hamiltonian function assigning to each state its total energy to the curves on the phase space encoding the dynamic content of the equations of motion of the theory. This strategy works for rigid bodies, systems of moving particles subject to many sorts of constraints, many field theories, and some theories of material continua such as fluids and elastic bodies.

SYMMETRIES IN THE HAMILTONIAN APPROACH

So under the Hamiltonian approach, a theory consists of a phase space (representing the possible dynamic states of the theory) equipped with a symplectic form (or generalization) and a Hamiltonian function. Below, this symplectic form will be referred to as the geometrical structure of the phase space, although it is important to keep in mind that this structure is different in kind from the sort of metric structure that is normally treated in geometry.

A symmetry of a Hamiltonian theory is a one-to-one mapping from the phase space onto itself that preserves the geometric structure of the phase space and the Hamiltonian. Because these latter two objects are smooth, it follows that symmetries are continuous and differentiable to all orders.

In the n-body problem, for instance, all symmetries are smooth maps from the phase space onto itself that correspond to some combination of the following actions: (a) shifting by some fixed amount the positions of all particles in the Euclidean space in which they move; (b) rotating the orientation of the system of particles in Euclidean space by some fixed amount; (c) shifting the temporal origin by some fixed amount (that is, associating each state with the state that normally precedes or follows it by the given amount of time); (d) applying related discrete symmetries, such as a mirror reflection of the positions of the particles or an interchange of negative and positive senses of time.

Because each symmetry of a Hamiltonian theory leaves invariant all of the structure on the phase space that was used to define the dynamics, it also leaves invariant the curves that encode the dynamics—as we should expect from our general account of dynamic symmetries above. (The operation of a Galileian boost is not a symmetry in the present sense. Boosting a system does not leave its Hamiltonian invariant. A boost changes the kinetic energy of each particle and in general alters the total kinetic energy of the system, while leaving the potential energy of the system unchanged. But Galileian boosts do leave invariant the set of dynamic curves of the n-body problem.)

NOETHER'S THEOREM

A remarkable consequence of the geometric structure of the phase space is that in any Hamiltonian system, the Hamiltonian is constant along each curve encoding the dynamics. That is, the total energy of the system is a conserved quantity of the dynamics: If one state evolves into another, each has the same total energy.

Are there additional conserved quantities—functions on our phase space that are constant along the curves encoding the dynamics? To find them, consider any one-parameter continuous family of symmetries of a Hamiltonian system closed under composition—such as the family of spatial translations by a varying amount in a given direction in the n-body problem. What happens if we allow such a family to act on a point in the phase space of a Hamiltonian system? To find out, we construct a curve in the phase space that describes how each symmetry in our one-parameter family acts on the initial state. By performing this operation for each point in the phase space, we construct partitions the phase space. For the sort of theories that arise in practice, we can then find a nice function on our phase space that the geometric structure associates with this family of curves. From the geometric structure and from the fact that the family of curves in question arises via the action of a family of symmetries that preserve the Hamiltonian, it follows that this function will itself be a constant of motion of the physical theory under consideration—that this new function, associated with our one-parameter family of symmetries, is constant along each of the dynamic curves associated with the Hamiltonian of our theory.

In this way, for any well-behaved Hamiltonian theory, we can construct a conserved quantity corresponding to each one-parameter family of symmetries of the theory. Indeed, we can find as many functionally independent conserved quantities as there are dimensions in the complete family of symmetries of the theory. In the case of the n-body problem, we find seven conserved quantities: the Hamiltonian, the components of the total linear momentum of the system, and the components of the total angular momentum of the system. These conserved quantities correspond, respectively, to the invariance of the system under time translations, to its invariance under spatial translations in each direction, and to its invariance under rotation.

These insights derive from work of Emmy Noether in 1918 (1971), though they assume a somewhat different form in her work, since she worked in the Lagrangian framework rather than the Hamiltonian framework.

See also Classical Mechanics, Philosophy of; Philosophy of Physics.

Bibliography

Brading, Katherine, and Elena Castellani, eds. *Symmetries in Physics: Philosophical Reflections.* Cambridge, U.K.: Cambridge University Press, 2003.

Descartes, René. *Principles of Philosophy* (1644). Translated by Valentine Miller and Reese Miller. Dordrecht, Netherlands: Kluwer, 1991.

Huygens, Christian. "The Motion of Colliding Bodies." Translated by Richard J. Blackwell. *Isis* 68 (1977): 574–597.

Noether, Emmy. "Invariant Variation Problems" (1918). Translated by M. Tavel. *Transport Theory and Statistical Physics* 1 (1971): 184–207.

Singer, Stephanie Frank. *Symmetry in Mechanics: A Gentle, Modern Introduction.* Basel, Switzerland: Birkhäuser, 2001.

Van Fraassen, Bas. *Laws and Symmetry.* Oxford: Oxford University Press, 1989.

Zuckerman, Gregg. "Action Principles and Global Geometry." In *Mathematical Aspects of String Theory*, edited by Shing-Tung Yau. Singapore: World Scientific, 1987.

Gordon Belot (2005)

CONSERVATISM

Conservatives hold that the aim of political arrangements is to make a society good, that a society is good if those living in it can make good lives for themselves, and that good lives are satisfying for oneself and beneficial for others. The political arrangements that make such lives possible are discovered by historical reflection, which discloses various enduring traditions. People participate in them because they conceive of good lives in terms of the beliefs, values, and practices these traditions provide. Conservatism is not an uncritical defense of all traditions but only ones that have endured because people have found participation in them satisfying and beneficial. The justification or criticism of traditions, therefore, is based on their success or failure in fostering good lives. Conservatism has different versions depending on the views held about history, values, the relation between individuals and their society, and between human nature and evil. Conservatives agree that these are the pivotal political topics and that political arrangements should be based on the views held about them, but they disagree about what these views should be.

HISTORY

Conservatives believe that the starting points of political thought should be the prevailing political arrangements, rather than a hypothetical contract, a theory about an ideal society, a conception of the common good for all of humanity, or some basic value that always overrides any other value that may conflict with it. Some conservatives, however, believe that it is not a coincidence that certain political arrangements have been historically conducive or detrimental to good lives. They hold that there is a metaphysical explanation of their success or failure: the existence of a moral order in reality. Lives are good if they conform to this moral order and bad if they do not, and the same is true of political arrangements. These conservatives recognize that there are serious disputes about whether the order is (a) hierarchical—having The Good at its pinnacle, as supposed by the ancient Greek philosopher Plato, (b) providential, embodied in natural law, as held in the thirteenth century by Saint Thomas Aquinas and his many followers since then, or (c) an unfolding of the dialectic of clashing forces culminating in the final unity of reason and action, as claimed by Georg W. F. Hegel in nineteenth-century Germany. They nevertheless all assume that there is a moral order. Their task is to find out what it is, or, if it has already been revealed in some canonical text, to find out how it should be interpreted. Disputes about these matters are taken to show only the infirmity of human understanding or motivation, not that the existence of the moral order is doubtful.

The historical record of societies whose political arrangements have been based on a supposed moral order, however, is most alarming. They have tended to indoctrinate unwilling or uninformed people, leaving them no opportunity for choice. Such societies have not been freer of misery than less dogmatic ones. But they have added the misery peculiar to themselves of recognizing authorities who have claimed privileged access to the true and the good and thought that only human shortcomings stand in the way of good lives. This was taken by them to justify coercion, silencing dissenters, and indoctrinating the rest. Many conservatives, such as Edmund Burke in the eighteenth century and Michael Oakeshott in the twentieth, have rejected this approach to politics because of its grave dangers.

Other conservatives, such as the Frenchman Joseph de Maistre (1753–1821), deny that the right political arrangements can be justified by reason. It makes no difference to them whether the proffered reasons are metaphysical, scientific, or historical. They believe that all reasons are ultimately based on assumptions accepted on faith. Their rejection of reason as a guide, however, leaves them with the problem of deciding what political arrangements they ought to favor. The solution they have offered is to be guided by their faith and perpetuate existing arrangements because familiarity makes them safer than untried alternatives.

The problems of this approach are as evident from the historical record as those of the preceding one. Faith breeds dogmatism, persecution of those who hold other faiths or none at all, and it provides no justification for regarding political arrangements based on one faith as better than contrary ones based on other faiths. Moreover, the perpetuation of political arrangements on account of their familiarity makes their improvement virtually impossible because even flawed familiar ones will be judged preferable to dangerous unfamiliar possibilities.

An alternative to relying on a moral order or on faith is the fallibilism of the Frenchman Michel de Montaigne in the sixteenth century, the Scottish David Hume in the eighteenth century, and, closer to our times, George Santayana (1863–1952) and Oakeshott. They do not deny that there may be a moral order, only that reliable knowledge of it can be had. They find the historical evidence testifying to humans' fallibility much more convincing than the success of efforts to overcome it. They think that the claims of revelation, canonical texts, or putative eternal verities stand in need of persuasive evidence. But the available evidence is as questionable as the claims based on it. Fallibilists believe that it is far more prudent to look to the historical record of various political arrangements than to endeavor to justify or criticize them by relying on metaphysical speculations or faith, either of which is more dubious than the historical record.

Fallibilism, however, does not commit conservatives to the denial that it is possible to adduce reasons for or against political arrangements. What they deny is that good reasons must be universal and timeless. They reject the fideistic repudiation of reason, accept the importance and desirability of being as reasonable as possible, and claim that political arrangements should be based on the historical evidence available for them. Fallibilists want political arrangements to be firmly rooted in the experiences of the people who are subject to them. Since these experiences are inevitably historical, it is to their history that these conservatives look for evidence. Thus they avoid basing political arrangements on metaphysical speculation about what lies beyond experience and suspecting reasonable evaluations because of a global distrust of reason.

It seems, then, that the most defensible conservative belief about history is the fallibilist one. There is a presumption in favor of the enduring political arrangements of a society because their endurance is prima facie reason for supposing that they foster satisfying and beneficial lives. In the absence of contrary reasons, the enduring political arrangements ought to be maintained. It is possible, of course, that the arrangements have endured because of coercion or manipulation. If the case for change is based on cogent evidence that the arrangements have endured for reasons other than fostering good lives, then it should be seriously considered. But if the case is inspired merely by metaphysical, contractarian, fideistic, or utopian speculations, then much stronger reasons are needed before they could mount a reasonable challenge to political arrangements that have stood the test of time and attracted the allegiance of many people.

VALUES

Commitment to political arrangements that make good lives possible requires a view about what makes lives good. But there are countless valued activities, obligations, virtues, and satisfactions, countless ways of combining them and evaluating their respective importance, and so there seem to be countless ways in which lives can be good. Conservatives, therefore, must have a view about the diversity of values because the arguments for or against particular political arrangements depend on it. The problem is that there are three incompatible views about the diversity of values: absolutist, relativist, and pluralist.

Absolutists believe that the diversity of values is apparent, not real. They concede that there are many values, but they think that there is a universal standard that can be used to rank them. This standard may be a highest value, such as Plato's Good; the tranquility of ancient Greek and Roman Stoics; the love of God postulated by Saint Augustine, the fifth-century Bishop of Hippo; or the idea of general happiness advanced by nineteenth-century English Utilitarians. Other values, then, can be ranked on the basis of their contribution to the realization of the highest value. Or the standard may be a principle, like the Ten Commandments of the Old Testament, the Golden Rule of the New Testament, or the categorical imperative formulated by the German philosopher Immanuel Kant in the eighteenth century. If a choice needs to be made among different values, the principle will determine which ought to take precedence. Contemporary absolutists—for instance, the English John Finnis, the American Germain Grisez, and the German-American Eric Voegelin—argue that some political arrangements are preferable to others because they conform more closely to the universal standard than the alternatives. However, the candidates for a universal standard are also numerous and face the same problems as the values whose diversity is supposed to be diminished by them. Absolutists acknowledge this problem and explain it in terms of human shortcomings that prevent people from recognizing the true standard. The history of religious wars, persecutions, and tyrannies, aiming to rectify human shortcomings, testifies to the dangers inherent in this explanation.

Relativism is opposed to absolutism. Relativists regard the diversity of values as real: There are many values; many ways of combining and ranking them; and there is no universal standard that could be appealed to in resolving disputes about them. A good society, however, requires some consensus about values, and political arrangements should reflect this consensus. If the consensus changes, the arrangements should change as well. According to relativists, then, what counts as a value and how important it is depends on the consensus of a society. A value is what is valued in a particular context; all values, therefore, are context-dependent.

Values and the political arrangements that reflect them can be reasonably justified or criticized, but, relativists believe, the reasons that can be given for or against them count as reasons only within the context of a society. Since reasons ultimately rest on the prevailing consensus, they will not and are not meant to persuade outsiders. The ultimate appeal of relativists is to point at their arrangements and say: This is what we do here. If relativism takes a conservative form, as in Burke, or in the nineteenth-century Germans Johann Gottfried Herder and Wilhelm Dilthey, it often results in the romantic celebration of national identity, of the spirit of a people and an age, of the shared landscape, historical milestones, ceremonies, stylistic conventions, manners, and rituals that unite a society.

Relativism may seem to avoid the dangers of dogmatism and repression that threaten absolutism, but it is, in fact, equally prone to them. That the values of a society are not thought to be binding outside of it does not mean that the values of other societies will be regarded tolerantly. Because the world is full of people and societies whose values are inimical to the relativist's, there is good reason to guard jealously the relativist's values. Furthermore, if the justification of the values of a society is the prevailing consensus, then any political arrangement becomes justifiable, provided a sufficiently large consensus favors it. Slavery, female circumcision, the maltreatment of minorities, child prostitution, the mutilation of criminals, blood feuds, bribery, and any other noxious political arrangement may be exempted from censure on the grounds that it happens to be valued in its context.

These pitfalls of absolutism and relativism make them unreliable guides to the evaluation of political arrangements. It is with relief, then, that some conservatives in the last and present century—for instance, Oakeshott, Gordon Graham, and John Kekes—have turned to pluralism as an alternative to these flawed views. Pluralists are in partial agreement and disagreement with both absolutists and relativists. According to pluralists, there is a universal standard, but it applies only to values that must be protected by all political arrangements if they are to foster good lives. This standard is universal and minimal. It is possible to establish with reference to it some values required by all good lives, but not all the values that may make lives good. This leads to recognizing some political arrangements as necessary and to allowing a generous plurality of possible political arrangements beyond the necessary minimum. The standard accommodates part of the universalism of absolutism and part of the contextualism of relativism.

The source of pluralism's standard is human nature. To understand human nature sufficiently for the purposes of this standard does not require scientific research or commitment to some metaphysical belief or to natural law. It is enough for it to concentrate on normal people in a commonsensical way. It will then become obvious that good lives depend on the satisfaction of basic physiological, psychological, and social needs such as nutrition, shelter, rest, companionship, self-respect, the hope for a good or better life, the division of labor, justice, predictability in human affairs, and so forth. The satisfaction of these basic needs is a universal requirement of all good lives, whatever may be their social context. If the political arrangements of a society foster their satisfaction, it is reasonable to support them; if they hinder their satisfaction, it is reasonable to reform them.

If absolutists merely asserted and relativists merely denied this requirement, then the former would be right and the latter wrong. But both go beyond this point: absolutists hold that all the values that make lives good are to be evaluated by a universal standard and relativists deny that there is any universal standard at all. Pluralists think that the minimum requirements of human nature set a universal standard, but beyond it there is a plurality of values, of ways of ranking them, and of good lives that embody these values and rankings. According to pluralists, then, the political arrangements of a society ought to protect minimum requirements of good lives and foster a plurality of values beyond the minimum.

The combination of pluralism and conservatism provides two important possibilities. The first is the justification of political arrangements that protect the minimum requirements and the criticism of political arrangements that violate them. This possibility sets the goal of political action and makes possible reasonable comparisons among different societies on the basis of how well they protect the conditions on which all good lives depend. This version of conservatism avoids the objection to relativism that it sanctions any political arrangement so long as a large consensus supports it. The second is that the best guide to the political arrangements a society ought to have beyond the minimum is the history of the society because it is most likely to provide the evidence for or against the prevailing political arrangements. This second possibility avoids the dangers of dogmatism and repression that beset absolutism.

The political arrangements favored by this version of conservatism are based on a familiar list of values: justice, freedom, the rule of law, order, legal and political equality, prosperity, peace, civility, happiness, and so forth. There is likely to be a significant overlap among the lists conservatives, liberals, and socialists may draw up. But there will also be a significant difference: conservatives are genuine pluralists, whereas the liberal and socialists are not. Liberals and socialists are committed to regarding some of these values as more important than the others. What makes them liberals or socialists is their claim that when the values they favor conflict with others on the list, then the favored ones should prevail. If they did not claim this, they would cease to be liberals or socialists. Conservatives reject this approach. Their concern is to protect the whole system of these values. This sometimes requires favoring a particular value over another, sometimes the reverse. Conservative pluralists hold this to be true of all values. They differ from liberals and socialists in refusing to make an a priori commitment to resolving conflicts in favor of any particular value in the prevailing system of values.

INDIVIDUALS AND SOCIETY

Good lives must be satisfying and beneficial, but these requirements often conflict because satisfying lives may not be beneficial and beneficial lives may not be satisfying. This raises the question of which requirement should be dominant, and it has far-reaching political consequences how it is answered. Some twentieth-century conservatives—for instance, Friedrich von Hayek, Shirley Letwin, and Robert Nozick—favor individual autonomy over social authority. Their position is virtually indistinguishable from classical liberalism or libertarianism. Other conservatives—such as James Fitzjames Stephen in nineteenth-century England, Voegelin, and the twentieth-century English thinker Roger Scruton—think that social authority should prevail over individual autonomy, if they conflict. As before, there is an intermediate view between these two extremes, namely, that of twentieth-century traditionalist conservatives, represented, among others, by Oakeshott, the American Edward Shils, and Kekes.

Conservatives who stress autonomy at the expense of authority face two serious problems. First, they assume that good lives must be autonomous and cannot involve the recognition of some form of authority over oneself. If this were so, no military or devoutly religious life, no life in static, traditional, hierarchical societies, no life that involves the subordination of individual will and judgment to what is regarded as a higher purpose could be good. This would require regarding of the vast majority of lives outside of modern Western societies as bad. The mistake involved is to slide from the reasonable view that autonomous lives may be good to the unreasonable view that a life cannot be good unless it is autonomous. Second, if a good society is one that fosters good lives, then the precedence of autonomy over authority cannot be right, since autonomous lives may be frustrated or harmful. It is obvious that social authority must prevail over the autonomy of fanatics, criminals, fools, and so on.

The problems of authoritarianism are no less serious. There is no guarantee that if social authority prevails over individual autonomy, the resulting lives will be satisfying. Lives cannot be pronounced satisfying by some authority. Whether they actually are satisfying must ultimately be judged by the individuals themselves. Their judgments, of course, may be influenced by social authority. But no matter how strong that influence is, it cannot override the judgment of individuals in finding what satisfies them. As the lamentable historical record shows, however, this has not prevented countless religious and ideological authorities from stigmatizing individuals who reject their prescriptions as heretics, pagans, maladjusted, or sinful. The result is a repressive society whose dogmatism is reinforced by specious moralizing.

How, then, is the question to be answered? There is no need to insist that either individual autonomy or social authority should systematically prevail over the other. Both are necessary for good lives, but neither is sufficient. Instead of engaging in futile arguments about their comparative importance, it is far more illuminating to understand that they are interdependent aspects of the same underlying activity of individuals trying to make good lives for themselves. The connecting link between them is tradition.

A tradition is a set of customary beliefs and practices that have endured from the past to the present and attracted the allegiance of people so that they wish to perpetuate it. Traditions may be religious, horticultural, scientific, political, stylistic, moral, aesthetic, commercial, medical, legal, military, educational, architectural, and so on. They permeate human lives. When individuals aim at a good life, part of what they are doing is deciding which traditions they should participate in. They may make conscious, deliberate, clear-cut yes-or-no choices, or they may unconsciously, unreflectively fall in with familiar patterns, or they may be at various points in between. The bulk of the activities of individuals concerned with living in ways that strike them as good is composed of participation in the various traditions of their society.

Participation involves the exercise of autonomy. Individuals choose and judge; their wills are engaged; they learn from the past and plan for the future. But they do so in the frameworks of various traditions that authoritatively provide them with a range of choices, with matters that are left to their judgments, and with standards that within a tradition determine what choices and judgments are reasonable or unreasonable. Their exercise of autonomy is the individual aspect of their conformity to their tradition's authority, which is the social aspect of what they doing. They act autonomously by following the authoritative patterns of the traditions to which they feel allegiance. When a Catholic goes to confession, a violinist gives a concert, or a football player scores a touchdown, then the individual and the social, the autonomous and the authoritative, the traditional pattern of doing it and an individual doing it are inextricably mixed. To understand what is going on in terms of individual autonomy is as one-sided as it is to do so in terms of social authority. Both play an essential role, and understanding what is going on requires understanding both the roles they play. Traditionalism rests on this understanding, and it is the political response to it to maintain political arrangements that foster participation in the various traditions that have endured in a society.

Traditions may be vicious, destructive, stultifying, nay-saying, and thus detrimental to good lives. Part of the purpose of political arrangements is to draw distinctions among traditions that are unacceptable (like slavery), suspect but tolerable (like pornography), and worthy of encouragement (like university education). Traditions that violate minimum requirements of good lives should be prohibited. Traditions that have shown themselves to make questionable contributions to good lives should be tolerated but not encouraged. Traditions whose record testifies to their importance for good lives should be cherished.

The obvious question is who should decide which tradition is which and how that decision should be made. Traditionalist conservatives say that the decision should be made by those who are legitimately empowered to do so through the political arrangements of their society and they should make the decisions by reflecting on the historical record of the tradition in question. From this three corollaries follow. First, those who are empowered to make the decisions ought to be able to view the prevailing political arrangements from a historical perspective. The process works well if it empowers people who are not ill-educated, preoccupied with some single issue, inexperienced, or have qualifications that lie in some other field of endeavor. Traditionalist conservatives are clearly not populists. Second, a society that proceeds in this manner is pluralistic because it fosters a plurality of traditions. It does so because it sees as the justification of its political arrangements that they foster good lives, and fostering them depends on fostering the traditions participation in which may make lives good. Third, the society is tolerant because it is committed to having as many traditions as possible. Its political arrangements place the burden of proof on those who wish to proscribe a tradition. If a tradition has endured, if it has the allegiance of enough people to perpetuate it, then there is a prima facie case for it. That case may be, and often is, defeated, but the initial presumption is in its favor.

This outlook leads traditionalists to favor limited government. They do not think that the purpose of its political arrangements is to impose a conception of a good life. The political arrangements of a limited government interfere as little as possible with the traditions that flourish among people subject to it. The purpose of its arrangements is to enable people to live as they please, not to force them to live in a particular way. One of the most important ways of accomplishing this is to have a wide plurality of traditions as a bulwark between individuals and the government that has power over them. Traditionalist conservatives thus believe that a good society should have political arrangements that balance the claims of individual autonomy and social authority. This balance is maintained by the mediation of the traditions of a society that make autonomy possible and provide many of the forms it might take.

HUMAN NATURE AND EVIL

Conservatives tend to take a dim view of progress. They are not so foolish as to deny that great advances in pure and applied science have changed human lives for the better. But they have also changed them for the worse. Advances have been both beneficial and harmful. They have certainly enlarged the stock of human possibilities, but the possibilities are for both good and evil, and new possibilities are seldom without new evils. Evil is an obstacle to the betterment of the human condition. Unjust war, genocide, tyranny, torture, terrorism, the drug trade, concentration camps, racism, the murder of religious and political opponents, easily avoidable epidemics and starvation are some familiar and widespread evils. If evil is understood as serious unjustified harm caused by human beings, then the conservative view is that the prevalence of evil is a permanent condition that cannot be significantly altered.

The prevalence of evil reflects not just a human propensity but also a contingency that influences what propensities people have and develop. The propensity for evil is itself a manifestation of deeper, more pervasive influences, which operate through genetic inheritance, environmental factors, the crimes, accidents, pieces of good or bad fortune, the historical period, society, family, and so on. The same contingency also affects people because others, whom they love, depend on, and with whom their lives are intertwined in other ways, are as subject to it as they are themselves.

Pessimistic conservatives, such as Thomas Hobbes in seventeenth-century England and Niccolo Machiavelli in sixteenth-century Florence, think that the prevalence of evil reveals that human nature is basically evil. Optimistic conservatives, such as Hume and Oakeshott, reject pessimism because they think that the right sort of political arrangements will make evil less prevalent. Opposed to both are realistic conservatives—for example, Montaigne, Stephen, and Santayana—who hold that whether the balance of good and evil propensities and their realization by people tilts one way or another is a contingent matter over which individuals and their political arrangements have insufficient control.

Realistic conservatives do not think that the human condition is devoid of hope, but they have no illusions about the limited control a society has over its future. Their view is not that evil propensities are uncontrollable. Rather, human beings have both good and evil propensities and neither they nor societies can exercise sufficient control to make good propensities reliably prevail over evil ones. The right political arrangements help of course, just as the wrong ones make matters worse. But even under the best political arrangements a great deal of contingency remains and it places beyond human control much good and evil. The chief reason for this is that the efforts to control contingency are themselves subject to the very contingency they aim to control. And that, of course, is the fundamental reason why realistic conservatives doubt the possibility of significant improvement of the human condition.

Realistic conservatives do not believe that it is a matter of indifference what political arrangements are made. Political arrangements cannot guarantee the victory of good over evil, but they can influence how things go. Whether that is sufficient at a certain time and place is itself a contingent matter insufficiently within human control. The attitude that results from realizing this combines the acceptance of the fact that not even the best political arrangements guarantee good lives with the motivation to make political arrangements as good as possible.

This view accounts for another significant difference between conservative and liberal or socialist politics: the insistence of conservatives on the importance of political arrangements that hinder evil. This difference is a result of the conservative rejection of the optimistic belief, shared by liberals and socialists, that the prevalence of evil is the result merely of bad political arrangements, which tend to corrupt people, and if political arrangements were good, evil would be much less prevalent. Realistic conservatives reject this optimism. They do not think that evil is prevalent merely because of bad political arrangements. They ask why political arrangements are bad. And the answer must be that political arrangements are made by people, and they are bound to reflect the propensities of their makers. Bad political arrangements are ultimately traceable to evil human propensities. Since the propensities are subject to contingencies over which human control is insufficient, there is no guarantee that political arrangements can be made good. Nor that, if they were made good, they would be sufficient to hinder evil.

Conservatives insist, therefore, on the necessity and importance of political arrangements that hinder evil: moral education, the enforcement of morality, the treatment of people according to what they deserve, the importance of swift and severe punishment for serious crimes, and so on. They oppose the prevailing attitudes that lead to agonizing over the criminal and forgetting the crime, the absurd fiction of a fundamental moral equality between habitual evildoers and their victims, guaranteeing the same freedom and welfare-rights to good and evil people, and so forth. Conservatives think that the aim of justice is to uphold the rule of law that assures that people get what they deserve.

Political arrangements that are meant to hinder evil are liable to abuse. Conservatives know and care about the historical record that testifies to the dreadful things that have been done on the many occasions when such arrangements have gone wrong. The remedy, however, cannot be to refuse to make the arrangements; it must be to learn from history, and try hard to avoid their abuse. Conservatives know that in this respect, as in all others, contingency will be a permanent obstacle to success. But this is precisely the reason why political arrangements are necessary for hindering evil. Realistic conservatives face the worst and try to deny scope to it, rather than endeavor to build a Utopia on optimistic illusions.

OVERVIEW

The most reasonable version of conservatism is fallibilist, pluralist, traditionalist, and realist. It avoids metaphysical and fideistic dogmatism. It denies that the content of good lives is given by a system of absolute values; accepts that good lives have some universal albeit minimal, requirements; and holds that some, but not all, values are context-dependent. It recognizes that both individual autonomy and social authority are necessary for good lives, and resolves their conflicts by balancing their claims. It rejects both optimism based on utopian illusions and pessimism that registers only human corruption. It sees human nature as having both good and evil propensities and strives for political arrangements that foster the first and curb the second. Conservatism is a view of politics guided by history and aiming at the betterment of society within the limits set by the contingency of life and human imperfection.

See also Augustine, St.; Burke, Edmund; Dilthey, Wilhelm; Evil; Hegel, Georg Wilhelm Friedrich; Herder, Johann Gottfried; Hobbes, Thomas; Human Nature; Hume, David; Kant, Immanuel; Liberalism; Machiavelli, Niccolò; Maistre, Comte Joseph de; Montaigne, Michel Eyquem de; Nozick, Robert; Oakeshott, Michael; Plato; Pluralism; Santayana, George; Social and Political Philosophy; Thomas Aquinas, St.; Value and Valuation.

Bibliography

Aquinas, Saint Thomas. *Summa Theologiae*. London: Eyre and Spottiswoode, 1963–1975.

Burke, Edmund. *Reflections on the Revolution in France*. Harmondsworth: Penguin, 1968.

Finnis, John. *Natural Law and Natural Rights*. Oxford: Clarendon Press, 1980.

Graham, Gordon. "True Conservatism—the Rejection of Ideology." In *Politics in Its Place*. Oxford: Clarendon Press, 1986.

Hayek, Friedrich von. *The Constitution of Liberty*. Chicago: Regnery, 1960.

Hegel, Georg W. F. *The Philosophy of Right*. Translated by T.M. Knox. Oxford: Oxford University Press, 1952.

Hobbes, Thomas. *Leviathan*. London: Dent, 1962.

Hume, David. *An Enquiry concerning the Principles of Morals*. Oxford: Clarendon Press, 1961.

Hume, David. *Essays Moral, Political, and Literary*. Indianapolis: Liberty Press, 1985.

Kekes, John. *A Case for Conservatism*. Ithaca: Cornell University Press, 1998.

Kirk, Russell. *The Conservative Mind*. South Bend, IN: Gateway, 1978.

Letwin, Shirley. *The Pursuit of Certainty*. Cambridge, U.K.: Cambridge University Press, 1965.

Letwin, Shirley. *The Gentleman in Trollope*. Cambridge, MA: Harvard University Press, 1982.

Machiavelli, Niccolo. *The Prince*. In *Selected Political Writings*. Translated and edited by David Wootten. Indianapolis: Hackett, 1994.

Montaigne, Michel de. *Essays*. In *The Complete Works of Montaigne*. Translated by Donald M. Frame. Stanford: Stanford University Press, 1958.

Muller, Jerry Z. ed. *Conservatism*. Princeton, NJ: Princeton University Press, 1997.

Nozick, Robert. *Anarchy, State, and Utopia*. New York: Basic Books, 1974.

Oakeshott, Michael. *The Politics of Faith and the Politics of Scepticism*, edited by Timothy Fuller. New Haven: Yale University Press, 1996.

Oakeshott, Michael. *Rationalism in Politics*, edited by Timothy Fuller. Indianapolis: Liberty Press, 1991.

O'Sullivan, Noel. *Conservatism*. New York: St. Martin's Press, 1976.

Plato. *The Republic*. Translated by Robin Waterfield. Oxford: Oxford University Press, 1993.

Santayana, George. *Dominations and Powers*. New York: Scribner's, 1951.

Scruton, Roger. *The Meaning of Conservatism*. Harmondsworth: Penguin, 1980.

Shils, Edward. *Tradition*. Chicago: University of Chicago Press, 1981.

Shils, Edward. *The Virtue of Civility*, edited by Steven Grosby. Indianapolis: Liberty Press, 1997.

Stephen, James Fitzjames. *Liberty, Equality, Fraternity*. Cambridge, U.K.: Cambridge University Press, 1967.

Voegelin, Eric. *Order in History*. Baton Rouge: Louisiana State University Press, 1954–1987.

John Kekes (2005)

CONSTRUCTIVISM, MORAL

Moral constructivism is a metaethical view about the nature of moral truth and moral facts (and properties), so called because the intuitive idea behind the view is that such truths and facts are human constructs rather than objects of discovery. More precisely, constructivism involves both a semantic thesis about moral sentences and a two-part metaphysical thesis about the existence and nature of moral facts and properties. According to the semantic thesis, ordinary moral sentences purport to be fact-stating sentences and thus purport to be genuinely true or false. And, according to the metaphysical thesis, there are moral facts whose existence and nature are in some sense dependent upon human attitudes, agreements, conventions, and the like. Thus, constructivism represents a metaethical view in partial agreement with versions of moral realism. Like the realist, the constructivist is a so-called cognitivist (descriptivist)—moral sentences have descriptive content and thus purport to be genuinely fact stating. Again, like the realist, the constructivist accepts the view that there are moral facts that serve as the truth makers of true moral sentences. But unlike the realist, the constructivist rejects the idea that there are moral facts (and properties) that are independent of human attitudes, conventions, and the like.

It is useful to distinguish between simple and sophisticated versions of constructivism as well as between nonrelativist and relativist versions. Simple versions of constructivism are represented by certain views that would construe moral truth in terms of the actual attitudes of individuals or actual agreements within cultures about matters of moral concern. More sophisticated versions of constructivism construe moral truths (and associated moral facts and properties) in terms of the hypothetical attitudes of individuals or perhaps hypothetical agreements among members of a group reached under suitably constrained circumstances. Nonrelativist versions of constructivism maintain that all individuals and groups whose attitudes, agreements, and so forth provide the basis for moral truths and facts do or would accept the same set of basic moral norms with the result that there is a single set of moral truths and facts. Usually, such views are wedded to some version or other of sophisticated constructivism.

Thus, a version of the ideal-observer view of moral truth—according to which basic moral truths are represented by the moral norms that would be accepted by an ideal observer, where the notion of an ideal observer is so characterized that all ideal observers will agree on the same set of basic moral norms—is a version of sophisticated nonrelativist constructivism. Relativist versions of constructivism allow that there may be more than one individual or group with differing attitudes and agreements that serve as the basis for different (and conflicting) sets of basic moral norms. Versions of moral relativism, according to which moral truths and facts are a matter of what basic moral norms a culture in fact accepts, represent versions of simple, relativistic constructivism; versions of relativism, according to which moral truths and facts are a matter of what would be accepted under conditions that are ideal for choosing such norms, represent sophisticated relativistic versions of constructivism. Versions of the ideal-observer view are relativistic if they allow that there can be ideal observers who would accept different (and conflicting) sets of moral norms. So-called Kantian constructivism of the sort elaborated and defended by John Rawls, which appeals to choices made by hypothetical individuals behind a veil of ignorance (a version of contractarianism), is yet another sophisticated and apparently nonrelativistic constructivist view.

Constructivism, at least in its sophisticated versions, is supposed to capture what is plausible about moral realism, leaving behind what is problematic about realist views. Thus, constructivism can accommodate quite well certain "objective pretensions" of commonsense moral thinking. Some of these pretensions have to do with the form and content of moral discourse. A good many moral sentences are in the declarative mood (e.g., "Abortion, except in cases of rape and incest, is wrong") and are thus naturally interpreted as genuinely fact-stating sentences. Moreover, some such sentences appear to make references to (putative) moral facts and properties (e.g., "The evil of American slavery was partly responsible for its demise as an institution"). Other objective pretensions have to do with such activities as moral deliberation, debate, and argument. These critical practices are seemingly aimed at arriving nonarbitrarily at true or correct moral views, ones that would ideally resolve intrapersonal and interpersonal conflict and uncertainty about moral issues. Like realism, constructivism is attractive in apparently being able to accommodate such objective pretensions of ordinary moral discourse. Moreover, it attempts to accommodate these features without endorsing the sorts of metaphysical commitments to independently existing moral properties and facts countenanced by the realist. In short, at least certain versions of constructivism boast a robust notion of moral objectivity without problematic metaphysical commitments.

One serious challenge to constructivism is represented by the argument from moral error. According to constructivism, moral truths and associated facts are to be understood in terms of the attitudes and agreements of individuals and groups. However, if we take ordinary moral discourse and argument seriously, then since such discourse and argument presuppose that there are right answers to moral questions whose correctness outstrips any actual or even ideal set of attitudes or agreements, the constructivist view cannot be correct. To understand this objection more clearly, it will be useful to distinguish between basic and nonbasic moral truths and facts. Basic moral truths and facts are of a quite general sort, properly expressed by moral principles, and are the direct objects of choice by those under ideal conditions of moral thought and deliberation. Nonbasic moral truths and facts are those truths and facts that, in some sense, follow from the basic ones together with nonmoral information.

Now the constructivist can allow for certain sorts of errors in moral judgment. For instance, simple moral relativism can allow that individuals and groups can be mistaken about particular moral judgments owing to misinformation about particular cases or perhaps to faulty reasoning from basic moral principles to concrete cases. This kind of moral relativism, however, cannot allow for error at the level of actual agreements, since such agreements constitute basic moral truths. The sophisticated constructivist can allow for error at the level of communal agreement, since it is possible on such views that the actual agreements of actual groups are at odds with those hypothetical choices constitutive of moral truth on this sort of view. However, the sophisticated constructivist cannot allow for error at the level of choice made under ideal conditions—call this "deep moral error." After all, the constructivist construes such choice as constitutive and not just evidence of basic moral truths and facts. But, so the objection goes, given our critical practices, we can sensibly raise questions about the truth of those moral principles and norms that are chosen under ideal circumstances. This indicates that moral truth is one thing and the norms and principles chosen even under the most ideal of circumstances is another. Hence, constructivism, in both its simple and sophisticated versions, is not acceptable.

In response, the constructivist can perhaps block the argument from moral error in the following way. First, the constructivist can note that it is dubious that our critical practices presuppose that deep moral error—error at the level of choice under ideal conditions—is possible. After all, our commonsense critical practices are not finely tuned to subtle differences in metaethical positions, and, in particular, common sense does not (so the constructivist might plead) make any distinction between the sort of realist objectivity that presupposes the possibility of deep moral error and a kind of constructivist objectivity that denies this possibility. Can we, for instance, really make sense of the idea that we might be mistaken about such basic moral principles as one that prohibits torture for fun? Furthermore, the constructivist can question the basic move featured in the argument from moral error—that is, the move from (1) it is quite sensible to raise questions about choices that purport to be made under ideal conditions to (2) an explanation of this phenomenon requires moral realism. Granted, the supposed gap between the truth of moral principles on the one hand and choice of such principles under ideal conditions on the other is one way to explain how we can sensibly raise questions about the truth of moral judgments made under ideal conditions, but this is not the only way to make sense of such critical stances.

The constructivist can note that in the context of everyday discussion where we have to judge whether or not to accept the moral judgments of others, one can sensibly raise questions about some judgment by raising questions about the judger herself. After all, whatever is involved according to the constructivist in being ideally well situated for choosing basic moral principles, it is not likely to involve features of the judger and her situation that are easy to detect. For example, part of being ideally well situated would seem to require having all sorts of factual information, being free from certain forms of bias, and properly weighing the interests of parties affected by the choice of principles. But it is difficult to determine that someone has satisfied these and other relevant desiderata for being well situated. So, even if it is not possible for someone who really is well situated to be mistaken in moral judgment, it is possible for critics who acknowledge that such error is not possible to raise sensible questions about the truth of a person's moral judgment. Hence, although the constructivist cannot allow for the possibility of deep moral error, she can plausibly argue that our commonsense critical practices do not presuppose that deep moral error is possible. Moreover, she can go on to accommodate the idea that it makes sense to criticize those who are ideally situated. The constructivist, it would appear, can plausibly respond to the argument from moral error.

See also Metaethics; Moral Realism; Rawls, John.

Bibliography

Brink, D. O. *Moral Realism and the Foundations of Ethics.* Cambridge, U.K.: Cambridge University Press, 1989. In chapter 2 Brink uses the argument from moral error against constructivism. Appendix 4 is a critical discussion of Rawlsian constructivism.

Firth, R. "Ethical Absolutism and the Ideal Observer." *Philosophy and Phenomenological Research* 12 (1952): 317–345. A classic statement of the ideal-observer version of constructivism.

Milo, R. "Skepticism and Moral Justification." *Monist* 76 (1993): 379–393. Milo defends a contractarian version of constructivism.

O'Neill, O. "Constructivisms in Ethics." In *Constructions of Reason.* Cambridge, U.K.: Cambridge University Press, 1990. O'Neill criticizes Rawls's version of constructivism and sketches what she takes to be a more plausible version of the view inspired by Immanuel Kant's writings.

Rawls, J. "Kantian Constructivism in Moral Theory." *Journal of Philosophy* 77 (1980): 515–572. An elaboration of a constructivist view that centrally involves a Kantian conception of persons.

Timmons, M. "Irrealism and Error in Ethics." *Philosophia* 22 (1993): 373–406. A critical discussion of the argument from moral error.

Wong, D. *Moral Relativity.* Berkeley: University of California Press, 1984. Wong both criticizes various versions of moral relativism and defends his own version.

Mark Timmons (1996)

CONSTRUCTIVISM AND CONVENTIONALISM

"Conventionalism" and "constructivism" are kindred, often overlapping positions, asserting that the subject matter of some area of inquiry is not fully mind-independent. Conventionalism and constructivism are not well-defined names of positions but labels adopted—as often by critics as by advocates—to emphasize one positive aspect of positions in a wide range of areas; consequently, these terms group together a variety of positions with varying motivations. In general, the label "conventionalism" is applied to positions that claim the truths in some area are so in virtue of the conventions of a linguistic or conceptual scheme, while "constructivism" emphasizes that a position assigns to the cognitive faculties of humans some role in "making" the objects or facts in the area in question.

CONVENTIONALISM

Conventionalists claim either that the truths of some subject matter—such as mathematics or logic, or of a certain sort, such as necessary truths, or some dispute, such as whether Euclid's parallel postulate holds of our physical world—are matters of convention rather than of how the world is independent of mind. Some extreme versions of conventionalism take the fact that it is a matter of convention what our words mean (we could have used *cat* to designate Napoleon Bonaparte) to show that all truth is conventional. However, its being a convention that "Napoleon" names Napoleon hardly makes it conventional that Napoleon was defeated at Waterloo. An interesting conventionalism must assert something more than the conventionality of word meaning and must rest on something more than wild inference from it.

One area in which conventionalism is familiar, though controversial, is necessary truth. This was one cornerstone of logical positivism; from the seeming a priori nature of necessary truths, the positivists argued (some would say claimed) that since a priori knowledge cannot be of (mind-independent) facts, necessary truths must be analytic, which they understood as true by definition. Given that mathematics is also a priori, their argument was applied there as well. This sort of epistemological argument is typical of conventionalist views: Arguing that our methods for ascertaining what is so in some area could not give us knowledge of a mind-independent world, they claim that this knowledge would not be problematic on the assumption that what is fundamentally under investigation are our conventions. Some sorts of conventionalism are also supported by metaphysical considerations such as naturalistic concerns about what, in the mind-independent world, could make for the relevant sort of truth. This sort of argument is common to necessary truths, mathematics, ethics, and other areas with normative import; plainly, such arguments need to be supplemented with an account of how it is that conventions can provide the relevant features.

Saul Kripke's arguments that there are necessary truths that are a posteriori—and, so, not analytic—seemed to some to undermine conventionalism about necessity (Kripke 1980). It has, however, been argued that conventions could explain the necessity of these truths without the truths themselves being analytic—that is, true by convention (Sidelle 1989). This may indicate that in general conventionalism, with respect to a subject matter, does not require that all target truths themselves be analytic but only that conventions be responsible for the features that purportedly cannot be adequately handled within a realistic interpretation.

Aside from the claim that certain truths are so by convention, another common conventionalist position is that some dispute is a conventional rather than factual matter. Jules Henri Poincaré's famous conventionalism about geometry is of this sort. He claims that the choice among systems of geometry, for describing the physical world, is not an issue of which is true but of which is most convenient or useful. By adopting any of them, we could modify our physics so as to have equally full and correct descriptions of the world; indeed, this last claim is the basis for his view that the issue is conventional rather than factual. Rudolf Carnap offers a similar view about ontological disputes between, for instance, phenomenalists and materialists. Both of these views illustrate that "conventional" does not as such imply "arbitrary," as pragmatic differences may be quite genuine; we can also see that the plausibility of conventionalism in some area depends largely on how implausible it is to claim that the issue, or truth in question, is a matter of mind-independent fact.

On a more local level, some disputes can appear "purely verbal," as perhaps whether some politician is conservative. When this is plausible, the issue may be said to be a matter of convention or choice rather than fact. The conventionalism of Poincaré, Carnap, and others is akin to this, only in a wider application. In book 3, chapters 7 and 11, of his *Essay,* John Locke speculates that many of the "great disputes" are of this sort.

As applied to areas in which the truths are well established (mathematics or logic, for instance), conventionalism is fundamentally a deflationary interpretive position, urging that we not mistake the metaphysical status of these truths. Applied to areas of controversy—ontological or essentialist claims, or whether whales are fish—conventionalism claims that disputes here can only be over what our conventions in fact are, or what they should be, either pragmatically or perhaps morally. In either case, if conventionalism is right, our focus and methods of investigation—and certainly our understanding of what is at stake—for the questions at hand would probably require alteration.

CONSTRUCTIVISM

Thomas Kuhn, by virtue of his *The Structure of Scientific Revolutions,* may be considered constructivism's leading protagonist of the mid-to-late twentieth century, despite not adopting the label himself and expressing unease at having it assigned to him. He writes of scientists within different paradigms—roughly, methodological and theoretical traditions or frameworks—as studying different worlds and of their paradigms as in "a sense … constitutive of nature" (Kuhn 1970, p. 110, chaps. 10, 13), at least suggesting a constructivism about the world studied by science. Kuhn's major concerns are epistemological; he argues that scientific procedure is deeply theory laden and encodes ontological and theoretical commitments that it is incapable of testing. How, then, can such a method give us knowledge of the world? Those who see a constructivist in Kuhn have him answer that the world under investigation is itself partly a product of the investigating paradigm. This puts Kuhn in the tradition of Immanuel Kant, except that the features we "impose" upon the phenomenal world are not (as for Kant) necessary for the possibility of experience, but, rather, contingent features of current science. It is important to note that, even as interpreted, this constructivism does not have scientists making the world out of whole cloth with their paradigms; rather, there is something mind-independent that "filters through" the conceptual apparatus of the paradigm. This is a central difference between constructivism and idealism. The object of scientific study is, however, not this mind-independent world, but rather that which results "through the filter."

Other philosophers, as well as historians and sociologists of science, have taken the supposedly arational or nonobjective features guiding scientific judgment to establish that scientific truth is relative to one's background theory or paradigm. This is sometimes then articulated as the view that these theories or paradigms in part "make" the objects of study—that is, as constructivism. Indeed, many positions that formerly would have simply been called relativist came, in the late twentieth century, to be called constructivist by their protagonists; arguments in their support tend to be of the familiar relativist sort and thus have the same strengths and problems. It should be noted that neither constructivism nor conventionalism need take a relativistic form.

Another philosopher associated with constructivism is Nelson Goodman, due largely to his *Ways of Worldmaking.* Goodman argues that no sense can be made of the notion "the (one) way the world is"; rather, there are lots of ways the world is, depending on the conceptual apparatus one brings. This sort of position is found in many philosophers since Kant, often argued on the trivial ground that one cannot describe or investigate the world without using a system of representation, therefore (*sic*) the world investigated is not mind-independent but partly constructed by our conceptual scheme. This is sometimes added to, or confused with, the relativistic considerations mentioned above. What needs to be explained is how we are supposed to get this substantive conclusion from the banal premise. Why can't the objects represented by the elements of a system of representation—by the name "Tabby," say—be wholly and utterly mind-independent? And even if we add the fact that there can be different schemes of representation, why can it not simply be that they pick out different features of a mind-independent reality? What gives Goodman his special place is that he supplements this argument with the claim that different schemes may be such that their claims conflict with each other, but there can be no grounds for maintaining that one is correct and the other not. Goodman uses as examples the claims that the planets revolve around the sun and that the sun and other planets revolve around Earth. Both, he claims, must be judged as correct (within the appropriately formulated total systems), but they cannot simply be seen as two notationally different descriptions of a single world (thus differing from Poincaré's conventionalism). The success of this argument depends on whether one can simultaneously make out that these claims genuinely do conflict with each other and that, so understood, neither of them can be judged to be true while the other is false.

PROSPECTS

While both Kuhn and Goodman offer relatively global constructivist positions, there are constructivists about essences, moral and aesthetic properties, mathematical objects, and in principle anything. The same is true of conventionalism. Both conventionalism and constructivism are motivated primarily by negative considerations against a realistic understanding of the subject matter in question; this is sometimes supplemented with positive arguments that by understanding the matter as concerning our conventions or choices we can get a better explanation of the phenomena at hand. Often, the negative arguments are very quick and fail to fully consider the range of options available to realists (Scheffler [1966] presents good discussion), and sometimes they fail to consider whether their positive proposals actually fare any better. Plainly, the plausibility of these positions depends on how well these arguments can be made out, and this may vary drastically across the different subject matters for which conventionalist and constructivist proposals have been offered. Additionally, if these positions are even to be candidates for serious consideration, defenders must be prepared to offer further proof. Conventionalists must specify some sense in which that which is purportedly so by convention would have been otherwise had our conventions been different, and constructivists must describe some sense in which the purportedly constructed objects would not have existed without our input.

See also A Priori and A Posteriori; Carnap, Rudolf; Conventionalism; Geometry; Goodman, Nelson; Kant, Immanuel; Kripke, Saul; Kuhn, Thomas; Locke, John; Logical Positivism; Poincaré, Jules Henri.

Bibliography

Carnap, R. "Empiricism, Semantics, and Ontology." In *Meaning and Necessity.* Chicago: University of Chicago Press, 1947. A classic exposition of the conventionalist's treatment of apparently ontological questions as fundamentally linguistic.

Dummett, M. *Frege: Philosophy of Language.* 2nd ed. Cambridge, MA: Harvard University Press, 1981. Chap. 16, esp. pp. 560–583. An interesting presentation of what may be seen as a constructivist position on objects or a conventionalist position on identity criteria.

Goodman, N. *Ways of Worldmaking.* Indianapolis: Hackett, 1978. For useful discussion, see C. G. Hempel, "Comments on Goodman's *Ways of Worldmaking,*" and I. Scheffler, "The Wonderful Worlds of Goodman," both in *Synthese* 45 (1980): 193–209.

Horwich, P. "A Defence of Conventionalism." In *Fact, Science and Morality,* edited by G. MacDonald and C. Wright. Oxford, 1986.

Knorr-Cetina, K. "The Ethnographic Study of Scientific Work: Towards a Constructivist Interpretation of Science." In *Science Observed: Perspectives on the Social Study of Science,* edited by K. Knorr-Cetina and M. Mulkay. London, 1983.

Kripke, S. *Naming and Necessity.* Cambridge, MA: Harvard University Press, 1980.

Kuhn, T. S. *The Structure of Scientific Revolutions.* 2nd ed. Chicago: University of Chicago Press, 1970.

Kyburg, H. E. "A Defense of Conventionalism." *Noûs* 11 (1977): 75–95.

Latour, B., and S. Woolger. *Laboratory Life: The Social Construction of Scientific Facts.* 2nd ed. Princeton, NJ: Princeton University Press, 1986.

Lewis, D. *Convention.* Cambridge, MA: Harvard University Press, 1969. Argues that sense can be made of the idea of nonexplicit conventions, *contra* Quine (1953).

Locke, J. *An Essay concerning Human Understanding* (1689). Locke's discussion of substance in book 3, chap. 7, classically expounds his conventionalism about essence and kinds.

Niiniluoto, I. "Realism, Relativism, and Constructivism." *Synthese* 89 (1991): 135–162. Critical discussion of constructivism in the social sciences.

Pap, A. *Semantics and Necessary Truth.* New Haven, CT: Yale University Press, 1958. An extended argument against conventionalism about necessity.

Poincaré, H. *Science and Hypothesis.* London: Walter Scott, 1905.

Putnam, H. "The Refutation of Conventionalism." In *Mind, Language, and Reality.* Cambridge, U.K.: Cambridge University Press, 1975.

Quine, W. V. O. "Truth by Convention." In *The Ways of Paradox and Other Essays.* New York: Random House, 1966. A classic argument against the possibility of truth by convention alone.

Quine, W. V. O. "Two Dogmas of Empiricism." In *From a Logical Point of View.* Cambridge, MA: Harvard University Press, 1953. Classical argument against the analytic-synthetic distinction and so against truth by convention.

Reichenbach, H. *Experience and Predication.* Chicago, 1938.

Scheffler, I. *Science and Subjectivity.* Indianapolis, IN: Bobbs-Merrill, 1967. Responds to arguments based on the history of science against objectivity in science, particularly Kuhn's, which are often used to bolster constructivist positions about the objects of scientific study.

Sidelle, A. *Necessity, Essence, and Individuation: A Defense of Conventionalism.* Ithaca, NY: Cornell University Press, 1989.

Alan Sidelle (1996)

CONTENT, MENTAL

Beliefs, desires, perceptions, and other mental states and events are said to possess content. We attribute such states and events with sentences such as

(1) Arabella believes that the cat is crying.

(1) contains a propositional attitude verb ("believes") and a sentence complement ("the cat is crying"). The verb specifies a type of mental state (belief), and the complement sentence indicates the content of the state. On most accounts this content is the proposition expressed by that sentence. Propositions have been variously conceived as abstract entities composed of modes of presen-

tation, sets of possible worlds, sets of synonymous sentences, and structured entities containing individuals and properties. All these accounts agree that propositions determine truth conditions. Some mental states and events (e.g., desiring to visit Paris) seem to have contents that are not propositions. However, for most of the current discussion, contents will be identified with propositions and contentful mental states with mental states that possess truth conditions.

Both natural-language sentences and mental states possess contents. The relation between content properties of the two items is controversial. Some philosophers think that natural-language expressions derive their contents from mental states, while others hold that, at least in some cases, the dependency goes the other way. In any case, it is plausible that there are mental states whose contents cannot be expressed or cannot be completely expressed by sentences of English (or other natural languages). For example, the full propositional content of a person watching the sun set is only partially captured by an attribution such as "*A* sees that the sun is setting." Also, some of the states posited by cognitive psychology and the mental states of animals plausibly have contents that fail to correspond to any contents expressible in English.

Content apparently endows mental states with a number of remarkable features. First, they or their constituents refer to extramental reality. When a person perceives that the sun is setting her perception refers to and thus puts her into contact with the sun. Second, they seem to be essentially normative. For example, a person ought to believe that the sun is setting only if the sun is setting, and if she believes that the sun is setting she ought not believe that the sun is not setting. Third, they apparently cause other mental states and behavior in virtue of their contents. For example, Arabella's belief that the cat is crying causes her to feed it. Fourth, a person can apparently know the contents of her own thought a priori and with an authority available only to her.

It is difficult to see how anything can exemplify all these features. The problem is especially difficult for philosophers who endorse naturalism, the view that all genuine properties are constituted by or realized by properties that are mentioned in true theories of the natural sciences. Content properties are prima facie so different from physical and biological properties as to raise the question of whether they are natural properties.

Hilary Putnam (1975) and Tyler Burge (1979) described thought experiments that have been taken to have important consequences for the nature of mental contents. Putnam imagined two thinkers, Oscar and twin-Oscar, who are identical with respect to their intrinsic neurophysiological properties but whose environments differ. Specifically. Oscar shares our environment, but twin-Oscar lives on twin-earth where the abundant substance that quenches thirst, fills the twin-earth oceans, and so forth is not H_2O but XYZ. H_2O's and XYZ's superficial properties are identical, and the two substances are indistinguishable without chemical analysis. Putnam claims that, while Oscar's sentence "Water is wet" and the thought he expresses with it are about H_2O, the same sentence in twin-Oscar's language and the thought he expresses with it are about XYZ. The two thoughts differ in their propositional contents, since one is true if and only if (iff) H_2O is wet and the other iff XYZ is wet. Putnam supports these conclusions with the intuition that, were Oscar and twin-Oscar to learn that the substances each refers to with the word *water* differ in their chemical natures, they would agree that their utterances of "Water is wet" possessed different truth conditions.

Putnam's thought experiment has been taken to establish the truth of content externalism, the thesis that the individuation conditions of mental content are partially external to the thinker. The point generalizes to other mental states whose contents are the same as the contents of sentences containing natural-kind terms such as *water*. Burge described further thought experiments that he thinks show that practically all thoughts expressible in natural language are externally individuated, and others have argued that all mental states that express extramental truth conditions are externally individuated (LePore and Loewer 1986).

Some philosophers (Fodor 1987, Loar 1987) react to content externalism by granting that mental states possess externally individuated contents but adding that they also possess narrow contents that are not externally individuated. Oscar's and twin-Oscar's beliefs possess the same narrow content. Philosophers sympathetic to narrow contents raise a number of considerations. One is the Cartesian intuition that thinkers in the same intrinsic state have the same mental lives. It seems essential to our conception of a mental life that it possess content, so there must be some kind of content that such thinkers share. The other consideration is that the causal powers of Oscar's and twin-Oscar's mental states seem to be, in an important way, the same. Jerry Fodor (1987) claims that if these causal powers involve the states' contents, then that content must be narrow.

Whether or not these considerations are persuasive, it has proved difficult to formulate a satisfactory notion of narrow content. If natural-language sentences express only externally individuated contents, then we do not attribute narrow content with sentences such as (1). While identity of intrinsic neurophysiological states is sufficient for identity of narrow content, it is not a plausible necessary condition. To adopt it as such would make it enormously unlikely that two people have ever shared the same narrow content state and impossible for a state to maintain its content in the course of reasoning. While some proposals for necessary and sufficient conditions for identity of narrow content have been forthcoming (Fodor 1987), there is little agreement concerning whether they are correct or, for that matter, whether a notion of narrow content is even needed.

Externalism seems to be in tension with our having a priori knowledge of the contents of our thoughts (Boghossian 1989). If the content of the thought (e.g., that water is wet) is individuated in part by external factors, then it seems that a person could know that she is thinking this thought only if she knows that those external factors obtain, and thus it is implausible that such knowledge is a priori. One response to this is to grant that we have a priori knowledge only of narrow contents. But a number of philosophers (Burge 1988, Warfield 1994) have responded that the tension is only apparent. Burge claims that judgments of the form "I am now thinking that water is wet" are self-verifying, since one cannot make the judgment without thinking the thought that the judgment is about. If this is correct, then externalism and a priori knowledge of content are not always incompatible. But such self-verifying thoughts seem to be a very special case of the thoughts whose contents we seem able to know a priori. It is likely that little progress concerning the epistemology of content can be made without an account of the nature of contentful mental states.

The dominant view in the philosophy of mind is that contentful mental states are functionally individuated internal states. Some philosophers (Dretske 1981, Fodor 1987) posit that these states are partially constituted by mental representations that are the bearers of propositional content. Mental representations are conceived of as picturelike (mental images), maps, or linguistic expressions. One view (Fodor 1979) is that mental representations are expressions in a language of thought, Mentalese. On this account thinking that the cat is crying involves tokening a Mentalese sentence with the content that the cat is crying. The thought inherits its content from the semantic properties of its constituent sentence, which in turn obtains its content from the semantic properties of its constituent expressions. Fodor identifies concepts with Mentalese expressions. So, for example, possessing the concept cat is being able to token a Mentalese expression that refers to cats. Some philosophers (Peacocke 1986) have argued that the contents of perceptual states are nonconceptual. If so, then the contents of these states are not borne by Mentalese expressions.

The nature of the bearers of mental content is best seen as an empirical issue. Fodor (1987) cites the fact that thought is productive and systematic as support for the language-of-thought hypothesis. Productivity is the capacity to produce complicated thoughts by combining simpler thoughts, and systematicity involves being able to think thoughts that are systematically related to each other, as are the thoughts that Bill loves Newt and that Newt loves Bill. Fodor argues that the language-of-thought hypothesis provides the best explanation of these phenomena, since languages are productive and systematic. Further, cognitive scientists have constructed theories of cognitive processes, language comprehension (Pinker 1994), perception (Marr 1982), and so forth that involve subpersonal contentful mental representations. For example, on one such theory understanding a natural-language sentence involves tokening a representation of its grammatical structure. These representations are not accessible to consciousness and have contents that are not usually available as the contents of a person's beliefs.

There have been various attempts to specify conditions in virtue of which mental states or mental representations possess their contents. Some of these are attempts to naturalize content properties. Following are brief descriptions of the main proposals.

According to interpretationist theories (ITs; Davidson 1984, Lewis 1974) our practices of interpreting one another partially constitute the contents of mental states. On Donald Davidson's approach interpretation is constrained by principles of rationality and charity. These principles say, roughly, that a person's mental states are generally rational and her beliefs are generally true. According to Davidson the evidential base for an assignment of contentful mental states to a person consists of her dispositions to hold true sentences under various conditions. She believes that *p* (desires that *p*, etc.) iff assignments of content to her sentences and to her mental states that systematize these holding true dispositions and that conform to the principles of charity and rationality assign to her the belief that *p* (desire that *p*, etc.).

On ITs, content properties are holistic, since whether or not a person exemplifies a particular contentful mental state depends on what other mental states she exemplifies and on their relations to each other and to environmental conditions. Davidson's IT is externalist, since a state's content is partially determined by relations to environmental conditions. But his account does not provide a naturalistic account of content, since it explains content in terms that presuppose content: holding true, rationality, truth. The primary difficulty with extant ITs is their vagueness. No one has formulated the principles of rationality and charity with sufficient clarity to permit an evaluation of proposed ITs.

According to conceptual role semantics (CRS), the content of a mental representation (or mental state) is determined by the inferential relations among representations and causal relations between representations and extramental events (Block 1986, Loar 1981, Sellars 1963). In this respect CRS is similar to IT. The difference is that, whereas ITs employ holistic principles of interpretations (rationality and charity), CRS attempts to spell out inferential patterns associated with particular concepts. CRS seems plausible for the logical connectives. For example, if a thinker is disposed to infer the representation *A#B* from *A* and *B* and vice versa, then # is the thinker's conjunction concept. Some philosophers (Peacocke 1992) have attempted to formulate conditions that are necessary and/or sufficient for possessing certain predicate concepts. It appears that any such account is committed to a substantial analytic-synthetic distinction, since it will hold that certain inferences involving a concept are necessary to having the concept (Fodor and LePore 1992). Willard Van Orman Quine's arguments (1960) that there are no analytic inferences poses an important problem for CRS.

Another approach is informational semantics (Dretske 1981, Stalnaker 1984). These theories are supposed to provide naturalizations of content; that is, they specify naturalistic properties that are claimed to be sufficient for possessing content. Informational theories claim that the content of a belief is constituted by the information the belief state carries under certain conditions. A state *S* carries the information that a property *P* is instantiated just in case the occurrence of *S* is caused by and nomically implies the instantiation of *P*. Informational theories have difficulty accounting for the possibility of error, since if a belief state has the content that *p* it carries the information that *p*. To solve this problem Fred Dretske proposed that the content of a belief is the information that it carries during what he calls "the learning period." A different suggestion (Stalnaker 1984) is to identify belief content with the information the belief state carries under epistemically optimal conditions. Barry Loewer (1987) has argued that these accounts are not successful as naturalizations, since they appeal to notions—learning, epistemic optimality—that themselves presuppose semantic notions.

Fodor has developed a sophisticated variant of informational theories that applies to the reference of Mentalese predicates. On this account, asymmetric dependency theory (ADT), a Mentalese predicate *C* refers to, for example, the property of being a cow if it is a law that cows cause *C*s, and any other causal relation between something other than cows and *C*s depends on this law but not vice versa. That is, if the other causal relations were to fail, it would still be a law that cows cause cows, but if the law were to fail, so would the other causal relation.

ADT is an atomistic account of content in that, contrary to CRS and ITs, it implies that the property of possessing a particular reference is metaphysically independent of inferential connections among thoughts and, indeed, independent of the existence of any other items with content. Whether or not one sees this as an advantage will depend on how one views the analytic-synthetic distinction. Obviously, ADT makes heavy use of metaphysical notions that are less than perspicacious, so one may wonder about its naturalistic credentials. It has also been argued (Boghossian 1991) that it is equivalent to an optimal-conditions account and is subject to the objections that show that account not to be a naturalization.

Teleological theories of content ground the contents of mental states in biological functions. The biological functions of a system in an organism are those of its features that increased the organism's fitness. Teleological accounts are quite elaborate, but the basic idea (Millikan 1984, Papineau 1992) is that there are desire-producing and belief-producing biological systems with certain biological functions. The desire-producing system has the function of producing states that tend to bring about certain effects. The effect associated with a particular desire is its content. The belief-producing systems have the function of producing states that tend to be tokened when certain states of affairs obtain. The state of affairs thus associated with a belief is its content.

Teleological accounts are appealing, since they are naturalistic, assign biological significance to contentful states, and seem to supply them with a kind of normativity. But various serious objections have been raised to teleological theories of content (Fodor 1992). The most serious is that it is doubtful that teleological considerations are sufficient to assign determinate contents to mental states. A desire state will typically tend to bring about a number of different advantageous effects. Natural selection does not select any one of these effects as the content of the desire. Similarly, natural selection will not single out one of the states of affairs a belief state will typically be associated with as its unique content.

Whether or not content properties can be naturalized is an open question. Some consider it a very important question, since they think that if content properties cannot be naturalized then they are unsuitable to appear in scientific theories or, even worse, that they do not exist or are uninstantiated (Stich 1983). The unsuitability of content properties for science would be a blow to the emerging cognitive sciences. But the nonexistence of content properties would be devastating to the way we think about ourselves and others, since these ways are permeated with attributions of contentful states. In fact, it has been argued (Boghossian 1990) that the thesis that there are no content properties is incoherent. Fortunately, no dire consequences strictly follow from the failure of naturalization. It may be that content properties are natural but not naturalizable (McGinn 1991). It is possible that, while content properties are natural, connections between them and properties that occur in the natural sciences are too unsystematic or too complicated for us to discern. But whether or not this is so is also an open question.

Following Gareth Evans's discussion (1982), there has been growing interest in the proposals that there is a distinction between *conceptual* and *nonconceptual* content and that the latter plays a significant role in perception (and perhaps imagination) and in subdoxastic (and so unavailable to consciousness) cognitive processing. Exactly what this distinction amounts to, whether there is nonconceptual content, and what its explanatory and epistemological roles may be are all controversial matters.

Beliefs and other propositional attitudes involve relations to thoughts (or propositions), and concepts are constituents of thoughts. It follows that for someone to have the belief, for example, that the Supreme Court is about to convene, he must have the concepts *supreme court*, *about to convene*, and so on. A widely held necessary condition for concept possession is that one has the concept *C* only if one can think an array of thoughts involving *C*. This is similar to the systematicity that Jerry Fodor (1987/1990) appealed to support his claim that mental representations involved in thought are languagelike. In fact, he and others (who do not necessarily share his views about meaning) think of concepts as words in the mental language deployed in thinking and in propositional attitudes. Evans observed that it is plausible that there are mental states whose contents are not conceptually articulated in this languagelike way. Visual perception seems to involve such states and processes. When one is looking at, for example, a sunset over a distant mountain range, one's perception seems much richer than what can be expressed in thought. There are particular colors and shapes represented in the perception that one is not able to represent in thought. Further, there do not seem to be components of visual representations that one can combine in the systematic ways in which concepts can be combined. In addition to perceptual states, the mental states of animals and the subdoxastic mental representations of humans posited by cognitive scientists are also said to have nonconceptual contents.

On some accounts of mental content, it is not clear that there can be nonconceptual content. For example, accounts like Donald Davidson's (1984), in which there is an intimate relationship between mental contents and the contents of public-language expressions and in which rationality constraints play a role in content determination, seem to preclude there being contents that cannot be expressed in public language. John McDowell (1994), who advocates such an account, has argued against the existence of nonconceptual content. Specifically, he thinks it is essential to mental states with content that they enter into rational and justifying relations with one another and claims that this requires that their contents be articulated conceptually. Famously, views like these resist attributing contentful mental states to animals and to subdoxastic mental processes, since animals and subdoxastic mental processes cannot harbor concepts.

Philosophers who think of mental content in terms of information (examples are Evans, Fodor, and Fred Dretske) can allow for states with nonconceptual content since non-conceptual representations can possess informational content. Dretske thinks that nonconceptual content is more basic than and prior to conceptual content, and that the latter is in some way derived from the former. Since information makes a division of possible worlds into those in which the information is correct and those in which it is not an informational state can stand in semantic relations of entailment and incompatibility with conceptual representations. On the other hand, it is not obvious how nonconceptualized information states can be involved in inference and reasoning.

There are a number of issues that advocates of nonconceptual content need to address. One is whether the distinction between conceptual and nonconceptual content is really a distinction between *kinds* of content or a distinction between different *ways* of representing content. Of course, this depends on what one takes content to be. As noted, states with nonconceptual content, like those with conceptual content divide possible worlds into those that are, and those that are not, in conformity with the content. However, conceptual content is often thought of as involving structure that reflects conceptual composition. The question is whether this structure is better understood as a species of content or belongs to the representation that represents the content. Those who think of contents solely in possible-world terms, such as Robert Stalnaker (1998), will see structure as belonging to the representation.

Another issue is that the alleged nonconceptual content of a perception seems to be informationally much more rich than the content of a thought. At the same time, it seems to be finer-grained in that there are distinctions that can be made in perception that we do not and perhaps cannot represent conceptually. It is not clear how these two features fit together. One idea is to think of nonconceptual content as analogous to pictorial or maplike content (Peacocke 2001). If this is correct, it raises the question of whether the pictorial structure belongs to the content or to the representation. Also, as mentioned above, there are issues concerning the epistemological role of nonconceptual content. Can a nonconceptual perceptual state justify a perceptual belief that it causes? Finally, it is not clear whether the contents involved in perception, the mental states of animals, and subdoxastic states and processes are all the same kind of nonconceptual contents. Indeed, theorists who appeal to subdoxastic states and processes often posit sentencelike representations as involved in mental computations. Their contents are nonconceptual only in that they are not available to thought and propositional attitudes.

See also Belief; Concept; Davidson, Donald; Internalism versus Externalism; Knowledge, A Priori; Language of Thought; Naturalism; Philosophy of Mind; Propositional Attitudes: Issues in the Philosophy of Mind and Psychology; Propositional Attitudes: Issues in Semantics; Putnam, Hilary; Quine, Willard Van Orman.

Bibliography

Block, N. "Advertisement for a Semantics for Psychology." In *Midwest Studies in Philosophy*. Vol. 10. Minneapolis: University of Minnesota Press, 1986.

Boghossian, P. "Content and Self-Knowledge." *Philosophical Topics* 17 (1989): 5–26.

Boghossian, P. "Naturalizing Content." In *Meaning and Mind*, edited by B. Loewer and G. Rey. Oxford, 1991.

Boghossian, P. "The Status of Content." *Philosophical Review* 99 (1990): 157–184.

Burge, T. "Individualism and Self-knowledge." *Journal of Philosophy* 85 (1988): 644–658.

Burge, T. "Individualism and the Mental." In *Midwest Studies in Philosophy*. Vol. 4. Minneapolis: University of Minnesota Press, 1979.

Davidson, D. *Inquiries into Truth and Interpretation*. Oxford: Clarendon Press, 1984.

Dretske, F. *Knowledge and the Flow of Information*. Cambridge, MA: MIT Press, 1981.

Evans, Gareth. *The Varieties of Reference*. Oxford, U.K.: Oxford University Press, 1982.

Fodor, J. *The Language of Thought*. Cambridge, MA, 1979.

Fodor, J. *Psychosemantics*. Cambridge, MA: MIT Press, 1987.

Fodor, J. *A Theory of Content and Other Essays*. Cambridge, MA: MIT Press, 1990.

Fodor, J., and E. LePore. *Holism: A Shopper's Guide*. Oxford: Blackwell, 1992.

Grice, P. "Meaning." *Philosophical Review* 66 (1957): 377–388.

LePore, E., and B. Loewer. "Solipsistic Semantics." *Midwest Studies in Philosophy* (1986).

Lewis, D. *Convention*. Cambridge, MA: Harvard University Press, 1969.

Lewis, D. "Radical Interpretation." *Synthese* 23 (1974): 331–344.

Loar, B. *Mind and Meaning*. Cambridge, U.K.: Cambridge University Press, 1981.

Loar, B. "Social Content and Psychological Content." In *Contents of Thought*, edited by R. Grimm and D. Merrill. Tucson: University of Arizona Press, 1986.

Loewer, B. "From Information to Intentionality." *Synthese* 70 (1987): 287–317.

Marr, D. *Vision*. San Francisco: Freeman, 1982.

McDowell, John. *Mind and World*. Cambridge, MA: Harvard University Press, 1994.

McGinn, C. *The Limits of Philosophy*. Oxford, 1991.

Millikan, R. *Language, Thought, and Other Biological Categories*. Cambridge, MA: MIT Press, 1984.

Papineau, D. *Naturalism*. Oxford, 1992.

Peacocke, C. "Does Perception Have a Non-conceptual Content." *Journal of Philosophy* 98 (2001): 239–264.

Peacocke, C. *A Study of Concepts*. Cambridge, MA: MIT Press, 1992.

Peacocke, C. *Thoughts: An Essay on Content*. New York: Blackwell, 1986.

Pinker, S. *The Language Instinct*. New York: Morrow, 1994.

Putnam, H. "The Meaning of Meaning." In his *Mind, Language, and Reality*. Cambridge, U.K.: Cambridge University Press, 1975.

Quine, W. V. O. *Word and Object*. Cambridge, MA: MIT Press, 1960.

Schiffer, S. *Meaning*. Oxford: Clarendon Press, 1972.

Sellars, W. *Science, Perception, and Reality*. New York: Humanities Press, 1963.

Stalnaker, R. *Inquiry*. Cambridge, MA: MIT Press, 1984.

Stalnaker, Robert. "What Might Non-conceptual Content Be?" In *Concepts: Philosophical Issues*, edited by Enrique Villanueva. Atascadero, CA: Ridgeview, 1998.

Stich, S. *From Folk Psychology to Cognitive Science*. Cambridge, MA: MIT Press, 1983.

Warfield, F. "Externalism and Self-Knowledge." *Analysis* (1994).

Barry Loewer (1996, 2005)

CONTEXTUALISM

The term "contextualism" has been used to denote many different philosophical theories. Within epistemology alone, there are two broad categories of theories that have been called "contextualist": subject contextualism and attributor contextualism.

SUBJECT CONTEXTUALISM

A few basic concepts are needed to explain subject contextualism. Let *S* be an epistemic subject, a being whose cognitive attitudes are proper targets of epistemic evaluation. Let *C* be a cognitive attitude that *S* has. *C* may be a belief, a judgment, a high degree of confidence, an affirmation or endorsement of some kind—any attitude that is a proper target of epistemic evaluation. *C* has a propositional content *p*. Finally, let *x* be the situation in which *S Cs* that *p*. We will hereafter specify the target of epistemic evaluation as "*S*'s *C*ing that *p* in *x*."

According to subject contextualism, whether *S Cs* that *p* in *x* constitutively depends on features of *x* that are metaphysically independent of *S*'s cognitive attitudes and of the truth-values of the propositional contents of *S*'s cognitive attitudes. As these features of *x* vary, so too does the epistemic status of (the degree of truth attached to) *S*'s *C*ing that *p*, even if *S*'s cognitive attitudes and the truth-values of their propositional contents all remain fixed. One or another version of such a view has been suggested in various passages in the writings of C. S. Peirce, Ludwig Wittgenstein, John Dewey, Karl Popper, W. V. Quine, and J. L. Austin. But only since the mid-1970s has subject contextualism been developed with any precision and generality.

The different versions of subject contextualism differ from each other in at least two ways. First, these different versions specify different features of *x* as relevant to constitutively determining whether *S Cs* that *p* in *x*. Second, these different versions of subject contextualism specify different ways in which the relevant feature of *x* can determine whether *S Cs* that *p*. By differences of the first kind, we can distinguish the various theories of subject contextualism that have been propounded into three broad groups.

According to one group of subject contextualist theories (Stine 1976, Goldman 1976, Dretske 1981), the epistemic status of *S C*ing that *p* in *x* constitutively depends on the objective probability of *p*'s being true in *x*. Other things being equal, the higher the objective probability of *p*'s being true in *x*, the higher the epistemic status of *S C*ing that *p* in *x*.

The most prominent argument in favor of this first variety of subject contextualism proceeds from consideration of case pairs such as the following (from Goldman 1976): Suppose that, in normal daylight, Henry, who has normal visual powers, has an unobstructed view of a barn right in front of him. Henry sees the barn, has a normal visual experience as of a barn, and believes that there is a barn in front of him. If there is nothing unusual about the case, then Henry knows that there is a barn in front of him. But now suppose that Henry's environment is full of barn facades that look exactly like barns from the angle and distance at which Henry is currently viewing the real barn in front of him. In this second case, just as in the first case, Henry has a true belief that there is a barn in front of him. And in both cases, this belief is based on Henry's seeing the barn, on his normal visual experience as of a barn. But in the second case, unlike the first, Henry does not know that there is a barn in front of him. What difference in the two cases could account for this difference in whether or not Henry knows? Subject contextualists of the first variety say that the difference in Henry's extrapsychological environment—in particular, the frequency of barn facades in his environment—is responsible for the difference in whether he knows.

Opponents of this first variety of subject contextualism typically respond to the preceding argument by offering an alternative explanation of why Henry knows, in the first case but not in the second case, that there is a barn in front of him. In each case, they contend, Henry believes that there is a barn in front of him partly because he believes that, in his environment, things that look like barns from his vantage point typically are barns. So his belief that there is a barn in front of him is partly based on the latter epistemic belief. And the epistemic belief is true in the first case and false in the second case. It is the difference in the truth-value of the epistemic belief that explains why Henry knows in the first case but does not know in the second case—or so say the opponents of this first variety of subject contextualism.

According to a second group of subject-contextualist theories (Annis 1978, Williams 1992, Henderson 1994, Klein 1999), whether *S Cs* that *p* in *x* constitutively depends on the inquiry that takes place in *x*. The inquiry fixes which considerations confer positive epistemic status upon *S*'s *C*ing that *p*. The main argument for this second variety of subject contextualism, propounded in different ways by Annis, Williams, and Klein, has to do with the regress of reasons. According to this argument, neither foundationalism nor coherentism offers a correct account of structure of epistemic reasons, or justifications. Foundationalism cannot offer a correct account, because it is committed to the unsustainable claim that some cognitive attitudes—the foundational beliefs—are intrinsically justified. And coherentism cannot offer a correct account, because it is committed to claiming either that circular reasoning provides justification or that each belief in a coherent set is a foundational belief. But if there are no foundational beliefs and if circular reasoning does not provide justification, then how can positive epistemic status accrue to *S*'s *C*ing that *p*? According to this second variety of subject contextualism, this question is best answered as follows: *S*, in a particular context of inquiry, makes certain presuppositions. These presuppositions can provide epistemic reasons, or justifications, for *S*'s other cognitive attitudes in that same inquiry. But when *S* moves into a different context of inquiry, some presuppositions in the earlier inquiry may be put into question in the new inquiry, and other propositions that were in question in the earlier inquiry may simply be presupposed in the new inquiry.

To the preceding argument, Henderson adds that because our cognitive competence is limited, in ways that can be empirically ascertained, we are incapable of forming beliefs about our environment without taking a great deal for granted. What we need to take for granted to form needed beliefs will vary from task to task. Since we are incapable of forming the beliefs that we need to form without taking a great deal for granted, we cannot be epistemically obligated to do otherwise. Our epistemic obligations cannot exceed our cognitive potential. Since our belief-forming processes require us to take more or less for granted, depending on the cognitive task at hand, our epistemic obligations must allow us to take more or less for granted, depending on the task.

Opponents of this second variety of subject contextualism typically respond to the preceding arguments by defending foundationalism or coherentism. While foundationalist and coherentist theories of justification might hold us to normative standards that we do not commonly meet, this is not a problem for those theories if, in the epistemological realm, "ought" does not imply "can."

According to a third group of subject-contextualist theories (Fantl and McGrath 2002, Hawthorne 2003, Stanley 2004), whether *S Cs* that *p* in *x* constitutively depends on how the truth-value of *p* affects *S*'s interests, or perceived interests, in *x*. Other things being equal, the higher the cost, or perceived cost, of *S*'s being wrong that *p*, the less likely that *S Cs* that *p*. The most prominent argument in favor of this third variety of subject contextualism considers pairs of cases such as the following (adapted from Fantl and McGrath 2002): Suppose that you are at the train station waiting for the train to New York. You would like to get on the express train so that you can be in New York by dinnertime, but it does not matter all that much to you whether you get there by dinnertime or not. You ask someone else on train platform, "Is the next train an express train, or a local?" and your honest and knowledgeable interlocutor sincerely tells you that it is an express. You believe her, and you have no reason to distrust her. In this situation, it seems that you know, and are justified and warranted in believing, that the next train is an express. But now suppose that the situation is exactly the same except that your life depends on your being in New York by dinnertime. In this case, the testimony of your honest and knowledgeable interlocutor does not justify or warrant—let alone give you knowledge—that the next train is an express. When so much depends on your being right, knowledge, justification, warrant, etc., all require more than they otherwise would require.

Opponents of this third variety of subject contextualism typically respond to the preceding argument by claiming that what depends on a subject's actual or perceived interests is not the epistemic status of the subject's *C*ing that *p*, but rather the rationality of the subject's acting as if *p* were true. For these opponents, whether *S Cs* that *p* is fixed independently of *S*'s actual or perceived interests.

These are the main varieties of subject contextualism, and the arguments concerning them. Some subject contextualists are also attributor contextualists, and almost all attributor contextualists are also subject contextualists.

ATTRIBUTOR CONTEXTUALISM

A few more basic concepts are needed to explain what attributor contextualism is. Let *A* be an epistemic attributor, someone who epistemically evaluates *S*'s *C*ing that *p* in *x*. *A*'s evaluation of *S*'s *C*ing that *p* in *x* will also be a cognitive attitude of some sort, either expressed (as in the case of an assertion) or not (as in the case of silent thought). *A*'s evaluation may concern whether *S* knows that *p* in *x*, or it may concern whether *S* is justified, reasonable, rational, or warranted in *C*ing that *p* in *x*, or it may concern whether *S* has adequate grounds, evidence, or reasons to *C* that *p* in *x*. More generally, an epistemic evaluation or appraisal of *S*'s *C*ing that *p* in *x* is a determination of whether *S Cs* that *p* in *x*. Let *y* be the situation that *A* is in when *A* evaluates whether *S Cs* that *p* in *x*. We will hereafter specify the act of epistemic evaluation as "*A*'s evaluation, in *y*, of *S*'s Cing that *p* in *x*."

According to attributor contextualism, the semantic value (the truth) of *A*'s evaluation (of *S*'s Cing that *p* in *x*) constitutively depends on features of *y*. As these features of *y* vary, so too does the semantic value of *A*'s evaluation, even with everything else held fixed. The earliest prominent statements of such a view appear in Lewis (1979) and Dretske (1981). The view gained widespread notice following the publication of Cohen (1988), DeRose (1995), and Lewis (1996).

Different versions of attributor contextualism specify different features of *y* as relevant to constitutively determining the semantic value of *A*'s evaluation of *S*'s Cing that *p* in *x*. And even if two attributor contextualists agree about which features of *y* are relevant to constitutively determining the semantic value of *A*'s evaluation, they might still disagree about precisely *how* those features of *y* are relevant. By differences of the first kind, we can distinguish the various attributor-contextualist theories on offer into several groups. Although there is thus some diversity among attributor-contextualist theories, a single line of argument has generally been used to support attributor contextualism.

The argument in question proceeds from consideration of cases similar to those commonly adduced to support the third variety of subject contextualism. Suppose that Jones and Smith are at the train station trying to catch a train to New York. They want to know whether the next train is an express. They ask a bystander if he knows whether the next train is an express. The bystander looks at a schedule and replies, "Yes, I know. It is an express." It turns out that Jones and Smith have to be in New York as soon as possible, and cannot afford the mistake of getting on a local train. Jones says, "That schedule could easily have been outdated. That guy does not really know that the next train is an express." So the bystander claims to know that the next train is an express, but Jones claims that the bystander does not know that the next train is an express. Who is right?

If the bystander is right that he knows, then is Jones making a false assertion when he says that the bystander does not know. Suppose that the bystander's warrant for thinking that the next train is an express is precisely what Jones takes it to be. If such warrant is strong enough to give the bystander knowledge, then, it seems, it is also strong enough to give Jones and Smith knowledge. But if Jones and Smith have warrant strong enough to give them knowledge that the next train is an express, they have no reason to check further whether the next train is an express. Since they clearly do have a reason to check further whether or not the next train is an express, their warrant cannot be strong enough to give them knowledge of whether or not it is. But if they do not have enough warrant for knowledge, then it seems that the bystander does not know, since he does not have any more warrant than they do.

Suppose that the bystander is wrong, that he does not know that the next train is an express. In this case, it seems that most of the knowledge attributions that we make in ordinary life are wrong as well, since our warrant for most of what we claim to know is no greater than is the bystander's warrant for the claim that next train is an express. So if the bystander does not know that the next train is an express, then most of us know very little of what we ordinarily claim to know.

How can we avoid simply granting that Jones and Smith are right to deny that the bystander knows, or that the bystander is right to claim to know? The attributor contextualist avoids granting this by claiming that the truth-values of knowledge attributions are relative to the context in which the attribution is made. Relative to the context in which the bystander claims to know, her claim is true. But relative to the context in which Jones claims that the bystander does not know, his claim is true. So both claims are true, and they do not contradict each other. These assertions only appear to contradict each other because we fail to notice that "knows" requires a higher standard (or signifies a more stringent epistemic relation) in one context of attribution than in the other context of attribution than in the other context of attribution. Analogous arguments may support the conclusion that ascriptions of other epistemic properties, not just ascriptions of knowledge, are semantically sensitive to context.

Opponents of attributor contextualism will typically reply to an argument like the preceding in one or both of the following two ways. First, like Bach (2005), they may claim that, although the bystander knows that the next train is an express, Jones and Smith do not know, and that is because knowledge requires sufficient confidence. Although the bystander is sufficiently confident that the next train is an express, Jones and Smith are not, and so they do not satisfy one of the necessary conditions of knowledge. If, without any further investigation, Jones and Smith claimed to be sufficiently confident of the bystander's claim, then, given how much is at stake in their being right, their degree of confidence would be irrational.

This suggests a second line of response to the attributor-contextualist argument above: Even if Jones and Smith, prior to doing any further investigation, are sufficiently confident that the next train is an express, their confidence is unreasonable, given how much is at stake. Knowing that *p* requires not simply that one be sufficiently confident that *p*, but moreover that one's level of confidence be reasonable. Since, without doing any further investigation, Jones and Smith cannot be reasonably confident that the next train is an express, they also cannot know that the next train is an express, even if they are sufficiently confident of it (by the bystander's standards), even if they share all of the bystander's evidence for it, and even if the bystander himself knows. On this second line of response, we resolve the problem set out by the attributor contextualist's argument by appealing to subject contextualism of the third variety distinguished above.

To bolster the argument for attributor contextualism in the face of these objections, attributor contextualists must now attempt to run their thought experiments while controlling for variation in *S*'s level of confidence and also in *S*'s level of reasonable confidence. To do this, they must focus on a particular epistemic subject *S* in a particular context *x*, and then find variation in the truth conditions for asserting that *S Cs* that *p* in *x*. To make the case for attributor contextualism, they must make sure that the variation they discover is variation in the truth conditions of an ascription of knowledge, and not simply in the conditions under which we are inclined to make, or are warranted in making, the ascription. DeRose (2004) undertook to do all this.

Three other sorts of argument that have commonly been used to support attributor contextualism. The first is an argument to the effect that attributor contextualism provides the best response to a skeptical argument like the following:

> Premise 1: I cannot possibly know that I am not a brain in a vat being electrochemically stimulated to have realistic experiences.
>
> Premise 2: If I knew that I have hands, then I could deduce, and thereby come to know, that I am not a brain in a vat being electrochemically stimulated to have realistic experiences.
>
> Conclusion: I do not know that I have hands.

While some philosophers would simply to deny one of the premises, attributor contextualists typically take such denial to be implausible. So how can attributor contextualists avoid accepting the skeptical conclusion of such an argument? They can do so by claiming that the skeptical conclusion is true *only relative* to contexts of attribution that we enter into by thinking (in some way or other) about premise 1. Relative to other, more commonplace, contexts of attribution, premise 1 is false, as is the skeptical conclusion of the argument. Attributor contextualists typically take this response to the skeptical argument above to be more plausible than any alternative response, and they take this to count as a point in favor of attributor contextualism concerning knowledge attributions. Analogous arguments have been adduced in favor of attributor contextualism concerning attributions of other epistemic properties.

A second style of argument in favor of attributor contextualism proceeds from premises concerning the epistemic properties in question. For instance, Dretske (1981) and Lewis (1996) both claim that knowledge that *p* involves having infallible grounds for one's belief that *p*. For them, one's grounds are infallible just in case all alternatives to *p* are ruled out. But "all," like other quantifiers, involves a contextually restricted domain of quantification. Ruling out "all" alternatives means ruling out all those that fall within the contextually restricted domain of quantification. So on this account, some form of attributor contextualism is true of knowledge attributions. Analogous arguments show that attributor contextualism is true of attributions of other epistemic properties as well.

Finally, a third style of argument in favor of attributor contextualism proceeds from premises concerning the conversational function of epistemic-property attributions and epistemic appraisal. Such arguments (e.g., Neta 2002, Schaffer 2004) claim that for attributions of epistemic properties to serve the function that they are supposed to serve, they must be semantically sensitive to contexts. For instance, if a knowledge attribution of the form "*S* knows why *p*" functions to signal to one's interlocutors that they can trust *S* on the topic of why it is that *p*, then whether it is appropriate to make such an attribution depends on whether one should signal to one's interlocutors that they can trust *S*, and this in turn depends on features of the conversational context. If this appropriateness depends on conversational context because the truth conditions depend on conversational context, then attributor contextualism is true of knowledge-why attributions. Analogous arguments may lead to attributor contextualism for attributions of other epistemic properties as well.

These are some of the main lines of argument that have been adduced in favor of one or another variety of attributor contextualism. Here is a review of those varieties:

According to one group of attributor-contextualist theories (Cohen 1986, 1988, 1999), what varies with the context of attribution is the threshold of evidential support for *p* that must be exceeded for *S* to *C* that *p* (for *S* to know, to be justified, to be warranted, etc.). In a particular context *x*, *S*'s evidence confers a certain level of epistemic support on the proposition that *p*. Does that level of support suffice to warrant asserting that *S Cs* that *p*? This first kind of attributor contextualism takes the answer to this question to depend on features of the context of attribution *y*.

According to a second group of attributor-contextualist theories (Dretske 1981, Lewis 1996, Schaffer 2004), what varies with the context of attribution is the range of relevant alternatives to *p* that *S*'s evidence must rule out for *S* to *C* that *p*. To say that *S*'s evidence must rule out these alternatives to *p* is not to say anything about what *S* does or does not know, or about what *S* does or does not believe. Rather, it is to say that *S* has adequate evidence only if these alternatives to *p* do not obtain. Epistemologists standardly assume that *S*'s evidence cannot rule out all alternatives to *p*—in particular, it cannot rule out the alternative that *p* is false but *S* is being deceived by a deceiving spirit into believing that *p*. But *S*'s evidence does not need to rule out all alternatives to *p* for *S* to *C* that *p*. Rather, for *S* to *C* that *p*, *S*'s evidence must rule out only the relevant alternatives to *p*. Which alternatives are relevant? That depends upon the context of attribution *y*.

According to a third group of attributor-contextualist theories (DeRose 1992, 1995; Heller 1995, 1999), what varies with the context of attribution is the range of possible situations throughout which, in order for *S* to count as knowing that *p*, *p* must be true if and only if *S Cs* that *p*. In a particular context *x* in which *S Cs* that *p*, *S* has the disposition to *C* that *p* just in case certain conditions obtain. *S Cs* that *p* if and only if there is an adequate range of conditions under which *S* is disposed to *C* that *p*. But what range of conditions is "adequate"? That is relative to a context of attribution *y*.

According to a third group of attributor-contextualist theories (DeRose 1992, 1995; Heller 1995, 1999), what varies with the context of attribution is the range of possible situations in which, for *S* to count as knowing that *p*, it is required that *p* is true if and only if *S Cs* that *p*. In a particular *x*, *S Cs* that *p*just in case certain conditions obtain (such as, for instance, *S*'s being an authority). What is the range of conditions throughout which this biconditional must hold for *S* to know that *p*? That is determined by the context of attribution *y*.

A view that combines features of the last two varieties of attributor contextualism is defended by Rieber (1998). According to Rieber, *S* knows that *p* if and only if the fact that *p* explains *S*'s belief that *p*. An explanation answers the question "Why?" "Why" questions are contrastive: To ask "Why is it that *p*?" is always, at least implicitly, to ask "Why is it that *p* rather than that *q*?" For Rieber, ascriptions of knowledge inherit the contrasts of explanation statements. Thus, for Rieber, for *S* to know that *p* is for there to be some contrast proposition *q* such that *S* knows that *p* rather than that *q*. And for the latter to hold true, on Rieber's account, the fact that *p*, rather than the fact that *q*, must explain *S*'s belief that *p*. On Rieber's view, then, *S* knows that *p* if and only if the fact that *p* (rather than the contrast proposition *q*) explains the fact that *S* believes that *p*. On Rieber's view, the context of attribution *y* determines the contrast proposition.

Finally, according to the most recently espoused version of attributor contextualism (Neta 2002, 2003a, 2004), what varies with the context of attribution is the range of propositions, or of psychological states, that count as part of *S*'s evidence set. Relative to some contexts of attribution, *S*'s evidence set may include nothing more than *S*'s own current states of consciousness. But relative to more ordinary contexts of attribution, *S*'s evidence set may include various propositions about, say, widely known results of experiments that took place completely independently of *S*. More generally, according to attributor contextualism concerning evidence, whether *S Cs* that *p* depends on *S*'s evidence for *p* for other epistemic properties *C* as well (e.g., knowing, being justified, having warrant).

THE RECENT CONTROVERSY OVER ATTRIBUTOR CONTEXTUALISM

Since the late 1990s, attributor contextualism has been subject to two sorts of objections. According to the first sort of objection, the problem with attributor contextualism is that it implausibly attributes to native speakers a significant level of semantic self-ignorance. We can see this either by thinking about attributor-contextualist responses to skeptical arguments, as Schiffer (1996) and Rysiew (2001) do, or by thinking about the consequences of attributor contextualism for our practices concerning disquotation of knowledge attributions, as Hawthorne (2003) and LePore and Cappellen (2004) do.

According to attributor-contextualist responses to skeptical arguments, such arguments gain their plausibility because, when going through these arguments, we confuse the propositions that our epistemic-property attributions express with the propositions that these attributions would express in certain other contexts. But, according to the proponents of this objection, it is implausible to claim that native speakers do indeed suffer from this confusion. Again, according to attributor contextualists, attributor *A* can, in some contexts, truthfully assert something of the following form: "*S* does not know that *p*, even though *S* speaks truthfully when *S* says, 'I know that *p*,' " or, more generally, "*S* is not justified or warranted in Cing that *p*, even though *S* speaks truthfully when *S* says, 'I am justified or warranted in Cing that *p*.' " But such assertions appear self-contradictory to native speakers. Thus, the attributor contextualist is committed to claiming that native speakers are wrong to think that such assertions are self-contradictory. Once again, the attributor contextualist is committed to attributing a significant level of semantic self-ignorance to native speakers.

In response to this first line of objection, Neta (2003b) raises the question of whether the level of self-ignorance that attributor contextualism posits is any greater than the level of self-ignorance about their own language that native speakers routinely display at other levels of linguistic analysis (e.g., pragmatics, syntax, phonology). If native speakers generally do not realize that there is a difference between the "t" sound in "butter" and the "t" sound in "putter," then why should they realize that there is a difference in the meaning of terms of epistemic appraisal, "*C*," as they occur in different contexts? Of course, naive speakers can be brought to notice the difference between the "t" sound in "butter" and the "t" sound in "putter." Can the attributor contextualist bring naive speakers (even if not theoretically invested philosophers) to discern a difference in the meaning of terms of epistemic appraisal as they occur in different contexts? This remains an open empirical question.

Stanley (2000, 2004), pursuing the second line of objection, has argued that attributor contextualism is empirically implausible because there is no well-established precedent for the particular kind of semantic context-sensitivity that attributor contextualists posit in our epistemic-property attributions. These empirical arguments have been rebutted most recently by Ludlow (2005) and DeRose (2005), but this issue, like many other empirical issues in semantics, remains unsettled. Indeed, Unger (1984, 1986) has argued that there is no empirically ascertainable fact of the matter as to whether attributor contextualism is true.

See also Austin, John Langshaw; Coherentism; Dewey, John; Dretske, Fred; Epistemology; Lewis, David; Peirce, Charles Sanders; Popper, Karl Raimund; Quine, Willard Van Orman; Skepticism, History of; Wittgenstein, Ludwig Josef Johann.

Bibliography

Annis, David. "A Contextualist Theory of Epistemic Justification." *American Philosophical Quarterly* 15 (1978): 213–219.

Austin, J. L. "Other Minds." *Proceedings of the Aristotelian Society*, supp. vol. 20 (1946): 149–187.

Bach, Kent. "The Emperor's New 'Knows.' " In *Contextualism in Philosophy*, edited by Gerhard Preyer and Georg Peter. Oxford, U.K.: Oxford University Press, 2005.

Cappelen, Herman, and Ernest LePore. *Insensitive Semantics: A Defense of Semantic Minimalism and Speech Act Pluralism.* Oxford, U.K.: Blackwell, 2004.

Cohen, Stewart. "Contextualism, Skepticism, and the Structure of Reasons." In *Epistemology, 1999*, edited by James E. Tomberlin. Atascadero, CA: Ridgeview, 1999.

Cohen, Stewart. "Knowledge and Context." *Journal of Philosophy* 83 (1986): 574–583.

Cohen, Stewart. "Knowledge, Context, and Social Standards." *Synthese* 73 (1987): 3–26.

Cohen, Stewart. "How to Be a Fallibilist." In *Epistemology, 1988*, edited by James E. Tomberlin. Atascadero, CA: Ridgeview, 1988.

DeRose, Keith. "Contextualism and Knowledge Attributions." *Philosophy and Phenomenological Research* 52 (1992): 913–929.

DeRose, Keith. "The Ordinary Language Basis for Contextualism and the New Invariantism." *Philosophical Quarterly* 55 (2005): 172–198.

DeRose, Keith. "The Problem with Subject Sensitive Invariantism." *Philosophy and Phenomenological Research* 68 (2004): 346–350.

DeRose, Keith. "Solving the Skeptical Problem." *Philosophical Review* 104 (1995): 1–51.

Dretske, Fred. "The Pragmatic Dimension of Knowledge." *Philosophical Studies* 40 (1981): 363–378.

Fantl, Jeremy, and Matthew McGrath. "Evidence, Pragmatics, and Justification." *Philosophical Review* 111 (2002): 67–94.

Gendler, Tamar, and John Hawthorne, eds. *Oxford Studies in Epistemology*. Vol. 1. Oxford, U.K.: Oxford University Press, 2005.

Goldman, Alvin. "Discrimination and Perceptual Knowledge." *Journal of Philosophy* 73 (1976): 771–791.

Hawthorne, John. *Knowledge and Lotteries*. Oxford, U.K.: Oxford University Press, 2003.

Heller, Mark. "Contextualism and Anti-luck Epistemology." In *Epistemology, 1999*, edited by James E. Tomberlin. Atascadero, CA: Ridgeview, 1999.

Heller, Mark. "The Simple Solution to the Problem of Generality." *Noûs* 29 (1995): 501–515.

Henderson, David. "Epistemic Competence and Contextualist Epistemology: Why Contextualism Is Not Just the Poor

Man's Coherentism." *Journal of Philosophy* 91 (1994): 627–649.

Klein, Peter. "Human Knowledge and the Infinite Regress of Reasons." In *Epistemology, 1999*, edited by James E. Tomberlin. Atascadero, CA: Ridgeview, 1999.

Lewis, David. "Elusive Knowledge." *Australasian Journal of Philosophy* 74 (1996): 549–567.

Lewis, David. "Scorekeeping in a Language Game." *Journal of Philosophical Logic* 8 (1979): 339–359.

Ludlow, Peter. "Contextualism and the New Linguistic Turn in Epistemology." In *Contextualism in Philosophy*, edited by Gerhard Preyer and Georg Peter. Oxford, U.K.: Oxford University Press, 2005.

Neta, Ram. "Contextualism and the Problem of the External World." *Philosophy and Phenomenological Research* 66 (2003a): 1–31.

Neta, Ram. "Perceptual Evidence and the New Dogmatism." *Philosophical Studies* 119 (2004): 199–214.

Neta, Ram. "Skepticism, Contextualism, and Semantic Self-Knowledge." *Philosophy and Phenomenological Research* 67 (2003b): 396–411.

Neta, Ram. "*S* Knows That *p*." *Noûs* 36 (2002): 663–681.

Preyer, Gerhard, and Georg Peter, eds. *Contextualism in Philosophy*. Oxford, U.K.: Oxford University Press, 2005.

Rieber, Steven. "Skepticism and Contrastive Explanation." *Noûs* 32 (1998): 189–204.

Rysiew, Patrick. "Contextualist Solutions to Scepticism." *Noûs* 35 (2001): 477–514.

Schaffer, Jonathan. "Contrastive Knowledge." In *Oxford Studies in Epistemology*. Vol. 1, edited by Tamar Gendler and John Hawthorne. Oxford, U.K.: Oxford University Press, 2005.

Schaffer, Jonathan. "From Contextualism to Contrastivism." *Philosophical Studies* 119 (2004): 73–103.

Schiffer, Stephen. "Contextualist Solutions to Scepticism." *Proceedings of the Aristotelian Society* 96 (1996): 317–333.

Stanley, Jason. "Context and Logical Form." *Linguistics and Philosophy* 23 (2000): 391–434.

Stanley, Jason. "On the Linguistic Basis for Contextualism." *Philosophical Studies* 119 (2004): 119–146.

Stine, Gail C. "Skepticism, Relevant Alternatives, and Deductive Closure." *Philosophical Studies* 29 (1976): 249–261.

Tomberlin, James E., ed. *Epistemology, 1988*. Atascadero, CA: Ridgeview, 1988.

Tomberlin, James E., ed. *Epistemology, 1999*. Atascadero, CA: Ridgeview, 1999.

Unger, Peter. "The Cone Model of Knowledge." *Philosophical Topics* 14 (1986): 125–178.

Unger, Peter. *Philosophical Relativity*. Minneapolis: University of Minnesota Press, 1984.

Williams, Michael. *Unnatural Doubts: Epistemological Realism and the Basis of Scepticism*. Oxford, U.K.: Basil Blackwell, 1992.

Ram Neta (2005)

CONTINENTAL PHILOSOPHY

Continental philosophy is a term that arose after the Second World War in English-speaking countries as a name for philosophical approaches that take as their point of departure the work of certain nineteenth and twentieth centuries figures from Continental Europe, especially Germany and France, whose themes and methods were different from those of the analytical philosophy common at most leading British and American philosophy departments at that time. As a general term it includes movements such as phenomenology, existentialism, critical theory, hermeneutics, psychoanalytically oriented philosophy, structuralism, deconstruction, and postmodernism as well as feminist theory, race theories, and other critical social theories to the extent that they draw on one or more of these other movements. Its themes can range across all of the traditional philosophical areas—from epistemology, metaphysics, and ethics to aesthetics, philosophy of language, philosophy of religion, philosophy of science, and studies in the history of philosophy, to name just a few.

General comparisons between the intellectual life in Britain and Continental Europe go back at least to the nineteenth century. However, the current opposition between analytical and continental philosophy can be traced back above all to polemical attempts on the part of leading English analytical philosophers, in particular those at Oxford, to justify their own approach to philosophy and distinguish it from the predominant philosophical movements in France and Germany during the 1950s such as phenomenology and existentialism. Gilbert Ryle (1971) and R. M. Hare (1960), for instance, were outspoken in contrasting the way they and their colleagues approached philosophy from philosophy as practiced in the rest of Europe, with a decidedly negative assessment of continental philosophy's Germanic roots. The primary targets at the time were Husserl, Heidegger, Sartre, and Merleau-Ponty, although it is not clear that their attackers had read many of their works closely.

The term became fairly common, however, only during the late 1960s and early 1970s when it was embraced, first in the United States and then later in Great Britain and other English-speaking countries, as a positive term by philosophers who used it as a name for their own work Continental philosophy was still defined in opposition to analytical philosophy, but without necessarily carrying the negative connotations it had for British and American analytical philosophers. Though discussions about the differences between analytic versus continental philosophy and the relative merits of each are still common, the term has increasingly become more of a commonly accepted, though still somewhat vague descriptive term used by both proponents and opponents of the different ways of doing philosophy that have been grouped together under the general heading of "continental" (often with a capital "C") in contrast to "analytical" philosophy.

From the outset, even though it suggests a geographical reference, the term "continental philosophy" has referred only to those figures from continental Europe whose approaches were not consistent with those of the project of earlier analytical philosophy. It specifically excluded thinkers such as Frege, Carnap, and Wittgenstein, whose work was viewed in a positive light by the English opponents of continental philosophy, because they were seen rather as precursors to or representatives of analytical philosophy. Moreover, even though the original point of difference goes back primarily to differences in philosophical work being conducted in Britain as opposed to continental European countries after the Second World War, these differences were projected backwards into the history of philosophy. Most observers agree that there were no clearly identifiable differences along geographic lines in philosophy as practiced in England and on the continent before the twentieth century. However, because analytic philosophy as practiced after World War II excluded idealistic philosophy and some other nineteenth-century movements that were originally from Germany or France from its lineage, the term continental philosophy soon came to include not only postwar and earlier twentieth-century philosophical movements from the continent, but also philosophers such as Kant, Hegel, Marx, Kierkegaard, Nietzsche, and others from eighteenth- and nineteenth-century European philosophy whose approaches were not consistent with the historical development of analytical philosophy.

Toward the end of the twentieth century it became common to speak of a "continental tradition" instead of simply referring to "continental philosophy." One reason for this is that many of the adherents and leading practitioners of these directions in philosophy come from countries all around the world instead of just Europe. Another reason is that, from the outset, the fate of this term has been tied to that of its opposite, namely "analytical philosophy," and critical developments within the latter movement led many of its adherents to refer to a "postanalytical" phase that is still part of an analytical tradition of philosophy. As philosophers from both traditions became increasingly familiar with each others' work and many of the original claims in both traditions have had to be modified, it became increasingly difficult to provide a simple characterization of what continental philosophy is and hence also of how it is and is not different from analytical philosophy. Increasingly, some scholars, especially those outside of English-speaking countries, have begun to draw on ideas and resources from both traditions to address philosophical problems across the differences that had previously divided them, so that it makes good sense to think of both continental and analytical philosophy as competing traditions of philosophy and less as two clearly delineated camps situated in different geographic locations.

See also Critical Theory; Deconstruction; Existentialism; Feminist Philosophy; Marxist Philosophy; Phenomenology; Postcolonialism.

Bibliography

Critchley, Simon. "Introduction: What Is Continental Philosophy?" In *A Companion to Continental Philosophy*, edited by Simon Critchley and William R. Schroeder, 1–17. Oxford, U.K.: Blackwell, 1998.

Glendinning, Simon. "Introduction: What is Continental Philosophy?" In *The Edinburgh Encyclopedia of Continental Philosophy*, edited by Simon Glendinning, 3–20. Edinburgh, U.K.: Edinburgh University Press, 1999.

Hare, R.M. "A School for Philosophers." *Ratio* 2 (1960): 107–120.

Rorty, Richard. *Philosophy and the Mirror of Nature*. Princeton, NJ: Princeton University Press, 1979.

Ryle, Gilbert. "Phenomenology versus *The Concept of Mind*." In *Collected Papers*. London: Hutchinson, 1971.

Sallis, John, Hugh Silverman, and Thomas M. Seebohm, eds. *Continental Philosophy in America*. Pittsburgh: Duquesne University Press, 1983.

West, David. *An Introduction to Continental Philosophy*. Cambridge, U.K.: Polity, 1966.

Thomas Nenon (2005)

CONTINUITY

In the decades bracketing the turn of the twentieth century, the real number system was dubbed the *arithmetic continuum* because it was held that this number system is completely adequate for the analytic representation of all types of continuous phenomena. In accordance with this view, the *geometric linear continuum* is assumed to be isomorphic with the arithmetic continuum, the axioms of geometry being so selected to ensure this would be the case. In honor of Georg Cantor (1845–1918) and Richard

Dedekind (1831–1916), who first proposed this mathematico-philosophical thesis, the presumed correspondence between the two structures is sometimes called the *Cantor-Dedekind axiom*.

Since their appearance, the late nineteenth-century constructions of the real numbers have undergone set-theoretical and logical refinement, and the systems of rational and integer numbers on which they are based have themselves been given a set-theoretic foundation. During this period the Cantor-Dedekind philosophy of the continuum also emerged as a pillar of standard mathematical philosophy that underlies the standard formulation of analysis, the standard analytic and synthetic theories of the geometrical linear continuum, and the standard axiomatic theories of continuous magnitude more generally.

Since its inception, however, there has never been a time at which the Cantor-Dedekind philosophy has either met with universal acceptance or has been without competitors. The period that has transpired since its emergence as the standard philosophy has been especially fruitful in this regard, having witnessed the rise of a variety of constructivist and predicativist theories of real numbers and corresponding theories of analysis as well as the emergence of a number of alternative theories that make use of infinitesimals. Whereas the constructivist and predicativist theories have their roots in the early twentieth-century debates on the foundations of mathematics and were born from critiques of the Cantor-Dedekind theory, the infinitesimalist theories were intended to either provide intuitively satisfying (and, in some cases, historically rooted) alternatives to the Cantor-Dedekind conception that have the power to meet the needs of analysis or differential geometry, or to situate the Cantor-Dedekind system of real numbers in a grander conception of an arithmetic continuum.

Speculation regarding the nature and structure of continua and of continuous phenomena more generally therefore naturally falls into three periods: the period of the emergence and eventual domination of the Cantor-Dedekind philosophy, and the periods before and after. These three periods are considered in this entry in historical turn.

THE ARISTOTELIAN CONCEPTION

Before the Cantor-Dedekind philosophy the idea of the continuum stood in direct opposition to the discrete and was generally thought to be grounded in our intuition of extensive magnitude, in particular of spatial or temporal magnitude, and of the motion of bodies through space. Some of the essential characteristics of what emerged as the standard ancient conception were already described by Anaxagoras of Clazomenae (c. 500–c. 428 BCE) when he observed that "Neither is there a smallest part of what is small, but there is always a smaller (for it is impossible that what is should cease be [no matter how far it is being subdivided])" (Kirk, Raven, and Schofield 1983, p. 360). Thus, not only is the continuum infinitely divisible, but through the process of division it cannot be reduced to discrete indivisible elements that are, as Anaxagoras picturesquely put it, "separated from one another as if cut off with an axe" (ibid. p. 371). However, while ingredients of the standard ancient conception are already found in the writings of some of the pre-Socratics, it was Aristotle (384–322 BCE), inspired by the writings of the geometers of his day, who provided its earliest systematic philosophical treatment.

Central to Aristotle's analysis is the distinction between discrete and continuous quantity; whereas the former lack, the latter have, a common boundary at which the parts join to form a unity. For Aristotle, number—by which he meant the positive integers greater than or equal to two—is discrete, whereas measurable magnitude—lines, surfaces, bodies, time, and place—are continuous. Lines, in particular, are continuous because "it is possible to find a common boundary at which its parts join together, a point" (*Categories* 6, 5^a1–2, in Aristotle 1984, p. 8); in the cases of surfaces and bodies, the common boundaries are lines, and lines or surfaces, respectively, and in the case of time they are moments.

Motion for Aristotle is also continuous, its continuity being a reflection of spatial and temporal continuity (*Physics* IV.11, 219^a10–13, in Aristotle 1984, p. 371). It is this reflection or isomorphism, for Aristotle, that endows continuous motion with its familiar characteristic properties such as the absence of spatial jumps and the absence of temporal pauses.

Aristotle's characterization of the continuous emerges as the culmination of the following series of definitions he offers in the third chapter of Book V of his *Physics*:

> Things are said to be *together* in place when they are in one primary place. … Things are said to be in *contact* when their extremities are together. … A thing is in *succession* when it is after the beginning in position or in form or in some other respect in which it is definitely so regarded, and when further there is nothing of the same kind as itself between it and that to which it is in succession. … A thing that is in succession and touches [i.e., is in contact] is *con-*

> *tiguous.* ... The *continuous* is a subdivision of the contiguous: things are called continuous when the touching limits become one and the same ... (*Physics* V.3, 226b22–227a12, in Aristotle 1984, pp. 383–384)

Aristotle maintains that the previous definition implies that

> nothing that is continuous can be composed of indivisibles: e.g. a line cannot be composed of points, the line being continuous and the point indivisible. For the extremities of two points can neither be *one* (since of an indivisible there can be no extremity as distinct from some other part) nor *together* (since that which has no parts can have no extremity, the extremity and the thing of which it is the extremity being distinct). ... Moreover, it is plain that everything continuous is divisible into divisibles that are always divisible; for if it were divisible into indivisibles, we should have an indivisible in contact with an indivisible, since the extremities of things that are continuous with one another are one and in contact. (*Physics* VI.1, 231a24–29, 231b15–19, in Aristotle 1984, pp. 390–391)

For Aristotle, the infinite divisibility of the continuous—a property, which on occasion, he appears to take to define the continuous—is a *potential* infinite. Indeed, for Aristotle, the infinite, which is a property of a process rather than of a collection or of a substance, is always potential as opposed to *actual* or completed; that is, no matter which finite stage of the process has been completed, in principle another such stage can be completed. Processes may be infinite with respect to addition or division. Moreover, in the case of spatial continua, in particular, it is the very process of division from which points arise. Thus, while a line segment contains an infinite number of points and an infinite number of parts, for Aristotle it does so only potentially. It is the infinite divisibility of the continuum in this sense that Aristotle appeals to in his treatment of the various paradoxes of Zeno of Elea that are intended to challenge the coherence of the continuity of space, time, matter, and motion. It was also this conception of the continuum that was the dominate conception among philosophers, scientists, and mathematicians alike until the time of Cantor and Dedekind.

NONSTANDARD ANCIENT CONCEPTIONS

However, while Aristotle's theory was the dominate theory until well into the nineteenth century, it never achieved hegemony. Among the ancients, in particular, there were a number of alternative conceptions of continua, including a variety of atomistic conceptions (Furley 1967, Sorabji 1983, White 1992) and the nonatomic conception of the *Stoics* (Sambursky 1959, White 1992). While atomic theories tended to apply solely to the physical realm, there appear to have been atomistic conceptions of geometrical continua as well. Democritus, for example, apparently held that a cone was made up of an infinite number of parallel sections, each of the same indivisible thickness; some who sought to square the circle, including Antiphon, also appear to have embraced atomic theories of geometrical objects. The Stoics, on the other hand, while continuing to adhere to the Aristotelian conception in the mathematical realm, and even to infinite divisibility in the physical realm, may well have distanced themselves from the standard conception in an important respect. According to the interpretation introduced by Shmuel Sambursky (1959) and championed by Michael J. White (1992), the Stoics maintained that there are no points, edges, and surfaces serving as sharp boundaries in physical continua, but rather regions of indeterminacy in which the parts of bodies and adjacent bodies blend. Sambursky (1959, p. 98) likens the physical continuum of the Stoics to the fluid intuitionistic conception of L. E. J. Brouwer, and White proposes instead that "[p]erhaps the best place to look for contemporary elucidation of the Stoic idea is the nonstandard mathematics based on L. A. Zadeh's fuzzy-set theory" (1992, p. 288).

Unlike the Stoics, Aristotle maintains that the physical continuum is a reflection of the geometrical continuum. Indeed, according to Aristotle, "geometry investigates natural [ie. physical] lines, but not qua natural" (*Physics* II.2, 194a9–10, in Aristotle 1984, p. 331). It was this widely held ancient view that the physical mirrors the geometrical that bequeathed to the geometers and their ideas regarding continua an influence far beyond the mathematical domain.

ANCIENT GEOMETRICAL CONCEPTIONS

Aspects of the distinction between discrete number and continuous magnitude are conspicuous in Euclid's *Elements.* Whether Euclid (flourished c. 300 BCE) was directly influenced by the Aristotelian corpus or by earlier geometric practice, however, is the subject of dispute. In any case, reminiscent of Aristotle's characterization, Euclid regards number as a multitude composed of units and believing that one is not itself a number but the unit of number, he appears to identify the numbers with the positive integers greater than one. Geometrical magnitude, on the contrary, for Euclid, is infinitely divisible. Line segments, in particular, can not only be bisected (Book 1, Proposition 10) *ad infinitum*, they can be divided into *n* congruent segments for each positive integer *n* (Book 6, Proposition 9).

Other ingredients of the Euclidean synthesis that shed important light on the nature of the classical conception of the geometrical continuum are the theories of proportions and incommensurable magnitudes presented in Books 5 and 10, respectively, and the so-called method of exhaustion that is developed in Book 12.

Though arguably the result of an evolutionary process (Knorr 1975, 1978), the theory of proportions developed in Book 5 is usually attributed in its entirety to Eudoxus (c. 400–c. 350 BCE), who, like his contemporaries Plato and Aristotle, lived about half a century before Euclid's *Elements* were compiled. Central to the theory is the concept of a *ratio*:

> A ratio [says Euclid] is a sort of relation in respect of size between two magnitudes of the same kind. … Magnitudes are said to have a ratio to one another which are capable, when multiplied [by a positive integer], of exceeding one another. … Magnitudes are said to be in the same ratio, the first to the second and the third to the fourth, when, if any equimultiples whatever be taken of the first and third, and any equimultiples whatever of the second and fourth, the former equimultiples alike exceed, are equal to, or alike fall short of the latter equimultiples respectively taken in corresponding order. (Book 5, Definitions 3–5 in Heath 1956, Volume 2, p. 114)

While Euclid never contends that two magnitudes of the same kind necessarily have a ratio to one another, his geometry (with the one possible exception of his treatment of horn angles [Book 3, Proposition 16]) is limited to systems of magnitudes for which this is the case. Following Otto Stolz (1842–1905), such systems are said to satisfy the axiom of Archimedes (although it is Eudoxus to whom Archimedes (c. 287–212 BCE) attributes the proposition). In contemporary parlance, if *A* and *B* are members of a given system of magnitudes, *A* is said to be *infinitesimal relative* to *B* if *A* and *B* do not have a ratio to one another and *A* is smaller than *B*. Collaterally, if *A* is infinitesimal relative to *B*, *B* is said to be *infinite relative* to *A*. Thus, in Euclid's geometry, no line segment is either infinitesimal or infinite relative to another segment, and analogous results hold for planer and solid figures as well. Moreover, as in the case of line segments, where there is a well-defined means of subtracting the smaller of two magnitudes of the same kind from the larger, the absence of infinitesimal magnitudes of a given kind precludes the existence, more generally, of magnitudes of a given kind that differ by an infinitesimal amount.

Among the virtues of the theory of proportions of Book 5 is that, unlike the older Pythagorean theory that was based on ratios of integers, it is applicable to both *commensurable* and *incommensurable* magnitudes. Following Euclid, "Those magnitudes are said to be *commensurable* which are measured by the same measure, and those *incommensurable* which cannot have any common measure" (Book 10, Definition 1 in Heath 1956, Volume 3, p. 10). The commensurable-incommensurable dichotomy is as close as the ancients came to the modern dichotomy of rational and irrational numbers, a dichotomy that is central to the Cantor-Dedekind conception of the continuum. The discovery of the existence of incommensurable magnitudes, which is usually attributed to the fifth-century Pythagoreans, was significant because it showed that not every pair of magnitudes of the same kind (straight line segments, rectilinear plane figures bounded by such segments, and so on) has a common measure that divides each an exact integral number of times. Thus, for example, since the side and diagonal of a square are incommensurable, it was not possible (given the ancients' conception of measure) to measure all the sides of even so simple a figure as an isosceles right triangle employing a common unit of measure. These and related discoveries, coupled with their conception of number as a multitude of units, convinced the ancients that it was impossible to bridge the gap between the discrete domain of number and the continuous domain of geometry.

Guided by their intuitions about geometrical continua, the Greeks assumed that simple curvilinear planer figures such as circles, ellipses, and segments of parabolas have areas and perimeters of the same kinds as those of polygons, and they made analogous assumptions about the surface areas and volumes of solids such as spheres, cylinders, and cones. The misleadingly term *exhaustion* was introduced by Gregory of St. Vincent (1584–1667) to describe the method devised by Eudoxus, incorporated into the *Elements* by Euclid, and later extended by Archimedes to measure these and other lengths, areas, and volumes in a rigorous fashion without appealing to either the infinitesimal techniques of the Newtonian and Leibnizian calculi or the passage to the limit concept that has been characteristic of the standard approach to calculus since its arithmetization during the latter part of the nineteenth century.

As early as 430 BCE Hippocrates of Chios established that the area of a lune (that is, a curvilinear area bounded by circular arcs) of a particular kind is equal to the area of a square. Soon thereafter, Antiphon contended it was possible to obtain a rectilinear figure having the same area as a circle by beginning with an inscribed regular polygon, say a square, and constructing successively more inclusive inscribed regular polygons until the area of the circle was exhausted. Surprisingly, however, he held that the area of the circle would be exhausted after a sufficiently large finite number of steps (perhaps believing that the side of the polygon would coincide with a small arc of the circumference of the circle). Bryson (c. 420 BCE) later developed an alternative account where he considered a circle C sandwiched between a finite series of successively more inclusive inscribed regular polygons, on the one hand, and a finite series of successively less inclusive circumscribed regular polygons, on the other. He maintained that for some positive integer n there is an n-sided regular polygon P, whose area equals the area of C, that properly contains and is properly contained within the aforementioned inscribed and the circumscribed polygons, respectively. To reach his conclusion he appears to have invoked a continuity principle to the effect that a magnitude passes from a smaller to a greater value solely through values of magnitudes of the same kind. The reliance on this principle, which was criticized by Proclus, John Philoponus, and others, was later obviated by the Eudoxean approach.

Central to the exhaustion approach is an alternative continuity principle—the so-called *bisection principle*—that, following Euclid, may be stated as follows:

> Two unequal magnitudes being set out, if from the greater there be subtracted a magnitude greater than or equal to its half, and from that which is left a magnitude greater than or equal to its half, and if this process is repeated continuously, there will be left some magnitude which will be less than the lesser magnitude set out. (Book 10, Proposition 1 in Heath 1956, Volume 3, p. 14)

Using the Archimedean axiom, Euclid proves the bisection principle for the case where the magnitudes subtracted are greater than half the given magnitude, and immediately thereafter observes that "the theorem can be similarly proved even if the parts subtracted be half" (Book 10, Proposition 1 in Heath 1956, Volume 3, p. 15).

The exhaustion method essentially consists of showing that the magnitude (or, more often, ratio of magnitudes) M in question is equal to another magnitude (or ratio of magnitudes) M' one already knows how to determine by showing—using a pair of *reductio ad absurdum* arguments, each of which employs the principle of bisection—that neither $M < M'$ nor $M' < M$. To draw the conclusion that $M' = M$, a tacit appeal is made the presupposition, alluded to earlier, that either $M < M'$, $M' < M$, or $M' = M$. In the version developed by Archimedes, by evoking the geometrical properties of the geometrical object whose perimeter, area, or volume is to be determined, two sequences $I_1, I_2, \dots, I_n$, and $C_1, C_2, \dots, C_n$, consisting respectively of inscribed and circumscribed lines, polygons, or polyhedrons are constructed whose corresponding perimeters, areas, or volumes are such that $I_n < M < C_n$ and $I_n < M' < C_n$ for all n. Using the principle of bisection, it is then either shown that, given $\varepsilon > 0$, $C_n - I_n < \varepsilon$ for n sufficiently large or that, given $\alpha > 1$, $C_n/I_n < \alpha$ for n sufficiently large.

Archimedes's version of the method of exhaustion resembles and, to some extent, inspired the technique of integration later employed in the calculus. Before the development of the calculus, however, a variety of the concepts and techniques inherited from the ancient geometers would undergo marked change. Of these perhaps none has had a more profound or lasting impact on theories of continua than the rethinking of the number concept and its relation to the geometrical continuum.

EARLY MODERN THEORY OF REAL NUMBERS

The early modern theory of real numbers began to emerge when mathematicians such as Simon Stevin (1548–1620) argued that not only is 1 also a number but that there is also a complete correspondence between (positive) number and continuous magnitude, as well as a parallelism between certain geometrical constructions and the now familiar arithmetic operations on numbers. In a number of his works, including his influential *L'Arithmétique* (1585), Stevin expresses the matter thus:

> I consider the relation between number and magnitude to be such that what can be done by the one can be done by the other. …
>
> … *these two quantities cannot be distinguished by continuity or discontinuity.*
>
> To a continuous magnitude corresponds the continuous number to which it is attributed. (Strong 1976, p. 105; Klein 1968, p. 195; Stevin 1585/1958, p. 501)

This viewpoint soon led to, and was implicit in, the analytic geometry of René Descartes (1596–1650), and was made explicit by John Wallis (1616–1703) and Isaac Newton (1643–1727) in their arithmetizations thereof. Influenced by work of Wallis, Isaac Barrow (1630–1677), and others, the (positive) numbers came to be associated with Eudoxian-Euclidean ratios that were assumed to exist between the magnitudes of a given kind and a selected unit magnitude of the same kind (compare Klein 1968, Pycior 1997). In accordance with the Eudoxian-Euclidean framework, no two such magnitudes of the same kind could differ by an infinitesimal amount. In his popular and influential *Arithmetica Universalis* (1707/1728), Newton extends the correspondence between numbers and ratios to include negative numbers and zero, but whereas some of his predecessors had identified the positive numbers with the symbolic representations of the ratios, Newton identifies numbers with the abstracted ratios themselves. Emphasizing his sharp break with the ancient conception of number, says Newton:

> By *Number* we understand not so much a Multitude of Unities, as the abstracted Ratio of any Quantity, to another Quantity of the same Kind, which we take for Unity. And this is threefold; integer, fracted, and surd: An *Integer* is what is measured by Unity, a *Fraction*, that which a submultiple Part or Unity measures, and a Surd, to which Unity is incommensurable. (Newton 1728/1967, p. 2)

That zero could not be a number in accordance with this definition did not preclude Newton from asserting it was, and the careful treatment that late nineteenth-century mathematicians would recognize to be required to handle ratios involving negative quantities is nowhere to be found.

THE CALCULUS OF NEWTON AND LEIBNIZ

During the sixteenth century the works of Archimedes were widely studied by Western mathematicians and served as the chief source of inspiration for the seventeenth-century development of the infinitesimal calculus, the branch of mathematics erected by Newton and Gottfried Wilhelm Leibniz (1646–1716) for the study of continuously varying magnitudes or quantities. The conception of the continuum embraced by most mathematicians of the period was geometrical or kinematical by nature and grounded in intuition. It was commonplace to consider a curve as a path of a moving point, the curve being continuous insofar as motion itself was presumed to be continuous. Moreover, perhaps as a result of the medieval speculations on the infinite and the continuum, the mathematicians of the day, unlike their mainstream Greek counterparts, were not adverse to employing infinitesimal techniques and appeals to the actual infinite in these and related works. Some authors, such as Galilei Galileo (1564–1642), following in the footsteps of such fourteenth-century thinkers as Henry of Harclay, Nicholas Bonet, Gerard of Odo, Nicholas of Autrecourt, and John Wyclif (Murdoch 1982), maintained that line segments, surfaces, and solids are made up of an actual infinite number of indivisible or infinitesimal elements. And similar ideas were employed by Johannes Kepler (1571–1630), Bonaventura Cavalieri (1598–1647), and others in their determinations of areas and volumes and by Barrow in his determinations of tangents to curves, determinations that would be the focus of the unifying algorithmic frameworks that would come to be called the calculus.

Following in the footsteps of their just-cited forerunners, infinitesimal techniques were employed by Newton and Leibniz in their treatments of the calculus, but unlike some of their predecessors neither of them attributed ontological status to either the actual infinite or the actual infinitesimal. Both regarded infinitesimals—or incomparables as Leibniz sometimes called them—as varying quantities in a state of approaching zero that serve as useful fictions to abbreviate their mathematical proofs. The abbreviated proofs in turn, they contended, could be replaced by limit-based proofs the latter of which not only constitute the rigorous formulation of calculus but are a direct version of the indirect method of exhaustion due to Archimedes. Newton and Leibniz also agreed that the justification for the limit-based proofs lay in the concept of continuity but they differed on the justification itself. Whereas Newton sought it in terms of one's intuition of continuous flow, Leibniz sought it in terms of his *law of continuity*, a philosophical principle to the effect that "[n]o transition is made through a leap" or that "nothing takes place suddenly." The natures of their respective attempts at justification, however, only begin to intimate that the limit-based proofs envisioned by Newton and Leibniz, while akin to, are by no means identical with the limit-based proofs that emerged during the nineteenth century.

Unlike the calculus of today, the calculi of Newton and Leibniz were not concerned with functions but with variable quantities, their rates of change, and so on. However, whereas Newton regarded these quantities as varying at finite rates with respect to time, Leibniz envisioned them as ranging over discrete sequences of values that successively differ by infinitesimal amounts. Underlying this difference was a difference in fundamental concepts: For Newton it was the *fluxion* or finite rate of change of the variable with respect to time, and for Leibniz it was the just-cited infinitely small differences or the differential. As a result, in Leibniz's treatment of the calculus the limit concept was suppressed or at least disguised, whereas it was explicit in Newton's formulation. In the case of differentiation, for example, since for Leibniz it is the distinct differentials *dx* and *dy* that are fundamental, their ratio *dy*/*dx* is of principal significance, whereas for Newton, especially in his later treatment, it is the derivative itself—as a ratio of fluxions or an ultimate ratio of evanescent quantities—that is of central importance.

That there were foundational difficulties with the science of continuously varying quantities was well known among seventeenth- and eighteenth-century mathematicians including Newton and Leibniz themselves. These difficulties were brought into sharp focus by George Berkeley (1685–1753) in his stinging critique of the logical and ontological foundations of the calculus titled *The Analyst* (1734/1992). According to Berkeley, there is no justification for attributing existence to either limits or infinitesimals: A limit of a ratio is either a limit of finite quantities, and therefore not an ultimate ratio, as Newton contended, or it is a mysterious indeterminate ratio 0/0; and if the infinitesimal quantities *dx* and *dy* are not equal to zero, one has the problem of explaining how it is possible that $x + dx = x$, and if they are equal to 0, once again one has the problem of explaining the meaning of the indeterminate 0/0. It was with these and related quandaries that mathematicians concerned with the study of continuously varying magnitude grappled well into the nineteenth century. Some eighteenth-century mathematicians, such as Colin Maclaurin (1698–1746) and Jean Le Rond d'Alembert (1717–1783), attempted to address the foundational worries with refinements of the limit approach of Newton, but it was the infinitesimal approach of Leibniz that emerged as the dominant approach of the day. Moreover, the remaining puzzlement over infinitesimals no longer applied solely to the fictional infinitesimals of Leibniz, but to the actual infinitely large and the actual infinitely small numbers and magnitudes employed to great effect throughout the eighteenth and early nineteenth century by a host of distinguished analysts working in the Leibnizian tradition including Jakob Bernoulli (1654–1705), Johann Bernoulli (1667–1748), Daniel Bernoulli (1700–1782), and Leonhard Euler (1707–1783), to name only a few.

THE ARITHMETIZATION OF ANALYSIS

During the nineteenth century, building on the work begun in 1821 by Augustin-Louis Cauchy (1789–1857) in his *Cours d'analyse*, the calculus was given a rigorous foundation that is still accepted today. By the middle of the century, developments in subject persuaded many mathematicians that the traditional concepts of the calculus were too imprecise, unreliable, and ineffective to provide such a basis. It was held that the traditional relation between real quantities and intuitively given continuous magnitudes such as straight lines was more of a hindrance than an aid in achieving that end as was the then familiar reliance on infinitesimals. In response, the modern *arithmetico-set-theoretic* conception of a real number emerged when a number of mathematicians including Cantor (1872/1939) and Dedekind (1872/1996) introduced systems of real numbers that were designed to dispense with the former and provide a basis for the calculus that made superfluous the latter.

Cantor's system is based on *Cauchy sequences* of rational numbers. A sequence $\{r_n\}$ of rational numbers (indexed over the natural numbers) is said to be a Cauchy sequence (or *fundamental sequence*, as Cantor called it) if for every rational number $\varepsilon > 0$ there is a natural number k such that $|r_m - r_n| < \varepsilon$ for all $m, n > k$. Two such sequences $\{r_n\}$ and $\{s_n\}$ are said to be equivalent if for every rational number $\varepsilon > 0$ there is a natural number k such that $|r_n - s_n| < \varepsilon$ for all $n > k$. In modern parlance, Cantor's construction amounts to identifying the set $\mathbb{R}$ of real numbers with the set of all equivalence classes of Cauchy sequences of rational numbers. If an equivalence class contains the Cauchy sequence $\{r_n\}$ where $r_n = r$ for all n, the equivalence class corresponds to the rational number r, otherwise it corresponds to an irrational number. Each irrational number is associated with the equivalence class containing the Cauchy sequence consisting of the initial segments of its unique nonperiodic decimal representation. For example, $\sqrt{2}$ is associated with the equivalence class containing the Cauchy sequence

$$r_0 = 1; r_1 = 1.4; r_2 = 1.41; r_3\ 1.414; \ldots$$

If α and β are real numbers represented by the Cauchy sequences $\{r_n\}$ and $\{s_n\}$, then the sum and product of α and β are represented by the Cauchy sequences $\{r_n + s_n\}$ and $\{r_n s_n\}$, respectively; and it is said that $\alpha > \beta$ if there is an $a > 0$ such that $r_n \geq s_n + a$ for sufficiently large n.

Dedekind's system, by contrast, is based on *cuts* of the ordered set $\mathbb{Q}$ of rational numbers. By a cut (A_1, A_2) of $\mathbb{Q}$ Dedekind means a partition of $\mathbb{Q}$ into two nonempty sets A_1 and A_2 in which every member of A_1 precedes every member of A_2. Dedekind identities $\mathbb{R}$ with the set of all cuts of $\mathbb{Q}$; if A_1 has a greatest member or A_2 has a least member, say, r, the cut (A_1, A_2) is associated with the rational number r; otherwise it defines an irrational number. $\sqrt{2}$, in particular, is defined by the cut

$$(\{a \in \mathbb{Q}: a < 0 \vee a^2 \leq 2\}, \{a \in \mathbb{Q}: a^2 > 2\}).$$

Given two real numbers $\alpha = (A_1, A_2)$ and $\beta = (B_1, B_2)$, Dedekind stipulates that $\alpha < \beta$ if A_1 is a proper subset of A_2. He also defines $\alpha + \beta = (C_1, C_2)$ where $C_2 = \mathbb{Q} - C_1$ and C_1 is the set of all $c \in \mathbb{Q}$ such that $c \leq a_1 + b_1$ for some $a_1 \in A_1$ and some $b_1 \in B_1$, and further observes that the remaining familiar arithmetic operations on real numbers can likewise be defined.

On the basis of Cantor's and Dedekind's systems of real numbers, whose equivalence (modulo the then tacitly emerging underlying set-theoretic assumptions) would soon be established, the classical concepts of the calculus, including Cauchy's and Bernhard Riemann's (1826–1866) modern definitions of the derivative and the integral, were reformulated in a rigorous fashion using the now familiar δ, ε-techniques, as were the concepts of convergence, sum of an infinite series, and continuity to name only a few. Central to this development was Karl Weierstrass's (1815–1897) replacement of Cauchy's dynamic conception of the limit concept, together with its Newtonian connotations of continuous motion, with a static purely arithmetical formulation. Instead of setting $\lim_{x \to \xi} f(x) = L$ provided that $f(x)$ approaches L as x approaches ξ, Weierstrass set $\lim_{x \to \xi} f(x) = L$ provided that, given a positive real number ε, there is a positive real number δ such that $|f(x) - L| < \varepsilon$ if $0 < |x - \xi| < \delta$. With the host of limit dependent concepts so reformulated, the calculus assumed the form that one still finds in the standard textbooks of the early twenty-first century.

CONTINUOUS FUNCTIONS

As was already noted, the calculus of Newton and Leibniz was not a calculus of functions. It was Euler in the middle of the eighteenth century who placed the concept of function and, in particular, the concept of continuous function at the center of analysis, and it was Cauchy in 1821, and independently Bernard Bolzano (1781–1848) in 1817, who gave the concept its now standard meaning. Following these authors, a function $f(x)$, defined in a neighborhood of a point ξ, is said to be *continuous at* ξ if $\lim_{x \to \xi} f(x) = f(\xi)$; and $f(x)$ is said to be *continuous in a closed interval* $[a, b]$ if it is continuous at each point of the interval, it being understood that the limits corresponding to the endpoints a and b are right-sided and left-sided limits, respectively. Thus, within the Weierstrassian framework, $f(x)$ is continuous in a closed interval iff for each member ξ of the interval and for each positive real number ε there is a positive real number δ such that $|f(x) - f(\xi)| < \varepsilon$ whenever $|x - \xi| < \delta$.

The Cauchy-Bolzano conception of continuity accords nicely with the intuition that the values of a continuous function f differ slightly when its arguments differ slightly and, hence, with its geometric analog that the graph of f does not have a *break* or *jump* in the interval in question. Indeed, using the Cauchy-Bolzano definition nineteenth-century mathematicians were able to show that formal replacements of a number of the familiar intuitions about continuous functions and curves could be established as theorems including the following two:

> The Intermediate Value Theorem. If f is a continuous function on a closed interval $[a, b]$ of $\mathbb{R}$ and $f(a) < \xi < f(b)$ for some ξ, then there is a $c \in (a, b)$ with $f(c) = \xi$;
>
> Extreme Value Theorem. If f is a continuous function on a closed interval $[a, b]$ of $\mathbb{R}$, then f has a maximum value at some $c \in [a, b]$ and f has a minimum value at some $d \in [a, b]$.

The Cauchy-Bolzano conception of continuity is local by nature, referring to the behavior of the function in the neighborhood of a point. Even the notion of continuity in a closed interval is defined in terms of continuity at every point of the interval. A more global conception of continuity that gradually emerged during the process of rigorization that implies but is not implied by the Cauchy-Bolzano conception is that of *uniform continuity*. Following Heinrich Heine (1821–1881), who carefully separated the two notions that had apparently been conflated by Cauchy, a function f is said to be uniformly continuous on a set A of real numbers if, for each positive real number ε, there is a positive real number δ such that for each pair of members ξ and ξ' of A, $|f(\xi) - f(\xi')| < \varepsilon$ whenever $|\xi - \xi'| < \delta$. Essentially, this asserts that for a given ε, the same δ for the continuity condition works for all members of A. The following result, which is of central importance in both standard analysis and a number of the nonstandard alternatives that will be discussed later on, is also due to Heine: f is uniformly continuous on a closed interval $[a, b]$ of $\mathbb{R}$, whenever f is continuous on $[a, b]$.

It is important to emphasize that the class of functions that are deemed to be continuous by standard analysts are more inclusive than those envisioned implicitly or explicitly by their seventeenth-, eighteenth-, and even early nineteenth-century predecessors. Basically, all the curves treated by seventeenth-century analysts were expressed everywhere by one and the same algebraic or transcendental equation and were, accordingly, continuous in the now standard sense. In the mid-eighteenth century so-called discontinuous functions were introduced into analysis by Euler, though they would not be recognized as such today. According to Euler's distinction, which was used up to the time it was replaced by that of Bolzano and Cauchy, a function is continuous if it is characterized by a single analytic expression, and it is discontinuous if it lacks any analytic expression, as in the case of freehand curves, or, if it is defined by different analytic expressions in a finite number of different intervals, the points at which the analytical expressions change being the points of discontinuity.

Euler's points of discontinuity correspond to points of the curve having no well-defined derivative. Accordingly, if one thinks of a continuous curve as the path of a moving point—an intuition that played an important heuristic role in the development of the calculus—Euler's points of discontinuity correspond to points at which the moving point has no well-defined direction. With this in mind it is not difficult to understand why during much of the nineteenth century it was widely believed that functions that are continuous in the Cauchy-Bolzano sense may fail to have derivatives at no more than a finite number of points. In fact, a number of mathematicians including Bolzano himself attempted to prove just this. Mathematicians were therefore surprised when in 1861 Weierstrass provided an example of a continuous function that is nowhere differentiable. A similar such function was constructed by Bolzano in 1834, but like the remainder of his work, it did not become known to the mathematical community till after the work of Weierstrass.

The Cauchy-Bolzano conception of discontinuity, by contrast with Euler's, is closer to that of *discontiguity*, an extreme case being P. G. Lejeune Dirichlet's (1805–1859) so-called monster function—the nowhere continuous function defined on the real line by the condition

$$f(x) = \begin{cases} 0, \text{ if } x \text{ is rational} \\ 1, \text{ if } x \text{ is irrational.} \end{cases}$$

Euler apparently was aware of the existence of discontinuous functions in the modern sense (Youschkevitch 1976, pp. 64–65), but they did not play a fundamental role in the calculus of his time. With the work of Riemann on the convergence of Fourier series during the middle of the nineteenth century, however, this all changed, and they have come to enjoy widespread application not only in analysis, but also in empirical science from where they came. Indeed, referring to their early nineteenth-century roots in the work of Joseph Fourier, the great philosopher-mathematician Jules Henri Poincaré (1854–1912) musingly observes:

> Fourier's series is a precious instrument of which analysis makes continual use, it is by this means that it has been able to represent discontinuous functions; Fourier invented it to solve a problem of physics relative to the propagation of heat. If this problem had not come up naturally, we should never have dared to give discontinuity its rights; we should still long have regarded continuous functions as the only true functions. (Poincaré 1913, p. 286)

THE CANTOR-DEDEKIND CONTINUUM

Central to Cantor's and Dedekind's constructions of the real number system was the underlying belief that only after providing a precise definition of a continuum based on the science of number would it be possible to lend precision to the idea of the continuity of the Euclidean straight line and of continuous magnitude more generally. For this purpose they turned to properties of $\mathbb{R}$ whose continuity they assumed as a *mathematico-philosophical thesis*. According to Cantor, the continuity of $\mathbb{R}$ consists in its being both *connected* and *Cauchy complete*; it is connected because whenever a and a' are elements of the system such that $a < a'$, then for any positive element ε of the system, there is a finite sequence $a_1, \ldots, a_n$ of elements of the system where $a < a_1 < \ldots < a_n < a'$ such that $a_1 - a, \ldots, a' - a_n < \varepsilon$; and it is Cauchy complete since every convergent sequence of elements of the system has a limit in the system. Dedekind, by contrast, identified the continuity of $\mathbb{R}$ with its being a totally ordered system having what is today called the Dedekind continuity property; that is, whenever the system is partitioned into two nonempty subsets X and Y such that every member of X precedes every member of Y, then either X has a greatest member or Y has a least member, but not both.

Connectivity, in Cantor's sense, was soon recognized to be equivalent the Archimedean axiom for a large class of structures including ordered fields, the latter of whose roots lie in analytic geometry. Indeed, since the time that Wallis and Newton incorporated directed segments into Cartesian geometry, it had been loosely understood that given a unit segment AB of a line L of a classical Euclidean space, the collection of directed segments of L emanating from A including the degenerate segment AA itself constitutes an Archimedean ordered field with AA and AB the additive and multiplicative identities of the field and addition and multiplication of segments suitably defined. These ideas were made precise by Giuseppe Veronese (1854–1917) in his *Fondamenti di geometria* (1891) and by David Hilbert (1862–1943) in his *Grundlagen der Geometrie* (1899), works on the foundations of geometry from which the modern conceptions of Archimedean and non-Archimedean ordered fields emerged. It was also these and related works on the foundations of geometry that gave rise to the following familiar characterizations of the arithmetic continuum whose continuity properties are associated with Cantor, Dedekind, Bolzano, and Hilbert, respectively:

(1) $\mathbb{R}$ is (up to isomorphism) the unique Archimedean ordered field that is Cauchy complete

(2) $\mathbb{R}$ is (up to isomorphism) the unique Dedekind continuous ordered field

(3) $\mathbb{R}$ is (up to isomorphism) the unique ordered field having the least upper bound property (that is, every subset of the system that is bounded above has a least upper bound)

(4) $\mathbb{R}$ is (up to isomorphism) the unique Archimedean ordered field that admits no proper extension to an Archimedean ordered field

Each of these characterizations of $\mathbb{R}$ makes use of metrical conceptions. However, in 1895 Cantor demonstrated that it is possible to provide a categorical characterization of the ordered set of real numbers and, hence, of a Cantor-Dedekind linear continuum, using order-theoretic concepts alone. Another such characterization that emerged soon thereafter is the following one given by Edward V. Huntington (1874–1952) that indicates what besides simple density—the set-theoretic analog of infinite divisibility—is required to characterize the order type of $\mathbb{R}$ (1917):

(1) $\langle K, <\rangle$ is a totally ordered set having neither a first element nor a last element;

(2) $\langle K, <\rangle$ is dense, that is, if a and b are elements of K such that $a < b$ there is an element x in K such that $a < x < b$;

(3) $\langle K, <\rangle$ is Dedekind complete, that is, if K_1 and K_2 are any two nonempty subsets of K, such that every element belongs either to K_1 or K_2 and every element of K_1 precedes every element of K_2, then there is at least one element x in K such that any element that precedes x belongs to K_1, and every element that follows x belongs to K_2;

(4) the class K contains a denumerable subset K' in such a way that between any two elements of K there is an element of K'.

Reflecting on the then newly developed order-theoretic conception of the mathematical continuum, the great philosopher-mathematician Jules Henri Poincaré perceptively remarks that:

> [t]he continuum so conceived is only a collection of individuals ranged in a certain order, infinite in number, it is true, but *exterior* to one another. This is not the ordinary conception, wherein is supposed between the elements of a continuum a sort of intimate bond which makes of them a whole, where the point does not exist before the line, but the line before the point. Of the celebrated formula, "the continuum is unity in multiplicity," only the multiplicity remains, the unity has disappeared. The analysts are none the less right in defining their continuum as they do, for they always reason on just this as soon as they pique themselves on rigor. But this is enough to apprise us that the veritable mathematical continuum is a very different thing from that of the physicist and that of the metaphysician. (1913, p. 43)

To some extent these views are a reflection of those of Cantor and Dedekind themselves. For example, distancing himself from a long line of metaphysicians, Cantor writes:

> The concept of the "continuum" has … always evoked the greatest differences of opinion and even vehement quarrels. This lies perhaps in the fact that, because the exact and complete definition of the concept has not been bequeathed to the dissentients, the underlying idea has taken on different meanings; but it may also be (and this seems to me the most probable) that the idea of the continuum had not been thought out by the Greeks (who may have been the first to conceive it) with the clarity and completeness which would have been required to exclude the possibility of different opinions among their posterity. Thus we see Leucippus, Democritus, and Aristotle consider the continuum as a composite which consists from parts divisible without end, but Epicurus and Lucretius construct it out of their atoms considered as finite things. Out of this a great quarrel arose among the

> philosophers, of whom some followed Aristotle, others Epicurus; still others, in order to remain aloof from this quarrel, declared with Thomas Aquinas that the continuum consisted neither of infinitely many nor of a finite Anzahl [number] of parts, but of *absolutely no* parts. … Here we see the *medieval-scholastic origin* of a point of view which we still find represented today, in which the continuum is thought to be an unanalysable concept, or as others express themselves, a pure a priori intuition which is scarcely susceptible to a determination through concepts. Every arithmetical attempt at determination of this *mysterium* is looked on as a forbidden encroachment and repulsed with due vigor. Timid natures thereby get the impression that with the "continuum" it is not a matter of a *mathematically logical concept* but rather of religious dogma. (1883/1996, p. 903)

Moreover, as to the necessity of even conceiving space as continuous, Dedekind remarks, "If space has at all a real existence it is not necessary for it to be continuous" (1872/1996, p. 772). Indeed,

> If anyone should say that we cannot conceive of space as anything else than continuous, I should venture to doubt it and call attention to the fact that a far advanced, refined scientific training is demanded in order to perceive clearly the essence of continuity and to understand that besides rational quantitative relations, also irrational, and besides algebraic, also transcendental quantitative relations are conceivable. (1888/1996, p. 793)

Bertrand Russell, who played the leading role in introducing the ideas of Cantor and Dedekind to the English-speaking philosophical world, goes even further when he remarks, "Whether the axiom of continuity be true as regards our actual space, is a question I see no means of deciding. For any such question must be empirical, and it would be quite impossible to distinguish empirically what may be called a rational space from what might be called a continuous space" (1903, p. 440).

However, despite these and other such pronouncements made in the years bracketing the turn of the twentieth century, and despite the ongoing speculation about quantized space and time that emerged soon thereafter with the advent of the quantum theory (compare Cepek 1961, pp. 223–243; Sorabji 1983, pp. 381–383, 447) and that was redirected toward overcoming the difficulties of harmonizing the quantum theory with the relativistic theory of gravity and space-time (compare Markopoulou 2004; Smolin 2001, 2004), it became and remains commonplace among philosophers and physicists to assume not only that space and time are continuous, as most of their modern predecessors had supposed, but also that they are continuous in the sense of Cantor and Dedekind. Whether this assumption should be construed instrumentally or realistically there is a multiplicity of views (compare Earman 1989, chapters 8 and 9; Maddy 1997, chapter 6; Hellman 1998), as are the views regarding the testable status of the thesis itself (compare Forrest 1995, Markopoulou 2004).

MODERN EUCLIDEAN GEOMETRY AND THE CONTINUUM

At least as far back as the seventeenth century there were thinkers who observed that there are places in the *Elements* where Euclid tacitly employs continuity assumptions that are not warranted by the axioms and common notions he assumes. For example, in his proof that given any segment, there is an equilateral triangle having the given segment as one of its sides (Book 1, Proposition 1), Euclid assumes

> *The Circular Continuity Principle*: If a circle C has one point inside and one point outside another circle C', then the two circles intersect in two points.

And in his proof that through a point outside a given line there is a line perpendicular to the given line (Book 1, Proposition 12), he assumes

> *The Line-Circle Continuity Principle*: If one endpoint of a segment is inside a circle and the other outside, then the segment intersects the circle at one point.

Among the thinkers who thus criticized Euclid was Leibniz in his *Specimen geometriae luciferae* (c. 1695/1962, p. 284). Such criticisms were significant not only because they drew attention to gaps in Euclid's reasoning but also because they intimated that, contrary to the ancient and the then still standard view, infinite divisibility is not sufficient for continuity. In fact, in the just-cited paper as Ernst Cassirer (1902, p. 183) importantly observes, Leibniz departed from his usual acceptance of the standard view and explicitly stated just this.

During the late nineteenth century geometers showed that by supplementing the then newly emerging refinements of Euclid's system of axioms with continuity axioms that ensured the satisfaction of the Cantor-Dedekind axiom, one could establish the circular continuity principle and the line-circle continuity principle and with these all of Euclid's continuity needs (compare Heath 1956, pp. 1:234–240; Greenberg 1993, pp. 93–101). However, as Cantor and Dedekind were aware, whereas the Cantor-Dedekind axiom suffices for the continuity needs of Euclid, it goes beyond those needs. Cantor makes this point, albeit only implicitly, when (following his proof-sketch that to each point of the Euclidean line there corresponds a real number) he maintains:

> In order to complete the connection of numerical quantity with the geometry of the straight line, one must only add an *axiom* which simply says that conversely every numerical quantity also has a determined point on the straight line, whose coordinate is equal to that quantity. … I call this proposition an *axiom* because by its nature it cannot be generally proved. (Cantor 1872/1932, p. 96)

And Dedekind makes the point more forcefully and explicitly when he revealingly observes:

> If we select three non-collinear points *A*, *B*, and *C* at pleasure, with the single limitation that the ratios of the distances *AB*, *AC*, *BC* are algebraic numbers, and regard as existing in space only those points *M*, for which the ratios of *AM*, *BM*, *CM* to *AB* are likewise algebraic numbers, then it is easy to see that the space made up of the points *M* is everywhere discontinuous. But in spite of this discontinuity, and despite the existence of gaps in this space, all constructions that occur in Euclid's *Elements*, can, so far as I can see, be just as accurately effected here as in a perfectly continuous space; the discontinuity of this space would thus not be noticed in Euclid's science, would not be felt at all. (1888/1996, p. 793)

The ordered field of real algebraic numbers to which Dedekind is referring is an instance of a *Euclidean ordered field*, that is, an ordered field in which every positive element is the square of some element of the field. Besides being Euclidean, the ordered field of real algebraic numbers is both countable and Archimedean. During the twentieth century it emerged that a model of all the axioms of (a modern refined version of) Euclidean geometry less the Archimedean axiom and the Cantor-Dedekind axiom satisfies the circular continuity principle iff it satisfies the line-circle continuity principle iff a line of the model is modeled by a Euclidean ordered field (compare Tarski 1959/1986; Hartshorne 2000, pp. 104–112, 144–145; Greenberg 1993, pp. 143–144). If, following Euclid, the Archimedean axiom is also assumed, the Euclidean ordered fields must be Archimedean as well. It is essentially for this reason that Euclidean ordered fields have been so named. For historically important examples of modern refined versions of Euclidean geometry, see David Hilbert (1899/1971) and Alfred Tarski (1959/1986); and for examples of non-Archimedean Euclidean ordered fields and their corresponding non-Archimedean Euclidean geometries, see Philip Ehrlich (1997a).

SET THEORY AND THE CONTINUUM

The Cantor-Dedekind theory of the continuum was originally formulated in a *naïve* set-theoretic framework, grounded in intuitions about sets that included the then radical assumption that infinitely many entities could be collected together in a set. Within this framework Cantor established the existence of an exhaustive hierarchy $\aleph_0$, $\aleph_1$, $\aleph_2$, … of increasingly large infinite cardinals, proved that the cardinality of the set of rational numbers is $\aleph_0$, that the cardinality of $\mathbb{R}$ is $2^{\aleph_0}$, and that $2^{\aleph_0}$ is greater than $\aleph_0$. In the early decades of the twentieth century Cantorian set theory was placed on an axiomatic basis that sidestepped a medley of paradoxes that had befallen the naïve theory. In honor of two of its principal architects, Ernst Zermelo (1871–1953) and Abraham A. Fraenkel (1891–1965), the theory has come to be designated ZFC, where ZF indicates the body of axioms outside the axiom of choice. Of the open problems inherited from the naïve theory none was regarded more important than that of deciding the veracity of the *continuum hypothesis* (CH)—Cantor's conjecture that the cardinality of the continuum is $\aleph_1$. However, in 1938 Kurt Gödel showed that ZFC + CH is consistent if ZFC is, and twenty-five years later Paul Cohen demonstrated if ZFC is consistent so is ZFC + ¬CH, thereby establishing the independence of CH from standard set theory. Since the work of Cohen there has been a good deal of speculation on the part of philosophers and logicians whether or not the axioms of ZFC should be supplemented with one or more additional axioms that would settle the matter one way or another (Kanamori 2003). Gödel (1947/1983), who held a platonist view of sets, maintained that CH is either objectively true or objectively false and, accordingly, promoted the search for additional axioms to settle the matter. Many set theorists, including Cohen (1990), however, believe that there is nothing in the intuitive concept of set that would recommend the adoption of an additional axiom that would conclusively settle CH one way or another. The views of Gödel and Cohen, however, only begin to indicate the range of opinion on the matter as is evident from the debate between Soloman Feferman et al. (2000), the writings of Donald Martin and H. G. Dales (Dales and

Oliveri 1998), and the intriguing though controversial views of W. Hugh Woodin (2001, 2002, 2004). Both models of ZFC + CH and ZFC + ¬CH are being explored by set theorists with perhaps a bit more attention being devoted to the latter. Mathematicians who are not set theorists, however, tend to use CH freely for the purpose of theorem proving, their reliance on CH being indicated in the statement of the theorem.

NONSTANDARD THEORIES OF CONTINUA

Although the Cantor-Dedekind theory of real numbers and philosophy of the continuum have occupied privileged positions in standard mathematical philosophy since the decades following the turn of the twentieth century, it has never enjoyed the complete allegiance of either philosophers or mathematicians. Early opponents such as Hermann Hankel (1839–1873) and Paul du Bois-Reymond (1831–1889) were critical of the attempts by Cantor, Dedekind, and others to treat irrational numbers formally and without the concept of continuous magnitude, and others such as Leopold Kronecker (1823–1891) complained, on the contrary, that the arithmetization had not gone far enough. Still others, including Emil Borel (1871–1956) and a young L. E. J. Brouwer (1881–1966), continued to regard the continuum as a primitive concept given to one directly by geometric intuition that was not amenable to analysis (compare Troelstra 1982); and others, including Hermann Weyl (1885–1955) (1918) as well as a more mature Brouwer (compare 1918, 1924, 1952), while embracing an analytical approach questioned one or another aspect of the logico-set-theoretic underpinnings of the Cantor-Dedekind theory. Another complaint that was, and to some extent still is, a stumbling block to the acceptance of the Cantor-Dedekind theory is the contention that the Cantor-Dedekind philosophy of the continuum is committed to the reduction of the continuous to the discrete, a program whose philosophical cogency, and even logical consistency, had been called into question over the centuries. Inspired by arguments originating with Aristotle, and reiterated and further developed by Immanuel Kant (1724–1804), Franz Brentano (1838–1917), Edmund Husserl (1859–1938), and others, a string of late nineteenth- and twentieth-century mathematicians and philosophers beginning with du Bois-Reymond (1882) maintained that unlike the unextended points that, by their lights, compose the Cantor-Dedekind continuum, the elements of a genuine continuum must themselves have extension if the continuum itself is to have extension. This view led Charles Sanders Peirce (1939–1914) to sketch a nonarithmetic theory of the continuum based on infinitesimals (1898/1992, 1900), and it played important contributing roles in the development of Brouwer's and Weyl's aforementioned intuitionist and predicativist alternatives to the standard conception as well.

Veronese (1889, 1891, 1894), however, while agreeing that the parts of a continuum must be intervals as opposed to points, held that for the sake of geometry the geometer may treat the line as an ordered collection of unextended points; moreover, holding that one's intuitive conception of the continuum is independent of the Archimedean axiom, he developed a general axiomatic theory of continua that was not only satisfied by the standard arithmetic continuum but by certain structures with infinitesimals as well, and he illustrated the latter by means of a synthetic construction of a non-Archimedean ordered field that is continuous in his sense. Veronese's non-Archimedean continuum was placed on a logically sound arithmetic foundation by Tullio Levi-Civita (1873–1941), who therewith provided the first analytic constructions of non-Archimedean ordered fields (1892–1993/1954, 1898/1954).

Building on the work of Levi-Civita, Hans Hahn (1879–1934) constructed non-Archimedean number systems (1907) having properties that generalize the aforementioned continuity properties of Dedekind and Hilbert, and he demonstrated that his number systems collectively provide a panorama of the finite, infinite, and infinitesimal numbers that can enter into a non-Archimedean theory of continua based on the concept of an ordered field (compare Ehrlich 1995, 1997, 1997a). Throughout the remaining first half of the twentieth century there continued to be important contributions to the theory of the continuum including the algebraic (Artin and Schreier 1926/1965) and logical (Tarski 1939/1986, 1948/1986) versions of the theory of elementary continuity. During the 1950s, under the influence of A. A. Markov (1856–1922), a Russian school of constructive analysis was developed based on a continuum consisting of real numbers with a *recursive* Cauchy sequence (compare Kushner 1984), and during the 1960s Errett Bishop (1928–1983) introduced an alternative constructive approach to analysis (1967) based on a model of the continuum whose theorems, unlike those of Brouwer and the Russian school, are all provable in classical mathematics.

Also during roughly the same period, interest in Weyl's predicative theory was rekindled by Feferman (1998), who developed his own predicative approach to analysis. In addition, since the late 1950s a number of nonstandard theories of continua have appeared that make use of infinitesimals including those arising from Abraham Robinson's (1918–1974) nonstandard approach to analysis (1961/1969, 1966/1974), those arising from F. W. Lawvere (1979, 1980) and Anders Kock's (1981) ideas on smooth infinitesimal analysis and synthetic differential geometry, the partially ordered continuum of Curt Schmieden and Detlef Laugwitz (1958), and Ehrlich's so-called absolute arithmetic continuum (1987, 1989, 1992) based on J. H. Conway's (1976) theory of *surreal numbers*. Still another theory that arose during this period is the theory of fuzzy real numbers based on Lofti Asker Zadeh's (1987) theory of fuzzy sets.

Of the nonstandard theories mentioned earlier, the intuitionist, Bishop-style constructivist, predicativist, and the Robinsonian and post-Robinsonian infinitesimalist theories have been given the most attention by philosophers. In the subsequent three sections these will be considered in turn with some attention paid to the Russian constructivist theory as well.

CONSTRUCTIVIST THEORIES

Constructivism is a rubric that has come to designate a family of approaches to the foundations of mathematics that are loosely united by their opposition to certain forms of mathematical reasoning employed in the mainstream mathematical community. However, as the term loosely suggests, there are significant differences between the various schools and substantial differences in attitude can be found even among the representatives of a given school or a single representative over time. However, whether the result of their rejection of actual infinities or the universal applicability of certain principles of classical logic, or their insistence on the use of algorithmic constructions of one form or another, constructivists have always found themselves at odds with the Cantor-Dedekind theory of the continuum and have sought to provide alternatives that are constructively sanctioned by their own particular lights. To distinguish the resulting intuitionist, Russian constructivist, and Bishop-style constructivist arithmetic continua from $\mathbb{R}$, from now on they will be denoted as $\mathbb{R}_I$, $\mathbb{R}_R$, and $\mathbb{R}_C$, respectively.

Before the late 1960s the constructivist theory of the continuum that attracted the greatest attention is the intuitionistic theory of Brouwer. Until 1914, Brouwer, like Borel before him, embraced a holistic view in which the continuum is regarded as a primitive notion given directly by intuition that cannot be understood as the totality of its individually definable elements. Thereafter, while still clinging to certain aspects of the irreducible conception, Brouwer adopted a more analytic view in which the continuum, while not a completed nondeumerable totality, can be more and more completely specified in a never-ending fashion with one's increasing knowledge as a medium of free development.

The basis of Brouwer's conception of the continuum is the concept of a *choice sequence*, a concept not acceptable to classical mathematics. According to Brouwer, the construction of such a potentially infinite sequence is always incomplete in the sense that at any given instant of its construction the sequence is limited to a finite number of terms. A choice sequence α is given by a fixed initial segment $\alpha_1, \alpha_2, \ldots, \alpha_n$ of mathematical objects along with a corresponding set of restrictions $R_1, R_2, \ldots, R_n$, where R_n restricts the range of possible choices for α_{n+1}. In particular, real numbers are introduced by Brouwer as choice sequences that are Cauchy sequences of rational numbers. Of course, being a choice sequence, the notion of a Cauchy sequence of rational numbers must be appropriately understood. More specifically, according to the intuitionist one can assert that a potentially infinite sequence $r_1, r_2, \ldots$ of rational numbers is a Cauchy sequence only if one knows there is a procedure that, given any positive integer k, effectively produces a natural number N along with a proof that N has the specified Cauchy property, for example, $|r_m - r_n| < 1/k$ for all $m, n < N$.

For Brouwer, such a choice sequence is not a technique for approximating some preexisting real number—it is the choice sequence itself, growing in time, that is the real number. Some such real numbers are introduced by letting the choices be prescribed by a fixed algorithm. These so-called *lawlike* sequences lead to the existence of real numbers such as e, π, and $\sqrt{2}$. Other real numbers arise from forbidding any restriction on the rational numbers one chooses outside of assuring that the choice sequence is Cauchy. Between these two extremes, however, there is a wide range of possibilities for introducing real numbers. Until 1927 Brouwer did not place any restrictions on choice sequences—having regarded them as sufficiently explained by the freedom of a supposed ideal mathematician generating them—but thereafter he became more specific and continued to revise his conception of permissible choice sequences until the early 1950s (compare Troelstra 1982, pp. 472–474).

The adoption of choice sequences forces a nonclassical logic on intuitionists that rejects the universal validity of the *law of excluded middle*. For example, given the incomplete nature of choice sequences the intuitionist has no right to assume for an arbitrary pair of choice sequences α and β having identical initial segments that α

$= \beta \vee \alpha \neq \beta$. The logic that has come to be embraced by intuitionists is a subtheory of classical logic called *intuitionistic logic* (compare Heyting 1971, chapter 7). For the intuitionist, logic does not provide a foundation for mathematics but emerges from one's mathematical practice. The adoption of intuitionistic logic leads intuitionists to a theory of real numbers and corresponding theory of continuity that differs markedly from their classical counterparts. For example, besides the just-cited deviation, it is not possible for intuitionists to prove precise analogs of the following classical results for their own system $\mathbb{R}_I$ of real numbers: $\forall x, y \in \mathbb{R}(xy = 0 \rightarrow (x = 0 \vee y = 0))$; $\forall x, y \in \mathbb{R}(x \leq y \vee x \geq y)$; $\forall x, y \in \mathbb{R}(x > y \vee x = y \vee x > y)$; every subset of $\mathbb{R}$ that is bounded above has a least upper bound; $\forall x \in \mathbb{R}(x \text{ is rational} \vee x \text{ is irrational})$. Nor can they prove the intermediate value theorem or the extreme value theorem. From Brouwer's perspective, this inability is not a limitation since each of the previous assertions implies an instance of the law of excluded middle that is not intuitionistically sanctioned (compare Bridges and Reeves 1999, pp. 72–73). This attitude, and the embrace of intuitionistic logic more generally (with the aforementioned implications for their own theories of real numbers and corresponding theories of continuity) is a common thread that binds constructive mathematicians. From the constructivist point of view, accepting the law of excluded middle as a universal principle would mean the existence of a universal procedure for generating for each proposition P, either a proof of P or a proof of $\neg P$, where a procedure for generating a proof of $\neg P$ is understood to be a method for generating a contradiction from a hypothetical proof of P. However, such a procedure is not available; if it were one could decide a proposition P—such as Goldbach's conjecture—the truth of which has not been decided.

Brouwer's concept of a choice sequence that is Cauchy corresponds, as Heyting notes, "to the intuitive concept of the continuum as a possibility of a gradual determination of points" (1971, p. 34). To develop an adequate theory of continuity and of analysis more generally, however, the mathematician must be able to talk about classes of such real numbers and functions. From the standpoint of the intuitionist, however, one cannot collect them together into a Cantorian set—there are simply too many of them. Rather, for the intuitionist, they are held together in a *spread*—roughly speaking, a growing tree, whose emerging paths through the tree correspond to the various ways an initial segment of a choice sequence can be continued (compare Heyting 1971, chapter 3).

Moreover, to obtain the central continuity theorems concerning such classes of real numbers and functions, Brouwer introduced two fundamental ideas governing the mathematical treatment of choice sequences: the *weak continuity principle for numbers* (compare Veldman 2001, Atten and Dalen 2002, Troelstra and Dalen 1988, chapter 5) and the *principle of bar induction* (compare Kushner 2001). The continuity principle makes choice sequences serviceable by contending that a total function from choice sequences to natural numbers never requires more input than an initial segment (of a choice sequence) to generate its output; and the induction principle ensures, among other things, that the entire intuitionistic continuum can be treated in a constructively manageable fashion (compare Atten 2004, chapters 3–4).

The adoption of the continuity principle and the induction principle gives the intuitionistic theory of continuity its own distinctive constructivist flavor and leads to even more striking deviations from the classical theory than those listed earlier. For example, in virtue of the continuity principle, the analogs of the aforementioned classical results that cannot be established as a result of the adoption of intuitionistic logic are now provably false (compare Bridges and Richman 1987, pp. 4–5; Troelstra and Dalen 1988, pp. 257–258). What is perhaps the most notorious such deviation, however, is that all functions from $\mathbb{R}_I$ to $\mathbb{R}_I$ are continuous, and uniformly continuous at that. This apparent absurdity arises in part from the fact that the contention "f is a function defined on all of $\mathbb{R}_I$" is substantially stronger construed intuitionistically than is the contention "f is a function defined on all of $\mathbb{R}$" construed classically. Consider, for example, the classical discontinuous function f defined by

$$f(x) = \begin{cases} 0, \text{ if } x < 0 \\ 1, \text{ if } x \geq 0. \end{cases}$$

From Brouwer's perspective, f is not a function at all since one cannot prove $\forall x \exists y (f(x) = y)$ by intuitionistically sanctioned means. In particular, one cannot prove $\forall x (x < 0 \vee x \geq 0)$ insofar as the definition of f does not tell one how to compute $f(x)$ if x is a number for which one cannot assert either $x < 0$ or $x \geq 0$. Closely related to this is still another striking deviation, the so-called *unsplittability* of the intuitionistic continuum; that is, unlike the Cantor-Dedekind arithmetic continuum, there do not exist two disjoint nonempty subsets of an interval of the intuitionistic continuum whose union is the given interval, nor are there such partitions of the intuitionistic continuum whose union is the continuum itself. Accordingly, for the intuitionist, as for Anaxagoras and Aristotle before them, it is not possible to separate out a point from their continuum or from an interval thereof.

While Brouwer's theory has attracted a good deal of attention from philosophers and logicians, it has received comparatively little attention from standard mathematicians. Whether this is because of the philosophical precepts underlying it, the highly nonclassical nature of the mathematical arguments it employs, the belief that the resulting mathematics is too impoverished, or simply the absence of a perceived need for it, is difficult to say. In 1967, however, Brouwer's theory was given an especially stinging critique, not by standard mathematicians, but by Bishop, whose treatise *Foundations of Constructive Analysis* is widely credited with having breathed new life into constructive mathematics. In the treatise's polemical opening chapter Bishop describes the construction and motivation underlying Brouwer's theory of the continuum in the following biting terms:

> Brouwer became involved in metaphysical speculation by his desire to improve the theory of the continuum. A bugaboo of both Brouwer and the logicians has been compulsive speculation about the nature of the continuum. In the case of the logicians this leads to contortions in which various formal systems, all detached from reality, are interpreted within one another in the hope that the nature of the continuum will somehow emerge. In Brouwer's case there seems to have been a nagging suspicion that unless he personally intervened to prevent it, the continuum would turn out to be discrete. He therefore introduced the method of free-choice sequences for constructing the continuum, a consequence of which the continuum cannot be discrete because it is not well enough defined. This makes mathematics so bizarre it becomes unpalatable to mathematicians, and foredooms the whole of Brouwer's program. This is a pity, because Brouwer had a remarkable insight into the defects of classical mathematics, and he made a heroic effort to set things right. (1967, p. 6)

Bishop sought to place analysis on a constructivist foundation that is free of the perceived difficulties mentioned earlier, a project that has been extended by a number of other mathematicians including Douglas Bridges and Fred Richman. In Bishop's arithmetic continuum $\mathbb{R}_C$ a real number is simply defined as a sequence $\{x_n\}$ of rational numbers that satisfies the condition $|x_m - x_n| \leq m^{-1} + n^{-1}$ (for all integers $m, n \geq 1$); though some authors, following Troelstra and Dirk van Dalen (1988, pp. 253–254), prefer to use equivalence classes of certain sequences of rational numbers in their place. Thus, for Bishop, as for Markov, every real number is a lawlike Cauchy sequence. Using a system of axioms for constructive ordered fields with a formulation of the Archimedean axiom and a constructive formulation of the least upper-bound principle, Bridges (1999) shows that $\mathbb{R}_C$ can be characterized in a manner that closely resembles one of the aforementioned standard axiomatizations of $\mathbb{R}$. Working independently, Alberto Ciaffaglione and Pietro Di Gianantonio (2002) and Herman Geuvers and Milad Niqui (2002) provide equivalent axiomatizations of $\mathbb{R}_C$ that employ constructive versions of Cauchy completeness in place of Bridges's least upper-bound condition. Assuming the axiom of countable choice (compare Troelstra and Dalen 1988, pp. 189–190)—an axiom that is frequently adopted by constructive mathematicians—Geuvers and Niqui (2002) further establish the categoricity of the axiomatizations. Absent the choice axiom (or some equivalent thereof), there are models of the axioms that are not isomorphic to $\mathbb{R}_C$—in particular, Troelstra and Dalen's version of the constructive continuum based on Dedekind cuts (1988, pp. 270–274).

Bishop tended to distinguish his theory of analysis from the classical theory by emphasizing the former's demand for algorithmic constructions. Following in the footsteps of Brouwer, Bishop took the concept of an algorithm as a primitive, undefined notion and was led to reject the universal validity of the law of excluded middle by interpreting mathematical existence strictly in terms of computability or constructivity. Bridges and, especially, Richman speculate that the theory of analysis that emerges from Bishop's approach may be regarded as the subtheory of the classical theory that is obtainable employing intuitionistic logic as opposed to classical logic as the underlying logic (Bridges and Richman 1987; Richman 1990, 1996; Bridges 1999). Since (in accordance with Heyting's axiomatization of intuitionistic logic [1971]) one passes from intuitionistic logic to classical logic by embracing the universal validity of the law of excluded middle, on their view Bishop's theory may be regarded as the subtheory of the classical theory that can be obtained without appealing to the instances of this classical law that are not intuitionistically sanctioned (Bridges and Richman 1987, p. 120).

Besides being a subtheory of the classical theory, Bishop's theory may be regarded as a subtheory of the intuitionist and Russian constructivist theories as well

(Bridges and Richman 1987, chapter 6). Whereas, in accordance with Bridges and Richman's view, one moves from Bishop's theory to the classical theory by embracing the universal validity of the law of excluded middle, to move from Bishop's theory to the intuitionistic theory one introduces Brouwer's weak continuity principle along with a seminal consequence of Brouwer's principle of bar induction called the *fan theorem*, and to pass from Bishop's theory to the Russian constructivist theory one adds a consequence of Church's thesis that all computable sequences of natural numbers are recursive (Bridges and Richman 1987, chapter 5). Talk of such passages, however, applies solely to theories in the logician's narrow sense of the term; it ignores the divergent philosophical motivations and mathematical trappings of the four theories. With respect to the Russian constructivist theory, for example, it ignores that every real number is a recursive real number, that algorithms are Markov algorithms, that functions are Gödel numbers of algorithms that compute them, and so on.

The differences between the classical, Russian constructivist, and intuitionist theories, however, go beyond their respective philosophical motivations and mathematical trappings; they have different theories of continuity, as is evident from the following theorems of the three respective theories:

(Classical): Some functions $f:[0, 1]\to\mathbb{R}$ are not continuous and, hence, not uniformly continuous

(Russian Constructivist): Whereas all functions $f:[0, 1]\to\mathbb{R}_R$ are continuous, some are not uniformly continuous

(Intuitionist): All functions $f:[0, 1]\to\mathbb{R}_I$ are not only continuous, they are uniformly continuous

Despite these differences, Bishop's theory manages to lie comfortably within the common core of the three theories in part because in Bishop's theory attention is restricted from the outset to functions that are assumed to be uniformly continuous on each closed interval of $\mathbb{R}_C$.

Restricting attention to the just-said functions, Bishop managed to obtain a surprisingly robust theory of analysis that includes among a wide range of other theorems constructive analogs of the intermediate value theorem and the extreme value theorem. Like many of the theorems of constructive analysis, the latter two theorems differ from their classical counterparts by having weakened conclusions or strengthened hypotheses. One constructive version of the intermediate value theorem asserts that a uniformly continuous function $f:[a, b]\to\mathbb{R}_C$ takes on a value as close to the given intermediate value as one pleases, and the constructive version of the extreme value theorem asserts that a uniformly continuous function $f:[a, b]\to\mathbb{R}_C$ does have a maximum (minimum), though the maximum (minimum) is not necessarily assumed. There is also a constructive version of the intermediate value theorem that asserts that in a particular class of cases (which includes all real-analytic functions), the intermediate value in question is in fact realized (compare Bishop and Bridges 1985, pp. 40–41; Troelstra and Dalen 1988, pp. 292–295).

However, despite the strength of Bishop's analysis and its compatibility with classical mathematics, Bishop's theory, like its intuitionist and Russian constructivist forerunner's, has not attracted the kind of attention from classical mathematicians its practitioners had hoped for (compare Bridges and Reeves 1999, p. 67). Moreover, while praising the significance of Bishop's accomplishment, some devotees of Brouwer's theory have questioned the adequacy of the analysis of the continuum that emerges from Bishop's approach. In particular, they are concerned that in Bishop's theory, like Markov's before it, the continuum of real numbers is restricted to those real numbers introduced by lawlike Cauchy sequences. For example, in his monograph devoted to Brouwer's theory, Mark van Atten remarks:

> One may, like Markov and Bishop, settle for just the lawlike sequences … but while practical, that also amounts to ducking the issue of how to model the full continuum. Brouwer's achievement is to have found a way to analyze the continuum that does not let it fall apart into discrete elements … and it is constructive to boot. (2004, p. 33)

PREDICATIVE THEORIES

Between classical mathematics, in which arbitrary sets are embraced, and Bishop's constructive mathematics, in which only algorithmically constructed objects are permissible, there is an intermediate approach called *predicativism*, in which only definable sets are considered, and in which quantifiers over sets are interpreted as ranging only over sets that have previously been defined. Although having its roots in Russell's and Poincaré's attempts to lay the blame for the paradoxes of set theory on definitions that define entities in terms of classes to which they belong—so-called *impredicative* definitions—it was Weyl, in his monograph *Das Kontinuum* (1918/1994), who first undertook the development of a theory of the arithmetic continuum and of analysis on it in a predicatively acceptable fashion.

Central to Weyl's critique of the classical theory is its dependence on the proposition that every nonempty set of real numbers that is bounded above has a least upper bound, the definition of the least upper bound of a set being inextricably impredicative. Weyl proposed overcoming this by employing the predicatively sanctioned proposition: Every nonempty sequence of reals having an upper bound has a least upper bound. Using this idea, Weyl constructed a restricted set of real numbers containing all reals that are expressible as Dedekind cuts definable in his system. Although the set of standard real numbers not definable in Weyl's system is everywhere dense, Weyl showed that on the basis of his continuum most, if not all, of the nineteenth-century analysis of piece-wise continuous functions can be carried out predicatively. On the other hand, as Weyl conceded, substantial and significant portions of modern analysis are not obtainable in his system including "the more far-reaching integration- and measure theories of Riemann, Darboux, Cantor, Jordan, Lebesque and Carathéodory" (Weyl 1918/1994, p. 86).

In the years following the publication of *Das Kontinuum* Weyl abandoned his own approach in favor of Brouwer's intuitionistic framework. Soon thereafter, however, he returned to the standard mathematical fold and distanced himself from Brouwer's school and from foundations work more generally. In the ensuing years, Weyl's predicative theory lay largely dormant until the 1960s, when a number of authors including, most prominently, Feferman undertook a formalization and systematic analysis of Weyl's system as well as the development of a variety of predicative extensions thereof (compare Feferman 1964, 1988/1998, 1993/1998). Unlike Weyl, who worried about the purported *vicious circles* associated with impredicative definitions, Feferman was motivated in part by the concern that the unbridled use of such definitions presupposed a strong form of platonic realism regarding sets, a view he found philosophically objectionable; he was also interested in providing an analysis of predicativity itself, as well as with the purely logical question of the extent to which analysis can be carried out by predicative means. One of Feferman's extensions, called W in honor of Weyl, has been proven to be sufficiently strong to permit the reconstruction of almost all of classical analysis as well as important portions of modern analysis that are not obtainable in Weyl's original system. Feferman maintains that:

> While there are clearly parts of theoretical analysis that cannot be carried out in W because they make essential use of the l.u.b. axiom applied to sets rather than sequences, or because they make essential use of transfinite ordinals or cardinals, or because they deal with nonseparable spaces, *the working hypothesis that all of scientifically applicable analysis can be developed in W has been verified in its core parts.* What remains to be done is to examine results closer to the margin to see whether this hypothesis indeed holds in full generality. (1993/1998, p. 294)

INFINITESIMALIST APPROACHES

Following Emil Artin (1898–1962) and Otto Schreier (1901–1929), an ordered field K may be said to be *real-closed* if it admits no extension to a more inclusive ordered field that results from supplementing K with solutions to polynomial equations with coefficients in K (1926/1965). Intuitively speaking, real-closed ordered fields are precisely those ordered fields having no holes that can be filled by algebraic means alone. Tarski demonstrated that real-closed ordered fields are precisely the ordered fields that are first-order indistinguishable from $\mathbb{R}$ or, to put this another way, they are precisely the ordered fields that satisfy the elementary (i.e., first-order) content of the Dedekind continuity axiom (1939/1986, 1948/1986). For this reason they are called *elementary continua.* While $\mathbb{R}$ is the best-known elementary continuum, it is hardly the only one.

Some elementary continua, like $\mathbb{R}$, are Archimedean, though most are non-Archimedean; and among the latter many are extensions of $\mathbb{R}$. In the early 1960s Robinson (1961, 1966) made the momentous discovery that among the real-closed extensions of the reals there are number systems that can provide the basis for a consistent and entirely satisfactory nonstandard approach to analysis based on infinitesimals. Robinson motivated his work with the following words:

> It is our main purpose to show that these models [i.e. number systems] provide a natural approach to the age old problem of producing a calculus involving infinitesimal (infinitely small) and infinitely large quantities. As is well known, the use of infinitesimals, strongly advocated by Leibnitz and unhesitatingly accepted by Euler fell into disrepute after the advent of Cauchy's methods which put Mathematical Analysis on a firm foundation. Accepting Cauchy's standards of rigor, later figures in the domain of nonarchimedean quantities concerned themselves only with small fragments of the edifice of Mathematical Analysis. We men-

> tion only du Bois-Reymond's Calculus of Infinites [1875] and Hahn's work on nonarchimedean fields [1907] which in turn were followed by the theories of Artin-Schreier [1926] and, returning to analysis, of Hewitt [1948] and Erdös, Gillman and Henriksen [1955]. Finally, a recent and rather successful effort at developing a calculus of infinitesimals is due to Schmieden and Laugwitz [1958] whose number system consists of infinite sequences of rational numbers. The drawback of this system is that it includes zero-divisors and that it is only partially ordered. In consequence, many classical results of the Differential and Integral calculus have to be modified to meet the changed circumstance. (1961/1979, p. 4)

Being elementary continua, Robinson's number systems do not have the just-cited drawbacks of the number system of Schmieden and Laugwitz. By analogy with Thoralf Skolem's (1934) *nonstandard model of arithmetic*, a number system from which Robinson drew inspiration, Robinson called his totally ordered number systems *nonstandard models of analysis*. These number systems, which are often called *hyperreal number systems* (Keisler 1976, 1994), may be characterized as follows: Let $\langle \mathbb{R}, S: S \in \mathfrak{F} \rangle$ be a relational structure where $\mathfrak{F}$ is the set of all finitary relations defined on $\mathbb{R}$ (including all functions). Furthermore, let $^*\mathbb{R}$ be a proper extension of $\mathbb{R}$ and for each n-ary relation $S \in \mathfrak{F}$ let $^*S$ be an n-ary relation on $^*\mathbb{R}$ that is an extension of S. The structure $\langle ^*\mathbb{R}, \mathbb{R}, ^*S{:}S \in \mathfrak{F} \rangle$ is said to be a hyperreal number system if it satisfies the *Transfer Principle*: Every n-tuple of real numbers satisfies the same first-order formulas in $\langle \mathbb{R}, S{:}S \in \mathfrak{F} \rangle$ as it satisfies in $\langle ^*\mathbb{R}, \mathbb{R}, ^*S{:}S \in \mathfrak{F} \rangle$.

The existence of hyperreal number systems is a consequence of the compactness theorem of first-order logic and there are a number of algebraic techniques that can be employed to construct such a system. One commonly used technique is the *ultapower* construction (Keisler 1976, pp. 48–57; Goldblatt 1998, chapter 3), though not all hyperreal number systems can be obtained this way. By results of H. Jerome Keisler (1963; 1976, pp. 58–59), however, every hyperreal number system must be (isomorphic to) a *limit ultapower*.

Using the transfer principle, one can develop satisfactory nonstandard conceptions and treatments of all of the basic concepts and theorems of the calculus including those from the theories of integration, differentiation, and continuity to name only a few (compare Keisler 1986, Goldblatt 1998, Loeb 2000). For example, it follows from the transfer principle that a real-valued function f is continuous at $a \in \mathbb{R}$ iff $^*f(x)$ is infinitesimally close to $^*f(a)$ whenever x is infinitesimally close to a, for all $x \in {}^*\mathbb{R}$. On the basis of this result one may prove various classical properties governing the continuity of real-valued functions including the intermediate and extreme value theorems (Goldblatt 1998, pp. 79–80). It should be emphasized, however, that Robinson's discoveries do not provide vindication of the Leibnizian formalism or of the seventeenth- and eighteenth-century preanalytic formalisms more generally. For example, whereas Leibniz conceived of differentiation and integration in terms of ratios of and infinite sums of infinitesimals, respectively, for Robinson they are real numbers that are infinitesimally close to such ratios and sums. On the other hand, nonstandard analysis not only demonstrates that the branch of mathematics erected for the study of continuously varying magnitude can be fully developed using infinitely large and infinitely small numbers as Leibniz and his followers had envisioned but it also provides one with an intuitively satisfying alternative to the standard picture of a continuum and of continuous phenomena more generally that is mathematically adequate and logically sound relative to classical mathematics.

Modern analysis, however, goes far beyond the traditional province of the calculus, dealing with arbitrary sets of reals, sets of sets of reals, sets of functions from sets of reals to sets of reals, and the like. Importantly, nonstandard analysis is entirely applicable to this expanded arena as well. However, the methods of superstructures (Robinson 1966) and internal set theory (Nelson 1977) that are most usually employed for this purpose are of little relevance here (compare Chang and Keisler 1990, §4.4; Robert 1988).

Unlike $\mathbb{R}$, the structures that may play the role of $^*\mathbb{R}$ in a hyperreal number system are far from being unique up to isomorphism. From a purely mathematical point of view this causes no difficulty and from the standpoint of varying applications can even be advantageous (compare Keisler 1994, p. 229). On the other hand, if one takes $^*\mathbb{R}$ to be a model of *the* continuous straight line of geometry—something practitioners of nonstandard analysis tend not to do—the absence of uniqueness is a bit disconcerting. Still, as several nonstandard analysts including Tom Lindstrøm (1988, p. 82) and Keisler (1994, p. 229) emphasize, even $\mathbb{R}$ is not as unique as one would like to think since its uniqueness up to isomorphism is in fact relative to the underlying set theory. In particular, by retaining the construction of $\mathbb{R}$ and supplementing the set theory with additional axioms, one can change the second-order theory of the real line. This leads Keisler (1994) to suggest that not only is ZFC not the appropriate underlying set theory for the hyperreal number system but also that set theory might have developed differently had it been developed with the hyperreal numbers rather than the real numbers in mind. According to Keisler, an appropriate set theory "should have the power set operation to insure the unique existence of the real number system, and another operation which insures the unique existence of the pair consisting of the real and hyperreal number systems" (p. 230).

Consistent with the previous observation, one type of axiom that is used to secure categoricity is a saturation axiom (Keisler 1976, pp. 57–60). As the name suggests, saturation axioms ensure that the line is extremely rich. A hyperreal number system $\langle {}^*\mathbb{R}, \mathbb{R}, {}^*S: S \in \mathfrak{F} \rangle$ is said to be *κ-saturated* if any set of formulas with constants from $^*\mathbb{R}$ of power less than κ is satisfiable whenever it is finitely satisfiable. If κ is the power of $^*\mathbb{R}$, the hyperreal number system is said to be *saturated.* Although there is a wide range of hyperreal number systems in ZFC that are saturated to varying degrees of power less than the power of $^*\mathbb{R}$, saturated hyperreal number systems do not exist in ZFC. In virtue of classical results from the theory of saturated models, however, there is (up to isomorphism) a unique saturated hyperreal number system of power κ whenever $\kappa > 2^{\aleph_0}$ and either κ is (strongly) inaccessible or the generalized continuum hypothesis (GCH) holds at κ (i.e., $\kappa = \aleph_{\alpha+1} = 2^{\aleph_\alpha}$ for some α). So, for example, by supplementing ZFC with the assumption of the existence of an uncountable inaccessible cardinal, one can obtain uniqueness (up to isomorphism) by limiting attention to saturated hyperreal lines having the least such power (Keisler 1976, p. 60).

However, as Ehrlich (2002, 2004) emphasizes, perhaps the most remarkable of all elementary continua that may play the role of $^*\mathbb{R}$ in a hyperreal number system (and bring categoricity to the hyperreal line to boot) is Conway's ordered field of *surreal numbers* (1976/2001), a system that was not created with nonstandard analysis in mind. This would correspond (to within isomorphism) of adopting a hyperreal number system that is the union of an elementary chain of ω_α-saturated hyperreal number systems where α ranges over the class *On* of all ordinals. Though such models do not exist in ZFC, they can be suitably characterized and shown to exist (up to isomorphism) in von Neumann–Bernays–Gödel (NBG) set theory with the axiom of global choice (Ehrlich 1989). Since NBG is a conservative extension of ZFC, its sets have the same properties as those of standard set theory (compare Fraenkel, Bar-Hillel, and Levy 1973). The idea of employing such a hyperreal number system to establish the categoricity of the hyperreal line appears to be due (at least implicitly) to Keisler (1976, p. 59; 1994, p. 233; theorem 3 of addendum to Ehrlich 1989), but guided by reasons of simplicity and convenience he chooses the least uncountable inaccessible cardinal approach instead.

The ordered field of surreal numbers, which Conway calls *No*, is so remarkably inclusive that, subject to the proviso that numbers—construed here as members of ordered (number) fields—be individually definable in terms of sets of NBG, it may be said to contain "All Numbers Great and Small." In this respect, *No* bears much the same relation to ordered fields as the system of real numbers bears to Archimedean ordered fields. Ehrlich (1987, 1989a, 1992, 2002) suggests that whereas the real number system may be regarded as an *arithmetic continuum modulo the Archimedean axiom*, the system of surreal numbers may be regarded as a sort of *absolute arithmetic continuum modulo NBG.* To lend credence to this thesis, Ehrlich provides a variety of categorical axiomatizations of $\mathbb{R}$ making use of novel continuity axioms (that are equivalent to any of the familiar continuity axioms) with axioms for Archimedean ordered fields (or Archimedean real-closed ordered fields) and shows that by simply deleting the Archimedean axiom one obtains categorical axiomatizations of *No* (Ehrlich 1992, theorems 1, 4, and 6). Ehrlich also introduces a natural generalization of Dedekind's conception of a gap, called a *set-gap*, and provides further evidence for the thesis by showing that whereas $\mathbb{R}$ is (up to isomorphism) the unique elementary continuum having no set-gaps that satisfies the Archimedean condition, *No* is (up to isomorphism) the unique elementary continuum having no set-gaps that satisfies the *On*-Archimedean condition, the latter being a natural generalization of the Archimedean condition that is appropriate for *No* (Ehrlich 1992, Lemma 1, Theorem 7; 2001, pp. 1255–1256). Critical to the proof of the latter result is Ehrlich's (1988, 1989, 2001) further characterization of *No* (up to isomorphism) as the unique elementary continuum such that for all subsets *X* and *Y* of the field where every member of *X* precedes every member of *Y* there is a member of the field lying strictly between those of *X* and those of *Y*. Intuitively, this characterizes *No* (up to isomorphism) as the unique ordered field having neither algebraic limitations nor order-theoretic limitations that are definable in terms of sets of standard set theory.

Besides its distinguished structure as an ordered field, *No* has a rich hierarchical structure that emerges from the recursive clauses in terms of which it is defined. This algebraico-tree-theoretic structure, or *simplicity hierarchy*, as Ehrlich (1994, 2001) calls it, depends on *No*'s structure as a lexicographically ordered binary tree and arises from the fact that the sums and products of any two members of the tree are the simplest possible elements of the tree consistent with *No*'s structure as an ordered group and an ordered field, respectively, it being understood that x is *simpler than* y just in case x is a predecessor of y in the tree. Among the remarkable consequences of this algebraico-tree-theoretic structure is that much as the surreal numbers emerge from the empty set of surreal numbers by a transfinite recursion that yields chains of increasingly less and less simpler numbers, the recursive process of defining *No*'s arithmetic in turn gives rise to chains of increasingly richer and richer numbers systems with the result that an isomorphic copy of every elementary continuum emerges in *No* as the union of a chain of elementary continua each of which is an initial subtree of *No* (Ehrlich 2001).

Conway (1976/2001) shows that besides the reals *No* contains a natural isomorphic copy of Cantor's ordinals, and hence, by virtue of the axiom of choice, the cardinals as well (Ehrlich 2001, pp. 1253–1256). Ehrlich (1988, 2001, 2002, 2004) notes that *No* also provides a natural setting for the non-Cantorian theories of the infinite (and infinitesimal) pioneered by Veronese, Levi-Civita, Hilbert, and Hahn in connection with their work on non-Archimedean-ordered algebraic and geometric systems and by du Bois-Reymond, Stolz, G. H. Hardy (1877–1947), and Felix Hausdorff (1868–1942) in connection with their work on the rate of growth of real functions (compare Ehrlich 1994, 1995, 2005; Fisher 1981). This, together with the observation about the relationship between *No* and hyperreal number systems, leads Ehrlich (2002, 2004) to observe that over and above providing a panorama of the entire set-theoretic spectrum of numbers great and small (modulo NBG), the purported absolute arithmetic continuum provides a unifying framework for many of the most important totally ordered systems of finite, infinite, and infinitesimal numbers that have played and continue to play prominent roles in mathematics since the days of Cantor and Dedekind.

Within a decade of the development of nonstandard analysis, Lawvere proposed a profound and novel approach to differential geometry based on infinitesimals. Unlike Robinson, who was stimulated by Leibniz's idea that the properties of infinitesimals should reflect the properties of the reals, Lawvere's ideas more closely mirror the heuristic ideas of geometers who envisioned a vector tangent to a surface at a point as a tiny arc of a curve having the vector tangent to it. Building on Lawvere's ideas, Kock (1981) presents a systematic treatment of the theory under the rubric *synthetic differential geometry* (SDG).

Unlike the nonzero infinitesimals employed in nonstandard analysis, the nonzero infinitesimal elements of SDG are *nilpotent*, that is, each such infinitesimal d satisfies the condition $d^2 = 0$. Nilpotent infinitesimals are not *invertible* (in the sense that they have no multiplicative inverses) and as such a line in SDG in not modeled by a field or a portion thereof. Rather, in SDG a line is modeled by a ring $\Re$ containing a subset $D = \{d \in \Re : d^2 = 0\}$ which satisfies the

Kock-Lawvere axiom: For every mapping $f: D \rightarrow \Re$, there is precisely one $b \in \Re$, such that for all $d \in D, f(d) = f(0) + d \cdot b$.

Geometrically speaking, the Kock-Lawvere axiom asserts that the graph of every function $f: D \rightarrow \Re$ is a piece of the unique straight line through $(0, f(0))$ with slope b. It is a consequence of this assumption that in SDG a tangent vector to a curve C at a point p is a nondegenerate infinitesimal line segment around p coincident with C.

Another consequence of the Kock-Lawvere axiom is that in SDG, unlike in Euclidean geometry, there are pairs of points in the plane that are connected by more than one straight line. In this regard, SDG resembles Johannes Hjelmslev's (1873–1950) *natural geometry* (compare Kock 2003), a geometry that was designed to mirror real (as opposed to ideal) sense experience and that also employs nilpotent infinitesimals. However, unlike in natural geometry, in SDG there are pairs of points in a plane that are not connected by any line at all. This arises in part from the fact that whereas the nilpotent infinitesimals in natural geometry have "a quantitative (linear ordered) character," those employed in SDG do not (Kock 2003, pp. 226–228). For an axiomatization of "Euclidean Geometry with Infinitesimals" inspired by SDG, see Succi Cruciani (1989).

A space X in SDG is said to be *indecomposable* if no proper nonempty part U of X is *detachable* in the sense that there is a part V such that $U \cup V = X$ where $U \cap V = \emptyset$. There are models of SDG in which a classical space $\mathbb{R}^n$ has a counterpart X that is indecomposable if X is *connected*. John Bell takes this to imply that "the connected continua of SDG are *true* continua in something like the Anaxagoran sense" (1995, p. 56). In this respect, they are also reminiscent of the unsplittable continuum of Brouwer; however, the similarity is not perfect and varies depending on the axioms adopted for SDG (Bell 2001).

Another respect in which SDG is similar to Brouwer's theory is the failure of the intermediate value theorem in its underlying theory of analysis. In fact, in SDG, unlike in Brouwer's system, the theorem even fails for some polynomials (Moerdijk and Reyes 1991, pp. 317–318), a failure that runs contrary to the thinking of Leibniz and Euler let alone Bolzano, Cauchy, and Weierstrass. Accordingly, while SDG may provide a viable alternative for differential geometry, its underlying analysis may not be as well suited to provide a natural alternative for classical analysis, at least not if it hopes to mirror the latter's most central ideas regarding continuity.

Unlike nonstandard analysis, which is developed in a set-theoretic setting, SDG is developed in a category-theoretic framework. Moreover, whereas the underlying logic employed in nonstandard analysis is classical logic, in SDG the underlying logic is intuitionistic logic. In SDG every function $f{:}\mathfrak{R}\rightarrow\mathfrak{R}$ is differentiable and, hence, infinitely differentiable (i.e. *smooth*) as well as continuous in the sense that it sends neighboring points to neighboring points. It is sometimes maintained (compare Bell 1995, p. 56) that it is the ubiquitous nature of continuity within SDG that forces the change from classical to intuitionistic logic. This, however, is apt to be misleading since it is possible to develop a theory of continua in which the continuity of functions from the continuum to the continuum is likewise ubiquitous though the underlying logic is classical (compare the so-called Cauchy continuum due to Schmieden and Laugwitz [1958; Laugwitz 2001, p. 134]). Rather, it is the Kock-Lawvere axiom that underlies the incompatibility of SDG with classical logic (compare Lavendhomme 1996, pp. 2–5). It is therefore interesting to note that Paolo Giordano (2001), by suitably modifying the axiom, presents a variation of SDG based on nilpotent infinitesimals in which the underlying logic is entirely classical, and he observes that the nilpotent infinitesimals could be supplemented with invertible infinitesimals as well. Earlier, Ieke Moerdijk and Gonzalo E. Reyes (1991), while retaining the underlying intuitionistic logic, also introduced an alternative approach in which invertible as well as nilpotent infinitesimals are employed. The work of Moerdijk, Reyes, and Giordano, much like the pioneering work of Lawvere and Kock, provides still other models of mathematical continua.

CONCLUDING REMARKS

"*Bridging the gap between the domains of discreteness and of continuity*, or between arithmetic and geometry, is a central, presumably even *the* central, problem of the foundations of mathematics." So write Fraenkel, Yehoshua Bar-Hillel, and Azriel Levy in their mathematico-philosophical classic *Foundations of Set Theory* (1973, p. 212). Cantor and Dedekind of course believed they had bridged the gap with the creation of their arithmetico-set theoretic continuum of real numbers, and it remains a well-entrenched tenet of standard mathematical philosophy that indeed they had. At the same time, Cantor was overly sanguine when in 1883 he seemed to suggest, or at least implied, that his theory of the continuum, unlike that of the ancients, had "been thought out … with the clarity and completeness … required to exclude the possibility of different opinions among [its] posterity" (Cantor 1883/1996, p. 903). Indeed, while Cantor and Dedekind had succeeded in replacing the vague ancient conception with a clear and complete arithmetico-set-theoretic conception, a conception that was adequate for the needs of analysis, differential geometry, and the empirical sciences, they did not, nor could not, free their theory of its logical, theoretical, and philosophical presuppositions, nor could they preclude the possibility that other adequate conceptual schemes, each self-consistent, could be devised offering alternative visions of the continuum.

However, it was critiques of the former that gave rise to some of its competitors and the realization of the logical possibility of the latter that gave rise to others. To some extent, the architects of each of its competitors were motivated by the belief, or at least the hope, that their respective theories are or with time would be adequate for the needs of analysis (or differential geometry), though in the cases of the constructivist and predicativist architects *analysis* was equated with *legitimate analysis* constructively and predicatively construed. Outside of the overarching question of the historical needs of analysis, the question of whether legitimate analysis thus understood is adequate for the needs of the empirical sciences and the physical sciences, in particular, is the subject of dispute (compare Fletcher 2002; Hellman 1993, 1993a, 1997, 1998; Bridges 1995; Billinge 2000; Bridges and Ishihara 2001; Feferman 1988/1998, postscript). Nonstandard analysis has bypassed all of these questions since from the standpoint of the standard domain it is as strong as or even stronger than standard analysis depending on what one assumes (Henson and Keisler 1986). Moreover, like their late nineteenth- and early twentieth-century non-Archimedean geometric forerunners, nonstandard analysis and the infinitesimalist approaches more generally have drawn attention to the possibility of physical continua whose logical cogency let alone physical possibility had long been in doubt. Whether empirical science will require such a theory, as some already contend (compare Fenstad 1987, 1988) and others, following Veronese (compare 1909/1994, p. 180), will not rule out, only time will tell. Nevertheless, while showing little sign of displacing the standard theory, the constructivist, predicativist, and infinitesimalist alternatives have performed, and continue to perform, important logical and philosophical service. Nonstandard analysis has also had real success in shedding important light on and establishing significant new results in various areas of analysis, theoretical physics, and economics (compare Albeverio, Luxemburg, and Wolff 1995; Arkeryd, Cutland, and Henson 1997; Loeb and Wolff 2000). However, whether nonstandard analysis or any of the other nonstandard theories canvassed earlier, together with its corresponding theory of the continuum, will eventually assume the status of the standard theory (or even stand alongside the standard theory as a co-standard theory) remains to be seen.

See also Infinity in Mathematics and Logic.

Bibliography

ANCIENT AND MEDIEVAL PHILOSOPHICAL AND COSMOLOGICAL THEORIES

Aristotle. *The Complete Works of Aristotle: The Revised Oxford Translation*, edited by Jonathan Barnes. Princeton, NJ: Princeton University Press, 1984.

Furley, David. J. *Two Studies in the Greek Atomists*. Princeton, NJ: Princeton University Press, 1967.

Kirk, Geoffrey Stephen; John Earle Raven, and Malcolm Schofield. *The Presocratic Philosophers: A Critical History with a Selection of Texts*. 2nd ed. Cambridge, U.K.: Cambridge University Press, 1983.

Kretzmann, Norman, ed. *Infinity and Continuity in Ancient and Medieval Thought*. Ithaca, NY: Cornell University Press, 1982.

Murdoch, John. "Infinity and Continuity." In *The Cambridge History of Later Medieval Philosophy*, edited by Norman Kretzmann, Anthony Kenny, and Jan Pinborg. New York: Cambridge University Press, 1982.

Pyle, Andrew. *Atomism and Its Critics: From Democritus to Newton*. Bristol, U.K.: Thoemme Press, 1995.

Sambursky, Shmuel. *Physics of the Stoics*. London: Routledge and Kegan Paul, 1959.

Sorabji, Richard. *Time, Creation, and the Continuum: Theories in Antiquity and the Early Middle Ages*. Ithaca, NY: Cornell University Press, 1983.

White, Michael J. *The Continuous and the Discrete: Ancient Physical Theories from a Contemporary Perspective*. Oxford, U.K.: Clarendon Press, 1992.

ANCIENT MATHEMATICAL THEORIES

Fowler, David. *The Mathematics of Plato's Academy*. 2nd ed. Oxford, U.K.: Clarendon Press, 1999.

Heath, Sir Thomas L., ed. *The Thirteen Books of Euclid's Elements: Translated from the Text of Heiberg*, Vols. 1–3. New York: Dover, 1956.

Knorr, Wilbur R. *The Ancient Tradition of Geometric Problems*. Boston: Birkhäuser, 1986.

Knorr, Wilbur R. "Archimedes and the Pre-Euclidean Proportion Theory." *Archives Internationales d'Histore des Sciences* 28 (1978): 183–244.

Knorr, Wilbur R. *The Evolution of the Euclidean Elements: A Study of the Theory of Incommensurable Magnitudes and Its Significance for Early Greek Geometry*. Dordrecht, Netherlands: D. Reidel, 1975.

Thiele, Rüdiger. "Antiquity." In *A History of Analysis*, edited by Hans Jahnke. Providence, RI: American Mathematical Society, 2003.

THE EARLY MODERN THEORY OF REAL NUMBERS

Klein, Jacob. *Greek Mathematical Thought and the Origin of Algebra*. Translated by Eva Brann. Cambridge, MA: MIT Press, 1968.

Newton, Isaac. "Universal Arithmetik." In *The Mathematical Works of Isaac Newton*. Vol. 2, edited by Derrk T. Whiteside. New York: Johnson Reprint Corporation, 1967.

Pycior, Helena. *Symbols, Impossible Numbers, and Geometric Entanglements*. New York: Cambridge University Press,1997.

Stevin, Simon. "Arithmetique." In *The Principal Works of Simon Stevin*, Volume 2B, edited by D. J. Struik. Amsterdam, Netherlands: C. V. Swets and Zeitlinger, 1958.

Strong, Edward W. *Procedures and Metaphysics: A Study in the Philosophy of Mathematical-Physical Science in the Sixteenth and Seventeenth Centuries*. Merrick, NY: Richwood Publishing Co., 1976.

HISTORY OF THE CALCULUS

Baron, Margret. *The Origin of the Infinitesimal Calculus*. New York: Oxford University Press, 1969.

Berkeley, George. *The Analyst* (1734). *De Motu and The Analyst: A Modern Edition with Introductions and Commentary by Douglas M. Josseph*. Dordrecht, Netherlands: Kluwer Academic, 1992. *The Analyst* was originally published in 1734.

Boyer, Carl. *The Concepts of the Calculus and Its Conceptual Development*. New York: Dover, 1959.

Edwards, C. H., Jr. *The Historical Development of the Calculus*. New York: Springer-Verlag, 1979.

Jahnke, Hans Niels, ed. *A History of Analysis*. Providence, RI: American Mathematical Society, 2003.

LEIBNIZ'S VIEWS

Bertoloni-Meli, Domenico. *Equivalence and Priority: Newton versus Leibniz*. Oxford, U.K.: Clarendon Press, 1993.

Bos, Henk J. M. "Differentials, Higher-Order Differentials, and the Derivative in the Leibnizian Calculus." *Archive for History of Exact Sciences* 14 (1974): 1–90.

Cassirer, Ernst. *Leibniz' Systeme in seinen wissenschaftlichen Grundlagen*. Marburg, Germany: N. G. Elwert, 1902.

Leibniz, Gottfried Wilhelm. *The Labyrinth of the Continuum: Writings on the Continuum Problem, 1672–1686*. Translated by Richard T. W. Arthur. New Haven, CT: Yale University Press, 2001.

Leibniz, Gottfried Wilhelm. "Specimen geometriae luciferae." (c. 1695). In *Leibniz Mathematische Schriften*. Vol. 7, edited by C. I. Gerhardt, 260–298. Hildesheim, Germany: G. Olms, 1962.

NEWTON VIEWS

Bertoloni-Meli, Domenico. *Equivalence and Priority: Newton versus Leibniz.* Oxford, U.K.: Clarendon Press, 1993.

Guicciardini, Niccolò. "Newton's Method and Leibniz's Calculus." In *A History of Analysis*, edited by Hans Niels Jahnke. Providence: American Mathematical Society, 2003.

Kitcher, Philip. "Fluxions, Limits, and Infinite Littleness." *Isis* 64 (221) (1973): 33–49.

GENERAL SET THEORY

Fraenkel, Abraham A., Yehoshua Bar-Hillel, and Azriel Levy. *Foundations of Set Theory*. 2nd ed. Amsterdam, Netherlands: North-Holland, 1973.

Levy, Azriel. *Basic Set Theory*. Berlin: Springer-Verlag, 1979.

THE CANTOR-DEDEKIND THEORY OF THE CONTINUUM

Cantor, Georg. "Grundlagen einer allgemeinen Mannigfaltigkeitslehre: Ein mathematischphilosophischer Versuch in der Lehre des Unendlichen" (1883). Translated by William B. Ewald as "Foundations of a General Theory of Manifolds: A Mathematico-Philosophical Investigation into the Theory of the Infinite." In *From Kant to Hilbert: A Source Book in the Foundations of Mathematics*. Vol. 2, edited by William B. Ewald. Oxford, U.K.: Clarendon Press, 1996.

Cantor, Georg. "Über die Ausdehnung eines Satzes der Theorie der trigonometrischen Reihen" (1872). In *Georg Cantor Gesammelte Abhandlungen mathematischen und philosophischen Inhalts*, edited by Ernest Zermelo. Berlin: J. Springer, 1932.

Dedekind, Richard. "Stetigkeit und irrationale Zahlen" (1872). Translated by W. W. Beman as "Continuity and Irrational Numbers." In *From Kant to Hilbert: A Source Book in the Foundations of Mathematics*. Vol. 2, edited by William B. Ewald (Oxford, U.K.: Clarendon Press, 1996).

Epple, Moritz. "The End of the Science of Quantity: Foundations of Analysis, 1860–1910." In *A History of Analysis*, edited by Hans Niels Jahnke. Providence, RI: American Mathematical Society, 2003.

Ferreirós, José. *Labyrinth of Thought: A History of Set Theory and Its Role in Modern Mathematics.* Berlin: Birkhäuser Verlag, 1999.

Hilbert, David. *Foundations of Geometry* (1899). 10th ed. Translated by Leo Unger. LaSalle, IL: Open Court, 1971.

Hilbert, David. *Grundlagen der Geometrie*. Leipzig, Germany: Teubner, 1899.

Huntington, Edward V. *The Continuum and Other Types of Serial Order: With an Introduction to Cantor's Transfinite Numbers*. 2nd ed. Cambridge, MA: Harvard University Press, 1917.

Poincaré, Henri. *Science and Hypothesis*. In *The Foundations of Science*. Translated by George Bruce Halsted. New York: Science Press, 1913. "Mathematical Magnitude and Experience" is a translation of a reprinting in modified form of "Le Continu Mathématique," *Revue de Métaphysique et de Morale* (1893).

Russell, Bertrand. *The Principles of Mathematics*. Cambridge, U.K.: Cambridge University Press, 1903.

THE CONTINUUM HYPOTHESIS

Cohen, Paul. "Conversation with Paul Cohen." In *More Mathematical People: Contemporary Conversations*, edited by Donald J. Albers, Gerald L. Alexanderson, and Constance Reid, 43–58. Boston: Harcourt, Brace, Jovanovich, 1990.

Cohen, Paul. "Independence of the Continuum Hypothesis." *Proceedings of the National Academy of Sciences* 50 (1963): 1143–1148; 51 (1964): 105–110.

Dales, H. G., and G. Oliveri. *Truth in Mathematics*. Oxford, U.K.: Clarendon Press, 1998.

Feferman, Solomon et al. "Does Mathematics Need New Axioms?" *Bulletin of Symbolic Logic* 6 (4) (2000): 401–446.

Gödel, Kurt. *The Consistency of the Continuum Hypothesis*. Princeton, NJ: Princeton University Press, 1940.

Gödel, Kurt. "What Is Cantor's Continuum Problem?" (1947). In *Philosophy of Mathematics: Selected Readings*. 2nd ed., edited by Paul Benacerraf and Hilary Putnam. New York: Cambridge University Press, 1983.

Kanamori, Akihiro. *The Higher Infinite*. 2nd ed. Berlin: Springer-Verlag, 2003.

Maddy, Penelope. *Naturalism in Mathematics*. Oxford, U.K.: Clarendon Press, 1997.

Woodin, W. Hugh. "The Continuum Hypothesis." *Notices of the American Mathematical Society* 48 (6) (2001): 567–576; (7) (2001): 681–690; 49 (1) (2002): 46.

Woodin, W. Hugh. "Set Theory after Russell: The Journey Back to Eden." In *De Gruyter Series in Logic and Its Applications (Number 6)*, edited by Godehard Link. Berlin: Walter de Gruyter, 2004.

CONSTRUCTIVIST APPROACHES: GENERAL BACKGROUND

Beeson, Michael J. *Foundations of Constructive Mathematics: Metamathematical Studies*. Berlin: Springer-Verlag, 1985.

Bridges, Douglas, and Fred Richman. *Varieties of Constructive Mathematics*. New York: Cambridge University Press, 1987.

Troelstra, A. S., and D. van Dalen. *Constructivism in Mathematics: An Introduction*. Amsterdam, Netherlands: North-Holland, 1988.

BROUWER'S INTUITIONISTIC APPROACH

Atten, Mark van. *On Brouwer*. Belmont, CA: Wadsworth, 2004.

Atten, Mark van, and Dirk van Dalen. "Arguments for the Continuity Principle." *Bulletin of Symbolic Logic* 8 (3) (2002): 329–347.

Brouwer, L. E. J., and Walter P. van Stigt. "Part I: L. E. J. Brouwer." In *From Brouwer to Hilbert: The Debate on the Foundations of Mathematics in the 1920s*, edited by Paolo Mancosu. New York: Oxford University Press, 1998.

Dalen, Dirk van, ed. *Brower's Cambridge Lectures on Intuitionism*. New York: Cambridge University Press, 1981.

Dummett, Michael. *Elements of Intuitionism*. 2nd ed. Oxford, U.K.: Clarendon Press, 2000.

Fraenkel, Abraham A., Yehoshua Bar-Hillel, and Azriel Levy. *Foundations of Set Theory*. 2nd ed. Amsterdam, Netherlands: North-Holland, 1973.

Heyting, Arend. *Intuitionism: An Introduction*. 3rd rev. ed. Amsterdam: North-Holland, 1971.

Kushner, Boris. "On Brouwerian Bar Induction." In *Reuniting the Antipodes: Constructive and Nonstandard Views of the Continuum*, edited by Peter Schuster, Ulrich Berger, and Horst Osswald. Dordrecht, Netherlands: Kluwer Academic, 2001.

McCarthy, David. "Intuitionism in Mathematics." In *The Oxford Handbook of Philosophy of Mathematics and Logic*, edited by Stewart Shapiro. New York: Oxford University Press, 2005.

Posy, Carl. "Intuitionism and Philosophy." In *The Oxford Handbook of Philosophy of Mathematics and Logic*, edited by Stewart Shapiro. New York: Oxford University Press, 2005.

Stigt, Walter P. van. *Brouwer's Intuitionism*. Amsterdam, Netherlands: North-Holland, 1990.

Troelstra, A. S. "On the Origin and Development of Brouwer's Concept of Choice Sequence." In *The L.E.J. Brouwer Centenary Symposium*, edited by A. S. Troelstra and Dirk van Dalen. Amsterdam, Netherlands: North-Holland, 1982.

Veldman, Wim. "Understanding and Using Brouwer's Continuity Principle." In *Reuniting the Antipodes: Constructive and Nonstandard Views of the Continuum*, edited by Peter Schuster, Ulrich Berger, and Horst Osswald. Dordrecht, Netherlands: Kluwer Academic, 2001.

BISHOP'S CONSTRUCTIVE APPROACH

Bishop, Errett. *Foundations of Constructive Analysis*. New York: McGraw-Hill, 1967.

Bishop, Errett, and Douglas Bridges. *Constructive Analysis*. New York: Springer-Verlag, 1985.

Bridges, Douglas. "A Constructive Look at the Real Number Line." In *Real Numbers, Generalizations of the Reals, and Theories of Continua*, edited by Philip Ehrlich. Dordrecht, Netherlands: Kluwer Academic, 1994.

Bridges, Douglas. "Constructive Mathematics: A Foundation for Computable Analysis." *Theoretical Computer Science* 219 (1–2) (1999): 95–109.

Bridges, Douglas, and Steve Reeves. "Constructive Mathematics in Theory and Programming Practice." *Philosophia Mathematica* (3) 7 (1999): 65–104.

Bridges, Douglas, and Fred Richman. *Varieties of Constructive Mathematics*. New York: Cambridge University Press, 1987.

Ciaffaglione, Alberto, and Pietro Di Gianantonio. "A Tour with Constructive Real Numbers." In *Types for Proofs and Programs (Durham, 2000)*, edited by Paul Callaghan et al., 41–52. Berlin: Springer-Verlag, 2002.

Geuvers, Herman, and Milad Niqui. "Constructive Reals in Coq: Axioms and Categoricity." In *Types for Proofs and Programs (Durham, 2000)*, edited by Paul Callaghan et al., 79–95. Berlin: Springer-Verlag, 2002.

Richman, Fred. "Interview with a Constructive Mathematician." *Modern Logic* (3) 6 (1996): 247–271.

Richman, Fred. "Intuitionism as Generalization." *Philosophia Mathematica* 5 (1990): 124–128.

RUSSIAN CONSTRUCTIVE APPROACH

Beeson, Michael J. *Foundations of Constructive Mathematics: Metamathematical Studies*. Berlin: Springer-Verlag, 1985.

Kushner, Boris A. *Lectures on Constructive Mathematical Analysis*. Translated by Elliott Mendelson. Providence, RI: American Mathematical Society, 1984.

CONTINUITY AND MATHEMATICAL PHYSICS

Billinge, Helen. "Applied Constructive Mathematics: On G. Hellman's 'Mathematical Constructivism in Spacetime.'" *British Journal for the Philosophy Science* 51 (2) (2000): 299–318.

Bridges, Douglas. "Constructive Mathematics and Unbounded Operators. Reply to: 'Constructive Mathematics and Quantum Mechanics: Unbounded Operators and the Spectral Theorem.'" *Journal of Philosophical Logic* 24 (5) (1995): 549–561.

Bridges, Douglas, and Hajime Ishihara. "Constructive Unbounded Operators." In *Reuniting the Antipodes: Constructive and Nonstandard Views of the Continuum*, edited by Peter Schuster, Ulrich Berger, and Horst Osswald. Dordrecht, Netherlands: Kluwer Academic, 2001.

Capek, Milic. *The Philosophical Impact of Contemporary Physics*. Princeton, NJ: D. Van Nostrand Company, Inc., 1961.

Earman, John. *World Enough and Space-Time*. Cambridge, MA: MIT Press, 1989.

Fletcher, Peter. "A Constructivist Perspective on Physics." *Philosophia Mathematica* 10 (1) (2002): 26–42.

Forrest, Peter. "Is Space-Time Discrete or Continuous? An Empirical Question." *Synthese* 103 (3) (1995): 327–354.

Hellman, Geoffrey. "Constructive Mathematics and Quantum Mechanics: Unbounded Operators and the Spectral Theorem." *Journal of Philosophical Logic* 22 (3) (1993): 221–248.

Hellman, Geoffrey. "Gleason's Theorem Is Not Constructively Provable." *Journal of Philosophical Logic* 22 (2) (1993a): 193–203.

Hellman, Geoffrey. "Mathematical Constructivism in Spacetime." *British Journal for the Philosophy Science* 49 (3) (1998): 425–450.

Hellman, Geoffrey. "Quantum Mechanical Unbounded Operators and Constructive Mathematics—A Rejoinder to Bridges." *Journal of Philosophical Logic* 26 (2) (1997): 121–127.

Markopoulou, Fotini. "Planck-scale Models of the Universe." In *Science and Ultimate Reality. Quantum Theory, Cosmology, and Complexity. In Honor of the 90th Birthday of John Archibald Wheeler*, edited by John D. Barrow, Paul C. W. Davies, and Charles L. Harper, Jr. Cambridge, U.K.: Cambridge University Press, 2004.

Poincaré, Henri. *The Value of Science. In The Foundations of Science*. Translated by George Bruce Halsted. New York and Garrison, NY: The Science Press, 1913. Reprinted in 1921. "Analysis and Physics," which is Chapter 5 of this book, is a translation of a reprinting in modified form of "Sur les Rapports de l'analyse pure et de la physique Mathématique," which was first published in *Acta Mathematica* 21 (1897): 331–341.

Smolin, Lee. *Three Roads to Quantum Gravity*. New York: Basic Books, 2001.

Smolin, Lee. "Quantum Theories of Gravity: Results and Prospects." In *Science and Ultimate Reality. Quantum Theory, Cosmology, and Complexity. In Honor of the 90th Birthday of John Archibald Wheeler*, edited by John D. Barrow, Paul C. W. Davies, and Charles L. Harper, Jr. Cambridge, U.K.: Cambridge University Press, 2004.

WEYL'S PREDICATIVE APPROACH AND ITS AFTERMATH

Bell, John L. "Hermann Weyl on Intuition and the Continuum." *Philosophia Mathematica* (3) 8 (2000): 259–273.

Feferman, Solomon. "Predicativity." In *The Oxford Handbook of Philosophy of Mathematics and Logic*, edited by Stewart Shapiro. New York: Oxford University Press, 2005.

Feferman, Solomon. "Systems of Predicative Analysis." *Journal of Symbolic Logic* 29 (1964): 1–30.

Feferman, Solomon. "Weyl Vindicated: Das Kontinuum 70 Years Later (1988)." In *In the Light of Logic*, edited by Solomon Feferman. New York: Oxford University Press, 1998.

Feferman, Solomon. "Why a Little Bit Goes a Long Way: Logical Foundations of Scientifically Applicable Mathematics (1993)." In *In the Light of Logic*, edited by Solomon Feferman. New York: Oxford University Press, 1998.

Parsons, Charles. "Realism and the Debate on Impredicativity, 1917—1944." In *Reflections on the Foundations of Mathematics: Essays in Honor of Solomon Feferman*, edited by Wilfried Sieg, Richard Sommer, and Carolyn Talcott. Natick, MA: A. K. Peters, 2002.

Scholz, Erhard. "Herman Weyl on the Concept of Continuum." In *Proof Theory: History and Philosophical Significance*, edited by Vincent F. Hendricks, Stig Andur Pedersen, and Klaus Frovin Jorgensen. Dordrecht, Netherlands: Kluwer Academic, 2000.

Weyl, Hermann. *Das Kontinuum* (1918). Translated by Stephen Pollard and Thomas Bole as *The Continuum: a Critical Examination of the Foundation of Analysis.* New York: Dover Publications Inc., 1994.

Weyl, Hermann, et al. "Part II: H. Weyl." In *From Brouwer to Hilbert: The Debate on the Foundations of Mathematics in the 1920s*, edited by Paolo Mancosu. New York: Oxford University Press, 1998.

ELEMENTARY CONTINUITY

Artin, Emil, and Otto Schreier. "Algebraische Konstruktion reeller Körper" (1926). In *The Collected Papers of Emil Artin*, edited by Serge Lang and John T. Tate. Reading, MA: Addison-Wesley, 1965.

Tarski, Alfred. *Completeness of Elementary Algebra and Geometry* (1939). In *Collected Papers of Alfred Tarski, Vol. 2, 1935–1944*, edited by Steven R. Givant and Ralph N. McKenzie. Basel, Switzerland: Birkhäuser Verlag, 1986.

Tarski, Alfred. *A Decision Method for Elementary Algebra and Geometry* (1948). In *Collected Papers of Alfred Tarski, Vol. 3, 1945–1957*, edited by Steven R. Givant and Ralph N. McKenzie. Basel, Switzerland: Birkhäuser Verlag, 1986.

Tarski, Alfred. "What Is Elementary Geometry?" (1959). In *Collected Papers of Alfred Tarski, Vol. 4, 1958–1979*, edited by Steven R. Givant and Ralph N. McKenzie. Basel, Switzerland: Birkhäuser Verlag, 1986.

Tarski, Alfred, and Steven Givant. "Tarski's System of Geometry." *Bulletin of Symbolic Logic* 5 (2) (1999): 175–214.

Sinaceur, Hourya. "Calculation, Order, and Continuity." In *Real Numbers, Generalizations of the Reals, and Theories of Continua*, edited by Philip Ehrlich. Dordrecht, Netherlands: Kluwer Academic, 1994.

Sinaceur, Hourya Benis. *Fields and Models: From Sturm to Tarski and Robinson*. New York: Springer-Verlag, 2006.

CONTINUITY AND EUCLIDEAN GEOMETRY

Ehrlich, Philip. "From Completeness to Archimedean Completeness: An Essay in the Foundations of Euclidean Geometry." In *A Symposium on David Hilbert*, edited by Alfred Tauber and Akihiro Kanamori. *Synthese* 110(1) (1997a): 57–76.

Greenberg, Marvin J. *Euclidean and Non-Euclidean Geometries: Development and History*. 3rd ed. New York: Freeman, 1993.

Hartshorne, Robin. *Geometry: Euclid and Beyond.* New York: Springer-Verlag, 2000.

Heath, Sir Thomas L. ed. *The Thirteen Books of Euclid's Elements: Translated from the Text of Heiberg*, Volumes 1–3. New York: Dover Publications, Inc., 1956.

Tarski, Alfred. "What is Elementary Geometry?" (1959). In *Collected Papers of Alfred Tarski, Vol. 4, 1958–1979,* edited by Steven R. Givant and Ralph N. McKenzie. Basel: Birkhäuser Verlag, 1986.

Tarski, Alfred, and Givant, Steven. "Tarski's System of Geometry." *Bulletin of Symbolic Logic* 5(2) (1999): 175–214.

INFINITESIMALIST APPROACHES: HISTORICAL BACKGROUND

Ehrlich, Philip. "Hahn's *Über die nichtarchimedischen Grössensysteme* and the Development of the Modern Theory of Magnitudes and Numbers to Measure Them." In *From Dedekind to Gödel: Essays on the Development of the Foundations of Mathematics*, edited by Jaakko Hintikka. Dordrecht, Netherlands: Kluwer Academic, 1995.

Ehrlich, Philip. "The Rise of Non-Archimedean Mathematics and the Roots of a Misconception I: The Emergence of Non-Archimedean Systems of Magnitudes." *Archive for History of Exact Sciences*, (Springer-Verlag Online) (2005).

Fisher, Gordon. "The Infinite and Infinitesimal Quantities of du Bois-Reymond and Their Reception." *Archive for History of Exact Sciences* 24 (2) (1981): 101–164.

DU BOIS-REYMOND'S CONCEPTION

Du Bois-Reymond, Paul. *Die allgemine Functionentheorie.* Tübingen, Germany: Verlag der H. Laupp'schen Buchhandlung, 1882.

Du Bois-Reymond, Paul. "Sur la grandeur relative des infinis des fonctions." *Annali di matematica pura ed applicata* 4 (1870–1871): 338–353.

Du Bois-Reymond, Paul. "Ueber die Paradoxen des Infinitärcalcüls." *Mathematische Annalen* 11 (1877): 149–167.

VERONESE'S NON-ARCHIMEDEAN CONTINUUM

Ehrlich, Philip. "Dedekind Cuts of Archimedean Complete Ordered Abelian Groups." *Algebra Universalis* 37 (2) (1997): 223–234.

Ehrlich, Philip. "General Introduction." In *Real Numbers, Generalizations of the Reals, and Theories of Continua*, edited by Philip Ehrlich. Dordrecht, Netherlands: Kluwer Academic, 1994.

Fisher, Gordon. "Veronese's Non-Archimedean Linear Continuum." In *Real Numbers, Generalizations of the Reals, and Theories of Continua*, edited by Philip Ehrlich. Dordrecht, Netherlands: Kluwer Academic, 1994.

Veronese, Giuseppe. *Fondamenti di geometria a più dimensioni e a più specie di unità rettilinee esposti in forma elementare.* Padua, Italy: Tipografia del Seminario, 1891.

Veronese, Giuseppe. *Grundzüge der Geometrie von mehreren Dimensionen und mehreren Arten gradliniger Einheiten in elementarer Form entwickelt. Mit Genehmigung des Verfassers nach einer neuen Bearbeitung des Originals übersetzt von Adolf Schepp.* Leipzig: Teubner, 1894.

Veronese, Giuseppe. "La geometria non-Archimedea" (1909). Translated by Mathieu Marion as "On Non-Archimedean Geometry." In *Real Numbers, Generalizations of the Reals, and Theories of Continua*, edited by Philip Ehrlich. Dordrecht, Netherlands: Kluwer Academic, 1994.

Veronese, Giuseppe. "Il continuo rettilineo e l'assioma V di Archimede." *Memorie della Reale Accademia dei Lincei, Atti della Classe di scienze naturali, fisiche e matematiche* (4) 6 (1889): 603–624.

THE NON-ARCHIMEDEAN CONTRIBUTIONS OF LEVI-CIVITA AND HAHN

Ehrlich, Philip. "From Completeness to Archimedean Completeness: An Essay in the Foundations of Euclidean Geometry." In *A Symposium on David Hilbert*, edited by Alfred Tauber and Akihiro Kanamori. *Synthese* 110 (1) (1997a): 57–76.

Ehrlich, Philip. "Hahn's *Über die nichtarchimedischen Grössensysteme* and the Development of the Modern Theory of Magnitudes and Numbers to Measure Them." In *From Dedekind to Gödel: Essays on the Development of the Foundations of Mathematics*, edited by Jaakko Hintikka. Dordrecht, Netherlands: Kluwer Academic, 1995.

Hahn, Hans. "Über die nichtarchimedischen Grössensysteme." *Sitzungsberichte der Kaiserlichen Akademie der Wissenschaften, Wien, Mathematisch - Naturwissenschaftliche* Klasse 116 (Abteilung IIa) (1907): 601–655.

Laugwitz, Detlef. "Tullio Levi-Civita's Work on Non-Archimedean Structures (with an Appendix: Properties of Levi-Civita Fields)." *Tullio Levi-Civita Convegno Internazionale Celebrativo Del Centenario Della Nascita, Accademia Nazionale Dei Lincei Atti Dei Convegni Lincei, Rome* 8 (1975): 297–312.

Levi-Civita, Tullio. "Sugli infiniti ed infinitesimi attuali quali elementi analitici" (1892–1893). In *Tullio Levi-Civita, Opere Matematiche, Memorie e Note, Volume primo 1893–1900.* Bologna, Italy: Nicola Zanichelli, 1954.

Levi-Civita, Tullio. "Sui Numeri Transfiniti" (1898). In *Tullio Levi-Civita, Opere Matematiche, Memorie e Note, Volume primo 1893–1900.* Bologna, Italy: Nicola Zanichelli, 1954.

NONSTANDARD ANALYSIS

Albeverio, Sergio A., Wilhelm A. J. Luxemburg, and Manfred P. H. Wolff, eds. *Advances in Analysis, Probability, and Mathematical Physics: Contributions of Nonstandard Analysis.* Dordrecht, Netherlands: Kluwer Academic, 1995.

Arkeryd, Leif O., Nigel J. Cutland, and C. Ward Henson, eds. *Nonstandard Analysis: Theory and Applications.* Dordrecht, Netherlands: Kluwer Academic, 1997.

Chang, C. C., and H. Jerome Keisler. *Model Theory.* 3rd ed. Amsterdam, Netherlands: North-Holland, 1990.

Di Nasso, Mauro, and Marco Forti. "On the Ordering of the Nonstandard Real Line." In *Logic and Algebra*, edited by Yi Zhang. Providence, RI: American Mathematical Society, 2002.

Fenstad, Jens Erik. "The Discrete and the Continuous in Mathematics and the Natural Sciences." In *L'Infinito Nella Scienza*, edited by Giuliano Toraldo di Francia. Rome: Istituto Della Enciclopedia Italiana, Fondata Di G. Treccani, 1987.

Fenstad, Jens Erik. "Infinities in Mathematics and the Natural Sciences." In *Methods and Applications of Mathematical Logic: Contemporary Mathematics.* Vol. 69, edited by Walter A. Carnielli and Luiz Paulo de Alcantara. Providence, RI: American Mathematical Society, 1988.

Goldblatt, Robert. *Lectures on the Hyperreals: An Introduction to Nonstandard Analysis.* New York: Springer-Verlag, 1998.

Henson, C. W., and H. Jerome Keisler. "On the Strength of Nonstandard Analysis." *Journal of Symbolic Logic* 51 (2) (1986): 377–1386.

Keisler, H. Jerome. *Elementary Calculus.* 2nd ed. Boston: Prindle, Weber and Schmidt, 1986.

Keisler, H. Jerome. *Foundations of Infinitesimal Calculus.* Boston: Prindle, Weber and Schmidt, 1976.

Keisler, H. Jerome. "The Hyperreal Line." In *Real Numbers, Generalizations of the Reals, and Theories of Continua*, edited by Philip Ehrlich. Dordrecht, Netherlands: Kluwer Academic, 1994.

Keisler, H. Jerome. "Limit Ultrapowers." *Transactions of the American Mathematical Society* 107 (1963): 383–408.

Lindstrøm, Tom. "An Invitation to Nonstandard Analysis." In *Nonstandard Analysis and Its Applications*, edited by Nigel Cutland. New York: Cambridge University Press, 1988.

Loeb, Peter A. "An Introduction to Nonstandard Analysis." In *Nonstandard Analysis for the Working Mathematician*, edited by Peter A. Loeb and Manfred Wolff. Dordrecht, Netherlands: Kluwer Academic, 2000.

Loeb, Peter A., and Manfred Wolff, eds. *Nonstandard Analysis for the Working Mathematician.* Dordrecht, Netherlands: Kluwer Academic, 2000.

Nelson, Edward. "Internal Set Theory: A New Approach to Nonstandard Analysis." *Bulletin of the American Mathematical Society* 83 (1977): 1165–1198.

Robert, Alain. *Nonstandard Analysis.* New York: Wiley, 1988.

Robinson, Abraham. "The Metaphysics of the Calculus" (1967). In *Abraham Robinson Selected Papers. Vol. 2, Nonstandard Analysis and Philosophy*, edited by W. A. J. Luxemburg and Stephan Körner. New Haven, CT: Yale University Press, 1979.

Robinson, Abraham. "Non-standard Analysis" (1961). In *Abraham Robinson Selected Papers. Vol. 2, Nonstandard Analysis and Philosophy*, edited by W. A. J. Luxemburg and Stephan Körner. New Haven, CT: Yale University Press, 1979.

Robinson, Abraham. *Non-standard Analysis.* Amsterdam, Netherlands: North-Holland, 1966.

Robinson, Abraham. *Non-standard Analysis.* Rev. ed. Amsterdam: North-Holland Publishing Company, 1974.

Skolem, Thoralf. "Über die Nichtcharakterisierbarkeit der Zahlenreihe mittels endlich oder abzählbar unendlich vieler Aussagen mit ausschliesslich Zahlenvariablen." *Fundamenta Mathematica* 23 (1934): 150–161.

Zakon, Elias. "Remarks on the Nonstandard Real Axis." In *Applications of Model Theory to Algebra, Analysis, and*

Probability, edited by W. A. J. Luxemburg. New York: Holt, Rinehart and Winston, 1969.

SMOOTH INFINITESIMAL ANALYSIS

Bell, John L. "The Continuum in Smooth Infinitesimal Analysis." In *Reuniting the Antipodes: Constructive and Nonstandard Views of the Continuum*, edited by Peter Schuster, Ulrich Berger, and Horst Osswald. Dordrecht, Netherlands: Kluwer Academic, 2001.

Bell, John L. "Infinitesimals and the Continuum." *The Mathematical Intelligencer* 17 (2) (1995): 55–57.

Bell, John L. *A Primer of Infinitesimal Analysis*. New York: Cambridge University Press, 1998.

Giordano, Paolo. "Nilpotent Infinitesimals and Synthetic Differential Geometry in Classical Logic." In *Reuniting the Antipodes: Constructive and Nonstandard Views of the Continuum*, edited by Peter Schuster, Ulrich Berger, and Horst Osswald. Dordrecht, Netherlands: Kluwer Academic, 2001.

Kock, Anders. "Differential Calculus and Nilpotent Real Numbers." *Bulletin of Symbolic Logic* 9 (2) (2003): 225–230.

Kock, Anders. *Synthetic Differential Geometry*. New York: Cambridge University Press, 1981.

Lavendhomme, René. *Basic Concepts of Synthetic Differential Geometry*. Dordrecht, Netherlands: Kluwer Academic, 1996.

Lawvere, F. William. "Categorical Dynamics." In *Topos Theoretic Methods in Geometry*, edited by Anders Kock. Aarhus Matematisk Institut: Various Publication Series, 1979.

Lawvere, F. William. "Toward the Description in a Smooth Topos of the Dynamically Possible Motions and Deformations of a Continuous Body." *Cahiers de Topologie et Géométrie Différentielle Catégoriques* 21(4) (1980): 377–392.

McLarty, Colin. "Defining Sets as Sets of Points." *Journal of Philosophical Logic* 17 (1988): 75–90.

Moerdijk, Ieke, and Gonzalo E. Reyes. *Models for Smooth Infinitesimal Analysis*. New York: Springer-Verlag, 1991.

Succi Cruciani, Rosanna. "Euclidean Geometry with Infinitesimals." *Rendiconti di Matematica e delle sue Applicazioni, Serie* (Serie VII) 8 (4) (1989): 557–578.

THE WORK OF SCHMIEDEN AND LAUGWITZ

Laugwitz, Detlef. "Kurt Schmieden's Approach to Infinitesimals: An Eye-Opener to the Historiography of Analysis." In *Reuniting the Antipodes: Constructive and Nonstandard Views of the Continuum*, edited by Peter Schuster, Ulrich Berger, and Horst Osswald. Dordrecht, Netherlands: Kluwer Academic, 2001.

Laugwitz, Detlef. "Leibniz's Principle and Omega Calculus." In *Le Continu Mathematique, Colloque de Cerisy*, edited by Hourya Sinaceur and Jean-Michel Salanskis. Paris: Springer-Verlag, 1992.

Laugwitz, Detlef. "Ω-Calculus as a Generalization of Field Extension—An Alternative Approach to Nonstandard Analysis." In *Nonstandard Analysis: Recent Developments*, edited by Albert Emerson Hurd. Berlin: Springer-Verlag, 1983.

Schmieden, Curt, and Detlef Laugwitz. "Eine Erweiterung der Infinitesimalrechnung." *Mathematische Zeitschrift* 69 (1958): 1–39.

SURREAL NUMBERS

Conway, J. H. *On Numbers and Games*. London: Academic Press, 1976.

Conway, J. H. *On Numbers and Games*. 2nd ed. Natick, MA: A.K. Peters, 2001.

Conway, J. H. "The Surreals and Reals." In *Real Numbers, Generalizations of the Reals, and Theories of Continua*, edited by Philip Ehrlich. Dordrecht, Netherlands: Kluwer Academic, 1994.

Ehrlich, Philip. "The Absolute Arithmetic Continuum and the Unification of All Numbers Great and Small." In *Philosophical Insights into Logic and Mathematics (Abstracts)*. Nancy, France: Université de Nancy Laboratoire de Philosophie et d'Histoire des Sciences, Archive Henri Poincaré (2002): 41–43.

Ehrlich, Philip. "The Absolute Arithmetic and Geometric Continua." In *PSA 1986*. Vol. 2, edited by Arthur Fine and Peter Machamer. Lansing, MI: Philosophy of Science Association, 1987.

Ehrlich, Philip. "Absolutely Saturated Models." *Fundamenta Mathematicae* 133 (1) (1989): 39–46.

Ehrlich, Philip. "All Number Great and Small." In *Real Numbers, Generalizations of the Reals, and Theories of Continua*, edited by Philip Ehrlich. Dordrecht, Netherlands: Kluwer Academic, 1994.

Ehrlich, Philip. "An Alternative Construction of Conway's Ordered Field No." *Algebra Universalis* 25 (1988): 7–16. Errata, *Algebra Universalis* 25 (1988): 233.

Ehrlich, Philip. "Number Systems with Simplicity Hierarchies: A Generalization of Conway's Theory of Surreal Numbers." *Journal of Symbolic Logic* 66 (3) (2001): 1231–1258. Corrigendum, 70 (3) (2005): 1022.

Ehrlich, Philip. "Surreal Numbers: An Alternative Construction (Abstract)." *Bulletin of Symbolic Logic* 8 (3) (2002a): 448.

Ehrlich, Philip. "Surreal Numbers and the Unification of All Numbers Great and Small." *Bulletin of Symbolic Logic* 10 (2) (2004): 253.

Ehrlich, Philip. "Universally Extending Arithmetic Continua." In *Le Continu Mathematique, Colloque de Cerisy*, edited by Hourya Sinaceur and Jean-Michel Salanskis. Paris: Springer-Verlag, 1992.

Ehrlich, Philip. "Universally Extending Continua." *Abstracts of Papers Presented to the American Mathematical Society* 10 (1989a): 15.

CAUCHY'S CONTINUUM

Cleave, J. P. "Cauchy, Convergence and Conitinuity." *British Journal for the Philosophy of Science* 22 (1971): 27–37.

Grabiner, Judith V. *The Origins of Cauchy's Rigorous Calculus*. Cambridge, MA.: MIT Press, 1981.

Lakatos, Imre. "Cauchy and the Continuum." *The Mathematical Intelligencer* (1) (1978): 151–161.

Laugwitz, Detlef. "Definite Values of Infinite Sums: Aspects of the Foundations of Infinitesimal Analysis around 1820." *Archive for History of Exact Sciences* 39 (1989): 195–245.

Laugwitz, Detlef. "Infinitely Small Quantities in Cauchy's Textbook." *Historia Mathematica* (14) (1987): 258–274.

Lützen, Jesper. "The Foundations of Analysis in the 19th Century." In *A History of Analysis*, edited by Hans Niels Jahnke. Providence, RI: American Mathematical Society, 2003.

Robinson, Abraham. "The Metaphysics of the Calculus" (1967). In *Abraham Robinson Selected Papers. Vol. 2, Nonstandard Analysis and Philosophy*, edited by W. A. J. Luxemburg and Stephan Körner. New Haven, CT: Yale University Press, 1979.

Robinson, Abraham. *Non-standard Analysis*. Rev. ed. Amsterdam, Netherlands: North-Holland, 1974.

Spalt, Detlef D. "Cauchys Kontinuum. Eine historiografische Annäherung via Cauchys Summensatz." *Archive for History of Exact Sciences* 56 (4) (2002): 285–338.

BERNARD BOLZANO

Rusnock, Paul. *Bolzano's Philosophy and the Emergence of Modern Mathematics*. Amsterdam, Netherlands: Editions Rodophi B. V., 2000.

Russ, Steve, ed. *The Mathematical Works of Bernard Bolzano*. New York: Oxford University Press, 2004.

CONTINUOUS FUNCTIONS

Youschkevitch, A. P. "The Concept of Function up to the Middle of the 19th Century." *Archive for History of Exact Sciences* 16 (1) (1976): 37–85.

CHARLES SANDERS PEIRCE

Ehrlich, Philip. "The Peircean Linear Continuum: A Surreal Model (Abstract)." *The Bulletin of Symbolic Logic* 11(4) (2005).

Herron, Timothy. "Charles Sanders Peirce's Theories of Infinitesimals." *Transactions of the Charles S. Peirce Society* 33 (3) (1997): 590–645.

Myrvold, Wayne. "Peirce on Cantor's Paradox and the Continuum." *Transactions of the Charles S. Peirce Society* 31 (3) (1995): 508–541.

Noble, N. A. Brian "Peirce's Definitions of Continuity and the Concept of Possibility." *Transactions of the Charles S. Peirce Society* 25 (2) (1989): 149–174.

Peirce, Charles Sanders. "Infinitesimals" (1900). In *Collected Papers of Charles Sanders Peirce*. Vol. 3, edited by Charles Hartshone and Paul Weiss. Cambridge, MA: Harvard University Press, 1935.

Peirce, Charles Sanders. "The Logic of Continuity." In *Reasoning and the Logic of Things: The Cambridge Conferences Lectures of 1898*, edited by Kenneth Laine Ketner. Cambridge, MA: Harvard University Press, 1992.

Potter, Vincent, and Paul Schields. "Peirce's Definitions of Continuity." *Transactions of the Charles S. Peirce Society* 13 (1) (1977): 20–34.

Putnam, Hilary. "Peirce's Continuum." In *Reasoning and the Logic of Things: The Cambridge Conferences Lectures of 1898*, edited by Kenneth Laine Ketner, with an Introduction by Kenneth Laine Ketner and Hilary Putnam. Cambridge, MA.: Harvard University Press, 1992: 37–54.

FUZZY REAL NUMBERS

Lowen, Robert. *Fuzzy Set Theory: Basic Concepts, Techniques, and Bibliography*. Dordrecht, Netherlands: Kluwer Academic, 1996.

Zadeh, Lotfi Asker. *Fuzzy Sets and Applications: Selected Papers*. Edited by R. R. Yager et al. New York: Wiley, 1987.

Philip Ehrlich (2005)

CONTINUUM PROBLEM

See *Set Theory*

CONTRACTUALISM

Contractualism, as a distinctive account of moral reasoning, was originally advanced by T. M. Scanlon in his widely admired paper "Contractualism and Utilitarianism" (1982) and was later elaborated on in detail in his book *What We Owe to Each Other* (1998). Drawing on an understanding of the significance of the social-contract metaphor that has its roots in Jean-Jacques Rousseau, rather than Thomas Hobbes, contractualism offers distinctive and interrelated answers to two central questions of philosophical theorizing about moral reasoning. First, what explains the importance of morality for people motivated to comply with the requirements of morality? Second, what kinds of reasons support judgments that particular acts or types of acts are right or wrong? Consequentialism provides what is undoubtedly the most familiar answer to this question. Contractualism seeks to provide a plausible alternative.

The contractualist account of why those who seek to comply with the requirements of morality care about being so guided presupposes a general approach to understanding the nature of value. The central idea of the presupposition is that to take something to be of value is to have reasons to regard it positively and reasons to act in certain ways with regard to it, some of which are required by the value of the thing in question. For instance, one's appreciation of the value of *The Last Supper* might take the form of planning trips to go and admire it, watching documentaries about it, reading scholarly works that deepen one's appreciation of it, worrying about its deterioration due to age, and debating the merits of various proposals to restore it with others who share one's passion.

Recognition of this value need not express itself in one's attitudes in these ways, though they are certainly rationally appropriate ways of responding to the value. But not all ways of engaging with something of value are optional. Some reasons for engaging with something of value in particular ways are reasons that all persons capable of making evaluative judgments are required to take account of in their practical deliberations. A person's indifference to *The Last Supper* does not alter the fact that he has reason not to ridicule or disparage it (even in his thoughts), not to urinate on it, not to attack it with a can of spray paint. These reasons, which are demanded by *respect* for the value of the *The Last Supper*, apply to all individuals irrespective of their particular tastes and inclinations. Such reasons can be usefully characterized as *categorical reasons*.

Just as there are categorical reasons that flow from the value of the *The Last Supper*, so there are categorical reasons that flow from the value of human life. The distinctive value of human life, on the contractualist account, lies in the human capacity to assess reasons and justifications, to select among various reasons for wanting one's life to go a certain way, and thus to actively live and govern one's life (Scanlon 1998, p. 105). We have reason, then, to have certain attitudes toward, and give consideration to, the interests of others in our practical deliberations, namely, out of respect for the value of others as rationally self-governing beings. Failure to do so is a rational mistake, a failure to respond appropriately to all the relevant reasons for our behavior. This conclusion follows from the theory of value presupposed by contractualism and a specific characterization of the value of human life, neither of which are distinctively contractualist.

In answering why complying with morality matters to people who are morally motivated, contractualism holds that there are more than just rational reasons for respecting the value of another human being. Intuitively, there is a significant difference between failing to respect the value of a human and the kind of failure of respect exhibited by, for instance, proposing to film a rock video in the Sistine Chapel or building a McDonald's on the Great Wall of China. What accounts for the difference, according to contractualism, is the value of *mutual recognition*. Rational creatures living their lives in ways respectful of one another's value as rational creatures creates a special relation between them, a moral community of the kind that Immanuel Kant called the "Kingdom of Ends" and "a systematic union of various rational beings through common laws" (1902–, 4: 433). It is the kind of moral community that John Stuart Mill had in mind when he spoke of "unity with our fellow creatures." Respecting the value of others as persons, then, has a special importance for the morally motivated because they value the kind of relationship with others created by so living. This ideal of a moral community is at the heart of the contractualist characterization of moral reasoning.

Standards must guide individuals in their deliberations if they are to live on terms of respect for one another's value as persons. Contractualism characterizes these standards as principles for the general regulation of how individuals ought to deliberate in various situations. It asserts that those who care about the justifiability of their conduct toward similarly motivated others cannot reasonably reject these standards as a basis for informed, unforced, general agreement. Thus, principles that the morally inclined cannot reasonably reject play an important interpersonal role in regulating how individuals should relate to one another. They do so by fixing the attitudes and treatment that individuals are entitled to legitimately demand, and have demanded, out of respect for each other's value as rational creatures. In other words, these principles fix legitimate expectations concerning how individuals should deliberate in various situations. On this account, one person *wrongs* another when he fails to regulate his deliberations as the other is legitimately entitled to expect.

Whether or not a principle cannot be reasonably rejected is assessed according to the implications (broadly construed) of licensing individuals to reason as required and permitted by the proposed principle. Contractualism is both more restrictive and more permissive than consequentialism concerning what counts as a relevant implication of a proposed principle. It is more restrictive in that it does not regard as relevant facts about the aggregate value of the outcome likely to result from general compliance with the principle. The only relevant considerations are those that have to do with the implications of a principle for the life of an *individual* with a particular point of view. Different relevant implications can emerge from consideration of a principle from different points of view. This restriction on relevant implications rules out appeals to the aggregate value of an outcome as relevant for assessing a principle. One outcome may be worse than another with respect to aggregate value without being worse from the point of view of each individual. Contractualism and consequentialism are thus diametrically opposed on the relevance of considerations having to do with the aggregate value of potential outcomes.

Contractualism is more permissive than consequentialism in counting, as relevant, considerations that have nothing do with what is likely to happen as a consequence of individuals being licensed to treat one another in certain ways. Consider, for example, a principle that licenses a designated authority periodically to force randomly chosen individuals to serve as test subjects for dangerous medical experiments. In addition to the consequences for the lives of some unlucky individuals, contractualism will also allow as relevant consideration of the fact that such a principle would turn the bodies of individuals into a form of public property. That is, it would undermine the exclusive authority of individuals concerning decisions about how their bodies are to be used, a prerogative that plays a fundamental role in an agent's understanding of his life as *his own*.

Assessing the validity of a principle requires both identifying the relevant considerations that ought to be taken into account in its assessment and combining them in a judgment about whether it is reasonable to reject the principle. Consequentialists claim that the right way to combine relevant implications of a principle is to aggregate their value. This sum is then compared to the aggregate value of the implications of possible alternatives. The valid principle is the one whose implications sum to the greatest aggregate value.

Contractualism adopts a different approach to this problem. Contractualism starts from the position that what the morally motivated person cares about is that his comportment toward another person be justifiable *to that person* as respectful of that person's value as a person. Justification *to another* requires that one's comportment toward the other be justified in light of what *that person cares about*. A principle is *justifiable to* a person, then, if he has reason to judge it to be justified (even if he himself does not recognize that reason) in light of the values that structure his particular point of view.

The central contractualist insight is that respect for the value of another as a person requires not merely that one take the implications of one's actions for that person's well-being into account, but that one be guided, in one's thinking about one's comportment toward that person, by a principle *justifiable to* that person. The impact of a possible principle on any person's well-being may be relevant to assessing the principle, but it will be so derivatively, as a consideration picked out as relevant by the master consideration of what is justifiable to that person. One's conduct may have negative implications for another, but if one has been guided by a principle justifiable to him, he has no grounds for complaint on the grounds that one has failed to give his interests the kind of consideration in one's deliberations that he is owed out of respect for his value as a person. If, in how one relates to another, one is guided by a principle that is justifiable to him, that principle can rightly be characterized as *authorized* by him.

Principles that no one can reasonably reject, then, enable individuals to relate to one another on terms of mutual respect for the value of one another as persons. They do so because a principle that no one can reasonably reject is justifiable to *any* individual from his point of view, provided at least that he values living with others on terms of mutual respect.

To arrive at a valid principle, we have to combine the implications of a proposed principle to arrive at an all-things-considered judgment about whether it is reasonable to reject the principle. At the heart of the contractualist approach to doing this is the requirement that a valid principle be justifiable to anyone from his own point of view. Assessing a proposed principle requires that one consider the point of view of the individual who stands to be most seriously burdened by it. Can such an individual reasonably reject the principle? On the contractualist account, that depends on the implications of a plausible alternative principle for those with other points of view. If every alternative principle to one that seriously burdens you will more seriously burden someone else, then you cannot reasonably reject the principle, as another individual's having to bear a burden that could be avoided by your bearing a lesser burden is justifiable *to you*. A valid principle is justifiable to the person who has the strongest reason for wanting to reject that principle.

This approach to how all the relevant implications of a principle are to be taken account of in an all-things-considered judgment of its validity stands in sharp contrast to that favored by consequentialist accounts. According to consequentialism, a principle that seriously burdens an individual can be justified by appeal to the aggregate value of the benefits secured under that principle for those with other points of view. Contractualism does not permit trade-offs of this kind among persons. A principle that seriously burdens you may secure benefits for others whose aggregate value outweighs the burden it places on you. But that fact has no bearing on whether the principle is justifiable *to you*, as it does not point to the viewpoint of another to whom any other principle, which does not so seriously burden you, would be justifiable. Under contractualism, our motivation for morality rules out aggregative considerations as relevant for the assessment of principles.

Consequentialism has a hard time making sense of commonsense prohibitions against treating others in certain abominable ways in circumstances where the consequences of doing so have great positive aggregate value. Nonconsequentialists argue that there is no problem in understanding the rationale for these prohibitions if one locates the basis for claims of wrongdoing in the very character of the prohibited way of treating others. One way of trying to articulate more clearly what the nonconsequentialist has in mind is the Kantian injunction to treat others, never as mere means, but always as ends in themselves. Contractualism, in locating the basis of a person's claim to have been wronged in his having been treated in a way not justifiable *to him*, powerfully illuminates the compelling insight to which Kant's injunction draws our attention.

See also Constructivism, Moral; Discourse Ethics; Hobbes, Thomas; Locke, John; Rawls, John; Rousseau, Jean-Jacques; Social Contract.

Bibliography

Kant, Immanuel. *Gesammelte Schriften*. Vols. 1–29. Berlin: G. Reimer, 1902–. Page numbers of this edition are printed in the margin of translations in the *Cambridge Edition of the Works of Immanuel Kant*.

Scanlon, T. M. "Contractualism and Utilitarianism." In *Utilitarianism and Beyond*, edited by Amartya Sen and Bernard Williams, 103–128. Cambridge, U.K.: Cambridge University Press, 1982.

Scanlon, T. M. *What We Owe to Each Other*. Cambridge, MA: Harvard University Press, 1998.

Rahul Kumar (2005)

CONVENTIONALISM

In the physical sciences, some very basic facts or principles appear to have a status that is difficult to categorize: not simply empirically discovered; not purely analytic (true by virtue of already established meanings); fundamental, but without quite being ordinary physical laws. Incompatible-looking alternative principles are conceivable; sometimes we can even see how an alternative physical framework could be built on them. Such principles are held, by some philosophers, to be true by *convention*. They are parts of our physical theories that had to be conventionally chosen by us over other incompatible postulates, whether or not we were overtly aware of this element of choice.

The most famous examples of putative conventional truths are to be found in our theories of space and time, and will be discussed below. But some are not directly related to space and/or time: in classical physics, Isaac Newton's famous 2nd law, F = ma, is an example. This law at first sight looks like it cannot be a convention, for surely, as the center of his mechanics, the 2nd law is far from true by stipulation. But in the Newtonian paradigm, the 2nd law served as ultimate arbiter of the questions (a) whether an external force is, in fact, acting on a given object; and (b) if so, what its magnitude was. While not necessarily immune to rejection or revision in the long run, this principle was nevertheless a postulate that helped constitute the meaning of other terms such as "force," and functioned as something *akin to* a definition, with a warrant *akin to* a priority.

Conventionalism of the Duhem-Quine sort holds that one can *always* maintain the truth of the 2nd law (or any other conventional truth), come what may. The backing for this claim comes from the *holism* of scientific theory testing (Pierre Duhem) or more generally, of conceptual frameworks (W. V. O. Quine): Since the things we hold true form an interconnected web, any one belief or postulate that faces apparent disconfirmation may be preserved as "true," as long as we are willing to make enough compensatory adjustments among other beliefs. (For example, the 2nd law may be held true in the face of motions that appear not to conform to it, as long as we are willing to postulate the existence of hitherto-undiscovered forces acting on the relevant bodies.)

However, one can usually imagine circumstances in which unbearable tensions arise in our conceptual frameworks from the insistence on retention of the putative conventional principle, and one is effectively forced to give it up. If this is right, then the original claim of conventionality—that the principle in question is a mere stipulation or definition—looks like something of an exaggeration. Are there in fact *any* choices in the creation of adequate physical theory that are genuinely free, conventional choices (as, for example, choice of units is), without being completely trivial (as, again, choice of units is)? Many philosophers have thought that space-time structures give us true examples of such conventionality. The debates over conventionalism form a significant fraction of twentieth-century philosophy of space and time, and work continues in a wave of recent books and papers (Friedman 1999, Ryckman 2004). We cannot hope to do justice to the depth and complexity of the arguments of the major thinkers here, but will limit ourselves to introducing the main themes and key arguments, directing the reader to further resources in the bibliography.

CONVENTIONALISM ABOUT SPACE

Before the eighteenth century all philosophers of nature assumed the Euclidean structure of space; it was thought that Euclid's axioms were true a priori. The work of Nikolai Lobachevsky, Bernhard Riemann, and Carl Friedrich Gauss destroyed this belief; they demonstrated, first, that consistent non-Euclidean constant-curvature geometries were possible, and later that even variably curved space was consistent and analytically describable. But what, exactly, does it mean to say that space is Euclidean or Riemannian? A naïve-realist interpretation can of course be given: there exists a *thing*, space, it has an intrinsic structure, and that structure conforms to Euclid's (or Riemann's) axioms. But space, so described, is not observable in itself; only the material phenomena governed by physical laws are. When philosophers gave attention to this fact, they realized that our physical theories always contain assumptions or postulates that *coordinate* physical phenomena with spatial and temporal structures. Light rays in empty space travel in straight lines, for example; rigid bodies moved through space without stresses do not change their length; and so on. So-called *axioms of coordination* are needed to give meaning and testability to claims about the geometry of space.

The need for axioms of coordination seems to make space for conventionalism. For suppose that, under our old axioms of coordination, evidence starts to accumulate that points toward a non-Euclidean space (triangles made by light rays having angles summing to less than 180 degrees, for example). We could change our view of the geometry of space; but equally well, say conventionalists, we could change the axioms of coordination. By eliminating the postulate that light rays in empty space travel in straight lines (perhaps positing some "universal force" that affects such rays), we could continue to hold that the structure of space itself is Euclidean. According to the strongest sorts of conventionalism, this preservation of a conventionally chosen geometry can always be done, come what may. Henri Poincaré (1902/1952) defended the conventionality of Euclidean geometry; but he also conjectured that it would always be *simpler* to construct mechanics on assumption of Euclidean geometry. (Poincaré argued, on the basis of the work of Hermann von Helmholtz and Sophus Lie on free-mobility mechanics, that the possible geometries among which we must make a conventional choice are just three: Euclidean, Riemannian, and Lobachevskian. He thus did not consider the possibility of the variably curved space-time introduced by Albert Einstein in 1912).

Poincaré did not defend a wide-ranging, Duhem-Quine style of conventionalism; rather his view might better be thought of as neo-Kantian (as was also true of Hans Reichenbach in his first book on space and time [1920[). The Euclidean status of space is a convention that plays the role of a constitutive, a priori axiom with respect to mechanics and the rest of physics. By contrast, although he held it to be synthetic, arithmetic was *not* conventional for Poincaré: we have no choice but to regard it as true. But when it comes to the choice between Euclidean and (say) Lobachevsky geometry for real space, Poincaré's defense of the tenability of the Euclidean convention becomes basically an instance of the Duhem-Quine thesis: by making compensatory adjustments in our physics (specifically, introducing "universal forces" of the right sort), we can continue to hold that space is Euclidean even if direct measurements with rods and light-rays do not conform to that geometry. We will explore this idea further via Reichenbach, its most vigorous proponent in the twentieth century.

Reichenbach introduces the basic argument for conventionalism with an example that has become a classic:

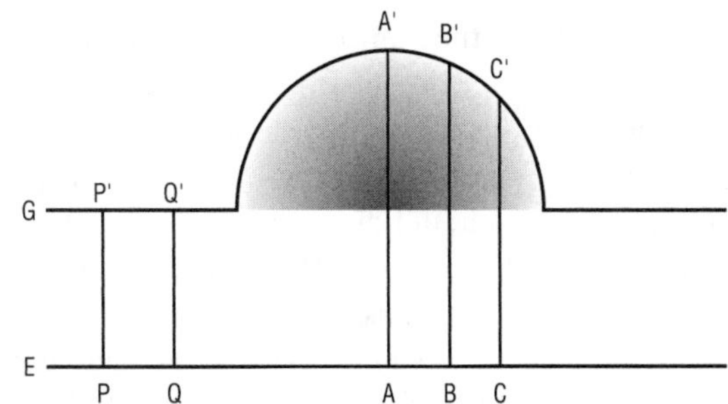

G represents a planar surface on which some 2-D beings live; we suppose that the surface is "really" flat almost everywhere, except for a non-flat hump centered around the point A'. The people on the plane can "know" that they have this hump in their space because of the way triangles' angles measure inside the hump. Using their measuring rods, they regard the segments A'B' and B'C' as equal in length.

Now we suppose that G is actually made of glass, and light shining from above casts shadows of everything on G onto the plane E below. People on E have their own measuring rods and so on. Let's suppose that, as it happens, the measuring rods on E behave exactly like the shadows of the E-rods: declaring AB congruent to BC, for example. Reichenbach has us suppose that there is a heating source under E that causes measuring rods to expand as they approach A, with no heat beyond the limits of the shadow of the hump. If the beings on E knew nothing of heat and how it expands measuring rods, what will they conclude? Like the G-people, they will conclude that their space has a non-Euclidean hump in it, centered on A.

The example brings to light the apparent impossibility—at least under the described circumstances—of determining whether one "really" lives in a curved space, or a flat Euclidean space with certain "universal" forces affecting things like measuring rods, light rays, and so on. (Reichenbach's "universal" forces affect every object in exactly the same way, and cannot be shielded out; they are clearly modeled on the force of gravity, for reasons we will see below.) Now Reichenbach makes the key move in arguing for his conventionalism about physical geometry, and it is based on his verificationist empiricism: given that there is no way in principle to determine which of these is the case, we should reject the question itself as a mistake based on false presuppositions. There is no fact of the matter, in the case discussed, about whether G is "really" flat or rather "really" has a hump. A conventional choice must be made concerning whether to keep the geometry flat or not; after that, one can determine the presence (or absence) of universal forces as required.

We should note the irony here: in order to introduce his conventionalism, Reichenbach had to present us with hypothetical cases in which there *is* a nonconventional fact of the matter about the intrinsic geometry of space, then argue that we should disbelieve in these facts after all. Realists about space (or space-time) respond to Reichenbach precisely on this point: The fact that we cannot determine the geometry of space beyond any possibility of doubt, due to the logical possibility of other physical theories postulating a different geometry, does not entail that there *is no* fact of the matter—unless, of course, one subscribes to the most far-reaching of verificationist views of meaning and truth.

But Reichenbach is not quite so easily dismissed. The "intrinsic" geometries of G and E were introduced as a crutch for the imagination, to get us ready to see how the combination of a geometry G and a set of physical postulates about forces, F, are only testable (hence meaningful) together. Once the point is understood, we realize that our "intrinsic" geometries by themselves had no significance. The combination of G and F together, by contrast, is both meaningful and testable: the E-residents can certainly tell that their world is such that *if held to have a Euclidean space, then there are universal forces acting in the A-region; or if held to have no universal forces, then space is non-Euclidean in the region around A*. Which they decide to adopt is up to them, and the decision is a conventional one (perhaps based on simplicity or convenience).

ANTI-CONVENTIONALIST RESPONSES. Roberto Torretti (1983) and others have criticized Reichenbach's notion of a universal force, arguing that (a) gravity does not meet the criteria established by Reichenbach; and (b) physicists would never take such a stipulated, truly-unverifiable concept seriously. Recalling the analogy used by Reichenbach (and Poincaré before him) of the deformation of a measuring rod by heat, notice that real material objects respond differently to temperature changes: steel expands while a ceramic contracts when heated, for example. The differential response of some materials to the physical "force" of heat is crucial to its playing a significant role in physics. Gravity, too, is a force that affects different objects differently: a meter-stick made of steel with ball-shaped ends will change its length little, if at all, when held vertical in a gravity field like the Earth's; but a meter-stick made of foam rubber with steel ball-shaped ends will change significantly in the same gravity field. The force of gravity is indeed universal in the sense of (1) affecting all massive bodies equally *per unit of mass*, and in (2) being un-shieldable. But the universal forces Reichenbach discusses would appear to be rather different, affecting all bodies equally on a *per unit volume* basis, so as to change their sizes by exactly the same amount, regardless of internal constitution. Torretti argues that there are no forces in real physics that act in such a way.

Interestingly, though it was not known to Reichenbach, there are illustrations of potentially conventional elements that may be discerned in classical Newtonian gravitation theory, though not involving Reichenbachean universal forces. The arguably conventional choices are in fact two-fold (see Friedman 1983). First, one may add an arbitrary (constant) universal acceleration to every body in space: This acceleration changes no observable phenomena, and in fact is implemented simply by adding a term to the gravitational potential Φ. This extra term in the potential generates a universal gravitational force that accelerates every object at the same rate—seemingly a real-science example of Reichenbach's universal forces, but in fact different: The force does not deform any body's shape or behavior relative to other bodies, hence does not change the Euclidean geometry of space. Physicists customarily chose Φ so as to make such overall-acceleration equal to zero.

Secondly, mathematicians in the early twentieth century discovered how to transform Isaac Newton's gravity theory into a curved-space-time theory analogous to Einstein's General Theory of Relativity (GTR, about which more below): in this formulation, there are no gravity forces and instead the local geometry of space-time is curved, non-Euclidean. (Note however that this is only true of space-*time*, not space on its own—that remains flat, i.e., Euclidean.) Still, the example illustrates the conventionalist point: we might have had to choose whether to consider space-time flat/Euclidean, and let gravity be a universal force explaining why things do not always move on straight-line paths (geodesics); or instead, eliminate the "force" of gravity, allow that our space-time is curved, and hold that all bodies follow geodesics of the curved geometry of space-time. If we imagine that physics had really turned out to show our world perfectly Newtonian, it is easy to see that we might find the conventionalist viewpoint attractive, compared to a realism that denies us the possibility of knowing what sort of space-time we live in, whether we are moving uniformly or instead with a frightful acceleration, and so forth.

Conventionalism and GTR. Discussions of conventionalism took a dramatic turn because of the work of Einstein. With its variably curved space-time, GTR obviously posed new challenges and opportunities for both sides on the conventionality of geometry. In the first half of the twentieth century GTR was widely viewed as vindicating a significant conventionalism or neo-Kantian "constitutive a priori" element in physics. In addition to Reichenbach, Ernst Cassirer, Moritz Schlick, and Adolf Grünbaum are some notable figures of twentieth-century philosophy who argued for the conventionality of space-time's geometry in the context of GTR (see Ryckman [2004] for an extensive and nuanced discussion of this early interpretive wave). Recent scholars have tended to be skeptical that any nontrivial conventionalist thesis is tenable in GTR; Friedman, Torretti and Hilary Putnam are prominent examples here.

Grünbaum, a student of Reichenbach's, recast the arguments for conventionalism in a non-epistemological form, more suited to the post-positivist climate of the 1960s and 1970s. He also brought forth a novel argument for the conventionality of geometry, based on the intrinsic *metrical amorphousness* of a continuous space. If space were composed of discrete atoms or chunks, it would thereby have a built-in metric. The distance between the ends of a meter stick would be determined by the number of space-atoms traversed by the line of its center, for example. But if, as most physical theories postulate, space(-time) is a continuum, then it cannot have any such built-in metric. (Grünbaum seems to be thinking of space as, intrinsically, just a topological manifold.) The metrical properties must be imposed extrinsically, by phenomena and bodies existing in the space (or space-time). And again, we must adopt conventions about which processes, bodies etc. are taken as constitutive for the geometry of space. See Grünbaum (1973) and Friedman (1983) for extensive discussion.

Einstein's GTR gave impetus to conventionalism in several ways; here we will mention just one. Consider Einstein's Equivalence Principle (EP), which says that a body that is uniformly accelerating (e.g., a rocketship) may consider itself as "at rest," but in the presence of a gravitational field that pulls everything downward. Conversely, according to the EP, a body freely "falling" under a gravitational force may equally well consider itself as "at rest" in a space without any gravitational forces. (The EP was, we see, implicit in our discussion of the two conventional elements in Newtonian gravity theory above.) A strong reading of this principle leads to the view that the existence or non-existence of a gravitational field is not a fact "out there" in the world, but rather something which we must arbitrarily decide. However, since gravitational fields (i.e., regions of local curvature of space-time) caused by bodies like planets and stars *can* be empirically distinguished from gravity-free regions—the EP is only true "locally," and to first approximation in small regions—the apparent freedom to choose turns out to be illusory.

Conventionality of Simultaneity. But it was in 1905, rather than 1915, that Einstein gave the greatest boost to conventionalism. In the astounding first few pages of "On the Electrodynamics of Moving Bodies," the paper that introduced the Special Theory of Relativity (STR) Einstein overthrew the Newtonian view of space-time structure—and, in passing, noted that *part* of the structure with which he intended to replace it had to be chosen by convention. That part was *simultaneity*. Einstein investigated the operational significance of a claim that two events at different locations happen simultaneously, and realized that it must be defined in terms of some clock synchronization procedure. The obvious choice for such a procedure was to use light-signals: Send a signal from event A for observer 1, have it be received and reflected back by observer 2 (at rest relative to 1), event B, and then received by 1 again at event C. The event B is then simultaneous with an event E, temporally midway between A and C.

Or is it? To suppose that it is, is to assume that the velocity of light on the trip from A to B is the same as its velocity from B to C (or, more generally, that light has the same velocity in a given frame, in all directions). This seems like a very good thing to assume. But can it be verified? Einstein thought not. All ways of directly measuring the one-way velocity of light seemed to require *first* having synchronized clocks at separated locations. But if this is right, we are going in circles: we need to know light's one-way velocity to properly synchronize distant clocks, but to know that velocity we need antecedently synchronized clocks.

To break the circle, Einstein thought we needed to make a conventional choice: We *stipulate* that event E is simultaneous with B (i.e., that light's velocity is uniform and direction-independent). Other choices are clearly possible, at least for the purposes of developing the dynamics and kinematics of STR. Following Reichenbach, these are synchronizations with ε ≠ ½ (ε being the proportion of the round-trip time taken on the outbound leg only, freely specifiable between 0 and 1 exclusive). Adopting one of these ε ≠ ½ choices is equivalent to stipulating that the velocity of light is different in different spatial directions, without offering any physical reason for the difference, which some philosophers and physicists would find objectionable. It is also a recipe for calculational misery of a very pointless kind. But the Einstein of 1905, and many philosophers since then, thought that such a choice cannot be criticized as objectively *wrong*. Ultimately, they say, distant simultaneity is not only frame-relative, but partly conventional. It is important to see how different the situation is from Newtonian physics, in which there is no upper limit to the velocity of causal signals. In Newtonian physics, as long as we prohibit objects from moving " backward" in time, the existence of arbitrarily high velocities means that, given a specific event *here*, only one instant of time *there* can be chosen as simultaneous; that is, there is no scope for conventionality of simultaneity at all.

Many philosophers have been skeptical of the conventionality of simultaneity in STR. In 1967 Brian Ellis and Peter Bowman argued that slow clock transport offers a means of synchronizing distant clocks that is independent of the velocity of light. Their idea was this: in STR, of course, when a clock is accelerated from rest in a given frame up to some constant velocity, then decelerated to rest again at a distant location, there are the notorious time-dilation effects that prevent us from regarding the clock as having remained in synch with clocks at its starting point (the accelerated clock will have fallen behind the rest-clock—though this can, again, only be *directly* verified if it is brought back to its starting place for comparison with the rest clock). And calculation of the size of the effect depends on having established a distant-simultaneity convention (i.e., a choice of ε). So it looks as though carrying a clock from observer 1 to observer 2 will not let us break the circle.

But Ellis and Bowman noted that the time dilation effect tends to zero as clock velocity goes to zero, and this is independent of ε-synchronization. Therefore, an "infinitely slowly" transported clock allows us to establish distant synchrony, and measure light's one-way velocity. Infinitely slow transport is not, of course, a practical method for synchronizing clocks. The point is rather this: Since we can prove mathematically that the time dilation effect goes to zero as velocity of transport approaches zero, we can establish the *conceptual* point that the one-way velocity of light is non-conventional. Conventionalists were not persuaded, and the outcome of the fierce debate provoked by Ellis and Bowman's paper was not clear (Norton 1986).

In 1977 David Malament took up the conventionalist challenge from a different perspective. One way of interpreting the claim of conventionalists such as Grünbaum is this: The observable *causal structure* of events in an STR-world does not suffice to determine a unique frame-dependent simultaneity choice. By "causal structure" we mean the network of causal connections between events; loosely speaking, any two events are causally connectable if they *could* be connected by a material process or light-signal. In STR, the "conformal structure" or light-cone structure at all points is the idealization of this causal structure. It determines, from a given event, what events could be causally connected to it (toward the past or toward the future). Grünbaum and others believed that the causal structure of space-time by no means singles out any preferred way of cutting up space-time into "simultaneity slices."

Malament showed that, in an important sense, they were wrong. The causal/conformal structure of Minkowski space-time *does* pick out a unique frame-relative foliation of events into simultaneity slices. Or rather, more precisely, the conformal structure suffices to determine a unique relation of *orthogonality*. If we think of an ε-choice as the choice of how to make simultaneity slices relative to an observer in a given frame, then Malament showed that the conformal structure is sufficient to define a unique, orthogonal foliation, which corresponds to Einstein's ε = ½ choice. But most conventionalists do not view Malament's result as a refutation of their view (Janis 1983), in part because Malament's proof starts from assumptions that are arguably already in violation of the spirit of the conventionalist's view.

In recent years philosophers have begun to consider whether quantum theories may shed light on the debates concerning simultaneity; see Gunn and Vetharaniam (1995) and Karakostas (1997) for arguments for and against the idea that quantum field theory refutes the conventionalist claim. Bain (2000) shows that while it is true that one can formulate quantum field physics in coordinate systems corresponding to ε ≠ ½ simultaneity, by choosing the *generally* covariant formulation of the theory (i.e., a formulation that is valid, roughly speaking, in any coordinate system whatsoever), doing so requires the introduction of a new mathematical object or "field," whose role is basically to represent the standard orthogonal simultaneity slices. That is, while one can nominally "choose" a simultaneity standard different from ε ≠ ½, the compensatory adjustments one is forced to introduce in order to make the theory work are such that one can see the "true" temporal structure lurking just under the surface. Conventionalists and anti-conventionalists disagree, of course, over whether the scare-quotes may be removed from the "true" in this verdict.

See also Philosophy of Physics; Space; Time.

Bibliography

Bain, J. "The Coordinate-Independent 2-Component Spinor Formalism and the Conventionality of Simultaneity." *Studies in History and Philosophy of Modern Physics 31B* (2000): 201–226.

DiSalle, R. "Spacetime Theory as Physical Geometry." *Erkenntnis* 42 (1995): 317–337.

Duhem, P. *The Aim and Structure of Physical Theory.* Translated by P. Wiener. Princeton, NJ: Princeton University Press, 1954.

Ellis, B., and P. Bowman. "Conventionality in Distant Simultaneity." *Philosophy of Science* 34 (1967): 116–136.

Friedman, M. *Foundations of Space-Time Theories: Relativistic Physics and Philosophy of Science.* Princeton, NJ: Princeton University Press, 1983.

Friedman, M. *Reconsidering Logical Positivism.* Cambridge, U.K.: Cambridge University Press, 1999.

Gunn, D., and I. Vetharaniam. "Relativistic Quantum Mechanics and the Conventionality of Simultaneity." *Philosophy of Science* 62 (1995): 599–608.

Janis, A. "Simultaneity and Conventionality." In *Physics, Philosophy and Psychoanalysis*, edited by R, Cohen, 101–110. Reidel: Dordrecht, 1983.

Karakostas, V. "The Conventionality of Simultaneity in the Light of the Spinor Representation of the Lorentz Group." *Studies in the History and Philosophy of Modern Physics* 28 (1997): 249–267.

Malament, D. "Causal Theories of Time and the Conventionality of Simultaneity." *Noûs* 11 (1977): 293–300.

Norton, J. "The Quest for the One Way Speed of Light." *British Journal for the Philosophy of Science* 37 (1986): 118–120.

Poincaré, H. *Science and Hypothesis* (1902). New York: Dover Books, 1952.

Putnam, H. "An Examination of Grünbaum's Philosophy of Geometry." In *Philosophy of Science: The Delaware Seminar*, Vol. 2, edited by B. Baumrin, 205–255. New York: Interscience, 1963.

Redhead, M. "The Conventionality of Simultaneity." In *Philosophical Problems of the Internal and External Worlds: Essays on the Philosophy of Adolf Grünbaum*, edited by J. Earman, A. Janis, G. Massey, and N. Rescher, 103–128. Pitsburgh, PA: University of Pitsburgh Press, 1993.

Reichenbach, H. *Philosophie der Raum-Zeit-Lehre.*Berlin and Leipzig: Walter de Gruyter, 1928. Translated by Maria Reichenbach and John Freund as *The Philosophy of Space and Time* (New York: Dover, 1957).

Reichenbach, H. *Relativitätstheorie und Erkenntnis apriori.* Berlin: Julius Springer1920. Translated by Maria Reichenbach as *The Theory of Relativity and A Priori Knowledge* (Berkeley and Los Angeles: University of California Press, 1965).

Ryckman, T. *The Reign of Relativity: Philosophy in Physics 1915–1925.* New York: Oxford University Press, 2004.

Torretti, R. *Relativity and Geometry.* Oxford, U.K.: Pergamon Press, 1983.

Carl Hoefer (2005)

CONVERSATIONAL IMPLICATURE

The concept of conversational implicature is due to the work of Paul Grice, and in particular to his paper "Logic and Conversation," which was delivered in 1967 and instantly became highly influential, although it was not published until 1975. A key goal of this paper was to defend the traditional logical understanding of connectives like *and* against what he saw as the excesses of ordinary language philosophy. He did this by drawing a sharp distinction between what is strictly speaking *said* and what is *conversationally implicated.* Consider sentence (1), below.

(1) Amanda and Beau fell in love and got married.

An utterance of (1) will typically suggest that the falling in love preceded the marriage. However, if *and* has its bare logical meaning, (1) may be true even if the marriage was initially loveless. According to Grice, (1) might indeed be true under these circumstances—because, strictly speaking, *and* contributes no more than its logical meaning to what is said. Grice claimed that the extra suggestion of temporal order was a conversational implicature. Conversational implicatures are an important part of communication, but (according to Grice) they have no effect on truth value. This is because they are not a part of what is strictly speaking said.

Grice argued that conversational implicatures arise from our adherence to (and presumption that others will adhere to) what he called the Cooperative Principle: "[m]ake your conversational contribution such as is required, at the stage at which it occurs, by the accepted purpose or direction of the talk exchange in which you are engaged" (1989b, p. 26). (He took this principle to govern conversation, but he also took it that the principle would have correlates in other cooperative endeavors.) In its broadest outline Grice's idea was that we presume that others are being cooperative—and we will generally make whatever supplementary assumptions are required to maintain this presumption. This presumption is what allows for the communication of conversational implicatures.

Grice takes it that we generally follow the Cooperative Principle by following four more specific maxims of cooperation (which, like the Cooperative Principle itself, he takes to have correlates in other endeavors):

> Quantity: Make your contribution as informative as (neither more nor less informative than) is required (1989b, p. 26).
>
> Quality: "Try to make your contribution one that is true": "do not say what you believe to be false" and "do not say that for which you lack adequate evidence" (1989b, p. 27).
>
> Relation: "Be relevant" (1989b, p. 27).
>
> Manner: "Be perspicuous": "1. Avoid obscurity of expression; 2. Avoid ambiguity; 3. Be brief (avoid unnecessary prolixity); 4. Be orderly" (1989b, p. 27).

Any of these maxims may play a role in generating conversational implicatures.

Grice characterizes conversational implicature as follows, and most scholars have followed him in this characterization.

> A man who, by (in, when) saying (or making as if to say) that *p* has implicated that *q* may be said to have conversationally implicated that *q*, provided that:
>
> (1) he is to be presumed to be following the conversational maxims, or at least the Cooperative Principle;
>
> (2) the supposition that he is aware that, or thinks that, *q* is required to make his saying or making as if to say *p* (or doing so in *those* terms) consistent with this presumption; and
>
> (3) the speaker thinks (and would expect the hearer to think that the speaker thinks) that it is within the competence of the hearer to work out, or grasp intuitively, that the supposition mentioned in (2) is required.
>
> (GRICE 1989, PP. 30–31)

To see how all of this machinery works in the generation of a conversational implicature, one must return to an utterance of (1).

(1) Amanda and Beau fell in love and got married.

Typically, the audience will assume that the speaker is being cooperative (so condition 1 is met). A cooperative speaker will follow the maxim of Manner, and the maxim of Manner dictates orderly presentation. If one is being orderly, one will generally present events in the order in which they occurred, so the audience must assume that the speaker thinks that Amanda and Beau's love predated their marriage. (Condition 2 is met). The speaker surely realizes that the audience is capable of working this out, so condition 3 is met. A typical utterance of (1), then, will implicate something like (1*).

(1*) Amanda and Beau fell in love and *then* got married.

There are a variety of ways that conversational implicatures may be generated. The above mechanism does not rely on the speaker's utterance being one whose explicit content would be uncooperative, but this latter sort of implicature (created by violating or flouting a maxim) is also an important one. It is crucial, for example, to irony, hyperbole, and understatement.

KINDS OF CONVERSATIONAL IMPLICATURE

Grice distinguished two main kinds of conversational implicature, *generalized* and *particularized*. Generalized conversational implicatures are ones that are *usually* carried by a certain word or phrase, while particularized conversational implicatures depend far more heavily on context. (Grice also allowed for nonconversational implicatures, such as *conventional* implicatures, with no role whatsoever for context. These are not of concern here.) The example discussed so far, involving (1), is that of a generalized conversational implicature: utterances of sentences involving *and* will usually carry the suggestion of temporal order that it is present in this example. Particularized implicatures depend far more heavily on context. Suppose you are hiring for a philosophy job, you ask me what I think of my student Charla, and I reply with nothing but (2).

(2) Charla reads a lot.

(2) is clearly not adequately informative, given your question—philosophy jobs require a great deal more than reading. By violating the maxim of Quantity in this way, I conversationally implicate that Charla is not a good philosopher. But in a different context, there would be no such implicature (consider, for example, a context in which I was asked for names of people who might like to join a book group). Because the implicature depends so heavily on context, it is particularized rather than generalized.

A great deal of work has been done, especially in linguistics, on generalized conversational implicatures, and various mechanisms for their generation. Some of the most important work on this topic is by Laurence Horn (1972) and Stephen Levinson (2000). Generalized conversational implicatures have also played a particularly important role in philosophy. For Grice, these implicatures were especially important for their role in explaining certain problematic intuitions—like the intuition that (1) is false if the marriage preceded the love. He argued that generalized conversational implicatures are especially difficult to distinguish from what is strictly speaking said and that they may therefore give rise to mistaken intuitions. Philosophers since Grice have followed up on this thought by using generalized conversational implicatures in explanations of recalcitrant intuitions in a wide variety of areas.

It is worth noting that many cases that Grice took to be ones of generalized conversational implicature are very much disputed. For example, Robyn Carston (1991) has argued for a notion of saying (or, in her preferred terminology, *explicating*) on which the meaning of *and* is just what Grice would have taken it to be, yet nonetheless an utterance of a sentence like (1) *says* (rather than implicates) that Amanda and Beau's love preceded their marriage.

(1) Amanda and Beau fell in love and got married.

Carston's work on such examples is a part of a broader debate on the notion of what is said, which is not addressed here. But for some other approaches that also result in examples like the above counting as said, see Jeffrey King and Jason Stanley (2005), François Recanati (1989), and Dan Sperber and Dierdre Wilson (1986). For objections to reconstruing such generalized conversational implicatures as a part of what is said, see Kent Bach (2001), Laurence Horn (1992), Stephen Levinson (2000), Michael O'Rourke (2003), and Jennifer Saul (2002b).

TESTING FOR IMPLICATURE

Grice does not offer necessary and sufficient conditions that would allow one to test conclusively whether a given claim is a conversational implicature. However, he does offer certain necessary conditions for conversational implicature that can provide partial tests, and these have been widely accepted. Two especially important ones are cancelability and calculability. For more on testing for conversational implicatures, see Jerrold Sadock (1978).

CANCELABILITY. Because all conversational implicatures depend at least to some extent on context, it is always possible to cancel a conversational implicature by indicating either explicitly or implicitly that the implicatures should not be taken as present. For example, one might utter (1C):

(1C) Amanda and Beau fell in love and got married, but not in that order. Because (1C) contains an explicit cancellation of the conversational implicature standardly carried by (1), that implicature will not be carried by an utterance of (1C).

This contrasts with the case of saying. An attempt to "cancel" something that is said results only in a contradiction. To see this, consider an utterance of (1C*):

(1C*) Amanda and Beau fell in love and got married, but they didn't get married.

Applying this test shows us that the claim that Amanda and Beau got married is definitely not a conversational implicature, while the claim that their love preceded their marriage may well be.

While failure of the cancelability test does indeed indicate that one is not dealing with a conversational implicature, passing the cancelability test cannot be taken to decisively established that one is dealing with a conversational implicature. There are at least two reasons for this. First, a case of disambiguation may resemble one of cancellation, as in (3):

(3) He is in the grip of a vice, but not the mechanical kind.

Second, speaking loosely may result in an appearance of cancellation. Grice's own example (1989a, p. 44) concerns the fact that one may acceptably say, "Macbeth saw Banquo, even though Banquo was not there to be seen," even if it is known by all that Banquo merely hallucinated. Because one might be using the verb "see" in a loose way, this apparent cancellation does not indicate that utterances involving "see" merely implicate that what is seen exists.

CALCULABILITY. According to Grice, a putative conversational implicature is not a conversational implicature unless it is possible for audience to work out that the presence of the implicature is required in order to understand the speaker as cooperative. This calculation is meant to draw on knowledge of the linguistic meaning of the sentence uttered, the maxims of conversation, relevant background information, and the specific context. If no explanation can be given of how an audience would perform a calculation like this, a hypothesis that a particular conversational implicature is present must be rejected.

This necessary condition is also widely accepted. But its exact interpretation is a matter of some controversy. In particular, there is disagreement over what it requires psychologically on the part of the hearer: must the hearer actually have distinct conscious representations of what is said and what is conversationally implicated (as argued by François Recanati in his work (1989)? Or are the requirements much more minimal (as argued by Kent Bach (2001), Manuel Garcia-Carpintero (2001), and Kenneth Taylor (2001)? The calculability requirement has proved very important: it has been used, for example, to argue for a more expansive conception of what is said (as in Recanati's work, as well as Robyn Carston's [1991]); to argue for and to object to particular invocations of conversational implicature; and (as in Wayne Davis's [1998]) to raise quite general concerns about the viability of Grice's theory of implicature.

GRICE'S TAXONOMY. It is very common to maintain that speaker meaning must divide exhaustively into what is said and what is implicated. Thus, any claim that the speaker means but does not say must be an implicature. (It need not, however, be a conversational implicature, since it could be a conventional implicature.) It is not entirely clear, however, that this is the right way to understand relationship between speaker meaning and implicature. For objections to this view of the relationship, see Kent Bach (1994) and Jennifer Saul (2002b).

See also Meaning; Pragmatics; Presupposition; Semantics.

Bibliography

Bach, Kent. "Conversational Impliciture." *Mind and Language* 9 (2) (1994): 124–161.

Bach, Kent. "You Don't Say?" *Synthese* 128 (2001): 15–44.

Carston, Robyn. "Implicature, Explicature, and Truth-Theoretic Semantics." In *Pragmatics: A Reader*, edited by Steven Davis. New York: Oxford University Press, 1991.

Davis, Wayne. *Implicature: Intention, Convention, and Principle in the Failure of Gricean Theory*. Cambridge, U.K.: Cambridge University Press, 1998.

Garcia-Carpintero, Manuel. "Gricean Rational Reconstructions and the Semantics/Pragmatics Distinction." *Synthese* 128 (2001): 93–131.

Grice, Paul. "Further Notes on Logic and Conversation." In *Studies in the Way of Words*, 41–57. Cambridge, MA: Harvard University Press, 1989a.

Grice, Paul. "Logic and Conversation." In *Studies in the Way of Words*, 3–21. Cambridge, MA: Harvard University Press, 1989b.

Horn, Laurence. "On the Semantic Properties of Logical Operators in English." Diss. University of California at Los Angeles, 1972.

Horn, Laurence. "The Said and the Unsaid." In *SALT II: Proceedings of the Second Conference on Semantics and Linguistic Theory*, 163–192. Columbus, OH: Ohio State University Department of Linguistics, 1992.

King, Jeffrey, and Jason Stanley. "Semantics, Pragmatics, and the Role of Semantic Content." In *Semantics versus Pragmatics*, edited by Zoltan Szabo, 111–164. New York: Oxford University Press, 2005.

Levinson, Stephen C. *Pragmatics*. Cambridge, U.K.: Cambridge University Press, 1983.

Levinson, Stephen C. *Presumptive Meanings: The Theory of Generalized Conversational Implicature*. Cambridge, MA: MIT Press, 2000.

O'Rourke, Michael. "The Scope Argument." *Journal of Philosophy* 100 (2003): 264–288.

Recanati, François. "The Pragmatics of What Is Said." *Mind and Language* 4 (1989): 295–329.

Sadock, Jerrold. "On Testing for Conversational Implicature." In *Syntax and Semantics*. Vol. 9: *Pragmatics*, edited by Peter Cole and Jerry Morgan. New York: Academic Press, 1978.

Saul, Jennifer. "Speaker Meaning, What Is Said, and What Is Implicated." *Noûs* 36 (2) (2002a): 228–248.

Saul, Jennifer. "What Is Said and Psychological Reality: Grice's Project and Relevance Theorists' Criticisms." *Linguistics and Philosophy* 25 (2002b): 347–372.

Sperber, Dan, and Dierdre Wilson. *Relevance: Communication and Cognition*. Cambridge, MA: Harvard University Press, 1986.

Taylor, Kenneth. "Sex, Breakfast, and Descriptus Interruptus." *Synthese* 128 (2001): 45–61.

Jennifer Saul (2005)

CONWAY, ANNE

(1631–1679)

Anne Conway (Anne Finch, Viscountess Conway), the English philosopher, was born in London. Her education was primarily informal and self-directed. Her associates included Henry More, Ralph Cudworth, Francis Mercury Van Helmont, William Harvey, and Robert Boyle, the latter two as physicians for her serious headaches. Later in life she scandalized More by becoming a Quaker.

WORK AND INFLUENCE

Conway's sole published work, *The Principles of the Most Ancient and Modern Philosophy*, published posthumously in 1690, shows the influence of the Cambridge Platonists, Kabbalism, and Neoplatonism. It criticized Thomas Hobbes, Benedict de Spinoza, and René Descartes, and influenced Gottfried Wilhelm Leibniz, who, during the year he was introduced to her work by Van Helmont in 1696, adopted her term *monad* and used it in a quite similar way (Merchant 1979). A notable difference between their uses of the term is that, while Leibniz's monads are purely spiritual, Conway's are both physical and spiritual.

Leibniz refers directly to Conway in his *New Essays* (book 1, chap. 1) as one of the better advocates of vitalism.

METAPHYSICS

Conway begins the *Principles* by asserting without proof the existence of a perfect God, the description of which is influenced by Neoplatonism and Kabbalism. Conway's God is one of three kinds of substance, each with its own essence. God is a complete, self-sufficient fountain that necessarily emanates Christ, the second kind of substance, and through the mediation of Christ, who shares some attributes with God, others with creatures, necessarily emanates creatures—the third kind of substance. Because emanative creation is creation "out of" God rather than "out of" nothing, creatures have a share of the divine attribute of life. Since all creatures are of the same kind of substance, they have a single essence, differing only modally from one another. Thus, spirit or mind and body are not "really distinct." There are many degrees of corporeity, and thus "a Thing may more or less approach to, or recede from the State and Condition of a body or a Spirit" (Conway 1982, p. 192). Conway draws the further conclusion that creatures are interconvertible: A horse, for example, can turn into a bird and spirits can turn into bodies (p. 177).

Not only God's creative act, but all of God's actions flow automatically from God's nature. Thus, God does whatever does not involve a contradiction. Conway's deity, like Leibniz', is timeless. Both Conway and Leibniz consider time to be relative to succession and motion; they consider succession and motion to be inferior analogues of eternity and the divine will, respectively, and thus to belong only to creatures (Conway 1982, p. 161).

Conway employs the concept of mediation, introduced in her account of creation, to explain action at a distance as well as causation between bodies and spirits. All created substances, in addition to sharing an essence, are interconnected by means of "Subtiler Parts," which are the "Emanation of one Creature into another." These mediated connections facilitate action at a distance and form "the Foundation of all Sympathy and Antipathy which happens in Creatures" (Conway 1982, p. 164). Conway offers, by contrast to the mechanical philosophy, a fairly direct account of the intelligibility of causation based on the concepts of similarity (or sympathy) and mediation. Similarity between cause and effect, as in the case of causation among bodies, renders causation directly intelligible, "because Things of one, or alike Nature, can easily affect each other." Mediation is required in the case of mind-body causation, because a soul is a "Spiritual Body" (pp. 214–215).

Since Conway regards interconnection as primitive, she requires no detailed explanations of causal interactions. Here she contrasts markedly with mechanistic philosophers' demands for explanations using motion and passive matter as primitives. Conway nonetheless incorporates causation by motion into her overall account of causation: Motion, especially vital motion, and divine emanation do not differ intrinsically from one another but are analogically related.

See also Boyle, Robert; Cambridge Platonists; Causation: Metaphysical Issues; Causation: Philosophy of Science; Cudworth, Ralph; Descartes, René; Harvey, William; Hobbes, Thomas; Kabbalah; Leibniz, Gottfried Wilhelm; More, Henry; Neoplatonism; Spinoza, Benedict (Baruch) de; Vitalism.

Bibliography

Conway, A. *The Principles of the Most Ancient and Modern Philosophy.* Edited by P. Lopston. The Hague: Nijhoff, 1982.

Duran, J. "Anne Viscountess Conway: A Seventeenth-Century Rationalist." *Hypatia* 4 (1989): 64–79.

Frankel, L. "Anne Finch, Viscountess Conway." In *A History of Women Philosophers,* Vol. 3, edited by M. E. Waithe. Dordrecht: Kluwer Academic, 1991.

Frankel, L. "The Value of Harmony." In *Causation in Early Modern Philosophy,* edited by S. Nadler. University Park: Pennsylvania State University Press, 1993.

Merchant, C. "The Vitalism of Anne Conway: Its Impact on Leibniz's Concept of the Monad." *Journal of the History of Philosophy* 17 (1979): 255–269.

Nicolson, M. H. *Conway Letters.* New Haven, CT: Yale University Press, 1930.

Lois Frankel (1996)

COPENHAGEN INTERPRETATION

The Copenhagen interpretation is the standard textbook interpretation of quantum mechanics. The term covers a range of divergent views, loosely related to Bohr's complementarity interpretation. The consensus of the physics community is that Einstein lost the debate to Bohr about the "completeness" of quantum mechanics at the Solvay conference of October 1927, and that Bohr's analysis of the experimental situation in quantum mechanics in terms of the notion of complementarity allows one to make sense of a universe that is indeterministic 'all the way down,' so that quantum states (that in general assign probabilities between 0 and 1 to the outcomes of experiments) are as complete as they can be.

It is difficult to pin down the Copenhagen interpretation. Heisenberg—who seems to have coined the term "Copenhagen interpretation" (see Howard's "Who Invented the Copenhagen Interpretation" for a discussion)—concedes differences between his own position and Bohr's, but concludes that "we really meant the same." The term is generally taken to cover such radical views as Wigner's, that "the quantum description of objects is influenced by impressions entering my consciousness" and John Wheeler's notion of a "participatory universe":

> The dependence of what is observed upon the choice of experimental arrangement made Einstein unhappy. It conflicts with the view that the universe exists 'out there' independent of all acts of observation. In contrast Bohr stressed that we confront here an inescapable new feature of nature, to be welcomed because of the understanding it gives us. In struggling to make clear to Einstein the central point as he saw it, Bohr found himself forced to introduce the word 'phenomenon.' In todays words Bohr's point—the central point of quantum theory—can be put into a single, simple sentence. 'No elementary phenomenon is a phenomenon until it is a registered (observed) phenomenon.' It is wrong to speak of the 'route' of the photon in the experiment of the beam splitter. It is wrong to attribute a tangibility to the photon in all its travel from the point of entry to its last instant of flight. A phenomenon is not yet a phenomenon until it has been brought to a close by an irreversible act of amplification such as the blackening of a grain of silver bromide emulsion or the triggering of a photodetector. In broader terms, we find that nature at the quantum level is not a machine that goes its inexorable way. Instead what answer we get depends on the question we put, the experiment we arrange, the registration device we choose. We are inescapably involved in bringing about that which appears to be happening.
>
> (WHEELER 1983, PP. 184–185)

It is doubtful that Bohr would have endorsed Wheeler's formulation as a friendly amendment to complementarity. In a cautionary remark about misleading terminology, he writes:

> In this connection I warned especially against phrases, often found in the literature, such as "disturbing of phenomena by observation" or "creating physical attributes to atomic objects by measurements." Such phrases, which may serve to remind of the apparent paradoxes in quantum theory, are at the same time apt to cause confusion, since words like "phenomena" and "observations," just as "attributes" and "measurements," are used in a way hardly compatible with common language and practical definition.
>
> (BOHR 1948, P. 237)

THE REJECTION OF EINSTEIN'S REALISM

The common strand linking these different positions is the rejection of Einstein's realism—the "ideal of the detached observer," as Pauli put it somewhat pejoratively in a letter to Max Born (dated March 30, 1954). Einstein's position can be characterized by two informal independence principles: A separability principle and a locality principle. The separability principle is the principle that if two physical systems are spatially separated (or, in a relativistic setting, space-like separated), then each system can be characterized by its own properties, independently of the properties of the other system. That is, each system separately has its own "being-thus," as Einstein put it: A characterization in terms of certain properties intrinsic to the system, insofar as it is a separable system. The locality principle is the requirement that no influence on a system can directly affect another system that is spatially separated from it. In particular, a measurement performed on a system cannot alter any properties of another system that is spatially separated from it. The Copenhagen idea is that, in some sense (notwithstanding Bohr's discomfort with the terminology), the dynamical variables of quantum mechanics—the so-called "observables" of the theory—"only have values when you look," where the notion of "looking" is understood in a certain way (depending on the version: As involving the specification of a classically describable experimental set-up, or an interaction with a macroscopic measuring instrument that does not involve an ultimate conscious observer, or a measurement process that does involve the activity of a conscious observer, etc.). This claim is justified by citing examples of quantum interference characterized by Heisenberg's uncertainty relations, such as the double-slit experiment, or beam splitter experiments, or by appealing to the irreducible disturbance of a measured system in a quantum mechanical measurement interaction.

MEASUREMENT AND INTERFERENCE

Now it is generally recognized that the mere fact that measurements disturb what we measure does not preclude the possibility that observables have determinate values, or even that measurements might be exploited to reveal these values in suitably designed measurement contexts. (The "disturbance" terminology itself suggests the existence of determinate values for observables, prior to measurement, that are "disturbed" or undergo dynamical change in physical interactions.) And there is no warrant in the theory for interpreting the Heisenberg uncertainty relations for observables like position and momentum as anything more than a constraint on the possibility of preparing ensembles of systems in which these observables are simultaneously "sharp"–that is, as anything more than a constraint on the reciprocal distribution of the determinate values of these observables in quantum measurements.

Even interference phenomena, by themselves, say nothing about whether or not observables have determinate values in the absence of measurements, unless some interpretative principle is introduced. The usual story, in the case of a double-slit photon interference experiment, for example, is that you get the wrong distribution of hits on the screen behind the slits if you calculate the distribution on the assumption that each individual photon goes through one or the other of the two slits, when the photon is prepared in a quantum state that is represented algebraically in the theory as a linear sum (superposition) of a state in which the photon goes through slit 1 and a state in which the photon goes through slit 2. The photon is supposed to exhibit "wave-particle duality" and "go through both slits at once" to produce the characteristic interference pattern on the screen, where the photon finally manifests its presence as a particle. In passing through the slits, the photon behaves like a wave, a physical influence spread out over both slits, but in hitting the screen, it behaves like a particle, something localized at a point.

The loophole in the argument is the assumption of a specific link between attributing a determinate value to a quantum observable (like position, in the case of a photon going through one of two slits), and attributing a specific quantum state to the photon. This depends on an interpretative principle, the so-called "eigenvalue-eigenstate link," that a quantum system has a determinate value (an "eigenvalue") for an observable if and only if the quantum state is in a specific state called the "eigenstate" of the observable associated with the specific eigenvalue. If we reject this principle, then we can attribute a determinate value (an eigenvalue) to the observable associated with the photon going through slit 1 or slit 2, exclusively, without assigning the associated state (the eigenstate) to the photon. This is precisely what observer-free hidden variable interpretations like Bohm's theory accomplish.

Interference *per se* represents no obstacle to the simultaneous determinateness of noncommuting observables. The justification for assuming constraints on the simultaneous determinateness of quantum mechanical observables comes, rather, from the hidden variable 'no go' theorems of Kochen and Specker (1967) and Bell (1964), which severely limit the assignment of values to observables.

IS THE COPENHAGEN INTERPRETATION INSTRUMENTALIST?

For Bohr, a quantum "phenomenon" is an individual process that occurs under conditions defined by a specific, classically describable experimental arrangement, and an observable can be said to have a determinate value only in the context of an experiment suitable for measuring the observable. The experimental arrangements suitable for locating an atomic object in space and time, and for a determination of momentum-energy values, are mutually exclusive. We can choose to investigate either of these "complementary" phenomena at the expense of the other, so there is no unique description of the object in terms of determinate properties.

Summing up a discussion on causality and complementarity, Bohr writes:

> Recapitulating, the impossibility of subdividing the individual quantum effects and of separating a behaviour of the objects from their interaction with the measuring instruments serving to define the conditions under which the phenomena appear implies an ambiguity in assigning conventional attributes to atomic objects which calls for a reconsideration of our attitude towards the problem of physical explanation. In this novel situation, even the old question of an ultimate determinacy of natural phenomena has lost its conceptual basis, and it is against this background that the viewpoint of complemenarity presents itself as a rational generalization of the very ideal of causality.
>
> (1949, p. 31)

Pauli characterizes Bohr's position this way:

> While the means of observation (experimental arrangements and apparatus, records such as spots on photographic plates) have still to be described in the usual 'common language supplemented with the terminology of classical physics,' the atomic 'objects' used in the theoretical interpretation of the 'phenomena' cannot any longer be described 'in a unique way by conventional physical attributes.' Those 'ambiguous' objects used in the description of nature have an obviously symbolic character.
>
> (1948, PP. 307–308)

The complementarity interpretation can be understood as the proposal to take the classically describable experimental arrangement (suitable for either a space-time or a momentum-energy determination) as defining what Bohr calls a quantum "phenomenon." A current approach is to refer to the macroscopic character of our measuring instruments, and to show that the nature of the interaction between such systems and the environment is of a specific sort that results in a physical process called "decoherence" that ensures the "classical" character of the instrument. Some version of this idea is incorporated into the Copenhagen interpretation, sometimes extended by claims such as Wheeler's. According to this view, then, the properties we attribute to a quantum object after a measurement depend partly on what we choose to measure, not solely on objective features of the system itself. To echo Pauli, the properties are "ambiguous" or merely "symbolic."

At first blush it would seem that the Copenhagen interpretation is thoroughly anti-realist, and in some contemporary versions straightforwardly instrumentalist. However, Don Howard in "Who Invented the Copenhagen Interpretation" has argued persuasively that Bohr's complementarity interpretation, as distinct from the Copenhgen interpretation, should be construed as a realist interpretation of quantum mechanics. For the contemporary philosophical debate on the Copenhagen interpretation, see Cushing (1994) and Beller (1999).

See also Bohr, Neils; Quantum Mechanics.

Bibliography

Bell, John S. "On the Einstein-Podolsky-Rosen Paradox." *Physics* 1 (1964): 195–200. Reprinted in *Speakable and Unspeakable in Quantum Mechanics*. Cambridge, U.K.: Cambridge University Press, 1987.

Beller, Mara. *Quantum Dialogue: The Making of a Revolution.* Chicago: University of Chicago Press, 1999.

Bohm, David, and Basil J. Hiley. *The Undivided Universe: An Ontological Interpretation of Quantum Mechanics*. London: Routledge, 1993.

Bohr, Niels. "Discussion with Einstein on Epistemological Problems in Modern Physics." In *Albert Einstein: Philosopher-Scientist*, edited by Paul A. Schilpp, 201–241. La Salle, IL: Open Court, 1949.

Bohr, Niels. "On the Notions of Causality and Complementarity." *Dialectica* 2 (1948): 312–319.

Born, Max, ed. *The Born-Einstein Letters*. London: Walker and Co: 1971.

Cushing, James T. *Quantum Mechanics, Historical Contingency and the Copenhagen Hegemony*. Chicago: University of Chicago Press, 1994.

Einstein, Albert. "Quantenmechanik und Wirklichkeit." *Dialectica* 2 (1948): 320–324. Translated as "Quantum Mechanics and Reality." In *The Born-Einstein Letters*, edited by Max Born, 170. See the accompanying letter from Einstein to Born dated April 5, 1948, and the letter dated March 18, 1948, on p. 164.

Fuchs, Christopher A., and Asher Peres. "Quantum Theory Needs No Interpretation." *Physics Today*, 70: 2000.

Heisenberg, Werner. "The Development of the Interpretation of Quantum Theory." In *Niels Bohr and the Development of Physics*, edited by Wolfgang Pauli, 12–29. London: Pergamon Press: 1955.

Heisenberg, Werner. "Quantum Theory and its Interpretation." In *Niels Bohr: His Life and Works as Seen by his Friends and Colleagues*, edited by S. Rozental, 94–108. New York: Wiley Interscience, 1967.

Howard, Don. "Who Invented the Copenhagen Interpretation?" Available at http://www.nd.edu/dhoward1/Papers.html.

Kochen, Simon, and E. P. Specker. "The Problem of Hidden Variables in Quantum Mechanics." *Journal of Mathematics and Mechanics* 17 (1967): 59–87.

Pauli, Wolfgang H. "Editorial on the Concept of Complementarity." *Dialectica* 2 (1948): 307–311.

Pauli, Wolfgang H. Letter to Max Born, dated March 30, 1954. In *The Born-Einstein Letters*, edited by Max Born, 218.

Wheeler, John A. "Law without Law." In *Quantum Theory and Measurement*, edited by John H. Wheeler and Wojciech H. Zurek, 183–213. Princeton, NJ: Princeton University Press, 1983.

Wigner, Eugene P. "Remarks on the Mind-Body Question." In *The Scientist Speculates*, edited by I. J. Good, 284–301. London: Heinemann, 1962.

Jeffrey Bub (2005)

COPERNICUS, NICOLAS

(1473–1543)

Nicolas Copernicus, or Mikolaj Kopernick, was a Polish clergyman, physician, and astronomer, and the propounder of a heliocentric theory of the universe. He was born at Torun (Thorn) on the Vistula. He studied liberal arts, canon law, and medicine at the universities of

Kraków (1491–1494), Bologna (1496–1500), and Padua (1501–1503) and received a doctorate in canon law from the University of Ferrara in 1503. Through the influence of his uncle, the bishop of Ermland, Copernicus was elected *in absentia* as a canon of the cathedral of Frauenburg in 1497. By 1506 he had returned to Poland, serving as physician to his uncle until 1512, when he took up his duties as canon. Copernicus's duties as canon involved him in the complex diplomatic maneuverings of the time and in the administration of the cathedral's large estates. In his own day he was more widely known as a physician than as an astronomer. He was one of the few persons in northeastern Europe to have a knowledge of the Greek language, and the one book he published without the urging of colleagues was a Latin translation of the poems of Theophylactus Simocatta, a seventh-century Byzantine poet. Copernicus's competence in economics was shown in some reports on money, presented to the Prussian diet, in which he anticipated a form of Gresham's law.

Copernicus's interest in astronomy was probably aroused at Kraków by the mathematician Wojciech Brudzewski and spurred on at Bologna by the astronomer Domenico Maria da Novara. Copernicus's first documented astronomical observation was made in Bologna in 1497. Twenty-seven such observations were used in his major treatise; others he recorded in the margins of books in his library. By 1514 he was so well known as an astronomer that he was asked by Pope Leo X to assist in the reform of the calendar, a task he declined because the motions of the sun and the moon had not yet been sufficiently determined.

Although Copernicus's major work, *De Revolutionibus Orbium Coelestium Libri IV,* was not published until 1543, the year of his death, he had been developing his theories at least from about 1512, the approximate date of his *Commentariolus* (a short outline of his system which he gave in manuscript copies to a few trusted friends). The first published account of his system was the *Narratio Prima* of his disciple and biographer (the biography is no longer extant), Georg Joachim Rheticus, in 1540. It was Rheticus who finally induced Copernicus to allow the publication of his major work.

LATE MEDIEVAL ASTRONOMY

The difference between Copernicus's theory and the then prevailing Ptolemaic system of astronomy can be stated briefly. The Copernican system was heliocentric rather than geocentric and geostatic; it placed the sun close to the center of the universe and Earth in orbit around the center, rather than postulating an immobile Earth at the center of the universe. But the full significance of this statement can be understood only via an examination of the *ad hoc* character of late medieval astronomy. Such late scholastic thinkers as Robert Grosseteste, Thomas Bradwardine, Jean Buridan, Nicholas Oresme, and Nicholas of Cusa had perceived the theoretical virtues and explanatory power of the heliocentric principle, as had Ptolemy himself long before. They understood the imperfections of the Ptolemaic techniques; yet they conceded that observational evidence did not clearly favor either theory—as was the case until the late sixteenth century. On scriptural grounds these thinkers accepted orthodox geocentrism; but they aired, more fully and deliberately than any of their predecessors, the arguments in support of terrestrial movement. They played *advocatus diaboli* with precision and imagination.

But prior to Copernicus astronomy was a piecemeal undertaking. Such problems as the prediction of a stationary point, or of an occultation, were dealt with one at a time, planet by planet. There was no conception that one planet's current stationary point might be related to another planet's later occultation. Techniques were employed as needed, and problem solving was not systematically integrated. Copernicus's theory changed this piecemeal approach forever. He effected a Kantian revolution in astronomy perhaps even more than Immanuel Kant effected a Copernican revolution in philosophy. Copernicus relocated the primary observational problem, that of explaining the apparent retrograde motions of the planets, by construing the motions not as something the planets "really" did "out there," but as the result of our own motion. Earth's flight around the sun makes other circling objects sometimes appear to move backward in relation to the fixed stars. Although either the Ptolemaic or the Copernican theory could be reconciled with sixteenth-century observations, Copernicus's view did not require investing those planets with queer dynamical properties, such as retrogradations-in-fact; a planet that actually halted, went into reverse, halted again, and then proceeded "forward" would be a strange physical object indeed. Rather, in Copernicus's view, all planets, including Earth, had the same kind of motion—a simple motion that explained the observed retrogradations.

It had been clear even to the ancients that the view that Earth was in the exact center of the universal system and that all celestial bodies moved about Earth in perfect circles could not generate predictions and descriptions even remotely close to the observed facts. In order to generate the right predictional numbers as well as tractable orbital shapes, the Ptolemaic astronomers made a number of ad hoc assumptions. They moved Earth from the exact center of the planetary array; they used the geometrical center of the system as a reference point from which to calculate planetary distances; and they invented a third point, the *punctum aequans* (a mere computational device without physical significance, a device that Copernicus described as "monstrous"), around which the centers of the planetary epicycles described equal angles in equal times. No mechanisms known in nature or in art, however, have one center from which distances are determined, another from which velocities are determined, and a third from which observations are made. Moreover, the location of all these points and the choice of angular velocities around them were fixed arbitrarily and ex post facto simply to cope with each new observation as it turned up.

Even had Ptolemaic astronomy achieved perfection in predicting and describing, it was still powerless to explain planetary motion. One might ask how a theory that could describe and predict perfectly could in any way lack explanatory power; but Copernicus would have distinguished between the mere capacity of a theory to generate accurate numbers, and its further ability to provide an intelligible foundation for comprehending the phenomena studied. Even had the Ptolemaic system been able to predict accurately any future position of each moving point of light, Copernicus would still have asked what these points of light were, and what systematic mechanical interconnections existed between them.

An imaginative scholar, aware of the many difficulties posed by the Ptolemaic system as it had been developed over the years, and knowing (as Copernicus did) the accounts of ancient heliocentric theorists, might have only been expected to continue to seek improvements within the Ptolemaic system by incorporating promising heliocentric devices from his Scholastic predecessors (if he knew them) and from the ancients. Any gifted astronomer of Copernicus's day bent on improving astronomy "from the inside" would thus have had to take heliocentrism seriously.

In fact, Copernicus's books and Rheticus's summary might be viewed as an articulate and systematic expression of much late medieval planetary thinking. The ties with fifteenth-century Scholastic thought are everywhere apparent. But the primary insight of *De Revolutionibus,* although not novel, was boldly carried out and very much sharpened in detail. It was a comprehensive attempt to make the science of that day work better; it was not explicitly a plan for a new science of tomorrow. The dramatic consequences, largely unanticipated by Copernicus, are a tribute to his thoroughness as a student of nature and not to any self-conscious desire to level the orthodoxy around him.

THE COPERNICAN ALTERNATIVE

Copernicus was led to conclude that, in view of the plethora of epicycles required by the Ptolemaic system to account for the observed motion of the heavenly bodies, it must contain some basic error. He found that the assumption of a moving Earth, however absurd and counterintuitive it appeared, led to a much simpler and aesthetically superior system. Imagine yourself on the outer edge of a merry-go-round, sitting in a swivel chair. The constant rotation of the chair, when compounded with the revolution of the chair around the center of the merry-go-round, would generate—to say the least—complex visual impressions. Those impressions are compatible either with the motion as just described or with the supposition that it is the chair which is absolutely fixed and that all of the visual impressions stem from the motion of the merry-go-round about the chair-as-center and of a like motion of the walls of the building in which it is housed. The actual observations could be accounted for by either hypothesis. But what is easy to visualize in this example was extraordinarily difficult to comprehend in astronomical terms. That it was Earth that rotated and twisted, and revolved around the sun, seemed contrary to experience, common sense, and Scripture. Yet it was this simple alternative hypothesis that, for reasons demanded by astronomy, Copernicus espoused.

COPERNICUS'S REVOLUTION

Fundamentally, then, Copernicus argued that the observational intricacies of planetary motion were not real, but merely apparent. This argument made planetary motion simpler to comprehend but our own motion more intricate and therefore harder to believe. That was the fundamental objection to Copernicus's innovation.

But one must be quite clear about the nature of the theory. It was not a celestial dynamics, even in the sense that Johannes Kepler's theory of the causes of planetary motion (in terms of primitive spokes of force radiating from the sun) was a celestial dynamics. Copernicus, like his predecessors, was no astrophysicist; he was concerned with positional astronomy—the kinematics of planetary appearances, the motions of stellar lights against the black bowl of the sky and the underlying geometry that would, with a minimum of ad hoc assumptions, make those motions intelligible. So, both the *Almagest* and the *De Rev-*

olutionibus were concerned with plantetary kinematics exclusively—the latter in a systematic way, the former in the manner of a recipe collection. And even as a kinematic theory, Copernicus's theory was less adequate than those of Tycho Brahe and Kepler. He believed that the planets moved in perfect circles, an assumption shattered by Kepler's discovery of elliptical orbits. There is nothing in Copernicus to compare with Kepler's second law—that planets sweep out equal circumsolar areas in equal times. Nor is there anything to compare to Kepler's third law, correlating the time a planet requires to circle the sun with its distance from the sun. (And only when Kepler's three laws were added to the Galileo-Descartes law of inertia, and Isaac Newton's law of universal gravitation, was there developed a genuine celestial mechanics.) Copernicus's contributions consisted in a redeployment of the established elements of Ptolemaic positional astronomy. It is in this sense that he has been, and should be, viewed as the last great medieval astronomer.

SIMPLICITY OF COPERNICUS'S THEORY

Copernicus's theory was not psychologically simpler than competing systems. A moving Earth, and a sun and stars that do not "rise" and "circle" us, seemed contrary to experience. Also, a theoretical apparatus that linked all astronomical problems instead of leaving them to be faced one at a time could not constitute an easier system of calculation. Indeed, in the sixteenth century, heliocentrism was psychologically far more complex than the theories men were accustomed to.

Was Copernicus's conception perhaps simpler in that, as a formal theoretical system, it did not require primitive new ideas for each new problem or for the times when old problems led to difficulties? It invoked nothing like a *punctum aequans*; that is, it invoked fewer independent conceptual elements (primitive terms) merely to explain aberrant calculations than did other astronomies. But this point is insufficient to explain the sense in which Copernicus's system manifests "simplicity." Computational schemes had been proposed by Caelio Calcagnini and Geronimo Fracastoro that were simpler in that they were built on smaller sets of primitive notions. But they were so inadequate to the observational tasks of astronomy that it would have been as idle to stress their simplicity as it would be today to press for the theoretical adoption of John Dalton's atom because of its simplicity; the issue of simplicity does not arise except between theories that are comparable in explanatory and predictional power.

It has been urged that Copernicus's theory was numerically simpler, in that it required only 17 epicycles to the Ptolemaic 83. But the Ptolemaist, because he addressed his problems singly and without regard for the configurational complexities of taking all planets at once, never had to invoke 83 epicycles simultaneously. The number was usually no more than 4 or 5 per individual calculation.

This error is analogous to that involved in referring to a Ptolemaic "system" at all. Such a system results only from taking all individual calculating charts for the separate planets, superimposing them, running a pin through the centric "Earthpoint," and then scaling the orbits up or down so they do not collide. This scaling is determined by a principle of order wholly unconnected with any part of the Ptolemaic epicycle-on-deferent technique. In contrast, Copernicus's system locates the planets in a circumsolar order such that their relative distances from, and their angular velocities around, the sun are in themselves sufficient in principle to describe and predict all stationary points, retrograde arcs, occultations, and the brightening and dimming of the planetary lights. Thus, since Copernicus linked all planets, and invented systematic astronomy, he had to invoke all the epicycles his theory needed en bloc. The number of epicycles in any calculation would tend to be greater, not less, than that required in a corresponding Ptolemaic problem.

Copernicus's scheme is systematically simpler. It required more independent concepts than some others, but these were deductively interlocked. Copernicus was astronomy's Euclid. He constructed out of the disconnected parts of astronomy as he found it a systematic monument of scientific theory. The *De Revolutionibus* is psychologically and quantitatively more complex than anything that had gone before, but it was deductively simpler. What Euclid had done for geometry, and what Newton was later to do for physics, Copernicus did for positional astronomy.

IMPORTANCE OF THE THEORY

It has been argued that, as formalizations, the Copernican and Ptolemaic theories were strictly equivalent (D. J. de S. Price 1959), geometrically equivalent (A. R. Hall), even "absolutely identical" (J. L. E. Dreyer). But characterizing the theory as no more than "an alternative frame of reference plus some anti-Aristotelian philosophy" obscures the sense in which the heliocentric system and the geocentric systems of the sixteenth century were really equivalent. They were not equivalent in the sense that every consequence of the one was also derivable from the other.

Even when construed as mere geometrical calculations on paper, what the Ptolemaist would generate within his theory as corresponding to a stationary point in Mars's orbit is not congruent with what the Copernican would generate. The orbits were accorded different shapes in both theories, so points on those shapes, although viewed at the same angle from Earth, will not be superimposable. Nonetheless, every line-of-sight observation inferable within the one theory is completely inferable in the other. As positional astronomy, the two theories were observationally equivalent; no astronomer then could distinguish the two by comparing them with known facts. (Even today the Nautical Almanac is virtually a textbook of geocentric observation-points.) But the theories were neither formally equivalent nor physically equivalent, and certainly not absolutely identical. This is a difference that should make a difference to a philosopher.

With Sigmund Freud, man lost his Godlike mind; with Charles Darwin his exalted place among the creatures on Earth; with Copernicus man had lost his privileged position in the universe. The general intellectual repercussions of this fact are more dramatic than any consequences within technical astronomy, where one can speak of the Keplerian "revolution" but of not more than a Copernican "disturbance."

For the broad history of ideas, however, the implications of Copernicanism can hardly be exaggerated. Even religious revolutionaries such as Martin Luther and Philipp Melanchthon came to view Copernicus's position with abhorrence. His views challenged the literal interpretation of Scripture, the philosophical and metaphysical foundations of moral theory, and even common sense itself. The result was a massive opposition, learned and lay, to the reported ideas of Copernicus. It was the slow, sure acceptance of the technical *De Revolutionibus* by natural philosophers that ultimately quieted the general clamor against heliocentrism. Without the riotous reaction against it, Copernicus's book might have been but a calm contribution to scholarship somewhat like Pierre Simon de Laplace's *Mécanique céleste.* In the sixteenth and seventeenth centuries, however, the name Copernicus became a battle cry against the establishment in religion, in philosophy, and in natural science. It was a cry amplified in the world of wider scholarship and theology—far beyond Copernicus's original pronouncements. For Copernicus epitomized the well-trained, thorough, and rigorous sixteenth-century natural philosopher. He sought to make the theories he had inherited work better than when he found them. The history of ideas is charged with such figures. The difference is that Copernicus was presented with a theory that was incapable of further internal revision and improvement. The only recourse was fundamental overhaul—the consequences of which we still feel today.

See also Bradwardine, Thomas; Buridan, Jean; Darwin, Charles Robert; Freud, Sigmund; Grosseteste, Robert; Kant, Immanuel; Kepler, Johannes; Laplace, Pierre Simon de; Luther, Martin; Melanchthon, Philipp; Nicholas of Cusa; Oresme, Nicholas.

Bibliography

WORKS BY COPERNICUS

Edward Rosen is the editor and translator of *Three Copernican Treatises* (New York: Columbia University Press, 1939), which contains a translation of the *Commentariolus,* a "Letter against Werner," and Rheticus's *Narratio Prima.*

De Revolutionibus Orbium Coelestium Libri IV is available in a facsimile text and a Latin printed text edited with notes by S. Kubach (1944). The translation by C. G. Wallis in *Great Books of the Western World,* Vol. 16 (Chicago: Encyclopaedia Britannica, 1952) is to be used with caution.

WORKS ON COPERNICUS

Armitage, Angus. *Copernicus, the Founder of Modern Astronomy.* London: Allen and Unwin, 1938.

Hanson, N. R. "Contra-Equivalence." *Isis* 55 (1964).

Hanson, N. R. "The Copernican Disturbance and the Keplerian Revolution." *Journal of the History of Ideas* 22 (1961): 169–184.

Kuhn, Thomas. *The Copernican Revolution.* Cambridge, MA: Harvard University Press, 1957.

Mizwa, S. P. *Nicholas Copernicus, 1543–1943.* New York: Kosciuszko Foundation, 1943.

Price, D. J. de S. "Contra-Copernicus." In *Critical Problems in the History of Science,* edited by Marshall Claggett. Madison: University of Wisconsin Press, 1959.

Prowe, Ludwig. *Nicolaus Coppernicus,* 3 vols. Berlin, 1883–1885.

Rudnicki, J. *Nicholas Copernicus.* Translated by B. W. A. Massey. London: Copernicus Quatercentenary Celebration Committee, 1943.

Norwood Russell Hanson (1967)

CORBIN, HENRY

(1903–1978)

The French Islamicist and philosopher Henry Corbin was born in Paris on April 14, 1903. He studied with such French scholars as Étienne Henry Gilson, Emile Brehier, and Louis Massignon. To expand the scope of his studies, he learned over a dozen classic and modern languages. His interest in philosophy took him to Germany where he made an acquaintance with Ritter, Karl Löwith, Alexander Kojve, and Martin Heidegger. He translated several works of Heidegger into French, including *What Is Metaphysics.*

Corbin's main philosophical interest during the 1930s was the relationship between philosophy and mysticism. This was a major factor in his decision to study Islamic philosophy. Louis Massignon, then the head of Islamic studies at Sorbonne, introduced him to the works of the twelfth century Muslim philosopher Shihāb al-Dīn Yahyā al-Suhrawardī (d. 1191). Suhrawardī founded a philosophical school called the School of Illumination and sought to combine philosophical analysis with mystical experience—a theme that runs through Corbin's works.

In 1940, during World War II, Corbin went to Istanbul, Turkey, to study the manuscripts of Suhrawardī's works. He stayed in Turkey for the next five years. Then in 1945 he went to Tehran, Iran, where he founded an institute of Iranian studies under the French-Iran Institute. This is the beginning of Corbin's lifelong involvement with what he came to call "Persian Islam" (*islam iranien*). Iran became a spiritual birthplace for him.

Corbin was a prolific writer. Even though his scholarly works are mostly devoted to the philosophical exposition of Islamic or "Oriental" thought, they are permeated by his lifelong concern to resuscitate the mystico-philosophical outlook of such mystical philosophers as Suhrawardī, Ibn al-ʿArabi, Mullā Ṣadrā, and Emmanuel Swedenborg. One key term in Corbin's thought is *mundus imaginalis* (the *ʿalam al-khayal* of the Muslim philosophers). Not to be confused with "imaginary" world, *mundus imaginalis* refers to an intermediary stage between the purely intellectual and empirical worlds. For Corbin, this is the realm of angels and spiritual visions where sensible forms become immaterial and intelligible forms take on an "imaginal" character and dimension. This is where heaven and earth meet in the metaphysical sense of the term. Corbin believed that the European intellectual tradition has lost sight of this crucial concept, severing its relation with the "angelic world" and lending religious justification to the Cartesian dualism of body and soul.

In his readings, Corbin followed the tradition of spiritual hermeneutics (*ta'wil*), "returning" words to their original meanings and thus going back to the "beginning." He called himself a phenomenologist in the sense of "removing the veils of ignorance," (*kashf al-mahjub*). In his philosophical quest, Corbin gave some of the best examples of what is sometimes called comparative philosophy, and his immense knowledge of European and Asian philosophies allowed him to do much more than simply compare or juxtapose different ideas and concepts.

See also Illuminationism; Nasr, Seyyed Hossein.

Bibliography

Jambet, Christian, ed., *Cahiers de l'Herne Henry Corbin.* Paris: Herne, 1981.

Nasr, Seyyed Hossein, ed. *Mélanges offerts à Henry Corbin.* Tehran, Iran: Institute of Islamic Studies, McGill University, Tehran Branch, 1977.

Shayegan, Daryush. *Henry Corbin: La topographie spirituelle de l'islam iranien.* Paris: Editions de la Difference, 1990.

Ibrahim Kalin (2005)

CORDEMOY, GÉRAUD DE

(1626–1684)

Géraud de Cordemoy, a French lawyer, historian, and philosopher, was born in Paris. From about 1657 on, he frequented Cartesian circles and soon developed some distinctive (but seemingly un-Cartesian) theses, such as atomism and occasionalism. He met Bishop Jacques Bénigne Bossuet in October 1668 and through him became *lecteur ordinaire* to the dauphin in 1673. During this period he was engaged, at Bossuet's order, on a biography of Charlemagne, which was understood as involving a complete history of the French monarchy. He did not finish the work, though it was completed and published posthumously in two volumes by his oldest son, Louis-Géraud, along with other unpublished manuscripts and a three-volume collection of his works. Cordemoy was elected to the Académie Française in 1675. His fame rests on his attempts to extend Cartesian philosophy to the fields of language and communication, in *Discours physique de la parole* (1668), and on his advocacy of Cartesian orthodoxy, such as the doctrine of animal-machines and the consistency of Cartesianism with Genesis in *Lettre écrite à un scavant religieux* (1668), but above all, Cordemoy is known for the views he defended in *Le discernement du corps et de l'ame* (1666).

For René Descartes, the principal attribute of body is extension and that of mind is thought. The first half of this tenet was thought to entail the impossibility of both atoms and the void: atoms, because extension was considered indefinitely divisible, and the void, because space was identified with the extension of bodies. Cordemoy offered a variation of Cartesian mechanical philosophy—everything in the physical world is explained in terms of the size, shape, and motion of particles—but one that required atoms and the void. He rejected the indefinite division of body and the Cartesian identification of space with extension. He distinguished body and matter, matter being an assemblage of bodies, and claimed that bodies as such were impenetrable and could not be divided or destroyed.

He even criticized the Cartesian principle of individuation of bodies as shared motion, pointing out that a body at rest between other bodies would have to constitute a single body with the other bodies, even though one has a clear and natural idea of a body at rest between other bodies. Cordemoy proposed that shape, rather than motion, distinguishes the indivisible atoms. Cordemoy further reduced all forms of motion to local motion, arguing that no body has motion by itself. The prime mover—ultimately God—is necessarily a mind, though one's mind is not capable to begin, stop, or accelerate a motion; it can only change its direction. According to Cordemoy, this change of direction or "determination" of motion is not a change in the quantity of motion. The application of this analysis to the problem of the union of the soul and body led Cordemoy to occasionalism: Changes in the soul occur on the occasion of motions in its body, and vice versa.

Cartesians, such as Robert Desgabets and Nicolas Malebranche, criticized Cordemoy's atomism, though others, such as Gottfried Wilhelm Leibniz, praised it. Leibniz rejected Cordemoy's physical atoms, but spoke of Cordemoy as recognizing something of the truth when he tried to save the substantial unity of bodies; according to Leibniz, something lacking extension is required for the substance of bodies, otherwise there would be no source for the reality of phenomena. Other aspects of Cordemoy's philosophy were options generally discussed at the time; Cartesians, such as Johannes Clauberg and Louis de La Forge, had already proposed versions of occasionalism. But Cordemoy produced a more systematic treatment, starting from the physics of motion, which anticipated a number of Malebranche's theses, including the soul knowing itself directly by consciousness, but without a clear idea, and the existence of the body being known only indirectly, as the object of faith.

See also Cartesianism.

Bibliography

WORKS BY CORDEMOY

Le monde de Mr Descartes ou le traité de la lumière et autres principaux objets des sens, avec un discours de l'action des corps et un autre des fièvres, composés selon les principes du même auteur. Paris: Jacques le Gras, 1664. The *Discours de l'action des corps* is the second *discours* of *Le discernement du corps et de l'ame.*

Le discernement du corps et de l'ame, en six discours. Paris: F. Lambert, 1666, with editions in 1670, 1671, 1679, 1680, and 1683.

Discours physique de la parole. Paris: F. Lambert, 1668, with editions in 1671, 1677, and 1704. English translation: *A Philosophical Discourse concerning Speech.* London: John Martin, 1668.

Copie d'une lettre écrite à un scavant Religieux de la Compagnie de Jesus: pour montrer, I. que le Systeme de Monsieur Descartes & son opinion touchant les bestes n'ont rien de dangereux, II. et que tout ce qu'il en a écrit semble estre tiré du premier Chapitre de la Genese. Paris: N.p., 1668. English translation: *A Discourse Written to a Learned Friar.* London: Moses Pitt, 1670.

Tractatus physici duo: I, de corporis et mentis distinctione; II, de loquela. Geneva: J. Pictetum, 1679. This is a Latin translation of *Le discernement du corps et de l'ame* and *Discours physique de la parole.*

Histoire de France. 2 vols. Published by Louis-Géraud de Cordemoy. Paris: J.-B. Coignard, 1685–1689.

Dissertations physiques sur le discernement du corps et de l'ame. 2 vols. Paris: Veuve D. Dion, 1689–90. This contains *Le discernement du corps et de l'ame, Discours physique de la parole,* and *Lettre écrite à un scavant religieux.*

Divers traitez de métaphysique, d'histoire et de politique. Published by Louis-Géraud de Cordemoy. Paris: Veuve de J.-B. Coignard, 1691.

Les oeuvres de feu monsieur de Cordemoy. 3 vols. Published by Louis-Géraud de Cordemoy. Paris: C. Remy, 1704.

Oeuvres philosophiques, edited by Pierre Clair and François Girbal. Paris: Presses Universitaires de France, 1968.

WORKS ABOUT CORDEMOY

Balz, Albert G. A. *Cartesian Studies.* New York: Columbia University Press, 1951.

Battail, Jean-François. *L'avocat philosophe Géraud de Cordemoy (1626–1684).* The Hague: Nijhoff, 1973.

Nicolosi, Salvatore. *Il dualismo da Cartesio a Leibniz: Cartesio, Cordemoy, La Forge, Malebranche, Leibniz.* Venice, Italy: Marsilio, 1987.

Prost, Joseph. *Essai sur l'atomisme et l'occasionalisme dans la philosophie cartésienne.* Paris: Henry Paulin, 1907.

Scheib, Andreas. *Zur Theorie individueller Substanzen bei Géraud de Cordemoy.* New York: Peter Lang, 1997.

Roger Ariew (2005)

CORDOVERO, MOSES BEN JACOB

(1522–1570)

Moses ben Jacob Cordovero, the Jewish legalist and mystic, was the outstanding systematizer of the kabbalah. The place of his birth is not known; his father probably was among the Jews expelled from Cordova, Spain. Cordovero's career centers in Safad, the little town in Palestine that had a period of glory in the sixteenth century. Here, after studying with three distinguished rabbinical teachers—Joseph Caro, Jacob Berab, and Moses di Trani—he was ordained at an early age and became one of the leading figures of the community. His kabbalistic studies were begun at the age of twenty, under the direction of his brother-in-law, Solomon Alkabez, and became the major concern of the remainder of his life. Isaac Luria, who was to become the key figure in a new, more theosophic version of kabbalistic teachings, was originally a pupil of Cordovero.

Cordovero wrote at least ten important kabbalistic books, of varying lengths, during his lifetime. From the philosophic point of view, the greatest of these was *Pardes Rimmonim* (A Garden of pomegranates; first printed at Kraków, 1591). This large book attempted to present a systematic exposition of kabbalistic ideas and to justify them by deductive rational argumentation instead of the usual methods of kabbalistic exegesis. The word *Pardes* (*PRDS*) in the title acrostically represents the four modes of interpretation of Scripture: *peshat,* literal interpretation; *remez,* allegorical, or hinting, interpretation; *derash,* homiletical interpretation; and *sod,* mystical interpretation. Among the subjects emphasized by Cordovero in his treatment are God's unity, God's will, God's knowledge and thought, God's wisdom and goodness, God's many names, and God's relation to creation; the emanations (*sephirot*), both individually and collectively, the reason for there being precisely ten emanations, and the mystery of their multiplicity in unity; the Shekinah; angels; soul; being; prophecy; the relation of correspondence between the upper and lower worlds and the necessity of each to the other; the Law and the commandments; the mysteries of the Law; the secrets of the Hebrew alphabet; man and Israel; righteousness; time; freedom and bondage; the service of God. Cordovero was one of the first writers to stress the idea of *zimzum,* the voluntary self-shrinkage of God to make room for the material world.

Because of his rational discussion of all these subjects and his successful philosophic justification of them, in terms of his own presuppositions, Cordovero may well be regarded as the climactic figure of the earlier period of kabbalistic speculation. To what extent he was also intrigued by the more practical or "magical" aspects of kabbalah, we cannot tell.

See also Kabbalah.

Bibliography

WORKS BY CORDOVERO

The Palm Tree of Deborah. Translated by Louis Jacobs. New York: Hermon Press, 1974.

WORKS ON CORDOVERO

Idel, M. *Language, Torah, and Hermeneutics in Abraham Abulafia.* Albany: State University of New York Press, 1989.

Robinson, Ira. "Moses Cordovero and Kabbalistic Education in the Sixteenth Century." *Judaism* 39 (1990): 155–162.

Robinson, Ira. *Moses Cordovero's Introduction to Kabbala.* New York: Yeshiva University Press, 1994.

Sack, Bracha. "The Influence of Cordovero on Seventeenth-Century Jewish Thought." In *Jewish Thought in the Seventeenth Century,* edited by Isadore Twersky and Bernard Septimus. Cambridge, MA: Harvard University Press, 1987.

Sack, Bracha. "Some Remarks on Rabbi Moses Cordovero's Shemu'ah be-'Inyan ha Gilgul." In *Perspectives on Jewish Thought and Mysticism,* edited by A. Ivry. E. Wolfson and A. Arkush. Amsterdam: Harwood Academic, 1998.

Scholem, G. *On the Mystical Shape of the Godhead: Basic Concepts in the Kabbalah.* New York: Schocken, 1991.

Tirosh-Samuelson, H. "Philosophy and Kabbalah." In *Cambridge Companion to Medieval Jewish Philosophy,* edited by D. Frank and O. Leaman, 218–257. Cambridge, U.K.: Cambridge University Press, 2003.

Wolfson, E. "Jewish Mysticism: A Philosophical Overview." In *History of Jewish Philosophy,* edited by D. Frank and O. Leaman, 450–498. London: Routledge, 1997.

J. L. Blau (1967)
Bibliography updated by Oliver Leaman (2005)

CORRESPONDENCE THEORY OF TRUTH

The term "correspondence theory of truth" has circulated among modern philosophical writers largely through the influence of Bertrand Russell, who sets the view (which he himself adopts) that "truth consists in some form of correspondence between belief and fact" against the theory of the absolute idealists that "truth consists in *coherence,*" that is, that the more our beliefs hang together in a system, the truer they are.

ANCIENT AND SCHOLASTIC VERSIONS OF THE THEORY

The origins of the word *correspondence,* used to denote the relation between thought and reality in which the truth of thought consists, appear to be medieval. Thomas Aquinas used *correspondentia* in this way at least once, but much more often he used other expressions and preferred most of all the definition of truth that he attributed to the ninth-century Jewish Neoplatonist Isaac Israeli:

Veritas est adaequatio rei et intellectus (truth is the adequation of things and the intellect). At one point he expanded this to *adaequatio intellectus et rei, secundum quod intellectus dicit esse, quod est, vel non esse, quod non est.* This is an echo of Aristotle's "To say of what is that it is not, or of what is not that it is, is false; while to say of what is that it is, and of what is not that it is not, is true." Other Scholastics sometimes said that a proposition is true when and only when *ita est sicut significat* ("the thing is as signified"); this too is in line with the Aristotelian account, in which "is" is not restricted to the meaning "exists"—the definition also covers the point that to say of what is so that it is not so, or of what is not so that it is so, is false; while to say of what is so that it is so, and of what is not so that it is not so, is true. This simple statement is the nerve of the correspondence theory; we shall continually return to it.

PLATO. Aristotle did not originate the correspondence theory but took it over from Plato's *Sophist.* There it was developed with an eye on a rejected alternative—not the coherence theory, which is a comparatively late invention (G. E. Moore is probably correct, in his "Truth" article in Baldwin's *Dictionary*, in tracing its vogue to Immanuel Kant), but one that we may call the existence theory, which also crops up in the *Theaetetus.* In this latter dialogue Socrates tries to find what differentiates true from erroneous belief, and the first suggestion he considers is that whereas true belief is directed toward what is, false belief is directed toward what is not. This view is rejected on the ground that just as to see or hear what is not is to see or hear nothing, and to see or hear nothing is just not to see or hear at all, so to "think what is not" is to think nothing, and that is just not to think at all, so that erroneous thought, on this view, would just not be thinking at all.

The same theory is considered in the *Sophist*, but here an alternative is put forward. Thought is compared with speech (it is the soul's dialogue with itself), and the important thing about speech is that in order to be true or false it must be complex—only complete statements are true or false, and these must consist of both nouns and verbs. (These points are also stressed by Aristotle.) As simple examples of complete statements, Plato gives "Theaetetus is-sitting-down" and "Theaetetus is-flying." The first of these is true because Theaetetus is sitting down, and the second is false because he is not flying. This escapes the difficulties of the existence theory because it abandons the suggestion that thinking is a simple direction of the mind toward an object—if it were that, its verbal expression would not have to be a complete sentence but could be just a name—and so opens up the possibility for thinking to be erroneous even though what is thought about, such as Theaetetus, is perfectly real.

The existence theory, however, dies hard and has continued to maintain itself, not merely as a rival to the correspondence theory but even more as something that theory is in constant danger of becoming. (The two views continually oscillate, for example, in the early work of Russell and Moore.) It is easy to equate the complexity of thinking with its having a complex object—for instance, Theaetetus's-sitting-down or Theaetetus's-flying—which exists if the thought is true and does not if it is not.

ARISTOTLE. There is no trace of the above slide or degeneration in Aristotle, nor even of a conscious resistance to it, but he has passages that have some bearing on it and that in any case develop a little further the correspondence theory itself. For example, having said that the distinguishing mark of a substance or individual thing is that it may have opposite qualities at different times, he resists a suggestion that statements and opinions would count as things by this criterion, since they may be at one time true and at another time false—for example, the statement or opinion that a person is sitting down will be true while he is doing so but false when he stands up. This, Aristotle suggests, is unfair, because what is in question here is not any genuine alteration in the statement or opinion itself, but rather in the facts outside it by which its truth or falsehood is measured. "For it is by the facts of the case, by their being or not being so, that a statement is called true or false."

Sometimes Aristotle represents the verification of statements by facts as a kind of causation. Causation, he says, differs from implication because even where implication is reciprocal we can distinguish the cause from the effect:

> The existence of a man, for instance, implies the truth of the statement in which we assert his existence. The converse is also the case. For if he exists, then the statement in which we assert his existence is true, and conversely, if the statement in which we assert his existence is true, he exists. But the truth of the statement is in no way the cause of his existence, though his existence is in a way the cause of the truth of the statement. For we call the statement true or false according as he exists or not.

(*CATEGORIES* 14B15–20)

(What Aristotle calls a cause here is perhaps something more like a criterion.)

MEGARIAN "LIAR" PARADOX. The Platonic–Aristotelian correspondence theory was not long formulated when a distressing consequence, or apparent consequence, of it was pointed out by Eubulides, a member of the school of Megara, which seems to have conducted constant warfare against various basic Platonic–Aristotelian positions. Eubulides invited his hearers to consider a man who says "I am lying" or "What I am now saying is false." According to the Platonic–Aristotelian view, this is true if what the man is saying *is* false—it is true if it is itself false—and false if what he is saying is *not* false—false if it is true. Therefore, in at least this one case, that view leads to the position that whatever we say about the truth or falsehood of an utterance entails its own opposite. We may note, too, that in this instance the Aristotelian one-sided dependence of the truth or falsehood of a proposition on the related matter of fact does not hold, since the related matter of fact in this instance *is* precisely the truth or falsehood of the proposition. This "paradox of the liar" was much discussed by both ancient and medieval writers and still presents a serious problem to anyone attempting to give a satisfactory general account of truth and falsehood.

STOICS. What is substantially the Platonic–Aristotelian account of truth is also found among the Stoics, but with modifications. The Stoics held that truth in the primary sense is a property of statements or *axiomata*, not in the sense of sentences but in the sense of what the sentences state or mean. These *axiomata* exist independently of their being expressed by sentences, and the "meanings" of false sentences exist just as much as the meanings of true ones—that is to say, *axiomata* include objective falsehoods as well as objective truths. (This is not, therefore, the existence theory.) Describing the Stoics' account of truth from this point on, Diogenes Laertius says that the *axioma* expressed by "It is day" is true if it is day and false if it is not. This is an example rather than a general theory; Sextus Empiricus says that the kind of *axioma* called simple and definite—the kind that would be expressed by a sentence of the form "This *X Y*'s" (for instance, "This bat flies")—is true when the predicate belongs to the object denoted by the demonstrative. This, however, only defines "true" for the simplest type of proposition. For other types we know that the Stoics laid down such rules as that an *axioma* of the form "Some *X Y*'s" is true if and only if there is some true *axioma* of the form "This *X Y*'s," and one of the form "*p* and *q*" is true if and only if both of its components are; but we do not know whether they regarded such rules as actually defining "true" for these forms. It is scarcely likely that they saw them as parts of a single "recursive" definition of truth, such as is found in Alfred Tarski, but they laid the foundations for such a development.

MEDIEVAL LOGICIANS. Such statements of truth conditions, as we now call them, were also laid down and discussed by the logicians of the later Middle Ages, although they generally treated truth as a property not of abstract *axiomata* but of spoken and written sentences. Besides the truth conditions of sentences containing "not," "or," and "some," they considered those of sentences containing such expressions as "possibly" and verbs in the past and future tenses. They observed, for example, that while in general a past-tense statement *is* true if and only if the corresponding present-tense statement *was* true, and a statement that something *could have been* so *is* true if and only if the statement that it *is* so *could have been* true, there are exceptions to such rules. For example, "Something white *was* black" *is* true, but "Something white *is* black" was never true. The rule here is that a past-tense predication *is* true if the corresponding predication *was* true of the individuals to which the subject term now applies; for instance, "Something white was black" is true if "It is black" could have been truly said in the past of a thing that is now white. "It could have been that no proposition is negative" is true, since God might have annihilated all negative propositions; but "No proposition is negative" could in no circumstances have been true, since the mere existence of this sentence (which is itself negative) falsifies it. The rule is rather that a sentence *de possibili* is true if and only if things could have been as the corresponding unqualified sentence says they are.

The later medieval logicians also implicitly modified the Platonic–Aristotelian theory in order to cope with the "liar" and similar paradoxes. John Buridan, for example, although he preserved the formula that a sentence is true when *ita est sicut significat*, gave a somewhat un-Aristotelian twist to the meaning of *significat*. According to Buridan, the man who says "I am saying something false," and says nothing else, really is saying something false, not because things are otherwise than as his sentence *significat formaliter* but because they are otherwise than as his sentence *significat virtualiter*. A sentence "virtually" signifies whatever follows from itself together with the circumstances of its utterance, and what follows from this particular sentence together with the circumstances of its utterance is that it is both true and false; since this is never the case, things are not as it "virtually" says they are, and it is false.

MOORE'S CORRESPONDENCE THEORY

In the twentieth century a particularly extended and fruitful discussion of the correspondence theory is found in a series of lectures given by G. E. Moore in 1910–1911. Here truth and falsehood first appear as properties of what are called propositions. Moore uses the term *proposition* to mean not an indicative sentence but what such a sentence *means*, an *axioma* in the Stoic sense. When we both hear and understand a spoken sentence, and both see and understand a written one, there is something apprehended by us over and above the sentence, and while this apprehension or understanding is the same kind of act in all cases, what is apprehended is in general different when different sentences (such as "Twice two are four" and "Twice four are eight") are involved and therefore is distinguishable from the act of apprehending. We also "constantly think of and believe or disbelieve, or merely consider, propositions, at moments when we are neither hearing nor seeing any words which express them"; for example, when we "apprehend a proposition, which we desire to express, before we are able to think of any sentence which would express it." In this lecture Moore is quite confident that "there certainly are in the Universe such things as propositions," and that it is propositions rather than sentences or acts of belief that are true or false in the primary sense. We often say that beliefs are true or false, but this is only because the word *belief* is often used not for an act of believing but for what is believed; for instance, if we say that two different people have the same belief, we mean to identify what they believe rather than their respective acts of believing, and what is believed is simply a proposition in Moore's sense. Acts of believing and sentences could, however, be said to be true or false in a secondary sense, when what is believed or expressed is a true or false proposition.

MOORE'S LATER POSITION. Moore returns to the subjects of true and false beliefs and the nature of propositions in later lectures in the series, but now he seems to move somewhat away from the position outlined above. He leads up to them with a problem he states as follows: "Suppose a man believes that God exists; … then to say that his belief is true seems to be exactly equivalent to saying that it *is a fact* that God exists or that God's existence is a fact" (*Some Main Problems in Philosophy*, p. 250). Quite generally it seems that "the difference between true and false beliefs is … that where a belief is true, there what is believed is a fact; whereas where a belief is false, there what is believed is not a fact" (ibid.). Even where a belief is false, however, there does seem to be something that is believed.

> A man believes in God's existence and it seems quite plain that he is believing in something—that there is such a thing as what he believes in, and that this something is God's existence. It seems quite plain, therefore, that there *is* such a thing as God's existence, *whether* his belief is true or false. But we have just seen that if his belief is false, then God's existence is *not* a fact. And what is the difference between saying that there is such a thing as God's existence and (saying) that God's existence is a fact? (ibid.)

This is the problem of the *Theaetetus* all over again—if a false belief has no real object, how can it be a belief at all?

DENIAL THAT PROPOSITIONS EXIST. Moore raises the above question with regard to a more certainly false proposition, namely, that the hearers of his lecture were at that time hearing the noise of a brass band; and he then restates, but no longer with conviction, his earlier theory. We *could* say that there was indeed such a thing as their hearing a brass band then but that this was a proposition, not a fact. But, Moore argues, this theory admits in the case of the phrase "the fact that they are hearing a brass band" that what looks like the name of a real object of a possible belief is not one, so why should we not say this also of the phrase "the proposition that they are hearing a brass band"? Moore is thus led to the view that the subject–verb–object form of assertions about beliefs is misleading. His new theory, he says, "may be expressed by saying that there simply are no such things as *propositions*. That belief does *not* consist … in a relation between the believer, on the one hand, and another thing which may be called the proposition believed" (ibid., p. 265). He cannot give any satisfactory alternative analysis of belief statements to supplant the one he has abandoned, but he thinks he can give an account of the truth and falsehood of beliefs without one.

FALSE BELIEF AND FACTS. In developing the account of truth and falsehood of beliefs, Moore considers the case of a friend believing that he has gone away for his holidays, and begins in a thoroughly Aristotelian vein. "If this belief of his is *true* then I *must* have gone away … and, conversely, … *if* I *have* gone away, then this belief of his certainly *is* true" (ibid., p. 274). And similarly, "if this belief is *false*, then I *can't* have gone away … and conversely, *if* I have not gone away, then the belief that I *have* gone away certainly *must* be false" (ibid., p. 275). However, this statement of necessary and sufficient conditions does not constitute a definition of truth and falsehood, for "when we assert: 'The belief that I have gone away is true,' we mean to assert that this belief has some property, which it shares with other true beliefs," whereas "in merely asserting 'I have gone away,' we are not attributing any property at all to this belief" (ibid., p. 276). For "Plainly I might have gone away without my friend believing that I had; and if so, his belief would not be true, simply because it would not exist." This objection, however, suggests that Moore's having gone away would not after all be a sufficient condition, but only a necessary one, of his friend's belief being true; and it could be met by defining the truth of his friend's belief, not simply as Moore's having in fact gone away but as this together with his friend's believing it.

The problem remains, however, of generalizing this to cover all cases, which Moore goes about solving as follows: "We can see quite plainly," he says, "that this belief, if true, has to the fact that I have gone away a certain relation which that belief has to no other fact," a relation which cannot be defined in the sense of being analyzed, but with which we are all perfectly familiar and which "is expressed by the circumstance that the name of the belief is 'the belief that I have gone away,' while the name of the fact is 'that I have gone away'" (ibid.). Moore proposes to call this relation correspondence, and "To say that this belief is true is to say that there is in the Universe *a* fact to which it corresponds, and to say that it is false is to say that there is *not* in the Universe any fact to which it corresponds" (ibid., p. 277).

FACTS RATHER THAN PROPOSITIONS. It is essential to Moore's final account that although there are no propositions, there are facts. A belief, even if true, does not consist in a relation between a person and a fact, but the truth of a belief does. He is also at pains to insist that facts "are" or exist in the very sense in which, say, chairs and tables do. He concedes that as a matter of usage we find it natural to say "It is a fact that bears exist," while we do not find it at all natural to say "That bears exist, is" (or "That bears exist, exists", or even "The existence of bears exists"), but he thinks this simply reflects our acute sense of the difference in kind between facts and other things—they are real objects but objects of a very special sort. We also express their character by calling them truths, or by prefixing "It is true that" to them as an alternative to "It is a fact that." This property of *being* a truth or fact is to be carefully distinguished from the "truth" which is possessed by some beliefs and which consists, as previously explained, in correspondence to a truth or fact.

RUSSELL'S CORRESPONDENCE THEORY

In Moore's account of truth and falsehood, it will be seen, there are two elements that are a little mysterious and that he is reluctantly compelled to leave in that condition—the correct analysis of belief statements and the nature of the correspondence that entitles us to use the same form of words in describing the content of a belief and in asserting the fact to which, if true, it corresponds.

Shortly before Moore gave these lectures, Russell had made an attempt to elucidate just these points. In the concluding section of a paper he gave before the Aristotelian Society in 1906, there is a hint of this explanation, which is more fully developed in various writings of the period 1910–1912. He suggests in the 1906 paper that a belief may differ from an idea or presentation in consisting of several interrelated ideas, whose objects will be united in the real world into a single complex or fact if the belief is true, but not otherwise, so that a false belief is indeed "belief in nothing, though it is not 'thinking of nothing,' because it is thinking of the objects of the ideas which constitute the belief." In the later versions this is expanded to the view that a belief consists in a many-termed relation, the number of terms always being two more than that occurring in the fact to which, if true, the belief corresponds. For example, if it is a fact that Desdemona loves Cassio, then in this fact the two terms Desdemona and Cassio are "knit together" by the relation of loving, while if it is a fact that Othello believes that Desdemona loves Cassio, then the four terms Othello, Desdemona, the relation of loving, and Cassio are "knit together" in this fact by the relation of believing. The correspondence between the belief and the fact, when the fact exists and the belief is therefore true, consists in a certain characteristic semiparallelism between the ordering of the last terms of the belief relation and the ordering of the terms by their ordering relation in the fact. Knowing and perceiving, on the other hand, really are relations between the knower or perceiver and the fact known or perceived (which of course must *be* a fact for knowledge or perception to occur).

CRITICISMS. The above theory is open to a number of objections, some of which have been particularly well stated by P. T. Geach, and one of which, due in essence to Ludwig Wittgenstein, had already led Russell to abandon the theory, in a course of lectures on logical atomism delivered in 1918.

Belief and what is the case. Russell's 1906–1912 theory—and indeed even Moore's more vague theory, of which it is a possible filling out—makes it altogether too mysterious that the very same words should be used to express what is believed and what is actually the case if the belief is true. (At most, there is in some languages a slight but regular formal alteration when the latter is put into *oratio obliqua* to give the former.) As Wittgenstein puts it (*Philosophical Investigations*, Para. 444), "One may have the feeling that in the sentence 'I expect he is coming' one is using the words 'he is coming' in a different sense from the one they have in the assertion 'He is coming.' But if it were so how could I say that my expectation had been fulfilled?"—that *the very thing* I expected had come to pass?

This severance of the senses of the *oratio obliqua* and *oratio recta* forms of the same sentence is exacerbated in Russell's account, as Geach points out, by its consequence that believing is not one relation but several, since the number of terms it requires differs with the number of terms required by the relation that occurs among its objects (for instance, while Othello's believing that Desdemona loves Cassio is a 4-termed relation, his believing that Desdemona gave Cassio a certain ring would be a 5-termed one). This difference arises even when we are only considering beliefs of which the apparent objects are simple relational propositions; still more radical differences would have to be admitted with believings apparently directed toward compound and general propositions. This point was, indeed, stressed by Russell himself from the outset and seems never to have been regarded by him as a serious objection to the theory, since in his 1918 lectures, even when he had abandoned the view that necessitated it, we find him saying that "belief will really have to have different logical forms according to the nature of what is believed" (*Logic and Knowledge*, p. 226), so that "the apparent sameness of believing in different cases is more or less illusory."

There is here, it seems, a remnant of the ramified theory of types that Russell at first thought necessary to deal with such paradoxes as that of the "liar." According to this theory, propositions are not only of different logical forms but also of different logical types, and "truth" and "falsehood" must be differently defined for each type; indeed, even such ordinary logical functions as negation and conjunction must be understood differently according to the types of propositions to which they are attached. Even by the time he was exercising the influence acknowledged in Russell's 1918 lectures, Wittgenstein had definitely abandoned this theory: "*Any* proposition can be negated. And this shews that 'true' and 'false' mean the same for all propositions (in contrast to Russell)" (*Notebooks 1914–1916*, p. 21).

Verbs in judgments. What Russell did successfully assimilate from Wittgenstein at this period was that in such judgments as that Othello believes that Desdemona loves Cassio, "both verbs have got to occur as verbs, because if a thing is a verb it cannot occur otherwise than as a verb." He also says:

> There are really two main things that one wants to notice in this matter that I am treating of just now. The *first* is the impossibility of treating the proposition believed as an independent entity, entering as a unit into the occurrences of the belief, and the *other* is the impossibility of putting the subordinate verb on a level with its terms as an object term in the belief. That is a point in which I think that the theory of judgment which I set forth once … was a little unduly simple, because I did then treat the object verb as if one could put it as just an object like the terms. (*Logic and Knowledge*, p. 226)

"Every right theory of judgment," as Wittgenstein puts it, "must make it impossible for me to judge that 'this table penholders the book' (Russell's theory does not satisfy this requirement)" (*Notebooks 1914–1916*, p. 96).

Propositions in judgments. Russell's objection ties up in two ways with Wittgenstein's that "a proposition itself must occur in the statement to the effect that it is judged." In the first place, it is by inserting the "proposition itself" into the "statement to the effect that it is judged" that we enable the subordinate verb to occur as a verb and not disguised as an abstract noun. (It looks, in fact, as if these "two main things" that Russell says we must notice cannot be observed together.) We might put the two objections together thus: Because the use of abstract nouns is *always* something to be explained, it is more illuminating to say that "Othello ascribes unfaithfulness to Desdemona" (where "ascribes" is apparently a 3-termed relation with "unfaithfulness" as one of its terms) means exactly what is meant by "Othello believes that Desdemona is unfaithful" than it is to say that the second means exactly what is meant by the first.

Facts as objects. The second way in which the two objections come together is more complicated, and it can be gathered from an extended discussion of what may at first seem another point: that Russell's 1906–1912 theory, like Moore's of 1910, still takes "facts" seriously as a special sort of object. On this point Russell's 1918 view is a little obscure. He seems not to have changed at all on this subject, and describes it as one of those truisms that "are so obvious that it is almost laughable to mention them," that "the world contains *facts*, … and that there are also *beliefs*, which have reference to facts, and by reference to facts are either true or false" (*Logic and Knowledge*, p. 182). He sharply contrasts facts with propositions in this respect. "If we were making an inventory of the world, propositions would not come in. Facts would, beliefs, wishes, wills would, but propositions would not" (ibid., p. 214). This last remark occurs in a criticism of an attempt by Raphael Demos to eliminate the *negative* fact that a certain piece of chalk is not red from the "inventory of the world" by equating it with the fact that the chalk has some other positive but incompatible color. "Even if incompatibility is to be taken as a sort of fundamental expression of fact," Russell says to this, "incompatibility is not between facts but between propositions. … It is clear that no two *facts* are incompatible" (ibid.). And since propositions do not have being independently, this "incompatibility of propositions taken as an ultimate fact of the real world will want a good deal of treatment, a lot of dressing up before it will do." However, Russell's own alternative, that there are irreducibly negative facts—for instance, the fact that it is not the case that this piece of chalk is red—equally involves the consequence that there are facts that contain real falsehoods as constituents. This Russell himself pointed out in his 1906 paper, and it led him then to be more hesitant than he was later about dismissing the notion of objective falsehoods. Even if, he says in this paper, we can remove the suggestion that false beliefs have objective falsehoods for their objects:

> There is … another argument in favour of objective falsehood, derived from the case of true propositions which contain false ones as constituent parts. Take, e.g., "Either the earth goes round the sun, or it does not." This is certainly true, and therefore, on the theory we are considering, it represents a *fact*, i.e. an objective complex. But it is, at least apparently, compounded of two (unasserted) constituents, … of which one must be false. Thus our fact seems to be composed of two parts, of which one is a fact, while the other is an objective falsehood. ("On the Nature of Truth," pp. 47–48)

The real moral of all this is surely that if propositions must go, facts must go, too; but Russell seems to shrink from this step.

Elsewhere in the 1918 lectures, however, he says that facts, although apparently real in a way in which propositions are not, have the extraordinary property that they cannot be named. In the first place, they are not named by propositions (sentences). For this he has a rather strange argument, taken from Wittgenstein. Whereas Moore thought of a false belief as one that corresponds to no fact at all, Wittgenstein held that a false statement does correspond to a fact, but in the wrong way. Hence, to quote Russell's exposition of the theory:

> There are *two* propositions corresponding to each fact. Suppose it is a fact that Socrates is dead. You have two propositions: "Socrates is dead" and "Socrates is not dead." And those two propositions corresponding to the same fact, there is one fact in the world, that which makes one true and one false. … There are two different relations … that a proposition can have to a fact: the one the relation that you may call being true to the fact, and the other being false to the fact. (*Logic and Knowledge*, p. 187)

This means that a proposition does not name a fact, since in the case of a name, there is only one relation that it can have to what it names. Further,

> You must not run away with the idea that you can name facts in any other way; you cannot. … You cannot properly name a fact. The only thing you can do is to assert it, or deny it, or desire it, or will it, or wish it, or question it. … You can never put the sort of thing that makes a proposition to be true or false in the position of a logical subject. (ibid., p. 188)

RAMSEY AND THE LATER WITTGENSTEIN

Russell's whole position, as it stands, is difficult to maintain. If there are really individual objects to which the common noun "fact" applies, and we can sometimes actually perceive them (Russell continued to hold this in the 1918 lectures), then if at the time of our perceiving one our language has no name for it, why can we not invent one and christen the thing on the spot? However, there is not just superstition, but something true and important, behind the statement of Russell and Wittgenstein that facts cannot be named, and they both identify it in the end. "When I say 'facts cannot be named,'" Russell admitted in 1924, "this is, strictly speaking, nonsense. What can be said without falling into nonsense is: 'The symbol for a fact is not a name.'" Or better, perhaps: to state a fact is not to name an object. Whatever may be the case with "that" clauses, *sentences* aren't names of anything; just as, whatever may be the case with abstract nouns, verbs are not names of anything—they are not names at all, but have other functions; naming is one thing, saying or stating another. Even Plato saw that this distinction was important.

But can we not *name what a sentence says*, for instance, by the corresponding "that" clause? Not really—"*what* a sentence says," although a good sense can be given to it, is a misleading expression; when it means anything, it means "*how* a sentence says things are" or, better, "how *we* say things are" when we use the sentence in question. To *name* what we are saying is to *say* what we are saying, and to name what we are thinking or wishing is similarly to say what we are thinking or wishing. "I think that bears exist" is, therefore, not to be analyzed as "I think (that bears exist)," which suggests that "that bears exist" is one term of the relation expressed by "think" but rather as "I think that (bears exist)," where "bears exist" does not even look like a name (it looks like, and is, a sentence) and "think that" does not look like the expression of a relation. If Othello thinks that Desdemona loves Cassio, there is indeed a 3-termed relation between Othello, Desdemona, and Cassio (not, as Russell thought, a 4-termed one between Othello, Desdemona, Cassio, and loving), but this relation consists in his *thinking that she loves him*, that is, the relation is expressed by the whole complex verb "——thinks that——loves——," not by the simple "——thinks that——," which does not express any relation at all, since its second gap is not filled by the name of an object but by a sentence, which does not name but *says* what he thinks (how he thinks things are). The plain "thinks," without the "that," means nothing at all. I may, indeed, use forms of expression like "I think something that Jones doesn't think" or "Something that Jones thinks is not true," but the "thing" in this "something" is no more to be taken seriously than the "what" in "what I say"—these sentences, respectively, mean simply "For some p, I *think that* p and Jones does not think that p" and "For some p, Jones thinks that p but it is not the case that p." The correspondence theory can now assume the simple form: "X says (believes) truly that p" means "X says (believes) that p, and p"; and "X says (believes) falsely that p" means "X says (believes) that p, and not p."

RAMSEY. The above position was very lightly sketched in 1927 by Frank Plumpton Ramsey, who says in effect that the words *fact* and *true* in their primary use are inseparable parts of the adverbial phrases "truly," "in fact," "it is a fact that," and "it is true that"; and these, attached to some sentence, say no more than this sentence says on its own. "It is false that p" or "That p, is contrary to fact" similarly says no more than the simple "Not p." Thus there are not only no falsehoods but no facts or truths either, any more than there is an entity called "the case" involved in the synonymous phrase "It is the case that." This part of Ramsey's view has led some writers to set it in opposition to the correspondence theory as a "no truth" theory, but Ramsey also discusses more complex uses of "true" in which there is something more like a juxtaposition of what a man says and what is so. In particular he considers the statement "He is always right"—"Whatever he says is true"—and renders this as "For all p, if he says that p, it is true that p," and this in turn as "For all p, if he says that p, then p." This may seem to require a further verb in its second clause, but there is already a "variable verb" implicit in the variable p.

WITTGENSTEIN. We may expand Ramsey's discussion of the more complex uses of "true" by taking up a suggestion of the later Wittgenstein (which, indeed, we have already used a bit). In the *Tractatus*, Wittgenstein says that "the general form of propositions is: this is how things are." In the *Investigations*, criticizing this identification, he reminds us that "This is how things are" is itself a proposition, an English sentence applied in everyday language, as in "He explained his position to me, said that this was how things were, and that therefore he needed an advance." "This is how things are" can be said to stand for any statement and can be employed as a propositional *schema*, but only because it already has the construction of an English sentence. Wittgenstein continues, "It would also be possible here simply to use a letter, a variable, as in symbolic logic. But no one is going to call the letter 'p' the general form of propositions."

"This is how things are," although a genuine proposition, is nevertheless being employed only as a propositional variable. "To say that this proposition agrees or does not agree with reality would be obvious nonsense." "This is how things are" is a propositional variable in ordinary speech in much the same way that a pronoun is a name variable in ordinary speech. In Wittgenstein's example, the "value" of this "variable" is given by a specific sentence uttered earlier, much as the denotation of a pronoun may be fixed by a name occurring earlier. "I'm desperate—that's how things are" is like "There's Jones—he's wearing that hat again." "This (that) is how things are" is a pro-sentence. But we may also obtain a specific statement by "binding" this variable, as in "However he says things are, that's how they are," that is, Ramsey's "For all p, if he says that p, then p." We speak truly whenever things are as we say they are, and falsely when they are not. There was a hint of this way of putting things when the later Scholastics equated *est vera*, said of a sentence, with *ita est sicut significat* or *qualitercumque significat, ita est*—"*however* the sentence signifies (that the case is), *thus* it is"—avoiding the possibly misleading "*What* the sentence says is so."

These "misleading" forms, however, *need* not mislead us, once the whole picture has been spread out, and we can soften our earlier skepticism by agreeing that after all there *are* facts, and that there are falsehoods, if all that is meant by "There are facts" is "For some *p*, *p*" and by "There are falsehoods" "For some *p*, not *p*." We can say, too, that there are both facts and falsehoods that have never been either thought or asserted, that is, we can insist on the objective or mind-independent character of propositions, if by this we mean that for some *p*, both *p* and it has never been thought or said that *p*. (We cannot, of course, give examples of such facts or falsehoods, for to do so would be to state them, and then they would not be unstated; but this is no more strange than that there should be people—as there certainly are—whose names we do not know, although we cannot in the nature of the case name any specific examples.) It is significant that Moore in his last years contrived to assimilate a Ramsey-like account of truth without losing any of his earlier sense of the mind-independent and speech-independent character of what is so. Propositions about propositions, he said in effect, are *not* propositions about sentences precisely because the words *proposition, true*, and *false* are eliminable—just because "The proposition that the sun is shining is true" is equivalent to and perhaps identical with the plain "The sun is shining," it neither says anything about sentences nor entails that there are such things, since the sun could obviously *be* shining even if no one ever said so.

TARSKI'S SEMANTIC THEORY

In the theories of Ramsey and the later Moore, truth is a quasi property of a quasi object. What is really defined in them is not a property of anything, but rather what it is to say with truth that something is so; it is an account of the adverbial phrase "with truth" rather than of the adjective "true." The late medieval treatment of "true" as a straightforward adjective applying to straightforward objects—sentences—was revived in the twentieth century, and developed with extraordinary precision, elegance, and thoroughness, in a paper by Alfred Tarski that is one of the classics of modern logic.

"TRUE" AS A METALINGUISTIC ADJECTIVE. A sentence, Tarski points out, is true or false only as part of some particular language. The Schoolmen were sensitive to this point also; Buridan, for example, observed that if we neglect it, we will be trapped by such arguments as the following: "A man is a donkey" is a true sentence if and only if a man is a donkey; but "A man is a donkey" could have been a true sentence (since we could have used it to mean what we now mean by "White is a color"); ergo it could have been that a man is a donkey. Moore was fond of making similar points.

Further, Tarski argues, a sentence asserting that some sentence *S* is a true sentence of some language *L*, cannot itself be a sentence of the language *L*, but must belong to a metalanguage in which the sentences of *L* are not used but are mentioned and discussed. He is led to this view by the paradox of the "liar" which he presents, after Jan Łukasiewicz, as follows: He uses the letter *c* as an abbreviation for the expression "the sentence printed on page 158 [of his paper], line 5 from the top," and the sentence printed there is "*c* is not a true sentence." By the ordinary Aristotelian criterion for the truth of sentences, we may say "'*c* is not a true sentence' is a true sentence if and only if *c* is not a true sentence." But "*c* is not a true sentence" is precisely the sentence *c*, so we may equate the preceding with "*c* is a true sentence if and only if *c* is not a true sentence," which is self-contradictory. The contradiction is eliminated if we put "of *L*" after "true sentence" throughout and deny the principle "'*c* is not a true sentence of *L*' is a true sentence of *L* if and only if *c* is not a true sentence of *L*" on the ground that *c* is not a true sentence of *L* under any conditions whatever, because it is not a sentence of the language *L* at all but of its metalanguage *M*.

Similar paradoxes lead to similar conclusions about such terms as "is a name of" or "signifies"—in fact, all terms that concern the relations between the expressions of a language and the objects which this language is used to describe or talk about. All such semantic terms must occur, not in the language that they concern, but in the associated metalanguage. This metalanguage must contain names for expressions in the object language and may also contain descriptions of the structure of such expressions; for instance, we might be able to say in it that one sentence is the negation of another, meaning by this that it is formed from that other by prefixing the expression "It is not the case that" to it. Tarski is attempting to state the conditions under which, for a given language *L*, we can define the term "true sentence" (and perhaps other semantic expressions) in terms of this basic metalinguistic apparatus, and in such a way as to entail all sentences, in the metalanguage *M*, of the form "*x* is a true sentence if and only if *p*," where *x* is a *name* of some sentence of *L* (we need not write "sentence of *L*" in the formula, since in *M* this is what "sentence" means), and *p* is the *translation* into *M* of this same sentence. (*M* could include *L* as a part of itself, in which case the sentences of *L* would be their own translations into *M*.) Note that this criterion of a satisfactory definition of truth, which Tarski calls the Convention *T*, is not itself such a definition in *M* of truth in *L*, since it talks *about* expressions of *M*, and about their relation to what they mean (they "name" sentences of *L*), and so is itself not in the metalanguage *M* but in the meta-metalanguage.

Since in many (meta)languages we form the name of an expression by putting that expression in quotation marks, the following might seem to meet Tarski's criterion: "For all *p*, '*p*' is a true sentence if and only if *p*." This, one might think, would immediately yield such individual cases as "'Snow is white' is a true sentence if and only if snow is white" (given, of course, that "Snow is white" is a sentence of *L*). This will not do, however, for by enclosing the fourteenth letter of the alphabet in quotation marks (however we use that letter elsewhere) we simply form the name of the fourteenth letter of the alphabet. Hence, what we get by instantiation of the proposed definition are, for example, the sentences "The fourteenth letter of the alphabet is a true sentence if and only if snow is white" and "The fourteenth letter of the alphabet is a true sentence if and only if snow is not white," which together entail that snow is white if and only if snow is not white, a contradiction.

"RECURSIVE" DEFINITION OF TRUTH. If the language *L* contained only the two simple sentences "Snow is white" and "Grass is green," plus such compounds as could be formed by prefixing "It is not the case that" to a sentence and by joining two sentences by "or," we might offer the following "recursive" definition of "true sentence":

(1) "Snow is white" is a true sentence if and only if snow is white, and "Grass is green" if and only if grass is green.

(2) The sentence formed by prefixing "It is not the case that" to a given sentence *S* is true if and only if *S* is not true.

(3) The sentence formed by placing "or" between the two sentences S_1 and S_2 is true if and only if either S_1 or S_2 is true.

There is a mathematical device for turning such "recursive" definitions into ordinary ones, so this feature of the above need not worry us; but we are clearly not very far along if we have to begin by listing all elementary sentences and defining "true" for each of them.

Suppose we enrich *L* by adding "Snow is green" and "Grass is white" to the elementary sentences, and enrich *M* by calling "snow" and "grass" names and "is green" and "is white" predicates, and defining an elementary sentence as a name followed by a predicate. We may then alter (1) above to "For any name *X* and predicate *Y*, the sentence *XY* is true if and only if the predicate *Y* applies to the object named by *X*." This, however, assumes that the metalanguage already contains the semantic expressions "names" and "applies to"; if it does not, we can only "define" them by saying that "snow" names snow, "grass" names grass, "is white" applies to *X* if and only if *X* is white, and "is green" applies to *X* if and only if *X* is green.

This is still not very satisfactory, but it is Tarski's basic procedure, except that for his simplest *L* he takes a language in which there is only one predicate, the relative or two-place predicate "is included in," and no names at all, but only variables standing for names of classes; sentences are formed from "sentential functions" by prefixing a sufficient number of universal quantifiers ("for all *x*," "for all *y*") to "bind" all the variables in the function. That is, the sentences in this language are ones like "For all *x*, *x* is included in *x*," and ones in which "not" and "or" are used either inside or outside the quantifiers or both—"For all *x* and *y*, either *x* is included in *y* or *y* is included in *x*" or "It is not the case that for all *x*, it is not the case that *x* is included in *x*" (this last can be abbreviated to "For some *x*, *x* is included in *x*"). Tarski so defines "sentential function" as to cover sentences as special cases (they are simply those sentential functions in which all the variables are bound by quantifiers) and defines the "satisfaction" of a sentential function by a class or classes (a notion very like that of a predicate's "applying to" an object) in such a way that the truth of a sentence becomes the satisfaction by *all* classes and groups of classes of the function which "is" the sentence in question.

To develop this in a little more detail: Tarski defines "sentential function" recursively, by saying that a variable followed by "is included in" followed by a variable is a sentential function, and so are expressions formed by joining sentential functions by "or" or by prefixing "It is not the case that" or a universal quantifier to a sentential function. "Satisfaction" is more complicated, for Tarski wishes to run together such cases as that the function "*x* is included in *x*" is satisfied by the class *A* if and only if *A* is included in A; "For all y, x is included in y" is satisfied by A if and only if for all y, A is included in y; "x is included in y" is satisfied by the pair of classes A and B if and only if A is included in B; "x is included in y or y in z" by the trio of classes A, B, and C if and only if A is included in B or B in C; and so on. To cover all such cases he introduces the notion of an infinite numbered sequence of classes, numbers his variables, and says that the sequence f satisfies the function "v_m is included in v_n" if and only if the mth member of f is included in the nth; the rest is done recursively—f satisfies the negation of a function Φ if and only if it does not satisfy Φ itself, the disjunction of Φ and Ψ if and only if it satisfies either Φ or Ψ, and the universal quantification of Φ with respect to the nth variable if and only if Φ is satisfied both by f itself and by all sequences that are like f except in having a different nth term.

This last part of the definition is difficult but crucial. How it works can best be seen by considering a simple example. The function "v_1 is included in v_2" is satisfied by all sequences such that the first member is included in the second. The function "For any v_2, v_1 is included in v_2" is satisfied by a sequence f if and only if f is one of the sequences satisfying the preceding function and the preceding function is still satisfied if we replace f by any sequence otherwise like it but with a different second term. This means, in view of what sequences satisfy the first function, that a sequence will satisfy the second function if and only if its first member is included in its second, whatever class that second member may be. Finally, consider the function "For all v_1, for all v_2, v_1 is included in v_2." This is satisfied by a sequence f if and only if f satisfies the preceding function (the second) and if the preceding function is still satisfied if we replace f by any sequence otherwise like it but with a different *first* term. This means, in view of what sequences satisfy the second function, that a sequence will satisfy the third only if its first member is included in its second, whatever class either of them may be, that is, if and only if every class is included in every class. It is clear that if this function were satisfied by any sequence at all, it would be satisfied by every sequence whatever. (In fact, of course, it is not satisfied by all, and therefore not by any.) In some cases a sentential function will be satisfied by any sequence whatever, even though it contains free variables—as is the case with "v_1 is included in v_1"—but if it is thus satisfied and has all its variables bound—that is, is not merely a sentential function but a sentence—it will be, in Tarski's sense, "true."

TRUTH AND CORRESPONDENCE. Tarski goes on to consider a more complicated language in which there are variables of two logical types, and an ingenious extension of the notion of a sequence enables him to define "true sentence" for this language also; but when he comes to consider "languages of infinite order," in which there are variables of an infinity of logical types, he has a proof (very similar to Gödel's proof of the incompletability of arithmetic) that any definition of either "truth" or "satisfaction" in terms of the basic material he allows himself would result in the provability of some sentence contravening his Convention T, that is, of the negation of some sentence of the form "x is a true sentence if and only if p," in which x is a name in the metalanguage of a sentence in the language studied and p is the translation into the metalanguage of the same sentence. Even with such a language, however, it is possible to introduce into the metalanguage the undefined semantic expression "true sentence" and so to axiomatize the metalanguage, thus enriched, that all sentences of the form indicated in the Convention T will be provable in it, and also desirable general theorems about truth, such as that "For any sentence x, either x is a true sentence or the negation of x is a true sentence." "Truth," introduced in this way, has something of the mysteriousness of the "correspondence" introduced without analysis by Moore, but Tarski has not merely a suspicion but a proof that, where "truth is understood as a property of sentences of the language in question, such acceptance of a semantic term without definition is inevitable.

See also Modal Logic; Negation.

Bibliography

Aristotle's definition of truth is in his *Metaphysics* 1011b26 ff., and there are further discussions in *Categories* 4a10–4b19 and 14b12–23, and *De Interpretatione* 16a10–19. As to Aristotle's Platonic sources, Plato states in the *Theaetetus* 188E–189A the problem solved in the *Sophist* 240D and 260C–263D.

Thomas Aquinas's echoes of Aristotle are in his *De Veritate*, Q. 1, A. 1, and *Summa contra Gentiles*, Book I, Ch. 59. Buridan's *Sophismata* unfortunately has not been reprinted in modern times, but there are accounts of his treatment of the "liar" and similar paradoxes in E. A. Moody, *Truth and Consequence in Mediaeval Logic* (Amsterdam: North-Holland, 1953), and A. N. Prior, "Some Problems of Self-Reference in John Buridan," in *Proceedings of the British Academy* 48 (1962): 115–126.

G. E. Moore's 1910–1911 lectures were published under the title *Some Main Problems of Philosophy* (London: Allen and Unwin, 1953); see especially Chs. 6 and 13–16. Bertrand Russell's multiple relation theory of truth is developed in his "On the Nature of Truth," in *PAS* (1906–1907): 28–49;

Philosophical Essays (London: Longmans, Green, 1910), Ch. 7; the introduction to the first edition of *Principia Mathematica* (Cambridge, U.K.: Cambridge University Press, 1910), pp. 42–45; and *Problems of Philosophy* (New York: Henry Holt, 1912). P. T. Geach's criticisms of the multiple relation theory are in his *Mental Acts* (London: Routledge and Paul, 1957), Sec. 13; Wittgenstein's, in his *Notebooks 1914–1916* (Oxford: Blackwell, 1961), pp. 21 and 96–97. Russell's recantation is in his 1918 lectures on *The Philosophy of Logical Atomism* (edited by R. C. Marsh), which is included in the collection *Logic and Knowledge*, also edited by R. C. Marsh (London: Allen and Unwin, 1956); see especially pp. 182, 187–188, 214, 218, 225–226. His "double correspondence" theory is in *The Analysis of Mind* (London: Allen and Unwin, 1921), Lecture 13. The more subtle views of the later Russell and Wittgenstein on propositions and facts appear in Russell's 1924 paper "Logical Atomism," included in his *Logic and Knowledge* and in Wittgenstein's *Blue and Brown Books* (Oxford: Blackwell, 1958), pp. 30–38, and *Philosophical Investigations* (Oxford: Blackwell, 1953), Paras. 134 and 444.

The key passage from F. P. Ramsey is in his paper "Facts and Propositions," included in *The Foundations of Mathematics*, edited by R. B. Braithwaite (London: K. Paul, Trench, Trubner, 1931), pp. 142–143. For later views of G. E. Moore, exhibiting some influence from Ramsey, see R. B. Braithwaite, ed., *The Commonplace Books of G. E. Moore* (London, 1962), pp. 228–231, 319, and especially 374–377. For the use of a Ramsey-type definition in the handling of paradoxes, see A. N. Prior, "On a Family of Paradoxes," in *Notre Dame Journal of Formal Logic* 2 (1961): 16–32, and J. L. Mackie, "Self-Refutation—A Formal Analysis," in *Philosophical Quarterly* (July 1964): 1–12.

Alfred Tarski's "The Concept of Truth in Formalized Languages" was first printed as a paper in 1931, then modified and enlarged in a German translation in 1935, of which there is an English version in his *Logic, Semantics, Metamathematics* (Oxford: Clarendon Press, 1956), Paper 7. Tarski states its main ideas less formally in "The Semantic Conception of Truth and the Foundations of Semantics," in *Philosophy and Phenomenological Research* 4 (1944): 341–376. Notable comments on it include Max Black, "The Semantic Definition of Truth," in *Analysis* 9 (March 1948): 49–63, and J. F. Thomson, "A Note on Truth," in *Analysis* 9 (April 1949): 67–72.

OTHER RECOMMENDED TITLES

Alston, William. *A Realist Conception of Truth*. Ithaca, NY: Cornell University Press, 1996.

Armstrong, D. M. *A World of States of Affairs*. Cambridge, U.K.: Cambridge University Press, 1997.

Austin, J. L. "Truth." In *Philosophical Papers*, edited by J. O. Urmson and G. J. Warnock. Oxford: Oxford University Press, 1950.

Bealer, George. *Quality and Concept*. Oxford: Clarendon Press, 1982.

Blackburn, Simon, and K. Simmons, eds. *Truth*. Oxford: Oxford University Press, 1999.

Coffa, Alberto. *The Semantic Tradition from Kant to Carnap*. Cambridge, U.K.: Cambridge University Press, 1991.

David, Marian. *Correspondence and Disquotation: An Essay on the Nature of Truth*. Oxford: Oxford University Press, 1994.

Davidson, Donald. "A Coherence Theory of Truth and Knowledge." In *Reading Rorty*, edited by Alan R. Malachowski. Cambridge, MA: Blackwell, 1990.

Davidson, Donald. "The Structure and Content of Truth." *Journal of Philosophy* 87 (1990): 279–328.

Devitt, M. *Realism and Truth*, 2nd ed. Oxford: Blackwell, 1991.

Forbes, Graham. "Truth, Correspondence, and Redundancy." In *Fact, Science and Morality: Essays on A. J. Ayer's Language, Truth & Logic*, edited by G. Macdonald and C. Wright. Oxford: Blackwell, 1986.

Kirkham, R. L. *Theories of Truth: A Critical Introduction*. Cambridge, MA: MIT Press, 1992.

Moser, Paul K. *Philosophy after Objectivity*. New York: Oxford University Press, 1993.

Pitcher, G., ed. *Truth*. Englewood Cliffs, NJ: Prentice Hall, 1964.

Rorty, Richard. *Philosophy and the Mirror of Nature*. Princeton, NJ: Princeton University Press, 1979.

Schmitt, F. F. *Truth: A Primer*. Boulder, CO: Westview Press, 1995.

Soames, Scott. *Understanding Truth*. Oxford: Oxford University Press, 1999.

Strawson, P. F. "Truth." In *Truth*, edited by G. Pitcher. Englewood Cliffs, NJ: Prentice Hall, 1964.

A. N. Prior (1967)

Bibliography updated by Benjamin Fiedor (2005)

COSMOGONY

See *Cosmology*

COSMOLOGICAL ARGUMENT FOR THE EXISTENCE OF GOD

The cosmological argument is actually a family of arguments that seek to demonstrate the existence of a sufficient reason or first cause of the existence of the cosmos. Among the proponents of the cosmological argument stand many of the most prominent figures in the history of western philosophy: Plato, Aristotle, Ibn Sīnā, al-Ghazālī, Maimonides, Anselm, Aquinas, Scotus, Descartes, Spinoza, Leibniz, and Locke, to name but some. The arguments offered by these thinkers can be grouped into three basic types: (1) what may be called the *kalam* cosmological argument for a first cause of the beginning of the universe; (2) the Thomist cosmological argument for a sustaining ground of being of the world; and (3) the Leibnizian cosmological argument for a sufficient reason why anything at all exists.

The *kalam* cosmological argument derives its name from the Arabic word designating medieval Islamic scholasticism, the intellectual movement largely responsible for developing this version of the cosmological argument. It originated in the efforts of Christian philosophers such as John Philoponus who, out of their commitment to the biblical teaching of *creatio ex nihilo*, sought to rebut the Aristotelian doctrine of the eternity of the universe. The argument aims to show that the universe had a beginning at some moment in the finite past and, because something cannot come out of nothing, must therefore have a transcendent cause that brought the universe into being.

By contrast the Thomist cosmological argument, named for the medieval philosophical theologian Thomas Aquinas, seeks a cause that is first—not in the temporal sense, but in the sense of rank. On Aquinas's Aristotelian-inspired metaphysic, every existing finite thing is composed of essence and existence and is therefore radically contingent. A thing's essence is a set of properties that serve to define what that thing is. Now if an essence is to be instantiated, there must be conjoined with that essence an act of being. This act of being involves a continual bestowal of being, or the thing would be annihilated. Essence is in potentiality to the act of being, and therefore without the bestowal of being the essence would not be instantiated.

For the same reason no substance can actualize itself; for in order to bestow being upon itself it would have to be already actual; a pure potentiality cannot actualize itself but instead requires some external cause. Although Aquinas argued that there cannot be an infinite regress of causes of being (because in such a series all the causes would be merely instrumental and so no being would be produced, just as no motion would be produced in a watch without a spring even if it had an infinite number of gears) and that therefore there must exist a first uncaused cause of being, his actual view was that there can be no intermediate causes of being at all, that any finite substance is sustained in existence immediately by the ground of being. This must be a being that is not composed of essence and existence and, hence, requires no sustaining cause. One cannot say that this being's essence includes existence as one of its properties, for existence is not a property, but an act, the instantiating of an essence. Therefore, one must conclude that this being's essence just *is* existence. In a sense, this being has no essence; rather it is the pure act of being, unconstrained by any essence. It is, as Thomas says, *ipsum esse subsistens*, the act of being itself subsisting. Thomas identifies this being with the God whose name was revealed to Moses as "I am" (Exod. 3.15).

The German polymath Gottfried Wilhelm Leibniz, for whom the third form of the argument is named, sought to develop a version of the cosmological argument from contingency without the Aristotelian metaphysical underpinnings of the Thomist argument. "The first question which should rightly be asked," he wrote, "will be, *Why is there something rather than nothing?*" ("The Principles of Nature and of Grace, Based on Reason," §7, p. 527). Leibniz meant this question to be truly universal, not merely to apply to finite things. On the basis of his principle of sufficient reason (PSR) that "no fact can be real or existent, no statement true, unless there be a sufficient reason why it is so and not otherwise" ("The Monadology," §32, p. 539), Leibniz held that this question must have an answer. It will not do to say that the universe (or even God) just exists as a brute fact. There must be an explanation why it exists. He went on to argue that the sufficient reason cannot be found in any individual thing in the universe, nor in the collection of such things which is the universe, nor in earlier states of the universe, even if these regress infinitely. Therefore, there must exist an ultramundane being that is metaphysically necessary in its existence, that is to say, its nonexistence is impossible. It is the sufficient reason for its own existence as well as for the existence of every contingent thing.

THE LEIBNIZIAN COSMOLOGICAL ARGUMENT

Undoubtedly, the most controversial premise in the Leibnizian cosmological argument is the PSR. The principle as stated in "The Monadology" has seemed, to many, evidently false. Not every fact can have an explanation, for there cannot be an explanation of what has been called the big conjunctive contingent fact (BCCF) that is itself the conjunction of all the contingent facts there are; for if such an explanation is contingent, then it, too, must have a further explanation; whereas if it is necessary, then the fact explained by it must also be necessary. But the explanation cannot have a further explanation, because the BCCF includes all the contingent facts there are; and the fact explained by it cannot be necessary, because the BCCF is contingent.

Some proponents of the cosmological argument have responded to this objection by abandoning the PSR and agreeing that one must ultimately come to some explanatory stopping point that is simply a brute fact, a being whose existence is unexplained. For example, Richard Swinburne (1991) argues that God, as the brute ultimate, is the best explanation of why everything else exists, because as a unique and infinite being God is simpler than the variegated and finite universe.

But other theists have sought to defend the Leibnizian argument without retreating to the dubious position that God is a contingent being. They have either challenged the assumption that there is a BCCF or sought to provide an acceptable explanation of it. It may well be that the existence of a BCCF is inherently paradoxical (compare the set of all truths), so that its existence cannot just be assumed. But if there is such a fact, then the claim that its explanation cannot be found in a necessary truth presupposes that explanations must entail the facts they serve to explain. If some fact is materially implied by a necessary truth, then it may be explained by that truth without itself being necessary.

Some theists have suggested that the BCCF may be explained by the necessary truth that God has weighed the reasons for creating each world and has freely chosen which world to create. Moreover, the claim that the BCCF cannot be explained by some contingent truth assumes, even more controversially, that no contingent truth can be self-explained. The reason why the BCCF is true may be simply because each of its conjuncts is true; nothing more is needed to explain why the BCCF is true than the truth of its atomic constituents, each of which has an explanation for its truth. Or again, it may be supposed that the explanation for the BCCF is that God freely wills the BCCF. Because that explanation is itself a contingent fact, it is also a constituent of the BCCF willed by God. It may then be regarded as self-explained or its explanation may be that God wills that he wills the BCCF, which fact will also be a constituent of the BCCF to be similarly explained in terms of yet another conjunct. This regress seems to be as innocuous as a series of entailments such as its being true that it is true that *p*. The entire regress is contained in the BCCF and so is willed by God.

This debate is, in any case, somewhat academic because the cosmological argument does not depend for its success on anything so strong as Leibniz's own version of the PSR. For example, in their discussion of Hartry Field's anti-Platonist claim that it is an inexplicable contingency whether mathematical objects exist, Crispin Wright and Bob Hale (1992), while rejecting the demand for an explanation of something such as the BCCF, nevertheless maintain that explicability is the default position and that exceptions to this rule have to be *explicable* exceptions—some explanation is needed for why no explanation is possible. For example, they claim that if physical existence is at issue, Leibniz's question, "Why is there something rather than nothing?" is an unanswerable question if a satisfactory explanation of why a physical state of affairs obtains has to advert to a causally prior situation in which it does not obtain, because a physically empty world would not cause anything. Wright and Hale believe that the demand for an explanation of the contingency of physical existence is preempted by the restrictive principle that "the explanation of the obtaining of a (physical) state of affairs must advert to a causally prior state of affairs in which it does not obtain" (Wright and Hale 1992, p. 128). Such a principle will be seen by the theist, however, as not at all restrictive, because the explanation of why the physical world exists can and should be provided in terms of a causally prior nonphysical state of affairs involving God's existence and will.

The proponent of the Leibnizian cosmological argument could generate an argument by holding, in conjunction with the above principle, that the obtaining of any physical state of affairs has an explanation. Or the proponent could claim that for any contingently existing thing, there is an explanation why that thing exists; or assert that everything that exists has an explanation of its existence, either in the necessity of its own nature or in an external cause; or, more broadly, maintain that in the case of any contingent state of affairs, there is either an explanation for why that state of affairs obtains or else an explanation of why no explanation is needed. All of these are more modest, nonparadoxical, and seemingly plausible versions of the PSR.

A simple statement of a Leibnizian cosmological argument might run as follows:

(1) Anything that exists has an explanation of its existence, either in the necessity of its own nature or in an external cause.

(2) If the universe has an explanation of its existence, that explanation is God.

(3) The universe exists.

(4) Therefore the explanation of the existence of the universe is God.

The version of the PSR in premise (1) is compatible with there being brute facts or states of affairs about the world. But there are two kinds of being: necessary beings, which exist of their own nature and so have no external cause of their existence, and contingent beings, whose existence is accounted for by causal factors outside themselves. Numbers might be prime candidates for the first sort of being, whereas familiar physical objects fall under the second kind of being.

Premise (2) is, in effect, the contrapositive of the typical atheist response to Leibniz that on the atheistic worldview the universe simply exists as a brute contingent thing. Atheists typically assert that, there being no God, the universe just exists inexplicably. Moreover, (2) seems plausible in its own right, for if the universe, by definition, includes all of physical reality, then the cause of the universe must (at least causally prior to the universe's existence) transcend space and time and therefore cannot be physical or material. But there are only two kinds of things that could fall under such a description: either an abstract object or else a mind. But abstract objects do not stand in causal relations. Therefore it follows that the explanation of the existence of the universe is an external, transcendent, personal cause—which is one meaning of "God."

Finally, premise (3) states the obvious—that there is a universe. Because the universe exists, it follows that God exists.

It is open to the nontheist to retort that whereas the universe has an explanation of its existence, that explanation lies not in an external ground but in the necessity of its own nature; in other words, (2) is false. The universe is a metaphysically necessary being. This is an extremely bold suggestion. One may safely say that there is a strong intuition of the universe's contingency. A possible world in which no concrete objects exist certainly seems conceivable. People generally trust their modal intuitions on other matters with which they are familiar; if they are to do otherwise with respect to the universe's contingency, then the nontheist needs to provide some reason for such skepticism other than the desire to avoid theism.

THE THOMIST COSMOLOGICAL ARGUMENT

Still, it would be desirable to have some stronger argument for the universe's contingency than modal intuitions alone. Could the Thomist cosmological argument help out here? If successful, it would show that the universe is a contingent being causally dependent upon a necessary being for its continued existence. The difficulty with appeal to the Thomist argument, however, is that it is difficult to show that things are, in fact, contingent in the special sense required by the argument. Certainly things are naturally contingent in that their continued existence is dependent upon myriad factors including particle masses and fundamental forces, temperature, pressure, entropy level, and so forth, but this natural contingency does not suffice to establish things' metaphysical contingency in the sense that being must continually be added to their essences lest they be spontaneously annihilated. Indeed, if Thomas's argument does ultimately lead to an absolutely simple being whose essence is existence, then one may well be led to deny that beings are metaphysically composed of essence and existence if the idea of such an absolutely simple being proves to be unintelligible.

THE *KALAM* COSMOLOGICAL ARGUMENT

But perhaps the *kalam* cosmological argument can reinforce the Leibnizian argument. For an essential property of a metaphysically necessary being is eternality, that is to say, existing without beginning or end. If the universe is not eternal, then, it could not be a metaphysically necessary being.

It may be countered that a being with a temporal beginning or end could be metaphysically necessary in that it exists in all possible worlds. But the notion of metaphysical necessity that underlies this suggestion fails to take tense seriously and may therefore seem inadequate. Metaphysicians have in recent years begun to appreciate the metaphysical importance of whether time is tensed or tenseless; that is to say, whether items in the temporal series are ordered objectively as past, present, or future, or whether, alternatively, they are ordered merely by tenseless relations of *earlier than*, *simultaneous with*, and *later than*. Possible worlds semantics is a tenseless semantics and so is incapable of expressing the significance of one's view of time and tense. In particular, it is evident that a truly necessary being, one whose nonexistence is impossible, must exist at every moment in every world. It is not enough for it to exist at only some moment or moments in every possible world; for the fact that there exist moments in various worlds at which it fails to exist shows that its nonexistence is not impossible. Furthermore, a truly metaphysically necessary being must exist either timelessly or sempiternally in any tensed world in which it exists, for otherwise its coming into being or ceasing to be would again make it evident that its existence is not necessary, even if it existed at every moment in worlds in which time had a beginning or end.

But it is precisely the aim of the *kalam* cosmological argument to show that the universe is not sempiternal but had a beginning. It would follow that the universe must therefore be contingent in its existence. Indeed, the *kalam* argument shows the universe to be contingent in a special way: It came into existence out of nothing. The nontheist who would answer Leibniz by holding that the existence of the universe is a brute fact, an exception to the PSR, is thus thrust into the awkward position of maintaining not simply that the universe exists eternally without explanation, but rather that for no reason at all it magically popped into being out of nothing, a position that might make theism look like a welcome alternative.

The *kalam* cosmological argument may be formulated as follows:

(1) Whatever begins to exist has a cause.

(2) The universe began to exist.

(3) Therefore, the universe has a cause.

Conceptual analysis of what it means to be a cause of the universe then helps to establish some of the theologically significant properties of this being.

Premise (1) seems obviously true—at the least, more so than its negation. It is rooted in the metaphysical intuition that something cannot come into being from nothing. Moreover, this premise is constantly confirmed in human experience. The conviction that an origin of the universe requires a causal explanation seems reasonable, for on the atheistic view, if the universe began at the big bang, there was not even the *potentiality* of the universe's existence prior to the big bang, because nothing is prior to the big bang. But then how could the universe become actual if there was not even the potentiality of its existence? It makes much more sense to say that the potentiality of the universe lay in the power of God to create it.

Often it is said that quantum physics furnishes an exception to premise (1), because on the subatomic level events are said to be uncaused. This objection, however, is based on misunderstandings. In the first place, not all scientists agree that subatomic events are uncaused. A great many physicists today are dissatisfied with this view (the so-called Copenhagen Interpretation) of quantum physics and are exploring deterministic theories like that of David Bohm (Cushing, et al, 1996). Thus, quantum physics is not a proven exception to premise (1). Second, even on the traditional, indeterministic interpretation, particles do not come into being out of nothing. They arise as spontaneous fluctuations of the energy contained in the subatomic vacuum, which constitutes an indeterministic cause of their origination. Thus, there is no basis for the claim that quantum physics proves that things can begin to exist without a cause, much less that the universe could have sprung into being uncaused from literally nothing.

Premise (2), the more controversial premise, may be supported by both deductive, philosophical arguments and inductive, scientific arguments. Classical proponents of the *kalam* argument contended that an infinite temporal regress of events cannot exist, because the existence of an actually infinite number of things leads to intolerable absurdities.

It is usually alleged that this sort of argument has been invalidated by Georg Cantor's work on the actual infinite and by subsequent developments in set theory (e.g., Sobel). But this allegation gratuitously presupposes a Platonistic view of mathematical objects that the argument's defender is at liberty to reject. Cantor's system and set theory may be taken to be simply a universe of discourse, a mathematical system based on certain adopted axioms and conventions. The argument's defender may hold that whereas the actual infinite may be a fruitful and consistent concept within the postulated universe of discourse, it cannot be transposed into the spatio-temporal world, for this would involve counterintuitive absurdities. A fictionalist understanding of abstract objects or a divine conceptualism combined with the simplicity of God's cognition is at least a tenable alternative to Platonism.

A second argument for the beginning of the universe offered by classical proponents of *kalam* is that the temporal series of past events cannot be an actual infinite because a collection formed by successive addition cannot be actually infinite, an argument that eventually became enshrined in the thesis of Kant's first antinomy concerning time. Sometimes the problem is described as the impossibility of traversing the infinite. In order for one to have "arrived" at today, temporal existence has, so to speak, traversed an infinite number of prior events. But before the present event could arrive, the event immediately prior to it would have to arrive; and before that event could arrive, the event immediately prior to it would have to arrive; and so on ad infinitum. No event could ever arrive, because before it could elapse there will always be one more event that has had to have happened first. Thus, if the series of past events were beginningless, the present event could not have arrived, which is absurd.

It is frequently objected that this sort of argument illicitly presupposes an infinitely distant starting point in the past and then pronounces it impossible to travel from that point to today. But if the past is infinite, then there would be no starting point whatever, not even an infinitely distant one. Nevertheless, from any given point in the past, there is only a finite distance to the present, which is easily traversed.

But proponents of the *kalam* argument have not in fact assumed that there was an infinitely distant starting point in the past. The fact that there is *no beginning* at all, not even an infinitely distant one, seems only to make the problem worse, not better. To say that the infinite past could have been formed by successive addition is like saying that someone has just succeeded in writing down all the negative numbers, ending at -1. And, one may ask, how is the claim that from any given moment in the past there is only a finite distance to the present even relevant to the issue? For the question is how the *whole* series can be formed, not a finite portion of it. To think that because every *finite* segment of the series can be formed by successive addition the whole *infinite* series can be so formed is to commit the fallacy of composition.

A third argument for the universe's beginning is an inductive argument based on contemporary evidence for the expansion of the universe. According to the standard big bang model, as time proceeds, the distances separating galactic masses become greater. It is important to understand that the model does not describe the expansion of the material content of the universe into a preexisting, empty space, but rather the expansion of space itself. This has the astonishing implication that as one reverses the expansion and extrapolates back in time, the universe becomes progressively denser until one arrives at a so-called singularity at which space-time curvature, along with temperature, pressure, and density, becomes infinite. It therefore constitutes an edge or boundary to space-time itself.

The history of twentieth-century cosmology has, in one sense, been a series of failed attempts to craft acceptable nonstandard models of the expanding universe in order to avert the absolute beginning predicted by the standard model. Whereas such theories are possible, it has been the overwhelming verdict of the scientific community than none of them is more probable than the big bang theory. There is no mathematically consistent model that has been so successful in its predictions or as corroborated by the evidence as the traditional big bang theory. For example, some theories, such as the oscillating universe (which expands and recontracts forever) or the chaotic inflationary universe (which continually spawns new universes), do have a potentially infinite future but turn out to have only a finite past. Vacuum fluctuation universe theories (which postulate an eternal vacuum out of which this universe is born) cannot explain why, if the vacuum was eternal, one does not observe an infinitely old universe. The no-boundary universe proposal of James Hartle and Stephen Hawking, if interpreted realistically, still involves an absolute origin of the universe even if the universe does not begin in a singularity, as it does in the standard big bang theory. More recently proposed ekpyrotic cyclic universe scenarios based on string theory or M-theory have also been shown not only to be riddled with problems, but, most significantly, to imply the origin of the universe that its proponents sought to avoid. Of course, scientific results are always provisional, but there is no doubt that the defender of the *kalam* argument rests comfortably within the scientific mainstream.

A fourth argument for the finitude of the past is also an inductive argument, appealing to implications of physical eschatology. According to the second law of thermodynamics, processes taking place in a closed system always tend toward a state of equilibrium. The universe is, on a naturalistic view, a gigantic closed system, because it is everything there is and there is nothing outside it. What this seems to imply is that, given the probability that the universe will expand forever, the universe will in the finite future degenerate into a cold, dark, lifeless, highly dilute condition, as it asymptotically approaches equilibrium. Now if, given enough time, the universe will reach such a condition, then why is it not in such a condition now, if it has existed forever, from eternity? Because it is not in such a state, the universe must have begun to exist.

Some have tried to escape this conclusion by proposing an oscillating model of the universe that restores an appearance of youth to an infinitely old cosmos. But even apart from the physical and observational problems plaguing such models, the thermodynamic properties of such a universe imply the very beginning that its proponents sought to avoid—for entropy increases from cycle to cycle in such a model, which has the effect of generating larger and longer oscillations with each successive cycle. Hence, the oscillating model has an infinite future, but only a finite past.

Even if this difficulty were avoided, a universe oscillating from eternity past would require an infinitely precise tuning of initial conditions in order to last through an infinite number of successive bounces. A universe rebounding from a single, infinitely long contraction is, if entropy increases during the contracting phase, thermodynamically untenable and incompatible with the initial low entropy condition of the expanding phase. Postulating an entropy decrease during the contracting phase in order to escape this problem would require one to postulate inexplicably special low entropy conditions at the time of the bounce in the life of an infinitely evolving universe. Such a low entropy condition at the beginning of the expansion is more plausibly accounted for by the presence of a singularity or some sort of quantum creation event.

From the two premises it follows logically that the universe has a cause. Protagonists of *kalam* maintain that a conceptual analysis of what properties must be possessed by such an ultramundane cause enables one to recover a striking number of the traditional divine attributes, revealing that if the universe has a cause, then an uncaused, personal creator of the universe exists who sans the universe is beginningless, changeless, immaterial, timeless, spaceless, and enormously powerful. This creator will be, as Leibniz maintained, the sufficient reason why anything at all exists.

See also Causation; Cosmology; Cosmos; God, Concepts of; Leibniz, Gottfried Wilhelm; Thomas Aquinas, St.

Bibliography

Adams, Fred C., and Gregory Laughlin. "A Dying Universe: The Long-Term Fate and Evolution of Astrophysical Objects." *Reviews of Modern Physics* 69 (2) (1997): 337–372.

Beck, W. David. "The Cosmological Argument: A Current Bibliographical Appraisal." *Philosophia Christi* 2 (2000): 283–304.

Burrill, Donald R. *The Cosmological Arguments*. Garden City, NY: Doubleday, 1967.

Craig, William Lane. *The Cosmological Argument from Plato to Leibniz*. New York: Barnes & Noble, 1980.

Craig, William Lane. *The* Kalam *Cosmological Argument*. London: Macmillan, 1979. Reprint, Eugene, OR: Wipf and Stock, 2000.

Craig, William Lane. "Naturalism and Cosmology." In *Analytic Philosophy without Naturalism*, edited by A. Corradini, S. Galvan, and J. Lowe. London: Routledge, 2005.

Craig, William Lane, and Quentin Smith. *Theism, Atheism, and Big Bang Cosmology*. Oxford: Clarendon Press, 1993.

Cushing, James T., Arthur Fine, and Sheldon Goldstein. *Bohmian Mechanics and Quantum Theory: An Appraisal*. Boston Studies in the Philosophy of Science 184. Dordrecht: Kluwer Academic Publishers, 1996.

Davis, Stephen T. *God, Reason, and Theistic Proofs*. Grand Rapids, MI: Eerdmans, 1997.

Gale, Richard M. *On the Existence and Nature of God*. New York: Cambridge University Press, 1991.

Harrison, Jonathan. *God, Freedom, and Immortality*. Avebury Series in Philosophy. Burlington, VT: Ashgate, 1999.

Hick, John. *Arguments for the Existence of God*. London: Macmillan, 1971.

Leibniz, G. W. "The Principles of Nature and of Grace, Based on Reason." In *Leibniz Selections*, edited by Philip P. Wiener, 522–533. New York: Charles Scribner's Sons, 1951.

Leibniz, G. W. "The Monadology." In *Leibniz Selections*, edited by Philip P. Wiener, 533–552. New York: Charles Scribner's Sons, 1951.

Mackie, John L. *The Miracle of Theism*. Oxford: Clarendon Press, 1982.

Martin, Michael. *Atheism: A Philosophical Justification*. Philadelphia: Temple University Press, 1990.

Pruss, Alexander. Ex Nihilo Nihil Fit: *A Study of the Principle of Sufficient Reason*. Cambridge, U.K.: Cambridge University Press, 2005.

Rowe, William L. "Circular Explanations, Cosmological Arguments, and Sufficient Reasons." *Midwest Studies in Philosophy* 21 (1997): 188–199.

Rowe, William L. *The Cosmological Argument*. Princeton, NJ: Princeton University Press, 1975.

Sobel, Jordan Howard. *Logic and Theism: Arguments for and against Beliefs in God*. Cambridge, U.K.: Cambridge University Press, 2004.

Swinburne, Richard. *The Existence of God*. Rev. ed. Oxford: Clarendon Press, 1991.

Vallicella, William. "On an Insufficient Argument against Sufficient Reason." *Ratio*10 (1997): 76–81.

Wright, Crispin, and Bob Hale. "Nominalism and the Contingency of Abstract Objects." *Journal of Philosophy* 89 (1992): 111–135.

William Lane Craig (2005)

COSMOLOGY

The term *cosmology* stands for a family of related inquiries, all in some sense concerned with the world at large. Two main subgroups of uses may be distinguished: those belonging to philosophy and those belonging to science.

"Cosmology" has received wide currency as a name for a branch of metaphysics, ever since Christian von Wolff, in his *Discursus Praeliminaris de Philosophia in Genere* (1728), gave cosmology a prominent place in his classificatory scheme of the main forms of philosophical knowledge and distinguished this branch from ontology, theology, and psychology. (See *Discourse on Philosophy in General*, translated by R. J. Blackwell, Indianapolis, 1963, Para. 77). Despite the severe strictures that Immanuel Kant leveled against the pursuit of rational cosmology in his *Critique of Pure Reason*, the term has continued to enjoy a standard use among many philosophers. For example, it occupies a central place in the manuals of scholastic philosophy; these adhere, for the most part, to the Wolffian scheme of classification of the branches of metaphysics. The term has been used, too, by many philosophers not in the scholastic tradition; for example, A. E. Taylor in his *Elements of Metaphysics* (London, 1903) assigns to cosmology the task of considering "the meaning and validity of the most universal conceptions of which we seek to understand the nature of the individual objects which make up the experienced physical world, 'extension,' 'succession,' 'space,' 'time,' 'number,' 'magnitude,' 'motion,' 'change,' 'quality,' and the more complex categories of 'matter,' 'force,' 'causality,' 'interaction,' 'thinghood,' and so forth" (p. 43). Cosmology is sometimes understood even more broadly, as being synonymous with speculative philosophy in its most comprehensive sense. Thus in Alfred North Whitehead's *Process and Reality* (New York, 1929), whose subtitle is "An Essay in Cosmology," the attempt is made to construct a categorial scheme of general ideas "in terms of which every element of our experience can be interpreted" (p. 4).

In its second major use, the term *cosmology* designates a science in which the joint efforts of the observational astronomer and the theoretical physicist are devoted to giving an account of the large-scale properties of the astronomical or physical universe as a whole. The task of constructing models of the universe that are suggested by and tested by appeals to the observational findings of the astronomer distinguishes the enterprise of scientific cosmology from the a priori investigations of rational cosmology (as a branch of metaphysics) and the purely conceptual and categorial analyses of the speculative philosopher. Nevertheless, even scientific cosmology poses a number of philosophical questions. The sum of these—and they are principally methodological and epistemological in character—constitutes the philosophy of scientific cosmology. The present entry is concerned with the philosophy of cosmology in this sense. Attention will be focused on a central theme in this area: the question whether cosmology must employ a method different from that employed in other empirical sciences because of its distinctive subject matter, namely, the universe as a unique system.

DESCRIPTION OR EXPLANATION?

Is the familiar distinction between description and explanation (or the corresponding one drawn between sciences still in the early stages that are primarily descriptive, and those that have progressed to the predominating use of the explanatory aspects of theory) a distinction that can be profitably applied in giving an account of the logic of cosmology? No simple and unqualified answer can be given. For, on the one hand, cosmology, in attempting to gain knowledge of the universe as a whole, certainly is not content to rest with the observational reports of the astronomer, and therefore cannot be classed with the descriptive sciences. On the other hand, in advancing to the level of theory, as cosmology in a qualified sense certainly does, it is not primarily concerned with the explanation of laws—as is the case with other explanatory sciences.

If by description is meant giving an account of some single event or object in observational terms, or (in an extended sense of "description") formulating a generalization (law) in observational terms which refers to the observable or measurable properties and relations of a class of events, then cosmology, which is interested in giving an account of the universe as a whole, is not engaged in description. Even if we recognize, as we must, the descriptive activities of observational cosmology as a branch of observational astronomy, these fall short of giving us an adequate account of the universe as a whole. All that astronomy can give us is a description of the domain of objects and events within the range of its most powerful instruments. At the present time, however, these instruments, have not reached the limit, if there is a limit, to what is in principle observable. Moreover, even if the universe were in some sense finite and wholly explorable by actually or theoretically available instruments, the statement that what is thus observationally explored is in fact the universe as a whole would not be warranted by observational evidence alone. Such a statement could not, therefore, be part of the description of the universe, insofar as this description is a report of what is found. The claim that the universe is open to complete inspection requires the support of theory. It is a statement which is not included in the description, but is a rider *to* the description—to the effect that the description as given is of the universe as complete; considerations other than purely observational ones are needed to support this claim.

If cosmology is not content with description, does it then aim at giving explanations? Here our answer must be qualified. In the case of ordinary empirical generalizations, where there are multiple instances of some phenomenon of which we have examined a limited number, we say that the law supported by this evidence may be used as a reliable rule of inference. Since the law applies to a kind of subject matter, or a type of phenomenon, it can be upheld as a useful means for predicting and explaining those instances that can be brought within its scope. But in cosmology, the primary goal is not to establish laws. The universe, by definition, is a unique object or system. Cosmology does not undertake to establish laws about universes; at best one can establish laws about the constituents of the universe. The relation that the observable portion of the universe bears to the universe is that of part to presumed whole, rather than that of instance to law. Hence, if to explain means to bring an instance under a law, this mode of explanation, which is a characteristic concern of other branches of physical science, does not characterize cosmology.

Can it be said, then, cosmology aims at giving explanations in the sense in which theories are employed to explain laws? Here our answer, once more, cannot be a straightforward "yes" or "no." The characteristic device employed by theoretical cosmology is a model of the universe, and a model in many respects functions precisely as a theory does. It is a conceptual construction that cannot be said to be a mere report of what is already found in observation, nor even an anticipated description of what might be found in future observations. Rather, it is a means for making the observational data themselves intelligible. However, the facts that the cosmologist wants to explain are not laws in the ordinary sense of the term, and so in this respect the purpose of a model of the universe is not identical with that of a theory in the ordinary sense.

Consider, for example, the question "Why is the apparent magnitude of galaxies correlated with their red shift?" This question asks for an explanation of an important datum of observation. The observed fact is sometimes called Hubble's "law," but it is a law only in the peculiar sense in which we refer to Kepler's laws as "laws." That is, Hubble's law tells us something about a particular distribution or process of a unique set of objects, namely the system of galaxies, just as Kepler's laws tell us something about the orbits of the planets in our solar system, not in any solar system. In general, however, laws of science are characterized by their universal form. They are unrestricted in scope and are not ostensibly tied to objects or events specifically located in some particular space-time region. Thus Newton's law of gravitation, for example, says that for *any* two bodies, the gravitational force that holds between them is inversely as the square of their distance apart and proportional to their masses. Now when we deal with the system of bodies and processes that constitute the unique configuration we call the universe, we are not dealing with *any* configuration of events and objects; we are dealing with the configuration actually observed and given.

An interesting and important question that can be raised here, however, is whether the unrestricted laws of ordinary physics are not themselves, in a more profound sense, relatively restricted, since they apply to bodies or phenomena within the ultimately unique configuration that constitutes the physical universe. From this point of view, the study of cosmology sets the environment and limiting framework for all other branches of physical science. Hence it is not unreasonable to expect—as E. A. Milne, D. W. Sciama, and others have pointed out—that one may hope to understand the laws of physics themselves in terms of the unique background making up the universe studied in cosmology. Such a claim, however, is associated only with certain specific models, namely, the kinematic model as worked out by Milne and the steady state model as sketched by Hermann Bondi and Sciama, and therefore this idea of explaining all laws by a cosmological model cannot be held up as a working goal for all cosmological models. In fact, the majority of models developed within the framework of general relativity theory have not been designed to embody this feature.

OBSERVATION AND THEORY

The study of cosmology has two lines of attack, that of the observational astronomer and that of the theoretical physicist. One might say that both the observational astronomer and the theoretical cosmologist are studying the universe, though from different vantage points, or that one supplies observational data about the universe that the other undertakes to interpret; but this is, at best, only a sketch of the situation and is in some ways seriously misleading. For it will not do to say that both the astronomer and the theoretical cosmologist are studying the universe, as if the universe is laid out for identification before them and the only difference between them is in approach and method. If we look more closely at the study of cosmology, the situation is rather different.

The observational astronomer is not confronted with the universe as an observationally complete whole. Instead, he obtains observational clues from various instruments about a large population of identifiable subsystems—namely, individual galaxies and clusters of galaxies. This population of observable entities is sometimes referred to as "the observable universe." However, this phrase is not to be understood in the sense that we have independent means for identifying the universe and that we wish to refer to it insofar as it is being observed. "The observable universe" is not the same as "the universe observed." What the astronomer reports on of relevance to cosmology is an observable population of galaxies and clusters of galaxies. These observational reports have to do with such matters as the spatial distribution of galaxies, their systematic motions, density, spectroscopic patterns, individual shapes, and stellar composition.

The population of subsystems that makes up the observable universe is now, as in a sense it must always be, a finite population. With the advance in the power and sensitivity of instruments, knowledge of the extent of this population and the refinement in the details of the reports about this population are improved. Although it is regarded as likely that further advances in observational resources will disclose a wider population of subsystems similar to those already observed, it must be remembered that it is always possible for further observations to disclose as basic constituents of the universe astronomical units of a higher degree of inclusiveness than galaxies or clusters of galaxies, or even entities of an altogether different type from those heretofore disclosed. Whatever may be the case in the future, it certainly is the case at present that what comes within the observational reaches of the astronomer is definitely not the universe as an absolute whole, if there is in fact such a whole.

When we say that the theoretical cosmologist studies the universe in order to understand it or make it intelligible, what is it that he studies? He does not study the universe in any direct way, if that means having before him a readily identified object which he tries to comprehend, for example by subsuming it under some law. Nor, as we have just seen, does the universe he studies consist of a complete population of entities about which the observational astronomer furnishes him detailed reports. The theoretical cosmologist is not given information about the universe as a whole, nor even about what lies beyond the immediate range of the astronomer's instruments.

What then does he study? A brief and simple answer is to say that he constructs a model of the universe and that he studies the way in which this model may be used to interpret the observational data already available. The cosmologist will use his model to interpret the data assembled by the observational astronomer and to guide the astronomer in the search for further data. Insofar as the use of theoretical models proves satisfactory, we may say that cosmology has helped us to understand the universe and to make it intelligible. This is not to be understood, however, as meaning that even at the end of a relatively successful course of inquiry, the cosmologist has been able to confront the universe directly as some kind of readily identifiable object, system, or class of objects. What is to be understood by "the universe," in short, can only be approached and identified through the use of models, not independently of them.

THE MODEL AND ITS CONSTRUCTION

The kind of model that the cosmologist constructs is wholly conceptual rather than material. It consists of different sorts of symbols including ordinary language, mathematical language, diagrams, and charts, all of which will normally be employed in presenting a given model. A model of the universe is not something that can be directly visualized or completely represented in a pictorial diagram. Consider, for example, a typical model in which use is made of a geometric mode of representation according to which the galaxies are treated as a set of mathematical points that trace out a set of geodesic curves in space-time. In this case, the metric of this set of points is given by the general Robertson-Walker expression for the space-time interval (ds):

$$ds^2 = dt^2 - \left(\frac{R^2(t)}{c^2}\right)\left\{\frac{dr^2 + r^2\,d\theta^2 + r^2 \sin^2\theta\,d\phi^2}{(1 + kr^2/4)^2}\right\}$$

where $R(t)$ is the expansion factor, k is a constant whose value determines whether space is Euclidean or non-Euclidean, c is the velocity of light, and r, θ, and ϕ are spatial coordinates. In addition to the specification of purely geometric or kinematic features, which are specified by introducing appropriate values for the curvature constant (k) and the expansion factor ($R(t)$), a model will also require some assignment of specific dynamic or gravitational properties to the entities thus represented. Additional formulas will then be required, and these will normally involve relativity theory or some equivalent branch of physics. It is clear that however much a simple diagram making use of dots and lines may serve to give us a visual representation of what we are talking about, this hardly suffices to encompass all those additional features of the model not included in the diagram.

Although the cosmologist cannot inspect the original, the universe itself, he nevertheless undertakes to make a model of it. How is this done? The answer is to be found by noting the various clues and sources to which the cosmologist appeals in determining the properties to be assigned to his model. These are of two principal types: observational clues provided by the astronomer, and theoretical principles thought to be of relevance to the cosmologic problem.

OBSERVATIONAL CLUES. In general, the observational data the astronomer gathers aid the cosmologist by suggesting ways of assigning certain idealized properties to the model, by providing empirically ascertained values for the constants and variables in the model, and by offering tests for the adequacy of the model as a tool for predicting observable matters of fact.

Idealized properties. The kinds of entities and their properties that the astronomer observes suggest to the cosmologist the lines to follow in developing a simplified and idealized conception of the universe. Let us take some examples. The galaxies, though of enormous physical bulk, may be considered for purposes of the model as particles making up a continuous and perfect fluid. The advantage of treating the galaxies in this fashion is that it permits a great simplification of the problem, to which readily available mathematical tools of representation and calculation may be applied. Here, of course, the cosmologist adopts a technique that is universally adopted in other branches of physical science and with similar justification. If necessary, suitable corrections to this idealization can always be introduced when application is made of the model to "describe" the actual universe.

An important feature of the domain of galaxies already observed is their spatial distribution. The actual spatial distribution of the galaxies is roughly homogeneous and isotropic when fairly large volumes of space are considered. On a smaller scale, departures from homogeneity become more noticeable, in the clustering of the galaxies, for example. When still smaller volumes of space are investigated, homogeneity breaks down altogether. In general, then, the claim to the uniformity of distribution of galaxies can be upheld only if one takes a sufficiently large unit of volume, say 3.5×10^8 parsecs in diameter. Yet in constructing his model, and as a first approximation, the cosmologist will assign a complete homogeneity to his model of the universe. The expression "cosmological principle" is commonly used to designate this feature of spatial homogeneity. Models that satisfy this cosmological principle, and thus possess the feature of spatial homogeneity, are known as uniform model universes.

When put into mathematical language, a uniform model universe is one possessing a constant curvature at a given moment of time. In the language of general relativity theory, since the density and pressure of material that make up the model are the same in all volumes of space at a given time, whatever their size, a geometric representation of this fact will involve the use of one or another of the spaces of constant curvature. All segments of space of the entire universe will have the same curvature. Such a model clearly requires a process of idealizing and simplifying the spatial distribution of bodies actually observed. For if we were to use the language of geometry to describe the actually observed spatial distribution, we should have to note the actual local departures from homogeneity or constancy of curvature.

In constructing a model of the universe that embodies the feature of spatial homogeneity or constancy of curvature, it is not enough to specify what that curvature is at the present moment of cosmic time. A fully determined model requires (in addition to other features) that the spatial properties of the universe be specified for any point in its past or future. Here there are, broadly speaking, two possibilities. According to one, the spatial properties of the universe remain the same at all times; this view is upheld by those who adhere to the "perfect cosmological principle" and use it to define the properties of the steady state model. A second alternative is to adopt the cosmological principle in its more restricted form as designating merely spatial uniformity, as is the case with the orthodox cosmological models of general relativity. For such models, the entire history of the universe, from a spatial point of view, could be specified if one knew just one thing—the rate at which the distance between any two galaxies changes with time. In a universe characterized simply by the cosmological principle, since an observer would always find a spatially isotropic distribution of particles about him, the only basic feature subject to change is a temporally noticeable feature, namely, changes in the density of the distribution of particles. Such changes in the density might then serve to define a cosmic "clock."

Empirically obtained values. A second important function that the appeal to observational data serves in the construction of cosmological models is that of yielding empirically obtained values for some of the constants and variables of theory. For example, in relativistic uniform models of the expanding universe, the defining characteristics of a particular model need to be specified by assigning values for the following quantities: the cosmological constant (λ), the temporal pattern of the universe as determined by evaluating the function $R(t)$, the values for the velocity factor and the acceleration factor in the velocity-distance relation that specify how the galaxies are moving, the density (ρ) and the pressure (p) of the material and energetic content that fills the universe, and the curvature constant (k). Observational evidence is, at present, either not available at all or not accurate enough to give sufficiently precise determinations for all of these terms. The cosmologist must, therefore, use whatever data is available to eliminate those models that are incompatible with present observations and to suggest lines of inquiry that will help to narrow the field down to those models that can be further tested by observation.

One overall condition for the acceptance of a model is, of course, the consistency of the empirically obtained values it proposes. In a particular model, a particular combination of empirically assigned curvature and density values, for example, may lead to a calculated "age of the universe" that will be inconsistent with an independently obtained estimate for the lower bound of such an "age"; the estimated time scale of the universe will be too short. In general what is sought is a model all of whose empirically ascertainable values are mutually consistent within the available limits of accuracy.

Empirical tests. Finally, as a natural extension of the point just made, we see how the data obtained by the astronomer serve to test the calculated numerical values for quantities appearing in the cosmologist's equations or other qualitative predictions made on the basis of a given model. Thus whether the extremely remote galaxies at the horizon of the now observable population of galaxies have roughly the same characteristics as those that are nearer is an important question much discussed at the present time as a means for evaluating the rival claims of the steady state and evolutionary theories. The steady state theory claims that galaxies that are at the outer limits of observability should have roughly the same characteristics as those at lesser distances. According to various "evolutionary" models, those same remote galaxies, from which we receive light and other forms of radiation emitted billions of years ago, could, in effect, tell us about the earlier stages of the evolution of the universe. Since conditions at the time of emission were presumably different from what they are now, these very remote galaxies should display differences from those that are nearer to us in at least some of their properties, and these differences should give us valuable clues about the course of development of the universe as a whole. In this regard a number of delicate questions that are the subject of much controversy have arisen in current research.

THEORETICAL IDEAS. A second major source of ideas in the construction of cosmological models is to be found in the conceptual resources of mathematical physics. Here there are two broad possibilities that confront the cosmologist.

Use of established principles. As a first possibility, the cosmologist may turn to some already established body of physical theory as expressed in fundamental principles and derived laws. Such theory will normally have already been found to be successful in dealing with a variety of physical problems of lesser scope than, and wide differences from, the purely cosmological problem. The cosmologist will nevertheless propose to see to what extent the same general body of ideas may be used when applied to the distinctive subject matter of cosmology. He will investigate to what extent the universe as a physical system has a detailed structure that may be articulated and specified by means of the selected physical theory. For example, he may use Newtonian mechanics to construct a model of the universe. Isaac Newton himself drew, in a general qualitative way, the cosmological consequences of using the inverse square law of gravitation as a guide. He argued that the universe, throughout its infinite space, must be filled by a more or less evenly distributed matter. For if all the matter that exists were to be confined to a finite "island" in an infinite "ocean" of space, it would have a center of mass toward which, in time, all matter would move by gravitational attraction. The fact is that no such motion is found, and Newton concluded, therefore, that matter is distributed uniformly throughout an infinite space.

At the present time, the primary and predominant source to which the cosmologist turns is the general theory of relativity as expressed in Albert Einstein's general field equations. These equations specify the relations between the space-time metric of any physical domain and its material or energetic content. The discovery of solutions to those field equations that are of special relevance to the cosmologic situation has led to the construction of several varieties of relativistic models. The other major use to which the field equations of general relativity have been put takes the form of the Schwarzschild solution. It was this solution that first afforded the opportunity for testing the predictive and explanatory powers of the theory as a whole. Karl Schwarzschild's solution is particularly applicable to a physical system such as we encounter in the solar system, namely, a single massive particle (the sun) in whose neighborhood we may study the behavior of much smaller masses (the planets) and light rays. The success of its predictions and explanations has been the primary basis for the confidence placed in the general theory.

To return then to cosmology: Within the broad class of homogeneous, or uniform, model universes we may distinguish the nonstatic models and the static models. Among the static models is Einstein's original model of 1917, which pictured the universe as finite and unbounded; in the light of the subsequent discovery of the mutual recession of the galaxies, it is no longer considered adequate. The nonstatic models include the ever-expanding-universe models that originate from zero or in some finite volume, and oscillating models that undergo alternate contractions and expansions. Within each of these groups, individuating characteristics for a particular model are to be found in the choice of values for the curvature, age, density, and cosmological constant. No single model has as yet been universally adopted.

Creation of new principles. The other broad possibility for furnishing theoretical ideas for cosmologic models is one in which the cosmologist, instead of appealing to already established principles or laws, for example those of relativistic mechanics, undertakes to create afresh basic principles thought to be of special relevance to the cosmologic problem. By way of illustration, there is the conflict of the 1930s and 1940s between the way in which E. A. Milne sought to establish his kinematic model and the more orthodox procedures of relativistic cosmology. Although Milne did use the formulas of special relativity, he did not take these over directly from Einstein's own presentation; Milne attempted instead to derive them from what he thought of as more basic and primitive postulates. These postulates, he claimed, state the conditions for the measurement of time and for the communication of results by different timekeepers and observers.

A more recent example of the same sort of procedure is the steady state model of the universe proposed by Bondi and Thomas Gold in 1948. In support of this model, it is argued that since the universe is unique, there is no reason to believe that the laws which apply to smaller-scale physical phenomena, for example in laboratory terrestrial physics, or even in the domain of gravitational phenomena in the solar system, need be expected to apply to the universe as a whole. Therefore, instead of taking such laws as the point of departure in investigating the physical properties of the universe as a whole, it is suggested that the cosmologist can actually enjoy a far greater freedom than is believed possible in orthodox relativistic cosmologies. Let the cosmologist adopt any "laws" or principles which he believes are appropriate to the study of the universe as a whole, even though these may not have been established or confirmed in other (smaller-scale) areas of physical phenomena. The important thing is to see whether using these laws and principles leads to confirmable empirical results and whether they help to increase and deepen our understanding of the universe.

Those who favor this view (Bondi and Gold among others) determine some of the major features of the steady state model by appeal to the specially introduced postulate known as the perfect cosmological principle. This principle was not in prior use in other branches of physics but was introduced because of its special relevance to cosmology. (Fred Hoyle's model of the steady state universe proceeds along more conventional lines, at least in this respect. Although it differs from the expanding universe models of general relativity in abandoning the principle of the conservation of matter—in order to make possible the idea of the continuous creation of matter—it appeals for its basic physical principles, although in modified form, to the field equations of general relativity.)

One general motive that seems to inspire the setting up of specially devised principles for cosmologic models is the desire to show that the science of cosmology is basic to all other physical sciences. Instead of appealing to other branches of physics for principles to be used in describing the features of the universe as a whole, it is thought desirable that one should be able, eventually, to show that the laws of ordinary physics can be linked with the properties of the universe as a whole. The universe would then disclose itself to be a unitary physical system within which it would be possible in principle to deduce ordinary physical laws from the principles of cosmology. Milne undertook to show how, for example, the inverse square law of gravitation, among other things, could be deduced from such more fundamental cosmological ideas. Similarly, within the framework of a steady state model, Sciama attempts to show how the local inertial properties of matter can be linked (as Ernst Mach originally proposed) with the distribution of masses in the universe at large.

From a logical point of view, there is no reason to discourage such efforts. On the contrary, the realization of such a goal would be of immeasurable significance for all of science, and one should in logic suspend judgment until such a program can be carried through with some fair degree of success.

Meanwhile, it is necessary to point out that some of the writers who favor this approach put methodological interpretations on the use and warrant for the specially devised principles that are not acceptable, whatever the eventual success or promise of the program as a whole. Thus Milne and Bondi, who support different models, are each concerned to stress what they take to be a special method for cosmology—as contrasted with other branches of physics. Milne, for example, thought of ordinary physics as employing an inductive method, whereas cosmology, he believed, should be based on a deductive method. Cosmology, he argued, should not employ the laws of ordinary physics to the extent that these are inductively warranted. This was his major complaint against what he took to be the faulty procedure of relativistic cosmologies founded on the "inductively established" principles of general relativity. In making this claim, Milne was in error, since the principles of general relativity theory are not, as he thought, ordinary inductive generalizations.

In fact, Milne's own appeal to "self-evidence" as the warrant for introducing his preferred cosmological principles must be rejected, for the appeal is groundless and fails to support the certainty and uniqueness which he claimed for his principles. In constructing a model of the universe, the cosmologist is engaged in setting up a theoretical tool for dealing with the facts of observation. Whether he gets his theoretical principles by "borrowing" them from some other branch of physics or whether he creates them especially for the problem at hand is of secondary importance to what he does with these principles once he has them and how he evaluates the results he achieves. There is a common method that characterizes cosmology regardless of the particular model being proposed or favored, and it is precisely the same method which is employed in other branches of physics. Moreover, the same criteria of evaluation need to be brought to bear in the appraisal of results in cosmology as in other areas of science. Far from including any appeal to self-evidence or to similar rationalistic demands, a satisfactory model requires the constant support provided by observational evidence.

COGNITIVE WORTH OF MODELS

Consideration of the goals set by scientific cosmology gives rise to a central philosophical question, that of determining the cognitive worth of any cosmological model. This is an epistemological question and may be put in terms of the traditional issues separating the realist and the conceptualist (or the instrumentalist). Should we say with the realist that cosmological models offer us an account of the structure of the independently existing universe, or, rather, should we say with the conceptualist that these models are simply useful means of presenting and interpreting observational data?

As a basis for clarifying the issue at hand, it will be helpful to point out a fundamental ambiguity in the use of the term *universe* itself. Employed without the qualifying adjectives "observed" or "observable," it may have at least two quite distinct senses. One meaning of *universe* is "that to which the observed universe belongs"; another is "that which is characterized by a cosmological model." So far as the realist is concerned, the two meanings are equivalent; in his view the universe defined by a cosmological model will be the same universe as the one described by the expression "that to which the observed universe belongs." But the realist's view of cosmological models cannot be assumed in advance to be the only tenable one. Thus the distinction suggested here has the merit of permitting us to keep this question open. If later a realist philosophy is accepted, the appropriate modifications can be made. Clearly, we do not need to commit ourselves to the position that everything properly said of "the universe" in the sense of "that which is characterized by a cosmological model" can also be said of "the universe" in the sense of "that to which the observed universe belongs." For example, we might want to attribute the property of being "a whole" or "an absolute totality" to the universe as characterized by a particular model, but not to the universe in the sense of that to which the observed universe belongs.

Cosmology aims at articulating the character of the universe *as* a whole. To that extent, then, it rests on the methodological postulate that the universe *is* a whole. The specific character of the whole will, of course, be variously described by various models. What remains fixed, however, is the assumption that the goal of cosmology is to characterize the universe *as* a whole. Therefore the statement "The universe is a whole" is in this context an analytic statement, a matter of definition. But note that it is a definition in which "the universe" is used to signify "that which is characterized by a cosmological model." Not only does cosmology require that, as a matter of definition, the universe be thought of as a whole (in the sense of being intelligible in the way that mathematical classes, geometrical relations, or physical systems are); it also postulates that the universe as a whole is unique or absolute. This means that there is just one such class, pattern, or system, and that all other physical processes or systems of lesser duration or spatial extent are to be taken only as parts of this all-embracing whole. Since each model will so define the universe, it would be a misuse of language to speak of a plurality of universes. Again, of course, the precise structure of this unique or absolute whole will, at least in some respects, vary from model to model.

But what if "the universe" means "that to which the observed universe belongs"? Is the statement "The universe is an absolute, unique whole" still analytic? To this the answer must be no. For when we use "the universe" in this sense, we move from methodology to ontology. In contrast to the case of the universe as defined by a cosmological model, we are no longer committed by the basic methodological postulate of cosmology to saying that the universe *is* a whole. True, in setting up a science, it may be necessary to presuppose the existence of some pervasive structure as the object of study. Yet such a presupposition need not be binding on what the universe is existentially. So long as "the universe" means simply "that to which the observed universe belongs," nothing in this meaning contains analytically the notion of its being a "whole" or an "absolute whole." Indeed, even if we grant that the observed universe is structured in some manner, this does not entail that the wider universe of which it is a part is also pervasively structured. Nor does the fact that we describe the observed universe as "part of" or "that which belongs to" something else require us to say that the universe to which it belongs is a unique or absolute whole. For our reliance on such terms as *part, whole*, and *belong* reveals merely that the mind, in reaching into the unfamiliar, must use analogies in order to relate the unfamiliar to what it already knows.

The universe as the "something more" than the observed universe may well be a complete, unique and intelligibly structured whole. But the claim that we are able to say so is something to which we need not commit ourselves. It is better left as an open question, since, strictly speaking, it is one on which we neither have nor can have any knowledge. Stipulating an affirmative answer by definition does not, of course, establish such knowledge.

See also Creation and Conservation, Religious Doctrine of; Einstein, Albert; Mach, Ernst; Newton, Isaac; Relativity Theory; Taylor, Alfred Edward; Time; Whitehead, Alfred North; Wolff, Christian.

Bibliography

HISTORICAL SURVEYS

De Sitter, W. *Kosmos*. Cambridge, MA: Harvard University Press, 1932.

Koyré, A. *From the Closed World to the Infinite Universe*. Baltimore: Johns Hopkins Press, 1957.

Kuhn, T. S. *The Copernican Revolution*. Cambridge, MA: Harvard University Press, 1957.

Munitz, M. K., ed. *Theories of the Universe from Babylonian Myth to Modern Science*. Glencoe, IL: Free Press, 1957.

SYSTEMATIC SURVEYS

Bondi, H. *Cosmology*. 2nd ed. Cambridge, U.K.: Cambridge University Press, 1961.

Bondi, H. et al. *Rival Theories of Cosmology*. London: Oxford University Press, 1960.

Bonnor, W. B. *The Mystery of the Expanding Universe*. New York: Macmillan, 1964.

Couderc, P. *The Expansion of the Universe*. London: Faber and Faber, 1952.

Eddington, A. *The Expanding Universe*. Cambridge, U.K.: Cambridge University Press, 1933.

Hubble, E. P. *Observational Approach to Cosmology*. Oxford, 1937.

Hubble, E. P. *The Realm of the Nebulae*. New Haven, CT: Yale University Press, 1936.

Lemaitre, G. *The Primeval Atom*. New York: Van Nostrand, 1950.

McVittie, G. C. *Fact and Theory in Cosmology*. London: Eyre and Spottiswoode, 1961.

Milne, E. A. *Modern Cosmology and the Christian Idea of God*. Oxford: Clarendon Press, 1952.

Milne, E. A. *Relativity, Gravitation, and World-Structure*. Oxford: Clarendon Press, 1935.

Sciama, D. *The Unity of the Universe*. Garden City, NY: Doubleday, 1959.

Tolman, R. C. *Relativity, Thermodynamics and Cosmology*. Oxford: Clarendon Press, 1934.

Whitrow, G. J. *The Structure and Evolution of the Universe*. London: Hutchinson, 1959.

PHILOSOPHICAL PROBLEMS

Bondi, H. "Fact and Inference in Theory and in Observation." In *Vistas in Astronomy*, edited by A. Beer. London: Pergamon Press, 1955. Vol. I.

Bondi, H. "Philosophical Problems of Cosmology." In *British Philosophy in the Mid-Century*, edited by C. A. Mace. London: Allen and Unwin, 1957.

Davidson, W. "Philosophical Aspects of Cosmology." *British Journal of the Philosophy of Science* 13 (50) (August 1962).

Dingle, H. "The Philosophical Aspects of Cosmology." In *Vistas in Astronomy*, edited by A. Beer. London: Pergamon Press, 1955. Vol. I.

Finlay-Freundlich, E. "Cosmology." In *International Encyclopedia of Unified Science* Vol. I, No. 8. Chicago: University of Chicago Press, 1951.

Harré, R. "Philosophical Aspects of Cosmology." *British Journal of the Philosophy of Science* 13 (50) (August 1962).

Johnson, M. *Time, Knowledge and the Nebulae*. London: Faber and Faber, 1945.

McVittie, G. C. "Rationalism and Empiricism in Cosmology." *Science* 133 (21) (April 1961).

Monist 47 (1) (Fall 1962). Entire issue.

Munitz, M. K. *The Mystery of Existence*. New York: Appleton-Century-Crofts, 1965.

Munitz, M. K. *Space, Time, and Creation*. Glencoe, IL: Free Press, 1957.

Toulmin, S. "Contemporary Scientific Mythology." In *Metaphysical Beliefs*, edited by S. Toulmin, R. W. Hepburn, and A. MacIntyre. London: SCM Press, 1957.

Milton K. Munitz (1967)

COSMOLOGY [ADDENDUM]

The key issue identified by Milton K. Munitz, whether cosmology should center on description or explanation, remains a central philosophical theme in the early twenty-first century. However, the context has changed dramatically since he wrote his entry, and that has changed the implications.

First, massive new data sets are available because of the extraordinary improvement of telescopes, detectors, and computer technology in the past three decades. Not only are optical, ultraviolet, and infrared observations of galaxies possible in determining luminosities and spectra with unprecedented sensitivity but radio, X-ray, and gamma ray sky surveys are also possible. Galaxies have been detected up to a redshift of 6 and many quasar-stellar objects as well as multiple images of distant gravitationally lensed galaxies have been identified. Besides large-scale number-count and redshift surveys, the background radiation spectrum at all wavelengths have been measured. A key feature has been identification of cosmic blackbody radiation (CBR) with a perfect 3 degrees Kelvin (K) blackbody spectrum, which is isotropic to one part in 104 after allowing for Earth's motion relative to the rest frame of the radiation. Detailed observations have mapped its anisotropies over the whole sky at a sensitivity of better than one part in 105. Cosmology has changed from a data-poor to a data-rich subject.

Second, theory has developed dramatically, largely in a symbiotic relation with the observations, being used both to interpret them and to suggest new observations. This has happened in relation to gravitational theory, as regards astrophysics, and in relation to various branches of high-energy physics. This has changed the texture of cosmology from being essentially an exercise in geometry with an admixture of philosophy, to being a rich theoretical subject with relations to many branches of physics.

The cosmological application of Albert Einstein's theory of gravitation has been developed simultaneously. This theory predicted there must have been a start to the universe, but it was not clear if this was simply because of the special geometry of the standard (Friedmann-Lemaître) models of the universe, which are exactly isotropic and spatially homogeneous. More realistic models might show the prediction was a mathematical artifact. The singularity theorems developed by Roger Penrose and Stephen Hawking showed this was not the case: even for realistic geometries, classical gravitational theory predicts a beginning to the universe at a space-time singularity. Sophisticated perturbation theory was developed to underlie the theory of structure formation in the expanding universe, and dynamical systems studies related the behavior of whole classes of anisotropic models in suitable phase spaces, enabling identification of generic patterns of behavior.

The cosmological constant is a possible repulsive force term in the Einstein field equations. After Einstein discarded it in the 1930s, it was usually assumed to be zero until a decade ago, when observations of supernovae in distant galaxies showed the expansion of the universe is speeding up. The gravitational equations then imply presence of a cosmological constant or some equivalent form of dark energy. There is no known physics reason why this force should exist at this level where it is just detectable—quantum field theory suggests it should be enormously larger. Perhaps the problem is that the wrong theory of gravity is being used.

Astrophysics studies the physics and evolution of galaxies, clusters of galaxies, and any intergalactic medium there may be. It has led to three important deductions. First, both the universe itself and the matter in it are evolving: Radio source counts preclude the steady state model proposed by Hermann Bondi, Thomas Gold, and Sir Fred Hoyle. Second, the dynamics of galaxies and clusters of galaxies is only compatible with observations if there is a large amount of dark matter present, felt by its gravitational effects but not emitting detectable radiation. In terms of the dimensionless density parameter, $\Omega_{dm} = 0.3$. This is less than the critical value = 1 separating universes that recollapse in the future ($\Omega < 1$) from those that expand forever ($\Omega > 1$) when the cosmological constant vanishes, but much greater than that for visible matter ($\Omega_{vm} = 0.02$). Third, the CBR is relic radiation from a hot early state of the universe, with matter and radiation held in tight equilibrium when the universe is ionized at redshifts greater than z_{dec} 1100, but separately evolving for lower redshifts when electrons and nuclei are combined into atoms. The matter at $z = z_{dec}$ formed the last scattering surface (LSS) in the early universe and emitted the CBR. The universe is opaque for $z > z_{dec}$ but transparent for $z < z_{dec}$. Thus, the LSS delineates the visual horizon: One is unable to see to earlier times than its occurrence (because the early universe was opaque) or to detect any matter at larger distances than that one sees on the LSS (because of the speed of light limit on propagation of information).

The physics of the early universe (before decoupling) can be thought of in three stages. The hot big bang stage is the last one, when matter and radiation cooled from a high temperature ($> 10^{12}$K) to 4000K on the LSS. Nuclear physics processes with pair production and weak interactions lead to a well-understood physical evolution. At about 109K nucleosynthesis took place: the creation of the light elements (deuterium, helium, and lithium) from protons and neutrons (heavy elements such as carbon only formed later in the interior of stars). Theory and observation are in excellent agreement provided the density of baryons is low: $\Omega^{bar} = 0.02$. This leads to an important conclusion: the much more abundant dark matter detected astrophysically cannot be ordinary matter made up of baryons. Many attempts have been made to identify its nature, but this is still unknown.

Particle physics processes dominated the preceding era when exotic processes took place such as combination of a quark-gluon plasma to produce baryons. Quantum field theory effects were significant then, and this leads to an important possibility: Scalar fields producing repulsive gravitational effects could have dominated the dynamics of the universe at those times. This leads to the theory of the inflationary universe, proposed by Alan Guth: an extremely short period of accelerating expansion preceding the hot big bang era, leading to a cold and smooth vacuum-dominated state and ending in reheating: conversion of the scalar field to radiation, initiating the hot big bang epoch. This inflationary process is claimed to explain some philosophical puzzles: why the universe is so special (with spatially homogeneous and isotropic geometry and a uniform distribution of matter) and why the space sections are so close to being flat (the sign of the spatial curvature is still unknown). This theory led to a major bonus: a proposal that initial tiny quantum fluctuations were expanded to such a large scale by inflation that they provided seeds initiating growth by gravitational attraction of large-scale structures such as clusters of galaxies. This theory makes clear observational predictions for the spectrum of CMB anisotropies, which have since been spectacularly verified.

Quantum gravity processes are presumed to have dominated the earliest times, preceding inflation. There are many theories of the quantum origin of the universe, but none has attained dominance. The problem is that there is not a good theory of quantum gravity, so all these attempts are essentially different proposals for extrapolating known physics into the unknown. A key issue is whether quantum effects can remove the initial singularity and make possible universes without a beginning. Preliminary results suggest this may be so.

Thus, the present dominant cosmological paradigm is a quantum gravity era followed by inflation, leading on to the hot big bang epoch and finally the observable universe domain. A wealth of observations supports this dominant theory, but some theoretical proposals are being made that have no observational support; sometimes it will be impossible to ever obtain such support. This happens both as regards physics and geometry.

The limits of physics testing are reached because accelerators on Earth attaining the energies relevant in the early universe cannot be constructed. Consequently, when considering physical processes at the time of inflation and earlier, the extrapolation of known physics into the unknown is relied on. Some things are assumed to be unchanged (e.g., the use of standard variational principles) and others as indefinitely mutable (any potential that is convenient may be used). Thus, the claimed link of cosmology to high-energy physics is potential rather than real. In particular, no specific particle or field has been identified as underlying inflation, and no experimental test is possible for the various mechanisms proposed for creation of the universe. There is only one universe, and what happens during a rerun with the same or different initial conditions cannot be observed.

The limits of what is observable is given by the visual horizon, as discussed by Munitz. However, most cosmological models make predictions of what lies beyond, and these predictions can never be observationally verified. This is particularly important in the case of the chaotic inflation theory proposed by Andrei Linde, which claims that the expanding universe domain is imbedded in a still-exponentially expanding inflationary universe in which there are embedded countless other expanding universe domains similar to this one, the whole forming a fractal-like structure. However those other domains cannot be seen, so this model is observationally unverifiable; furthermore, the underlying physics is experimentally untested. Adherence to this model implies the victory of theory over experimental tests and observational verification.

There is one case where this kind of spatial observational limit does not obtain. This is when a small universe occurs, that is, a universe that closes up on itself spatially for topological reasons and does so on such a small scale that one can see right round the universe since the time of decoupling. Then one can see all the matter that exists, with multiple images of many objects occurring. This possibility is observationally testable, and indeed there are weak hints in the CMB anisotropies that this could actually be the case. Checking if this is possible or not is an important task; the nature of the observational relationship to the universe is fundamentally different if it is true.

A key issue is whether the universe is special in geometrical and physical terms. The assumption that the universe is geometrically special was encoded in Edward Arthur Milne's cosmological principle, taken as a founding principle in cosmology until the 1960s. Then Charles W. Misner introduced the idea of a universe with generic initial conditions that was isotropized at later times by physical processes, giving a physical cause for its special geometry. This concept became central to the inflationary universe paradigm, but is only partially successful because universes that are anisotropic enough may never inflate and may not lead to ordinary thermodynamics. Some degree of geometric specialty must have occurred.

As regards physics, the key point is that only a restricted set of physical laws and boundary conditions will allow life to exist. This has led to the anthropic question: Why does the universe have that special character that is favorable to life? The only physically based answer is that there physically exists a multiverse: an ensemble of numerous universes with varying properties. If there is a large enough ensemble with enough variation, it becomes virtually certain that some of them will just happen to get things right so that life can exist. However, despite various ingenious suggestions, this proposal is observationally and experimentally untestable. Adherence to the multiverse idea to gain explanatory power is another triumph of theory and explanation over observational testing and description. There is no way to determine the properties of any other universe in the multiverse if they do indeed exist, for they are forever outside observational reach.

Some proposals claim there may be an infinite number of universes in a multiverse and many cosmological models have spatial sections that are infinite, implying an infinite number of particles, stars, and galaxies. This proposal involves, however, an idea that some have argued is incoherent. Thus, David Hilbert (1964), for example, argues that infinity is quite different from a very large number: The word *infinity* denotes a quantity or number that can never be attained, and so will never occur in physical reality. If so, then this last proposal is not only unverifiable, but such as cannot be true. On the contrary, many other scholars—such as José A. Benardete (1964)—argue that an actual infinity of things is possible.

See also Einstein, Albert; Hilbert, David; Infinity in Mathematics and Logic; Quantum Mechanics; Philosophy of Physics.

Bibliography

Barrow, John D., and Frank J. Tipler. *The Anthropic Cosmological Principle.* New York: Oxford University Press, 1986.

Benardete, José A. *Infinity: An Essay in Metaphysics.* Oxford, U.K.: Clarendon Press, 1964.

Harrison, Edward. *Cosmology: The Science of the Universe.* 2nd ed. New York: Cambridge University Press, 2000.

Hawking, Stephen W., and George F. R. Ellis. *The Large Scale Structure of Space Time.* Cambridge, U.K.: Cambridge University Press, 1973.

Hilbert, David. "On the Infinite." In *Philosophy of Mathematics,* edited by Paul Benacerraf and Hilary Putnam, 134–151. Englewood Cliffs, NJ: Prentice-Hall, 1964.

Leslie, John. "Anthropic Principle, World Ensemble, and Design." *American Philosophical Quarterly* 19 (1982): 141–152.

George F. R. Ellis (2005)

COSMOPOLITANISM

When the Cynic philosopher Diogenes of Sinope (c. 412–c. 323 BCE) was asked where he came from, he said "I am a citizen of the world" (Diogenes Laertius, *Lives of Eminent Philosophers*, bk. 6, chap. 63). The Greek term is "kosmopolitēs," the source of the English word "cosmopolitan." Cosmopolitanism is actually a range of views—moral, political, and cultural—affirming the importance and value of the community of all human beings. Against particular and local allegiance to the polis, city-state, or modern nation-state, the cosmopolitan would emphasize a general and far-reaching concern for humanity.

It remains unclear whether Diogenes' own view was meant to affirm a positive duty to humanity or only to deny the conventional obligations of citizenship associated with the polis. But the Greek Stoics, such as Zeno of Citium and Chrysippus in the third century BCE, developed the tradition by identifying the law of the cosmos with divine reason and extending world citizenship to everyone who lives in accordance with it. Roman Stoicism—especially as developed by Cicero, Seneca, Epictetus, and Marcus Aurelius—strongly influences modern cosmopolitanism by counting the possession of reason as a sufficient condition of membership in this foremost ethical community. Marcus Aurelius developed the idea of natural law as the common law of the polis of which all human beings are fellow citizens (*Meditations*, bk. 4). Nonetheless, the Roman Stoics readily acknowledged duties to one's country along with duties to humanity as a whole.

With advances of natural-law theory in the seventeenth century, international law, or the law of nations, got its first explicit modern statement in the theories of Hugo Grotius and Samuel Von Pufendorf. In the eighteenth century, Immanuel Kant, partly inspired by Stoicism, viewed all persons as members of a single community of rational agents, each of whom is free, equal, and independent. On these grounds he strongly criticized European colonialism and imperialism. In *Perpetual Peace* (1795), Kant argued for a federation of republics, each recognizing the human rights of all persons. (See Heater 1996 for a history of cosmopolitan thought.)

Cosmopolitanisms, as sets of moral, political, and cultural views, have developed significantly in the late twentieth century. Below are some of the most important arguments and distinctions made in recent debates, with particular emphasis on the core moral claims.

MORAL COSMOPOLITANISM

Moral cosmopolitanism is characterized by three basic commitments. First, it is a species of moral individualism, maintaining that the basic units of moral concern are human individuals rather than groups or other collectivities. Second, it is egalitarian, holding that each individual counts equally from a moral perspective, that is, that no person is worth more than any other and that every person is entitled to equal consideration. Finally, cosmopolitans are moral universalists, who believe that the proper scope of moral concern encompasses all persons, regardless of their ethnic, racial, cultural, religious, and national affiliations. In short, moral cosmopolitanism affirms the equal worth of every human individual, quite apart from any subgroup to which they might belong, along with a commitment to impartial concern.

The great interest in these ideas is for their possible implications for an account of the basic moral and political obligations of persons. A dominant puzzle is the apparent contradiction between (1) widely recognized special obligations and associative duties, for example, ties to one's family members, friends, fellow citizens, and compatriots, and (2) general duties to individual human beings, regardless of membership in any of these communities. How are special duties compatible with the requirement of equal concern?

To address this question, it will be useful to flag two truths about cosmopolitanism. First, it can be defended by a deeper moral theory, including utilitarianism, a theory of human rights, contractarianism, and a Kantian account of fundamental obligations explained ultimately by the categorical imperative. Such defenses are exemplified by some of the most notable recent thinkers in this tradition: the utilitarian Peter Singer, the human-rights theorists Henry Shue and Thomas Pogge, the contractarian Brian Barry, and the Kantian Onora O'Neill. Charles Beitz is less easily classified: His moral cosmopolitanism at times has drawn on contractarian thought and lately has issued in a sustained focus on human rights as the appropriate language of international justice.

The second truth about cosmopolitanism is that it can come in strong and moderate varieties, both sharing a commitment to helping other human beings regardless of citizenship, nationality, ethnicity, race, religious affiliation, and geographical location (Scheffler 2001). Strong moral cosmopolitans believe that universalist, egalitarian individualism entails that the basic moral claims of all human beings are the same, and that any special regard for some persons over others must be justified by the role such regard plays in promoting the good of the human community as a whole. As the prominent cosmopolitan Martha Nussbaum has said, the reason a cosmopolitan should show additional concern for the locals or fellow nationals "is not that the local is better per se, but rather that this is the only sensible way to do good" (1996, pp. 135–136). Moderate moral cosmopolitans, on the other hand, believe both that there are basic obligations toward all other human beings that each of us must recognize, and that particular affiliations—to family, nation, state, and so on—give rise to special duties justified independently of any instrumental value for promoting the good of humanity. On this view, associated duties do not derive from our universal duties to human beings in general.

David Miller's defense of nationality (1995, 2002) is a good example of a view strongly opposed to the idea that we have the same duties to each person in the world. For Miller, a nation is a community of belief, extended in history, active in character, tied to a particular homeland, and associated with a distinctive public culture. Compatriots share a common national identity and possess special reasons for recognizing duties to one another beyond those to persons generally. For one thing, nation-states involve institutionalized reciprocity, in which members contribute their efforts and wealth to the community for the benefit of fellow members. For another thing, nation-states pursue collective cultural projects involving distinctive choices about work, religion, and culture more generally, and these projects give rise to nationally different mixtures of burdens and benefits. The upshot of these two points is that fellow nationals owe to one another a range of duties that they do not owe to nonmembers, but these duties are compatible with the view that each person is due equal concern in virtue of their being human.

This dispute about the nature of cosmopolitan morality becomes especially acute in matters concerning just distribution. Here a range of views seem to deny the force or extent of cosmopolitan justice. Theorists such as Michael Walzer (1983) claim that these duties of distributive justice make sense only within the context of a community, such as a nation, within which the goods to be distributed are produced and shared. David Miller (1998) has defended the related view that some principles of distributive justice are comparative and some are noncomparative, and the comparative principles can apply only within communities and not globally. John Rawls (1999) has argued that the scope of distributive justice should be limited to the basic structure of a particular society conceived of as a self-contained cooperative venture for mutual advantage. On his view, justice beyond the nation-state is concerned with interstate rules aimed at promoting toleration and peace worldwide, but questions about the distributive entitlements of particular individuals considered as such can gain no footing.

Such views seem to go beyond merely rejecting strong moral cosmopolitanism; they offer positive views that seem to minimize the substance of global duties of distributive justice. But it is precisely on the basic justice-related claims of individuals that something like strong cosmopolitanism appears most plausible. If one believes that all human beings possess the same rights to be free from torture, persecution, hunger, and homelessness, it seems natural to infer that our duties as human beings include aiming to bring about a world in which these rights are protected and promoted to the same extent for each and every person in the world. No amount of reciprocity between fellow nationals in one country can generate special duties to each other when there are countless foreign nationals suffering from deprivations of their basic interests. Moral cosmopolitanism and the idea of justice itself seem to share a fundamental commitment to impartial concern for all persons affected by an institutional framework. In a worldwide network of social, political, and economic institutions, distributive justice demands that each human being on the planet be entitled to concern from a perspective that includes their interests on a par with everyone else's. Special treatment for insiders is legitimate only if it can be justified to those excluded from it (Barry 1998, p. 145).

These sorts of considerations have led cosmopolitans to argue for strong obligations to alleviate the continuing dire suffering and death of millions of our fellow human beings. Peter Singer (1972) has defended the utilitarian view that we are morally required to stop such suffering where we can do so without sacrificing anything of comparable moral importance. The argument emphasizes the moral irrelevance of distance. A dying child on another continent obligates us just as much as a dying child next door. This cosmopolitan aspect of the case has been more readily accepted than the specifically utilitarian aspect of maximizing benefits, the demand for which has seemed difficult to square with commonsense views about the limits of moral obligation.

One influential line of argument proposed by Brian Barry (1973), Thomas Pogge (1989), and Charles Beitz (1999) has suggested that a consistent application of John Rawls's justly famous original-position argument for principles of distributive justice would lead in the direction of strong moral cosmopolitanism. If the Rawlsian veil of ignorance rules out knowledge of facts about oneself that unfairly skew one's choice of principles, then—along with sex, race, class, and conception of the good—citizenship too ought to be obscured from the contractors' considerations. If principles of distributive justice should not privilege or disadvantage people on the basis of characteristics they possess for which they are not responsible, then their citizenship should not affect their life prospects. If Rawls is correct that inequalities should be allowed only when they maximally benefit the worst-off group, the scope of principles of justice should encompass the least advantaged in the world.

POLITICAL COSMOPOLITANISM

There is a long tradition of favoring political institutions beyond the local or national—a view often allied with the need to promote global peace. While the positions of moral and political cosmopolitanism are distinct, political and legal proposals tend nonetheless to be linked to underlying moral views that emphasize the universal scope of concern for the interests of persons. Options for political cosmopolitanism take various forms, each an instance of the general institutional view that authority should be shifted from individual states to supranational political institutions (Beitz 1994, p. 124).

One option would be a single state encompassing the whole world. Immanuel Kant's rejection of a world state has been followed by later theorists, including John Rawls, who concurs with Kant's judgment that such a state would be either a global despotism or the backdrop for unending civil wars. But if duties to other persons have global scope, it seems reasonable to think that global institutions of some sort will be necessary to make sure that those duties are fairly distributed and that they achieve the goal of protecting human beings from avoidable harm.

Another approach is David Held's model of "cosmopolitan democracy" (2004), which envisages not a single world government but a range of reforms of international political and economic institutions in the name of democratic accountability, consent, and inclusiveness. Held's approach is distinctive in its appeal to democracy as the core value of global political legitimacy, but this is questioned by those who rank justice, rather than democracy, as the highest-ranking value underpinning any assessment of global political institutions.

CULTURAL COSMOPOLITANISM

Cultural cosmopolitanism is a view about the conditions under which individuals can generate an identity and live a good life. It emphasizes that cultures are constantly changing and that individuals can benefit from mixing elements from different cultural traditions. Strong cultural cosmopolitans believe that individuals can live well only by drawing on a range of cultural traditions and practices, while moderate cultural cosmopolitans hold that a range of good lives can be grounded in both this sort of openness to cultural variation and a more traditional, inward-looking existence with its settled cultural commitments (Scheffler 2001, Waldron 1992).

While the strong position is more contentious, both views deny that lives can be good only when lived within the confines of a particular cultural or national tradition. Consequently, this form of cosmopolitanism is relevant to evaluating cultural nationalism and its attendant claim to political self-determination (Caney 2005)

CONCLUSION

The recent flourishing of cosmopolitan thought signals a recognition that any plausible account of politics, morality, distributive justice, and the good life for human beings should take seriously the idea that humanity is a community whose claims on us are both fundamental and far-reaching. A significant project for the future is developing a comprehensive account of the basis and implications of cosmopolitan political morality.

See also Chrysippus; Cicero, Marcus Tullius; Diogenes of Sinope; Epictetus; Grotius, Hugo; Kant, Immanuel; Marcus Aurelius Antoninus; Multiculturalism; Nussbaum, Martha; Postcolonialism; Pufendorf, Samuel von; Rawls, John; Republicanism; Seneca, Lucius Annaeus; Stoicism; Zeno of Citium.

Bibliography

Barry, Brian. "International Society from a Cosmopolitan Perspective." In *International Society: Diverse Ethical Perspectives*, edited by David Mapel and Terry Nardin, 144–163. Princeton, NJ: Princeton University Press, 1998.

Barry, Brian. *The Liberal Theory of Justice*. Oxford: Clarendon Press, 1973.

Beitz, Charles. "Cosmopolitan Liberalism and the States System." In *Political Restructuring in Europe: Ethical Perspectives*, edited by Chris Brown, 123–136. London: Routledge, 1994.

Beitz, Charles. *Political Theory and International Relations*. 2nd ed. Princeton, NJ: Princeton University Press, 1999.

Caney, Simon. *Justice beyond Borders: A Global Political Theory*. Oxford, U.K.: Oxford University Press, 2005.

Heater, Derek. *World Citizenship and Government: Cosmopolitan Ideas in the History of Western Political Thought*. Basingstoke, U.K.: Macmillan, 1996.

Held, David. *Global Covenant*. Cambridge, U.K.: Polity, 2004.

Miller, David. "Cosmopolitanism: A Critique." *Critical Review of International Social and Political Philosophy* 5 (2002): 80–85.

Miller, David. "The Limits of Cosmopolitan Justice." In *International Society: Diverse Ethical Perspectives*, edited by David Mapel and Terry Nardin, 164–181. Princeton, NJ: Princeton University Press, 1998.

Miller, David. *On Nationality*. Oxford, U.K.: Clarendon Press, 1995.

Nussbaum, Martha. "Patriotism and Cosmopolitanism" and "Reply." In *For Love of Country*, edited by Joshua Cohen, 3–17, 131–144. Boston: Beacon Press, 1996.

O'Neill, Onora. *Bounds of Justice*. Cambridge, U.K.: Cambridge University Press, 2000.

Pogge, Thomas. *Realizing Rawls*. Ithaca, NY and London: Cornell University Press, 1989.

Pogge, Thomas. *World Poverty and Human Rights: Cosmopolitan Responsibilities and Reforms*. Cambridge, U.K.: Polity, 2002.

Rawls, John. *The Law of Peoples*. Cambridge, MA: Harvard University Press, 1999.

Scheffler, Samuel. "Conceptions of Cosmopolitanism." In his *Boundaries and Allegiances*, 111–130. Oxford, U.K.: Oxford University Press, 2001.

Shue, Henry. *Basic Rights: Subsistence, Affluence, and U.S. Foreign Policy*. 2nd ed. Princeton, NJ: Princeton University Press, 1996.

Singer, Peter. "Famine, Affluence, and Morality." *Philosophy and Public Affairs* 1 (1972): 229–243.

Waldron, Jeremy. "Minority Cultures and the Cosmopolitan Alternative." *University of Michigan Journal of Law Reform* 25 (1992): 751–792.

Walzer, Michael. *Spheres of Justice*. Oxford, U.K.: Basil Blackwell, 1983.

Charles Jones (2005)

COSMOS

From Anaximander on, early Greek philosophers regarded the structure and regular processes of the world as central to their accounts of nature. However, their understanding of this order differed considerably. These processes might be viewed as harmony or balance and as the result of growth or conflict or an intelligence, or they might be considered the result of random collisions of particles. The order might involve cycles or it might be a single continuous development from a primal state. In some philosophers, order itself exemplifies the goodness of the world. Many of these elements can be found in nonphilosophical cosmologies as well, such as the emergence of the world from waters in the Babylonian *Enuma Elish*, or the Genesis creation story. What distinguishes Greek philosophers is the variety of their attempts to describe the world as ordered, their reflection on what such an account must consist in, their consideration of the role of divinity in their accounts, and the depth of their attempts to provide rich, unified, explanatory accounts of the world. Scholars do not know who first used the word "kosmos" to describe arrangements of the world or parts of it, but it came to be a common word in denoting this central concept.

Kosmos normally means "fine or beautiful arrangement or order" and can refer to an array of warriors, a hairdo, or a government; by extension, it can apply to cosmetic accessories or even to each of the ten officials in a Cretan senate (that is, the components of an arrangement). In Aristotle's *Poetics*, it is a technical term for the spectacle of a play and also for ornamental diction. Early philosophers used the word to describe an order or arrangement in the world, but later "the kosmos" could refer to the world itself or at least to the most organized part of it, the heaven: "The kosmos is a system consisting of heaven and earth and the natures enclosed in these" (ps. Aristotle, *De mundo* 2).

The oldest extant, philosophical use of the word, to describe the balance of changes, occurs in Heraclitus (fr. 30), although a late doxographer, Aetius, says that Pythagoras was the first to name the enclosure of all things "kosmos." Even if Aetius is right (the claim is rejected by most modern scholars), it is indeterminate whether in each case the philosopher meant to speak of all changing elements, or even all things, as an order (the general use) or instead of the arrangement of all things, the world (the privileged use). The latter seems unlikely in early authors, but becomes probable when Empedocles (fr. 134) speaks of intellect darting through the kosmos, and almost certain in Democritus, Diogenes of Apollonia, and Philolaus at the end of the fifth century. Hence, Xenophon could say around 385 BCE that Socrates did not discuss the nature of "the kosmos as the wise call it." Similarly, Plato could have Socrates say that the wise call "kosmos" the whole of heaven, earth, gods, and man, as sharing community and friendship (*Gorgias* 507E–8A). A fundamental presupposition of the privileged use of "kosmos" is that the world is orderly and well arranged.

There is, however, a fundamental ambiguity even in the privileged use of "kosmos," which also reflects philosophical debates about the nature of the world. In the fourth century BCE, "the kosmos" can be used to refer to the entire world or just the system of stars, planets, sun, and moon. For Plato and Aristotle, the sublunary world is unorderly in comparison with the heaven and one task of the philosopher is to find the order it. The heaven is a better kosmos. But, depending on the interests of the text, the kosmos in some discussions might signify the entire world. Thus Aristotle can also speak of "the kosmos encompassing the earth," the region between the earth and the heaven (*Meteor.* A 2–8).

For Aristotle, as for most scientists until the sixteenth century, the world was spherical, consisting of three concentric layers, an outermost spherical shell for the fixed stars, then, contained within it, a spherical shell with the planets, sun, and moon and the apparatus by which they move (for Aristotle, an elaborate system of concentric spheres), and the sublunary sphere which has the earth as its center. Hence he distinguishes three senses of heaven (*De caelo* 9, 278b9–21), the limit of the periphery of the heaven or the spherical shell of the fixed stars (the first heaven), the spherical shell for the planets, sun, and moon are (the lower heavens), the sphere contained by the first heaven or the universe (all three layers). To these one may add the obvious first and lower heavens. It is plausible that in its privileged use, "the kosmos" could refer to any of these.

However, the universe need not be a kosmos, as is clear from ancient discussions of those philosophers who believed in many worlds, Democritus, Diogenes of Apollonia, and Epicurus. The many different systems of stars and earth are all "kosmoi," but neither the disordered universe composed out of all of them nor what lies in between them is itself a kosmos. So too, for the Stoics, the universe is not a kosmos since the universe includes not just the finite world sphere, but also an infinite void outside. Only what they call "the whole," the finite sphere encompassing the heaven and earth, is a kosmos (though within this "whole" there are three different arrangements they describe as a "kosmos": god or the divine moving principle; the ordering produced by this god; and the unity of the two).

In Greek mathematical astronomy, the kosmos is just a mathematical object, so that the connotations of orderliness are irrelevant. The primary goal of Greek astronomers from Eudoxus (fourth century BCE) on include mapping the heavens, determining the sizes and distances of all the bodies of the world, and constructing geometrical models that explain the apparent motions and phases of the heavenly bodies. With few exceptions, such as heliocentric theories (Aristarchus, c. 270 BCE), the kosmos will be a rotating sphere with the earth as center and whose poles determine the daily rotation of the stars.

See also Anaximander; Aristotle; Cosmology; Diogenes of Apollonia; Empedocles; Epicurus; Heraclitus of Ephesus; Leucippus and Democritus; Philolaus of Croton; Plato; Pre-Socratic Philosophy; Pythagoras and Pythagoreanism; Socrates; Stoicism; Xenophon.

Bibliography

Finkelberg, Aryeh, "On the History of the Greek Kosmos," *Harvard Studies in Classical Philology* 98 (1998): 103–136.

Kahn, Charles H. *Anaximander and the Origins of Greek Cosmology*. New York: Columbia University Press, 1960.

Kahn, Charles H. *The Art and Thought of Heraclitus*. Cambridge, U.K.: Cambridge University Press, 1979.

Kerschensteiner, Jula. *Kosmos; quellenkritische Untersuchungen zu den Vorsokratikern*. Munich: Beck, 1962.

Henry Mendell (2005)

COSTA, URIEL DA
(1585–1640)

Uriel da Costa, or Gabriel Acosta, an opponent of traditional religion, was born in Portugal to a New Christian family, that is, one forced to convert to Catholicism from Judaism. After completing studies at Coimbra, he held a minor church office. According to his autobiography, biblical studies led him back to Judaism, which he then expounded to his family as he deduced it from the Bible. The family fled to Amsterdam to escape the Inquisition and to practice their religion freely. Da Costa soon found that his biblical Judaism was in conflict with actual practices, which he claimed were too rigid and ritualistic. He attacked "the Pharisees of Amsterdam" and wrote a book arguing that the doctrine of the immortality of the soul was doubtful and unbiblical. The next year da Costa completed his *Examen dos tradiçoens Phariseas conferidas con a ley escrita* (Examination of the Traditions of the Pharisees Compared with the Written Law; 1624), a work considered so dangerous that the author was excommunicated by the Jews and arrested by the Dutch authorities as a public enemy of religion. He was fined, and the book was publicly burned. (Its contents can be reconstructed from a reply by Samuel da Silva.) In 1633 he sought readmission to the Jewish community. Though he had not changed his views, he needed the communal life, and so, he said, he would "become an ape among apes," and submit to the synagogue. However, he soon found himself doubting whether the Mosaic law was really God's law, and asking whether all religions were not human creations. He transgressed all sorts of Jewish regulations and observances, and finally was condemned for discouraging two Christians from becoming Jews. He was again excommunicated. In 1640 he submitted once more and underwent the most severe penance, first recanting before the whole synagogue, then receiving thirty-nine lashes, and finally lying prostrate while the congregation walked over him. He then went home, wrote his autobiography (*Exemplar Humanae Vitae*), and shot himself.

Da Costa's tragic career has made him a symbol of the dangers of religious intolerance, as well as a precursor of modern naturalism and higher criticism. One romantic painting shows him as a kindly scholar, holding young Benedict de Spinoza on his knee, teaching him.

Almost all our information about da Costa comes from his autobiography, published in 1687 from a Latin manuscript. It is not known if it is the original text or an altered version. Very little other data have turned up concerning his actual relations with Amsterdam Jewry or Spinoza. I. S. Révah's 1962 study, based on Portuguese Inquisition records, indicates that da Costa's initial conversion was not, in fact, from Catholicism to biblical Judaism, but rather to a peculiar Iberian form of crypto-Judaism. Then, Révah suggests, in Amsterdam da Costa developed first a biblical Judaism, and later a variety of deism or natural religion.

Da Costa's influence, from the eighteenth century onward, has been mainly on religious liberals opposing traditional orthodoxies. It is his martyrdom, rather than his doctrines (which we hardly know), that has affected people. Considering the many intellectuals gruesomely killed by Protestants and Catholics, it is odd that da Costa has stood out as *the* example of a freethinker destroyed by religious bigotry. Possibly Enlightenment and romantic thinkers could better accept a hero victimized by Judaism than one victimized by their own previous Christian traditions.

Bibliography

WORKS BY DA COSTA

Die Schriften des Uriel da Costa. With introduction, translation, and index, edited by Carl Gebhardt. Amsterdam: Hertzberger, 1922. Bibliotheca Spinozana Tomus II.

Une vie humaine. Translated, with a study of the author, by A.-B. Duff and Pierre Kann. Paris, 1926.

Examination of Pharisaic Traditions. Translated by H. Salomon and I. Sassoon. Leiden: Brill, 1993.

WORKS ON DA COSTA

"Acosta, Uriel." In *Jewish Encyclopedia,* Vol. I, 167–168.

Bayle, Pierre. "Acosta." In *Dictionnaire philosophique et critique.* Rotterdam, 1695–1697.

Israel, J., and D. Katz, eds. *Sceptics, Millenarians and Jews.* Leiden: Brill, 1990.

Popkin, R. "The Jewish Community of Amsterdam." In *History of Jewish Philosophy,* edited by D. Frank and O. Leaman, 600–611. London: Routledge, 1997.

Révah, I. S. "La Religion d'Uriel da Costa." *Revue de l'histoire des religions* 161 (1962): 45–76.

Révah, I. S. *Uriel da Costa et Les Marranes de Porto.* Paris: Centre Culturel Calouste Gulbenkian, 2004.

Salomon, H. "A Copy of Uriel da Costa's *Examen des tradicoes phariseas* Located in the Royal Library of Copenhagen." *Studia Rosenthaliana* 24 (1990): 153–168.

Richard H. Popkin (1967)
Bibliography updated by Oliver Leaman (2005)

COUNTERFACTUALS

See Appendix, Vol. 10

COUNTERFACTUALS IN SCIENCE

The term *counterfactual* is short for "counter-to-fact conditional," a statement about what would have been true, had certain facts been different—for example, "Had the specimen been heated, it would have melted." On the face of it, claims about what would or could have happened appear speculative or even scientifically suspect because science is an investigation of reality grounded in experimental evidence, and by definition people have experimental access only to the actual universe. Yet, despite their implicit reference to alternative possibilities, many counterfactuals are scientifically respectable because the criteria determining whether they are true depend wholly on facts about the actual universe. Counterfactuals are often important in science because they appear implicitly in the definitions of certain specific concepts such as "solubility" and "biological fitness," and because they are closely related to general scientific notions such as "law of nature" and "causation."

The exact definition of *counterfactual* is controversial. In philosophy, a counterfactual is a statement that can be paraphrased in the form, "If *A* were true, then *C* would be true." They are distinguished from indicative conditionals, which take the form, "If *A* is true, then *C* is true." The difference in meaning consists roughly in the kind of facts one keeps fixed when considering the hypothetical situation *A*. To evaluate "If Napoleon Bonaparte had been born in Spain, France would have been ruled by democrats," one imagines Napoleon for some reason being born in Spain instead of Corsica and then speculates about alternative histories for France, ignoring what is known about the specifics of Napoleon's actual reign of power. But when evaluating the indicative, "If Napoleon was born in Spain, France was ruled by democrats," one can imagine that somehow historians have made a mistake on this one issue of Napoleon's birth and retain other things known about Napoleon, such as his undemocratic rule of France.

Despite the clear difference in meaning between these two particular sentences, there is significant controversy about whether the distinction between indicatives and counterfactuals makes sense in general and whether it is the best way to categorize conditionals. Associated with such debates are subtleties regarding how truth applies to counterfactuals. For example, the name "counterfactual" is misleading in that one can use counterfactuals for situations that are known to be true. Believing "If the fish had mutated, it would have survived," is consistent with believing the fish did mutate. So, counterfactuals are not only about counter-to-fact possibilities, but sometimes about actual situations as well.

RELATION TO LAWS

What makes counterfactuals especially suitable for science is that the truth of counterfactuals depends largely on the general patterns that science aims to describe. One can reasonably say that a particular sample of salt is soluble in water even when the salt has never been dissolved and never will, on the grounds that because of its chemical structure, had it been placed in a sufficient amount of pure water, it would have dissolved. One is justified in making claims about what the salt counterfactually would have done in virtue of what other similar samples of salt have actually done and that person's knowledge of nature's regularities. In this way, the laws of nature can be understood as governing not only actual happenings but also what may have happened.

In one early philosophical treatment, Nelson Goodman tried to explain counterfactuals as a kind of elliptical expression. He thought counterfactuals such as, "Had I struck this match, it would have lit," should be understood as, "I struck this match and the laws of nature are true and … logically entails that the match lit," where the ellipses represent some unstated but true facts. In a typical situation one may complete the sentence as, "I struck this match, and the laws of nature are true, and the match was dry, and there was sufficient oxygen in the air, and the match had the proper chemicals in the tip, entails that the match lit." The value of Goodman's account is that it captures the idea that counterfactuals in science express consequences of actual or hypothetical facts following from the laws of nature.

A major problem with this account, as Goodman himself recognized, is that it fails to give any constructive advice about how to pick out the right facts to insert into the ellipses. Why should one insert the fact that the match was dry and infer that the match would have lit, rather than insert that the match did not light and infer that the match would have been wet? Because there is no principled way of answering this question, Goodman's theory is of limited value as a guide to determining the truth of counterfactual statements. Also, because many counterfactuals have nothing to do with laws ("If the circumference were only half as large, the radius would be …") and some require the actual laws to be abandoned ("If there were no friction …"), the elliptical account is not a general account of counterfactuals, and it was not immediately obvious how it would fit into a larger account.

SIMILARITY APPROACHES

The dominant approach to elucidating the meaning of counterfactuals is to think of them as having truth conditions given by similarity relations among possible worlds—that is, hypothetical universes—and more controversially that some more or less tractable notion of similarity tells how to evaluate specific counterfactuals. The justification for this is primarily formal. Robert Stalnaker and David Lewis developed a compelling family of logic systems describing counterfactual conditionals that do a remarkable job of justifying a wide range of intuitively plausible reasoning patterns. It is a feature of the logic that it can be interpreted using a notion of similarity among possible worlds. The way it works roughly is that the counterfactual "If *A* were the case, then *C* would be the case," is true when the worlds most similar to actuality among those where *A* is true are also worlds where *C* is true. Consider, "If this bird had three legs, it would have more legs than wings." The worlds where *A* is true are all the worlds where the bird has three legs, including worlds where it has three legs and three wings, worlds where it has three legs and four wings, and worlds where it has three legs, two wings, transparent feathers and a metallic beak. Intuitively, the minimal departure from actuality is for it to have one extra leg without any change to its wings, and so using common sense, one would say this counterfactual is true.

This illustration of how to determine whether a counterfactual is true involves an appeal to one's offhand, pretheoretical judgements of similarity, an appeal not mandated by the role similarity plays in the formal logic. It is a significant speculative leap to suppose that which counterfactuals are true depends on what human beings find similar. Nevertheless, inspired by David Lewis's work, there has been a serious philosophical research program dedicated to finding a plausible refinement of people's ordinary similarity concept to justify the usage of counterfactuals and more important to use counterfactuals in elucidating other concepts, such as causation.

CAUSATION

A large part of science is figuring out what causes what. The role of counterfactuals in this project is to express dependencies among logically independent elements of reality, dependencies that are often causal. In the vast literature on causation, counterfactuals appear in different roles, not all of them central. One tradition concerning causation is to take causal connections between facts or events to be primitive elements of reality holding together the pattern of various particular facts. In this tradition, counterfactuals are not crucial to the formulation or definition of causation, although they are useful for expressing consequences of causal relations.

Where counterfactuals become most important are in theories where causes are understood as the byproduct of physical processes that are themselves not fundamentally causal in nature. This tradition is compelling because fundamental physics uses equations establishing mathematical relationships between physical entities in a way that does not obviously indicate what causes what. Here a theory about counterfactual relationships between events can be constructed as part of a story that tells how the mathematical relations in physics could possibly account for truths such as "Lightning causes thunder."

Some theories of causation are literally counterfactual accounts of causation. They argue that the causal connection is really due to a counterfactual dependence relation. An event *E* counterfactually depends on the event *C* whenever if *C* had not happened, *E* would not have happened. In one famous version of the theory—by David Lewis—causation is identified with having a chain of events that are counterfactually dependent on one another, but other variations on the connection between causation and counterfactual dependence are possible. While counterfactual accounts need to successfully explain many aspects of causation, for them to be even superficially plausible, they need to explain the causal asymmetry—why in ordinary circumstances causes precede their effects. In counterfactual accounts, the difficult part of that explanation is to say why in an ordinary case of causation such as lightning causing thunder, one does not also have the lightning counterfactually depending on the thunder, wrongly entailing that thunder causes lightning.

Explaining why thunder does not cause lightning is difficult if one followsthe orthodoxy of using anthropocentric ideas of similarity as a guide to counterfactual truth. It is plausible that lightning counterfactually does depend on thunder because a possible world with a bolt of perfectly silent lightning is intuitively stranger than a world with just one less bolt of lightning. This shortcoming for the counterfactual account of causation may be corrected by giving up on using naive judgements of similarity and instead concocting a suitable theory of similarity that fits the needs of causation. David Lewis's theory in "Counterfactual Dependence and Time's Arrow" (1979) has been a popular model for developing such an account. In following this strategy, the attempt is to defend the more general hypothesis that counterfactuals ordinarily exhibit a temporal asymmetry that in turn explains the difference between cause and effect.

COUNTERFACTUAL ASYMMETRY

When one considers how things may have been had only *X* not happened, typically one envisions alternate histories with an identical past where for some reason *X* did not happen. one then speculates how these alternate histories may have played out, leaving the future as open as the laws and circumstances allow. The practice of evaluating counterfactuals this way is asymmetric, treating the future but not the past as counterfactually dependent on the present.

Because there are counterfactuals having nothing to do with time, such as "If the variable x had been equal to three, then $x+1$ would have been equal to four," it is known that time asymmetry is not a part of the logic or meaning of counterfactuals per se. In a sense, it is wholly up to a person to choose whether he or she evaluate a given counterfactual symmetrically or asymmetrically. Nevertheless, it is an objective fact that nature tends to reward people for using the asymmetric ones. For example, it is sometimes useful to think, "If I were to shield myself now, I would avoid the next volley of arrows," and not so useful to think, "If I were to shield myself now, I would have avoided the previous volley." In this sense, counterfactual asymmetry is a natural fact perhaps amenable to scientific explanation. The project is to determine which physical structures vindicate the practice of evaluating counterfactuals asymmetrically. This includes determining to what extent the asymmetry is an aspect of people's particular perspective on nature, and to what extent the asymmetry is a feature of broader physical conditions and laws.

One idea is that there are fundamentally random processes that make the future chancy in a way that the past is not. This is problematic because although chances seem to imply a sense of openness for the future, it is not clear how chances imply a fixed past. Perhaps the intuition about chance in this case presupposes a theory where the past is given special fundamental significance as being in some sense more real than the future, or real in a different way. Spelling out such a deep metaphysical difference between past and future has proven difficult in itself, and clarification of its connection to chances has been problematic because the application of chances in science does not seem to require any such distinction.

Another group of proposed candidates for the explanation do not take counterfactual asymmetry to be a fundamental fact about reality or time itself, but as a contingent feature of the particular environment. A suggestion by Lewis is that typical processes exhibit a pattern where future facts "overdetermine" past facts in the sense that they give redundant evidence of the past. For example, after an explosion, there are many fragments around, each of which individually suggests an explosion, but there are often only a few facts beforehand that imply an explosion will occur—for example, a burning fuse.

Another idea is that counterfactual asymmetry is explained by cosmological facts, such as the universe is expanding from a smooth distribution of matter just after the big bang. This idea draws some plausibility from nature's two classes of time asymmetries. The first kind is a local asymmetry—a fact that applies directly to the physical process taking place. Examples of this first kind include chancy transitions in the physical state, and time-asymmetric evolutions such as one sees in certain high energy particle experiments involving weak decays. The second kind is an asymmetry in the boundary conditions. Irreversible phenomena such as mixing gasses or a hot and cool object settling to a single temperature are explained only when one posits special boundary conditions. Specifically, the explanation for why people regularly see thermodynamic asymmetries comes by way of the physics of the distant past being constrained in a way that the future is not. The connection to counterfactuals is that one's reason for thinking that causation is asymmetric comes from one's experience with asymmetric macroscopic phenomena, exactly the kind of phenomena whose asymmetries are explained by boundary conditions and not by local asymmetries. Hence, it is plausible to think that special facts about the beginning of the universe are a critical component of why counterfactuals and causation treat the past as more fixed—that is, why nature rewards people for evaluating counterfactuals in a way that treats the past as fixed.

These strategies that attempt to explain counterfactual asymmetry by way of contingent physical circumstances are interesting in that they allow for at least some counterfactual dependence of the past on the future. This seems reasonable because one wants to allow for counterfactual differences that arise from ordinary processes. If the population were greater right now than it actually is, this would have been because people would have had more children, not because people would have magically popped into existence. While having some counterfactual dependence of the past on the present is good for matching up the theory of counterfactual evaluation with pretheoretical intuitions about counterfactuals, it highlights a difficulty with the desired uses of counterfactual asymmetry. If the past counterfactually depends on the present, and the difference between cause and effect is purely given by the counterfactual asymmetry, then one would seem to have backwards causation, such as thunder causing lightning. So either counterfactual asymmetry can't do the job of grounding the cause-effect asymmetry or causation is a less robust notion than is ordinarily thought, defined with respect to a temporal asymmetry that at best is justified only in certain special cases—for example, human decisions—where there is little or no significant backwards dependence.

See also Causation: Philosophy of Science; Conditionals; Counterfactuals; Philosophy of Statistical Mechanics.

Bibliography

Goodman, Nelson. "The Problem of Counterfactual Conditionals." *The Journal of Philosophy* 44 (1947): 113–128.

Lewis, David. "Causation," *The Journal of Philosophy* 70 (1973): 556–567.

Lewis, David. "Counterfactual Dependence and Time's Arrow." *Noûs* 13 (1979): 455–476.

Lewis, David. *Counterfactuals.* Oxford: Blackwell, 1973.

Stalnaker, Robert. "A Theory of Conditionals." In *Studies in Logical Theory: American Philosophical Quarterly Monograph Series*, no. 2, edited by Nicholas Rescher. Oxford: Basil Blackwell, 1968.

Douglas Kutach (2005)

COUNTERPART THEORY

See *Modality, Philosophy and Metaphysics of*

COURNOT, ANTOINE AUGUSTIN

(1801–1877)

Antoine Augustin Cournot, the French mathematician, economist, philosopher, and educator was born in Gray, Haute Saône. He was educated at *collèges* at Gray (which now bears his name) and Besançon, and at the École Normale Supérieur in Paris. In addition to teaching at the universities of Lyon and Paris, he was head of the *Académie* at Grenoble and rector of the *Académie* at Dijon and succeeded André Marie Ampère as inspector general of studies. An able student of mechanics (including astronomy) and of mathematics, he applied probability theory to problems in both the physical and the social sciences. His work in economics early secured his reputation in that field, and he is now generally regarded as a founder of econometrics; as a philosopher he remains much less known.

Cournot is identified by Jean de la Harpe as a critical realist. This designation would be peculiarly appropriate were it not for the fact that this name has been taken by a group of American philosophers whose position is notably unlike that of Cournot in important respects. Since the term *critical realist* is equivocal, it may be advisable to refer to Cournot as a critical rationalist. Cournot is a realist of sorts in his metaphysics and more rationalist (albeit critically so) than empiricist or positivist in his epistemology. For him knowledge is a function of reason. The senses furnish neither the basis nor the criteria of knowledge, which not only can but does extend beyond their limits. Yet the senses do make important contributions to knowledge, especially by restraining its claims by challenging overextended speculations by confronting them with what William James aptly called "brute facts." Cournot rejects all dogmatic philosophies, whether rationalist or empiricist. Knowledge requires a continuing appraisal of all principles to determine both their grounds and the range of their legitimate applications. Specifically, he examines the established sciences to see whether they have any basic concepts in common. He discovers three such concepts—order, chance, probability. These three concepts lie at the heart of Cournot's philosophy and suffice to account for his rejection of many earlier and contemporary alternative positions. He rejects the idealistic basis and implications of Immanuel Kant's philosophy, but he accepts the critical intent of the Kantian program.

For Cournot, order is a basic category which, as "objective reason," relates to the nature of things and, as "subjective reason," to the means through which we apprehend that nature. The major function of philosophy is to examine and criticize the efforts of subjective reason to know objective reason, making sure among other things that such closely related and often confused principles as "reason" and "cause," "rational order" and "logical order," are clearly differentiated in both their meaning and their function. We have knowledge when we apprehend the objective reason of things, but such knowledge is rarely complete and certain. Therefore, our knowledge is relative and probable, not absolute and apodictic, but it nonetheless rests on objective grounds, not on forms or categories native to the mind itself.

Cournot's unusual and cogent use of probability draws attention to a fundamental moderating element in his philosophy. His treatment of probability is developed most extensively in his *Exposition* (1843) and is used ingeniously and productively in his *Essai* (1851), *Traité* (1861), and *Matérialisme, vitalisme, rationalisme.* Long before putting these views to philosophic use, Cournot had applied them to problems in astronomy and in various fields of social studies, notably in economics, where he applied them with lastingly important results.

The calculus of probabilities is related to both order and chance. Both order and probability have plural meanings. Order as a category of the objective reason of things must not be confused either with logical order—that is, with the order essential to a formal system of ideas—or with causal order, by which Cournot means essentially what Aristotle called "efficient cause." The reason for a phenomenon must be distinguished from its cause, from the conditions or circumstances which give rise to it. *Cause* is related to the particular and unique; *reason* is related to the universal and abstract aspects of phenomena that are the ground for laws of general and fundamental relations among them, relations that are necessary, but not in themselves sufficient, conditions for the production of specific phenomena. Probability is of two sorts, mathematical and philosophical. Mathematical probability applies to those relatively rare situations in which the number and relative frequency of various possibilities can be numerically determined. Philosophical probability—which may attain practical, but never demonstrable, certainty—applies to the vastly more numerous cases in which such numerical determination is not possible. It involves an appraisal of evidence in terms of rational cogency where probabilities persuade and win the acquiescence of reasonable persons even though the relevant evidence is neither quantifiably manipulatable nor conclusive. We live continuously and inescapably with such probabilities; philosophical criticism is also largely concerned with them. In either case probability is a function of objective factors and conditions and not solely of our ignorance or other subjective factors, although these do contribute to our need to deal with probabilities of both types.

Of Cournot's three basic ideas, that of chance is least adequately developed. It is unfortunate that there is no specific and clear definition of this concept in its theoretical function, yet what the concept refers to is not at all unclear. Numerous examples leave no doubt about the meaning of the term as Cournot uses it. A chance occurrence is one in which there is an unpredictable conjunction of independent series of events, each series being internally related and having a determinable nature. However complete our knowledge of each independent series, events resulting from unpredictable conjunctions among them are contingent, unpredictable, fortuitous. Such events have causes, but they are not reducible to laws. The absence of reasons for such events is irreducible, chance, like order, being an objective feature of the nature of things. This doctrine is one source of the pluralism in Cournot's philosophy. In it he anticipates Émile Boutroux and suggests certain aspects of the philosophies of C. S. Peirce (for example, his "tychism") and M. R. Cohen (whose general philosophical position is not unlike Cournot's critical rationalism).

Another pluralistic aspect of Cournot's thought is indicated in the title of his last philosophic work, *Matérialisme, vitalism, rationalisme.* Countering the principles of Darwinian evolution, Cournot holds to the principle that living beings are distinguished from nonliving things by a unity and form suggestive of finality and by a vital principle inexplicable in physical and chemical terms. Here Cournot anticipates both Henri Bergson and the emergent evolutionists, notably Samuel Alexander and C. Lloyd Morgan.

In his consideration of such concepts as form, unity, simplicity, and symmetry, Cournot moves toward a transrationalism—that is, toward a view in which ideas that go beyond normal rational analysis and use, such as finality, purpose, and God, find a place. This development is consistent with, indeed perhaps it is a consequence of, his pluralism and his implied doctrine of levels and with his rejection of any reductionist view as these are evidenced by his assertion that the phenomena of life involve something not present in nonliving phenomena. Such ideas as simplicity and symmetry are relevant to rational investigation, to the discovery of the order and reason of things, as in the probabilistic assessment and choice between otherwise equally adequate alternative hypotheses. In this sense such concepts are regulative ideas of reason. But Cournot argues that they are more than this, and in his treatment of these concepts he moves from a logic of reason toward an aesthetic of reason, in which the concept of order has a connotation more extensive than reason can explore. What effect does such a transrationalism have on the claimed objective existence of chance, the second concept so fundamental to Cournot's philosophy as a whole? None. Why this is the case is not adequately developed in Cournot's works, although a hint is found in *Exposition*: God lays out the laws or rational elements of reality and leaves to objective and inexpugnable chance the details of fortuitous occurrences. Therefore, even such a superior intelligence would, like man, be unable to foresee contingent events, although unlike man its assessment of what is contingent would not be complicated by subjective factors of the sort which inescapably limit and affect human judgment.

In developing his philosophy, Cournot deals with the nature of language, ethics, and aesthetics and with various social institutions and factors which contribute to civilization. He also discusses the nature of science, history, and philosophy and considers at some length the irreducible distinctions between them. His *Considérations* is a peculiarly interesting account of his handling of various historical matters.

See also Alexander, Samuel; Ampère, André Marie; Aristotle; Cohen, Morris Raphael; Critical Realism; Kant, Immanuel; Morgan, C. Lloyd; Peirce, Charles Sanders.

Bibliography

WORKS BY COURNOT

Mémoire sur le mouvement d'un corps rigide soutenu par un plan fixe. Paris, 1829.

Recherches sur les principes mathématiques de la théorie des richesses. Paris: Hachette, 1838. Translated into English by N. I. Bacon as *Researches into the Mathematical Principles of the Theory of Wealth.* Economic Classics series. London: Macmillan, 1897.

Traité élémentaire de la théorie des fonctions et du calcul infinitesimal. 2 vols. Paris: Hachette, 1841; 2nd ed., revised and corrected, 1857.

Exposition de la théorie des chances et des probabilités. Paris, 1843.

De l'origine et des limites de la correspondance entre l'algèbre et la géometrie. Paris, 1847.

Essai sur les fondements de nos connaissances et sur les caractères de la critique philosophique. 2 vols. Paris: Hachette, 1851; 2nd ed., 1912; 3rd ed., 1 vol., 1922. Translated into English by Merritt H. Moore as *An Essay on the Foundations of Our Knowledge.* New York: Liberal Arts Press, 1956.

Traité de l'enchaînement des idées fondamentales dans les sciences et dans l'histoire, 2 vols. Paris: Hachette, 1861; 2nd ed., 1 vol., 1911; 3rd ed., 1 vol., 1922. The 1911 and 1922 editions include a foreword by L. Lévy-Bruhl.

Principes de la théorie des richesses. Paris: Hachette, 1863.

Des institutions d'instruction publique en France. Paris: Hachette, 1864.

Considérations sur la marche des idées et des événements dans les temps modernes. 2 vols. Paris: n.p., 1872; republished with introduction by M. Mentré, 2 vols., Paris: Boivin, 1934.

Matérialisme, vitalisme, rationalisme: Études sur l'emploi des données de la science en philosophie. Paris, 1875; Paris: Hachette, 1923.

Revue sommaire des doctrines économiques. Paris: Hachette, 1877.

Souvenirs: 1760 à 1860. Paris: Hachette, 1913. Written in 1859; published with introduction and notes by E. P. Bottinelli.

WORKS ON COURNOT

Bottinelli, E. P. *A. Cournot métaphysicien de la connaissance.* Paris: Hachette, 1913.

Darbon, A. *Le concept du hasard dans la philosophie de Cournot.* Paris: Alcan, 1911.

Harpe, Jean de la. *De l'ordre et du hasard: Le Réalisme critique D'Antoine Augustin Cournot.* Memoirs of the University of Neuchâtel, Vol. IX. Neuchâtel: Secrétariat de l'Université, 1936.

Lévèque, R. *L' "élément historique" dans la connaissance humaine d'après Cournot.* Publications of the Faculty of Letters of the University of Strasbourg, No. 82. Paris: La Société d'édition Les Belles lettres, 1938.

Mentré, F. *Cournot et la renaissance du probabilisme au XIXe siècle.* Paris: Rivière, 1908.

Milhaud, G. *Études sur Cournot.* Paris: J. Vrin, 1927.

Revue de métaphysique et de morale 13 (3) (1905): 293–543. A special number dedicated to A. Cournot, with portrait. Articles by H. Poincaré, G. Milhaud, G. Tarde, C. Bouglé, A. Anpetit, F. Faure, A. Darlu, F. Vial, D. Parodi, R. Audierne, H.-L. Moore.

Ruyer, R. *L'humanité de l'avenir d'après Cournot.* Paris: F. Alcan, 1930.

Segond, J. *Cournot et la psychologie vitaliste.* Paris: Alcan, 1911.

Merritt Hadden Moore (1967)

COUSIN, VICTOR

(1792–1867)

Victor Cousin, the French philosopher and historian, was born in Paris and educated at the Lycée Charlemagne and the École Normale, where he studied under Pierre Laromiguière. He began his teaching career in 1815, assisting Pierre Paul Royer-Collard in his course on the history of philosophy at the University of Paris. Cousin studied German and read Immanuel Kant and F. H. Jacobi; but he was especially attracted to the works of Friedrich Wilhelm Joseph von Schelling, whose thought had a permanent influence upon him. A trip to Germany in 1817 brought him into personal contact with both Schelling and G. W. F. Hegel, a fact which was later responsible for the accusation that he had rejected French philosophy in favor of Germany's. In 1821 Cousin was removed from his position because of his supposed antigovernmental views, and he used his freedom to make another trip to Germany. While there he was imprisoned, on charges that have never been entirely clear, but was freed after six months. Returning to France, he spent his time writing his philosophical and historical works and editing the works of other philosophers, including Proclus (6 vols., 1820–1827) and René Descartes (1826, 11 vols.), and beginning his translation of Plato (13 vols., 1822–1840). In 1828 he was restored to his post and from then on had an influential career as lecturer. He became a spokesman for the *juste milieu,* as he called it, which in philosophy meant eclecticism. Cousin's power increased when in 1840 he became minister of public instruction, director of the École Normale, and a member of the Institut de France. He was not only the most famous French philosopher of his time but also supreme dictator of who should teach philosophy and what should be taught. He had become, moreover, a power in the whole educational system of France when he published a report on Prussian education (1833). (This report was later translated into English in 1834 and distributed to the schools of Massachusetts by an act of the legislature.) At the advent to power of Louis Napoleon in 1848 Cousin retired from active teaching and spent his time in literary studies.

ECLECTICISM

Though Cousin started his career as a pupil of Laromiguière, it was the commonsense philosophy of Thomas Reid, as interpreted by Royer-Collard, that was the source of his own doctrine. To Cousin common sense was a fusion of the best that had been done in philosophy, combining the empiricism of sensationalism in epistemology with the spiritualism of religion. The epistemology of Étienne Bonnot de Condillac and his school, Cousin felt, because it made the spirit of man a simple passive victim of external forces, had led them to atheism and materialism, both of which were to be condemned. Atheism and materialism could not give men those permanent principles that would guide their moral life. Such principles were to be found only if men realized that their minds were active as well as passive, their activity consisting in their use of their a priori categories of substance and causality.

Though it is likely that Cousin got the idea of the complementary active and passive aspects of mentality from Schelling, he himself attributed it to Maine de Biran's self-scrutiny. This gave him a French origin for doctrines which were to guide French professors. Maine de Biran's active will, Cousin maintained, was balanced by sensibility, which "implies" the existence of an external world. Sensibility and active will were accompanied by reason, and thus Cousin revived the traditional threefold analysis of the mind. Corresponding to the three faculties was a threefold division of philosophical problems into that of the good, the beautiful, and the true. In his book *Du vrai, du beau et du bien* (1853) Cousin argued that these problems were united in a whole which absorbed what was valid in sensation (John Locke), reason (Plato), and the heart (for which he named no sponsor). These three parts of the soul are not independent of one another. Reason requires both sensation and the heart, sensation requires reason and the heart, and the heart requires both reason and sensation. By analogy epistemology, ethics, and aesthetics are all intertwined and inseparable except for purposes of exposition.

POLITICAL PHILOSOPHY

The political philosophy of Cousin was expressed in *Justice et charité,* a brief tract that he wrote as one of a series published by members of the Académie des Sciences Morales et Politiques in 1848. This tract is based on the same metaphor of the interdependence of separate things. The purpose of all the tracts in this series was to substantiate the right to property, the well-being of family life, popular freedom, and progress. Cousin opposed the idea of equality, the right to work, and governmental aid. Justice is the protection of natural rights, but every right implies a complementary duty. Men are all free, but their freedom resides only in the search for truth, in religious beliefs and practices, and in property. Justice demands that these rights be respected and protected by the state. On the other hand, charity demands that we abuse none of these rights, that we individually seek the truth and not perpetuate error, that we give others the religious freedom that we demand for ourselves, that we respect others' property as we would have them respect ours. In short, law is futile if it is not obeyed, and we cannot obey a law that is not enforced. Respect for the law is like charity in that it has no limits; for charity extends to all men and to liberty in all its forms.

AESTHETICS

Cousin was a strong believer in absolute beauty. His ideal work of art was the Apollo Belvedere. Art, he believed, is neither an imitation of nature (sensationalism) nor edification (moralism), but rather a vision of "the infinite." Though all arts utilize matter, they communicate to it "a mysterious character which speaks to the imagination and to the soul, liberates them from the real, and bears them aloft either gently or violently to unknown regions." These unknown regions are the country of God, the world of the ideal. Though this passage might seem to ally Cousin with the Romantic school, in fact it led him to give highest praise to the classicists of the seventeenth century. He was clearly under the influence of J. J. Winckelmann, who also admired the Apollo Belvedere as the *summum* of all ideal beauty and believed that all praiseworthy artists put into their works of art the ideal beauty of Plotinus. Cousin saw in beauty, as did Hegel, a sensuous manifestation of the Absolute, though he expressed it in different language.

At the same time Cousin admitted that one must not exaggerate the idealism of a work of art. All works of art speak to the senses as well as to the heart. The ideal must be presented to us in sensible form and it must also be agreeable to our feelings. A work of art that is beautiful was for Cousin a concrete presentation of the unity he found in eclecticism. Consequently, art that did not realize the potentialities of the sensuous, the rational, and the sentimental would not be of as high a rank as art that did. The conclusion was that poetry was the highest of all the arts. Its power of words is such that it can stimulate images, feelings (affections), and thoughts at one and the same time. It is thus a synthesis of all human powers.

HISTORIOGRAPHY

The pioneering editorial work of Cousin, mentioned above, made accessible to the public manuscripts that had been previously hidden in libraries. His eclecticism served him well in this field, for with the exception of the sensationalists of the eighteenth century, there were few philosophers of the past in whom he could not find some truth.

Cousin's *Philosophie sensualiste au XVIIIe siècle* (1819), a course of lectures, is the most biased of his historical studies, but still treats of Locke, Condillac, Claude-Adrien Helvétius, Saint-Lambert, and Thomas Hobbes in an interesting manner. His criticism of Locke, that Locke was unable by the very nature of his epistemology to account for universal and necessary ideas, Cousin's analysis of Condillac's notion that deduction is always tautological, and even Cousin's attacks on Helvétius are carefully based on the texts and are far from superficial. Fundamentally his objection to these thinkers was the pragmatic, moral, and religious consequences of their premises, an objection which obviously sprang from his own moral and religious convictions. His *Cours de l'histoire de la philosophie* (1829) was considered a work serious enough to be analyzed and commented upon by Sir William Hamilton in the *Edinburgh Review,* and, indeed, its exposition of the technique of historiography was thorough and based on a perception of genuine historical problems.

Cousin made the mistake of dividing all possible philosophies into four kinds—sensualism, idealism, skepticism, and mysticism—and thus helped to influence his successors in this area toward thinking of philosophies as always productive of systems. This division led Cousin to look for a unitary idea pervading each system, though the idea in question might be a simple metaphor or a theory of the origin of ideas which exfoliated into an ethics, aesthetics, theology, or other theoretical construct. Like Hegel, Cousin was given to envisioning philosophical systems as "expressive" of ages and peoples, as if an age or a people were homogeneous. Yet at the same time he admitted the heterogeneity of what he called populations as distinguished from peoples, the latter being unified in their beliefs and outlooks on the world's problems, the former being diversified or, as he would put it, not yet unified. Where there was diversity, there was nevertheless a predominant idea in every epoch, but alongside of it existed other ideas "playing a secondary but real role."

Each people, Cousin maintained, was given, presumably by God or by the inevitable course of history, an idea to represent, and its history was the realization of this idea. This idea expresses itself in all human concerns—in philosophy, religion, science, art, and morals. It is almost certain that Hegel was the source of this theory, though Cousin made no mention of his influence. He was willing, however, to give great credit to J. J. Brucker, Dietrich Tiedemann, and W. G. Tennemann; these last two, he believed, expressed a history of philosophy associated with Locke and Kant, respectively. As for the nineteenth century, Cousin held that it would not have its own history of philosophy until it had a representative philosophy. That philosophy would be a union of the two traditions referred to by Cousin as the nucleus of a "vast and powerful eclecticism."

It is customary to treat Cousin with patronizing disdain, and it is true that he was always ready to compromise with political power and adjust his conclusions and, indeed, his methods of research to what he believed to be expedient. He succeeded in excluding from his "regiment," as he called it, philosophers whose views were not harmonious with his own. Thus neither Auguste Comte nor J. G. F. Ravaisson-Mollien nor Charles Renouvier, to cite but three names, were able to become members of the teaching staff of the University of Paris. On the other hand, Cousin did stimulate research into the classics of philosophy, and his very chauvinism turned men's attention to such neglected figures as Maine de Biran. His eclecticism was not real, for he rejected any philosophy whose supposed religious and ethical effects he thought were undesirable. Yet his notion that every philosophy contained some truth induced his pupils to look into them all and gave them a catholicity of interest that was unusual and almost unique.

See also Absolute, The; Art, Interpretation of; Comte, Auguste; Condillac, Étienne Bonnot de; Descartes, René; Hamilton, William; Hegel, Georg Wilhelm Friedrich; Helvétius, Claude-Adrien; Hobbes, Thomas; Idealism; Jacobi, Friedrich Heinrich; Kant, Immanuel; Laromiguière, Pierre; Locke, John; Maine de Biran; Mysticism, Nature and Assessment of; Plato; Ravaisson-Mollien, Jean Gaspard Félix; Reid, Thomas; Renouvier, Charles Bernard; Royer-Collard, Pierre Paul; Schelling, Friedrich Wilhelm Joseph von; Winckelmann, Johann Joachim.

Bibliography

With the omission of his editions of classical authors and literary studies, Cousin's works include *Fragments philosophiques* (Paris: A Sautelet, 1826); *Cours de l'histoire de la philosophie,* 3 vols. (Paris: Pichon et Didier, 1829), which together with *Cours de l'histoire de la philosophie moderne,* 5 vols. (Paris: Ladrange, 1841) contains many titles also published separately; *Justice et charité* (Paris: Pagnerre, 1848); and *Du Vrai, du beau et du bien* (Paris: Didier, 1853).

For literature on Cousin, see P. F. Dubois, *Cousin, Jouffroy, Damiron, souvenirs publiés avec un introduction par Adolphe Lair* (Paris: Perrin and Cie, 1902); Paul Janet, *Victor Cousin et son oeuvre* (Paris: Calmann Lévy, 1885); and Jules Simon, *Victor Cousin* (Paris: Hachette et Sie, 1887), which has been translated under the same title by M. B. Anderson and E. P. Anderson (Chicago: A.C. McClurg, 1888). For a generally hostile approach, from a positivistic point of view, see Lucien Lévy-Bruhl, *History of Modern Philosophy in France,* translated by G. Coblence (Chicago and London: Open Court, 1924), Ch. 12; for a favorable account see John Veitch and X, "Cousin, Victor," in *Encyclopaedia Britannica,* 11th ed. (Chicago, 1910).

George Boas (1967)

COUTURAT, LOUIS

(1868–1914)

Louis Couturat, the French philosopher and logician, studied at the École Normale Supérieure and earned an *agrégé* in philosophy and a licentiate in mathematics. He taught philosophy at the universities of Toulouse and Caen but soon gave up teaching in order to devote all of his time to his own researches.

Couturat first attracted attention with his important doctoral thesis, *L'infini mathématique* (Paris, 1896). At a time when the mathematicians were still questioning the validity of Georg Cantor's theories and when the majority of French philosophers, led by Charles Renouvier, were resolute advocates of finitism, Couturat presented a vigorous case in behalf of an actual infinite. In opposition to the formalist theories of number of Julius Dedekind, Leopold Kronecker, and Hermann Helmholtz, he bases number on magnitude—not on a strictly spatial intuition but on magnitude considered as the object of a "rational intuition." This is why, of the various generalizations of number—the arithmetical, the algebraic, the geometrical—he regards the geometrical as the most rational. His reasoning consisted of offering the actual infinite as a new generalization of number, analogous to those that resulted in signed numbers, fractions, irrationals, and imaginaries. All of these numbers at first seemed to be arithmetical nonsense, but they took on meaning once they were recognized as suitable for representing new magnitudes and for allowing various operations on them that were hitherto impossible. The justification for infinite numbers is that they are indispensable for maintaining the continuity of magnitudes.

From this point on, Couturat's studies proceeded in three areas closely associated in his mind—the history of philosophy, logic and the philosophy of mathematics, and the development of a universal language.

After writing an essay (his Latin complementary thesis) on the myths of Plato, he devoted himself to Gottfried Wilhelm Leibniz, the great infinitist, whose reinterpretation he undertook independently of Bertrand Russell but at the same time and in the same sense. As indicated by the title of his book *La logique de Leibniz* (Paris, 1901), Couturat had at first intended simply to study the precursor of modern logistic. He soon perceived, however, that Leibniz's "logic was not only the heart and soul of his system, but the center of his intellectual activity, the source of all his discoveries, … the obscure or at least concealed hearth from which sprang so many *fulgurations.*" The manuscripts he discovered at

Hanover, a copious collection of which he published in *Opuscules et fragments inédits de Leibniz* (Paris, 1903), further strengthened Couturat in this conviction. Considering only Leibniz's known, celebrated works, if we wish to find the real root of his system, we must look not to the *Monadology* or the *Theodicy* but to the *Discourse on Metaphysics,* together with the *Correspondence with Arnauld,* which is, as it were, a commentary on the *Discourse.* Taking the old formula *praedicatum inest subjecto* in all its rigor, Leibniz held that every true proposition can be resolved into identities provided one pursues its analysis to the end. Contingent or factual truths differ from the necessary truths of reason only in respect to the infinite length of the analysis, an analysis which God alone is able to complete. Couturat showed, with supporting texts, that all the theses of the Leibnizian metaphysics are obtained from this position and derive their unity from it. The system thus appears as a panlogism.

It is likewise to his interest in Leibniz that we may ascribe, indirectly, Couturat's important study "La philosophie des mathématiques de Kant," published in the *Revue de métaphysique* (1904) on the centennial of Immanuel Kant's death. In *L'infini mathématique* Couturat had already criticized the Kantian antinomies that claim to establish the impossibility of an actual infinite. He now concluded that "the progress of logic and mathematics in the nineteenth century has invalidated the Kantian theory and decided the issue in favor of Leibniz" and his ideal of a completely "intellectualized" mathematics. The majestic edifice of the three *Critiques* lacks the indispensable basement of a logic on a level with science. "The brass colossus has feet of clay."

Deploring the fact that C. I. Gerhardt, in editing Leibniz, had separated the mathematical writings from the philosophical, Couturat could not but associate himself with the task assumed by the newly founded *Revue de métaphysiqu?* of working for a *rapprochement,* unfortunately broken off in the nineteenth century, between philosophers and scientists. After the establishment of the *Revue* in 1893, scarcely a year passed when he did not publish one or more articles in this spirit (some thirty at the time of his death, plus three that appeared posthumously). Rather than present original views, he dedicated himself with great disinterestedness to making known the views of others, mainly foreigners. He explained to French philosophers the mathematical logic of Guiseppe Peano, the universal algebra of Alfred North Whitehead, and the foundations of geometry and the principles of mathematics according to Russell. He vigorously defended both the new logic (to whose diffusion he contributed with his *L'algèbre de la logique,* Paris, 1905) and the Russellian logistic. This involved him in a celebrated controversy with his former teacher Jules Henri Poincaré. Although at the time Poincaré was often able to score against his opponent, subsequent developments in logic and mathematics have been more favorable to Couturat on many points.

Couturat's admiration for Leibniz, who dreamed of a universal language; his adherence to logistic that he saw as the source of an algorithm disengaged from the contingencies and irregularities of the natural languages; his participation in the organization of the first International Congress of Philosophy (Paris, 1900); his active collaboration with André Lalande in the preparation of the *Vocabulaire technique et critique de la philosophie* (Paris, 1926); and his rationalism, which one may characterize as militant in the sense that his purpose was less to rediscover reason in things than to work to make it rule among men—all these converging concerns led him to devote himself more exclusively to a task which became a veritable apostolate for him—the creation and adoption of an international auxiliary language by the rationalization of Esperanto and Ido. He prepared himself for this mission first by studying and then by publishing, in collaboration with Léopold Léau, the *Histoire de la langue universelle* (Paris, 1903). After 1900, Couturat was the moving spirit of the Délégation pour l'Adoption d'une Langue Auxiliaire Internationale, initiated by Léau, and later of the Akademie di la Lingue Internaciona Ido. In 1908 he founded and directed until his death the monthly review *Progreso,* written in the reformed language and designed to propagate it. The opposition of many Esperantists and the death of Couturat, which happened to come at the very moment when a war that exacerbated national particularisms was breaking out, caused the abandonment of the project. His friends and admirers have often regretted that Couturat should have expended so much effort in vain and sacrificed his wide talent to a noble dream.

See also Cantor, Georg; Helmholtz, Hermann Ludwig von; History and Historiography of Philosophy; Kant, Immanuel; Leibniz, Gottfried Wilhelm; Plato; Poincaré, Jules Henri; Renouvier, Charles Bernard; Russell, Bertrand Arthur William; Whitehead, Alfred North.

Bibliography

WORKS BY COUTURAT

L'algèbre de la logique. Paris: Gauthier-Vill, 1905. The 1914 edition (Paris) was republished at Hildesheim, Germany, in 1965, Georg Olms edition.

Les principes des mathématiques. Paris: Alcan, 1905. Republished under the same title with the addition of the article "La philosophie des mathématiques de Kant" in Hildesheim, Germany, in 1965.

La logique de Leibniz. Georg Olms edition. Hildesheim, Germany, 1961.

WORKS ON COUTURAT

Cassirer, Ernst. "Kant und die moderne Mathematik. Mit Bezug auf Russells und Couturats Werke über die Prinzipien der Mathematik." *Kantstudien* (1907).

Lalande, André. "L'Oeuvre de Louis Couturat." *Revue de métaphysique* 22 (1914): 644–688. Includes a detailed bibliography.

Robert Blanché (1967)
Translated by Albert E. Blumberg

CRAIG'S THEOREM

In mathematical logic, Craig's Theorem—not to be confused with Craig's Interpolation Theorem—states that any recursively enumerable theory is recursively axiomatizable. Its epistemological interest lies in its possible use as a method of eliminating "theoretical content" from scientific theories.

PROOF OF CRAIG'S THEOREM

Assume that S is a deductively closed set of sentences, the elements of which may be recursively enumerated thus $F(0)$, $F(1)$, …, $F(n)$, … where F is a recursive function from natural numbers to sentences (we assume that expressions, sentences, etc., have been Gödel-coded in some manner). The set of theorems of an axiomatic theory is automatically recursively enumerable. But in general a recursively enumerable set is not automatically recursive. An example of a recursively enumerable set that is non-recursive is the set of logical truths in a first-order language with a single dyadic predicate. This follows from Church's Theorem, which states that the general notion of first-order validity is undecidable. However, through a trick devised by Craig, we can define a recursive set Craig(S) whose deductive closure is S. Let A be a sentence and n a natural number. Let A^n be the $(n+1)$-fold conjunction $A \wedge \ldots \wedge A$. The sentence A^n is logically interdeducible with A. Next consider sentences of the form $F(n)^n$. Define Craig(S) to be $\{F(n)^n\colon n \in N\}$. The deductive closure of Craig(S) must be S, since each element of Craig(S) is equivalent to an element of S. Next we give an informal decision procedure for membership in Craig(S). Given a sentence A, to decide whether $A \in$ Craig(S), first check if A has the form B^n, for some sentence B and number n. Through unique readability this is checkable, and if A is not of this form then $A \notin$ Craig(S). So suppose that A is of the form B^n. We calculate $F(n)$, and if B is indeed $F(n)$ then $A \in$ Craig(S). And otherwise $A \notin$ Craig(S). The existence of a decision procedure for membership in Craig(S) implies that Craig(S) is recursive. The set Craig(S) is therefore a recursive axiomatization of the theory S.

CRAIGIAN ELIMINATION. The logical positivists held that, under a logical reconstruction, a scientific theory is an axiom system formulated in a language $L(O, T)$, in which extra-logical predicates and function symbols are classified as either O-terms, for observational properties, or T-terms, for theoretical properties. Statements in $L(O, T)$ can be classified as observational, theoretical, or mixed, depending upon the presence or absence of O-terms or T-terms. Deleting theoretical terms yields a sublanguage $L(O)$ whose sentences express observational or empirical claims about the world. Assume that the property of being an $L(O)$-sentence is recursive. Consider a recursively enumerable theory S in $L(O, T)$. The empirical content of S is the set of $L(O)$-theorems of S. This is a subtheory of S obtained by a restriction on a recursive property. So it is recursively enumerable too. According to Craig's Theorem there is a recursive set of $L(O)$-sentences whose deductive closure is the empirical content of S. According to these assumptions we can therefore recursively axiomatize the empirical content of any given scientific theory S, obtaining a recursive axiom system Craig(S), known as the Craigian reaxiomatization of S's empirical content.

PHILOSOPHICAL SIGNIFICANCE OF CRAIGIAN ELIMINATION

Instrumentalism or positivism about science involves a scepticism towards the non-observational content of a scientific theory. Lacking such content the Craigian reaxiomatization Craig(S) provides an object of rational belief compatible with instrumentalist or positivist scruples. Note that this elimination method need not be based on an observation/theory distinction. With obvious modification it can be used as a way of eliminating, for example, the mathematical content from a scientific theory formulated using mathematical predicates and quantification over sets, functions, and so forth, or as a way of eliminating theoretical content from a psychological theory that refers to mental states, and so on. Craigian reaxiomatization offers a possible elimination strategy for a variety of instrumentalist positions.

CRITICISMS OF CRAIGIAN ELIMINATION

Of the aforementioned there are two methodological criticisms. First, even if the original theory *S* is presented in a simple manner, the reaxiomatization Craig(*S*) will be complex and thus will violate the canon of *simplicity* which we might impose on admissible theories. Second Craig(*S*) is *parasitic* upon the original theory *S* and so does not really stand alone from the original theory. Indeed Craig(*S*) is a bizarre theory, having infinitely many axioms of the form A'', where *A* is an empirical consequence of *S*. Hartry Field refers to Craigian reaxiomatization as "bizarre trickery" and complains that Craig(*S*) is "obviously uninteresting, since [it] does nothing towards explaining the phenomenon in question in terms of a small number of basic principles" (Field 1980, p. 8). A third criticism is that Craigian elimination rests on a mistaken conception of scientific theories, namely a *syntactic view* of theories. This criticism has been urged by Bas van Fraassen, who writes "empirical import cannot be isolated syntactically … the reduced theory [Craig(*S*)] is not a description of the observable part of the world of *S*; rather it is a hobbled and hamstrung version of *S*'s description of everything" (van Fraassen 1976, pp. 87–88). A final criticism attacks the tenability of the observation/theory distinction required. A simple example of this is that although "red" seems a paradigmatic observational term, we can nonetheless speak of red blood cells, which are too small to be visible to the naked eye (see Putnam 1962).

With respect to certain assumptions discussed above concerning the notion of "empirical content," Craig's Theorem tells us that we can reaxiomatize the empirical content of a scientific theory, thereby eliminating apparent reference to unobservable objects and properties. However this elimination procedure has not found many adherents, and it seems safe to say that the significance of Craigian elimination is primarily pedagogical.

See also Field, Hartry.

Bibliography

Craig, William. "On Axiomatizability Within a System." *Journal of Symbolic Logic* 18 (1953): 30–32.

Field, Hartry. *Science without Numbers*. Princeton, NJ: Princeton University Press, 1980.

Putnam, Hilary "What Theories Are Not." In *Logic, Methodology and Philosophy of Science*, edited by Ernest Nagel, Patrick Suppes, and Alfred Tarski. Stanford University Press, 1962. Reprinted in Hilary Putnam *Mathematics, Matter and Method: Philosophical Papers*, Vol. 1, Cambridge University Press, 1979.

van Fraassen, B. C. "To Save the Phenomena. " *Journal of Philosophy* 73 (1976): 623–632 (page references to the reprint in David Papineau, ed. *Philosophy of Science*. New York: Oxford University Press, 1996).

Jeffrey Ketland (2005)

CRATYLUS

Cratylus, an Athenian, was contemporary with Socrates but was probably considerably younger. He was, according to Aristotle, a follower of the doctrines of Heraclitus, and Plato, in his youth, was closely associated with him. Aristotle implies that this was before he came under Socrates' influence, although later sources put the influence of Cratylus upon Plato after the death of Socrates.

Cratylus took as his starting point the doctrine of the flux of phenomena (here assumed to have been a genuine doctrine of Heraclitus, despite G. S. Kirk's objections), and he capped Heraclitus's saying that one cannot step twice into the same river by adding "nor once either." His reason clearly was his contention that the river is changing even as you step into it. He ended by coming to the view that one ought not to say anything, but only move the finger, since no true statement can be made about a thing that is always changing. According to Aristotle, upon whose evidence the above account rests, Plato took from Cratylus the belief, which he maintained even in later years, that all sensible things are always in a state of flux and that there is no knowledge about them.

Plato in the *Cratylus* attributes to him the doctrine that everything has a right name of its own, fixed by nature, and somehow or other this one right name will point to the nature of the thing named.

At an early stage it became clear to modern critics that the contention that there is a right name that indicates the true nature of a thing is apparently inconsistent with the doctrine of a Heraclitean flux in phenomena, since this flux would prevent a thing from having an abiding nature. Attempts to explain this contradiction in Cratylus's position have been numerous. Frequently it has been supposed that Cratylus either did not have a doctrine of words at all or else did not believe in the flux doctrine.

All such explanations seem misguided. Aristotle makes it clear that the final step—the refusal to use words—came after a previous period when Cratylus was already a Heraclitean. The implications of Plato's account are also clear; Cratylus at the time of the dialogue had long been interested in the doctrines of Heraclitus, and he also held the theory of words attributed to him. It might be that he failed to realize the inconsistency at the stage represented by the dialogue, and, when the inconsistency became clear, subsequently proposed to abandon speech. More probably, at the time of the dialogue he inclined to the view to which he is clearly attracted when Socrates mentions it, namely, that words themselves in some sense flow, and so point to the flowing nature of the objects to which they refer (*Cratylus,* 437D).

See also Aristotle; Heraclitus of Ephesus; Plato; Socrates.

Bibliography

Testimonia in Diels-Kranz, *Fragmente der Vorsokratiker,* Vol. II, 10th ed. (Berlin: Weidmann, 1961). See also V. Goldschmidt, *Essai sur le Cratyle* (Paris: H. Champion, 1940); G. S. Kirk, "The Problem of Cratylus," in *American Journal of Philology* 72 (1951): 225–253; D. J. Allan, "The Problem of Cratylus," ibid., 75 (1954): 271–287; H. Cherniss, "Aristotle, Metaphysics 987a32–b7," ibid., 76 (1955): 184–186.

G. B. Kerferd (1967)

CREATION AND CONSERVATION

Many religions view the universe as the creation of a divine being or beings. The value of such a view is manifold. Among other things, it implies that the world is at least partly a product of divine planning and governance. To the extent that this is so, the world can be expected to be an orderly place, made for a purpose and ruled by providence. Thus, humans can anticipate that what befalls them in earthly life will not have occurred by accident, that their fortunes and destiny are, at least in some measure, divinely ordained. The idea of divine governance of the world also offers a possible basis for grounding principles of moral conduct; finally, if human destiny is in the hands of a higher power, there is at least hope of a life beyond the grave.

The doctrine of creation characteristic of the Judeo-Christian-Islamic tradition is a very strong one, for at least three reasons. First, these religions understand the universe to be entirely the product of one God. Second, creation is understood to be *ex nihilo*—that is, the universe is not fashioned out of any preexisting thing. Third, the world is not just created by God "in the beginning," but is also sustained in being by him for its entire existence; thus, the fact that the world is able to persist beyond the present moment is as much owing to the creative action of God as is the fact that it exists at all. Taken together, these claims indicate that divine governance of the world is unified, close, and thorough, with implications about both the nature of the world and God's relation to it. These implications are related in turn to a number of problems in philosophical theology and to certain aspects of contemporary scientific cosmology.

THE COSMOLOGICAL ARGUMENT

No single account of creation could ever portray the richness of the Western philosophical tradition on the matter. There are, however, a number of common themes. Typically, treatments of God as creator begin with an argument for the existence of God—usually some version of either the teleological argument, which is based on premises about order or purpose in the universe, or the so-called cosmological argument, which invokes God as an uncaused first cause of all things. The latter argument shall be examined first.

The cosmological argument is traditionally presented as a deductive argument. Put very roughly, it asserts the following:

(1) The universe of our experience need not have existed—that is, that its existence is contingent.

(2) The existence of contingent things must have an explanation.

(3) The only or best explanation for the existence of the universe is the creative activity of a necessarily existing "first cause."

(4) Therefore, there is such an entity or being.

Further, it is held, this being is in fact the personal God of traditional Western monotheism.

Of the premises of this argument, the first seems plausible. The second is a version of the principle of sufficient reason. It is needed if the argument is to be deductively valid, but in the end it is probably damaging to the argument. The principle of sufficient reason is not a necessary truth, and so cannot be known a priori; any effort to establish its truth a posteriori is apt to be inconclusive, in part because the truth of the principle depends precisely on whether it holds with regard to cases such as the existence of the universe, which is precisely the point at issue.

Suppose, then, that premise number two is dropped. What remains is best interpreted as a kind of inductive argument, an inference to the best explanation, according to which the existence of the universe is a result of the causal activity of a necessary being. In such an argument, it is best to separate two claims that are implicit in the third premise above:

(3a) The creative activity of a necessarily existing first cause is sufficient to explain the existence of the universe.

(3b) No alternative hypothesis is sufficient to do the job.

With this clarification, and premise number two now out of the way, an appropriate conclusion might now be something like:

(5) Relative to the evidence of experience, we have better reason for thinking there is a necessarily existing first cause of the universe than for thinking otherwise.

Because this is an inductive argument, the conclusion no longer follows necessarily from the premises. In this, however, it is no different from any inductive argument, including many that we find quite persuasive—for example, arguments for the existence of subatomic particles or even for exotic and unexpected phenomena such as quantum entanglement. No doubt, a skeptic may treat this feature as a reason for denying the conclusion, but that is not a point of interest. A skeptic can find a reason to deny any conclusion. A second important point is that the God postulated in the argument is described as a necessary being—that is, a being whose existence is necessary or a being that exists by its very nature. Some philosophers have questioned whether such a being is possible, and that is an issue worthy of consideration. It would, however, be logically misguided to greet this argument with the question, "What caused God?" By definition, a necessary being is existentially self-sufficient: It neither has nor requires a cause. Admittedly, it is not obvious that a necessarily existing first cause of the universe ought to be identified with the personal God of traditional belief. Proponents of cosmological arguments have, however, been well aware of this point; medieval demonstrations of a creator—that of Thomas Aquinas, for example—were often followed by lengthy consideration of what characteristics might appropriately be attributed to such a being.

Perhaps the most interesting issues about the cosmological argument concern premises 3a and 3b. Whether, as 3a asserts, the activity of a creator God explains the existence of the word will depend on how we understand that activity. Presumably, it does not consist in a sequence wherein God first commands that the universe exist, and the command then causes its existence. For if, as is usually supposed, causal relations are themselves contingent, then God would first have to create the causal mechanism by which his commands gain efficacy. This would require another command, and a vicious regress would ensue. How, then, should the activity of creation be understood? One attractive possibility is an analogy with human creation: for example, a writer envisioning a drama, a composer inventing a melody, or a scientist coming up with a hypothesis. On this kind of view, the first cause would indeed have to be conceived as personal, since the world would owe its existence to a knowing will, of which it would be the *content* as well as the product. That is to say, unlike the products of human creation, the universe would have its existence in God both as a concrete reality and as something known.

Premise 3b must itself be established inductively: That is, we must canvas the known alternatives to the hypothesis of a creator and show that they do not work. Of course, even if we succeed, it may be that some as yet undiscovered explanation for the existence of the world will be found superior to any invoking a creator God. Still, the cosmological argument is greatly strengthened if alternative hypotheses can be eliminated. Historically, the most favored alternative by far has been the hypothesis that the world had no temporal beginning but rather is infinite in duration, its existence at each moment being a causal consequence of the immediate past, from which it is generated in accordance with scientific law. In fact, however, this alternative is all but indefensible. Scientific laws, classically at least, are not diachronic: That is, they do not speak of causes that occur at one moment and effects at another. Action and reaction are simultaneous in Newton's scheme. The application of net force produces acceleration at the instant of application; if at t an object is not acted upon by a net force, then it is at rest or in uniform rectilinear motion at t.

We can, of course, deduce the state of a closed system at a later time if we know its state at t, but only if we *assume* as a premise that the mass/energy of which it is constituted will continue to exist. Nor will it do at this point to invoke conservation principles. For, again, the law that mass/energy is conserved holds only of closed systems—that is, systems in which, *ex hypothesi*, mass/energy is neither gained nor lost. Conservation laws are not, however, mere tautologies. They tell us something very important: that physics is not about things just *being*, but about how they change; and that although we may learn a great deal from science about the development of the universe over time, and the ways in which the items of our experience combine and separate and change, physics has next to nothing to tell us about the existence of things.

A second difficulty with the alternative hypothesis is that we have no idea what it would be like for the universe to be able to bootstrap itself into the future by sustaining its own existence. No one has ever described a mechanism by which this could occur; and if one should deny the need to do so—invoking, say, a principle of "existential inertia" by which, once in existence, things "naturally" tend to continue existing— the explanation becomes empirically vacuous, a mere redescription of the phenomenon to be explained. Finally, even if one temporal stage of the universe could give rise to a succeeding one, the question that drives the cosmological argument would go unanswered.

For the problem is not why the universe exists at this moment, but why it exists at all. If I ask you why the bordelaise sauce in the upper container of a double boiler is hot, you may fairly explain that it is heated by the boiling water in the lower container. If I ask you why the water is boiling, you could in principle reply that this is in fact a triple boiler: that the water is heated by still further water, boiling merrily another level below. But if I ask you how heat gets into the system at all, it will not do to postulate an infinity boiler, for water is never anything but contingently hot. You have to come to something essentially hot—fire, perhaps—to answer my question. Similarly, if the problem is to explain the existence of contingent things, an infinite sequence of them is of no avail. Only if we postulate a necessary being will an explanation be possible.

CONSERVATION

If these points are correct, then the traditional cosmological argument is in a considerably stronger position than is often supposed. Its plausibility is the same, moreover, whether the past duration of the universe is finite or infinite. If there is never a natural accounting for the existence of contingent things, then at any moment of their existence, only the activity of a necessary being can explain them. This is the essence of the religious doctrine of conservation, according to which God is as much responsible for the persistence of the universe as for its being there at all. Many have thought, however, that the doctrine of conservation leads to a serious difficulty. If God is, at each moment, the cause of all that exists, what place can there be for natural causes? It is unreasonable to think God is causally responsible for the present existence of my chair unless he is also responsible for its properties. Indeed, the seventeenth-century philosopher Nicolas Malebranche argued that nothing else is possible, that it is self-contradictory to suppose God could create a chair that is neither at rest nor in motion, and has no color or mass or any other property characteristic of a chair. But if God is creatively responsible for all the properties of the chair at each moment of existence, are not natural causes simply redundant? God's will as creator must, after all, be presumed completely efficacious. But if it is, what efficacy is left to natural causes?

Malebranche's answer was blunt: none. He held a doctrine known as *occasionalism*, according to which the events we ordinarily take to be causes (for example, my pushing on the chair) are only occasions for God to exercise his own causal power (to create the chair in motion), the only causal power that is legitimately efficacious. But occasionalism has uncomfortable consequences. Perhaps the worst is that if it is true, we do not perceive the world in the way we think we do—that is, by the action of the things in it on our senses. Rather, our sensations are caused in us by God so as to match what is going on in the world. And then we are only a step away from the idealism of George Berkeley: that is, from moving to the conclusion that the so-called physical universe must be superfluous to God's plan, then denying its existence and attempting to reduce its contents to nothing but sets of ideas.

It is possible, however, to avoid occasionalism if the suggestion of the previous section is correct: that natural causation is not a matter of conferring existence to begin with. Much more plausible accounts are possible. In the realm of physical action in particular, causal interaction may be viewed as a matter of energy transfer, wherein quantities presumed to be conserved—motion, momentum, charge, and the like—are transmitted from one entity to another. As such, what we normally take to be causal processes (one billiard ball imparting motion to another, to cite the classic example) count as genuine exercises of causal power yet do not carry the suggestion of one event conferring existence on another. The case of perception, where what is caused is something mental, is notoriously more difficult. But if a similar solution can be found there, we have every reason to think both natural and divine causation can be accepted without setting up a false competition between them.

CREATION AND SCIENTIFIC COSMOLOGY

Philosophical arguments for the existence of God are widely understood to be reinforced by two recent developments in scientific cosmology. The first is the so-called big bang theory, according to which the universe of our observation constitutes a kind of continuous explosion that commenced some 15 billion years ago from an initial singularity in which the entirety of space-time was compressed to a state so dense as to be indescribable by any known principles of physics. This theory is now well confirmed, and it implies that the universe did indeed have a temporal beginning—so radical a beginning, in fact, that it would be scientifically meaningless to speak of a time prior to the big bang.

That the universe had a temporal beginning is in line with many religious creation narratives. Theists have therefore tended to treat the big bang theory as confirmation of their views, holding that it is far more plausible to postulate a creator to explain the world's beginning than to claim it "just happened." Opponents have found the appeal to such a cause unscientific. Some have argued that, in fact, a divine act of creation is not possible, because even a divine cause must precede its effect, and the big bang allows for no time prior to itself. Others have posed mathematical models for the universe's origin that would avoid the claim of an initial singularity and the attendant implication of a temporal beginning.

The suggestion that a proper science ought not to be postulating a creator has much to be said for it; science is fairly taken to be solely concerned with natural phenomena and natural explanations of them. Theists who take comfort from big bang theories need not, however, be deterred by such a delimitation of scientific purview, given that they seek an explanation for the existence of the entire natural order—something a science thus delimited cannot in principle provide. As for the claim that even a divine cause must precede its effect, that seems mistaken. On the contrary: if, as is argued above, the laws that govern natural processes are synchronic rather than diachronic, then even natural causation must be understood in a way that makes cause and effect simultaneous—in which case any support for the claim that a divine cause must precede its effect vanishes. Humans may eventually come to understand the genesis of the cosmos according to some model other than the standard big bang. But the alternatives presently available face problems of internal coherence and of testability, and so have yet to offer strong competition.

The second development in cosmology that is often taken to support claims of a creator is the realization that living beings of the sort with which we are familiar owe their existence to a wondrously exacting fine-tuning of various physical parameters. For example, if the ratio of the universe's rate of expansion to its total mass were increased or decreased by only one part in a million, there would be no stars and planets to support life. If the strong nuclear force were increased by just 1 percent, it would have been impossible for carbon to form; an increase of 2 percent would have ruled out the formation of protons from quarks. On the opposite side, a decrease of 4 percent would have allowed no atoms other than hydrogen to form.

Examples like this can be multiplied at considerable length, and the likelihood that all the requirements for life that they embody should be satisfied in one universe is exceedingly remote. The fact that our universe does exactly that has therefore been held to justify a teleological argument for the existence of God. That is, it is argued that the only way to explain the fine-tuning of our universe for life is to postulate an intelligent creator who designed it to be so. Opponents have countered that the universe visible to us may be only one of a great many worlds, perhaps even an infinite number, in which many or even all possible combinations of basic parameters are displayed. If so, then the fine-tuning of our world might be "explained," at least in the weak sense that the appearance of such a universe would be made more likely, or even certain. In addition to being plainly ad hoc in character, these speculations too present problems of testability—not to mention the difficulty of truly explaining the existence of such an ensemble of worlds by specifying a mechanism that could cause it to appear, and guarantee its exhaustiveness. Like the big bang, however, the issue of fine-tuning is a subject of intense interest, and there is doubtless a good deal more to be said about both.

See also Berkeley, George; Cosmological Argument for the Existence of God; Cosmology; Laws, Scientific; Malebranche, Nicolas; Teleological Argument for the Existence of God; Thomas Aquinas, St.

Bibliography

Barrow, John, and Frank Tipler. *The Anthropic Cosmological Principle*. Oxford: Clarendon Press, 1986.

Craig, William L. "Professor Grünbaum on Creation." *Erkenntnis* 40 (1994): 325–341.

Craig, William L., and Quentin Smith. *Theism, Atheism, and Big Bang Cosmology*. Oxford: Clarendon Press, 1993.

Dowe, Phil. *Physical Causation*. Cambridge, U.K.: Cambridge University Press, 2000.

Freddoso, Alfred J. "Medieval Aristotelianism and the Case Against Secondary Causation in Nature." In *Divine and Human Action: Essays in the Metaphysics of Theism*, edited by Thomas V. Morris. Ithaca, NY: Cornell University Press, 1988.

Grünbaum, Adolf. "Creation as a Pseudo-Explanation in Current Physical Cosmology." *Erkenntnis* 35 (1991): 233–254.

Hawking, Stephen. *A Brief History of Time*. New York: Bantam Books, 1988.

Kvanvig, Jonathan L., and Hugh J. McCann. "Divine Conservation and the Persistence of the World." In *Divine and Human Action: Essays in the Metaphysics of Theism*, edited by Thomas V. Morris. Ithaca, NY: Cornell University Press, 1988.

Mackie, J. L. *The Miracle of Theism*. Oxford: Clarendon Press, 1982.

Malebranche, Nicolas. *Dialogues on Metaphysics*. Translated by Willis Doney. New York: Abarus Books, 1980.

Quinn, Philip L. "Divine Conservation, Secondary Causation, and Occasionalism." In *Divine and Human Action: Essays in the Metaphysics of Theism*, edited by Thomas V. Morris. Ithaca, NY: Cornell University Press, 1988.

Rowe, William L. *The Cosmological Argument*. Princeton, NJ: Princeton University Press, 1975.

Thomas Aquinas. *Summa Contra Gentiles*, Bk. III, Chs. 64–70. Translated by Vernon J. Bourke. Notre Dame, IN: University of Notre Dame Press, 1975.

Thomas Aquinas. *Summa Theologiae* I, Ques. 1–11. London: Blackfriars, 1964.

Hugh J. McCann (2005)

CREATIVITY

It has often been claimed that genuine creativity is largely if not entirely a matter of inspiration—the sudden, involuntary, and inexplicable outpouring of innovative ideas and actions. In many expressions of this thesis, including Plato's, the source of this outpouring is a sacred instance—a spirit or muse—while in other versions it is the unconscious mind. The antithesis to such inspirationist theses is the rationalist doctrine that all creativity is ultimately reducible to a form of calculation or more or less deliberate problem-solving.

Although both the extreme inspirationist thesis and the rationalist antithesis have adherents, many investigators find an intermediary position more tempting. Inspirationist theses are hard to square with basic, naturalist inclinations and with a commitment to scientific research. That creative behavior is complex and hard to explain does not mean that it is essentially mysterious or could never be modeled with some modest measure of accuracy. Inspirationism is further challenged by evidence that most if not all significant episodes of innovation require industry, rational thought, and action. Extreme rationalist accounts, on the other hand, confront testimony regarding the involuntary and sudden onslaught of important new ideas, such as vivid accounts of inspiration's "sudden illumination" offered by Pyotr Il'ich Tchaikovsky (1970 [1878]), Henri Poincaré (1952 [1908]), Albert Einstein, and scores of other impressive informants. Yet some of these same sources identify rational elements of creativity, as when Tchaikovsky goes on to underscore the necessity of daily, strenuous efforts. How to balance such divergent insights and data in a synthetic account of creativity remains a matter of great controversy.

UNDERSTANDING CREATIVITY AND CREATION

A nontrivial problem is that of specifying how the terms *creativity* and *creation* are to be understood in the first place. While there is widespread agreement that creative acts and their products must be new or innovative, there is disagreement as to the sense in which this is true, as well as with regard to other conditions on creativity. In what way are all creative acts novel or original? Although every particular action is new in the sense that this particular event never happened before, genuine creativity involves something far less common. Saying that creative acts must never have been performed before is not only vague, but overly restrictive. Is not someone's wholly independent repetition of a great discovery creative? With this question in view, Margaret A. Boden distinguishes between historical and psychological creativity. An act is *historically* creative, she proposes, only if it has never been had before by anyone else in all of human history. In contrast, *psychologically* creative acts may replicate previous inventions.

Even if one agrees to focus on what Boden calls psychological creativity—a move disputed by some theorists, including Mihály Csikszentmihályi—there remains the problem of coming up with a nontrivial elucidation of the novelty clause. To that end, Boden attempts to characterize radical psychological novelty in terms of the creative act's transformation of "a conceptual space," by which she means the principles that unify and structure a given domain of thinking and action. She contrasts the relatively uncreative writer who produces a new and interesting novel while conforming entirely to the rules of some established genre, to a genuinely creative writer who creates a strikingly new work that transforms generic patterns and establishes a new literary category. Boden further contends that what sets off the genuinely creative transformations of conceptual spaces is that their results could not have been thought before by the person working within that space. Given that a conceptual space is governed by a system of constitutive rules, its transformation entails that at least one of these rules is dropped or violated in a genuinely creative act. Jon Elster (2000) also explores the relation between creativity and rules or constraints of various sorts, arguing that originality—which may be either sterile or of genuine value—involves not merely a rebellious violation, but the revolutionary replacement of constraints.

David Novitz (2003) challenges Boden's proposal and identifies counterexamples. Some inventions, such as Thomas Edison's creation of the phonograph and Henri Matisse's use of color in his paintings, are not plausibly described as having arisen within a rule-governed conceptual space. Matisse, after all, was playing around with color combinations he found pleasing, hardly a pursuit organized by a system of rules. And some actions that do arise within a rule-governed practice or "space," such as a chess player's invention of a new opening, may nonetheless be genuinely creative. Thus if Boden's discussion offers insight into some forms of creativity, it does not adequately cover all of them.

Novitz defends an alternative, "recombination" theory of creativity. He proposes that creative acts are novel in the sense that they are not predicted by, and are surprising to a given population. Alternately, creative acts are those which would have been surprising had the members of the population become aware of them. Novitz does not specify how the population in question is to be identified, but does remark that the members of the population must have some familiarity with some of the ideas or objects that get recombined in the creative act. Another alternative is to say that it is the invention's creator or creators who must be surprised by the discovery.

Novitz argues that it is a mistake to associate creativity with the making of art. Many creative acts and inventions have nothing to do with the fine arts, and much art-making, or creation, is routine and devoid of creativity. Novitz joins a long tradition in specifying that genuine creativity must, in addition to manifesting a novel or surprising recombination of ideas or objects, bring forth a result having some real, positive value: "Creative acts are valued positively because they are intended to, and have the potential to, satisfy actual human needs and desires" (2003, p. 186). Novitz also allows that creative acts may also display a form of intrinsic value in addition to such instrumental value. These points are not, however, uncontroversial, as some authors are willing to allow that a fiendish or malicious invention, or intentionally immoral act, could be creative. Some forms of creativity may be useless. Nor is it clear that a viable conception of creativity need entail strong, realist commitments in the theory of value.

THE NATURE OF THE CREATIVE PROCESS

Additional controversy surrounds proposals concerning the nature or basic structure of the creative process or processes. One key issue has to do with the question whether the expression "the creative process" really refers to a single type of process or activity. Francis Sparshott (1981), John Hospers (1984–1985), and others state that there is no such thing as a single, determinate process involved in all creative acts, but instead, different sorts of processes having little or nothing in common. Another controversy concerns the extent to which creative activity can be adequately described as a species of problem-solving or means-end rationality. Vincent Tomas rejects the idea that artistic creation is "a paradigm of purposive activity" (1958, p. 2).David Ecker's description of the creation of art as "qualitative problem-solving" (1963) is critiqued by Monroe C. Beardsley (1965), who deems it a mistake to think that creative thinking, in the arts at least, is characteristically a matter of means-end calculations. Even if the sought-for aesthetic and artistic effects do depend on the artist's manipulation of some medium or media, creative work is not throughout guided by the effort to realize some preconceived goal or end: it would be unusual if the precise quality of the final painting were in the painter's mind from the start.

Various investigators have contended that there is a characteristic creative process having a hybrid nature. In an account popularized by Graham Wallas in *The Art of Thought* (1926), this process breaks down into four discrete stages. Creativity requires, first of all, apprenticeship and preparation: even the most brilliant innovator must learn his or her craft.Second comes "incubation," a stage in which the creative person stops working consciously on some problem, allowing unconscious processes to predominate. The result, when circumstances are favorable, is illumination or inspiration, the moment when some unexpected and innovative idea "pops" into mind. In the final stage of "verification," the creator assesses and revises what inspiration has yielded. As Beardsley observes, it would be wiser to replace talk of four linear stages with the idea of an interplay between two alternating phases, namely, preconscious invention and conscious criticism and selection of the latter phase's results. This is similar to Paul Valéry's contention that creative art-making is always a matter of both the spontaneous emergence of ideas, and conscious, means-end adjustments and rearrangements of the latter (1957–1960 [1938]). Only their relative proportion varies, he adds.

Psychologists and cognitive scientists continue to attempt to provide models of complex creative processes in various domains, including musical composition, the formation of scientific hypotheses, the visual arts, and storytelling (for surveys, see Albert and Runco 1999; Boden 2004). The greatest challenge is perhaps that of providing detailed explanations and effective simulations of the processes that underlie and generate moments of inspiration, or "popping." Psychologists working in a range of traditions, including Gestalt theory, psychoanalysis, associationism, cognitive psychology, interactionism, systems theory, and so on, have devised elaborate labels for the mind's unconscious generation and selection of novel ideas. Some of these traditional insights have been revived in the development of computer simulations using connectionist and other approaches (Martindale 1995). And in a philosophical vein, Berys Gaut (2003) explores the Kantian connection between creativity, genius, and the imagination, taking metaphor's linking of diverse domains as a paradigm.

See also Imagination.

Bibliography

Albert, Robert S., and Mark A. Runco. "A History of Research on Creativity." In *Handbook of Creativity*, edited by Robert J. Sternberg. Cambridge, U.K.: Cambridge University Press, 1999.

Beardsley, Monroe C. "On the Creation of Art." *Journal of Aesthetics and Art Criticism* 23 (1965): 291–304.

Boden, Margaret A. *The Creative Mind: Myths and Mechanisms*. London: Weidenfeld and Nicholson, 1990. 2nd rev. ed., London: Routledge, 2004.

Boden, Margaret A. "What is Creativity?" In *Dimensions of Creativity*, edited by Margaret A. Boden. Cambridge, MA: MIT, 1994.

Ecker, David. "The Artistic Process as Qualitative Problem Solving." *Journal of Aesthetics and Art Criticism* 21 (1963): 283–90.

Elster, Jon. *Ulysses Unbound: Studies in Rationality, Precommitment, and Constraints*. Cambridge, U.K.: Cambridge University Press, 2000.

Feyerabend, Paul. "Creativity—A Dangerous Myth." *Critical Inquiry* 13 (1986–1987): 700–711.

Gaut, Berys. "Creativity and Imagination." In *The Creation of Art: New Essays in Philosophical Aesthetics*, edited by Berys Gaut and Paisley Livingston. Cambridge, U.K.: Cambridge University Press, 2003.

Ghiselin, Brewster, ed. The *Creative Process: A Symposium*. New York: Mentor, 1952.

Halper, Edward. "Is Creativity Good?" *British Journal of Aesthetics* 29 (1989): 47–56.

Hospers, John. "Artistic Creativity." *Journal of Aesthetics and Art Criticism* 43 (1984–1985): 243–255.

Kant, Immanuel. *Critique of Judgment* [1790]. Translated by Werner S. Pluhar. Indianapolis: Hackett, 1987.

Martindale, Colin. "Creativity and Connectionism." In *The Creative Cognition Approach*, edited by Steven M. Smith, Thomas B. Ward, and Ronald A. Finke. Cambridge, MA: MIT, 1995.

Novitz, David. "Creativity and Constraint." *Australasian Journal of Philosophy* 77 (1999): 67–82.

Novitz, David. "Explanations of Creativity." In *The Creation of Art: New Essays in Philosophical Aesthetics*, edited by Berys Gaut and Paisley Livingston. Cambridge, U.K.: Cambridge University Press, 2003.

Poincaré, Henri. *Science et méthode*. Paris: Flammarion, 1908. Translated by Francis Maitland as *Science and Method.* New York: Dover, 1952.

Sparshott, Francis. "Every Horse has a Mouth: A Personal Poetics." In *The Concept of Creativity in Science and Art*, edited by Denis Dutton and Michael Krausz. The Hague: Martinus Nijhoff, 1981.

Tchaikovsky, Pyotr Il'lich. "Letters" [1878]. In *Creativity: Selected Readings*, edited by P. E. Vernon. Harmondsworth, U.K.: Penquin, 1970.

Tomas, Vincent. "Creativity in Art." *The Philosophical Review* 67 (1958): 1–15.

Valéry, Paul. "L'invention esthétique" [1938]. In *Oeuvres.* 2 vols. Edited by Jean Hytier. Paris: Gallimard, 1957–1960.

Wallas, Graham. *The Art of Thought.* London: Jonathan Cape, 1926.

Paisley Livingston (2005)

CREIGHTON, JAMES EDWIN

(1861–1924)

James Edwin Creighton, an American idealist philosopher, was born in Pictou, Nova Scotia. Creighton was educated at Dalhousie College, Halifax (A.B., 1887), where one of his teachers was Jacob Gould Schurman, whom he later followed to Cornell University. He was appointed fellow in philosophy there in 1888 and studied in Leipzig and Berlin, returning to Cornell in 1889 as an instructor. He received his Ph.D. in 1892 with the thesis "The Will; Its Structure and Mode of Operation," and became associate professor. In 1895 he was elected Sage professor of logic and metaphysics, succeeding Schurman, and held that chair until his death. He received LL.D. degrees from Queens University (1903) and from Dalhousie (1914). While Creighton was dean of the graduate school at Cornell from 1914 to 1923, his flexible policies stimulated student initiative, but the administrative demands on his time limited his literary output. He was coeditor of the *Philosophical Review* from 1892 until 1902, when he became sole editor, and he was American editor of *Kantstudien* from 1896 until his death.

Convinced that the intellectual life is a social venture, Creighton was a cofounder of the American Philosophical Association and in 1902 became its first president. His vigorous instruction influenced the development of philosophy in American education through the efforts of his students, twenty-two of whom honored him with a volume of articles, *Philosophical Essays* (New York, 1917), commemorating twenty-five years of his teaching.

Creighton's "speculative idealism" grew out of his view that philosophical inquiry must occur in the context of the history of ideas and must begin with "the standpoint of experience." But experience is not a simple, isolated particular which can be understood by analysis. Finite individuality has system implicit in it, and can be understood as a part of the order of the universe. It is unity in plurality and identity in difference. It is permeated with meaning. In short, Creighton identified it as the "concrete universal."

Thus, with Bernard Bosanquet, Creighton held that philosophical judgments are ways in which experience progresses toward its goal of intelligibility, and the task of such judgments is to disclose the implications of the dynamic coordinates of experience: mind, nature, and other selves. Reality cannot be identified with mind, will, or personality but must be comprehended as a system in which each entity plays a part as an individual and as a significant function of the purposeful whole. Epistemological problems traceable to Immanuel Kant's emphasis on the centrality of the knowing subject are artificial because mind by its very nature is already in touch with reality. Subject and object cannot be viewed as ontologically discrete but are correlative. Accordingly, Creighton dissociated himself from neorealism, which regards truth as a quality of single propositions; from pragmatism, which fails to see that thought modifies the internal structure of experience itself; and from Berkeleianism and other "mentalistic" idealisms, which interpret nature as a phase of mind, thereby transforming experience unnecessarily into an order of ideas instead of accepting objective reality as a direct intuition. Such idealisms, even Josiah Royce's absolutism, issue in subjectivism and thus deny the objective world. Creighton maintained that this conclusion would render all thought chaotic because the objective order is the presupposition of all rationality.

Appointed to the Carus lectureship in 1924, Creighton planned to develop his views on historical method in philosophy, but death intervened. He wrote virtually nothing on ethics, aesthetics, or religion, unlike his idealist contemporaries, but certain details of his system can be inferred from his excellent critical discussions of competing movements.

See also Bosanquet, Bernard; Idealism; Kant, Immanuel; Pragmatism; Royce, Josiah.

Bibliography

WORKS BY CREIGHTON

Translator with E. B. Titchener, of W. Wundt, *Lectures on Human and Animal Psychology.* London: S. Sonnenschein, 1894.

Translator with A. Lefevre, of F. Paulsen, *Immanuel Kant.* New York: Scribners, 1902.

An Introductory Logic. New York: Macmillan, 1909. The fifth edition (New York: Macmillan, 1932) was revised by one of Creighton's colleagues, H. R. Smart.

Studies in Speculative Philosophy, edited by H. R. Smart. New York: Macmillan, 1925. Fourteen of his 38 major articles were posthumously published in this volume, which is the best single source for his views, containing a select bibliography and his most representative essay, "Two Types of Idealism."

WORKS ON CREIGHTON

Blau, Joseph L. *Men and Movements in American Philosophy.* New York: Prentice-Hall, 1952.

Cunningham, G. Watts. *The Idealist Argument in Recent British and American Philosophy.* New York: Century, 1933.

Townsend, Harvey G. *Philosophical Ideas in the United States.* New York: American, 1934.

Critical discussions of Creighton's work can be found in the three books listed above.

Warren E. Steinkraus (1967)

CRESCAS, HASDAI
(1340–1410)

The Spanish rabbi and philosopher Hasdai Crescas was born in Barcelona, the scion of a distinguished family. He exercised considerable influence both in the Jewish community and at the Aragonese court. After the 1391 persecution of the Jews, in which his only son perished, Crescas moved to Saragossa, where he engaged in literary activity until his death.

Crescas's purpose was to defend Judaism from both internal and external subversion. To this end he composed his Spanish "Refutation of the Principles of Christianity" (extant only in Hebrew translation), a rational critique of Christian dogmatic theology, and his masterwork, *The Light of the Lord* (*Or Adonai*), conceived as an introduction to a legal code that was never composed. Crescas wrote in the tradition of those thinkers, such as Judah Halevi and Nahmanides, who rejected the rationalistic compromising of Judaism with the teachings of Aristotle, but he differed from them in that he chose to combat the philosophers on their own ground. In this respect his position may be compared with that of Muhammad al-Ghazālī in Islamic philosophy. The *Light* is arranged as a dogmatic treatise, beginning with an exposition of the primary concept of God's existence and unity and followed by expositions of certain fundamental and subordinate doctrines. The first section, in which Crescas presents and criticizes the twenty-six basic propositions of physics which Maimonides (*Guide,* Part II, Introduction) culled from Aristotle, is concerned less with advancing a new system than with indicating the inadequacy of those of his forerunners. Crescas conceived of time as duration independent of motion and insisted on the possibility of a vacuum based on a conception of space as extension independent of body. These two notions enabled him to establish the existence of infinite time and space, thereby destroying the concept of the Aristotelian prime mover. Furthermore, the debate over creation ex nihilo is dismissed as futile since, in any event, all is derivative from God, who is the only necessary existent.

Crescas maintained both the literalness of the Biblical attributes and God's unity by advancing the Kalam-like theory of essential attributes compatible with God's absolute simplicity. These attributes are related to the subject as light rays are to the source of luminescence, one being inconceivable without the other, and are bound together by the unifying principle of the divine goodness. It is this goodness or perfection which characterizes the Divinity, rather than the Aristotelian concept of self-thinking thought.

The return of Crescas to the biblical conception of God is best exemplified in his treatment of the problem of the conflict between divine foreknowledge and human free will. Maimonides had taken refuge in the notion that God's knowledge has nothing in common with humanity's while Gersonides sacrificed divine knowledge of the future and the particulars to unconditional human free will. Rejecting both points of view, Crescas felt it unnecessary to reconcile divine knowledge (which he considered absolute) with free will but rather free will with causality. Definitely inclined toward determinism, he maintained that an act is contingent when considered in relation to itself but necessary in relation to its causes and to God's knowledge. Human consciousness of free will consists in the pleasure or disapproval felt when an act is committed.

Divine providence, prophecy, and immortality are not dependent on intellectual perfection, as in Maimonides and Gersonides, but rather on love and reverence for God, which is the purpose of the Divine Law and the universe. It is the substance of the soul itself, rather than the acquired intellect, which survives death.

Crescas's independence of Aristotle helped pave the way for such Renaissance thinkers as the younger Pico della Mirandola and Giordano Bruno. Of particular interest is Crescas's influence on the thought of Benedict (Baruch) de Spinoza, who knew his work well.

See also al-Ghazālī, Muhammad; Aristotle; Bruno, Giordano; Gersonides; Halevi, Yehuda; Islamic Philosophy; Jewish Philosophy; Maimonides; Spinoza, Benedict (Baruch) de.

Bibliography

The *editio princeps* of the *Or Adonai* (*Light of the Lord*) appeared at Ferrara in 1556 and has since been published several times. The first section, which deals with the 26 propositions, has been edited and translated into English by H. A. Wolfson in *Crescas' Critique of Aristotle* (Cambridge, MA: Harvard University Press, 1929). The section on free will was rendered into German by Philipp Bloch in *Die Willensfreiheit von Chasdai Crescas* (Munich, 1879).

Crescas's thought has been surveyed in M. Waxman, *The Philosophy of Don Hasdai Crescas* (New York: Columbia University Press, 1920) and M. Joel, *Don Hasdae Crescas' religionsphilosophische Lehren in ihrem geschichtlichen Einflusse dargestellt* (Breslau: Schletter, 1866). His influence on Spinoza has been discussed by Joel in *Zur Genesis der Lehre Spinozas* (Breslau: Schletter, 1871) and by D. Neumark in "Crescas and Spinoza," in *Essays in Jewish Philosophy* (Cincinnati, OH, 1929). For a full bibliography, see *Encyclopedia Judaica* (Berlin: Eschkol, 1928), Vol. V, pp. 698ff., 708.

Frank Talmage (1967)

CRESCAS, HASDAI [ADDENDUM]

Hasdai Crescas takes a radical anti-Aristotelian position, and yet he himself presents conclusions that are threatening to the traditional understanding of religion. For example, in attacking the views on the creation of the world by Maimonides and Gersonides he ends up presenting a theory that allows for an eternal world. The world could be eternal in the sense that it would be eternally dependent on God. According to Crescas there is no difficulty about the existence of a vacuum before the creation of the world, and so it is no good objecting to Aristotle that something could not come from nothing. He even contemplates the possibility of this world being only one of a number of worlds, each existing along with the others.

Crescas is unusual also in accepting the existence of the infinite, a concept that many Aristotelians think suggests an absurdity, and the discovery of which is taken by Aristotelians to indicate an impossibility in the argument. The concept of infinity allows Crescas to envisage an infinite space in which a vast variety of worlds could exist.

Still, the qualms about infinity that his predecessors held had allowed them to argue for the necessity of a first cause, since otherwise the series of causes and effects would continue infinitely. Crescas's attack on Aristotle led him to propose a range of ideas and arguments that were to play a major part in the acceptance of new ways of thinking not only in philosophy but also in science.

Bibliography

Frank, Daniel H., and Oliver Leaman. *History of Jewish Philosophy*. London: Routledge, 1997.

Kellner, Menachem. *Dogma in Medieval Jewish Thought: From Maimonides to Abravanel*. New York: Oxford University Press, 1986.

WORKS BY CRESCAS

"Or Adonai (Light of the Lord)." In *With Perfect Faith: The Foundations of Jewish Belief*, edited by J. David Bleich. New York: Ktav, 1983.

The Refutation of Christian Principles by Hasdai Crescas. Translated by Daniel J. Lasker. Albany: SUNY Press, 1992.

WORKS ON CRESCAS

Robinson, James T. "Hasdai Crescas and Anti-Aristotelianism." In *Cambridge Companion to Medieval Jewish Philosophy*, edited by Daniel H. Frank and Oliver Leaman. New York: Cambridge University Press, 2003.

Oliver Leaman (2005)

CRITERIOLOGY

"Science of criteria" or "criteriology" is a term, originally neoscholastic, for a theory of knowledge in which judgments are warranted or justified simply by conforming to certain criteria for correct judgment. These criteria are general principles that specify what sorts of considerations ultimately confer warrant on some judgments and that tend (tacitly) to guide self-reflective persons in checking and correcting their judgments. The epistemologist's task is to formulate these principles by reflecting on the considerations present and absent in various judgments we intuitively think of as warranted and unwarranted.

Different criteria may deal with different subject matters, degrees, and sources of warrant (e.g., in perception, memory, inference). Ultimately, there must be warranting considerations other than inferability from other warranted judgments. These must be internally accessible through introspection or reflection without relying on further warranted judgments. They will not be considerations such as whether nature designed us to be reliable judges but ones such as whether we ostensibly see or recall something or intuitively grasp or clearly and distinctly conceive something.

Many epistemologists argue that critical considerations need not guarantee truth or confer certainty, and whatever warrant they confer may be defeated. For instance, if one ostensibly sees something red, one is prima facie or defeasibly warranted in judging that one actually sees something red. The judgment might not be warranted when, despite ostensibly seeing something red, one has evidence that the illumination makes everything look red. We need additional principles specifying what considerations defeat warrant.

However, if criterial considerations do not guarantee truth, what makes a set of principles genuinely warranting? Putative common contingent features such as their overall reliability rest warrant on something beyond mere conformity to these principles and may allow for alternative principles. Criteriologists (e.g., Pollock 1974, 1986) often appeal to controversial, nonscholastic, views about concepts and truth influenced by Ludwig Wittgenstein. Criteria are internalized norms (rules) about when to make and correct judgments ascribing a concept. They characterize what persons must, in order to have a particular concept, tacitly know how to do in their judging and reasoning and be tacitly guided by. Criteria individuate our concepts and thus are necessarily correct. Although warranted judgments need not be true, we have no idea of their truth completely divorced from what undefeated criterial considerations warrant. Critics often respond: Surely this norm conformity must have a purpose beyond itself, like accurately representing the world?

See also Epistemology; Wittgenstein, Ludwig Josef Johann.

Bibliography

CRITERIOLOGIES

Coffey, P. *Epistemology or the Theory of Knowledge: An Introduction to General Metaphysics.* 2 vols. London: Longmans Green, 1917.

Pollock, John. *Contemporary Theories of Knowledge*. Totowa, NJ: Rowman & Littlefield, 1986; 2nd ed. (with J. Cruz), 1999.

Pollock, John. *Knowledge and Justification*. Princeton, NJ: Princeton University Press, 1974.

CRITICAL DISCUSSIONS

Lycan, W. G. "Non-inductive Evidence: Recent Work on Wittgenstein's 'Criteria.'" *American Philosophical Quarterly* 8 (1971): 109–125.

Millikan, R. "Truth Rules, Hoverflies, and the Kripke-Wittgenstein Paradox." *Philosophical Review* 99 (1990): 323–353.

Plantinga, A. *Warrant: The Current Debate*. New York: Oxford University Press, 1993.

Wright, C. J. G. "Second Thoughts about Criteria." *Synthese* 58 (1984): 383–405.

Bruce Hunter (1996)
Bibliography updated by Benjamin Fiedor (2005)

CRITICAL PHILOSOPHY

See *Kant, Immanuel; Neo-Kantiansim*

CRITICAL REALISM

Critical Realism is the title of a book by Roy W. Sellars published in 1916. The name was adopted by a group of philosophers who shared many of his views on the theory of knowledge. *Essays in Critical Realism: A Cooperative Study of the Problem of Knowledge* by Durant Drake, A. O. Lovejoy, J. B. Pratt, A. K. Rogers, George Santayana, C. A. Strong, and Sellars was published in 1920.

BACKGROUND

Much of the epistemological debate since the seventeenth century stems from the matter-mind dualism of René Descartes, who argued that what we know first and most surely is not a physical world but the existence of our own minds, and of John Locke, who argued that we are immediately acquainted only with our own ideas. Starting from these assumptions, how can one know a physical world external to the mind, if, indeed, such a world exists at all? Critical Realism is a chapter in this long debate. Some philosophers, finding it impossible to bridge the gap from a mental world to a material reality that transcends it, turned to some form of subjectivism or idealism; at the beginning of the twentieth century the dominant philosophy in Britain was the Neo-Hegelian idealism of F. H. Bradley and Bernard Bosanquet, and in America it was the voluntarism of Josiah Royce, the personalism of George H. Howison and Borden Parker Bowne, or the pragmatism of William James. But idealism, uncongenial to common sense and to ordinary interpretations of physical science, was followed by a reaction. Scientific knowledge seemed to support philosophical realism rather than idealism.

Shortly before the emergence of Critical Realism a group of philosophers, calling their view the New Realism, argued that even if it is true that whenever something is being perceived, it is an object for a mind, it does not follow that it has no existence except by being perceived. Hence, the idealist commits a fallacy if he concludes that the whole world is nothing but ideas from the truism that when something is known, it is an object for a mind. The American new realists, then—and here they could claim the support of such important British thinkers as G. E. Moore and Bertrand Russell—maintained that elements in perception can at the same time be elements in the physical world. Things do not cause ideas in us, as Locke would have said, so that we first know only ideas and then try to infer from them the nature of the real world which is never directly perceived. Rather, knowing is more akin to selecting, or throwing a light upon, aspects or parts of a world already there to be selected or illuminated by the light of consciousness.

THE CRITICAL REALIST POSITION

The critical realist agrees with the new realist in holding that there is an objective physical world; their disagreement is chiefly on the question of the relation of the datum of knowledge to its object. Physical things, or parts of them, cannot be directly presented to us in perception. Considering the great variety of what is perceived—the double image, the partially submerged bent stick, the toe that is felt after the leg has been amputated—under various conditions by both normal persons and those who are, for example, inebriated or color-blind, are we to say that the real world actually contains all that is disclosed in all these circumstances? And is there no such thing as error? The trouble is that the "direct" realist, by identifying the immediate data of knowledge with elements of the physical world, is trying to account for the universe with an insufficient number of categories or kinds of entities. The knower, whether he is conceived as an organism and a part of nature or as a mind, does not "take in" the physical world. According to Santayana, the datum is an essence, a Platonic universal, which has an identity by being just the character it is, whether it characterizes one or many things in nature or characterizes no existent whatsoever. The datum, the immediately intuited evidence of reality, cannot be numerically identical with any part of that reality.

It is on this epistemological point that the critical realist opposes both the idealist and the direct realist. Whatever exists and whatever its character may be, no datum, or essence, given in experience exists, at least not in the sense in which we say that the objects of perception exist. As Santayana says in *Scepticism and Animal Faith*, "Existence is never given." When the astronomer talks about the moon, he does not mean by "the moon" the yellow disk image that may come to your mind; no doubt, a different image will come to the mind of your companion. If both of you understand the astronomer, "the moon" will mean to both of you, and to the astronomer, the same object to which your thoughts or perceptions are referred—namely, the distant satellite of Earth to which you ascribe certain physical properties. The words or images are the symbols of a meaning, but the essence of the word or image is not, in general, the essence of its meaning. The essence of the meaning is intended to be, but in cases of error will not be, the essence of the actual moon in the sky. This distinction, perhaps difference, between the nature of an image or sense datum and the nature of the object known by means of it is still more obvious when we consider feelings instead of visual images. When sympathizing with a person who has a toothache, we do not say, "I feel the way you feel"; we say, "I know how you feel." Knowing about another person's toothache is not having a toothache.

In perception, as distinguished from thought or conception, there is a tendency to identify image with meaning, so that an effort of analysis is required to separate image, meaning, and object. Paradoxically, the meaning is often psychologically prior to the image. For example, we may perceive a penny as round and as "out there" before noting that in the given perspective it presents an elliptical image. We can then analyze the situation into the image (elliptical), the meaning (round), and the belief that a round object was out there. Error is possible because there may be no object having the same essence as that contemplated in the meaning we have given to the elliptical image that was presented to us. A resolute skeptic who doubts all existence cannot be proved to be mistaken, but if he is consistent, he should be as skeptical of the existence of other minds and even of his own living self as he is of a physical world. Since the idea of change is no guarantee of actual change or process, he should arrive at an inarticulate solipsism of the present moment.

Yet there is no doubt that philosophers as well as laypeople normally believe in the existence of themselves and other minds and ascribe at least some of the characters they intuit to things that exist in space at present or past times. In memory and in the belief in history, the referent of present thoughts is a world of things and events believed to be existentially real and independent of any intuitions, present or past. An actual past or future is not given in any datum, but when one speaks, as David Hume did, of having or of being a succession of perceptions, one posits the existence of a temporal series of events and thereby instantiates in existence one or more essences. To ascribe existence to an essence as such would be a logical or categorial error; it would equally be a logical error to assert that an essence had been intuited by some mind or that some event or perception had occurred and at the same time deny that there is any factual temporal existence. The ontological status proper to essences is timeless subsistence. Actual intuitions come to exist on particular occasions, but knowledge of what they mean, says Santayana, "involves a leap of faith and action from the symbol actually given in sense or thought, to some ulterior existing object."

In *Essays in Critical Realism* Santayana argued that a child reaching for the moon is in quest of an object deployed in a physical world along with the outstretched arm and other bodies. If the moon did not transcend experience, if what is experienced were itself the object striven for, it would already be attained, and there would be no biological need to employ the presently intuited essence as a symbol for an existence still to be reached. There would be no knowledge about anything nor any need for it. If there is any validity in our scientific and commonsense beliefs, our intuitions are engendered in a biological organism by a natural environment. Matter in flux embodies now one essence, now another, and the set of propositions that describes all that exists at all times constitutes the realm of truth. Truth is therefore that part of the realm of essence that happens to characterize existence, and to have knowledge is to believe what is true.

But believing a proposition does not guarantee its truth, beyond the truth of the fact that it is believed. The terms of our beliefs are, in general, symbolic rather than literal representations of nature. Does it make any difference, then, if we clothe nature with intuited essences that are more fanciful than true as long as they are signals for successful action? If a pragmatist at this point suggests that truth means no more than the verification in later experience of the anticipated result of action guided by the earlier experience, the realist cannot agree. The pragmatist does agree with the realist that in knowing there is a reference beyond the immediate having of perceptions, but for the pragmatist the consummation of knowing, the successful working of an idea, does not go beyond experience; the referent of an idea is another experience. This avoids the problems of a mind-matter dualism and avoids the unanswerable question: How can we know when our ideas correctly represent external things? But the realist sees the pragmatist position as a reversion to idealism and subjectivism and will have none of it. If the pragmatist, to escape idealism, speaks in naturalistic terms, he admits all that the realist asks for. Lovejoy quotes William James: "Practically our minds meet in a world of objects which they share in common" (*Essays in Radical Empiricism*, New York, 1912, p. 79) to show that the practical man, going about his business of solving problems, must assume the existence of an external world; it is important that he discover what its properties were antecedent to and independent of the inquiry in which that discovery is made. Phenomenalism and positivism, sharing with pragmatism the view that the referent of all that can be meaningfully said about real existence must be, in principle, capable of being found in direct experience, are likewise rejected by the critical realist.

How, then, is knowledge of an external reality possible? The critical realist maintains that Locke erred in taking his own ideas to be the objects of knowledge. Knowledge, Locke said, is nothing but the perception of the agreement or disagreement of our ideas. When he comes to a discussion of "knowledge of real existence," however, he is forced to abandon his own definition, and true knowledge becomes the correspondence between ideas and external things. The critical realist argues that Locke should have recognized that when ideas are used in knowing, as distinguished from being merely entertained or had as an experience, there is always reference to an object other than themselves. But merely insisting that data have a referent beyond themselves does not tell us why we should believe one interpretation of them to be a truer description of the facts than any other interpretation. In his more skeptical mood Santayana tells us that knowledge is only faith mediated by symbols, yet in *The Realm of Matter* he sets forth what he takes to be the "indispensable properties of substance." Presumably, he means literally true properties. Substance has parts external to one another and, being in flux and unequally distributed, constitutes a spatial and temporal field of action. These are very nearly those primary qualities that Locke had said resemble the ideas the mind has of them, and if the critical realist seems to have a better case for his position than Locke had, it is chiefly because the sciences have supplied us with a detailed account of the mechanism of perception.

The scientist finds by actual experiment that the date of emission of light from the star, the distorting intervening media between the star and the observer, and the physiological peculiarities of the observer's body all condition what turns up at what time in the experience of the observer. But this scientific account cannot be used by the critical realist to support his position without begging the question. What is proved is that whenever something is found in our world, we can also find something else related to it; scientific knowledge consists of finding what is related to what. This supports the critical realist's thesis that experience depends upon a reality outside all possible experience only if it is assumed from the outset that the experimental data used by the astronomer and by the physiologist are experienced effects of a physical star and a physical organism. The scientist could interpret his explanatory theories on idealist or pragmatist, instead of on critical realist, assumptions. Hence, it is not what the scientist finds, but the epistemology he happens to assume, that supports critical realism. The best that can be said for this realist assumption is that it may be the most economical way to predict and control our experiences and that it may even be the truth about reality.

DIFFERENCES AMONG CRITICAL REALISTS

Some of the critical realists, including Sellars, believe that their position is not best interpreted, even by some within their own camp, when a curtain of essences, ideas, or sense data is drawn between the perceiver and the objects he wants to know by means of such data. For in that case, as in Locke's representative perception theory, the essences or ideas are themselves the only possible objects of knowledge. Sellars would escape this difficulty by what he believes to be a more adequate account of perceiving. When a biological organism has sensations—that is, is affected by an object in the environment with which it must come to terms—the sensation functions as information about the object that caused it. Perception is a response; it is an act of taking the sensation as the appearance of the external object. It is not the sensation or the sense datum that appears; it is by means of the sensation that the object appears. A sophisticated analyst might make the qualities of the sensation the object of his study, but then he is no longer using them to decipher things.

Sellars finds an ally in the English philosopher Gilbert Ryle, who follows common sense in the belief that we perceive trees and hands, not sense data. Here it would seem that Sellars has left the critical realists to join the direct realists, but he would insist that he is not taking either a direct presentational view or a Lockean representational view. The mediating role of sensation, which determines how the object will look, is not to be ignored. We look *with* our sensations but not *at* them.

In addition to some differences about the role of essences and of sense data, the critical realists are not all in accord on questions of metaphysics. Sellars and Santayana could be called metaphysical monists because for them only one kind of substance—matter—exists. The psyche of which Santayana speaks is the conscious material organism. Sellars thinks of the so-called mental functions not as being carried on by a substantial mind but as ways in which biological organisms, after a long evolutionary development, have learned to respond to stimuli.

Lovejoy, on the other hand, maintains that only a psychophysical dualism is a tenable corollary of an epistemological dualism; only a mind could have sensations and thoughts and intend or mean objects by them.

There has, then, been considerable divergence in the views of thinkers who were, and many who still are, called critical realists. Some have drawn closer to the positions of the direct realists in America or in Britain, and it may be that the label will cease to characterize a definite epistemology.

Bibliography

Boyd, Richard. "Scientific Realism and Naturalistic Epistemology." In *PSA 1980: Proceedings of the 1980 Biennial Meeting of the Philosophy of Science Association*. Vol. 2, edited by Peter D. Asquith and Ronald N. Giere, 613–662. East Lansing, MI: Philosophy of Science Association, 1982.

Chisholm, Roderick. *Perceiving: A Philosophical Study*. Ithaca, NY: Cornell University Press, 1957.

Churchland, Paul M. *Scientific Realism and the Plasticity of Mind*. Cambridge, U.K.: Cambridge University Press, 1979.

Drake, Durant. *Mind and Its Place in Nature*. New York: Macmillan, 1925.

Drake, Durant et al. *Essays in Critical Realism: A Cooperative Study of the Problem of Knowledge*. London, 1920.

Dretske, Fred. *Seeing and Knowing*. London: Routledge and Kegan Paul, 1969.

Goldman, Alan. *Empirical Knowledge*. Berkeley: University of California Press, 1989.

Haack, Susan. *Evidence and Inquiry: Towards Reconstruction in Epistemology*. Oxford: Blackwell, 1993.

Hanley, Richard. "Much Ado about Nothing: Critical Realism Examined." *Philosophical Studies* 115 (2) (2003): 123–147.

Kulp, Christopher, ed. *Realism/Antirealism and Epistemology*. Lanham, MD: Rowman & Littlefield, 1997.

Lovejoy, A. O. *The Revolt against Dualism*. New York: Norton, 1930.

Moser, Paul K. *Knowledge and Evidence*. New York: Cambridge Unversity Press, 1989.

Murphy, A. E. "The Fruits of Critical Realism." *Journal of Philosophy* 34 (1937): 281–292.

Pratt, J. B. *Personal Realism*. New York: Macmillan, 1937.

Quinton, Anthony. *The Nature of Things*. London: Routledge and Kegan Paul, 1977.

Santayana, George. *Realms of Being*. 4 vols. New York: Scribners, 1927–1940.

Santayana, George. *Scepticism and Animal Faith*. New York: Scribners, 1923.

Schilpp, Paul A., ed. *The Philosophy of George Santayana*. Evanston, IL: Northwestern University, 1940.

Sellars, Roy W. "American Critical Realism and British Theories of Sense Perception." *Methodos* 14 (55–56) (1962): 61–108.

Sellars, Roy W. *Critical Realism*. Chicago: Rand, McNally 1916.

Sellars, Roy W. *The Philosophy of Physical Realism*. New York: Macmillan, 1932.

Sellars, Wilfrid. *Science, Perception, and Reality*. Atascadero, CA: Ridgeview Press, 1991.

A. G. Ramsperger (1967)
Bibliography updated by Benjamin Fiedor (2005)

CRITICAL THEORY

"Critical theory" is used to refer to the diverse body of work produced by members and associates of the Frankfurt Institute for Social Research after Max Horkheimer became its director in 1930. The first generation of what came to be called the Frankfurt school included, in addition to Horkheimer, such prominent figures as Theodor Adorno, Herbert Marcuse, Walter Benjamin, Erich Fromm, Leo Löwenthal, Franz Neumann, Otto Kirchheimer, and Frederick Pollock. The most influential members of the second generation are Jürgen Habermas, Karl-Otto Apel, and Albrecht Wellmer. As the variety of backgrounds and interests might suggest, critical social theory was conceived as a multidisciplinary program linking philosophy to history and the human sciences in a kind of "philosophically oriented social inquiry," as Horkheimer put it. Though very strongly influenced by Immanuel Kant and neo-Kantianism, Georg Wilhelm Friedrich Hegel and German idealism, Max Weber and Sigmund Freud, it was understood as a renewal of Marxism inspired in part by the earlier work of Georg Lukács and Karl Korsch. This updated Marxism would take account of the altered historical realities of advanced capitalism and integrate areas of inquiry neglected by traditional Marxism, such as philosophy and political theory, cultural studies (including studies of mass culture), and social psychology (appropriating psychoanalysis for social theory). With the rise of National Socialism, the institute moved briefly to Geneva and Paris in 1933 and then in 1934 to Columbia University in New York, where its journal, the *Zeitschrift für Sozialforschung,* continued to be published until 1941, the last volume in English. Early in the 1950s, Horkheimer and Adorno reestablished the institute in Frankfurt. Habermas became an assistant there in 1955.

The original project of a critical social theory advanced by Horkheimer was a version of Karl Marx's *Aufhebung* of philosophy in social theory and practice. Philosophy was to become a sociohistorical, practically oriented critique of reason and its claimed realizations. While the dominant forms of reason were often distorted in the interests of dominant classes, the aim of critical theory was, not simply to negate them, but, by examining their genesis and functions, to transform them and enlist them in the struggle for a better world. The insistence on the "truth content" of the "bourgeois ideals" of freedom, truth, and justice, the refusal to abandon them as mere ideology, was severely tested by the horrors of World War II. Early in the 1940s, in their collaborative reflections on the "dialectic of enlightenment," Horkheimer and Adorno offered a much more pessimistic view of the history of reason. Keying on a tendency that Weber had emphasized, the relentless spread of "instrumental" rationality, they revered Marx's positive evaluation of scientific-technological progress. It was now seen as the core of a domination that had spread to all spheres of life and, in the process, had immobilized the potential agents of social change. In this "totally administered society" with what Marcuse later called its "one-dimensional man," critical theory could at best reveal the unreason at the heart of what passed for reason, without offering any positive account of its own.

Habermas's work since the 1960s might be viewed as an attempt to avoid this impasse by introducing into critical theory a fundamental shift in paradigms from the philosophy of the subject to the theory of communication and from means-ends rationality to communicative rationality. This serves as the basis for an altered diagnosis of the ills of modernity—as rooted, not in rationalization as such, but in a one-sided rationalization driven by economic and administrative forces—and an altered prescription for their cure, the democratization of public opinion and will formation in an effectively functioning public sphere, where issues of general concern are submitted to rational, critical public debate.

See also Adorno, Theodor; Apel, Karl-Otto; Benjamin, Walter; Freud, Sigmund; Habermas, Jürgen; Hegel, Georg Wilhelm Friedrich; Horkheimer, Max; Kant, Immanuel; Lukács, Georg; Marxist Philosophy; Marx, Karl; Neo-Kantianism; Weber, Max.

Bibliography

Arato, A., and E. Gebhardt, eds. *The Essential Frankfurt School Reader.* New York: Urizen Books, 1978.

Bronner, S., and D. Kellner, eds. *Critical Theory and Society: A Reader.* New York: Routledge, 1989.

Ingram, D., and J. Simon-Ingram, eds. *Critical Theory: The Essential Readings.* New York: Paragon House, 1992.

Jay, M. *The Dialectical Imagination.* Boston: Little Brown, 1973.

Wiggershaus, R. *The Frankfurt School.* Translated by M. Robertson. Cambridge, MA: MIT Press, 1994.

Thomas McCarthy (1996)

CROCE, BENEDETTO

(1866–1952)

Benedetto Croce was the best-known Italian philosopher of the twentieth century. His universally and justly celebrated book on aesthetics, *Estetica come scienza dell'espressione e linguistica generale* (1902), which became the first volume of his systematic "philosophy of the spirit," was a foundation stone in the great revival of historical idealism in Italy between 1900 and 1920. In a long and diligent life devoted almost entirely to scholarly studies, Croce gained an international reputation in the fields of aesthetics, literary criticism, cultural history, and historical methodology; and he exercised in these areas an influence so pervasive that it cannot yet be definitively estimated.

LIFE AND WORKS

Born at Pescasseroli, in the Abruzzi, of a family of wealthy landowners, Croce never needed to earn a living. He displayed an early bent for literary and historical research but never seriously entered on an academic career, preferring to be master of his own course of study. From 1883—when his parents were killed, and he himself buried and injured, in an earthquake—until 1886 he lived with his uncle Silvio Spaventa (brother of the philosopher Bertrando) in Rome, and for a time he attended the university there. At the university he came under the influence of Antonio Labriola, who led him to the study of Johann Friedrich Herbart and, later, of Karl Marx. These studies left a lasting mark on his philosophy. After 1886 he lived permanently in Naples.

In 1893 Croce published his first philosophical essay, "La storia ridotto sotto il concetto generale dell'arte"

(History brought under the general concept of art), a title that foreshadowed the main concerns of his mature thought. In 1898, while working on a book on Marx (*Materialismo storico ed economia marxista*), he entered into correspondence with his younger contemporary, Giovanni Gentile, who was similarly occupied. Thus began a friendly collaboration that lasted twenty-five years. In 1900 came the first sketch of Croce's *Aesthetic.* In 1903 he founded the journal *La critica,* and in 1904 he became an editorial adviser to the publishers Laterza of Bari. For the rest of his life he exercised an ever-increasing influence on the literary and academic world through these two channels.

Even as the volumes of Croce's philosophy of spirit were being published, his association with Gentile was leading him to a reexamination of G. W. F. Hegel. He published his results in 1907 (*Ciò che è vivo e ciò che è morto nella filosofia di Hegel*) and made appropriate revisions in his *Estetica* and in his *Logica come scienza del concetto puro* (1905). *Filosofia della pratica, economia ed etica* appeared at Bari in 1909. In 1911 he published *La filosofia di Giambattista Vico*—Giambattista Vico was the other major influence on his thought—and in the succeeding years he wrote the essays that appeared at Bari in 1917 as the culminating volume of his system, *Teoria e storia della storiografia.*

In 1910 Croce was made a life member of the Italian senate, but he was not then actively involved in politics. He was a neutralist prior to Italy's entry into World War I in 1915; and in the postwar crisis, he became minister of public instruction in Giovanni Giolitti's last cabinet (1920–1921). With Gentile's help, Croce drafted a reform of the school system, rejected at the time but later incorporated in the fascist *Riforma Gentile* of 1923–1924. Naturally, therefore, he regarded the first fascist administration with some benevolence. His breach with fascism (and with Gentile) came with the establishment of an overt dictatorship in January 1925. He drafted a celebrated "Protest" against Gentile's "Manifesto of Fascist Intellectuals" and thus became identified as the chief antifascist intellectual, a role he worthily maintained through more than fifteen years of almost complete political isolation and retirement. He emerged briefly in 1929 to speak in the senate against the concordat with the Vatican. After the fall of fascism he became a leader of the revived Liberal Party and served once more as a cabinet minister for a short period in 1944.

During his years of isolation, Croce wrote voluminously and his thought developed significantly. His aesthetics reached its final form only in *La poesia* (1936). His opposition to fascism is often apparent in his literary criticism, but it expressed itself more naturally in his historical writing and in theoretical reflection on politics and history, where it led to vital developments in his thought.

Croce celebrated his eightieth birthday by founding and endowing the Institute for Historical Studies, which is still located in his former home. In spite of a serious stroke in 1950, he went on working right up to his death.

AESTHETICS

When Croce's philosophical interests were first aroused in 1893, he was a historical and literary scholar who accepted most of the assumptions of the French positivism then dominant in the circles in which he moved. But controversy led him to ask himself whether history was an art or a science, and he made a decisive choice in favor of the idealist view of the great Hegelian philosopher of art and literary historian Francesco De Sanctis (1817–1883). Initially, his idealist aesthetics was set in a context of a realistic metaphysics, of which there were still some signs in the *Aesthetic* of 1902; but the attempt to expound his view systematically, combined with his discovery of Vico and rediscovery of Hegel, led to the development of his full-fledged idealism. Thus, his aesthetic theory was the original foundation of his philosophy of spirit, although it might fairly be argued that the theory of moral judgment became more fundamental in the final form of his system. Croce himself distinguished four phases in his reflections on aesthetics. Some critics have held one or more of the later phases to be inconsistent with his system as a whole, but they will here be viewed as part of a continuous and essentially consistent evolution.

AESTHETIC INTUITION. It is characteristic of idealist aesthetics to regard aesthetic experience as a kind of cognition. Following Vico and De Sanctis, Croce regarded it as the primitive form of cognitive experience. Intuition is a nonconceptual form of knowledge; it is the awareness of a particular image either of outward sense (a person or a thing) or of inner sense (an emotion or a mood). Intuitions possess a kind of ideal being and validity that is independent of and ontologically prior to any question of existence or nonexistence. Croce's use of the term *intuition* derived directly from Immanuel Kant's use of *Anschauung,* and he originally thought of the external world as a Kantian manifold of sensation, which we organize into distinct perceptions through the intuitive faculty of imagination. Thus, history was initially "subsumed under the general concept of Art," as the subform of art that is concerned with the ordering of intuitions of actual existence. He soon abandoned this position, but if Kant's theory of space and time as the "forms of intuition" through which the sensible manifold is organized is recalled, it can be seen how Croce's view applies to the plastic arts, which he often seemed to ignore. His own background and interests were predominantly literary, and his theory frequently seems specifically devised to meet the needs of literary critics who have to deal with poems, which are uniquely individual entities created in the conceptual (or logically universal) medium of language. Croce himself fostered this illusion by insisting that aesthetics was "the general science of language." This is a very Pickwickian contention on his part, since the conceptual function of words and symbols in factual communication—which must surely be regarded as fundamental in a general theory of *language*—is specifically excluded from his "science of expression"; and all forms of nonconceptual communication—even nonverbal ones—are included in it.

LYRICAL INTUITION. If it had not been for his overriding concern with poetry, Croce might never have advanced to the second phase of his aesthetics, the theory that all intuition is "lyrical" in character. The problem he faced was essentially one of defining what it is that is nonconceptually communicated in poetry by way of language. His answer was that poetry communicates emotions and moods, it expresses for cognitive contemplation different aspects of the practical personality of man. Here the "circle of the spirit," the doctrine that man's theoretical activity has his practical reality as its one and only object, comes into view. By means of this doctrine, Croce was able to dispense with the last residues of naive realism present in his basically Kantian epistemology. Some doctrine of this sort was certainly needed if the view that art is nonconceptual cognition was to be maintained. As Croce said in 1908, in his lecture announcing the doctrine, "An image that does not express a state of mind has no theoretical value." But the need might well have appeared less pressing, and the solution less natural and obvious, if he had not always thought primarily about poetry.

It is easy—especially if one reads only the *Breviary of Aesthetics* (1912), as many English-speaking students do—to misinterpret Croce's theory that all art is lyrical as a type of romanticism, which he was, in fact, absolutely opposed to. His doctrine was that art is the expression of emotion, not just for its own sake but as a special kind of cognitive awareness. He was seeking a middle way between the intellectualist errors of classical theorists, with their artificial canons, rules, and genres (all of which he categorically rejected), and the emotional excesses of the romantics, with their glorification of immediate feeling. His critique of classical intellectualism is easily grasped; but it is a mistake to think, as some critics have, that his "lyricism" is radically inconsistent with his own systematic rationalism. Unlike Gentile, Croce always refused to identify intuitions as "feelings" or to formulate his theory in terms of "feeling" at all, because he held that "feeling" was an ambiguous concept which when clarified referred to the practical impulse that is the content of intuition.

COSMIC INTUITIONS. How can the expression of emotion produce cognitive awareness? This was the problem that Croce faced in the third phase of his thought—his theory that all intuition has a "cosmic" aspect. Again, some doctrine of the sort was required by his basic thesis that intuition is cognitive of particulars without reference to their existential status. Simply as images they provide experience of the universal human spirit. This self-validating character, this reference to universal humanity (not as an abstract nature or essence but as the activity of the spirit revealing itself in personal experience and in history as a whole) is what Croce called the cosmic aspect of genuine intuition. Some intuitions, however, are more directly cosmic than others and are hard to characterize in terms of specific emotions; this was the classical counterweight against lyrical romanticism in Croce's thought. It was apparently suggested to him by an essay of Wilhelm von Humboldt on Johann Wolfgang von Goethe, and he applied it in critical studies of such masterpieces as *Faust* and the *Divine Comedy.* Oddly enough, however, it was neither Dante Alighieri nor Goethe, but Ariosto, who served as Croce's paradigm of the cosmic poet. Croce earnestly desired to avoid confusion between the proper lyrical unity of a poem and the logical coherence of a philosophical system. His own critical practice even provides some justification for the view that the whole cosmic phase of his theory was an aberration. The truth is rather that it was an inescapably necessary complement of his general view and that his critical practice suffered from an antiphilosophical bias.

LITERATURE AND ART. The final phase of Croce's aesthetic theory is the theory of literature in *La poesia,* which forms the negative corollary of his theory of intuition. Much that is ordinarily classified as art was, in Croce's view, not properly art at all because in it the purity of intuitive cognition is subordinated to various practical ends, such as entertainment or intellectual and moral instruction. For instance, he declared the *De Rerum*

Natura to be a work of literature, not of art; and although this is an extreme case of his critical bias, it is easy to see what led him to it, since the passionate conviction and practical aim of Lucretius are evident in every line of the poem.

LOGIC OF HISTORY AND THE SCIENCES

As aesthetics is the science of pure intuition, so logic is the science of pure concept; and as pure intuition is the form in which we imaginatively express some particular aspect of the human spirit, so pure conception is the form in which we rationally evaluate these particular manifestations and relate them to one another and to the spirit as a systematic unity. Thus on the one hand, conceptual cognition presupposes intuition because it requires intuitions as its material; and on the other hand, aesthetics, the science of intuitive cognition, is only a subdivision of logic because beauty is a form of the pure concept. Concepts presuppose intuitions but are not derivable from them; and any evaluation or correlation of intuitions—even the categorizing of them as intuitions—presupposes concepts. This is the "dialectic of the distincts," which Croce insisted was more ultimate and fundamental than the Hegelian dialectic of opposites. His model here was Kant, rather than the often-cited Vico. For Vico, as for Hegel, poetic cognition was already an immature form of reason, or, in other words, reason develops out of it; whereas for Croce, as for Kant, the two functions were quite distinct and interdependent, although not equally primitive. Croce's aesthetics was a new transcendental analytic, and his logic was a new deduction of the categories.

KNOWLEDGE. For Croce, however, the words *reason* and *knowledge* meant something very different from what they meant to Kant. Croce's work was a "critique of historical reason," and the knowledge that he regarded as genuine was historical knowledge. It is only to historical judgments that the predicates "true" and "false" are properly applicable. According to Croce, the scientific knowledge of Kant's *Critique* was a myth, and belief in this myth was one type of logical error. (Croce offered an exhaustive analysis of the types of logical error as a sort of negative proof of his own deduction.) Science and scientific investigation are forms of practical activity, not of cognition. They cannot be genuinely cognitive because they are founded on pseudo concepts, not on the genuine forms of the pure concept.

Thus, for example, if a child reports that "the cat is on the mat," this is a statement of historical fact and its truth or falsity can be established. But if a scientist says, "The cat is a mammal with such and such properties," the words *cat* and *mammal,* together with all the property-terms, are abstract universals, artificial summaries of actual aesthetic and historical experience. These abstractions are enormously useful in practical experience—indeed, they are vital to the intelligent planning of our lives—but they could only be the basis of genuine knowledge if we were endowed with the kind of rational intuition into the "real essences" of things that is described in Plato's myths.

The forms of the pure concept are the distinct forms of the spirit itself, since only a proof that some form of the spirit is "distinct" in Croce's sense could establish the a priori validity of a proposed category or standard of judgment. There are four such forms and, hence, four ways in which our experience can be cognitively categorized and evaluated. Any proper element of experience can be considered from two theoretical and two practical points of view; it can be evaluated intuitively, rationally, economically, or morally.

ERROR. In his theory of error, Croce followed René Descartes and Antonio Rosmini. He regarded all genuine error as caused by the intrusion of practical motives into theoretical contexts. He was primarily concerned with philosophical errors, such as the belief that science is knowledge or the belief in myth (a historical narrative possessing absolute significance), which he took to be the origin of religion. About mistakes in historical interpretation, his view appears to have been that (if the historian advances his hypotheses in a properly tentative spirit) they are not really errors but stages in the development of truth.

PHILOSOPHY AND HISTORY. Under the influence of Gentile, Croce accepted the Hegelian identification of philosophy with the history of philosophy and reduced even the a priori judgments of his own logic (for example, that there are four forms of the spirit) to the status of historical judgments. He did this because he held that no one could "close the gates of truth" against further progress. Yet he never accepted Gentile's view that this formal concession to the future meant that all deductions of "the forms of the spirit" were mistaken; he remained convinced that his logic possessed an eternal validity. In his view, the unity of philosophy and history was a unity of distincts.

ECONOMICS AND LAW

The most fundamental of all distinctions in Croce's philosophy is the distinction between theory and practice. Goaded by the actual idealists who sought to unify theory and practice in the "pure act," Croce tried to justify this distinction by arguments that were largely wasted, because his opponents did not really deny the distinction any more than he denied the unity. The only point at issue was the more general question of whether the unity arose from a dialectic of opposed moments or of distinct forms.

ECONOMIC UTILITY AND VITALITY. It has already been shown how the circle of the spirit first appeared when Croce recognized practical impulse as the presupposed content of intuition. It would seem to follow that the practical manifestation of the spirit is somehow more primitive than the spirit's theoretical functions; but the implication is, at best, only a partial truth, for Croce claimed also that the primitive form of practical activity—economic volition—presupposes both forms of theoretical activity. He had learned from his long study of Marx and of the English classical economists that the calculation of economic utility is a rational process and that economic action involves historical judgment. The practical impulse that intuition presupposes, considered in itself, is not yet the conscious action of the spirit; it is only the blind urge of organic life out of which the spirit emerges. But the origin of volition in vitality is what accounts for the independence that Croce always ascribed to economic utility as a distinct spiritual form. Critics objected from the beginning that there was a paradox involved in treating utility as an autonomous form of value. There is no such thing as simple usefulness; there is only usefulness for some purpose. It is really life or vitality that is the primitive category of action. In later writings Croce recognized this, but he continued to hold that economic action is the first form of action in the true sense.

In spite of Croce's insistence that the "utility" of the economists is a fundamental philosophical category, his logic does not allow the admission of economics itself as a genuine philosophical science. The work of economists, like that of all other scientists, belongs to the category of utility itself, not to that of truth. "Economic man" is a paradigm case of a pseudo concept.

LAW AND UTILITY. It is more surprising, perhaps, to find the concept of law subsumed under that of utility in Croce's system. The Kantian model, which we have appealed to several times, might lead us to expect moral law as the universal form of practical consciousness. Law in fact functions as a transitional notion in Croce's system because it may be obeyed either from motives of duty or from motives of expediency. Croce held, however, that in the making and execution of law we should be guided strictly by considerations of social utility, since no one can make a genuinely moral judgment about what is right for a whole class of cases defined abstractly. Laws are of necessity framed in terms of the pseudo concepts of economics and social science; even the moral habits and rules we adopt as our own guides are similarly abstract. They belong among the instruments of life, not among its purposes. Because so much of the work of government is also instrumental, Croce tried at first to formulate a purely economic theory of political action in general. This view he subsequently abandoned.

ETHICS AND POLITICS

Moral action and moral judgment are the distinct universal forms of practical consciousness corresponding to economic action and economic rationality. The dialectic of the distinction is closely analogous to that of the two theoretical forms. There can be economic acts that are not moral (for example, historical explanation of an *im*moral act is bound to be at the economic level); but there cannot be moral acts that have no vital utility (asceticism or abstract moralism is a moral error). On the other hand, practical activity cannot concretely achieve rationality at the economic level without superseding that level. There can be no theory of economic life except from an independent ethical point of view. This is shown by the inconsistency of utilitarian ethics, which attempts to justify individual self-sacrifice by smuggling in moral principles that have not themselves been accounted for. Confined strictly to the economic level, rational people would live in the Hobbesian state of nature, and all the consequences of Hobbesian philosophy would follow.

Moral, as distinct from economic, consciousness is the awareness of some definite act as a duty overriding private inclinations. Moral judgment declares the act to be a duty because it embodies some universal spiritual value (which may fall under the category of beauty, truth, or social utility or be a distinctively moral good). Whatever category the value belongs to, if the act is a moral duty, there is always a sense of "harmony with the Universe." The moral point of view is the final all-embracing awareness of the spirit as a whole, in its wholeness; hence this is the point of view from which true history can be written.

FREEDOM. Because he held that all true judgment is historical, Croce could do little except offer historical illustrations of his view. Reflection on the nature of history itself and on the reason for rejecting scientific concepts as pseudo concepts, however, throws further light on goodness as a distinct category of the spirit. Science fails to be genuine knowledge because the spirit in all its forms always exhibits spontaneity and individual uniqueness. At the moral level, this spontaneity becomes conscious freedom and self-possession. History is "the story of liberty," and freedom is another name for the good as a distinct form of value.

ETHICO-POLITICAL HISTORY. Gentile buttressed an ethical theory similar to Croce's with the Hegelian conception of the national state as an ethical organism and as the bearer of the spirit in history. Croce admitted that if one interpreted the concept "state" broadly enough, this was a legitimate way of viewing it. But he was initially more inclined to think of politics as an economic art or technique of directing selfish passions into orderly channels (as if there were no conflicting moral ideals in political life). The advent of fascism taught him that both of these extreme views were mistaken. Politics does involve moral consciousness, but the absorption of all morality into the "ethical state" is a "governmental concept of morality" unacceptable in a society of free men. The true bearer of the spirit is the individual moral agent, and the state contains the dialectic of practical life as a whole (economics and ethics). The ethical universal is only fully revealed in the history of the state so conceived. Political life, as the unity in which all spiritual activities (even poetry) have a place, is raised to the ethical level in the consciousness of the historian who writes ethico-political history. This is the complete expression of the spirit in which philosophy and history are unified. Croce's work as a historian, particularly in *La storia del regno di Napoli* (History of the Kingdom of Naples; 1925), illustrated how this concept applies to periods of decadence as well as periods of progress.

The "circularity of the spirit" might seem to require that this form of historical consciousness become the content of poetic intuition. But Croce never made this point, and he does not seem to have held this view. The circle of the spirit, as he describes it, closes by returning from vitality to poetry. Ethico-political history transcends the circle altogether because it is the perfected consciousness of the spirit in its circularity.

See also Aesthetics, History of; Aesthetics, Problems of; Dante Alighieri; De Sanctis, Francesco; Descartes, René; Error; Gentile, Giovanni; Goethe, Johann Wolfgang von; Hegel, Georg Wilhelm Friedrich; Herbart, Johann Friedrich; Humboldt, Wilhelm von; Idealism; Intuition; Kant, Immanuel; Marx, Karl; Rosmini-Serbati, Antonio; Spaventa, Bertrando; Vico, Giambattista.

Bibliography

WORKS BY CROCE

Croce's *Opere complete* as of 1965 consists of 67 volumes.

La storia ridotto sotto il concetto generale dell'arte. Naples, 1893.

Materialismo storico ed economta marxista. Palermo, 1900. Translated by C. M. Meredith as *Historical Materialism and the Economics of Karl Marx.* New York: Macmillan, 1914.

Estetica come scienza dell'espressione e linguistica generale. Bari: Laterza, 1902. Translated by Douglas Ainslie as *Aesthetic.* New York, 1909; 2nd complete ed., 1922.

Logica come scienza del concetto puro. Naples, 1905. Translated by Douglas Ainslie as *Logic.* New York, 1917.

Ciò che è vivo e ciò che è morto nella filosofia di Hegel. Bari, 1907. Translated by Douglas Ainslie as *What Is Living and What Is Dead in the Philosophy of Hegel.* London: Macmillan, 1915.

Filosofia della pratica, economia ed etica. Bari: Laterza, 1909. Translated by Douglas Ainslie as *Philosophy of the Practical.* New York, 1913.

La filosofia di Giambattista Vico. Bari: Laterza, 1911. Translated by R. G. Collingwood as *The Philosophy of Giambattista Vico.* New York: Macmillan, 1913.

Breviario di estetica. Bari: Laterza, 1913. Translated by Douglas Ainslie as *The Essence of Aesthetic.* London: Heinemann, 1921. First published in *The Book of the Opening of the Rice Institute.* Houston, TX, 1912.

Teoria e storia della storiografia. Bari: Laterza, 1917. Translated by Douglas Ainslie as *History—Its Theory and Practice.* New York: Harcourt Brace, 1921.

Contributo alla critica di me stesso. Naples, 1918. Translated by R. G. Collingwood as *Autobiography.* Oxford: Clarendon Press, 1927.

Frammenti di etica. Bari: Laterza, 1918. Translated by Arthur Livingston as *The Conduct of Life.* New York: Harcourt Brace, 1924.

Goethe. Bari: Laterza, 1919. Translated by E. Anderson. London: Methuen, 1923.

Ariosto, Shakespeare, Corneille. Bari: Laterza, 1920. Translated by Douglas Ainslie. New York, 1920.

La poesia di Dante. Bari: Laterza, 1921. Translated by Douglas Ainslie as *The Poetry of Dante.* New York: Holt, 1922.

Elementi di politica. Bari: Laterza, 1922. Translated by Salvatore Castiglione as *Politics and Morals.* London: Allen and Unwin, 1946.

La storia del regno di Napoli. Bari: Laterza, 1925.

Aesthetica in nuce. Bari, 1928. Translated by R. G. Collingwood as "Aesthetics," in *Encyclopaedia Britannica,* 14th ed. New York and London, 1929. Vol. VII.

Storia d'Italia dal 1871 al 1915. Bari: Laterza, 1928. Translated by Cecilia M. Ady as *History of Italy 1871–1915.* Oxford: Clarendon Press, 1929.

Storia d'Europa nel secolo XIX. Bari: Laterza, 1932. Translated by Henry Furst as *History of Europe in the Nineteenth Century.* New York: Harcourt Brace, 1933.

La poesia. Bari: Laterza, 1936.

La storia come pensiero e come azione. Bari: Laterza, 1938. Translated by Sylvia Sprigge as *History as the Story of Liberty.* London: Allen and Unwin, 1941.

My Philosophy. London: Allen and Unwin, 1949. Essays selected by R. Klibansky and translated by E. F. Carritt.

WORKS ON CROCE

Borsari, Silvano. *L'opera di Benedetto Croce.* Naples: Istituto Italiano per gli Studi Storici, 1964.

Caponigri, A. R. *History and Liberty.* London: Routledge and Paul, 1955. A study of the historical works.

Nicolini, Fausto. *Benedetto Croce.* Turin, 1962. A definitive biography.

Orsini, G. N. G. *Benedetto Croce, Philosopher of Art and Literary Critic.* Carbondale: Southern Illinois University Press, 1961. A masterly survey of Croce's aesthetic writings.

Piccoli, R. *Benedetto Croce.* London: J. Cape, 1922. Still the best general introduction to Croce, but it covers only the period from 1893 to 1920.

H. S. Harris (1967)

CRUSIUS, CHRISTIAN AUGUST

(1715?–1775)

Christian August Crusius, the German Pietist philosopher and theologian, was born at Leuna, Saxony. Educated in Leipzig, he was appointed extraordinary professor of philosophy there in 1744, and professor of theology in 1750. Crusius initiated the third wave of Pietist attacks on Wolffianism by a series of dissertations (1739–1745), and continued it in his four main philosophical works (1744–1749). He later turned to theological studies, lost interest in philosophy, and founded a new theological school, the Biblicoprophetic school, which partially diverged from Pietism. He later became *canonicus* at the Meissen Theological Seminary.

Crusius's reputation in his own time and his influence on his contemporaries was second among Pietist philosophers only to Christian Thomasius. The collaboration of his close follower, A. F. Reinhard, with Pierre-Louis Moreau de Maupertuis and the Berlin Academy in their polemics against Wolffianism established a link between Christian Wolff's Pietist and academic opponents. Several later philosophers acknowledged Crusius as their teacher, although they combined a Crusian background with more advanced trends of French and English origin. These thinkers contributed considerably to the renewal of German philosophy after the dissolution of the Wolffian school. In theology Crusius's influence was even stronger.

Crusius's importance was forgotten or suppressed soon after his death, especially among theologians, and has not yet been fully reestablished because of the hostility of the subsequently dominant rationalist and philological schools to the trend of his theology. As a philosopher, Crusius was nearly voted into oblivion, along with most other minor eighteenth-century philosophers, by idealistic historiographers. He was rediscovered by the new philological historiographers, chiefly in connection with his influence on Immanuel Kant.

ORIGIN OF CRUSIUS'S THOUGHT

After 1730, Wolff and his school began to recover from his expulsion from Halle University in 1723, and from the loss by most of his pupils of their professorships, an attack launched for personal and political reasons by his Pietist opponents. The Pietists were gradually deprived of official support and were more and more restricted to theoretical controversy with Wolff. However, Wolff's system of philosophy was a much more modern, comprehensive, and technically refined body of doctrines than those in the obsolete and clumsy treatises of Thomasius, Franz Budde, and Andreas Rüdiger. A far-reaching reform in the doctrine and quality of Pietist philosophy was needed for it to face the Wolffian doctrine and counteract it successfully. Crusius's teacher, A. F. Hoffman (1703–1741), developed the logical doctrines of Thomasius and Rüdiger, taking into account Wolff's new philosophical techniques and achievements and accepting some of his doctrines, in his own *Vernunft-Lehre* (Leipzig, 1737). Crusius's own logic was inspired by Hoffman's refined and comprehensive handbook, whose quality and thoroughness substantially met the most modern requirements. Hoffman's early death prevented him from publishing the treatises on the other branches of philosophy that he had announced in 1734, but Crusius proceeded along Hoffman's lines, both improving and completing his lifework. Crusius provided the Pietist school with a renewed, efficient, and modern theoretical platform that temporarily assured its philosophical survival, outlived orthodox Wolffianism, and led to a far-reaching change in German philosophy.

METHODOLOGY AND LOGIC

Crusius's methodology, the foundation of his philosophical attitude, was based on two central ideas, both originating in the Pietist tradition. Philosophy is not, as it was for Wolff, a pure "science of possible things insofar as they are possible," but is based on existing things. Second, human understanding has very narrow limits; theoretical certainty is impossible concerning many fundamental points whose only foundation is moral certitude or revelation. The mysteries of religion are not only beyond human reason, as Wolff claimed, but also contradict it. Something may be unthinkable for human reason that is not so for God or in itself.

Crusius held that the most general principle of human knowledge is neither the principle of identity nor the principle of contradiction, but a principle concerning what we can and cannot think: What cannot be thought at all is false, and what cannot be thought of as false is true. Our notions of identity and contradiction are based on this principle, which he called the principle of *cogitabilitas*. It is an inner criterion, depending on the nature of the human understanding.

Crusius further held that human reason cannot reach ultimate truth. Knowledge begins with experience, both inner and outer, and in many cases is stopped in its analysis of an order of facts by certain notions that, although they are not simple in themselves, cannot be further analyzed by man. Even if an analysis is completed and man does reach some simple basic notion, this notion cannot be demonstrated or deduced from a unique source. Each notion must be intuited singly by connecting it with concrete examples.

It is therefore impossible, according to Crusius, to assume that the method of philosophy is identical with the method of mathematics. Mathematics deals with very simple properties of things and its objects are exhaustively defined, whereas many notions relating to objects of philosophical thought can neither be known with intuitive distinctness nor analyzed by man. Again, mathematics proceeds only by demonstration and solely on the basis of the principle of identity. Philosophy, on the other hand, frequently must revert to moral certainty and is based on several different principles and on the knowledge of fact.

The main characteristics of Crusian logic, as expounded in his *Weg zur Gewissheit und Zuverlässigkeit der menschlichen Erkenntnis* (Way to certainty and reliability of human knowledge; Leipzig, 1747), follow from these views. Crusius connected logic with methodology. His logic contained much empirical psychology and many informal concrete and practical rules for obtaining or verifying knowledge, including rules for experimentation. Because Crusius so limited the field of theoretical demonstration, he presented a highly developed logic of probability (which he called moral certitude), covering, among other topics, induction, hypothesis, and the reliability of testimony. The last was essential in the justification of revelation.

Both for Crusius and for Wolff, knowledge derived only from the senses, but the main characteristics of Crusius's methodology allowed his successors to be much more receptive to English and French empiricism, sensationalism, and commonsense philosophy than were orthodox Wolffian rationalists. This receptivity was partially due to John Locke's strong influence on Thomasius, but the ethical and mystical sources of these Pietistic attitudes was most important.

METAPHYSICS

Crusius, in his *Entwurf der nothwendigen Vernunftwahrheiten* (Sketch of necessary rational truths; Leipzig, 1745), divided metaphysics into ontology, theology, cosmology, and pneumatology, in explicit opposition to Wolff's ordering of the metaphysical sciences.

ONTOLOGY. Ontology begins, not with first principles, but with the notion of a thing in general, directly connected with the notion of a "really given thing." Only after introducing these notions did Crusius discuss essence, existence, and causality. Crusius regarded existence as indefinable and as a primary notion arising from sensation.

In his discussion of causality, Crusius expounded a principle of determining reason, his version of Gottfried Wilhelm Leibniz's principle of sufficient reason. Crusius held, against Wolff, that a sufficient reason suffices only for free actions insofar as they are free. Rational truths and natural events not depending on free causes need a more cogent foundation, a determining reason. This principle does not derive from the principle of identity, but rather from what we must conceive or what we cannot conceive as united or separate, and thus from a new case of the principle of *cogitabilitas*. Crusius, aiming at a sharper distinction between mechanism and free actions, held that the real nature of causality is unknown and that our knowledge of causal connections is based on the constant conjunction of two events in experience. This, of course, cleared the path for the members of his school to accept the Humean critique of the causal connection.

Crusius's ontology reveals a general characteristic of his metaphysics. His was not a monolithic system beginning with a single principle and deducing from it all subsequent notions and propositions, as was Wolff's. Rather, it was founded both on several independent principles and on a multitude of elementary notions that could be defined only by an appeal to reality (by their concrete representation)—notions such as existence, space, time, and force; or, in psychology, the particular powers of the soul, some mental faculties, and pleasure and pain. Through Hoffman Crusius derived this view from Locke's doctrine of simple ideas, but he supposed that the number of elementary notions (which he once called categories) could be infinite.

THEOLOGY. Rational theology followed immediately after ontology, instead of being—as for Wolff—the final section of metaphysics, because Crusius held that God's existence is a necessary foundation for cosmology and pneumatology. Crusius denied the Ontological Argument: God's existence can be proved by moral evidence only, and his attributes cannot, properly speaking, be understood by humankind—among other things, positive infinity is beyond human reason. The human notion of God is partially relative and partially negative; nevertheless, it is certain. God is different from created beings both in degree and in essence. Among the attributes of God, Crusius stressed his free will, which is limited by the principle of contradiction and by his goodness. In God and God alone, intellect and will are a single power.

COSMOLOGY. Crusius held that matter is composed of a multitude of simple substances. Simple material substances are extended, and the infinite divisibility of matter is impossible. Simple substances have an essential, though not absolutely necessary, force. They act upon each other only by motion and contact. Physical space and time are real, but they are neither independent beings (substances), nor properties, nor relations (all of these concern the metaphysical essence of things). Space and time are intimately connected with existence; they are conditions of things insofar as such things exist. There is no real space or time without substance to fill it; outside the real world there is only possible (not sensible) space or time, which is infinite and filled by God. There are empty spaces in the world (otherwise movement would be impossible), but they are only physically—and not metaphysically—empty, because they are filled with God's presence. Mathematical space and time are distinct from physical space and time, and are abstracted from the relations of things.

Crusius was trying to offer a new set of solutions to the difficulties of the traditional doctrines of substance, of space and time and their limits, and of the void, while avoiding the concepts of *res extensa*, Leibnizian monads, and atoms, as well as the contradictions presented by the real space and time of René Descartes and Isaac Newton and the ideal space and time of Leibniz and Wolff. His doctrine resembled that of Locke, but it was a mixture of well-chosen elements of the traditional views connected by doubtful subtleties.

PNEUMATOLOGY. In his pneumatology, or rational psychology, Crusius rejected Thomasius's spiritual materialism but retained some of its characteristics. He held that finite spirits are simple unextended substances, but that they fill a space and share with material substances the power of motion. Thus, a real interaction between spiritual and material substances is possible, and the doctrines of preestablished harmony and occasionalism are unnecessary. The human soul is an independent substance with two fundamental powers, thinking and willing, both of which are a complex of several independent lesser powers.

Crusius was, in general, very cautious in his pneumatology, and frequently appealed to the limitations of human reasoning. For instance, he held that the immortality of the soul could be proved only if God's existence were presupposed—that is, by an appeal to moral certitude.

NATURAL PHILOSOPHY

Crusius's treatise on natural philosophy, *Anleitung, über natürliche Begebenheiten ordentlich und vorsichtig nachzudenken* (Introduction to regular and prudent reflections on natural events; 2 vols., Leipzig, 1749), was by far the least original of his works. Nevertheless, he was the first important Pietist philosopher to accept mechanism. In this work, Pietist philosophy finally renounced animism and adopted the more modern Cartesian and Leibnizian views, although it was still opposed to Newton's theory of gravitation. Crusius stressed the difficulties of physics and the purely hypothetical character of much of our knowledge of the particular laws of nature.

ETHICS

Crusius's first major work was a treatise on ethics, *Anweisung, vernunftig zu leben* (Instructions for a Reasonable Life; Leipzig, 1744). Hoffman's influence on Crusius is clear. Ethics, for Crusius, is not based on reason alone, but also on revelation. Natural duties have been imposed on humanity through God's free choice.

THE WILL. Crusius split Wolff's empirical psychology into two parts. He incorporated the first part, concerned with the cognitive power, into logic. The second, concerned with the will, he placed in ethics. Moral goodness consists in the conformity of the human will with God's will. The human will is a power to act on the understanding, on the body, and on the will itself, but its connection with the understanding is not altogether clear. We are immediately conscious of freedom, which is the main property of the human will. The will is moved by sufficient reason, which does not necessitate, and therefore the will is free.

DUTY. The second section of the *Anweisung*, on ethics proper, discusses human duties. An action is moral if it is done out of obligation only, and not in quest of happiness. Virtue is formally conditioned by a coincidence of human will and divine law, and is materially conditioned by love for God. Divine law is known through conscience, which is an immediate power of moral judgment founded on a sort of common sense called moral taste. Evil originates in a wrong use of free will, which, when it submits to unreasonable impulses, corrupts human understanding and the true representation of goodness.

A third section of the *Anweisung* was devoted to moral theology; a fourth, to natural law; and a fifth, to prudence, which was closely studied in Thomasius's school and partially corresponded to Kant's technical imperatives.

REVEALED THEOLOGY

In his revealed theology Crusius united orthodox Pietist doctrines with those of a dissident Pietist, J. A. Bengel (1687–1752). Bengel and Crusius carried to an extreme the Pietist belief that the Bible is an organic whole inspired by God and historically true throughout. The Pietists held that Scripture is the only source of theological truth, and rejected all exegetical developments, even those of Protestant divines. No rational criticism of the Bible was permitted; its meaning could be penetrated only by a kind of empathy or inner light. Crusius stressed a theology of history, founded on biblical prophecies, that tried to explain the whole history of Christianity and to reveal its future aim in a second coming of Christ.

CRUSIUS'S INFLUENCE ON KANT

Recent historical scholarship has stressed Crusius's importance in Kant's development, and the view that Kant's philosophy was rooted in Wolff's system has been more and more questioned. Recent research has shown that Kant, educated in the Pietistic, eclectic, and anti-Wolffian milieu of Königsberg University, was mainly trying in his precritical development (1745–1768)—despite the nonorthodox Wolffian influence of his teacher, Martin Knutzen—to counteract Wolffian philosophy in an increasingly original way. He therefore appealed both to recent anti-Wolffian trends—to Maupertuis and his Berlin circle and through Maupertuis to Newton—and to Crusius, the new leader of Pietist philosophy and only nine years his senior, whose reputation grew tremendously from 1744 on.

Crusius's influence on Kant consists in six main points, some of which were also held by other Pietist philosophers or by Maupertuis. Crusius stressed the limits of human understanding, a theme that recurs in Kant's writings under different forms from 1755 on. He rejected the Ontological Argument, as did Kant after 1755, and he later rejected all theoretical proofs of God's existence. He assumed a multiplicity of independent first principles; Kant did so after 1755. He denied the importance of formal logic, and simplified it. He rejected the possibility of defining existence, and accepted a multiplicity of simple notions. He rejected the mathematical method as applied to philosophy. Kant adopted these last three positions in 1762.

Kant's Crusianism reached its climax in his *Untersuchung über die Deutlichkeit der Grundsätze der naturlichen Theologie und der Moral* (Investigations concerning the Distinctness of the Fundamental Principles of Natural Theology and Morals; Berlin, 1764), written in 1762. By 1763 Kant's enthusiasm for Crusius's philosophy was waning, but he did not reject the six tenets above and was still influenced by Crusius on individual points as late as the 1770s. J. Bohatec has claimed that Crusius's doctrines in revealed theology exerted some influence on Kant's late works in religion.

See also Descartes, René; Kant, Immanuel; Knutzen, Martin; Leibniz, Gottfried Wilhelm; Locke, John; Maupertuis, Pierre-Louis Moreau de; Newton, Isaac; Ontological Argument for the Existence of God; Pietism; Probability and Chance; Revelation; Rüdiger, Andreas; Sensa; Thomasius, Christian; Wolff, Christian.

Bibliography

ADDITIONAL WORKS BY CRUSIUS

Die philosophischen Hauptschriften, edited by Giorgio Tonelli. Hildesheim, 1964–.

Dissertations

De Corruptelis Intellectus a Voluntate Pendentibus. Leipzig, 1740.

De Appetitibus Insitis Voluntatis Humanae. Leipzig, 1742.

De Usu et Limitibus Principii Rationis Determinantis, Vulgo Sufficientis. Leipzig, 1743.

Opuscula Philosophico-Theologica. Leipzig, 1751. Reprint of above three dissertations.

Theological Work

Hypomnemata ad Theologiam Propheticam. Leipzig, 1764–1778.

WORKS ON CRUSIUS

Adickes, Erich. *Kantstudien.* Kiel and Leipzig, 1895.

Bohatec, J. *Die Religionsphilosophie Kants.* Hamburg, 1938.

Burkhardt, Hans. "Modalities in Language, Thought and Reality in Leibniz, Descartes and Crusius." *Synthese* 75 (1988): 183–215.

Campo, Mariano. *La genesi del criticismo kantiano.* Varese, 1953.

Delitzsh, Fr. *Die biblisch-prophetische Theologie, ihre Fortbildung durch Christian August Crusius, und ihre neueste Entwicklung seit der Christologie Hengstenbergs.* Leipzig, 1845.

Festner, C. *Christian August Crusius als Metaphysiker.* Halle, 1892.

Heimsoeth, Heinz. "Metaphysik und Kritik bei Chr. Aug. Crusius" (1926). Reprinted in his *Studien zur Philosophie Immanuel Kants.* Cologne, 1956.

Marquardt, A. *Kant und Crusius.* Kiel, 1885.

Schmalenbach, H. *Leibniz,* 553–560. Munich, 1921.

Schmucker, J. *Die Ursprünge der Ethik Kants.* Meisenheim an der Glan, 1951.

Seitz, A. von. *Die Willensfreiheit in der Philosophie des Christian August Crusius.* Würzburg, 1899.

Tonelli, Giorgio. *Elementi in Kant precritico.* Turin, 1959. Vol. I.

Tonelli, Giorgio. "Kant, dall'estetica metafisica all'estetica psicoempirica." *Memorie della Academia delle scienze di Torino,* Series 3, Vol. 3, Part 2 (1955).

Tonelli, Giorgio. "La question des bornes de l'entendement humain au XVIIIe siècle." *Revue de metaphysique et de morale* (1959): 396–427.

Tonelli, Giorgio. "Der Streit über mathematische Methode in der Philosophie in der ersten Hälfte des XVIII Jahrhunderts." *Archiv für Philosophie* 9 (1959).

Watkins, Eric. "The Development of Physical Influx in Early Eighteenth Century Germany: Gottsched, Knutzen, and Crusius." *Review of Metaphysics* 49(2) (1995): 295–339.

Watkins, Eric. "Forces and Causes in Kant's Early Pre-Critical Writings." *Studies in History and Philosophy of Science* 34a(1) (2003): 5–27.

Wundt, Max. *Die deutsche Schulphilosophie im Zeitalter der Aufklärung,* 254–264. Tübingen, 1945.

Wundt, Max. *Kant als Metaphysiker,* 60–81. Stuttgart: Enke, 1924.

Giorgio Tonelli (1967)
Bibliography updated by Tamra Frei (2005)

CUDWORTH, RALPH

(1617–1688)

Ralph Cudworth was one of the leading figures among the Cambridge Platonists, a group of seventeenth-century philosopher theologians. He was born in Aller, Somerset, to a minister who had been a fellow of Emmanuel College, Cambridge. Educated at home by his stepfather, John Stoughton, until 1632, he then entered Emmanuel College. There he was influenced by Benjamin Whichcote, founder of the Cambridge Platonist school. In 1639 he was elected a fellow of Emmanuel, and received the bachelor of divinity degree in 1645, defending for his examination Whichcote's thesis that good and evil are eternal and immutable. This examination, with its opposition to any system that makes morality contingent on will, whether human or divine, already betrays Cudworth's distance from the rigorous Calvinism with which Emmanuel College had always been associated. Nevertheless, Cudworth did have some sympathy with political aspects of the Puritan cause. He was appointed by Parliament master of Clare College and Regius professor of Hebrew in 1645, and served as advisor to Oliver Cromwell's secretary of state on several government appointments. In 1647 he was invited to preach to a sharply divided House of Commons.

In his sermon of March 31, 1647, Cudworth urged parliamentarians not to legislate on doctrinal matters, arguing that salvation depends not on speculative details but on living a life of Christlike love and forbearance. This emphasis on morality over doctrine was characteristic of the Cambridge Platonists and influential for the later Latitudinarian divines. Cudworth was appointed master of Christ's College in 1654, and succeeded in retaining his appointment at the time of the Restoration. He remained in the post until his death in 1688. In 1654 Cudworth was married. None of his sons survived him, but his daughter, Damaris, later Lady Masham (1658–1708), took custody of her father's writings and became a philosopher in her own right. Intimate friend and correspondent of John Locke, she published *A Discourse concerning the Love of God* in 1696.

METAPHYSICS

Cudworth's massive *True Intellectual System of the Universe* (1678) was the only one of Cudworth's principal writings to be published during his lifetime. Lengthy as it is, the published volume represents only the first installment of a three-part project originally sketched by Cudworth, with the parts devoted respectively to attacking mechanistic or atomistic determinism, theological determinism (Calvinism), and Stoic determinism. The *True Intellectual System of the Universe* in its published form constitutes a defense of theistic atomism and an attack on "Hylopathic" atheism. Hylopathic atheism, which claims that all things can be explained by reference to material atoms, with no need to invoke spirit or incorporeal substance, was an important target because it was represented in Cudworth's own day by Thomas Hobbes. A secondary target of the book is "Hylozoic" atheism, differing from Hylopathic in attributing life to matter, but still materialistic, and worthy of Cudworth's notice because of its recent revival by Benedict Spinoza. Rather than engage directly with Hobbes or Spinoza, Cudworth's argument is directed against ancient schools of philosophy, and much of it consists in a *consensus gentium* argument; atheism is an anomaly or aberration from an original truth that has been acknowledged from the beginning. This original true system accepted atomism, but only as an account of matter or corporeal reality. Properly understood, atomism reveals matter to be essentially passive or inert, thus making clear that only the existence of incorporeal substance can explain the origin, motion, and organization of matter.

While interested in the *ancient theology* argument that Plato's insights (particularly what Cudworth regarded as a concept of the Trinity in Plato) derived originally from divine revelation through Moses, Cudworth was finally content to claim that there is a natural *prolepsis* or anticipation of the idea of God existing throughout all times and places. Atheism is thus a willful destruction of this prolepsis, and Hobbes and Spinoza are not new threats, but reincarnations of old foes. The other leading philosophical thinker among the Cambridge Platonists, Henry More (1614–1687), devoted more direct attention to Spinoza's thought than did Cudworth, and differed from Cudworth as well in seeking, along with Joseph Glanvill (1636–1680), empirical evidence for the existence of incorporeal substances in cases of witchcraft and demonic possession.

In embracing atomism, Cudworth was making common cause with Cartesian dualism and rejecting scholastic accounts of substantial forms. Mind cannot be simply a property of material objects. For Cudworth, though, it is passivity, not extension, that essentially constitutes matter, and it is activity, rather than self-consciousness, that essentially constitutes incorporeal substance. The key challenge facing Cartesian dualism was to account for the interaction between body and soul, corporeal and incorporeal substance. Cudworth's solution was to appeal to active incorporeal powers that mediate between wholly passive matter and self-conscious soul, creating a vital union between them. Each finite soul has a finite field of action—its own body.

An analogous solution allows Cudworth to articulate the relationship between God and the world. While God is not bound to physical creation as a finite soul is bound to its body, Plastic Nature does serve as an intermediary between God and world that, like the lower powers of the soul, allows for a vital connection between the two. Critical of Descartes's suggestion that the existing ordered universe could have originated from a single initiating divine act, Cudworth argued that an ongoing divine influence was necessary if the material universe was to maintain an ordered motion. At the same time, God is not required, as in *occasionalism*, to attend directly to each and every detail of order in the universe. *Plastic Nature*, an unconscious power that pursues not its own but divine purposes, imposes order and finality on the material world. Nothing works according to mere chance, but according to final causes, divine intentions mediated by Plastic Nature.

Cudworth's Plastic Nature is similar to More's *Hylarchic Principle*, but Cudworth did not follow More's contentions that both material and immaterial substance are extended and that space is infinite. The concept of Plastic Nature was influential for biologist John Ray and for philosophical biology generally up through Darwin. Pierre Bayle attacked Cudworth's plastic powers as atheistic in tendency in eliminating the need for direct divine action to account for purpose displayed in the physical world. Denis Diderot and Jean d'Alembert's *Encyclopédie* (1751–1772) included a detailed account of Cudworth's theory, and the theory may, via Paul Janet, have influenced modern doctrines of the unconscious.

On the one hand, Cudworth cannot be finally understood as opposing the new philosophies of Hobbes and Spinoza merely on the basis of allegiance to an outmoded neoplatonism; his *consensus gentium* argument advances at the same time a contemporary position. On the other hand, the baroque erudition displayed in the *True Intellectual System of the Universe* was out of step with the leaner philosophical style of his contemporaries. This did not prevent the work from achieving significant influence in its own day, and in fact the text served for several generations as a key resource on Greek philosophy. But it did in the nineteenth and twentieth centuries often mean that Cudworth's importance as an interlocutor of Hobbes, Spinoza, and Descartes was not fully appreciated.

EPISTEMOLOGY

Cudworth's Platonist epistemology is developed at length in *A Treatise of Eternal and Immutable Morality*. The *Treatise* was published in 1731 at the behest of Cudworth's grandson, Lady Masham's son. Cudworth argues against empiricism that knowledge is more than a mirroring or representation of reality, and that the mind is more than a blank sheet of paper upon which the objects of sense are inscribed. Knowledge can never arise solely out of sense experience. When we sense, we sense particulars, but when we know, we know by means of universals. Cudworth insists that universals must precede the empirical particulars that they organize and make sense of; they are not abstracted from particulars, for this act of abstraction would be unmotivated and undirected unless one already knew the universal at which one was aiming. Sense allows the soul to perceive the appearances of things, but not clearly to comprehend them.

The universals of which we have knowledge are eternal and immutable. But the fragmented nature of human nature points beyond itself to God. Given the eternal and immutable nature of intelligible ideas, they cannot solely be modifications of limited and finite intellects, which only come to know them in time, if at all. It is God's infinite and eternal mind that, in perceiving itself, eternally perceives these ideas. Rather than innate ideas, human souls possess innate activities or tendencies, a capacity to exert themselves so as to participate in a limited way in divine self-knowledge. Human persons do not, though, arrive at knowledge by comparing their ideas with ideas in the mind of God. Pointing out the impossibility of such a comparison, Cudworth insists simply on clear intelligibility as the criterion of truth. Descartes, Cudworth argues, fell into circularity in seeking further to defend the criteria of clarity and distinctness by proving that God is not a deceiver. The criterion of clear intelligibility is self-evident and depends on no external support.

ETHICS

As the title of *A Treatise* suggests, among the eternal and immutable ideas that may be known as clearly intelligible are moral principles. In fact, Cudworth's epistemological discussion is occasioned and motivated by his concern to defeat voluntarist and relativist accounts of morality. This concern reached back to Whichcote, but Cudworth was both much more learned than Whichcote about ancient and more recent Platonism and much more connected to contemporary philosophical discourse. As in the *True Intellectual System of the Universe*, one of Cudworth's key targets is Hobbes, who argues that right and wrong are relative concepts, based solely in convention. Cudworth also attacks "diverse modern theologers" who argue that morality is created by divine fiat, naming among them William of Ockham and Pierre d'Ailly and one contemporary theologian, the Polish Jan Szydlowski. The Calvinistic theology of Cudworth's Puritan contemporaries is a looming unnamed target. Descartes's argument that the natures and essences of things, including moral good and evil, must depend on the contingent will of God in order not to be independent of God, receives particular criticism. Following Plato's *Euthyphro*, Cudworth argues that things are not good because they are willed by God; rather, God wills things because they are good. It is either eternally true or eternally false that something is good; no act of will can change this. The good is not, though, an external constraint on divine freedom, but God's essential nature.

If the *True Intellectual System of the Universe* was originally intended as a comprehensive critique of all forms of determinism, Cudworth's many manuscripts defending "freewill" represent his efforts to articulate a positive account of free human action and a moral psychology to accompany that. None of these manuscript treatises were published during Cudworth's lifetime, and it is unclear how widely they may have circulated. Lady Masham may well have shared them with Locke and Shaftesbury. The shortest of the manuscripts was published in 1838 as *A Treatise of Freewill*, testifying to ongoing interest in Cudworth's thought. In an innovative move, Cudworth rejects traditional faculty psychology; the will and understanding are not distinct faculties in the soul, but activities of the soul. Drawing on Stoic terminology, Cudworth argues that the soul's *hegemonikon* or ruling power "is the soul as comprehending itself, all its concerns and interests, its abilities and capacities, and holding itself, as it were in its own hand, as it were redoubled upon itself" (p. 178). It is through this reflexive capacity that the soul is able to adjudicate among conflicting passions, dictates of conscience, and inferences of reason, and act as a unified self. Cudworth considers that in identifying this capacity for reflexive deliberation he has successfully shown that persons are not determined by any "antecedent necessary causes" (p. 179). It is far from clear that this is so, although Cudworth's account of the *hegemonikon* does make it possible to speak intelligibly of the soul's self-determination and moral responsibility.

For Cudworth, moral agency and thus moral responsibility rest on the capacity to survey in a comprehensive way possible courses of action and to pass judgment on which is best. Only action that issues from such reflection can properly be regarded as one's own. God neither has nor needs a *hegemonikon*, being simple and unified. God's freedom consists in unfailingly acting according to God's own perfect nature, and God's self-determination in the fact that nothing outside of God determines divine action. Insofar as human self-determination takes the form of an active pursuit of the good, human persons come to participate increasingly fully in God and God's goodness. Thus human "freewill" can be employed in order to arrive at a more perfect, more godlike, freedom.

See also Cambridge Platonists; Epistemology; Ethics; Metaphysics.

Bibliography

WORKS BY CUDWORTH

The True Intellectual System of the Universe. Stuttgart-Bad Cannstatt, Germany: Friedrich Fromann Verlag, 1964. Facsimile of 1678 edition.

"A Sermon Preached Before the House of Commons." In *The Cambridge Platonists*, edited by C. A. Patrides. Cambridge, MA: Harvard University Press, 1970.

A Treatise concerning Eternal and Immutable Morality, with *A Treatise of Freewill.* Edited by Sarah Hutton. Cambridge, U.K.: Cambridge University Press, 1996.

WORKS ABOUT CUDWORTH

Darwall, Stephen. "Cudworth: Obligation and Self-Determining Moral Agency." In *The British Moralists and the Internal Ought, 1640–1740.* Cambridge, U.K.: Cambridge University Press, 1992.

Hutton, Sarah. "Ralph Cudworth, God, Mind and Nature." In *Religion, Reason and Nature in Early Modern Europe*, edited by Robert Crocker. Dordrecht, Netherlands: Kluwer, 2001.

Passmore, J. A. *Ralph Cudworth: An Introduction.* Cambridge, U.K.: Cambridge University Press, 1951.

Scott, D. "Platonic Recollection and Cambridge Platonism." *Hermathena* 149 (1990): 73–97.

Thiel, Udo. "Cudworth and Seventeenth-Century Theories of Consciousness." In *The Uses of Antiquity: The Scientific Revolution and the Classical Tradition*, edited by Stephen Gaukroger. Dordrecht, Netherlands: Kluwer, 1991.

Jennifer A. Herdt (2005)

CULVERWEL, NATHANAEL
(1618?–1651?)

Nathanael Culverwel, the religious and moral philosopher commonly if rather misleadingly described as a Cambridge Platonist, was probably a son of Richard Culverwel, rector of St. Margaret's, in London, although neither his parentage nor the date of his birth is certain. He certainly grew up in a Calvinist atmosphere. In 1633 he was admitted to Emmanuel College, Cambridge, where he encountered the teachings of Benjamin Whichcote, the spiritual leader of Cambridge Platonism. Ralph Cudworth was slightly junior to him as an undergraduate at Emmanuel but was elected to a fellowship three years before Culverwel's election in 1642. John Smith was of the same generation. Culverwel's contemporaries refer in somewhat obscure terms to troubles that beset him in later life; these may have included some sort of mental breakdown. He died not later than 1651.

Culverwel published nothing during his lifetime. Shortly after his death, however, William Dillingham prepared for publication a discourse titled, in Culverwel's typically metaphorical style, *Spiritual Opticks: or a Glasse discovering the weaknesse and imperfection of a Christians knowledge in this life* (1651). This was sufficiently successful to encourage Dillingham to proceed to the publication of a manuscript by Culverwel, composed, Dillingham says, about 1646, which was obviously intended, although incomplete, to be a book—*An Elegant and Learned Discourse of the Light of Nature.* In the same volume Dillingham included a number of Culverwel's sermons. Prefixed to the *Discourse* is an essay by Culverwel's brother Richard that asserts that in its present form the *Discourse* is somewhat misleading, since the praise of reason which it contains was to have been followed by another section in which the limitations of reason would have been more strongly insisted upon. That judgment is borne out by the tone of Culverwel's sermons, which are severely Calvinist.

The *Discourse*, as it stands, is an elaboration of Whichcote's favorite quotation (from Proverbs 20:27), which Culverwel translates as "The understanding of a man is the candle of the Lord." Insofar as it is critical of those who "blaspheme reason," the *Discourse* is written in Whichcote's spirit. However, its philosophical tone is in many respects Aristotelian rather than Platonic; Culverwel sharply criticizes the "fanciful ideas" of "the Platonists," under which heading he almost certainly includes his Emmanuel colleagues. (None of them had yet published, so that although—unusually for his time—Culverwel makes precise references to such near-contemporaries as Lord Herbert of Cherbury, Lord Brooke, and Sir Kenelm Digby, he could not refer to the Cambridge Platonists in similarly definite terms.) When Culverwel speaks with enthusiasm of Plato, it is of the *Laws* or the *Republic* rather than of John Smith's favorite, the *Phaedo*; quite unlike Smith or Cudworth he rarely pays any attention to the Neoplatonists. On the other hand, he writes with great approval not only of Aristotle but also of the Scholastics, especially Thomas Aquinas and Francisco Suárez, and even of Francis Bacon, to whom the Platonists were generally strongly opposed.

He differs from the Platonists on four crucial points. The first is epistemology; he disagrees with them, as he puts it, about "the time at which the candle of the Lord is lighted." It is true that at an early stage in the *Discourse* (Ch. 7) he writes: "There are stamped and printed upon the being of man some clear and indelible principles, some first and alphabetical notions, by putting together of which it can spell out the law of nature," a passage which it is natural to read as a defense of innate ideas. Later, however, in Chapter 11, he argues quite explicitly against the doctrine of innateness, even in the modified form in which Platonists like Cudworth held it. First principles—which he describes as having "so much of certainty in them, that they are near to a tautology and identity"—arise, he argues, "from the observing and comparing of objects"; these principles are not inherent in our minds. He strongly criticizes Plato and René Descartes in Chapter 14 for "too much scorning and slighting" of sensations. Sensation, he admits, is no more than "the gate of certainty," but only through this gate can certainty enter the soul. Otherwise, the soul would remain "a blank sheet."

Second, he criticizes the Platonist tendency to diminish the gap between human and divine by treating the human soul as having a degree of divinity, as being, insofar as it is rational, an ingredient in divine reason. The candle of the Lord, he argues, is lit by God but is no part of God's light. God's light is like the sun; a candle is but a wavering, imperfect light even when it is at its brightest. Men cannot hope to be godlike, the ideal the Platonists set before themselves.

This is connected with the third point of difference. Culverwel continued to be a Calvinist; he continued to believe, therefore, that no human being is worthy of salvation. In a sermon titled "The Act of Oblivion," addressed to a congregation presumed to belong to the elect, he says that God "might have written thy name in his Black Book, with fatal and bloody characters, and made his justice glorious in thy misery and damnation"; God had chosen otherwise because he so chose, not because any members were deserving of a higher destiny. If God has chosen to save Socrates, he argues, this can only be because God gave a private revelation to him, not because Socrates was a worthy man. God may well have chosen to save Aristophanes rather than Socrates. God's decrees, Culverwel insists, are absolute; it is ridiculous to suppose that a man can save himself from the damnation decreed for him merely by exercising an act of choice, by choosing to be good. Nothing could be further from the spirit of Cambridge Platonism than Culverwel's unmitigated Calvinism.

Finally, and this again is connected with his Calvinism, Culverwel's emphasis as a moral philosopher is on law rather than on reason. He agrees with the Platonists, it is true, that some acts are good in their own nature and that some relationships are peculiarly just and rational; however, the performance of such acts, he argues, does not constitute a moral good. Essentially, he says, morality is a matter of obedience to rule, and there can be rules only when there is a lawgiver. The obligatoriness of moral laws depends upon the fact that they are commanded by God. Even though the lawgiving is itself a rational act, even though moral laws are based upon the lawgiver's apprehension of "the eternal relations of things," even though it is by our reason that we discover their nature, command, not reason, is still the foundation of morality. A capacity for obeying rules, he suggests, is the distinguishing mark of a rational being; moral rules apply to men, not to animals, just because men are capable of following rules. But human rationality does not in any way constitute the obligatoriness of the rules.

Following Hugo Grotius, Culverwel devotes a great deal of attention to the concept of a natural law and its relation to the laws of nations. In the *Discourse*, as his argument proceeds, the importance of law comes more and more to the fore, and the importance of reason recedes, although Culverwel takes the two to be intimately connected. For Culverwel, as for so many of his antirationalist successors, Abraham's sacrifice of Isaac is the crucial case. This was decreed, and the decree had to be obeyed, he argues, even though it goes against all our concepts of a rational morality; "the candle durst not oppose the sun."

One can discern a tension in Culverwel's work between his Calvinism and the Platonism he had learned from Whichcote. A very similar tension between empiricism and rationalism, between the concept of law and the concept of reason, is manifest in John Locke, and it is more than likely that Locke was strongly influenced by Culverwel's *Discourse*, most obviously, but by no means exclusively, in the *Essays on the Law of Nature*, which he wrote in 1660.

See also Aristotelianism; Aristotle; Bacon, Francis; Cambridge Platonists; Cudworth, Ralph; Descartes, René; Grotius, Hugo; Herbert of Cherbury; Locke, John;

Neoplatonism; Plato; Platonism and the Platonic Tradition; Socrates; Suárez, Francisco; Thomas Aquinas, St.; Whichcote, Benjamin.

Bibliography

The best edition of the *Elegant and Learned Discourse of the Light of Nature* is edited by John Brown, with a critical essay by John Cairns (Edinburgh: Constable, 1857). The sermons, including *Spiritual Opticks*, can be read in the 1652 edition of the *Discourse* (London: John Rothwell; reprinted, 1654). There are extracts in John Wesley, *Christian Library*, Vols. IX–X (London, 1819–1827); and Ernest Trafford Campagnac, *The Cambridge Platonists* (Oxford: Clarendon Press, 1901).

See also William Cecil de Pauley, *The Candle of the Lord, Studies in the Cambridge Platonists* (London: Society for Promoting Christian Knowledge, 1937); A. C. Scupholme, "Nathanael Culverwel—a Cambridge Platonist," in *Theology* 38 (225) (1939); Wolfgang von Leyden, *John Locke: Essays on the Law of Nature* (Oxford: Clarendon Press, 1954); Jay G. Williams, "Nathaniel Culverwel (1619?–1651?)," in *British Philosophers, 1500–1799 (Dictionary of Literary Biography, Vol. 252)*, edited by Peter Fosl (Farmington Hills, MI: Thomson Gale, 2002); and the bibliography to the *Cambridge Platonists* entry.

John Passmore (1967)
Bibliography updated by Tamra Frei (2005)

CUMBERLAND, RICHARD

(1631–1718)

Richard Cumberland, the bishop and moral philosopher, was born in London, the son of a London citizen. Educated at St. Paul's School, in 1648 he entered Magdalene College, Cambridge, where, distinguishing himself both by his scholarship and by his capacity for friendship, he was elected a fellow in 1656. He first studied medicine, but he finally decided to enter the church, accepting preferment in 1658 to the rectory of Brampton, Northamptonshire, and in 1667 to the rectory of All Hallows at Stamford, Lincolnshire. In 1661, Cambridge appointed him one of its twelve official preachers, and he kept in close touch with Cambridge intellectual life. Cumberland earned the reputation of being an exceptionally staunch Protestant. Report has it that the attempt of James II to reintroduce Roman Catholicism into England produced in him a dangerous fever. Such zeal did not go unrewarded under William III, and although quite without personal ambition, Cumberland was consecrated as bishop of Peterborough on July 5, 1691. He performed his episcopal duties with diligence until his death in 1718.

Jewish history was Cumberland's main interest. In 1686 he published *An Essay towards the Recovery of the Jewish Measures and Weights*. His domestic chaplain and son-in-law Squier Payne published in 1720 *Sanchoniatho's Phoenician History*, translated with a commentary by Cumberland. This monument of misplaced scholarly ingenuity derived its immediate inspiration from Hugo Grotius. With no qualms about the authenticity as history of Sanchoniatho's cosmogony, Cumberland devoted himself to identifying its personages with characters in the Old Testament. A sequel, *Origines Gentium Antiquissimae; or Attempts for Discovering the Times of the First Planting of Nations*, appeared in 1724.

Cumberland's sole philosophical work, *De Legibus Naturae* (1672), was designed, as the subtitle explains, as a refutation of Thomas Hobbes—the first full-length philosophical reply to Hobbes to be published. Written in an inelegant Latin, badly printed, ill-organized, intolerably diffuse, Cumberland's treatise did not attract much contemporary attention. In 1692, with Cumberland's approval, James Tyrrell prepared an abridgment and translation as *A Brief Disquisition of the Law of Nature*, hoping to draw attention to Cumberland's main ideas. But the abridgment was a poor one (in addition, Tyrrell's own views were mingled with Cumberland's) and failed in its main purpose. Eighteenth-century philosophers were more interested in Cumberland's work than his contemporaries had been; he anticipated their ambitions and preoccupations. A complete English translation was prepared by John Maxwell in 1727, and what has become the standard translation was published, with copious annotations by John Towers, in 1750. A French translation by Jean Barbeyrac (1744) ran into two editions.

Cumberland's point of departure is Grotius's *De Iure Belli et Pacis* (1625). Grotius, or so Cumberland interprets him, had based his demonstration of the existence and binding force of natural laws upon the consensus of civilized opinion. Very conscious of Hobbes, Cumberland sets out to supplement Grotius by demonstrating that natural laws are founded on "the nature of things," as distinct from the commands of sovereign rulers. To that extent Cumberland's aims coincide with Ralph Cudworth's, but unlike Cudworth he does not base his argument on Platonic metaphysics. Nor does he criticize, as did the Cambridge Platonists, the mechanical worldview; indeed, he wholeheartedly accepts it. He thinks of his approach as scientific and nonmetaphysical. He sets out to construct an ethics that, although Christian, is independent of revelation and, although demonstrating that morality is eternal and immutable, is based on "the evidence of sense and experience." These were to be the typical eighteenth-century specifications for a satisfactory moral theory.

Cumberland begins by arguing that there is a single natural law from which all moral laws can be derived—the law, namely, that an agent secures his own good by the promotion of the good of the whole to which he belongs. If this single law is based on "the nature of things," if its truth can be demonstrated from experience, then, he thinks, morality rests secure. And, he argues, experience reveals to us—he draws upon his medical training to illustrate the point—that the parts of a whole secure their own welfare only when they work for the good of the whole to which they belong. A bodily organ, for example, is at its healthiest when it is most effectively securing the health of the body. This truth men could recognize, so Cumberland argues against Hobbes, even in a state of nature. Thus, the foundation of moral laws is not the will of the sovereign.

Benevolence, Cumberland further maintains, is natural to humankind. Even brute animals, indeed, devote themselves to the welfare of their fellow brutes. A state of nature, therefore, would not be, as Hobbes suggested, a war of all against all; their human instincts, not the pressure of a sovereign will, lead men to cooperate with their fellow men in society. Certainly, Cumberland admits, men sometimes act in opposition to the good of the whole, just as an organ of the body will sometimes infect, rather than work toward the health of, the organism of which it forms a part. The fact remains, however, that the "natural impetus of man" is toward securing the common good, just as the general tendency of a bodily organ is to make the body healthier. The legislator's rewards and punishments, like medicine, are directed toward correcting abnormalities; they are not the original springs of moral action.

All moral concepts, Cumberland tries to show, are definable in terms of the single natural law that men secure their own welfare by pursuing the common good. An act is "naturally good" if by virtue of its own nature it tends toward the common good; it is "right" if it is the shortest way to that end; it is "morally good" if it conforms to the natural law. Particular virtues are similarly deducible from the obligation of pursuing the common good; to show that the common good ought to be our objective is at the same time to show that we ought to be law-abiding, just, temperate, and obedient to God.

Most of what were to be the leading eighteenth-century moral theories can be found somewhere suggested, if nowhere fully worked out, in *De Legibus Naturae*. Cumberland argues in detail that moral principles are analogous to the propositions of mathematics, and Samuel Clarke learned much from him on this point. Cumberland also sketches a moral calculus of the sort Francis Hutcheson was to employ; there are many resemblances between his moral philosophy and the third earl of Shaftesbury's; he has been described as the first systematic utilitarian; the organic theory of morality and of the state is conspicuous in his work; resemblances between Cumberland and Benedict de Spinoza are easy to detect.

Accounts of his moral philosophy differ widely, depending on which of the manifold tendencies in his thinking commentators stress. In Cumberland's own eyes, however, the crucial points are (1) there is a law of nature, defined as a proposition of "unchangeable truth and certainty … which lays firm obligations upon all outward acts of behaving, even in a state of nature"; (2) this law enjoins upon us the pursuit of the common good and assures us that by pursuing the common good we achieve happiness and personal perfection; (3) observation of the world, including man's nature, demonstrates the truth of this law; (4) all other moral precepts are applications of the law of nature to particular forms of human action.

See also Cambridge Platonists; Clarke, Samuel; Cudworth, Ralph; Ethics, History of; Grotius, Hugo; Hobbes, Thomas; Hutcheson, Francis; Shaftesbury, Third Earl of (Anthony Ashley Cooper); Spinoza, Benedict (Baruch) de.

Bibliography

The best edition of Cumberland's *De Legibus Naturae* is John Tower's 1750 translation (Dublin), which also includes, as Appendix IV, Squier Payne 's *Life of Cumberland*, the main biographical source. For commentaries, see Frank Elsworth Spaulding, *Richard Cumberland als Begründer der englischen Ethik* (Leipzig: Fock, 1894); Ernest Albee, *A History of English Utilitarianism* (London: Allen and Unwin, 1902); Frank Chapman Sharp, "The Ethical System of Richard Cumberland, and Its Place in the History of British Ethics," in *Mind* 21 (83) (1912): 371–398; James Clarke, *Richard Cumberland and Natural Law: Secularisation of Thought in Seventeenth-Century England* (Cambridge, U.K.: James Clarke, 1987); William Ewald, "The Biological Naturalism of Richard Cumberland." *Jahrbuch fur Recht und Ethik* (8 [2000]: 125–141); Murray Forsyth, "The Place of Richard Cumberland in the History of Natural Law." *Journal of the History of Philosophy* (20 [1982]: 23–42); M. A. Stewart, M. A., ed. *English Philosophy in the Age of Locke* (New York: Oxford University Press, 2000).

John Passmore (1967)
Bibliography updated by Tamra Frei (2005)

CUSANUS

See *Nicholas of Cusa*

CYNICS

"Cynics," the "dog philosophers" of the Greek and Roman world, so called almost certainly from the nickname of Diogenes of Sinope, were not a continuous school of theoretical philosophy but an erratic succession of individuals who from the fourth century BCE to the sixth century CE preached, through ascetic practice and mordant denunciation of established convention, a more or less similar way of life designed to lead to the happiness of the individual. Consequently there is no established doctrinal canon by which to define an "orthodox" Cynic, and the ancient but still lively debate as to whether Antisthenes or Diogenes was the founder of Cynicism is an unreal one. Nevertheless, despite marked variations of stress and tone in individual exponents, Diogenes was always regarded as the arch-Cynic, and a sufficient number of characteristic attitudes recur to identify the movement.

The nature of the existing evidence of Cynicism is highly unsatisfactory. The written works with which Diogenes was credited have not survived, and doxographies are few and of uncertain origin (for example, Diogenes Laërtius, Bk. 6, 70–73). Since Diogenes's life was his main testament, the largest class of evidence is anecdotal, with all the uncertainties and elaborations of an oral tradition. Information of his pupils and of Cynics of the third century BCE is tantalizingly fragmentary. Even the comparatively abundant material on contemporary Cynicism from the first century CE comes from outside the movement, from sympathizers of such diverse interests as Epictetus, Dio Chrysostom, and Julian, or from satirists such as Lucian.

TEACHING

The Cynics believed that happiness was found in "virtuous" action, which was the practical expression of self-realization (*arete* and "know thyself"). This state was in turn produced by a rational awareness of the distinction between natural and artificial values. External and physical goods such as wealth, reputation, pleasure, conventional duties arising from family, property, or state, and all traditional inhibitions, whether social or religious, were condemned as unnatural tyrannies that fettered a man through desire, indulgence, and the ignorance of a confused and corrupt society—the three causes of human misery. Freedom was secured by "following nature" by means of self-discipline whose end was self-sufficiency (*autarkeia*); since man was vulnerable and perverted through his emotions and desires, happiness could be guaranteed only by the understanding and strength of mind to want nothing, lack nothing. And since the artificial currency of human standards was thought to be, not an indifferent factor, but an active corruption to be eradicated, Cynics wished not merely to devalue the coin (like Socrates and the Stoics), but to deface it (*paracharattein*); hence, the most characteristic feature of Cynicism was an asceticism that sought to reduce physical wants to a minimum, as in the case of the animals after which Cynics were named, and to achieve spiritual independence like gods.

Independence was not to be achieved, however, by the withdrawal of a hermit; the Cynic engaged in an active crusade that required a continual training (*askesis*) to harden the body and temper the spirit in the very face of temptation, and thus to free the natural "perceptions" and capacities for virtuous actions. The toiling, painful effort of this moral struggle (*ponos*) was categorized as a good, the steep short cut to virtue, which evoked the only natural pleasure; and the legend of Herakles's life of service spent in successfully overcoming labors was sanctified as an ideal of freedom and self-fulfillment. He and the Cynic, whether slave or oppressed, ruled himself as his own master and, therefore, was the ideal king among men. Essentially individualistic and largely antisocial in advocating independence from any community, Cynicism was the most radical philosophy of spiritual security offered to fill the social and moral vacuum created in the fourth century BCE by the dissolution of the city-state political organism. Yet there was a strong philanthropic impulse in the movement in the sense that the gospel of Herakles, the ideal king, was a spiritual evangel for all men, to be preached by personal example. The Cynic saw himself as "scout and herald of God," dedicating his own labors as a reconnaissance for others to follow; he was the "watchdog of mankind" to bark at illusion, the "surgeon" whose knife sliced the cancer of cant from the minds of others. Cynics deliberately adopted shamelessly shocking extremes of speech and action to jolt the attention and illustrate their attack on convention.

Fearlessness in criticism was a virtue, useful to further Cynic ideals, but it was also open to abuse, as was the license of affected shamelessness. There was always a real danger that the negative, denunciatory side of Cynicism would predominate, the more so since happiness was most often described as freedom from misery, and virtue, practical wisdom, and right reason remained somewhat nebulous terms. The Cynics did not offer arguments to intellectuals, whose theories they despised as useless. Rather, they offered the ideal practical example of autonomy of will through their own actions, bringing by the very vilification of luxury and sensual indulgence and by the justification of poverty, spiritual hope to the poor, disenchanted and oppressed. Thus the more formal types of philosophical instruction were abandoned and three new literary genres fostered: the *chreia*, or short anecdotal quip with a pungent moral tang; the diatribe, or popular sermon in conversational style; and Menippean satire.

HISTORY OF THE MOVEMENT

The most influential of Diogenes's converts was Crates of Thebes. Joined by his wife in a life devoted to Cynic ideals, he earned by his humanity and good works the affectionate name of "Door-Opener." He wrote philosophical tragedies and poetry about a Cynic paradise named the island of Pera. In the third century BCE. Bion of Borysthenes, a wandering preacher, was "the first to tart up philosophy" by popularizing the diatribe; Menippus of Gadara initiated a new type of satire mingling seriocomic themes in prose and verse (his works are lost); Cercidas of Megalopolis applied Cynic ideas to practical politics by proposing reforms attacking social inequalities in the refounding of his city; the fragments of Teles, a dull Megarian schoolmaster, throw some light on Bion and earlier Cynics. After a quieter, although not dormant, period Cynicism revived in the first century CE with some encouragement from Stoicism: Demetrius was prominent in the Stoic-flavored opposition to the emperor in the seventh decade; Dio Chrysostom found solace for his exile in an amalgam of Cynic and Stoic practice; Epictetus, the Stoic, admired Diogenes.

The second century records the apogee of Cynic influence and extravagance. The leading figures differed sharply. The philanthropy and popularity of Demonax of Cyprus contrasted with the brutal scorn of Oenomaus of Gadara. Peregrinus Proteus, a convert from Christianity, was an irrepressible radical with a touch of the mystic; he burned himself to death before huge crowds at the Olympic festival. These were men of ideals; but Lucian and Julian also record with disgust a riffraff of confidence tricksters and professional beggar-preachers masquerading under the Cynic uniform of cloak, knapsack, and stick. The peculiar animal-divine polarity of Cynicism attracted both saints and rogues. In the history of Greek thought Cynicism was most influential on the development of Stoicism, first through Zeno and then much later with Epictetus, who gave noble expression (3.22) to the most uncompromisingly radical ethic that anyone attempted to put into practice in the ancient world.

It is tempting to recognize Cynic traits in other civilizations, as Onesicratus, the admiral and historian of Alexander, did on encountering the gymnosophist Indian fakirs. In medieval times, the mendicant friars are more apposite than anchorites, especially when one considers the complementary virtues of Franciscans and Dominicans (*Domini canes*).

See also Antisthenes; Asceticism; Diogenes of Sinope; Epictetus; Lucian of Samosata; Megarians; Socrates; Stoicism; Zeno of Citium.

Bibliography

SOURCES, COMMENTARIES, AND TRANSLATIONS

Giannantoni, G. *Socratis et Socraticorum Reliquiae*. 4 vols. Naples: Bibliopolis, 1990.

For Crates: Diehl, E. *Anthologia Lyrica Graeca* I. Leipzig, 1958.

For Teles: Hense, O. *Teletis Reliquiae*. Freiburg, 1889.

Malherbe, A. J. *The Cynic Epistles*. Missoula: Scholars Press for the Society of Biblical Literature, 1977.

Müseler, E. *Die Kynikerbriefe*. 2 vols. Paderborn: F. Schöningh, 1994.

Caizzi, F. D. *Antisthenis Fragmenta*. Milan, 1966.

Von Fritz, K. *Quellenuntersuchungen zur Leben und Philosophie des Diogenes von Sinope*. Philologus Suppl. 18, Leipzig, 1926.

STUDIES

Billerbeck, M. *Die Kyniker in der modernen Forschung*. Amsterdam: B. R. Grüner, 1991.

Caizzi, F. D. "Antistene." *Studi Urbinati* 1 (1964) 25–76.

Downing, F. G. *Cynics and Christian Origins*. Edinburgh: T & T Clark, 1992.

Dudley, D. R. *A History of Cynicism from Diogenes to the Sixth Century A.D.* London: Methuen, 1937.

Goulet-Cazé, M.-O. "Le cynisme à l'époque impériale." *Aufstieg und Niedergang der Römischen Welt* 2.36.4. Berlin: W. de Gruyter, 1990.

Goulet-Cazé, M.-O. *Sophiês Maiêtores*. In *Chercheurs de Sagesse: Hommage à Jean Pepin*. Collection des Études Augustiniennes, Serie Antiquité 131 (1992) 5–36.

Goulet-Cazé, M.-O., and R. Goulet, eds. *Le cynisme ancien et ses prolongements: Actes du Colloque intérnational du C.N.R.S.* Paris: Presses universitaires de France, 1993.

Hahm, D. "Diogenes Laertius VII: On the Stoics." *Aufstieg und Niedergang der Römischen Welt* 2.36.6. Berlin: W. de Gruyter, 1992.

Mansfeld, J. "Diogenes Laertius on Stoic Philosophy." *Elenchos* 7 (1986) 296–382.

I. G. Kidd (1967)

Bibliography updated by Scott Carson (2005)

CYRANO DE BERGERAC, SAVINIEN DE

(1619–1655)

Savinien de Cyrano de Bergerac, a soldier, man of letters, and freethinker, was born in Paris, where he died thirty-six years later; he resembled only superficially the hero of Edmond Rostand's romanticized drama (1897). Hostile to the formal authoritarian education to which he had been subjected at the Collège de Beauvais, he was persuaded to serve in the army, where he gained a considerable reputation as a duelist and writer of verses. His military career came to an end when he was wounded at the siege of Arras in 1640. Between 1642 and 1651 he studied philosophy assiduously, with special stress on Pierre Gassendi and René Descartes, and was, according to some, a pupil of Gassendi himself. Descartes's principle of methodical doubt, Gassendi's rehabilitation of Epicurus, and the attendant influence of a newly translated Lucretius were all forces providing a common philosophical denominator which drew Cyrano closer to his fellow *libertins*—Gabriel Naudé, François La Mothe Le Vayer, and Molière, among others. At the same time he was emerging as a burlesque poet of consequence and a redoubtable political writer who first attacked and then defended the Machiavellian statecraft of Cardinal Mazarin. In 1652 he entered the service of the Duc d'Arpajon under whose protection he brought out in 1654 his *Oeuvres diverses,* which included the boldly rational *Lettre contre les sorciers* and a farcical comedy, *Le pédant joué,* from which Molière borrowed two passages for *Les fourberies de Scapin.* In 1654 Cyrano also published an intellectually challenging and ideologically daring tragedy, *La mort d'agrippine.* A falling beam, dislodged by accident—or perhaps intentionally—brought death a year later.

Cyrano's reputation as an intellectual libertine, propagator of subversive ideas, satirist of man and his foibles, and as a figure in the vanguard of scientific thought—already firmly established before 1655—received increased notoriety with the posthumous appearance of *L'autre monde, ou les états et empires de la lune et du soleil,* which described imaginary voyages to the moon and the sun, respectively. The first of the two parts of this work was made public in truncated form by the author's friend Le Bret in 1657. The second part, either unfinished or censored (the original manuscript has vanished), was published in 1762.

Despite borrowings and suggestions from a variety of sources, Cyrano's work, particularly when compared with that of many of his contemporaries, is strikingly original. Subscribing to the still little known and highly controversial Copernican theory, he adhered to the principle that all is relative in the universe and attacked religious and philosophical anthropocentrism. In fact he was the first to link closely together a criticism of the religion of Moses and the philosophy of Aristotle. In the man-machine–beast-machine debate, he stressed the idea of continuity among all living creatures. A forerunner of Denis Diderot's materialism, he outlined a calculation of probability according to which atoms, by means of chance and infinite time alone, could, in their innumerable combinations, create the organized world known to man. Furthermore he demonstrated an awareness of the forces of gravitation, the laws of which Isaac Newton was to discover and define several decades later. But he did not have Gassendi's gift for observation and experimentation or Descartes's aptitude for mathematics. He was more a popularizer of science than a true scientist. Indeed, he was the originator of science fiction.

The chief significance of Cyrano lies in the fact that he epitomized the general mental attitudes among the freethinkers of his period: enmity toward tradition, interest in ethical and scientific progress, and fondness for philosophical abstractions. As such he was eminently representative of those engaged in a protracted intellectual struggle which revealed the great trend of the French critical spirit—a spirit that was to gain increased momentum in the eighteenth century and to approach fulfillment with the publication of Diderot's encyclopedia.

See also Aristotle; Descartes, René Gassendi, Pierre; La Mothe Le Vayer, Francois de; Newton, Isaac.

Bibliography

WORKS BY CYRANO

Modern editions of de Bergerac's works include F. Lachèvre, ed., *Les oeuvres libertines de Cyrano de Bergerac* (Paris: E. Champion, 1921); H. Weber, ed., *Cyrano de Bergerac. L'autre monde* (Paris: Editions Sociales, 1959); and Richard Aldington, ed. and tr., *Voyages to the Moon and Sun* (New York: Orion, 1962).

WORKS ON CYRANO

See P.-A. Brun, *Savinien de Cyrano Bergerac. Sa vie et ses oeuvres* (Paris: A. Colin, 1893); René Pintard, *Le libertinage érudit dans la premiere moitié de XVIII*[e] *siècle* (Paris: Boivin, 1943); J.-J. Bridenne, "A la recherche du vrai Cyrano de Bergerac," *Information littéraire* (November–December 1953).

Otis Fellows (1967)

CYRENAICS

The Cyrenaics were a school of philosophy founded by Aristippus of Cyrene in the first quarter of the fourth century BCE. Although he had two sons, Aristippus designated his daughter Arete as his intellectual heiress. She in turn bestowed the succession on her son Aristippus, called "the Mother-taught." Apparently it was mainly he, a contemporary of Aristotle, who developed the more technical aspects of Cyrenaic doctrines. Cyrenaics were always included in lists of philosophical schools drawn up by the historians even though they had no fixed headquarters (unlike the Academy, the Lyceum, the Garden, etc.). There were several subschools referred to by the names of individuals, as Hegesiacs, Annicerians, and so on. They seem to have carried on the tradition of the Sophists of Socrates' time, being loosely associated itinerant teachers offering, for fees, instruction in general culture and on particular philosophical doctrines. Their pupils were supposed to learn from them how to live the good life, specifically, how to get along with anybody in any circumstances, as their founder put it.

The Cyrenaics were hedonists. They regarded it as self-evident that pleasure is the goal of life, for pleasure and avoidance of pain are what all living creatures seek by nature. The sage best knows how to attain a life of as many pleasures, interspersed with as few pains, as feasible and how to bear the pains when they come, as come they must. Unlike the Epicureans, the Cyrenaics regarded pleasure not negatively as mere absence of pain—dead people are in that condition—but as positive feeling, notably what is experienced in eating, drinking, and sex.

The younger Aristippus formulated a physiological analysis. There are three kinds of internal bodily motions: rough, smooth, and intermediate, which he compared to a tempestuous sea, a gently undulating sea, and doldrums respectively. Pleasure is the perception, by "internal feeling," of smooth motion; pain, of rough motion. Pleasures thus are particular present-moment happenings in individuals. These motions and their perceptions include satisfactions and dissatisfactions not so obviously internal to the body, such as gratitude and the pleasure one takes in the prosperity of one's country. The Cyrenaics noted that thought, not simply perception, enters into pleasure/pain distinctions. For example, watching a man really dying is painful, but to see an actor "die" on stage may be pleasurable. Nevertheless, plainly corporeal pleasures and pains are, in general, more intense, which is why they are prescribed as rewards and punishments.

Like his teacher Socrates, the elder Aristippus did not concern himself with natural science, which he deemed useless for furthering the good life. His grandson justified this rejection by advancing a skeptical theory of knowledge, of greater present-day interest perhaps than Cyrenaic ethics, for it is the closest ancient forerunner of modern phenomenalism and subjectivism. The only things one knows infallibly and certainly, he held, are one's feelings. These are internal states of the body. Things outside us produce the feelings—the Cyrenaics never doubted the external world—but one cannot know what those things are in themselves and how they operate. Something not yellow in itself may produce the sensation of yellow in a person with jaundice, and so on through the usual litany. Strictly, then, when in the presence of snow, one ought to say not "I see something white" but rather "I am being whitened" or, even better, "I am being affected whitely." Statements of these forms are the only ones knowable as absolutely true or false. Furthermore, if someone else in the same situation says—sincerely, let us assume—that he too is being affected whitely, then he speaks the truth, but from this it cannot be inferred that his feeling is identical to one's own. We apply the word "white" conventionally in the context of snow, but we have no way of knowing that the feeling it refers to is identical in everyone. Thus although the Cyrenaics did not explicitly raise the problem of other minds, in maintaining this possibility of an inverted spectrum they came close.

Cyrenaic skepticism helped also to justify Cyrenaic hedonism. Choices, as Socratics insisted, should be based on knowledge, not opinion or conjecture. But the scope of knowledge is limited to feelings, including pleasure and pain. Therefore, it is not only natural but rational to base our choices on pleasure and pain.

The most notable later Cyrenaics were Hegesias, Anniceris, and Theodorus, all active at the turn of the fourth to third century BCE. Hegesias, called "the Death Persuader," was an ancient Schopenhauer. From hedonism, surprisingly but straightforwardly, he deduced an unmitigated pessimism. The only good is pleasure; the only evil is pain. But as things are and must be, pains so predominate over pleasures that a life adding up to a pleasurable net balance is impossible. Therefore, suicide is eminently rational. Hegesias wrote a book, *The Man Starving Himself to Death*, in which the title character describes in detail the unavoidable ills of life. It was said that he lectured on this theme with such eloquence that some of his auditors killed themselves, whereupon the Greek king of Egypt, Ptolemy I Soter ("the Savior"), forbade him to deliver any more such addresses. Thus Hegesias perhaps had the dubious honor of being the first professor to have had his academic freedom curtailed by the government. He did not kill himself. There is a further similarity to Arthur Schopenhauer in his counsel "We should not hate people, but educate them."

Anniceris altered Cyrenaic hedonism by putting mental pleasures on a par with bodily ones, or even preferring them. Moreover, he softened the Cyrenaic egoism, declaring that the sage might forgo particular pleasures for the sake of friendship (as Epicurus maintained). He was credited with having ransomed Plato when that philosopher was for sale in the slave market of Aegina, though there are chronological and other difficulties with the story.

Theodorus, Anniceris's pupil, took free speech and the flouting of conventional pieties to an extreme even for the Greeks. He said that the sage would not fight for his country, for why should he put his wisdom at risk of extinction for the sake of the stupid masses? (Theodorus, unlike Hegesias, did not say no to life.) Aristippus had said that if all the laws were abrogated, the sage would continue to behave as before. Theodorus turned this proto-Kantian ethic all the way around, declaring that the sage might steal, commit adultery, even pillage temples if the occasion demanded—such acts being evil not by nature but only supposedly so to restrain the stupid. Extending his teacher's view on precedence among pleasures, for pleasure/pain he substituted joy/sorrow (primarily mental feelings) as the basic ethical contrast. He even went so far as to hold, as the Cynics did, that matters of the body are "indifferent." Threatened with crucifixion after he insulted Lysimachus, king of Macedon and in consequence ruler of Athens at the time, Theodorus contemptuously replied that it did not matter to him whether he rotted in the ground or in the air. (The threat apparently was not carried out.) But in place of Anniceris's amiability he reinstated hard-boiled egoism, claiming that the sage, being self-sufficient, has no need of friends.

With Diagoras of Melos and Euhemerus of Tegea, also a Cyrenaic, Theodorus was one of only three Greek thinkers who unequivocally proclaimed that there are no gods or demons at all, thereby earning the sobriquet "the Atheist." At a party in Athens, Hipparchia, wife of Crates the Cynic and a philosopher in her own right, chopped logic with him, saying, "What would not be wrong when done by Theodorus would not be wrong when done by Hipparchia. Now, it would not be wrong for Theodorus to strike himself. Therefore it would not be wrong for Hipparchia to strike Theodorus." Theodorus made no answer but instead pulled up her dress. (Doing so was not, or not merely, a display of classical male chauvinism, for it would not have been wrong for Hipparchia to pull up her own dress.)

The modifications by Anniceris and Theodorus brought the Cyrenaics so close to Epicurean views that it is not surprising that we hear no more of them as a distinct school after the first half of the third century BCE, when it was displaced by the Epicurean school.

See also Aristippus of Cyrene; Epicurus; Hedonism; Schopenhauer, Arthur.

Bibliography

Giannantoni, Gabriele. *I Cirenaici*. Florence, Italy: G. C. Sansoni, 1958.

Mannebach, Erich, ed. *Aristippi et Cyrenaicorum fragmenta*. Leiden, Netherlands: E. J. Brill, 1961.

Tsouna, Voula. *The Epistemology of the Cyrenaic School*. Cambridge, U.K.: Cambridge University Press, 1998.

Wallace Matson (2005)

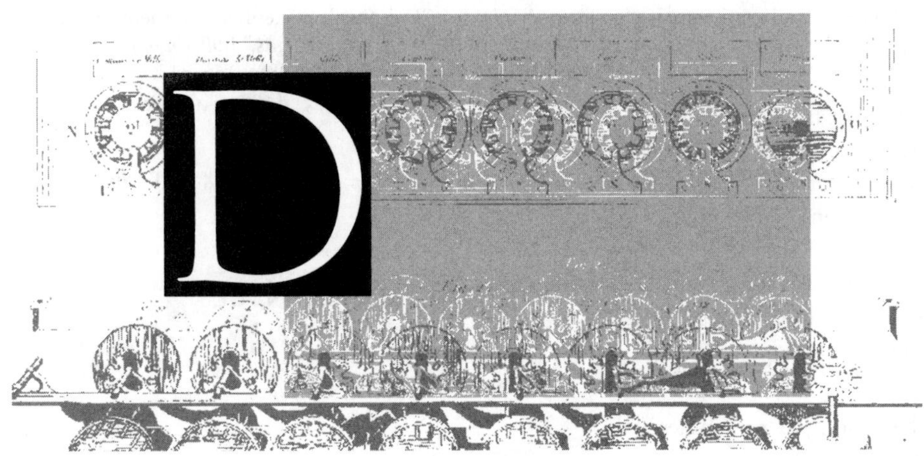

DAI ZHEN

(1723–1777)

Dai Zhen, styled Dongyuan, was a critical-minded neo-Confucian in the Qing period. He is noted as a critic of neo-Confucianism of the Song (960–1279) and Ming (1368–1644) periods and made original contributions to the critical exposition of the philosophy of Mencius (c. 371–c. 289 BCE). Even though not known as a philosopher in his own time, his work in neo-Confucian criticism and exposition received more attention after Hu Shi wrote about his philosophy in the 1930s.

Dai Zhen was born in the Huizhou area of Anhui Province at a place known as Longfu (Tunxi) of Xiuling County. Although Huizhou was prosperous and produced outstanding academic talents, Dai Zhen, coming from a poor family with no academic traditions, received no good formal schooling. His success as a scholar derived from his own dedication to self-study.

Dai Zhen wrote *Yuan shan* (*Inquiry into Goodness*), his first philosophical treatise, from age 33 to age 41. With this work as a foundation, Dai Zhen then introduced quotations from the classics to support his philosophical points, and this later work, together with *Yuan shan*, became *Xuyan* (Prefatory words). Consolidating and concentrating on *Mengzi* (The book of Mencius), he sorted out and expanded *Xuyan* into a philosophical commentary on the key notions of *Mengzi*, producing *"Mengzi" ziyi shuzheng* (Commentary on the meanings of terms in *Mengzi*). This was his last work, which he completed at age 44.

Although Dai Zhen strongly objected to the abstract use of principles (*li*), he did not deny the importance of reason when applied correctly to concrete matters. But how does one acquire an understanding of reason and principle? The answer is twofold: by correctly reading the classical texts on which doctrines of moral reasoning are based and by clearly reflecting on what reason and principle concretely signify. One must first authenticate the classical texts and semantically and philologically determine their meaning. Only then can one correctly read and interpret them. In this sense textual criticism is highly relevant to understanding the principles and moral reasoning embodied in the texts of the classical philosophers.

The usefulness of textual criticism for understanding reasons and principles is, of course, no explanation of the rise of textual criticism in the Qing period. Most well-known textual critics were not interested in discovering or rediscovering the principles and moral reasoning of the classical texts. But for Dai Zhen, textual criticism is essential for such discovery. He wrote, "The ultimate idea of the classics is the Way. We use words [*ci*] to understand the Way. We use the linguistic study of the text [*xiaoxue wenzi*] to understand the words. From such study we come to understand the discourse, from the discourse we come to understand the mind and intent of the ancient sages" (1995, p. 378). Hence, for Dai Zhen, the purpose of textual criticism of a classic is to retrieve the original meaning of the text. On this basis one can then come to understand the moral reasoning and principles behind the texts.

Dai Zhen was perhaps the first modern Chinese scholar to formulate a textual hermeneutics that combines historical linguistics with philosophical reflection for reading classical texts. He was also one of the earliest pioneers in philosophical hermeneutics in the whole world.

Another important philosophical contribution of Dai Zhen's was his objection to separating reason from feelings and desires in Song and Ming neo-Confucianism and hence his stress on understanding in terms of human feelings and desires. This position came from his deep appreciation of the naturalistic cosmology of the *Yijing* (Book of changes), where he found sources of human nature and human reason. He took the productivity of life (*shengsheng*) as the most basic fact of reality. The purpose of this productivity gives purpose to the interplay of yin and yang and is called the Way, he explained. This interplay results in the unceasing transformation of life and the ordering of things (*tiaoli*) in heaven and on earth. From the productivity of life and the ordering of things Dai Zhen derives the virtues of humanity (*ren*) and moral reason (*yi*), which he regards as inherent in these two processes.

See also Chinese Philosophy. Confucius; Cosmology; Human Nature; Hu Shi; Mencius; Reason.

Bibliography

WORKS BY DAI ZHEN

Tai Chên's "Inquiry into Goodness." Translated by Chung-ying Cheng. Honolulu, HI: East-West Center Press, 1968.

Dai Zhen wenji. Beijing: Zhonghua shuju, 1980.

Dai Dongyuan quanji. Beijing: Qinghua daxue chubanshe, 1993.

"Gujing jie Gou Chen xu." In *Dai Zhen quanshu.* Vol. 6. Hefei, China: Huangshan shushe, 1995.

WORKS ON DAI ZHEN

Hu Shi. *Dai Dongyuan de zhexue.* Taipei: Yuanliu chuban gongsi, 1968.

Torbjoern Loden. "Dai Zhen's Evidential Commentary on the Meaning of the Words of Mencius." *Bulletin of the Museum of Far Eastern Antiquities* 60 (1988): 165–313.

Yu Yingshi. *On Dai Dongyuan and Zhang Xuecheng.* Hong Kong, 1976.

Chung-ying Cheng (2005)

D'ALEMBERT, JEAN LE ROND

See *Alembert, Jean Le Rond d'*

DAMASCIUS

(c. 462–c. 538)

Damascius was a neoplatonic philosopher and the last head of the Academy in Athens. He was born around 462 CE in Damascus and studied in Alexandria and Athens. In 515 he became head of the Academy, which, through his reforms and teaching, would see a final flourishing. After the closing down of the Academy by Emperor Justianus in 529, Damascius and six colleagues went into exile at the court of King Chosroes in Persia. They returned in 532, having been granted the freedom to continue their philosophical work. Damascius died in Syria sometime after 538.

His writings include the "Life of Isidore" (Isidore was his teacher and predecessor), in which he offers a privileged insight in the history of the pagan Platonic school in the fifth century CE; and commentaries on Plato (preserved are those on the *Parmenides*, the *Philebus*, and the *Phedo*). He is, however, mainly known for his treatise "On the First Principles" (*De principiis*), an ingenious philosophical speculation about the first causes of all things.

Damascius had no ambition to develop a better metaphysical system than his predecessors. His own thought is primarily aporetic: He raises critical questions in the margin of the doctrine of the principles, as it had been developed in the neoplatonic tradition, and confronts the doctrine with all sorts of difficulties. When he ventures a solution—and on many issues he can be original (for instance, his doctrine on time)—he again puts that solution into a question with new aporias (or doubts). Damascius's work is in many ways a critical analysis of the position of Proclus, who, in his view, was too preoccupied with logical coherence and system building. He raises questions about the One and multiplicity, about procession and return, about triads of principles, and about concepts such as power—not in order to discredit all philosophical discourse skeptically, but to clarify what is inadequate in the formulations of his predecessors.

The most fundamental aporia is discussed at the beginning of the treatise: Is the first principle itself a part of the whole of which it is the principle? But if it is a part, how could it still have the status of a principle? If it is outside the whole, how can we understand that the whole originates from it? The first principle, it seems, is neither principle nor cause, nor does it fit in any other category used to explain relations between beings: It is an ineffable "nothing" we have to postulate beyond the one whole. This "ineffable" is even beyond the "One" that is the first principle of all things.

More than any other Platonic philosopher, Damascius is aware of the precarious nature of all rational discourse when people deal with questions that go beyond the limits of what they can experience. More than any other, he explored the boundaries of rationality; he tried, by all means, to say what could not be said, because about the first principles one can only speak using analogies and "indications" (*endeixeis*), which are as such unfitting to indicate divine realities.

Damascius's sharp critical mind does not, however, bring him to skepticism. If philosophical systems remain tentative and fragile, there is also the mythological tradition and religious practice, to which Damascius remains devoted. Damascius is, together with Proclus, our main source on Chaldean and Orphic theologies. In many ways his work is a wonderful swan song of pagan Hellenism.

See also Greek Academy; Neoplatonism; Plato; Proclus.

Bibliography

WORKS BY DAMASCIUS

Damascius: Traité des premiers principes. 3 vols, edited by Leendert Westerink and Joseph Combès. Paris: Les Belles Lettres, 1986–1991.

Damascius: Commentaire du Parménide de Platon. 4 vols, edited by Leendert Westerink and Joseph Combès. Paris: Les Belles Lettres, 1997–2003.

WORKS ABOUT DAMASCIUS

Athanassiadi, Polymnia, ed. *Damascius: The Philosophical History.* Athens: Apamea Cultural Assocation, 1999.

Hoffmann, Philippe. "Damascius." In *Dictionnaire des philosophes antiques.* Vol. 2, 541–593. Paris: CNRS, 1994.

Carlos Steel (2005)

DANTE ALIGHIERI

(1265–1321)

Dante Alighieri, the author of the *Divine Comedy,* was born in Florence of a middle-class family with some pretensions to nobility. It is likely that he frequented the church schools, and he probably spent a year at the University of Bologna. He fought in the battle of Campaldino (1289) and a few years later married Gemma Donati, by whom he had at least three children. He took part in the government of his native city, serving on various city councils (1295–1297, 1301), as prior (1300), and as ambassador to San Gimignano (May 1300) and later to Rome (October 1301), where his mission was to negotiate with the pope to bring about a just peace between the warring factions of White Guelphs and Black Guelphs. Aided by the intervention of Charles of Valois, the Blacks took over the city and Dante, a White, went into exile. He wandered from court to court of medieval Italy, with especially long sojourns at Verona and at Ravenna, where he spent the last three years of his life. He seems to have served his patrons as adviser and on occasion specifically as ambassador; it was after an embassy to Venice on behalf of Guido da Polenta, Lord of Ravenna, that the poet died.

By choice Dante might well have devoted himself to political life: circumstance deprived him of this opportunity and constrained him to put his great gifts to the service of letters; his masterpiece, the *Divine Comedy,* is generally regarded as the supreme poetic achievement of the Western tradition and has assured his fame. His *Vita Nuova* is the story of his idealistic love for Beatrice, presumably of the Portinari family, who married Simone de' Bardi and died in 1290. The *Convivio*, composed after the author went into exile, is a didactic work; the *De vulgari eloquentia* is a milestone in the history of linguistics, being the first serious study of a vernacular tongue; and the *De monarchia* is the vehicle for Dante's expression of his political theory. Mention should also be made of his *Rhymes,* a collection of verses of varying kinds—some purely lyrical, some moralistic, and some, one might say, philosophical.

To what extent Dante may properly be considered a philosopher depends on one's definition of the term. Richard McKeon does not consider him such "by the crucial test that, despite the philosophic doctrines that crowd his poems, scholars have been unable to agree concerning what his attitude toward the philosophers he uses is." But this is to make a very special category of philosophers. The best statement of Dante's attitude is found at the beginning of the *Convivio* (Banquet), where he represents himself not as one of the great (scholars and philosophers) who actually sit at the banquet table but rather as one who, sitting at their feet, passes on to others the crumbs that he is able to pick up. This would make him on the one hand at least an eager student of philosophy and on the other what we should now call a popularizer, if the term may be used without disparagement. And within the great area of philosophy his major interest was in ethics and politics. Let us concede that in the field of pure speculation his mind was alert and curious rather than original. Like his contemporaries he was for the most part content to follow Aristotle as interpreted by Thomas Aquinas, with recourse to what he thought of as "Platonic" where it suited him. His use of his authority, his stature as a poet, and his influence, which still endures, make it worthwhile to study his philosophical posture in some detail.

THE *VITA NUOVA* AND *CONVIVIO*

If a drive to seek eternal truth, permanent universals, and order in things is the proper attribute of a philosopher, as it would seem to be, then Dante's claim to the cherished title is reasonable. Perhaps his first work, the *Vita Nuova,* is the most dramatic example of this precisely because, paradoxically, it is not a philosophical work at all. It is a love story of intimate and personal nature, grounded, it would seem, in historical fact but taking on the air of a spiritual parable; its immediate sources are not in works of philosophy but in the love cult of the Middle Ages. Yet the construction and the apparatus betray a disciplined intent; the prose and poetry are mingled in a strict architectural pattern; and each of the poems is followed by an analysis composed in the tradition of Scholasticism. Digressions on the nature of personification and the meaning of certain terms are evidence of what one might fairly call the philosophical manner. Beatrice herself becomes in the course of the confessional narrative something very close to a theological and thus a quasi-philosophical concept.

It is, however, the *Convivio* that is the most purposefully "philosophical" of Dante's canon. It was inspired, the author tells us, by the reading of Cicero and Boethius, and Dante in fact seems to see himself as having much in common with the latter, also a victim of political injustice, and as turning to the same source for consolation. It is noteworthy, too, that Dante, like Boethius, attempts—consciously, one suspects—to set philosophy free from its entanglement with Christian theology. His definition of philosophy in the third tractate goes back to Pythagoras, and in Book IV, in the course of enumerating the virtues appropriate to the successive ages of man, he turns to the pagans (such as Aeneas and, very strikingly, Cato), to exemplify such virtues. All but startling is his eulogy: "And what earthly man was more worthy than Cato to signify God? Truly none." Such an attitude toward the "ideal pagan" dramatizes the author's celebrated exposition of the two beatitudes (II, 4): one in speculation and contemplation, the other in proper conduct of the active life; the former is "higher" than the latter, which, however, clearly is not "subordinate": "It is typical of Dante," says Étienne Gilson, "to base the autonomy of an inferior order on its very inferiority."

In this connection the plan of the *Convivio* (if it may be called a plan, for, unlike most of Dante's works, the book seems to have grown of itself) is very revealing of the author's concept of the uses, if not the nature, of philosophy. The first tractate is highly personal, stating that the genesis of his interest was his need for consolation in his exile and his feeling that his "image" in Italy had suffered somewhat from the youthful and impassioned portrait that emerged from the pages of the *Vita Nuova.* In the second tractate he avows that in effect philosophy, "the fairest and noblest daughter of the universe," is the new lady who has replaced Beatrice in his heart. In the third tractate he discusses the meaning of philosophy, which he finds to signify "love of and zeal for wisdom," adding that philosophy has "as its subject understanding and as its form an almost divine love of the thing understood." Presumably "understanding" can be applied to the various fields of study Dante had enumerated in the second tractate, composing an ingenious correlation between the sciences and the heavens of the Ptolemaic system. Of these branches the highest for any medieval theologian (theology itself is in the empyrean, beyond the physical cosmos) would be metaphysics, but it is significant that Dante brackets it with physics in the starry heaven and puts ethics in the loftiest physical sphere, the primum mobile, morality being "the science that disposes us rightly for the other sciences" even as the crystalline heaven sets in motion all the other spheres. In fact, the largest part of the work, the fourth treatise, is given over to a study of true nobility, its source and its effects.

Dante finds this human excellence to be not the Aristotelian "inherited wealth and good manners" but rather a God-given grace, the nature of which is evident in its fruits. The fruits, which are enumerated in chronological order, are all of such a nature as to be properly called social virtues. Dante's ideal is not a mystic or a visionary but, in the best sense of the term, a man of the world, living in a community and serving it to the best of his ability—certainly an Aristotelian concept. Only in the stage of "decrepitude" does Dante say that the good man's thoughts should turn to God and the afterlife, and even this passage, beautiful as it is, has about it a tone more pagan than Christian. It is noteworthy that all the men chosen to exemplify the appropriate virtues are men of action, in many cases pagans but also including such ambiguous characters as Lancelot and Guido da Montefeltro, the *condottiere.* Thus the *Convivio*, dedicated to the glorification of philosophy, ends by being a rule of good living, high-minded, to be sure, but practical as well. Noteworthy too is the rather lengthy excursus of Book IV (Chs. 4–5) that is inserted to justify the Roman Empire. Dante finds historical correspondences between the empire and the church, affirms that Christ chose to come to Earth at the time the world was best governed and at peace (that is, under Augustus), and concludes with a panegyric to Rome. This is the more interesting because some of his data are traceable to St. Augustine, whose view of imperial Rome was quite opposite.

THE *DE MONARCHIA*

The *De monarchia,* developing the latent and the tentative attitudes of the *Convivio,* may well contain Dante's most original contribution to philosophical thought. Written, it seems likely, either during or shortly after Henry VII of Luxembourg's descent into Italy (c. 1313), it is an eloquent defense of the imperial cause or, more accurately, principle. The work is divided into three parts: in the first Dante shows the necessity for the rule of one monarch in temporal affairs; in the second he argues that for historical reasons such a monarch should be the Roman emperor; and in the third he defends the thesis that the emperor, although he owes deference to the pope, should not be subordinate to the pontiff in temporal matters.

It is the first book that is the most fascinating to the student of Dante the philosopher. Briefly, the main argument is that peace is a necessity if humanity is to actualize its potential intellect in the highest degree; and there can be no assurance of peace, national rivalries being what they are and greed being as strong as it is, unless the world is governed by one prince, supreme above all nations and beyond the temptations of *cupiditas.* In the course of defining the collective potential intellect, Dante invokes the name of Averroes, thus laying himself open to a charge of heresy (and indeed the *De monarchia* was solemnly burned and remained on the Index for many years).

Gilson, however, has well made the point that the collective potential intellect of humanity as conceived by Dante was not a "being," as was the "possible intellect" (or kind of oversoul) of Averroes, but rather a "community." Indeed, in the course of his arguments in the first book Dante follows Thomistic reasoning, but unlike Thomas, who never so much as mentioned the word *emperor,* he applies it to secular purposes. Conceding the superiority of contemplation over action and, by inference, of the spiritual over the temporal, he nevertheless stresses the importance of the machinery necessary to perfect the fulfillment of man's proper endowment in the active life and his happiness in this world. So too at the end he readily concedes that the emperor owes the pope the respect of a younger brother, but while thus indicating that the spiritual life is superior, he seems also to imply that it is separate and independent; both pope and emperor would, in his theory, derive their authority directly from God. The result is in fact a kind of political facet of the Averroistic double truth, as contemporary critics were quick to point out. Gilson, for whom Dante is no Averroist, nevertheless commends him for seeing clearly "that one cannot entirely withdraw the temporal world from the jurisdiction of the spiritual world without entirely withdrawing philosophy from the jurisdiction of theology" and adds that Dante's perception of this fact gives him "a cardinal position in the history of mediaeval political philosophy." In this sense and with a practical intent characteristic of Dante, the *De monarchia* reaffirms the underlying thesis of the *Convivio.*

THE *DIVINE COMEDY*

It has been argued by some critics that the *Divine Comedy* is in essence a repudiation of the secular and independent *Convivio* and *De monarchia* and is evidence of a kind of "Conversion" of the poet, resulting either from some inner crisis or from his despair at the defeat of Henry VII. Perhaps if we say that in the *Comedy* the substance of the earlier works is utilized as a preparation for the vision, a basis for the mystic superstructure rather than as a finality in itself, we may speak of "conversion," but not, in the opinion of this writer, if the word carries any suggestion of rejection. It is true that the devotional element is novel and important: the intercession of the Virgin Mary makes it possible for the poet to undertake the supernatural journey and to enjoy the vision that crowns it. The vision itself is of a mystical nature, adumbrated perhaps in the *Vita nuova* but totally absent from the "philosophical" works. Concern with purely theological matters—the Incarnation, predestination, divine justice, and the like—

bulk large in the *Comedy,* which also contains (in *Paradiso* XI) a very interesting example of the *contemptus mundi* posture, otherwise quite uncharacteristic of Dante. The poet is also very careful to point out the error of the belief in Averroistic oversoul (*Purgatorio* XXV). Such elements have led to discussion of Dante's Augustinianism as opposed to his Thomism. (T. K. Swing has argued that in his manipulation of these doctrines "Dante is the first to accomplish a consistent elucidation of the teleological destiny of the Christian soul through a metaphysical scheme.") It is true that the presence of St. Bernard as Dante's last guide and, as it were, sponsor for his ultimate vision, gives dramatic emphasis to the Neoplatonic or Augustinian strain. But if the substitution of rapture for reason represents the victory of Augustine over Thomas, it also carries us beyond the limits of philosophy and perhaps out of the area of our proper concern here.

We may yet affirm, in the face of all such elements as noted, that the *Comedy* is, in the author's intent, primarily an exposition of ethics; the letter to Can Grande specifically defines it as having for its subject "man, liable to the reward or punishment of Justice, according as through the freedom of the will he is deserving or undeserving." And in this area the frame of reference is, as it was in the *Convivio,* Aristotelian and Thomistic—not without some original sallies of Dante's own. The presence in the *Paradiso* of the Latin Averroist Siger of Brabant, for example, may be interpreted as an affirmation of the autonomy and dignity of the "contemporary profane science" (Pierre Mandonnet) of Aristotelian philosophy. But from the point of view of ethical investigation, the *Inferno* is the most interesting part of the work, for here, dealing not with the way of salvation, which is no longer possible to the damned, nor with the ultimate doctrines, interesting only to saints, Dante is in a sense free to formulate his own code of morality. Clearly his inclusion of pagans and other non-Christians in hell indicates his intent to establish a code of behavior for all men; his hell is nonsectarian, broadly speaking. His main divisions of incontinence, violence, and fraud are ingeniously worked out from a combination of Aristotle, Cicero, and Thomas; interesting too is his creation of the "vestibule" for the lukewarm spirits and his peopling of the limbo with the souls of the virtuous pagans. Nor does the "converted" Dante abandon his appreciation of the second beatitude; not only do the pagans in limbo enjoy quite a comfortable immortality but Cato, so much revered in the *Convivio,* reappears as the guardian of purgatory, where he symbolizes free will; and, most startling of all, in the heaven of Jupiter the Trojan Ripheus is shown as an example of the "baptism of desire" that would make it possible for a good man, totally ignorant of the Mosaic or Christian message, to win salvation. To be sure, this is rare and does not avail to save Vergil or Aristotle, but on the other hand salvation in Christian terms also is ultimately a matter of predestined grace: without being unorthodox, Dante, in the example of Ripheus, has revealed his deep concern for ultimate justice. Indeed, the analysis of sin in the *Inferno,* as Kenelm Foster has pointed out, has its genesis in a conception of justice and presupposes society. The souls in the *Inferno* have "injured" others, have broken the social fabric in one way or another; even the heretics seem to be there because they have misled their followers rather than because of their own arrogant pride (a sin not specifically classified in the *Inferno*). We may also remark that Dante's concern for the good life on Earth does not desert him: The theory of the two "suns" necessary for the proper illumination of humankind reappears in the *Purgatory*; the emperor is glorified (a reserved seat awaits Henry VII in the celestial rose); and certain cabalistic prophecies indicate Dante's hope for a *dux* who will lead the temporal world back to order and sanity. "The *Divine Comedy* is as much a political as it is a religious poem," says A. Passerin d'Entrèves, and surely in that climactic work both politics and religion are seen *sub specie philosophiae.* If Dante is not a true philosopher, he is certainly a magnificent amateur.

See also Aristotelianism; Aristotle; Augustine, St.; Augustinianism; Averroes; Boethius, Anicius Manlius Severinus; Cicero, Marcus Tullius; Continental Philosophy; Gilson, Étienne Henry; Love; Neoplatonism; Pythagoras and Pythagoreanism; Siger of Brabant; Thomas Aquinas, St.; Thomism.

Bibliography

WORKS BY DANTE

Convivio. Translated by Philip Wicksteed. London, 1903.

Epistolae. With English translation by Paget Toynbee. Oxford, 1920.

Le opere di Dante. Florence: R. Bemporad, 1921; 2nd ed., 1960.

The Portable Dante. Edited by Paolo Milano. New York: Viking, 1947. Selected translations.

Divine Comedy. Translated by H. R. Huse. New York: Rinehart, 1954. A useful, prose, line-for-line version.

Monarchy. Translated by Donald Nicholl. London: Weidenfeld and Nicolson, 1954.

WORKS ON DANTE

Davis, C. T. *Dante and the Idea of Rome.* Oxford: Clarendon Press, 1957.

Entrèves, A. P. d'. *Dante as a Political Thinker.* Oxford: Clarendon Press, 1952.

Foster, Kenelm. "The Theology of the 'Inferno.'" In *God's Tree.* London: Blackfriars, 1957.

Gilson, Étienne. *Dante et la philosophie.* Paris: J. Vrin, 1939. Translated by David Moore as *Dante the Philosopher.* New York: Sheed and Ward, 1949.

Mandonnet, Pierre. *Dante le théologien.* Paris, 1935.

Mazzeo, J. A. *Medieval Cultural Tradition in Dante's Comedy.* Ithaca, NY: Cornell University Press, 1960.

Mazzeo, J. A. *Structure and Thought in the Paradiso.* Ithaca, NY: Cornell University Press, 1958.

McKeon, Richard. "Poetry and Philosophy in the Twelfth Century." In *Critics and Criticism: Ancient and Modern,* edited by R. S. Crane et al. Chicago: University of Chicago Press, 1952.

Nardi, Bruno. *Dante e la cultura medievale.* Bari, Italy, 1949.

Santayana, George. *Three Philosophical Poets.* Cambridge, MA: Harvard University Press, 1910; New York, 1953. Latter edition is paperback.

Swing, T. K. *The Fragile Leaves of the Sibyl: Dante's Master Plan.* Westminster, MD: Newman Press, 1962.

Thomas Goddard Bergin (1967)

DANTO, ARTHUR

(1924–)

Arthur Danto's contributions to the philosophy of art have been shaped by his experiences as art maker, art critic, and art lover. He earned a bachelor's degree in fine arts from Wayne State University in 1948. For the next decade, his woodcuts were shown in such important venues as the Art Institute of Chicago, the Detroit Institute of Arts, Los Angeles County Museum, the Museum of Fine Arts in Boston, and the National Gallery of Art in Washington, D.C. During this period of active art-making, he completed a doctorate in philosophy at Columbia University in 1952 and began his half-century-long appointment in the Columbia philosophy department.

One of Danto's central aims for the first thirty years of his career was to render the ideas of nineteenth- and twentieth-century continental philosophers such as Hegel, Nietzsche, and Sartre accessible and useful to analytical philosophers. Danto's writing about these figures is clear and often critical. He has also published penetrating overviews of core fields such as the philosophy of science, the philosophy of action, the theory of knowledge, the philosophy of history, and philosophical psychology.

Nevertheless, this philosopher remained an artist and passionate art lover. He had come to New York to study philosophy just when that city emerged as the center of innovative achievement in the art world. The art Danto encountered in the museums and galleries he frequented was conceptually challenging.

Andy Warhol's 1964 work *Brillo Box* provoked a key question: What makes *Brillo Box*—a replica of the box used to ship packages of Brillo pads—a work of art, suitable for display in a museum or gallery, when perceptually indiscernible objects—the actual Brillo boxes created en masse by the manufacturer—are relegated to grocery displays or storerooms? This is a philosophical query, but also an integral part of experiencing *Brillo Box* as art, for the art lover encountering *Brillo Box* is initially transfixed by questions about its status.

Danto's famous essay "The Art World" (1964) initiated an answer that he refined and elaborated over the ensuing fifteen years. Danto asked how commonplace objects that never could have been art in earlier times not only had gained the possibility of being art by 1964 but also appeared to be the art necessary for that time. Danto presumes that philosophy should accept, not correct, the phenomena of art-world practice and discourse. Therefore, the traditional questions of philosophy of art and philosophical aesthetics must be transformed to fit the art world's realities.

Danto's more fully elaborated position, first presented in full in *The Transfiguration of the Commonplace* (1981), is that art history and art theory contribute experiential (albeit not sensuous) properties to certain objects. These properties make the difference in experiencing objects as art. Absent being experienced at the appropriate art-historical moment, and through the lens of compelling art-theoretical understandings that offer illuminating interpretive hypotheses, objects do not rise to the status of art.

Seeing affinities between Danto's focus on art-world practice and his own view that it is artists, critics, and curators who decree which objects should be treated as art, George Dickie heralded the advent of the institutional theory of art. Danto's view differs from Dickie's in many ways, however. For example, a key idea in Danto's, but not in Dickie's, thought is that art distinctively embodies meaning, or at least embodies questioning.

Danto takes modern art's history to be a quest for answers about the general (transhistorical) nature and identity of art. Art in our time has achieved a philosophical self-consciousness that acknowledges rather than veils ontological questions about its own nature. But in pursuing its own ontology, art transcends its limits and is transfigured into philosophy. Persisting in this transgressive aim, art subsequently executes its own end, turning its back on philosophical anxiety about what art must be. Art thereby is liberated to place itself freely in the service of a multiplicity of values rather than to embrace a single value that is uniquely aesthetic. Danto's theory of the end of art is empirical, not prescriptive. He explains where art has arrived, and why, rather than directing where art should go. In such a pluralistic age as our own, when everything is possible, what principles should guide the art critic? This question, traditionally a concern of philosophical aesthetics, is of special interest to Danto because of another artworld role he fills, that of art critic. In 1984 Danto became the art critic for *The Nation* magazine. Much of his writing since that time has been criticism of works of art or reflections on art criticism. His *Encounters and Reflections: Art in the Historical Present*, a collection of art criticism, won the National Book Critics Circle Prize for Criticism in 1990.

In general, Danto's art criticism is about understanding artistic processes, not assessing aesthetic outcomes. Some philosophers fault him for stamping his philosophy of art with his style of art criticism and thereby giving artistic considerations priority over aesthetic values. Others praise him for developing a philosophical theory of art into which enlightening art criticism is tightly woven. Danto seeks to explain rather than steer the direction of art. Art criticism, as Danto understands the practice, deploys artistic judgment to detect an object's content and explain how the object embodies or presents what it is about. Yet Danto himself offers no developed philosophical analysis of artistic embodiment, neither of the process nor of the criteria of success. His signature stance is to observe from the intersect of philosophy and criticism. His strategy is to gently and genially compel art criticism to confront its own implicit abstractions and generalizations, while persuasively propelling philosophy to engage with the puzzling particulars of the world of art.

See also Art, Expression in; Art, Style and Genre in.

Bibliography

Danto, Arthur C. *After the End of Art*. Princeton, NJ: Princeton University Press, 1997.

Danto, Arthur C. "The Art World." *Journal of Philosophy* 61 (1964): 571–584

Danto, Arthur C. *Encounters and Reflections: Art in the Historical Present*. New York: Farrar, Straus & Giroux, 1990.

Danto, Arthur C. *Narration and Knowledge, Including the Integral Text of Analytical Philosophy of History*. New York: Columbia University Press, 1990.

Danto, Arthur C. *The Transfiguration of the Commonplace*. Cambridge, MA: Harvard University Press, 1981.

"Danto and His Critics: Art History, Historiography, and After the End of Art." *History and Theory* 37 (1998): 1–143.

Dickie, George. *Art and the Aesthetic: An Institutional Analysis*. Ithaca, NY: Cornell University Press, 1974.

Rollins, Mark, ed. *Danto and His Critics*. Cambridge, MA: Basil Blackwell, 1993.

Anita Silvers (2005)

DAOISM

See *Chinese Philosophy: Daoism; Laozi; Mysticism, History of*

DARWIN, CHARLES ROBERT

(1809–1882)

Charles Robert Darwin, the British biologist whose theory of organic evolution revolutionized science, philosophy, and theology, was born at Shrewsbury. He attended the universities of Edinburgh and Cambridge but was not attracted by his medical studies at the first or by his theological studies at the second. Near the end of his undergraduate days he formed a friendship with J. T. Henslow, professor of botany at Cambridge, "a man who knew every branch of science" (*Autobiography of Charles Darwin*). This association, together with an enthusiasm for collecting beetles and a reading of works by Wilhelm von Humboldt and John Herschel, generated in him "a burning zeal to contribute to the noble structure of Natural Science." The opportunity to do so on a large scale arose when Henslow secured for him the post of naturalist "without pay" aboard the H.M.S. *Beagle,* then about to begin a long voyage in the Southern Hemisphere. Thus, between 1831 and 1836 Darwin was able to make extensive observations of the flora, fauna, and geological formations at widely separated points on the globe. This experience determined the course of his life thereafter and laid the foundation for many of his fundamental ideas. On his return he lived in London for six years, where he became acquainted with leading scientists of the day. Sir Charles Lyell, Sir Joseph Hooker, and T. H. Huxley were among his most intimate friends. In 1842 he took up residence at Down, a secluded village in Kent. Here, during the forty years until his death, he conducted the researches and wrote the works that made him famous. He was buried in Westminster Abbey close to the grave of Sir Isaac Newton.

Darwin's productivity, despite recurrent bouts of illness, was prodigious. His publications ranged over such diverse subjects as volcanic islands, coral reefs, barnacles, plant movement, the fertilization of orchids, the action of earthworms on the soil, the variation of domesticated animals and plants, and the theory of evolution. Even if he had never written *The Origin of Species* (1859) and *The Descent of Man* (1871), he would still be regarded as one of the great biologists of the nineteenth century. Of course, it was these two books that made him the initiator of a revolution in thought more far-reaching than that ushered in by Nicolas Copernicus. He established beyond reasonable doubt that all living things, including man, have developed from a few extremely simple forms, perhaps from one form, by a gradual process of descent with modification. Furthermore, he formulated a theory (natural selection), supporting it with a large body of evidence, to account for this process and particularly to explain the "transmutation of Species" and the origin of adaptations. As a result, the biological sciences were given a set of unifying principles, and man was given a new and challenging conception of his place in nature.

It was characteristic of Darwin that he came to these conclusions by his own observations and reflections. When he embarked on the *Beagle*, his outlook was "quite orthodox." He accepted without question the fixity of species and their special creation as depicted in Genesis. Doubts began to arise in his mind during the ship's visit to the Galápagos Archipelago in 1835, when he noticed that very small differences were present in the so-called species inhabiting separate islands. The doubts were reinforced by his observation of fossils on the Pampas and the distribution of organisms on the South American continent as a whole. He was "haunted" by the idea that such facts "could be explained on the supposition that species gradually became modified." In July 1837 he "opened his first notebook" to record additional facts bearing on the question, but it was not until he happened to read Thomas Robert Malthus's *Essay on Population* in October 1838 that he found an explanatory theory from which the above "supposition" followed. He then proceeded to formulate the principle of natural selection, which is simply "the doctrine of Malthus applied with manifold force to the whole animal and vegetable kingdoms." Darwin never professed to have invented the idea of organic evolution, of the mutability of species, or even of natural selection. What he did profess was to have produced the first scientific proof that these ideas apply to the living world.

Unlike some lesser men of science, Darwin was not inclined to rush into print in order to establish a proprietary right to his theory. His modesty and single-minded desire to find out the truth forbade any such action. Accordingly, the theory underwent several preliminary formulations. It was first set down in a short abstract in 1842 and two years later was expanded into an essay that both Lyell and Hooker read. Early in 1856 Lyell advised Darwin to write a full-length account of his views. It was when this manuscript, which would have been "three or four times as extensive" as *The Origin of Species,* was about half finished that Alfred Russel Wallace's paper, which contained virtually the same ideas that Darwin was working out, arrived at Down from the Malay Archipelago. The resulting crisis was resolved by having a joint communication from the two men read at a meeting of the Linnaean Society on July 1, 1858. Between September of that year and November 1859, Darwin "abstracted" the large manuscript and produced his classic. *The Origin of Species* appeared on November 24 in an edition of 1,250 copies, all of which were sold on the first day. Ultimately, six editions containing many revisions were published.

Despite the interest that *The Origin of Species* excited, it was by no means universally approved at first. In the scientific world support for it came from Darwin's friends, but others expressed opposition that often took the form of objections to the modes of explanation and proof employed in the work. Darwin's use of historical or genetic explanations, his implicit adoption of statistical conceptions ("population thinking," as it is now called), and his practice of introducing conjectures or "imaginary illustrations" to buttress his argument were repugnant to biologists who held that scientific explanation must consist in bringing directly observed phenomena under general laws. Believers in this oversimplified model also disliked his notion of "chance" variations and his repudiation of "any law of necessary development." Before long, however, the cumulative force of Darwin's arguments, augmented by the case put forward in *The Descent of Man,* convinced the great majority of biologists, so that opposition from this quarter had disappeared by 1880.

The popular reaction to Darwin's theory focused on its religious and ideological implications. These were recognized to be hostile to the Establishment. Hence, Darwin found himself enthusiastically supported by radicals, rationalists, and anticlericals and vehemently attacked by reactionaries, fundamentalists, and priests. He shrank from entering into this controversy, which was altogether distasteful to him, but T. H. Huxley, who enjoyed crossing swords with theologians, took a different stand. Appointing himself "Darwin's bulldog," he relentlessly pursued such antievolutionists as Bishop Wilberforce and W. E. Gladstone. His efforts had a good deal to do with creating the image of Darwin as an enemy of the Bible, the church, and Christianity.

This image was, in fact, fairly close to the truth. Darwin's religious beliefs, as he relates in his *Autobiography,* underwent a change from naive acceptance of Christian doctrines to reluctant agnosticism. In the two years following his return from the voyage of the *Beagle* he was "led to think much about religion." Doubts were engendered in his mind about the historical veracity of the Gospels, the occurrence of miracles, and the dogma of everlasting damnation of unbelievers (which he calls "a damnable doctrine"). By reflection on such matters he "gradually came to disbelieve in Christianity" and wondered how anybody could wish it to be true.

A similar erosion occurred in connection with his belief in the existence of a personal God. When he wrote *The Origin of Species,* Darwin accepted a vague theism or deism. In the last chapter he speaks of laws having been "impressed on matter by the Creator" and of life's powers "having been breathed by the Creator into a few forms or into one." He was thus able at the time to deny that it was his intention "to write atheistically." Yet it was also clear to him that the theory of natural selection exploded the old argument for theism based on the presence of design in the organic world. The vast amount of suffering and misery that exists seemed to him a strong argument against any belief in a beneficent First Cause. He had moods in which it seemed difficult or impossible to conceive that "this immense and wonderful universe, with our conscious selves, arose through chance." In the end, however, he concluded "that the whole subject is beyond the scope of man's intellect. … The mystery of the beginning of all things is insoluble by us; and I for one must be content to remain an Agnostic."

Darwin's reflections on religion, although not systematic, provide a good example of his intellectual integrity. "I have steadily endeavored," he wrote in his *Autobiography,* "to keep my mind free, so as to give up any hypothesis, however much beloved (and I cannot resist forming one on every subject), as soon as facts are shown to be opposed to it." That statement might well serve as his epitaph.

See also Copernicus, Nicolas; Darwin, Erasmus; Darwinism; Evolutionary Ethics; Evolutionary Theory; Herschel, John; Humboldt, Wilhelm von; Huxley, Thomas Henry; Malthus, Thomas Robert; Newton, Isaac; Philosophy of Biology; Wallace, Alfred Russel.

Bibliography

WORKS BY DARWIN

The Autobiography of Charles Darwin (London, 1958) was edited by his granddaughter Nora Barlow, who restored the material omitted from the original. The original *Autobiography* was first published in 1887 as part of the *Life and Letters of Charles Darwin,* but many passages of the manuscript were omitted because they contained candid and caustic judgments of persons and of the Christian religion. These omitted passages, amounting to nearly six thousand words, were restored in the 1958 edition.

The *Life and Letters of Charles Darwin* (2 vols., New York: Basic Books, 1959) was edited by Francis Darwin. The 1959 edition has an introduction by George Gaylord Simpson.

Among the many editions of *On the Origin of Species* are a facsimile of the first edition, with an illuminating introduction by Ernst Mayr (Cambridge, MA: Harvard University Press, 1964), and a variorum text of the six editions, edited by Morse Peckham (Philadelphia: Univ. of Pennsylvania Press, 1959). The *Origin* is also available in paperback with a foreword by George Gaylord Simpson (New York, 1962).

For the voyage of the *Beagle* see *Charles Darwin's Diary of the Voyage of H.M.S. Beagle* (Cambridge, U.K.: Cambridge University Press, 1933), which was edited from the manuscript by Nora Barlow, and Nora Barlow's edition of *Charles Darwin and the Voyage of the Beagle* (London: Pilot Press, 1945), for which she has written an introduction.

Darwin and Wallace's *Evolution by Natural Selection* (London: Cambridge University Press, 1958) has been edited, with an introduction, by Gavin De Beer. This volume contains the Linnaean Society papers.

WORKS ON DARWIN

For works on Darwin see Alvar Ellegård's *Darwin and the General Reader* (Göteborg, Sweden, 1958) and Gavin De Beer's excellent *Charles Darwin: Evolution by Natural Selection* (London: T. Nelson, 1963).

T. A. Goudge (1967)

DARWIN, ERASMUS

(1731–1802)

Erasmus Darwin, an English physician, man of science, and poet, was the grandfather of Charles Darwin, whose evolutionary views he partly anticipated, and of Francis Galton. Like Charles he was educated at Cambridge, where he took the M.B. degree in 1755. For more than forty years he practiced medicine at Lichfield and Derby and gained a wide reputation for his skill, intellectual vigor, and originality of character. Among his friends were Jean-Jacques Rousseau, whom he met in 1766, and Joseph Priestley. He corresponded with both men. In 1784 he founded the Philosophical Society at Derby to stimulate interest in the sciences. He wrote copiously, with varying degrees of success. His chief prose works are *Zoonomia or the Laws of Organic Life* (2 vols., London, 1794–1796) and *Phytologia or the Philosophy of Agriculture and Gardening* (London, 1799). Two long poems embodying his views about the origin and development of life, *The Botanic Garden* (London, 1789) and *The Temple of Nature* (London, 1803), were not taken seriously by his contemporaries, although Darwin himself was rather proud of them. Samuel Taylor Coleridge likened the poems to "mists that occasionally arise at the foot of Parnassus" and coined the word *darwinizing* to describe their biological speculations. After his death Erasmus Darwin was forgotten until interest in his ideas revived as a result of the fame of his grandson Charles.

An important feature of Erasmus Darwin's work is the relation it establishes between early evolutionary theory and the embryological controversy of the preformationists and the epigenesists. In "Of Generation," Chapter 39 of *Zoonomia,* Darwin argues against the doctrine that each new individual is already "preformed" on a minute scale in the reproductive cell from which it is developed. He defends an epigenetic position according to which new individuals develop by utilizing material from the environment to generate new parts. Hence, there is a transformation of a relatively undifferentiated egg into a complex organism. From this position it is only a short step to the view that life in general has evolved by a similar transformation.

Darwin actually took this step but did not provide a systematic justification of it. His writings are a curious mixture of observed facts, sober scientific judgments, and extravagant speculations, all designed to support the conclusion that living things, different from one another as they now are, originated from one "primal filament" that existed long ago. Through the ages organisms have altered to meet altered conditions of life. The result has been a continuous perfecting of their capacities. "This idea of the gradual formation and improvement of the animal world accords with the observations of some modern philosophers" (*Zoonomia,* Vol. I). An evolution of life has undoubtedly occurred.

Among the items of evidence adduced to support this contention are some that anticipate matters later embodied in *The Origin of Species.* Thus, Erasmus Darwin calls attention to such phenomena as the metamorphosis of tadpoles into frogs, the changes produced by the domestic breeding of animals, the specialized adaptations to climatic conditions, and, above all, "the essential unity of plan in all warm-blooded animals." These things oblige us to believe that all organisms have been derived from "a single living filament."

Embedded in Darwin's work are the rudiments of a theory about the causes of evolution. What he says foreshadows the more finished theory of the Chevalier de Lamarck. Environmental stimuli act on organisms that are endowed with the unique power of "irritability or sensibility." The organisms respond in accordance with their wants, desires, and dislikes. Thus, the bodily characteristics required to satisfy the organisms' demands are produced. These characteristics are inherited by some members of succeeding generations and favor them in the struggle for existence, which is depicted in lurid terms by Darwin in *The Temple of Nature.*

The facts that man's body bears traces of his evolution from lower forms of life and that Earth itself appears to have come into being gradually by the operation of natural processes in no way led Darwin to doubt the existence of "the Great Architect" of the cosmos. His solid and complacent deism enabled him to regard God as simply "the Great First Cause," who infused spirit and life into the primal filament and gave it the potentiality to evolve. "The whole of nature may be supposed to consist of two essences or substances, one of which may be termed spirit and the other matter" (*Zoonomia,* Vol. I, Section 1). The "whole of nature" was designed by the Great Architect. Indeed, God "has infinitely diversified the works of His hands, but has at the same time stamped a certain similitude on the features of nature, that demonstrates to us, that the whole is one family of one parent."

Darwin's views mark the close of the era of romantic speculation about natural history and the advance into an era of systematic observation and generalization. He did not, however, succeed in formulating any enduring principles. Perhaps his major achievement was acquiring the characteristics of scientific curiosity, independence of mind, and intellectual power that were transmitted to his descendants.

See also Coleridge, Samuel Taylor; Darwin, Charles Robert; Evolutionary Theory; Lamarck, Chevalier de; Priestley, Joseph; Rousseau, Jean-Jacques.

Bibliography

For material bearing on the once notorious controversy between Charles Darwin and Samuel Butler, in which the assessment of Erasmus Darwin's ideas played a part, see Charles Darwin, *Life of Erasmus Darwin: An Introduction to an Essay on His Works by Ernst Krause* (London, 1879), and Samuel Butler, *Evolution, Old and New* (London, 1879), Chs.

12–14. The complex story of the controversy is given in the complete edition of *The Autobiography of Charles Darwin*, edited by Nora Barlow (London, 1958), Appendix, Part 2, pp. 167–219.

See also Hesketh Pearson, *Doctor Darwin: A Biography* (London: Dent, 1930), and Desmond King-Hele, *Erasmus Darwin* (New York: Scribners, 1964).

T. A. Goudge (1967)

DARWINISM

The term *Darwinism* has both a narrow and a broad meaning. In the narrow sense, it refers to a theory of organic evolution presented by Charles Darwin (1809–1882) and by other scientists who developed various aspects of his views; in the broad sense, it refers to a complex of scientific, social, theological, and philosophical thought that was historically stimulated and supported by Darwin's theory of evolution. Biological Darwinism—the first sense—was the outstanding scientific achievement of the nineteenth century and is now the foundation of large regions of biological theory. Darwinism in the second sense was the major philosophical problem of the later nineteenth century. Today, Darwinism no longer provides the focus of philosophical investigation, largely because so much of it forms an unquestioned background to contemporary thought.

Darwin's theory is an example of scientific innovation that has had reverberations into the farthest reaches of human thought. It is fair to say that every philosophical problem appears in a new light after the Darwinian revolution. In order to outline the connections between biological and philosophical Darwinism, it will first be necessary to describe Darwin's own views and to discuss various criticisms that were directed against them. It will then be possible to describe Darwinism in the broader sense, and to distinguish the various ways in which the scientific theory has afforded material for philosophical inquiry.

DARWIN'S THEORY

The theory of the origin of species by means of natural selection was the discovery of Darwin and Alfred Russel Wallace (1823–1913). Both Darwin and Wallace had stated the theory in a series of papers delivered before the Linnaean Society on July 1, 1858. The members of the Linnaean Society listened without enthusiasm and apparently without much understanding, but in fairness to them, it should be observed that Wallace and Darwin did not present their theory forcefully on this occasion. Some of the shattering implications of the theory were not drawn in detail, and the evidence in its support, which Darwin in particular had amassed, was barely hinted at. Wallace's paper "On the Tendency of Varieties to Depart Indefinitely from the Original Type" was a discussion of a widely accepted argument in favor of the "original and permanent distinctness of species," namely, that the varieties that are produced by artificial selection in domesticated species never vary beyond the limits of the original wild species, and that whenever artificial selection is relaxed, the domesticated varieties revert to the ancestral form. These facts were interpreted by naturalists as evidence for an innate conservative tendency in nature that kept all variation within the bounds defined by the unbridgeable gaps between species.

But, Wallace argued, the view that artificial selection can produce only new varieties, never new species, rests on the false assumption that naturalists possess a criterion for distinguishing the species from the variety. Moreover he stated, "This argument rests entirely on the assumption that varieties occurring in a state of nature are in all respects analogous to … those of domestic animals, and are governed by the same laws as regards their permanence or further variation. But it is the object of the present paper to show that this assumption is altogether false." Overproduction, together with heritable variations, some of which are better adapted to the circumstances of life, will tend to make varieties depart indefinitely from the ancestral type, bringing about changes that will eventually amount to the origin of a new species. Wallace accounted for the reversion of domestic varieties by pointing out that the ancestral type is better adapted to life "in a state of nature," and consequently the very same principles that bring about progress in nature also bring about the reversion of domestic varieties.

Wallace aimed his argument precisely at the philosophical presupposition that for so long had stood in the way of a proper interpretation of natural selection, namely, that the species—being the exemplar of a divine archetype—is as well adapted as it could be and, consequently, that variation away from the type will automatically be selected against. Natural selection, according to this interpretation, is an agency of permanence, not change. One of Wallace's, as well as Darwin's, most original contributions consisted in breaking the hold of this idea.

Wallace's argument is implicit in Darwin's Linnaean Society papers, but the focus is different. Instead of challenging accepted opinion, Darwin added up well-known facts. With great eloquence he described the prevalent overproduction of animals and plants: "Nature may be compared to a surface on which rest ten thousand sharp wedges touching each other and driven inwards by incessant blows." The wedges are held back by large numbers of "checks" that bring about the death, or prevent the mating, of individuals. "Lighten any check in the least degree, and the geometrical powers of increase in every organism will almost instantly increase the average number of the favored species." He called attention to the extreme heritable variability of animals under domestication. In nature there is also variation, although no doubt not as much. Some variants will be better adapted to their environments than others and will tend to survive and propagate. "Let this work of selection on the one hand, and death on the other, go on for a thousand generations, who will pretend to affirm that it would produce no effect?" To the effects of this natural selection, Darwin added the effect of "the struggle of males for females."

Both Wallace and Darwin had stated the essence of the theory of the *Origin of Species* (1859). The *Origin* itself is mainly a sober, scrupulously fair, and thoroughly documented elaboration and defense of the doctrine of natural selection presented in the Linnaean Society papers. Darwin set out to accomplish three things: (*a*) to show that evolution has in fact occurred; (*b*) to describe the mechanism of evolution; and (*c*) to account for the major facts of morphology, embryology, biogeography, paleontology, and taxonomy on the evolutionary hypothesis.

THE FACT OF EVOLUTION. Darwin freely admitted that we do not directly observe the process of evolution. The time needed even for the origin in nature of a new variety is far too long. Consequently, the case for the occurrence of evolution is simply the same as the case for its scope and mechanism, and Darwin did not have access to direct evidence for the efficacy of natural selection—a gap that was not filled until the twentieth century. Darwin argued that life is too short for direct evidence but that certain facts force the conclusion upon us that there must be evolution; and if we adopt the hypothesis, a wide range of hitherto unconnected facts may be given a uniform explanation.

THE MECHANISMS OF EVOLUTION. Darwin described three mechanisms that tend to effect the evolution of populations. These are natural selection, sexual selection, and the inheritance of characteristics acquired during the lifetime of the individual organism.

Natural selection. In the *Origin* Darwin placed the greatest weight on evolution by natural selection. It operates in conjunction with sexual selection and the inheritance of acquired characters and, Darwin argued, there are some features of organisms that could have developed only by natural selection. Indeed, it seems that the theory of natural selection was partially inspired by his observations on the *Beagle* voyage (1831–1836) of local variations, particularly in the islands of the Galápagos Archipelago, that could not be accounted for on Lamarckian grounds.

The theory of natural selection as Darwin presented it may be summarized as follows: (1) Populations of animals and plants exhibit variations. (2) Some variations provide the organism with an advantage over the rest of the population in the struggle for life. (3) Favorable variants will transmit their advantageous characters to their progeny. (4) Since populations tend to produce more progeny than the environment will support, the proportion of favorable variants that survive and produce progeny will be larger than the proportion of unfavorable variants. (5) Thus, a population may undergo continuous evolutionary change that can result in the origin of new varieties, species, genera, or indeed new populations at any taxonomic level. Darwinian natural selection may accordingly be defined as a differential death rate between two variant subclasses of a population, the lesser death rate characterizing the better-adapted subclass.

Darwin was careful to present evidence for every hypothesis in his account of natural selection. It was especially necessary to argue that natural populations do exhibit the requisite amount of variation and that the variation is heritable. He cited, among other things, the extreme variability of domestic plants and animals and the well-known fact that new varieties can be propagated. He admitted that the causes of variation were unknown; but he argued that changing environmental conditions greatly increase variability by action on the reproductive system, thereby providing material for natural selection when it is most needed. This is "indefinite variability." In addition, there is "definite variability," due to the direct action of the environment on the body of the organism. "Definite variations" are heritable; they provide material for natural selection and, being responsive to the environment, are more likely than chance variations to be adaptive.

"The laws governing inheritance," he remarked, "are for the most part unknown." This lack of knowledge turned out to be the most serious obstacle to the further development of the theoretical foundations of selection theory in the nineteenth century; but, as Darwin noted, although the laws of inheritance were unknown, a number of the phenomena of inheritance were known, and those were probably all that were required for the theory of natural selection. Most important is the obvious fact that progeny bear an overwhelming resemblance to their parents, although they differ in some degree. In addition, Darwin was familiar with the intermittent appearance of hereditary characters, with sex-linked and sex-influenced characters, and with the tendency for a character to appear in the progeny at the same developmental stage that it appears in the parents.

For natural selection to be an agency of change rather than an agency of permanence, it is necessary that some variations from the ancestral type represent better adaptations. Darwin pointed out that, in fact, every organism could be better adapted to its ordinary environment; and that, moreover, environments change.

Pre-Darwinian taxonomy ascribed a very special significance to the species, as against varieties, genera, and the higher taxonomic groups. The species was regarded by the pious as the unalterable work of God; the limits laid down by the diagnostic features of any species established the limits of possible variation within the species. Thus, although any biologist would be willing to countenance the origin of new varieties or subspecies, brought about by the operation of biological laws, most were unwilling to admit the possibility of the origin of new species by natural processes. The title of Darwin's book was aimed precisely at this conception. Like Wallace, he argued that there is no difference in principle between the diagnostic characters of varieties and species; therefore, to admit the origin of new varieties amounts to admitting the possibility of new species—and if new species appear, so may new genera, families, and so on. He cited the existence of "doubtful species"—groups that cannot be definitely placed at either the variety or species level—and the general inconsistency of taxonomists in the identification of species.

Sexual selection. In the Linnaean Society papers Darwin described the second mechanism of evolution as the "struggle of males for females." The theory was developed further in the *Origin,* and it occupied some two-thirds of the pages of his *Descent of Man and Selection in Relation to Sex* (1871). In these later statements of the theory, the struggle of males for females is a special case of a more general phenomenon. Suppose that a population is divided in some proportion between males and females and suppose for the sake of simplification that all of the males and females are equally well endowed for the struggle for survival. Now, Darwin argued, it may happen that either the males or females are unequally endowed with some characteristic that will increase their propensity to leave progeny. There will then be selection in favor of that characteristic, even though it will not be favored by natural selection. All such cases Darwin calls "sexual selection." It is clear that different sorts of characteristics can influence the probability of having offspring. Some individuals, for example, may possess behavior patterns that lead to the fertilization of a larger percentage of eggs or have more efficient organs of copulation. Or they may have some advantage in the competition for mates—migratory male birds may arrive early at the breeding grounds and be ready to receive the more vigorous females, leaving the culls for their tardy brothers; or the females may for some reason prefer plumage or displays of a certain character; or some males may aggressively drive away other males; and so on. Finally, some characteristics that are also useful in the struggle for survival might also be useful in the competition for mates; for example, the antlers of male deer may do double duty against both rivals and predators.

Darwin appeals to sexual selection in order to account for the evolution of such things as mating rituals and secondary sexual characteristics, such as breeding plumage in birds. He regards it as especially significant in the evolution of man. The loss of body hair, for example, is attributed to systematic choice among man's ancestors of mates that exhibited large regions of bare skin.

The inheritance of acquired characters. Darwin's work was plagued by ignorance and misinformation concerning the laws of heredity. The principles of segregation and independent assortment, which form a cornerstone of contemporary evolution theories, were discovered by Gregor Mendel in 1864; but his paper remained unnoticed until 1900. Moreover, although "sports" were well known to biologists, the concept of mutation had not been clearly formulated. Consequently, the modern theory of the origin of genetic variation in populations was not available to Darwin; instead, he suggested that some variations are due to the action of the environment on the germplasm and that others are due to the effects of use and disuse. For example, if an animal's skin is tanned by sunlight, this may induce changes in its germplasm that will result in its progeny possessing pretanned skin; or if a wolf develops his muscles by chasing rabbits, his pups may inherit larger muscles. These mechanisms, if they exist, would account for some variability. But they would also account for some evolutionary change even in the absence of natural or sexual selection. Since, accordingly, there seemed to be no sound reason for rejecting the inheritance of acquired characters and since the doctrine would aid in explaining both variability and evolutionary change, Darwin was led to adopt it and to give it increasing weight in his later years. This aspect of Darwin's views is often labeled Lamarckism, but the Chevalier de Lamarck himself, although he did accept the inheritance of the effects of use and disuse, did not accept the doctrine of the direct action of environmental factors on the germplasm.

THE SCOPE OF EVOLUTIONARY THEORY. It is clear that Darwin regarded his theory as revolutionary. He believed that all the traditional branches of biology would be transformed and deepened; familiar phenomena would take on a new significance; apparently unconnected facts could be regarded as mutually related. Even the vocabulary of the older biology would acquire new meanings: "The terms used by naturalists, of affinity, relationship, community of type, paternity, morphology, adoptive characters, rudimentary and aborted organs, etc., will cease to be metaphorical, and will have a plain signification." Natural history would acquire the fascination, not of a catalog of *curiosae,* but of a labyrinth that may be charted.

> When we no longer look at an organic being as a savage looks at a ship, as something wholly beyond his comprehension; when we regard every production of nature as one which has had a long history; when we contemplate every complex structure and instinct as the summing up of many contrivances, each useful to the possessor, … when we thus view each organic being, how far more interesting—I speak from experience—does the study of natural history become!

And not only would the old biology be put on a new foundation; whole new fields of research would become possible. For example, "Psychology will be securely based on the foundation … of the necessary acquirement of each mental power and capacity by gradation. Much light will be thrown on the origin of man and his history."

The major part of the *Origin* is devoted to the detailed application of the theory of natural selection to a range of biological phenomena. It is impossible to give more than a general impression of the thoroughness, detail, and diversity of Darwin's evidence. The modern reader cannot fail to be impressed not only by Darwin's immense learning but also by his subtlety of insight—his ability to locate those phenomena that lend his theory the most striking support.

The *Origin* as a whole provides, on the one hand, a sweeping portrait of the history and biology of living things, a portrait whose internal balance and consistency are easily discernible. On the other hand, Darwin fills selected regions of his portrait with careful detail, exhibiting the applicability of his theory to a variety of phenomena. These two aspects of his work constitute both the argument for the fact of evolution and the argument for the truth of his account of its mechanisms.

In the broad portrait Darwin shows how the main facts of known fossil successions, the relation of living fauna and flora to recent fossil forms, the geographical distribution of species, the connection between morphology and function, and the major features of embryological development are explicable by his theory. He applies it in detail to such phenomena—to mention only a few—as rudimentary organs, insect metamorphosis, the divergence of island and mainland forms, and sexual dimorphism. He provides us with a discussion of taxonomy that is philosophically superior to many contemporary accounts, arguing, among other things, in favor of the special significance for the taxonomist of embryological and phylogenetic studies.

Darwin was always sensitive to the effect that his views might have on the general public. In composing the *Origin* he decided to avoid the whole topic of man's evolution; the book would be a sufficiently bitter pill without explicitly treating a subject that was "so surrounded with prejudices." His only explicit reference to man was the remark quoted above, that "light will be thrown on the origin of man and his history." Darwin's successors, however, were not so cautious. Sir Charles Lyell (1797–1875) discussed the question in 1863. Shortly thereafter, Wallace published his paper "The Origin of Human Races and the Antiquity of Man Deduced from the Theory of Natural Selection." T. H. Huxley (1825–1895) and a number of Continental morphologists, particularly Ernst Haeckel (1834–1919), produced a series of studies aimed at showing the similarity of man and the anthropoid apes and giving speculative reconstructions of man's ancestry. Thus, by the date of Darwin's *Descent of Man* (1871), the controversy over man was in full swing, and there were already a number of alternative theories that Darwin had to consider, such as whether the races of men are distinct species.

Darwin showed a wise unwillingness to acknowledge any known nonhuman species, living or extinct, as ancestral to man. We have so far examined, he argued, only animals that have diverged from the prehuman stock. For instance, the anthropoid apes and man have a common ancestor, but its remains have not been found. Nor did he identify species that are ancestral to the primates, the mammals, or even the vertebrates. He did trace a general line of descent: Old World ape, a lemurlike animal, some "forms standing very low in the mammalian series," marsupials, and monotremes. No true reptile is an ancestor of man. All the classes of vertebrates may have been derived from a remote ancestor similar to the larvae of the tunicates. With a flash of romanticism, Darwin wrote: "In the lunar or weekly recurrent periods of some of our functions we apparently still retain traces of our primordial birthplace, a shore washed by the tides."

In the *Descent of Man* evolution by the inheritance of acquired characters and by sexual selection plays a larger role than in the *Origin.* Darwin admitted that he had been accused of overrating the importance of natural selection, but added, "whether with justice the future will decide." His relative retreat from natural selection was probably occasioned by two factors: first, his doubts as to whether Earth is old enough for evolution by natural selection without substantial help from faster mechanisms; second, his belief that man is in many ways less the child of violent nature than his ancestors, a belief that requires considerable appeal to sexual selection and to the development of moral and spiritual qualities through social usage.

CRITICISMS OF DARWIN'S THEORY

In spite of the resistance that Darwin's theory aroused on other than scientific grounds, the weight of his arguments was largely—but with many notable exceptions—sufficient for the younger generation of biologists. In 1872, in the sixth edition of the *Origin,* Darwin was in a position to write, "At the present day almost all naturalists admit evolution under some form." It was, like any novel and important theory, carefully scrutinized for empirical weaknesses. We shall describe the major ones and indicate how they were dealt with.

The most damaging scientific objections were the following:

(1) Darwin had no direct evidence for the effectiveness of natural selection, let alone for the origin of new species.

(2) Darwin could not show a single species that was transitional between two known species.

(3) Complex organs, such as the vertebrate eye, could not have evolved by stages, since they would have been useless at any preliminary stage and hence would have given their possessor no selective advantage.

(4) If evolution has taken place, then some evolutionary trends must have continued past the point of usefulness to the organism. Such trends could not be accounted for by Darwinian selection.

(5) Earth is not old enough for evolution to have taken place.

(6) Evolution by natural selection is incompatible with the laws of inheritance.

(7) There is no inheritance of acquired characters.

The first two objections were commonly raised in the nineteenth century; they are genuine questions that require some sort of answer. Darwin, however, was not in a position to answer them in a way that would satisfy everybody, since the weight that one assigns to them depends in part upon personal preference.

INDIRECT EVIDENCE. With regard to the first objection Darwin pointed out that natural selection cannot be directly observed; we can only present indirect evidence in its favor. On this point he was mistaken. Natural selection has been directly studied in the twentieth century, both experimentally (in fruit fly populations, for example) and in nature (for instance, the development of so-called industrial melanism). But even today Darwin's and Wallace's contention that evolution by natural selection can pass the species limit has no direct support. Darwin recognized, however, that it is no fatal objection to a theory if some of its components are not subject to direct verification.

TRANSITIONAL SPECIES. On the second criticism—the absence of forms intermediate between species—Darwin had a double-barreled answer. He admitted that, for instance, we know of no forms intermediate between man and the apes. But we have innumerable examples of species that are in process of giving rise to new species, namely, those that have varieties or subspecies. These polytypic species (as they are now called) are intermediate between other species which, to be sure, have not yet evolved, but which are in process of evolving.

When it was further objected that we ought to have better examples of demonstrable ancestors of existing species, Darwin appealed to the incompleteness of the fossil record. This is the correct answer, but one that is hardly satisfying to a skeptic. Again, the weight that one would assign to the objection depends upon personal preference.

DEVELOPMENT OF COMPLEX ORGANS. Darwin was well aware of the difficulty in accounting for the origin of structures that would be useless, even deleterious, until they were essentially complete. The eye, he wrote, gave him "a cold shudder." In such cases as the eye, however, he had no alternative but to appeal to natural selection. Therefore, he was compelled to argue that in point of fact all the earlier stages in the evolution of the eye were useful in the struggle for survival. Darwin himself provided us with the standard textbook example: he constructed a plausible sequence of stages that could have led to the human eye. Each stage is a functional eye; and something similar to each stage does exist in one or another living species. The criticism has the form, "Such and such *could not* have happened." It can be countered piecemeal, by showing in a variety of cases how it *could* have happened.

ORTHOGENETIC TRENDS. A great many of Darwin's critics accepted the fact of evolution but entered reservations concerning his account of the mechanisms of the process. The reservations were of several types. Some rejected "Lamarckism," by which they meant simply the inheritance of acquired characters; they were known as the Neo-Darwinians. Others doubted that there was such a process as sexual selection. Still others, however, believed that there must be an evolutionary process that Darwin had not identified at all. The evidence consisted in the existence of apparently nonfunctional evolutionary trends. Trends that continue over long periods and that are relatively straight-lined—for example, increasing size in horses and increasing length of sabers in the saber-toothed cat—came to be called orthogenetic trends. The question was whether orthogenetic trends could be accounted for on Darwinian principles.

Wallace argued (in "Geological Climates and the Origin of Species," *Quarterly Review,* 1869) that the development of man's brain could not be so accounted for. Man's apelike ancestors, he argued, had reached a certain stage of evolution and then, over a period of some ten million years, remained largely unchanged except for a steady orthogenetic increase in the size and complexity of the brain. This was an unprecedented episode in the history of life, for it freed man from those ordinary pressures of natural selection that so often led to close specialization and ultimate extinction. Moreover, the brain acquired abilities that could not have been exercised in a primitive environment, such as the power to construct speculative systems of ideas or the insight into spiritual reality. These are present in modern man, but would have been useless in man's primitive ancestors. Natural selection operates only on abilities that are actually so exercised as to give an advantage in the struggle for life. "An instrument," Wallace concluded about the brain, "has been developed in advance of the needs of its possessor." Later he wrote: "A superior intelligence has guided the development of man in a definite direction, and for a special purpose, just as man guides the development of many animal and vegetable forms." Thus we avoid the "hopeless and soul-deadening belief" that man is the product of "blind eternal forces of the universe."

Darwin looked upon this as a failure of nerve, a hankering after miraculous origins for man. "I can see no necessity for calling in an additional and proximate cause in regard to man," he wrote in a letter to Wallace. Nevertheless, Wallace's position, fitting as it did the efforts of many theologians to come to grips with Darwinism, gained a number of adherents, and although the main line of evolutionary theory has bypassed it, even now versions of Wallace's position turn up from time to time.

Wallace had argued that the evolution of the brain was an orthogenetic trend that outstripped its usefulness. Others argued that trends sometimes continued even after they had become positively deleterious. A favorite example was the teeth of the saber-toothed cat, which, it was alleged, were valuable as weapons up to a certain length, but which finally became detrimental by interfering with feeding. There would be selection against increased tooth length under these conditions; consequently, it was argued, some cause other than natural selection must have operated. A variety of theories were proposed—for example, those of Karl Nägeli (1817–1891) and E. D. Cope (1840–1897). These theories posited an otherwise unknown internal principle of change, which was compared to the laws of embryological development, to the principle of inertia, or, as with Henri Bergson, to creative spiritual activity. Since the theories accounted for nothing other than the alleged orthogenetic trends, they have always had a peripheral position in the history of evolutionary thought. Moreover, subsequent analysis of orthogenesis has shown that in most cases the trends are in fact adaptive; and in those cases where they are not adaptive, contemporary theory provides various possible sorts of explanation compatible with the doctrine of natural selection, such as the explanation that if a trend affects only adults past the breeding age, it will not be selected against.

AGE OF EARTH. In 1865 William Thomson, Lord Kelvin, published a paper titled "The Doctrine of Uniformity in Geology Briefly Refuted." Its argument was aimed at Lyell and his followers, who had maintained that Earth as we now find it is not the result of a series of catastrophes, but is the outcome of the ages-long operation of geological processes that we can still observe. This viewpoint, known as uniformitarianism, was widely accepted among geologists even before the publication of the *Origin,* having been impressively established in Lyell's *Principles of Geology* (1834). It was in fact an earlier application of the idea of evolution. But uniformitarianism required vast reaches of time; consequently, Kelvin was prodding its weakest point when he argued that Earth could not be as old as the geologists supposed. Grant, Kelvin argued, that Earth was once a molten sphere; then it could not have solidified much over twenty million years ago, or it would now be cooler, through dissipation of its heat, than we actually find it. The biological consequences were clear: there was not enough time for evolution to have produced the forms we now see.

Darwin was deeply concerned by this reasoning. As far as he could tell, it was perfectly sound; on the other hand, he was perfectly convinced that Earth had supported life for a much longer time. His later emphasis on Lamarckism was probably an attempt to provide an evolutionary process that was swifter than natural selection. But this was a half measure; in fact, Darwin simply swallowed what he believed to be a contradiction—a not uncommon occurrence in the history of science. It turned out that Kelvin's argument was mistaken, since he was unaware of an additional source of heat within Earth, namely radioactive decay.

LAWS OF INHERITANCE. As noted above, the evolutionists of the nineteenth century worked in ignorance of the principles of genetics discovered by Mendel; this lack was by far the most serious theoretical gap in the Darwinians' arguments. It now appears that no fundamental innovation in evolutionary theory was possible until the gap was filled. Biologists of the nineteenth century accepted a rough theory of blending inheritance, that is, the view that the characteristics of the progeny of sexual crosses were intermediate between the characteristics of the parents. This theory was seldom explicitly defended, since everyone was familiar with a variety of phenomena that were incompatible with it, for example, blue-eyed children of brown-eyed parents. Nevertheless, when biologists theorized at all on the subject, the theory produced was ordinarily a vague and suitably guarded version of the theory of blending inheritance.

In 1867 Fleeming Jenkin ("The Origin of Species," *North British Review*) pointed out that the blending theory was incompatible with the theory of natural selection as ordinarily presented by the Darwinians. He argued that if favorable variations appeared in a population, their characteristics, even if favored by natural selection, would soon be lost in the vast population pool by crossing with individuals of the normal type. Assume, for instance (as Jenkin did), that a white man is greatly superior to a black man and that a white man is shipwrecked on a black-populated island. "He would kill a great many blacks in the struggle for existence; he would have a great many wives and children.… But can anyone believe that the whole island will gradually acquire a white, or even a yellow population?" Jenkin's argument in essence is this: the white man's children will be darker than their father; and it is impossible on the blending theory that their descendants could become lighter, whatever the effects of natural selection might be.

Again, Darwin was forced to admit the strength of a powerful objection that he was unable to counter directly. At best, he could only argue that natural selection would be effective if adaptive variations were sufficiently common; the black island could become white, for example, if there were a steady influx of shipwrecked sailors. He actually had no evidence that adaptive variations were sufficiently common; instead, he retreated more and more to the Lamarckian theory that variation is due to the effects of activity in the environment and would accordingly be largely adaptive.

Unlike the answer to Kelvin's objection, which could not have been offered in the nineteenth century, the answer to Jenkin was available but remained unknown except to a few, who did not see its significance. Mendel's paper on plant hybridization established an alternative to the blending theory of inheritance. Mendel showed that there were discrete genetic factors that pass unchanged from generation to generation and are hence not subject to Jenkin's swamping effect. Mendel had established that the character of these factors (genes) is not changed by other factors in the germplasm and that the factors segregate independently of one another in gamete formation. (He was unaware of the phenomenon of linkage.) Researchers of the literature on heredity recovered Mendel's work in 1900; and in 1904 William Bateson (1861–1926), in *Genetics and Evolution,* applied Mendel's laws to the theory of natural selection, thus answering Jenkin's objection.

The new genetics turned out to be far more significant for the theory of evolution than merely answering Jenkin's objection. The history of scientific Darwinism in the twentieth century was mainly the story of a series of advances in genetics, and the working out of their consequences for evolution. Mendel's laws were correlated with the behavior of the chromosomes in meiosis; the concepts of chromosome and gene mutation were introduced; linkage was discovered and understood; and statistical methods were employed in the analysis of the dynamics of genetic change in natural populations. One major gain of these developments was a systematic understanding of the origin and maintenance of genetic variability—the question that was so troublesome for Darwin. Another was the final decline of the Lamarckian aspect of Darwinism.

ACQUIRED CHARACTERS. The Neo-Darwinians had already denied the inheritance of acquired characters, but their evidence against it, like the Neo-Lamarckians' evidence in its favor, was largely anecdotal. August Weismann (1834–1914) had presented the theory that life is essentially a continuous stream of germplasm that from time to time gives rise to whole organisms; the organisms die but the germplasm is immortal. The stream can divide (gamete formation) and merge (fertilization), thus accounting for variability. This view was employed by Weismann and others as a theoretical argument against the inheritance of acquired characters, for it is an easy step from the continuity of the germplasm to its independence of somatic influences. The emergence of Mendelism shed a new light on Weismann's theory. The mechanism of "immortality"—self-replication of chromosomes—was elucidated, and evidence accumulated that the chromosomes were indeed uninfluenced, or influenced only randomly, by somatic factors.

PHILOSOPHICAL DARWINISM

We have considered Darwinism as a biological theory; we may now consider its wider intellectual connections. These are many and complex, so it will be necessary to select the most important—those which now seem to be enduring ingredients of speculative thought or those which struck the people of the later nineteenth century with the greatest force. The differences between the climate of opinion—the ordinary presuppositions, ideas about the proper pattern of argument, assumptions as to proper method, in short, the worldview—of the mid-nineteenth and twenty-first centuries is large, comparable in degree to the differences between the Middle Ages and the Renaissance. Of course the change had many causes, but the advent and absorption of Darwinism, while in part an effect of other currents, was also one major cause.

We shall consider the connections of Darwin's theory in three major regions: scientific cosmology, theology, and social doctrine.

SCIENTIFIC COSMOLOGY. Scientists have general views about the way things are. The scientists of any historical period are likely to share a common set of views, with, of course, individuals differing over one or another point to some degree. These general views, insofar as they concern a subject matter of professional scientific interest and insofar as they are capable of influencing method, methodology, or empirical formulations, may be called cosmological. They differ from the ordinary statements of a science (for example, "organisms overproduce," "acquired characters are not inherited") in degree of determinateness. They are so formulated that they are exempt from immediate verification and falsification but subject to specification, by means of a series of semantical decisions, into determinate, verifiable propositions. A good example of such a cosmological proposition is "Nature makes no jumps," or "Nature has no gaps." Darwin, unlike many of his contemporaries, was fond of making this remark (in Latin); he employs it in the Linnaean Society papers and subsequently quotes it again and again. It constitutes part of Darwin's cosmology and is a point on which the nineteenth century was deeply divided. It is clear that the sense of the proposition is not sufficiently determinate, as it stands, for verification. But it can be construed to mean, for instance, that evolution is gradual or that the apparent gaps between living species can be filled if we consider a sufficient stretch of history.

These properties of cosmological belief have important implications. First, it is possible to arrive at a cosmology by a process akin to generalization—an empirical statement can be construed as the determinate form of an indeterminate proposition, which in turn can be applied to new subject matters. This is the formal pattern of the influence of science on cosmology. Second, the precise verbal formulation of a cosmological belief is relatively unimportant; indeed, it can affect thought without being explicitly formulated at all. For cosmological beliefs do not function as premises of empirical arguments; rather, they impart color to empirical argument, affecting its form and conceptual materials.

Darwin's biological theory was itself supported by prior developments in cosmological belief. The theory of evolution by natural selection did not occur to Darwin in an intellectual vacuum. Most important of these cosmological beliefs was uniformitarianism, the belief that nature operates everywhere and always by the same sorts of law. This view Darwin had imbibed from Lyell's *Principles of Geology*; it became cosmological by construing the geological theory as exhibiting a general truth about the way things, including livings things, are. This particular belief is already a powerful stimulus to look at organic nature as the outcome of a historical process, although, to be sure, the belief does not entail this conclusion.

A second belief, which Darwin inherited and was seen to support, was the necessity of taking time seriously. This meant, among other things, that the past is long. By the date of the *Origin* there was little actual evidence on the age of Earth, let alone the age of the universe. Outside scientific circles, the prevailing view was that Earth and universe were the same age, something on the order of thousands of years. As long as this is accepted, evolution is evidently most improbable. Some geologists, in particular James Hutton (1726–1797), had, on the other hand, argued that Earth is infinitely old—an important argument, since it helped to accustom scientists to the possibility of vast stretches of time and change. Geologists after Hutton were willing to help themselves to as much time as they needed, and Darwin gladly followed suit.

Taking time seriously, however, gained a deeper meaning after the publication of the *Origin,* namely, that change is a fundamental feature of nature. This constituted part of the cosmology of every Darwinian. It meant that the process of change is not merely the reshuffling of preexisting materials in accordance with physical law but that the materials themselves are subject to alteration. For instance, as applied to biology it meant that the fundamental form, the species, did not merely exhibit eternal law but changed in such a way that new regularities of behavior replaced the old. In the favored terminology of the nineteenth century, we may say that taking time seriously meant that the laws of nature are subject to change.

Structures and patterns of behavior, then, have to be regarded as historically conditioned. This is the cosmological aspect of the most characteristic post-Darwin view of method, the insistence upon the investigation of origins, together with the view that such investigation can be scientific. Thus, we find the development of the idea of a human prehistory, the application of elaborate schemes concerning, as they were called, stages of development—spiritual, social, political, moral—and the belief that, at least in outline, the future of man may be successfully charted.

Pre-Darwinian biological theory was strongly influenced by the view that all living things are patterned after an eternal idea or archetype. This was held not only for the species but also for other taxonomic categories and for anatomical structures as well. Taxonomists were fond of describing, for example, the ideal vertebrate or mollusk; and morphologists described the ideal organ. One of the achievements of Darwinism was to break the hold of this notion on taxonomic and anatomical theory. Darwin was finally able to write, in *Descent of Man,* "A discussion of the beau ideal of the liver, lungs, kidneys, etc., as of the human face divine, sounds strange to our ears."

THEOLOGY. The expressed doctrines of theology are related to empirical propositions as cosmological doctrines are related to the natural sciences. The role of Darwin's theory as a generator of such indeterminate beliefs naturally is well exemplified in theology. On the one hand it was immediately taken to be in prima facie opposition to a number of theological doctrines, especially the following: the uniqueness of man as God's supreme creation; the importance of natural theology; and the dominant theory, in Protestant circles, that the Bible is an authoritative source of beliefs about the natural world.

The first theological reaction to Darwinism can only be described as one of outrage; but by the close of the century, theologians having decided that since they must live with Darwinism, they ought to love it, the outlines of a reconciliation had been sketched. Even further, Darwinism was allowed to guide the formation of a new brand of theology. We shall consider first the reaction.

As we have seen, Darwin's readers were quick to grasp the consequences of the *Origin* for man himself. These consequences immediately aroused the most intense feelings. These feelings were quite justified, for Christian theology demands that man be considered unique; and his uniqueness was universally interpreted as ontological separateness from the rest of creation. The geologist Adam Sedgwick (1785–1873), for example, spoke no more than common opinion when he wrote in 1850 that man is a barrier to "any supposition of zoological continuity—and utterly unaccounted for by what we have any right to call the laws of nature." The Darwinians not only argued that man is continuous with the animal kingdom and subject to the laws of nature; they also asserted that his mental, moral, and spiritual qualities evolved by precisely the same processes that gave the eagle its claws and the tapeworm its hooks. Such opinions were a threat to the deepest level of Christian doctrine, and were bound to be, until man's uniqueness could be given a new theological interpretation.

Moreover, the furor over the animal nature of man was heightened, especially in Britain, by local circumstances. T. H. Huxley compared man and the ape with endless zest, knowing how the comparison annoyed his opponents. For apes and monkeys were thought to be oversexed and obscene; in addition, the British took very seriously the principle that a man's standing in the world is dependent on the standing of his ancestors. Thus the literature of the period is enlivened by comic remarks, such as, "Are you descended from an ape, Mr. Huxley, from your mother's or your father's side?" (Bishop Wilberforce) and "You can't wash the slugs out of a lettuce without disrespect to your ancestors" (John Ruskin). But the symbol of the ape squatting in one's family tree was no more than an expression of dismay at being swallowed up in the infinite forms of nature. The twentieth century did not fully regain its equanimity on this point. Pius XII wrote that a Catholic may accept a doctrine of evolution, but should beware of doubting that there was a first man and woman. And consider this passage from the speech of William Jennings Bryan at the Scopes trial (1925): "We are told just how many species there are, 518,900. … and then we have mammals, 3,500, and there is a little circle and man is in the circle, find him, find man."

The edifice of traditional theology was touched at other points. Early-nineteenth-century theologians placed heavy weight on the cooperation of science and religion. The clergyman-naturalist was a familiar figure. It was thought that the intricacy and systematic interconnections of nature exhibited the handiwork of God; to study them was an act of piety. More specifically, natural teleology was the mainstay of natural theology. William Paley's *Natural Theology* (1802) is a good example. He holds that God's creation is totally good, that the organs of living things are almost perfect, that all animals have their just share of happiness, and that all this demonstrates with thousandfold certainty the existence and beneficence of God. An older natural theology tended to see evidences of God's design throughout nature; but Paley, and others after him, such as Thomas Chalmers in the *Bridgewater Treatises* (1834), rest their case on the structure of living things: consider, they suggest, the hand, the heart, the eye (especially the eye); they are complex and adapted for their functions to a degree that transcends all possibility of chance correlation.

By hindsight this attitude appears curiously self-defeating as well as vulnerable. The religiously inspired examination of organic adaptation was precisely one factor that led to Darwin's account of the origin of adaptation. His theory made the last citadel of divine teleology in nature untenable except, of course, for a few holdouts; but it was also widely interpreted as refuting all natural teleology, especially by the German materialists. "Chance" had been defined by Paley as "the operation of causes without design," and on this definition Darwinism leaves the origin of species to chance.

Theology in the middle half of the nineteenth century was especially vulnerable to Darwinism on a second point, namely, its extreme Biblicism and, even further, its literalism in biblical interpretation. It hardly needs saying that Darwinism is incompatible with any literal construction put upon either the Old Testament or the New Testament. The laity and most of the clergy, however, insisted upon such constructions. Matthew Arnold quotes the following as prevailing opinion in England: "Every verse of the Bible, every word of it, every syllable of it, every letter of it, is the direct utterance of the Most High"—a view Coleridge describes as "Divine ventriloquism." The matter was not so extreme outside of Britain, but the fact remains that Protestant education and practice relied heavily on the study and interpretation of the Bible.

The intellectual compromise that gradually emerged seems obvious today; the problem was not to think of it but to accept it. It consists in admitting that man is part of nature and that he is indeed, even in his spiritual aspects, the outcome of an evolutionary process. But lowly origins do not detract from a unique present. And the process of evolution is either guided, as Wallace suggested, or is itself the mode and manner of God's creation. Indeed, it was sometimes argued that Darwinism provides us with an elevated conception of God. Canon Charles Kingsley, for example, wrote to Darwin as follows: "I have gradually learnt to see that it is just as noble a conception of the Deity to believe that he created primal forms capable of self-development …, as to believe that He required a fresh act of intervention to supply the *lacunas* which He Himself had made." This passage is quoted by Darwin with some changes in later editions of the *Origin.* As Kingsley also put it, Darwin allows us to get "rid of an interfering God—a master-magician, as I call it" in favor of a "living, immanent, ever-working God."

The final step in this direction was to give God an even more intimate metaphysical connection with natural process. This step had been taken by previous philosophers—Benedict (Baruch) de Spinoza and G. W. F. Hegel, for example; but it was repeated under the aegis of Darwinism by Bergson, Alfred North Whitehead, and a number of Protestant thinkers. The problem of a divine nature that is both perfect and yet incomplete is one contemporary heritage of Darwinism.

SOCIAL DOCTRINE. The social thought of the later nineteenth century drew so heavily from the theories of evolution that its major ideas became known as social Darwinism. The 1850s were a period of revolutionary fervor in the streets as well as the academies, and political ideologists seized on Darwin as their major intellectual spokesman. His views, or rather selected aspects of them, presented ideal material for application to ethical, economic, and political problems.

It is convenient to divide social Darwinism into a political right and left, using these terms in their rough, contemporary editorial-page sense. In adopting Darwinism to social questions, it must be admitted that the right wing had the best of the bargain. In Europe these were the men whose interests were vested in hereditary privilege and in the factories and institutions of the industrial revolution. On the grounds of these interests they defended themselves against any attempt to justify social revolution, governmental control, unionism, or socialism in any of its many nineteenth-century forms. The ideology that was developed, with the help of Darwinism, in order to facilitate this defense also committed them, in various combinations, against such things as child-labor legislation, poor laws, compulsory safety regulations, and public education. A similar ideology provided the United States with its justification for the undisturbed economic expansion, speculation, and competition that we associate with the robber barons.

On the other hand, Darwinism was employed by the social reformers. Karl Marx wanted to dedicate the first volume of *Das Kapital* to Darwin. George Bernard Shaw, although he criticized the theory* of natural selection, defended his socialism with the help of his version of Bergson's creative evolutionism. The reformers saw Darwinism as the final demonstration that no particular economic or political institution—however hallowed by tradition or supported by existing theories—need be regarded as unalterable. The forms of society, like the forms of life, are local, temporary, and functional and may accordingly be changed (for the better) without shaking the foundations of the cosmos.

In short, the biology and cosmology of Darwinism was capable of being all things to all men. It enjoyed this status by virtue of its ability to inspire and lend a measure of apparent scientific support to the following major ideas:

(1) The vision of a science that was historical, and at the same time a rigorous application of natural law, inspired a new vision of a science of society. Herbert Spencer (1820–1903), whose evolutionism antedated the *Origin*, became the symbol of this ideal wedding of history and sociology. He drew elaborate comparisons between social structures and the forms of living organisms and saw societies as undergoing a progressive evolution in which egoism would be gradually replaced by altruism through a mechanism analogous to the inheritance of acquired characters. Sociology stood in relation to society as evolutionary biology stood to the phenomena of organic nature.

(2) The process of natural selection, interpreted as the survival of the fittest, provided a means for explaining social process. The American political economist William Graham Sumner (1840–1910), for example, saw society as the outcome of a social struggle in which each man, in pursuing his own good, can succeed only at the expense of others. The fittest in this social struggle are the ruthless, the imaginative, the industrious, the frugal. They climb to the top, and it is right that they should do so. The idle, infirm, and extravagant are losers, not adapted to the realities of their world, and thus legitimately subject to elimination by "social selection." Sumner presents society with an alternative: either "liberty, inequality, survival of the fittest," or "not-liberty, equality, survival of the unfittest." Self-made millionaires are the paradigm of the fittest. They are "a product of natural selection, acting on the whole body of men to pick out those who can meet the requirement of certain work to be done."

This doctrine of the financially successful as the cream of the universe naturally had a sympathetic audience. John D. Rockefeller, Andrew Carnegie, and Theodore Roosevelt were supporters, although Roosevelt believed that the unfit were entitled to some protection.

(3) Darwinism provided a rationale for Adam Smith's doctrine of the "Invisible Hand." Smith had supposed that while each man follows his innate tendency to "truck, barter, and trade," men's efforts would automatically dovetail in such a way that the economic good of society as a whole would be served. And Darwin had shown that the net result of each organism's engaging in a struggle for its own welfare was continuous evolution of the species as a whole in the direction of better adaptation to its environment. The political implications of this viewpoint are clear.

The central ethical question raised by the social Darwinists is this: granted that man is subject to natural law, and even granted further that he is subject to some form of natural or social selection, can one legitimately derive from this such policies as laissez-faire? Alfred Russel Wallace had argued that with the advent, under divine guidance, of man's brain, the evolution of man was no longer controlled by natural selection, so that inference from the doctrine of natural selection to ethical policy would be illegitimate. Huxley provided a similar argument: Man represents an island of cultural evolution in a sea of Darwinian change. These issues have largely passed into history, however, due to the philosophical point that whether or not to support a law of nature is not a question for decision.

The fate of Darwinism since the twentieth century has been mixed. Social Darwinism is of no more than historical interest. It is rightly regarded as philosophically naive and, moreover, as concerned with social questions that are not of contemporary interest. The same is largely true of the theological battles over the significance of evolution. Current theology exhibits a sublime indifference to the questions that agitated Huxley and Bishop Wilberforce. It must be pointed out, however, that modern theology is free to pursue other problems because of the clarification of the status of man and of the relation of science to theology that emerged from the Darwinian debate.

In biological theory proper, Darwin's theory remains secure. His Lamarckism is no longer accepted, if we discount some periodic revivals in the former Soviet Union; and the doctrine of sexual selection is still a matter of some debate. But the major theory of the *Origin,* evolution by natural selection, is the framework of modern evolutionary theory. This modern account—sometimes called the synthetic theory and sometimes, rather confusingly, Neo-Darwinism—accepts in toto the doctrine of natural selection as described above but develops it in a manner that Darwin himself could not have envisaged. The synthetic theory may fairly be described as Darwin's theory of natural selection, deepened by the absorption of twentieth-century genetics and systematically applied to the whole range of biological phenomena.

The absorption of genetics accounts for the novel developments in the doctrine of natural selection itself. Darwin thought of natural selection fundamentally as differential survival, and he regarded the organism as the natural unit that is subjected to selective pressures. With the advent of Mendelian genetics, and especially of the statistical study of the genetics of populations, these two Darwinian conceptions underwent a significant change. From the geneticist's point of view, differential survival is subordinate to differential reproduction of genetic materials; evolution is simply temporal change in the genetic constitution of a population. The simplest model of evolutionary change would be the following: Suppose that we have in a population two alleles, a_1 and a_2, of a gene a, and that a_1 is present in the proportion p, and a_2 in the proportion $1-p$. Then any temporal change in the value of p would be a case of reproductive differential between a_1 and a_2; and it would be an evolutionary change in the population. Some biologists simply identify such differential reproduction with natural selection, in which case sexual selection is a special case of natural selection. The natural unit of selection becomes the gene rather than the whole organism.

This conception of natural selection is not incompatible with Darwin's. Differential survival is still the major cause of differential reproduction of genes; and there is still a clear and obvious sense in which the organism is the fundamental unit of natural selection. But the new conception of natural selection facilitates the discussion of a large range of questions, for example, the roles of isolation and migration in evolution; the effectiveness of very small selective advantages; the roles of gene mutations, sex-linkage, and dominance; and so on. The modern theory has much to say on these topics that could not have been foreseen by Darwin, but nothing that he could not readily endorse.

See also Arnold, Matthew; Bergson, Henri; Darwin, Charles Robert; Darwin, Erasmus; Ethics, History of; Evolutionary Ethics; Evolutionary Theory; Good, The; Haeckel, Ernst Heinrich; Hegel, Georg Wilhelm Friedrich; Huxley, Thomas Henry; Lamarck, Chevalier de; Laws of Nature; Marx, Karl; Paley, William; Racism; Ruskin, John; Smith, Adam; Spinoza, Benedict (Baruch) de; Sumner, William Graham; Teleology; Wallace, Alfred Russel; Whitehead, Alfred North.

Bibliography

DARWIN AND WALLACE

Darwin, Charles Robert. *On the Origin of Species by means of Natural Selection, or the Preservation of Favoured Races in the Struggle for Life.* London, 1859. A variorum text, edited by Morse Peckham (Philadelphia, 1959), was published in paperback with an introduction by G. G. Simpson (New York, 1962). There is also a Modern Library edition (New York, 1949).

Darwin, Charles Robert. *The Descent of Man, and Selection in Relation to Sex.* London: J. Murray, 1871.

Darwin, Charles Robert. *The Voyage of the Beagle.* London and New York, n.d. A reissue by J. M. Dent and E. P. Dutton of their 1906 edition of the *Journal of Researches into the Geology and Natural History of the Various Countries Visited by H. M. S. Beagle, 1832–1836.*

Darwin, Charles Robert, and Alfred Russel Wallace. *Evolution by Natural Selection.* Cambridge, U.K.: Cambridge University Press, 1958. This contains Darwin's sketch of

1842, his essay of 1844, and the Darwin and Wallace papers read before the Linnaean Society in 1848.

Wallace, Alfred Russel. *Contributions to the Theory of Natural Selection.* London: Macmillan, 1870.

Wallace, Alfred Russel. *Darwinism.* London: Macmillan, 1889.

Wallace, Alfred Russel. "The Origin of Human Races and the Antiquity of Man Deduced from the Theory of Natural Selection." *Journal of the Anthropological Society of London* (1864).

CULTURAL ASPECTS OF DARWINISM

Dewey, John. *The Influence of Darwinism on Philosophy.* New York, 1910.

Eiseley, Loren. *Darwin's Century; Evolution and the Men Who Discovered It.* Garden City, NY: Doubleday, 1958. Contains many illuminating discussions of the interplay of philosophical and scientific theories.

Fothergill, Philip. *Historical Aspects of Organic Evolution.* London: Hollis and Carter, 1952. A history of evolutionary theories.

Goudge, T. A. *Ascent of Life; a Philosophical Study of Evolution.* Toronto: University of Toronto Press, 1961.

Gray, Asa. *Natural Science and Religion.* New York: Scribners, 1880. A topical discussion of the way theism looked to an evolutionist.

Himmelfarb, Gertrude. *Darwin and the Darwinian Revolution.* Garden City, NY: Doubleday, 1959.

Hofstadter, Richard. *Social Darwinism in American Thought, 1860–1915.* Philadelphia, 1944.

Huxley, Thomas Henry. *Evolution and Ethics, and Other Essays.* New York, 1898.

Schneider, Herbert. "The Influence of Darwin and Spencer on American Philosophical Theology." *Journal of the History of Ideas* 6 (1945).

MODERN EVOLUTIONARY THEORY

Darlington, C. D. *The Evolution of Genetic Systems.* Cambridge, U.K.: Cambridge University Press, 1939.

De Beer, Gavin. *Embryology and Evolution.* Oxford: Clarendon Press, 1930.

Dobzhansky, Theodosius. *Genetics and the Origin of Species,* 3rd ed. New York: Columbia University Press, 1951.

Fisher, R. A. *The Genetical Theory of Natural Selection.* Oxford: Clarendon Press, 1930. This is the classic application of statistical methods to the dynamics of evolving populations; together with the Darlington and Dobzhansky works, it affords a good introduction to the crucial relations between evolution and population genetics.

Mayr, Ernst. *Systematics and the Origin of Species.* New York: Columbia University Press, 1942.

Ross, H. H. *A Synthesis of Evolutionary Theory.* Englewood Cliffs, NJ: Prentice-Hall, 1962.

Simpson, G. G. *The Meaning of Evolution.* New York: New American Library, 1951. The best general introduction to the modern synthetic theory, this is a revised and abridged paperback edition of *The Meaning of Evolution: A Study of the History of Life and Its Significance for Man.* New Haven, CT, 1949.

Simpson, G. G. *The Major Features of Evolution.* New York: Columbia University Press, 1953. This and the above work by Simpson are the best nontechnical introductions for the general reader.

Morton O. Beckner (1967)

DAVID BEN MERWAN AL-MUKKAMMAS

See *Muqammis, David ben Merwan al-*

DAVID OF DINANT

The materialistic pantheist of the Middle Ages David of Dinant taught at Paris near the beginning of the thirteenth century. Apart from this fact, almost nothing is known of his life. It is uncertain whether he derived his name from Dinant in Belgium or Dinan in Brittany. His major work, *De Tomis, Hoc Est de Divisionibus,* is probably identical with the *Quaternuli* condemned at a provincial council in Paris in 1210, and his writings were among those banned at the University of Paris in 1215 by the papal legate, Robert de Courçon. Our knowledge of his ideas is largely derived from Albert the Great, Thomas Aquinas, and Nicholas of Cusa.

David developed his philosophy at a time when Latin Christian thought was facing an almost unprecedented challenge from rival world views. Neoplatonism, introduced into the medieval West by John Scotus Erigena and popularized in the twelfth century by numerous translations of Arabic works, was the first great non-Christian system to impress the medieval mind, but by the early thirteenth century Aristotelianism loomed large, and other Greek philosophies were not unknown. Attempts were made to blend the Christian doctrine of creation with these doctrines, notably with the Neoplatonic theory of emanation, with the result that the distinctive character of the biblical conception of the relation between the world and God was at least occasionally obscured.

The title of David's *De Tomis* suggests some indebtedness to Erigena's *De Divisione Naturae,* and David's pantheism may well have been inspired to some extent by his reading of Erigena's work. His thought seems, however, to have been more strongly influenced by ancient Greek materialism, as described in Aristotle's *Physics* and *Metaphysics,* and by certain Aristotelian ideas dialectically manipulated in the manner of the early medieval logicians.

David's interpretation of reality was essentially monistic. He first divided the objects of knowledge into three classes and then presented individual objects within each class as mere modes of a primary reality. Thus, bodies are modes of matter (*hyle*), souls are modes of mind (*nous*), and eternal substances or separated forms are modes of God. Furthermore, these three primary realities are themselves essentially one being or substance.

David supported this doctrine by a dialectical argument based on the logical notion of a "difference" (*differentia*) that, when added to a genus, forms a species. Such *differentiae,* he argued, can be predicated only of composite beings. God, mind, and prime matter, however, are all simple realities, and can therefore include no *differentiae.* Consequently, they must be substantially identical.

David's monism may be further characterized as materialistic. In his view, neither God nor matter possesses form, since beings determined by form are individual, composite substances. God and matter, therefore, cannot be known by an assimilation of their forms through abstraction. If in fact the intellect knows both God and matter, the explanation must be that it is already identical with them. Furthermore, if both God and matter are unformed, they are nothing but being in potentiality. Being in potentiality, however, is the definition of prime matter. Properly speaking, then, the ultimate reality, which is at once God, mind, and matter, is best described as matter.

See also Albert the Great; Aristotelianism; Aristotle; Erigena, John Scotus; Medieval Philosophy; Neoplatonism; Nicholas of Cusa; Pantheism; Thomas Aquinas, St.

Bibliography

Gabriel Théry, *David de Dinant. Étude sur son panthéisme matérialiste* (Paris, 1925), is the only book on David of Dinant. See also A. Birkenmajer, "Découverte de fragments manuscrits de David de Dinant," in *Revue néo-scolastique de philosophie* 35 (1933): 220–229, which does not, however, affect the accepted picture.

Eugene R. Fairweather (1967)

DAVIDSON, DONALD

(1917–2003)

Donald Davidson was born in 1917 in Springfield, Massachusetts, and graduated from Harvard in 1939. After serving in the United States Navy, Davidson returned to Harvard, where he wrote his doctoral dissertation on Plato's *Philebus* (1990a). After he received his PhD in 1949, Davidson went on to do extensive work in decision theory, in collaboration with Patrick Suppes and others. After many years at Stanford, and somewhat shorter stays at Princeton, Rockefeller, and Chicago, Davidson in 1981moved to the University of California at Berkeley, where he was appointed Willis and Marion Slusser Professor of Philosophy. Davidson lived in Berkeley for the rest of his life, continuing to produce important work until his death in 2003.

The early confrontation with the methodological challenges of giving empirical application to rational-choice theory had a lasting influence on Davidson. It is apparent in his later formulation of philosophical questions regarding action, the mental and linguistic meaning. Davidson's views on these matters have gradually come to articulation through a series of papers presenting detailed arguments pertaining to specific problems. In each of three areas of philosophy, Davidson elaborated a set of closely interconnected and highly influential doctrines. This entry looks briefly at each area in turn, emphasizing certain general features characteristic of Davidson's philosophical approach. The entry concludes with a glance at key themes of Davidson's later work, in which he elaborates an anti-representationalist conception of mind and of philosophy.

THE CAUSAL THEORY OF ACTION

Davidson's view, first set out in print in *Actions, Reasons, and Causes* (1963), is that individuals must consider the reasons for their actions—combinations of propositional attitudes, paradigmatically belief-desire pairs—to be also their causes. In this and related papers Davidson granted a main premise of the anti-causalist view prevailing at the time, that the teleological form of action-explanation makes such explanation irreducibly different from the nomological form characteristic of explanation in the natural sciences. What is distinctive about action-explanation is that it identifies the events involved (the action and its explanatory antecedent) in terms that reveal them to be part of a rational pattern. Davidson proceeded to challenge anti-causal orthodoxy, however, by arguing that it does not follow from this irreducible difference that action explanation is not a species of causal explanation.

A striking aspect of Davidson's view is the claim that the appeal to reason on which action explanations turn will be genuinely explanatory only insofar as the particular events thus rationally related are also related as cause and effect, and hence, for Davidson, may also be characterized by nomologically related descriptions. But Davidson insisted that the explanatory efficacy of a reason-explanation in no way depends on one possessing the law-evincing descriptions of the particular events in question. Indeed, in the typical case one enjoys the full benefits of effective action explanation without the slightest idea of what those descriptions might be. Davidson's work thus reconciles the following three fundamental claims.

First, when an event is cited in successful explanation of another event, the former is a cause of the latter. Second, causal relations between events entail nomological relations between them. Third, *explanans* and *explanandum* in action explanations are captured in terms that cannot be subsumed under strict law. This reconciliation trades on a particular conception of the relation between cause and law. If two events are causally related, they are so related no matter how described. The nomological relation, however, obtains between kinds of events; laws, as Davidson said, are linguistic, and so while causal relations are extensional, and causally related events necessarily fall under what he terms strict laws (that is, laws that are "free from caveats and *ceteris paribus* clauses … treating the universe as a closed system" (1993 [2005a], p. 191), they instantiate such law only under some appropriate description. Hence, the descriptions under which two causally related events appear in successful action explanation may be such that no amount of knowledge of strict causal law would allow one to infer the action from knowledge of the conditions cited in the explanation of it (1963a; 1993; 1995).

ANOMALOUS MONISM

A crucial element in Davidson's account of action is the distinction between a particular event and the descriptions that sort particular events under kinds. This same distinction is central also to his claims about the nature of the mental and its relation to the physical. In "Mental Events" (1970) and subsequent papers (1991b, 1993), Davidson argued that what it is to be a mental event is to be an event that falls under a mental predicate; that is to say, for Davidson, an event is mental just in case it falls under a description that ineliminably involves an intentional term. Correspondingly, what it is to be a physical event is to fall under a physical predicate. Physical predicates are of diverse kinds; a subset of physical terms are the predicates of developed physics. They form an ideal vocabulary the constitutive purpose of which is to track the causal structure of the world by displaying all events as they fall under maximally strict laws.

Since Davidson conceived of events as extensionally identified spatio-temporal particulars constituting nodes in the causal network, W. v. O. Quine's basic ontological dictum expresses also for Davidson an important truth; it is the unique business of physics to aim for full coverage. What this means for Davidson is that all events, qua nodes in the causal network, must be describable in the terms of physics. Yet some events are also mental, and Davidson argued that his physicalism supports no reductivist or eliminativist conclusions. For while all particular mental events are also particular physical events, no particular *kind* of mental event is a particular *kind* of physical event. The reason for this is that intentionality, which for Davidson is the mark of the mental, is constituted, in his view, by one's efforts to characterize fellow creatures as rational according to an inter-subjective standard. One is able to view fellow language-users thus because an individual has at his or her disposal two kinds of conceptual resources. One keeps track of other people by keeping tabs on objective environmental relations in which human beings are all embroiled in various and changing ways. At the same time, one is able to deploy a set of concepts—of belief, desire, and so on—which allows one to construct accounts not just of objective environmental relations, but also of how these relations appear to someone to be.

This system of double bookkeeping allows an individual to absorb a great deal of variation and irregularity in human behavior by accounting for objective anomalies in terms of subjective variables. But this strategy remains informative and useful only insofar as the essential discrepancies between subjective perspective and objective reality that interpretation exploits are prevented from becoming arbitrary or chaotic—were that to happen, the subjective would lose its explanatory purpose, it would simply mark the place where explanation ends.

This is why the interpretive construction of the subjective perspective must be tightly constrained; as Davidson stated, making sense of others "we will try for a theory that finds [them] consistent, believer[s] of truths, and lover[s] of the good (all by our own lights, it goes without saying)" (1970 [1980a], p. 222). This constraint on the application of intentional terms is often referred to as the "principle of charity." It reflects the fact that only the attitudes (though not only the rational attitudes) of a recognizably rational subject may be invoked in a genuinely explanatory way to account for the subject's behavior. Moreover, as Davidson later emphasized, because rationality considerations govern an individual's application of propositional-attitude concepts, these concepts are irreducibly causal, "identified in part by the sorts of action they are prone to cause, given the right conditions" (1991b [2001], p. 216).

As he further pointed out, "the right conditions" are themselves not independently characterizable. The phrase, marking the interdependence of the application conditions of mental predicates, remains an ineliminable qualification of the sort of platitudinous generalizations that express the content of our psychological terms. By contrast, Davidson argued, the application of the predicates of physics—aimed at the formulation of strict law—cannot itself depend on causal concepts (1991b). The application conditions of terms related by strict empirical law must be independently specifiable. The real difference, then, between the mental and the physical, and the reason for the irreducibility of one to the other, stems from the fact that the vocabulary of physics and the vocabulary of psychology have evolved under the pressure of distinctively different interests. What one wants from the former are modes of description that allow people to interact with each other as persons. What one wants from the latter are laws "as complete and precise as we can make them; a different aim" (1991b [2001], p. 217).

TRUTH AND MEANING

In the philosophy of language, Davidson is associated with the view that an individual may account for linguistic competence by appropriately characterizing the evidence available to and resources required by an idealized interpreter (1973). There are two fundamental aspects to this position. What, Davidson asked, might one know such that by knowing it one would be able to say what a speaker of a given language meant by some arbitrary utterance? His answer is a theory of truth for that language, an account of the logical structure of a language of the sort that Alfred Tarski demonstrated how to construct (1967a; 1990b; 2005b). The condition of adequacy for such a theory is an adaptation of what Tarski called "convention T." One has, Davidson proposed, a theory of meaning for a given language L provided one has a theory that entails for each sentence of L an instance of the schema, "s is true in L if and only if p." In this schema, s would be replaced by an expression that mentions a sentence of L (for example by means of quotation marks), and p replaced with any sentence of the language in which the theory is stated that is true if and only if the sentences mentioned by s is true. Such a theory provides, based on finite resources, a recursive characterization of the truth conditions for any sentence of L. While all that is demanded by convention T is that the theorems of the theory—known as T-sentences—capture co-extension of truth-values, "the hope," as Davidson said, "is that by putting appropriate formal and empirical restrictions on the theory as a whole, individual T-sentences will in fact serve to yield interpretations." (1973, [1984], p 124).

This proposal has spawned a great deal of work in formal semantics, guided by the aim of accounting for natural-language idioms in terms of their deep structure, or logical form, which makes explicit their truth-theoretical composition. For Davidson, the notion of logical form is extremely powerful; constrained on the one hand by one's intuitions concerning entailment relations, and on the other by the logical resources of Tarskian truth-theory construction, the uncovering of logical form functions as a crucible within which crystallize the ontological categories human language commits a person to. So for example, support for an ontology of events takes the form of an argument that one cannot account for the entailment relations intuitively characteristic of action sentences within the logical confines of a Tarskian theory of truth for a language unless one is willing to see such sentences as quantifying over events (1967b).

If a theory of truth is to serve as a theory of meaning for a language, tone needs to know how an interpreter may arrive at such a theory for a language she does not know. What is required for a recursive truth-theory to have empirical application? This question points to the other main aspect of Davidson's conception of linguistic understanding, an aspect where Quine's influence is most apparent. Observing the utterances of a speaker but knowing neither what the speaker means nor what the speaker believes, the interpreter will face endless alternative explanations of any observed piece of behavior. However, she can narrow the range of possibilities dramatically, by assuming that the speaker's behavior, including the speaker's linguistic behavior, embodies a rational response to salient features of her environment. This assumption of rationality is defeasible with respect to any particular attribution within the context of the construction of a theory of the meanings of someone's words and the contents of the person's thoughts. Davidson's point is emphatically not that one is never irrational, or that the irrational cannot be interpreted. Rather, the lesson is that irrationality is conceptually parasitic, diagnosable only against a background of reason (1982b; 1985). Thus, in what Davidson called radical interpretation, the interpreter may inductively construct a theory of truth for the speaker based on observations of behavior only by assuming that the speaker's mental life—her thoughts, actions and utterances—constitutes a largely rational whole (1973; 1980b). This assumption, compulsory for the radical interpreter, is often referred to as the principle of charity.

Even while minimizing the irrationality of her subject in accordance with charity, the radical interpreter will be able to produce for a speaker alternative theories of belief and meaning, theories that comport equally well with the empirical evidence (i.e., with the speaker's utterances and their contexts). This indeterminacy Davidson regards as innocuous; the salient facts about meaning and mind are what such differing theories have in common. If alternative theories are empirically equivalent, this means that there is more than one way of stating the facts that interpretive theories are designed to capture. This is no threat to the viability of interpretation (1974a; 1979; 1990b; 1991b).

CHALLENGES

With respect to Davidson's view of action, the most serious objection holds that Davidson's theories cannot indicate how action explanation actually can be explanatory at all. The point of the objection is that one cannot reconcile the three fundamental claims regarding explanation, cause, and law to which Davidson's work is committed (see aforementioned text). One claim—advanced, for example, by Jerry Fodor—is that informative action explanation must somehow draw on the explanatory power of nomic relations, in which case Davidson's irreducibility-claim would be threatened. An alternative view—defended by anti-causalists like George Wilson—is that the explanatory force of reason-explanation is *sui generis*, and does not depend on reasons being causes. This would jeopardize Davidson's conception of event monism.

With regard specifically to anomalous monism, Jaegwon Kim and others have argued that Davidson's view renders the mental causally inert. So reason explanations cannot really be explanations at all, since Davidson believed that any genuine explanation of an event, including an action, must pick out actual causal relations. Partly because of their different views on the individuation of events, this conflict is difficult to assess. However, if one grants Davidson his fundamental claims—that is, that the difference between the mental and the physical is a matter of vocabulary of description, and that events should be extensionally conceived—then his concept of supervenience ensures that a change in the truth value of the relevant kind of mental predicate ascription will entail some difference or other in causal relations. Naturally, alternatives to Davidson's Humean conception of causality and of the relations between causality and law are frequently at play in criticisms of Davidson's account. Davidson relied on this conception both in arguing for anomalous monism and in reconciling the irreducibility of action-explanation with a causal view of action.

As for Davidson's philosophy of language, there have been objections at various levels to the idea that a theory of meaning for a language must take the form of a Tarskian truth-theory. Even while accepting the proposal that a theory of meaning should take the form of a theory of truth, one may ask, for example, why theorists should restrict themselves, in producing a formal semantics for a language, to the resources of first-order predicate calculus. A great majority of scholars now doubt the prospects of an account of natural language semantics couched in purely extensional terms.

ANTI-REPRESENTATIONALISM

Davidson's contention that theories of truth as Tarski defined them give the structure of theories of meaning is best viewed as a pragmatic methodological commitment. What supports Davidson's most innovative philosophical conclusions is the more general point that one must understand meaning in terms of truth, in conjunction with his insistence—following Quine—on a third-person perspective to meaning and mind. This view makes the conditions of interpretation constitutive of content. Together, these commitments yield an account of the concept of truth constrained by the methodological requirements of interpretation. This account contrasts both with traditional correspondence theories and with epistemic accounts of the sort advanced, for example, by Hilary Putnam. It is also distinct from disquotationalist or deflationist theories such as that of Paul Horwich (1990b; 2005b).

The significance of these core commitments is readily apparent in Davidson's argument aimed to discredit the duality of representational scheme and empirical content on the grounds that it presupposes the notion of an untranslatable language (1974b). If truth and meaning are interlocking concepts whose features are illuminated by an account of the methodology of an ideal interpreter, the idea of alternative representations of reality that are mutually semantically impenetrable is not coherent. This argument also marks a dividing line between Davidson and Quine. For the metaphysical opposition between what is given to the mind on the one hand, and the processes brought to bear on that given, on the other hand, is the very duality in terms of which empiricism faces its defining challenge, namely to articulate a coherent notion of sensory evidence (1982a). On this fundamental score, Quine has remained within the bounds of empiricism (1990c). Davidson, on the other hand, has gone on explicitly to reject the basic metaphor of mind as inner space on which empiricism rests. For Davidson the hold of this metaphor reveals itself in the persistence of the interdependent notions of mental states as representational and of truth as correspondence, which, in turn, inextricably entangle philosophy in the problems of relativism and skepticism (1986a; 1987; 1988; 1990b; 2005b).

Davidson's alternative to the representational view of mind is most succinctly expressed in the thesis that there is thought only when there is actual communication (1989a; 1989b; 1991a; 1991b; 1992). On this controversial view, knowledge of one's own mental state, knowledge of the so-called external world, and knowledge of the mental states of others appear mutually interdependent (1991b). This blocks the very possibility of a skeptical or relativist challenge from arising, insofar as these are typically constructed around arguments that purport to show the impossibility of deriving any one of the three kinds of knowledge from either or both of the other two. This impossibility is something Davidson's work accepts—indeed insists on. Against the skeptic or relativist his claim is simply that the three forms of knowledge stand or fall together; denying one is to deny all, and to deny all is just to deprive our intentional concepts of any application.

This position rests on two key claims. One is that shared linguistic understanding is a prerequisite for any standard of objectivity (1991b). Such a standard gives content to the very distinction exploited by the propositional-attitude verbs between what is and what seems from some perspective to be, and hence, on Davidson's conception, is a prerequisite of thought. The other is the claim that the idea of shared linguistic understanding presupposes actual communication (1986b). The mental is thus what one reveals when one subjects a certain vaguely delimited range of causal relations to a particular kind of description, the terms of which presuppose the mutual recognition of subjects interacting in a shared world.

This view carries with it the commitments to event monism, to the constitutive role of rationality for content, and to a view of human agents as an integral part of the natural world, that have always been evident in Davidson's work. The distinction between extensionally conceived particulars and their descriptions remains pivotal. But the upshot is fundamentally at odds with the governing metaphors of modern epistemology-centered philosophy: "A community of minds," Davidson concluded, "is the basis of all knowledge; it provides the measure of all things." And he added: "It makes no sense to question the adequacy of this measure, or to seek a more ultimate standard" (1991b [2001], p. 218). However one assesses the plausibility of the considerations Davidson offers in support of this position, cognizance of the thorough-going externalism on which it is based should lead one to see it not as a species of antirealism or idealism, but as a profound rejection of foundationalist aspirations. Systematically linking the content of one's concepts to one's communicative practices as agents in the world, Davidson's work articulates a recognizably pragmatist view of mind, nature, and philosophy.

See also Action; Anomalous Monism; Philosophy of Language; Philosophy of Mind; Semantics; Supervenience.

Bibliography

WORKS BY DAVIDSON

Essays

The following essays have been reprinted in the works following this list, as indicated by year of publication:

"Actions, Reasons and Causes" (1963). Reprinted in 1980a.

"Truth and Meaning" (1967a). Reprinted in 1984.

"The Logical Form of Action Sentences" (1967b). Reprinted in 1980a.

"Mental Events" (1971). Reprinted in 1980a.

"Radical Interpretation" (1973). Reprinted in 1984.

"Belief and the Basis of Meaning" (1974a). Reprinted in 1984.

"On the Very Idea of a Conceptual Scheme" (1974b). Reprinted in 1984.

"The Inscrutability of Reference" (1979). Reprinted in 1984.

"A Unified Theory of Thought, Meaning and Action" (1980b). Reprinted in 2004.

"Empirical Content" (1982a). Reprinted in 2001.

"Paradoxes of Irrationality" (1982b). Reprinted in 2004.

"Incoherence and Irrationality" (1985). Reprinted in 2004.

"A Coherence Theory of Truth and Knowledge" (1986a). Reprinted with "Afterthoughts, 1987" in 2001.

"A Nice Derangement of Epitaphs" (1986b). Reprinted in 2005a.

"Knowing One's Own Mind" (1987). Reprinted in 2001.

"The Myth of the Subjective" (1988). Reprinted in 2001.

"What is Present to the Mind?" (1989a). Reprinted in 2001.

"The Conditions of Thought" (1989b). Reprinted in 2001.

"The Structure and Content of Truth" (Journal of Philosophy, Vol. 97. 1990b.

"Meaning, Truth and Evidence" (1990c). Reprinted in 2005a.

"Epistemology Externalized" (1991a). Reprinted in 2001.

"Three Varieties of Knowledge" (1991b). Reprinted in 2001.

"The Second Person" (1992). Reprinted in 2001.

"Thinking Causes" (1993). Reprinted in 2005a.

"Laws and Cause" (1995). Reprinted in 2005a.

Works

Essays on Action and Events. Oxford: Oxford University Press, 1980a.

Inquiries into Truth and Interpretation. Oxford: Oxford University Press, 1984.

Plato's Philebus. New York: Garland, 1990a.

Subjective, Intersubjective, Objective. Oxford: Oxford University Press, 2001.

Problems of Rationality. Oxford: Oxford University Press, 2004.

Truth, Language, and History. Oxford: Oxford University Press, 2005a.

Truth and Predication. Cambridge, MA: Harvard University Press, 2005b.

WORKS ABOUT DAVIDSON

Brandl, J., and W. Gombocz, eds. *The Mind of Donald Davidson*. Amsterdam: Rodopi, 1989.

Dazenbrock, W. R., ed. *Literary Theory after Davidson*. University Park, PA: Penn State Press, 1989.

Evnine, Simon. *Donald Davidson*. Palo Alto, CA: Stanford University Press: 1991.

Hahn, L. ed. *The Library of Living Philosophers*. Vol. 27: *The Philosophy of Donald Davidson*. Lasalle, IL: Open Court, 1999.

Joseph, M. *Donald Davidson*. Kingston, ON: McGill-Queen's University Press, 2004.

Kotatko, P., P. Pagin, and G. Segal, eds. *Interpreting Davidson*. Palo Alto, CA: CSLI Publications, 2001.

LePore, E., ed. *Truth and Interpretation: Perspectives on the Philosophy of Donald Davidson*. Oxford: Blackwell, 1986.

LePore, E., and K. Ludwig. *Donald Davidson: Meaning, Truth, Language, and Reality*. Oxford: Oxford University Press, 2005.

LePore, E., and B. McLaughlin, eds. *Actions and Events: Perspectives on the Philosophy of Donald Davidson*. Oxford: Blackwell, 1985.

Ludwig, K., ed. *Donald Davidson*. Cambridge, U.K.: Cambridge University Press.

Malpas, J. E. *Donald Davidson and the Mirror of Meaning*. Cambridge, U.K.: Cambridge University Press, 1992.

Preyer, G., F. Siebelt, and A. Ulfig, eds. *Language, Mind and Epistemology: On Donald Davidson's Philosophy*. Dordrecht: Kluwer Academic Publishers, 1994.

Ramberg, B. *Donald Davidson's Philosophy of Language: An Introduction*. Oxford: Blackwell, 1989.

Stoecker, R., ed. *Reflecting Davidson*. Berlin: De Gruyter, 1993.

Vermazen, B., and M. Hintikka, eds. *Essays on Davidson: Actions and Events*. Oxford: Oxford University Press, 1985.

Bjørn T. Ramberg (1996, 2005)

DA VINCI, LEONARDO

See *Leonardo da Vinci*

DEATH

Although most of the great philosophers have touched on the problem of death, few have dealt with it systematically or in detail. Frequently, as in the case of Benedict (Baruch) de Spinoza, an author's views on the subject are known to us from a single sentence; and at almost all stages in Western history we are likely to discover more about the topic in the writings of men of letters than in those of technical philosophers. Whether this relative reticence on the part of philosophers should be attributed to a general lack of interest or to other causes is a moot point. Arthur Schopenhauer, who was the first of the major philosophers to deal extensively with the subject, declared that death is the muse of philosophy, notwithstanding that the muse is seldom avowed. And the existentialist philosophers from Søren Kierkegaard to the present have more or less consistently endorsed Schopenhauer's contention; Albert Camus's declaration in *The Myth of Sisyphus* (1942) that suicide is the only genuine philosophical issue is an extreme but notable case in point. On the other hand, most contemporary Anglo-American analytic philosophers probably regard the paucity of materials on death as evidence of the subject's resistance to serious philosophical inquiry. In general, they wish to exclude the subject of death from the area of legitimate philosophical speculation, either as a part of their campaign against metaphysics or on the grounds that the subject can be more adequately dealt with by psychologists and social scientists. The psychologists and social scientists have, in fact, recently given signs of a willingness to explore the question. One such indication was a symposium on the psychology of death at the 1956 American Psychological Association Convention, which resulted in the publication in 1959 of an anthology including contributions from scholars in a wide variety of fields. Unfortunately, as several of the contributors to this volume lamented, the number of experimental studies actually undertaken has been disappointingly small.

THE KNOWLEDGE OF DEATH

The primary concern of most philosophers who have dealt with the question of death has been to discover ways in which we may mitigate or overcome the fear it tends to inspire. There are, however, several other loosely related problems that have also tended to excite interest or controversy and that it will be advisable to discuss first. How does man learn of death? Is death a natural phenomenon, or does it require explanation in nonnatural terms? What specific psychological or social conditions tend to heighten the awareness and fear of death?

AWARENESS OF DEATH. The clearest and simplest answer to the first of these questions was given by Voltaire, who stated: "The human species is the only one which knows it will die, and it knows this through experience" (*Dictionnaire philosophique*). Although some persons have questioned whether man is the only animal who knows he will die, arguing that certain of the lower animals appear to show some vague presentiment of approaching extinction, it appears to be unquestioned that man alone has a clear awareness of death and that man alone regards death as a universal and inevitable phenomenon. The interesting question is how man knows he will die. The view that experience alone gives knowledge of death derives support from the ignorance of death displayed by many children and from anthropological data indicating that many primitive peoples refuse even as adults to regard death as necessary or universal. However, a number of twentieth-century philosophers contested this view, especially Max Scheler and Martin Heidegger, who argue that the awareness of death is an immanent, a priori structure of human consciousness. Although neither of these authors offers anything in the nature of scientific evidence for his position, it is not easily refuted; for, if one grants current notions about levels of consciousness, apparent ignorance of death may be interpreted as merely superficial and attributed to some form of repression. Moreover, the imperfect knowledge of death among primitive peoples is a fact that could be used against those who argue that the knowledge of death comes from experience, since the hazards of their lives expose primitive peoples to an earlier and greater experience of death than is common among civilized men. At the very least it must be granted that the knowledge of death depends not only upon experience but also upon a level of mental culture that makes it possible to interpret experience accurately.

Ironically, Sigmund Freud, who more than anybody else has habituated us to think in terms of levels of consciousness and has thereby rendered credible the idea that knowledge of death may exist despite apparent ignorance, stated that the consciousness, not the apparent ignorance, of death is merely superficial, the unconscious being firmly convinced of its immortality. How Freud could reconcile this belief, which dates from the period of World War I, with his later belief in the unconscious death wish is not clear.

DEATH: A NATURAL PHENOMENON? Is death a natural phenomenon? Most persons today tend to find this question a bit foolish. It is noteworthy, however, that most primitive peoples attribute death to the agency of gods or demons who are jealous of human achievements. Equally significant is the Christian explanation of death as punishment for the sins of Adam. It should also be observed that if by a "natural" phenomenon one means a fact that can be fully understood and explained by empirical inquiry, death is not a natural phenomenon for Heidegger or Scheler. This reluctance to explain death in terms of natural causes has an interesting parallel in the reluctance to explain life itself naturalistically, and the religious or metaphysical perspectives that give rise to nonnaturalistic interpretations of life tend also to occasion nonnaturalistic interpretations of death.

VARIATIONS IN CONSCIOUSNESS OF DEATH. Are there great variations in the awareness or fear of death from person to person, from epoch to epoch, from culture to culture? If so, how are these variations to be explained? Surprisingly, very little attention has been given to these questions. The most interesting and almost the only hypothesis on this topic is that of Johan Huizinga and Paul-Louis Landsberg, who, each in his own way, link the consciousness of death to individualism. According to these authors, the consciousness of death has been most acute in periods of social disorganization, when individual choice tends to replace automatic conformity to social values; they point especially to classical society after the disintegration of the city-states; to the early Renaissance, after the breakdown of feudalism; and to the twentieth century. This hypothesis has yet to be fully confirmed or disconfirmed by careful historical and anthropological study. However, it is true that late antiquity, the early Renaissance, and the twentieth century made unusually great contributions to the literature on death.

THE FEAR OF DEATH

With respect to the fear of death, the great divide is between those who argue that only the hope of personal immortality will ever reconcile men to death and those who argue that the fear of death may be mitigated or overcome even when death is accepted as the ultimate extinction of the individual person. The second group, which is remarkably heterogeneous, may be subdivided according to the techniques recommended for allaying fears.

THE EPICUREANS. One of the oldest of the "solutions" to the fear of death was that of Epicurus and his followers. According to Epicurus, the fear of death is based upon the beliefs that death is painful and that the soul may survive to experience pain or torture in an afterlife.

Since both of these beliefs are mistaken, it suffices to expose them as such. Although death may be precipitated by painful disease, death itself is a perfectly painless loss of consciousness, no more to be feared than falling asleep. And since the soul is merely a special organization of material atoms, it cannot survive physical destruction. "Death," Epicurus said, "is nothing to us. … It does not concern either the living or the dead, since for the former it is not, and the latter are no more" (*Letter to Menoeceus*). It is hardly necessary to point out that many persons have questioned Epicurus's conception of the soul and consequently have rejected his views with respect to its immortality. The principal criticism, however, is that the Epicureans have falsely diagnosed the cause of humankind's fear of death. Death terrorizes us, not because we fear it as painful, but because we are unwilling to lose consciousness permanently. The twentieth-century Spanish existentialist philosopher Miguel de Unamuno reports that "as a youth and even as a child, I remained unmoved when shown the most moving pictures of hell, for even then nothing appeared to me quite so horrible as nothingness itself."

THE STOICS. The later Stoics, especially Seneca, Epictetus, and Marcus Aurelius, offered a more complicated and elusive view of death. Seneca said that to overcome the fear of death we must think of it constantly. The important thing, however, is to think of it in the proper manner, reminding ourselves that we are but parts of nature and must reconcile ourselves to our allotted roles. He recurrently compared life to a banquet from which it is our obligation to retire graciously at the appointed time, or to a role in a play whose limits ought to satisfy us, since they satisfy the author. The fear of death displays a baseness wholly incompatible with the dignity and calm of the true philosopher, who has learned to emancipate himself from finite concerns. Essential to the Stoic outlook was the Platonic view that philosophizing means learning to die; that is, learning to commune with the eternal through the act of philosophic contemplation.

Although much of Stoic thinking on death crept into later Christianity, the contemporary Christians saw in this thinking a sinful element of pride. Death, Augustine said, is a punishment for human sin, and the fear of death cannot be overcome except through divine grace. Others find it highly questionable whether one can reasonably accept the metaphysical underpinnings of the Stoic view, most especially the belief in a providential order of Nature.

SPINOZA. A third solution is that of Spinoza. He wrote: "A free man thinks of nothing less than of death, and his wisdom is not a meditation upon death but upon life" (*Ethics,* Prop. LXVII). Since Spinoza did not elaborate, it is possible to argue almost endlessly about the precise import of this famous remark. Most often, however, it is interpreted to mean that men can and should allay the fear of death simply by diverting their attention from it, and some persons have argued that by his nature man tends to—perhaps must—follow this advice. François de La Rochefoucauld, for instance, averred that man can no more look directly at death than he can look directly at the sun. One fundamental criticism of this position comes from the Stoics and the existentialists, both of whom maintain that the fear of death can be allayed only by facing it directly. A second criticism consists in pointing out that the fear of death is frequently an involuntary sentiment that cannot be conquered by a merely conscious decision or a bare act of will. It is not enough to tell people not to think of death; one must explain how they can avoid thinking of it.

DEATH AND THE GOOD LIFE. This brings us to a fourth view on death, a view that was felicitously put by Leonardo da Vinci. Just as a day well spent brings happy sleep, so, he said, a life well spent brings happy death. Painful preoccupation with death has its source in human misery; the cure is to foster human well-being. A happy man is not seriously pained by the thought of death, nor does he dwell on the subject. This view was held by many Enlightenment thinkers, most notably the Marquis de Condorcet. It also appears to be the view of most pragmatists and of Bertrand Russell.

There are two counterarguments. The first is the theme prevalent in several branches of Christianity concerning the total impossibility of attaining happiness on Earth. The second is the even more familiar and prevalent Christian theme that in order to achieve happiness in this life, one must first conquer the fear of death. Happiness, therefore, is not a cure; it is a consequence of the cure.

DEATH WITHOUT CONSOLATION. In sharp contrast to this last position is that of a long line of nineteenth-century and more recent philosophers, from Schopenhauer to contemporary existentialists. For them human well-being or happiness, at least as traditionally conceived, is totally impossible to achieve; and if the individual is to experience such rewarding values as life does permit, he must uncompromisingly embrace the tragedy of the human condition, clearheadedly acknowledging such evils as death. Like the Stoics, these authors would have us think constantly of death. Unlike the Stoics, however, they do not offer us the consolation of belief in a providential order of nature. From the standpoint of Being or Nature, the death of the individual is totally meaningless or absurd.

For Schopenhauer the finite, empirical self is a manifestation of a cosmic will that has destined man to live out his life in suffering or painful striving. The only remedy is to achieve a state of indifference or pure will-lessness—a state best known in moments of pure aesthetic contemplation but to which the awareness of death substantially contributes.

According to Friedrich Nietzsche, the superior man will not permit death to seek him out in ambush, to strike him down unawares. The superior man will live constantly in the awareness of death, joyfully and proudly assuming death as the natural and proper terminus of life.

Heidegger and Jean-Paul Sartre, like most existentialists, urge us to cultivate the awareness of death chiefly as a means of heightening our sense of life. The knowledge of death gives to life a sense of urgency that it would otherwise lack. The same point has been made by Freud, who compared life without the consciousness of death to a Platonic romance or to a game played without stakes.

Heidegger makes the additional claim, although here Sartre parts company with him, that the awareness of death confers upon man a sense of his own individuality. Dying, he says, is the one thing no one can do for you; each of us must die alone. To shut out the consciousness of death is, therefore, to refuse one's individuality and to live inauthentically.

See also Augustine, St.; Camus, Albert; Epictetus; Epicurus; Euthanasia; Existentialism; Freud, Sigmund; Heidegger, Martin; Immortality; Kierkegaard, Søren Aabye; La Rochefoucauld, Duc François de; Leonardo da Vinci; Life, Meaning and Value of; Marcus Aurelius Antoninus; Nietzsche, Friedrich; Platonism and the Platonic Tradition; Reincarnation; Sartre, Jean-Paul; Scheler, Max; Schopenhauer, Arthur; Seneca, Lucius Annaeus; Spinoza, Benedict (Baruch) de; Stoicism; Unamuno y Jugo, Miguel de; Voltaire, François-Marie Arouet de.

Bibliography

Jacques Choron, *Death and Western Thought* (New York: Collier, 1963), is a fairly comprehensive review of what Western philosophers have had to say on the subject of death. It is especially recommended for its wealth of quotations. Herman Feifel, ed., *The Meaning of Death* (New York: McGraw-Hill, 1959), is an anthology containing many contemporary essays by psychologists, sociologists, and workers in allied fields.

Russell's views on death may be found in "The Art of Growing Old," in his *Portraits from Memory and Other Essays* (London: Allen and Unwin, 1956) and in "What I Believe," in his *Why I Am Not a Christian* (London: Allen and Unwin, 1957).

Heidegger's views will be found in his *Being and Time* (New York: Harper, 1962), Part II, Ch. 1; Sartre's in his *Being and Nothingness* (New York: Philosophical Library, 1956), pp. 531–553.

An interesting work by a Roman Catholic existentialist is Paul-Louis Landsberg, *Essai sur l'experience de la mort* (Paris, 1951).

Freud's views are expressed in "Thoughts for the Times on War and Death," in *Standard Edition of the Complete Psychological Works of Sigmund Freud,* edited by James Strachey and Anna Freud (London: Hogarth Press, 1957), Vol. XIV, 288–317.

Johan Huizinga, *The Waning of the Middle Ages* (London, 1952), provides the best account of that author's reflections.

For an analysis of primitive attitudes toward death, see Lucien Lévy-Bruhl, *Primitive Mentality,* translated by Lilian A. Clare (London: Allen and Unwin, 1923).

Robert G. Olson (1967)

DEATH [ADDENDUM]

In recent decades death has garnered considerable philosophical attention in three principal areas: medical ethics, value theory, and metaphysics.

In medical ethics, interest has centered on determining the criterion of death. The most common criterion for the death of human beings is irreversible loss of consciousness, but this postulate remains controversial for those who see humans principally as animals rather than as conscious beings. A human animal may be said to be alive even if he or she is not conscious. The meaning of "irreversibility" is also controversial. Would Jane Doe be dead if she lost consciousness but her consciousness could be recovered if she were injected with a serum that will not be invented for another thousand years? Medical ethicists have also debated the relevance of the principle of double effect regarding situations in which a doctor is the cause of death. Followers of the principle of double effect will allow morphine to be administered to a patient in order to stop his suffering, even allowing for the possibility that the morphine will kill the patient. But this outlook does not countenance such an injection if the patient's death is the main objective of the act.

In the theory of values, the argument of Epicurus (341–270 BCE) still engenders controversy. Epicurus argued that if death is the annihilation of a person, then the death cannot be bad for that person. For something to be bad, there must be some thing or person for whom it is bad, but if the person who has died has ceased to be, then (for that person) there is no bad or evil. Epicurus employed this argument to alleviate the fear of death. Epicurus also argued that just as one does not fear or bemoan one's nonexistence before birth, one ought not to lament one's nonexistence after death.

Epicurus's reasoning has elicited a number of counterarguments. Some have argued that death is bad for the person insofar as it involves missed opportunities or possibilities. The death of a person involves his absence, and such an absence can be a bad state of affairs even if it is not bad for the person or for others. It has also been suggested that the Epicurean bid for a symmetry of neither regretting past nonexistence or future nonexistence is not plausible because a person may well wish she had been alive in some earlier era.

Philosophical reflection on death has implications for an overall theory of values, involving questions about rights (if the dead have ceased to be, do they have any rights whatsoever?), promise-keeping (do you have a duty to keep a promise to someone who has ceased to be?), and the environment (should environmental harms be understood principally in terms of the death of individual animals and plants or of species)?

Still other thinkers have wrestled with the issue of whether or not the death of humans is in fact a case of annihilation. This debate has unfolded mainly among specialists in the metaphysics of personal identity, philosophy of mind, and philosophy of religion. Dualist conceptions of human nature—according to which there is a distinction between a person or soul or mind on the one hand and his or her body on the other—allow for the possibility that the physical body may be annihilated without destroying the person or soul or mind. The case for dualism and the coherence of disembodiment has been bolstered by reports of out-of-the-body experiences (OBE). Even if the empirical testing of such OBEs is inherently problematic, some dualists have appealed to the apparent coherence of such reports in arguing that disembodiment is a bona fide possibility. Philosophical speculation on the afterlife contains a great deal of debate on the coherence of competing thought experiments. It may appear that materialist accounts of persons, according to which a person *is* his or her body, are ill-suited to lending any credibility to an afterlife scenario, but late-twentieth-century philosophers have challenged this conclusion. Some have argued that a physical object (such as a human body) can cease to exist and then be re-created. This process entails what has been called a "gap inclusive" or "intermittent" identity, for it posits an interval when a person temporarily ceases to exist.

Philosophers have also advanced a constitutional argument, according to which human beings are material objects because they are constituted exclusively by material objects. The constitutional relationship is not one of strict identity, so it is possible for the same thing (a person) to survive the change of his or her constitutive parts. Some argue that a person (understood as a material body) can survive the loss of his or her present body or perhaps come to have a new body or even be reconstituted by nonphysical individuals. The philosophical investigation into the possibility of an afterlife is often located in the broader philosophical enterprise of weighing the merits of naturalism, theism, and various nontheistic religious traditions.

Bibliography

Almeder, Robert. *Beyond Death: The Evidence for Life After Death.* Springfield, IL: Charles C. Thomas, 1987.

Baker, Lynne Rudder. *Persons and Bodies.* Cambridge, U.K.: Cambridge University Press, 2000.

Feldman, Fred. *Confrontations with the Reaper: A Philosophical Study of the Nature and Value of Death.* New York: Oxford University Press, 1992.

Hick, John. *Death and Eternal Life.* Louisville, KY: Westminster John Knox, 1994).

Moody, Raymond. *Life After Life: The Investigation of a Phenomenon—Survival of Bodily Death.* Bantam Doubleday Dell, 1976.

Nagel, Thomas. *Mortal Questions.* Cambridge, U.K.: Cambridge University Press, 1979.

Taliaferro, Charles. *Consciousness and the Mind of God.* Cambridge, U.K.: Cambridge University Press, 1994.

Taliaferro, Charles. "Sensibility and Possibilia: A Defense of Thought Experiments." *Philosophia Christi* 3:2, 201 (2001): 403–420.

Rick Fairbanks (2005)
Charles Taliaferro (2005)

DECISION THEORY

Decision theory provides a general, mathematically rigorous account of decision making under uncertainty. The subject includes rational choice theory, which seeks to formulate and justify the normative principles that govern optimal decision making, and descriptive choice theory, which aims to explain how human beings actually make decisions. Within both these areas one may distinguish individual decision theory, which concerns the choices of a single agent with specific goals and knowledge, and game theory, which deals with interactions among individuals. This entry will focus on rational choice theory for the single agent, but some descriptive results will be mentioned in passing.

DECISION PROBLEMS

It is standard to portray decision makers as facing choices among acts that cause desirable or undesirable consequences when performed in various states of the world. Acts characterize those aspects of the world that an agent can directly control. States specify contingencies beyond her control that might influence the consequences of acts. Each combination of an act A and state S fixes a unique consequence $A(S)$ that describes the result of doing A in S. When there are only finitely many acts and states the decision situation can be represented as a matrix:

	S_1	$S_2 \ldots$	S_n
A_1	$A_1(S_1)$	$A_1(S_2) \ldots$	$A_1(S_n)$
A_2	$A_2(S_1)$	$A_2(S_2) \ldots$	$A_2(S_n)$
A_3	$A_3(S_1)$	$A_3(S_2) \ldots$	$A_3(S_n)$
$\vdots$	$\vdots$	$\vdots$	$\vdots$
A_m	$A_m(S_1)$	$A_m(S_2) \ldots$	$A_m(S_n)$

The agent decides the row, the world decides the column, and these together determine the consequence.

In any well-formed decision problem (1) the value of each consequence is independent of the act and state that bring it about, (2) each consequence is sufficiently detailed to settle every matter about which the agent intrinsically cares, (3) neither acts nor states have any value except as a means for producing consequences, and (4) the agent will not believe that she has the ability to causally influence which state obtains. When these conditions are met, the agent's goals and values affect her decision only via her desires for consequences, and her beliefs influence her choice via her uncertainty about which state obtains. The agent will use her beliefs about states to select an act that provides the best means for securing a desirable consequence.

For theoretical purposes, it is useful to idealize the decision setting by assuming that the repertoire of actions is rich. Specifically, for each consequence c there is a constant act $[c]$ that produces c in every state of the world, and, for any acts A and B, and any disjunction of states E, there is a mixed act $A_E \cup B_{\sim E}$ that produces A's consequence when E holds and B's consequence when $\sim E$ holds. While real agents will typically be unable to realize such recherché prospects as these, imagining that decision makers have attitudes toward them often helps one determine which realistic acts should be performed.

This model applies to one-choice decisions made at a specific time. Early decision theorists believed that sequences of decisions made over time could be reduced to one-shot decisions among contingency plans, or strategies, but this view now has few adherents. The topic of dynamic decision making lies beyond the scope of this entry. For relevant discussions, see Peter Hammond (1988), Edward McClennen (1990), and James M. Joyce (1995).

SUBJECTIVE EXPECTED UTILITY

The central goal of rational choice theory is to identify the conditions under which a decision maker's beliefs and desires rationalize the choice of an action. According to the standard model of decision-theoretic rationality, an action is rational just in case, relative to the agent's beliefs and desires, it has the highest subjective expected utility of any available option. This subjective expected utility (SEU) theory has its roots in the work of Blaise Pascal, Daniel Bernoulli, Vilfredo Pareto, and Frank P. Ramsey, and finds its fullest expression in Leonard J. Savage's *Foundations of Statistics* (1972). According to SEU a rational agent's basic desires can be represented by a utility function $\boldsymbol{u}$ that assigns a real number $\boldsymbol{u}(c)$ to each consequence c. The value of $\boldsymbol{u}(c)$ measures the degree to which c would satisfy the agent's desires and promote his or her aims.

Likewise, the agent's beliefs can be characterized by a subjective probability function $\boldsymbol{P}$ whose values express the agent's subjective degrees of confidence, or credences, in the states of the world. $\boldsymbol{P}$ is assumed to be unique, and $\boldsymbol{u}$ is unique once the choice of a unit and a zero for measuring utilities are fixed. Given $\boldsymbol{P}$ and $\boldsymbol{u}$, the expected utility of each act A is a weighted average of the utilities of its consequences, so that $\boldsymbol{Exp}_{P,u}(A) = \sum_{i=1} \boldsymbol{P}(S_i)\boldsymbol{u}(A(S_i))$. According to the core doctrine of SEU, the choice of an act is rational only if it maximizes the chooser's subjective expected utility, so that $\boldsymbol{Exp}_{P,u}(A) \geq \boldsymbol{Exp}_{P,u}(B)$ for all acts B. This should not be taken to suggest that the agent sees herself as maximizing expected utility, or even that she has the concept of expected utility. SEU does not propose expected utility maximization as a decision procedure, but as a way of assessing the results of such procedures. Rational decision makers merely act as if they maximize subjective expected utility; they need not explicitly do so.

REPRESENTATION OF RATIONAL PREFERENCE

A central challenge for SEU is to find a principled way of characterizing credences and utilities. Following the lead of Ramsey (1931), the standard solution involves proving a representation theorem that shows how an agent's beliefs about states and desires for outcomes are related to her all-things-considered preferences for acts. The agent is assumed to make three sorts of comparative evaluations between acts: She might strictly prefer A to B, written $A > B$, weakly prefer A to B, $A \geq B$, or be indifferent between them, $A \approx B$. These relations hold, respectively, just in case the agent judges that, on balance, A will do more than, at least as much as, or exactly as much as, B will to satisfy her desires and promote her aims. The totality of such evaluations is the agent's preference ranking.

Early decision theorists, motivated by a misguided scientific methodology, thought of preferences as operationally defined in terms of overt choices, so that, by definition, an agent prefers A to B if and only if (iff) she will incur a cost to choose A over B. Even though this sort of behaviorism remains firmly ensconced in some areas of economics, it has been widely and effectively criticized (Sen 1977, Joyce 1999). In the end, preferences are best thought of as subjective judgments of the comparative merits of actions as promoters of desirable outcomes. While such judgments are closely tied to overt choice behavior, the relationship between the two is nowhere near as direct and unsophisticated as behaviorism suggests.

The representation theorem approach seeks to justify SEU by (1) imposing a system of axiomatic constraints on preference rankings, (2) arguing that these express requirements of rationality, and then (3) proving that any preference ranking that satisfies the axioms can be associated with a probability P and a utility u such that each of $A >, \geq, \approx B$ hold iff, respectively, $\mathbf{Exp}_{P,u}(A) >, \geq, = \mathbf{Exp}_{P,u}(B)$. An agent whose preferences can be represented in this way evaluates acts as if she were aiming to maximize expected utility relative to $\mathbf{P}$ and $\mathbf{u}$.

FRAME INVARIANCE

All versions of SEU share a common set of core principles. The first says that logically equivalent redescriptions of prospects should not alter preferences.

> *SEU_1 Frame Invariance.* The evaluation of an act should not depend on how its consequences happen to be described.

People often violate this constraint. Consider the following two decision framings due to E. Shafir and A. Tversky (1995):

- You receive \$300, and are then given a choice between getting another \$100 for sure or getting \$200 or \$0 depending on the toss of a fair coin.
- You receive \$500, but are then forced to choose between returning \$100 for sure or returning \$200 or \$0 depending on the toss of a fair coin.

Since both decisions offer a sure \$400 or a fifty-fifty chance of \$300 or \$500, SEU_1 requires agents to make the same choice in each case (though it does not tell them which choice to make). As it turns out, most people make the safe choice in the first case and take the sure \$400, but they make risky choice in the second case by taking the fifty-fifty gamble. Cognitive psychologists attribute this violation of SEU_1 to the following two irrational tendencies of human decision makers:

> Divergence from Status Quo. People are more concerned with incremental gains and losses, seen as changes in the status quo, than with total well-being or overall happiness.

> Asymmetrical Risk Aversion. People eschew risk when pursuing gains, but to seek risk when avoiding losses.

Under the first description, where the status quo is \$300, people see themselves as trying to secure an additional gain, and so opt for the safe alternative. Under the second description, where the status quo is \$500, people see themselves avoiding losses, and so incline toward the risky choice. These divergent attitudes are irrational given that the options are effectively identical.

VALUE INDEPENDENCE

The second principle requires each act to have a value that depends only on the values and probabilities of the outcomes it might cause.

> SEU_2 *Value Independence.* If the agent prefers A to B in a decision where C is not an option, then she should still prefer A to B even if C is an option, provided that C's inclusion does not provide any information about state probabilities.

Apparent counterexamples to SEU_2 as a requirement of rationality always involve violations of the proviso. For example, R. Duncan Luce and Howard Raiffa (1957) discuss a diner who, thinking he is in a greasy spoon, prefers salmon to steak, but then orders steak when told that snails are on the menu. SEU_2 is vindicated by the observation that the availability of snails provides the diner with evidence for thinking that he is in fine restaurant, and this alters his views about the comparative merits of the salmon and steak. Other common violations of SEU_2 are clearly irrational. For example, D. Redelmeier and E. Shafir (1995) show that physicians are less likely to prescribe ibuprofen to patients in pain when they have the option of prescribing the inferior drug piroxicam than when piroxicam is unavailable. While this sort of behavior does not discredit SEU_2 as a normative principle, it does show that it is inaccurate as a description of human behavior.

ORDERING

The third principle rules out preference cycles in which $A \gtrsim B$, $B \gtrsim C$, but $A > C$, and it requires that the preference ranking be complete in the sense that exactly one of $A > B$, $A \approx B$ or $B > A$ always hold.

> SEU_3 *Ordering.* Preference rankings completely order the set of acts.

Though some dispute anticyclicality, and Peter C. Fishburn (1991) even develops an acyclic decision theory, the prohibition against cycles remains among the most widely accepted principles of rational preference. On views that equate preferences and choices, preference cycles are irrational because they leave the agent open to exploitation as a "money pump": she will freely trade C for B and B for A, and then pay a fee to exchange C for A, thereby getting nothing for something. Even if choice is not equated with preference, cycles are still problematic. Many seemingly rational cycles treat preferences as partial, rather than all-things-considered evaluations. For instance, one might prefer an expensive shirt to a moderately priced one on the basis of style, and prefer the moderately priced shirt to a cheap shirt on the basis of durability, but prefer the cheap shirt to the expensive one on the basis of price. Here what seems to be a rational preference cycle is really a failure to integrate considerations of style, durability, and price into an all-things-considered value judgment.

Failures of evaluative discrimination can also seem to generate rational preference cycles. Suppose a vinophile, who cares only about how his wine tastes, cannot taste any difference between wine A and wine B, or between wine B and wine C, but can taste that C is better than A. It is tempting to think that the vinophile should be indifferent between A and B and between B and C, but should prefer C to A. A clearer understanding of the situation shows that this is incorrect. A person should only be indifferent between prospects when he lacks any reason, on balance, for preferring one to the other. The vinophile, however, has reason to favor B over A since B is indistinguishable in taste from a wine superior to A. He also has reason to favor C over B since B is indistinguishable from a wine inferior to C. Properly speaking, then, the vinophile is not indifferent between A and B or between B and C: his preferences run $B \gtrsim A$, $C \gtrsim B$, and $C > A$, but neither $A \approx B$ nor $B \approx C$ is true.

One might worry that the vinophile's reasons seem insufficient to justify strict preferences. It would, for example, be silly for him to pay anything to trade a bottle of A for a bottle of B (unless he could convert the latter into a bottle of C for a small enough fee). While this is a legitimate concern, it tells against completeness rather than anticyclicality. When an agent cannot precisely discriminate the qualities of prospects on which his evaluations depend, or when these qualities are themselves vague or indeterminate, his preference ranking will be incomplete: for certain options, all three of $A > B$, $A \approx B$, and $B > A$ will fail. Sometimes both $A \gtrsim B$ and $B \gtrsim A$ will fail as well, in which case the agent has no views about the comparative merits of A and B. Alternatively, as in the vinophile example, the agent might determinately weakly prefer B to A even though he neither strictly prefers B to A nor is indifferent between them. So, while $A \approx B$ and $B > A$ each entail $B \gtrsim A$, the latter is consistent with the falsity of both $A \approx B$ and $B > A$. Besides indeterminacy or vagueness in values, incompleteness in preferences can arise via an imprecision in credences. In both sorts of cases it can be perfectly rational to have an incomplete preference ranking.

One response to these considerations, which is advocated in Isaac Levi (1980), Richard Jeffrey (1983), and Mark Kaplan (1983), is to construe SEU_3's completeness clause as a requirement of coherent extendibility. Instead of asking an agent to completely order acts, one demands merely that there be at least one complete preference ranking (usually there will be many) that satisfies all other requirements of rationality, and that agrees with the agent's preferences whenever she has definite preferences. One then represents vague or indeterminate preferences by giving up the idea that the agent's attitudes can be modeled by a single probability/utility pair (given a unit and zero for utility). Rather, there will be a representing set $\boldsymbol{R}$ of $(\boldsymbol{P}, \boldsymbol{u})$ pairs that agree with the agent's preferences in the sense that, for any options A and B, each of $A >, \gtrsim, \approx B$ hold iff, respectively, $\boldsymbol{Exp}_{P,u}(A) >, \geq, = \boldsymbol{Exp}_{P,u}(B)$ holds for every $(\boldsymbol{P}, \boldsymbol{u})$ pair in $\boldsymbol{R}$. Act A is unambiguously choice worthy only if maximizes expected utility relative to every $(\boldsymbol{P}, \boldsymbol{u})$ pair in $\boldsymbol{R}$. It is admissible when it maximizes expected utility relative to some such pair. There is no generally accepted procedure for handling situations where no admissible act is unambiguously choice worthy. Some theorists would say that the agent's beliefs and desires are too indefinite to justify any choice as rational. Others, most notably Levi (1980), maintain that principles of decision making that outrun expected utility maximization come into play in this situation. For example, Levi allows agents to decide among admissible options using *maximin*, that is, by selecting the act whose worst consequence is at least as good as the worst consequence of any alternative.

COMPARATIVE PROBABILITY

The next principle of SEU forges a link between rational preference and rational belief. A wager on event E is an act of the form $[c]_E \cup [d]_{\text{-}E}$ where $[c] > [d]$. Such a wager produces the desirable consequence c in every state consistent with E and the undesirable consequence d in every state consistent with $\tilde{}E$. Intuitively, a person should prefer such a wager more strongly the more likely she takes E to be. More precisely, given any events E and F, $[c]_E \cup [d]_{\text{-}E}$ should be preferred to $[c]_F \cup.\ [d]_{\text{-}F}$ exactly if E as more probable than F. The following axiom is meant to ensure that this is so.

> SEU_4 *Comparative Probability*. Assuming $[c] > [d]$, if the agent prefers $[c]_E \cup [d]_{\text{-}E}$ to $[c]_F \cup [d]_{\text{-}F}$, she must also prefer $[c^*]_E \cup [d^*]_{\text{-}E}$ to $[c^*]_F \cup [d^*]_{\text{-}F}$ for any consequences such that $[c^*] > [d^*]$.

SEU_4 can seem implausible when the values of consequences vary with the world's state. Suppose, for example, that c and d are monetary fortunes that one might have in ten years, say c = \$500,000 and d = \$400,000. Let E and F be hypotheses about the cumulative rate of inflation over the decade: E puts the figure at 60 percent, while F puts it at 10 percent. Even if one regards E as the more probable hypothesis, one might still prefer to wager on F since one's fortune will be worth more if F is true.

There are two standard responses to this problem. Savage (1972) maintains that decision problems of this sort, in which the values of consequences depend on states, are ill formed. He argues any such problem could be transformed into a well-formed decision by a suitable subdivision of consequences. In the previous example, c would be split into c_1 = "\$500,000 after cumulative inflation of 60 percent," and c_2 = "\$500,000 after cumulative inflation of 10 percent." Alternatively, one might opt for a state-dependent utility theory, which replaces SEU_4 by a weaker condition and allows the values of consequences of vary with states (for details, see Karni 1993; Schervish, Seidenfeld, and Kadane 1990).

INDEPENDENCE AND THE SURE-THING PRINCIPLE

The most controversial tenet of SEU is the independence axiom:

> SEU_5 *Independence.* Preference among acts that have exactly the same consequences when E is false should depend exclusively on whathappens when E is true. If $A_E \cup C_{\text{-}E}$ is preferred to $B_E \cup C_{\text{-}E}$ forsome act C, then $A_E \cup D_{\text{-}E}$ is preferred to $B_E \cup D_{\text{-}E}$ for all acts D.

To illustrate, consider the following act types, where c, d, c^* and d^* are known consequences, and x ranges over possible consequences.

	S_1	S_2	S_3
A_x	c	d	x
B_x	c^*	d^*	x

SEU_5 says that an agent's preference between A_x and B_x should not depend on x's value. More generally, it requires agents to have well-defined conditional preferences: A is preferred to B in the event of E just in case $A_E \cup C_{\text{-}E} > B_E \cup C_{\text{-}E}$ for some (hence any) C.

SEU_5 has the following intuitive consequence:

> *Sure-Thing Principle*: Let $E_1, E_2, \ldots, E_n$ be mutually exclusive, collectively exhaustive events. If A is weakly preferred to B conditional on each E_i, then A is weakly preferred to B simpliciter. Moreover, if A is strictly preferred to B conditional on some event that is not judged certainly false, then A is strictly preferred to B.

Independence and the sure-thing principle have been quite controversial. Some apparent failures of SEU_5 arise in ill-formed decision problems whose states are not independent of acts. For example, imagine a man who has to drive home from a party where alcohol is being served. He likes to drink, but worries about getting home safely. Suppose he frames his decision like this:

	Car accident	No accident
Drink	−100	1
Teetotal	−101	0

Since the consequences of drinking are better that those of refraining both in the event of an accident and otherwise, it looks as if the sure-thing principle advocates drinking, which is clearly bad advice given that drinking increases the probability of an accident. Problems of this sort led Jeffrey (1983) to develop an evidential version of decision theory in which independence is only valid for decisions in which acts provide no evidence about the occurrence of any state. Reflections on Newcomb problems, in which acts and states are causally independent but evidentially correlated, led causal decision theorists like Robert Stalnaker (1981), Allan Gibbard and William Harper (1978), and Brian Skyrms (1980) to insist that the two principles be restricted to decisions in which the choice of an act has no causal influence over states.

The most famous objections to SEU_5 are the paradoxes of Maurice Allais (1953) and Daniel Ellsberg (1961), which seem to show that SEU rules out certain rational attitudes toward risk and uncertainty. An act involves risk when the agent knows the objective probabilities with which its consequences will obtain. It involves uncertainty when the agent's information allows a range of possible risk profiles for consequences. SEU_5 entails that, insofar as decision making is concerned, all legitimate considerations of risk and uncertainty are fully captured in expected utilities. The Allais and Ellsberg paradoxes suggest, to the contrary, that risk and uncertainty are nonseparable quantities: one cannot express them as weighted averages of their values conditional on disjoint events. If this is correct, then an agent need not have any fixed preference between the act types A_x and B_x because x's value might provide information about the relative risk or uncertainty of the two options, and this information might justifiably influence the agent's preferences.

The Allais paradox envisions an agent who chooses between A and A^* and then between B and B^* (with the know probabilities listed).

	0.10	0.01	0.89
A	$1,000,000	$1,000,000	$1,000,000
A^*	$5,000,000	$0	$1,000,000
B	$1,000,000	$1,000,000	$0
B^*	$5,000,000	$0	$0

Empirical studies show that people systematically violate independence when presented with such choices. They "play it safe" and select A over A^* in the first choice, but favor the riskier option B^* over B in the second. The standard rationale for these choices assumes (1) that there is more risk involved in choosing A^* over A than there is in choosing B^* over B, and (2) that it is rational minimize this risk even when doing so violates independence.

Ellsberg's paradox shows something similar with respect to judgments of uncertainty. Suppose a ball will be drawn at random from an urn that holds thirty red balls and sixty white or blue balls in an unknown proportion. One chooses between C and C^* and then between D and D^*.

	Red	White	Blue
C	$100	$0	$0
C^*	$0	$100	$0
D	$100	$0	$100
D^*	$0	$100	$100

Here most people prefer C to C^* and D^* to D. Interestingly, when gains are replaced by losses, people still violate independence, but both choices are reversed. People thus seem to prefer risk to uncertainty when they have something to gain, but prefer uncertainty to risk when they have something to lose. Those who regard Ellsberg's paradox as a counterexample to SEU maintain that such nonseparable preferences for risk over uncertainty or uncertainty over risk are entirely rational.

Some proponents of SEU (see Broome 1991) respond by arguing that the consequences in the Allais and Ellsberg paradoxes are underdescribed. For example, the standard pattern of preferences in Allais can be rationalized by noting that, when the 0.01 event occurs, agents who choose A^* over A may feel regret (because they passed up a sure thing), while those who choose B^* over B will feel no regret (because they probably would have ended up with nothing anyhow). For such agents, the decision matrix really looks like this:

	0.10	0.01	0.89
A	$1,000,000	$1,000,000	$1,000,000
A^*	$5,000,000	$0 with regret	$1,000,000
B	$1,000,000	$1,000,000	$0
B^*	$5,000,000	$0 without regret	$0

Likewise, if an agent feels uneasy when gains ride on uncertain prospects (or losses ride on risky prospects), then the correct description of the Ellsberg problem is this:

	Red	White	Blue
C	$100	$0	$0
C^*	$0 with uneasiness	$100 with uneasiness	$0 with uneasiness
D	$100 with uneasiness	$0 with uneasiness	$100 with uneasiness
D^*	$0	$100	$100

If these matrices accurately describe the decisions, then neither the Allais or Ellsberg paradoxes provide a genuine counterexample to SEU_5.

These sorts of rationalizing responses are weakened by their dependence on substantive assumptions about the psychology of risk, uncertainty, and regret that are not universally accepted (see Loomes and Sudgen 1982, Weber 1998). An alternative is to argue that the usual preferences in the Allais and Ellsberg paradoxes are simply irrational. In Allais, for example, agents assume that the disparity in risk between A and A^* exceeds the disparity in risk between B and B^*. This may be a mistake. One way to determine differences in risk is to consider the costs of insuring against the incremental risk one incurs by trading one option for another. Someone who switches from A^* to A in Allais can offset this risk by purchasing an insurance policy that pays out $1,000,000 contingent on the 0.01 event. Notice, however, that the risk incurred by switching from B^* to B can be offset by the same policy. Since a single policy eliminates both risks there is reason to think that the actual change in risk is the same in each case. Similar things can be said about the Ellsberg choosers, who implicitly assume that they decrease their uncertainty more by switching from C^* to C than they do by switching from D^* to D. So, if one measures disparities in risk or uncertainty by the costs of insuring against it, then SEU is safe from the Allais and Ellsberg examples.

Opponents of SEU will, of course, deny that risks should be measured by the costs of insuring against them. Ultimately, the issue will be resolved by the development of a convincing measure of risk. While there is a well-known theory of risk aversion within SEU, there is no universally accepted method for quantifying risk itself. The best work in this area, which builds on M. Rothschild and J. E. Stiglitz (1970), suggests that risk is indeed separable.

ALTERNATIVES TO SEU

While subjective expected utility theory remains firmly ensconced as the standard model of rational decision making for individuals, a number of alternatives have been developed. One kind of approach seeks to relax independence while preserving most other aspects of SEU. Especially noteworthy here is the "generalized expected utility analysis" of Mark Machina (1982), and the "weighted utility model" of Soo-Hong Chew and Kenneth R. MacCrimmon (1979). Alternatively, one can reject maximizing conceptions of rationality altogether and see decision making as matter of *satisficing* relative to fixed constraints. For example, G. Gigerenzer et al. (1999) seek to replace the single all-purpose prescription to maximize expected utility by an ecological model of rationality in which decision makers employ a set of simple, highly localized decision heuristics. These heuristics efficiently generate choices that produce desirable consequences in the contexts where they tend to be employed, but they can go badly awry when used in out of context. For discussion of further nonstandard decision theories, see Robert Sugden (2004).

Interesting though these alternatives are, none has seriously challenged the normative status of SEU. Though highly idealized, and far from adequate as a description of human behavior, SEU remains the best overall account of rational decision making.

See also Bayes, Bayes' Theorem, Bayesian Approach to Philosophy of Science; Game Theory; Pareto, Vilfredo; Pascal, Blaise; Probability and Chance; Ramsey, Frank Plumpton; Savage, Leonard; Sen, Amartya; Statistics, Foundations of.

Bibliography

Allais, Maurice. "Le comportement de l'homme rationnel devant le risque: Critique des postulats et axiomes de l'École Americaine." *Econometrica* (1953).

Broome, John. *Weighing Goods: Equality, Uncertainty, and Time.* Cambridge, MA: Basil Blackwell, 1991.

Chew, Soo-Hong, and Kenneth R. MacCrimmon. "Alpha-nu Theory: A Generalization of Expected Utility Thoery." *Working Paper* 669 (1979). University of British Columbia, Vancouver.

Ellsberg, Daniel. "Risk, Ambiguity, and the Savage Axioms." *Quarterly Journal of Economics* 75 (1961): 643–669.

Fishburn, Peter C. 1991. "Nontransitive Preferences in Decision Theory." *Journal of Risk and Uncertainty* 4 (1991): 113–134.

Gibbard, Allan, and William Harper. "Counterfactuals and Two Kinds of Expected Utility." In *Foundations and Applications of Decision Theory*, edited by C. Hooker, J. Leach, and E. McClennen. Dordrecht, Netherlands: D. Reidel, 1978.

Gigerenzer, G, et al. *Simple Heuristics that Make Us Smart.* New York: Oxford University Press, 1999.

Hammond, Peter. "Consequentialist Foundations for Expected Utility." *Theory and Decision* 25 (1988): 25–78.

Jeffrey, Richard. *The Logic of Decision.* 2nd ed. Chicago: University of Chicago Press, 1983.

Joyce, James M. *The Foundations of Causal Decision Theory.* New York: Cambridge University Press, 1999.

Kaplan, Mark. "Decision Theory as Philosophy." *Philosophy of Science* 50 (1983): 549–577.

Karni, E. "Subjective Expected Utility Theory with State-Dependent Preferences." *Journal of Economic Theory* 60 (1993): 428–438.

Levi, Isaac. *The Enterprise of Knowledge.* Cambridge, MA: MIT Press, 1980.

Loomes, Graham, and Robert Sugden. "Regret Theory: An Alternative Theory of Rational Choice under Uncertainty." *Economic Journal* 92 (1982): 805–824.

Luce, R. Duncan, and Howard Raiffa. *Games and Decisions*. New York: Wiley, 1957.

Machina, Mark. "'Expected Utility' Analysis without the Independence Axiom." *Econometrica* 50 (1982): 277–323.

McClennen, Edward. *Rationality and Dynamic Choice: Foundational Explorations*. New York: Cambridge University Press, 1990.

Ramsey, Frank P. "Truth and Probability." In *The Foundations of Mathematics and Other Logical Essays*, edited by Richard Braithwaite. London: Kegan Paul, 1931.

Redelmeier, D., and E. Shafir. "Medical Decision Making in Situations that Offer Multiple Alternatives." *Journal of the American Medical Association* 273 (4) (1995): 302–305.

Rothschild, M., and J. E. Stiglitz. "Increasing Risk: I. A Definition." *Journal of Economic Theory* 2 (1970): 225–243.

Savage, Leonard J. *The Foundations of Statistics*. 2nd ed. New York: Dover, 1972.

Schervish, M., T. Seidenfeld, and J. Kadane. "State-Dependent Utilities." *Journal of the American Statistical Association* 85 (1990): 840–847.

Sen, Amartya. "Rational Fools: A Critique of the Behavioral Foundations of Economic Theory." *Philosophy and Public Affairs* 6 (1977): 317–344.

Shafir, E., and A. Tversky. "Decision Making." In *An Invitation to Cognitive Science*. Vol. 3, *Thinking*. 2nd ed., edited by Edward Smith and Daniel Osherson, 77–100. Cambridge, MA: MIT Press, 1995.

Skyrms, Brian. *Causal Necessity*. New Haven, CT: Yale University Press, 1980.

Stalnaker, Robert. "Letter to David Lewis, May 21, 1972." In *IFs: Conditionals, Belief, Decision, Chance, and Time*, edited by Robert Stalnaker, William Harper, and Glen Pearce. Dordrecht, Netherlands: D. Reidel, 1981.

Sugden, Robert. "Alternatives to Expected Utility: Formal Theories." In *Handbook of Utility Theory*. Vol. 2, edited by Peter Hammond, Salvador Barberà, and Christian Seidl. Dordrecht, Netherlands: Kluwer Academic, 2004.

Weber, Michael. "The Resilience of the Allais Paradox." *Ethics* 109 (1998): 94–118.

James M. Joyce (2005)

DECONSTRUCTION

Deconstruction is a philosophical-critical approach to textual analysis that is most closely associated with the work of Jacques Derrida in philosophy and the Yale School (Paul DeMan, J. Hillis Miller, Geoffrey Hartman) in literary theory and criticism. Derrida draws the term *déconstruction* from his interpretation of Martin Heidegger as a way to translate two Heideggerian terms: *Destruktion*, which means not destruction but a destructuring that dismantles the structural layers in a system; and *Abbau*, which means to take apart an edifice in order to see how it is constituted or deconstituted. For Derrida, then, deconstruction, in the context of philosophy, refers to a way to think the structured genealogy of philosophy's concepts while exposing what the history of these concepts has been able to obscure or exclude. By displaying those concepts that the philosophical tradition both authorizes and excludes, a deconstructive reading seeks to work within the closed field of metaphysical discourse without at the same time confirming that field. Instead, it allows a text to dismantle itself by exposing the internal inconsistencies and implicit significations that lie concealed within the language of the text.

One way to understand deconstruction is in terms of a critique of the binary, oppositional thinking that, for Derrida, is central to the history of philosophy. This is to say, each term in the Western philosophical/cultural lexicon is accompanied by its binary opposite: intelligible/sensible, truth/error, speech/writing, reality/appearance, mind/body, culture/nature, good/evil, male/female, and so on. These oppositions do not peacefully coexist, however: one side of each binary opposition has been privileged and the other side devalued. A hierarchy has been established within these oppositions, as the intelligible has come to be valued over the sensible, mind has come to be valued over body, and so on. The task of deconstruction is to dismantle or deconstruct these binary oppositions: to expose the foundational choices of the philosophical tradition and to bring into view what the tradition has repressed, excluded, or—to use the Derridean terminology—marginalized.

As a critical practice, the deconstruction of these oppositions involves a double movement of overturning and displacement. The first phase initiates an overturning of the hierarchy that valorizes the term traditionally subordinated by the history of philosophy: for example, privileging writing over speech, signifier over signified, or the figurative over the literal. But this privileging is temporary and strategic, for in overturning a metaphysical hierarchy, deconstruction seeks to avoid reappropriating the same hierarchical structure; it is the hierarchical oppositional structure itself that underwrites the metaphysical tradition, and to remain within the binary logic of metaphysical thinking will only reestablish and affirm these oppositions. The second phase of deconstruction destabilizes the inversion by showing the arbitrary nature of the process of hierarchical valorization itself and displaces the hierarchy altogether by intervening with a new "undecidable" term—for example, *difference*, *trace*, *pharmakon*, *supplement*—that resists the formal structure imposed by the binary logic of philosophical opposition. Much of Derrida's early work involves elucidating the play of these undecidables: the play of *différence*, which both differs and defers; the play of the trace, which is both present and absent; the play of the *pharmakon*, which is both poison and cure; the play of the supplement, which is both surplus and lack. By displaying the choices by means of which the philosophical tradition constitutes itself *as* a tradition, Derridean deconstruction opens the possibility to think difference other than as opposition and hierarchy.

Within literary criticism, the deconstructive method is used to show that the meaning of a literary text is not fixed and stable. Instead, by exploring the dynamic tension within a text's language, literary deconstruction reveals the literary work to be not a determinate object with a single correct meaning but an expanding semantic field that is open to multiple, sometimes conflicting interpretations.

See also Structuralism and Post-structuralism.

Bibliography

Bloom, Harold, Paul DeMan, Jacques Derrida, Geoffrey Hartman, and J. Hillis Miller. *Deconstruction and Criticism*. London: Continuum, 1979.

Culler, Jonathan D. *On Deconstruction: Theory and Criticism in the 1970s*. Ithaca, NY: Cornell University Press, 1982.

DeMan, Paul. *Allegories of Reading: Figural Language in Rousseau, Nietzsche, Rilke, and Proust*. New Haven, CT: Yale University Press, 1979.

DeMan, Paul. *Blindness and Insight: Essays in the Rhetoric of Contemporary Criticism*. 2nd ed. Minneapolis: University of Minnesota Press, 1983.

Derrida, Jacques. *Dissemination*. Translated by Barbara Johnson. Chicago: University of Chicago Press, 1981. Originally published as *La Dissémination* (Paris: Du Seuil, 1972).

Derrida, Jacques. *Margins of Philosophy*. Translated by Alan Bass. Chicago: University of Chicago Press, 1982. Originally published as *Marges de la Philosophie* (Paris: Éditions de Minuit, 1972).

Derrida, Jacques. *Of Grammatology*. Translated by Gayatri Chakravorty Spivak. Baltimore, MD: Johns Hopkins University Press, 1976. Originally published as *De la Grammatologie* (Paris: Éditions de Minuit, 1967).

Derrida, Jacques. *Positions*. Translated by Alan Bass. Chicago: University of Chicago Press, 1981. Originally published as *Positions: Entretiens avec Henri Ronse, Julia Kristeva, Jean-Louis Houdebine, Guy Scarpetta* (Paris: Éditions de Minuit, 1972).

Derrida, Jacques. *Speech and Phenomena, and Other Essays on Husserl's Theory of Signs*. Translated by David B. Allison. Evanston, IL: Northwestern University Press, 1973. Originally published as *La voix et le phénomène: Introduction au problème du signe dans la phénoménologie de Husserl* (Paris: Presses Universitaires de France, 1967).

Derrida, Jacques. *Writing and Difference*. Translated by Alan Bass. Chicago: University of Chicago Press, 1978. Originally published as *L'écrituré et la difference* (Paris: Éditions de Seuil, 1967).

Gasche, Rodolphe. *The Tain of the Mirror: Derrida and the Philosophy of Reflection*. Cambridge, MA: Harvard University Press, 1988.

Hartman, Geoffrey. *Criticism in the Wilderness*. New Haven, CT: Yale University Press, 1982.

Miller, J. Hillis. *The Ethics of Reading: Kant, De Man, Eliot, Trollope, James, and Benjamin*. New York: Columbia University Press, 1989.

Miller, J. Hillis. *The Linguistic Moment: From Wordsworth to Stevens*. Princeton, NJ: Princeton University Press, 1985.

Norris, Christopher. *Deconstruction: Theory and Practice*. London: Methuen, 1982.

Alan D. Schrift (2005)

DEDUCTION

See *Logic, History of: Modern Logic: From Frege to Gödel*

DE FINETTI, BRUNO

(1906–1985)

Bruno de Finetti, an Italian mathematician, was born in Innsbruck, Austria. On the death of his father, the six-year-old de Finetti and his mother moved to Trento (then in Austrian possession). At thirteen he suffered severe osteomyelitis in the left leg; surgery left him permanently lame. In 1923 he entered the Politecnico di Milano to study engineering, his father's and grandfather's profession. In his third year he transferred to the new University of Milan, from which he graduated in 1927 with a degree in applied mathematics. While still an undergraduate he published the first of a series of articles on Mendelian population genetics, developing the first mathematical model with overlapping generations.

From graduation until 1931 de Finetti worked at Rome's Istituto Centrale di Statistica. This was a period of intense and productive research, resulting in publication of a series of mathematical and foundational works on probability. The mathematical works made his name internationally known. The foundational works set out the subjectivist interpretation of probability that he was to advocate all his life. Two stand out: "Sul significato soggetiva della probabilità" (1931) and the remarkable "Probabilismo" (1931), remarkable not least, but certainly not only, for its fascist peroration.

Between 1931 and 1946 de Finetti worked in the actuarial office of the Assicurazioni Generali insurance company in Trieste. At the same time he taught at the Universities of Padua and Trieste. In this period de Finetti's range widened to include actuarial and financial mathematics, economics, the automation of actuarial procedures (an interest reflected in the postwar years in his advocacy of computing and the use of simulation methods in statistics), and mathematics education. From the early 1950s his works became better known in the English-speaking world, thanks to the advocacy of the American statistician Leonard Savage. In 1947 de Finetti was appointed to the chair of financial mathematics in Trieste. In 1954 he moved to the Faculty of Economics at the University of Rome "La Sapienza"; in 1961 he transferred to the Faculty of Sciences in which he was a professor of the theory of probability until his retirement in 1976. De Finetti died in 1985.

In the 1970s de Finetti was active in Italian politics, standing as a parliamentary candidate for the Radical Party; for a while he edited the party's *Notizie Radicali*. On one occasion a judge ordered his arrest for antimilitarist campaigning.

What de Finetti's life exhibits is a concern for the tying of ideas to applications. The cornerstone of the radical subjectivist interpretation of probability, summed up in de Finetti's claim (in the preface to the English translation of his *Teoria delle probabilità* [1974]), "PROBABILITY DOES NOT EXIST" is that only concepts that can be given an operational, practical significance are meaningful. The radical subjectivist denies the meaningfulness of talk of objective, unknown probabilities. Probability is degree of belief/credence/conviction. De Finetti, as Frank Plumpton Ramsey before him (in work unknown to de Finetti), gave a Dutch book argument to show that a rational person's degrees of belief satisfy the axioms of the probability calculus: degrees of belief are revealed in the betting odds the person considers fair; a rational person does not bet so as to lose money with certainty; fair betting quotients avoid certain loss just if they satisfy the axioms of the probability calculus. Conditional probabilities are handled by conditional bets, bets that are canceled if a given event does not occur. (This led de Finetti to a logic of conditional events: $B|A$ is true if A and B are both true, false if A is true and B is false, and neither if A is false, corresponding to the cases when the bet on B conditional on A is won, lost, and canceled. The idea has resurfaced from time to time in work on the indicative conditional of natural language and on production rules in computer science.)

One axiom is the subject of dispute. In Andrei Nikolajevich Kolmogorov's (1903–1987) *Foundations of the Theory of Probability* (1933) the axiom that probabilities add across a countably infinite partition is adopted as mathematically expedient. De Finetti urged its rejection. Much is known of the consequences of giving up this axiom, but de Finetti's line has not won general acceptance.

Not a philosopher by training, de Finetti found parallels to his thought in the Italian pragmatists Mario Calderoni and Giovanni Vailati (a mathematician), and the man-of-letters Giovanni Papini. Later he saw Humean connections in his influential work on exchangeable and partially exchangeable sequences of events and random variables. A sequence of events of N types is partially exchangeable if the probability that n_1 events of the first type, n_2 events of the second type, … , and n_N events of the Nth type all occur depends only on the numbers $n_1, n_2, \ldots, n_N$. For exchangeability, $N = 1$. De Finetti sees this notion as the subjective analogue of (and correction to) talk of independent trials with unknown probability and as making mathematically precise David Hume's account of induction and causation. This comes about through representation theorems. Take the case of an infinite sequence of exchangeable events. From the probability, for various n, that n events all yield favorable outcomes, one can infer the probabilities of r favorable outcomes in n trials, $0 \leq r \leq n$. The distributions of these relative frequencies for different n tend, as n increases, to a limit distribution that functions exactly as a distribution over an unknown probability, so that the probability of any definable event is the expectation with respect to this distribution of the probability it would have were one dealing with a sequence of independent events of constant probability. Exchangeability is preserved as one conditionalizes on the outcomes of any finite number of trials, so, provided the initial limit distribution assigns a nonzero probability to an interval containing it, one obtains a sequence of limit distributions increasingly weighted toward the observed relative frequency as the number of observed instances increases. This encapsulates de Finetti's account of learning from experience and inductive inference, his "translation into logic-mathematical terms of Hume's ideas" (1938, p. 194).

With the acceptance by today's philosophers of science of semantic realism and, increasingly, pluralism in the philosophy of probability, de Finetti's eliminativist reading of what is now called the de Finetti representation theorem is little in favor. But there has been a huge increase in the application both to scientific reasoning generally and to statistics in particular of the subjectivist interpretation of probability, usually under the name Bayesianism.

See also Bayes, Bayes' Theorem, Bayesian Approach to Philosophy of Science; Calderoni, Mario; Hume, David; Mathematics, Foundations of; Papini, Giovanni; Probability and Chance; Ramsey, Frank Plumpton; Savage, Leonard; Vailati, Giovanni.

Bibliography

WORKS BY DE FINETTI

"Probabilismo: Saggio critico sulla teoria della probabilità e sul valore della scienza." *Logos* (Naples) 14 (1931): 163–219. Translated by R. C. Jeffrey, M. C. DiMaio, and M. C. Galavotti as "Probabilism: A Critical Essay on the Theory of Probability and on the Value of Science." *Erkenntnis* 31 (2–3) (1989): 169–223.

"Sul significato soggetiva della probabilità." *Fundamenta Mathematicae* 17 (1931): 298–329. Translated as "On the Subjective Meaning of Probability." In *Probabilità e induzione/Induction and Probability*, edited by Paolo Monari and Daniela Cocchi, 291–321 (Bologna, Italy: Editrice Clueb, 1993).

"La logique de la probabilité." In *Actes du congrès international de philosophie scientifique*. Vol. 4, 31–39. Paris: Hermann, 1936. Translated by R. B. Angell as "The Logic of Probability." *Philosophical Studies* 77 (1995): 181–190.

"La prévision: ses lois logiques, ses sources subjectives." *Annales de l'Institut Henri Poincaré* 7 (1937): 1–68. Translated by Henry E. Kyburg Jr. as "Foresight: Its Logical Laws, Its Subjective Sources." In *Studies in Subjective Probability*. 2nd ed., edited by Henry E. Kyburg Jr. and Howard E. Smokler, 57–118. Huntington, NY: Robert E. Krieger, 1980.

"Sur la condition d'équivalence partielle." *Actualités scientifiques et industrieles No. 739 (Coloque Genève d'Octobre 1937 sur la Théorie des Probabilités, 6ième partie)*, 5–18. Paris: Hermann, 1938. Translated by P. Benacerraf and R. C. Jeffrey as "On the Condition of Partial Exchangeability." In *Studies in Inductive Logic and Probability*, Vol. 2., edited by Richard C. Jeffrey, 193–205. Berkeley: University of California Press, 1980.

Teoria delle probabilità: Sintesi introdutiva con appendice critica. 2 vols. Turin, Italy: Einaudi, 1970. Translated by Antonio Machí and Adrian Smith as *Theory of Probability: A Critical Introductory Treatment.* 2 vols. New York: Wiley, 1974–1975.

Probability, Induction, and Statistics: The Art of Guessing. New York: Wiley, 1972.

"Probability and My Life." In *The Making of Statisticians*, edited by J. Gani, 3–12. New York: Springer-Verlag, 1982.

Probabilità e induzione/Induction and Probability, edited by P. Monari and D. Cocchi. Bologna, Italy: Editrice CLUEB, 1993.

Filosofia dela probabilità, edited by A. Mura. Milan, Italy: Il Saggiatore, 1995.

WORKS ABOUT DE FINETTI

Cifarelli, Donato Michele, and Eugenio Regazzini. "De Finetti's Contribution to Probability and Statistics." *Statistical Science* 11 (4) (1996): 253–282.

Diaconis, Persi, and David Freedman. "De Finetti's Generalizations of Exchangeability." In *Studies in Inductive Logic and Probability*. Vol. 2, edited by Richard C. Jeffrey, 233–249. Berkeley: University of California Press, 1980.

Hintikka, Jaakko. "Unknown Probabilities, Bayesianism, and de Finetti's Representation Theorem." In PSA 1970 *In Memory of Rudolf Carnap*, edited by Roger C. Buck and Robert S. Cohen, 325–341. Dordrecht, Netherlands: D. Reidel, 1971.

Howson, Colin, and Peter Urbach. *Scientific Reasoning: The Bayesian Approach*. 2nd ed. Chicago: Open Court, 1993.

Jeffrey, Richard. *Subjective Probability: The Real Thing*. New York: Cambridge University Press, 2004.

Jeffrey, Richard C., and Maria Carla Galavotti, eds. "Bruno de Finetti's Philosophy of Probability." *Erkenntnis* 31 (2–3) (1989).

Milne, Peter. "Bruno de Finetti and the Logic of Conditional Events." *British Journal for the Philosophy of Science* 48 (1997): 195–232.

Peter Milne (2005)

DEFINITION

The problems of definition are constantly recurring in philosophical discussion, although there is a widespread tendency to assume that they have been solved. Practically every book on logic has a section on definition in which rules are set down and exercises prescribed for applying the rules, as if the problems were all settled. And yet, paradoxically, no problems of knowledge are less settled than those of definition, and no subject is more in need of a fresh approach. Definition plays a crucial role in every field of inquiry, yet there are few if any philosophical questions about definition (what sort of thing it is, what standards it should satisfy, what kind of knowledge, if any, it conveys) on which logicians and philosophers agree. In view of the importance of the topic and the scope of the disagreement concerning it, an extensive reexamination is justified. In carrying out this conceptual reexamination, this article will summarize the main views of definition that have been advanced, indicate why none of these views does full justice to its subject, and then attempt to show how the partial insights of each might be combined in a new approach.

All the views of definition that have been proposed can be subsumed under three general types of positions, with, needless to say, many different varieties within each type. These three general positions will be called "essentialist," "prescriptive," and "linguistic" types, abbreviated as "E-type," "P-type," and "L-type," respectively. This classification is not intended as a precise historical summary, but merely as a useful schema for stating some of the problems and disputes. Thus, some outstanding philosophers may very clearly belong to one of these types. Others who, for the purposes of this article, are placed in a certain class hold positions varying considerably from the presentation to be given. It must therefore be borne in mind that not all the criticisms that will be made apply to all philosophers included in the class being criticized. Writers whose accounts of definition fall largely under the E-type include Plato, Aristotle, Immanuel Kant, and Edmund Husserl. Those who support P-type views include Blaise Pascal, Thomas Hobbes, Bertrand Russell, W. V. Quine, Nelson Goodman, Rudolf Carnap, C. G. Hempel, and most contemporary logicians. Supporters of L-type views include John Stuart Mill (in part), G. E. Moore (in part), Richard Robinson, and most members of the school of linguistic analysis.

According to essentialist views, definitions convey more exact and certain information than is conveyed by descriptive statements. Such information is acquired by an infallible mode of cognition variously called "intellectual vision," "intuition," "reflection," or "conceptual analysis." Prescriptive views agree with essentialism that definitions are incorrigible, but account for their infallibility by denying that they communicate information and by explaining them as symbolic conventions. Although linguistic views agree with essentialism that definitions communicate information, they also agree with prescriptivism in that they reject claims that definitions communicate information that is indubitable. The linguistic position is that definitions are empirical (and therefore corrigible) reports of linguistic behavior.

ESSENTIALISM

An essentialist account was first proposed by Socrates and Plato. Socrates is renowned for having brought attention to the importance of definitions. His favorite type of question, "What does (virtue, justice, etc.) mean?," became the characteristic starting point of philosophical inquiry. But Socrates did not make clear what kind of answer he was looking for. In Plato's *Euthyphro* Socrates is reported to have said that the kind of answer he expected to his question "What is piety?" was one giving an explanation of "the general idea which makes all pious things to be pious" and "a standard to which I may look and by which I may measure actions." He did not explain, however, what he meant by "idea" and "standard" nor how one produces an "idea" or a "standard" when one is defining a term. Richard Robinson, in his book *Plato's Earlier Dialectic* (p. 62), has suggested that the question "What is *X?*" is more ambiguous than Socrates realized and that it may be answered in all sorts of ways, depending on the context in which it is asked.

PLATO. Plato's attempts in his later dialogues to explain the meaning of the Socratic question "What is *X?*" constitute the celebrated Theory of Forms, the trademark of Platonic metaphysics and epistemology. In a passage of central importance (*Republic* VI), Plato distinguished two kinds of objects of knowledge (sensible things and forms) and two modes of knowledge (sense perception and intellectual vision). Sensible things are objects of opinion, while abstract forms are objects of philosophical knowledge. Physical objects, shadows, and images are imperfect and ephemeral copies of forms; our perceptual knowledge of them is an inaccurate approximation to our knowledge of their abstract archetypes. Definitions describe forms, and since forms are perfect and unchanging, definitions, when arrived at by the proper procedure, are precise and rigorously certain truths. Empirical statements describe objects of perception and are therefore only more or less reliable approximations to truth.

Models and copies. Plato's analogy between definitions and empirical descriptions—an analogy upon which all E-type theories of definition rest—is supplemented by a second analogy between the relation of a model to a copy and the relation of a definition to an individual predication. This analogy was suggested by Socrates when he asked for "a standard to which I may look and by which I may measure actions." Plato describes the process of coming to know as if it were like the procedure of a craftsman producing a piece of sculpture or a house. The sculpture is a "copy" of the subject who models for it; the house is in one sense a "copy" of the architect's blueprint, in a somewhat different sense a "copy" of a small-scale model, and in still a third sense a "copy" of the idea in the mind of the builder. Plato's frequent references to the arts and crafts in his exploration of conceptual problems indicate that the analogy of the model-copy relation plays a central role in his theory of knowledge.

Thus, Platonic essentialism provides two sets of answers (both of which rest on metaphors) to the questions "What kind of statements are definitions?" "What purpose do they serve?" and "How are they to be judged as good or bad?" It suggests primarily that definitions are descriptions of objects that are somehow analogous to tables, chairs, and other familiar things; that these definitions serve the purpose of providing descriptive information about their objects; and that they are confirmed by a mode of cognition somehow analogous to sense perception, yet independent of the sensory organs. Secondarily, Platonic essentialism specifies the relation between the objects of definitions and those of empirical descriptions by characterizing the former as models of which the latter are "copies."

Adequacy of the model metaphor. Metaphors are apt or inapt, illuminating or misleading, according to two criteria: (1) the number and importance of the known points of resemblance between the things compared; and (2) the number and importance of previously unnoted facts suggested by the metaphor. To what extent does Plato's metaphor of the unseen model satisfy these criteria?

The primary term of comparison in Plato's metaphor is the abstract form or universal that a definition allegedly describes. The secondary term is the model for a painting or, alternatively, a tailor's pattern. As the painter looks to his model and the tailor to his pattern, the philosopher can look to the forms for the specifications that identify things as instances of one class rather than another, as well as for exact information about the properties of that class.

What are the known points of resemblance between forms and models, on which this metaphor is grounded? Merely to ask this question is already to see that the metaphor is defective from the start, since there cannot possibly be *any* literal points of comparison. The Platonic forms, unlike models and patterns, have no observable properties by virtue of which they can be said to "resemble" anything at all. Thus, if the model metaphor has any value, it must lie entirely in what the metaphor suggests, rather than in its literal grounds.

Primarily, the model metaphor suggests that definitions and their corollaries constitute all there is to knowledge. Whenever a question of fact or of judgment is raised in the Platonic dialogues, it is treated as a problem of definition. For example, when, in the *Euthyphro,* Socrates and Euthyphro argue about the propriety of a son's prosecuting his father for murder, Socrates proceeds as though the issue could be settled by arriving at a clear definition of piety—as though one could then look at the definition, look at the action, and decide whether they coincide. We can identify a portrait or a garment by comparing it with its model or its pattern, but we cannot classify and judge an action in the same way. Description and evaluation are seldom matters of identification by comparison with a pattern. In this respect Plato's essentialism is misleading rather than illuminating.

The metaphor of the unseen model also suggests that definitions provide us with precise and rigorous knowledge in the way that blueprints make possible a high degree of uniformity and precision in productive arts such as architecture. But definitions increase precision only when they change the original meanings of words for technical purposes. Generally speaking, a definition can be no more precise than the concept it defines, at the risk of shifting to a different concept. Our concept of what constitutes an adult is vague; if we try to make it precise by specifying an exact age at which childhood is divided from adulthood, we merely lose sight of what we started out to talk about by replacing the concept of maturity with that of having passed a certain birthday.

The model metaphor is not entirely misleading; it suggests at least one genuine resemblance between the terms it compares. The relation between definitions and empirical descriptions is, in one respect, rather similar to the relation between portraits and their models. We judge a portrait (to some extent) by noting whether the portrait looks like the model; we verify the empirical description "This table is round" by looking at the table to see whether it has the properties definitive of tables and of roundness. But if we are asked, "Is that person a good model?" or "Is that definition a good definition?" we cannot look toward anything of which the model is himself a portrait, and we cannot look at a definitional form of which the particular definition is itself an instance. Definitions are not evaluated in the same way as empirical descriptions, just as models are not judged in the same way as their portraits. Thus the analogy between definitions and empirical descriptions from which Platonic essentialism starts eventually contradicts itself.

ARISTOTLE. One can find in Aristotle's works anticipations of every later theory of definition, but he gave high priority to his own brand of essentialism, whereby he explained the nature of "real" as distinguished from "nominal" (that is, prescriptive or linguistic) definition. Like Plato, Aristotle stressed the similarity between definitions and statements of fact, and he assumed that definitions convey precise and certain information. But Aristotle employed a different supporting metaphor to explain the special nature of definitions. The most noteworthy feature of his many discussions of definition is his insistence that a real definition should provide a causal explanation of the thing defined. In the *Physics,* Aristotle distinguished four types of causes—formal, material, final, and efficient. He characterized the first three types as "internal," while efficient causes are (usually) "external" to their effects. Internal causes are not available to public inspection, but must be discovered in abstract intuition. The causal explanation provided by a real definition is in terms of one or more of these three internal types of cause.

Definition and causality. It is not easy to explain just what Aristotle meant by "internal cause." Part of what he seems to have meant is that, unlike "incidental" causes, internal causes are necessary for their effects. But it is by no means clear what sense of necessity is involved in this instance. To explain this necessity as causal would be a case of circular reasoning. On the other hand, to say that the necessity is logical seems only another way of saying that the effect is definable in terms of its cause, which is again circular reasoning. As an example of a causal definition, Aristotle defined a lunar eclipse as the privation of the moon's light because of the interposition of the earth between the moon and the sun (*Posterior Analytics* 90a). This example confirms the suggestion that for something to be an internal causal is for it to be part of a definition. But the difficulty then arises that definition has been explained by internal causality, internal causality by necessity, and necessity by definition. Thus, Aristotle's eclipse leaves us in the dark about definition.

Classification and explanation. The trouble is that the idea of internal causality is a metaphor. An essential cause is not "internal" to the thing defined as a kernel is inside a nut, but only metaphorically "inside."

This metaphor suggests two important but dubious principles: that scientific knowledge consists entirely of definitions and their corollaries and that systematic classification is identical with theoretical explanation. If to define a term is, at the same time, to provide a causal explanation of what it denotes and if the classification of a thing in terms of its species and differentia is sufficient for deducing the laws of its behavior, then the work of scientific inquiry is completed when a comprehensive system of classification has been constructed. Thus, Aristotle wrote in the *Posterior Analytics* (90b) that "Scientific knowledge is judgment about things that are universal and necessary, that the conclusions of demonstration *and all scientific knowledge* follow from the first principles" and that "the first principles of demonstration are definitions" (italics added).

That scientific knowledge is not entirely derivable from a set of definitions and that systematic classification is only one small aspect of scientific procedure need hardly be argued. Aristotelian concepts of causality and explanation have been almost completely expunged from modern science, and causes are conceived of in quite different ways. But it is not the archaic character of Aristotle's use of "cause" and "explanation" that concerns us here. It is largely a matter of terminological convenience whether we continue to use these words in the Aristotelian manner or confine them to the procedures of modern physical science. In regard to the problem of clarifying the functions and criteria of definitions, however, Aristotle's claim that definitions reveal the internal causes of their definienda must be criticized not as a false, but as a misleading, metaphor, for it dissolves the very distinctions which it is intended to explain—namely, the distinction between definitions and empirical statements of fact, that between the method of evaluating definitions and the method of confirming factual hypotheses, and that between the distinctive functions of definition and the general aims of scientific inquiry.

IDEAS AND CONCEPTS. A third metaphor that has been employed in the support of E-type views of definition originated in Cartesian dualism. René Descartes himself leaned toward a prescriptive account of definition, which will be considered later. But John Locke, Kant, Husserl, and other philosophers who accepted the Cartesian division between the "inner world" of the mind and the "outer world" of physical events took the essentialist position that philosophical inquiry should provide information about a special set of objects ("ideas" for Locke, David Hume, and Husserl; "concepts" for Kant, Heinrich Rickert, and G. E. Moore) discoverable by an infallible mode of cognition ("reflection" for Locke and Husserl; "analysis" for Hume, Kant, Rickert, and Moore).

According to Locke, the outer world of material objects and their motions is describable by the laws of physics, while the inner world of ideas is describable by the laws of psychology that are discovered by reflection on the contents of the mind. These contents are simple and complex ideas; the task of philosophy is to analyze complex ideas into their simple elements and to describe their mode of combination.

Kant distinguished between "analytical" and "synthetic" definitions, regarding the former as the identification of the simple elements (predicates) out of which concepts are formed by the understanding and the latter as the formation of rules of serial order that provide the synthetic a priori postulates of mathematics and physics.

The philosophers under consideration, like their predecessors, assumed that definitions convey knowledge of objects (ideas, images, essences, concepts, or meanings) whose special nature guarantees precision and certainty and that this remarkable kind of knowledge is acquired through a special mode of cognition (reflection, introspection, intuition, or conceptual analysis). The literal content of the private-world metaphor thus seems to be identical with that of the essentialist metaphors already considered. The differences between the private-world and essentialist metaphors (other than terminological ones) must be sought in the suggestive implications of the metaphor. But there is an important difference between philosophers such as Locke, Hume, and Husserl, who reserve the word *definition* for conventions of word usage and do not consider their introspective analyses of ideas to be definitions, and those such as Kant, Rickert, and C. I. Lewis, who regard philosophical definitions as products of conceptual analysis.

Both groups employ the Aristotelian distinction between real and nominal definitions, except that members of the first group avoid calling the results of their introspective studies "definitions" because they think of them as descriptions of the workings of the mind analogous to descriptions of a clock that has been taken apart for inspection. They think of the special mode of cognition by means of which they discover how simple ideas are organized into complex ideas as inner vision or grasp, which is analogous to sight and touch. But members of the more abstractly minded group compare the special faculty by which real (or analytic or explicative) definitions are discovered to the experience (familiar to logicians and mathematicians) of recognizing logical relation, rather than comparing it to any type of sense perception. They speak of "understanding the meanings of words," of "logical analysis," of "understanding what is contained in a concept," rather than of seeing or grasping the "contents of the mind." There are, then, two kinds of world imagined by these theorists: a world of privately visible or tangible ideas, sense data, secondary qualities, and so forth and a world of abstract concepts or meanings. Some, like Kant, Husserl, and, most systematically, C. I. Lewis, posit both kinds of worlds.

What then do these two metaphors suggest, and how illuminating are their implications? The metaphor of the private world of sense data that is allegedly described by definitions of complex ideas suggests that such definitions, like reports of hallucinations, dreams, and other private experiences, must be taken at face value (provided that they are sincerely and consistently expressed), since they cannot be checked by public observation. This would account for the unchallengeable character of definitions and their analytic corollaries, in contrast to the corrigibility of empirical statements. But this view deprives definitions of any claim to objective validity and entails that every person has a right to his own definitions, in the same way that everyone has a right to his own dreams.

The metaphor of the world of concepts and meanings also attributes a self-certifying character to definitions but fares better with respect to the commonsense fact that we balk at some definitions and accept others—for the recognition of logical relations, no matter how intuitive, is a socially shared experience. We immediately and privately understand, see, or grasp that a statement of the form $P \cdot Q$ implies a statement of the form Q, but we can also argue the fact and summon evidence (in the form of postulates of a logical system) to prove it. But this metaphor, which of all those we have considered comes closest to not being a metaphor at all and blends imperceptibly into a prescriptive concept of definition, suggests both too much and too little. It suggests that definitions are logical truths and possess logical certainty. But although some definitions are worse than others, all logical truths are normatively equal. Moreover, the metaphor fails to indicate how definitions can be evaluated other than by their formal consistency (the standard by which we confirm a system of logical truths). Yet a definition of a cow as a three-legged animal would be universally rejected on grounds having nothing to do with inconsistency. The denial of a logical truth can be shown to involve a contradiction, but the denial of a definition leads to contradiction only if one has already accepted the definition. Although consistency is a sufficient condition for a system of logical truths, it is merely a necessary condition for sound definitions; yet no additional conditions are provided by logistic phenomenalism.

PRESCRIPTIVISM

E-type views claim that definitions are statements and that they make assertions that can be pronounced true or false. Essentialists, however, have difficulty explaining how and why definitions differ from ordinary statements of fact, and hence they fall back on metaphors. P-type theories avoid this trouble by denying that definitions are statements of any kind. The prescriptivist assimilates definitions to imperative sentences rather than to declarative sentences and endows them with the function of syntactic or semantic rules for prescribing linguistic operations.

There are two main varieties of prescriptivism. The nominalist variety explains definitions as semantic rules for assigning names to objects, while the formalist variety regards definitions as syntactic rules for abbreviating strings of symbols. P-type views of definition can be traced back to the Greek Sophists and Skeptics, but this article will concentrate on the modern sources of these views. The rebirth of science in the seventeenth century was accompanied by a sweeping rejection of medieval thought, in particular the medieval concept of definition as the penetration by metaphysical intuition into a realm of changeless forms. The nominalist theories of language employed by Sophist and Cynic contemporaries of Plato to undermine belief in the objectivity of knowledge, and again by the more radical medieval Scholastics to subvert the control of theology over science, became, in the seventeenth century, a cornerstone of the reconstruction of knowledge on a new scientific foundation.

Seventeenth-century writings on definition are not entirely free of the influence of classical essentialism. Seventeenth-century prescriptive theories of definition try to avoid the obscurities of essentialism by repudiating the informative role of definitions, but they cannot provide adequate criteria for distinguishing good definitions from bad without presupposing some sort of informative role for them.

NOMINALISM. For Francis Bacon and Hobbes, definitions possessed a therapeutic function, as a means of clearing up or avoiding ambiguous, vague, and obscure language. Regarding semantic confusion as the main source of intellectual trouble, they proposed to clear the way for a new system of knowledge by subjecting existing concepts to the test of definitional reduction to observable and measurable properties. Definition was thus a surgical knife for cutting away metaphysical encrustations, as described by Bacon in paragraph 59 of the *Novum Organum*:

> But the idols of the market-place are the most troublesome of all: idols which have crept into the understanding through the alliances of word and names, and this it is that has rendered philosophy and the sciences sophistical and inactive. Whence it comes to pass that the high and formal discussions of learned men end oftentimes in disputes about words and names: with which it would be more prudent to begin, and so by means of definitions reduce them to order.

Thomas Hobbes also stressed the clarifying role of definitions, taking geometry as his model. In the *Leviathan* he wrote:

> Seeing then that truth consists in the right ordering of names in our affirmations, a man that seeketh precise truth had need to remember what every name he useth stands for … or else he will find himself entangled in ffords as a bird in lime twigs. And therefore in geometry, which is the only science which it hath pleased God hitherto to bestow on mankind, men begin at settling the significations of their words: which settling of significations they call *definitions,* and place them in the beginning of their reckoning.

Definitions thus clear up ambiguities and "settle significations," rather than communicate information about a realm of essences. They are introduced at the beginning of inquiry, as in geometry, rather than at the culmination of inquiry, as in metaphysics and Aristotelian natural science.

According to Hobbes, all knowledge consists in the "right ordering of names in affirmation." A proposition connects one name to another, and an inference adds or subtracts one proposition from another. The structure of scientific thought thus maps the structure of the physical world. It would seem then that, for Hobbes, all scientific knowledge is derivable from definitions. Yet Hobbes also stressed the role of perception in knowledge. The solution to this paradox lies in Hobbes's conception of naming. All inquiry is deductive except for the assignment of names to things, and it is to the assignment of names that we must look for the empirical sources of knowledge. But it follows that definitions as assignments of names must be as informative for Hobbes as they are for Plato or Aristotle. This conclusion leads to a further paradox, for, according to Hobbes, definitions provide no information at all; they express conventional decisions to use particular signs as names of particular objects.

There is an ambiguity in Hobbes's account of definitions that must hamper any attempt to reduce definitions to assignments of names. In order to make definitions entail all the propositions of scientific knowledge, Hobbes had to include, in the notion of naming, all the cognitive functions that we ordinarily distinguish from naming. He first compared the highly abstract and sophisticated definitions of concepts in mathematics and natural science to simple naming procedures such as baptism. Then, in order to account for the conspicuous differences between the two kinds of procedures, he was compelled to reinject into the notion of naming the very distinctions he set out to eliminate. The reduction of definitions to assignments of names only *appears* to solve the problem of whether definitions are informative: It first suggests that definitions are as arbitrary as acts of naming and then suggests that naming is, after all, not always arbitrary.

EARLY FORMALISM. Although the language used by the Cartesians of the seventeenth century in discussing definitions was similar to that of Bacon and Hobbes, their emphasis and direction of interest was different. Bacon and Hobbes were primarily concerned with the role of definitions in achieving semantic clarity, the Cartesians were more interested in the role of definitions in deductive inference. They developed a conception of definitions as theoretically dispensable abbreviations whose value lies solely in the notational economy they make possible. Cartesian references to "names" are rather misleading since, unlike Hobbes, the Cartesians did not regard assignment of names as the initial and fundamental process of inquiry from which the rest of knowledge is derived. This role was taken over by axioms and postulates that relate "simple" (i.e., indefinable) terms to each other, definitions then being introduced as rules for substituting brief expressions for logical complexes of simple terms.

Descartes did not give much attention to the subject of definition. In rejecting classical syllogistic logic as the framework of scientific inference, he abandoned the emphasis on terms or classes as the basic units of inference in favor of propositional units. The simplest inference became, for Descartes, the intuitive recognition of the implication of one proposition by another. Consequently, postulates replaced definitions as the foundation of deductive science, and essential definitions ceased to represent the highest goal of knowledge.

Pascal's analysis of the nature and function of definitions made explicit the view of definition implicit in Descartes's theory of knowledge. The main elements of Pascal's discussion are formalistic. However, it is not free of ambiguity with respect to the purely notational role of definitions as against the informative role ascribed to them by essentialists.

Pascal's theory of definition is expounded in a brief essay, *De l'esprit géométrique* (*Oeuvres,* 14 vols., Léon Brunschvicg and E. Boutroux, eds., Paris, 1904–1914). He began by distinguishing two types of definition, *définitions de nom,* which he claimed to be the only type appropriate in science, and an unnamed type that seems to be what Aristotle called "real," the type favored by essentialists, about which he thereafter says nothing more.

Définitions de nom are said to be "mere impositions of names upon things that have been clearly indicated in perfectly intelligible terms," as, for example, the definition of "even number" as "number that can be divided by two without remainder." Such definitions, Pascal claimed, are conventional labels that need have nothing in common with the things they name. They communicate no information about their *nominata,* expressing merely the decision of the writer to use them in the prescribed manner. The sole limitation on *définitions de nom* is that they be internally and mutually consistent.

When he discussed the methodology of definition, Pascal no longer regarded the relation between language and reality as purely conventional. We must make sure "not to define things that are clear and are understood by everyone." Geometry provides the model for definitional procedure. "It does not define such things as *space, time, motion, number, equality* … because these terms so naturally designate the things to which they refer, for those who understand the language, that the intended clarification would be more likely to obscure them than to instruct." One might think that, in saying "space naturally designates" its referent, Pascal meant that the word *space* is so familiar that everyone understands what it signifies. But why, then, should he interdict any definition of "space"? If definitions are notational conventions, there could be no objection to stipulating a new use of the word. Indeed, the ordinary use of "space" is quite different from its technical use in mathematics. Why, then, is it improper to define either the ordinary or the mathematical use? Surely, Pascal was not thinking of the word *space,* but of space itself as an irreducible entity that cannot be analyzed into simpler components, and if so, then he was thinking of definition not as a notational convenience, but as an informative mode of analysis.

The Cartesian theory of knowledge by which Pascal was guided conceives of the world as a system of elements combined according to mathematical laws to form complex objects and events. While Descartes stressed the analytical reduction of complex propositions to simple ones (i.e., axioms), Pascal joined definitions to axioms as the basis from which the deductive reconstruction of science should start. But common to all the Cartesians is the assumption that knowledge is a mathematical mapping of the structure of nature. In the light of this epistemological atomism, the conventional character attributed to definitions contrasts sharply with the requirement that they correspond to an antecedent natural order—a requirement that leads back to essentialism.

MODERN FORMALISM. The formalistic conception of definitions as rules of notational abbreviation was only vaguely anticipated by seventeenth-century philosophers, who failed to separate this purely syntactic procedure from epistemological considerations such as mapping the order of nature. Only in recent times have formalistic discussions of definition been purified of epistemological assumptions, by (among others) Russell, Alfred North

Whitehead, W. V. Quine, Rudolf Carnap, C. G. Hempel, and Nelson Goodman. But it remains doubtful whether this purely formalistic view either is or can be consistently maintained.

Russell and Whitehead, in *Principia Mathematica* (Vol. I, p. 11), define a definition as follows:

> A definition is a declaration that a certain newly introduced symbol or combination of symbols is to mean the same as a certain other combination of symbols of which the meaning is already known. … It is to be observed that a definition is, strictly speaking, no part of the subject in which it occurs. For a definition is concerned wholly with the symbols, not with what they symbolize. Moreover, it is not true or false, being the expression of a volition, not of a proposition.

This characterization of definition is not consistently syntactical. It defines *definition* in terms of sameness of meaning, while claiming that a definition "is concerned wholly with the symbols, not with what they symbolize." Later in the same passage, Russell and Whitehead declare:

> In spite of the fact that definitions are theoretically superfluous, it is nevertheless true that they often convey more important information than is contained in the propositions in which they are used. This arises from two causes. First, a definition usually implies that the *definiens* is worthy of careful consideration. … Secondly, when what is defined is … something already familiar …, the definition contains an analysis of a common idea. (p. 12)

The first and last sentence in the passage above express a nonsyntactical attitude toward definitions. Definitions turn out to be highly informative, and we seem to have returned to an essentialist view of the matter. But a further qualification has been attached, namely, "when what is defined is … something already familiar." In fact, two types of definition are being considered, one being a rule of notational abbreviation and the other an "analysis of an idea." But if some definitions are "analyses of ideas" and are highly informative, then these are the important kinds of definitions, and the formalist view proclaimed at the outset loses its force.

Similar difficulties attend the efforts of other modern logicians to deal with the problem of definition from a purely formal point of view. Thus, W. V. Quine, after asserting that "a definition is a convention of notational abbreviation," qualified his statement as follows:

> Although signs introduced by definition are formally arbitrary, more than such arbitrary notational convention is involved in questions of definability; otherwise any expression might be said to be definable on the basis of any expressions whatever. … To be satisfactory … a definition … not only must fulfill the formal requirement of unambiguous eliminability, but must also conform to the traditional usage in question. ("Truth by Convention," in *Readings in Philosophical Analysis,* edited by H. Feigl and W. Sellars, New York, 1949, p. 252)

Nelson Goodman took the same position and fell into the same difficulties:

> In a constructional system … most of the definitions are introduced for explanatory purposes. … In a formal system considered apart from its interpretation, any such definitional formula has the formal status of a convention of notational interchangeability once it is adopted; but the terms employed are ordinarily selected according to their usage, and the correctness of the interpreted definition is legitimately testable by examination of that usage. (*The Structure of Appearance,* p. 3)

In common with many other logicians, Quine and Goodman distinguish between the function of definitions "in a formal system" and their function when the system is interpreted—that is, when definite meanings are assigned to the symbols of the system. But this distinction overlooks the fact that from a purely formal standpoint, there is no such thing as a definition at all. Before it is interpreted, the formula that we interpret as a definition is just a string of marks. From a "purely formal standpoint," not only is there no difference between a definition and a notational abbreviation, but there is no difference between a definition and *any* other kind of formula. There are only various strings of marks, some permitted by the rules of formation of the system, others excluded by these rules. Consequently, the distinction made by Quine and Goodman between definitions in a formal system and those in an interpreted system is seriously misleading.

Rudolf Carnap and C. G. Hempel have tried to clarify the difference between informative definitions and mere notational abbreviations by distinguishing between "old" and "new" concepts. Definitions of old concepts are called "explications" by Carnap and "rational reconstructions" by Hempel, while both call definitions of new concepts "notational conventions." When we are "explicating" or "reconstructing" a concept, our definitions are subject to evaluation by the criteria of conformity to usage and increase of precision (Rudolf Carnap, *The Logical Syntax of Language,* p. 23). When definitions are introduced solely for the purpose of abbreviation, only the criterion of consistency applies. One must therefore wonder why Carnap and Hempel should bother to call notational abbreviations "definitions," since they have nothing whatever in common with explications.

Perhaps the answer to this question lies in the logical difficulties lurking within the notion of explication. What does it mean to "reconstruct" or "explicate" a concept, and what precisely is the difference between "old" and "new" concepts? If definitions of old concepts must conform to established usage, are they not true or false statements about language usage, in which case the distinction between definitions and empirical statements disappears? These problems lead naturally into the linguistic theory of definition.

LINGUISTIC THEORIES

Anticipations of a linguistic view of definition may be found in classical writings (for example, in Aristotle's discussion of "nominal definition") and in the nominalist and formalist positions previously considered. But while early nominalism attempted to reduce all the varied functions of words to that of proper names and thus to reduce meaning to the arbitrary assignment of a name to an object, formalism added linguistic considerations as an inessential afterthought. The first step from nominalism to an L-type view proper was taken by John Stuart Mill, although his formulations are permeated with elements of both nominalism and essentialism. A further step was taken by G. E. Moore, but Moore's discussion also contains a heavy strain of essentialism. The clearest formulation of the linguistic view was provided by Richard Robinson in his book *Definition,* which has the distinction of being the only book in the English language devoted to this subject.

In his *System of Logic,* J. S. Mill defined "definition" as follows: "The simplest and most correct notion of a Definition is, a proposition declaratory of the meaning of a word: namely, either the meaning which it bears in common acceptation, or that which the speaker or writer … intends to annex to it" (10th ed., p. 86).

Mill then explained that a definition is a "verbal proposition" that "adds no information to that which was already possessed by all who understood the name (defined)"—a tautology that Mill mistook for an important observation. But, unlike the thoroughgoing prescriptivist, Mill did not regard definitions as purely conventional stipulations, at least insofar as terms in general use are concerned:

> It would, however, be a complete misunderstanding of the proper office of the logician in dealing with terms already in use, if we were to think that because a name has not at present an ascertained connotation, it is competent to anyone to give it such a connotation at his own choice. The meaning of a term actually in use is not an arbitrary quantity to be fixed, but an unknown quantity to be sought. (p. 91)

At this point, Mill conceded that some definitions are not mere "declarations" but convey some kind of information about "unknown quantities to be sought." Mill gave two reasons for this departure from prescriptivism. The first consideration involves him in a tug of war between nominalist and linguistic theories. "Since names and their significations are entirely arbitrary, such (verbal) propositions are not, strictly speaking, susceptible of truth or falsity, but only of conformity or disconformity to usage or convention; and all the proof they are capable of is proof of usage" (p. 92).

In this instance, Mill first denied and then asserted that definitions are informative. If "all the proof they are capable of is proof of usage," then they *are* capable of proof after all, despite his initial disclaimer of this possibility.

Mill's second reason for ascribing at least a quasi-informative function to some definitions resembles, to some extent, the phenomenalist conception of definition as analysis of complex ideas into simple constituents. Mill wrote:

> A name, whether concrete or abstract, admits of definition, provided we are able to analyze, that is, to distinguish into parts, the attribute or set of attributes which constitutes the meaning both of the name and of the corresponding abstract. … We thus see that to frame a good definition of a name in use is not a matter of choice but of discussion … not merely respecting the usage of language, but respecting the properties of things, and even the origin of these properties. (p. 91)

The source of Mill's shifts of emphasis and inconsistencies lies in the ambiguity of his notion of meaning. At times he identified the meaning of a term with the object it "names," at other times with the customary usage of the word, and at still other times with an abstract object or "idea" capable of being divided into simpler parts. Thus, depending on which conception of meaning he had in mind, he thought of a definition as the stipulation of a name, a report of linguistic usage, or the analysis of a complex idea into its constituent parts.

G. E. MOORE. The extent to which G. E. Moore's approach to definitions can properly be called "linguistic" is debatable. Moore placed less stress on the linguistic aspect of definition than later philosophers such as Gilbert Ryle, Peter Frederick Strawson, and Robinson, who were influenced by Moore's analytical method. For Moore, as for Socrates, the clarification of language was only a means toward the discovery of deeper philosophical truths. But there can be no doubt that Moore inspired others to concern themselves with language and that his painstaking attention to the nuances of words was the most distinctive feature of his work.

In his *Principia Ethica,* Moore characterized "analytical" definitions (the kind produced by philosophical analysis) as follows: "Definitions of the kind that I was asking for, definitions which describe the real nature of the object or notion denoted by a word and which do not merely tell us what the word is used to mean, are only possible when the object or notion is complex" (p. 7).

In order to indicate the kind of descriptive information that he expected philosophical definitions to provide, Moore offered an example that is as misleading as it is famous: "When we say … 'The definition of horse is "a hoofed quadruped of the genus Equus"' … we may mean that a certain object, which we all of us know, is composed in a certain manner: that it has four legs, a head, a heart, a liver, etc., all of them arranged in definite relations to one another" (p. 8).

This passage is curious; it suggests that an analytical definition lists the physical parts of the thing defined. The example, however, gives the species and differentia of the class of horses but does *not* mention any physical parts. In commenting on this passage in his *Reunion in Philosophy* (p. 184), Morton White has observed that Moore shifted inadvertently from logical to physical complexity.

In later writings, Moore maintained that concepts are the proper subject matter of definition. "To define a concept," he wrote, "is the same thing as to give an analysis of it" ("Reply to My Critics," in *The Philosophy of G. E. Moore,* pp. 664–665). It is not easy to tell just what Moore meant by "concept analysis." For the analysis of a concept, he offered three criteria that add up to the relation of synonymity of expressions. Thus, despite his explicit effort to find an informative function for definitions that goes beyond the explanation of how words are used, it is not unreasonable to conclude that all that his obscure notion of "analyzing a concept" finally comes to is linguistic clarification. In denying that analytic definitions "merely tell us what the word is used to mean," Moore was rejecting the view that definitions are generalizations about common usage and suggesting that they have a more explanatory function. But he never made clear what that function is.

In the only full-length volume in English devoted to the study of definition, Richard Robinson formulated a purely linguistic account of definitions as reports of word usage. But he thought it necessary to supplement his main view with a "stipulative," or prescriptive, account. The reasons for his vacillation are that reports of usage are empirical generalizations, while definitions are, if acceptable at all, necessary truths, and that stipulations are uninformative, while definitions are highly informative. Thus, neither the linguistic nor the prescriptive interpretation accounts for all features of definitions. But the mere juxtaposition of the two can hardly overcome the defects of each taken separately.

A PRAGMATIC-CONTEXTUAL APPROACH

Linguistic theories of definition brought needed attention to the close relation between definitions and the meanings of words, but they erred in identifying meanings either with objects or concepts allegedly denoted by words or with linguistic usage. A correct theory of definition would unite the partial insights of E-type, P-type, and L-type views without relying on misleading metaphors, denying the obvious informative value of definitions, or reducing definitions to historical reports of linguistic behavior.

Why should essentialists and linguistic philosophers claim that definitions convey knowledge, while prescriptivists deny that they do? In some sense of the word *knowledge,* anyone would agree that definitions communicate knowledge. The problem is to identify a special sense of "knowledge" that is appropriate to definitions but does not require us to postulate obscure essences or to reduce definitions to historical reports. This special kind of knowledge may be knowledge of how to use words effectively. Use, unlike usage, is functional. As Gilbert Ryle has observed, there are misuses and ineffective uses, but there is no such thing as a misusage or ineffective usage ("Ordinary Language," in *Philosophical Review* 42 [1953]). Usage is what people *happen* to do with words and is determined by habits, while use is what *should* be done with words and is governed by rules. To explain the right use of a word, as distinct from merely reporting its usage, a definition must give the rules that guide us in using it. In this respect definitions are rules, rather than descriptions or reports.

All three traditional theories of definition assume, mistakenly, that if definitions convey knowledge, then the knowledge they convey is of the same type as that conveyed by ordinary statements of fact. Essentialists conclude that the knowledge conveyed by definitions is descriptive knowledge of essences, linguistic philosophers conclude that it is descriptive knowledge of language usage, while prescriptivists maintain that definitions do not convey knowledge of any kind. There has been a strikingly similar three-way dispute over the status of value judgments: nonnaturalists hold that value judgments convey knowledge of an abstract realm of "values"; naturalists maintain that they convey knowledge of observable causal relations; and emotivists assert that they convey no knowledge whatsoever. Arguments about whether definitions and value judgments convey true or false information mistakenly presuppose that all information must be of the descriptive type, thus overlooking the fact that cookbooks, military manuals, Sunday sermons, and do-it-yourself instruction sheets all convey, in various ways, the kind of normative information that Ryle has called "knowledge-how" in *The Concept of Mind* (Ch. 2). Practical or ethical advice may be regarded as stating rules that inform us how to act effectively, while definitions provide rules that inform us how to speak or write effectively. In either case it may be said that the information conveyed is subject to being evaluated as good or bad, but not to being verified as true or false.

APPLICATIONS OF A CONTEXTUALIST VIEW. The three views of definition distinguished above fail to provide adequate criteria for distinguishing good definitions from bad ones. They assume that the criteria of a good definition can be stated independently of the specific context in which the definition is offered and the purpose it is intended to serve. But no brief list of criteria can be given that would enable us to judge at sight whether a definition is adequate. The most we can do on a general level is to classify the kinds of rules of use that definitions provide and the kinds of discursive purposes they serve, and to say generally that definitions are good if and only if they serve the purpose for which they are intended.

Thus, an evaluation of a definition must begin with the identification of the point or purpose of the definition, and this requires knowledge of the discursive situation in which the need for the definition arises. We use words to incite ourselves and others to action, to express and share emotions, to draw attention to things, to memorize, to make inferences, to evoke and enjoy images, to perform ceremonies, to teach, to exercise, and to show off. It is when we are unsure of the most effective use of an expression for one of these purposes that we seek a definition.

LINGUISTIC RULES. Rules governing the uses of words can be sorted into three main types: (1) referring rules, which aid us in identifying the things or situations to which a word may be applied; (2) syntactical rules, which govern the ways in which a word may be combined with other words to form phrases and sentences; and (3) discursive rules (the most difficult to formulate), which indicate when we may use language metaphorically (as in poetry) and when we must use it literally (as in science), as well as indicating differences of category or logical type (for example, the rule that one cannot predicate human qualities such as intelligence of inanimate things such as machines) and indicating when a word should be used in one sense rather than another (for example, *space* in mathematics as distinguished from physics). Discursive rules are the genuinely philosophical rules.

Rules for defining. The practical value of any account of the nature of definition is to be found in the clarity of the standards it provides for judging when a definition is good or bad. How does the pragmatic-contextualist account fare in this respect?

A number of rules of thumb for evaluating definitions have become canonical in the literature on the subject despite the fact that they make no clear sense in terms of any of the traditional views. The following rules can be found in practically every textbook on logic. They were first suggested by Aristotle in his *Topica* and have survived without change by sheer weight of tradition:

(1) A definition should give the essence or nature of the thing defined, rather than its accidental properties.

(2) A definition should give the genus and differentia of the thing defined.

(3) One should not define by synonyms.

(4) A definition should be concise.

(5) One should not define by metaphors.

(6) One should not define by negative terms or by correlative terms (thus, one should not define north as the opposite of south, or parent as a person with one or more children).

Significance of the rules. Rule 1, which makes sense only according to the essentialist theory, is nevertheless accepted by many writers who hold a prescriptive or linguistic view of definition, although these writers usually mean that a definition should indicate the properties that *define* the meaning of the term in question rather than those that just happen to hold true of the objects to which the term applies. But in such a case, the rule is vacuous; it asserts only that a definition should define rather than describe.

Rule 2 deserves its high status only if one accepts Aristotle's extension of biological classification to metaphysics, but it retains a limited value when it is reinterpreted in linguistic terms. We may understand "genus" to mean what Ryle has called the logical grammar of a term. The term defined need not be the name of any natural species or, for that matter, any object whatsoever. In defining words such as *function,* we do not identify a class of objects. We define a function as a certain type of relation, thus indicating that whatever can be said about relations in general can also be said about functions in particular. We thus provide a rule of syntax governing the word *function,* indicating with what other words it may be combined. The differentia of function—namely, that the relation is many-one between two variables—is a referring rule (criterion of identification) that helps us to identify the situations or formulas to which the term *function* may be applied. But it is wrong to think that the genus and differentia are necessary for a good definition. What must be stated in a definition varies with the definition's purpose. The genus may already be known and only the differentia needed or vice versa. Moreover, there are types of definition, such as contextual and recursive definition, that cannot be expressed in genus-differentia form. Contextual and recursive definitions provide rules for substituting a simpler expression for each of an infinite number of complex expressions of a given type.

Synonyms. The rule that forbids defining by a synonym makes sense only on the contextualist view of definitions as rules of use, although it has long been cited by supporters of the traditional views. The same books that cite this rule also insist that the definiendum must be logically equivalent to the definiens. But a synonym is just an expression that is logically equivalent to a given expression. The trouble seems to be that the term *synonym* is employed in a vaguely restricted sense to signify not just any logically equivalent expression, but a very brief one. Thus, we often find the injunction, "Do not define a word by a single other word." But this formulation, while sufficiently clear, is misleading. Is a two-word definition, such as "phonograph disc" for "record," a case of defining by a synonym or not? Just how many words may the definiens contain if it is not to violate this rule?

To make matters worse, the prohibition of synonyms is inconsistent with rule 4, which demands that a definition be concise; indeed, the more concise the definiens, the more it looks like a synonym. However, we can understand a rule only if we know what specific purpose the rule is intended to serve. A contextualist view of definitions provides the following solution to the conflict between conciseness and nonsynonymity:

Single-word definitions are seldom useful because a person who does not know the rules governing the definiendum, is not likely to know the rules governing the definiens. The more words there are in the definiens, the more likely it is that those for whom the definition is offered are familiar with some of the words and thus understand some of their rules of use. Everyone has experienced the frustration of looking up a word in a dictionary and being confounded by some equally unfamiliar synonym.

But why should definitions be concise if the greater the number of words, the greater are our chances of at least partial comprehension? One obvious answer is that brief explanations are easier to remember. A second answer is that a lengthy definiens is more likely to suggest some rules of use that are inessential to the definiendum. But the most important consideration has to do with the kind of discursive context in which the definition is employed. In mathematics and in other formal contexts such as jurisprudence and contractual language, the purpose of most definitional equations is to abbreviate discourse or notation. In such cases it is a virtue rather than a defect for the definiens to be long and complicated, since it is precisely this fact that makes the definiendum worth introducing as an abbreviation. Moreover, the complexity of the definiens is less likely to produce confusion in technical contexts because of the great pains taken to preserve consistency and precision of language. In contrast, the rule of conciseness is more appropriate to informal discourse, in which definitions are intended to translate or otherwise clarify an expression unfamiliar to some of the participants. In informal discourse, the definiens should be brief, while in formal contexts, the longer and more complicated the definiens, the more useful the definition. Clearly, one can make little sense of criteria of good definitions without specifying the context in which and the purpose for which a definition is needed.

Figurative language. Why should a definition avoid figurative language? This traditional injunction is probably a result of the concentration of classical philosophy on formal discursive contexts such as mathematics and natural science, in which figures of speech are usually out of place. But in informal contexts such as conversation, literature, public debate, and even the less technical discussions of scientists, figurative language may well be the most effective way of getting a point across, and it is certainly the only way to define expressions whose meaning is essentially figurative (for example, *fathead* may be defined as "a fool puffed up with vanity"). No literal definiens can do justice to the nuances of natural discourse, as every translator knows from bitter experience.

Negative and correlative terms. Why not define by the use of negative or correlative terms? This injunction, in contrast to rule 5, holds for informal discourse and becomes senseless when applied to formal discourse. It is perfectly proper in mathematics or logic to define "$-p$" as "the negation of p" or to define "$F^{-1}(x)$" as "the inverse of the function $F(x)$." The reason for prohibiting negative and correlative definitions in informal contexts is that a person who is unclear about the rules of use of the definiendum would be just as puzzled about the rules of use of a negative or correlative definiens.

Meaning equations. In light of the preceding discussion, it is advisable to look again at the problem of synonymity. It has already been noted that every meaning equation—that is, every definition of the form "*E*" means (or means the same as) "*x, y, z*"—provides a definiens that is synonymous with its definiendum. The very point of the definition is to assert this synonymity and thus to transfer the rules of use already known to govern the definiens to the presumably less familiar definiendum. In order to make sense of the traditional injunction against synonymous definitions, we found it necessary to interpret the synonymity in question as a special and restricted subtype of synonymity, measured by the number of words in the definiens. But although it is absurd to require that a meaning equation must not offer synonyms (in the general sense of "synonym"), it is quite sensible to cast doubt on the usefulness of meaning equations. Meaning equations provide a kind of definition misleadingly called "explicit," in contrast to axioms and postulates, which are frequently regarded as "implicit" or "partial" definitions.

It is unfortunate that meaning equations have come to be called "explicit" definitions, because their function, as we have seen, is to transfer rules of use from definiens to definiendum without articulating the rules in question, so that the rules remain implicit. The most explicit kind of definition, the kind that actually states the rules governing the use of an expression, is a very complicated matter. Outside of technical contexts, it is doubtful whether complete definitions of this kind can ever be provided. On the other hand, it is just as doubtful whether a complete articulation of all the rules of use of the definiendum need be given. We seldom, if ever, require more than one or a few rules of reference, logical grammar, or relevant discourse that happen to be obscure to us in a particular context. Thus, meaning equations are frequently neither the most valuable nor the most appropriate kind of definition. In technical discourse, contextual, recursive, and operational definitions play a far more important role than mere notational abbreviations. And in nontechnical contexts, such as teaching a child or a foreigner the use of a word, definitions by illustration, by enumeration of instances or enumeration of subclasses, and by an indefinite number of other devices (depending on the ingenuity and linguistic sensitivity of the parties concerned) are usually more appropriate and effective than meaning equations. The evaluation of specific definitional procedures remains an important task for philosophically minded experts in each field of discourse and inquiry.

See also Aristotle; Art, Definitions of; Bacon, Francis; Brunschvicg, Léon; Carnap, Rudolf; Descartes, René; Essence and Existence; Geometry; Goodman, Nelson; Hempel, Carl Gustav; Hobbes, Thomas; Hume, David; Husserl, Edmund; Intuition; Kant, Immanuel; Language, Philosophy of; Lewis, Clarence Irving; Locke, John; Logical Terms, Glossary of; Medieval Philosophy; Mill, John Stuart; Moore, George Edward; Pascal, Blaise; Plato; Proper Names and Descriptions; Quine, Willard Van Orman; Rickert, Heinrich; Russell, Bertrand Arthur William; Ryle, Gilbert; Semantics; Socrates; Strawson, Peter Frederick; Universals, A Historical Survey; Whitehead, Alfred North.

Bibliography

Aristotle. *Works.* Edited by W. D. Ross. Oxford, 1928. See especially *Physics* 192–195, *Metaphysics* 982–984, *Posterior Analytics* 90, *Topics.*

Ayer, A. J. *Language, Truth, and Logic,* 2nd ed. London: Gollancz, 1946. Chs. 3 and 4.

Bacon, Francis. *Novum Organum.* In *Works,* edited by J. Spedding. London, 1901. Vol. IV.

Black, Max. *Problems of Analysis.* Ithaca, NY: Cornell University Press, 1954. Ch. 2.

Carnap, Rudolf. *Introduction to Semantics.* Cambridge, MA: Harvard University Press, 1942. Secs. 6, 24.

Carnap, Rudolf. "Testability and Meaning." *Philosophy of Science* 3 (1936): 419–471 and 4 (1937): 1–40.

Carnap, Rudolf. "The Two Concepts of Probability." *Philosophy and Phenomenological Research* 5 (1945): 513–532.

Carré, M. H. *Realists and Nominalists.* Oxford: Oxford University Press, 1946.

Church, Alonzo. "Definition." In *Dictionary of Philosophy,* edited by D. D. Runes. New York: Philosophical Library, 1942.

Copi, I. M. *Introduction to Logic.* New York, 1948. Ch. 4.

Descartes, René. *Rules for the Direction of the Understanding.* In *Works.* Translated by E. S. Haldane and G. R. T. Ross. Cambridge, U.K., 1911. Vol. I.

Dewey, John, and A. F. Bentley. "Definition." *Journal of Philosophy* 44 (1947): 281–306.

Dubs, Homer H. *Rational Induction.* Chicago: University of Chicago Press, 1930.

Frege, Gottlob. *Translations from the Writings of Gottlob Frege,* edited by P. T. Geach and Max Black. Oxford, 1952.

Goodman, Nelson. *The Structure of Appearance.* Cambridge, MA: Harvard University Press, 1951. Ch. 1.

Hempel, C. G. *Fundamentals of Concept Formation in Empirical Science.* Chicago: University of Chicago Press, 1952. Ch. 1, Parts 2–4.

Hobbes, Thomas. *Leviathan.* Book I, Secs. 3–5.

Husserl, Edmund. *Erfahrung und Urteil.* Hamburg: Claassen and Goverts, 1948. Pp. 410 ff.

Husserl, Edmund. *Ideas.* Translated by W. R. Boyce Gibson. New York: Macmillan, 1931. Vol. I.

Kant, Immanuel. "Introduction." In *Critique of Pure Reason,* translated by Norman Kemp Smith. London, 1929.

Kaplan, Abraham. "Definition and Specification of Meaning." *Journal of Philosophy* 43 (1946): 281–288.

Lenzen, Victor. "Successive Definition." In *Procedures of Empirical Science.* Chicago, 1938.

Lewis, C. I. *An Analysis of Knowledge and Valuation.* La Salle, IL: Open Court, 1946. Pp. 105 ff.

Locke, John. *Essay concerning Human Understanding.* Edited by A. C. Fraser. Oxford, 1894. Vol. I.

Maritain, Jacques. *Philosophy of Nature.* Translated by I. Byrne. New York: Philosophical Library, 1951.

Mill, John Stuart. *A System of Logic.* London, 1879. Pp. 72ff., 436ff.

Moore, G. E. *Principia Ethica.* Cambridge, U.K., 1913. Ch. 1.

Moore, G. E. "Reply to My Critics." In *The Philosophy of G. E. Moore,* edited by P. A. Schilpp, 660–667. Evanston, IL: Northwestern University Press, 1942.

Pepper, S. C. "The Descriptive Definition." *Journal of Philosophy* 43 (1946): 29–36.

Plato. *The Dialogues of Plato.* Translated by Benjamin Jowett. See especially *Charmides, Euthyphro, Meno, Republic, Sophist,* and *Theaetetus.*

Quine, W. V. "Truth by Convention." In *Philosophical Essays for A. N. Whitehead.* London and New York: Longmans, Green, 1936.

Rickert, Heinrich. *Zur Lehre von der Definition.* Tübingen, 1929.

Robinson, Richard. *Definition.* Oxford, 1954.

Robinson, Richard. *Plato's Earlier Dialectic.* Ithaca, NY: Cornell University Press, 1941.

Russell, Bertrand, and A. N. Whitehead. *Principia Mathematica.* Cambridge, U.K.: Cambridge University Press, 1910. Vol. I.

Scriven, Michael. "Definitions, Explanations, and Theories." In *Minnesota Studies in the Philosophy of Science II,* edited by H. Feigl, G. Maxwell, and M. Scriven, 99–195. Minneapolis: University of Minnesota Press, 1958.

Scriven, Michael. "Definitions in Analytical Philosophy." *Philosophical Studies* 5 (1954).

Wittgenstein, Ludwig. *Philosophical Investigations.* Translated by G. E. M. Anscombe. New York: Macmillan, 1953.

Raziel Abelson (1967)

DEGREES OF PERFECTION, ARGUMENT FOR THE EXISTENCE OF GOD

The proof for the existence of God from degrees of perfection, sometimes called the Henological Argument, finds its best-known expression as the fourth of Thomas Aquinas's "Five Ways" in his *Summa Theologiae* Ia, 2, 3. It is here quoted in full:

> The fourth way is based on the gradation observed in things. Some things are found to be more good, more true, more noble, and so on, and other things less. But comparative terms describe varying degrees of approximation to a superlative; for example, things are hotter and hotter the nearer they approach what is hottest. Something therefore is the truest and best and most noble of things, and hence the most fully in being; for Aristotle says that the truest things are the things most fully in being. Now *when many things possess some property in common, the one most fully possessing it causes it in the others: fire,* to use Aristotle's example, *the hottest of all things, causes all other things to be hot.* There is something therefore which causes in all other things their being, their goodness, and whatever other perfections they have. And this we call God.

COMPARATIVES AND SUPERLATIVES

A distinctive feature of the Fourth Way is the principle that "comparative terms describe varying degrees of approximation to a superlative"; for example, suppose "whiter than" is such a comparative term. The judgment that bond paper is whiter than newsprint would then be more adequately expressed as "The color of bond paper is closer to *pure white* than is the color of newsprint." However, the new comparative term "closer to" (that is, "more closely resembles," "more similar to") is used in exactly the same sense when none of the things compared is a superlative, for example, in "The color of bond paper is closer to the color of newsprint than the color of newsprint is close to the color of lemons," and here "closer to" obviously does not describe a degree of approximation to pure white. If "closer to," used to compare colors, does describe degrees of approximation to a superlative, the superlative must be the greatest possible similarity between colors, that is, qualitative identity of colors. Perhaps the initial judgment should then be expressed "The similarity between the color of bond paper and pure white is closer to the *greatest possible similarity* than is the similarity between newsprint and pure white." But here there is still a comparative term, "closer to," used to compare similarities between colors. It seems impossible to define a comparative term by means of a superlative without using another comparative term, and we are on our way to an infinite regress. If all comparative terms describe degrees of approximation to a superlative, then any comparative judgment implicitly refers to infinitely many superlatives.

But perhaps not all comparative terms describe degrees of approximation to a superlative. Suppose "closer to" (as used to compare colors) does not, and therefore the infinite regress can be cut short. Then "closer to" can be used to define "whiter than," and the definition need not refer to pure white, or to any other superlative. This is a reason for denying that "whiter than" describes a degree of approximation to a superlative. The definition runs as follows:

First it must be given, perhaps simply by fiat, that color *B* is whiter than color *A*. *B* need not be pure white, or superlatively white. Then any color *X* is between *A* and *B* if and only if both *X* is closer to *A* than *A* is close to *B* and *X* is closer to *B* than *B* is close to *A*. If *X* is between *A* and *B*, then *X* is whiter than *A*, and *B* is whiter than *X*. If *X* is different from both *A* and *B* and is not between *A* and *B*, then (1) *X* is whiter than *B* if and only if *X* is closer to *B* than *X* is close to *A* and (2) *A* is whiter than *X* if and only if *X* is closer to *A* than *X* is close to *B*. Two colors, *X* and *Y*, can be compared with respect to whiteness by (1) comparing *X* with the initially given pair in the manner just described and (2) similarly comparing *Y* with either the pair *A* and *X* or the pair *B* and *X*.

Superlative terms can be defined by means of comparatives more easily than comparative terms can be defined by means of superlatives. For example, "Brand *X* is the whitest bond paper if and only if Brand *X* is whiter than any other bond paper." Or "Brand *X* is the whitest bond paper if and only if no other bond paper is whiter than Brand *X*." On the second definition there can be more than one whitest bond paper. On the first definition there can be only one; and it is therefore possible that nothing satisfies the first definition. Such nonequivalent forms of definition are possible whatever the kind of superlative term defined; either form may be used if it is not confused with the other. Both definitions above define a relative superlative term. *Whitest* is defined with respect to a certain class, the class of bond papers. Since not only bond paper is white, neither definition rules out the possibility that something other than bond paper is whiter than the whitest bond paper. A universal superlative term is defined with respect to the class of everything of which the corresponding comparative term is predicable. For example, "*X* is the whitest thing if and only if nothing is whiter than *X*." Both relative and universal superlative terms can be absolute superlative terms. An absolute superlative term is defined by means of a modal term such as *possible* or *can*. "*X* is pure white if and only if it is not *possible* for anything to be whiter than *X*." There are as many senses of an absolute superlative term as there are relevant senses of *possible*.

Any comparative term can be used to define some superlative term. For example, "greater than" can be used to define "greatest prime number": *n* is the greatest prime number if and only if *n* is a prime number and there is no prime number greater than *n*. But it has been proved that there is no greatest prime number—that the predicate "greatest prime number" cannot be truly predicated of any number. This raises a general question: How can we know whether a particular superlative term could possibly be truly predicated of something? One can define "pure white," but this gives no assurance that there might possibly be something that is pure white. Perhaps we do not know what we are talking about when we talk about "pure white"; for perhaps there can be nothing to talk about, just as there can be nothing to talk about when we talk about "the greatest prime number." A superlative term should be suspected of not being truly predicable of anything possible unless there is a reason to think otherwise, and such a reason is not provided by the fact that the superlative term can be defined by a perfectly understandable comparative term.

Such a reason is sometimes provided when the superlative term can be defined without using any corresponding comparative or superlative terms. Definitions of this sort will usually, perhaps always, employ a universal quantifier. For example, "An object is (absolutely) *pure gold* if and only if *all* its atoms are atoms of gold. A *perfect* reflector is one that reflects *all* the light falling on it." Definitions of the form "Something is pure ______ if and only if it contains no impurities" or "something is a perfect ______ if and only if it has *no* imperfections" will not do by themselves. The terms "contains *no* impurities" and "has *no* imperfections" are as problematic as the particular superlative terms they define and should be used without qualms only if they can be characterized independently. "Absolutely pure minestrone soup" can be defined as "minestrone soup completely free of impurities," but this is no help until we have a complete list of possible impurities. Aniline dyes are definitely impurities in soups. Some batches of minestrone soup are therefore definitely purer than others. But starting from an incomplete list of possible impurities, there is no obvious way, other than by arbitrary stipulation, of making a complete list. It seems that "absolutely pure minestrone soup" can therefore be given a clear sense only by stipulation. We do not need to give it a clear sense in order to talk sensibly about some batches of soup being purer than others.

A comparative term is often much clearer than the corresponding superlative term; one can often know how to use a comparative term without at all knowing how to use the corresponding superlative term. It seems reasonable to deny that such comparative terms describe degrees of approximation to a superlative.

PERFECTIONS

Thomas stated his principle quite generally, but presumably he would have been willing to qualify it. He argued himself that there can be nothing that is unlimited in size (*Summa Theologiae* Ia, 7, 3) and he would deny, reasonably, that the comparative term "longer than," for example, describes degrees of approximation to a superlative. The argument from degrees of perfection does not lead to the heretical conclusion that God is pure white or pure red. Still less does it lead to the impossible conclusion that God is both pure white and pure red or that God is both perfectly circular and perfectly triangular. The argument is concerned only with perfections whose predication does not imply any sort of imperfection. If a thing is white, it must be extended; if extended, it must be divisible; and if divisible, it must be perishable. Perishability is an imperfection, and therefore whiteness, like all other properties that exist only in something extended, can exist only in things less than completely perfect. Perfections that involve absolutely no imperfection are sometimes called "transcendental perfections." The traditional list includes being, unity, truth, goodness, nobility, and sometimes beauty and intelligence. Thomas thought that anything, a member of any genus, and God, who is not a member of any genus, could have these perfections. For Thomas's argument the principle about comparison need be true only of the transcendental perfections.

The principle about comparison is generally dubious, and it is particularly dubious with the transcendental perfections. Goodness, for example, is sensibly predicated of something only when it is understood as being of some kind. One who asserts of something "It is good" should be prepared always to answer the question "A good *what*?" Things of a certain kind are good in virtue of having certain characteristics; things of another kind in virtue of having others. Thus, if comparisons of goodness describe degrees of approximation to a superlative, then comparison with respect to any of the different characteristics admitting of degrees in virtue of which different kinds of things are good must also describe degrees of approximation to a superlative. The restriction of the comparative principle to transcendental perfections is not much of a restriction.

Those who do not subscribe to a Thomistic metaphysics, or to one like it, will not find any reason to accept the principle that comparisons of perfections describe degrees of approximation to a superlative. It is not surprising that Thomas's philosophy contains enough material to construct more arguments for God's existence than he formulated explicitly. Some of these back up the Fourth Way. For example, Thomas's philosophical theology makes great use of the Aristotelian distinction between act and potency: "Each thing is perfect according as it is in act, and imperfect as it is in potency" (*Summa contra Gentiles* I, 28, 6). Furthermore, something whose actuality is less than complete must be caused by something else with at least as much actuality (I, 28, 7). Bearing these two principles in mind, the argument from degrees of perfection can be reformulated as follows:

> Some things are found to be more perfect than others. Thus, some things have less than the superlative degree of perfection. Since a thing's perfection is its actuality, these things have less than the superlative degree of actuality. Something whose actuality is less than complete must be caused by something else with at least as much actuality. The resulting hierarchy of causes cannot be infinite, so there must be a first cause whose actuality is complete, who is pure act, and who therefore has all perfections in a superlative degree. And this we call God.

Thus reformulated, the Fourth Way resembles the First Way, the argument from efficient causality, and the Second Way, the argument from change. And it is susceptible to the same sorts of familiar objections raised against them. These objections, however, may seem less forceful against the Fourth Way than against the other arguments. A modern reader who is untroubled by the idea of an infinite hierarchy of efficient causes may well balk at the idea of an infinite hierarchy of increasing perfection. And one who claims that a proof of a first cause does not prove *God's* existence may admit that a proof of an absolutely perfect being does. However, this does not make the argument from degrees of perfection more convincing than the other proofs. The argument is now generally neglected, and a modern nonbeliever is not likely to be much influenced by it. For its premises will seem plausible only to one who accepts metaphysical principles, which in turn will seem plausible only to one who has a prior belief in the existence of God.

The reformulation of the Fourth Way given earlier brings out the relevance of the relation between comparative and superlative to other parts of Thomas's system. A central doctrine of Thomas's philosophical theology is that God is *pure act,* that there neither is nor could be any potency in him. Even if it is granted that we can learn, from Aristotle's and Thomas's examples, how to compare some things as being more or less in act, this gives us no reason to suppose that the superlative term "pure act" is intelligible or that it could possibly apply to something.

See also Aristotle; Perfection; Popular Arguments for the Existence of God; Thomas Aquinas, St.

Bibliography

The Fourth Way seems the most Platonic of Thomas Aquinas's Five Ways. See, for example, Plato, *Phaedo,* 100–101. Two books in English on Thomas's relation to Plato are Arthur Little, *The Platonic Heritage of Thomism* (Dublin, 1950), and R. J. Henle, *Saint Thomas and Platonism* (The Hague: Nijhoff, 1956). The Fourth Way is the major topic of Little's book. Henle's book has a very complete bibliography.

The principle that comparative terms describe varying degrees of approximation to a superlative appears several times in Thomas's *Summa contra Gentiles* (I, 28, 8, I, 42, 19; I, 62, 5). It does not, however, appear in the very compressed argument for God's existence (I, 13, 34), where an argument from degrees of truth is attributed to Aristotle. Aristotle's *Metaphysics* II, 993b25–30, a passage mentioned in both the *Summa Theologiae* and the *Summa contra Gentiles* versions of the argument, does seem adaptable to Thomas's purposes. *Metaphysics* IV, 1008b31–1009a5, mentioned only in the *Summa contra Gentiles* version, does not. Aristotle probably should not be counted among the philosophers who employed or would be willing to employ the argument from degrees of perfection to prove the existence of a perfect being.

Several arguments from degrees of perfection appear in the writings of Augustine; see, for example, Bk. V, Sec. 11, and Bk. VIII, Sees. 4 and 5, of *De Trinitate,* the work of Augustine's referred to in the preface of Anselm's *Monologion.* Anselm's arguments from degrees of perfection appear in the first four chapters of the *Monologion.*

The Blackfriars edition of Thomas's *Summa theologiae* (New York: McGraw-Hill, 1964–; only a few of the projected 60 vols. have been published so far) has the Latin text, along with a new English translation. The second volume, Ia. 2–11 (New York McGraw-Hill, 1964), translated by Timothy McDermott, contains appendices by Thomas Gilby, "The Fourth Way" and "Perfection and Goodness."

Thomas's doctrine of "analogical" predication is usually invoked to explain the notion of a transcendental perfection. This, as well as the act-potency distinction, is discussed in Knut Tranøy, "Thomas Aquinas," in *A Critical History of Western Philosophy,* edited by D. J. O'Connor (New York: Free Press of Glencoe, 1964), and further references are given.

The Fourth Way is the least widely accepted of Thomas's proofs for the existence of God. References to the disputes are given in Étienne Gilson, *The Christian Philosophy of St. Thomas Aquinas* (New York: Random House, 1956). See also Gilson's *Elements of Christian Philosophy* (New York: Doubleday, 1960).

René Descartes presented a proof for the existence of God from the degrees of perfection found in ideas. See his *Third Meditation,* his *Principles of Philosophy,* I. xviii., Objection II of the second set of *Objections to the Meditations,* and his *Reply* to this objection.

Bobik, Joseph. "Aquinas's Fourth Way and the Approximating Relation." *The Thomist* 51 (1987): 17–36.

Brady, Jules. "Note on the Fourth Way." *New Scholasticism* 48 (1974): 219–232.

Catan, John, ed. *St. Thomas Aquinas on the Existence of God: Collected Papers of Joseph Owens.* Albany: State University of New York Press, 1980.

Dewan, Lawrence. "St. Thomas's Fourth Way and Creation." *The Thomist* 59 (1995): 371–378.

Kenny, Anthony. *The Five Ways: St. Thomas Aquinas' Proofs of God's Existence.* London: Routledge and Kegan Paul, 1969.

Morreall, John. "Aquinas' Fourth Way." *Sophia* 18 (1979): 20–28.

Urban, Linwood. "Understanding St. Thomas's Fourth Way." *History of Philosophy Quarterly* 1 (1984): 281–296.

Wippel, John. *The Metaphysical Thought of Thomas Aquinas: From Finite Being to Uncreated Being.* Washington, DC: Catholic University of America Press, 2000.

David Sanford (1967)

Bibliography updated by Christian B. Miller (2005)

DEISM

Deism (Lat. *deus,* god) is etymologically cognate to theism (Gr. *theos,* god), both words denoting belief in the existence of a god or gods and, therefore, the antithesis of atheism. However, as is customary in the case of synonyms, the words drifted apart in meaning; theism retained an air of religious orthodoxy, while *deism* acquired a connotation of religious unorthodoxy and ultimately reached the pejorative. Curiously, however, the earliest known use of the term *deist* (1564) already had this latter intent, although it was by no means consistently retained thereafter. The situation is complicated by a late eighteenth- and nineteenth-century technical metaphysical interpretation of deism, in which the meaning is restricted to belief in a God, or First Cause, who created the world and instituted immutable and universal laws that preclude any alteration as well as divine immanence—in short, the concept of an "absentee God." A further complication has been the acceptance of natural religion (religion universally achievable by human reason) by many eminent Christian theologians throughout the course of many centuries. Such theologians also believed in revelation and in personal divine intervention in the life of man, a position that had been made clear and authoritative by St. Thomas Aquinas. No sharp line can be drawn between the doctrines of such rationalistic theologians and those of deists, especially those who termed themselves "Christian deists." Nor is it accurate to maintain that the historical deists (mainly of the seventeenth and eighteenth centuries), like the philosophical deists, altogether denied the immanence of God, even though they did tend to become more and more critical of the necessity of any revelation and of the Hebraic-Christian revelation in particular. It is therefore necessary to distinguish between the two types of deists. The remainder of this entry will be devoted to a survey of historical deism.

EARLY HISTORY OF DEISM

To attempt to disentangle the antecedents of historical deism—intertwined as they are with rationalistic natural religion on the one hand, and with skepticism on the other—would indeed be foolhardy. Skepticism itself might end in Pyrrhonism or atheism or fideism. It is safe to generalize, however, that any tendency away from religious dogmatism, implicit faith and the mysterious, and in the direction of freedom of thought on religious matters, was in some measure a premonitory symptom of deism.

The earliest known use of the word *deist* was by Pierre Viret, a disciple of John Calvin, in his *Instruction chrétienne* (Geneva, 1564), Vol. II, "Epistre" (signed, Lyons, December 12, 1563). Viret regarded it as an entirely new word that (he claimed) the deists wished to oppose to *atheist:* According to him, the deist professes belief in God as the creator of heaven and earth but rejects Jesus Christ and his doctrines. Although those unidentified deists were learned men of letters and philosophy, they were bitterly attacked by Viret as monsters and atheists. This definition and commentary was given wide circulation through Pierre Bayle's citation in his article on Viret in the *Dictionnaire historique et critique* (1697; English translation, 1710). The word *deist* remained unknown in England until 1621, when it appeared in Robert Burton's *Anatomy of Melancholy* (III. iv. II. i). After discussing atheists and near-atheists, Burton continues: "Cousin-germans to these men are many of our great Philosophers and Deists," who, although good and moral, are yet themselves atheists. These "great Philosophers and Deists" likewise remain unidentified. A century and a half later, David Hume (1711–1776), in his *History of England,* ventured to name James Harrington, Algernon Sidney, and Sir John Wildman, among others, as the reputed leaders of the deists under the Commonwealth. The first interpretation of *deist* in both French and English as a euphemism for *atheist* was not followed by Dr. Samuel Johnson, who, in his *Dictionary* (1755), defined *deist* as "a man who follows no particular religion but only acknowledges the existence of God, without any other article of faith."

The first appearance of *deism* seems to have been in John Dryden's preface to his poem *Religio Laici* of 1682, where he equated it with natural religion. Dr. Johnson agreed: "The opinion of those that only acknowledge one God, without the reception of any revealed religion." Neither Dryden nor Johnson, evidently, regarded deism as disguised atheism. The notion of deism, however, if not the word itself, is to be found in one form or another throughout the Renaissance until, in the late seventeenth century, the Englishman Charles Blount openly acknowledged that he was a deist.

Beginning in the early sixteenth century, general contributions to the development of deism include such broad movements as anti-Trinitarianism, Unitarianism, secularism, anticlericalism, Erastianism, Arminianism, and Socinianism, the rise of the sects, and the general revolt against authority. It may be argued that all of these currents and undercurrents were united in the increasing trend away from religious persecution and toward religious toleration, the glorification of the natural powers of man, and the endorsement of the right to think and to publish freely on all religious and political subjects.

DEISM IN BRITAIN

The British deists constituted no conspiracy and formed no school of thought; they were highly individualistic, frequently unknown to one another, and sometimes at odds with one another. They were less systematic philosophers than thoughtful writers on practical moral, religious, and political issues. In 1704 the rationalist Anglican theologian Samuel Clarke distinguished four varieties of deists: those who denied providence; those who acknowledged providence in natural religion but not in morality; those who, while denying a future life, admitted the moral role of the deity; and finally, those who acknowledged a future life and the other doctrines of natural religion. The following summary of the leading deists will testify to the general truth of Clarke's subtle distinctions.

LEADING BRITISH DEISTS AND THE RISE OF DEISM.

Lord Herbert of Cherbury. Lord Herbert (1583–1648) never called himself a deist and had but a single acknowledged disciple, Charles Blount; nevertheless, he exerted considerable influence and deserves the title of "the father of English deism" bestowed on him in 1714 by Thomas Halyburton in *Natural Religion Insufficient.* Lord Herbert's *De Veritate, Prout Distinguitur a Revelatione, a Verisimili, a Possibili, et a Falso* was published in Paris in 1624, in London in 1633, and again in 1645. The first edition, therefore, postdated Burton's avowal of the existence of many deists by three years. In the expanded London edition of 1645, Herbert laid down the religious Common Notions that constitute the rationalistic basis of deism and that were to be assumed, if not always acknowledged, by virtually all succeeding deists. These principles are (1) that there is one supreme God; (2) that he ought to be worshiped; (3) that virtue and piety are the chief parts of divine worship; (4) that man ought to be sorry for his sins and repent of them; (5) that divine goodness dispenses rewards and punishments both in this life and after it. These truths, he argued, are universal, and may be apprehended by reason. Revelation is not openly repudiated, but by implication is rendered supererogatory. (Somewhat incongruously, however, Herbert prayed for a sign from Heaven that would grant permission to publish *De Veritate,* and was satisfied that he had received it.) Herbert treated Scripture as ordinary history, ridiculed bibliolatry, and overtly attacked priestcraft, and disavowed faith as a basis for religion. His *De Religione Gentilium* (1663) is one of the earliest studies of comparative religion.

Propagation of Deism. Although precise documentation is not available, deism was ripening between the time of Herbert and Blount, through such various and overlapping influences as humanism in general, the philosophy of Thomas Hobbes, the idealism of Harrington, the naturalistic biblical exegesis of Benedict de Spinoza and others, the corruption of the clergy, the widespread religious rationalism of the Cambridge Platonists and other Latitudinarians, the "sweet reasonableness" of John Locke, and the scientific approach of Isaac Newton—all of which were contributing to religious and political toleration. By the close of the seventeenth century, a new and memorable influence was added—the pervasive presence of the skepticism of Bayle. The first direct attack on British deism, Bishop Stillingfleet's *Letter to a Deist* (1677), acknowledges that owning to the being and providence of God but expressing "a mean esteem" of the Scriptures and the Christian religion had become a common theme.

Charles Blount. Beginning in 1679, Blount (1654–1693) was an indefatigable propagandist who, in the battle for freedom on all fronts, learned to resort to indirect methods in order to keep clear of the law. His *Summary Account of the Deist's Religion* (1693), which appeared posthumously during the same year in which he committed suicide, is his most outspoken work.

The year 1610 marks the last burning of heretics in England. Yet the matter of legal suppression of heterodox works is of vital importance in understanding and assessing the writings of the deists. The strict Press Licensing Act of 1662 was allowed to drop by 1695, but the blasphemy laws were still in effect. The ecclesiastical courts had the power to imprison heretics for a period of six months; in 1676 Lord Chief Justice Hale ruled that through common law the Court of King's Bench had jurisdiction over blasphemy, because Christianity is "parcel of the laws of England"; and finally, in 1698 a vicious statute was enacted under which any acknowledged Christian who made any accusation whatsoever against the Christian religion could be rendered incapable of holding office, of taking legal action, of purchasing land, and, if the blasphemy was repeated, would be made to suffer three years' imprisonment without bail. Such repressive measures drove the heterodox into various evasive techniques. Irony, innuendo, ridicule, raillery, allegorical interpretation of the Scriptures, fictitious analogies, frequent use of the dialogue and epistolary forms, the claim to be "Christian deists," pseudonymity, and anonymity not only successfully hampered legal prosecution but also made it difficult for modern historians to ascertain the genuine beliefs of the writers.

After Herbert and Blount, the foremost British deists were John Toland, Anthony Collins, and Matthew Tindal, and of somewhat less consequence, William Wollaston, Thomas Woolston, Thomas Chubb, Thomas Morgan, Henry St. John Bolingbroke, and Peter Annet. Others, such as the earl of Shaftesbury and Bernard Mandeville, have been labeled deists with some justification, and many others without justification, even including orthodox clergymen who emphasized natural religion, expressed scruples about specific biblical passages or voiced doubts about specific biblical miracles.

John Toland. Toland (1670–1722) produced in 1696 his most famous deistical work, the very title of which spells out its major thesis: *Christianity not Mysterious: Or a treatise Shewing That there is nothing in the Gospel Contrary to Reason, Nor above it: And that no Christian Doctrine can be properly call'd a Mystery.* The treatise is basically rationalistic and is reminiscent of Herbert's *De Veritate.* It opposes not only biblical mysteries, but also challenges the validity of the biblical canon and points out corruptions in biblical texts. It mocks the implicit faith of the Puritans and their bibliolatry, and severely censures the vested interests of priests of all denominations. Philosophically, Toland was in the tradition of Giordano Bruno, René Descartes, Spinoza, Gottfried Wilhelm Leibniz, and, to a lesser extent, of Locke. Eclectic and somewhat inconsistent in his opinions, he was a freethinker and a deist, a materialist and a pantheist (the first use of the word *pantheist* is found in 1705 in his *Socinianism truly stated*). With his great learning, Toland became a figure of international renown, for the first time bringing deism to a wide reading public through a profusion of bold controversial publications.

Anthony Collins. Collins (1676–1729) was a well-to-do and well-educated gentleman and magistrate. At the age of twenty-seven he earned the respect and friendship of Locke. Two early works, *An Essay concerning the Use of Reason* (1707) and *Priestcraft in Perfection* (1709), prepared the way for the more famous *Discourse of Free-Thinking* (1713), in which the right to think and publish freely is examined chiefly as it pertains to religion. Enthusiasm and superstition are considered more evil than atheism; modern science and the Protestant Reformation are presented as examples of courageous freethinking that have relieved many from age-old errors, including witchcraft; and priests are blamed for trivial quarreling among themselves over biblical interpretations and are held responsible for many corrupt texts. An impressive list of freethinkers is furnished from the ancient Greeks, Romans, and Hebrews; from the Church Fathers; and from the moderns, ranging from Michel Eyquem de Montaigne to John Tillotson and Locke.

Collins defended his style of writing in *A Discourse concerning Ridicule and Irony in Writing* (1727); his philosophical doctrine of necessitarianism (wherein he differs from the doctrine of free will espoused by most deists) is developed in a *Philosophical Inquiry concerning Human Liberty* (1715) and a *Dissertation on Liberty and Necessity* (1729); and his biblical criticism, mainly of the supposed fulfillment of Old Testament prophecies in the New Testament, in the *Discourse of the Grounds and Reasons of the Christian Religion* (1724) and the *Scheme of Literal Prophecy Considered* (1725). Collins is unquestionably the most readable and urbane of the British deists.

Matthew Tindal. A law fellow at All Souls College, Oxford, and advocate at Doctors' Commons, Tindal (1657?–1733) was the most learned of the British deists, as well as the most significant historically. His *Christianity as Old as the Creation: Or, The Gospel A Republication of the Religion of Nature* (1730), composed in dialogue form, was at once recognized as "The Deist's Bible," and elicited over 150 replies, the most famous of which is Bishop Joseph Butler's *The Analogy of Religion* (1736). Although a declared admirer of Locke, Tindal deduces the being and attributes of God by a priori reason. As man reasons downward from the knowledge of the attributes of God to knowledge of himself, the religion of nature, including all the moral precepts requisite for leading the life of virtue and achieving ultimate salvation, then follows. Scripture, replete with ambiguities, is not only unnecessary but is actually confusing to men of reason; and according to Tindal, all men of whatever education or status in life are capable of Right Reason. Some Old Testament heroes are inspected in detail and are found wanting in virtue; even some New Testament parables are subjected to critical comment. Tradition is repudiated as a basis for Christianity, since it can be used equally as the basis for any and all religions. The customary deistical castigation of priestcraft is combined with this repudiation of tradition. Tindal, a rationalist, always maintained the title of "Christian deist."

LESSER ENGLISH DEISTS. The remaining British deists, already named, each made some personal contribution to the movement, however small.

William Wollaston. A graduate of Sidney Sussex College, Cambridge, Wollaston (1660–1724) took holy orders, but through the unexpected inheritance of a large fortune he was able to devote himself to moral philosophy and general learning. His *The Religion of Nature Delineated* (1724) was well received by Queen Caroline the Illustrious, as well as by the public at large. It was attacked, however, by the American deist Benjamin Franklin and was subjected to ridicule by Lord Bolingbroke, the British deist. Unlike most deistical treatises, it contains no biblical criticism of any sort. Almost purely rationalistic, it has obvious affinities, in a simplified form, with Herbert of Cherbury's religious Common Notions. Man knows truth (that is, things as they are) by means of reason; vice, or the denial of things as they are, is a lie. To seek happiness is man's duty, because happiness, or the excess of pleasure over pain, is part of man's approach to truth. Man is by nature not fundamentally selfish; his search for truth must take into account the happiness of others. It is altogether likely that Bishop Butler, in *The Analogy of Religion,* had Wollaston at least partly in mind when he reproved extreme religious rationalism as "that idle and not very innocent employment of forming imaginary models of a world, and schemes of governing it."

Thomas Woolston. Woolston (1670–1731), fellow of Sidney Sussex College, Cambridge, and Christian divine, was a deist of another stamp. A disciple of Anthony Collins, who had spearheaded the assault on biblical prophecies, Woolston extended the assault to biblical miracles. Influenced by the writings of the Greek Church Father Origen, he interpreted Scripture allegorically, was subsequently deemed out of his mind by his adversaries and, as a result, in 1720 was deprived of his fellowship. In 1705 he first employed the allegorical method in *The Old Apology for the Truth of the Christian Religion against the Jews and Gentiles Revived,* and later published a series of anticlerical tracts against those who spurned it. But it was a series of six *Discourses On the Miracles of our Saviour, In View of the Present Contest between Infidels and Apostates* (1727–1729) that brought prosecution by the government, ending in 1729 with a conviction of blasphemy. Sentenced to a fine of £100, imprisonment for one year, and security for good behavior during life, he died in jail in 1731, unable to pay the fine. A fighter for freedom of thought and publication for all, Woolston ironically fell the victim of his own principles. The six *Discourses* take a colloquial and frequently witty dialogue form, with a fictitious learned Jewish rabbi presenting Woolston's queries concerning fifteen New Testament miracles. Woolston's madness may possibly have been real (in which case his sentence was truly infamous), but his tracts read more like the strong convictions of a strong mind. He was one of two of the leading British deists (the other being Annet) to suffer punishment by the government.

Thomas Chubb. An Arian and "Christian deist," Chubb (1679–1746) was a self-educated and humble artisan. Writing for the common people, Chubb was also able to hold his own with the educated upper classes, divines, and scholars. He mastered the widespread rationalism of the early eighteenth century and propagated its basic ideas through prolific publication, as is observable in such works as *A Discourse concerning Reason, With Regard to Religion and Divine Revelation* (1731) and *An Enquiry Into the Ground and Foundation of Religion. Wherein is shewn, that Religion is founded in Nature* (1740). Another approach is taken in *A Discourse on Miracles, Considered as evidence to prove the Divine Original of a Revelation* (1741), a work influenced by Toland and Woolston. Although he is skeptical of the Hebrew revelation, Chubb is never skeptical of the Christian, as is manifested in *The True Gospel of Jesus Christ asserted* (1732) and *The True Gospel of Jesus Christ Vindicated* (1739). In these two tracts, Chubb employs natural religion as proof of Christian religion. He defends the miraculous propagation of primitive Christianity against the aspersions of the deist Tindal. A believer in free will, Chubb was answered at considerable length by the eighteenth-century American theologian Jonathan Edwards in *A Careful and Strict Enquiry into The modern prevailing Notions of the Freedom of Will* (1754).

Thomas Morgan. A Welsh "Christian deist," divine, and medical doctor, Morgan (d. 1743) came from a poor family (as did Chubb and Annet). Morgan combined the religious Common Notions of Lord Herbert with some of the principles of historical biblical criticism found in the writings of Toland and Chubb. He opposed Chubb, however, on the question of free will. Morgan's chief contributions to the deistical controversy are to be found in *The Moral Philosopher, in a Dialogue between Philalethes, a Christian Deist, and Theophanes, a Christian Jew* (1737), and its two sequels. His general historical criticism of Scripture stresses the many ambiguities that permit many different interpretations of biblical texts by believers who truly attempt to understand their significance. All history, therefore, is simply probability, and infallibility is fostered by priestcraft for selfish purposes. Toleration, reasonableness, and freedom are necessary to combat superstition and persecution.

Henry St. John, Viscount Bolingbroke. Tory statesman, historian, deist, and wit, Bolingbroke (1678–1751) left his philosophical and religious compositions to be published posthumously in 1754 by David Mallet. Regarded by Dr. Johnson as a "blunderbuss" against religion and morality, Bolingbroke's *Works* were regarded by

Hume as unoriginal and feeble. In the twentieth century, Voltaire's long-alleged great indebtedness to Bolingbroke has been discredited, and the claim that Alexander Pope's *Essay on Man* was founded on Bolingbroke's *Fragments or Minutes of Essays* has been vigorously challenged. As a philosopher Bolingbroke is a rationalist, but a curiously inconsistent one. In one passage he states that only Right Reason can demonstrate the Being of Deity, yet in another, that only empiricism can prove the Being of Deity. Paradoxes abound: No universal revelation has ever been made, but modern religion can benefit by the study of primitive religions—for example, of China and Egypt. Like all the deists, Bolingbroke regarded the baneful influence of priestcraft as a major cause of the corruption of religious texts and religious traditions. With Bolingbroke, the course of British rationalistic deism, stemming from that of Lord Herbert in the middle of the seventeenth century, up to the middle of the eighteenth century, had been pretty well played out, but there was always opportunity for remorseless repetition and intensified publicity.

Peter Annet. Schoolmaster Annet (1693–1769) may be regarded as the last of the old-line deists. An outspoken freethinker, Annet advocated the freedom to divorce and, in a long series of tracts, attacked the Resurrection of Jesus and the character and conversion of St. Paul. His truculent assault on the credibility of all miracles in general, and those of the Old Testament in particular, carried on in *The Free Enquirer* of 1761, brought a governmental charge of blasphemous libel to which Annet pleaded guilty. The inhumane sentence against a man aged seventy included imprisonment for a month, two pilloryings, hard labor for a year, a fine, and bonds of security for good behavior during life. Annet survived this flagrant miscarriage of justice with its attendant humiliation and returned to schoolmastering until his death. The ascription to him of the authorship of the notorious *History of the Man after God's own Heart* (1761) has been disproved by modern scholarship. Although he contributed little fresh to the deistical movement, Annet, like Chubb, wrote directly to the people in their own language.

THE RATIONALISTIC CLIMATE OF OPINION. Little has been said so far about the rationalistic "orthodox" of the seventeenth and eighteenth centuries, those Latitudinarians, who were closely akin to the deists, except on the one crucial point of raising objections against Christian revelation. Nevertheless, both groups were united in a contemptuous rejection of Tertullian's dictum, *credo quia impossibile est*; in this respect, there was no warfare between reason and religion. In a 1670 defense of the orthodox rationalists, a Latitudinarian was succinctly defined as "a gentleman of a wide swallow."

Ralph Cudworth. Cudworth (1617–1688) may be taken as representative of the small but important band of Cambridge Platonists who sought to synthesize the spirit of Christianity with that of Greek philosophy by affirming that reason is spiritual as well as intellectual. Cudworth distinguishes between fundamental and nonfundamental religious doctrines: "I perswade myself, that no man shall ever be kept out of heaven, for not comprehending mysteries that were beyond the reach of his shallow understanding; if he had but an honest and good heart, that was ready to comply with Christ's commandments" (*A Sermon before the House of Commons, March 31, 1647.*) In *The True Intellectual System of the Universe* (1678), Cudworth argues cogently against fatalism. His posthumous *Treatise concerning Eternal and Immutable Morality* (1731) derives morality from natural law rather than from the positive precepts of revelation. Another member of the group, Benjamin Whichcote, states their position admirably: "If you would be religious, be rational in your religion." In short, the Cambridge Platonists stood for reason and moderation.

John Tillotson. Tillotson (1630–1694), archbishop of Canterbury and great champion of Anglicanism, employed rationalistic arguments against the Catholic use of tradition and authority. Observing that these same arguments could be turned against Christianity itself, the deists frequently seized upon Tillotson's authority and quoted his arguments in this new context. Collins went so far as to name him the man "whom all English freethinkers own as their head."

THE NEW SCIENCE. It might be expected that the New Science, which had made such great strides from Nicolas Copernicus to Newton, would have precipitated warfare between science and religion as it did in the nineteenth century, following Charles Darwin's *Origin of Species* (1859). But insofar as Britain was concerned, such was not the case, for Francis Bacon had enunciated the principle of a rigid dichotomy between science and religion that, on the whole, was adhered to during the seventeenth century. Indeed, science was more generally used as a bulwark for Christianity than the reverse—notably, in the case of the Latitudinarians. Newton himself was a student of Old Testament prophecies and believed in the Scriptures as inerrant guides.

The "skeptical chemist" Robert Boyle wrote orthodox religious tracts, one of which had the ancillary purpose of proving that by being "addicted" to experimental philosophy, a man is assisted rather than indisposed to being a good Christian. In 1691 Boyle endowed a lectureship for the proof of the Christian religion against the attacks of infidels. Great efforts were made to replace a priori reasoning with the argument from design. Richard Bentley, the first Boyle Lecturer, corresponded with Newton in preparing *The Folly of Atheism and what is now called Deism* (1692). William Derham's two lectures, *Physico-Theology* (1713) and *Astro-Theology* (1715), continued the effort. Nevertheless, the bulk of the Boyle Lectures, from the beginning to 1732, are almost purely rationalistic, as, for example, Clarke's *Demonstration of the Being and Attributes of God* (1704) and *Discourse concerning the Unchangeable Obligations of Natural Religion, and the Truth and Certainty of the Christian Religion* (1705). Collins gibed that until Clarke's "demonstration" of the existence of God, nobody had doubted the fact; and Franklin, in his autobiography, acknowledged that he became a deist after reading some of the Boyle Lectures. The New Science, in effect, had relatively little influence on the course of the deistical controversy, since neither side squarely faced the problem of the relationship of science to religion.

THE DECLINE AND FALL OF REASON. Rationalistic refutations of deism were prolific and formidable but achieved relatively little because they had so much in common with those of deism. Tindal had forced upon the apologists acceptance of the natural sufficiency of reason in theology. Thus, if deism was to be defeated, it had to be from a citadel other than that of an infallible and universal reason. One of the infrequent replies to Tindal's direct challenge, "Dare any say that God is an Arbitrary Being, and His laws not founded on the eternal reason of things?" (*Christianity as Old as the Creation*) was *The Case of Reason, Or Natural Religion Fairly and Fully Stated* (1731). Its pietistic author, William Law (1686–1761), better remembered for his *A Serious Call to a Devout and Holy Life* (1729) and as a forerunner of John Wesley (1703–1791), totally disavowed Right Reason in the areas of morality and religion, and argued for historical evidence and implicit faith.

Bishop Joseph Butler (1692–1752) offered in the *Rolls Sermons* (1726) an important revaluation of the authority of conscience and in the *Analogy of Religion* (1736) a matter-of-fact defense of Christianity; he sought to prove by analogy that all deistical objections against revelation were equally applicable to natural religion. The danger of this argument (which employed some of the methods of science and of Lockean empiricism) was that it might conceivably drive readers to become skeptical of both kinds of religion, to espouse atheism, or to retreat into implicit faith.

Bishop George Berkeley's (1685–1753) *Alciphron, or the Minute Philosopher* (1732), with its subtitle "Containing an Apology for the Christian religion against those who are called Freethinkers," is a brilliant series of polemical dialogues, but it contains little of his highly controversial and much misunderstood philosophical denial of abstract ideas and of "matter," for which Berkeley was frequently accused of being a skeptic. His *The Analyst* (1734), addressed to an "infidel mathematician" (presumably Edmund Halley), adopts the hazardous method of defending orthodoxy by asserting that the axioms of mathematics are as irrational and incomprehensible as the mysteries of Christianity.

Law and Butler had paved the way for antirationalistic assaults on deism, the former through faith, the latter through matter of fact. The argument for faith was implemented in *Christianity Not Founded on Argument* (1742) by Henry Dodwell ("the younger"), who had as little use for historical proofs as for intellectual proofs. According to Dodwell, the Boyle Lectures, like all rationalistic efforts, had only succeeded in spreading infidelity; external proofs have no real evidential value; probability reigns; so in the final analysis, there is no other way to approach religion, than to believe because you wish to believe. With Dodwell's appeal to emotionalism, the "enthusiasm" of Wesley was just around the corner.

Conyers Middleton (1683–1750), Anglican clergyman, and equally antirationalistic, pressed the historical argument against external proof of the validity of religious claims in his *Free Inquiry into the Miraculous Powers which are supposed to have subsisted in the Christian Church from the Earliest Ages through several successive Centuries* (1749). Professedly denying the supernatural powers associated with the growth of Catholicism, Middleton could scarcely have been unaware that the same arguments could also be used to attack Gospel miracles, and that there is in actuality no breach between sacred and profane history.

Fatal blows to the Age of Reason (as differentiated from the Age of Enlightenment) came simultaneously on two levels—intellectually, from Hume and emotionally, from Wesley. What might be termed the deistical side of Hume can most readily be seen in "Of Miracles" and "Of a Particular Providence and of a Future State" (1748), "The Natural History of Religion (1757), and *Dialogues concerning Natural Religion* (1779), the last of which comes to the purposefully lame conclusion "that the cause or causes of order in the universe probably bear some remote analogy to human intelligence." Natural religion, whether of the rationalistic or matter-of-fact variety, can lead only to doubt, uncertainty, and suspension of judgment. In reality, of course, Hume was no deist, but rather an antideist, a skeptic who destroyed the vulnerable a priori basis of deism.

At about the same time, Wesley attacked deism through "enthusiasm," the doctrine of continuous personal inspiration and inner conversion of the soul: "By grace are ye saved through faith." The fatal blows had been delivered; the Age of Reason had fallen and deism was dead. Or was it? The question will be taken up after brief considerations of deism in France, Germany, and America.

DEISM ON THE CONTINENT

The term *Enlightenment* was unknown in Britain during the eighteenth century, although its spirit was plainly manifest. When it did appear in the nineteenth century, it was employed in the derogatory sense of shallow and pretentious intellectualism coupled with unreasonable contempt for tradition and authority. In eighteenth-century France and Germany, on the contrary, full-fledged movements of *Éclaircissement* and *Aufklärung* were under way and were winning important intellectual and political victories. The present section will confine itself, insofar as possible, to religion and will deal with only a few predominant thinkers.

VOLTAIRE. Without stopping to investigate such sixteenth-century precursors as Jean Bodin, Rabelais, Pierre Charron, and Montaigne, or such seventeenth-century precursors as Descartes, Pierre Gassendi, Bernard Le Bovier de Fontenelle, and Bayle, it is well to proceed directly to François-Marie Arouet, universally known as Voltaire (1694–1778), the greatest of the French deists. Banishment to England (1726–1729) by order of the ancien régime put the already widely known poet, playwright, *philosophe* (and later, historian and novelist) into the scientific atmosphere of Newton, the philosophical and religious atmosphere of Locke and some of the earlier deists (Voltaire had already known Bolingbroke in France), and the literary neoclassical atmosphere of Jonathan Swift and Pope. Much impressed by the relatively tolerant attitudes of the English as compared to the rigid censorship of the ancien régime, Voltaire published in London in 1733 *Letters concerning the English Nation.* A surreptitiously arranged French version of 1734, *Lettres philosophiques,* speedily burned by the common hangman, was Voltaire's first bombshell against governmental and church tyranny. Thereafter, his remorseless battle cry of *Écrasez l'infâme!* was to be heard throughout a long life of polemic.

Although he consistently used the word *theist* in reference to himself, Voltaire was a deist in the tradition of the British deists, never attacking the existence of Deity but always the corruptions of church and priestcraft. As late as 1770, in a letter to Frederick the Great voicing strong disapproval of the avowed atheism of many of the *philosophes,* Voltaire repeated his conviction that if God did not exist, it would be necessary to invent him. The *Lettres philosophiques* eulogizes the Quakers as ideal deists for their freedom of thought and their freedom from dogmatism and clericism; attacks Blaise Pascal's Pyrrhonism, which leaves man only the alternative of implicit faith; praises the philosophical empiricism and religious reasonableness of Locke; and seeks to convert the scientists of France to the Newtonian system. Other writings on religion and morality, *Poème sur la loi naturelle* and *Poème sur le désastre de Lisbonne,* both of 1756, as well as the famous novel *Candide* (1759), assail the doctrine of philosophical optimism and, indeed, of divine benevolence. Believing as he did in a natural religion based on reason, Voltaire's chief onslaughts were upon dogmatism, superstition, fanaticism, and tyranny. His *Traité sur la tolérance* (1763), a classic denunciation of oppression, occasioned by the infamous Calas *affaire* of 1762, was followed in 1764 by the witty and effective *Dictionnaire philosophique.* Like most of the so-called deists, Voltaire was fundamentally a humanist seeking to better the condition of humankind.

JEAN-JACQUES ROUSSEAU. Novelist, political writer, deist, *philosophe* and anti-*philosophe,* Rousseau (1712–1778) remains one of the most inscrutable literary and philosophical geniuses of all time—a supreme individualist doting upon his own uniqueness. Born a Protestant, he became a Catholic, and finally a deist. His *Confessions* reveals that it was the reading of Voltaire's *Lettres philosophiques* that first incited him to study, to think, and to become a dedicated man of letters.

In touching solely upon Rousseau's role as a deist, it is fitting to examine the "Profession of Faith of a Savoyard Vicar," part of the fourth book of *Émile, ou de l'éducation* (1762). The first book had opened with the affirmation that everything is good as it comes from the Author of all things, but that everything degenerates in the hands of man. The fourth book seeks to develop and clarify this thesis, using, for prudential purposes, a vicar as spokesman. Jettisoning metaphysical proofs of God and subscribing to no strict system, the vicar simply feels God within himself, as a world governor of will, intelligence, power, and goodness. This beneficent deity is to be worshiped from the heart, and not through artificial forms. Yet it is paradoxically evident that while mere animals are happy, superior man is miserable. Why? asks the vicar. He replies to his own question that far from being a simple uncompounded creature, man is actually a being of contradictions. Self-love is natural to him, but a sense of justice or conscience or inner light is innate; he has the power to will things, but does not always exert this power to enforce his will.

Man, therefore, is the author of evil: Born good, he acquires vice. God, infinitely powerful, is infinitely good and supremely just. To emulate God in seeking justice is man's only source of happiness. In this respect, natural religion, learned through conscience, is sufficient. Christian revelation, on the one hand, is fraught with difficulty, mystery, obscurity, and dogma. Its majesty, sublimity, and beauty, on the other hand, bear witness to its divinity: It is not a manmade invention; indeed, it remained Rousseau's "pillow-book" throughout life. Rousseau, in brief, is a sentimental and primitivistic, rather than a "hard," rationalistic deist. Yet, in substance, his "soft" sentimental deism is actually not far removed from the religious Common Notions of Lord Herbert or even from Spinoza's Doctrines of Universal Faith.

Rousseau's device of using the Savoyard vicar as spokesman for his own deism was unsuccessful; *Émile* was publicly burned and an order was issued for the arrest of the author, who was forced to flee the country. Except for his much later autobiographical writings, *Émile* was Rousseau's last major work.

ATHEISM. Aside from Voltaire, who subscribed to "hard" deism, and Rousseau, who dispensed the "soft" variety, the *philosophes* were not deists at all. To them, deism was but the starting point on the road to atheism. Their militant atheism, as well as their dogmatic belief in constant and inevitable progress and the perfectibility of man, shocked Gibbon and Hume, and greatly disturbed both Voltaire and Rousseau. The names of Jean Le Rond d'Alembert and Denis Diderot (editors of the *Encyclopédie*), Baron d'Holbach (and his "atheistical club"), Claude-Adrien Helvétius, F. M. Grimm, Julien Offray de La Mettrie, …tienne Bonnot de Condillac, and Marquis de Condorcet can hardly be excluded from the list of atheistical *philosophes* or, at least, those well on the road to atheism. Deism in France, although considerably influenced by deism in England, was much more extreme both religiously and politically, simply because England had already made considerable social progress. In France, deism was part and parcel of the general move toward materialism, freedom of thought and publication, freedom from the tyranny of the ancien régime in the affairs of state and church, that ultimately exploded in the Revolution.

DEISM IN GERMANY. The course of the *Aufklärung* differed in major respects from the analogous movements in Britain and France, and developed later. Under the domination of the earlier Leibniz-Wolff philosophy, rational supernaturalism generally prevailed. After 1740 (the year of the accession of Frederick the Great, the first modern freethinking king), numerous translations of the British deists and of their orthodox refuters (as indicated in G. W. Alberti's *Briefe betreffend den allerneusten Zustand der Religion und der Wissenschaften in Gross-Brittannien* of 1752–1754, J. A. Trinius's *Freydenker-Lexicon* of 1759, and U. G. Thorschmid's *Freidenker-Bibliothek* of 1765–1767) introduced a new influence. Although the German *philosophes* were widely read, there was little of French radicalism in either their religious or political thinking. Among out-and-out deists (called *Freidenkers,* or Freethinkers), the names of Karl Bahrdt, Johann Eberhard, Johann Edelmann, and Hermann Samuel Reimarus must be mentioned.

Hermann Samuel Reimarus. The apology of Reimarus (1694–1768) for natural religion as opposed to atheism and materialism, written in 1755, was Englished in 1766 as *The Principal Truths of Natural Religion Defended and Illustrated.* His direct attacks on Christianity, through a painstaking study of New Testament texts, included "On the Object of Jesus and His Apostles" and "On the Story of the Resurrection," and were published posthumously (1774–1778) by Gotthold Ephraim Lessing as *Fragments of an Anonymous Work found at Wolfenbüttel.*

Gotthold Ephraim Lessing. Lessing (1729–1781), distinguished man of letters and author of the *Laokoon* (1766) and *Nathan the Wise* (1779), was a freethinker in the nonabusive sense of the term. He should probably not be classified as a typical deist, since he professed belief in natural revelation in his last publication, *The Education of the Human Race* (1780), and at the close of his life he is said to have privately acknowledged pantheistic beliefs. Lessing's lifelong friend Moses Mendelssohn (1729–1786), a Jewish freethinker, is customarily classified as a deist in the loose usage of the term.

Immanuel Kant. The case of Immanuel Kant (1724–1804), the greatest of the German philosophers, is highly instructive. Born and educated as a religious Pietist, he came under the influence of Newtonian physics and always remained interested in science. In theology his three most famous critiques, stimulated by the "mitigated scepticism" of Hume, agree with Hume in principle. The *Critique of Pure Reason* (1781) presses beyond Hume in criticizing proofs of the existence of God; the *Critique of Practical Reason* (1788) is concerned with moral experience in natural religion; and the *Critique of Judgement* (1790), in a sense, mediates between the first two. Kant's position as a "Christian deist," however, is best expressed in *Religion within the Limits of Reason Alone* (1792–1794). The limits of religion, basically naturalistic, are set in conscience or practical religion. Christianity is stripped of mystery and tradition and is treated as a purely moral religion—in fact, the only purely moral one; God is the moral Creator of the world, and it is the duty of the good man to worship him. Kant's transcendental philosophy is beyond the scope of this entry, but it is relevant to say that Kant was the leader of the *Aufklärung,* which he defined as the freeing of man from the self-imposed bondage of the mind, and proclaimed as its motto *sapere aude* ("dare to know").

DEISM IN THE UNITED STATES

The works of the British deists, as well as those of the defenders of the faith, were well known in American intellectual circles, commencing with the second quarter of the eighteenth century. In the latter half of the century, Voltaire's "hard" deism and, especially, Rousseau's "soft" deism were widely disseminated; but the atheism of the *philosophes* made little headway. The Great Awakening, triggered by the preaching of Edwards in 1734 and bolstered by the preaching of the English Methodist George Whitefield, militated against orthodox Puritanism and in favor of republicanism both in religion and politics, but the atmosphere of rationalism still prevailed. Before the Revolution, however, deism made relatively little progress. Among the intelligentsia at Harvard, nevertheless, the Dudleian Lectures were established in 1755 for the purpose of explicating natural religion. Alarms sounded by the orthodox that deism was sweeping the country were unjustified. However, the Treaty of Paris in 1763 and the French alliance at the time of the Revolution undeniably quickened the spread of radical Gallic ideas.

MAJOR AMERICAN DEISTS.

Benjamin Franklin. Franklin (1706–1790), man of letters, scientist, and diplomatist, as early as 1723 acknowledged himself a deist to intimate friends but circumspectly continued church attendance throughout life, thereby setting the conservative pattern followed by most of the leaders of the colonial and Revolutionary periods. In London in 1725 Franklin published his *Dissertation on Liberty and Necessity, Pleasure and Pain* in opposition to the free-will doctrine of the British deist Wollaston. However, Franklin shortly repudiated and suppressed this juvenile work. When he was about twenty-two, he drafted "Articles of Belief and Acts of Religion," a creed not unlike Lord Herbert of Cherbury's religious Common Notions and one that sustained him for life. Prudence and practicality characterize all of Franklin's publications and actions. *Poor Richard's Almanack* (1732–1757) is the essence of common sense, or how to get along in the world without unduly disturbing society; his list of virtues by no means coincides with the Christian virtues.

Thomas Jefferson. Framer of the Declaration of Independence, diplomatist, vice president and twice president of the United States, and member of the Episcopal Church, Jefferson (1743–1826) was in reality a deist, rationalist, and, above all, a humanitarian. He compiled but never published what later came to be known as *The Jefferson Bible, being The Life and Morals of Jesus Christ of Nazareth.* This little work, a cento of clippings from the Gospels of Matthew, Mark, Luke, and John pasted in a blankbook, extols Jesus as a man for his moral teachings, omits ambiguous and controversial passages, and, while rejecting many of the supernatural elements, presents the core of Christian morality and is genuinely religious in tone. Religion, for Jefferson as well as for Franklin, was essentially a utilitarian moral code.

George Washington. Washington (1732–1799), general and first president of the United States, was a deist of a similar stripe. Although he always maintained a church pew, he was one of the leading statesmen who advocated total separation of state and church and who saw to it that no reference to Christianity or even to Deity was made in the Constitution. In answer to a direct question from a Muslim potentate in Tripoli, Washington acquiesced in the declaration of Joel Barlow, then American consul in Algiers, that "the Government of the United States of America is not in any sense founded on the Christian religion."

Thomas Paine. Born in England, Paine (1737–1809) arrived in America in 1774, bearing a letter of introduction from Franklin. A political theorist, diplomatist, and man of letters, Paine was a deist, but not overtly until the publication in Paris of his *The Age of Reason: Being an Investigation of True and Fabulous Theology* (1794–1796). The first of its two books, intended to rescue deism from the reigning French atheism, is a more or less scientific assault upon revealed religion in general as being supererogatory to natural religion. The second book carries the attack directly to both the Old and New Testaments, arguing that the Bible is not the word of God and depicting Christianity as a species of atheism. Paine wrote vigorously and extensively and was outspoken in carrying his message to the common people, whose battles he had fought on the political, social, and economic fronts as well. In *The Age of Reason* the battleground was not new but was considerably enlarged from that of any earlier British deist. The work offended readers in France and shocked many in England and America who were laboring under the delusion that the deistical controversy was over and that orthodoxy had triumphed. Paine was rewarded for his efforts by banishment from England and by social obloquy in America. The patriot who throughout a long and turbulent career had accomplished so much for the new country, the man who had so vigorously combated atheism, was held to be an atheist, infidel, radical, and drunkard.

LESSER AMERICAN DEISTS. Paine was not the first acknowledged American deist, for the year 1784 produced *Reason the Only Oracle of Man, or a Compendious System of Natural Religion.* Its author, Ethan Allen (1738–1789), Revolutionary hero and leader of the Green Mountain Boys, had acquired his deism through early reading of the British deists. His book is flagrantly anticlerical and anti-Christian; he argues that a rationalistic universal religion of nature that provides the fundamentals of morality is all-sufficient and needs no supplementation. Both the Hebraic and the Christian testaments are subjected to ridicule. Like Paine, Allen was not so much an original thinker as a fearless propagandist.

Beginning in 1793, the blind ex-Baptist preacher Elihu Palmer (1764–1806) led a fiery deistical campaign from the lecture platform and by publication against the divine authority of the Bible. In 1794 he rushed to the defense of Paine's *Age of Reason* and in 1801–1802 published *Principles of Nature; or, a Development of the Moral Causes of Happiness and Misery among the Human Species.* From 1803 to 1805 he edited a weekly deistical paper, *Prospect; or, View of the Moral World.* Palmer also organized the Deistical Society of New York. With his many speeches and tracts designed to disseminate deism among the lower classes, Palmer was a most unusual deist, in that he was deliberately leading a popular crusade.

Philip Freneau (1752–1832), writer of patriotic verse, was also the American poet of the religion of nature and humanity, and his ideas were close to those of Paine. The very titles of such poems as "Belief and Unbelief: Humbly recommended to the serious consideration of creed makers," "On the Uniformity and Perfection of Nature," "On the Religion of Nature," tell their own story, without need of commentary.

DECLINE OF DEISM. During the eighteenth century, Puritanism in America had begun to crumble under the combined attacks of the Great Awakening, Methodism, and deism. "The Triumph of Infidelity" (1788), the poem by Timothy Dwight, orthodox president of Yale University, bears weak witness to the strength of deism. Shortly after 1800 deism became submerged in a revival of enthusiastic evangelism, particularly in the frontier areas, where intellectual attainments were hardly predominant. In New England, Unitarianism began making headway under the influence of Joseph Priestley, who in 1794 had immigrated from England. But elsewhere emotionalism, conservatism, reaction, and fideism were triumphant.

THE LEGACY OF DEISM

Historical deism, a term of many connotations, was essentially rationalism applied to religion, and as such was the counterpart to literary neoclassicism. Deism and neoclassicism flourished at approximately the same time, both stressing universality and shying away from particularity. In deism, this cardinal point meant that from the very beginning the Hebraic and Christian revelations were suspect, if not invariably attacked. Deism primarily put forth the view that the aim of religion is morality and that anything traditionally taught beyond morality is superfluous. The widely accepted distinction between constructive deism and critical deism, or, as it has also been put, deism before Locke and deism after Locke, or humanistic deism as opposed to scientific deism, will not survive the careful scrutiny and evaluation of leading deistical texts. Yet the prime position of Right Reason in deism did not prevent empiricism, in the form of scholarly examination of Scriptural texts and historicism, from assuming increasingly important roles. Edward Gibbon's purely naturalistic investigation into the early progress and establishment of the Christian religion in the famous (or infamous) fifteenth and sixteenth chapters of his *Decline and Fall of the Roman Empire* (Vol. I, 1776) was manifestly influenced, not only by the philosophical skepticism of Hume, but also by the somewhat crude historical investigations of a number of the deists themselves.

One general development of the deistical movement, therefore, was the rise of "the higher criticism": The Bible was no longer deemed sacrosanct, and its verbal inspiration no longer dogmatically assumed. A second development was the greatly intensified study of comparative religion. A third development was the rise of "the philosophy of religion," spurred on by Hume's demonstration that no matter of fact, including the existence of God, can be proved a priori.

In actuality, deism did not die; it did not even fade away, and it still exists in fact, though perhaps not in name, for those who say (with Voltaire) that there must be a God and those who say (with Rousseau) that they know there is a God. Nor was deism vanquished, as has so often been asserted, by the superior talents of its orthodox opponents, by the exhaustion of the subject, or by the incapacities of its protagonists: Certainly, among the English, at least, Toland, Collins, and Tindal were the intellectual equals of most of their adversaries. By and large, both orthodox and heterodox alike were rational theists of a somewhat naive variety. Charles Leslie's *Short and Easy Method with the Deists* of 1696 proved, in actuality, neither short nor easy. The deists were long subjected to the *odium theologicum,* and the historians of the movement have almost without exception downgraded or slandered them socially as well as intellectually since the time of John Leland in the mid-eighteenth century. Even the foremost rationalists of the nineteenth century, Mark Pattison and Leslie Stephen (the latter produced the most complete and erudite history to date) are condescending. Rarely have the achievements of deism been acknowledged and appreciated, and then only in passing, in brief comments from specialized monographs, articles, and encyclopedia entries. No really satisfactory, complete, impartial, and scholarly account of the significance of the movement has as yet appeared.

Deism had somewhat different effects in different countries, depending on the different national cultural situations. By the close of the eighteenth century in England, it seemed, superficially at least, to have disappeared or gone underground. Yet in 1790, when Burke triumphantly asked, "Who born within the last forty years has read one word of Collins and Toland, and Tindal, and Chubb, and Morgan, and that whole race who called themselves Freethinkers? Who now reads Bolingbroke? Who ever read him through?" he was historically mistaken and premature in his inference. For in the nineteenth century, radical publishers such as William Benbow, William Hone, and, most notably, Richard Carlile (1790–1843), all of whom were political as well as religious reformers, flooded the popular market with periodicals (for example, *The Deist; or Moral Philosopher,* 1819–1820), pamphlets, and cheap reprints and excerpts from freethinkers of all ages, including the whole range of the British deists, the skeptical Hume, Voltaire and Rousseau of France, and Paine and Palmer of America. The campaign was continued by others throughout the nineteenth century and survives in the present century on a higher intellectual level by affiliations with Unitarianism, Fabian socialism, and rationalist and humanistic societies, among others.

In France, the true deism of Voltaire and Rousseau was overwhelmed by the atheism of most of the *philosophes,* a doctrine which inevitably contributed to the upheaval of the French Revolution. The course of these eighteenth-century developments may be said to be paralleled today, on the one hand, by widespread atheism and, on the other, by the militant anticlericism of even many of the devout. In Germany, early intellectual deism was followed by both the fideism of Friedrich Heinrich Jacobi and a new post-Humean variety of rationalism which began with Kant and the romanticists of the following century.

In America, deism was long submerged by evangelism among the semiliterate masses and by Unitarianism among the well educated. An aggressive antireligionism resurged in the 1870s with Robert Ingersoll, "the great agnostic," and a host of followers, such as William Brann in Texas in the 1890s with his world-famous newspaper *Brann's Iconoclast.* Today, rationalist and humanistic societies and Unitarianism are omnipresent.

With few exceptions, deists in all countries have been interested in political and social reform, and with the passage of time it has become virtually impossible to isolate the purely religious aspects. Deism remains a symptom of revolt against orthodoxy and dogmatism.

By way of summary and possible oversimplification, deism is the individual's affirmation of his right to think for himself on all subjects and to communicate his thoughts to others for the general welfare. It is the affirmation of the principle of the oneness of humanity. It marks the rise of secularism and the beginning of modernity in theology. In this sense it is still viable, and although freethinking today claims a philosophical substratum different from the simple rationalism of the seventeenth and eighteenth centuries, it is akin in spirit to historical deism. The early rise of deism in all countries was strongly abetted by the growth of the spirit of toleration, and deism, in its turn, has strongly contributed to the continued growth and acceptance of toleration of other views. Perhaps, in the most universal sense, this is the major legacy of historical deism to the modern world.

Bibliography

USEFUL ANTHOLOGIES

Berlin, Isaiah, ed. *The Age of Enlightenment.* New York: New American Library, 1956.

Brinton, Crane, ed. *The Portable Age of Reason Reader.* New York: Viking Press, 1956.

Creed, John M., and John S. Boys Smith, eds. *Religious Thought in the Eighteenth Century.* Cambridge, U.K., 1934.

Fellows, Otis E., and Norman L. Torrey, eds. *The Age of Enlightenment.* New York: Crofts, 1942.

Gay, Peter, ed. *Deism: An Anthology.* Princeton, NJ: Van Nostrand, 1968.

Hampshire, Stuart, ed. *The Age of Reason: The 17th Century Philosophers.* Boston: Houghton Mifflin, 1956.

Torrey, Norman L., ed. *Les philosophes.* New York: Capricorn, 1960.

GENERAL HISTORIES

Betts, C. J. *Early Deism in France: From the So-Called "Déistes" of Lyon (1564) to Voltaire's "Lettres Philosophiques."* (1734). Boston: Martinus Nijhoff Publishers, 1984.

Byrne, Peter. *Natural Religion and the Nature of Religion: The Legacy of Deism.* London: Routledge, 1989.

Herrick, James. *The Radical Rhetoric of the English Deists: The Discourse of Skepticism, 1680–1750.* Columbia: University of South Carolina Press, 1997.

Lechler, Gotthard V. *Geschichte des englischen Deism.* Stuttgart, 1841.

Leland, John. *A View of the Principal Deistical Writers that have appeared in England in the last and present Century.* 3rd ed. 3 vols. London, 1754–1756. Early, voluminous, and vituperative apologetics.

Orr, John. *English Deism: Its Roots and Its Fruits.* Grand Rapids, MI: Eerdmans, 1934. Discursive, not too sound.

Sayous, Edouard. *Les déistes anglais et le christianisme, 1696–1738.* Paris, 1882.

Stephen, Leslie. *English Thought in the Eighteenth Century.* 2 vols. London, 1876; revised, 1902; paperback, New York, 1963. Vol. I is most scholarly study available but with a curious personal animus.

Walters, Kerry. *The American Deists: Voices of Reason and Dissent in the Early Republic.* Lawrence: University of Kansas Press, 1992.

GENERAL HISTORICAL BACKGROUND

Abbey, C. J., and J. H. Overton. *The English Church in the Eighteenth Century.* 2 vols. London, 1878.

Becker, Carl L. *The Heavenly City of the Eighteenth-Century Philosophers.* New Haven, CT: Yale University Press, 1932. Becker's brilliant paradox has dimmed over the years.

Bury, J. B. *A History of Freedom of Thought.* New York: Holt, 1913.

Cassirer, Ernst. *The Philosophy of the Enlightenment.* Princeton, NJ: Princeton University Press, 1951, and Boston, 1955.

Colie, R. L. *Light and Enlightenment: A Study of the Cambridge Platonists and the Dutch Arminians.* Cambridge, U.K.: Cambridge University Press, 1957.

Cragg, G. R. *From Puritanism to the Age of Reason.* Cambridge, U.K.: Cambridge University Press, 1950.

Farrar, A. S. *Critical History of Free Thought.* London: Murray, 1862.

Hall, Thomas C. *The Religious Background of American Culture.* Boston: Little Brown, 1930.

Havens, George R. *The Age of Ideas.* New York: Holt, 1955.

Hazard, Paul. *La crise de la conscience européenne.* 3 vols. Paris: Boivin, 1935.

Hazard, Paul. *La pensée européenne au XVIIIe siècle.* 3 vols. Paris, 1946. Both of Hazard's works are brilliantly comprehensive.

Humphreys, A. R. *The Augustan World.* London: Methuen, 1954. Useful survey.

Hunt, John. *Religious Thought in England from the Reformation to the End of the Last Century.* 3 vols. London: Strahan, 1870–1873.

Jordan, Wilbur K. *Development of Religious Toleration in England,* 4 vols. Cambridge, MA: Harvard University Press, 1932–1940. Highly important.

Lecky, W. E. M. *History of the Rise and Influence of the Spirit of Rationalism in Europe.* 2 vols. in one. London, 1910. Valuable.

Martin, Kingsley. *French Liberal Thought in the Eighteenth Century.* Boston, 1929.

M'Giffert, Arthur C. *Protestant Thought before Kant.* London, 1919.

Parrington, Vernon L. *Main Currents in American Thought.* 3 vols. New York: Harcourt Brace, 1927–1930.

Popkin, Richard, and Argo Vanderjagt, eds. *Scepticism and Irreligion in the Seventeenth and Eighteenth Centuries.* Leiden, Netherlands: Brill, 1993.

Robertson, J. M. *A History of Freethought in the Nineteenth Century.* 2 vols. London: Watts, 1929.

Robertson, J. M. *A Short History of Freethought Ancient and Modern.* 3rd ed. 2 vols. London, 1915. Both works are indispensable.

Smith, Preserved. *A History of Modern Culture.* 2 vols. New York, 1930–1934. Wide coverage.

Tulloch, John. *Rational Theology and Christian Philosophy in England in the Seventeenth Century.* 2 vols. Edinburgh: Blackwood, 1872.

Urwin, Kenneth. *A Century for Freedom.* London: Watts, 1946.

Willey, Basil. *The Eighteenth Century Background.* London: Chatto and Windus, 1940. Somewhat superficial.

SPECIALIZED STUDIES

Aldridge, Alfred O. "Shaftesbury and the Deist Manifesto." *Transactions of the American Philosophical Society,* n.s. 41 (2) (1951): 297–385.

Biddle, John. "Locke's Critique of Innate Principles and Toland's Deism." *Journal of the History of Ideas* 37 (1976): 411–422.

Boller, Paul F., Jr. *George Washington & Religion.* Dallas, TX: Southern Methodist University Press, 1963.

Bushell, Thomas. *The Sage of Salisbury: Thomas Chubb, 1679–1747.* New York: Philosophical Library, 1967.

Cole, G. D. H. *Richard Carlile.* London: Gollancz, 1943.

Courtines, Leo P. *Bayle's Relations with England and the English.* New York: Columbia University Press, 1938.

Cunliffe, Christopher, ed. *Joseph Butler's Moral and Religious Thought: Tercentenary Essays.* Oxford: Clarendon Press, 1992.

Daniel, Stephen. *John Toland: His Methods, Manners and Mind.* Montreal: McGill-Queen's University Press, 1984.

Fruchtman, Jack. *Thomas Paine and the Religion of Nature.* Baltimore: Johns Hopkins University Press, 1993.

Harkness, Douglas. *Bolingbroke: The Man and his Career.* London: Staples Press, 1957.

Hefelbower, S. G. *The Relation of John Locke to English Deism.* Chicago: University of Chicago Press, 1918.

Koch, G. Adolf. *Republican Religion: The American Revolution and the Cult of Reason.* New York: Holt, 1933. Indispensable.

Lovejoy, A. O. "The Parallel of Deism and Classicism." *Modern Philology* 29 (1932): 281–299. Important.

Luke, Hugh J., Jr. *Drams for the Vulgar: A Study of Some Radical Publishers and Publications of Early Nineteenth-Century London.* Unpublished PhD dissertation. University of Texas, 1963.

Merrill, Walter. *From Statesman to Philosopher: A Study in Bolingbroke's Deism.* New York: Philosophical Library, 1949.

Morais, Herbert M. *Deism in Eighteenth Century America.* New York: Columbia University Press, 1934.

Mossner, Ernest C. *Bishop Butler and the Age of Reason.* New York: Macmillan, 1936.

Noack, Ludwig. *Die Freidenker in der Religion.* 3 vols. Bern, 1853–1855.

Pattison, Mark. "Tendencies of Religious Thought in England." In *Essays and Reviews.* London, 1860.

Popkin, Richard H. "Scepticism in the Enlightenment." *Studies on Voltaire and the Eighteenth Century,* Geneva, xxiv/xxvii (1963): 1321–1345.

Redwood, J. "Charles Blount (1654–93), Deism, and English Free Thought." *Journal of the History of Ideas* 35 (1974): 490–498.

Russell, Bertrand. *Why I Am Not a Christian and Other Essays on Religion and Related Subjects,* edited by Paul Edwards. London: Allen and Unwin, 1957.

Salvatorelli, Luigi. *From Locke to Reitzenstein: The Historical Investigation of the Origins of Christianity.* Cambridge, MA, 1930.

Stromberg, Roland N. *Religious Liberalism in Eighteenth-Century England.* London: Oxford University Press, 1954. Sound survey.

Sullivan, Robert E. *John Toland and the Deist Controversy: A Study in Adaptations.* Cambridge, MA: Harvard University Press, 1982.

Tennant, F. R. *Miracle & Its Philosophical Presuppositions.* Cambridge, U.K.: Cambridge University Press, 1925.

Torrey, Norman L. *Voltaire and the English Deists.* New Haven, CT: Yale University Press, 1930. Indispensable.

Webb, Clement C. J. *Studies in the History of Natural Theology.* Oxford: Clarendon Press, 1915.

Winnett, A. R. "Were the Deists 'Deists'?" *Church Quarterly Review* 161 (1960): 70–77. Makes distinction between philosophical and historical deists.

Yolton, John W. *John Locke and the Way of Ideas.* London: Oxford University Press, 1956.

Ernest Campbell Mossner (1967)
Bibliography updated by Christian B. Miller (2005)

DELEUZE, GILLES
(1925–1995)

Gilles Deleuze, one of the most influential and prolific French philosophers of the postwar period, was born in Paris, and lived there, with a few exceptions, for the rest of his life. The son of a conservative, middle-class engineer, a veteran of World War I, Deleuze received his early elementary education in the French public school system. When the Germans invaded France, Deleuze's family was on vacation in Normandy, and he spent a year being schooled there. Deleuze traced his own initiation into literature and philosophy to his encounter with a teacher at Deauville named Pierre Halwachs (son of the sociologist Maurice Halwachs), who introduced him to writers such as André Gide and Charles Baudelaire. Early on, he later recalled, philosophical concepts struck him with the same force as literary characters, having their own autonomy and style, and he soon began to read philosophical works with the same animation and engagement as literary texts. During the occupation, Deleuze's older brother was arrested by the Nazis for resistance activities and deported; he died on the train to Auschwitz.

After the Liberation, Deleuze returned to Paris and undertook his khâgne (an intensive year of preparatory studies) at the prestigious Lycée Henri IV, and then studied the history of philosophy at the Sorbonne. He was taught by Jean Hippolyte and Ferdinand Alquié ("two professors I loved and admired enormously" [Deleuze, 1977, p. 12]), as well as Georges Canguilheim and Maurice de Gandillac, though like many of his peers he was as influenced by the writings of Jean-Paul Sartre as by the work of his academic mentors. He published his first book, *Empiricism and Subjectivity*, on David Hume, in 1953, when he was twenty-eight. In an era dominated by phenomenology and "the three Hs" (Hegel, Husserl, Heidegger), Deleuze's decision to write on empiricism and Hume was already a provocation, early evidence of the heterodox tendencies of his thought.

During the decade between 1953 and 1962—which he later referred to as "a hole in my life" (Deleuze 1990, p. 138)—Deleuze published little, moved among various teaching positions in Paris and the provinces, and contracted a recurring respiratory ailment that would plague him for the rest of his life. In 1956 he married Fanny (Denise Paul) Grandjouan, a French translator of D. H. Lawrence, with whom he would have two children. In 1962 his groundbreaking study *Nietzsche and Philosophy* was published to considerable acclaim, cementing Deleuze's reputation in academic circles. In the decade that followed, Deleuze more or less published a book per year, most of them devoted to the work of a particular philosopher or writer: Kant (1963), Proust (1964), Nietzsche (1965), Bergson (1966), Sade and Masoch (1967), Spinoza (1968), and later Kafka (1975), Francis Bacon (1981), Michel Foucault (1986), and Leibniz (1988). *Difference and Repetition*, his magnum opus, appeared in 1968, followed by *Logic of Sense* in 1969.

In the same year, he met Félix Guattari, a militant psychoanalyst, with whom he wrote a number of influential books, including the two volumes of *Capitalism and Schizophrenia* (1972, 1980), which were overtly political texts written in the wake of the ferment of May 1968. The first volume, *Anti-Oedipus*, was a best-seller in France, and thrust Deleuze into the limelight as a public intellectual. In 1969 Deleuze took up a teaching post at the experimental campus of the University of Paris VII (at Vincennes and, later, St. Denis), where he gave weekly seminars until his retirement in 1987. Like Kant, he traveled little, and devoted his time to teaching and writing: Paris was his Konigsberg, France was his Prussia. He shunned academic conferences and colloquia, insisting that the activity of thought took place primarily in writing, and not in dialogue and discussion. By 1993 his pulmonary illness had confined him severely, making it increasingly difficult to read or write; he took his own life on November 4, 1995.

Deleuze's writings were strongly grounded in the history of philosophy, but he read widely in contemporary science and mathematics, and was well known for his interactions with the various arts. His early work was in part a reaction against Hegel, and more generally against the then-dominant post-Kantian tradition in philosophy. Kant's genius, for Deleuze, was to have conceived of a purely *immanent* critique of reason—a critique that did not seek, within reason, "errors" produced by external causes, but rather "illusions" that arise internally from within reason itself by the illegitimate (transcendent) uses of the syntheses of consciousness. Deleuze characterized his own work as a philosophy of immanence, but argued that Kant himself had failed to fully realize the immanent ambitions of his critique, for at least two reasons.

First, Kant made the immanent field immanent *to* a transcendental subject, thereby reintroducing an element of transcendence, and reserving all power of synthesis to the activity of the subject. In his first book, *Empiricism and Subjectivity* (1953), on Hume, Deleuze pointed to an empiricist reversal of this relation: whereas Kant's question had been "How can the given be given to a subject?" Hume's question had been "How is the subject (human nature) constituted within the given?" Deleuze would later characterize his own position as a "transcendental empiricism": the determination of an impersonal and pre-individual transcendental field in which the subject is itself the result or product of *passive syntheses* (of the body, habit, desire, the unconscious). Just as there is no universal reason but only historically variable processes of "rationalization" (Max Weber), so there is no universal or transcendental subject, but only diverse and historically variable processes of "subjectivation." Deleuze summarized his empiricism in terms of two characteristics: the abstract does not explain, but must itself be explained; the aim of philosophy is not to rediscover the eternal or the universal, but to find the singular conditions under which something new is produced (creativity).

Second, Kant had simply presumed the existence of certain "facts" (knowledge, morality) and then sought their conditions of possibility in the transcendental. But already in 1789, Salomon Maimon, whose early critiques of Kant helped generate the post-Kantian tradition, had argued that Kant's critical project required a method of *genesis*—and not merely a method of conditioning—that would account for the production of knowledge, morality, and indeed reason itself—a method, in other words, that would be able to reach the conditions of *real* and not merely *possible* experience. Maimon found a solution to this problem in a principle of difference: Whereas identity is the condition of possibility of thought in general, it is *difference* that constitutes the genetic and productive principle of real thought.

These two Maimonian exigencies—the search for *the genetic conditions of real experience* and *the positing of a principle of difference*—reappear like a leitmotif in almost every one of Deleuze's early monographs. *Nietzsche and Philosophy* (1962), for instance, suggests that Nietzsche completed and inverted Kantianism by bringing critique to bear, not simply on false claims to knowledge or morality, but on true knowledge and true morality, and indeed on truth itself: "genealogy" constituted Nietzsche's genetic method, and the will to power was his principle of difference. *Bergsonism* (1966) argues that Bergson's concepts of duration, memory, and *élan vital* constitute the dimensions of the multiplicities of the real. Against the "major" post-Kantian tradition of Fichte, Schelling, and Hegel, Deleuze in effect posited his own "minor" post-Kantian trio of Maimon, Nietzsche, and Bergson. In rethinking the post-Kantian heritage, Deleuze would also retrieve the work of a well-known trio of pre-Kantian philosophers—Hume, Spinoza, and Leibniz—although from a decidedly post-Kantian viewpoint.

Deleuze's historical monographs were, in this sense, preliminary sketches for the great canvas of *Difference and Repetition* (1968), which marshaled these resources from the history of philosophy in an ambitious project to construct a metaphysics of difference. Normally, difference is conceived of as an empirical relation between two terms each of which has a prior identity of its own ("x is different from y"). In Deleuze, this primacy is inverted: identity persists, but it is now a secondary principle produced by a prior relation between differentials (*dx* rather than not-x). Difference is no longer an empirical relation but becomes a *transcendental* principle that constitutes the sufficient reason of empirical diversity as such (for example, it is the difference of potential in a cloud that constitutes the sufficient reason of the phenomenon of lightning). In Deleuze's ontology, the different is related to the different through difference itself, without any mediation. Although he was indebted to metaphysical thinkers such as Spinoza, Leibniz, and Bergson, Deleuze appropriated their respective systems of thought only by pushing them to their "differential" limit, purging them of the three great terminal points of traditional metaphysics (God, World, Self).

Deleuze's subsequent work was, to some degree, a working out of the metaphysics developed in *Difference and Repetition*. Deleuze considered himself a classical philosopher and conceived of his philosophy as a system—albeit an open and *heterogenetic* (non-totalizing) system—which might be summarized in terms of the following traditional rubrics, derived largely from Kant.

DIALECTICS (THEORY OF THE IDEA)

Difference and Repetition attempts to formulate a theory of Ideas (dialectics) based neither on an essential model of identity (Plato), nor a regulative model of unity (Kant), nor a dialectical model of contradiction (Hegel), but rather on a problematic and genetic model of difference. Ideas are what define the "essence" of a thing, but one cannot attain an Idea through the Socratic question "What is … ?" (which posits Ideas as transcendent and eternal), but rather through "minor" questions such as "Which one?" "Where?" "When?" "How?" "How many?" "In which case?" "From which viewpoint?"—all of which allow one to define the spatio-temporal coordinates of Ideas that are purely immanent and differential. The formal criteria Deleuze uses to define Ideas are largely derived from Leibniz and the model of the differential calculus, which provides a mathematical symbolism for the exploration of the real: things or beings are virtual and problematic multiplicities composed of singularities-events, which are prolonged in converging and diverging series, forming zones of indiscernibility where the multiplicities entering into perpetual becomings.

AESTHETICS (THEORY OF SENSATION)

What are the implications of a principle of difference for aesthetics? Kant had dissociated aesthetics into two halves: the theory of sensibility as the form of possible experience (the "Transcendental Aesthetic"), and the theory of art as a reflection on real experience (the "Critique of Aesthetic Judgment"). In Deleuze's work, these two halves of aesthetics are reunited: If the most general aim of art is to "produce a sensation," then the genetic principles of sensation are at the same time the principles of composition for works of art; conversely, it is works of art that are best capable of revealing these conditions of sensibility. Deleuze's writings on the various arts—including the cinema (*Cinema* I and II), literature (*Essays Critical and Clinical*), and painting (*Francis Bacon: The Logic of Sensation*)—must be read, not as works of criticism, but rather as philosophical explorations of this transcendental domain of sensibility. Deleuze locates the conditions of sensibility in an *intensive* conception of space and a *virtual* conception of time, which are necessarily actualized in a plurality of spaces and a complex rhythm of times (for instance, in the nonextended spaces and non-linear times of modern mathematics and physics).

ETHICS (THEORY OF AFFECTIVITY)

Deleuze has similarly developed a purely immanent conception of ethics, an "ethics without morality." If morality implies an appeal to transcendent values as criteria of judgment (as in Kant's moral law), ethics evaluates actions and intentions according to the immanent mode of existence they imply. One says or does this, thinks or feels that: What mode of existence does it imply? This is the link Deleuze establishes between Spinoza and Nietzsche, his two great precursors as philosophers of immanence: each of them argued, in his own manner, that there are things one cannot do or think except on the condition of being base or enslaved, unless one harbors a *ressentiment* against life (Nietzsche), unless one remains the slave of passive affections (Spinoza); and there are other things one cannot do or say except on the condition of being noble or free, unless one affirms life or attains active affections. The transcendent moral opposition (Good/Evil) is in this way replaced by an immanent ethical difference (good/bad). A bad or sickly life is an exhausted and degenerating mode of existence, one that judges life from the perspective of its sickness, which devalues life in the name of higher values. A good or healthy life, by contrast, is an overflowing or ascending mode of existence, capable of transforming itself depending on the forces it encounters, always opening up new possibilities of life, new becomings.

POLITICS (SOCIO-POLITICAL THEORY)

This immanent conception of ethics leads directly into Deleuze's political philosophy, which he developed most fully in the two volumes of *Capitalism and Schizophrenia*, with Félix Guattari. *Anti-Oedipus* (1972), under the guise of a critique of psychoanalysis, is in effect an immanent reworking of Kant's theory of desire in the *Critique of Practical Reason*. Since the capacities and affectivity (desire) of individuals is always effectuated within concrete socio-political "assemblages"—one of Deleuze's fundamental political concepts—the political philosophy presented in *A Thousand Plateaus* (1980) takes the form of a typology of social assemblages (primitive societies, the State, nomadic war machines, capitalism) that provide conceptual tools for analyzing the complex dimension of the actual situation: How are its mechanisms of power organized? What are the "lines of flight" that escape its integration? What new modes of existence does it make possible? What relations does it sustain between desire and power?

ANALYTICS (THEORY OF THE CONCEPT)

Finally, Deleuze's dialectic (the constitution of problems) leads directly into his analytic (concepts as cases of solution), which he presented in his late book *What Is Philosophy?* (1991, co-authored with Guattari). Deleuze defines philosophy as the art of creating concepts, as knowledge through pure concepts. But for Deleuze, the highest concepts are not a priori universals applicable to objects of possible experience (categories), but singularities that correspond to the structures of real experience. Concepts are self-referential—they posit their object in being posited—and are defined in terms of their consistency of their components (endo-consistency) and their relation to other concepts (exo-consistency). Deleuze's analytic should be evaluated critically in relation to competing theories of the concept (Frege, Russell), which often make use of scientific functions or logical propositions as their model. His analysis of the concepts of "sadism" and "masochism" in his 1967 book *Coldness and Cruelty* (and his concomitant critique of the notion of "sado-masochism") provides an excellent case study of his differential approach to concepts.

See also Hegel, Georg Wilhelm Friedrich; Hume, David; Kant, Immanuel; Nietzsche, Friedrich.

Bibliography

WORKS BY GILLES DELEUZE

Empiricism and Subjectivity: An Essay on Hume's Theory of Human Nature (1953). Translated by Constantin V. Boundas. New York: Columbia University Press, 1991.

Nietzsche and Philosophy (1962). Translated by Hugh Tomlinson. New York: Columbia University Press, 1983.

Kant's Critical Philosophy (1963). Translated by Hugh Tomlinson and Barbara Habberjam. Minneapolis: University of Minnesota Press, 1984.

Proust and Signs (1964). Translated by Richard Howard. London: Athlone Press, 2000.

Bergsonism (1966). Translated by Hugh Tomlinson and Barbara Habberjam. Minneapolis: University of Minnesota Press, 1988.

Masochism: Coldness and Cruelty (1967). Translated by Jean McNeil. New York: Zone Books, 1989.

Difference and Repetition (1968). Translated by Paul Patton. New York: Columbia University Press, 1994.

Expressionism in Philosophy: Spinoza (1968). Translated by Martin Joughin. New York: Zone Books, 1990.

The Logic of Sense (1969). Translated by Mark Lester, with Charles Stivale; edited by Constantin V. Boundas. New York: Columbia University Press, 1990.

Capitalism and Schizophrenia. With Félix Guattari. Vol. 1: *Anti-Oedipus* (1972). Translated by Robert Hurley, Mark Seem, and Helen Lane. Vol. 2: *A Thousand Plateaus* (1980). Translated by Brian Massumi. Minneapolis: University of Minnesota Press, 1983, 1987.

Kafka: Toward a Minor Literature (1975). With Félix Guattari. Translated by Sean Hand. Minneapolis: University of Minnesota Press, 1986.

Dialogues (1977). With Claire Parnet. Translated by Hugh Tomlinson and Barbara Habberjam. New York: Columbia University Press, 1987.

Francis Bacon: The Logic of Sensation (1981). Translated by Daniel W. Smith. London: Athlone Press, 2003.

Cinema. Vol. 1: *The Movement-Image* (1983). Vol. 2: *The Time-Image* (1985). Translated by Hugh Tomlinson, Barbara Habberjam, and Robert Galeta. Minneapolis: University of Minnesota Press, 1986, 1989.

Foucault (1986). Translated by Sean Hand. Minneapolis: University of Minnesota Press, 1986.

The Fold: Leibniz and the Baroque (1988). Translated by Tom Conley. Minneapolis: University of Minnesota Press, 1988.

Negotiations, 1972–1990 (1990). Translated by Martin Joughin. New York: Columbia University Press, 1995.

What Is Philosophy? (1991). With Félix Guattari. Translated by Hugh Tomlinson and Graham Burchell. New York: Columbia University Press, 1991.

Essays Critical and Clinical. (1993). Translated by Daniel W. Smith and Michael A. Greco. Minneapolis: University of Minnesota Press, 1997.

Daniel W. Smith (2005)

DEL VECCHIO, GIORGIO

(1878–1970)

Giorgio Del Vecchio, the Italian legal philosopher, was born in Bologna, the son of the economist Giulio Salvatore Del Vecchio. He studied in Italy and Germany and taught in Ferrara, Sassari, Messina, Bologna, and at Rome, where he was a professor from 1920, rector of the university from 1925 to 1927, and dean of the faculty of law from 1930 to 1938. He was dismissed by the fascists in 1938 because of his Jewish background. He resumed teaching in 1944 but was dismissed again in 1945, this time as a former fascist; he taught again from 1947 to 1953. He was named professor emeritus in 1955. Del Vecchio founded the *Rivista internazionale di filosofia del diritto* in 1921 and was its editor; he founded the Istituto di Filosofia del Diritto of the University of Rome in 1933 and the Società Italiana di Filosofia del Diritto in 1936.

Del Vecchio was influential in turning Italian legal thought from nineteenth-century positivism. His own position has been described as neo-Kantian idealism and as humanist ethical idealism. According to Del Vecchio, the thinking subject is necessarily conscious of the *other,* not merely as object, but as itself a subject. Hence, mutual recognition and respect are necessary, and it is possible to deduce for the mutual relations of subjects not merely a logical form but also an ideal content of justice based on respect for personality. Law is the objective coordination of possible actions between subjects according to an ethical principle, which in its highest expression is the principle of justice. Psychologically, the idea of justice is a necessary aspect of consciousness, found in rudimentary form even among animals. Historically, the idea has been realized with varying degrees of positivity in human societies, and continual effort is needed to realize it in the changing specific conditions of life. There are instances of "involution" (regression), but history on the whole shows a progressive evolution toward the understanding and realization of justice. These main ideas, stated in Del Vecchio's early writings, were developed with a wealth of historical learning in his *Lezioni di filosofia del diritto* and *La giustizia*; in other writings he applied them to particular problems of legal and political philosophy.

Del Vecchio, like other veterans of World War I, joined the fascist movement when it arose because he saw it as a defense against Bolshevism, and it is unjust to consider him a representative of fascist philosophy. For a time he did hope, mistakenly, that the fascist "strong state" might realize the "ethical state" that, by harmonizing individual freedoms, would enhance individual personality. Throughout the fascist period, however, Del Vecchio's fundamental teaching was unchanged; and he continued to assert the validity of natural law and to defend individual freedom against the statolatry of official fascist doctrine.

See also Continental Philosophy; Idealism; Justice; Legal Positivism; Political Philosophy, History of; Positivism.

Bibliography

PRIMARY WORKS

Presupposti, concetto e principio del diritto (The formal bases of law). Translated by John Lisle. New York: Macmillan, 1921.

La giustizia, 3rd ed. Rome: Editrice Studium, 1946.

Lezioni di filosofia del diritto, 6th ed. Milan: Giuffrè, 1948.

Sui principi generali del diritto (General principles of law). Translated by Felix Forte. Boston: Boston University Press, 1956.

Studi sullo stato. Milan, 1958.

Studi su la guerra e la pace. Milan, 1959.

Contributi alla storia del pensiero giuridico e filosofico. Milan: Giuffrè, 1963.

Humanité et unité de droit. Paris, 1963.

Man and Nature; Selected Essays. Edited by Ralph A. Newman; translated by A. H. Campbell. Notre Dame, IN: University of Notre Dame Press, 1969.

SECONDARY WORKS

Orecchia, Rinaldo. *Bibliografia di Giorgio Del Vecchio,* 2nd ed. Bologna, 1949.

Vela, Luis. *El Derecho Natural en Giorgio Del Vecchio.* Rome: Libreria editrice dell'Università Gregoriana, 1965.

Vidal, Enrico. *La filosofia giuridica di Giorgio Del Vecchio.* Milan: Giuffrè, 1951.

A. H. Campbell (1967)
Bibliography updated by Philip Reed (2005)

DEMIURGE

Demiurge, an anglicized form of δημιουργός, the ordinary Greek word for a workman, craftsman, or artificer, is commonly used in Greek literature from Homer onward. In Homer it is applied to heralds, soothsayers, and physicians as well as to manual workers; but in later Greek it primarily means a craftsman or maker, such as a carpenter or a smith. Its importance in the history of philosophy derives almost entirely from Plato's *Timaeus*, in which a Demiurge, or Craftsman, is represented as ordering and arranging the physical world and bringing it as far as possible into conformity with the best and most rational pattern. In two other places (*Republic* 530A and *Sophist* 265C) Plato uses the word δημιουργος, or the corresponding verb, in connection with divine creation; and it occurs in one passage in Xenophon's Socratic discourses (*Memorabilia* 1.4.9), but these are all casual and isolated references. For our understanding of Plato's conception of creation we must rely almost exclusively on the *Timaeus.*

The *Timaeus* is, in fact, Plato's only substantial essay in physical theory and cosmology. There is disagreement about the date of the dialogue and about its place in the chronological order of Plato's writings; but it is generally agreed to be later than the great group of middle dialogues, from the *Phaedo* and *Symposium* to the *Republic* and *Phaedrus,* in which Plato expounds his most characteristic metaphysical and ontological doctrines. The substance of these doctrines is repeated and underlined in the *Timaeus* itself, which makes a sharp division between the eternal, transcendent, intelligible, unchanging world of true being or reality and the temporal, phenomenal, sensible, unstable world of mere becoming. It was this very contrast between the world of Forms and the world of sense that had led Plato to neglect physical research and speculation; and when he does turn to this subject in the *Timaeus,* he repeatedly insists that even his own best efforts in this field cannot produce more than an εἰκὼς μυθός—a "likely tale"—falling far short of the certainty and exactness that can be sought in mathematics and pure philosophy. He speaks of the whole doctrine of the *Timaeus* in the provisional, tentative manner in which he presents the eschatological myths of the *Gorgias, Phaedo, Republic,* and *Phaedrus.*

Against this background it may appear surprising that Plato ventured on these topics at all. His motives become plainer if we remember his own comments in the *Phaedo* (97C–99D) on the cosmology of Anaxagoras. Socrates first praises Anaxagoras for holding that νοῦς—Intelligence or Reason—ordered and arranged the world, imposing a rational plan on a preexisting chaos. He then complains that Anaxagoras did not pursue this line of thought to its proper conclusion: He uses Reason as a mere deus ex machina to explain the origin of the cosmic process as a whole but does not give detailed teleological explanations of particular things and events, showing that everything is arranged for the best. Anaxagoras resorts instead to the purely physical explanations that had been used by his Ionian predecessors, which is like trying to explain why Socrates does not escape from prison wholly in terms of bones and sinews, without reference to intelligence, intention, motive, and morality. Aristotle makes a similar comment in *Metaphysics* I,3: Anaxagoras stands out among his contemporaries and predecessors "like a sober man among drunkards," but he does not make proper use of his concept of cosmic νοῦς.

The *Timaeus* is Plato's attempt to carry out the program of rationalist cosmology that Anaxagoras had promised but had failed to fulfill. The Demiurge is portrayed as the agent who turns the initial chaos into a cosmos. Like a human craftsman, he arranges existing materials and does not create them. The conception of creation ex nihilo is foreign to the whole tradition of Greek thought. The Demiurge shapes his materials to conform as much as possible to the eternal intelligible model of the Forms. First, he makes other gods, the world soul that the cosmos requires as its motive principle, and the immortal part of the human soul. The created gods then complete the work by making physical things, including human bodies. The Demiurge's success is necessarily limited: the Reason that constitutes his pattern is opposed by a recalcitrant Necessity (ἀνάγκη) that hinders his work in something like the way in which a human craftsman may be frustrated by intractable materials—and no material is perfectly tractable. This obstacle to a faultless achievement by the Demiurge is also the main reason why Plato cannot hope to give more than a "likely tale" of the Demiurge's work.

It has been widely believed, from ancient times to the present day, that the Demiurge is a mythical figure and that Plato did not believe in the literal existence of such a creator-god. He is a personification of the Reason whose requirements he is represented as trying to embody in the nature of the cosmos. Even if he is literally meant, he must still be sharply contrasted with the creator-god of the Judeo-Christian tradition, not only because he is not in that sense a creator, but also because he is in no sense an object of worship.

It is more difficult to decide whether the process of creation is also mythical; whether Plato believed that the imposition of order on the physical world was a definite event that took place at some time in the past, or whether the narrative of the *Timaeus* is a presentation in chronological form of Plato's views about the relative value and ontological priority of the various elements in the universe. According to this latter view, the story that bodies were created after souls would be a pictorial way of marking the inferiority of the body to the soul. Aristotle reports (*De Caelo* 279b33) that this was the tradition in Plato's Academy. The chronological picture is said to be used only for purposes of exposition, like a figure in geometry. Aristotle himself took the chronology literally, and he was followed in this by Plutarch; but the ancient authorities were nearly all on the other side.

Most modern scholars have disagreed with Aristotle, but he has had some notable supporters; and the question is still being debated. In support of the usual interpretation one may quote the parallel case of the *Republic,* where the building and dissolution of the ideal community is a pictorial means of presenting a logical analysis in chronological terms. Defenders of the opposite view point out that the word γέγονεν ("it came into being") gives an emphatic answer to the crucial question "Has the cosmos always been, or has it come to be, starting from some beginning?" (28B). However, the imagery of the *Republic* is equally emphatic. Once a man has chosen to represent one thing by painting a picture of another, the fact that he uses firm brush strokes and bright colors does not destroy its claims to be a picture.

The concept of the Demiurge was taken over by the Neoplatonists and by some Gnostic writers. To the Gnostics he was the evil lord of the lower powers, creator of the despised material world, and entirely separate from the supreme God. Their parody of the Demiurge as a clumsy imitator is blended with hostile satire of the Old Testament creator-God. Plotinus protested against their conception of the Demiurge as a source of positive evil in the world.

There is no clear case of any notable modern thinker whose teaching has been closely or directly influenced by the concept of the Demiurge, although there are hints of a similar idea in J. S. Mill's essay "Theism," where the word *Demiurgos* is applied to a God whose creative power is limited by the nature of his materials.

See also Anaxagoras of Clazomenae; Aristotle; Gnosticism; Greek Academy; Homer; Mill, John Stuart; Neoplatonism; Plato; Xenophon.

Bibliography

Archer-Hind, R. D. *The Timaeus of Plato.* London and New York, 1888. Text, translation, introduction, and notes.

Bury, R. G. *Plato, Timaeus, Critias, Clitopho, Menexenus, Epistulae.* Loeb Classical Library. London and New York, 1929. Text and translation.

Cornford, Francis M. *Plato's Cosmology.* London: K. Paul, Trench, Trubner, 1937. Translation of the *Timaeus,* with a running commentary.

Crombie, I. M. *An Examination of Plato's Doctrines.* London and New York: Humanities Press, 1963. Vol. II, *Plato on Knowledge and Reality,* Ch. 2.

Grube, G. M. A. *Plato's Thought.* London: Methuen, 1935. Ch. 5.

Hackforth, R. "Plato's Cosmogony." *Classical Quarterly,* n.s., 9 (1959): 17–22.

Taylor, A. E. *A Commentary on Plato's Timaeus.* Oxford: Clarendon Press, 1928. Prolegomena and notes.

Renford Bambrough (1967)

DEMOCRACY

Democracy is difficult to define, not only because it is vague, like so many political terms, but more importantly, because what one person would regard as a paradigm case another would deny was a democracy at all. The word has acquired a high emotive charge in the last hundred years; it has become good tactics to apply it to one's own favored type of regime and to deny it to rivals. The most diverse systems have been claimed as democracies of one sort or another, and the word has been competitively redefined, to match changes in extension by appropriate changes in intention. However, there is still this much agreement: Democracy consists in "government by the people" or "popular self-government." As such, it would still be universally distinguished from, say, a despotism that made no pretense of popular participation—the despotism of Genghis Khan or of Louis XIV, for instance—or from a theocracy, like the Vatican. There remains plenty of room for disagreement, however, about the conditions under which the people can properly be said to rule itself.

In the first place, what is "the people"? In ancient Greece, the *demos* was the poorer people; democracy meant rule of the poor over the rich. This is still the usage of those who identify the people with the proletariat and democracy with the rule of the working class. The word *people,* however, is often used to differentiate the subject mass from the ruling elite, as, for instance, when John Locke speaks of a tyrannical government putting itself into a state of war with the people. In this sense, "the people" necessarily means the ruled. Can the people, however, be said *to rule itself* in the same sense as it is said to be ruled by monarchs, oligarchs, and priests? To rule is, generally, to prescribe conduct for someone else. There is a sense, it is true, in which moralists speak of ruling oneself, when by a kind of metaphor they speak of reason governing the passions. Again, a former colony becomes self-governing when its people is no longer ruled by outsiders; but this is not inconsistent with its still being ruled by *native* masters.

The usual paradigm of a people governing itself is the direct democracy of ancient Athens. Admittedly, citizenship was a hereditary privilege, excluding slaves and metics, and it is very doubtful whether, without this limitation, the citizen body would have been small enough for it to have operated as it did. Aside from this, however, the Athenian people governed itself in the sense that every individual could participate personally in policy decisions by discussion and voting, in a face-to-face situation. Athenian procedures are held to have been democratic in the sense that everyone was supposed to have an equal opportunity to state a case and influence decisions, even if, in some cases, individuals had ultimately to accept decisions that they had previously resisted. So today, in a similar sense, if a school or a department is said to be democratically run, we should expect its head to consult his staff on important issues and to concur in decisions to which he himself is opposed when the weight of opinion is against him. Self-government for a small group consists in general participation in the deliberative process, in which each person's voice carries a weight appropriate not to his status but to the merits, in the judgment of others, of what he has to say. If, despite continuing disagreement, a decision is essential, then it must be arrived at by majority vote. For it is not consistent with equal participation in decision making for any one individual to be privileged to say in advance that regardless of the distribution of opinions, his own or that of his group must prevail. That privilege excluded, decisions may be reached by lot or by vote; and if by vote, the opinion of either the lesser or the greater number may prevail. Deciding by lot was in fact used in Athens to fill certain public offices; it is a way of giving everyone an equal chance where advantages or privileges cannot be equally and simultaneously enjoyed; but to decide policy by lot would make nonsense of the procedure of public discussion, which is as integral to the democratic process as the idea of equality. The same would apply to a rule whereby whatever opinion received the fewest votes would prevail; for what point would there be in persuasion if it had no effect on the outcome or, still worse, if it actually reduced the chance of one's view being implemented? If a democratic decision is thought of, then, as the result of a fair confrontation of opinions, it must, at best, be generally agreed upon, and at worst, agreed upon by the majority.

CONDITIONS OF POLITICAL DEMOCRACY

Obviously, the conditions of face-to-face democracy, with direct participation, cannot be fulfilled within the political structure of modern states, both because of the size of their populations and because of the specialized knowledge needed to govern them. So although everyone may agree on what makes a small group democratic, when it comes to applying the concept to mass organizations, there is plenty of room for different interpretations of the principles to be applied and of the way to realize them under these very different conditions. Democracy now becomes representative government, that is, government by persons whom the people elect and thereby authorize to govern them.

Election and *representation* are themselves complex notions, however. In one sense, to be representative of a group may mean no more than to possess salient characteristics common to and distinctive of most of its members. In another, quasi-legal sense, one person may be said to represent another if, according to some code of rules, the consequences attached to an act of the representative are precisely those that would be attached to the act had it been performed by the principal himself; the representative can, in this case, *commit* the represented. In yet a third sense, one may represent another by looking after his interests, with or without his authorization (for example, the representation of infants in law). Now, democratic representation need not imply representation in the first sense, that of resemblance. Since an elected member of a legislature is taken to represent those who voted against as much as those who voted for him, he need not resemble those he represents, even in his opinions. Nor does he commit them as if they themselves had acted; the fact of their having legal duties does not depend on the fiction that, if their representative votes for a law, they have personally agreed to it. Their legal duties remain even if their representative voted against it. Nor must we necessarily accept moral responsibility for what is done by those who politically represent us, for in voting against them, we may have done the only thing open to us to disavow them.

Political representation is closer to the third sense of the term—the representation of interests; a democratic representative is usually thought to have the duty to watch over either the interests of his constituents or, as a member of an assembly representing the whole people, the interests of the people at large. Nevertheless, he could still represent the interests of a group of people without their having had any part in choosing him. Some members of colonial legislatures in Africa used to be nominated by the governor to represent the interests of the unenfranchised native population. Precisely analogous, from the standpoint of the liberal democrat, is the case of a single-party system, where the ruling party invites the electors to endorse the candidate it has chosen to represent them. No matter how zealously the representative watched their interests, this would not count as democratic representation, precisely because the electors had had no part in selecting him. This view of democracy, therefore, is not compatible with tutelage; it implies the possibility not only of rejecting but also of freely proposing candidates, if none put forward by others is acceptable. Choosing and rejecting representatives is, indeed, the central act of participation by the citizens of a mass democracy, from which any effectiveness that they might have in other respects derives.

Closely related to election is the notion of the *responsibility* of the democratic representative. This means, in practice, that representatives must submit themselves periodically for reelection and, as a corollary, that they must be prepared to justify their actions and to attend to the experience and needs of their constituents, whose good will they must retain so long as they wish to remain in office.

DEMOCRACY AND POPULAR SOVEREIGNTY

It is often said that in a democracy the people's will is sovereign. But can the people be said to have a will? Opinions are divided on most things; there may be ignorance and apathy; on many questions only sectionally interested groups may have any clear opinions at all. Small groups, like committees, may reach agreed policies to which everyone feels committed; or in time of grave national danger, whole nations may discover a collective devotion to a single objective, overriding all conflicts of interests. However, although it might be intelligible to speak of a collective will in such cases, they are too limited or too rare to provide a framework for a general theory of democratic government. Such cases apart, one may speak of action, will, or decision in relation to collectivities only if their collective acts can be identified by some more or less formal procedure or if there are rules authorizing some identifiable individual to act *in the name of* the whole group. Thus, "Parliament has decided …" presupposes rules determining who are members of Parliament, defining their roles, and giving their several actions a collective significance and validity as "legislation." Are there analogous procedures, by virtue of which the people can be said to act or to express a will? Only by voting and by applying the majority principle in elections and referenda. And of course, applied to any particular collection of individual votes, different systems of voting or different arrangements of constituency boundaries can yield quite different results, each in its own rule context expressing "the people's will." Nevertheless, some people consider a system democratic to the extent that it approximates to government by referendum, though they would agree that this could not work as a day-to-day procedure. The doctrine that a government ought not to initiate policy changes without putting them to a vote in a general election (or, in a stronger form, that having done so, it is entitled—or obliged—to implement them forthwith) is a practical application of the popular-sovereignty view of democracy. A possible corollary sometimes derived from this last view is that it is undemocratic to oppose or impede any government acting with the people's mandate. Moreover, since the people is sovereign, the traditionally important safeguards against the abuse of power become otiose; for, in Jean-Jacques Rousseau's words, "the sovereign, being formed wholly of the individuals who compose it, neither has nor can have any interest contrary to theirs." Popular-sovereignty theory is always, therefore, on the brink of totalitarianism, since—as the French Jacobin party showed—it is only a short step from proclaiming the sovereignty of the people to claiming the unlimited authority of its elected representatives, to proscribing opposition, and to denying individuals any rights other than those which the government with majority support deems fit.

There is, of course, another view, closer to the tradition of liberal individualism, which sees democracy as a way of safeguarding and reconciling individual and group interests. For James Madison, the virtue of the new Constitution of the United States was that it permitted no faction, not even a majority, to deprive minorities of their natural rights, since it demanded the concurrence in action of independent authorities. The constitution was designed to balance diverse interests against one another, so that none might ever become a dominant and entrenched majority. More recent pluralistic accounts of democracy (or of what R. A. Dahl calls "polyarchy"), while more sophisticated, follow a similar approach. To be democratic, policy-making agencies must be sensitive to a wide range of pressures, so that no interest significantly affected by a decision will be left out of account. Popular participation consists not merely in voting, but also in wide consultation with interest groups and in the whole process of public criticism and governmental self-justification. Democracy, according to this view, requires the dispersal, not the concentration, of power; every voter has his quantum, making him worth the attention of those who want to govern. The people is not homogeneous, but a highly diversified complex of interest groups with crisscrossing memberships. It rarely makes sense to talk of the majority, except with reference to the result of a particular election or referendum, to describe how the votes were cast. A sectional majority, if there were one, would have no intrinsic claim to rule. To govern, a party would have to piece together an electoral majority; but every elector would have his own reasons for voting as he did, and no party could say in advance that, since it had no potential supporters among the members of some particular group, that group could, therefore, be safely neglected. Admittedly, wherever group divisions coincide over a wide range of interests (as, for instance, in many polyethnic societies), these conditions might not be fulfilled, and there might be a built-in majority and minority. In such a case, no party aiming at majority support could afford to uphold a minority interest, and democracy would tend to give way to majority tyranny. Thus, where popular-sovereignty theorists see the majority as the expression of the supreme will of the people, writers such as Madison, Alexis de Tocqueville, J. S. Mill, and, more recently, Walter Lippmann and the pluralists have seen it as either a myth or a potential tyrant.

THE POSSIBILITY OF DEMOCRACY

According to elitist sociologists like Vilfredo Pareto, Gaetano Mosca, and Robert Michels, there is always, behind the democratic facade, an oligarchy, even though its members take turns at playing the key governing roles. Now obviously, in every organization leaders initiate action and followers concur, but the power relations between leader and led are not on that account always the same. Precisely because democracy is a form of political organization, it *must* also be a pattern of leadership; nevertheless, the way leaders gain and retain their authority; the extent to which their initiatives respond to the interests of those they lead; their need to listen to and answer criticism—these things distinguish a democracy in important ways from what we usually mean by an oligarchy.

For the Marxist, bourgeois democracy is a sham because equal political rights cannot equalize political power where economic power is unequal. This does not amount to saying that democracy is *necessarily* impossible, only that economic equality and a classless society are necessary conditions for it.

According to other critics, popular self-government is delusory because government calls for expertise that few voters possess. Most accept the directions of some party, to whose image they are irrationally committed, and are incapable of a rational choice of policy. However, except in the popular-sovereignty variant, democracy does not require the electors to choose policies. Their role is merely to choose governors whom they trust to deal fairly and efficiently with problems as they emerge, and to look for new governors when they are disillusioned. A party's public image need not be an irrational construct; it may accurately epitomize deep-rooted tendencies and traditional preferences and be a reliable guide to the spirit in which the party would govern.

JUSTIFICATION OF DEMOCRACY

Democracy, it is sometimes said, asks too much of ordinary men, who would never be prepared to maintain the lively and informed interest in politics that ideally it demands. This, however, presupposes a particular view of the purpose and justification of democratic government. For some writers, as J. S. Mill, men and women cannot be fully responsible, adult, moral persons unless they are "self-determining," that is, concerned about the ways in which their lives are to be controlled. This view is a development from an older natural-rights theory of democracy, according to which (in the words of Colonel Rainborough, the Leveller), "Every man that is to live under a government ought first by his own consent put himself under that government," this being a condition for preserving his natural autonomy as a rational being. Or again, for democrats in the tradition of Rousseau, men achieve moral fulfillment only as participants in the collective self-governing process, helping to give expression to the "General Will" for the "Common Good"; failure in this constitutes failure in one's moral duty as a citizen.

There is, however, a more strictly utilitarian theory, sketched by Jeremy Bentham and James Mill and implicit in a good deal of the work of democratic political scientists today. According to this view, the test of the adequacy of a political system is whether it tends to provide for the interests of the governed and protect them against the abuse of power. Democracy, they maintain, is likely to do this better than other systems. Active participation has no intrinsic virtue. Mill would have limited the franchise to men over forty, on the grounds that the interests of women and younger men would be adequately safeguarded by their husbands and fathers, and therefore universal suffrage would be an unnecessary expense. For many modern writers, politics is a second-order activity: if things are going well, there is really no reason for people who prefer to spend their time on other things to devote it to politics. Political activity, indeed, is often most vigorous, as in Germany before 1933, when passions are high and democracy is in imminent danger of collapse. Apathy may be a sign of political health, indicating that there are no irreconcilable conflicts nor serious complaints. If there is ground for disquiet, it is only that apathy may become so habitual that democracy's defenses may be found unmanned in the face of some future attack.

This is a prudential model of democracy, in which satisfaction is maximized and conflicts reconciled by pressures bringing countervailing pressures into operation. It leaves out of account, perhaps, the sense in which democracy moralizes politics. Because decisions have to be publicly justified, political debate is conducted in moral terms, reviewing the impact of decisions on all interests affected, not just on this or that pressure group. Moreover, the quantum of power one has as a citizen can be represented not simply as a lever for personal or sectional protection or advantage, but also as a public responsibility; for even when one's own interests are not affected, one is still a member of a court of appeal. The bystanders in a democracy are, in a sense, the guarantors that a political decision shall not simply register the strongest pressure but shall be a reasoned response to diverse claims, each of which has to be shown to be *reasonable,* in the light of whatever standards are widely accepted in the community.

See also Authority; Bentham, Jeremy; Civil Disobedience; Communism; Locke, John; Marxist Philosophy; Mill, James; Mill, John Stuart; Mosca, Gaetano; Pareto, Vilfredo; Political Philosophy, History of; Republicanism; Rousseau, Jean-Jacques; Social and Political Philosophy; Socialism; Sovereignty.

Bibliography

GENERAL

Benn, S. I., and R. S. Peters. *Social Principles and the Democratic State.* London: Allen and Unwin, 1959. Reissued as *Principles of Political Thought.* New York: Collier, 1964.

Dahl, Robert Alan. *Preface to Democratic Theory.* Chicago: University of Chicago Press, 1956. A formal analysis of types of democratic theory.

De Grazia, Alfred. *Public and Republic.* New York: Knopf, 1951. On theories of representation, with useful annotated bibliography.

Mayo, Henry B. *An Introduction to Democratic Theory.* New York: Oxford University Press, 1960.

Pennock, J. Roland. *Liberal Democracy: Its Merits and Prospects.* New York: Rinehart, 1950. Includes an extensive bibliography.

Sartori, G. *Democrazia e definizione,* 2nd ed. Bologna, 1958. Translated by the author as *Democratic Theory.* Detroit, 1962. Notes include extensive bibliographical references.

Wollheim, R. "Democracy." *Journal of the History of Ideas* 19 (1958): 225–242. Includes brief history and bibliographical references.

ON THE SEMANTICS OF "DEMOCRACY"

McKeon, R., ed. *Democracy in a World of Tensions.* Chicago: University of Chicago Press, 1951. Edited for UNESCO.

Naess, A., J. A. Christopherson, and K. Kvalø. *Democracy, Ideology, and Objectivity.* Oslo: Norwegian Research Council for Science and the Humanities by University Press, 1956. A semantic analysis of the McKeon volume.

ON THE HISTORY OF DEMOCRATIC IDEAS

Crosa, E. *La sovranità popolare dal medioevo alla rivoluzione francese.* Turin: Bocca, 1915.

Glover, T. R. *Democracy in the Ancient World.* Cambridge, U.K.: Cambridge University Press, 1927.

Gooch, G. P. *English Democratic Ideas in the Seventeenth Century* edited by H. J. Laski. Cambridge: Cambridge University Press, 1927.

Mill, James. *Essay on Government.* London, 1821; Cambridge, U.K.: Cambridge University Press, 1937.

Mill, John Stuart. *Considerations on Representative Government.* London: Parker, 1861. More recent edition by R. B. McCallum. Oxford: Blackwell, 1946.

Rousseau, J. J. *Political Writings of Jean-Jacques Rousseau.* Edited by C. E. Vaughan. Oxford, 1962. In French.

Rousseau, J. J. *Rousseau: Political Writings.* Translated and edited by F. Watkins. New York: B. Franklin, 1971.

Spitz, D. *Patterns of Antidemocratic Thought.* New York, 1949.

Talmon, J. L. *Origins of Totalitarian Democracy.* London: Secker and Warburg, 1952.

Tocqueville, Alexis de. *De la démocratie en Amérique,* 2 vols. Brussels: Meline, Cans, 1835–1840. Translated by H. Reeve as *Democracy in America,* edited by P. Bradley, 2 vols. New York: Knopf, 1945.

Woodhouse, A. S. P. *Puritanism and Liberty.* London: Dent, 1938.

Stanley I. Benn (1967)

DEMOCRACY [ADDENDUM]

It is widely agreed that democracy is a system of government in which the people rule. Since the term "democracy" is often also used to describe nonpolitical communities—such as religious congregations, clubs, and athletic teams—democracy may be understood more generally to be a system in which the community is governed through the participation of its members. Thoroughly understanding democracy therefore requires answers to five key questions about this process of participation: What does democracy *presuppose*? What are the principal *instruments* that democracies must employ? What *conditions* are critical for its success? How can democracies be *appraised*? How can democracy be *theoretically defended*?

PRESUPPOSITIONS OF DEMOCRACY

For a democracy to be realized in any context, the community to be governed must self-consciously recognize itself as such, those entitled to participate in its government must be identified as citizens or members, and the extent of the community's concerns, both geographical and theoretical, must be at least roughly agreed upon. In short, democracy presupposes *community*.

Democratic government is possible only if members of the community can participate in decision making. They must be able to communicate effectively and to grasp the relations of means to ends. Participating citizens will not always be rational, of course, but at a minimum, democracy presupposes that members of the community have a *capacity for rationality*.

INSTRUMENTS OF DEMOCRACY

Democracies with many members must devise systems by which those members can reasonably effect their wills. All cannot speak; therefore some must speak and act for others. There are many kinds of representation (geographic, institutional, proportional, etc.). Whatever the manner of representation, every democracy of substantial size must have some *system of representation*.

Since there will be continuing and often serious disagreements among the participating members, every democracy must employ some *decision-making rules*. The rule of the majority, of the greatest number, is foremost among these, but other rules (qualified majorities, the rule of consensus, etc.) are also used in some contexts. A *system of representation* and *decision-making rules* within that system are essential instruments of every democracy.

CONDITIONS FOR THE SUCCESS OF DEMOCRACY

Self-government will not be sustainable unless some conditions are widely (but not necessarily universally) met within the community that aims to be democratic.

Some *material* conditions must be realized, chiefly a degree of economic well-being sufficient to permit its members to devote the needed time and energy to self-government. Ideally, the economic system should support, and even encourage, general participation. Yet which economic systems best do this is a topic of unending controversy.

Some *constitutional* conditions are essential for democratic participation in decision making. Among these the most essential are universal (or almost universal) protection of the *right to vote* and the *right to speak freely*. Thus a central condition of democratic success is a widely respected and legally protected liberty of all to publish with little or no restraint, to engage in robust political debate, to criticize intensely and vigorously those presently in authority.

Some *intellectual* conditions must be realized if general participation is to be reasonably successful. *Information* needed for decision making must be widely available; secrecy must be minimized. Citizens must be able to use this information. Thus an inevitable goal of every democracy will be *education*, broad and deep.

Some *psychological* conditions must also be realized. Citizens must permit intense opposition and debate while retaining good will. Citizens must be generally disposed to keep their expectations reasonable, to invite experimentation, and above all to encourage and accept compromise. A democracy is not likely to succeed unless its members, by and large, have the flexibility and resilience to bear defeat with patience when all does not go their way.

In a perilous world, political democracies require some *protective* conditions. A democratic state must be able to ward off international enemies, and therefore must sometimes rely on (while carefully controlling) military forces that themselves are not democratically organized. There must be security against attacks from without and subversion from within, but to achieve such security without sacrificing constitutional liberties is the greatest modern challenge for political communities that hope to become or remain democratic.

APPRAISING DEMOCRACIES

Self-government is a method of achieving the objectives of the members of a community. What they will seek cannot be known in advance. So appraising a democracy cannot depend on its goals, which we may despise. Democracies often make bad laws and sometimes behave immorally. The extent to which a community has achieved a democracy may be appraised by estimating *the degree to which the will of its members is genuinely realized by its government.*

This yardstick of achievement has two principle dimensions. First, how *broadly* within the community is participation realized in fact? Excluding from participation any substantial fraction of the community directly undermines the self-government of the community as a whole. Breadth of participation is fundamental; universal participation is the ideal, never perfectly realized. Democracy is crippled when breadth is restricted by law, as when women could not vote or when serfs or slaves had no voice in community affairs. But democracy is also undermined when segments of the community are excluded in fact, even if not by law, as when ethnic minorities are oppressed in nations that profess democracy but informally limit participation. And when apathetic citizens ignore or abandon the process of participation, democracy is wounded.

Second, how *deep* is community participation? To gauge a democracy, one must estimate not only the number of citizens who vote, but also the quality of their interaction and discussion for the eventual vote. In a healthy democracy, elections are not the only manifestation of participation; member participation unceasingly goes on in the informal workings of its representative system.

Great breadth combined with substantial depth is exceedingly difficult to achieve, especially when the political community is very large, as most nations are. But that combination is the ideal against which every democracy (whatever its particular objectives) must be appraised.

THE THEORETICAL DEFENSE OF DEMOCRACY

Even when the instruments of democracy are well devised and the conditions of its success are realized in good measure, there remains the question, Why should we want democracy? Answers of two kinds may be given: We may *vindicate* the process by showing that the outcomes of self-government tend to be more beneficial than those of its alternatives. We may *justify* the process by showing that democracy is the form of government most nearly in accord with our most fundamental moral convictions, that is, by showing that universal participation in government is morally right.

VINDICATION. Democracy, its proponents contend, is the one system most likely to achieve the objectives we seek through government. Among the alternatives, it is the most likely to enact just laws, because all (or most) members are represented in the law-making process. It is the most likely to reach wise decisions (though, of course, it does not always or universally do so), because it provides maximal opportunities for all to contribute. Of all forms of government, it is the most likely to avoid violence and disorder, because all have opportunity to speak. And it is most likely to safeguard the freedoms of speech and conduct, just because those freedoms are so central to the democratic process itself. Democracies behave stupidly and badly at times, but all things considered and over the long run, they are likely to produce better outcomes for community members than those of any alternative system of government.

JUSTIFICATION. Democracy can be justified by showing that it is the one form of government that most fully gives to community members what they deserve, what is most fair to them. Democracy presupposes that community members are roughly equal—equal not in skill or strength, but in being persons with lives to live, and therefore equally entitled to a voice in community affairs. Only democracy can give them that voice. The autonomy that individuals prize in their lives is prized in the larger social sphere as well. In that larger sphere, autonomy can realized only when the members of a community, through participation in common affairs, govern themselves.

See also Civil Disobedience; Cosmopolitanism; Equality, Moral and Social; Multiculturalism; Postcolonialism; Republicanism.

Bibliography

Andersen, Kristi. *After Suffrage: Women in Partisan and Electoral Politics before the New Deal.* Chicago: University of Chicago, 1996.

Anderson, Christopher J., A. Blais, S. Bowler, et al., eds. *Losers' Consent: Elections and Democratic Legitimacy.* Oxford, U.K.: Oxford University Press, 2005.

Avritzer, Leonardo. *Democracy and the Public Space in Latin America.* Princeton, NJ: Princeton University Press, 2002.

Bird, Colin. *The Myth of Liberal Individualism.* Cambridge, U.K.: Cambridge University Press, 1999.

Calhoun, John C. *A Disquisition on Government* (1851). In his *"A Disquisition on Government," and Selections from the "Discourse"*. New York: Liberal Arts Press, 1953.

Carter, April, and Geoffrey Stokes, eds. *Democratic Theory Today: Challenges for the 21st Century.* Cambridge, U.K.: Polity Press, 2002.

Cohen, Carl. *Democracy.* New York: Free Press, 1973.

Elkin, Stephen, and Karol Soltan, eds. *Citizen Competence and Democratic Institutions.* University Park: Pennsylvania State University Press, 1999.

Friedman, Milton. *Capitalism and Freedom*. Chicago: University of Chicago Press, 1962.

Green, Thomas Hill. "Liberal Legislation and Freedom of Contract." In *Works of T. H. Green*, edited by R. L. Nettleship. Vol. 3. London: Longmans Green, 1888.

Gutmann, Amy, and Dennis Thompson. *Democracy and Disagreement*. Cambridge, MA: Harvard University Press, 1996.

Hayek, Friedrich. *The Road to Serfdom*. Chicago: University of Chicago Press, 1944.

Klosko, George. *Democratic Procedures and Liberal Consensus*. Oxford, U.K.: Oxford University Press, 2000.

Laski, Harold. *A Grammar of Politics*. London: G. Allen and Unwin, 1925.

MacDonald, J. Ramsay. *Parliament and Democracy*. London: National Labour Press, 1920.

Madison, James. "The Union as a Safeguard against Domestic Faction and Insurrection." *The Federalist*, no. 10 (1787). Available from http://www.constitution.org/fed/federa10.htm.

Meiklejohn, Alexander. *Political Freedom* (1948). New York: Harper, 1960.

Mill, John Stuart. *On Liberty* (1859). New Haven, CT: Yale University Press, 2003.

Paine, Thomas. *The Rights of Man* (1792). In his *"Rights of Man"; "Common Sense"; and Other Political Writings*. Oxford, U.K.: Oxford University Press, 1995.

Perry, Ralph Barton. *Puritanism and Democracy*. New York: Vanguard Press, 1944.

Rawls, John. *A Theory of Justice*. Cambridge, MA: Harvard University Press, 1971.

Richardson, Henry. *Democratic Autonomy: Public Reasoning about the Ends of Policy*. Oxford, U.K.: Oxford University Press, 2003.

Shapiro, Ian. *The State of Democratic Theory*. Princeton, NJ: Princeton University Press, 2003.

Sharansky, Natan. *The Case for Democracy: The Power of Freedom to Overcome Tyranny and Terror*. New York: Public Affairs Press, 2004.

Thomas, Norman. *Democratic Socialism*. New York: League for Industrial Democracy, 1953.

U.S. Supreme Court. *Schenck v. United States*, 249 U.S. 47 (1919). *Abrams v. United States*, 250 U.S. 616 (1919). *Gitlow v. New York*, 268 U.S. 652 (1925). *Whitney v. California*, 274 U.S. 357 (1927). *W. Va. State Board of Education v. Barnette*, 319 U.S. 624 (1943). *United States v. Dennis*, 341 U.S. 494 (1951). *Brown v. Board of Education*, 347 U.S. 483 (1954). *Yates v. United States*, 354 U.S. 298 (1957). *Barenblatt v. United States*, 360 U.S. 109 (1959). *Baker v. Carr*, 369 U.S. 186 (1962). "U.S." is an abbreviation for *United States Supreme Court Reports*.

Carl Cohen (2005)

DEMOCRITUS

See *Leucippus and Democritus*

DEMONSTRATIVES

Demonstratives are one type of *indexical*. Like other indexicals, demonstratives can be used to refer to different objects on different occasions. Some examples of demonstratives are *that, this, you, he, she, there, then, this dog* and *that yellow house.*

INDEXICALS AND DEMONSTRATIVES

Philosophers of language commonly distinguish between the *meaning* of a linguistic expression and its *referent*. For example, the definite descriptions *the president of the United States in 2003* and *the husband of Laura Bush in 2003* refer to the same individual (namely, George W. Bush), but differ in meaning. Indexicals (also known as *context-sensitive expressions*) lead many philosophers to distinguish between two different sorts of meaning. Consider the paradigm indexical *I* and suppose that Al and Bob both utter the sentence *I live in Chicago*. Their utterances of *I* have the same meaning, in one sense of *meaning*. Let us call the type of meaning that their utterances share *linguistic meaning*. But there are reasons to think that their utterances also differ in some other type of meaning. Al's utterance of *I* refers to Al, whereas Bob's utterance refers to Bob. Al and Bob also say different things: Al says that Al lives in Chicago, whereas Bob says that Bob does. Finally, one of their utterances may be true while the other is false. Let us call the type of meaning that their utterances do not share *content*. All utterances of *I* have the same linguistic meaning, but utterances that are produced by different speakers have different contents. Similarly for the sentence *I live in Chicago*.

A speaker's utterance of *I* refers to that speaker no matter what object he might want to refer to, even if he intends to refer to Napoleon Bonaparte as he utters *I* (because he mistakenly thinks that he is Napoleon) and even if he points at someone else as he produces his utterance. By contrast, the referent of a speaker's utterance of *he* depends on the speaker's intentions or pointing gestures. If Al intends to refer to George W. Bush, and points at Bush as he utters *He is a Republican*, then his utterance of *he* refers to Bush. If Al instead intends to refer to Bill Clinton, and points at Clinton, then his utterance of *he* refers to Clinton. Indexicals, such as *he*, whose reference and content depend on the actions or intentions of the speaker are commonly called *demonstratives*. Those that do not, such as *I*, are often called *pure indexicals*. David Kaplan (1989a, 1989b), whose work on indexicals is highly influential, claims that *he, she, this*, and *that* are demonstratives, whereas *I, today, tomorrow, yesterday, now*, and *here* are pure indexicals.

The pronouns *he* and *she* are often used as demonstratives, but they also have nondemonstrative uses. For instance, the pronoun *he* is used in roughly the same way as a bound variable of formal logic in the sentence *Every man thinks that he is handsome* (on the interpretation "for every man *x*, *x* thinks that *x* is handsome"). The pronoun *she* is used as an anaphor in *Fiona sat down. She picked up a pencil.* It is controversial how these uses of *he* and *she* are related to their demonstrative uses.

REFERENCE-FIXING FOR DEMONSTRATIVES

We previously observed that the reference of a demonstrative utterance depends on the speaker's intentions or pointing gestures. Kaplan's early work (1989b) tends to emphasize the importance of pointing gestures in determining reference. In this early work Kaplan says that an utterance of a demonstrative is typically accompanied by a demonstra*tion*, which is a public presentation of an object that is typically, though not always, a pointing gesture. The demonstration determines a demonstrated object (a demonstra*tum*) in a context, and the demonstratum is the referent of the demonstrative, in the context. Kaplan's later work (1989b) tends to emphasize the role of speakers' intentions. According to it demonstrations are directed towards objects by *directing intentions* and it is directing intentions that determine the referents of demonstrative utterances.

One difficulty for the view that pointing gestures determine reference is that not all utterances of demonstratives are accompanied by pointing gestures. Kaplan's early theory allows there to be demonstrations that are not pointing gestures, but unfortunately leaves unclear what demonstrations (in general) are. A problem for the view that directing intentions determine reference is that it is not clear what directing intentions are. Speakers typically have many different intentions when they utter demonstratives. When Gail utters *he*, she may simultaneously (1) intend to refer to Hal, (2) intend to refer to the man she sees, and (3) intend to refers to the man to whom others are referring with *he*. But these intentions may conflict, and it is unclear which of them (if any) is a directing intention.

KAPLAN'S SEMANTICS FOR PURE INDEXICALS

Kaplan (1989b) presents a semantics for indexicals that attempts to describe their various meanings. We shall first consider how his theory works with pure indexicals, and then consider how to extend it to simple demonstratives. (The following text concentrates on Kaplan's informal remarks about the semantics of indexicals. His formal logical system uses the apparatus of possible-worlds semantics.)

Kaplan's theory begins with the idea that a linguistic expression has a *content with respect to*, or *in*, a *context* of utterance. For instance, the word *I* has a content in every context, depending on who the agent of the context is. For every context *C*, there is an agent of *C*, a location of *C*, a time (or day) of *C*, and a possible world of *C*. The content of the word *I* in any context *C* is the agent of *C*, the content of *here* at *C* is the location of *C*, and the content of *now* and *today* at *C* is the time (day) of *C*. The linguistic meaning, or *character*, of an expression is a function whose value at any context *C* is its content in *C*. For instance, the character of *I* is a function on contexts whose value at any context *C* is the agent of *C*.

The content of a declarative sentence in a context is a *proposition*, which is an entity that can be an object of attitudes such as belief, doubt, and assertion. When a speaker assertively utters a sentence, she asserts the proposition that is the content of her sentence in her context, and if she is sincere, then she believes that proposition. On Kaplan's (informal) semantics, propositions have constituent structures that resemble the constituent structures of sentences: Just as sentences have words as parts or constituents, so propositions have individuals, properties, and relations as parts or constituents. If the content of sentence *S* in context *C* is proposition *P*, then the constituents of *P* are (roughly) the contents, in *C*, of the words in *S*. For example, suppose that *C** is a context in which Inga is the agent. Then the content of *I laugh* with respect to *C** is a proposition whose constituents are Inga and the property of laughing. If Inga laughs in the possible world of context *C**, then *I laugh* is true in context *C**.

The sentence *I am speaking* is false in some contexts, according to Kaplan, because there are contexts in which the agent is not speaking. However, every agent of every context exists in the possible world of that context. Therefore, *I exist* is true in every context. Thus, Kaplan (1989b) claims that *I exist* is a logical truth. But the content of *I exist* in a context is (usually) not a necessary truth. For example, the content of *I exist* with respect to context *C** above is the proposition that Inga exists. This is not a necessary proposition. Therefore on Kaplan's theory, the sentence *I exist* is a logical truth that fails to express a necessary truth in many contexts.

EXTENDING KAPLAN'S THEORY TO SIMPLE DEMONSTRATIVES

One way to extend Kaplan's (1989a, 1989b) theory to simple demonstratives involves adding more items to contexts. (A second way, which will not be discussed here, involves Kaplan's dthat-terms.) For instance, one can suppose that every context has a sequence of demonstrata, and that the content of $that_1$ with respect to context *C* is the first demonstratum of *C*, the content of $that_2$ is the second demonstratum of *C*, and so on. One can then say that the character of $that_1$ is a function whose value at every context *C* is the first demonstratum of *C*, the character of $that_2$ is a function whose value at every context *C* is the second demonstratum of *C*, and so on. Similarly, one can suppose that every context has a sequence of addressees and that the content of you_1 is the first addressee, the content of you_2 is the second addressee, and so on.

There are two difficulties with this extension. First, We saw earlier that the referent of a demonstrative in a context is determined, somehow, by the pointing gestures and intentions of the speaker. The preceding theory assumes that every context has a sequence of demonstrata. But as Kaplan (1989b) points out, the agents of many contexts are not pointing at any objects and do not have any intentions that are relevant to determining a referent for a demonstrative. So it is highly artificial to suppose that every context contains a sequence of demonstrata. Second, the English word *that* is a single linguistic expression with a single linguistic meaning. But the previous theory instead provides an infinite number of distinct subscripted demonstratives ($that_1$, $that_2$, …), each with its own character (Braun 1994).

BELIEF AND DEMONSTRATIVES

Propositions that have individuals as constituents are known as *singular propositions*. Kaplan's theory says that singular propositions can be asserted and believed. This claim is problematic. Suppose that John is wearing a shirt with a large stain on its back. Suppose that he sees the back of his shirt in a mirror, but does not realize that he is viewing his own shirt. Then he may sincerely say *I am wearing a clean shirt and he is not wearing a clean shirt*, as he points at the person reflected in the mirror. On Kaplan's theory, John asserts and believes the contradictory singular proposition that John is wearing a clean shirt and John is not wearing a clean shirt. But surely he does not believe a contradictory proposition.

Gottlob Frege gives similar reasons for thinking that the content of a proper name is not its referent, but is instead a sense that determines a referent. Kaplan (1989b) and John Perry (2000) respond to Fregean criticisms of Kaplan's theory and criticize Frege's theory of demonstratives.

COMPLEX DEMONSTRATIVES

Complex demonstratives are expressions of the form *that CN*, where *CN* is a common noun phrase. Examples are *that car*, *that man who is wearing a baseball hat*, and *that yellow house*. Kaplan's theory does not mention complex demonstratives, and it is not entirely clear how they should be integrated into a theory of demonstratives. The major issue concerns the property expressed by the common noun phrase inside a complex demonstrative. Is this property a part of the content of the entire complex demonstrative? For instance, does the content of an utterance of *that yellow house* include the property of being yellow? Or, alternatively, is the content of the complex demonstrative simply the object to which the utterance refers?

On the one hand, it seems that a speaker's intentions and demonstrations are relevant to determining the referent of *that yellow house*. In this respect, *that yellow house* resembles the simple demonstrative *that*. We concluded earlier that the content of a simple demonstrative is just its referent. Therefore, We have some reason to think that the content of a complex demonstrative is also its referent and to think that the property of being yellow is not a part of the content of *that yellow house*. David Braun (1994) and Nathan Salmon (2002) argue for this view of complex demonstratives. On the other hand, the complex demonstrative *that yellow house* has a syntactic form much like the syntactic forms of the definite description *the yellow house* and the quantifier phrase *some yellow house*. Most philosophers think that the contents of *the yellow house* and *some yellow house* include the property of being yellow. That is some reason to think that the content of *that yellow house* also includes the property of being yellow. Jeffrey C. King (2001) argues for this latter view.

See also Anaphora; Frege, Gottlob; Indexicals; Logical Form; Meaning; Modality and Quantification; Proper Names and Descriptions; Propositional Attitudes; Propositions; Sense.

Bibliography

Braun, David. "Demonstratives and Their Linguistic Meanings." *Noûs* 30 (1996): 145–173.

Braun, David. "Indexicals." In *Stanford Encyclopedia of Philosophy*, edited by Edward N. Zalta. Stanford, CA: Metaphysics Research Lab, Center for the Study of Language and Information, Stanford University, 2001.

Braun, David. "Structured Characters and Complex Demonstratives." *Philosophical Studies* 74 (1994): 193–219.

Kaplan, David. "Afterthoughts." In *Themes from Kaplan*, edited by Joseph Almog, John Perry, and Howard Wettstein, 565–614 . New York: Oxford University Press, 1989a.

Kaplan, David. "Demonstratives." In *Themes from Kaplan*, edited by Joseph Almog, John Perry, and Howard Wettstein, 481–563 . New York: Oxford University Press, 1989b.

King, Jeffrey C. *Complex Demonstratives: A Quantificational Account*. Cambridge: MIT Press, 2001.

Perry, John. *The Problem of the Essential Indexical and Other Essays*. Expanded ed. Stanford, CA: CSLI Publications, 2000.

Salmon, Nathan. "Demonstrating and Necessity." *Philosophical Review* 111 (3) (2002): 497–537.

David Braun (2005)

DE MORGAN, AUGUSTUS

(1806–1871)

A British mathematician and logician, Augustus De Morgan was born at Madura, India, where his father was an army officer. After early education in the west of England, he entered Trinity College, Cambridge, in 1823 and graduated fourth wrangler in 1827. His refusal to subscribe to the religious tests then in force precluded him from further advancement at Cambridge, but he was fortunate enough to be appointed first professor of mathematics at the newly opened University of London. Because of his habit of resigning on matters of principle, he twice vacated this chair, once at the beginning and once at the end of his career; but he enjoyed, in the interval, the highest repute and affection as a teacher and had many pupils who later achieved distinction.

In addition to numerous important papers on the foundations of algebra and the philosophy of mathematical method, De Morgan was the author of several excellent elementary textbooks; a standard bibliography, *Arithmetical Books* (London, 1847); a large treatise on the calculus (London, 1842); and an enormous quantity of learned journalism, mostly in the shape of review articles in the London *Athenaeum* and contributions on mathematical and astronomical subjects to the *Companion to the Almanac* (1831–1857) and to the *Penny* (later *English*) *Cyclopaedia.* His best-known work in this line is the posthumously assembled *Budget of Paradoxes* (London, 1872), a still-diverting miscellany from the lunatic fringes of science and mathematics, originally serialized in the *Athenaeum.* Despite many years' service as secretary of the Royal Astronomical Society, De Morgan was in general suspicious of official bodies and distinctions, never sought membership in the Royal Society, and declined an Edinburgh LL.D. Indifferent to politics and society—and professedly hostile to the animal and vegetable kingdoms as well—he nonetheless maintained an extensive scientific correspondence with such friends as William Whewell, George Boole, Sir John Herschel, Sir William Rowan Hamilton (the mathematician), and John Stuart Mill. His crotchets did little to disguise his exceptional benevolence and firmness of character or to inhibit his talents as a humorist and a wit.

De Morgan's outlook was that of a philosophical mathematician and historian of science; he did not claim to be a philosopher in any narrow sense of the term. He admired Berkeley and followed him to the extent of holding the existence of minds to be more certain, as a fact of experience, than that of a material world. But his general attitude to such questions may be gathered from his remark that, while he would not dissuade a student from metaphysics, he would warn him, "when he tries to look down his own throat with a candle in his hand, to take care that he does not set his head on fire."

In common with other mathematicians of his time, De Morgan realized that algebra could be conceived as a system of symbols whose laws could be codified independently of any arithmetical or other interpretation that might be given to them. His logic had a similar aim. Deeply versed in the history of logic, he was able to freshen and illuminate the subject by generalizing its traditional principles along mathematical lines. In this respect he ranks as the chief precursor of Boole; but his views attained notice chiefly through the controversy that arose when Sir William Hamilton (of Edinburgh) accused him of plagiarizing the doctrine of a quantified predicate.

De Morgan's *Formal Logic* (London, 1847) represents the best-known, though by no means the most mature, statement of his logical views. Among its many excellences, the chapter on fallacies is worthy of mention. De Morgan's later work is dispersed in pamphlets and periodicals, most notably in five memoirs contributed to the *Cambridge Philosophical Transactions* (Vols. 8–10, 1847–1863) and in his *Syllabus of a Proposed System of Logic* (London, 1860, reprinted in *On the Syllogism* (London, 1964). Though too largely concerned with polemics against Hamilton, and hampered by a notation that found no acceptance, these writings display much originality in the handling of negative terms, compound propositions, and numerous unorthodox varieties of syllogistic reasoning. Apart from the well-known "De Morgan laws" for the negation of conjunctions and disjunctions (or logical sums and products), the most important development was the recognition that the copula performs its function in the syllogism solely by virtue of its character as a transitive and convertible relation. De Morgan was led by this to examine the logic of relations in general and so paved the way not only for Peirce's "logic of relatives" but for all that has since been done in this branch of the subject.

As a skilled actuary, who was often in demand as a consultant to insurance companies, De Morgan was not unnaturally interested in the mathematical theory of probability and the problems of applying it to the hazards of mortality and other types of experience. His treatise "Theory of Probabilities," in the *Encyclopaedia Metropolitana* (London, 1837) and the more popular *Essay on Probabilities* (London, 1838) were among the earlier discussions of this topic in English (see further relevant chapters of *Formal Logic* and the papers on the evaluation of argument and testimony attached to the first two Cambridge memoirs above). De Morgan's conception of probability was largely derived from Pierre Simon de Laplace, whose ideas (and errors) he was thus instrumental in propagating among his nineteenth-century successors. His method of approach was to construe the theory as an extension of formal logic, that is, as an investigation of the rules whereby propositions not absolutely certain affect the certainty of other propositions with which they are connected. He also employed the "inverse" procedures founded on Bayes's theorem, whereby, from known factual premises, it is sought to conjecture the probabilities of their likely or possible antecedents. In attempting to quantify the degree of uncertainty involved, De Morgan identified it with the amount of belief that is, or rather, that ought to be attached to it by a rational person, and proceeded on this basis to discuss the compounding and derivation of partial beliefs in accordance with the mathematical rules of the calculus of chances. His view of the matter was thus both a priori and subjective, though not in the objectionably psychological sense that has sometimes been ascribed to him. There are better reasons for censuring the technical errors he fell into through uncritical reliance on the Laplacean "rule of succession" and "principle of indifference"; even here, however, his confidence in the mathematical apparatus was often less blindly trusting than that of the writers who preceded him.

De Morgan's conception of scientific method may be gathered primarily from a review of Francis Bacon's works inserted in the *Budget of Paradoxes.* He there embraced what is essentially the modern "hypothetico-deductive" view of the subject; but one has to go to William Whewell before him or to W. S. Jevons after him to see it worked out in full.

See also Bacon, Francis; Bayes, Bayes' Theorem, Bayesian Approach to Philosophy of Science; Berkeley, George; Boole, George; Hamilton, William; Herschel, John; Jevons, William Stanley; Laplace, Pierre Simon de; Logic, History of; Logic, Traditional; Logical Terms, Glossary of; Mill, John Stuart; Scientific Method; Whewell, William.

Bibliography

Apart from the works mentioned under the History of Logic entry there is not much literature on De Morgan. The best general accounts are in A. Macfarlane, *Ten British Mathematicians* (New York, 1916) and J. A. Passmore, *A Hundred Years of Philosophy* (London: Duckworth, 1957). The *Memoir* by his wife, Sophia Elizabeth De Morgan (London: Longmans, Green, 1882), contains an excellent account of him. The details of the quarrel with Hamilton may be found in Hamilton's *Letter to Augustus De Morgan* (Edinburgh, 1847) and De Morgan's *Statement in Answer* (London, 1847) or more readily in the appendices to De Morgan's *Formal Logic.*

P. L. Heath (1967)

DENNETT, DANIEL CLEMENT

(1942–)

Daniel Clement Dennett obtained his first degree at Harvard, where, as he tells us in *Brainchildren* (1998), he vigorously resisted the most influential American philosopher of the twentieth century, Willard van Orman Quine. He then did a D. Phil. in Oxford in a brief two years under Gilbert Ryle, the most influential Oxford philosopher of his time, finishing in 1966.

His first book was *Content and Consciousness* (1969). These two words, *content* and *consciousness*, encapsulate much of Dennett's mission. *Content* refers to the contents of the mind—all the beliefs, desires, values, emotions, hopes, expectations, memories, and so forth that make up the mind. *Consciousness* refers, of course, to consciousness. In Dennett's view, the correct order in which to examine these topics is content first and then consciousness. Dennett's central project is already clear in this book, the project of "naturalizing the mind." This is the project of showing that mind and consciousness are simply aspects of brain and behavior, just as much open to investigation by cognitive psychology and neuroscience as other aspects of cognition. He has never waivered in this commitment.

CONTENT

Dennett's next book was a collection of essays, *Brainstorms*, written during the 1970s. This work helped launch a unique publishing enterprise, Bradford Books. Founded by Harry and Betty Stanton and subsequently absorbed by MIT Press, the Bradford insignia has become one of the most important collections of books in philosophy of mind and cognitive science in the English language.

Brainstorms begins with the first full articulation of Dennett's distinctive approach to mental content, the approach that he calls the intentional stance. According to Dennett, we can approach something in order to explain it from three stances: the physical stance, the design stance, and the intentional stance. Each has its own advantages and costs, but none is describing reality from the one correct perspective.

After editing, with Douglas Hofstadter, a charming collection of works by others on the mind, *The Mind's I* (1981), Dennett next turned to decision making and responsibility in an idiosyncratic little book called *Elbow Room: The Varieties of Free Will Worth Wanting* (1984). The book began life as John Locke Lectures in Oxford and espouses a brisk compatibilism between decisions being causally determined and decisions being free in any way that is "worth wanting." Interestingly, he returned to the topic of free will nearly twenty years later in *Freedom Evolves*(2003).

The year 1987 saw his second major collection of papers on content, *The Intentional Stance*. The papers in this collection are probably the most influential papers that Dennett has written. Near the end of the collection are two papers on evolutionary theory, a topic that was to loom large in his thinking in the 1990s.

Dennett's work on mental content has led him to questions about such topics as artificial content (AI [artificial intelligence]), the evolution of content, the relationship of content to the environment and brain (neuroscience), content in nonhumans (cognitive ethology), the nature of explanation in psychology and science generally, how content is represented and the different styles of mental representation, the relationship of representations to the brain, and how we ascribe mental content to ourselves and others.

CONSCIOUSNESS

At this point Dennett turned to consciousness, and a large book, *Consciousness Explained* (1991), ensued. For the first time, Dennett wrote a book deliberately aimed at a wide audience (it was not the last). Dennett laid out methods for studying consciousness, built a model of consciousness as a cognitive system, and discussed the nature of introspection (the consciousness we have of ourselves and our own mental states). He considered how consciousness evolved, pathologies of consciousness such as dissociative identity disorder (formerly multiple personality disorder), whether there is any real difference between how a mental state functions in us and how it feels to us (what philosophers call *qualia* or felt quality), what selves might be, the neural implementation of consciousness, and so on—just about every issue pertaining to consciousness.

This book has two main targets. One is the picture of conscious states that the tradition received from Descartes. This is the idea that there is something to a conscious state, some felt quality, that is unmistakably clear and clearly different from anything else in the world. The other is what Dennett calls the Cartesian theater, the idea that the conscious system is a kind of screen on which conscious states play before a little homunculus sitting in the middle of the theater. To replace the Cartesian picture in both its parts, Dennett proposed what he calls a Multiple Drafts Model (MDM) of consciousness. MDM treats consciousness as a kind of mental content, almost a matter of programming.

Dennett next wrote a shorter book pulling the two sides of his work together: *Kinds of Minds* (1996). Then he turned to a task that had been awaiting him for a long time: evolutionary theory. *Darwin's Dangerous Idea* (1995) was also published as a trade book and also enjoyed phenomenal success. Here Dennett argues for two main claims: (1) Darwin's theory of evolution is a "universal acid" that dissolves all manner of intellectual "skyhooks" and other pseudoscientific props that philosophers (and not just philosophers) have dreamed up to try to patch up hopeless theories; (2) yet contrary to those who see Darwin as the destroyer of all morality, the theory of evolution leaves one perfectly satisfactory approach to morality and political philosophy untouched: traditional western liberalism. Among the most important claims introduced in this book is that it is language that makes it possible for us to have our kind of mind, a kind of mind that, by being able to cooperate with other minds and record the results of cooperation for others to build on, can figure out the physics of the universe, find cures for serious diseases, build Hubble telescopes and the Channel tunnel, and so on.

The book set off a stormy debate with Steven Jay Gould and others in the *New York Review of Books* in 1997. Gould insisted that Dennett had espoused an ultra-adaptionist position, assigning change in species to natural selection (selection on the basis of survival and reproductive fitness) over almost all other sources of change over time, such as cataclysmic changes in weather, exhaustion of habitats. Despite the heat that the debate generated (and some astonishingly uncollegial language), with the passage of time it now seems clear that the elements of agreement between the two of them are far greater than the elements of disagreement.

In the late 1990s, Dennett published another collection of essays, *Brainchildren* (1998), a remarkably diverse array of pieces mostly on consciousness and artificial intelligence. His most recent book is *Freedom Evolves* (2003). He is working on a book on religion. There are many sides to Dennett's contribution, but one of the most important is the way he challenges orthodoxies. He is a master at showing what is wrong with points of view with which he disagrees. One of his most characteristic techniques is to go after comfortable ideas with what he calls intuition pumps. Following is an example, the case of Mr. Chase and Mr. Sanborn:

> Mr. Chase and Mr. Sanborn both used to like a certain coffee. More recently it has lost its appeal. The reasons they give seem to differ markedly. Chase: "The flavor of the coffee hasn't changed but I just don't like that flavor very much now." Sanborn: "No, no, you are quite wrong. I would still like *that* flavor as much as ever. The problem is that the coffee *doesn't* taste that way anymore." (reconstructed from Dennett 1988, p. 50)

Dennett's target is the idea that there is always a clear distinction between a conscious state, in this case how something tastes to us, and how we react to it. When we read about Mr. Chase and Mr. Sanborn, we are meant to say to ourselves, "Hmmm, maybe the distinction is not so clear after all." One is then meant to see that similar doubts arise all over the place.

An expert high-seas sailor and an accomplished pianist and choral singer, Dennett is far from retirement. In addition to his prolific authorship of books, Dennett has written an average of ten papers per year for thirty-five years. He has taught at Tufts University for more than thirty years.

See also Cognitive Science; Consciousness.

Bibliography

WORKS BY DENNETT

Content and Consciousness. London: Routledge, 1969.

Brainstorms. Montgomery, VT: Bradford Books, 1978.

The Mind's I, edited with Douglas Hofstadter. New York: Basic Books, 1981.

Elbow Room: The Varieties of Free Will Worth Wanting. Cambridge, MA: MIT Press/A Bradford Book, 1984.

The Intentional Stance. Cambridge, MA: MIT Press/A Bradford Book, 1987.

"Quining qualia." In *Consciousness in Contemporary Society,* edited by A. Marcel and E. Bisiach, 42–47 Oxford: Oxford University Press: 1988.

Consciousness Explained. Boston: Little Brown, 1991.

Darwin's Dangerous Idea. New York: Simon and Schuster, 1995.

Kinds of Minds. New York: Basic Books, 1996.

Brainchildren. Cambridge, MA: MIT Press/A Bradford Book, 1998.

Freedom Evolves. New York: Penguin Books, 2003.

WORKS ABOUT DENNETT

Brook, Andrew, and Donald Ross. *Daniel Dennett: Contemporary Philosophy in Focus.* New York and Cambridge, U.K.: Cambridge University Press, 2002.

Dahlbom, Dagmar, ed. *Dennett and His Critics: Demystifying Mind.* Oxford: Blackwell, 1995.

Quine, Willard v. O. *Word and Object (Studies in Communication).* Cambridge, MA: MIT, 1964.

Ross, Don, Andrew Brook, and David Thompson, eds. *Dennett's Philosophy: A Comprehensive Assessment.* Cambridge, MA: MIT Press/A Bradford Book, 2000.

Ryle, Gilbert. *The Concept of Mind.* London: Hutchinson, 1949.

Andrew Brook (2005)

DEONTIC LOGIC

See *Modal Logic*

DEONTOLOGICAL ETHICS

Deontology is the view that because there are moral constraints on promoting overall best consequences, sometimes the right action is not the one whose consequences are best. The constraints that deontological theories emphasize are familiar from our everyday experience of morality: One ought to keep one's promises and be loyal to one's friends; one ought not to inflict unnecessary suffering or to ignore one's debts of gratitude, and so on. Some deontological theorists see a unified basis for all such duties; others are frankly pluralist.

THE MEANING OF "DEONTOLOGY"

Apparently coined by Jeremy Bentham in the nineteenth century, the term "deontology" initially was used to refer, quite widely, to the "science of duty." This wide usage reflects the word's two Greek roots: *deon*, meaning "needful" or "fitting," and *logos*, meaning "science" or "discourse." Within a century, the term gained its narrower meaning; even this wide use of the term, however, carries some definite commitments. These stem from each of its two roots: (1) It is fitting to be virtuous; but it is not part of the concept of virtue that virtue is always needful or morally necessary. In focusing on the needful, deontology may thus either leave the moral virtues to one side or demote them to a derivative status. In its concern with duty, deontology also either ignores, or treats as peripheral, the nature of moral success—described by some as happiness or *eudaimonia*, by others as perfected moral worth. Deontology's principal terms of assessment are, instead, deontic: they concern what ought to be the case and, more specifically, what people ought (morally) to do. (2) It is possible to speak or discourse about almost anything; but holding that there is a *logos* of duty suggests that moral duties may be correctly described in general terms. This suggestion runs contrary to the views of at least some contemporary moral particularists, who deny that there are any general truths about what people ought to do.

By the middle of the twentieth century, "deontology" acquired its more specific meaning, which refers to a particular conception or theory of our moral duties. To say that something is one's duty is to represent a type of action as necessary in some way, but how? C. D. Broad noted that there are at least two ways. One way is to represent the action as a means best suited to our attaining some good end that we ought, unconditionally, to pursue: This he called "teleological necessity" (from the Greek word *telos*, meaning "end"). Another is to represent the action as one that we ought, unconditionally, to take, irrespective of the consequences: This he called "deontological necessity." Of course, it is perfectly possible to embrace both of these types of moral necessity—as did, for instance, Immanuel Kant, who recognized both obligatory ends and strictly prohibited actions. Yet this contrast between two types of moral necessity may also be used to divide moral theories into two groups.

"Teleological" theories, as it has become commonplace to say, hold that the rightness and wrongness of actions is *wholly* determined by their tendencies to generate good. "Deontological" theories deny this, holding that the right action at least *sometimes* expresses deontological necessity, which stands independent of teleology—even a teleology that tots up *overall* goodness. As we have seen, the initial, wide use of "deontology" suggests that there are general ethical truths. In keeping with that suggestion, the more specific idea of deontological theory, as it is usually presented, invokes the idea of a general type of duty. One or more generally statable moral *constraints* prohibits certain ways of pursuing good results. In this way, we arrive at the conception of deontology stated at the outset: Deontology is the ethical theory, or family of ethical theories, according to which there are constraints on promoting overall best consequences that imply that sometimes the right act is not the one whose consequences are best.

This distinction between teleological and deontological theories does not cover all possible ethical theories—not even all of the non-particularist ones that focus on duty rather than virtue or happiness. On the one hand, there are other ways of resisting the idea that the right act is the one whose consequences are best. Philippa Foot (1985) and others have questioned the coherence of this apparently all-purpose notion of overall goodness: Does it really make sense to ask, for any two states of affairs or any two alternative actions, which is "better?" Another possibility (emphasized by Samuel Scheffler [1982]) is to hold that the basis for deviating from what is for the best is not a set of constraints or duties, but rather a set of prerogatives or permissions: Perhaps we sometimes have moral latitude to act in some merely acceptable ways. On the other hand, there are ways of developing consequentialism that drop any reference to teleological necessity: Perhaps we simply rank (some) alternative actions as better or worse, on the basis of whatever considerations apply, interpreting "consequentialism" simply as holding that we ought to take the best available alternative. If this abstract understanding of consequentialism is taken to the limit, the contrast between deontology and consequentialism will blur. To see why, we must shift from the meaning of deontology to the merits of the view.

THE MERITS OF DEONTOLOGY

Deontological constraints are often called "agent-centered." The negative ones, for instance, direct people not to *do* certain things while not directing them to minimize the extent to which certain kinds of action *are done*.

Although these constraints are typically conceived as applying to everyone, that does not mean that they apply in the latter, impersonal, way, but only that they apply to each agent in the former, personal way. This distinction is implicit in St. Paul's principle from Romans 3:8, central in Alan Donagan's (1977) deontological theory: "Thou shalt not do evil in order that good may come of it." The principal difficulty in justifying deontology is to explain why agent-centered restrictions make sense. If breaking a promise or unnecessarily harming someone is a bad thing, then would not rationality dictate minimizing this type of bad, other things equal? Niccolò Machiavelli infamously wrote that princes need to learn how not to be good. They must be ready to use cruelty well in order to minimize cruelty in the long run; but perhaps the advice applies not only to princes. Should one not suffocate the crying child so as to prevent the evil soldiers from finding the refugees in the attic and killing them all? Such cases present what are known as "paradoxes of deontology."

Some deontological theorists simply deny that the paradoxes pose any problem: The deontological constraints stand on their own—as self-evident, a priori, or resting on divine authority—and entail nothing about minimizing bads. Others do attempt to defend deontology from the challenge posed by the paradoxes, in three ways. One is to defend the moral significance of the distinction between doing ill and allowing ill effects to happen. The doctrine of doing and allowing holds that, across a wide range of cases, there is a morally significant difference between the two. As Warren Quinn's (1993) sympathetic discussion reveals, it is not easy to explain why the bare difference between doing something and allowing something to happen should make a fundamental moral difference; a first step is to concede that the distinction matters only in certain contexts.

A second way to attempt to defend deontology is to develop Thomas Nagel's (1986) idea of "agent-centered" (or "agent-relative") *reasons*, which explain the point of deontological constraints. We can understand how certain moral reasons may not apply to everyone, but only to some people. This may be because of special relationships in which some people stand to others (friend, physician) or it may be because of the moral leeway we have to pursue what we care about. Perhaps the reasons that underwrite deontological constraints are similarly agent-relative. W. D. Ross (1988) suggested that each important deontological constraint reflects a different special relationship in which we can stand to others: as past benefactors, promisors, and so on. Alternatively, agent-relative reasons can be given a systematic place in moral theory. For example, T. M. Scanlon's (1998) contractualist theory holds that the rightness of actions is determined by principles that could not be reasonably rejected by anyone motivated to reach reasonable agreement on principles. The reasons that individuals might reject proposed principles, he suggests, will naturally include some agent-relative ones. In either sort of deployment, however, there are grounds for worrying that the agent-relative reasons presuppose deontological constraints rather than really justifying them.

A third way to defend deontological constraints is to deny that all goods call for one to promote them. Some goods—some valuable things—may instead call upon us to respect or honor them. Kant's seminal contribution to deontological thinking was his insistence that rational persons are to be respected, as having a dignity that is beyond all price. Having said that, one *might* turn around and argue that human rational dignity, as an agent-neutral value, is to be promoted. That would be to turn away from deontology. In contrast, one might hold that the appropriate attitude to human dignity is, in turn, to respect *it*. Frances Kamm (1992) has argued that human dignity is best respected by ensuring the inviolability of persons' basic rights.

THE PRIORITY OF RIGHT

As Kamm herself points out, resting deontological constraints on the value of human dignity begins to efface the distinction between deontology and consequentialist views. A fully abstract consequentialism can look to *any* relevant basis for holding that one alternative action is better or worse than another. Jamie Dreier (1993) has argued that the strictness of deontological constraints can easily be recast in a consequentialist mode by stipulating that some actions be ranked *lexically* better than others. Such an abstract consequentialism gives up the title to being a teleological view, as it does not develop its content on the basis of observed teleological necessities; but it remains recognizably consequentialist. Maintaining a firm contrast between deontological theories and consequentialist theories, therefore, depends upon resisting such an abstract recasting of consequentialism. Friends of deontology may want to understand "goods" or "goodness" somewhat more narrowly, as referring only to features of states of affairs or to values towards which the correct stance is promotion rather than respect, such as human well-being. The values that do not fall within the good—or at least some of them—may then be thought of as belonging to "the right"—the domain of rightness.

Accepting that there are values proper to the right, whose role is not to be promoted but rather to be honored and respected by the structure of duty, opens up many additional possible ways of defending deontology. Such an approach helps ground deontological constraints by relating them to some value, but in a non-teleological way; and this helps explain why we should care about acting morally. Barbara Herman (1993) has emphasized this layer in Kant's moral theory. Kant (1998) held that the a priori concepts of morality determine the content of the one unconditionally valuable thing, namely the good will, the will that acts from respect for the moral law. Although this value cannot, in Kant's view, be directly promoted, it helps characterize the value of acting morally. Our capacity to achieve this value also underwrites our dignity: We are worthy of respect because we are capable of acting with a good will. A contemporary example of this approach is Scanlon's contractualism. As noted above, Scanlon (1998) holds that the rightness of actions depends on whether they accord with principles that no one duly motivated to find agreement on principles could reasonably reject. What motivates us to act morally, on this interpretation? Scanlon's answer in *What We Owe to Each Other* is that it is "the positive value of living with others on terms that they could not reasonably reject" (1998, p. 162). This value seems to belong to the right, not to the good insofar as it is distinct from the right. Yet it is nonetheless something we might intelligibly care about. According to deontologists such as Kant and Scanlon, then, these considerations of rightness have a kind of structural priority over other types of value.

See also Categorical Imperative; Contractualism; Divine Command Theories of Ethics; Duty; Ethics; Kant, Immanuel; Kantian Ethics; Moral Rules and Principles; Ross, William David; Teleological Ethics.

Bibliography

Bentham, Jeremy. *Deontology, Together with a Table of the Springs of Action and the Article on Utilitarianism*, edited by A. Goldworth. Oxford: Clarendon Press, 1983.

Broad, C. D. *Five Types of Ethical Theory*. London: Routledge & Kegan Paul, 1930.

Darwall, Stephen, ed. *Deontology*. Malden, MA: Blackwell, 2003.

Donagan, Alan. *The Theory of Morality*. Chicago: University of Chicago Press, 1977.

Dreier, Jamie. "Structures of Normative Theories." *Monist* 76 (1993): 22–40.

Foot, Philippa. "Utilitarianism and the Virtues." *Mind* 94 (1985): 196–209.

Herman, Barbara. "Leaving Deontology Behind." In *The Practice of Moral Judgment*. Cambridge, MA: Harvard University Press, 1993.

Kamm, Frances. "Non-Consequentialism, the Person as an End-in-Itself, and the Significance of Status." *Philosophy and Public Affairs* 21 (1992): 354–389.

Kant, Immanuel. *Groundwork of the Metaphysics of Morals*, edited and translated by M. Gregor. Cambridge, U.K.: Cambridge University Press, 1998.

Louden, Robert B. "Toward a Genealogy of 'Deontology.'" *Journal of the History of Philosophy* 34 (1996): 571–592.

Nagel, Thomas. *The View from Nowhere*. New York: Oxford University Press, 1986.

Quinn, Warren. *Morality and Action*. Cambridge, U.K.: Cambridge University Press. 1993.

Ross, W. D. *The Right and the Good* (1930). Indianapolis: Hackett, 1988.

Scanlon, T. M. *What We Owe to Each Other*. Cambridge, MA: Harvard University Press, 1998.

Scheffler, Samuel. *The Rejection of Consequentialism*. Oxford: Clarendon Press, 1982.

Henry S. Richardson (2005)

DERRIDA, JACQUES

(1930–2004)

Although he was not altogether happy with the fact, Jacques Derrida's name has become synonymous with deconstruction. Derrida was born in El-Biar, near Algiers, in 1930. In 1949 he left for Paris and in 1952 began to study at the École Normale Supérieure, where he taught from 1964 to 1984. Beginning in 1975, Derrida spent a few weeks each year teaching in the United States. While at Yale University Derrida collaborated with Paul de Man (1919–1983), leading to the extraordinary impact that deconstruction has had on the study of literature in the United States, an impact that quickly spread to other disciplines and countries.

Derrida's record of publications is remarkable. In 1962 he wrote an introduction to a translation of Husserl's *Origin of Geometry* that in many respects anticipates the later works. In 1967 he published a further study of Edmund Husserl, *Speech and Phenomena*; a collection of essays, *Writing and Difference*; and a reading of Ferdinand de Saussure, Claude Lévi-Strauss, and Jean-Jacques Rousseau, *Of Grammatology*. A rapid succesion of publications ensued, among the most important of which are *Dissemination* (1972), *Glas* (1974), *The Post Card* (1980), *Psyché* (1987), *Given Time* (1991), and *The Politics of Friendship* (1994). Derrida also published extensively on an increasingly broad range of subjects from literature and politics to art and architecture.

STYLES OF DECONSTRUCTION

Deconstruction is neither a method nor a negative critique. It is better understood as a strategy for reading texts under the influence of Husserl, Martin Heidegger, Friedrich Nietzsche, Sigmund Freud, Emmanuel Levinas, and Saussure. In the early years of deconstruction many of the most important readings were devoted to these thinkers, all of whom, except for Husserl, were treated in Derrida's 1968 lecture "Différance." Derrida justified this cross-fertilization of disparate authors by saying that their names served to define contemporary thought. This practice came to be generalized as *intertextuality* and came to be further enhanced as Derrida, in each new text, drew heavily on his previous readings. Because Derrida's language is both cumulative and parasitic on the texts that he is reading, attempts to formulate Derridean doctrines are often misleading. Hence it is more appropriate to focus on his strategies.

Most of Derrida's writings operate by close reading, and their impact depends on the capacity of this reading to account for details that more conventional readings either ignore or explain away. In clear contrast, not only with most modern trends in philosophy, but also with a widespread image of him, Derrida was immersed in the history of philosophy. For Derrida this was the only way to avoid unwittingly repeating the most classic gestures of philosophy, a danger that threatens every attempt to ignore that history and begin philosophy anew. Deconstruction locates itself within traditional conceptuality in order to find the radical fissures that it believes can be traced in every work of philosophy. Derrida was drawn to the apparent contradictions of the tradition and made them the starting point of his readings, whereas a more conventional treatment tends to stop short as soon as a contradiction is identified. Much that is strange, and to some even offensive, about Derrida's analyses arises because he attempted to uncover the structures that organize and so transcend or exceed conventional reason.

Particularly in his early writings, Derrida presented his deconstructive readings of individual works in the history of Western philosophy as directed against a certain understanding of that history as one in which presence had been privileged. The priority of presence was reflected throughout the binary oppositions that structured Western thought: presence over absence, speech over writing, inside over outside, and so on. Derrida's strategy was to show that those texts that were supposed to have exhibited this privilege of presence also reflected a certain counter-tendency. So, for example, texts that on the surface appear to privilege speech over writing also have moments in which the hierarchy was reversed. Following this reversal, Derrida sought to pass beyond the opposition to that which exceeds it: Hence, in the example given, he identifies what he calls a proto-writing, which is neither speech nor writing in the conventional sense, but that which is the condition of all forms of language.

Derrida drew his account of history of Western metaphysics in terms of presence from Heidegger, but in so far as Heidegger's account was directed toward the overcoming of metaphysics, Derrida located within that project an opposition between what was inside and outside metaphysics. He thus identified within the project of leaving metaphysics behind, a hierarchical opposition that was itself still metaphysical. By contrast, Derrida's own position was that one cannot stand unequivocally either within or outside metaphysics. This was reflected in his strategy of double reading. To any text that was conventionally conceived of as belonging to Western metaphysics, he added a new reading that showed how that same text could be understood as exceeding Western metaphysics, and to texts, such as those by Heidegger and Levinas, that presented themselves as passing beyond Western metaphysics, Derrida added a reading that drew them back into the conceptuality of Western metaphysics. The deconstruction lay not in the new reading alone, but in its juxtaposition with previous readings, which were not thereby supplanted so much as understood as belonging to the history of the text. This means that Derrida does not so much oppose the dominant reading, as that he adds another reading to it, so that the so-called double reading combats any attempt to locate the text in question either within or outside Western metaphysics.

There is, however, another style of deconstruction that has become increasingly widespread in Derrida's thought. It proceeds by the exploration of *aporias*, as will be illustrated later in a discussion of Derrida's conception of the gift. Because Derrida sometimes seems to give the aporias he investigates a universal status, deconstruction in this sense is no longer as attached to the conception of the history of philosophy as the history Western metaphysics, as was the case with his textual readings of philosophy. However, Derrida did not consider these two styles of deconstruction as independent of each other, so that it would be a mistake to suppose that he had abandoned the genealogical component of his work.

THE SUPPLEMENT

Supplement is one of the key terms of Derrida's challenge to Western metaphysics, understood as a unified body of thought that privileges presence. He used this term to problematize the philosophical quest for a simple origin as a self-sufficient source. He identified a "logic of supplementarity," which is said to be "inconceivable to reason," according to which the supplement, by delayed reaction, produces that onto which it is said to be added (*Of Grammatology*, pp. 179 and 259). The force of Derrida's analysis relies heavily on the close readings of philosophical texts in which he uncovered this logic, most notably his reading of Jean-Jacques Rousseau in *Of Grammatology*.

The logic of supplementarity uncovers the rules that structure some of the apparent contradictions found in the texts of metaphysics. In the case of an author who courts paradox as readily as Rousseau, the task is particularly demanding. Derrida's diagnosis is that Rousseau wants to resist the conclusions he nevertheless cannot avoid. As a result, Rousseau's descriptions do not match with the declarations that reveal what he wants those descriptions to say. For example, Rousseau wants to identify the origin of language with speech and thereby make writing a "mere" supplement, but speech is itself a substitute for gesture, which is thereby, in a phrase whose apparent incoherence Derrida underlines, the primordial supplement. Derrida argued that instead of distinguishing Rousseau's use of "supplement" as addition from its use as "substitute," one should see the two senses as operating together (pp. 144–165). So, to continue with the example, much of what appeared contradictory in Rousseau's account of the origin of languages is found to arise because Rousseau wanted to locate the origin of language in the languages of the south but found himself having to draw constantly on the supplementary principles that he had associated with the languages of the north. The languages of the north were, therefore, not simply an external addition, but an alterity that must have been lodged within the system from the outset.

Derrida has exhibited the logic of supplementarity in other metaphysical texts. For example, in *Speech and Phenomena* (1973), Derrida located this operation in Edmund Husserl's account of language. Derrida identified a double tendency in Husserl, like that found in Rousseau. On the one hand Husserl wants to separate indication from solitary life, the strata of expression. On the other hand there are suggestions in Husserl's text that indication is constitutive of expression. The deconstruction of Husserl performed by this double reading is not a critique any more than the reading of Rousseau is. Neither thinker is criticized for failing to recognize the logic of supplementarity as such, not least because this logic has to be understood in terms of what metaphysics represses. The effacement of the primordial supplement is the condition of metaphysics, which thus can no longer be seen as a unity, as it was for Heidegger.

THE TRACE

That *trace* is another notion that Derrida employed as part of his contestation of the tradition of Western metaphysics understood in terms of the priority of presence is clear from his use of the phrase "a past that has never been present" to explicate it. The phrase itself is already found in Maurice Merleau-Ponty's *Phenomenology of Perception*, where it describes the unreflective fund of experience on which reflection draws. Derrida adopted the phrase in "Violence and Metaphysics" to explicate the notion of trace in the work of Levinas, who immediately introduced it into his own account.

Derrida employed various strategies to show that the trace challenges conventional thought. For example, in *Of Grammatology* (1976), when he introduced the concept of an originary trace or arche-trace, he underlined that it represents a contradiction because a trace, which is ordinarily possible only as an effect, is here posited as an origin. The point is to problematize the language and procedures of transcendental philosophy, especially transcendental phenomenology, on which the thought of the trace nevertheless depends for its articulation. This was already Levinas's aim when he appealed to the trace in his account of the possibility of ethics in terms of the face of the Other. The trace is more than a sign of remoteness; it is an irrecuperable absence. Levinas was serving notice that the face surpasses the limits of phenomenology and yet can be approached only through phenomenology. Similarly, even though Derrida makes Freud's failure to apply the effaceability of the trace to all traces a critical element of his reading, at the same time he explicitly recognizes Freud's unconscious as transcending transcendental phenomenology, just as the structure of delay in the sense of deferred effect (*Nachträglichkeit*) cannot be construed as a variation on the present.

These examples show how in the 1960s Derrida developed his account of the trace by gathering together the thought of such thinkers as Levinas and Freud, but he subsequently moved away from this largely parasitic approach. Most notably in *Cinders*, Derrida took the impossible thought of the trace to a different level by explicating it as ashes, with clear reference to the Holocaust. In this way the trace comes to define our epoch even more definitively, than when he drew on the thinkers who, as he had put it earlier, had helped to define our epoch.

CRITICISM AND RESPONSES

If deconstruction's initial impact within the United States has been strongest in literature departments, this is in part because Derrida's conviction that absolute univocity is impossible is more readily welcomed by literary critics, who have always celebrated the multiplicity or meaning, than by philosophers, whose discipline has tended to encourage a reduction on controlling of equivocity. Whereas the dominant tendency in philosophy has been to mark different uses of a term in an effort to control the ambiguity, the deconstructive approach is to question the basis of any attempt to limit the associations of language. This approach has sometimes been confused with an invitation to so-called free play, in the sense of arbitrariness in interpretation, although Derrida has often rejected this way of reading his work. In exploring equivocity, Derrida is acknowledging and not ignoring the ambiguity of words. In the literary context the constraints of deconstruction are sometimes neglected for the freedom of literacy experimentation. This is less common in Derrida than in some of his followers, but it has given ammunition to the critics of deconstruction.

The most persistent criticism of Derrida arises from his claim in *Of Grammatology* that "there is nothing outside the text" (p. 158). This has sometimes been understood to mean that all reference to the social and historical context is ruled out, and even that the text has no referent. It is easy to show that Derrida has never practiced such an extreme aestheticization of the text. What he did mean is explained in "Living On," in which he sets out the concept of a text as a differential network that overruns all the limits assigned to it (p. 84). This, the so-called general text, is not conceived as a totality. It does not have an outside, anymore than it has an inside. As Derrida explained in the 1988 afterword to *Limited Inc.*, there is nothing outside context, which is almost the opposite of what he is often accused of saying by many who do not share his philosophical background in phenomenology, psychoanalysis, or structural linguistics and yet fail to make allowance for that fact.

One of the most persistent criticisms raised against Derrida in the 1970s and 1980s was that his thought was ill-placed to address ethical and political issues. The understanding, widespread at that time, that Derrida's 1964 essay "Violence and Metaphysics," subsequently reprinted with revisions in the collection *Writing and Difference*, was critical of Levinas for his evocation of ethics after Nietzsche and after Heidegger's *Letter on Humanism* seemed to block him from making any such contribution. This interpretation has now been abandoned in the face of Derrida's repeated invocations of Levinas in the course of his own efforts to contribute to an understanding of ethics. It is here that a form of deconstruction as the exploration of certain aporias has come into his own. Derrida takes up the idea of a duty to go beyond one's duty. So, for example, in *Given Time* Derrida introduced the aporia of the gift whereby a gift is only a gift and not a form of exchange if there is no return on the gift. Derrida pursued these conditions to the point where even being aware that one is making a gift of something would constitute a form of return, thereby making the gift impossible. Parallel studies of hospitality and forgiveness followed. However, it should always be remembered that, for Derrida, the impossibility of the gift or of hospitality, for example, does not mean that giving and hospitality do not happen. It means rather that they are singular events that exceed, and so cannot be explained in terms of what precedes them.

See also Deconstruction; Freud, Sigmund; Heidegger, Martin; Husserl, Edmund; Language; Levinas, Emmanuel; Merleau-Ponty, Maurice; Metaphysics; Nietzsche, Friedrich; Phenomenology; Rousseau, Jean-Jacques.

Bibliography

A complete list of works by Derrida in French and English up to 1992, established by Albert Leventure and Thomas Keenan, is available in *Derrida: A Critical Reader*, edited by D. Wood (Oxford: Blackwell, 1992).

DERRIDA'S MAJOR PHILOSOPHICAL WORKS

De la grammatologie. Paris: Édtions de Minuit, 1967. Translated by G. Spivak as *Of Grammatology* Baltimore: The John Hopkins University Press, 1976.

La carte postale. Paris, 1980. Translated by A. Bass as *The Post Card* Chicago: Chicago University Press, 1987.

La dissémination. Paris, 1972. Translated by B. Johnson as *Dissemination* Chicago: Chicago University Press, 1981.

La voix et le phénomène. Paris, 1967. Translated by D. Allison as *Speech and Phenomena* Evanston, IL: Northwestern University Press, 1973.

L'écriture et la différence. Paris, 1967. Translated by A. Bass as *Writing and Difference* Chicago: Chicago University Press, 1978.

Glas. Paris, 1974. Translated by J. Leavey, Jr., and R. Rand as *Glas* Lincoln, NE: University of Nebraska Press, 1986.

Introduction to *L'origine de la géométrie* by Edmund Husserl. Translated by J. Leavey, Jr., as Edmund Husserl's *Origin of Geometry*. Lincoln, NE: Nebraska University Press, 1989.

Limited Inc. Translated by Samuel Weber and Jeffrey Mehlman. Evanston: Northwestern University Press, 1988.

"Living On." In *Deconstruction and Criticism*. New York: Seabury Press, 1979, pp. 75–176.

Marges de la philosophie. Paris, 1972. Translated by A. Bass as *Margins of Philosophy* Chicago: Chicago University Press, 1982.

Psyché: Inventions de l'autre. Paris: Galilée, 1987.

WORKS ON DERRIDA

Bennington, G., and J. Derrida. *Jacques Derrida*. Paris: Seuil, 1991. Translated by Geoffrey Bennington as *Jacques Derrida* Chicago: Chicago University Press, 1993.

Direk, Z., and L. Lawlor, eds. *Jacques Derrida: Critical Assessments of Leading Philosophers*. 3 vols. London: Routledge, 2002.

Gasché, R. *The Tain of the Mirror*. Cambridge, MA: Harvard University Press, 1986.

Lawlor, L. *Derrida and Husserl: The Basic Problem of Phenomenology*. Bloomington, IN: Indiana University Press, 2002.

Llewelyn, J. *Derrida on the Threshold of Sense*. London: Macmillan, 1986.

Robert Bernasconi (1996, 2005)

DE SANCTIS, FRANCESCO
(1817–1883)

Francesco De Sanctis, the Italian liberal politician and political and literary critic, was born near Naples. Although trained for the law, he turned to the study of Italian culture. He taught at the Military School of Naples, but his participation in the Revolution of 1848 led to his dismissal, a three-year prison sentence, and banishment. He taught and lectured in Turin and Zürich, and returned to Naples in 1860 as governor of the province of Avellino. As director of the Ministry of Public Instruction he brought scholars of great repute to the University of Naples and fought for the secularization of the public schools. After becoming editor of the newspaper *Italia* in 1863, he continued to champion reforms and helped to establish the modern Italian tradition of combining philosophy and worldly affairs. In 1868 De Sanctis returned to literary criticism. Several years later he completed his *Storia della letteratura italiana* (History of Italian literature). He accepted the chair of comparative literature at the University of Naples in 1872, but in 1877 he resumed his political career as organizer of a liberal opposition party, vice-president of the Chamber of Deputies, and minister of public instruction.

De Sanctis developed no systematic aesthetics or political philosophy. His principles of criticism are implicit in his essays. Literary truth, for De Sanctis, is realized in form, but literature's connection with political and social life is the substance of its meaning and the true source of formal beauty. Form transforms an idea into art and is the instrument by which artistic truth is achieved; it is art itself. Content and ideas are, for artistic purposes, without truth. Form provides truth, artistic integrity, the capacity to project an experience or idea so as to bring it subjectively alive for an observer. It does so successfully when it is naturally wedded to the content and seems fused with it. Successful form is derived from the concrete vision of the poet as he reflects on a living experience of the language and forms of his age. This tie between the artist and his immediate image is the deepest source of true art. The language and ideas of art spring from and are shaped by the social and historical events against which they act in the mind of the artist. De Sanctis sought, by grasping history and language, to grasp the work of art as conceived by the artist. History, and specifically political history, provides the framework in which ideas are tested against each other and find concrete representation in artistic form.

Traditional criticism saw technical skill as the essence of poetry, but poetry is involved with the values of the moral, historical, and social orders it expresses and reflects. The philosophical commitments of the poet, his moods and personal objectives, are the stimuli, the raw materials from which an ordered piece of art is shaped. The essence of art is form, but form into which content has passed and fulfilled itself.

De Sanctis believed that the poet must be immersed in the life of his national community. The subject and object of art is the human being. The artist must study man, exhort him, laugh at him, understand him. The artist's manner of picturing human life gives art its truth; this truth is gained by mastery of the language of the age and absorption of its combinations and formal possibilities.

Although art is measured by aesthetic criteria, as a historical phenomenon it is subject to social and moral considerations. Therefore, De Sanctis was led from literary criticism to literary history to the history of Italian culture and ultimately to the relation and debt of Italian culture to Italian politics.

Politics, De Sanctis believed, is a reflection of the moral fiber of a nation. Political activities reflect a wider cultural context and have a special responsibility for that culture, through the power to stimulate or repress it. Politics is a national dialogue between the various sectors of the population. The capacity of the popular classes to participate in and guard a national political organism, to preserve its morality in the face of the tasks of national destiny, to absorb the style and content of past national leaders imprints the national style and goal on political behavior.

Many of De Sanctis's political essays are exhortations, expressions of concern over apathy and loss of morality in political life, as well as attempts to express the inner urgings of Italy. For De Sanctis morality and culture were intimately connected. Moral political activity carried out Italy's destiny, which its previous culture had marked for restored greatness. The politics of a great nation reflects its culture and is perpetually open to self-renewal through the participation of the bearers of that culture. If they cease to participate in the nation's political activity, the culture breaks down, and politics becomes immoral, politicians self-aggrandizing, and the people apathetic.

See also Aesthetics, History of; Aesthetics, Problems of; Art, Truth in; Political Philosophy, History of.

Bibliography

PRIMARY WORKS

Scritti rarii inediti o rari, 2 vols. Naples, Italy: Morano, 1898.

Scritti politici, 3rd ed. Naples, Italy: Morano, 1900.

Saggi critici, 3 vols. Bari, Italy: Laterza, 1952.

La scuola liberale e la scuola democratica. Bari, Italy: Laterza, 1953.

Storia della letteratura italiana (History of Italian literature), 2 vols. Translated by Joan Redfern. New York: Barnes and Noble, 1968.

SECONDARY WORKS

Cione, Edmondo. *Francesco de Sanctis,* 2nd ed. Milan: Casoni, 1944.

Croce, Benedetto. *Estetica (Aesthetics),* 2nd ed. Translated by Douglas Ainslie. London: Macmillan, 1922.

Davis, John A., and Paul Ginsborg, eds. *Society and Politics in the Age of the Risorgimento: Essays in Honour of Denis Mack Smith.* Cambridge, U.K.: Cambridge University Press, 1991.

Holliger, Max. *Francesco De Sanctis: Sein Weltbild und seine Ästhetik.* Freiburg: Paulusdruckerei, 1949.

Landucci, Sergio. *Cultura e ideologia in Francesco De Sanctis.* Milan: Feltrinelli Economica, 1964.

Muscetta, Carlo. *Francesco De Sanctis.* Rome: Laterza, 1975.

Russo, Luigi. *Francesco De Sanctis e la cultura napoletana.* Venice: La Nuova Italia, 1928.

Irving Louis Horowitz (1967)
Bibliography updated by Philip Reed (2005)

DESCARTES, RENÉ
(1596–1650)

In *Discourse on Method* (1637), his first published work, French philosopher and scientist René Descartes combined an intellectual autobiography with a popular presentation of the system he was to develop more rigorously in his *Meditations* (1641) and *Principles of Philosophy* (1644). *Meditations* begins with a radical attempt to doubt all past beliefs, but finds a proposition that resists doubt in the existence of the self as a thinking thing. It then uses this initial certainty as a basis for arguing that God exists, that mind and body are distinct, and that we can achieve certainty in the sciences if we assent only to clear and distinct ideas, provided we have first shown that God would not deceive us about those ideas. The *Principles* uses the metaphysics and epistemology laid out in the *Meditations* as the foundation for an ambitious attempt to provide a scientific account of the entire world.

CHILDHOOD AND FORMAL EDUCATION (1596–1618)

Descartes was born on March 31, 1596, in the village of La Haye, in Touraine, at the home of his maternal grandmother, with whom he lived after his mother's death in 1597. His father, Joachim Descartes, was a member of the gentry and a councilor in the parliament of Brittany whose duties required him to spend several months each year in Rennes. When René was four, his father remarried and moved to Rennes; René and two older siblings remained with his grandmother. We do not know much about his earliest years, but it appears that he was never close to his father, either as a child or as an adult. His grandmother died when he was about fourteen.

At ten, Descartes entered the Royal College at La Flèche, founded two years earlier by Henry IV and run by the Jesuit order. The first five years of the program were guided by the ideals of Renaissance humanism, and thus were devoted to studying Latin, Greek, and classical literature (especially Latin and the works of Cicero). The last three years were dedicated to instruction in numerous subjects, including:

- Thomistic-Aristotelian philosophy, including dialectic (Aristotle's *Organon*), natural philosophy (Aristotle's *Physics*; *On the Heavens* [*De caelo*]; and *On Generation and Corruption* [*De generatione et corruptione*], book I);
- Mathematics (arithmetic, geometry, and topics in applied mathematics, such as astronomy);
- Metaphysics (Aristotle's *On Generation and Corruption*, book II; *On the Soul* [*De anima*]; and *Metaphysics*);
- Moral philosophy (Aristotle's *Nicomachean Ethics* and the work of Jesuit casuists).

Study of Aristotle and Aquinas made extensive use of late-sixteenth- and early-seventeenth-century commentaries, especially those by the Jesuits at the University of

Coimbra. Sometimes the curriculum ignored aspects of Aristotle's thought difficult to reconcile with Christian doctrine. Instead of reading the theological portions of Aristotle's *Metaphysics*, whose remote God is not the creator of the universe, students read a creationist treatise from the first century CE, *On the World* (*De mundo*), which was mistakenly ascribed to Aristotle. In other cases the problems were faced. Thomas Aquinas had interpreted Aristotle's teaching about the soul as consistent with the Christian doctrine of personal immortality. In the sixteenth century Pietro Pomponazzi had argued persuasively that Aquinas misread Aristotle and that Aristotle in fact held the soul to be mortal. Pomponazzi himself did not deny immortality; his official position was that philosophy could neither prove nor disprove the immortality of the soul, but that revelation made it certain. However, since he tended to identify Aristotle's views with those views that human reason would naturally reach unaided by revelation, he came perilously close to the doctrine of double truth associated with the Averroist tradition—the idea that philosophical truth and theological truth may conflict irreconcilably. The Jesuit curriculum called for the teachers in its colleges to attack the authority of such commentators.

Descartes may have drawn an unintended conclusion from these disputes. When he first began to work out his own theory of knowledge, he wrote, "Whenever two people make contrary judgments about the same thing, it is certain that at least one of them is wrong, and it seems that neither of them has knowledge. For if one had a certain and evident argument, he would be able to propose it to the other in a way which would in the end convince his intellect" (Adam and Tannery X, p. 363). The persistence of the dispute about whether immortality was consistent with an Aristotelian theory of the soul probably encouraged Descartes to develop his own anti-Aristotelian theory. His studies in mathematics may also have encouraged skepticism about Aristotelian natural philosophy. At La Flèche the teachers used the texts of the Jesuit mathematician Christopher Clavius (1538–1612), who argued that mathematics was superior to the other supposed sciences, because it succeeded in eliminating all doubt, and that the other so-called sciences demonstrated their uncertainty by their inability to elicit consensus.

At the time, the Jesuit colleges dominated secondary education in France and had an immense influence on the formation of a generation of leaders in politics, philosophy, and religion. Their primary mission was to combat the Protestant heresy, but they also reciprocated the King's support, defending his claims to absolute power. The colleges required total immersion in the Jesuit educational program, permitting little contact with the outside world (parents included). Descartes had mixed feelings about this education. In his *Discourse on Method* he was quite critical of it, claiming it had not provided him with what he had hoped for—clear and certain knowledge of everything useful in life—but had instead left him embarrassed by many doubts and errors. It seemed to him that he gained nothing from his studies but an increasing awareness of his own ignorance. Still, he was careful to say he thought his school had given him as good an education as was then available, and he later recommended it to friends for their children.

Descartes completed the program at La Flèche in 1614. In *Discourse* he wrote that as soon as he was old enough to leave the control of his teachers, he completely quit the study of letters and sought what knowledge he could find either in himself or in the great book of the world. This is not entirely true. We do not know much about what he did in the years between 1614 and 1618, but we do know that he completed a degree in law at the University of Poitiers in 1616. His earliest biographer, Adrien Baillet, reports that Descartes spent the first year after leaving La Flèche in St. Germain-en-Lay, a village outside Paris. The Royal Gardens there contained remarkable statues, designed to move, play music, and even speak. Seeing these machines mimic the behavior of living, intelligent creatures may have helped make plausible to Descartes his later doctrine that animals are nothing but machines.

INFORMAL EDUCATION: ENCOUNTERING BEECKMAN (1618–1619)

In the summer of 1618 Descartes left France to join the army of Maurice of Nassau in the Netherlands. His legal studies would more naturally have led to a career in the law or government, possibilities he considered at various times in the next several years. But in 1618 military life was more enticing, with its opportunities to travel and to learn about the practical application of scientific theories. Maurice encouraged scientific research and employed one of the leading scientists in the Netherlands, Simon Stevin, to oversee his army's education in military technology. Among Stevin's scientific accomplishments were an experimental refutation (anticipating Galileo Galilei) of the Aristotelian theory that heavy bodies fall faster than light ones and his discovery of the "hydrostatic paradox": that the downward pressure of a liquid depends only on the height and base of its vessel and is independent of its shape. As a military engineer, Stevin developed a system of sluices to flood the fields, giving the Dutch a critical (if Pyrrhic) means of defense against invading armies. In 1618 the Dutch were still enjoying an extended truce in their war for independence from Spain, so Descartes saw no combat. In a letter from this period he wrote that he spent his time learning drawing, military architecture, and Dutch. But he also mentioned plans to write books.

The stimulus for this last ambition was his encounter with Isaac Beeckman, a Dutch scientist, several years his elder, whom he met in November 1618. In a letter to Beeckman, Descartes credits Beeckman with having roused him from his laziness, recalled to his mind the learning he had almost forgotten, and brought him back to serious pursuits. By the spring of 1619 Descartes was contemplating two works, one in mechanics, the other in geometry. In his enthusiasm, Descartes wrote to Beeckman and promised to embrace him as "the promoter and first author of my studies" (Adam and Tannery X, p. 162). Their later relations were not so cordial. In 1630 Descartes was to write Beeckman complaining that the older man was claiming too much credit for having been Descartes's teacher. Though they later reconciled, Descartes makes no mention of Beeckman in the *Discourse.*

Why was Descartes's encounter with Beeckman so important? First, as Beeckman put it, they shared a desire to "combine physics with mathematics in an exact way" (Gaukroger 1995, p. 69). Beeckman had been working on problems in this manner for some years and was delighted to find a like-minded colleague. One result was a short treatise that Descartes wrote on music, attempting to work out a mathematical relationship between the various sounds that appear pleasing to us in combination. He may have begun this treatise before he met Beeckman, but he finished it in December and presented it to Beeckman as a gift on New Year's Day, 1619.

Their more normal pattern of interaction was that Beeckman would set up Descartes with a problem in mechanics or some related area, and invite him to solve it. For example, Beeckman recognized that bodies falling freely in a void would accelerate uniformly. So he posed the following problem: Suppose that a body moving in a void will move eternally (in opposition to Aristotelian physics, Beeckman assumed a version of the principle of inertia). Suppose further (again in opposition to Aristotle) that there is a void between a falling stone and the Earth, and that the stone covers a given distance in a given time. How far will it fall in half that time? As early as 1604 Galileo had worked out the correct law governing the free fall of bodies, which implied that the velocity of the falling body is proportional to the duration of time that it falls, but he did not publish this result until 1638. Descartes concluded that the velocity was proportional to the distance covered, a mistake that Galileo had also made in his first attempt to solve the problem. What is important here is that Beeckman was encouraging Descartes to engage in the Galilean project of discovering laws governing the motion of bodies, expressible in mathematical formulas.

Another area where Beeckman influenced Descartes involved his program of explaining macroscopic physical phenomena in terms of the mechanical properties of the microscopic particles composing them. This program—generally now called "the corpuscularian hypothesis" or "the mechanical philosophy"—had connections with ancient atomism, but differed from atomism in important respects. It did not assume that the component particles were indivisible, and as Descartes was to develop it, it did not assume the existence of a void. Moreover, whereas ancient atomism had regarded the size and shape of the atoms as the primary explanatory factors, the corpuscularians emphasized the speed of the particles and direction of motion.

One problem that Beeckman set for Descartes was to explain in corpuscular terms Stevin's hydrostatic paradox. Descartes postulated that the weight of the column of water can be reduced to the force exerted by its particles in their tendency to downward motion and that each particle of water on the bottom of the container is connected with a particle on the surface by a unique line of particles along which the force (tendency to motion) is transmitted. It is surprising that Descartes thought this explanation worked. It seems plausible where the area at the surface and the area at the base are equal in size, but not in the cases that most require explanation, cases where the area at the surface is smaller (or larger) than the area at the base.

These examples give us an idea of the sort of study that Descartes might have included in the work on mechanics he was contemplating. His work in mathematics seems to foreshadow his discovery of analytic geometry, his most enduring contribution to the sciences. In a letter to Beeckman in March 1619, Descartes excitedly wrote that he hoped to discover "a completely new science," one that would "provide a general solution of all possible equations, involving any sort of quantity, whether continuous or discrete" (Adam and Tannery X, pp. 156–157). The path to solving these geometric or arithmetic problems seems to have involved using complex instruments, "proportional compasses." Descartes devised compasses that not only solved the problem of dividing an angle into any number of equal smaller angles, but also solved cubic equations of varying degrees of complexity. He had not yet formulated the program, which he was to develop in his *Geometry*, of using algebraic means to solve geometric problems. But he had taken a step toward unifying arithmetic and geometry.

FINDING A VOCATION IN GERMANY (1619–1620)

In the spring of 1619, as the Thirty Years War was just beginning, Descartes set out for Germany to join the army of Maximilian of Bavaria, the leader of the Catholic League. In the *Discourse* he tells us he attended the coronation of Ferdinand II as Holy Roman Emperor. As he was returning to the army, the onset of winter detained him in a place where he had no one to talk to and no cares to trouble him. Shut up all day in a stove-heated room, he was alone with his thoughts. This isolation produced the first of two major turning points in his life. In a document now lost that Baillet saw and preserved (apparently in a mixture of paraphrase and quotation), Descartes wrote that on November 10, 1619, while "full of enthusiasm," he discovered "the foundations of a wonderful science." Descartes left behind conflicting indications of what this discovery was.

The account in the *Discourse*, written seventeen years later, implies that Descartes's discovery involved a decision that to make firm judgments in the sciences, he would have to rid himself of all his previous opinions and reconstruct his system of beliefs on new foundations, accepting nothing he had previously believed until he had squared it with reason. Too much of what he believed was based on uncritical acceptance in his youth of the opinions of others. The document Baillet saw—an account of three dreams that Descartes reported having had on the night of November 10, probably written not long after the event—doesn't suggest a project of ridding himself of all his past opinions. Nor does Descartes's earliest methodological work, *Rules for the Direction of the Mind*, which he apparently began around this time.

Of the three dreams, the most important was the last. In that dream Descartes found two books on a table. One he describes as a dictionary; the other was an anthology of poetry. When he opened the anthology, he found a poem by Decimus Magnus Ausonius (c. 310–395) that opens with the sentence *Quod vitae sectabor iter?* ("What path shall I follow in life?") Descartes said that while he was still asleep, he recognized he had been dreaming and began to interpret his dreams. He construed his discovery of the poem by Ausonius as indicating that he must choose the proper direction for his life. And the dictionary, which we should probably think of as more like an encyclopedia, he interpreted as representing a collection of all the sciences. The dream as a whole he took to indicate that the path he should choose in life was to pursue the sciences and demonstrate their fundamental unity. A fragment preserved from this period expresses that idea vividly: "The sciences now are masked, but if the masks were taken off, they would appear most beautiful. Someone who sees how the sciences are linked together will find them no harder to retain in his mind than the series of numbers" (Adam and Tannery X, p. 215). Descartes's vocation was to unmask the sciences. The ambition to construct a unified system of all scientific knowledge was to guide him for the rest of his life.

RULES FOR THE DIRECTION OF THE MIND (EARLIEST STAGES, 1619–1620)

Among the unfinished works Descartes left behind at his death was a treatise on methodology, which he apparently worked at, off and on, between 1619 and 1628: *Rules for the Direction of the Mind* (*Regulae*, for short). He intended the *Regulae* to be a three part work, each part of which would consist of twelve rules. Although he completed only the first part and about half of the second part, this is the most substantial work we have from the period before 1629. Its parts often seem inconsistent with one another, apparently reflecting different stages of the work's composition and the lack of any unifying revision. Nevertheless, the work sheds light on Descartes's development and later thought. Our best current theory of its composition—resulting from the analyses of Jean-Paul Weber (1964) and John Schuster (1980)—holds that Descartes wrote a part of Rule Four first, perhaps before the night of the three dreams, that he completed most of Part One sometime during the period from 1619 to 1620, and that he then set the work aside for several years, returning to it in the period between 1626 and 1628, when he added Rules Twelve through Twenty-One. After that, he abandoned the work, for reasons we can only guess.

The second half of Rule Four ("Rule IV-B," as it is now called, beginning at the bottom of Adam and Tannery X, p. 374) recounts Descartes's first investigations of mathematics and his disappointment with the ancient mathematicians. He found in them many propositions about numbers that he recognized as true after doing his own calculations and many conclusions about figures that his authors reached by logical arguments. But they did not explain why these things should be true or how they had discovered them. Descartes conjectured that the ancient mathematicians possessed an algebraic method of discovery they concealed because it made the discovery of mathematical truths too easy. They feared that revealing their method would diminish people's respect for their accomplishments. Rule IV-B is entirely concerned with the project of developing a general method for discovering mathematical truth.

The second stage of the *Regulae* is more ambitious, aiming to formulate a methodology that applies to *all* the sciences. They are all, he says, "nothing but human wisdom, which always remains one and the same, however much its objects may differ" (Adam and Tannery X, p. 360). The sciences are so interconnected and interdependent that it is easier to learn them together than separately. What someone seeking truth in the sciences must first do is to consider how to increase his "natural light of reason," the cognitive abilities he is naturally endowed with. ("Ingenium," the term traditionally translated as "mind" in the title, *Regulae ad directionem ingenii*, might more happily be translated as "native cognitive powers.") Negatively, this means that we should rely only on intuition and deduction—that is, on propositions whose truth we can see distinctly, with certainty, when we attend to them carefully, without being confused by what our senses and imagination tell us, and on propositions that can be inferred from propositions of the first kind by a process of inference equally clear and certain.

Descartes claimed that the only genuine sciences discovered thus far were arithmetic and geometry. But he denied that these were the only areas where we could achieve absolute certainty by intuition and deduction. There are more intuitively certain truths than most people suspect. He gave as examples the propositions that he exists, that he thinks, and that a triangle is bounded by just three lines, among others. If we make proper use of such truths, not mixing them up with probable assumptions, we will be able to extend the certainty of mathematics to other areas. This was an attack, not only on reliance on the senses or imagination, but also on the scholastic use of "probable syllogisms," whose premises needed only the support of a majority of the wise to be acceptable. Descartes thought that in difficult matters the minority is more likely to be right than the majority.

Positively, Descartes's central message is that we must conduct our investigations in an orderly way, gradually reducing complex and obscure propositions to simpler ones, until we reach propositions simple enough that we can know them intuitively, that we can *see* their truth without the aid of other propositions. Once we have completed that reduction, we can work our way back, step by step, to the proposition whose truth or falsity we originally wished to determine. Suppose that the problem is to find the three mean proportionals between 3 and 48. We might not have any intuitions about the answer. But if we look for the single mean proportional between those numbers, 12, then we will have reduced the original problem to something more manageable, finding the mean proportionals between 3 and 12 and between 12 and 48. We can see easily enough that 3 is to 6 as 6 is to 12, and that 12 is to 24 as 24 is to 48. Seeing this enables us to see that 6, 12, and 24 are the numbers sought.

The visual metaphor here is deliberate. "Intuitus," the Latin noun translated as "intuition" is derived from a verb, "intueri," whose basic reference was to visual perception, though it was commonly extended to mental acts of consideration and contemplation in classical Latin. Descartes thought that we can learn how to better use our mental power of intuition by comparing it to vision. If we try to look at many physical objects at once, we see none of them distinctly. Likewise if we try to attend to many propositions in a single act of thought. We can improve our vision, both physical and mental, by focusing our attention on one simple object at a time.

Descartes emphasized that intuition is required not only for our knowledge of the premises of our inferences, but also in the inferential process itself. To have scientific knowledge of the conclusion of an inference, we must intuit not only the premises of the inference, but also the connection between the premises and the conclusion. To know by deduction that $2 + 2 = 3 + 1$, we must see not only that $2 + 2 = 4$ and that $3 + 1 = 4$, but also that our conclusion follows necessarily from these premises. We cannot avoid relying on intuition by insisting, with the Scholastics, that our arguments possess formal validity. Descartes accepted the classical skeptical critique of syllogistic reasoning: that it is useless as a means of acquiring knowledge, because the formalization of the argument—the addition of a suppressed conditional or universal premise to transform an enthymeme into a formally valid syllogism—accomplishes nothing. If the suppressed premise is evident, it is unnecessary for the argument's validity. If the suppressed premise is not evident, then all that the formalization of the inference accomplishes is to increase the number of assumptions requiring proof.

WANDERER YEARS (1621–1625)

After the initial burst of energy that produced the earliest stages of the *Regulae*, Descartes appears to have set the project aside for a while and to have produced no significant work. He traveled here and there, returning to France, visiting Italy (perhaps more than once), and finally returning to France for an extended stay in Paris. He sold the property that he had inherited from his mother, using the proceeds to secure a modest but regular income. This freed him from the need to earn a living. He probably made a pilgrimage to Loreto, Italy, fulfilling a promise made after the night of the three dreams. Apparently, he did not visit Galileo when he passed through Florence. But during this period he seems to have made the acquaintance of Marin Mersenne (a member of the Order of Minims, residing at a convent in Paris), who shared his interest in mathematics and the new mechanical philosophy.

In these years Mersenne was preoccupied with arguing against the radical, Pyrrhonian skepticism that Michel de Montaigne had popularized, which he regarded as a serious threat to religion and society. His "refutation," summed up in *La vérité des sciences contre les sceptiques ou pyrrhoniens* (*The Truth of the Sciences*; [1625]), conceded to the skeptic that we cannot have certain knowledge of the essences of physical things, but insisted that we can have certain knowledge in mathematics (including such applied mathematical disciplines as geometrical optics). He also argued that sense experience provided the basis for knowledge of the physical world, so long as it claimed to be no more than knowledge of appearances, not of the essences of things. If Descartes was not familiar with the Pyrrhonian skeptical challenge before his association with Mersenne in the 1620s, he must have been aware of it by then.

LIFE IN LIBERTINE PARIS (1625–1628)

When Descartes returned to Paris in 1625, he encountered a contentious intellectual scene. Not only were men like Mersenne concerned about the threat of Pyrrhonism, but Paris had just seen the trial of Théophile de Viau, a protestant poet whose writings contained suggestions of Lucretian atomism, a celebration of sensuality, and an advocacy of free thought. Only a few years earlier Giulio Cesare Vanini had been burned in Toulouse for spreading doctrines alleged to be materialistic. The "libertines," as these and other freethinkers were called, were accused of holding scandalous religious opinions and of leading a debauched, hedonistic way of life—the natural consequence of their denial of (or skepticism about) the afterlife. One of Mersenne's projects in this period was a lengthy attack on religious unorthodoxy, *L'impiété des déistes, athées et libertins de ce temps* (The Impiety of the Deists, Atheists, and Libertines of Our Time [1624]). Using, no doubt, a very generous criterion for atheism, Mersenne estimated that in Paris alone there were then at least 50,000 atheists (the population of the whole city at the time was only about 300,000).

Whether or not the threat was as grave as Mersenne claimed, it provoked a response that sought to repress any kind of unorthodoxy. In 1624 three men attempted to hold a public debate in which they would have challenged various theses in Aristotelian natural philosophy. There was apparently considerable public interest in the proposed debate, for it is said to have attracted a crowd of eight or nine hundred people. But the Theology Faculty at the Sorbonne prevented it from occurring. The men were banished from Paris on pain of death; the *parliament* prohibited anyone from holding or teaching theses "contrary to the ancient approved authors, and from holding any public debate other than those approved by the doctors of the Theology Faculty" (Gaukroger 1995, p. 136). The penalty for violating this edict would be death.

Descartes does not seem, at this stage of his life, to have engaged in these culture wars. His main preoccupations, apparently, were with solving problems in geometrical optics and resuming work on the *Regulae*. Sometime during these Paris years he evidently discovered the law of refraction known as Snell's law: When light passes from one medium to another, the sine of the angle of incidence is proportional to the sine of the angle of refraction. (Though Willebrord Snell discovered this law before Descartes, Descartes's discovery was independent of Snell's.) Knowledge of this law is required to solve a practical problem in optics, that of finding the anaclastic curve, the shape that the surface of a lens must have to collect parallel rays of light into a single focus. This knowledge was necessary to design a telescope that would provide a clearer image than existing telescopes did. When Descartes was doing this work, the telescope was a recent invention, dating back only to his years at La Flèche. Descartes was quite excited about the potential of the new scientific instrument for extending our knowledge of nature.

In his treatise on *Optics*, published in 1637 with *Discourse on Method*, Descartes tried to explain Snell's law micromechanically, in terms of the tendencies to motion of the particles involved in the transmission of light rays and the laws of motion, which he held applied to tendencies to motion as well as to motions. He also proposed a solution to the problem of the anaclastic curve: that the lenses should have a hyperbolic shape. His new studies in optics also had an impact on his revision of the *Regulae*, providing him with an example of the use of the method that extended its range from mathematics to physics.

THE LATER *REGULAE* (1626–1628)

According to our best current theory of the composition of the *Regulae*, one change that Descartes made when he returned to this work was to add two examples of the method to Rule Eight in a passage now generally designated as "Rule Eight-C" (Adam and Tannery X, p. 393–396).

The first example deals with the problem of determining the anaclastic curve. Earlier rules prescribed that we gradually reduce complex and obscure propositions to simpler ones, till we reach an intuition of the simplest propositions, from which we can then retrace our steps till we achieve intuitive knowledge of the proposition we originally wished to know. Someone who follows this advice is supposed to see, first, that determining the anaclastic line depends on determining the relation between the angles of refraction and the angles of incidence. He will not be able to determine that relation by conjecture or by appeal to experience or by learning it from the philosophers. But he will make progress if he realizes that the relation depends on the change made in the angles by the difference of the media, and that this change depends on how a ray of light penetrates a transparent medium. Knowing how it penetrates that medium requires knowing the nature of light. Understanding light requires, finally, knowledge of what a natural power is in general.

In this passage Descartes did not say what a natural power is. Here he limited himself to claiming that because this is "the most absolute thing in the whole series," the most basic item in the investigation, which does not depend on anything more fundamental, it is something we will be able to grasp intuitively. Once we have done that, we will be able to retrace our steps—using our understanding of natural powers to understand the nature of light, our understanding of light to understand how it penetrates transparent media, and our understanding of light penetration to understand how a change in the medium changes the path of a light ray—until we are finally able to answer the question about the anaclastic curve. Elsewhere in the *Regulae* (Adam and Tannery X, p. 402), Descartes suggests that understanding the concept of a natural power requires reflection on the local motion of bodies—the idea apparently being that bodies always act on one another by transmitting motion from one body to another through contact.

The frequent talk of intuition and deduction in the *Regulae* is apt to suggest—what many people are inclined to believe on other grounds anyway—that Descartes's scientific methodology is wholly a priori. But this is not true, even in the *Regulae*. Although Descartes says in Rule Eight-C that we cannot determine by experience the relation of the angle of refraction to the angle of incidence, the reason seems to have been that the question is too complex to be resolved by an appeal to experience. "We can have certain experiential knowledge," he said, "only of things completely simple and absolute." We might infer that we derive from experience our intuition of what in this case is most simple—of what a natural power is, of how bodies naturally act on one another in cases where this action is immediately intelligible.

When Descartes was developing his theory of light in the *Optics*, he frequently used analogies from experience. The transmission of light from a luminous body to the object of illumination is like the transmission of resistance through a blind man's cane from the object in his path to his hand. The reflection of light from a shiny surface is like the motion of a tennis ball when it bounces off an impermeable surface. Refraction is like the motion of a tennis ball when it encounters a permeable surface. Not everything we observe is as immediately intelligible as these analogical cases are. The movement of iron filings subjected to the power of a magnet is mysterious. But it's part of Descartes's scientific program to try to understand such phenomena by reducing them to others that are readily intelligible. Insofar as Descartes appeals to common experience in support of these intuitions, his method in the sciences is not wholly a priori.

The other example that Descartes added when he returned to Rule Eight he describes as "the most notable of all." Everyone who loves truth in the slightest degree, he said, should, set himself, once in his life (*semel in vita*), the task of determining what truths human reason is capable of knowing and what questions are beyond our cognitive powers. This will prevent him from always being uncertain about what the mind can do and save him from wasting time on matters our faculties are not capable of dealing with. Someone who undertakes this task will discover that nothing can be known prior to the intellect, since knowledge of all other things depends on it, and it does not depend on knowledge of them. But though Descartes asserted the priority of the pure intellect, he also acknowledged that we have other instruments of knowledge in addition to the intellect. In Rule

Eight-C Descartes said that there are two such instruments: the imagination and the senses. In the text that follows (from Adam and Tannery X, p. 396, 26, to the end of Rule Eight, commonly dubbed "Rule Eight-D" and apparently a rewrite of Eight-C), he added a third instrument: memory.

What is most striking about this passage is its difference from well-known later texts to which it is in other respects quite similar. Three times in Rule Eight (once in Eight-C, twice in Eight-D) Descartes used the phrase "semel in vita" to refer to a project that everyone who wants to use his cognitive powers well should undertake once in his life. Each time he describes the project, with minor variations, in Lockean terms, as one which requires us to determine the limits of the human understanding. Descartes used the same phrase, "semel in vita," in the opening sentence of the First Meditation, also to refer to a project one should undertake once in one's life. But in the *Meditations* the project involves, not determining the limits of the human understanding, but *overthrowing all the opinions he has haphazardly acquired over the years, so he can start anew, from firm foundations*. Three years later, in *Principles of Philosophy*, he used the same phrase, "semel in vita," to again call all seekers after truth to the same overthrow of any past opinion in which they find even the smallest suspicion of uncertainty. As Descartes develops this project in the *Meditations*, it becomes clear that among the opinions to be rejected, at least provisionally, are those involving even the simplest truths of mathematics, which in the *Regulae* were paradigms of certainty. The call to radical doubt, undertaken in the hope of achieving absolute certainty—the most characteristic feature of Descartes's published works—is nowhere present in the *Regulae*.

SEEKING SOLITUDE IN THE NETHERLANDS (1629–1633)

Toward the end of the Paris years Descartes attended a meeting that was to become the second major turning point in his life. The meeting, attended by many of Paris's leading intellectuals, occurred at the palace of the papal nuncio. The speaker was a chemist/alchemist named Chandoux, who attacked Aristotelian natural philosophy as an inadequate basis for chemistry and apparently proposed a mechanistic approach in its place. Contrary to what we might have expected from the ban on criticisms of Aristotle in 1624, most of those present, who included Mersenne and Cardinal Pierre de Bérulle, received Chandoux's speech well. Descartes did not.

Bérulle noticed that Descartes did not share the group's enthusiasm and asked why. After politely trying to excuse himself from saying what he thought, Descartes gave an extended critique of Chandoux, praising his desire to rescue philosophy from "the perplexity of the schoolmen" (Baillet, p. 69), but faulting him for replacing it with something merely probable. If merely probable arguments are allowed, he contended, it is easy to make the false appear true and the true false. He then challenged the company to give him an example of an incontestable truth. When they did, he produced a dozen probable arguments designed to prove its falsity. Then he asked them for an example of an evident falsehood. When they provided one, he showed the falsehood to be credible by another dozen probable arguments. The group then asked him whether there was any infallible way of avoiding sophisms. He replied that he knew of no more certain way than to use the method he commonly followed, which was derived from mathematics, and which he thought sufficient to provide a clear demonstration of all truths.

Descartes's dialectical ingenuity made a deep impression on his audience, especially Cardinal Bérulle, who asked to see him privately. When they met later, Descartes claimed that if he continued his inquiries, the benefits to the public would be considerable. He could achieve results in medicine that would greatly improve people's health and results in mechanics that would greatly lessen people's labor. Bérulle replied that since God had given Descartes this extraordinary talent, he owed it to God and his fellow men to make full use of it. Descartes had been thinking about leaving Paris for some time. This conversation tipped the balance. He resolved to take up residence in the Netherlands, where he would find a more congenial climate and, more important, the solitude that would allow him to meditate without constant interruptions by his friends.

There is nothing up to this point to indicate that Descartes had entertained radical skepticism as a serious possibility. He must have been aware of the debates about Pyrrhonism and of some of the Pyrrhonist literature. But Baillet's account of the Chandoux episode and Descartes's own description of the event in 1631 both suggest a Descartes whose epistemology is very like that of the *Regulae*: dismissive of scholastic philosophy and of any reliance on probable arguments, confident of the certainty of mathematics and of the method he had modeled on his discoveries in mathematics. In his first years in the Netherlands, Descartes's attitude on these issues changed, it seems.

We know from a letter to Mersenne in November 1630 that soon after Descartes moved there (probably during the winter of 1628–1629), he began what he described as "a little treatise on metaphysics," in which he set out to prove "the existence of God and of our souls when they are separate from the body, from which their immortality follows" (Adam and Tannery I, p. 182). This "little treatise" sounds like an early version of the *Meditations*. It was evidently not complete at that point, and we do not know much about its specific content, but from an earlier letter to Mersenne (April 15, 1630) it appears that Descartes worked on this treatise for the first nine months that he was in the Netherlands.

In that letter of April 15, Descartes also described what seems to be a different "little treatise," begun more recently. To provide himself with an extra incentive to finish it as soon as possible, he promises to send it to Mersenne by the beginning of 1633. Mersenne will be amazed, he says, that he is taking such a long time to write a treatise so short that it requires only an afternoon to read. This treatise was apparently focused on physics. But Descartes said that he would not have been able to discover the foundations of his physics if he had not approached them by first trying to know God and himself, and that he had discovered how to prove metaphysical truths in a way more evident than the proofs of geometry. This suggests, for the first time, that Descartes was trying to ground physics on metaphysics, specifically on a metaphysics that focuses on a knowledge of God and the self. It also suggests, for the first time, that there may be something defective about geometrical proofs, that considered apart from a metaphysical foundation, they may be less certain than the metaphysical proofs Descartes discovered.

Why did Descartes then think geometrical proofs might need a metaphysical foundation? The letter of April 15 contains a possible clue. For the first time Descartes stated a doctrine for which he was to become notorious: the creation of the eternal truths. He wrote to Mersenne that in his treatise on physics he would discuss several metaphysical topics; in particular, he would defend the view that the eternal truths of mathematics have been established by God just as a king establishes laws in his kingdom, that they depend entirely on him, no less than does the rest of his creation.

There has been much debate about what this doctrine means and why Descartes held it. But our present concern is its relation to the certainty of mathematics. When Descartes argued, in the First Meditation, that even mathematical truths are subject to doubt, he did not invoke this doctrine that God created them. He simply appealed to the idea of God as an omnipotent being who created him, and who *could*, if God had chosen, have created him so imperfectly that his cognitive apparatus might lead him astray, even in the things that seem most evident to him. In the correspondence and elsewhere, we can see that Descartes thinks a proper understanding of omnipotence would conclude that it requires the ability to determine what the eternal truths are. But Descartes knows this was an unusual, controversial conception of omnipotence, and he did not deploy it in the First Meditation. In the *Discourse*, as he was about to justify his skepticism about mathematics, Descartes would write, "I don't know whether I should tell you of the first meditations that I had [in the Netherlands], for they are perhaps too metaphysical and uncommon for everyone's taste."

Since Aquinas, the dominant view among Scholastics was that God has the power to determine, by his will, what contingent truths are true, but that his will does not determine what necessary truths are true. Those truths were supposed to be grounded in God's intellect, in the ideas he has, not in his will. The meditator of the First Meditation approaches the question of what things are subject to doubt from the perspective of someone just beginning to philosophize, who presumably holds conventional views about what God's omnipotence implies. Moreover, the ability to interfere with his creatures' cognitive faculties would not seem to require God to have the power to create eternal truths. Surely, anyone with enough power to create the world of contingent beings must have the power to make one species of contingent being defective in its perception of necessary truths.

Skeptics nevertheless suggested that God's power might extend to eternal truths and used that thought to ground a doubt about mathematics and any other truths we might think necessary. In his *Apology for Raymond Sebond*, one of Montaigne's arguments for Pyrrhonian skepticism involves the claim that because God's power is incomprehensibly great, we speak irreverently if we say that there is something he cannot do. Among the things that Montaigne suggested it would be impious to say God cannot do are to make two times ten not equal twenty, to go back on his word, to cause a man who has lived not to have lived. Montaigne did not say that God *created* the eternal truths. But he did say it is arrogance on man's part to claim that God *cannot render false* the truths commonly classed as eternal. This category includes not only simple mathematical truths, but also metaphysical truths (such as "The past is immutable" and "Nothing is made of nothing") and moral truths (such as "A perfect being would not go back on his word"). And he uses these accusations of irreverence and arrogance to justify his claim that we ought to suspend judgment about everything, including these supposedly incontestable truths.

Descartes agreed with Montaigne that we do not do justice to God's power if we say that there is something God cannot do. "We can assert that God can do everything within our grasp, but not that he cannot do what is beyond our grasp" (Adam and Tannery I, p. 146). To say that God's power is limited to what we can comprehend would be rash and disrespectful. Descartes did not want to say that God can render the eternal truths false. They are immutable. But they are immutable because God's will is immutable. So by the spring of 1630 Descartes thought there was a need to ground physics (including the truths of mathematics) in metaphysics, and his perception of this need was connected with his view that God's power is incomprehensibly great. He thought that he had a way to accomplish this grounding, and he began, but did not complete, a draft of a treatise on metaphysics like the *Meditations* that would accomplish that.

THE WORLD (1629–1633)

Descartes never did publish the treatise on physics he referred to in his correspondence as "*The World*" (or "my *World*"), but he used material from it in his *Optics* (1637) and *Meteorology* (1637) and *Principles of Philosophy* (1644). And portions of the work appeared after his death: one under the title *Le monde, ou Traité de la lumière* (The World, or Treatise on Light [1664/1979]), which reproduced the beginning of the treatise, another titled *Traité de Homme* (Treatise of Man [1662/1972]), which reproduced a later part of it. Here the entire physical treatise, as projected in the early 1630s, will be referred to as *The World*, and the title *Treatise on Light* will refer to the opening portion published in 1664.

The World originated in Descartes's concern with the problem of explaining parhelia, the bright spots that sometimes appear in a solar halo, caused by the refraction of sunlight through ice crystals in the atmosphere. In the summer of 1629 a friend had shown him a description of this phenomenon and asked him what he thought of it. Descartes set aside work on his treatise on metaphysics to see what he could make of it:

> My mind is not so strong that I can devote it to many tasks at once, and as I never make any discoveries except through a long train of diverse considerations, I must devote myself wholly to a subject when I wish to investigate some particular aspect of it" (Adam and Tannery I, p. 22–23).

His curiosity about parhelia led him first to inquire into meteorological phenomena in general (including the rainbow, another effect of refraction in the atmosphere) and then to the incredibly ambitious project of explaining "all the phenomena of nature, that is, the whole of physics."

The Treatise on Light begins by arguing that there can be a difference between the visual sensation we have of something and what there is in the object that produces this sensation. The common view, he claimed, is that our ideas are completely like the objects from which they proceed. But there are many experiences which should cast doubt on this. For example, in the case of sound, most philosophers think that the cause of our auditory sensations is a vibration in the air, which does not resemble those auditory sensations at all. Descartes proposed that something similar is true of light.

The first step in discovering the nature of light is to identify the bodies that we know produce light. These seem to be the stars and fire. Because the stars are too remote to be easily observable, Descartes concentrated on fire. When we watch fire burning a piece of wood, we observe that it sets the minute parts of the wood in motion and separates them from one another. It transforms the smallest particles into fire, air, and smoke, and leaves the grosser particles as ash. Scholastic philosophers might have supposed that in addition to these mechanical processes, there is a form of fire or a quality of heat involved. But Descartes (applying Ockham's razor) limited himself to what he saw as necessarily part of the process and did not postulate anything unnecessary to explain the phenomena. Since it is inconceivable that one body should move another except through its own motion, Descartes inferred that the body of the flame is composed of particles so small as not to be observable but moving so rapidly that, in spite of their small size, the force with which they act on the wood is great enough to disperse its particles. The motions of the flame particles cause both the light the flame produces and its heat, depending on which sense organs they encounter. But in neither case is there any resemblance between the cause and the idea.

Descartes observed that there is nothing anywhere in nature that is not changing. He suggested that the changes involved in combustion are not unusual: In many cases the cause of observable changes will lie in the motions of unobservable particles. The principle at the core of the mechanical philosophy is that all physical change is reducible to change of place in bodies, if not in bodies large enough to be observable, then in bodies so small as to be unobservable. The fundamental differences among bodies are in the size, shape, and motion of their constituent particles.

Descartes distinguished three elements, which he called "fire," "air," and "earth." These are not to be identified with the elements traditionally so-called or with the familiar substances commonly so called. Fire is a very subtle liquid, made up of the smallest, fastest moving particles, which have no determinate size or shape. This permits them to fill the gaps between the particles of the other elements and makes it unnecessary to allow for the existence of a void. Air too is a subtle liquid. Its particles are small and fast-moving compared with those of earth, but large and slow-moving compared with those of fire. They have a determinate size and shape; almost all of them are round. The particles of earth are the largest and have little or no movement. Descartes emphasized that he did not attribute the traditional qualities of heat and cold, moisture and dryness, to his elements. He took those qualities to require explanation themselves, by appeal to the size, shape, and motion of bodies or their constituent particles.

Having explained the basic elements of his physics, Descartes then asked us to imagine that God has created, somewhere in space, a new world, made only of such matter, and has distinguished the different bodies in this world from one another only by the different motions he has given to the different parts of its matter. There is no order in the initial state of this imaginary world. Descartes's project was to show how a world like ours could emerge from this chaos, given only the laws of nature that God established when he created this world. (Genesis, of course, tells us how the world we are familiar with *was* created. Descartes professed to be interested only in exploring other ways God could have done it.)

The language Descartes used here—that God *established* the laws of nature—is reminiscent of the language he used in his letter to Mersenne, where he said that God established the eternal truths (referred to as "laws in nature") as a king establishes laws in his kingdom. The comparison to a king suggests that there is something arbitrary about this act and may also suggest that the laws are subject to change. Descartes wanted the suggestion of arbitrariness, but he did not want the suggestion of mutability. Writing to Mersenne in 1630, he anticipated an objection that Mersenne might encounter when he publicized Descartes's view (as Descartes encouraged him to do):

> They will tell you that if God had established these truths, he could change them, as a king makes his laws. To which one must reply: Yes, if his will can change.—'But I understand them as eternal and immutable.'—And I make the same judgment about God" (Adam and Tannery I, p. 145–146).

In the correspondence of 1630, Descartes invoked the immutability of God's will to explain the immutability of the eternal truths. In *The World* he used it to give content to the laws of nature.

God, "as everyone must know," is immutable. (Presumably, this could have been established by an argument from God's perfection in the 1629 treatise on metaphysics.) This entails that he always acts in the same way. This, in turn, entails that he continues to preserve the objects he created in the same way he created them. That does not mean that things do not change. On the contrary, since God endowed some of these things with motion when he created them, it means that he preserves that motion. This fact, combined with the absence of a void, entails that when beginning to move, bodies also begin to change and diversify their movements through their encounters with other bodies.

Descartes claimed to derive three principal laws of nature from God's immutability: (1) Each part of matter always continues to exist in the same state, so long as encounters with other bodies do not cause it to change. (2) When bodies push against one another, the total quantity of motion is preserved (one body cannot increase the motion of another body without losing as much of its own motion as it transfers to the other body). (3) Although the motion of a body is usually in a curved line, it always *tends to move* in a straight line. Because Descartes denied the existence of a void, he insisted that all motion must be "in some way circular." Since there is no empty space for a body to move into, it can move only by displacing other bodies. Ultimately, each moving body must be part of a chain of moving bodies that forms a closed curve of some sort. Though Descartes deduced these laws from God's immutability, which he presumably knew a priori, he also insisted that they agree well with what we find in experience. Aristotelian physics, he pointed out, assumes that motion will continue only as long as force continues to be applied to the moving object; so it has difficulty accounting for projectile motion.

From these assumptions about the nature of matter and the laws according to which matter moves, Descartes developed a theory about how a world like ours might have evolved from the chaos that he supposed God originally created in the hypothetical new world. Since that world is a plenum, whose parts must displace other parts to move at all, and all motion must be in a closed curve, matter will naturally organize itself into vortices, masses of matter swirling, whirlpool-like, around a center. The element of fire will tend to concentrate at the centers of the vortices, composing the Sun and the stars; the element of earth will tend to form into large clusters, rotating around the centers of their vortices and carried along by particles of the second element. The planets are formed from such clusters, as are the comets. But the planets remain in one vortex, whereas the comets have motions that carry them from one vortex to another. This clearly heliocentric system implies not only that Earth rotates around the Sun, but also that our solar system is only one of many in the universe, each forming around the various stars, which are no longer embedded in a single sphere, as in the Aristotelian-Ptolemaic cosmology.

Descartes went on to offer explanations for the planets' rotations around their axes, the motions of satellites (moons) around their planets, the movement of the tides, weight, and light. The last he interpreted as resulting from the rotation of the Sun and the matter around it. This generates a radial pressure, which spreads outward from the Sun along straight lines from its center. He enumerated a dozen properties of light that he claimed this theory can account for: that it is propagated from all sides of the luminous body, to any distance, instantaneously, normally in a straight line, but subject to reflection when it encounters a body it cannot penetrate, and subject to refraction when it encounters a medium it can penetrate, and so on. The treatise as it has come down to us does not explain reflection and refraction but instead refers us to his *Optics*, published in 1637. In another work, *Meteorology* (1637), Descartes offered explanations of rainbows and of parhelia.

The work commonly known as the *Treatise of Man* was to have been part of *The World*, though it appears that it would not have come immediately after the *Treatise on Light*. We do not know how many intervening chapters are missing, but we can have a fair idea of their intended contents from the description of *The World* in Part Five of the *Discourse*. Among the topics covered would have been the formation of mountains, seas, springs, and rivers on Earth; the formation of metals in the earth and plants in the fields; and the nature of fire and its various properties, such as its ability to form glass from the ashes of the material it has burned.

The *Treatise of Man* was to have included accounts of both the body and the soul, though only the chapters dealing with the body survive. These chapters begin by asking us to imagine that God created a statue or machine made of earth (the element), which he intended to make as much as possible like us. Just as the *Treatise on Light* tries to show that God could have produced a world that would look just like ours, using only the materials and mechanisms Descartes described, so the *Treatise of Man* tries to show that God could have produced machines that would have looked and behaved just like the human body, using only such means. Though an exception would be the functions that Descartes thinks need to be attributed to the rational soul, notably the intelligent use of language, he claimed to give a mechanistic explanation of all the animal functions that Aristotelian philosophy attributed to vegetative and sensitive souls: the digestion of food; the beating of the heart; the nourishment and growth of members; waking and sleeping; the reception of light, sounds, smells, heat, and so on, by the sense organs; the transmission of ideas of these qualities to the brain; the retention of these ideas in memory; the internal movements of the appetites and passions; and the external movements of the limbs (insofar as their explanation does not depend on the actions of the soul).

We cannot go into these explanations here, but two points about them deserve notice. First, we know from his correspondence that Descartes spent a lot of time during these years dissecting animals to learn anatomy. However much works like the *Regulae* encourage the picture of Descartes as a purely a priori scientist, and however much justice there may be in that picture, it is clear that in practice Descartes believed it was necessary for scientists to do a great deal of data collection. When Mersenne wrote saying that he knew people so dedicated to advancing the sciences that they were willing to make all kinds of experiments at their own expense, Descartes replied,

> It would be very useful if some such person were to write the history of celestial phenomena, according to the Baconian method, describing exactly for us the present appearance of the heavens, without any explanations or hypotheses, reporting the positions of each fixed star in relation to its neighbors, and their differences in size, color, visibility, brilliance, and so on. He should tell us how far this accords with what ancient astronomers have written about it and what differences there are; for I have no doubt that the stars are constantly changing their relative position somewhat, in spite of being called fixed. (Adam and Tannery I, p. 251–252)

Descartes himself regularly offered hypotheses to explain phenomena. But he knew that a satisfactory explanation of phenomena required good descriptions of the phenomena to be explained and that such descriptions required empirical inquiry. He might also have acknowledged that the necessary empirical inquiries would be guided by intuitions about what the ultimate explanation of the phenomena was likely to be. In this case, his call for a Baconian history seems to be guided by his conviction that the so-called fixed stars are not really fixed.

Second, although it may not be obvious that Descartes's scientific procedure in *The World* exemplifies his method, we can regard it as an extension of the method described in Rule Eight-C of the *Regulae*. Reflection on the problem of determining the anaclastic curve had persuaded Descartes that solving that problem would require understanding refraction, which would require understanding the nature of light and its transmission, and ultimately, understanding what a natural power is. In the *Regulae* Descartes was vague about what a natural power might be, suggesting only that it had something to do with local motion. When he began to write *The World*, his starting point was a similar problem in optics, explaining parhelia, which he must have realized would also involve understanding refraction. He already believed that understanding refraction required understanding the nature of light, and that understanding light required understanding what a natural power is. He then saw that understanding the concept of a natural power requires a full-fledged theory of the nature of bodies and the laws governing their motion, and that getting this right should enable him to explain all kinds of phenomena, both in the heavens and on Earth.

THE GALILEO AFFAIR AND ITS AFTERMATH (1633–1637)

Descartes never published *The World*, despite having worked hard on it for years and having achieved results he was very proud of. In 1616 the Church condemned as false and contrary to Scripture the Copernican doctrines that Earth moves and that the Sun is motionless. It prohibited a book by Paolo Foscarini that taught this doctrine, and suspended Nicolaus Copernicus's *On the Revolutions of the Heavenly Spheres* "until it should be corrected." Also, Cardinal Robert Bellarmine, in a private meeting with Galileo Galilei, ordered him to abandon the Copernican view. Descartes knew that the Copernican view had been censured. He probably did not know about Galileo's meeting with Bellarmine. He seems to have heard rumors that, in spite of the censure, some continued to teach the Copernican view "publicly, even in Rome."

In 1623 a Florentine cardinal friendly to Galileo became Pope Urban VIII. After discussions with the new pope, Galileo got permission to write a treatise on the Copernican system, provided he treat it as a mathematical hypothesis, no more than a convenient predictive device. Galileo apparently decided to test the limits of this permission. He wrote a dialogue in which one participant defended the Copernican theory, another defended the Ptolemaic theory, and a third played the role of uncommitted inquirer. His spokesman in the dialogue does not claim certainty for the Copernican theory. Moreover, he permitted his representative of orthodoxy to have the last word, proclaiming that, however plausible the pro-Copernican arguments might be, we can never know with certainty what the true explanation of the phenomena is. God, in his infinite power and wisdom, might have produced the phenomena in any number of ways. Finally, in the preface he claimed that his work treated the heliocentric theory as "a pure mathematical hypothesis," adopted for astronomical convenience, and that he was writing only to demonstrate that Italians were well aware of the scientific case *for* Copernicanism, and that the prohibition of 1616 had not been issued in ignorance. After long negotiations with the censors, he secured permission to publish his *Dialogue Concerning the Two Chief World Systems* in 1632.

But his precautions proved insufficient. It was evident to careful readers that he had crossed the line between hypothetical consideration and advocacy. In the spring of 1633 he was tried by the Inquisition on the charge of "vehement suspicion of heresy." What this language meant, in this case, was that he had presented views contrary to Scripture as if they were probable, but that there was some doubt as to whether he had the evil intention necessary for conviction of formal heresy. Found guilty in June, he was sentenced to house arrest for the rest of his life and required to abjure his errors.

In November 1633 Descartes wrote to Mersenne that he had tried to buy a copy of Galileo's *Dialogue*, which he heard had been published the year before. But when he looked for it, he learned that it had been confiscated and burned. He was so astonished, he said, "that I almost decided to burn all my papers, or at least, to let no one see them. For I could not imagine that he, who is an Italian, and even (as I hear) favored by the Pope … could have been made a criminal simply because he wanted (as doubtless he did) to establish the movement of the earth" (Adam and Tannery I, p. 270–271). The doctrine of the Earth's movement, Descartes writes, is so connected with the other parts of his own *World* that he could not detach it without making the remainder very unsatisfactory. If that doctrine is false, "all the foundations of my philosophy are, too, for they demonstrate it quite evidently." When he learned several months later that Galileo had been condemned "even though he pretended that he proposed [the Copernican system] only hypothetically" (Adam and Tannery I, p. 271) he was especially concerned, since he had adopted a similar device himself, representing himself as merely telling a story about how God *could have* created a world like ours, while conceding that Genesis tells us how he *did* create it.

It is not clear what stage *The World* was in at this time. Descartes said that he had been on the point of sending it to Mersenne as a New Year's present, if it could be copied in time. Perhaps it was nearer completion than the surviving parts would suggest. For a while Descartes held out hope that there may be a way to publish it. Perhaps this action of the Inquisition had not yet been ratified by the pope or by a Church council. If so, it may not have the full authority of the Church behind it. But eventually Descartes decided to abandon his treatise for the time being and adopt a different plan. He decided to publish a semiautobiographical treatise on method, to be supplemented by three short treatises demonstrating the power of his method: *Optics*, *Meteorology*, and *Geometry*.

THE *DISCOURSE ON METHOD* AND ITS ESSAYS (1637)

At age forty-one, with only thirteen more years to live, Descartes published his first works. Thus began the public career that would earn him a reputation as the father of modern philosophy. As we have noted, Descartes's *Discourse on the Method of Conducting One's Reason Well and Searching for Truth in the Sciences* is partly autobiographical, but it is not very reliable in this regard, for it omits important events (such as his relation with Beeckman, his three dreams, and his encounter with Chandoux); it projects into the past ideas that Descartes probably had only at a later date (such as the idea of overturning all his past opinions to reconstruct his beliefs on firmer foundations); and it is silent on ideas that Descartes feared might cause his readers to raise objections he did not want to deal with (such as the creation of the eternal truths). Descartes himself warned us not to take his work too seriously as autobiography when he wrote that he was presenting it "only as a history, or, if you prefer, a fable." Descartes wanted us to read his work for its moral, for examples of conduct to imitate or avoid. But he also cautioned us that both fables and history have their dangers: Fables may make us think that something is possible when it is not, and even the most accurate histories, because of their selectivity, may make us conceive plans beyond our powers.

Examples of conduct to imitate would be examples of how to conduct our reason when we seek truth in the sciences. Descartes offered four rules that he said he found sufficient in this search:

> 1) never accept anything as true which he did not know evidently to be true, including nothing in his judgments except what has presented itself so clearly and distinctly to his mind that he had no reason to doubt it;
>
> 2) divide the difficulties he was examining into as many parts as possible;
>
> 3) conduct his thoughts in an orderly way, beginning with the simplest objects, and ascending gradually to the most complex; and
>
> 4) make enumerations so complete and reviews so comprehensive that he was sure he had not left anything out. (Adam and Tannery VI, p. 18–19)

Presented thus baldly, these rules probably do not give enough direction to be very useful. And in a letter to Mersenne in February 1637, Descartes disclaimed any intention to *teach* his method in the *Discourse*. His purpose there was only to *talk* about it, and his purpose in the scientific essays that accompanied the *Discourse* was to show what could be accomplished through its use. Even the essays do not, for the most part, purport to show the method at work. As Descartes explained in a letter to Antoine Vatier in February 1638, "I could not show the use of this method in [the three scientific treatises] because it prescribes an order for investigating things which is rather different from the one I thought I had to use to explain them" (Adam and Tannery I, p. 559). But Descartes made one exception to this generalization. He told Vatier he had given a sample of the method in his discussion of rainbows in the eighth chapter of *Meteorology*.

In that chapter Descartes began by noting that rainbows occur not only in the sky but also in the air near us, whenever there are many drops of water in the air illuminated by the Sun. We know this from our experience with fountains. He inferred from this that the rainbow arises only from the way light rays interact with drops of water, and from there move toward our eyes. Previously in the *Meteorology* he had shown that these drops are round; he also knew, presumably from experience, that the occurrence of a rainbow is independent of the size of the drops.

These reflections suggested an experiment that enabled him to examine the phenomenon close up, in circumstances he could control.

He filled a large, round flask with water and positioned it so that the Sun was coming from behind him as he faced it. Then he situated himself in relation to the flask so that he observed a bright red spot at its bottom. He discovered that a line drawn from his eye to the bottom of the flask made about a 42-degree angle with a line drawn from the Sun to the flask's bottom. Furthermore, no matter how he moved—nearer to the flask or further away, to the right or to the left, even if he made the flask revolve around his head—he always saw a red spot at the bottom, so long as the angle between his line of vision and the line of the Sun's rays remained about 42 degrees. If he increased the angle, the red disappeared. If he decreased it slightly, the spot did not cease to be colored, but divided into two less brilliant parts of different colors (yellow, blue, etc.). From this he inferred that if all the air in that direction were filled with such round drops of water, a red spot would appear in each drop where the angle between the Sun's rays and the line of vision was about 42 degrees, producing a continuous circle of red spots. Similar circles of other colors would be generated in drops that were at slightly more acute angles.

Through further experiments with the flask, Descartes discovered that the red spot did not disappear when the light source was blocked, so long as light was permitted to enter at the top of the flask and leave at the bottom, and so long as certain paths within the flask were not blocked. He inferred that the appearance of red at the bottom was caused by refraction of the Sun's rays as they enter at the top of the flask, their reflection from a point at the back of the flask, and their refraction again at the bottom of the flask as they leave it to move toward the eye. He proposed a similar explanation for the production of the secondary bow, which appeared at an angle of about 52 degrees and had its colors arranged in reverse order. This, he inferred, arises from a combination of two refractions and two reflections.

So far the phenomena Descartes was trying to account for depended essentially on the refractive index of water in relation to air, a figure that he could calculate accurately. And so far his explanation of the phenomena was basically right. But he still had not explained what he called the principal difficulty: Why do only those rays refracted at a certain angle cause certain colors to appear? To resolve this difficulty, he undertook a series of experiments with a prism, a similar object also known to produce a spectrum of colors. The prism differed in various ways from his flask, and these differences enabled him to eliminate as irrelevant certain features of the flask. To produce a spectrum of colors, it is not necessary that the medium through which the light passes have a curved surface, or that the light strike that medium at a particular angle, or that it be reflected, or that it be refracted more than once. But it is necessary that the light be refracted at least once.

At this point Descartes invoked his theory of the nature of light, that it is the action or movement of particles of air (the element), which must be imagined as little balls. These balls have two motions, one in the direction of their propagation, the other rotational. Different degrees of rotational motion produce different color sensations when they strike the eye. The differences in the colors produced when light is refracted arise from the fact that the refractive process imparts different degrees of rotational motion to the light particles. (For further details, see Gaukroger 1995, chap. 6.)

This part of Descartes's explanation has not fared well. But the example remains interesting in a number of respects. First, it illustrates Descartes's second and third rules: dividing a complex problem into as many parts as possible till you reach something simple and easy to understand, and then retracing your steps back to the complex phenomenon you were originally interested in. The complex phenomenon is the rainbow. The simple object is the individual drop of water seen to have one of the colors of the rainbow. By using a model of the simple object, which we can observe close up and manipulate, we can determine the conditions for its being seen as having the color it has, and we can determine how changing those conditions might produce different colors (or no colors at all). We then reconstruct the complex phenomenon from the simple model by recognizing that if we observed a mass of such simple objects in the sky, the ones observed at the right angle for producing a particular color would form a continuous circle of that color, and that other concentric circles of different colors would also be produced at different angles.

But this example also warns us that if we use the concepts of intuition and deduction to analyze our solution of this problem, we need to understand those concepts very broadly. Our understanding of how the simple objects behave involves a priori elements, insofar as we make use of geometry to deal with certain aspects of the problem (such as the shape of the bow). But it also involves numerous appeals to experience. It is by careful experiment that we determine that the same color is produced so long as the same angle is preserved, or that a double refraction, combined with reflection, is involved in producing the primary bow, or that the refractive index of water in relation to air has the particular value it has. Our ordinary experience of fountains initially suggests a way of breaking the complex phenomenon down into simple elements. Experience is also involved, no doubt, in the theory of matter that Descartes's theory of light invokes. There is no a priori reason why there must be exactly three elements, having the properties that Descartes assumed they have. A priori considerations of simplicity and intelligibility speak for this theory when it is compared with the scholastic forms and qualities. But those considerations would not be sufficient to warrant acceptance of the theory if it were not capable of explaining a wide range of phenomena, as Descartes clearly thought it is.

The rules of the *Discourse*, then, are quite similar to the rules of the *Regulae*, provided that we interpret the concepts of the *Regulae* freely. But one notable feature of the *Discourse* is the absence of any explicit discussion of intuition and deduction. The ghosts of these concepts are present in the first rule, insofar as Descartes advises us to never accept as true anything we don't know to be evidently true, making no judgments except those that present themselves so clearly and distinctly to our minds that we have no reason to doubt them. This excludes reliance on merely probable assumptions. But it does not explicitly mention intuition or deduction. And it suggests a problem we have so far not considered, because so far it has not seemed to arise in the writings we have considered.

Throughout his work Descartes was clearly a foundationalist, at least in the minimal sense that he thought some of our beliefs are based on other beliefs we have, whereas some are not based on others. We can call the ones not based on others *basic beliefs*. Our basic beliefs provide the foundations for our system of beliefs; our derivative beliefs, the superstructure. This metaphor of our system of beliefs as like a building, which has foundations and a superstructure and might collapse if the foundations are not solid, is prominent in the *Discourse* and in the *Meditations*, but is only implicit in the *Regulae*, where Descartes presents arithmetic and geometry as the only genuine sciences yet discovered, superior to all other alleged sciences because of the certainty of their initial assumptions and the care with which mathematicians derive from those assumptions only conclusions clearly seen to follow from them.

But the *Regulae* does not have a criterion for distinguishing the absolutely certain from the merely probable. It assumes that mathematics is more certain than the other sciences because it is concerned with objects so pure and simple that it need make no assumptions that experience has rendered uncertain. At that point, that is all that Descartes thought it necessary to say to justify reliance on the assumptions of mathematics. But in the *Discourse* (and the *Meditations*), he is concerned with a problem his earlier work had not considered. It is not the problem of the creation of the eternal truths, but a different skeptical problem.

We are not born with fully mature cognitive faculties. Rather our faculties develop gradually as we grow to adulthood. While they are developing, we accept, uncritically, many propositions from parents, teachers, and others whose authority we have come to respect. Then we learn, sadly, that these are not perfectly reliable sources. The propositions we accepted in this way can seem quite obvious. Nevertheless, they lack a firm foundation, and we can be mistaken about them, even when they seem most obvious. This reflection gives us a reason, not only for doubting the specific propositions we have accepted from others and everything based on them, but also for wondering whether our cognitive faculties, our basic capacities for distinguishing truth from falsity, are as reliable as we thought they were.

The *Discourse* not only identifies this problem; it offers a solution for it. Descartes was not content, in this work, simply to say that the basic beliefs we acquire through intuition are indubitable or evident. He wanted to show that we perceive some propositions so clearly and distinctly that there is no reason to doubt them, even on a generous conception of what might constitute a reason for doubt. So in Part IV of the *Discourse* he embarked on a project of rejecting as false anything in which he could "imagine the least doubt." This is what is called the method of doubt. He was very permissive in what he counted as a ground of doubt. He was prepared to allow that even "the most extravagant suppositions of the skeptics" provide some ground for doubt. If a belief can survive that permissive a test, we cannot reasonably demand anything more certain as a foundation for our beliefs. If we are to doubt, we must have some reason to doubt. But if we want what survives our attempt to doubt to be absolutely certain, we must be thorough about the attempt; we must allow even the most improbable possibilities to count as reasons for doubt.

This might seem to be a quixotic quest if Descartes had not apparently discovered something that resists his attempts to doubt it: that he, who is engaged in this methodical doubt, and thus is thinking, exists. So we encounter what is commonly referred to as "Descartes's *cogito*," a label deriving from the Latin version ("*Cogito, ergo, sum*") of an inference that appears in the *Discourse* in French: "*Je pense, donc, je suis*" ("I think; therefore, I exist").

Though there is something very compelling about that inference, it is not clear exactly what Descartes was claiming as his initial certainty. In the *Regulae* he had cited both "I think" and "I exist" as truths known certainly by intuition; if that's their status, then either proposition might be a suitable foundation for demonstrations. In the *Discourse* he seems to be inferring his existence from his thought, as if he can be certain of his existence because he can be certain that he thinks—and, moreover, certain that to think, it is necessary to exist (Adam and Tannery VI, p. 32–33). This suggests that his affirmation of his existence is the conclusion of the following demonstration:

(1) To think, it is necessary to exist.

(2) I think.

(3) Therefore, I exist.

This way of thinking about the *cogito* naturally raises the question of how Descartes can be certain of the premises of this demonstration. The *Discourse* does not explicitly ask that question, but it does have what looks like an answer to it, as far as the first premise is concerned, where Descartes says that he sees very clearly that (1) is true. Though the *Discourse* has not offered any *theory* of intuition, this looks like an appeal to intuition, a faculty whose reliability we might have thought was put in doubt when Descartes questioned the certainty of simple mathematical truths.

The *Discourse* does not even *seem* to answer the question as it concerns the certainty of the second premise. But in a letter that Descartes wrote to Henri Reneri in 1638, the answer seems to be that when we are thinking, we cannot doubt that we are thinking (Adam and Tannery II, p. 38). This may suggest the following argument for the certainty of (2):

(4) When we think, we cannot doubt that we think.

(5) I am thinking.

(6) Therefore, I cannot doubt that I am thinking.

But though Descartes often seems to accept (4), or propositions equivalent to it, there are times when he seems to reject such claims. Earlier in the *Discourse* he had written that "many people don't themselves know what they believe; for the act of thought by which one believes a thing being different from the act by which one knows that one believes it, the one often occurs without the other" (Adam and Tannery VI, p. 23). Moreover, the argument consisting of propositions (4) to (6), if offered as a demonstration of the certainty of (2), looks hopelessly question-begging: it assumes the truth (and certainty) of the proposition whose certainty it claims to prove. So the *cogito* argument of the *Discourse*, in spite of its fame and wide appeal, is problematic. Fortunately, the argument takes a different, and more attractive, form in the *Meditations*, as we shall see below.

The remainder of part IV gives a quick sketch of the argument Descartes would develop more fully and accurately in the *Meditations*. Having found one proposition that he knew to be true and certain, he provisionally formed a general rule: Whatever we conceive very clearly and very distinctly is true. Reflecting on his nature as a doubter, and hence as imperfect, he asked how he could have acquired his ideas of things other than himself. Most of them, he thought, he could have generated himself. But the idea of God is an exception. An imperfect being cannot cause itself to have the idea of a perfect being. So God must be the cause of his idea of God. God, therefore, must exist. To this causal argument he added a version of the ontological argument: If God is a perfect being, as we conceive him to be, then he cannot lack the perfection of existence. Having established the existence of God, he proceeded to argue that because everything real and true in us comes from a perfect being, the general rule he had provisionally adopted is correct: All our clear and distinct ideas must be true. And even those ideas that are not clear and distinct must have *some* foundation in truth. This account of Descartes's metaphysics raises issues that are best pursued in the discussion below of the *Meditations*.

Parts V and VI of the *Discourse* are primarily concerned with Descartes's *World*, which, he wrote, "certain considerations" prevent him from publishing. He tantalizes us with a summary of its contents, omitting any explicit mention of its Copernicanism, but strongly hinting that the Church's condemnation of Galileo is the reason that he could not publish at that time. He did not mention either the Church or Galileo by name, but what he did say must have left little doubt in the minds of informed readers: "People to whom I defer and who have no less authority over my actions than my reason has over my thoughts have disapproved an opinion in physics, published not long ago by someone else" (Adam and Tannery VI, p. 60). Descartes did not say whether he accepted this opinion, but he did say that before the authorities' censure he had not noticed anything in the work "prejudicial either to religion or to the state," so nothing would have prevented him from publishing this opinion himself if his reason had convinced him it was true. This censure, he said, made him fear that he might have made some mistake in his own theories. And that, combined with a fear of getting involved in time wasting controversies, made him decide not to publish, at least at that time.

Descartes had clearly not given up all hope of publishing *The World* during his lifetime. He even suggested that he had a duty to publish it: If, as he thought, he was on the path to developing a correct and comprehensive physics, giving an account not only of the heavens, but of all the principal kinds of bodies here on Earth, the potential benefits would be enormous. Such a science would enable us to become "the masters and possessors of nature." It would offer the hope of discovering new ways to maintain our health and prolong our lives. He saw only two obstacles to his achieving this goal: the brevity of life and the lack of observations. Though he presented the foundations of his physics as a priori ("To discover in general the principles or first causes of everything that exists or can exist in the world … , I considered nothing but God alone, who created the world"), he reported that as he proceeded from the first causes, through the first and most ordinary effects deducible from them, to more particular things, he found that the only way he could discover the causes of the particular effects was to construct what Bacon called crucial experiments.

Descartes's principles were so general that there were many ways he could deduce the effects from them. To determine which, among many possible ways to produce the effects, was the one God had chosen, he needed to set up situations where the alternative theories would have different observable consequences. To do that he would need money for research. Part 6 of the *Discourse* was, among other things, an appeal for money from public-spirited citizens who saw the value of his work and wished to aid him. But the whole project of the *Discourse* and its essays was also intended to generate such interest in his project that the Church would feel obliged to permit him to publish his *World* during his lifetime. Failing that, he would publish posthumously.

Other matters in Parts V and VI of the *Discourse* merit more discussion than they can receive here: Descartes's discoveries regarding the circulation of the blood, which he made independently of William Harvey, and his affirmation that the fundamental laws of nature are necessary truths that must be observed in any world that God might have created. Here we must limit ourselves to noting his provocative doctrine that animals are nothing but machines. In the portions of *The World* dealing with humankind, Descartes had tried to show that God could have produced machines that would have looked and behaved just as the human body does, using only matter of the kind Cartesian physics allows and the laws that follow from God's nature. Descartes aimed to give a mechanistic explanation of many different animal functions, all the functions, in fact, that humans share with the lower animals. He did not think mechanism could explain all human activities. Some, notably the intelligent use of language, could be explained only by the presence of a rational soul embedded in the machine. We can be certain from their language use, Descartes thought, that the human-looking bodies around us are inhabited by rational souls. (He was not troubled by the problem of other minds.) But nonhuman animals, which do not display intelligent language use, lack a rational soul; they are nothing but complex machines, lacking even sensations of the kind we have.

This doctrine had a strong impact, most of it in ways that Descartes would not have welcomed. Some thought it absurd to draw such a sharp distinction between humans and the rest of the animal kingdom. Some accused the Cartesians of being cruel to animals, or at least of having no good reason not to be. And some argued that Descartes was right about lower animals, but wrong to think that humans are fundamentally different. They too are nothing but very complex machines.

THE START OF CONTROVERSY (1637–1641)

After publishing the *Discourse* and its essays in June 1637, Descartes spent the next few years responding to criticisms of his work and, toward the end of the period, preparing to publish his *Meditations*. The criticism of the 1637 publications tended to focus, not on metaphysics or epistemology, but on his commitment to mechanistic explanations in science: of light, of the circulation of the blood, of animal behavior. In the early part of this period he tried to reassure friends in the Jesuit order that his work does not contain dangerous innovations. He boasted to Vatier (Adam and Tannery I, p. 564) that the faith had never been so strongly supported by human reasons as it was by his, and that transubstantiation, "which the Calvinists criticize as impossible to explain by the ordinary philosophy, is very easily explained by mine." But by 1640, the Jesuit priest Pierre Bourdin's criticism of his *Optics* had persuaded Descartes that he had to 'go to war with the Jesuits' (Adam and Tannery III, p. 752).

By that point Descartes had already begun revising his "little treatise" on metaphysics (the future *Meditations on First Philosophy*) and planned to circulate it privately among twenty or thirty theologians before making it public so that he could learn from their criticisms what needed to be corrected or added before publication (Adam and Tannery II, p. 622). Descartes told Mersenne that his book on metaphysics was to contain "all the foundations of my physics," but cautioned him not to tell people that, "for those who favor Aristotle might make more difficulty about approving them. I hope that readers will gradually get used to my principles, and recognize their truth, before they notice that they destroy Aristotle's principles" (January 28, 1641; Adam and Tannery III, p. 298).

Descartes was particularly keen to have the Sorbonne's approval of his work. This may seem out of character, for in the *Discourse* he said that since God has given each of us some capacity for distinguishing truth from falsity, he felt obliged not to be content with accepting the opinions of others (Adam and Tannery VI, p. 27). Presumably this is an obligation we all have. But experience had persuaded him that he needed the support of the authorities to get people to read his work carefully and to free himself from having to reply to quibbling, malicious critics (Adam and Tannery III, p. 184, 237–238).

When the *Meditations* first appeared in August 1641, the original plan had changed. Instead of circulating his work first among twenty or thirty theologians to get objections that might lead to changes, Descartes delegated most of the preliminary circulation of the work to Mersenne, who selected a smaller number of critics, not all theologians. Instead of modifying the text in the light of this criticism, Descartes left the text largely untouched, publishing the objections he received and his replies after the main text. Each critic could see the preceding objections and replies in composing his own.

The author of the first set of objections was a Dutch Catholic theologian named Johan van Kater (Johannes Caterus). Mersenne himself is generally credited with having written some or all of the anonymous second and sixth sets of objections. The third, fourth, and fifth sets of objections were written by Thomas Hobbes, Antoine Arnauld, and Pierre Gassendi, respectively. Those were the only objections included in the first edition. When the second edition appeared in 1642, there was an additional set of objections, by Father Bourdin, accompanied by Descartes's irate replies. Descartes was not a man to suffer fools gladly, and he found it easy to believe that his critics were fools. Sometimes he was right.

MEDITATIONS ON FIRST PHILOSOPHY (1641)

The title page of the first edition claims that Descartes was publishing it "with the approval of the learned" and that in his work he would demonstrate both the existence of God and the immortality of the soul. Neither of these claims was true. Though he and Mersenne tried, they were not able to get the approval of the Theology Faculty at the Sorbonne. While Descartes did offer several arguments for the existence of God, he did not even attempt to prove the immortality of the soul. Both these mistakes were corrected on the title page of the second edition, which appeared in the following year. But it is puzzling that they were made in the first place. Some have blamed them on Mersenne, who saw the work through the press. He is supposed to have hastily inferred from the Dedicatory Letter to the Theology Faculty that Descartes intended to prove the immortality of the soul. But in December 1640 Descartes warned Mersenne not to expect a proof of immortality in the *Meditations*. Descartes thought the most he could prove was that the mind is distinct from the body, not subject to die when the body does. Since God is omnipotent, he can always annihilate the mind (Adam and Tannery III, p. 265–266). The title page of the second edition claimed only a proof that mind and body are really distinct, and it dropped any claim to be approved by the learned.

The *Meditations* is a work with multiple agendas. No reasonable interpreter doubts that Descartes wanted to establish the religious conclusions announced on the title page of the second edition. But the First Meditation emphasizes a different aim: establishing something firm and lasting in the sciences. It is that project that has preoccupied most English-language students of Descartes and made the *Meditations* one of the most commonly used texts in modern universities. The project involves more than just validating our reliance on clear and distinct ideas. As Descartes said in a letter to Mersenne (January 28, 1641), he also wanted to accustom people to the foundations of his physics and destroy Aristotelian natural philosophy.

The First Meditation begins by recalling the project of the *Discourse*: ridding ourselves of all past beliefs. Descartes assumed that if a belief survives a thorough attempt to doubt it, and is permissive in what it counts as a valid ground of doubt, it will qualify as indubitable and provide a proper foundation for reconstructing our system of beliefs. If the fact that a belief is indubitable is to make it a proper foundation for a new system of beliefs, that indubitability cannot be a merely psychological matter. But facts about what we can and cannot believe are relevant to determining what is indubitable. We cannot doubt a belief at will. We must have *some reason* for doubt. That reason need not be probable enough to make the belief improbable. But if, after a thorough search for some reason, we cannot find even a slight reason for doubt, our inability to doubt the proposition is more than just a psychological fact about us.

How are we to proceed? If we had to question each of our beliefs individually, it would be an endless task to doubt them all. Fortunately, many of our beliefs are based on other beliefs. If we shake the foundation, we shake everything that rests on it. Most, if not all, of our beliefs are based on trust in the senses. Descartes actually said, early in the First Meditation, that *all* his past beliefs were. But when Frans Burman questioned him about this, he explained that the "I" who speaks to us in the *Meditations* is a man who is first beginning to philosophize, someone who holds the opinions anyone might hold, if he has not reflected critically on his beliefs. Call this fictional person "the meditator." Descartes does not endorse all the opinions the meditator expresses, any more than the author of a dialogue endorses all the opinions his characters express. Before the First Meditation is over, reflection will lead the meditator to drop this empiricist assumption. but in the beginning, empiricism rules.

The meditator briefly considers common cases of sense deception as a ground of doubt, but dismisses them because they support doubts only about small or distant objects, not a more general doubt about all material objects. More serious, he thinks, are the skeptical implications of dreaming. Each night, when he falls asleep, he dreams. In those dreams he has experiences just as vivid as his most vivid waking experiences. Or at least if there is a difference between his dreams and his most vivid waking experiences, it is not discernible during the dream. Only afterward, when he wakes up, does he realize that he was dreaming. So it is possible, for all he knows, that he is dreaming *now*, no matter how convincing his present experience seems to be. If this doubt can be raised about *any* sense experience, no matter how vivid, then no belief based on sense experience can be certain. And if all justified beliefs are based on sense experience, then no belief is certain.

That seems to be the conclusion the meditator reaches during the first stage of his reflections. But the *Meditations* are a dialogue within the meditator's mind, a dialogue between his skeptical side and his dogmatic side. After reflection it occurs to the meditator that perhaps arithmetic and geometry, those sciences that deal with the simplest and most general objects and care little whether their objects exist in nature, might not be affected by the dream argument. Sense experience is our primary means of knowing what is in nature. But if the mathematical sciences do not require objects actually existing in nature, they may not depend on sense experience. If they do not, they will not be impugned by an argument that shows sense experience to be unreliable. Moreover, it seems impossible that truths so clear should be suspected of falsity.

The meditator then reflects on the implications of a belief he has long held: that there is a God, who can do all things, and who has made him what he is. If there is such a being, it seems he might have created him (the meditator), not only with deceptive perceptions of everything around him (so that he seems to see Earth, a sky, and other extended objects even though there are no such things), but also with mistaken beliefs about even the simplest truths of mathematics—so that it seems evident that two added to three makes five, though this proposition is false. Of course, the meditator also believes that God is supremely good, and that such a being would not want him to be deceived. But the meditator does, after all, make mistakes. Evidently, if the meditator was created by a good God, it is consistent with God's goodness to permit him sometimes to be deceived. Couldn't it be consistent with God's goodness to make him always be deceived? Moreover, dropping the assumption that God created the meditator does not help. The less perfect his cause, the less reason he has to think that his cognitive faculties are not flawed.

The meditator has no answer to these arguments. He concludes that a legitimate doubt can be raised about *all* his former beliefs and that he has powerful (*validas*) and carefully considered (*meditatas*) reasons for these doubts. The reasons are powerful not because of their probability, but because of their scope, because they cast doubt on all kinds of beliefs, sense-based or not. The meditator insists that his former beliefs remain highly probable, more reasonable to believe than to deny. Later he will characterize the doubt based on the possibility of a deceiving God as "slight (*tenuis*) and … metaphysical." Many critics have asked how Descartes *knows* that the premises of his skeptical arguments are true. The answer is that he does not, and *need not*, claim to know that. Since the meditator is seeking absolute certainty, the only epistemic requirement for a legitimate ground of doubt is that the doubt not be one that he has compelling reasons to reject.

In the Second Meditation, having resolved to set aside as false anything that admits even the slightest doubt, Descartes claims to finds his Archimedean point, a proposition that resists all attempts to doubt it, on which he can build his revised system of beliefs. His initial certainty is the existence of the self. But the argument for the certainty of his existence takes a different form than it had in the *Discourse*. The famous inference—"I think; therefore, I exist"—does not appear. Instead, the *cogito* paragraph concludes with the words "This proposition, *I am, I exist*, is necessarily true as often as I utter it or conceive it in my mind" (Adam and Tannery VII, p. 25).

This formulation, combined with the absence of any explicit inference and some obscure remarks Descartes makes in the second set of replies, has led some readers to think Descartes is claiming intuitive certainty for the proposition "I exist." But we must remember that in the *Discourse* and the *Meditations* Descartes was writing for readers who had not read the *Regulae*. In neither the *Discourse* nor the *Meditations* does he introduce intuition as a central concept in his epistemology. Moreover, like the *Discourse*, but unlike the *Regulae*, the *Meditations* has raised as yet unresolved doubts about those paradigms of intuitive knowledge, the simplest truths of mathematics.

There is an alternative to seeing the existence of the self as something which, if known at all, must be known either by intuition or by inference from intuitions. As the *cogito* paragraph opens, the meditator is reviewing his situation. He has rejected the existence of all bodies, but perhaps there is something incorporeal whose existence he cannot doubt. God, perhaps? But God does not yet qualify as an indubitable being; at this stage the meditator thinks he himself might be the cause of his thoughts about God. What about himself? Is his existence so bound up with the existence of his body that he cannot exist without it? No. *If he has convinced himself of something* (say that there are no bodies), *then he must exist*, whether bodies exist or not. Perhaps a supremely powerful deceiver is deceiving him about everything (including his own existence). But *if the deceiver is deceiving him, then he exists.*

The italics here emphasize two *cogito*-like conditionals that each have an antecedent hypothesizing some thought process that the meditator *may* be involved in (convincing himself, being deceived by the deceiver) and a consequent affirming his existence. The meditator does not commit to either of the antecedents. The point is that whatever skeptical hypothesis he entertains, and whether he is responsible for his beliefs or the deceiver is, it follows from that hypothesis that he exists. Descartes hit on a way to justify accepting something as a first principle without incurring reasonable accusations of dogmatism: if the truth of a proposition follows from any skeptical hypothesis that could validly be invoked to cast doubt on it, then it's permissible to accept that proposition as certain without other argument, specifically, without having to deduce it from some prior certainty and without having to appeal to an infallible faculty of intuition.

Any valid ground of doubt must entail the existence of the doubter. Although valid doubts need to satisfy only a weak epistemic requirement (that we not have compelling reasons to reject them), there is another condition they must also satisfy: They must explain, conjecturally at least, how the person engaged in the search for truth could be mistaken. But if they do that, they must say something of the form "Perhaps, but you could be mistaken because God is deceiving you, or you are dreaming, or you are yourself the source of this thought, etc." The skeptic, if he is rationally, and not dogmatically, skeptical in his attempt to cast doubt on our beliefs, must argue that there is some reason why things seem to us as they do, even though things are not as they seem. As soon as he does that, he concedes that we are thinking, and hence that we exist.

Descartes used the same procedure when he took up the next problem in the Second Meditation: What is this self whose existence the meditator is now certain of? The meditator starts from the beliefs that he assumes a beginner in philosophy would have and asks which of them, if any, can survive radical doubt. The meditator thinks that he is something that has both a body (something with shape and location, occupying space so as to exclude other bodies, perceptible to the senses, and movable by other bodies that come in contact with it) and a soul (a fine substance, like air or fire, infused throughout the body and responsible for nutrition, motion, sensation, and thinking).

Not many of these prereflective beliefs can survive the hypothesis that some supremely powerful malicious being is deceiving him. The meditator has already rejected, until it can be reestablished on firmer ground, the belief that there are bodies. So the self whose existence he is certain of is apparently not something corporeal, nor can it engage in functions requiring the existence of a body. Nutrition and movement must go. At first it seems that sensation too must go, since sensation apparently presupposes the existence of sense organs. Only thought remains. Just as the existence of the self follows from any hypothesis entertained to cast doubt on it, so (trivially) does its thinking. If Descartes's procedure for identifying indubitable first principles is sound, he could have taken "I think" as a first principle and demonstrated "I exist" from that principle. Perhaps that is why he sometimes gives the appearance of doing that.

To say that the meditator is a thinking being is to attribute a number of different activities to him: that he understands many propositions, affirms some, denies others, and suspends judgment about still others. All this is implicit in the dialogue between his skeptical side and his dogmatic side. And on reflection, even sensation is something whose occurrence he cannot deny. Not having a body, he may not have sense organs, but he cannot deny that it sometimes *seems* to him *as if* he were perceiving something through some organ of the body he thought he had. And such seeming is a purely mental occurrence, immune to skeptical doubt. The skeptic assumes it in his attempt to explain why we had the ill-founded beliefs we had about bodies.

Toward the end of the Second Meditation, Descartes indulges in what looks like a digression. Though the meditator has not yet resolved his doubts about the existence of bodies, he says that he will give in to his natural inclination to believe that he knows bodies (which he can imagine and sense) more distinctly than he knows this mysterious self (which he can neither imagine nor sense). So he decides to examine one particular body, a piece of wax, to see what he knows distinctly in that object. He describes its properties: size, shape, color, hardness, temperature, taste, fragrance, etc. Then he takes the wax near a fire and notes the changes it undergoes in these changed circumstances. All its sensible properties change. What was cold becomes warm; what was hard becomes soft; and so on. But the wax, he says, remains (numerically) the same, in spite of its qualitative changes. No one doubts this. He concludes that the wax is not to be identified with any of its changing sensible properties. What he imagines distinctly in the wax is nothing but an extended something, capable of changing its shape, and capable of change in general.

Descartes draws a number of conclusions from this experiment. First, the wax, and bodies in general, are known, not by the senses or the imagination, but by the mind alone. The wax is capable of changing in many more ways than either the meditator's senses or imagination can encompass. Only the mind can grasp the wax. Second, the mind is better known than the body. Whenever the meditator judges, on the basis of sense evidence, that the wax exists, those sensations do not establish the existence of the wax. But they do establish the existence of the thinking being that judges that the wax exists.

What appears here to be a digression, not necessary to establish the main announced conclusions of the *Meditations*, does serve Descartes's unannounced purpose of insinuating the foundations of his physics. Just as the middle section of the Second Meditation clarified our prereflective concept of the soul, or mind, paring away the inessential to lay bare the essential property of thought, so the concluding section clarifies our prereflective concept of body. After the wax passage we know not to think of the sensible properties of bodies as essential to them. The only first-order property essential to any body is that it is extended. We also know not to think of bodies as inherently perceptible by the senses.

The wax passage serves another nonobvious purpose. It is characteristic of Descartes's method in the *Meditations* that he does not formally define his central concepts, but lets them emerge in informal ways. One of Descartes's central concepts is that of a clear and distinct idea, which he first mentioned prominently at the beginning of the Third Meditation, where he proposed his criterion of truth: Whatever he perceives clearly and distinctly is true. He did not define "clarity" and "distinctness" until he wrote his *Principles of Philosophy* (and even then the definitions are not very helpful). But the wax passage gives us a paradigm of what it is to acquire a clear and distinct idea. When the meditator begins to reflect on the wax, his idea of it is imperfect and confused. After he considers more attentively what the wax consists in and eliminates the inessential, his idea is clear and distinct.

The Third Meditation illustrates another way in which the process of acquiring clear and distinct ideas can work. When the meditator introduced the idea of God in the First Meditation, he explained the content of that idea by enumerating several attributes that he took God to have, among them that he created the meditator, that he can do all things, that he is supremely good, and that he is a source of truth. The problem the meditator faced was that he was not sure that all these attributes are united in one being. Perhaps he was created by an omnipotent being who is not supremely good and, far from being a source of truth, is a deceiver.

The idea of God is central to both arguments for the existence of God in the Third Meditation. At the heart of those arguments is the contention that the only possible explanation for the meditator's possessing an idea of God is that God does exist and has implanted an idea of himself in the meditator, much as a craftsman might stamp his mark on his work. But what exactly is the content of that idea? Descartes offers three answers to that question in the Third Meditation. The first two involve lists of divine attributes: God is supreme, eternal, infinite, omniscient, omnipotent, and the creator of all things apart from himself (Adam and Tannery VII, p. 40); God is an infinite substance, independent, supremely intelligent, supremely powerful, and has created the meditator and everything else that exists, if there is anything else (Adam and Tannery VII, p. 45). The French translation of the *Meditations*, which appeared in 1647, adds immutability to both lists.

These varying lists have several notable features: All three include the idea that God is the creator and that he is omnipotent. The two lists in the Third Meditation both omit the attributes that gave trouble in the First Meditation, that God is supremely good and the source of truth. And the Third Meditation lists both include infinity, an attribute that will play an important part in the arguments for God's existence. But no two lists are identical. This highlights a problem to which the Third Meditation will suggest a solution. We cannot adequately explain the content of the idea of God by listing his attributes. We may know where to begin: with his being the creator and being omnipotent. But we do not know where to stop. If God is absolutely infinite, not only are his individual attributes infinite in themselves, he must have infinitely many of them. No finite mind will be able to list them all. And as we learned in the First Meditation, there may be disagreement about some candidates. If God created the meditator and is omnipotent but the meditator makes mistakes and is imperfect in other ways, is God supremely good and a source of truth?

The solution that the Third Meditation proposes is that God is best understood as a supremely perfect and infinite being (Adam and Tannery VI, p. 46), where this implies that he must have *all* perfections and *only* perfections. This formula is a generalization from the various lists of attributes, each of which is a perfection. It is a useful way of summing up those lists, since it covers attributes that may have been omitted, either inadvertently or because of the limitations of the mind compiling the list. But most important, it provides a criterion for deciding what should be on the list and what should not. If an attribute is a perfection, it should be; if it is not, it shouldn't be.

Is there such a perfect being? Descartes first addressed this question in the Third Meditation, mounting two arguments, each starting from the assumption that we have an idea of God of the kind described. In the third set of objections Thomas Hobbes challenged the claim that we have an idea of God. But Descartes replied that Hobbes's challenge depends on confusing ideas with images. Since God is an infinite being, we can, of course, have no image of God. But that does not mean that we cannot have an idea of him. "Whenever I express something in words and understand what I am saying, it is certain, from this very fact, that there is in me an idea of the thing the words signify" (Adam and Tannery VII, p. 160). If a theist affirms, and an atheist denies, the existence of God, and if they both understand what they are saying, they both have an idea of God.

But how can the mere fact that we have an idea of God lead to a proof of his existence? In the Third Meditation the arguments are causal. They depend first on the general causal maxim that there must be at least as much reality in the total efficient cause as there is in the effect (Adam and Tannery VII, p. 40). It was an axiom of ancient philosophy, which Descartes endorsed, that something cannot come from nothing. A stone that previously did not exist cannot now begin to exist unless it is produced by something in which there exists, "either formally or eminently," whatever is in the stone. Descartes never really explained what the quoted qualification means. It's clear that he did not think that the cause needs to have the same properties as the effect. If it did, then God, who is incorporeal, would not be able to create extended objects. It is also clear that if the cause does not have the same properties, it must have properties "of at least equally great perfection." There cannot be heat in an object not previously hot except from something that is "of an order at least as perfect as is the heat" (Adam and Tannery VII, p. 41). That language clearly does not mean that the cause needs to have heat in it. But it is unclear what restriction the language does place on possible causes.

From this general causal maxim the meditator infers a causal principle applying specifically to ideas: The cause of an idea must contain at least as much formal reality as the idea contains objective reality. If we understood what formal reality is, we would understand what objective reality is, since objective reality can be defined in terms of formal reality. Objective reality is a property of ideas as representative entities that is correlated with the formal reality of their objects. An idea that represents its object as possessing a very high degree of formal reality will have more objective reality than one that represents its object as possessing a lower degree of formal reality. To say that an idea has objective reality is *not* to say that its object exists. All ideas have some degree of objective reality, even though some ideas have non-existent objects. Similarly, all objects have some degree of formal reality, even though some objects do not exist.

Descartes's point is that all ideas have some content, and their content requires causal explanation. In the first set of replies, he illustrates this with the example of someone who has the idea of a machine with a highly intricate design. The person might have acquired the idea of that machine by observing a real machine with that design. But perhaps there is no such machine. If not, we must seek some other cause for his conception of that object, perhaps in his extensive knowledge of mechanics. If he derived his idea of the machine neither from having observed such a machine nor from his knowledge of mechanics, he may have derived it from someone who had seen such a machine or had the requisite knowledge of mechanics. But whatever the cause, there must be a cause sufficient to produce that effect. The idea of God, as the idea of an infinite being possessing all the perfections that God is supposed to possess, has more objective reality than the idea of a finite substance does. Indeed, it has as much objective reality as it is possible for an idea to have, since its object has as much perfection as it is possible for an object to have.

Stripped to its essentials, the argument is as follows: 1) Each idea must have a cause possessing at least as much formal reality as the idea represents its object as having. 2) The idea of God represents its object as having the maximum possible formal reality. 3) Therefore, the only possible cause of our idea of God is a being that has the maximum possible formal reality (that is, equals all possible perfections). 4) Therefore, the idea of God must have God as its cause. 5) Therefore, God exists. This argument has generally not been well received by Descartes's readers, partly because of the obscurity of the causal principles involved, and partly because Descartes seems to have precluded himself from ever using such an argument.

The argument appeals to causal principles that Descartes said are known by natural light, a cognitive faculty whose deliverances cannot be doubted in any way. (Adam and Tannery VII, p. 38). As an example of one of the things so known, he gave the proposition: "From the fact that I doubt, it follows that I am." But just before he entered on this argument, he said that until he knew whether God exists and can be a deceiver, he could not be certain of anything (Adam and Tannery VII, p. 36). And he seemed there to regard the possibility of God's deception as a reason for doubting, not only simple truths of mathematics, but also the proposition "If I think that I am something, I am something"—a proposition that would presumably be known by that natural light whose deliverances are beyond doubt. It looks as though, to prove the reliability of the natural light, Descartes needs to construct a proof of the existence of a nondeceiving God. And to construct that proof, he needs to deploy premises known by the natural light, which he cannot be sure of until he is sure of his conclusion. The reasoning looks circular. The difficulty is known, therefore, as the Cartesian circle.

We will not have the materials to respond to this objection until we have considered the Fourth Meditation. But first we must note briefly that Descartes offers a second causal argument in the Third Meditation, beginning at the top of Adam and Tannery VII, p. 48. The focus of this argument is not on explaining the existence of the meditator's idea of God, but rather the meditator's own existence as a being possessing this idea. This argument has not persuaded many readers either, partly because it involves some of the same conceptual difficulties as the first argument. But it does introduce another restriction on causality, which had interesting consequences.

At one point in the argument the meditator considers the possibility that his existence as a being possessing the idea of God that he has, might be explained by saying that he has always existed, as he does now. This might not seem a plausible hypothesis, since few people are likely to think they have always existed. But Descartes's reason for rejecting it is curious. He replied that each person's life can be divided into countless parts, each completely independent of the others. From the fact that the meditator exists at one moment, it does not follow that he will exist at the next moment. Apparently he will not exist then, unless some cause creates him again at that time. The meditator thus requires a cause to sustain him in existence from one moment to the next, much as he requires a cause to bring him into existence, if he has not always existed. And that cause, of course, must be God.

What is interesting about this position is the assumption that for a cause to explain an effect, the existence of the effect must follow logically from the existence of the cause. The will of an omnipotent being can satisfy this requirement on causality. It is part of the notion of omnipotence that if an omnipotent being wills something, what it wills must occur. But no finite being appears able to satisfy the condition. For any supposed finite cause, it will always be possible for that being to exist without having the effect we suppose it to have. This restriction on causality looks like it will lead quickly to the occasionalist doctrine that no finite being is ever truly a cause, that God is the only real cause of anything that happens, apparent finite causes being merely occasions for his willing things to happen as they do. It is unclear whether Descartes saw that his argument might have these consequences.

At the end of the Third Meditation, having devoted most of his longest meditation to elaborating two complex arguments for the existence of God, Descartes makes a quick argument that God cannot be a deceiver. The God whose existence he has proven is a supremely perfect being, possessing all perfections and no defects. It is manifest by the natural light that all deception involves some defect. So God cannot be a deceiver. Of course, there is the awkward fact, noted in the First Meditation, that God's creatures do sometimes make mistakes. Not until the next meditation will Descartes attempt to reconcile his awareness of that with his conviction that a supremely perfect being created him.

The main line of response to this difficulty in the Fourth Meditation is a variation of a standard approach to the problem of evil: Though God created the meditator as he is, God is not responsible for the meditator's errors, because they arise from the meditator's misusing the free will God has given him. Free will is a good great enough to compensate for whatever evil is involved in the meditator's mistakes. If the meditator exercised his free will properly, he would not make mistakes.

In the Third Meditation, Descartes classified his thoughts into three kinds: ideas, which, though *not* images, are *like* images insofar as they represent their objects as possessing certain properties; volitions or emotions, which involve having an idea of an object and also having some affective attitude toward it (wanting it, disliking it, fearing it, etc.); and judgments, which involve having an idea of an object and affirming or denying something about that object. Only judgments can be true or false. The most common mistake the meditator makes is to judge that things outside him are as his ideas represent them. When they are not, as is often the case, he errs. But error, like any judgment, always involves an act of the will, either affirming something or denying it. The meditator makes judgments he does freely. If he makes a mistake, it is his fault, not God's.

The notion of freedom used here requires some examination. Within one sentence, Descartes suggests two very different conceptions of freedom. The sentence reads as follows:

> The will, or freedom of choice … , consists only in this, that we can do something or not do it (that is, affirm or deny, pursue or flee, the same thing), *or rather*, only in this, that when the intellect proposes something to us for affirmation or denial, pursuit or avoidance, we are so inclined that we do not feel we are determined to it by any external force. (Adam and Tannery VII, p. 57; emphasis added)

This puzzling sentence presents difficulties both of translation and of interpretation. But what Descartes seems to mean by it is that the first clause (before "or rather") describes one (indeterminist) way we can be free, and the second clause (after "or rather") describes another way we can be free (without assuming indeterminism).

Descartes's view seems to be this: *Much of the time*, when we affirm something, we could have denied it, and when we deny it, we could have affirmed it (or neither affirmed it nor denied it). This will be true under a variety of circumstances: We might have no evidence one way or the other; we might have evidence each way, but the evidence might not favor one way over the other; or the evidence for the proposition might outweigh the evidence against it, perhaps quite strongly, without being conclusive. In all these cases we will have the power to decide either way, and will be free under the first clause of Descartes's definition. This is often called a *liberty of indifference*, though that term has misleading connotations. It may suggest either that we have no evidence one way or the other, or that our evidence one way is no stronger than our evidence the other way. As Descartes conceived this liberty, that will not always be true. In cases where our evidence for a proposition is strong but inconclusive, as is our sense evidence for the existence of material objects, denial or suspension of judgment will be difficult, but not impossible.

But *sometimes*, Descartes thought, we find that we cannot help judging as we do. In the Second Meditation, when the meditator was examining whether there was anything in the world and noticed that it followed from the fact that he was examining this that he existed, he could not but judge that what he understood so clearly was true. He was not aware of any external force compelling him to judge thus. Rather, a great inclination of his will followed from a great light in his intellect. He seemed to be all the more free the less indifferent he was. This is what is sometimes called a *liberty of spontaneity*, a notion that suggests that the absence of external constraint is sufficient for freedom. It is not necessary for our freedom that we have the power to act differently than we do.

Descartes wanted to allow both a liberty of indifference and a liberty of spontaneity. When we do not have clear and distinct ideas, we possess a liberty of indifference. We can judge either way. When we do have clear and distinct ideas, we cannot judge otherwise, but we are still judging spontaneously, and not under any kind of coercion. The absence of external coercion does not imply that there is no external causation of our judgments. Descartes explicitly allowed that God might be disposing the meditator's innermost thoughts to judge the way he did. That will not diminish his liberty of spontaneity, though it will mean that he no longer has a liberty of indifference.

Some critics have found Descartes's theory of judgment highly implausible. Benedict de Spinoza argued that Descartes was confusing judgments with utterances when he supposed that we might have a liberty of indifference in some of the cases where he claimed it. It is one thing to *say* that one's experiences of the external world might have no more basis than a dream, and quite another to actually *believe* it. The first is easy; the second may well be impossible. Again, is the liberty of indifference that Descartes requires to relieve God of responsibility for our errors compatible with his doctrine that God is continuously creating us at each moment of time? The doctrine of continuous creation seems to make us completely dependent on God; a liberty of indifference seems to make us at least partially independent of God.

For all the time that Descartes spent arguing that we have a liberty of indifference with respect to some ideas, in the final analysis he seems not to have relied on that liberty to reconcile God's goodness with the occurrence of error. At the end of the Fourth Meditation he conceded that God could easily have brought it about that the meditator would never make a mistake without losing his freedom. All God would have to do is to give the meditator clear and distinct ideas about everything he would ever have to make judgments about, or to implant in him a firm resolution to make judgments only about things he perceived clearly and distinctly. In the closing paragraphs of the Fourth Meditation it looks like Descartes's solution to the problem of error does not depend on free will at all, but on the thought that, although the *meditator* might be better if he never made mistakes, it is possible that the *world as a whole* is better for having in it beings who make mistakes. Variety is the spice of the universe.

Nevertheless, the doctrine of judgment in the Fourth Meditation has considerable systematic importance. The method of doubt requires that we suspend judgment about everything we have the slightest reason to doubt, that we withhold our assent from things we do not perceive clearly and distinctly. Moreover, it is arguable that Descartes's vindication of reason depends on our *in*ability to refrain from assenting to things we *do* perceive clearly and distinctly. As noted above, when Descartes was arguing in the Third Meditation that God exists and is not a deceiver, he frequently justified the assumptions of those arguments as things "manifest by the natural light." And it's not clear how, given the arguments of the First Meditation, he can repose confidence in that, or any other, cognitive faculty until he has first determined whether God exists and is a deceiver.

Since the mid-twentieth century, at least, commentators have been reluctant to accuse Descartes of blatant circularity. But there is no consensus about how he escapes the accusation. Here is one try. It is not controversial that Descartes thought that our clear and distinct ideas compel assent when we are attending to them. We may be able to doubt simple propositions of mathematics when we consider them under some general rubric, like "the things which seem most evident to me." But when we are actually focusing on a particular simple proposition of mathematics, we cannot in fact doubt it. It compels our assent. The same is true, Descartes thought, of some metaphysical propositions, such as "So long as I think I am something, I am something," and "If I exist now, then it will not be true at some later time that I never existed."

The arguments for God's existence and nondeception in the Third Meditation are constructed from two kinds of propositions. One kind reports the contents of the meditator's consciousness, specifically, the fact that he has an idea of God. This is a presupposition of the dialogue with the skeptic and amenable to the defense offered above for the propositions "I exist" and "I think." The other kind are general propositions, such as "A cause must have at least as much reality or perfection as its effect," and "Deception is a defect." If we perceive these things clearly and distinctly, we will not be able to doubt them when we attend to them. Descartes may not have thought that they are self-evident, in the sense that they command assent as soon as we understand the terms. But if they do not command assent, then we have not yet perceived them clearly and distinctly. We are confused in some way, perhaps by badly understood experiences that seem to refute the principles.

Suppose that we are able to construct an argument that God exists and is not a deceiver, relying entirely on propositions about contents of our consciousness that we cannot doubt and on general propositions that we perceive clearly and distinctly, which we also cannot doubt when we attend to them. If we perceive all these premises clearly and distinctly, and see equally clearly their connection with the conclusion, we cannot doubt the conclusion.

A skeptic might now say, "I understand that you *cannot* doubt that God exists and is not a deceiver. But that's just a fact about you. It doesn't mean the proposition is not worthy of doubt. Perhaps your creator is an omnipotent demon and this conviction of yours is just another of his tricks." On the interpretation offered here, Descartes would say that once he has a compelling argument to the conclusion that he has been created by a God who is not a deceiver, it is no longer enough to offer the mere supposition that a demon might be deceiving us when we assent to ideas that we cannot in fact doubt. In the First Meditation the hypothesis that an omnipotent creator might deceive us, even about matters most evident to us, constituted a valid ground of doubt, because we had no compelling argument against it. By the end of the Fourth Meditation we do have a compelling argument against it. So it no longer constitutes a valid ground of doubt. The validity of a ground of doubt is situational. What constitutes a valid ground of doubt at one stage of the argument, when we have no compelling argument against it, will no longer be valid when we do have such an argument. Descartes makes this clear in his reply to the seventh set of objections (Adam and Tannery VII, p. 473–474).

It may help to consider the Pyrrhonian skepticism that we find in Montaigne's *Apology for Raymond Sebond.* The Pyrrhonist advocates what Montaigne calls the principle of equipollence: For every argument in favor of a proposition, there is an equally strong argument against it. Montaigne's criterion for the strength of an argument is psychological persuasiveness. When someone who holds the principle of equipollence is confronted with a compelling argument that we have been created by a nondeceiving god, he can no longer cast doubt on that conclusion simply by hypothesizing the possibility of deception by an omnipotent being. He must produce an equally strong and compelling argument for the opposite conclusion. Absent such an argument, Descartes is entitled to his conclusion.

There is one other respect in which the situation at the end of the Fourth Meditation is different from the situation at the beginning of the Third Meditation. Now we have a clear and distinct idea of God. At the beginning of the Third Meditation we conceived of God simply as an omnipotent creator who was supposed to be supremely good and is the source of all truth. But we didn't see any necessary connection between these attributes, and we worried that we might have been created by a being who possessed some of these attributes, but not all of them. By the end of the Fourth Meditation we understand that what God is, essentially, is a supremely perfect being, who has all the perfections and no defects. Once we have seen this, we see that the hypothesis of an omnipotent deceiver is incoherent. It is not even a hypothesis that we can consider as a possibility.

In the Fifth Meditation, Descartes had two items on his agenda: considering the nature of material things and arguing once more for the existence of God. His most urgent task if he is to recover from his doubts, he said, is to determine whether he can have any certainty about material things. Before he could decide whether such things really exist, he needed to consider what distinct ideas he had of them. He prepared the ground for this consideration in the Second Meditation, where he identified extension as the one first-order property that remains constant in the wax as it changes. There his focus was on a particular body. Here it is on what he calls "continuous quantity … or the extension of this quantity—or rather, of the thing quantified—in length, breadth and depth" (Adam and Tannery VII, p. 63). So we are to think of geometrical space (continuous quantity) as a material substance extended in three dimensions, of which particular bodies are parts, each possessing its own size, shape, and position, and distinguished from the other parts by their varying motions. (Here again, Descartes is insinuating fundamental propositions of his physics.)

When Descartes reflected on his ideas of extended objects, he realized that he had countless ideas of geometrical objects, objects that may not exist anywhere outside his mind but that nevertheless have a definite nature, "a true and immutable nature," independent of his mind. He could demonstrate properties of these shapes, even though he might never have observed any shapes of the kind whose properties he was demonstrating. He may have observed triangles; it's unlikely that he ever observed a chiliagon (a thousand-sided polygon). But he could determine what its properties are, even if there are no chiliagons to observe. Whenever he saw clearly and distinctly that some property belongs to the true and immutable nature of some thing, that property really does belong to that thing. He had a clear and distinct idea of God as a supremely perfect being. He understood that to be supremely perfect, a being must possess all perfections, and that existence is a perfection. He inferred, then, that God must possess the perfection of existence.

This version of the ontological argument depends on a Platonic philosophy of mathematics, which Pierre Gassendi criticized in the fifth set of objections. Gassendi complained first that it seemed to him that it is hard to maintain that there are true and immutable natures apart from God. He imagined Descartes replying that he was only saying what they say in the schools, that the essences of things are eternal, and that there can be true propositions about them. But Gassendi did not understand how there can be an essence of something—his example is man—if there are no things of that kind. At one point he seemed willing to concede that there is a sense in which "Man is an animal" can be true even if no men exist. But he said that the statement is true only if it is understood conditionally: "If something is a man, it is an animal." And he gave an analysis of that conditional that makes its truth apparently require the existence of some men:

> When man is said to be of such a nature that he cannot exist without being an animal, it is not on that account to be imagined that such a nature is something or is somewhere outside the intellect. The meaning is only that for something to be a man, he must be like the rest of those things to which we give the same name, man, on account of their mutual similarity. (Adam and Tannery VII, p. 320)

Gassendi also questioned whether existence is a perfection: "Existence is not a perfection either in God or in anything else; it is that without which no perfections can be present. … What does not exist has no perfections or imperfections. … If a thing lacks existence, we do not say it is imperfect … but say instead that it is nothing at all" (Adam and Tannery VII, p. 323). Though Gassendi focused on the idea that existence might be a perfection, his reasoning would seem to exclude its being a property of any kind. He treated existence not as something which is predicated of a thing, but as a precondition of any predication.

When Descartes replied, he was puzzled about what category Gassendi wanted to put existence in. Existence seemed to him analogous to omnipotence, something that can be predicated of a thing, and that therefore is a property. But then he rejected Gassendi's conditional analysis of essential predications. Gassendi's example, man, was one of the "universals of the dialecticians," that is, the Scholastic philosophers. Descartes preferred to focus on essences that we understand clearly and distinctly, like those of geometric figures. We cannot understand the latter essences the way the Scholastics and Gassendi did, as based on concepts abstracted from experience of instances of the concept, because there are no instances for us to experience. This is true not only for such unfamiliar figures as chiliagons, but also for such apparently common figures as triangles. The problem is that nothing in our experience strictly satisfies the definition of a triangle, which requires, among other things, that it be composed of straight lines. The lines we experience turn out, when examined closely, not to be perfectly straight. But we can recognize the figures we experience as approximations of the ideal geometric figures because we have ideas of the ideal figures from another source.

Descartes's objections to Gassendi's analysis of essential predication probably go deeper than his opposition to the scholastic theory that our concepts are formed by abstraction from experience. It seems likely that he would reject any conditional analysis of essential predications, even if it was not spelled out in abstractionist terms. Gassendi had complained that the essences Descartes was talking about could not have an immutable and eternal nature apart from God. Descartes replied that he did not claim that the essences of things exist independently of God. He conceived of them rather as depending on the will of God, and as being immutable only because God's will is immutable. Although Descartes did not explicitly invoke his doctrine of the creation of the eternal truths in the body of the *Meditations* itself –(he *may* have presupposed it in the Third Meditation), he did make it explicit in his replies to objections. (It comes up again in the sixth set of replies.) Reflection on the reasons that may have led Descartes to his doctrine of the creation of the eternal truths may also suggest a reason why he would reject Gassendi's conditional analysis of essential predications.

One problem that scholastic philosophers faced when they thought about essential predications was that, according to the orthodox theory of universal propositions, they have existential import. "All men are animals" entails that there are men. But if "All men are animals" is a necessary truth, so are its entailments. However, "There are men" is supposed to be a contingent truth, made true at the creation by God's will. Descartes may have been moved to compare the eternal truths with the laws that a king establishes in his kingdom because a king's laws depend for their validity not on the existence of violators of those laws, but only on the authority of their source. The king's prohibition on dueling does not depend on there being any duelists. Descartes may have felt that a conditional analysis of essential predications avoided one problem only to raise another equally difficult problem. On the hypothesis that there are no men, "If anything is a man, it is an animal" is a conditional whose antecedent is false. If this is a material conditional, it is true in such circumstances, as is the conditional "If anything is a man, it is a plant." If it is a modal conditional, it is unclear what the truth conditions for such conditionals are (if they have any).

Gottfried Wilhelm Leibniz raised an equally serious problem when he argued that Descartes needed to supplement his ontological argument with a proof that the concept of God is consistent. Arguably, that is what Descartes was trying to do, in a limited way, in the Fourth Meditation. That meditation tried to resolve an inconsistency that had threatened his concept of God since the First Meditation: that God was a perfect being who was nonetheless supposed to have created a very imperfect being. But emphasizing human freedom as a solution to that problem, even if it is not Descartes's final solution, only raised the question of whether human freedom is compatible with God's omnipotence, a problem Descartes would address in his *Principles of Philosophy*.

In the Sixth Meditation there are two announced items on the agenda: establishing the existence of bodies and proving that mind and body are distinct. The first step in approaching the latter problem is to recognize (1):

> (1) Whatever I clearly and distinctly understand can be made by God as I understand it.

The thought here seems to be that if I understand something clearly and distinctly, it must be free of contradiction, and that God, being omnipotent, can create anything that does not involve a contradiction. From (1) it follows that (2):

> (2) If I clearly and distinctly conceive myself as a thinking, non-extended thing, then God can create me as a thinking, nonextended thing.

Similarly, (3) also follows from (1):

> (3) If I clearly and distinctly conceive of body as an extended, non-thinking thing, God can create it as an extended, nonthinking thing.

In the Second Meditation Descartes' meditator, in his reasoning, achieved a state in which he satisfied the antecedents of (2) and (3). He had a clear and distinct idea of the wax as an extended thing, to which he did not ascribe any thought, and a clear and distinct idea of himself as a thinking thing, to which he did not ascribe anything corporeal. So he infers (4) and (5):

> (4) God can create me as a thinking thing, apart from my or any other body.

> (5) God can create my or any other body as an extended thing, apart from me or any other thinking thing.

To show that two things are really distinct, it does not matter what power is required to create them as separate substances. *According to the definition of a real distinction, two things are really distinct if they are substances and it's possible for each to exist without the other.* So this is sufficient to prove that:

> (6) I and my body are really distinct substances.

It is not obvious what is wrong with this argument, though it certainly has not lacked critics.

In the fourth set of objections Antoine Arnauld proposed the following counterexample. An individual might clearly and distinctly perceive that a triangle inscribed in a semicircle is right-angled, but not be aware of the Pythagorean theorem, according to which the square on the hypotenuse of a right-angled triangle must equal the sum of the squares on the other two sides. So he might doubt or deny that a particular triangle inscribed in a semicircle has the Pythagorean property. From Descartes's first assumption (1), he might infer (2'):

> (2') If I clearly and distinctly conceive the triangle inscribed in a semicircle as right-angled, but doubt or deny that this triangle has the Pythagorean property, then God can create a triangle inscribed in a semicircle that does not have that property.

The antecedent of this conditional might well be true, it seems, but the consequent attributes to God a power he cannot have, even if we accept Descartes's doctrine of the creation of the eternal truths. Even if God *could have* created a different nature for triangles, the immutability of his will entails that he *cannot now* create a triangle with a different nature (Adam and Tannery V, p. 160). Descartes replied at length to Arnauld's objection without ever seeming to meet the point. It is not obvious what he should have said to defend himself.

Though Descartes regarded mind and body as substances capable of existing apart from one another, he was also anxious to insist that he is very closely united to his body, "as it were, intermingled with it" (Adam and Tannery VII, p. 81), so that he composes one thing with it. His bodily sensations taught him this: He feels pain when this body is damaged, hunger when it needs food, thirst when it needs drink. He does not feel these sensations when similar things happen to other bodies. So, he said, nature taught him that he is not merely present to his body as a sailor is present to his ship. He thereby rejected what the medievals regarded as the excessive dualism of Plato. Bodily sensations are nothing but confused modes of thinking arising from the union of mind and body. It is not clear that this doctrine of mind-body union is compatible with the doctrine that mind and body are distinct. This was to become a major topic of debate after the publication of the *Meditations*, as we shall see.

Descartes's attempt to prove the existence of bodies has generated not so much debate as dismissal. God, he said, had given him a great propensity to believe that his sensations are caused by material things and no faculty for recognizing any alternative source for them. So Descartes did not see how God could be cleared of the charge of being a deceiver if his sensations were caused by something incorporeal. There must be corporeal things. They may not have all the properties he grasped by sensation, since there is much in those properties that is obscure and confused. But they must have all the properties he understands clearly and distinctly, that is, all the properties that are the subject of pure mathematics.

It is indeed hard to see how a perfectly good God could permit such a massive delusion. But Descartes here has weakened the conditions under which God can be judged to be a deceiver. In the Fourth Meditation, God would have been a deceiver if we had false beliefs that we could not help having. Now God is a deceiver even if we have false beliefs that we can help having, provided we are strongly inclined to believe them and have no way of telling that they are false. Perhaps the proper conclusion from this argument is that it is improbable that our belief in material objects is false. When we are dealing with beliefs that we *could* help having, we probably need to know something about God's purposes before we can decide whether or not he would be a deceiver if we held false beliefs under those circumstances. Descartes did not think that we can know what God's ends are. But probably the main reason the argument has not found much favor is that it does not seem that we should have to accept this complex theistic argument to see the existence of bodies as certain.

We should note an important negative conclusion that Descartes reaches in the Sixth Meditation: Even if we have been created by a nondeceiving God, we have no justification for believing that the things we perceive by the senses have *all* the properties we are inclined to ascribe to them. The properties of which we have confused and obscure ideas—the heat we attribute to hot bodies, the color we attribute to green bodies, and in general what later philosophers were to call "the secondary qualities of things"—these properties, insofar as we think of them as properties of external objects, need not resemble in any way the ideas we have of them. There must be some differences in the things themselves, between a hot object and a cold one, or between a red object and a green one. But so long as there is a systematic correlation between the differences in external objects and the differences in our sensations, we needn't suppose that there is anything in the objects themselves resembling color or heat. This was one of the fundamental principles of Descartes's physics that he slipped into the *Meditations.*

CONTINUED CONTROVERSY (1641–1644)

Even before the publication of the *Meditations* in August 1641, Descartes had begun work on his next major publication, his *Principles of Philosophy* (1644), which he sometimes referred to in the correspondence as his "*summa* of philosophy" or as his "philosophy" or as his "physics." His aim was to produce "a complete textbook" of his philosophy, combining metaphysics, physics, and biology, in the form of theses, "where, without any excess words, I will just present all my conclusions, with the true premises from which I derive them" (Adam and Tannery III, p. 233). There would be none of the false starts that gave the *Meditations* their dialectical character. When he first began planning this work, he thought of publishing it with a standard textbook of scholastic philosophy on which he would comment. He had selected Eustachius of St. Paul's *Summa philosophiae* for this purpose, but gave up that aspect of the project after Eustachius's death in December 1640. Clearly, he had decided that he could be more open about his anti-Aristotelianism, and could present his cosmology in a way that would escape condemnation.

When the second edition of the *Meditations* appeared in May 1642, it added not only Father Bourdin's objections and Descartes's replies, but also a letter from Descartes to Father Jacques Dinet, a former teacher at La Flèche and now the head of the Jesuit order in France, complaining about his treatment by Bourdin. Descartes had reason to be upset by Bourdin: He was long-winded, sarcastic, and unsympathetic in his interpretation of Descartes's views. Descartes said he showed the acumen of a bricklayer, not a Jesuit priest. And he wrote bad Latin. Though Descartes seems to have had a genuine affection for some members of the Jesuit order and respect for the quality of education the society provided in its schools, he was prone to see conspiracy in its members' actions. He worried that Bourdin's critique was not the opinion of one Jesuit priest, but represented a consensus among the Jesuits. He urged Dinet to read the *Meditations* himself—or if he did not have the time for that, to assign the task to members of the society more competent than Bourdin—and to let him know if they saw problems in his project. Dinet delegated the task to Father Etienne Charlet, formerly the rector at La Flèche and later Dinet's successor as head of the Jesuits in France, who was to write to Descartes about his works. It appears that Charlet eventually demonstrated his personal good will toward Descartes and his work, but left him uncertain about the attitude of the society as a whole.

Descartes also included in his letter to Dinet an account of a controversy he was embroiled in at the University of Utrecht. In 1641 a follower of his, Henricus Regius, professor of medicine at the University, had engaged in a disputation there in which he presented his version of Cartesian natural philosophy, going further than Descartes judged it wise to go. Regius said that the union of mind and body was an accidental one, rather than substantial, and also denied the existence of substantial forms, those formal aspects of things that in scholastic natural philosophy were supposed to make them the kinds of things they are and explain their characteristic behavior. For these positions Regius came under attack from the rector of the university, Gisbert Voetius, who took the opportunity to hurl a few barbs in Descartes's direction as well.

Regius felt he needed to reply publicly, and Descartes advised him on what to say. Though Descartes thought Regius meant something acceptable when he declared that the union of soul and body was accidental—namely that mind and body are really distinct from one another, each capable of existing without the other—he warned Regius that the Scholastics would interpret this language differently, and that the best thing would be to claim ignorance of scholastic terminology and to say that the disagreement between them was only verbal. Regarding substantial forms, Descartes thought Regius should say that he did not wish to reject them absolutely, and that he meant merely that he had no need to invoke them in his scientific explanations. Saying that fire possesses the form of fire does not help us in any way to understand its ability to burn wood. This was the stance Descartes had taken, leaving it to his readers to draw the conclusion that if substantial forms were explanatorily useless, there was no reason to postulate them.

When Regius published his reply, he only made matters worse. The university condemned the new philosophy and forbade Regius to teach his course on physical problems. "Utrecht University, the first in the world to allow one of its professors to teach Cartesianism, was also the first that forbade its teaching" (Verbeek 1992, p. 19). When Descartes criticized Voetius in his letter to Father Dinet, Voetius responded by arranging for Martin Schoock, a professor at Groningen and a disciple of his, to write a book that accused Descartes, among other things, of atheism and of fathering numerous illegitimate children. (Descartes did, in fact, have one illegitimate child, a daughter whom he was quite fond of but who died in 1640, at the age of five.) The full story of the Utrecht affair—which ultimately involved lawsuits for libel, charges of perjury, and a prohibition on any discussion of Descartes, pro or con—is too complex to tell here (for further details, see Verbeek 1992).

PRINCIPLES OF PHILOSOPHY (1644)

The *Principles* was Descartes's most systematic work and the one his contemporaries went to for a definitive statement of his philosophy. It consists of four parts, the first dealing with metaphysics and epistemology, the second with general principles of physics, the third with celestial phenomena, and the fourth with terrestrial phenomena. Since Descartes himself preferred the exposition of his metaphysics and epistemology in the *Meditations* to the one he gave in Part I of the *Principles*, and since the science that dominates the remainder of the work is primitive by modern standards, most recent students of Descartes have neglected the *Principles*. Here we must limit ourselves to noting only a few of the many things it adds to what we know from our survey of Descartes's other works.

Among the additions is a metaphor that Descartes used in the Preface to the French translation of 1647: "The whole of philosophy is like a tree, whose roots are metaphysics, whose trunk is physics, and whose branches are all the other sciences, which reduce to three principal sciences, medicine, mechanics and morals" (Adam and Tannery IX-B, p. 14). This passage illustrates Descartes's conception of the close connection among disciplines that we now regard as quite separate, his ambition to found the sciences in metaphysics, and his hope that his foundational work would have practical consequences. Particularly intriguing is his ambition to derive a moral philosophy from his metaphysics and physics. We will see what that led to when we come to his last major work, *The Passions of the Soul.*

One delicate issue the *Principles* raises is the question of the extent of the universe. Copernicus had not claimed that the world was infinite, but later Copernicans, such as Giordano Bruno, did. Though we do not know the specific grounds for the Church's execution of Bruno in 1600, it seems likely that this was one of them. Since Descartes identified matter with (Euclidean) space, it might seem that he too would be committed to the infinity of the physical universe. But in the *Principles* (pt. I, secs. 26–27), he said that he was not. He reserved the term "infinite" for God alone and designated things in which he could discover no limits—such as the extension of the world and the divisibility of matter—indefinite. Nevertheless, later in the *Principles* (pt. II, sec. 21), he passed from denying knowledge that there are any limits to the extent of the world to affirming knowledge that there are no limits to its extent. When he later began to develop his moral philosophy, he listed, as one of the truths most useful to us, the proposition that we must beware of supposing that there are limits to the extent of the world God created (*Principles*, pt. III, sec. 1). Descartes supposed that an appreciation of the vastness of God's creation would aid us in detaching ourselves from the things of this world (Adam and Tannery IV, p. 292).

Another theologically sensitive issue that Descartes dealt with in Part 1 is the problem of reconciling human freedom with God's omnipotence (secs. 37–41). Descartes's conception of freedom here seems to be more single-mindedly indeterminist than it was in the *Meditations*. If we are to deserve praise for our actions, we must be in some special way the author of those actions, and not have been determined to so act by our maker. We must have been able to do otherwise. That we have the power to assent or not to assent in many cases is as evident as any first principle, though this is not innate knowledge, but something we learn from what we experience within ourselves. On the other hand, now that we know God, we see that his power is so immense that it would be impious to think we could ever do something he had not foreordained.

Recent discussion of the problem of reconciling human freedom with God's attributes has tended to focus on showing that human freedom is consistent with divine foreknowledge. Descartes was more worried about showing it to be consistent with God's omnipotence. Perhaps Descartes thought that his identification of God's will with his intellect ruled out the possibility that he might foreknow without foreordaining. In any case, the solution that Descartes proposed is that we should maintain both our freedom and God's foreordination, even though we do not see how they could be compatible. God's power is infinite; our intellects are finite. So we should not expect to understand how they can be compatible, and we cannot give up two such certain truths merely because of a defect in our understanding. Had Descartes continued to allow the liberty of spontaneity that he recognized in the Fourth Meditation, it seems that he would not have needed to take this position.

In part II of the *Principles*, Descartes laid the groundwork for a version of Copernicanism that was supposed to avoid the censured claim that Earth moves. In sections 13 and 24 he gave a relativistic account of what we ordinarily mean when we say that a body moves: It changes its place, which is defined as its position relative to other bodies taken to be at rest. We will get different answers to the question of whether something is moving, depending on which other bodies we take as our frame of reference. Suppose that a man is sitting on the stern of a ship headed down river to the sea. We say that he is at rest if we consider his constant relation to the part of the ship where he is sitting. We say that he is moving if we consider his relation to the shore, since he is continually moving away from some parts and toward others. If we think that Earth is rotating on its axis and moving just as much from west to east as the ship is moving from east to west, we say that he is not moving—our frame of reference now being certain bodies in the heavens that we suppose to be motionless. But if we think that there are no such motionless points anywhere in the universe, we will conclude that nothing has a permanent place, except insofar as it is determined by our thought. In part II, section 13, Descartes foreshadowed an argument that, he said, makes it probable that there are no genuinely fixed points in the universe. We get that argument in part III, section 29, where he contended that if we follow ordinary usage, there is no reason to say it is the stars that are at rest rather than Earth.

Descartes seems to reject ordinary usage. In part 2, section 25, he said that if we want to understand motion "according to the truth of the matter," we ought to define it as "a transfer of one part of matter, or of one body, *from the neighborhood of those bodies immediately touching it*, considered as resting, *to the neighborhood of other bodies*" (emphasis added). So he treats the immediately surrounding bodies as a privileged reference frame. On this definition, Earth, strictly speaking, is at rest, even though there is admittedly a sense in which it is moving round the Sun. In Descartes's cosmology, it is at rest in relation to the fluid matter immediately surrounding it, which carries it round the Sun, just as a ship, neither driven by the wind nor hindered by an anchor, might be at rest in relation to the water around it, though it is imperceptibly carried out to sea by the tide (pt. III, sec. 26–28). Of course, as Descartes noted, the same thing can be said of all the other planets.

Cartesian scholars have often suspected Descartes of adopting this strict definition of motion simply because he could then claim that in his cosmology the Earth did not move, permitting him to adopt a basically Copernican astronomy without suffering the fate of Galileo. Descartes anticipated that his denial that the Earth moves might be judged to be "merely verbal," intended to avoid censure. But he said that a careful reading of his work should remove that suspicion (Adam and Tannery V, p. 550). In any event, it is arguable that he had serious reasons, internal to his philosophy, for wanting to define motion in a way that would escape the relativism he saw in the common conception of motion. Motion is supposed to do a great deal of work in his mechanistic physics. As he said in the *Principles*, "All the variety in matter, all the diversity of its forms, depends on motion" (pt. II, sec. 23). To make that kind of explanatory use of motion, he needed it to be something that really exists in bodies, not something that is in them or not, depending on how you look at them. But his solution to the problem is highly problematic, and not only because it did not in the end protect him from condemnation by the Church. (For more on this complex issue, see Garber 1992, chap. 6.)

We cannot leave this all-too-brief discussion of the *Principles* without noting that at the end Descartes commented on the epistemological status he took his scientific theories to have. He claimed that they are *at least morally certain*, that is, certain enough that it would be reasonable to act on them (or perhaps unreasonable not to act on them), even if they are not absolutely or metaphysically certain (pt. IV, sec. 205). His principles explain so many phenomena that it hardly seems possible that they could be false. And some of his principles, he thought, are absolutely certain, because they are grounded in his certainty that God is supremely good and is not a deceiver (pt. IV, sec. 206). He mentioned mathematical demonstrations, the existence of material things, and "all evident reasonings about material things." He clearly hoped that his readers would find even more of his conclusions metaphysically certain.

ROYAL ADMIRERS, CONTINUING CONFLICTS (1644–1648)

Descartes dedicated his *Principles of Philosophy* to Princess Elisabeth, the daughter of Frederick V (formerly the Elector Palatine and briefly King of Bohemia) and Elisabeth Stuart (sister of Charles I of England). They had begun to correspond in 1643, after Descartes learned that the princess, who was living in exile in the Hague, had read his *Meditations* with approval. She pressed him with acute questions about the relation between mind and body, eliciting some surprising answers. Later their correspondence turned to questions of ethics and psychology, which prompted Descartes to write his last major work, *The Passions of the Soul* (1649), also dedicated to her. Though the extravagant mutual flattery that pervades their correspondence may be mere courtly etiquette, readers have sometimes wondered if Descartes did not harbor an affection for this sad, lovely, intelligent young woman that might have led to a romance, had not the difference in their ages, social station, and religion made that impossible. In any event, she proved to be a stimulating student.

Elisabeth began their correspondence by raising an issue that was to become central in the subsequent development of Cartesianism: How, in voluntary motion, can the mind, as a nonextended thing, cause its body, an extended thing, to move (Adam and Tannery III, p. 661)? Her paradigm for an intelligible causation of motion—and Descartes's paradigm too, we might have thought—involves the impact of one body on another, with the cause transmitting some of its motion to the body that begins to move. Impact requires contact, which requires extension in both cause and effect. A nonextended thing cannot have an impact on an extended one.

Descartes replied by saying that what explains the mind's power to move the body is its union with the body (Adam and Tannery III, p. 664). The notion of the union of mind and body is a primitive one, like extension and thought, which cannot be explained in terms of anything more fundamental. But Descartes thought that we demonstrate our possession of this notion when we attribute to so-called "real qualities," like weight, a force that moves bodies toward the center of Earth. Although we have no knowledge of weight, except as a force of a sort that has this effect, we find no difficulty in thinking of it as moving a body, even though we do not think that it does so by actually touching one surface against another. We find this easy to conceive because we experience in ourselves a power to move the body, and we infer that bodies possess qualities that have analogous powers. We call these qualities "real," meaning thereby that we conceive of them as being really distinct from the body that has them, and hence as a kind of substance. (In fact, as Descartes explained elsewhere, we think of them as a kind of spiritual substance, since we attribute goal-oriented behavior to them.)

Unsatisfied with this explanation, Elisabeth pointed out that real qualities are a disreputable part of scholastic natural philosophy that Cartesian physics aims to replace (Adam and Tannery III, p. 684). Descartes promised to give a proper mechanical explanation of such phenomena as the fall of heavy bodies to Earth, so that it will not be necessary to explain the mind's power to move the body in terms of occult qualities, powers known only by their effects. Since Elisabeth did not really understand weight, she could not use its supposed causal powers to help her understand how the soul might act on the body. It would be easier for her, she confessed, to grant extension to the soul than to suppose that an immaterial being has the ability to move and be moved by a material one. In his reply (Adam and Tannery III, p. 694), Descartes gave her permission to do just that: to think of the soul as an extended being! Thinking of the soul as extended is just thinking of it as united to the body. Elisabeth was not satisfied with this reply either, which hardly seems consistent with saying that we have a clear and distinct idea of the mind as a thinking, nonextended substance. But she got no more from Descartes on this subject.

Later their correspondence turned to ethical questions, and Descartes recommended that they discuss Seneca's "De Vita Beata" (On the happy life). Elisabeth's life as a princess in exile was not a happy one. Descartes hoped that reading Seneca would help her overcome her depression. Evidently, he had not read Seneca, or had not read him recently, when he made that suggestion. When he did, he did not find much useful there. But when he made his own recommendations for achieving happiness, they had a distinctly Stoic flavor: We should use our reason to consider without passion the value of all the perfections, both of body and of soul, so that we can always choose the better. We should cultivate a firm and constant resolution to carry out what reason recommends as best without being diverted by our passions. Virtue consists in sticking to this resolution, and virtue, Descartes thought, is the path to contentment. But before long he decided that he needed to examine the passions in more detail, so that he could define them. This led to the first draft of his *Passions of the Soul*, written in the winter of 1645–1646.

While these positive developments were occurring, the controversy with Voetius continued and spread to the University of Leiden, where Jacob Revius, the dean of the Staten college at the University, attacked Descartes, and Adriaan Heereboord, Revius's subdean in the college, defended him. This time the principal issues were not so much Descartes's rejection of key ideas in scholastic philosophy as the positive doctrines of his own philosophy:

- Whether the method of doubt leads to skepticism—a reasonable concern, considering the problems Descartes faced in getting beyond the *cogito*
- Whether Descartes was guilty of blasphemy even to suggest the possibility that God might be a deceiver—not so reasonable, it seems, since Descartes had shown sensitivity to the issue by substituting the demon for God at the end of the First Meditation and had gone on to argue that the hypothesis of a deceiving God involves a contradiction
- Whether Descartes was guilty of atheism in rejecting the Thomistic versions of the cosmological argument for God's existence and replacing them with less satisfactory arguments of his own—a possibly reasonable concern, though the details of the critic's arguments show a poor understanding of Descartes's conception of an idea of God
- Whether Descartes was guilty of Pelagianism for excessively exalting free will

The principal basis for this last accusation was Descartes's claim, in the Fourth Meditation, that he experienced within himself a freedom of choice so great that he could not conceive of the idea of a greater freedom (Adam and Tannery VII, p. 57). It is above all in virtue of his freedom that he understood how he might have been made in the image of God.

The accusation of Pelagianism had come up in the correspondence with Mersenne as early as 1637 (Adam and Tannery I, p. 366). Descartes was always puzzled by it, since he understood the Pelagian heresy to involve the claim that an individual, using only his own natural powers, without a special act of divine grace, can achieve salvation. He knew that he had never made this claim, and he was happy to reject it when the situation required (Adam and Tannery III, p. 544). Nevertheless, when the curators at the University of Leiden forbade any discussion of Descartes's views, pro or con, and Descartes appealed to them, complaining that he must be permitted to defend himself against misrepresentation, the rector of the University, who was well disposed to Descartes, advised him to drop the appeal. The matter might be brought before an ecclesiastical council, where his opponents would surely win, not because of what he had said about freedom of the will, but "because they believe he is a Jesuit in disguise" (Verbeek 1992, p. 47). This was ironic, in view of the trouble Descartes was having with the Jesuits in France, but it was not the last of the ironies arising from Descartes's ambiguous position on free will, as we shall see later.

These were busy years for Descartes. One matter that occupied him was seeing that his principal Latin works were translated into French, so that they could be read by a broader audience. Various friends did the translations: Louis Charles d'Albert, Duke of Luynes, did the *Meditations*; Claude Clerselier, *Objections and Replies*; and the abbot Claude Picot, the *Principles*. The translations were published in 1647. In each case Descartes is supposed to have reviewed them, presumably correcting anything he found faulty and occasionally adding text to explain his views more clearly. In principle, this means we might prefer the French translations of his works to the Latin originals. But it is not clear how much weight we can put on the French variations. We cannot know how carefully he reviewed the translations. Substantial variations almost certainly come from his hand. Smaller ones are doubtful. Older translations of Descartes into English blended the Latin and French texts. The now standard translation listed in the bibliography (Cottingham, Stoothoff, Murdoch, and Kenny) properly takes the Latin as the primary text, noting variations in the French.

In 1647 or 1648 Descartes initiated a quarrel with his former follower, Henricus Regius, who had developed positions at odds with Cartesian philosophy. Descartes first criticized Regius in the preface he wrote for the French translation of the *Principles* and later in the short work *Notae in programma quoddam* (Notes on a Program; also known as Comments on a Certain Broadsheet), published in 1648 and notable for its clarification of Descartes's views on innate ideas. Also in 1648, Descartes sat down for a long interview with a young Dutch theology student named Frans Burman. Burman prepared well for the interview, carefully reading Descartes's published works and asking probing questions about them. His record of Descartes's answers is a valuable source of information about Descartes's views, though sometimes it is not clear that Burman accurately transcribed what Descartes said.

Toward the end of this period, Descartes entered into a correspondence with Queen Christina of Sweden, who was making her court in Stockholm a center for learning. Most of their correspondence was conducted through Pierre-Hector Chanut, the French ambassador, and there is none of the give and take that makes his correspondence with Elisabeth so interesting. But Descartes's relationship with Christina was momentous in other ways, as we shall see.

THE PASSIONS OF THE SOUL (1649)

The Passions of the Soul is Descartes's most serious attempt to provide the moral philosophy promised in the preface to the French edition of the *Principles*. In a prefatory letter, Descartes said that he will treat the passions "only as a natural philosopher," not "as a rhetorician, or even as a moral philosopher." But this is somewhat misleading. Although the work begins with a quick course in Cartesian physiology (secs. 1–16), and broader and narrower definitions of the passions that emphasize their close connection with the body (secs. 17, 25, 27–29), it ends by making a moral evaluation of the passions that smacks more of Aristotelian moderation than Stoic rigor: The passions are all good in their nature; all we need do is to avoid their excess and misuse (sec. 211). Indeed, all the good and evil of this life depend only on the passions (sec. 212).

In the broad sense, the passions of the soul are perceptions the soul receives from the things they represent (sec. 17). Sometimes the things these perceptions represent are in the soul itself, as when we perceive our volitions, imaginations, etc. (sec. 19). Sometimes the things they represent are either in our body or in some external object that acts on our body. This category includes bodily sensations, sensations of external objects, and passions in the narrow sense. These last are defined as excitations of the soul that, though in fact proximately caused by some movement of the animal spirits, are not perceived as having that proximate cause, but are referred to the soul itself (sec. 27).

Descartes maintained that there are six "simple and primitive" passions: wonder, love, hatred, desire, joy, and sadness (sec. 69). All other passions are either combinations of the primitive passions or particular species of them. Like sensations, the passions help to preserve the mind-body union: Their use "consists in this alone, they dispose the soul to will the things nature tells us are useful and to persist in this volition" (sec. 52). They are nature's way of telling us what is useful to us and what is harmful, motivating us to pursue what is useful and avoid what is harmful. The sensation of fear incites the will to flight; the sensation of boldness incites the will to fight.

The connection between the movements of the animal spirits and the excitations of the soul they cause and sustain is no more perspicuous here than it was in the correspondence with Elisabeth. Descartes identified the locus of interaction as the pineal gland, selected for this role, it seems, because it is the only part of the brain that is not double, and because a slight movement of this gland can greatly alter the movements of the animal spirits and, conversely, a slight movement of the animal spirits can greatly alter the movement of this gland (secs. 31–32). But how a particular movement of the pineal gland can affect the soul and how an action of the soul can move the pineal gland are mysteries shrouded in silence. The connections, apparently, are established "by nature" (secs. 44, 50), that is, we assume, the will of God.

Descartes, it seems, thought that for the most part the regularities God has put in place work well for us. But just as in the Sixth Meditations, our bodily sensations can sometimes lead us astray, causing us to want drink, say, when drink would be harmful to us, so can our passions sometimes lead us astray. "When we feel the blood stirred up, we should be warned and remember that everything which presents itself to the imagination tends to deceive the soul, and to make the reasons favoring the object of its passion appear much stronger than they are, and the opposing reasons much weaker" (sec. 211). If the passion favors some object that does not require immediate action, we should refrain from making any immediate judgment and distract ourselves with other thoughts, until our blood has cooled. If it incites us to an action requiring immediate action, we should reflect on the reasons that oppose that action, and follow them even if they seem weaker. This, Descartes said, is "the general remedy for all the excesses of the passions, and the easiest to put into practice" (sec. 211). Descartes is not at his best when he is doing moral philosophy.

DEATH AND CONDEMNATION (1649–1663)

In July 1649, in response to an invitation from Queen Christina, Descartes embarked for Stockholm, where he was to enhance the reputation of her court as an intellectual center and provide the queen with lessons in philosophy. This Swedish adventure did not end happily. When Descartes first arrived in October, his duties were minimal. But by mid-January he was required to give Christina five-hour lessons in philosophy, three mornings a week, beginning at five in the morning. Within two weeks he came down with pneumonia. By February 11, 1650, he had died.

Thirteen years later Descartes's works were placed on the Catholic Church's Index of Prohibited Books. For a long time it was unclear what the grounds for this condemnation were, but recently the Archives of the Congregation for the Doctrine of the Faith have been opened, permitting a clearer view of the Church's reasons and procedures. The Holy Office assigned two outside consultants to read Descartes's works and report on them: Joannes Tartaglia, to read the *Discourse on Method* (and its essays) and the *Meditations* (with the *Objections and Replies*); and Stephanus Spinula, to read *The Principles of Philosophy* and *The Passions of the Soul.* On the whole, the censors (especially Tartaglia) seem to have done their work carefully, attributing to Descartes only doctrines he actually held, or at least doctrines that might reasonably be inferred from what he wrote.

The censors found much to object to. Some were propositions in Cartesian physics where Descartes knew he was pushing the bounds of orthodoxy: the denial of substantial forms and real qualities; the doctrine that Earth moves, while the Sun is immobile; the doctrine that the physical universe has no limits. Others were fundamental doctrines of Cartesian epistemology: that the existence of the self as a thinking thing is the first evident truth, from which all other evident truths derive; that we cannot clearly understand what is true unless we know clearly that God exists and cannot deceive us; and that the standard Thomistic versions of the cosmological argument are unsatisfactory ways of proving God's existence.

Particularly interesting are the objections to two doctrines relating to human freedom: that the soul can easily acquire an absolute power over all its passions; and that freedom of the will does not require freedom from necessity, but only freedom from constraint. The first of these was a proposition that Spinoza also sharply criticized, in the Preface to part V of his *Ethics*. The second was one of five Jansenist propositions that the Church had censured in 1653. So while the Dutch Protestants accused Descartes of Pelagianism, the Catholic Church condemned him for Jansenism, that is, for siding with those within the Church who thought that in their reaction against Lutheran/Calvinist denial of free will the Jesuit theologians had succumbed to Pelagianism. The gate to doctrinal orthodoxy is narrow indeed.

See also Anselm, St.; Aristotelianism; Aristotle; Arnauld, Antoine; Augustine, St.; Berkeley, George; Cartesianism; Cosmological Argument for the Existence of God; Degrees of Perfection, Argument for the Existence of God; Galileo Galilei; Gassendi, Pierre; Hintikka, Jaakko; Hobbes, Thomas; Husserl, Edmund; Kant, Immanuel; Leibniz, Gottfried Wilhelm; Locke, John; Malebranche, Nicolas; Matter; Mind-Body Problem; More, Henry; Newton, Isaac; Nicholas of Cusa; Ontological Argument for the Existence of God; Pascal, Blaise; Plato; Reid, Thomas; Ryle, Gilbert; Skepticism; Spinoza, Benedict (Baruch) de; Wittgenstein, Ludwig Josef Johann.

Bibliography

WORKS BY DESCARTES

Discourse on Method, Optics, Geometry, and Meteorology. Translated by Paul Olscamp. Indianapolis, IN: Library of Liberal Arts, 1965. The only complete English translation of the scientific essays published with the *Discourse.*

Oeuvres. 11 vols., edited by Charles Adam and Paul Tannery. Paris: J. Vrin, 1974–1986. This is the standard edition of the texts in their original languages. All references to Descartes's works in this entry are to volume and page of this edition, cited as "Adam and Tannery."

Treatise of Man. Cambridge, MA: Harvard University Press, 1972. The French text with translation and commentary by Thomas Steele Hall.

Descartes' Conversation with Burman. Translated by John Cottingham. Oxford, U.K.: Clarendon Press, 1976.

Descartes: His Moral Philosophy and Psychology. Translated by John Blom. New York: New York University Press, 1978. The only English language edition of Descartes's correspondence with Elisabeth that gives her letters to Descartes as well as his replies to her.

Le monde, ou Traité de la lumière (*The World*). French text with English translation by Michael Mahoney. New York: Abaris, 1979.

Principles of Philosophy. Translated by Valentine Rodger Miller and Reese P. Miller. Dordrecht, Netherlands: D. Reidel, 1983. The only complete English translation of this work.

Philosophical Writings. 3 vols. Translated by John Cottingham, Robert Stoothoff, Dugald Murdoch, and (in vol. 3), Anthony Kenny. Cambridge, U.K.: Cambridge University Press, 1985–1991. The best comprehensive English language edition. It gives the volume and page numbers of the Adam and Tannery edition in the margins.

The Passions of the Soul. Translated by Stephen Voss. Indianapolis, IN: Hackett, 1989.

BIOGRAPHY

Baillet, Adrien. *The Life of Monsieur Descartes*. Translated by S. R. London: 1653. Available through Early English Books Online (http://eebo.chadwyck.com/home).

Gaukroger, Stephen. *Descartes: An Intellectual Biography*, Oxford, U.K.: Clarendon Press, 1995.

WORKS ON DESCARTES

Alanen, Lilli. *Descartes' Concept of Mind*. Cambridge, U.K.: Harvard University Press, 2003.

Ariew, Roger. *Descartes and the Last Scholastics*. Ithaca, NY: Cornell University Press, 1999.

Ariew, Roger, John Cottingham, and Tom Sorell. *Descartes' "Meditations": Background Source Materials*. Cambridge, U.K.: Cambridge University Press, 1998.

Ariew, Roger, Dennis Des Chene, Douglas Jesseph, Tad Schmaltz, and Theo Verbeek. *Historical Dictionary of Descartes and Cartesian Philosophy*. Lanham, MD: Scarecrow Press, 2003.

Ariew, Roger, and Marjorie Grene. *Descartes and His Contemporaries, "Meditations," Objections and Replies*. Chicago: University of Chicago Press, 1995.

Armogathe, Jean-Robert, and Vincent Carraud. "The First Condemnation of Descartes' *Oeuvres*: Some Unpublished Documents from the Vatican Archives." *Oxford Studies in Early Modern Philosophy* 1 (2003): 67–109.

Baker, Gordon, and Katharine Morris. *Descartes' Dualism*. London: Routledge, 1996.

Broughton, Janet. *Descartes' Method of Doubt*. Princeton, NJ: Princeton University Press, 2002.

Clarke, Desmond. *Descartes' Philosophy of Science*. Manchester, U.K.: Manchester University Press, 1982.

Cottingham, John, ed. *The Cambridge Companion to Descartes*. Cambridge, U.K.: Cambridge University Press, 1992.

Cottingham, John, ed. *Reason, Will, and Sensation*. Oxford, U.K.: Clarendon Press, 1994.

Curley, Edwin. *Descartes against the Skeptics*. Cambridge, MA: Harvard University Press, 1978.

Frankfurt, Harry. *Demons, Dreamers, and Madmen*. Indianapolis, IN: Bobbs-Merrill, 1970.

Garber, Daniel. *Descartes' Metaphysical Physics*. Chicago: University of Chicago Press, 1992.

Garber, Daniel. *Descartes Embodied: Reading Cartesian Philosophy through Cartesian Science*. Cambridge, U.K.: Cambridge University Press, 2001.

Gaukroger, Stephen, ed. *Descartes: Philosophy, Mathematics, and Physics*. Sussex, U.K.: Harvester Press, 1980.

Hatfield, Gary. *Routledge Philosophy Guidebook to Descartes and the "Meditations."* London: Routledge, 2003.

Kenny, Anthony. *The Anatomy of the Soul: Historical Essays in the Philosophy of Mind*. Oxford, U.K.: Basil Blackwell, 1973.

Kenny, Anthony. *Descartes: A Study of His Philosophy*. New York: Random House, 1968.

Koyré, Alexandre. *From the Closed World to the Infinite Universe*. Baltimore: Johns Hopkins University Press, 1957.

Matthews, Gareth. *Thought's Ego in Augustine and Descartes*. Ithaca, NY: Cornell University Press, 1992.

Menn, Stephen. *Descartes and Augustine*. Cambridge, U.K.: Cambridge University Press, 1998.

Rorty, Amélie Oksenberg, ed. *Essays on Descartes' "Meditations."* Berkeley: University of California Press, 1986.

Schuster, John. "Descartes' *mathesis universalis*, 1619–1628." In *Descartes: Philosophy, Mathematics, and Physics*, edited by Stephen Gaukroger. Sussex, U.K.: Harvester Press, 1980.

Verbeek, Theo. *Descartes and the Dutch: Early Reactions to Cartesian Philosophy, 1637–1650*. Carbondale: Southern Illinois University Press, 1992.

Voss, Stephen, ed. *Essays on the Philosophy and Science of Descartes*. Oxford, U.K.: Oxford University Press, 1993.

Weber, Jean-Paul. *La constitution du texte des "Regulae."* Paris: Société d'édition d'enseignement supérieur, 1964.

Williams, Bernard. *Descartes: The Project of Pure Enquiry*. Harmondsworth, U.K.: Penguin, 1978.

Williston, Byron, and André Gombay, eds. *Passion and Virtue in Descartes*. Amherst, NY: Humanity Books, 2003.

Wilson, Margaret Dauler. *Descartes*. London: Routledge and Kegan Paul, 1978.

Edwin Curley (2005)

DESCRIPTIONS

See *Proper Names and Descriptions*

DESCRIPTIONS, THEORY OF

See *Analysis, Philosophical; Existence*

DESGABETS, ROBERT

(1610–1678)

Robert Desgabets was a French Benedictine who offered a form of Cartesianism that departs from René Descartes's own account of the nature of substance and of one's knowledge of the self and of the external world. These departures are indicated in the two book-length texts from Desgabets published during his lifetime, but they are explicated most fully in manuscripts published only during the mid-1980s, in a definitive edition of his philosophical writings sponsored by *Studia Cartesiana*.

Desgabets was born in Ancemont in Verdun, a region annexed by France in 1552, to Jean des Gabets and Barbe Richard. He entered the Benedictine order in 1636 and taught philosophy and theology for over a decade at Saint-Evre in Toul. In 1648 he was named the Benedictine procurer general in Paris, and the following year he took up the position of professor of philosophy at Saint-Arnold in Metz. From 1653 to 1657 he served in administrative posts in various Lorraine abbeys. It was during this time that Claude Clerselier attempted to draw him into a defense of Descartes by sending him copies of Descartes's discussion in unpublished correspondence of the Catholic doctrine that the Eucharist involves the "transubstantiation" of bread and wine into Christ's body and blood. Desgabets endorsed Descartes's proposal that such transubstantiation occurs by means of the union of Christ's soul with the matter of the Eucharistic elements. What he added to this proposal was an argument against the possibility of the annihilation of this matter that appeals to the result in his 1654 manuscript "Traité de l'indéfectibilité des creatures," that material substance has an existence that is "indefectible," that is, indestructible and immutable.

In 1658 Desgabets spent a brief time in Paris on official business, and while there he participated in public discussions of Cartesian natural philosophy. He also offered for consideration a brief *Discours* on the transfusion of blood, which the French physician Jean-Baptiste Denis included in his 1668 *Lettre à Sorbière* in part to draw the attention of the English Royal Society to French research in this area.

Following his return to the Lorraine provinces in 1659, Desgabets worked to spread the teaching of Cartesianism in local Benedictine abbeys. In the mid-1660s he also became involved in the controversies in France over Jansenist theology associated most prominently with the convent of Port-Royal. Desgabets took the risky step of siding with the Jansenists and Port-Royal against the religious and political establishment.

Even so, Desgabets later split with the Port-Royalists on the issue of the Eucharist. One occasion for the rupture was the publication in 1671 of his *Considérations sur l'état présent de la controverse*. Jean Ferrier, the royal confessor, promptly condemned the work to Louis XIV as heretical, and Louis ordered François de Harlay de Champvallon, the archbishop of Paris, to censure it. When Harlay questioned the Port-Royalist solitaires Antoine Arnauld and Pierre Nicole about this text, they denounced it in no uncertain terms. In an audience with Clerselier Harlay also insinuated that Desgabets's tract was responsible for a 1671 decree from Louis to the University of Paris that marked the start of the official campaign against the teaching of Cartesianism in France. Pressure from above led Desgabets's Benedictine superiors to interrogate him the following year and to prohibit him from speaking on the issue of the Eucharist. The effects of the censure were felt even into the mid-eighteenth century, when the Benedictine authorities refused the request of some admirers of Desgabets to publish an edition of his writings.

Despite the 1672 censure, Desgabets subsequently became underprior and then prior of the provincial abbey of Breuil. Moreover, the censure did not bring about the end of his philosophical activity. In 1674 he engaged in correspondence with Nicolas Malebranche after the latter sent him a copy of the first volume of his *Recherche de la verité*. When Simon Foucher wrote *Critique de la recherche de la verité* that cast doubt on claims in Malebranche's text that mind and body are distinct substances and that ideas represent external objects, Desgabets composed a Cartesian refutation of Foucher's skeptical position. Desgabets's *Critique de la critique de la recherche de la verité* appeared in 1675, and like his 1671 *Considérations*, it was published anonymously. Desgabets further defended the fundamental tenets of his *Critique* in a manuscript commentary on the *Meditations*, the 1675 "Supplément à la philosophie de Monsieur Descartes."

In 1677 there was a series of conferences concerning Desgabets's distinctive version of Cartesianism that took place at the chateau of the Cardinal de Retz (Jean-François-Paul de Gondi) in Commercy. Around this same time Retz's secretary, Jean Corbinelli, led a discussion of the results of the conferences at a special meeting of Cartesians in Paris that included Malebranche. Shortly after these discussions, in March 1678, Desgabets died at his home abbey of Breuil, near Commercy.

MATTER, SUBSTANCE, AND THE COGITO

In commentary published with his 1840 edition of the Commercy conferences, Victor Cousin noted that "if dom Robert, in metaphysics, is a disciple of Descartes revolting against all the principles of his master, he is not so in physics. There he is a faithful Cartesian" (cited in Retz 1887, p. 345). The fidelity to Descartes in physics is indicated in a 1666 letter to Clerselier, in which Desgabets criticized as schismatic the attempt of the French Cartesian Géraud de Cordemoy to introduce a version of Cartesian physics that posits indivisible atoms and the void. Desgabets also argued against the atomist admission of vacua by appealing to Descartes's claim in the *Principles* that matter by its nature occupies all imaginable space.

However, Desgabets went further than Descartes in connecting the claim that matter fills all space to the conclusion that this matter is "indefectible" since not even God can annihilate any part of it. There may seem to be a similarity here to Descartes's view in the Synopsis to the *Meditations* that "body taken in general" is incorruptible since it cannot be destroyed by natural means. Still, Descartes argued in the *Meditations* that since creatures have a duration divisible into distinct parts, God can reduce them to nothing at any moment by refraining from conserving them. Desgabets explicitly rejected this line of argument when he charged Descartes with confusing the modes of a substance with the substance itself. In the case of the material world Desgabets allowed that particular bodies can and do go out of existence. However, he claimed that these bodies are merely modes of extended substance that exist only "secundum quid" as particular temporal determinations of that substance. Desgabets insisted that substance itself exists "simpliciter" in a manner that is wholly indivisible, and so not subject to temporal change (1675, p. 77f).

Desgabets's opposition to Descartes's view that substance has a divisible temporal duration is a clear case of his revolt "against the principles of the master." Another such case is provided by his charge that it is a "principal fault" in Descartes that he took the certainty of the cogito argument to show that the existence of the self is better known than and independent of the existence of body. In Descartes this conclusion is supported by the possibility of a hyperbolic doubt of the existence of the material world. In the "Supplément," however, Desgabets objected to the possibility of such doubt. In the first part of this text he urged that the cogito itself undermines this sort of doubt since it reveals that one's thoughts bear an essential connection to bodily motion (1983–1985, p. 5:183f). His argument stresses that reflection on the cogito occurs in a continuous time that is not intrinsic to thought as such but derives from the union of one's thought with motion. Desgabets relied explicitly here on the traditional Aristotelian definition of time as "the measure of motion." He also held, with other Cartesians, that the only motion is local motion, and further claimed, in orthodox Cartesian fashion, that local motion itself presupposes the existence of the particular bodies that are in motion.

These various premises help to explain his conclusion that the temporality revealed by reflection on the cogito could not exist if there were no bodies external to mind. This argument is somewhat reminiscent of the later appeal in Immanuel Kant to the temporality of consciousness in his "refutation" of a "problematic idealism" in Descartes that takes consciousness to reveal with certainty only the existence of the self. Whereas Kant emphasized that the existence of "outer things" is required for the determination of the temporal succession of inner experience, Desgabets held that the existence of bodies in motion is required for the presence of the temporal duration of one's thoughts.

Desgabets's "Cartesian refutation of idealism," as one might call it, is connected to his endorsement in his *Critique* of Foucher's rejection of Malebranche's orthodox Cartesian claim that one has a "pure intellect" that operates independently of the body. For Desgabets, that all one's thoughts are temporal reveals that they all involve a union with motion. Since he adopted the traditional view that the soul is united to the body through the senses, he accepted the scholastic maxim *Nihil est in intellectu quod prius non fuerit in sensu* (Nothing is in the intellect that was not first in the senses). Pierre Gassendi also had appealed to this maxim in response to Descartes's claim that one has a pure intellect, and this resemblance has led some commentators to label Desgabets as a Gassendist. Unlike Gassendi, however, Desgabets was firmly committed to a Cartesian dualism that distinguishes mind as thinking substance from body as extended substance.

IDEAS, EXTERNAL OBJECTS, AND ETERNAL TRUTHS

In the second part of the "Supplément" Desgabets argued that skepticism concerning the existence of extended substance is overturned by "the most simple, the best known, and the most evident of all principles," namely, that all simple ideas or conceptions correspond to real objects (1983–1985, p. 6:223). Desgabets took this principle to be linked to the claim that to perceive nothing is not to perceive. He admitted that one can make false judgments about what one perceives. Indeed, he pointed to the scholastic claim that sensible qualities exist in bodies as a paradigmatic example of such a judgment, one that is to be corrected by "the great discovery of M. Descartes" that these qualities exist only in us (1983–1985, p. 5:164f). However, Desgabets's "intentionality principle," as commentators have called it, requires that ideas that succeed in representing extramental objects, such as the idea of body, presuppose that their objects actually exist in some sense. The qualification is required by Desgabets's distinction, which informs his discussion of the indefectibility of matter, between modes and the substances they modify. Desgabets allowed that one can conceive of modes that do not actually exist insofar as one can conceive of them as only possibly modifying an existing substance. In this way the nonexistent modes have a "true possibility" conferred on them by substance. Since substance cannot be conceived through any other feature of created reality, however, the possibility of its existence also cannot be conceived through anything else. Desgabets concluded that one cannot even conceive of a substance that is "purely possible" and does not actually exist. For him, then, the mere fact that one has an idea of extended substance, and so can conceive of it, suffices to show that this substance exists external to mind.

Desgabets admitted "an extreme difference between the thoughts of M. Descartes and mine" concerning the issue of the existence of the external material world, since Descartes allowed for the possibility that extended substance exist not in extramental reality but only "objectively" in one's mind (1983–1985, 6:223). However, one reason for Desgabets's extreme opposition derives from his development of Descartes's doctrine of the creation of the eternal truths. Descartes had introduced this doctrine in 1630 in correspondence with Marin Mersenne, in which he insisted that God's free and indifferent will is the efficient cause of the eternal truths. Desgabets took this position to indicate that there are no preexisting truths concerning creatures that constrain divine creation. But he also insisted that if eternal truths concerning bodies were grounded in a mental objective reality, then those truths would seem to be as contingent and mutable as one's mind. In Desgabets's version of the Cartesian doctrine the truths are grounded rather in an extended substance with an atemporal existence that is completely indefectible. Thus, the necessity and immutability of the relevant truths are assured, even given that God has freely created the indefectible substance that provides the foundation for these truths.

The juxtaposition in Desgabets of a strong voluntarism and a firm commitment to substantial indefectibility is found also in the work of the French Cartesian Pierre-Sylvain Regis, who called Desgabets "one of the greatest metaphysicians of our age." Regis endorsed Desgabets's arguments both for the claim that one's idea of extended substance reveals immediately the extramental existence of that substance and for the conclusion that temporal human thought requires a union with and thus presupposes the existence of bodily motion. In both Desgabets and Regis, then, radical doctrines concerning the indefectibility of substance, the intentionality of ideas, and the union of all human thought with motion constitute an unusual but philosophically sophisticated version of Cartesianism.

See also Cartesianism.

Bibliography

WORKS BY DESGABETS

Considérations sur l'état présent de la controverse touchant le Très Saint-Sacrement de l'autel, où il est traité en peu mots de l'opinion qui enseigne que la matière du pain est changé en celle du corps de Jésus-Christ par son union substantielle à son âme et à sa personne divine. Hollande: Sphère, 1671.

Critique de la critique de la recherche de la verité, ou l'on découvre le chemin qui conduit aux connoissances solides. Pour servir de reponse à la lettre d'un academicien. Paris: du Puis, 1675.

Dom Robert Desgabets: Oeuvres philosophiques inédites. 7 vols, edited by Joseph Beaude. Amsterdam: Quadratures, 1983–1985.

WORKS ABOUT DESGABETS

Armogathe, Jean-Robert. *Theologia cartesiana: l'explication physique de l'Eucharistie chez Descartes et dom Desgabets.* The Hague: Nijhoff, 1977.

Beaude, Joseph. "Cartésianisme et anticartésianisme de Desgabets." *Studia cartesiana* 1 (1979): 1–24.

Cook, Monte. "Desgabets's Representation Principle." *Journal of the History of Philosophy* 40 (2) (2002): 189–200.

Denis, Jean-Baptiste. *Lettre escrite à M. Sobière, with an "Extrait d'une lettre de Dom Robert des Gabets et Discours de la communication ou transfusion du sang pronouncé à Paris chez Montmor … en juillet 1658."* Paris: Cusson, 1668.

Easton, Patricia. "Desgabets, dom Robert." In *The Stanford Encyclopedia of Philosophy*, edited by Edward N. Zalta. Stanford, CA: Metaphysics Research Lab, Center for the Study of Language and Information, Stanford University, 1995–. (http://plato.stanford.edu/).

"Journée D. Robert Desgabets du CNRS." *Revue de synthèse* 74 (1974).

Retz, Jean-François-Paul de Gondi, cardinal de. "Dissertations sur le cartésianisme, par le cardinal de Retz et le bénédictin dom Robert Des Gabets." In *Oeuvres de cardinal de Retz*, vol. 9. Edited by R. de Chantelauze. Paris: Hachette, 1887.

Rodis-Lewis, Geneviève. *L'anthropologie cartésienne.* Paris: Presses Universitaires de France, 1990.

Rodis-Lewis, Geneviève. "Robert Desgabets." In *Grundriss der Geschichte der Philosophie, begründet von Friedrich Ueberweg, völlig neubearbeitete Ausgabe. Die Philosophie des 17. Jahrhunderts. Vol. 2, Frankreich, und Niederlande, vol. 1,* edited by Jean-Pierre Schobinger. Basil: Schwabe, 1993.

Schmaltz, Tad M. *Radical Cartesianism: The French Reception of Descartes.* New York: Cambridge University Press, 2002.

Tad M. Schmaltz (2005)

DESIGN

See *Philosophy of Technology*

DESTUTT DE TRACY, ANTOINE LOUIS CLAUDE, COMTE

(1754–1836)

Comte Antoine Louis Claude Destutt de Tracy, the French philosopher and propounder of the doctrine of Ideology, was born in Paris. Educated at the University of Strasbourg, he entered the army and served later as deputy of the Bourbonnais nobility to the States-General. Despite his noble rank he was a fervent partisan of reform in monarchical government, but by 1792 he had become disgusted with the extremists among the revolutionaries and retired from politics to Auteuil, where he joined the celebrated group of philosopher-scientists that found its center at the home of Madame Helvétius. Among his intimates were Pierre-Jean-Georges Cabanis and Marquis de Condorcet, Comte de Volney and Dominique Joseph Garat. Imprisoned for a year under the Terror, he began to study the works of Étienne Bonnot de Condillac and John Locke, the result of which was his elaboration of the discipline he called Ideology. The group associated with Destutt de Tracy took the name *Idéologues* from his doctrine. They became influential in 1795 in two new institutions, the École Normale and the Institut National, especially in the Second Class of the Institut National.

Ideology, according to Destutt de Tracy, is the analysis of ideas into the sensory elements of which he believed them to be composed. Training in this new science would replace classical logic, and, he maintained, if a man learned how to analyze his ideas, he would then discover which of them were founded in experience and which were groundless. Destutt de Tracy held that Ideology was a branch of zoology; all ideas had a physiological determinant. The child, with its weak sense organs, has nothing but sensation and memory; the adult, whose sense organs have become strengthened through use, has the powers of judgment and intelligence. It was therefore to be asked what the effect of habit would be on judgment. This question was put to the Second Class of the Institut National on 15 Vendémiaire, An VIII (October 6, 1799). The winning *mémoire* was that of Maine de Biran, at that time a young disciple of the *Idéologues,* and his *Mémoire sur l'habitude* (1802) formed the link between the French epistemological tradition of the eighteenth century and that of the nineteenth-century "spiritualists."

The word *thinking* in the works of Destutt de Tracy means, as it did for René Descartes, all conscious processes. Any immediate apprehension is called "feeling," whether it be sensory, emotional, or intellectual. Even memory and the perception of relations were "felt." But the feelings were not images; they were merely the awareness of whatever content might be before one. Destutt de Tracy called these contents ideas, following Locke. They were of four kinds: sensations, memories, judgments, and desires.

The question that puzzled Destutt de Tracy and, for that matter, most of the philosophers of this period in France was whether all consciousness is passive or whether some is active. If all were passive, then we should have no reason to believe in the existence of an external world. There is, however, according to Destutt de Tracy, one idea that gives us an intimation of a reality beyond ourselves, the idea of touch. When we put pressure upon an object, it resists. We cannot, at the same time, desire both a feeling and its annihilation. The feeling of resistance annihilates the desire to penetrate. Therefore, when we feel resistance, we are forced to conclude that there is a resisting object. In this way an element of activity was introduced into Destutt de Tracy's epistemology, an element that was to form the logical nucleus of the theories of his successors, Maine de Biran and Pierre Laromiguière.

Destutt de Tracy thought that the analysis of general ideas into elementary feelings would destroy the analyzer's faith in many of the teachings of religion. For if an idea could not be found to be either an elementary feeling or to be composed of such, it must be discarded. But many religious ideas cannot be so analyzed and therefore must be discarded.

Although the *Idéologues* had favored Napoleon Bonaparte's coup d'état of 1799, they soon opposed him, and in 1803 Napoleon suppressed the Second Class of the Institut. Destutt de Tracy's antireligious views, which directly clashed with Napoleon's reestablishment of religion, were a major factor in Napoleon's act of suppression. The soon-to-be emperor, moreover, could not tolerate Destutt de Tracy's view that every man has the power to determine the truth and falsity of his ideas without recourse to authority and that among those ideas are those of right and wrong, both moral and political.

See also Cabanis, Pierre-Jean Georges; Condillac, Étienne Bonnot de; Condorcet, Marquis de; Continental Philosophy; Descartes, René; Ideology; Laromiguière, Pierre; Locke, John; Maine de Biran; Volney, Constantin-François de Chasseboeuf, Comte de.

Bibliography

PRIMARY WORKS

Quels sont les moyens de fonder la morale chez un peuple? Paris, 1798.

Observations sur le système d'instruction publique. Paris, 1801.

Eléments d'idéologie, 4 vols. Paris, 1801–1815.

Grammaire générale. Paris, 1803.

Logique. Paris, 1805.

Traité de la volonté et de ses effets. Paris, 1805.

Commentaire sur l'esprit des lois de Montesquieu (*A Commentary and Review of Montesquieu's Spirit of Laws*). Translated by Thomas Jefferson. Philadelphia, 1811.

De l'Amour. Edited by Gilbert Chinard. Paris, 1926.

A Treatise on Political Economy. Translated by Thomas Jefferson. Detroit: Center for Health Education, 1973.

SECONDARY WORKS

Boas, George. *French Philosophies of the Romantic Period.* Baltimore: Johns Hopkins Press, 1925.

Chinard, J. *Jefferson et les idéologues.* Baltimore: Johns Hopkins Press, 1925.

Head, Brian William. *Ideology and Social Science: Destutt de Tracy and French Liberalism.* Dordrecht: Nijhoff, 1985.

Kennedy, Emmet. *A* Philosophe *in the Age of Revolution, Destutt de Tracy and the Origins of "Ideology."* Philadelphia: American Philosophical Society, 1978.

Picavet, François. *Les idéologues.* Paris: Alcan, 1891.

Van Duzen, C. *The Contributions of the Idéologues to French Revolutionary Thought.* Baltimore, 1935.

Welch, Cheryl B. *Liberty and Utility: The French Ideologues and the Transformation of Liberalism.* New York: Columbia University Press, 1984.

George Boas (1967)
Bibliography updated by Philip Reed (2005)

LOWER MERION LIBRARY SYSTEM
30043004863555